C++ HOW TO PROGRAM

— Sixth Edition —

W9-COU-989

CYBER CLASSROOM STUDENT ACCESS CARD

Thank you for purchasing a new copy of *C++ How to Program* Sixth Edition, by Deitel and Deitel. The access code below provides you with full access to the Cyber Classroom that accompanies this text. You will now have full access to all student support areas, including:

- Hours of detailed, expert audio descriptions of thousands of lines of code that help to reinforce important concepts.
- An abundance of self-assessment material, including practice exams, hundreds of programming exercises, and self-review questions and answers.
- A lab manual featuring lab exercises as well as pre- and post-lab activities.
- Student solutions to approximately half of the exercises in the textbook.

To access the *C++ How to Program Cyber Classroom* for the first time:

You will need to register online using a computer with an Internet connection and a Web browser. The registration process takes just a few minutes and only needs to be completed once.

1. Go to http://www.prenhall.com/deitel/cyberclassroom
2. Find the appropriate title and click "**Access the Cyber Classroom**"
3. Click "**register**" under the student area.
4. Use a coin to scratch off the gray coating below and reveal your student access code.
   ** *Do not use a knife or other sharp object, which can damage the code.*

5. On the registration page, enter your student access code. Do not type the dashes. You can use lower or uppercase letters.
6. Follow the on-screen instructions. If you need help during the online registration process, simply click the **Need Help?** icon.
7. Once your personal Login Name and Password are confirmed, you can begin using the *C++ How to Program Cyber Classroom*!

To login to the *C++ How to Program Cyber Classroom* for the first time after you register:

Please visit http://www.prenhall.com/deitel/cyberclassroom and click "**Access the Cyber Classroom**" under the appropriate book title. Click "login" under the student section. When prompted, provide your login name and password created during the registration process.

Note to Instructors: For access to Instructor Resources, contact your Prentice Hall Sales Representative.

PEARSON
Education

Upper Saddle River, NJ 07458
www.prenhall.com

C++

HOW TO PROGRAM

SIXTH EDITION

Deitel® Ser

How To Program Series

Advanced Java™ 2 Platform How to Program

C How to Program, 5/E

C++ How to Program, 6/E

e-Business and e-Commerce How to Program

Internet and World Wide Web How to Program, 3/E

Java How to Program, 7/E

Small Java™ How to Program, 6/E

Perl How to Program

Python How to Program

Visual C++® .NET How to Program

Visual Basic® 6 How to Program

Visual Basic® 2005 How to Program, 3/E

Visual C#® 2005 How to Program, 2/E

XML How to Program

Simply Series

Simply C++: An Application-Driven Tutorial Approach

Simply C#: An Application-Driven Tutorial Approach

Simply Java™ Programming: An Application-Driven Tutorial Approach

Simply Visual Basic® .NET: An Application-Driven Tutorial Approach (Visual Studio .NET 2003 Edition)

Simply Visual Basic® 2005, 2/E: An Application-Driven Tutorial Approach

ies Page

To follow the Deitel publishing program, please register for the free *Deitel® Buzz Online* e-mail newsletter at:

> www.deitel.com/newsletter/subscribe.html

To communicate with the authors, send e-mail to:

> deitel@deitel.com

For information on corporate on-site seminars offered by Deitel & Associates, Inc. worldwide, visit:

> www.deitel.com

or write to

> deitel@deitel.com

For continuing updates on Prentice Hall/Deitel publications visit:

> www.deitel.com
> www.prenhall.com/deitel
> www.InformIT.com/deitel

Check out our Resource Centers for valuable web resources that will help you master C++, other important programming languages and Web 2.0 topics:

> www.deitel.com/ResourceCenters.html

Library of Congress Cataloging-in-Publication Data
On file

Vice President and Editorial Director, ECS: *Marcia J. Horton*
Associate Editor: *Carole Snyder*
Supervisor/Editorial Assistant: *Dolores Mars*
Director of Team-Based Project Management: *Vince O'Brien*
Senior Managing Editor: *Scott Disanno*
Managing Editor: *Bob Engelhardt*
Production Editor: *Marta Samsel*
A/V Production Editor: *Greg Dulles*
Art Studio: *Artworks, York, PA*
Art Director: *Kristine Carney*
Cover Design: *Abbey S. Deitel, Harvey M. Deitel, Francesco Santalucia, Kristine Carney*
Interior Design: *Harvey M. Deitel, Kristine Carney*
Manufacturing Manager: *Alexis Heydt-Long*
Manufacturing Buyer: *Lisa McDowell*
Director of Marketing: *Margaret Waples*

© 2008 by Pearson Education, Inc.
Upper Saddle River, New Jersey 07458

10 9 8 7 6 5 4 3 2 1

ISBN 0-13-615250-3

Pearson Education Ltd., *London*
Pearson Education Australia Pty. Ltd., *Sydney*
Pearson Education Singapore, Pte. Ltd.
Pearson Education North Asia Ltd., *Hong Kong*
Pearson Education Canada, Inc., *Toronto*
Pearson Educación de Mexico, S.A. de C.V.
Pearson Education–Japan, *Tokyo*
Pearson Education Malaysia, Pte. Ltd.
Pearson Education, Inc., *Upper Saddle River, New Jersey*

MULTIMEDIA CYBER CLASSROOMS

DEITEL® *Multimedia Cyber Classrooms* include:

- The full text, illustrations and program listings of its corresponding *How to Program* book.

- Hours of detailed, expert audio descriptions of hundreds of lines of code that help to reinforce important concepts.

- An abundance of self-assessment material, including practice exams, hundreds of programming exercises and self-review questions and answers.

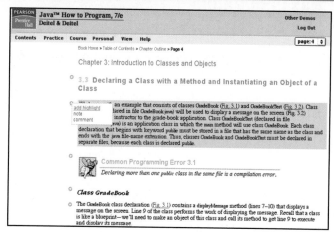

DEITEL® Multimedia Cyber Classrooms *offer a host of interactive features, such as highlighting of key sections of the text...*

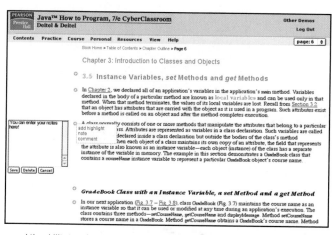

...*and the ability to write notes in the margin of a given page for future reference.*

- Intuitive browser-based interface designed to be easy and accessible.

- A Lab Manual featuring lab exercises as well as pre- and post-lab activities.

- Student Solutions to approximately one-half of the exercises in the textbook.

Students receive 12-month access to a protected Web site via access code cards packaged with these new textbooks. (Simply tear the strip on the inside of the Cyber Classroom package to reveal access code.)

For more information, please visit:
www.prenhall.com/deitel/cyberclassroom

PearsonChoices

For Instructors and Students using DEITEL® Publications

Today's students have increasing demands on their time and money, and they need to be resourceful about how, when and where they study. Pearson Education has responded to that need by creating PearsonChoices, which allows faculty and students to choose from a variety of formats and prices.

Visit www.pearsonchoices.com for more information.

We are pleased to announce PearsonChoices for our leading DEITEL publications:

- SafariX eTextbooks—We are pleased to offer students ten DEITEL SafariX eTextbooks available at 50% off the print version's price!
  - — *Java How to Program, Seventh Edition*
  - — *Small Java How to Program, Sixth Edition*
  - — *C++ How to Program, Sixth Edition*
  - — *Small C++ How to Program, Fifth Edition*
  - — *Simply C++: An Application-Driven Tutorial Approach*
  - — *Visual C# 2005 How to Program, Second Edition*
  - — *SafariX for Visual Basic 2005 How to Program, Third Edition*
  - — *SafariX for C How to Program, Fifth Edition*
  - — *SafariX for Simply Visual Basic 2005 How to Program*

SafariX eTextbooks Online is an exciting new service for college students looking to save money on required or recommended textbooks for academic courses!

This secure eTextbooks platform creates a new option in the higher education market: an additional choice for students alongside conventional textbooks and online learning services. By eliminating the costs relating to printing, manufacturing and retail distribution for the physical textbook, Pearson provides students with an eTextbook at 50% of the cost of its conventional print equivalent. Students can choose to purchase a print edition textbook or subscribe to the same textbook content through SafariX eTextbooks Online.

SafariX eTextbooks are digital versions of print textbooks enhanced with features such as high-speed search, note taking and bookmarking. SafariX eTextbooks are viewed through a Web browser connected to the Internet. SafariX eTextbooks Online requires no special plug-ins and no applications download to your computer. Students just log in, purchase access and begin studying!

With SafariX eTextbooks Online students will be able to search the text, make notes online, print out reading assignments that incorporate your lecture notes and bookmark important passages they want to review later. They can navigate easily to a page number, reading assignment or chapter. The Table of Contents of each eTextbook appears in the left hand column alongside the text.

Visit www.safarix.com for more information!

C++

HOW TO PROGRAM

SIXTH EDITION

P. J. Deitel

Deitel & Associates, Inc.

H. M. Deitel

Deitel & Associates, Inc.

Upper Saddle River, New Jersey 07458

Trademarks

To the victims of the tragedy at Virginia Tech,
their families, their friends and the
Virginia Tech community.

Paul and Harvey Deitel

Deitel Resource Centers

Our Resource Centers focus on the vast amounts of free content available online. Start your search here for resources, downloads, tutorials, documentation, books, e-books, journals, articles, blogs, RSS feeds and more on many of today's hottest programming and technology topics. For the most up-to-date list of our Resource Centers, visit:

www.deitel.com/ResourceCenters.html

Let us know what other Resource Centers you'd like to see! Also, please register for the free *Deitel® Buzz Online* e-mail newsletter at:

www.deitel.com/newsletter/subscribe.html

Programming
.NET
.NET 3.0
Ajax
Apex On-Demand
 Programming
 Language
ASP.NET
C
C#
C++
C++ Boost Libraries
C++ Game
 Programming
Code Search Engines
 and Code Sites
Computer Game
 Programming
CSS 2.1
Flash 9
Flex
Java
Java Certification and
 Assessment Testing
Java Design Patterns
Java EE 5
Java SE 6
JavaFX
JavaScript
OpenGL
Perl
PHP
Programming Projects
Python
Ruby
Silverlight

Visual Basic
Visual C++
Web Services
Web3D Technologies
XML

Software
Apache
DotNetNuke (DNN)
Eclipse
Firefox
Internet Explorer 7
Linux
MySQL
Open Source
Search Engines
Wikis
Windows Vista

Microsoft
.NET
.NET 3.0
ASP.NET
C#
DotNetNuke (DNN)
Internet Explorer 7
Silverlight
Visual Basic
Visual C++
Windows Vista

Java
Java
Java Certification and
 Assessment Testing
Java Design Patterns

Java EE 5
Java SE 6
JavaFX
JavaScript

Web 2.0
Alert Services
Attention Economy
Blogging
Building Web
 Communities
Community
 Generated Content
Google Base
Google Video
Google Web Toolkit
Internet Video
Joost
Mashups
Microformats
Ning
Recommender
 Systems
RSS
Skype
Social Media
Social Networking
Software as a Service
 (SaaS)
Virtual Worlds
Web 2.0
Web 3.0
Widgets
Wikis

Internet Business
Affiliate Programs
Google Adsense
Google Analytics
Google Services
Internet Advertising
Internet Business
 Initiative
Internet Public
 Relations
Link Building
Podcasting
Search Engine
 Optimization
Sitemaps
Web Analytics
Website Monetization

Open Source
Apache
DotNetNuke (DNN)
Eclipse
Firefox
Linux
MySQL
Open Source
Perl
PHP
Python
Ruby

Other Topics
Computer Games
Computing Jobs
Gadgets and Gizmos
Sudoku

Contents

13 Object-Oriented Programming: Polymorphism 693

23   Game Programming with Ogre   1148

H UML 2: Additional Diagram Types 1355

I Using the Visual Studio Debugger 1357

J Using the GNU C++ Debugger 1373

Bibliography 1390

Index 1396

Preface

"The chief merit of language is clearness ... "
—Galen

Welcome to C++ and *C++ How to Program, Sixth Edition*! At Deitel & Associates, we write programming language textbooks and professional books for Prentice Hall, deliver corporate training worldwide and develop Web 2.0 Internet businesses. This book reflects significant changes to the C++ language and to the preferred ways of teaching and learning programming. All the chapters have been significantly tuned. The *Tour of the Book* section of the Preface gives instructors, students and professionals a sense of *C++ How to Program, 6/e's* coverage of C++ and object-oriented programming.

New and Updated Features

Here's a list of updates we've made to the fifth and sixth editions of *C++ How to Program*:

- **Game Programming.** We've added a new chapter on game programming. The computer-game industry's revenues are already greater than those of the first-run movie business, creating lots of opportunities for students interested in game-programming careers. Chapter 23, Game Programming with Ogre, introduces game programming and graphics with the open source Ogre 3D graphics engine. We discuss basic issues involved in game programming. Then we show how to use Ogre to create a simple game featuring a play mechanic similar to the classic video game Pong®, originally developed by Atari in 1972. We demonstrate how to create a scene with colored 3D graphics, smoothly animate moving objects, use timers to control animation speed, detect collisions between objects, add sound, accept keyboard input and display text output.

- **Future of C++.** We've added Chapter 24, which considers the future of C++—we introduce the Boost C++ Libraries, Technical Report 1 (TR1) and C++0x. The free Boost open source libraries are created by members of the C++ community. Technical Report 1 describes the proposed changes to the C++ Standard Library, many of which are based on current Boost libraries. The C++ Standards Committee is revising the C++ Standard. The main goals for the new standard are to make C++ easier to learn, improve library building capabilities, and increase compatibility with the C programming language. The last standard was published in 1998. Work on the new standard, currently referred to as C++0x, began in 2003. The new standard is likely to be released in 2009. It will include changes to the core language and, most likely, many of the libraries in TR1. We overview the TR1 libraries and provide code examples for the "regular expression" and "smart pointer" libraries. Regular expressions are used to match specific character patterns in text. They can be used to validate data to ensure that it is in a particular format, to replace parts of one string with another, or to split a string. Many common bugs in C and C++ code are related to pointers, a powerful programming capability you'll study in Chapter 8, Pointers and Pointer-Based Strings. Smart pointers help you avoid errors by providing additional functionality to standard pointers.

- **Major Content Revisions.** All the chapters have been significantly updated and upgraded. We tuned the writing for clarity and precision. We also adjusted our use of C++ terminology in accordance with the ISO/IEC C++ standard document that defines the language.

- **Early Classes and Objects Approach.** Students are introduced to the basic concepts and terminology of object technology in Chapter 1 and begin developing customized, reusable classes and objects in Chapter 3. This book presents object-oriented programming, where appropriate, from the start and throughout the text. The early discussion of objects and classes gets students "thinking about objects" immediately and mastering these concepts more completely. Object-oriented programming is not trivial by any means, but it's fun to write object-oriented programs, and students can see immediate results.

- **Integrated Case Studies.** We provide several case studies spanning multiple sections and chapters that often build on a class introduced earlier in the book to demonstrate new programming concepts later in the book. These case studies include the development of the GradeBook class in Chapters 3–7, the Time class in several sections of Chapters 9–10, the Employee class in Chapters 12–13, and the optional OOD/UML ATM case study in Chapters 1–7, 9, 13 and Appendix G.

- **Integrated GradeBook Case Study.** The GradeBook case study reinforces our early classes presentation. It uses classes and objects in Chapters 3–7 to incrementally build a GradeBook class that represents an instructor's grade book and performs various calculations based on a set of student grades, such as calculating the average grade, finding the maximum and minimum, and printing a bar chart.

- **Unified Modeling Language™ 2 (UML 2).** The Unified Modeling Language (UML) has become the preferred graphical modeling language for designers of object-oriented systems. All the UML diagrams in the book comply with the UML 2 specification. We use UML class diagrams to visually represent classes and their inheritance relationships, and we use UML activity diagrams to demonstrate the flow of control in each of C++'s control statements. We make especially heavy use of the UML in the optional OOD/UML ATM case study

- **Optional OOD/UML ATM Case Study.** The optional OOD/UML automated teller machine (ATM) case study in the Software Engineering Case Study sections of Chapters 1–7, 9 and 13 is appropriate for first and second programming courses. The nine case study sections present a carefully paced introduction to object-oriented design using the UML. We introduce a concise, simplified subset of the UML 2, then guide you through a first design experience intended for the novice object-oriented designer/programmer. Our goal in this case study is to help students develop an object-oriented design to complement the object-oriented programming concepts they begin learning in Chapter 1 and implementing in

Chapter 3. The case study was reviewed by a distinguished team of OOD/UML academic and industry professionals. The case study is not an exercise; rather, it is a fully developed end-to-end learning experience that concludes with a detailed walkthrough of the complete 877-line C++ code implementation. We take a detailed tour of the nine sections of this case study later in the Preface.

- **Compilation and Linking Process for Multiple-Source-File Programs.** Chapter 3 includes a detailed diagram and discussion of the compilation and linking process that produces an executable application.

- **Function Call Stack Explanation.** In Chapter 6, we provide a detailed discussion (with illustrations) of the function call stack and activation records to explain how C++ is able to keep track of which function is currently executing, how automatic variables of functions are maintained in memory and how a function knows where to return after it completes execution.

- **C++ Standard Library string and vector Classes.** The string and vector classes are used to make earlier examples more object-oriented.

- **Class string.** We use class string instead of C-like pointer-based char * strings for most string manipulations throughout the book. We continue to include discussions of char * strings in Chapters 8, 10, 11 and 21 to give students practice with pointer manipulations, to illustrate dynamic memory allocation with new and delete, to build our own String class, and to prepare students for working with char * strings in C and C++ legacy code.

- **Class Template vector.** We use class template vector instead of C-like pointer-based array manipulations throughout the book. However, we begin by discussing C-like pointer-based arrays in Chapter 7 to prepare students for working with C and C++ legacy code and to use as a basis for building our own customized Array class in Chapter 11, Operator Overloading; String and Array Objects.

- **Tuned Treatment of Inheritance and Polymorphism.** Chapters 12–13 have been carefully tuned using an Employee class hierarchy to make the treatment of inheritance and polymorphism clearer and more accessible for students who are new to OOP.

- **Discussion and Illustration of How Polymorphism Works "Under the Hood."** Chapter 13 contains a detailed diagram and explanation of how C++ can implement polymorphism, virtual functions and dynamic binding internally. This gives students a solid understanding of how these capabilities really work. More importantly, it helps students appreciate the overhead of polymorphism—in terms of additional memory consumption and processor time. This helps students determine when to use polymorphism and when to avoid it.

- **Standard Template Library (STL).** This might be one of the most important topics in the book in terms of your appreciation of software reuse. The STL defines powerful, template-based, reusable components that implement many common data structures and algorithms used to process those data structures. Chapter 22 introduces the STL and discusses its three key components—containers, iterators and algorithms. We show that using STL components provides tremendous expressive power, often reducing many lines of code to a single statement.

- **ISO/IEC C++ Standard Compliance.** We have audited our presentation against the most recent ISO/IEC C++ standard document for completeness and accuracy. [*Note:* If you need additional technical details on C++, you may want to read the C++ standard document. A PDF copy of the C++ standard (document number INCITS/ISO/IEC 14882-2003) can be purchased at `webstore.ansi.org/ansidocstore/default.asp`.]

- **Debugger Appendices.** We include two Using the Debugger appendices—Appendix I, Using the Visual Studio Debugger, and Appendix J, Using the GNU C++ Debugger.

- **Code Testing on Multiple Platforms.** We tested the code examples on various popular C++ platforms. For the most part, all of the book's examples port easily to all popular standard-compliant compilers.

- **Errors and Warnings Shown for Multiple Platforms.** For programs that intentionally contain errors to illustrate a key concept, we show the error messages that result on several popular platforms.

All of this has been carefully reviewed by distinguished academics and industry developers who worked with us on *C++ How to Program, 5/e* and *C++ How to Program, 6/e.*

We believe that this book and its support materials will provide students and professionals with an informative, interesting, challenging and entertaining C++ educational experience. The book includes a comprehensive suite of ancillary materials that help instructors maximize their students' learning experience.

As you read this book, if you have questions, send an e-mail to `deitel@deitel.com`; we'll respond promptly. For updates on this book and the status of all supporting C++ software, and for the latest news on all Deitel publications and services, visit `www.deitel.com`. Sign up at `www.deitel.com/newsletter/subscribe.html` for the free *Deitel*® *Buzz Online* e-mail newsletter and check out our growing list of C++ and related Resource Centers at `www.deitel.com/ResourceCenters.html`. Each week we announce our latest Resource Centers in the newsletter. Please let us know of other Resource Centers you'd like to see.

Teaching Approach

C++ How to Program, 6/e contains a rich collection of examples. The book concentrates on the principles of good software engineering and stresses program clarity. We teach by example. We are educators who teach leading-edge topics in industry classrooms worldwide. Dr. Harvey M. Deitel has 20 years of college teaching experience and 18 years of industry teaching experience. Paul Deitel has 16 years of industry teaching experience. The Deitels have taught courses at all levels to government, industry, military and academic clients of Deitel & Associates.

Live-Code Approach. *C++ How to Program, 6/e* is loaded with "live-code" examples—by this we mean that each new concept is presented in the context of a complete working C++ application that is immediately followed by one or more actual executions showing the program's inputs and outputs. This style exemplifies the way we teach and write about programming; we call this the "live-code approach."

Syntax Coloring. We syntax color all the C++ code, similar to the way most C++ integrated-development environments and code editors syntax color code. This improves code readability—an important goal, given that this book contains about 20,000 lines of code in complete, working C++ programs. Our syntax-coloring conventions are as follows:

```
comments appear in green
keywords appear in dark blue
errors appear in red
constants and literal values appear in light blue
all other code appears in black
```

Code Highlighting. We place gray rectangles around the key code segments in each program.

Using Fonts and Colors for Emphasis. We place the key terms and the index's page reference for each defining occurrence in bold blue text for easier reference. We emphasize on-screen components in the **bold Helvetica** font (e.g., the **File** menu) and emphasize C++ program text in the Lucida font (e.g., int x = 5).

Web Access. All of the source-code examples for *C++ How to Program, 6/e* are available for download from:

```
www.deitel.com/books/cpphtp6/
```

Site registration is quick and easy. Download all the examples, then run each program as you read the corresponding text discussions. Making changes to the examples and seeing the effects of those changes is a great way to enhance your C++ learning experience.

Objectives. Each chapter begins with a statement of objectives. This lets you know what to expect and gives you an opportunity, after reading the chapter, to determine if you have met the objectives.

Quotations. The learning objectives are followed by quotations. Some are humorous; some are philosophical; others offer interesting insights. We hope that you enjoy relating the quotations to the chapter material.

Outline. The chapter outline helps you approach the material in a top-down fashion, so you can anticipate what is to come and set a comfortable and effective learning pace.

Illustrations/Figures. Abundant charts, tables, line drawings, programs and program output are included. We model the flow of control in control statements with UML activity diagrams. UML class diagrams model the fields, constructors and methods of classes. We make extensive use of six major UML diagram types in the optional OOD/UML 2 ATM case study.

Programming Tips. We include programming tips to help you focus on important aspects of program development. These tips and practices represent the best we have gleaned from a combined six decades of programming and teaching experience. One of our students— a mathematics major—told us that she feels this approach is like the highlighting of axioms, theorems and corollaries in mathematics books; it provides a basis on which to build good software.

Good Programming Practices

Good Programming Practices *call attention to techniques that will help you produce programs that are clearer, more understandable and more maintainable.*

Common Programming Errors

Students tend to make certain kinds of errors frequently. Pointing out these Common Programming Errors *reduces the likelihood that you'll make the same mistakes.*

Error-Prevention Tips

These tips contain suggestions for exposing bugs and removing them from your programs; many describe aspects of C++ that prevent bugs from getting into programs in the first place.

Performance Tips

Students like to "turbo charge" their programs. These tips highlight opportunities for making your programs run faster or minimizing the amount of memory that they occupy.

Portability Tips

We include Portability Tips *to help you write code that will run on a variety of platforms and to explain how C++ achieves its high degree of portability.*

Software Engineering Observations

The Software Engineering Observations *highlight architectural and design issues that affect the construction of software systems, especially large-scale systems.*

Wrap-Up Section. Each of the chapters ends with a brief "wrap-up" section that recaps the chapter content and transitions to the next chapter.

Summary Bullets. Each chapter ends with additional pedagogical features. We present a thorough, bullet-list-style summary of the chapter, section by section.

Terminology. We include an alphabetized list of the important terms defined in each chapter. Each term also appears in the index, with its defining occurrence highlighted with a bold, blue page number.

Self-Review Exercises and Answers. Extensive self-review exercises and answers are included for self-study.

Exercises. Each chapter concludes with a substantial set of exercises including simple recall of important terminology and concepts; identifying the errors in code samples; writing individual C++ statements; writing small portions of functions and classes; writing complete C++ functions, classes and programs; and writing major term projects. The large number of exercises enables instructors to tailor their courses to the unique needs of their students and to vary course assignments each semester. Instructors can use these exercises to form homework assignments, short quizzes, major examinations and term projects. See our Programming Projects Resource Center (www.deitel.com/ProgrammingProjects/) for many additional exercise and project possibilities.

[*NOTE:* **Please do not write to us requesting access to the Prentice Hall Instructor's Resource Center. Access is limited strictly to college instructors teaching from the book. Instructors may obtain access only through their Prentice Hall representatives.**]

Thousands of Index Entries. We have included an extensive index which is especially useful when you use the book as a reference.

"Double Indexing" of C++ Live-Code Examples. For every source-code program in the book, we index the figure caption both alphabetically and as a subindex item under "Examples." This makes it easier to find examples using particular features.

Tour of the Book

You'll now take a tour of the C++ capabilities you'll study in *C++ How to Program, 6/e*. Figure 1 illustrates the dependencies among the chapters. We recommend studying the topics in the order indicated by the arrows, though other orders are possible. This book is widely used in all levels of C++ programming courses. Search the Web for "syllabus," "C++" and "Deitel" to find syllabi used with recent editions of this book.

Chapter 1, Introduction to Computers, the Internet and the World Wide Web, discusses what computers are, how they work and how they are programmed. The chapter gives a brief history of the development of programming languages from machine languages to assembly languages and high-level languages. The origin of the C++ programming language is discussed. The chapter includes an introduction to a typical C++ programming environment. We walk readers through a "test drive" of a typical C++ application on Windows and Linux platforms. This chapter also introduces basic object technology concepts and terminology and the Unified Modeling Language.

Chapter 2, Introduction to C++ Programming, provides a lightweight introduction to programming applications in the C++ programming language. The chapter introduces nonprogrammers to basic programming concepts and constructs. The programs in this chapter illustrate how to display data on the screen and how to obtain data from the user at the keyboard. Chapter 2 ends with detailed treatments of decision making and arithmetic operations.

Chapter 3, Introduction to Classes and Objects, provides a friendly early introduction to classes and objects. Chapter 3 gets students working with object orientation comfortably from the start. It was developed with the guidance of a distinguished team of industry and academic reviewers. We introduce classes, objects, member functions, constructors and data members using a series of simple real-world examples. We develop a well-engineered framework for organizing object-oriented programs in C++. First, we motivate the notion of classes with a simple example. Then we present a carefully paced sequence of seven complete working programs to demonstrate creating and using your own classes. These examples begin our **integrated case study on developing a grade-book class** that instructors can use to maintain student test scores. This case study is enhanced over the next several chapters, culminating with the version presented in Chapter 7, Arrays and Vectors. The GradeBook class case study describes how to define a class and how to use it to create an object. The case study discusses how to declare and define member functions to implement the class's behaviors, how to declare data members to implement the class's attributes and how to call an object's member functions to make them perform their tasks. We introduce C++ Standard Library class string and create string objects to store the name of the course that a GradeBook object represents. Chapter 3 explains the differences between data members of a class and local variables of a function, and how to use a constructor to ensure that an object's data is initialized when the object is created. We

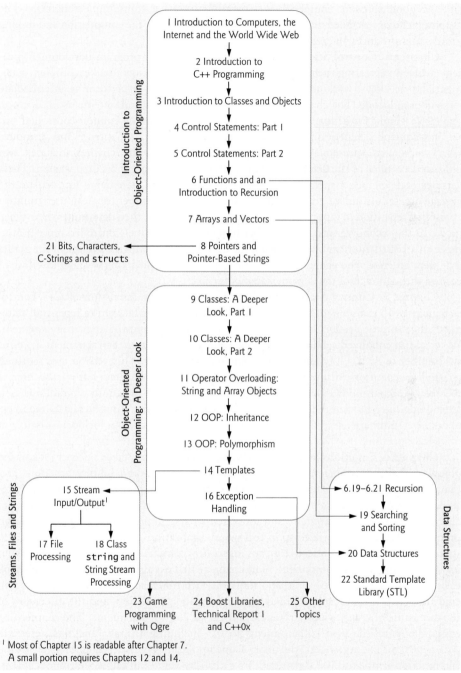

Fig. 1 | *C++ How to Program, 6/e* chapter dependency chart.

show how to promote software reusability by separating a class definition from the client code (e.g., function main) that uses the class. We also introduce another fundamental principle of good software engineering—separating interface from implementation. The chapter includes a detailed diagram and discussion explaining the compilation and linking process that produces an executable application.

Chapter 4, Control Statements: Part 1, focuses on the program-development process involved in creating useful classes. The chapter discusses how to take a problem statement and develop a working C++ program from it, including performing intermediate steps in pseudocode. The chapter introduces some simple control statements for decision making (if and if...else) and repetition (while). We examine counter-controlled and sentinel-controlled repetition using the **GradeBook class** from Chapter 3, and introduce C++'s increment, decrement and assignment operators. The chapter includes **two enhanced versions of the GradeBook class**, each based on Chapter 3's final version. These versions each include a member function that uses control statements to calculate the average of a set of student grades. In the first version, the member function uses counter-controlled repetition to input 10 student grades from the user, then determines the average grade. In the second version, the member function uses sentinel-controlled repetition to input an arbitrary number of grades from the user, then calculates the average of the grades that were entered. The chapter uses simple UML activity diagrams to show the flow of control through each of the control statements.

Chapter 5, Control Statements: Part 2, continues the discussion of C++ control statements with examples of the for repetition statement, the do...while repetition statement, the switch selection statement, the break statement and the continue statement. We create an **enhanced version of class GradeBook** that uses a switch statement to count the number of A, B, C, D and F grades entered by the user. This version uses sentinel-controlled repetition to input the grades. While reading the grades from the user, a member function modifies data members that keep track of the count of grades in each letter grade category. Another member function of the class then uses these data members to display a summary report based on the grades entered. The chapter includes a discussion of logical operators.

Chapter 6, Functions and an Introduction to Recursion, takes a deeper look inside objects and their member functions. We discuss C++ Standard Library functions and examine more closely how students can build their own functions. The techniques presented in Chapter 6 are essential to the production of properly organized programs, especially the kinds of larger programs and software that system programmers and application programmers are likely to develop in real-world applications. The "divide and conquer" strategy is presented as an effective means for solving complex problems by dividing them into simpler interacting components. The chapter's first example continues the **GradeBook class case study** with an example of a function with multiple parameters. Students will enjoy the chapter's treatment of random numbers and simulation, and the discussion of the dice game of craps, which makes elegant use of control statements. The chapter discusses the so-called "C++ enhancements to C," including inline functions, reference parameters, default arguments, the unary scope resolution operator, function overloading and function templates. We also present C++'s call-by-value and call-by-reference capabilities. The header files table introduces many of the header files that you'll use throughout the book. In this new edition, we provide a detailed discussion (with illustrations) of the function call stack and activation records to explain how C++ is able to keep track of which function is currently executing, how automatic variables of functions are maintained in memory and how a function knows where to return after it completes execution. The chapter then offers a solid introduction to recursion and includes a table summarizing the recursion examples and exercises distributed throughout the remainder of the book. Some texts leave recursion for a chapter late in the book; we feel this topic is best covered gradually throughout the text. The extensive collection of exercises at the end of the chapter includes several classic recursion problems, including the Towers of Hanoi.

Chapter 7, Arrays and Vectors, explains how to process lists and tables of values. We discuss the structuring of data in arrays of data items of the same type and demonstrate how arrays facilitate the tasks performed by objects. The early parts of this chapter use C-style, pointer-based arrays, which, as you'll see in Chapter 8, can be treated as pointers to the array contents in memory. We then present arrays as full-fledged objects, introducing the C++ Standard Library vector class template—a robust array data structure. The chapter presents numerous examples of both one-dimensional arrays and two-dimensional arrays. Examples in the chapter investigate various common array manipulations, printing bar charts, sorting data and passing arrays to functions. The chapter includes the **final two GradeBook case study sections**, in which we use arrays to store student grades for the duration of a program's execution. Previous versions of the class process a set of grades entered by the user, but do not maintain the individual grade values in data members of the class. In this chapter, we use arrays to enable an object of the GradeBook class to maintain a set of grades in memory, thus eliminating the need to repeatedly input the same set of grades. The first version of the class stores the grades in a one-dimensional array and can produce a report containing the average of the grades, the minimum and maximum grades and a bar chart representing the grade distribution. The second version (i.e., the final version in the case study) uses a two-dimensional array to store the grades of a number of students on multiple exams in a semester. This version can calculate each student's semester average, as well as the minimum and maximum grades across all grades received for the semester. The class also produces a bar chart displaying the overall grade distribution for the semester. Another key feature of this chapter is the discussion of elementary sorting and searching techniques. The end-of-chapter exercises include a variety of interesting and challenging problems, such as improved sorting techniques, the design of a simple airline reservations system, an introduction to the concept of turtle graphics (made famous in the LOGO language) and the Knight's Tour and Eight Queens problems that introduce the notion of heuristic programming widely employed in the field of artificial intelligence. The exercises conclude with many recursion problems including selection sort, palindromes, linear search, the Eight Queens, printing an array, printing a string backwards and finding the minimum value in an array.

Chapter 8, Pointers and Pointer-Based Strings, presents one of the most powerful features of the C++ language—pointers. The chapter provides detailed explanations of pointer operators, call by reference, pointer expressions, pointer arithmetic, the relationship between pointers and arrays, arrays of pointers and pointers to functions. We demonstrate how to use const with pointers to enforce the principle of least privilege to build more robust software. We discuss using the sizeof operator to determine the size of a data type or data items in bytes during program compilation. There is an intimate relationship between pointers, arrays and C-style strings in C++, so we introduce basic C-style string-manipulation concepts and discuss some of the most popular C-style string-handling functions, such as getline (input a line of text), strcpy and strncpy (copy a string), strcat and strncat (concatenate two strings), strcmp and strncmp (compare two strings), strtok ("tokenize" a string into its pieces) and strlen (return the length of a string). In this new edition, we frequently use string objects (introduced in Chapter 3, Introduction to Classes and Objects) in place of C-style, char * pointer-based strings. However, we include char * strings in Chapter 8 to help you master pointers and prepare for the professional world in which you'll see a great deal of C legacy code that has been implemented over the last three decades. Thus, you'll become familiar with the two most prevalent methods of creating and manipulating strings in C++. Many people find that the topic of pointers is, by far, the most difficult part of an introductory programming course. In C and "raw C++" arrays and strings are pointers to array and string contents in memory (even function names are pointers). Studying this chapter carefully should reward you with a deep understanding of pointers. The chapter is loaded with challenging exercises. The chapter exercises include a simulation of the classic race between the tortoise and the hare, card-shuffling and dealing algorithms, recursive quicksort and recursive maze traversals. A **special section entitled Building Your Own Computer** also is included. This section explains machine-language programming and proceeds with a project involving the design and implementation of a computer simulator that leads the student to write and run machine-language programs. This unique feature of the text will be especially useful to readers who want to understand how computers really work. Our students enjoy this project and often implement substantial enhancements, many of which are suggested in the exercises. A second special section includes challenging string manipulation exercises related to text analysis, word processing, printing dates in various formats, check protection, writing the word equivalent of a check amount, Morse Code and metric-to-English conversions.

   Chapter 9, Classes: A Deeper Look, Part 1, continues our discussion of object-oriented programming. This chapter uses a rich Time class case study to illustrate accessing class members, separating interface from implementation, using access functions and utility functions, initializing objects with constructors, destroying objects with destructors, assignment by default memberwise copy and software reusability. Students learn the order in which constructors and destructors are called during the lifetime of an object. A modification of the Time case study demonstrates the problems that can occur when a member function returns a reference to a private data member, which breaks the encapsulation of the class. The chapter exercises challenge the student to develop classes for times, dates, rectangles and playing tic-tac-toe. Students generally enjoy game-playing programs. Mathematically inclined readers will enjoy the exercises on creating class Complex (for complex numbers), class Rational (for rational numbers) and class HugeInteger (for arbitrarily large integers).

   Chapter 10, Classes: A Deeper Look, Part 2, continues the study of classes and presents additional object-oriented programming concepts. The chapter discusses declaring and using constant objects, constant member functions, composition—the process of building classes that have objects of other classes as members, friend functions and friend classes that have special access rights to the private and protected members of classes, the this pointer, which enables an object to know its own address, dynamic memory allocation, static class members for containing and manipulating class-wide data, examples of popular abstract data types (arrays, strings and queues), container classes and iterators. In our discussion of const objects, we mention keyword mutable which is used in a subtle manner to enable modification of "non-visible" implementation in `const` objects. We discuss dynamic memory allocation using `new` and `delete`. When `new` fails, the program terminates by default because `new` "throws an exception" in standard C++. We motivate the discussion of `static` class members with a video-game-based example. We emphasize how important it is to hide implementation details from clients of a class; then, we discuss proxy classes, which provide a means of hiding implementation (including the `private` data in class headers) from clients of a class. The chapter exercises include developing a savings-account class and a class for holding sets of integers.

Chapter 11, Operator Overloading; String and Array Objects, presents one of the most popular topics in our C++ courses. Students really enjoy this material. They find it a perfect complement to the detailed discussion of crafting valuable classes in Chapters 9 and 10. Operator overloading enables you to tell the compiler how to use existing operators with objects of new types. C++ already knows how to use these operators with objects of built-in types, such as integers, floats and characters. But suppose that we create a new `String` class—what would the plus sign mean when used between `String` objects? Many programmers use plus (+) with strings to mean concatenation. In Chapter 11, you'll learn how to "overload" the plus sign, so when it is written between two `String` objects in an expression, the compiler will generate a function call to an "operator function" that will concatenate the two `String`s. The chapter discusses the fundamentals of operator overloading, restrictions in operator overloading, overloading with class member functions vs. with nonmember functions, overloading unary and binary operators and converting between types. Chapter 11 features a collection of substantial case studies including an array class, a `String` class, a date class, a huge integer class and a complex numbers class (the last two appear with full source code in the exercises). Mathematically inclined students will enjoy creating the `polynomial` class in the exercises. This material is different from most programming languages and courses. Operator overloading is a complex topic, but an enriching one. Using operator overloading wisely helps you add extra "polish" to your classes. The discussions of class `Array` and class `String` are particularly valuable to students who have already used the C++ Standard Library `string` class and `vector` class template that provide similar capabilities. The exercises encourage the student to add operator overloading to classes `Complex`, `Rational` and `HugeInteger` to enable convenient manipulation of objects of these classes with operator symbols—as in mathematics—rather than with function calls as the student did in the Chapter 10 exercises.

Chapter 12, Object-Oriented Programming: Inheritance, introduces one of the most fundamental capabilities of object-oriented programming languages—inheritance: a form of software reusability in which new classes are developed quickly and easily by absorbing the capabilities of existing classes and adding appropriate new capabilities. In the context of an **Employee hierarchy** case study, this substantially revised chapter presents a five-example sequence demonstrating `private` data, `protected` data and good software engineering with inheritance. We begin by demonstrating a class with `private` data members and `public` member functions to manipulate that data. Next, we implement a second class with additional capabilities, intentionally and tediously duplicating much of the first example's code. The third example begins our discussion of inheritance and software reuse—we use the class from the first example as a base class and quickly and simply inherit its data and functionality into a new derived class. This example introduces the inheritance mechanism and demonstrates that a derived class cannot access its base class's `private` members directly. This motivates our fourth example, in which we introduce protected data in the base class and demonstrate that the derived class can indeed access the protected data inherited from the base class. The last example in the sequence demonstrates proper software engineering by defining the base class's data as private and using the base class's public member functions (that were inherited by the derived class) to manipulate the base class's private data in the derived class. The chapter discusses the notions of base classes and derived classes, protected members, public inheritance, protected inheritance, private inheritance, direct base classes, indirect base classes, constructors and destructors in base classes and derived classes, and software engineering with inheritance. The chapter also compares inheritance (the *is-a* relationship) with composition (the *has-a* relationship) and introduces the *uses-a* and *knows-a* relationships.

Chapter 13, Object-Oriented Programming: Polymorphism, deals with another fundamental capability of object-oriented programming: polymorphic behavior. The completely revised Chapter 13 builds on the inheritance concepts presented in Chapter 12 and focuses on the relationships among classes in a class hierarchy and the powerful processing capabilities that these relationships enable. When many classes are related to a common base class through inheritance, each derived-class object may be treated as a base-class object. This enables programs to be written in a simple and general manner independent of the specific types of the derived-class objects. New kinds of objects can be handled by the same program, thus making systems more extensible. Polymorphism enables programs to eliminate complex switch logic in favor of simpler "straight-line" logic. A screen manager of a video game, for example, can send a draw message to every object in a linked list of objects to be drawn. Each object knows how to draw itself. An object of a new class can be added to the program without modifying that program (as long as that new object also knows how to draw itself). The chapter discusses the mechanics of achieving polymorphic behavior via virtual functions. It distinguishes between abstract classes (from which objects cannot be instantiated) and concrete classes (from which objects can be instantiated). Abstract classes are useful for providing an inheritable interface to classes throughout the hierarchy. We demonstrate abstract classes and polymorphic behavior by revisiting the **Employee hierarchy** of Chapter 12. We introduce an abstract Employee base class, from which classes CommissionEmployee, HourlyEmployee and SalariedEmployee inherit directly and class BasePlusCommissionEmployee inherits indirectly. In the past, our professional clients have insisted that we provide a deeper explanation that shows precisely how polymorphism is implemented in C++, and hence, precisely what execution time and memory "costs" are incurred when programming with this powerful capability. We responded by developing an illustration and a precise explanation of the *vtables* (virtual function tables) that the C++ compiler builds automatically to support polymorphism. To conclude, we introduce run-time type information (RTTI) and dynamic casting, which enable a program to determine an object's type at execution time, then act on that object accordingly. Using RTTI and dynamic casting, we give a 10% pay increase to employees of a specific type, then calculate the earnings for such employees. For all other employee types, we calculate their earnings polymorphically.

Chapter 14, Templates, discusses one of C++'s more powerful software reuse features, namely templates. Function templates and class templates enable you to specify, with a single code segment, an entire range of related overloaded functions (called function template specializations) or an entire range of related classes (called class-template specializations). This technique is called generic programming. Function templates were introduced in Chapter 6. This chapter presents additional discussions and examples on function template. We might write a single class template for a stack class, then have C++ generate separate class-template specializations, such as a "stack-of-int" class, a "stack-of-float" class, a "stack-of-string" class and so on. The chapter discusses using type parameters, nontype parameters and default types for class templates. We also discuss the relationships between templates and other C++ features, such as overloading, inheritance, friends and static members. The exercises challenge the student to write a variety of function templates and class templates and to employ these in complete programs. We greatly enhance the treatment of templates in our discussion of the Standard Template Library (STL) containers, iterators and algorithms in Chapter 22.

Chapter 15, Stream Input/Output, contains a comprehensive treatment of standard C++ input/output capabilities. This chapter discusses a range of capabilities sufficient for performing most common I/O operations and overviews the remaining capabilities. Many of the I/O features are object oriented. This style of I/O makes use of other C++ features, such as references, function overloading and operator overloading. The various I/O capabilities of C++, including output with the stream insertion operator, input with the stream extraction operator, type-safe I/O, formatted I/O, unformatted I/O (for performance). Users can specify how to perform I/O for objects of user-defined types by overloading the stream insertion operator (<<) and the stream extraction operator (>>). This extensibility is one of C++'s most valuable features. C++ provides various stream manipulators that perform formatting tasks. This chapter discusses stream manipulators that provide capabilities such as displaying integers in various bases, controlling floating-point precision, setting field widths, displaying decimal point and trailing zeros, justifying output, setting and unsetting format state, setting the fill character in fields. We also present an example that creates user-defined output stream manipulators.

Chapter 16, Exception Handling, discusses how exception handling enables you to write programs that are robust, fault tolerant and appropriate for business-critical and mission-critical environments. The chapter discusses when exception handling is appropriate; introduces the basic capabilities of exception handling with try blocks, throw statements and catch handlers; indicates how and when to rethrow an exception; explains how to write an exception specification and process unexpected exceptions; and discusses the important ties between exceptions and constructors, destructors and inheritance. The exercises in this chapter show the student the diversity and power of C++'s exception-handling capabilities. We discuss rethrowing an exception, and we illustrate how new can fail when memory is exhausted. Many older C++ compilers return 0 by default when new fails. We show the new style of new failing by throwing a bad_alloc (bad allocation) exception. We illustrate how to use function set_new_handler to specify a custom function to be called to deal with memory-exhaustion situations. We discuss how to use the auto_ptr class template to delete dynamically allocated memory implicitly, thus avoiding memory leaks. To conclude this chapter, we present the Standard Library exception hierarchy.

Chapter 17, File Processing, discusses techniques for creating and processing both sequential files and random-access files. The chapter begins with an introduction to the data hierarchy from bits, to bytes, to fields, to records and to files. Next, we present the C++ view of files and streams. We discuss sequential files and build programs that show how to open and close files, how to store data sequentially in a file and how to read data sequentially from a file. We then discuss random-access files and build programs that show how to create a file for random access, how to read and write data to a file with random access and how to read data sequentially from a randomly accessed file. The case study combines the techniques of accessing files both sequentially and randomly into a complete transaction-processing program. Students in our industry seminars have mentioned that, after studying the material on file processing, they were able to produce substantial file-processing programs that were immediately useful in their organizations. The exercises ask the student to implement a variety of programs that build and process both sequential files and random-access files.

Chapter 18, Class `string` and String Stream Processing, The chapter discusses C++'s capabilities for inputting data from strings in memory and outputting data to strings in memory; these capabilities often are referred to as in-core formatting or string stream processing. Class `string` is a required component of the Standard Library. We preserved the treatment of C-like, pointer-based strings in Chapter 8 and later for several reasons. First, it strengthens your understanding of pointers. Second, for the next decade or so, C++ programmers will need to be able to read and modify the enormous amounts of C legacy code that has accumulated over the last quarter of a century—this code processes strings as pointers, as does a large portion of the C++ code that has been written in industry over the last many years. In Chapter 18 we discuss `string` assignment, concatenation and comparison. We show how to determine various `string` characteristics such as a `string`'s size, capacity and whether or not it is empty. We discuss how to resize a `string`. We consider the various "find" functions that enable us to find a substring in a `string` (searching the `string` either forwards or backwards), and we show how to find either the first occurrence or last occurrence of a character selected from a `string` of characters, and how to find the first occurrence or last occurrence of a character that is not in a selected `string` of characters. We show how to replace, erase and insert characters in a `string` and how to convert a `string` object to a C-style `char *` string.

Chapter 19, Searching and Sorting, discusses two of the most important classes of algorithms in computer science. We consider a variety of specific algorithms for each and compare them with regard to their memory consumption and processor consumption (introducing Big O notation, which indicates how hard an algorithm may have to work to solve a problem). Searching data involves determining whether a value (referred to as the search key) is present in the data and, if so, finding the value's location. In the examples and exercises of this chapter, we discuss a variety of searching algorithms, including: binary search and recursive versions of linear search and binary search. Through examples and exercises, Chapter 19 discusses the recursive merge sort, bubble sort, bucket sort and the recursive quicksort.

Chapter 20, Data Structures, discusses the techniques used to create and manipulate dynamic data structures. The chapter begins with discussions of self-referential classes and dynamic memory allocation, then proceeds with a discussion of how to create and maintain various dynamic data structures, including linked lists, queues (or waiting lines), stacks and trees. For each type of data structure, we present complete, working programs and show sample outputs. The chapter also helps the student master pointers. The chapter includes abundant examples that use indirection and double indirection—a particularly difficult concept. One problem when working with pointers is that students have trouble visualizing the data structures and how their nodes are linked together. We have included illustrations that show the links and the sequence in which they are created. The binary-tree example is a superb capstone for the study of pointers and dynamic data structures. This example creates a binary tree, enforces duplicate elimination and introduces recursive preorder, inorder and postorder tree traversals. Students have a genuine sense of accomplishment when they study and implement this example. They particularly appreciate seeing that the inorder traversal prints the node values in sorted order. We include a substantial collection of exercises. A highlight of the exercises is the special section Building Your Own Compiler. The exercises walk the student through the development of an infix-to-postfix-conversion program and a postfix-expression-evaluation program. We then modify the postfix-evaluation algorithm to generate machine-language code. The compiler places this code in a file (using the techniques of Chapter 17). Students then run the machine language produced by their compilers on the software simulators they built in the exercises of Chapter 8! The numerous exercises include recursively searching a list, recursively printing a list backwards, binary-tree node deletion, level-order traversal of a binary tree, printing trees, writing a portion of an optimizing compiler, writing an interpreter, inserting/deleting anywhere in a linked list, implementing lists and queues without tail pointers, analyzing the performance of binary-tree searching and sorting, implementing an indexed-list class and a supermarket simulation that uses queueing. After studying Chapter 20, you are prepared for the treatment of STL containers, iterators and algorithms in Chapter 22. The STL containers are prepackaged, templatized data structures that most programmers will find sufficient for the vast majority of applications they will need to implement. The STL is a giant leap forward in achieving the vision of reuse.

Chapter 21, Bits, Characters, C Strings and structs, presents several important features. This chapter begins by comparing C++ structures to classes, then defining and using C-like structures. We show how to declare structures, initialize structures and pass structures to functions. The chapter features a high-performance card-shuffling and dealing simulation. This is an excellent opportunity for the instructor to emphasize the quality of algorithms. C++'s powerful bit-manipulation capabilities enable you to write programs that exercise lower-level hardware capabilities. This helps programs process bit strings, set individual bits and store information more compactly. Such capabilities, often found only in low-level assembly languages, are valued by programmers writing system software, such as operating systems and networking software. As you recall, we introduced C-style char * string manipulation in Chapter 8 and presented the most popular string-manipulation functions. In Chapter 22, we continue our presentation of characters and C-style char * strings. We present the various character-manipulation capabilities of the <cctype> library—such as the ability to test a character to determine whether it is a digit, an alphabetic character, an alphanumeric character, a hexadecimal digit, a lowercase letter or an uppercase letter. We present the remaining string-manipulation functions of the various string-related libraries; as always, every function is presented in the context of a complete, working C++ program. The numerous exercises encourage the student to try out most of the capabilities discussed in the chapter. The feature exercise leads the student through the development of a spelling-checker program. This chapter presents a deeper treatment of C-like char * strings for the benefit of C++ programmers who are likely to work with C legacy code.

Chapter 22, Standard Template Library (STL), Throughout this book, we discuss the importance of software reuse. Recognizing that many data structures and algorithms are commonly used by C++ programmers, the C++ standard committee added the Standard Template Library (STL) to the C++ Standard Library. The STL defines powerful, template-based, reusable components that implement many common data structures and algorithms used to process those data structures. The STL offers proof of concept for generic programming with templates—introduced in Chapter 14 and demonstrated in detail in Chapter 20. This chapter introduces the STL and discusses its three key components—containers (popular templatized data structures), iterators and algorithms. The STL containers are data structures capable of storing objects of any data type. We'll see that there are three container categories—first-class containers, adapters and near containers. STL iterators, which have similar properties to those of pointers, are used by programs to manipulate the STL-container elements. In fact, standard arrays can be manipulated as STL containers, using standard pointers as iterators. We'll see that manipulating containers with iterators is convenient and provides tremendous expressive power when combined with STL algorithms—in some cases, reducing many lines of code to a single statement. STL algorithms are functions that perform common data manipulations such as searching, sorting and comparing elements (or entire containers). There are approximately 70 algorithms implemented in the STL. Most of these use iterators to access container elements. We'll see that each first-class container supports specific iterator types, some of which are more powerful than others. A container's supported iterator type determines whether the container can be used with a specific algorithm. Iterators encapsulate the mechanism used to access container elements. This encapsulation enables many of the STL algorithms to be applied to several containers without regard for the underlying container implementation. As long as a container's iterators support the minimum requirements of the algorithm, then the algorithm can process that container's elements. This also enables you to create algorithms that can process the elements of multiple different container types. Chapter 20 discusses how to implement data structures with pointers, classes and dynamic memory. Pointer-based code is complex, and the slightest omission or oversight can lead to serious memory-access violations and memory-leak errors with no compiler complaints. Implementing additional data structures such as deques, priority queues, sets, maps, etc. requires substantial additional work. In addition, if many programmers on a large project implement similar containers and algorithms for different tasks, the code becomes difficult to modify, maintain and debug. An advantage of the STL is that you can reuse the STL containers, iterators and algorithms to implement common data representations and manipulations. This reuse results in substantial development-time and resource savings. This is a friendly, accessible chapter that should convince you of the value of the STL and encourage further study.

Chapter 23, Game Programming with Ogre, introduces game programming with 3D graphics using Ogre (Object-oriented Graphics Rendering Engine). Ogre is one of the leading open source graphics engines. It has been used in commercial applications including several computer games. We discuss the basic concepts of 3D game programming including graphics, 3D models, sound, user input, collision detection and controlling game speed. We provide a complete working example of a simple game featuring a play mechanic similar to the classic video game Pong®, originally developed by Atari in 1972. The chapter walks through the example, explaining key concepts and functions as they are encountered. We discuss the various resources used by Ogre and how to create them using scripts. Students will learn how to move, position and resize objects in a 3D environment, perform simple collision detection, display text within the game and respond to user input from the keyboard. We also demonstrate how to use OgreAL, a wrapper for the OpenAL audio library, to add sound effects to the game.

Chapter 24, Boost Libraries, Technical Report 1 and C++0x, focuses on the future of C++. We introduce the Boost Libraries, a collection of free, open source C++ libraries. The Boost libraries are carefully designed to work well with the C++ Standard Library. We then discuss Technical Report 1 (TR1), a description of proposed changes and additions to the Standard Library. Many of the libraries in TR1 were derived from libraries currently in Boost. The chapter briefly describes all the libraries included in TR1. We provide in-depth code examples for two of the most useful libraries, `Boost.Regex` and `Boost.Smart_ptr`. The `Boost.Regex` library provides support for regular expressions. We demonstrate how to use the library to search a string for matches to a regular expression, validate data, replace parts of a string and split a string into tokens. The `Boost.Smart_ptr` library provides smart pointers to help manage dynamically allocated memory. We discuss the two types of smart pointers included in TR1—`shared_ptr` and `weak_ptr`. We provide examples to demonstrate how these can be used to avoid common memory management errors. This chapter also discusses the upcoming release of the new standard for C++, currently referred to as C++0x. We describe the goals for the new standard and overview the core language changes most likely to be standardized.

Chapter 25, Other Topics, is a collection of miscellaneous C++ topics. This chapter discusses one additional cast operator—`const_cast`. This operator, along with `static_cast` (Chapter 5), `dynamic_cast` (Chapter 13) and `reinterpret_cast` (Chapter 17), provide a more robust mechanism for converting between types than do the original cast operators C++ inherited from C (which are now deprecated). We discuss namespaces, a feature particularly crucial for software developers who build substantial systems, especially for those who build systems from class libraries. Namespaces prevent naming collisions, which can hinder such large software efforts. The Chapter discusses the operator keywords, which are useful for programmers who have keyboards that do not support certain characters used in operator symbols, such as !, &, ^, ~ and |. These keywords can also be used by programmers who do not like cryptic operator symbols. We discuss keyword `mutable`, which allows a member of a const object to be changed. Previously, this was accomplished by "casting away const-ness", which is considered a dangerous practice. We also discuss pointer-to-member operators .* and ->*, multiple inheritance (including the problem of "diamond inheritance") and `virtual` base classes.

Appendix A, Operator Precedence and Associativity Chart, presents the complete set of C++ operator symbols, in which each operator appears on a line by itself with its operator symbol, its name and its associativity.

Appendix B, ASCII Character Set. All the programs in this book use the ASCII character set, which is presented in this appendix.

Appendix C, Fundamental Types, lists C++'s fundamental types.

Appendix D, Number Systems, discusses the binary, octal, decimal and hexadecimal number systems. It considers how to convert numbers between bases and explains the one's complement and two's complement binary representations.

Appendix E, C Legacy Code Topics, presents additional material including several advanced topics not ordinarily covered in introductory courses. We show how to redirect program input to come from a file, redirect program output to be placed in a file, redirect the output of one program to be the input of another program (piping) and append the output of a program to an existing file. We develop functions that use variable-length argument lists and show how to pass command-line arguments to function main and use them in a program. We discuss how to compile programs whose components are spread across multiple files, register functions with atexit to be executed at program termination and terminate program execution with function exit. We also discuss the const and volatile type qualifiers, specifying the type of a numeric constant using the integer and floating-point suffixes, using the signal-handling library to trap unexpected events, creating and using dynamic arrays with calloc and realloc, using unions as a space-saving technique and using linkage specifications when C++ programs are to be linked with legacy C code. As the title suggests, this appendix is intended primarily for C++ programmers who will be working with C legacy code as most C++ programmers are almost certain to do at one point in their careers.

Appendix F, Preprocessor, discusses the preprocessor's directives. The appendix includes more complete information on the #include directive, which causes a copy of a specified file to be included in place of the directive before the file is compiled and the #define directive that creates symbolic constants and macros. The appendix explains conditional compilation, which enables you to control the execution of preprocessor directives and the compilation of program code. The # operator that converts its operand to a string and the ## operator that concatenates two tokens are discussed. The various predefined preprocessor symbolic constants (__LINE__, __FILE__, __DATE__, __STDC__, __TIME__ and __TIMESTAMP__) are presented. Finally, macro assert of the header file <cassert> is discussed, which is valuable in program testing, debugging, verification and validation.

Appendix G, ATM Case Study Code, contains the implementation of our case study on object-oriented design with the UML. This appendix is discussed in the overview of the case study (presented shortly).

Appendix H, UML 2: Additional Diagram Types, overviews the UML 2 diagram types that are not found in the OOD/UML Case Study.

Appendix I, Using the Visual Studio Debugger, demonstrates key features of the Visual Studio Debugger, which allows a programmer to monitor the execution of applications to locate and remove logic errors. The appendix presents step-by-step instructions, so students learn how to use the debugger in a hands-on manner.

Appendix J, Using the GNU C++ Debugger, demonstrates key features of the GNU C++ Debugger, which allows a programmer to monitor the execution of applications to locate and remove logic errors. The appendix presents step-by-step instructions, so students learn how to use the debugger in a hands-on manner.

Bibliography. The Bibliography lists many books and articles to encourage the student to do further reading on C++ and OOP.

Index. The comprehensive index enables you to locate by keyword any term or concept throughout the text.

Object-Oriented Design of an ATM with the UML: A Tour of the Optional Software Engineering Case Study

In this section, we tour the book's optional case study of object-oriented design with the UML. This tour previews the contents of the nine Software Engineering Case Study sections (in Chapters 1–7, 9 and 13). After completing this case study, you'll be thoroughly familiar with a carefully reviewed object-oriented design and implementation for a significant C++ application.

The design presented in the ATM case study was developed at Deitel & Associates, Inc. and scrutinized by a distinguished developmental review team of industry professionals and academics. We crafted this design to meet the requirements of introductory course sequences. Real ATM systems used by banks and their customers worldwide are based on more sophisticated designs that take into consideration many more issues than we have addressed here. Our primary goal throughout the design process was to create a simple design that would be clear to OOD and UML novices, while still demonstrating key OOD concepts and the related UML modeling techniques. We worked hard to keep the design and the code relatively small so that it would work well in the introductory course sequence.

Section 1.21, Software Engineering Case Study: Introduction to Object Technology and the UML—introduces the object-oriented design case study with the UML. The section introduces the basic concepts and terminology of object technology, including classes, objects, encapsulation, inheritance and polymorphism. We discuss the history of the UML. This is the only required section of the case study.

Section 2.8, (Optional) Software Engineering Case Study: Examining the ATM Requirements Specification—discusses a *requirements specification* that specifies the requirements for a system that we'll design and implement—the software for a simple automated teller machine (ATM). We investigate the structure and behavior of object-oriented systems in general. We discuss how the UML will facilitate the design process in subsequent Software Engineering Case Study sections by providing several additional types of diagrams to model our system. We include a list of URLs and book references on object-oriented design with the UML. We discuss the interaction between the ATM system specified by the requirements specification and its user. Specifically, we investigate the scenarios that may occur between the user and the system itself—these are called *use cases*. We model these interactions, using *use case diagrams* of the UML.

Section 3.11, (Optional) Software Engineering Case Study: Identifying the Classes in the ATM Requirements Specification—begins to design the ATM system. We identify its classes, or "building blocks," by extracting the nouns and noun phrases from the requirements specification. We arrange these classes into a UML class diagram that describes the class structure of our simulation. The class diagram also describes relationships, known as *associations*, among classes.

Section 4.13, (Optional) Software Engineering Case Study: Identifying Class Attributes in the ATM System—focuses on the attributes of the classes discussed in Section 3.11. A class contains both *attributes* (data) and *operations* (behaviors). As we'll see in later sections, changes in an object's attributes often affect the object's behavior. To determine the attributes for the classes in our case study, we extract the adjectives describing the nouns and noun phrases (which defined our classes) from the requirements specification, then place the attributes in the class diagram we created in Section 3.11.

Section 5.11, (Optional) Software Engineering Case Study: Identifying Objects' States and Activities in the ATM System—discusses how an object, at any given time, occupies a specific condition called a *state*. A *state transition* occurs when that object receives a message to change state. The UML provides the *state machine diagram*, which identifies the set of possible states that an object may occupy and models that object's state transitions. An object also has an *activity*—the work it performs in its lifetime. The UML provides the *activity diagram*—a flowchart that models an object's activity. In this section, we use both types of diagrams to begin modeling specific behavioral aspects of our ATM system, such as how the ATM carries out a withdrawal transaction and how the ATM responds when the user is authenticated.

Section 6.22, (Optional) Software Engineering Case Study: Identifying Class Operations in the ATM System—identifies the operations, or services, of our classes. We extract from the requirements specification the verbs and verb phrases that specify the operations for each class. We then modify the class diagram of Section 3.11 to include each operation with its associated class. At this point in the case study, we will have gathered all information possible from the requirements specification. However, as future chapters introduce such topics as inheritance, we'll modify our classes and diagrams.

Section 7.12, (Optional) Software Engineering Case Study: Collaboration Among Objects in the ATM System—provides a "rough sketch" of the model for our ATM system. In this section, we see how it works. We investigate the behavior of the simulation by discussing *collaborations*—messages that objects send to each other to communicate. The class operations that we discovered in Section 6.22 turn out to be the collaborations among the objects in our system. We determine the collaborations, then collect them into a *communication diagram*—the UML diagram for modeling collaborations. This diagram reveals which objects collaborate and when. We present a communication diagram of the collaborations among objects to perform an ATM balance inquiry. We then present the UML *sequence diagram* for modeling interactions in a system. This diagram emphasizes the chronological ordering of messages. A sequence diagram models how objects in the system interact to carry out withdrawal and deposit transactions.

Section 9.11, (Optional) Software Engineering Case Study: Starting to Program the Classes of the ATM System—takes a break from designing the system's behavior. We begin the implementation process to emphasize the material discussed in Chapter 9. Using the UML class diagram of Section 3.11 and the attributes and operations discussed in Section 4.13 and Section 6.22, we show how to implement a class in C++ from a design. We do not implement all classes—because we have not completed the design process. Working from our UML diagrams, we create code for the Withdrawal class.

Section 13.10, (Optional) Software Engineering Case Study: Incorporating Inheritance into the ATM System—continues our discussion of object-oriented programming. We consider inheritance—classes sharing common characteristics may inherit attributes and operations from a "base" class. In this section, we investigate how our ATM system can benefit from using inheritance. We document our discoveries in a class diagram that models inheritance relationships—the UML refers to these relationships as *generalizations*. We modify the class diagram of Section 3.11 by using inheritance to group classes with similar characteristics. This section concludes the design of the model portion of our simulation. We fully implement this model in 877 lines of C++ code in Appendix G.

Appendix G, ATM Case Study Code—The majority of the case study involves designing the model (i.e., the data and logic) of the ATM system. In this appendix, we implement that model in C++. Using all the UML diagrams we created, we present the C++ classes necessary to implement the model. We apply the concepts of object-oriented design with the UML and object-oriented programming in C++ that you learned in the chapters. By the end of this appendix, students will have completed the design and implementation of a real-world system, and should feel confident tackling larger systems, such as those that professional software engineers build.

Appendix H, UML 2: Additional Diagram Types—Overviews the UML 2 diagram types that are not found in the OOD/UML Case Study.

Student Resources Included with *C++ How to Program, 6/e*

Many C++ development tools are available. We wrote *C++ How to Program, 6/e* primarily using Microsoft's free Visual C++ Express Edition (which is included on the CD that accompanies this book) and the free GNU C++, which is already installed on most Linux systems and can be installed on Mac OS X systems as well. You can learn more about Visual C++ Express at `msdn.microsoft.com/vstudio/express/visualc`. You can learn more about GNU C++ at `gcc.gnu.org`. Apple includes GNU C++ in their Xcode development tools, which Max OS X users can download from `developer.apple.com/tools/xcode`.

Additional resources and software downloads are available in our C++ Resource Center:

    www.deitel.com/cplusplus/

and at the website for this book:

    www.deitel.com/books/cpphtp6/

For a list of other compilers that are available free for download, visit the following sites:

    www.thefreecountry.com/developercity/ccompilers.shtml
    www.compilers.net

Warnings and Error Messages on Older C++ Compilers
The programs in this book are designed to be used with compilers that support standard C++. However, there are variations among compilers that may cause occasional warnings or errors. In addition, though the standard specifies various situations that require errors to be generated, it does not specify the messages that compilers should issue. Warnings and error messages vary among compilers—this is normal.

Some older C++ compilers, such as Microsoft Visual C++ 6, Borland C++ 5.5 and various earlier versions of GNU C++ generate error or warning messages in places where newer compilers do not. Although most of the examples in this book will work with these older compilers, there are a few examples that need minor modifications to work with older compilers.

Notes Regarding **using** *Declarations and C Standard Library Functions*
The C++ Standard Library includes the functions from the C Standard Library. According to the C++ standard document, the contents of the header files that come from the C Standard Library are part of the "`std`" namespace. Some compilers (old and new) generate error messages when `using` declarations are encountered for C functions.

C++ Multimedia Cyber Classroom, 6/e

C++ How to Program, 6/e includes a free, web-based, audio-intensive interactive multimedia ancillary to the book—*The C++ Multimedia Cyber Classroom, 6/e*—available with new books purchased from Prentice Hall. If you have a used book, you can purchase standalone access to the *Cyber Classroom* at MyPearsonStore.com. Our Web-based *Cyber Classroom* includes audio walkthroughs of code examples in Chapters 1–14, solutions to about half of the exercises in the book, a lab manual and more. For more information about the web-based *Cyber Classroom*, please visit

> www.prenhall.com/deitel/cyberclassroom/

Students who use our Cyber Classrooms like its interactivity and reference capabilities. Professors tell us that their students enjoy using the Cyber Classroom and consequently spend more time on the courses, mastering more of the material than in textbook-only courses.

Instructor Resources for C++ *How to Program, 6/e*

C++ How to Program, 6/e has extensive instructor resources. The Prentice Hall *Instructor's Resource Center* contains the *Solutions Manual* with solutions to the vast majority of the end-of-chapter exercises, a *Test Item File* of multiple-choice questions (approximately two per book section) and PowerPoint® slides containing all the code and figures in the text, plus bulleted items that summarize the key points in the text. Instructors can customize the slides. If you are not already a registered faculty member, contact your Prentice Hall representative or visit vig.prenhall.com/replocator/.

Deitel® *Buzz Online* Free E-mail Newsletter

Each week, the *Deitel® Buzz Online* newsletter announces our latest Resource Center(s) and includes commentary on industry trends and developments, links to free articles and resources from our published books and upcoming publications, product-release schedules, errata, challenges, anecdotes, information on our corporate instructor-led training courses and more. It's also a good way for you to keep posted about issues related to *C++ How to Program, 6/e*. To subscribe, visit

> www.deitel.com/newsletter/subscribe.html

The Deitel Online Resource Centers

Our website www.deitel.com provides Resource Centers on various topics including programming languages, software, Web 2.0, Internet business and open source projects (Fig. 2). The Resource Centers evolved out of the research we've done for our books and business endeavors. We've found many exceptional resources including tutorials, documentation, software downloads, articles, blogs, videos, code samples, books, e-books and more. Most of them are free. In the spirit of Web 2.0, we share these resources with the worldwide community. The Deitel Resource Centers are a starting point for your own research. We help you wade through the vast amount of content on the Internet by providing links to the most valuable resources. Each week we announce our latest Resource Centers in our newsletter, the *Deitel® Buzz Online* (www.deitel.com/newsletter/subscribe.html). The following Resource Centers may be of interest to you as you study *C++ How to Program, 6/e*:

- C++
- C++ Boost Libraries

Deitel Resource Centers

Programming
.NET
.NET 3.0
Ajax
Apex On-Demand Programming Language
ASP.NET
C
C#
C++
C++ Boost Libraries
C++ Game Programming
Code Search Engines and Code Sites
Computer Game Programming
CSS 2.1
Flash 9
Flex
Java
Java Certification and Assessment Testing
Java Design Patterns
Java EE 5
Java SE 6
JavaFX
JavaScript
OpenGL
Perl
PHP
Programming Projects
Python
Ruby
Silverlight
Visual Basic
Visual C++
Web Services
Web 3D Technologies
XML

Software
Apache
DotNetNuke (DNN)
Eclipse
Firefox
Internet Explorer 7

Linux
MySQL
Open Source
Search Engines
Wikis
Windows Vista

Microsoft
.NET
.NET 3.0
ASP.NET
C#
DotNetNuke (DNN)
Internet Explorer 7
Silverlight
Visual Basic
Visual C++
Windows Vista

Java
Java
Java Certification and Assessment Testing
Java Design Patterns
Java EE 5
Java SE 6
JavaFX
JavaScript

Web 2.0
Alert Services
Attention Economy
Blogging
Building Web Communities
Community Generated Content
Google Base
Google Video
Google Web Toolkit
Internet Video
Joost
Mashups
Microformats
Ning
Recommender Systems
RSS

Skype
Social Media
Social Networking
Software as a Service (SaaS)
Virtual Worlds
Web 2.0
Web 3.0
Widgets
Wikis

Internet Business
Affiliate Programs
Google Adsense
Google Analytics
Google Services
Internet Advertising
Internet Business Initiative
Internet Public Relations
Link Building
Podcasting
Search Engine Optimization
Sitemaps
Web Analytics
Website Monetization

Open Source
Apache
DotNetNuke (DNN)
Eclipse
Firefox
Linux
MySQL
Open Source
Perl
PHP
Python
Ruby

Other Topics
Computer Games
Computing Jobs
Gadgets and Gizmos
Sudoku

Fig. 2 | Deitel Resource Centers.

- C++ Game Programming
- Code Search Engines and Code Sites
- Computer Game Programming
- Computing Jobs
- Open Source
- Programming Projects
- Eclipse
- Linux
- .NET
- Windows Vista

Acknowledgments

It is a great pleasure to acknowledge the efforts of many people whose names may not appear on the cover, but whose hard work, cooperation, friendship and understanding were crucial to the production of the book. Many people at Deitel & Associates, Inc. devoted long hours to this project—thanks especially to Abbey Deitel and Barbara Deitel.

We'd also like to thank one of the participants in our Honors Internship program who contributed to this publication—Greg Ayer, a computer science major at Northeastern University.

We are fortunate to have worked on this project with the talented and dedicated team of publishing professionals at Prentice Hall. We appreciate the extraordinary efforts of Marcia Horton, Editorial Director of Prentice Hall's Engineering and Computer Science Division. Carole Snyder and Dolores Mars did an extraordinary job recruiting the book's review team and managing the review process. Francesco Santalucia (an independent artist) and Kristine Carney of Prentice Hall did a wonderful job designing the book's cover; we provided the concept, and they made it happen. Vince O'Brien, Scott Disanno, Bob Engelhardt and Marta Samsel did a marvelous job managing the book's production.

We wish to acknowledge the efforts of our reviewers. Adhering to a tight time schedule, they scrutinized the text and the programs, providing countless suggestions for improving the accuracy and completeness of the presentation.

We sincerely appreciate the efforts of our fifth edition post-publication reviewers and our sixth edition reviewers:

C++ How to Program 6/e Reviewers
Academic and Industry Reviewers: Dr. Richard Albright (Goldey-Beacom College), William B. Higdon (University of Indianapolis), Howard Hinnant (Apple), Anne B. Horton (Lockheed Martin), Terrell Hull (Logicalis Integration Solutions), Rex Jaeschke (Independent Consultant), Maria Jump (The University of Texas at Austin), Geoffrey S. Knauth (GNU), Don Kostuch (Independent Consultant), Colin Laplace (Freelance Software Consultant), Stephan T. Lavavej (Microsoft), Amar Raheja (California State Polytechnic University, Pomona), G. Anthony Reina (University of Maryland University College, Europe), Daveed Vandevoorde (C++ Standards Committee), Jeffrey Wiener (DEKA Research & Development Corporation, New Hampshire Community Technical College), and Chad Willwerth (University of Washington, Tacoma). **Ogre Reviewers:** Casey Bor-

ders (Sensis Corp.), Gregory Junker (Author of *Pro OGRE3D Programming*, Apress Books), Mark Pope (THQ, Inc.), and Steve Streeting (Torus Knot Software, Ltd.). **Boost/C++OX Reviewers:** Edward Brey (Kohler Co.), Jeff Garland (Boost.org), Douglas Gregor (Indiana University), and Björn Karlsson (Author of *Beyond the C++ Standard Library: An Introduction to Boost*, Addison-Wesley/Readsoft, Inc.).

C++ How to Program 5/e Reviewers
Academic Reviewers: Richard Albright (Goldey-Beacom College), Karen Arlien (Bismarck State College), David Branigan (DeVry University, Illinois), Jimmy Chen (Salt Lake Community College), Martin Dulberg (North Carolina State University), Ric Heishman (Northern Virginia Community College), Richard Holladay (San Diego Mesa College), William Honig (Loyola University), Earl LaBatt (OPNET Technologies, Inc./University of New Hampshire), Brian Larson (Modesto Junior College), Robert Myers (Florida State University), Gavin Osborne (Saskatchewan Institute of Applied Science and Technology), Wolfgang Pelz (The University of Akron), and Donna Reese (Mississippi State University). **Industry Reviewers:** Curtis Green (Boeing Integrated Defense Systems), Mahesh Hariharan (Microsoft), James Huddleston (Independent Consultant), Ed James-Beckham (Borland Software Corporation), Don Kostuch (Independent Consultant), Meng Lee (Hewlett-Packard), Kriang Lerdsuwanakij (Siemens Limited), William Mike Miller (Edison Design Group, Inc.), Mark Schimmel (Borland International), Vicki Scott (Metrowerks), James Snell (Boeing Integrated Defense Systems), and Raymond Stephenson (Microsoft). **OOD/UML Optional Software Engineering Case Study Reviewers:** Sinan Si Alhir (Independent Consultant), Karen Arlien (Bismarck State College), David Branigan (DeVry University, Illinois), Martin Dulberg (North Carolina State University), Ric Heishman (Northern Virginia Community College), Richard Holladay (San Diego Mesa College), Earl LaBatt (OPNET Technologies, Inc./University of New Hampshire), Brian Larson (Modesto Junior College), Gavin Osborne (Saskatchewan Institute of Applied Science and Technology), Praveen Sadhu (Infodat International, Inc.), Cameron Skinner (Embarcadero Technologies, Inc./OMG), and Steve Tockey (Construx Software).

These reviewers scrutinized every aspect of the text and made countless suggestions for improving the accuracy and completeness of the presentation.

Well, there you have it! Welcome to the exciting world of C++ and object-oriented programming. We hope you enjoy this look at contemporary computer programming. Good luck! As you read the book, we would sincerely appreciate your comments, criticisms, corrections and suggestions for improving the text. Please address all correspondence to:

deitel@deitel.com

We'll respond promptly, and post corrections and clarifications on:

www.deitel.com/books/cpphtp6/

We hope you enjoy reading *C++ How to Program, Sixth Edition* as much as we enjoyed writing it!

Paul J. Deitel
Dr. Harvey M. Deitel
Maynard, Massachusetts
July 2007

About the Authors

Paul J. Deitel, CEO and Chief Technical Officer of Deitel & Associates, Inc., is a graduate of MIT's Sloan School of Management, where he studied Information Technology. He holds the Java Certified Programmer and Java Certified Developer certifications, and has been designated by Sun Microsystems as a Java Champion. Through Deitel & Associates, Inc., he has delivered Java, C, C++, C# and Visual Basic courses to industry clients, including IBM, Sun Microsystems, Dell, Lucent Technologies, Fidelity, NASA at the Kennedy Space Center, the National Severe Storm Laboratory, White Sands Missile Range, Rogue Wave Software, Boeing, Stratus, Cambridge Technology Partners, Open Environment Corporation, One Wave, Hyperion Software, Adra Systems, Entergy, CableData Systems, Nortel Networks, Puma, iRobot, Invensys and many more. He has also lectured on Java and C++ for the Boston Chapter of the Association for Computing Machinery. He and his father, Dr. Harvey M. Deitel, are the world's best-selling programming language textbook authors.

  Dr. Harvey M. Deitel, Chairman and Chief Strategy Officer of Deitel & Associates, Inc., has 45 years of academic and industry experience in the computer field. Dr. Deitel earned B.S. and M.S. degrees from the MIT and a Ph.D. from Boston University. He has 20 years of college teaching experience, including earning tenure and serving as the Chairman of the Computer Science Department at Boston College before founding Deitel & Associates, Inc., with his son, Paul J. Deitel. He and Paul are the co-authors of several dozen books and multimedia packages and they are writing many more. With translations published in Japanese, German, Russian, Spanish, Traditional Chinese, Simplified Chinese, Korean, French, Polish, Italian, Portuguese, Greek, Urdu and Turkish, the Deitels' texts have earned international recognition. Dr. Deitel has delivered hundreds of professional seminars to major corporations, academic institutions, government organizations and the military.

About Deitel & Associates, Inc.

Deitel & Associates, Inc., is an internationally recognized corporate training and content-creation organization specializing in computer programming languages, Internet and World Wide Web software technology, object technology education and Internet business development through its Internet Business Initiative. The company provides instructor-led courses on major programming languages and platforms, such as C++, Java, Advanced Java, C, C#, Visual C++, Visual Basic, XML, Perl, Python, object technology and Internet and World Wide Web programming. The founders of Deitel & Associates, Inc., are Dr. Harvey M. Deitel and Paul J. Deitel. The company's clients include many of the world's largest companies, government agencies, branches of the military, and academic institutions. Through its 30-year publishing partnership with Prentice Hall, Deitel & Associates, Inc. publishes leading-edge programming textbooks, professional books, interactive multimedia *Cyber Classrooms*, *Complete Training Courses*, Web-based training courses and e-content for the popular course management systems WebCT, Blackboard and Pearson's CourseCompass. Deitel & Associates, Inc., and the authors can be reached via e-mail at:

    deitel@deitel.com

To learn more about Deitel & Associates, Inc., its publications and its worldwide *Dive Into*® Series Corporate Training curriculum, visit:

www.deitel.com

and subscribe to the free *Deitel*® *Buzz Online* e-mail newsletter at:

www.deitel.com/newsletter/subscribe.html

Check out the growing list of online Deitel Resource Centers at:

www.deitel.com/resourcecenters.html

Individuals wishing to purchase Deitel publications can do so through:

www.deitel.com/books/index.html

Bulk orders by corporations, the government, the military and academic institutions should be placed directly with Prentice Hall. For more information, visit

www.prenhall.com/mischtm/support.html#order

Before You Begin

Please follow the instructions in this section to download the book's examples before you begin using this book.

Downloading the C++ *How to Program, 6/e* Example Code

The examples for *C++ How To Program, Sixth Edition* can be downloaded as a ZIP archive file from www.deitel.com/books/cpphtp6/. After you register and log in, click the link for the examples under **Download Code Examples and Other Premium Content for Registered Users**. Save the ZIP file to a location that you'll remember. Extract the example files to your hard disk using a ZIP file extractor program, such as WinZip (www.winzip.com). [*Note:* If you are working in a computer lab, please consult your instructor to determine where you can save the example code.]

Installing/Choosing a Compiler

The CD that accompanies this book includes the version of Microsoft® Visual C++® Express integrated development environment (IDE) that was available at the time of this printing. To get the most recent release of this IDE, visit msdn.microsoft.com/vstudio/express/visualc/default.aspx.

If you have a computer running Windows XP or Windows Vista, you can install Visual C++ Express to edit, compile, execute, debug and modify your programs. When you insert the CD in your computer, the Visual C++ Express installation program will start automatically. Follow the on-screen instructions to install Visual C++ Express. We recommend that you use the default installation options and select the option to install the documentation as well.

If your computer has Linux or Mac OS X, then you probably already have the GNU C++ command-line compiler installed. There are many other C++ compilers and IDEs. We provide links to various free C++ development tools for Windows, Linux and Mac OS X platforms in our C++ Resource Center at

    www.deitel.com/cplusplus/

This Resource Center also links to online tutorials that will help you get started with various C++ development tools.

You are now ready to begin your C++ studies with *C++ How to Program*. We hope you enjoy the book! You can reach us easily at deitel@deitel.com. If you have any questions, please feel free to email us at deitel@deitel.com. We'll respond promptly.

1

Introduction to Computers, the Internet and the World Wide Web

OBJECTIVES

In this chapter you will learn:

- Basic hardware and software concepts.
- Object-technology concepts, such as classes, objects, attributes, behaviors, encapsulation and inheritance.
- The different types of programming languages.
- A typical C++ program development environment.
- The history of the industry-standard object-oriented system modeling language, the UML.
- The history of the Internet and the World Wide Web, and the Web 2.0 phenomenon.
- To test-drive C++ applications in two popular C++ environments—GNU C++ running on Linux and Microsoft's Visual C++® on Windows® XP.
- What open source is, and two popular C++ open source libraries—Ogre for graphics and game programming, and Boost for broadly enhancing the capabilities of the C++ Standard Library.

1.1 Introduction

Welcome to C++! We've worked hard to create what we hope you'll find to be an informative, entertaining and challenging learning experience. C++ is a powerful computer programming language that is appropriate for technically oriented people with little or no programming experience and for experienced programmers to use in building substantial information systems. *C++ How to Program, Sixth Edition*, is an effective learning tool for each of these audiences. We've added a new game programming chapter, which students, instructors and professionals alike should enjoy. We'd love to see the games you develop!

The core of the book emphasizes achieving program clarity through the proven techniques of object-oriented programming. This is an "early classes and objects" book—nonprogrammers will learn programming the right way from the beginning. The presentation is clear, straightforward and abundantly illustrated. We teach C++ features in the context of complete working C++ programs and show the outputs produced when those programs are run on a computer—we call this the live-code approach. You may download the example programs from www.deitel.com/books/cpphtp6/.

The early chapters introduce the fundamentals of computers, computer programming and the C++ computer programming language, providing a solid foundation for the deeper treatment of C++ in the later chapters. Experienced programmers tend to read the early chapters quickly, then find the treatment of C++ in the remainder of the book both rigorous and challenging.

Most people are at least somewhat familiar with the exciting things computers do. Using this textbook, you'll learn how to command computers to do those things. Computers (often referred to as hardware) are controlled by software (i.e., the instructions you write to command the computer to perform actions and make decisions). C++ is one of today's most popular software development languages. This text provides an introduction to programming in the version of C++ standardized in the United States through the American National Standards Institute (ANSI) and worldwide through the efforts of the International Organization for Standardization (ISO).

Computer use is increasing in most fields of endeavor. Computing costs have decreased dramatically due to rapid developments in both hardware and software technologies. Computers that might have filled large rooms and cost millions of dollars a few decades ago can now be inscribed on silicon chips smaller than a fingernail, costing a few dollars each. (Those large computers were called mainframes and current versions are widely used today in business, government and industry.) Fortunately, silicon is one of the most abundant materials on earth—it's an ingredient in common sand. Silicon chip technology has made computing so economical that about a billion general-purpose computers are in use worldwide, helping people in business, industry and government, and in their personal lives.

Over the years, many programmers learned the programming methodology called structured programming. You'll learn structured programming and an exciting newer methodology, object-oriented programming. Why do we teach both? Object orientation is the key programming methodology used by programmers today. You'll create and work with many software objects in this text. You'll discover, however, that their internal structure is often built using structured-programming techniques. Also, the logic of manipulating objects is occasionally expressed with structured programming.

To keep up to date with C++ developments at Deitel & Associates, please register for our free e-mail newsletter, *the Deitel® Buzz Online,* at

    www.deitel.com/newsletter/subscribe.html

Please check out our growing list of C++ and related Resource Centers at

    www.deitel.com/ResourceCenters.html

Some Resource Centers that will be valuable to you as you read this book are C++, C++ Game Programming, C++ Boost Libraries, Code Search Engines and Code Sites, Computer Game Programming, Programming Projects, Eclipse, Linux, Open Source and Windows Vista. Each week we announce our latest Resource Centers in the newsletter. Errata and updates for this book are posted at

    www.deitel.com/books/cpphtp6/

You are embarking on a challenging and rewarding path. As you proceed, if you have any questions, please send e-mail to

    deitel@deitel.com

We'll respond promptly. We hope that you'll enjoy learning with C++ *How to Program, Sixth Edition.*

1.2 What Is a Computer?

A computer is a device that can perform computations and make logical decisions billions of times faster than human beings can. For example, many of today's personal computers can perform several billion additions per second. A person operating a desk calculator could spend an entire lifetime performing calculations and still not complete as many calculations as a powerful personal computer can perform in one second! (Points to ponder: How would you know whether the person added the numbers correctly? How would you know whether the computer added the numbers correctly?) Today's fastest supercomputers can perform trillions of additions per second!

Computers process data under the control of sets of instructions called computer programs. These programs guide the computer through orderly sets of actions specified by people called computer programmers.

A computer consists of various devices referred to as hardware (e.g., the keyboard, screen, mouse, hard disk, memory, DVDs and processing units). The programs that run on a computer are referred to as software. Hardware costs have been declining dramatically in recent years, to the point that personal computers have become a commodity. In this book, you'll learn proven methods that are reducing software development costs—object-oriented programming and (in our optional Software Engineering Case Study on building an automated teller machine in Chapters 2–7, 9 and 13) object-oriented design.

1.3 Computer Organization

Regardless of differences in physical appearance, virtually every computer may be envisioned as divided into six logical units or sections:

1. **Input unit.** This is the "receiving" section of the computer. It obtains information (data and computer programs) from input devices and places this information at the disposal of the other units for processing. Most information is entered into computers through keyboards and mouse devices. Information also can be entered in many other ways, including by speaking to your computer, scanning images, uploading digital photos and videos, and receiving information from a network, such as the Internet.

2. **Output unit.** This is the "shipping" section of the computer. It takes information that the computer has processed and places it on various output devices to make the information available for use outside the computer. Most information output from computers today is displayed on screens, printed on paper or used to control other devices. Computers also can output their information to networks, such as the Internet.

3. **Memory unit.** This is the rapid-access, relatively low-capacity "warehouse" section of the computer. It stores computer programs while they are being executed. It retains information that has been entered through the input unit, so that it will be immediately available for processing when needed. The memory unit also retains processed information until it can be placed on output devices by the output unit. Information in the memory unit is typically lost when the computer's power is turned off. The memory unit is often called either memory or primary memory. [Historically, this unit has been called "core memory," but that term is fading from use today.]

4. **Arithmetic and logic unit (ALU).** This is the "manufacturing" section of the computer. It is responsible for performing calculations, such as addition, subtraction, multiplication and division. It contains the decision mechanisms that allow the computer, for example, to compare two items from the memory unit to determine whether they are equal.

5. **Central processing unit (CPU).** This is the computer's "administrative" section. It coordinates and supervises the other sections' operations. The CPU tells the input unit when information should be read into the memory unit, tells the ALU when information from the memory unit should be used in calculations and tells the output unit when to send information from the memory unit to certain output devices. Many of today's computers have multiple CPUs and, hence, can perform many operations simultaneously—such computers are called multiprocessors.

6. **Secondary storage unit.** This is the computer's long-term, high-capacity "warehousing" section. Programs or data not actively being used by the other units normally are placed on secondary storage devices, such as your hard drive, until they are needed, possibly hours, days, months or even years later. Information in secondary storage takes much longer to access than information in primary memory, but the cost per unit of secondary storage is much less than that of primary memory. Other secondary storage devices include CDs and DVDs, which can hold hundreds of millions and billions of characters, respectively.

1.4 Early Operating Systems

Early computers could perform only one job or task at a time. This is often called single-user batch processing. The computer runs a single program at a time while processing data in groups or batches. In these early systems, users generally submitted their jobs to a computer center on decks of punched cards and often had to wait hours or even days before printouts were returned to their desks.

Operating systems were developed to make using computers more convenient. Early operating systems smoothed and speeded up the transition between jobs, and hence increased the amount of work, or throughput, computers could process.

As computers became more powerful, it became evident that single-user batch processing was inefficient, because so much time was spent waiting for slow input/output devices to complete their tasks. It was thought that many jobs or tasks could *share* the computer's resources to achieve better utilization. This is achieved by multiprogramming. Multiprogramming involves the simultaneous operation of many jobs that are competing to share the computer's resources. With early multiprogramming operating systems, users still submitted jobs on decks of punched cards and waited hours or days for results.

In the 1960s, several groups in industry and the universities pioneered timesharing operating systems. Timesharing is a special case of multiprogramming in which users access the computer through terminals, typically devices with keyboards and screens. Dozens or even hundreds of users share the computer at once. The computer actually does not run all the user's programs simultaneously. Rather, it runs a small portion of one user's job, then moves on to service the next user, perhaps providing service to each user several times per second. Thus, the users' programs *appear* to be running simultaneously. An advantage of timesharing is that user requests receive almost immediate responses.

1.5 Personal, Distributed and Client/Server Computing

In 1977, Apple Computer popularized personal computing. Computers became so economical that people could buy them for their own personal or business use. In 1981, IBM, the world's largest computer vendor, introduced the IBM Personal Computer. This quickly legitimized personal computing in business, industry and government organizations, where IBM mainframes were heavily used.

These computers were "stand-alone" units—people transported disks back and forth between them to share information (this was often called "sneakernet"). Although early personal computers were not powerful enough to timeshare several users, these machines could be linked together in computer networks, sometimes over telephone lines and sometimes in local area networks (LANs) within an organization. This led to the phenomenon of distributed computing, in which an organization's computing, instead of being performed only at some central computer installation, is distributed over networks to the sites where the organization's work is performed. Personal computers were powerful enough to handle the computing requirements of individual users as well as the basic communications tasks of passing information between computers electronically.

Today's personal computers are as powerful as the million-dollar machines of just a few decades ago. The most powerful desktop machines—called workstations—provide individual users with enormous capabilities. Information is shared easily across computer networks, where computers called servers (file servers, database servers, web servers, etc.) offer a common data store that may be used by client computers distributed throughout the network, hence the term client/server computing. C++ has become widely used for writing software for operating systems, for computer networking and for distributed client/server applications. Today's popular operating systems such as UNIX, Linux, Mac OS X and Microsoft's Windows-based systems provide the kinds of capabilities discussed in this section.

1.6 The Internet and the World Wide Web

The Internet—a global network of computers—was initiated almost four decades ago with funding supplied by the U.S. Department of Defense. Originally designed to connect the main computer systems of about a dozen universities and research organizations, the Internet today is accessible by computers worldwide.

With the introduction of the World Wide Web—which allows computer users to locate and view multimedia-based documents on almost any subject over the Internet—the Internet has exploded into the world's premier communication mechanism.

The Internet and the World Wide Web are surely among humankind's most important and profound creations. In the past, most computer applications ran on computers that were not connected to one another. Today's applications can be written to communicate among the world's computers. The Internet mixes computing and communications technologies. It makes our work easier. It makes information instantly and conveniently accessible worldwide. It enables individuals and local small businesses to get worldwide exposure. It is changing the way business is done. People can search for the best prices on virtually any product or service. Special-interest communities can stay in touch with one another. Researchers can be made instantly aware of the latest breakthroughs.

1.7 Web 2.0[1]

In 2006, *TIME Magazine*'s "Person of the Year"[2] was "you." In this article, Web 2.0 and the associated social phenomena were recognized as a shift away from a powerful few to an empowered many. Web 2.0 has no single definition but can be explained through a series of Internet trends, one being the empowerment of the user. Companies, such as eBay, are built almost entirely on community-generated content. Web 2.0 takes advantage of collective intelligence, the idea that collaboration will result in intelligent ideas. For example, wikis, such as the encyclopedia Wikipedia, allow users access to edit content. Tagging, or labeling content, is another key part of the collaborative theme of Web 2.0, which can be seen in sites such as Flickr, a photo sharing site, and del.icio.us, a social bookmarking site.

Social networking sites, which keep track of users' interpersonal relationships, have experienced extraordinary growth as part of Web 2.0. Sites such as MySpace, Facebook and LinkedIn rely heavily on network effects, attracting users only if their friends or colleagues are also members. Similarly, social media sites, such as YouTube (an online video site) and Last.fm (a social music platform), have gained immense popularity, partly due to the increased availability of broadband Internet, often referred to as high-speed Internet.

Blogs—websites characterized by short postings in reverse chronological order—have become a major social phenomenon within Web 2.0. Many bloggers are recognized as part of the media, and companies are reaching out to the blogosphere, or blogging community, to track consumer opinions.

The increased popularity of open source software—a style of developing software in which individuals and companies develop, maintain and evolve software in exchange for the right to use that software for their own purposes—has made it cheaper and easier to start Web 2.0 companies. Web services—software components accessible by applications (or other software components) over the Internet—are on the rise, favoring the "webtop" over the desktop in much new development. Mashups combine two or more existing web applications to serve a new purpose and are dependent on open access to web services. For example, housingmaps.com is a mashup of Google Maps and real-estate listings on Craigslist. In our book *Internet & World Wide Web How to Program, 4/e* we describe key Web 2.0 technologies, including XML, RSS, Ajax, RIA, Podcasting, Internet video and others. We also mention many of the key companies of Web 2.0.

Many Web 2.0 companies use advertising as their main source of monetization. Internet advertising programs such as Google AdSense match advertisers with website publishers. Another website monetization model is premium content, providing additional services or information for a fee.

Web 3.0 refers to the next movement in web development—one that realizes the full potential of the web. The Internet in its current state is a giant conglomeration of single websites with loose connections. Web 3.0 will resolve this by moving toward the Semantic Web—or the "web of meaning"—in which the web becomes a giant database meaningfully searchable by computers.

See our Web 2.0 Resource Center at www.deitel.com/web2.0/ for more information.

---

1. O'Reilly, T. "What is Web 2.0: Design Patterns and Business Models for the Next Generation of Software." September 2005 <http://www.oreillynet.com/pub/a/oreilly/tim/news/2005/09/30/what-is-web-20.html?page=1>.
2. Grossman, L. "Time's Person of the Year: You." *Time*, December 2006 <http://www.time.com/time/magazine/article/0,9171,1569514,00.html>.

1.8 Machine Languages, Assembly Languages and High-Level Languages

Programmers write instructions in various programming languages, some directly understandable by computers and others requiring intermediate translation steps. Hundreds of computer languages are in use today. These may be divided into three general types:

1. Machine languages

2. Assembly languages

3. High-level languages

Any computer can directly understand only its own machine language. Machine language is the "natural language" of a computer and as such is defined by its hardware design. [*Note:* Machine language is often referred to as object code. This term predates "object-oriented programming." These two uses of "object" are unrelated.] Machine languages generally consist of strings of numbers (ultimately reduced to 1s and 0s) that instruct computers to perform their most elementary operations one at a time. Machine languages are machine dependent (i.e., a particular machine language can be used on only one type of computer). Such languages are cumbersome for humans, as illustrated by the following section of an early machine-language program that adds overtime pay to base pay and stores the result in gross pay:

```
+1300042774
+1400593419
+1200274027
```

Machine-language programming was simply too slow, tedious and error prone for most programmers. Instead of using the strings of numbers that computers could directly understand, programmers began using English-like abbreviations to represent elementary operations. These abbreviations formed the basis of assembly languages. Translator programs called assemblers were developed to convert early assembly-language programs to machine language at computer speeds. The following section of an assembly-language program also adds overtime pay to base pay and stores the result in gross pay:

```
load    basepay
add     overpay
store   grosspay
```

Although such code is clearer to humans, it is incomprehensible to computers until translated to machine language.

Computer usage increased rapidly with the advent of assembly languages, but programmers still had to use many instructions to accomplish even the simplest tasks. To speed the programming process, high-level languages were developed in which single statements could be written to accomplish substantial tasks. Translator programs called compilers convert high-level language programs into machine language. High-level languages allow programmers to write instructions that look almost like everyday English and contain commonly used mathematical notations. A payroll program written in a high-level language might contain a statement such as

```
grossPay = basePay + overTimePay;
```

From your standpoint, obviously, high-level languages are preferable to machine and assembly language. C, C++, Microsoft's .NET languages (e.g., Visual Basic, Visual C++ and Visual C#) and Java are among the most widely used high-level programming languages.

The process of compiling a high-level language program into machine language can take a considerable amount of computer time. Interpreter programs were developed to execute high-level language programs directly, although much more slowly.

1.9 History of C and C++

C++ evolved from C, which evolved from two previous programming languages, BCPL and B. BCPL was developed in 1967 by Martin Richards as a language for writing operating systems software and compilers for operating systems. Ken Thompson modeled many features in his language B after their counterparts in BCPL and used B to create early versions of the UNIX operating system at Bell Laboratories in 1970.

The C language was evolved from B by Dennis Ritchie at Bell Laboratories. C uses many important concepts of BCPL and B. C initially became widely known as the development language of the UNIX operating system. Today, most operating systems are written in C and/or C++. C is available for most computers and is hardware independent. With careful design, it is possible to write C programs that are portable to most computers.

The widespread use of C with various kinds of computers (sometimes called hardware platforms) unfortunately led to many variations. This was a serious problem for program developers, who needed to write portable programs that would run on several platforms. A standard version of C was needed. The American National Standards Institute (ANSI) cooperated with the International Organization for Standardization (ISO) to standardize C worldwide; the joint standard document was published in 1990 and is referred to as *ANSI/ISO 9899: 1990*.

C99 is the latest ANSI standard for the C programming language. It was developed to evolve the C language to keep pace with today's powerful hardware and with increasingly demanding user requirements. The C99 Standard is more capable (than earlier C Standards) of competing with languages like Fortran for mathematical applications. C99 capabilities include the `long long` type for 64-bit machines, complex numbers for engineering applications and greater support of floating-point arithmetic. C99 also makes C more consistent with C++ by enabling polymorphism through type-generic mathematical functions and through the creation of a defined boolean type. For more information on C and C99, see our book *C How to Program, Fifth Edition* and our C Resource Center (located at www.deitel.com/C).

 Portability Tip 1.1

Because C is a standardized, hardware-independent, widely available language, applications written in C often can be run with little or no modification on a wide range of computer systems.

C++, an extension of C, was developed by Bjarne Stroustrup in the early 1980s at Bell Laboratories. C++ provides a number of features that "spruce up" the C language, but more importantly, it provides capabilities for object-oriented programming.

A revolution is brewing in the software community. Building software quickly, correctly and economically remains an elusive goal, and this at a time when the demand for new and more powerful software is soaring. Objects are essentially reusable software components that model items in the real world. Software developers are discovering that a modular, object-oriented design and implementation approach can make them much more productive than can previous popular programming techniques. Object-oriented programs are easier to understand, correct and modify.

For this reason, we changed to an early-classes-and-objects pedagogy. You'll be introduced to the basic concepts and terminology of object technology in Section 1.21. You'll begin developing customized, reusable classes and object in Chapter 3, Introduction to Classes and Objects. This new edition of the book is object oriented, where appropriate, from the start and throughout the text. Moving the discussion of objects and classes to earlier chapters gets you "thinking about objects" immediately and mastering these concepts more completely. Object-oriented programming is not trivial by any means, but it's fun to write object-oriented programs, and students can see immediate results.

We also provide an optional automated teller machine (ATM) case study in the Software Engineering Case Study sections of Chapters 1–7, 9 and 13, and Appendix G, which contains a complete C++ implementation. The nine case study sections present a carefully paced introduction to object-oriented design using the UML—an industry standard graphical modeling language for developing object-oriented systems. We guide you through a first design experience intended for the novice object-oriented designer/programmer. Our goal is to help you develop an object-oriented design to complement the object-oriented programming concepts you learn in this chapter and begin implementing in Chapter 3.

1.10 C++ Standard Library

C++ programs consist of pieces called classes and functions. You can program each piece that you may need to form a C++ program. However, most C++ programmers take advantage of the rich collections of existing classes and functions in the C++ Standard Library. Thus, there are really two parts to learning the C++ "world." The first is learning the C++ language itself; the second is learning how to use the classes and functions in the C++ Standard Library. Throughout the book, we discuss many of these classes and functions. P. J. Plauger's book, *The Standard C Library* (Upper Saddle River, NJ: Prentice Hall PTR, 1992), is a must read for programmers who need a deep understanding of the ANSI C library functions that are included in C++, how to implement them and how to use them to write portable code. The standard class libraries generally are provided by compiler vendors. Many special-purpose class libraries are supplied by independent software vendors.

Software Engineering Observation 1.1

Use a "building-block" approach to create programs. Avoid reinventing the wheel. Use existing pieces wherever possible. Called software reuse, this practice is central to object-oriented programming.

Software Engineering Observation 1.2

When programming in C++, you typically will use the following building blocks: classes and functions from the C++ Standard Library, classes and functions you and your colleagues create and classes and functions from various popular third-party libraries.

We include many Software Engineering Observations throughout the book to explain concepts that affect and improve the overall architecture and quality of software systems. We also highlight other kinds of tips, including Good Programming Practices (to help you write programs that are clearer, more understandable, more maintainable and easier to test and debug—or remove programming errors), Common Programming Errors (problems to watch out for and avoid), Performance Tips (techniques for writing programs that run faster and use less memory), Portability Tips (techniques to help you write programs that can run, with little or no modification, on a variety of computers— these tips also include general observations about how C++ achieves its high degree of portability) and Error-Prevention Tips (techniques for removing programming errors— also known as bugs—from your programs and, more important, techniques for writing bug-free programs in the first place). Many of these tips and observations are only guidelines. You'll, no doubt, develop your own preferred programming style.

The advantage of creating your own functions and classes is that you'll know exactly how they work. You'll be able to examine the C++ code. The disadvantage is the time-consuming and complex effort that goes into designing, developing and maintaining new functions and classes that are correct and that operate efficiently.

> **Performance Tip 1.1**
>
> *Using C++ Standard Library functions and classes instead of writing your own versions can improve program performance, because they are written carefully to perform efficiently. This technique also shortens program development time.*

> **Portability Tip 1.2**
>
> *Using C++ Standard Library functions and classes instead of writing your own improves program portability, because they are included in every C++ implementation.*

1.11 History of Java

Microprocessors are having a profound impact in intelligent consumer electronic devices. Recognizing this, Sun Microsystems in 1991 funded an internal corporate research project code-named Green. The project resulted in the development of a C++-based language that its creator, James Gosling, called Oak after an oak tree outside his window at Sun. It was later discovered that there already was a computer language called Oak. When a group of Sun people visited a local coffee shop, the name Java was suggested and it stuck.

The Green project ran into some difficulties. The marketplace for intelligent consumer electronic devices did not develop in the early 1990s as quickly as Sun had anticipated. The project was in danger of being canceled. By sheer good fortune, the World Wide Web exploded in popularity in 1993, and Sun saw the immediate potential of using Java to add dynamic content (e.g., interactivity, animations and the like) to web pages. This breathed new life into the project.

Sun formally announced Java at an industry conference in May 1995. Java garnered the attention of the business community because of the phenomenal interest in the World Wide Web. Java is now used to develop large-scale enterprise applications, to enhance the functionality of web servers (the computers that provide the content we see in our web browsers), to provide applications for consumer devices (e.g., cell phones, pagers and personal digital assistants) and for many other purposes.

1.12 Fortran, COBOL, Pascal and Ada   *high-level procedural programming*

Hundreds of high-level languages have been developed, but only a few have achieved broad acceptance. FORTRAN (FORmula TRANslator) was developed by IBM Corporation in the mid-1950s to be used for scientific and engineering applications that require complex mathematical computations. Fortran is still widely used, especially in engineering applications.

COBOL (COmmon Business Oriented Language) was developed in the late 1950s by computer manufacturers, the U.S. government and industrial computer users. COBOL is used for commercial applications that require precise and efficient manipulation of large amounts of data. Much business software is still programmed in COBOL.

During the 1960s, many large software development efforts encountered severe difficulties. Software deliveries were often late, costs greatly exceeded budgets and the finished products were unreliable. People realized that software development was a more complex activity than they had imagined. Research in the 1960s resulted in the evolution of structured programming—a disciplined approach to writing programs that are clearer and easier to test, debug and modify than large programs produced with previous techniques.

One of the more tangible results of this research was the development of the Pascal programming language by Professor Niklaus Wirth in 1971. Named after the seventeenth-century mathematician and philosopher Blaise Pascal, it was designed for teaching structured programming and rapidly became the preferred programming language in most colleges. Pascal lacks many features needed in commercial, industrial and government applications, so it was not widely accepted outside academia.

The Ada programming language was developed under the sponsorship of the U.S. Department of Defense (DoD) during the 1970s and early 1980s. Hundreds of separate languages were being used to produce the DoD's massive command-and-control software systems. The DoD wanted a single language that would fill most of its needs. The Ada language was named after Lady Ada Lovelace, daughter of the poet Lord Byron. Lady Lovelace is credited with writing the world's first computer program in the early 1800s (for the Analytical Engine mechanical computing device designed by Charles Babbage). One important capability of Ada, called multitasking, allows programmers to specify that many activities are to occur in parallel. Java, through a technique called *multithreading*, also enables programmers to write programs with parallel activities. Although multithreading is not part of standard C++, it is available through various add-on class libraries such as Boost (www.boost.org).

1.13 BASIC, Visual Basic, Visual C++, C# and .NET

The BASIC (Beginner's All-purpose Symbolic Instruction Code) programming language was developed in the mid-1960s at Dartmouth College as a means of writing simple programs. BASIC's primary purpose was to familiarize novices with programming techniques. Microsoft's Visual Basic language, introduced in the early 1990s to simplify the development of Microsoft Windows applications, has become one of the most popular programming languages in the world.

Microsoft's latest development tools are part of its corporate-wide strategy for integrating the Internet and the web into computer applications. This strategy is implemented in Microsoft's .NET platform, which provides the capabilities developers need to create and run computer applications that can execute on computers distributed across the Internet. Microsoft's three primary programming languages are Visual Basic (based on the original BASIC), Visual C++ (based on C++) and Visual C# (a new language based on C++ and Java that was developed expressly for the .NET platform). Developers using

.NET can write software components in the language they are most familiar with, then form applications by combining those components with others written in any .NET language.

1.14 Key Software Trend: Object Technology

One of the authors, Harvey Deitel, remembers the great frustration felt in the 1960s by software development organizations, especially those working on large-scale projects. During his undergraduate years, he had the privilege of working summers at a leading computer vendor on the teams developing timesharing, virtual memory operating systems. This was a great experience for a college student. But, in the summer of 1967, reality set in when the company "decommitted" from producing as a commercial product the particular system on which hundreds of people had been working for many years. It was difficult to get this software right—software is "complex stuff."

Improvements to software technology did emerge, with the benefits of structured programming (and the related disciplines of structured systems analysis and design) being realized in the 1970s. Not until the technology of object-oriented programming became widely used in the 1990s, though, did software developers feel they had the necessary tools for making major strides in the software development process.

Actually, object technology dates back to the mid 1960s. The C++ programming language, developed at AT&T by Bjarne Stroustrup in the early 1980s, is based on two languages—C, which initially was developed at AT&T to implement the UNIX operating system in the early 1970s, and Simula 67, a simulation programming language developed in Europe and released in 1967. C++ absorbed the features of C and added Simula's capabilities for creating and manipulating objects. Neither C nor C++ was originally intended for wide use beyond the AT&T research laboratories. But grass roots support rapidly developed for each.

What are objects and why are they special? Actually, object technology is a packaging scheme that helps us create meaningful software units. These can be large and are highly focused on particular applications areas. There are date objects, time objects, paycheck objects, invoice objects, audio objects, video objects, file objects, record objects and so on. In fact, almost any noun can be reasonably represented as an object.

We live in a world of objects. Just look around you. There are cars, planes, people, animals, buildings, traffic lights, elevators and the like. Before object-oriented languages appeared, procedural programming languages (such as Fortran, COBOL, Pascal, BASIC and C) were focused on actions (verbs) rather than on things or objects (nouns). Programmers living in a world of objects programmed primarily using verbs. This made it awkward to write programs. Now, with the availability of popular object-oriented languages such as C++ and Java, programmers continue to live in an object-oriented world and can program in an object-oriented manner. This is a more natural process than procedural programming and has resulted in significant productivity gains.

A key problem with procedural programming is that the program units do not effectively mirror real-world entities, so these units are not particularly reusable. It's not unusual for programmers to "start fresh" on each new project and have to write similar software "from scratch." This wastes time and money, as people repeatedly "reinvent the wheel." With object technology, the software entities created (called classes), if properly designed, tend to be reusable on future projects. Using libraries of reusable componentry can greatly reduce effort required to implement certain kinds of systems (compared to the effort that would be required to reinvent these capabilities on new projects).

Software Engineering Observation 1.3

Extensive class libraries of reusable software components are available on the Internet. Many of these libraries are free.

Some organizations report that the key benefit object-oriented programming gives them is not software reuse but, rather, that the software they produce is more understandable, better organized and easier to maintain, modify and debug. This can be significant, because perhaps as much as 80 percent of software costs are associated not with the original efforts to develop the software, but with the continued evolution and maintenance of that software throughout its lifetime.

Whatever the perceived benefits, it's clear that object-oriented programming will be the key programming methodology for the next several decades.

1.15 Typical C++ Development Environment

Let's consider the steps in creating and executing a C++ application using a C++ development environment (illustrated in Fig. 1.1). C++ systems generally consist of three parts: a program development environment, the language and the C++ Standard Library. C++ programs typically go through six phases: edit, preprocess, compile, link, load and execute. The following discussion explains a typical C++ program development environment.

Phase 1: Creating a Program
Phase 1 consists of editing a file with an editor program (normally known simply as an editor). You type a C++ program (typically referred to as source code) using the editor, make any necessary corrections and save the program on a secondary storage device, such as your hard drive. C++ source code filenames often end with the .cpp, .cxx, .cc or .C extensions (note that C is in uppercase) which indicate that a file contains C++ source code. See the documentation for your C++ compiler for more information on file-name extensions.

Two editors widely used on UNIX systems are vi and emacs. C++ software packages for Microsoft Windows such as Microsoft Visual C++ (msdn.microsoft.com/vstudio/express/visualc/default.aspx) and Code Gear C++Builder (www.codegear.com) have editors integrated into the programming environment. You can also use a simple text editor, such as Notepad in Windows, to write your C++ code. We assume you know how to edit a file.

Phases 2 and 3: Preprocessing and Compiling a C++ Program
In phase 2, you give the command to compile the program. In a C++ system, a preprocessor program executes automatically before the compiler's translation phase begins (so we call preprocessing phase 2 and compiling phase 3). The C++ preprocessor obeys commands called preprocessor directives, which indicate that certain manipulations are to be performed on the program before compilation. These manipulations usually include other text files to be compiled, and perform various text replacements. The most common preprocessor directives are discussed in the early chapters; a detailed discussion of preprocessor features appears in Appendix F, Preprocessor. In phase 3, the compiler translates the C++ program into machine-language code (also referred to as object code).

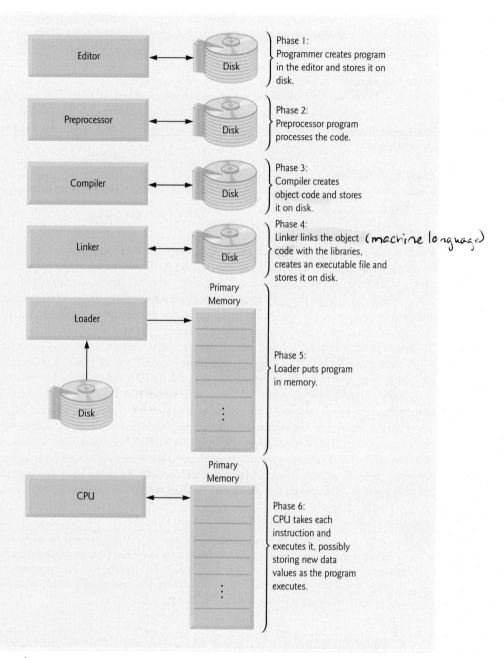

Phase 1:
Programmer creates program in the editor and stores it on disk.

Phase 2:
Preprocessor program processes the code.

Phase 3:
Compiler creates object code and stores it on disk.

Phase 4:
Linker links the object *(machine language)* code with the libraries, creates an executable file and stores it on disk.

Phase 5:
Loader puts program in memory.

Phase 6:
CPU takes each instruction and executes it, possibly storing new data values as the program executes.

Fig. 1.1 | Typical C++ environment.

Phase 4: Linking

Phase 4 is called linking. C++ programs typically contain references to functions and data defined elsewhere, such as in the standard libraries or in the private libraries of groups of programmers working on a particular project. The object code produced by the C++ compiler typically contains "holes" due to these missing parts. A linker links the object code with the code for the missing functions to produce an executable image (with no missing pieces). If the program compiles and links correctly, an executable image is produced.

Phase 5: Loading
Phase 5 is called loading. Before a program can be executed, it must first be placed in memory. This is done by the loader, which takes the executable image from disk and transfers it to memory. Additional components from shared libraries that support the program are also loaded.

Phase 6: Execution
Finally, the computer, under the control of its CPU, executes the program one instruction at a time.

Problems That May Occur at Execution Time
Programs do not always work on the first try. Each of the preceding phases can fail because of various errors that we discuss throughout the book. For example, an executing program might attempt to divide by zero (an illegal operation for whole number arithmetic in C++). This would cause the C++ program to display an error message. If this occurs, you would have to return to the edit phase, make the necessary corrections and proceed through the remaining phases again to determine that the corrections fix the problem(s).

   Most programs in C++ input and/or output data. Certain C++ functions take their input from cin (the standard input stream; pronounced "see-in"), which is normally the keyboard, but cin can be redirected to another device. Data is often output to cout (the standard output stream; pronounced "see-out"), which is normally the computer screen, but cout can be redirected to another device. When we say that a program prints a result, we normally mean that the result is displayed on a screen. Data may be output to other devices, such as disks and hardcopy printers. There is also a standard error stream referred to as cerr. The cerr stream (normally connected to the screen) is used for displaying error messages. It is common for users to assign cout to a device other than the screen while keeping cerr assigned to the screen, so that normal outputs are separated from errors.

Common Programming Error 1.1

Errors such as division by zero occur as a program runs, so they are called runtime errors *or* execution-time errors. Fatal runtime errors *cause programs to terminate immediately without having successfully performed their jobs.* Nonfatal runtime errors *allow programs to run to completion, often producing incorrect results.* [Note: On some systems, divide-by-zero is not a fatal error. Please see your system documentation.]

1.16 Notes About C++ and C++ *How to Program, 6/e*
Experienced C++ programmers sometimes take pride in being able to create weird, contorted, convoluted uses of the language. This is a poor programming practice. It makes programs more difficult to read, more likely to behave strangely, more difficult to test and debug, and more difficult to adapt to changing requirements. This book is geared for novice programmers, so we stress program *clarity*. The following is our first "good programming practice."

Good Programming Practice 1.1

Write your C++ programs in a simple and straightforward manner. This is sometimes referred to as KIS ("keep it simple"). Do not "stretch" the language by trying bizarre usages.

You have heard that C and C++ are portable languages, and that programs written in C and C++ can run on many different computers. *Portability is an elusive goal.* The ANSI C standard document contains a lengthy list of portability issues, and complete books have been written that discuss portability.

Portability Tip 1.3

Although it's possible to write portable programs, there are many problems among different C and C++ compilers and different computers that can make portability difficult to achieve. Writing programs in C and C++ does not guarantee portability. You often will need to deal directly with compiler and computer variations. As a group, these are sometimes called platform variations.

We have audited our presentation against the ISO/IEC C++ standard document for completeness and accuracy. However, C++ is a rich language, and there are some features we have not covered. If you need additional technical details on C++, you may want to read the C++ standard document, which can be ordered from ANSI at

    webstore.ansi.org/ansidocstore/default.asp

The title of the document is "Information Technology – Programming Languages – C++" and its document number is INCITS/ISO/IEC 14882-2003.

We have included an extensive bibliography of books and papers on C++ and object-oriented programming. We also lise many websites relating to C++ and object-oriented programming in our C++ Resource Center at www.deitel.com/cplusplus/. We list several websites in Section 1.23, including links to free C++ compilers, resource sites, some fun C++ games and game programming tutorials.

Good Programming Practice 1.2

Read the documentation for the version of C++ you are using. Refer to this documentation frequently to be sure you are aware of the rich collection of C++ features and that you are using them correctly.

Good Programming Practice 1.3

Your computer and compiler are good teachers. If, after reading your C++ language documentation, you still are not sure how a feature of C++ works, experiment using a small test program and see what happens. Set your compiler options for "maximum warnings." Study each message that the compiler generates and correct the program to eliminate the messages.

1.17 Test-Driving a C++ Application

In this section, you'll run and interact with your first C++ application. You'll begin by running an entertaining guess-the-number game, which picks a number from 1 to 1000 and prompts you to guess it. If your guess is correct, the game ends. If your guess is not correct, the application indicates whether your guess is higher or lower than the correct number. There is no limit on the number of guesses you can make. [*Note:* For this test drive only, we have modified this application from the exercise you'll be asked to create in Chapter 6,

Functions and an Introduction to Recursion. Normally this application randomly selects the correct answer as you execute the program. The modified application uses the same correct answer every time the program executes (though this may vary by compiler), so you can use the same guesses we use in this section and see the same results as we walk you through interacting with your first C++ application.

We'll demonstrate running a C++ application in two ways—using the Windows XP **Command Prompt** and using a shell on Linux (similar to a Windows **Command Prompt**). The application runs similarly on both platforms. Many development environments are available in which readers can compile, build and run C++ applications, such as Code Gear's C++Builder, GNU C++, Microsoft Visual C++, etc. Consult your instructor for information on your specific development environment.

In the following steps, you'll run the application and enter various numbers to guess the correct number. The elements and functionality that you see in this application are typical of those you'll learn to program in this book. Throughout the book, we use fonts to distinguish between features you see on the screen (e.g., the **Command Prompt**) and elements that are not directly related to the screen. Our convention is to emphasize screen features like titles and menus (e.g., the **File** menu) in a semibold **sans-serif Helvetica** font and to emphasize filenames, text displayed by an application and values you should enter into an application (e.g., `GuessNumber` or `500`) in a `sans-serif Lucida` font. As you have noticed, the defining occurrence of each term is set in blue, heavy bold. For the figures in this section, we highlight the user input required by each step and point out significant parts of the application. To make these features more visible, we have modified the background color of the **Command Prompt** window (for the Windows test drive only). To modify the **Command Prompt** colors on your system, open a **Command Prompt**, then right click the title bar and select **Properties**. In the **"Command Prompt" Properties** dialog box that appears, click the **Colors** tab, and select your preferred text and background colors.

Running a C++ Application from the Windows XP Command Prompt

1. *Checking your setup.* Read the *Before You Begin* section at the beginning of this book to make sure that you have copied the book's examples to your hard drive correctly.

2. *Locating the completed application.* Open a **Command Prompt** window. For readers using Windows 95, 98 or 2000, select **Start > Programs > Accessories > Command Prompt**. For Windows XP users, select **Start > All Programs > Accessories > Command Prompt**. To change to your completed **GuessNumber** application directory, type `cd C:\examples\ch01\GuessNumber\Windows`, then press *Enter* (Fig. 1.2). The command cd is used to change directories.

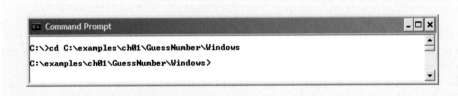

Fig. 1.2 | Opening a **Command Prompt** window and changing the directory.

3. *Running the GuessNumber application.* Now that you are in the directory that contains the **GuessNumber** application, type the command **GuessNumber** (Fig. 1.3) and press *Enter*. [*Note:* GuessNumber.exe is the actual name of the application; however, Windows assumes the .exe extension by default.]

4. *Entering your first guess.* The application displays "Please type your first guess.", then displays a question mark (?) as a prompt on the next line (Fig. 1.3). At the prompt, enter **500** (Fig. 1.4).

5. *Entering another guess.* The application displays "Too high. Try again.", meaning that the value you entered is greater than the number the application chose as the correct guess. So, you should enter a lower number for your next guess. At the prompt, enter **250** (Fig. 1.5). The application again displays "Too high. Try again.", because the value you entered is still greater than the number that the application chose as the correct guess.

6. *Entering additional guesses.* Continue to play the game by entering values until you guess the correct number. The application will display "Excellent! You guessed the number!" (Fig. 1.6).

7. *Playing the game again or exiting the application.* After you guess correctly, the application asks if you would like to play another game (Fig. 1.6). At the "Would

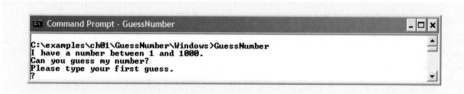

Fig. 1.3 | Running the **GuessNumber** application.

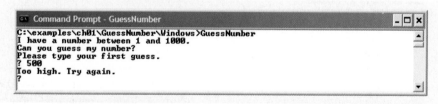

Fig. 1.4 | Entering your first guess.

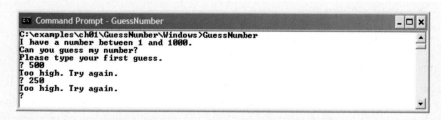

Fig. 1.5 | Entering a second guess and receiving feedback.

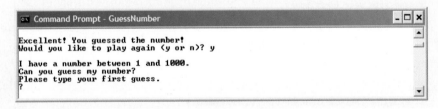

```
Command Prompt - GuessNumber                              _ □ ×
Too high. Try again.
? 125
Too low. Try again.
? 187
Too high. Try again.
? 156
Too high. Try again.
? 140
Too high. Try again.
? 132
Too high. Try again.
? 128
Too low. Try again.
? 130
Too low. Try again.
? 131

Excellent! You guessed the number!
Would you like to play again (y or n)?
```

Fig. 1.6 | Entering additional guesses and guessing the correct number.

you like to play again (y or n)?" prompt, entering the one character **y** causes the application to choose a new number and displays the message "Please type your first guess." followed by a question mark prompt (Fig. 1.7) so you can make your first guess in the new game. Entering the character **n** ends the application and returns you to the application's directory at the **Command Prompt** (Fig. 1.8). Each time you execute this application from the beginning (i.e., *Step 3*), it will choose the same numbers for you to guess.

8. *Close the* **Command Prompt** *window.*

```
Command Prompt - GuessNumber                              _ □ ×
Excellent! You guessed the number!
Would you like to play again (y or n)? y

I have a number between 1 and 1000.
Can you guess my number?
Please type your first guess.
?
```

Fig. 1.7 | Playing the game again.

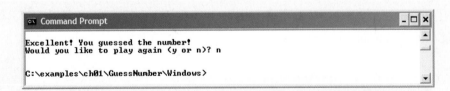

```
Command Prompt                                            _ □ ×
Excellent! You guessed the number!
Would you like to play again (y or n)? n

C:\examples\ch01\GuessNumber\Windows>
```

Fig. 1.8 | Exiting the game.

Running a C++ Application Using GNU C++ with Linux

For this test drive, we assume that you know how to copy the examples into your home directory. Please see your instructor if you have any questions regarding copying the files to your Linux system. Also, for the figures in this section, we use a bold highlight to point out the user input required by each step. The prompt in the shell on our system uses the tilde (~) character to represent the home directory, and each prompt ends with the dollar sign ($) character. The prompt will vary among Linux systems.

1. *Locating the completed application.* From a Linux shell, change to the completed **GuessNumber** application directory (Fig. 1.9) by typing

   ```
   cd Examples/ch01/GuessNumber/GNU_Linux
   ```

   then pressing *Enter*. The command cd is used to change directories.

2. *Compiling the GuessNumber application.* To run an application on the GNU C++ compiler, you must first compile it by typing

   ```
   g++ GuessNumber.cpp -o GuessNumber
   ```

   as in Fig. 1.10. This command compiles the application and produces an executable file called GuessNumber.

3. *Running the GuessNumber application.* To run the executable file GuessNumber, type ./GuessNumber at the next prompt, then press *Enter* (Fig. 1.11).

4. *Entering your first guess.* The application displays "Please type your first guess.", then displays a question mark (?) as a prompt on the next line (Fig. 1.11). At the prompt, enter **500** (Fig. 1.12). [*Note:* This is the same application that we modified and test-drove for Windows, but the outputs could vary based on the compiler being used.]

5. *Entering another guess.* The application displays "Too high. Try again.", meaning that the value you entered is greater than the number the application chose as the correct guess (Fig. 1.12). At the next prompt, enter **250** (Fig. 1.13). This time

```
~$ cd examples/ch01/GuessNumber/GNU_Linux
~/examples/ch01/GuessNumber/GNU_Linux$
```

Fig. 1.9 | Changing to the **GuessNumber** application's directory after logging in to your Linux account.

```
~/examples/ch01/GuessNumber/GNU_Linux$ g++ GuessNumber.cpp -o GuessNumber
~/examples/ch01/GuessNumber/GNU_Linux$
```

Fig. 1.10 | Compiling the **GuessNumber** application using the g++ command.

```
~/examples/ch01/GuessNumber/GNU_Linux$ ./GuessNumber
I have a number between 1 and 1000.
Can you guess my number?
Please type your first guess.
?
```

Fig. 1.11 | Running the **GuessNumber** application.

```
~/examples/ch01/GuessNumber/GNU_Linux$ ./GuessNumber
I have a number between 1 and 1000.
Can you guess my number?
Please type your first guess.
? 500
Too high. Try again.
?
```

Fig. 1.12 | Entering an initial guess.

```
~/examples/ch01/GuessNumber/GNU_Linux$ ./GuessNumber
I have a number between 1 and 1000.
Can you guess my number?
Please type your first guess.
? 500
Too high. Try again.
? 250
Too low. Try again.
?
```

Fig. 1.13 | Entering a second guess and receiving feedback.

the application displays "Too low. Try again.", because the value you entered is less than the correct guess.

6. *Entering additional guesses.* Continue to play the game (Fig. 1.14) by entering values until you guess the correct number. When you guess correctly, the application displays "Excellent! You guessed the number." (Fig. 1.14).

```
Too low. Try again.
? 375
Too low. Try again.
? 437
Too high. Try again.
? 406
Too high. Try again.
? 391
Too high. Try again.
? 383
Too low. Try again.
? 387
Too high. Try again.
? 385
Too high. Try again.
? 384

Excellent! You guessed the number.
Would you like to play again (y or n)?
```

Fig. 1.14 | Entering additional guesses and guessing the correct number.

7. *Playing the game again or exiting the application.* After you guess the correct number, the application asks if you would like to play another game. At the "Would you like to play again (y or n)?" prompt, entering the one character **y** causes the application to choose a new number and displays the message "Please type your first guess." followed by a question mark prompt (Fig. 1.15) so you can make your first guess in the new game. Entering the character **n** ends the application and returns you to the application's directory in the shell (Fig. 1.16). Each time you execute this application from the beginning (i.e., *Step 3*), it will choose the same numbers for you to guess.

```
Excellent! You guessed the number.
Would you like to play again (y or n)? y

I have a number between 1 and 1000.
Can you guess my number?
Please type your first guess.
?
```

Fig. 1.15 | Playing the game again.

```
Excellent! You guessed the number.
Would you like to play again (y or n)? n

~/examples/ch01/GuessNumber/GNU_Linux$
```

Fig. 1.16 | Exiting the game.

1.18 Software Technologies

In this section, we discuss a number of software engineering buzzwords that you'll hear in the software development community. We've created Resource Centers on most of these topics, with many more on the way.

Agile Software Development is a set of methodologies that try to get software implemented quickly with fewer resources than previous methodologies. Check out the Agile Alliance (www.agilealliance.org) and the Agile Manifesto (www.agilemanifesto.org).

Refactoring involves reworking code to make it clearer and easier to maintain while preserving its functionality. It's widely employed with agile development methodologies. Many refactoring tools are available to do major portions of the reworking automatically.

Design patterns are proven architectures for constructing flexible and maintainable object-oriented software. The field of design patterns tries to enumerate those recurring patterns, encouraging software designers to reuse them to develop better quality software with less time, money and effort.

Game programming. The computer game business is larger than the first-run movie business. College courses and even majors are now devoted to the sophisticated software techniques used in game programming. Check out our Resource Centers on Game Programming, C++ Game Programming and Programming Projects.

Open source software is a style of developing software in contrast to proprietary development that dominated software's early years. With open source development, individuals and companies contribute their efforts in developing, maintaining and evolving software in exchange for the right to use that software for their own purposes, typically at no charge. Open source code generally gets scrutinized by a much larger audience than proprietary software, so bugs get removed faster. Open source also encourages more innovation. Sun recently announced that it is open sourcing Java. Some organizations you'll hear a lot about in the open source community are the Eclipse Foundation (the Eclipse IDE is popular for C++ and Java software development), the Mozilla Foundation (creators of the Firefox browser), the Apache Software Foundation (creators of the Apache web server) and SourceForge (which provides the tools for managing open source projects and currently has over 150,000 open source projects under development).

Linux is an open source operating system and one of the greatest successes of the open source movement. MySQL is an open source database management system. PHP is the most popular open source server-side "scripting" language for developing Internet-based applications. LAMP is an acronym for the set of open source technologies that many developers used to build web applications—it stands for Linux, Apache, MySQL and PHP (or Perl or Python—two other languages used for similar purposes).

Ruby on Rails combines the scripting language Ruby with the Rails web application framework developed by the company 37Signals. Their book, *Getting Real*, is a must read for today's web application developers; read it free at `gettingreal.37signals.com/toc.php`. Many Ruby on Rails developers have reported significant productivity gains over using other languages when developing database-intensive web applications.

Software has generally been viewed as a product; most software still is offered this way. If you want to run an application, you buy a software package from a software vendor. You then install that software on your computer and run it as needed. As new versions of the software appear, you upgrade your software, often at significant expense. This process can become cumbersome for organizations with tens of thousands of systems that must be maintained on a diverse array of computer equipment. With Software as a Service (SaaS) the software runs on servers elsewhere on the Internet. When those servers are updated, all clients worldwide see the new capabilities; no local installation is needed. You access the service through a browser—these are quite portable, so you can run the same applications on different kinds of computers from anywhere in the world. Salesforce.com, Google, and Microsoft's Office Live and Windows Live all offer SaaS.

1.19 Game Programming with the Ogre Libraries

Ogre (Object-Oriented Graphics Rendering Engine), one of the leading graphics engines, has been used in many commercial products including video games. It provides an object-oriented interface for 3D graphics programming, and runs on the Windows, Linux and Mac platforms. Ogre is an open-source project maintained by the Ogre team at `www.ogre3d.org`. OgreAL is a wrapper around the OpenAL audio library. The wrapper allows you to integrate sound functionality into Ogre code.

Chapter 23, Game Programming with Ogre, introduces game programming and graphics with the Ogre 3D graphics engine. First, we discuss basic issues involved in game programming. Then we show how to use Ogre to create a simple game featuring a play mechanic similar to the classic video game Pong®, originally developed by Atari in 1972.

We demonstrate how to create a scene with colored 3D graphics, smoothly animate moving objects, use timers to control animation speed, detect collisions between objects, add sound, accept keyboard input and display text output.

1.20 Future of C++: Open Source Boost Libraries, TRI and C++0x

Bjarne Stroustrup, the creator of C++, has expressed his vision for the future of C++. The main goals for the new standard are to make C++ easier to learn, improve library building capabilities, and increase compatibility with the C programming language.

Chapter 24, Boost Libraries, Technical Report 1 and C++0x considers the future of C++—we introduce the Boost C++ Libraries, Technical Report 1 (TR1) and C++0x. The Boost C++ Libraries are free, open source libraries created by members of the C++ community. Boost has grown to over 70 libraries, with more being added regularly. Today there are thousands of programmers in the Boost open source community. Boost provides C++ programmers with useful, well-designed libraries that work well with the existing C++ Standard Library. The Boost libraries can be used by C++ programmers working on a wide variety of platforms with many different compilers. We overview the libraries included in TR1 and provide code examples for the "regular expression" and "smart pointer" libraries.

Regular expressions are used to match specific character patterns in text. They can be used to validate data to ensure that it is in a particular format, to replace parts of one string with another, or to split a string.

Many common bugs in C and C++ code are related to pointers, a powerful programming capability you'll study in Chapter 8, Pointers and Pointer-Based Strings. Smart pointers help you avoid errors by providing additional functionality to standard pointers. This functionality typically strengthens the process of memory allocation and deallocation.

Technical Report 1 describes the proposed changes to the C++ Standard Library, many of which are based on current Boost libraries. These libraries add useful functionality to C++. The C++ Standards Committee is currently revising the C++ Standard. The last standard was published in 1998. Work on the new standard, currently referred to as C++0x, began in 2003. The new standard is likely to be released in 2009. It will include changes to the core language and, most likely, many of the libraries in TR1.

1.21 Software Engineering Case Study: Introduction to Object Technology and the UML

Now we begin our early introduction to object orientation, a natural way of thinking about the world and writing computer programs. Chapters 1–7, 9 and 13 all end with a brief Software Engineering Case Study section in which we present a carefully paced introduction to object orientation. Our goal here is to help you develop an object-oriented way of thinking and to introduce you to the Unified Modeling Language™ (UML™)— a graphical language that allows people who design object-oriented software systems to use an industry-standard notation to represent them.

In this required section, we introduce basic object-oriented concepts and terminology. The optional sections in Chapters 2–7, 9 and 13 present an object-oriented design and implementation of the software for a simple automated teller machine (ATM) system. The Software Engineering Case Study sections at the ends of Chapters 2–7

- analyze a typical requirements specification that describes a software system (the ATM) to be built
- determine the objects required to implement that system
- determine the attributes the objects will have
- determine the behaviors these objects will exhibit
- specify how the objects interact with one another to meet the system requirements

The Software Engineering Case Study sections at the ends of Chapters 9 and 13 modify and enhance the design presented in Chapters 2–7. Appendix G contains a complete, working C++ implementation of the object-oriented ATM system.

Although our case study is a scaled-down version of an industry-level problem, we nevertheless cover many common industry practices. You'll experience a solid introduction to object-oriented design with the UML. Also, you'll sharpen your code-reading skills by touring the complete, carefully written and well-documented C++ implementation of the ATM.

Basic Object Technology Concepts

We begin our introduction to object orientation with some key terminology. Everywhere you look in the real world you see objects—people, animals, plants, cars, planes, buildings, computers, monitors and so on. Humans think in terms of objects. Telephones, houses, traffic lights, microwave ovens and water coolers are just a few more objects we see around us every day.

We sometimes divide objects into two categories: animate and inanimate. Animate objects are "alive" in some sense—they move around and do things. Inanimate objects do not move on their own. Objects of both types, however, have some things in common. They all have attributes (e.g., size, shape, color and weight), and they all exhibit behaviors (e.g., a ball rolls, bounces, inflates and deflates; a baby cries, sleeps, crawls, walks and blinks; a car accelerates, brakes and turns; a towel absorbs water). We'll study the kinds of attributes and behaviors that software objects have.

Humans learn about existing objects by studying their attributes and observing their behaviors. Different objects can have similar attributes and can exhibit similar behaviors. Comparisons can be made, for example, between babies and adults, and between humans and chimpanzees.

Object-oriented design (OOD) models software in terms similar to those that people use to describe real-world objects. It takes advantage of class relationships, where objects of a certain class, such as a class of vehicles, have the same characteristics—cars, trucks, little red wagons and roller skates have much in common. OOD takes advantage of inheritance relationships, where new classes of objects are derived by absorbing characteristics of existing classes and adding unique characteristics of their own. An object of class "convertible" certainly has the characteristics of the more general class "automobile," but more specifically, the roof goes up and down.

Object-oriented design provides a natural and intuitive way to view the software design process—namely, modeling objects by their attributes, behaviors and interrelationships just as we describe real-world objects. OOD also models communication between objects. Just as people send messages to one another (e.g., a sergeant commands a soldier to stand at attention), objects also communicate via messages. A bank account object may receive a message to decrease its balance by a certain amount because the customer has withdrawn that amount of money.

OOD encapsulates (i.e., wraps) attributes and operations (behaviors) into objects—an object's attributes and operations are intimately tied together. Objects have the property of information hiding. This means that objects may know how to communicate with one another across well-defined interfaces, but normally they are not allowed to know how other objects are implemented—implementation details are hidden within the objects themselves. We can drive a car effectively, for instance, without knowing the details of how engines, transmissions, brakes and exhaust systems work internally—as long as we know how to use the accelerator pedal, the brake pedal, the steering wheel and so on. Information hiding, as we'll see, is crucial to good software engineering.

Languages like C++ are object oriented. Programming in such a language is called object-oriented programming (OOP), and it allows computer programmers to implement object-oriented designs as working software systems. Languages like C, on the other hand, are procedural, so programming tends to be action oriented. In C, the unit of programming is the *function.* In C++, the unit of programming is the *class* from which objects are eventually *instantiated* (an OOP term for "created"). C++ classes contain functions that implement operations and data that implements attributes.

C programmers concentrate on writing functions. Programmers group actions that perform some common task into functions, and group functions to form programs. Data is certainly important in C, but the view is that data exists primarily in support of the actions that functions perform. The *verbs* in a system specification help the C programmer determine the set of functions that will work together to implement the system.

Classes, Data Members and Member Functions

C++ programmers concentrate on creating their own *user-defined types* called *classes.* Each class contains data as well as the set of functions that manipulate that data and provide services to clients (i.e., other classes or functions that use the class). The data components of a class are called *data members.* For example, a bank account class might include an account number and a balance. The function components of a class are called *member functions* (typically called *methods* in other object-oriented programming languages such as Java). For example, a bank account class might include member functions to make a deposit (increasing the balance), make a withdrawal (decreasing the balance) and inquire what the current balance is. You use built-in types (and other user-defined types) as the "building blocks" for constructing new user-defined types (classes). The *nouns* in a system specification help the C++ programmer determine the set of classes from which objects are created that work together to implement the system.

Classes are to objects as blueprints are to houses—a class is a "plan" for building an object of the class. Just as we can build many houses from one blueprint, we can instantiate (create) many objects from one class. You cannot cook meals in the kitchen of a blueprint; you can cook meals in the kitchen of a house. You cannot sleep in the bedroom of a blueprint; you can sleep in the bedroom of a house.

Classes can have relationships with other classes. For example, in an object-oriented design of a bank, the "bank teller" class needs to relate to other classes, such as the "customer" class, the "cash drawer" class, the "safe" class, and so on. These relationships are called associations.

Packaging software as classes makes it possible for future software systems to reuse the classes. Groups of related classes are often packaged as reusable components. Just as realtors often say that the three most important factors affecting the price of real estate are "location, location and location," some people in the software development community say that the three most important factors affecting the future of software development are "reuse, reuse and reuse."

Software Engineering Observation 1.4

Reuse of existing classes when building new classes and programs saves time, money and effort. Reuse also helps programmers build more reliable and effective systems, because existing classes and components often have gone through extensive testing, debugging and performance tuning.

Indeed, with object technology, you can build much of the new software you'll need by combining existing classes, just as automobile manufacturers combine interchangeable parts. Each new class you create will have the potential to become a valuable software asset that you and other programmers can reuse to speed and enhance the quality of future software development efforts.

Introduction to Object-Oriented Analysis and Design (OOAD)

Soon you'll be writing programs in C++. How will you create the code for your programs? Perhaps, like many beginning programmers, you'll simply turn on your computer and start typing. This approach may work for small programs (like the ones we present early in this book), but what if you were asked to create a software system to control thousands of automated teller machines for a major bank? Or suppose you were asked to work on a team of 1000 software developers building the next U.S. air traffic control system. For projects so large and complex, you could not simply sit down and start writing programs.

To create the best solutions, you should follow a detailed process for analyzing your project's requirements (i.e., determining *what* the system is supposed to do) and developing a design that satisfies them (i.e., deciding *how* the system should do it). Ideally, you would go through this process and carefully review the design (or have your design reviewed by other software professionals) before writing any code. If this process involves analyzing and designing your system from an object-oriented point of view, it is called an object-oriented analysis and design (OOAD) process. Experienced programmers know that analysis and design can save many hours by helping them to avoid an ill-planned system-development approach that has to be abandoned part of the way through its implementation, possibly wasting considerable time, money and effort.

OOAD is the generic term for the process of analyzing a problem and developing an approach for solving it. Small problems like the ones discussed in these first few chapters do not require an exhaustive OOAD process. It may be sufficient to write pseudocode before we begin writing C++ code. Pseudocode is an informal means of expressing program logic. It is not actually a programming language, but we can use it as a kind of outline to guide us as we write our code. We introduce pseudocode in Chapter 4, Control Statements: Part 1.

As problems and the groups of people solving them increase in size, the methods of OOAD become more appropriate than pseudocode. Ideally, members of a group should agree on a strictly defined process for solving their problem and a uniform way of communicating the results of that process to one another. Although many different OOAD processes exist, a single graphical language for communicating the results of *any* OOAD process has come into wide use. This language, known as the Unified Modeling Language (UML), was developed in the mid-1990s under the initial direction of three software methodologists—Grady Booch, James Rumbaugh and Ivar Jacobson.

History of the UML

In the 1980s, increasing numbers of organizations began using OOP to build their applications, and a need developed for a standard OOAD process. Many methodologists—including Booch, Rumbaugh and Jacobson—individually produced and promoted separate processes to satisfy this need. Each process had its own notation, or "language" (in the form of graphical diagrams), to convey the results of analysis and design.

By the early 1990s, different organizations, and even divisions within the same organization, were using their own unique processes and notations. At the same time, these organizations also wanted to use software tools that would support their particular processes. Software vendors found it difficult to provide tools for so many processes. A standard notation and standard processes were needed.

In 1994, James Rumbaugh joined Grady Booch at Rational Software Corporation (now a division of IBM), and the two began working to unify their popular processes. They soon were joined by Ivar Jacobson. In 1996, the group released early versions of the UML to the software engineering community and requested feedback. Around the same time, an organization known as the Object Management Group™ (OMG™) invited submissions for a common modeling language. The OMG (www.omg.org) is a nonprofit organization that promotes the standardization of object-oriented technologies by issuing guidelines and specifications, such as the UML. Several corporations—among them HP, IBM, Microsoft, Oracle and Rational Software—had already recognized the need for a common modeling language. In response to the OMG's request for proposals, these companies formed UML Partners—the consortium that developed the UML version 1.1 and submitted it to the OMG. The OMG accepted the proposal and, in 1997, assumed responsibility for the continuing maintenance and revision of the UML. The UML version 2 now available marks the first major revision of the UML since the 1997 version 1.1 standard. We present UML 2 terminology and notation throughout this book.

What Is the UML?

The UML is now the most widely used graphical representation scheme for modeling object-oriented systems. It has indeed unified the various popular notational schemes. Those who design systems use the language (in the form of diagrams) to model their systems.

An attractive feature of the UML is its flexibility. The UML is extensible (i.e., capable of being enhanced with new features) and is independent of any particular OOAD process. UML modelers are free to use various processes in designing systems, but all developers can now express their designs with one standard set of graphical notations.

The UML is a complex, feature-rich graphical language. In our Software Engineering Case Study sections, we present a simple, concise subset of these features. We then use this subset to guide you through a first design experience with the UML intended for novice object-oriented programmers in first- or second-semester programming courses.

UML Web Resources

For more information about the UML, refer to the websites listed below. For additional UML sites, refer to the web resources listed at the end of Section 2.8.

`www.uml.org`
This UML resource page from the Object Management Group (OMG) provides specification documents for the UML and other object-oriented technologies.

`www.ibm.com/software/rational/uml`
This is the UML resource page for IBM Rational—the successor to the Rational Software Corporation (the company that created the UML).

Recommended Readings

The following books provide information about object-oriented design with the UML:

Ambler, S. *The Object Primer: Agile Model-Driven Development with UML 2.0, Third Edition.* New York: Cambridge University Press, 2005.

Arlow, J., and I. Neustadt. *UML and the Unified Process: Practical Object-Oriented Analysis and Design, Second Edition.* Boston: Addison-Wesley Professional, 2006.

Fowler, M. *UML Distilled, Third Edition: A Brief Guide to the Standard Object Modeling Language.* Boston: Addison-Wesley Professional, 2004.

Rumbaugh, J., I. Jacobson and G. Booch. *The Unified Modeling Language User Guide, Second Edition.* Boston: Addison-Wesley Professional, 2006.

Section 1.21 Self-Review Exercises

1.1   List three examples of real-world objects that we did not mention. For each object, list several attributes and behaviors.

1.2   Pseudocode is _____.
   a)   another term for OOAD
   b)   a programming language used to display UML diagrams
   c)   an informal means of expressing program logic
   d)   a graphical representation scheme for modeling object-oriented systems

1.3   The UML is used primarily to _____.
   a)   test object-oriented systems
   b)   design object-oriented systems
   c)   implement object-oriented systems
   d)   Both a and b

Answers to Section 1.21 Self-Review Exercises

1.1   [*Note:* Answers may vary.] a) A television's attributes include the size of the screen, the number of colors it can display, its current channel and its current volume. A television turns on and off, changes channels, displays video and plays sounds. b) A coffee maker's attributes include the maximum volume of water it can hold, the time required to brew a pot of coffee and the temperature of the heating plate under the coffee pot. A coffee maker turns on and off, brews coffee and heats coffee. c) A turtle's attributes include its age, the size of its shell and its weight. A turtle walks, retreats into its shell, emerges from its shell and eats vegetation.

1.2   c.

1.3   b.

1.22 Wrap-Up

This chapter introduced basic hardware and software concepts. You studied the history of the Internet and the World Wide Web and learned about the Web 2.0 phenomenon. We discussed the different types of programming languages, their history and which programming languages are most widely used. We also discussed the C++ Standard Library which contains reusable classes and functions that help C++ programmers create portable C++ programs.

We presented basic object technology concepts, including classes, objects, attributes, behaviors, encapsulation and inheritance. You also learned about the history and purpose of the UML—the industry-standard graphical language for modeling object-oriented software systems.

You learned the typical steps for creating and executing a C++ application. You "test-drove" a sample C++ application similar to the types of applications you'll learn to program in this book.

We discussed several key software technologies and concepts, including open source, and looked to the future of C++. In later chapters, you'll study two open source libraries—Ogre for graphics and game programming, and Boost for broadly enhancing the C++ Standard Library's capabilities.

In the next chapter, you'll create your first C++ applications. You'll see several examples that demonstrate how programs display messages on the screen and obtain information from the user at the keyboard for processing. We analyze and explain each example to help you ease your way into C++ programming.

1.23 Web Resources

This section provides many web resources that will be useful to you as you learn C++. The sites include C++ resources, C++ development tools for students and professionals and some links to fun games built with C++. This section also lists our own websites where you can find downloads and resources associated with this book.

Deitel & Associates Web Sites

www.deitel.com/books/cpphtp6/
The Deitel & Associates *C++ How to Program, 6/e* site. Here you'll find links to the book's examples and other resources, such as our *Dive Into™ guides* that help you get started with several C++ integrated development environments (IDEs).

www.deitel.com/cplusplus/
www.deitel.com/cplusplusgameprogramming/
www.deitel.com/cplusplusboostlibraries/
www.deitel.com/codesearchengines
www.deitel.com/programmingprojects
The Deitel C++ and related Resource Centers currently available on www.deitel.com. Start your search here for resources, downloads, tutorials, documentation, books, e-books, journals, articles, blogs, RSS feeds and more that will help you develop C++ applications.

www.deitel.com
Please check the Deitel & Associates site for updates, corrections and additional resources for all Deitel publications.

www.deitel.com/newsletter/subscribe.html
Please visit this site to subscribe for the *Deitel® Buzz Online* e-mail newsletter to follow the Deitel & Associates publishing program, including updates and errata to *C++ How to Program, 6/e*.

Compilers and Development Tools

www.thefreecountry.com/developercity/ccompilers.shtml
This site lists free C and C++ compilers for a variety of operating systems.

`msdn.microsoft.com/vstudio/express/visualc/default.aspx`
The *Microsoft Visual C++ Express* site provides a free download of *Visual C++ Express* edition, product information, overviews and supplemental materials for Visual C++.

`www.codegear.com/products/cppbuilder`
This is a link to the *Code Gear C++Builder* site.

`www.compilers.net`
Compilers.net is designed to help users locate compilers.

`developer.intel.com/software/products/compilers/cwin/index.htm`
An evaluation download of the *Intel C++ compiler* is available at this site.

Resources

`www.hal9k.com/cug`
The *C/C++ Users Group (CUG)* site contains C++ resources, journals, shareware and freeware.

`www.devx.com`
DevX is a comprehensive resource for programmers that provides the latest news, tools and techniques for various programming languages. The *C++ Zone* offers tips, discussion forums, technical help and online newsletters.

`www.acm.org/crossroads/xrds3-2/ovp32.html`
The Association for Computing Machinery (ACM) site offers a comprehensive listing of C++ resources, including recommended texts, journals and magazines, published standards, newsletters, FAQs and newsgroups.

`www.accu.informika.ru/resources/public/terse/cpp.htm`
The Association of C & C++ Users (ACCU) site contains links to C++ tutorials, articles, developer information, discussions and book reviews.

`www.cuj.com`
The *C/C++ User's Journal* is an online magazine that contains articles, tutorials and downloads. The site features news about C++, forums and links to information about development tools.

`www.research.att.com/~bs/homepage.html`
This is the site for Bjarne Stroustrup, designer of the C++ programming language. This site provides a list of C++ resources, FAQs and other useful C++ information.

Games and Game Programming

`www.codearchive.com/list.php?go=0708`
This site has several C++ games available for download.

`www.mathtools.net/C_C__/Games/`
This site includes links to numerous games built with C++. The source code for most of the games is available for download.

`www.gametutorials.com/gtstore/c-3-c-tutorials.aspx`
This site has tutorials on game programming in C++. Each tutorial includes a description of the game and a list of the methods and functions used in the tutorial.

Summary

Section 1.1 Introduction

- Computers (often referred to as hardware) are controlled by software (i.e., the instructions you write to command the computer to perform actions and make decisions).
- C++ is one of today's most popular software development languages.

- Computing costs have been decreasing dramatically due to rapid developments in both hardware and software technologies.
- Silicon chip technology has made computing so economical that about a billion general-purpose computers are in use worldwide.
- Object orientation is the key programming methodology used by programmers today.

Section 1.2 What Is a Computer?
- A computer is capable of performing computations and making logical decisions at speeds billions of times faster than human beings can.
- Computers process data under the control of sets of instructions called computer programs, which guide the computer through orderly sets of actions specified by computer programmers.
- The various devices that comprise a computer system are referred to as hardware.
- The computer programs that run on a computer are referred to as software.

Section 1.3 Computer Organization
- The input unit is the "receiving" section of the computer. It obtains information from input devices and places it at the disposal of the other units for processing.
- The output unit is the "shipping" section of the computer. It takes information processed by the computer and places it on output devices to make it available for use outside the computer.
- The memory unit is the rapid-access, relatively low-capacity "warehouse" section of the computer. It retains information that has been entered through the input unit, making it immediately available for processing when needed, and retains information that has already been processed until it can be placed on output devices by the output unit.
- The arithmetic and logic unit (ALU) is the "manufacturing" section of the computer. It is responsible for performing calculations and making decisions.
- The central processing unit (CPU) is the "administrative" section of the computer. It coordinates and supervises the operation of the other sections.
- The secondary storage unit is the long-term, high-capacity "warehousing" section of the computer. Programs or data not being used by the other units are normally placed on secondary storage devices (e.g., disks) until they are needed, possibly hours, days, months or even years later.

Section 1.4 Early Operating Systems
- Early computers could perform only one job or task at a time. This is often called single-user batch processing.
- Operating systems were developed to help make it more convenient to use computers.
- Multiprogramming involves the sharing of a computer's resources among the jobs competing for its attention, so that the jobs appear to run simultaneously.
- Timesharing is a special case of multiprogramming in which users access the computer through terminals, typically devices with keyboards and screens. Dozens or even hundreds of users share the computer at once. The computer actually does not run them all simultaneously. Rather, it runs a small portion of one user's job, then moves on to service the next user, perhaps providing service to each user several times per second. Thus, the users' programs appear to be running simultaneously.

Section 1.5 Personal, Distributed and Client/Server Computing
- Apple Computer popularized personal computing.

- IBM's Personal Computer quickly legitimized personal computing in business, industry and government organizations, where IBM mainframes were heavily used.

- Although early personal computers were not powerful enough to timeshare several users, these machines could be linked together in computer networks, sometimes over telephone lines and sometimes in local area networks (LANs) within an organization. This led to the phenomenon of distributed computing.

- Today's personal computers are as powerful as the million-dollar machines of just a few decades ago, and information is shared easily across computer networks.

- C++ has become widely used for writing software for operating systems, for computer networking and for distributed client/server applications.

Section 1.6 The Internet and the World Wide Web
- The Internet—a global network of computers—was initiated almost four decades ago with funding supplied by the U.S. Department of Defense.

- With the introduction of the World Wide Web—which allows computer users to locate and view multimedia-based documents on almost any subject over the Internet—the Internet has exploded into the world's premier communication mechanism.

Section 1.7 Web 2.0
- Web 2.0 has no single definition but can be explained through a series of Internet trends, one being the empowerment of the user. Companies, such as eBay, are built almost entirely on community-generated content.

- Web 2.0 takes advantage of collective intelligence, the idea that collaboration will result in intelligent ideas.

- Tagging, or labeling content, is another key part of the collaborative theme of Web 2.0.

- Social networking sites, which keep track of users' interpersonal relationships, have experienced extraordinary growth as part of Web 2.0.

- Social media sites have also gained immense popularity due to the increased availability and use of broadband Internet, often referred to as high-speed Internet.

- Blogs, websites characterized by short postings in reverse chronological order, have become a major social phenomenon within Web 2.0. Many bloggers are recognized as part of the media, and companies are reaching out to the blogosphere to track consumer opinions.

- The increased popularity of open source software has made it cheaper and easier to start Web 2.0 companies. Web services are on the rise, favoring the "webtop" over the desktop in much new development.

- Mashups combine two or more existing web applications to serve a new purpose and are dependent on small modular pieces and open access to web services APIs, which allow developers to integrate other web services into their applications.

- Many Web 2.0 companies use advertising as their main source of monetization.

Section 1.8 Machine Languages, Assembly Languages and High-Level Languages
- Any computer can directly understand only its own machine language, which generally consist of strings of numbers that instruct computers to perform their most elementary operations.

- English-like abbreviations form the basis of assembly languages. Translator programs called assemblers convert assembly-language programs to machine language.

- Compilers translate high-level language programs into machine-language programs. High-level languages (like C++) contain English words and conventional mathematical notations.

- Interpreter programs directly execute high-level language programs, eliminating the need to compile them into machine language.

Section 1.9 History of C and C++
- C++ evolved from C, which evolved from two previous programming languages, BCPL and B.
- C++ is an extension of C developed by Bjarne Stroustrup in the early 1980s at Bell Laboratories. C++ enhances the C language and provides capabilities for object-oriented programming.
- Objects are reusable software components that model items in the real world. Using a modular, object-oriented design and implementation approach can make software development groups more productive than with previous programming techniques.

Section 1.10 C++ Standard Library
- C++ programs consist of pieces called classes and functions. You can program each piece you may need to form a C++ program. However, most C++ programmers take advantage of the rich collections of existing classes and functions in the C++ Standard Library.

Section 1.11 History of Java
- Java is used to create dynamic and interactive content for web pages, develop enterprise applications, enhance web server functionality, provide applications for consumer devices and more.

Section 1.12 Fortran, COBOL, Pascal and Ada
- FORTRAN (FORmula TRANslator) was developed by IBM Corporation in the mid-1950s for scientific and engineering applications that require complex mathematical computations.
- COBOL (COmmon Business Oriented Language) was developed in the late 1950s by a group of computer manufacturers and government and industrial computer users. COBOL is used primarily for commercial applications that require precise and efficient data manipulation.
- Ada was developed under the sponsorship of the United States Department of Defense (DoD) during the 1970s and early 1980s. Ada provides multitasking, which allows programmers to specify that many activities are to occur in parallel.

Section 1.13 BASIC, Visual Basic, Visual C++, C# and .NET
- The BASIC (Beginner's All-Purpose Symbolic Instruction Code) programming language was developed in the mid-1960s at Dartmouth College as a language for writing simple programs. BASIC's primary purpose was to familiarize novices with programming techniques.
- Microsoft's Visual Basic was introduced in the early 1990s to simplify the process of developing Microsoft Windows applications.
- Microsoft has a corporate-wide strategy for integrating the Internet and the web into computer applications. This strategy is implemented in Microsoft's .NET platform.
- The .NET platform's three primary programming languages are Visual Basic (based on the original BASIC), Visual C++ (based on C++) and Visual C# (a new language based on C++ and Java that was developed expressly for the .NET platform).
- .NET developers can write software components in their preferred language, then form applications by combining those components with components written in any .NET language.

Section 1.14 Key Software Trend: Object Technology
- Not until object-oriented programming became widely used in the 1990s did software developers feel they had the tools to make major strides in the software development process.
- Object technology dates back to the mid 1960s. The C++ programming language, developed at AT&T by Bjarne Stroustrup in the early 1980s, is based on two languages—C, which initially

was developed at AT&T to implement the UNIX operating system in the early 1970s, and Simula 67, a simulation programming language developed in Europe and released in 1967. C++ absorbed the features of C and added Simula's capabilities for creating and manipulating objects.

- Neither C nor C++ was originally intended for wide use beyond the AT&T research laboratories, but grass roots support rapidly developed for each.

- Object technology is a packaging scheme that helps us create meaningful software units.

- A key problem with procedural programming is that the program units do not effectively mirror real-world entities, so these units are not particularly reusable.

- With object technology, the software entities created (called classes), if properly designed, tend to be reusable on future projects. Using libraries of reusable componentry can greatly reduce effort required to implement certain kinds of systems.

- Some organizations report that the key benefit object-oriented programming gives them is the production of software which is more understandable, better organized and easier to maintain, modify and debug. It has been estimated that as much as 80 percent of software costs are associated not with the original efforts to develop the software, but with the continued evolution and maintenance of that software throughout its lifetime.

Section 1.15 Typical C++ Development Environment
- C++ systems generally consist of three parts: a program development environment, the language and the C++ Standard Library.

- C++ programs typically go through six phases: *edit, preprocess, compile, link, load* and *execute*.

- C++ source code filenames often end with the .cpp, .cxx, .cc or .C extensions.

- A preprocessor program executes automatically before the compiler's translation phase begins. The C++ preprocessor obeys commands called preprocessor directives, which indicate that certain manipulations are to be performed on the program before compilation.

- The object code produced by the C++ compiler typically contains "holes" due to references to functions and data defined elsewhere. A linker links the object code with the code for the missing functions to produce an executable image (with no missing pieces).

- The loader takes the executable image from disk and transfers it to memory for execution.

- Most programs in C++ input and/or output data. Data is often input from cin (the standard input stream) which is normally the keyboard, but cin can be redirected from another device. Data is often output to cout (the standard output stream), which is normally the computer screen, but cout can be redirected to another device. The cerr stream is used to display error messages.

Section 1.18 Software Technologies
- Agile Software Development is a set of methodologies that try to get software implemented quickly with fewer resources then previous methodologies.

- Refactoring involves reworking code to make it clearer and easier to maintain while preserving its functionality.

- Design patterns are proven architectures for constructing flexible and maintainable object-oriented software.

- The computer game business is larger than the first-run movie business. College courses and even majors are now devoted to the sophisticated software techniques used in game programming.

- Open source software is a style of developing software in contrast to the proprietary development that dominated software's early years. With open source development, individuals and companies develop, maintain and evolve software in exchange for the right to use that software for their own purposes. Open source code generally gets scrutinized by a much larger audience than proprietary software, so bugs get removed faster. Open source also encourages more innovation.

- Linux is an open source operating system.
- MySQL is an open source database management system.
- PHP is the most popular open source server-side "scripting" language for developing Internet-based applications.
- LAMP is an acronym for the set of open source technologies that many developers used to build web applications—it stands for Linux, Apache, MySQL and PHP (or Perl or Python—two other languages used for similar purposes).
- Ruby on Rails combines the scripting language Ruby with the Rails web application framework developed by the company 37Signals.
- With Software as a Service (SaaS) the software runs on servers. When those servers are updated, all clients worldwide see the new capabilities; no local installation is needed. You access the service through a browser.

Section 1.19 Game Programming with the Ogre Libraries
- Ogre is an open-source project maintained by the Ogre team at `www.ogre3d.org`.
- Ogre (Object-Oriented Graphics Rendering Engine), one of the leading graphics engines, has been used in many commercial products including video games. It provides an object-oriented interface for 3D graphics programming, and runs on the Windows, Linux and Mac platforms.
- OgreAL is a wrapper around the OpenAL audio library. The wrapper allows us to integrate sound functionality into Ogre code.

Section 1.20 Future of C++: Open Source Boost Libraries, TR1 and C++0x
- Bjarne Stroustrup, creator of the C++ programming language, has expressed his vision for the future of C++. The main goals for the new standard are to make C++ easier to learn, improve library building capabilities, and increase compatibility with the C programming language.
- The Boost C++ Libraries are free, open source libraries created by members of the C++ community. Boost provides C++ programmers with useful, well-designed libraries that work well with the existing C++ Standard Library. The Boost libraries can be used by C++ programmers working on a wide variety of platforms with many different compilers.
- Technical Report 1 describes the proposed changes to the C++ Standard Library, many of which are based on current Boost libraries. These libraries add useful functionality to C++.
- C++0x is the working name for the next version of the C++ Standard. It includes some changes to the core language and many of the library additions described in TR1.
- Boost has grown to over 70 libraries, with more being added regularly. Today there are thousands of programmers in the Boost community.

Section 1.21 Software Engineering Case Study: Introduction to Object Technology and the UML
- The Unified Modeling Language (UML) is a graphical language that allows people who build systems to represent their object-oriented designs in a common notation.
- Object-oriented design (OOD) models software components in terms of real-world objects. It takes advantage of class relationships, where objects of a certain class have the same characteristics. It also takes advantage of inheritance relationships, where newly created classes of objects are derived by absorbing characteristics of existing classes and adding unique characteristics of their

own. OOD encapsulates data (attributes) and functions (behavior) into objects—the data and functions of an object are intimately tied together.

- Objects have the property of information hiding—objects normally are not allowed to know how other objects are implemented.

- Object-oriented programming (OOP) allows programmers to implement object-oriented designs as working systems.

- C++ programmers create their own user-defined types called classes. Each class contains data (known as data members) and the set of functions (known as member functions) that manipulate that data and provide services to clients.

- Classes can have relationships with other classes. These relationships are called associations.

- Packaging software as classes makes it possible for future software systems to reuse the classes. Groups of related classes are often packaged as reusable components.

- An instance of a class is called an object.

- With object technology, programmers can build much of the software they will need by combining standardized, interchangeable parts called classes.

- The process of analyzing and designing a system from an object-oriented point of view is called object-oriented analysis and design (OOAD).

Terminology

action	COBOL (COmmon Business
Ada	Oriented Language)
Agile Software Development	collective intelligence
American National Standards Institute (ANSI)	community-generated content
analysis	compile phase
ANSI/ISO standard C	compiler
arithmetic and logic unit (ALU)	component
assembler	computer
assembly language	computer program
association	computer programmer
attribute of an object	core memory
BASIC (Beginner's All-Purpose	data
Instruction Code)	data member
batch processing	debug
behavior of an object	decision
blog	design
blogosphere	design patterns
Booch, Grady	distributed computing
Boost C++ Libraries	dynamic content
broadband Internet	edit phase
C	editor
C++	encapsulate
C++ Standard Library	executable image
C++0x	execute phase
C#	extensible
central processing unit (CPU)	file server
class	Fortran (FORmula TRANslator)
client	function
client/server computing	game programming

Google AdSense
hardware
hardware platform
high-level language
information hiding
inheritance
input device
input unit
input/output (I/O)
instantiate
interface
International Organization for Standardization (ISO)
Internet
interpreter
ISO/IEC standard C++
Jacobson, Ivar
Java
LAMP
link phase
linker
Linux
live-code approach
load phase
loader
local area networks (LANs)
logical unit
machine dependent
machine independent
machine language
mashups
member function
memory
memory unit
method
multiprocessor
multiprogramming
multitasking
multithreading
MySQL
.NET platform
network effects of social networking
object
object code
Object Management Group (OMG)
object-oriented analysis and design (OOAD)
object-oriented design (OOD)
object-oriented programming (OOP)
Ogre (Object-Oriented Graphics Rendering Engine)

OgreAL
open source
open source software
OpenAL audio library
operating system
operation
output device
output unit
personal computing
PHP
platform
portable
premium content
preprocess phase
preprocessor directives
primary memory
procedural programming
pseudocode
Rational Software Corporation
refactoring
requirements specification
Ruby on Rails
Rumbaugh, James
runtime errors or execution-time errors
secondary storage unit
Semantic Web
smart pointers
social networking
Software as a Service (SaaS) software
software reuse
source code
structured programming
structured systems analysis and design
supercomputer
tagging
task
Technical Report 1
throughput
timesharing
translation
translator program
Unified Modeling Language (UML)
user-defined type
Visual Basic
Visual C++
Web 3.0
web services
wiki
workstation
World Wide Web

Self-Review Exercises

1.1   Fill in the blanks in each of the following:

a) The company that popularized personal computing was _____.

b) The computer that made personal computing legitimate in business and industry was the _____.

c) Computers process data under the control of sets of instructions called computer _____.

d) The six key logical units of the computer are the _____, _____, _____, _____, _____ and the _____.

e) The three classes of languages discussed in the chapter are _____, _____, and _____.

f) The programs that translate high-level language programs into machine language are called _____.

g) C is widely known as the development language of the _____ operating system.

h) The _____ language was developed by Wirth for teaching structured programming.

i) The Department of Defense developed the Ada language with a capability called _____, which allows programmers to specify that many activities can proceed in parallel.

j) _____, or labeling content, is another key part of the collaborative theme of Web 2.0.

k) With Internet applications, the desktop evolves to the _____.

l) _____ involves reworking code to make it clearer and easier to maintain while preserving its functionality.

m) With _____ development, individuals and companies contribute their efforts in developing, maintaining and evolving software in exchange for the right to use that software for their own purposes, typically at no charge.

n) _____ are used to match specific character patterns in text. They can be used to validate data to ensure that it is in a particular format, to replace parts of one string with another, or to split a string.

1.2   Fill in the blanks in each of the following sentences about the C++ environment.

a) C++ programs are normally typed into a computer using a(n) _____ program.

b) In a C++ system, a(n) _____ program executes before the compiler's translation phase begins.

c) The _____ program combines the output of the compiler with various library functions to produce an executable image.

d) The _____ program transfers the executable image of a C++ program from disk to memory.

1.3   Fill in the blanks in each of the following statements (based on Section 1.21):

a) Objects have the property of _____—although objects may know how to communicate with one another across well-defined interfaces, they normally are not allowed to know how other objects are implemented.

b) C++ programmers concentrate on creating _____, which contain data members and the member functions that manipulate those data members and provide services to clients.

c) Classes can have relationships with other classes. These relationships are called _____.

d) The process of analyzing and designing a system from an object-oriented point of view is called _____.

    e) OOD also takes advantage of _____ relationships, where new classes of objects are derived by absorbing characteristics of existing classes, then adding unique characteristics of their own.

    f) _____ is a graphical language that allows people who design software systems to use an industry-standard notation to represent them.

    g) The size, shape, color and weight of an object are considered _____ of the object.

Answers to Self-Review Exercises

1.1   a) Apple. b) IBM Personal Computer. c) programs. d) input unit, output unit, memory unit, arithmetic and logic unit, central processing unit, secondary storage unit. e) machine languages, assembly languages and high-level languages. f) compilers. g) UNIX. h) Pascal. i) multitasking. j) Tagging. k) webtop. l) Refactoring. m) open source. n) Regular expressions.

1.2   a) editor. b) preprocessor. c) linker. d) loader.

1.3   a) information hiding. b) classes. c) associations. d) object-oriented analysis and design (OOAD). e) inheritance. f) The Unified Modeling Language (UML). g) attributes.

Exercises

1.4   Categorize each of the following items as either hardware or software:

    a) CPU
    b) C++ compiler
    c) ALU
    d) C++ preprocessor
    e) input unit
    f) an editor program

1.5   Why might you want to write a program in a machine-independent language instead of a machine-dependent language? Why might a machine-dependent language be more appropriate for writing certain types of programs?

1.6   Fill in the blanks in each of the following statements:

    a) Which logical unit of the computer receives information from outside the computer for use by the computer? _____.

    b) The process of instructing the computer to solve specific problems is called _____.

    c) What type of computer language uses English-like abbreviations for machine-language instructions? _____.

    d) Which logical unit of the computer sends information that has already been processed by the computer to various devices so that the information may be used outside the computer? _____.

    e) Which logical units of the computer retain information? _____.

    f) Which logical unit of the computer performs calculations? _____.

    g) Which logical unit of the computer makes logical decisions? _____.

    h) The level of computer language most convenient for you to write programs quickly and easily is _____.

    i) The only language that a computer directly understands is called that computer's _____.

    j) Which logical unit of the computer coordinates the activities of all the other logical units? _____.

1.7   Why is so much attention today focused on object-oriented programming in general and C++ in particular?

1.8   Distinguish between the terms fatal error and nonfatal error. Why might you prefer to experience a fatal error rather than a nonfatal error?

1.9   Give a brief answer to each of the following questions:
  a) Why does this text discuss structured programming in addition to object-oriented programming?
  b) What are the typical steps (mentioned in the text) of an object-oriented design process?
  c) What kinds of messages do people send to one another?
  d) Objects send messages to one another across well-defined interfaces. What interfaces does a car radio (object) present to its user (a person object)?

1.10   You are probably wearing on your wrist one of the world's most common types of objects—a watch. Discuss how each of the following terms and concepts applies to the notion of a watch: object, attributes, behaviors, class, inheritance (consider, for example, an alarm clock), abstraction, modeling, messages, encapsulation, interface, information hiding, data members and member functions.

1.11   Fill in the blanks in each of the following statements (based on Section 1.18, Software Technologies):
  a) The open source database management system used in LAMP development is _____.
  b) A key advantage of Software as a Service (SaaS) is _____.
  c) _____ are proven architectures for constructing flexible and maintainable object-oriented software.
  d) _____ is the most popular open source server-side "scripting" language for developing Internet-based applications.

2

Introduction to C++ Programming

OBJECTIVES

In this chapter you'll learn:

- To write simple computer programs in C++.
- To write simple input and output statements.
- To use fundamental types.
- Basic computer memory concepts.
- To use arithmetic operators.
- The precedence of arithmetic operators.
- To write simple decision-making statements.

2.1 Introduction

We now introduce C++ programming, which facilitates a disciplined approach to program design. Most of the C++ programs you'll study in this book process information and display results. In this chapter, we present five examples that demonstrate how your programs can display messages and obtain information from the user for processing. The first three examples simply display messages on the screen. The next obtains two numbers from a user, calculates their sum and displays the result. The accompanying discussion shows you how to perform various arithmetic calculations and save their results for later use. The fifth example demonstrates decision-making fundamentals by showing you how to compare two numbers, then display messages based on the comparison results. We analyze each program one line at a time to help you ease your way into C++ programming. To help you apply the skills you learn here, we provide many programming problems in the chapter's exercises.

2.2 First Program in C++: Printing a Line of Text

C++ uses notations that may appear strange to nonprogrammers. We now consider a simple program that prints a line of text (Fig. 2.1). This program illustrates several important features of the C++ language. We consider each line in detail.
   Lines 1 and 2

```
// Fig. 2.1: fig02_01.cpp
// Text-printing program.
```

each begin with //, indicating that the remainder of each line is a comment. You insert comments to document your programs and to help other people read and understand them. Comments do not cause the computer to perform any action when the program is run—they are ignored by the C++ compiler and do not cause any machine-language object code to be generated. The comment Text-printing program describes the purpose of the program. A comment beginning with // is called a single-line comment because it terminates at the end of the current line. [*Note:* You also may use C's style in which a comment—possibly containing many lines—begins with /* and ends with */.]

```
 1   // Fig. 2.1: fig02_01.cpp
 2   // Text-printing program.
 3   #include <iostream> // allows program to output data to the screen
 4
 5   // function main begins program execution
 6   int main()
 7   {
 8      std::cout << "Welcome to C++!\n"; // display message
 9
10      return 0; // indicate that program ended successfully
11
12   } // end function main
```

```
Welcome to C++!
```

Fig. 2.1 | Text-printing program.

Good Programming Practice 2.1

Every program should begin with a comment that describes the purpose of the program, author, date and time. (We are not showing the author, date and time in this book's programs because this information would be redundant.)

Line 3

```
#include <iostream> // allows program to output data to the screen
```

is a **preprocessor directive**, which is a message to the C++ preprocessor (introduced in Section 1.15). Lines that begin with # are processed by the preprocessor before the program is compiled. This line notifies the preprocessor to include in the program the contents of the **input/output stream header file <iostream>**. This file must be included for any program that outputs data to the screen or inputs data from the keyboard using C++-style stream input/output. The program in Fig. 2.1 outputs data to the screen, as we'll soon see. We discuss header files in more detail in Chapter 6 and explain the contents of <iostream> in Chapter 15.

Common Programming Error 2.1

Forgetting to include the <iostream> header file in a program that inputs data from the keyboard or outputs data to the screen causes the compiler to issue an error message, because the compiler cannot recognize references to the stream components (e.g., cout).

Line 4 is simply a blank line. You use blank lines, space characters and tab characters (i.e., "tabs") to make programs easier to read. Together, these characters are known as white space. White-space characters are normally ignored by the compiler. In this chapter and several that follow, we discuss conventions for using white-space characters to enhance program readability.

Good Programming Practice 2.2

Use blank lines, space characters and tabs to enhance program readability.

Line 5

```
// function main begins program execution
```

is another single-line comment indicating that program execution begins at the next line.
Line 6

```
int main()
```

is a part of every C++ program. The parentheses after main indicate that main is a program building block called a function. C++ programs typically consist of one or more functions and classes (as you'll learn in Chapter 3). Exactly one function in every program must be main. Figure 2.1 contains only one function. C++ programs begin executing at function main, even if main is not the first function in the program. The keyword int to the left of main indicates that main "returns" an integer (whole number) value. A keyword is a word in code that is reserved by C++ for a specific use. The complete list of C++ keywords can be found in Fig. 4.3. We'll explain what it means for a function to "return a value" when we demonstrate how to create your own functions in Section 3.5 and when we study functions in greater depth in Chapter 6. For now, simply include the keyword int to the left of main in each of your programs.

The left brace, {, (line 7) must begin the body of every function. A corresponding right brace, }, (line 12) must end each function's body. Line 8

```
std::cout << "Welcome to C++!\n"; // display message
```

instructs the computer to perform an action—namely, to print the string of characters contained between the double quotation marks. A string is sometimes called a character string, a message or a string literal. We refer to characters between double quotation marks simply as strings. White-space characters in strings are not ignored by the compiler.

The entire line 8, including std::cout, the << operator, the string "Welcome to C++!\n" and the semicolon (;), is called a statement. Every C++ statement must end with a semicolon (also known as the statement terminator). Preprocessor directives (like #include) do not end with a semicolon. Output and input in C++ are accomplished with streams of characters. Thus, when the preceding statement is executed, it sends the stream of characters Welcome to C++!\n to the standard output stream object—std::cout—which is normally "connected" to the screen. We discuss std::cout's many features in detail in Chapter 15, Stream Input/Output.

Notice that we placed std:: before cout. This is required when we use names that we've brought into the program by the preprocessor directive #include <iostream>. The notation std::cout specifies that we are using a name, in this case cout, that belongs to "namespace" std. The names cin (the standard input stream) and cerr (the standard error stream)—introduced in Chapter 1—also belong to namespace std. Namespaces are an advanced C++ feature that we discuss in depth in Chapter 25, Other Topics. For now, you should simply remember to include std:: before each mention of cout, cin and cerr in a program. This can be cumbersome—in Fig. 2.13, we introduce the using declaration, which will enable us to omit std:: before each use of a name in the std namespace.

The << operator is referred to as the stream insertion operator. When this program executes, the value to the operator's right, the right operand, is inserted in the output stream. Notice that the operator points in the direction of where the data goes. The right operand's characters normally print exactly as they appear between the double quotes.

However, the characters \n are not printed on the screen (Fig. 2.1). The backslash (\) is called an escape character. It indicates that a "special" character is to be output. When a backslash is encountered in a string of characters, the next character is combined with the backslash to form an escape sequence. The escape sequence \n means newline. It causes the cursor (i.e., the current screen-position indicator) to move to the beginning of the next line on the screen. Some common escape sequences are listed in Fig. 2.2.

Common Programming Error 2.2

Omitting the semicolon at the end of a C++ statement is a syntax error. (Again, preprocessor directives do not end in a semicolon.) The syntax of a programming language specifies the rules for creating proper programs in that language. A syntax error occurs when the compiler encounters code that violates C++'s language rules (i.e., its syntax). The compiler normally issues an error message to help you locate and fix the incorrect code. Syntax errors are also called compiler errors, compile-time errors or compilation errors, because the compiler detects them during the compilation phase. You cannot execute your program until you correct all the syntax errors in it. As you'll see, some compilation errors are not syntax errors.

Line 10

```
return 0; // indicate that program ended successfully
```

is one of several means we'll use to exit a function. When the `return` statement is used at the end of `main`, as shown here, the value 0 indicates that the program has terminated successfully. In Chapter 6 we discuss functions in detail, and the reasons for including this statement will become clear. For now, simply include this statement in each program, or the compiler may produce a warning on some systems. The right brace, }, (line 12) indicates the end of function `main`.

Good Programming Practice 2.3

Many programmers make the last character printed by a function a newline (\n). This ensures that the function will leave the screen cursor positioned at the beginning of a new line. Conventions of this nature encourage software reusability—a key goal in software development.

Escape sequence	Description
\n	Newline. Position the screen cursor to the beginning of the next line.
\t	Horizontal tab. Move the screen cursor to the next tab stop.
\r	Carriage return. Position the screen cursor to the beginning of the current line; do not advance to the next line.
\a	Alert. Sound the system bell.
\\	Backslash. Used to print a backslash character.
\'	Single quote. Use to print a single quote character.
\"	Double quote. Used to print a double quote character.

Fig. 2.2 | Escape sequences.

Good Programming Practice 2.4

Indent the entire body of each function one level within the braces that delimit the body of the function. This makes a program's functional structure stand out and makes the program easier to read.

Good Programming Practice 2.5

Set a convention for the size of indent you prefer, then apply it uniformly. The tab key may be used to create indents, but tab stops may vary. We recommend using either 1/4-inch tab stops or (preferably) three spaces to form a level of indent.

2.3 Modifying Our First C++ Program

This section continues our introduction to C++ programming with two examples, showing how to modify the program in Fig. 2.1 to print text on one line by using multiple statements, and to print text on several lines by using a single statement.

Printing a Single Line of Text with Multiple Statements

`Welcome to C++!` can be printed several ways. For example, Fig. 2.3 performs stream insertion in multiple statements (lines 8–9), yet produces the same output as the program of Fig. 2.1. [*Note:* From this point forward, we use a darker shade of gray than the code table background to highlight the key features each program introduces.] Each stream insertion resumes printing where the previous one stopped. The first stream insertion (line 8) prints `Welcome` followed by a space, and the second stream insertion (line 9) begins printing on the same line immediately following the space. In general, C++ allows you to express statements in a variety of ways.

Printing Multiple Lines of Text with a Single Statement

A single statement can print multiple lines by using newline characters, as in line 8 of Fig. 2.4. Each time the \n (newline) escape sequence is encountered in the output stream, the screen cursor is positioned to the beginning of the next line. To get a blank line in your output, place two newline characters back to back, as in line 8.

```
1   // Fig. 2.3: fig02_03.cpp
2   // Printing a line of text with multiple statements.
3   #include <iostream> // allows program to output data to the screen
4
5   // function main begins program execution
6   int main()
7   {
8      std::cout << "Welcome ";
9      std::cout << "to C++!\n";
10
11     return 0; // indicate that program ended successfully
12
13  } // end function main
```

```
Welcome to C++!
```

Fig. 2.3 | Printing a line of text with multiple statements.

```
1   // Fig. 2.4: fig02_04.cpp
2   // Printing multiple lines of text with a single statement.
3   #include <iostream> // allows program to output data to the screen
4
5   // function main begins program execution
6   int main()
7   {
8      std::cout << "Welcome\nto\n\nC++!\n";
9
10     return 0; // indicate that program ended successfully
11
12  } // end function main
```

```
Welcome
to

C++!
```

Fig. 2.4 | Printing multiple lines of text with a single statement.

2.4 Another C++ Program: Adding Integers

Our next program uses the input stream object `std::cin` and the stream extraction operator, `>>`, to obtain two integers typed by a user at the keyboard, computes the sum of these values and outputs the result using `std::cout`. Figure 2.5 shows the program and sample inputs and outputs. Note that we highlight the user's input in bold.

The comments in lines 1 and 2

```
// Fig. 2.5: fig02_05.cpp
// Addition program that displays the sum of two numbers.
```

state the name of the file and the purpose of the program. The C++ preprocessor directive

```
#include <iostream> // allows program to perform input and output
```

in line 3 includes the contents of the `<iostream>` header file in the program.

The program begins execution with function `main` (line 6). The left brace (line 7) marks the beginning of `main`'s body and the corresponding right brace (line 25) marks the end of `main`.

Lines 9–11

```
int number1; // first integer to add
int number2; // second integer to add
int sum; // sum of number1 and number2
```

are declarations. The identifiers `number1`, `number2` and `sum` are the names of variables. A variable is a location in the computer's memory where a value can be stored for use by a program. These declarations specify that the variables `number1`, `number2` and `sum` are data of type `int`, meaning that these variables will hold integer values, i.e., whole numbers such as 7, –11, 0 and 31914. All variables must be declared with a name and a data type before they can be used in a program. Several variables of the same type may be declared in one

```
1    // Fig. 2.5: fig02_05.cpp
2    // Addition program that displays the sum of two integers.
3    #include <iostream> // allows program to perform input and output
4
5    // function main begins program execution
6    int main()
7    {
8       // variable declarations
9       int number1; // first integer to add
10      int number2; // second integer to add
11      int sum; // sum of number1 and number2
12
13      std::cout << "Enter first integer: "; // prompt user for data
14      std::cin >> number1; // read first integer from user into number1
15
16      std::cout << "Enter second integer: "; // prompt user for data
17      std::cin >> number2; // read second integer from user into number2
18
19      sum = number1 + number2; // add the numbers; store result in sum
20
21      std::cout << "Sum is " << sum << std::endl; // display sum; end line
22
23      return 0; // indicate that program ended successfully
24
25   } // end function main
```

```
Enter first integer: 45
Enter second integer: 72
Sum is 117
```

Fig. 2.5 | Addition program that displays the sum of two integers entered at the keyboard.

declaration or in multiple declarations. We could have declared all three variables in one declaration as follows:

```
int number1, number2, sum;
```

This makes the program less readable and prevents us from providing comments that describe each variable's purpose. If more than one name is declared in a declaration (as shown here), the names are separated by commas (,); this is referred to as a comma-separated list.

Good Programming Practice 2.6

Place a space after each comma (,) to make programs more readable.

Good Programming Practice 2.7

Some programmers prefer to declare each variable on a separate line. This format allows for easy insertion of a descriptive comment next to each declaration.

We'll soon discuss the data type double for specifying real numbers, and the data type char for specifying character data. Real numbers are numbers with decimal points, such as 3.4, 0.0 and −11.19. A char variable may hold only a single lowercase letter, a single uppercase letter, a single digit or a single special character (e.g., $ or *). Types such as int, `double` and `char` are often called fundamental types, primitive types or built-in types. Fundamental-type names are keywords and therefore must appear in all lowercase letters. Appendix C contains the complete list of fundamental types.

A variable name (such as `number1`) is any valid identifier that is not a keyword. An identifier is a series of characters consisting of letters, digits and underscores (_) that does not begin with a digit. C++ is case sensitive—uppercase and lowercase letters are different, so `a1` and `A1` are different identifiers.

Portability Tip 2.1

C++ allows identifiers of any length, but your C++ implementation may impose some restrictions on the length of identifiers. Use identifiers of 31 characters or fewer to ensure portability.

Good Programming Practice 2.8

Choosing meaningful identifiers makes a program self-documenting—a person can understand the program simply by reading it rather than having to refer to manuals or comments.

Good Programming Practice 2.9

Avoid using abbreviations in identifiers. This promotes program readability.

Good Programming Practice 2.10

Avoid identifiers that begin with underscores and double underscores, because C++ compilers may use names like that for their own purposes internally. This will prevent names you choose from being confused with names the compilers choose.

Error-Prevention Tip 2.1

Languages like C++ are "moving targets." As they evolve, more keywords could be added to the language. Avoid using "loaded" words like "object" as identifiers. Even though "object" is not currently a keyword in C++, it could become one; therefore, future compiling with new compilers could break existing code.

Declarations of variables can be placed almost anywhere in a program, but they must appear before their corresponding variables are used in the program. For example, in the program of Fig. 2.5, the declaration in line 9

```
int number1; // first integer to add
```

could have been placed immediately before line 14

```
std::cin >> number1; // read first integer from user into number1
```

the declaration in line 10

```
int number2; // second integer to add
```

could have been placed immediately before line 17

```
std::cin >> number2; // read second integer from user into number2
```

and the declaration in line 11

```
int sum; // sum of number1 and number2
```

could have been placed immediately before line 19

```
sum = number1 + number2; // add the numbers; store result in sum
```

Good Programming Practice 2.11

Always place a blank line between a declaration and adjacent executable statements. This makes the declarations stand out in the program and contributes to program clarity.

Good Programming Practice 2.12

If you prefer to place declarations at the beginning of a function, separate them from the executable statements in that function with one blank line to highlight where the declarations end and the executable statements begin.

Line 13

```
std::cout << "Enter first integer: "; // prompt user for data
```

prints the string Enter first integer: on the screen. This message is called a prompt because it directs the user to take a specific action. We like to pronounce the preceding statement as "std::cout *gets* the character string "Enter first integer: "." Line 14

```
std::cin >> number1; // read first integer from user into number1
```

uses the input stream object cin (of namespace std) and the stream extraction operator, >>, to obtain a value from the keyboard. Using the stream extraction operator with std::cin takes character input from the standard input stream, which is usually the keyboard. We like to pronounce the preceding statement as, "std::cin *gives* a value to number1" or simply "std::cin *gives* number1."

Error-Prevention Tip 2.2

Programs should validate the correctness of all input values to prevent erroneous information from affecting a program's calculations.

When the computer executes the preceding statement, it waits for the user to enter a value for variable number1. The user responds by typing an integer (as characters), then pressing the *Enter* key (sometimes called the *Return* key) to send the characters to the computer. The computer converts the character representation of the number to an integer and assigns (i.e., copies) this number (or value) to the variable number1. Any subsequent references to number1 in this program will use this same value.

The std::cout and std::cin stream objects facilitate interaction between the user and the computer. Because this interaction resembles a dialog, it is often called conversational computing or interactive computing.

Line 16

```
std::cout << "Enter second integer: "; // prompt user for data
```

prints Enter second integer: on the screen, prompting the user to take action. Line 17

```
std::cin >> number2; // read second integer from user into number2
```

obtains a value for variable number2 from the user.

The assignment statement in line 19

```
sum = number1 + number2; // add the numbers; store result in sum
```

calculates the sum of the variables number1 and number2 and assigns the result to variable sum using the assignment operator =. The statement is read as, "sum *gets* the value of number1 + number2." Most calculations are performed in assignment statements. The = operator and the + operator are called binary operators because each has two operands. In the case of the + operator, the two operands are number1 and number2. In the case of the preceding = operator, the two operands are sum and the value of the expression number1 + number2.

Good Programming Practice 2.13

Place spaces on either side of a binary operator. This makes the operator stand out and makes the program more readable.

Line 21

```
std::cout << "Sum is " << sum << std::endl; // display sum; end line
```

displays the character string Sum is followed by the numerical value of variable sum followed by std::endl—a so-called stream manipulator. The name endl is an abbreviation for "end line" and belongs to namespace std. The std::endl stream manipulator outputs a newline, then "flushes the output buffer." This simply means that, on some systems where outputs accumulate in the machine until there are enough to "make it worthwhile" to display them on the screen, std::endl forces any accumulated outputs to be displayed at that moment. This can be important when the outputs are prompting the user for an action, such as entering data.

Note that the preceding statement outputs multiple values of different types. The stream insertion operator "knows" how to output each type of data. Using multiple stream insertion operators (<<) in a single statement is referred to as concatenating, chaining or cascading stream insertion operations. It is unnecessary to have multiple statements to output multiple pieces of data.

Calculations can also be performed in output statements. We could have combined the statements in lines 19 and 21 into the statement

```
std::cout << "Sum is " << number1 + number2 << std::endl;
```

thus eliminating the need for the variable sum.

A powerful feature of C++ is that users can create their own data types called classes (we introduce this capability in Chapter 3 and explore it in depth in Chapters 9 and 10). Users can then "teach" C++ how to input and output values of these new data types using the >> and << operators (this is called operator overloading—a topic we explore in Chapter 11).

2.5 Memory Concepts

Variable names such as number1, number2 and sum actually correspond to locations in the computer's memory. Every variable has a name, a type, a size and a value.

In the addition program of Fig. 2.5, when the statement

```
std::cin >> number1; // read first integer from user into number1
```

in line 14 is executed, the characters typed by the user are converted to an integer that is placed into a memory location to which the name number1 has been assigned by the C++

compiler. Suppose the user enters the number 45 as the value for `number1`. The computer will place 45 into location `number1`, as shown in Fig. 2.6.

Whenever a value is placed in a memory location, the value overwrites the previous value in that location; thus, placing a new value into a memory location is said to be destructive.

Returning to our addition program, when the statement

```
std::cin >> number2; // read second integer from user into number2
```

in line 17 is executed, suppose the user enters the value 72. This value is placed into location `number2`, and memory appears as in Fig. 2.7. Note that these locations are not necessarily adjacent in memory.

Once the program has obtained values for `number1` and `number2`, it adds these values and places the sum into variable `sum`. The statement

```
sum = number1 + number2; // add the numbers; store result in sum
```

that performs the addition also replaces whatever value was stored in `sum`. This occurs when the calculated sum of `number1` and `number2` is placed into location `sum` (without regard to what value may already be in `sum`; that value is lost). After `sum` is calculated, memory appears as in Fig. 2.8. Note that the values of `number1` and `number2` appear exactly as they did before they were used in the calculation of `sum`. These values were used, but not destroyed, as the computer performed the calculation. Thus, when a value is read out of a memory location, the process is nondestructive.

number1	45

Fig. 2.6 | Memory location showing the name and value of variable `number1`.

number1	45
number2	72

Fig. 2.7 | Memory locations after storing values for `number1` and `number2`.

number1	45
number2	72
sum	117

Fig. 2.8 | Memory locations after calculating and storing the `sum` of `number1` and `number2`.

2.6 Arithmetic *Operators*

Most programs perform arithmetic calculations. Figure 2.9 summarizes the C++ arithmetic operators. Note the use of various special symbols not used in algebra. The asterisk (*) indicates multiplication and the percent sign (%) is the modulus operator that will be discussed shortly. The arithmetic operators in Fig. 2.9 are all binary operators, i.e., operators that take two operands. For example, the expression number1 + number2 contains the binary operator + and the two operands number1 and number2.

Integer division (i.e., where both the numerator and the denominator are integers) yields an integer quotient; for example, the expression 7 / 4 evaluates to 1 and the expression 17 / 5 evaluates to 3. Note that any fractional part in integer division is discarded (i.e., truncated)—no rounding occurs.

C++ provides the modulus operator, %, that yields the remainder after integer division. The modulus operator can be used only with integer operands. The expression x % y yields the remainder after x is divided by y. Thus, 7 % 4 yields 3 and 17 % 5 yields 2. In later chapters, we discuss many interesting applications of the modulus operator, such as determining whether one number is a multiple of another (a special case of this is determining whether a number is odd or even).

Common Programming Error 2.3

Attempting to use the modulus operator (%) with noninteger operands is a compilation error.

Arithmetic Expressions in Straight-Line Form

Arithmetic expressions in C++ must be entered into the computer in straight-line form. Thus, expressions such as "a divided by b" must be written as a / b, so that all constants, variables and operators appear in a straight line. The algebraic notation

$$\frac{a}{b}$$

is generally not acceptable to compilers, although some special-purpose software packages do support more natural notation for complex mathematical expressions.

Parentheses for Grouping Subexpressions

Parentheses are used in C++ expressions in the same manner as in algebraic expressions. For example, to multiply a times the quantity b + c we write a * (b + c).

C++ operation	C++ arithmetic operator (binary operators)	Algebraic expression	C++ expression
Addition	+	$f + 7$	f + 7
Subtraction	-	$p - c$	p - c
Multiplication	*	bm or $b \cdot m$	b * m
Division	/	x / y or $\frac{x}{y}$ or $x \div y$	x / y
Modulus	%	$r \bmod s$	r % s

Fig. 2.9 | Arithmetic operators.

Rules of Operator Precedence

C++ applies the operators in arithmetic expressions in a precise sequence determined by the following rules of operator precedence, which are generally the same as those followed in algebra:

1. Operators in expressions contained within pairs of parentheses are evaluated first. Parentheses are said to be at the "highest level of precedence." In cases of nested, or embedded, parentheses, such as

   ((a + b) + c)

   the operators in the innermost pair of parentheses are applied first.

2. Multiplication, division and modulus operations are applied next. If an expression contains several multiplication, division and modulus operations, operators are applied from left to right. Multiplication, division and modulus are said to be on the same level of precedence.

3. Addition and subtraction operations are applied last. If an expression contains several addition and subtraction operations, operators are applied from left to right. Addition and subtraction also have the same level of precedence.

The set of rules of operator precedence defines the order in which C++ applies operators. When we say that certain operators are applied from left to right, we are referring to the associativity of the operators. For example, in the expression

   a + b + c

the addition operators (+) associate from left to right, so a + b is calculated first, then c is added to that sum to determine the value of the whole expression. We'll see that some operators associate from right to left. Figure 2.10 summarizes these rules of operator precedence. This table will be expanded as additional C++ operators are introduced. A complete precedence chart is included in Appendix A.

Operator(s)	Operation(s)	Order of evaluation (precedence)
( )	Parentheses	Evaluated first. If the parentheses are nested, the expression in the innermost pair is evaluated first. If there are several pairs of parentheses "on the same level" (i.e., not nested), they are evaluated left to right.
*, /, %	Multiplication, Division, Modulus	Evaluated second. If there are several, they are evaluated left to right.
+ -	Addition Subtraction	Evaluated last. If there are several, they are evaluated left to right.

Fig. 2.10 | Precedence of arithmetic operators.

Sample Algebraic and C++ Expressions

Now consider several expressions in light of the rules of operator precedence. Each example lists an algebraic expression and its C++ equivalent. The following is an example of an arithmetic mean (average) of five terms:

Algebra: $m = \dfrac{a + b + c + d + e}{5}$

C++: `m = ( a + b + c + d + e ) / 5;`

The parentheses are required because division has higher precedence than addition. The entire quantity (a + b + c + d + e) is to be divided by 5. If the parentheses are erroneously omitted, we obtain a + b + c + d + e / 5, which evaluates incorrectly as

$a + b + c + d + \dfrac{e}{5}$

The following is an example of the equation of a straight line:

Algebra: y = mx + b

C++: `y = m * x + b;`

No parentheses are required. The multiplication is applied first because multiplication has a higher precedence than addition.

The following example contains modulus (%), multiplication, division, addition, subtraction and assignment operations:

Algebra: $z = pr\,\%q + w/x - y$

C++: `z = p * r % q + w / x - y;`

          6   1   2   4   3   5

The circled numbers under the statement indicate the order in which C++ applies the operators. The multiplication, modulus and division are evaluated first in left-to-right order (i.e., they associate from left to right) because they have higher precedence than addition and subtraction. The addition and subtraction are applied next. These are also applied left to right. Then the assignment operator is applied.

Evaluation of a Second-Degree Polynomial

To develop a better understanding of the rules of operator precedence, consider the evaluation of a second-degree polynomial ($y = ax^2 + bx + c$):

`y = a * x * x + b * x + c;`

     6   1   2   4   3   5

The circled numbers under the statement indicate the order in which C++ applies the operators. There is no arithmetic operator for exponentiation in C++, so we have represented x^2 as x * x. We'll soon discuss the standard library function pow ("power") that performs exponentiation. Because of some subtle issues related to the data types required by pow, we defer a detailed explanation of pow until Chapter 6.

Common Programming Error 2.4

*Some programming languages use operators ** or ^ to represent exponentiation. C++ does not support these exponentiation operators; using them for exponentiation results in errors.*

Suppose variables a, b, c and x in the preceding second-degree polynomial are initialized as follows: a = 2, b = 3, c = 7 and x = 5. Figure 2.11 illustrates the order in which the operators are applied.

As in algebra, it is acceptable to place unnecessary parentheses in an expression to make the expression clearer. These are called redundant parentheses. For example, the preceding assignment statement could be parenthesized as follows:

```
y = ( a * x * x ) + ( b * x ) + c;
```

Good Programming Practice 2.14

Using redundant parentheses in complex arithmetic expressions can make the expressions clearer.

2.7 Decision Making: Equality and Relational Operators

This section introduces a simple version of C++'s if statement that allows a program to take alternative action based on the truth or falsity of some condition. If the condition is met, i.e., the condition is true, the statement in the body of the if statement is executed. If the condition is not met, i.e., the condition is false, the body statement is not executed. We'll see an example shortly.

Step 1.   y = 2 * 5 * 5 + 3 * 5 + 7;   (Leftmost multiplication)
           2 * 5 is 10

Step 2.   y = 10 * 5 + 3 * 5 + 7;   (Leftmost multiplication)
           10 * 5 is 50

Step 3.   y = 50 + 3 * 5 + 7;   (Multiplication before addition)
                3 * 5 is 15

Step 4.   y = 50 + 15 + 7;   (Leftmost addition)
           50 + 15 is 65

Step 5.   y = 65 + 7;   (Last addition)
           65 + 7 is 72

Step 6.   y = 72   (Last operation—place 72 in y)

Fig. 2.11 | Order in which a second-degree polynomial is evaluated.

Conditions in `if` statements can be formed by using the equality operators and relational operators summarized in Fig. 2.12. The relational operators all have the same level of precedence and associate left to right. The equality operators both have the same level of precedence, which is lower than that of the relational operators, and associate left to right.

Common Programming Error 2.5

A syntax error will occur if any of the operators ==, !=, >= and <= appears with spaces between its pair of symbols.

Common Programming Error 2.6

Reversing the order of the pair of symbols in any of the operators !=, >= and <= (by writing them as =!, => and =<, respectively) is normally a syntax error. In some cases, writing != as =! will not be a syntax error, but almost certainly will be a logic error that has an effect at execution time. You'll understand why when you learn about logical operators in Chapter 5. A fatal logic error causes a program to fail and terminate prematurely. A nonfatal logic error allows a program to continue executing, but usually produces incorrect results.

Common Programming Error 2.7

Confusing the equality operator == with the assignment operator = results in logic errors. The equality operator should be read "is equal to," and the assignment operator should be read "gets" or "gets the value of" or "is assigned the value of." Some people prefer to read the equality operator as "double equals." As we discuss in Section 5.9, confusing these operators may not necessarily cause an easy-to-recognize syntax error, but may cause extremely subtle logic errors.

The following example uses six `if` statements to compare two numbers input by the user. If the condition in any of these `if` statements is satisfied, the output statement associated with that `if` statement is executed. Figure 2.13 shows the program and the input/output dialogs of three sample executions.

Standard algebraic equality or relational operator	C++ equality or relational operator	Sample C++ condition	Meaning of C++ condition
Relational operators			
>	>	x > y	x is greater than y
<	<	x < y	x is less than y
≥	>=	x >= y	x is greater than or equal to y
≤	<=	x <= y	x is less than or equal to y
Equality operators			
=	==	x == y	x is equal to y
≠	!=	x != y	x is not equal to y

Fig. 2.12 | Equality and relational operators.

Lines 6–8

```
using std::cout; // program uses cout
using std::cin; // program uses cin
using std::endl; // program uses endl
```

are using declarations that eliminate the need to repeat the std:: prefix as we did in earlier programs. Once we insert these using declarations, we can write cout instead of std::cout, cin instead of std::cin and endl instead of std::endl, respectively, in the remainder of the program. [*Note:* From this point forward in the book, each example contains one or more using declarations.]

```
 1   // Fig. 2.13: fig02_13.cpp
 2   // Comparing integers using if statements, relational operators
 3   // and equality operators.
 4   #include <iostream> // allows program to perform input and output
 5
 6   using std::cout; // program uses cout
 7   using std::cin; // program uses cin
 8   using std::endl; // program uses endl
 9
10   // function main begins program execution
11   int main()
12   {
13      int number1; // first integer to compare
14      int number2; // second integer to compare
15
16      cout << "Enter two integers to compare: "; // prompt user for data
17      cin >> number1 >> number2; // read two integers from user
18
19      if ( number1 == number2 )
20         cout << number1 << " == " << number2 << endl;
21
22      if ( number1 != number2 )
23         cout << number1 << " != " << number2 << endl;
24
25      if ( number1 < number2 )
26         cout << number1 << " < " << number2 << endl;
27
28      if ( number1 > number2 )
29         cout << number1 << " > " << number2 << endl;
30
31      if ( number1 <= number2 )
32         cout << number1 << " <= " << number2 << endl;
33
34      if ( number1 >= number2 )
35         cout << number1 << " >= " << number2 << endl;
36
37      return 0; // indicate that program ended successfully
38
39   } // end function main
```

Fig. 2.13 | Comparing integers using if statements, relational operators and equality operators. (Part 1 of 2.)

```
Enter two integers to compare: 3 7
3 != 7
3 < 7
3 <= 7
```

```
Enter two integers to compare: 22 12
22 != 12
22 > 12
22 >= 12
```

```
Enter two integers to compare: 7 7
7 == 7
7 <= 7
7 >= 7
```

Fig. 2.13 | Comparing integers using `if` statements, relational operators and equality operators. (Part 2 of 2.)

Good Programming Practice 2.15

Place using declarations immediately after the #include to which they refer.

Lines 13–14

```
int number1; // first integer to compare
int number2; // second integer to compare
```

declare the variables used in the program. Remember that variables may be declared in one declaration or in separate declarations.

The program uses cascaded stream extraction operations (line 17) to input two integers. Remember that we are allowed to write `cin` (instead of `std::cin`) because of line 7. First a value is read into variable `number1`, then a value is read into variable `number2`.

The `if` statement in lines 19–20

```
if ( number1 == number2 )
    cout << number1 << " == " << number2 << endl;
```

compares the values of variables `number1` and `number2` to test for equality. If the values are equal, the statement in line 20 displays a line of text indicating that the numbers are equal. If the conditions are `true` in one or more of the `if` statements starting in lines 22, 25, 28, 31 and 34, the corresponding body statement displays an appropriate line of text.

Notice that each `if` statement in Fig. 2.13 has a single statement in its body and that each body statement is indented. In Chapter 4 we show how to specify `if` statements with multiple-statement bodies (by enclosing the body statements in a pair of braces, { }, creating what is called a **compound statement** or a **block**).

Good Programming Practice 2.16

Indent the statement(s) in the body of an `if` statement to enhance readability.

Good Programming Practice 2.17

For readability, there should be no more than one statement per line in a program.

Common Programming Error 2.8

Placing a semicolon immediately after the right parenthesis after the condition in an if statement is often a logic error (although not a syntax error). The semicolon causes the body of the if statement to be empty, so the if statement performs no action, regardless of whether or not its condition is true. Worse yet, the original body statement of the if statement now becomes a statement in sequence with the if statement and always executes, often causing the program to produce incorrect results.

Note the use of white space in Fig. 2.13. Recall that white-space characters, such as tabs, newlines and spaces, are normally ignored by the compiler. So, statements may be split over several lines and may be spaced according to your preferences. It is a syntax error to split identifiers, strings (such as "hello") and constants (such as the number 1000) over several lines.

Common Programming Error 2.9

It is a syntax error to split an identifier by inserting white-space characters (e.g., writing main as ma in).

Good Programming Practice 2.18

A lengthy statement may be spread over several lines. If a single statement must be split across lines, choose meaningful breaking points, such as after a comma in a comma-separated list, or after an operator in a lengthy expression. If a statement is split across two or more lines, indent all subsequent lines and left-align the group of indented lines.

Figure 2.14 shows the precedence and associativity of the operators introduced in this chapter. The operators are shown top to bottom in decreasing order of precedence. Notice that all these operators, with the exception of the assignment operator =, associate from left to right. Addition is left-associative, so an expression like x + y + z is evaluated as if it had been written (x + y) + z. The assignment operator = associates from right to left, so an expression such as x = y = 0 is evaluated as if it had been written x = (y = 0), which, as we'll soon see, first assigns 0 to y, then assigns the result of that assignment—0—to x.

Operators	Associativity	Type
()	left to right	parentheses
* / %	left to right	multiplicative
+ -	left to right	additive
<< >>	left to right	stream insertion/extraction
< <= > >=	left to right	relational
== !=	left to right	equality
=	right to left	assignment

Fig. 2.14 | Precedence and associativity of the operators discussed so far.

Good Programming Practice 2.19

Refer to the operator precedence and associativity chart when writing expressions containing many operators. Confirm that the operators in the expression are performed in the order you expect. If you are uncertain about the order of evaluation in a complex expression, break the expression into smaller statements or use parentheses to force the order of evaluation, exactly as you would do in an algebraic expression. Be sure to observe that some operators such as assignment (=) associate right to left rather than left to right.

2.8 (Optional) Software Engineering Case Study: Examining the ATM Requirements Specification

Now we begin our optional object-oriented design and implementation case study. The Software Engineering Case Study sections at the ends of this and the next several chapters will ease you into object orientation. We'll develop software for a simple automated teller machine (ATM) system, providing you with a concise, carefully paced, complete design and implementation experience. In Chapters 3–7, 9 and 13, we'll perform the various steps of an object-oriented design (OOD) process using the UML, while relating these steps to the object-oriented concepts discussed in the chapters. Appendix G implements the ATM using the techniques of object-oriented programming (OOP) in C++. We present the complete case study solution. This is not an exercise; rather, it is an end-to-end learning experience that concludes with a detailed walkthrough of the C++ code that implements our design. It will acquaint you with the kinds of substantial problems encountered in industry and their potential solutions.

We begin our design process by presenting a requirements specification that specifies the overall purpose of the ATM system and *what* it must do. Throughout the case study, we refer to the requirements specification to determine precisely what functionality the system must include.

Requirements Specification

A local bank intends to install a new automated teller machine (ATM) to allow users (i.e., bank customers) to perform basic financial transactions (Fig. 2.15). Each user can have only one account at the bank. ATM users should be able to view their account balance, withdraw cash (i.e., take money out of an account) and deposit funds (i.e., place money into an account).

The user interface of the automated teller machine contains the following hardware components:

- a screen that displays messages to the user
- a keypad that receives numeric input from the user
- a cash dispenser that dispenses cash to the user and
- a deposit slot that receives deposit envelopes from the user.

The cash dispenser begins each day loaded with 500 $20 bills. [*Note:* Owing to the limited scope of this case study, certain elements of the ATM described here do not accurately mimic those of a real ATM. For example, a real ATM typically contains a device that reads a user's account number from an ATM card, whereas this ATM asks the user to type an account number using the keypad. A real ATM also usually prints a receipt at the end of a session, but all output from this ATM appears on the screen.]

Fig. 2.15 | Automated teller machine user interface.

The bank wants you to develop software to perform the financial transactions initiated by bank customers through the ATM. The bank will integrate the software with the ATM's hardware at a later time. The software should encapsulate the functionality of the hardware devices (e.g., cash dispenser, deposit slot) within software components, but it need not concern itself with how these devices perform their duties. The ATM hardware has not been developed yet, so instead of writing your software to run on the ATM, you should develop a first version of the software to run on a personal computer. This version should use the computer's monitor to simulate the ATM's screen, and the computer's keyboard to simulate the ATM's keypad.

An ATM session consists of authenticating a user (i.e., proving the user's identity) based on an account number and personal identification number (PIN), followed by creating and executing financial transactions. To authenticate a user and perform transactions, the ATM must interact with the bank's account information database. [*Note:* A database is an organized collection of data stored on a computer.] For each bank account, the database stores an account number, a PIN and a balance indicating the amount of money in the account. [*Note:* For simplicity, we assume that the bank plans to build only one ATM, so we do not need to worry about multiple ATMs accessing this database at the same time. Furthermore, we assume that the bank does not make any changes to the information in the database while a user is accessing the ATM. Also, any business system like an ATM faces reasonably complicated security issues that go well beyond the scope of a first- or second-semester computer science course. We make the simplifying assumption, however, that the bank trusts the ATM to access and manipulate the information in the database without significant security measures.]

Upon first approaching the ATM, the user should experience the following sequence of events (shown in Fig. 2.15):

1. The screen displays a welcome message and prompts the user to enter an account number.

2. The user enters a five-digit account number, using the keypad.

3. The screen prompts the user to enter the PIN (personal identification number) associated with the specified account number.

4. The user enters a five-digit PIN, using the keypad.

5. If the user enters a valid account number and the correct PIN for that account, the screen displays the main menu (Fig. 2.16). If the user enters an invalid account number or an incorrect PIN, the screen displays an appropriate message, then the ATM returns to *Step 1* to restart the authentication process.

After the ATM authenticates the user, the main menu (Fig. 2.16) displays a numbered option for each of the three types of transactions: balance inquiry (option 1), withdrawal (option 2) and deposit (option 3). The main menu also displays an option that allows the user to exit the system (option 4). The user then chooses either to perform a transaction (by entering 1, 2 or 3) or to exit the system (by entering 4). If the user enters an invalid option, the screen displays an error message, then redisplays to the main menu.

If the user enters 1 to make a balance inquiry, the screen displays the user's account balance. To do so, the ATM must retrieve the balance from the bank's database.

The following actions occur when the user enters 2 to make a withdrawal:

1. The screen displays a menu (shown in Fig. 2.17) containing standard withdrawal amounts: $20 (option 1), $40 (option 2), $60 (option 3), $100 (option 4) and $200 (option 5). The menu also contains an option to allow the user to cancel the transaction (option 6).

Fig. 2.16 | ATM main menu.

Fig. 2.17 | ATM withdrawal menu.

2. The user enters a menu selection (1–6) using the keypad.

3. If the withdrawal amount chosen is greater than the user's account balance, the screen displays a message stating this and telling the user to choose a smaller amount. The ATM then returns to *Step 1*. If the withdrawal amount chosen is less than or equal to the user's account balance (i.e., an acceptable withdrawal amount), the ATM proceeds to *Step 4*. If the user chooses to cancel the transaction (option 6), the ATM displays the main menu (Fig. 2.16) and waits for user input.

4. If the cash dispenser contains enough cash to satisfy the request, the ATM proceeds to *Step 5*. Otherwise, the screen displays a message indicating the problem and telling the user to choose a smaller withdrawal amount. The ATM then returns to *Step 1*.

5. The ATM debits (i.e., subtracts) the withdrawal amount from the user's account balance in the bank's database.

6. The cash dispenser dispenses the desired amount of money to the user.

7. The screen displays a message reminding the user to take the money.

The following actions occur when the user enters 3 (while the main menu is displayed) to make a deposit:

1. The screen prompts the user to enter a deposit amount or to type 0 (zero) to cancel the transaction.

2. The user enters a deposit amount or 0, using the keypad. [*Note:* The keypad does not contain a decimal point or a dollar sign, so the user cannot type a real dollar amount (e.g., $1.25). Instead, the user must enter a deposit amount as a number of cents (e.g., 125). The ATM then divides this number by 100 to obtain a number representing a dollar amount (e.g., $125 \div 100 = 1.25$).]

3. If the user specifies a deposit amount, the ATM proceeds to *Step 4*. If the user chooses to cancel the transaction (by entering 0), the ATM displays the main menu (Fig. 2.16) and waits for user input.

4. The screen displays a message telling the user to insert a deposit envelope into the deposit slot.

5. If the deposit slot receives a deposit envelope within two minutes, the ATM credits (i.e., adds) the deposit amount to the user's account balance in the bank's database. [*Note:* This money is not immediately available for withdrawal. The bank first must physically verify the amount of cash in the deposit envelope, and any checks in the envelope must clear (i.e., money must be transferred from the check writer's account to the check recipient's account). When either of these events occurs, the bank appropriately updates the user's balance stored in its database. This occurs independently of the ATM system.] If the deposit slot does not receive a deposit envelope within this time period, the screen displays a message that the system has canceled the transaction due to inactivity. The ATM then displays the main menu and waits for user input.

After the system successfully executes a transaction, the system should redisplay the main menu (Fig. 2.16) so that the user can perform additional transactions. If the user chooses to exit the system (option 4), the screen should display a thank you message, then display the welcome message for the next user.

Analyzing the ATM System

The preceding statement is a simplified example of a requirements specification. Typically, such a document is the result of a detailed process of requirements gathering that might include interviews with potential users of the system and specialists in fields related to the system. For example, a systems analyst who is hired to prepare a requirements specification for banking software (e.g., the ATM system described here) might interview financial experts to gain a better understanding of *what* the software must do. The analyst would use the information gained to compile a list of system requirements to guide systems designers.

The process of requirements gathering is a key task of the first stage of the software life cycle. The software life cycle specifies the stages through which software evolves from the time it is first conceived to the time it is retired from use. These stages typically include: analysis, design, implementation, testing and debugging, deployment, maintenance and retirement. Several software life-cycle models exist, each with its own preferences and specifications for when and how often software engineers should perform each of these stages. Waterfall models perform each stage once in succession, whereas iterative models may repeat one or more stages several times throughout a product's life cycle.

The analysis stage of the software life cycle focuses on defining the problem to be solved. When designing any system, one must certainly *solve the problem right*, but of equal importance, one must *solve the right problem*. Systems analysts collect the requirements that indicate the specific problem to solve. Our requirements specification describes our ATM system in sufficient detail that you do not need to go through an extensive analysis stage—it has been done for you.

To capture what a proposed system should do, developers often employ a technique known as use case modeling. This process identifies the use cases of the system, each of which represents a different capability that the system provides to its clients. For example,

ATMs typically have several use cases, such as "View Account Balance," "Withdraw Cash," "Deposit Funds," "Transfer Funds Between Accounts" and "Buy Postage Stamps." The simplified ATM system we build in this case study allows only the first three of these use cases (Fig. 2.18).

Each use case describes a typical scenario in which the user uses the system. You have already read descriptions of the ATM system's use cases in the requirements specification; the lists of steps required to perform each type of transaction (i.e., balance inquiry, withdrawal and deposit) actually described the three use cases of our ATM—"View Account Balance," "Withdraw Cash" and "Deposit Funds."

Use Case Diagrams

We now introduce the first of several UML diagrams in our ATM case study. We create a use case diagram to model the interactions between a system's clients (in this case study, bank customers) and the system. The goal is to show the kinds of interactions users have with a system without providing the details—these are provided in other UML diagrams (which we present throughout the case study). Use case diagrams are often accompanied by informal text that describes the use cases in more detail—like the text that appears in the requirements specification. Use case diagrams are produced during the analysis stage of the software life cycle. In larger systems, use case diagrams are simple but indispensable tools that help system designers remain focused on satisfying the users' needs.

Figure 2.18 shows the use case diagram for our ATM system. The stick figure represents an actor, which defines the roles that an external entity—such as a person or another system—plays when interacting with the system. For our automated teller machine, the actor is a User who can view an account balance, withdraw cash and deposit funds from the ATM. The User is not an actual person, but instead comprises the roles that a real person—when playing the part of a User—can play while interacting with the ATM. Note that a use case diagram can include multiple actors. For example, the use case diagram for a real bank's ATM system might also include an actor named Administrator who refills the cash dispenser each day.

We identify the actor in our system by examining the requirements specification, which states, "ATM users should be able to view their account balance, withdraw cash and deposit funds." Therefore, the actor in each of the three use cases is the User who interacts with the ATM. An external entity—a real person—plays the part of the User to perform financial transactions. Figure 2.18 shows one actor, whose name, User, appears below the actor in the diagram. The UML models each use case as an oval connected to an actor with a solid line.

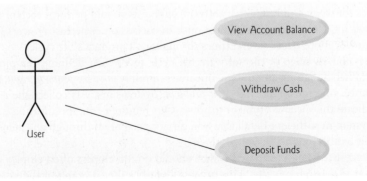

Fig. 2.18 | Use case diagram for the ATM system from the User's perspective.

Software engineers (more precisely, systems analysts) must analyze the requirements specification or a set of use cases and design the system before programmers implement it. During the analysis stage, systems analysts focus on understanding the requirements specification to produce a high-level specification that describes *what* the system is supposed to do. The output of the design stage—a design specification—should specify clearly *how* the system should be constructed to satisfy these requirements. In the next several Software Engineering Case Study sections, we perform the steps of a simple object-oriented design (OOD) process on the ATM system to produce a design specification containing a collection of UML diagrams and supporting text. Recall that the UML is designed for use with any OOD process. Many such processes exist, the best known of which is the Rational Unified Process™ (RUP) developed by Rational Software Corporation (now a division of IBM). RUP is a rich process intended for designing "industrial strength" applications. For this case study, we present our own simplified design process.

Designing the ATM System

We now begin the design stage of our ATM system. A system is a set of components that interact to solve a problem. For example, to perform the ATM system's designated tasks, our ATM system has a user interface (Fig. 2.15), contains software that executes financial transactions and interacts with a database of bank account information. System structure describes the system's objects and their interrelationships. System behavior describes how the system changes as its objects interact with one another. Every system has both structure and behavior—designers must specify both. There are several distinct types of system structures and behaviors. For example, the interactions among objects in the system differ from those between the user and the system, yet both constitute a portion of the system behavior.

The UML 2 specifies 13 diagram types for documenting the models of systems. Each models a distinct characteristic of a system's structure or behavior—six diagrams relate to system structure; the remaining seven relate to system behavior. We list here only the six types of diagrams used in our case study—one of these (class diagrams) models system structure—the remaining five model system behavior. We overview the remaining seven UML diagram types in Appendix H, UML 2: Additional Diagram Types.

1. Use case diagrams, such as the one in Fig. 2.18, model the interactions between a system and its external entities (actors) in terms of use cases (system capabilities, such as "View Account Balance," "Withdraw Cash" and "Deposit Funds").

2. Class diagrams, which you'll study in Section 3.11, model the classes, or "building blocks," used in a system. Each noun or "thing" described in the requirements specification is a candidate to be a class in the system (e.g., "account," "keypad"). Class diagrams help us specify the structural relationships between parts of the system. For example, the ATM system class diagram will specify that the ATM is physically composed of a screen, a keypad, a cash dispenser and a deposit slot.

3. State machine diagrams, which you'll study in Section 3.11, model the ways in which an object changes state. An object's state is indicated by the values of all the object's attributes at a given time. When an object changes state, that object may behave differently in the system. For example, after validating a user's PIN, the ATM transitions from the "user not authenticated" state to the "user authenticated" state, at which point the ATM allows the user to perform financial transactions (e.g., view account balance, withdraw cash, deposit funds).

4. **Activity diagrams**, which you'll also study in Section 5.11, model an object's activity—the object's workflow (sequence of events) during program execution. An activity diagram models the actions the object performs and specifies the order in which it performs these actions. For example, an activity diagram shows that the ATM must obtain the balance of the user's account (from the bank's account information database) before the screen can display the balance to the user.

5. **Communication diagrams** (called **collaboration diagrams** in earlier versions of the UML) model the interactions among objects in a system, with an emphasis on *what* interactions occur. You'll learn in Section 7.12 that these diagrams show which objects must interact to perform an ATM transaction. For example, the ATM must communicate with the bank's account information database to retrieve an account balance.

6. **Sequence diagrams** also model the interactions among the objects in a system, but unlike communication diagrams, they emphasize *when* interactions occur. You'll learn in Section 7.12 that these diagrams help show the order in which interactions occur in executing a financial transaction. For example, the screen prompts the user to enter a withdrawal amount before cash is dispensed.

In Section 3.11, we continue designing our ATM system by identifying the classes from the requirements specification. We accomplish this by extracting key nouns and noun phrases from the requirements specification. Using these classes, we develop our first draft of the class diagram that models the structure of our ATM system.

Internet and Web Resources
The following URLs provide information on object-oriented design with the UML.
www-306.ibm.com/software/rational/uml/
Lists frequently asked questions (FAQs) about the UML, provided by IBM Rational.
www.douglass.co.uk/documents/softdocwiz.com.UML.htm
Hosts the Unified Modeling Language Dictionary. Lists and defines all terms used in the UML.
www-306.ibm.com/software/rational/offerings/design.html
Provides information about IBM Rational software available for designing systems. Provides downloads of 30-day trial versions of several products, such as IBM Rational Rose® XDE Developer.
www.embarcadero.com/products/describe/index.html
Provides a free 14-day license to download a trial version of Describe™—a UML modeling tool from Embarcadero Technologies®.
www.borland.com/us/products/together/index.html
Provides a free 30-day license to download a trial version of Borland® Together® Control-Center™—a software-development tool that supports the UML.
www.ilogix.com/sublevel.aspx?id=53
Provides a free 30-day license to download a trial version of I-Logix Rhapsody®—a UML 2 based model-driven development environment.
argouml.tigris.org
Contains information and downloads for ArgoUML, a free open-source UML tool written in Java.
www.objectsbydesign.com/books/booklist.html
Lists books on the UML and object-oriented design.
www.objectsbydesign.com/tools/umltools_byCompany.html
Lists software tools that use the UML, such as IBM Rational Rose, Embarcadero Describe, Sparx Systems Enterprise Architect, I-Logix Rhapsody and Gentleware Poseidon for UML.

`www.ootips.org/ood-principles.html`
Provides answers to the question, "What Makes a Good Object-Oriented Design?"
`parlezuml.com/tutorials/umlforjava.htm`
Provides a UML tutorial for Java developers that presents UML diagrams side by side with the Java code that implements them.
`www.cetus-links.org/oo_uml.html`
Introduces the UML and provides links to numerous UML resources.
`www.agilemodeling.com/essays/umlDiagrams.htm`
Provides in-depth descriptions and tutorials on each of the 13 UML 2 diagram types.

Recommended Readings

The following books provide information on object-oriented design with the UML.

Booch, G. *Object-Oriented Analysis and Design with Applications*. 3rd ed. Boston: Addison-Wesley, 2004.

Eriksson, H., et al. *UML 2 Toolkit*. New York: John Wiley, 2003.

Fowler, M. *UML Distilled*. 3rd ed. Boston: Addison-Wesley Professional, 2004.

Kruchten, P. *The Rational Unified Process: An Introduction*. Boston: Addison-Wesley, 2004.

Larman, C. *Applying UML and Patterns: An Introduction to Object-Oriented Analysis and Design*. 2nd ed. Upper Saddle River, NJ: Prentice Hall, 2002.

Roques, P. *UML in Practice: The Art of Modeling Software Systems Demonstrated Through Worked Examples and Solutions*. New York: John Wiley, 2004.

Rosenberg, D., and K. Scott. *Applying Use Case Driven Object Modeling with UML: An Annotated e-Commerce Example*. Reading, MA: Addison-Wesley, 2001.

Rumbaugh, J., I. Jacobson and G. Booch. *The Complete UML Training Course*. Upper Saddle River, NJ: Prentice Hall, 2000.

Rumbaugh, J., I. Jacobson and G. Booch. *The Unified Modeling Language Reference Manual*. Reading, MA: Addison-Wesley, 1999.

Rumbaugh, J., I. Jacobson and G. Booch. *The Unified Software Development Process*. Reading, MA: Addison-Wesley, 1999.

Schneider, G. and J. Winters. *Applying Use Cases: A Practical Guide*. 2nd ed. Boston: Addison-Wesley Professional, 2002.

Software Engineering Case Study Self-Review Exercises

2.1   Suppose we enabled a user of our ATM system to transfer money between two bank accounts. Modify the use case diagram of Fig. 2.18 to reflect this change.

2.2   _____ model the interactions among objects in a system with an emphasis on *when* these interactions occur.
   a) Class diagrams
   b) Sequence diagrams
   c) Communication diagrams
   d) Activity diagrams

2.3   Which of the following choices lists stages of a typical software life cycle in sequential order?
   a) design, analysis, implementation, testing
   b) design, analysis, testing, implementation
   c) analysis, design, testing, implementation
   d) analysis, design, implementation, testing

Answers to Software Engineering Case Study Self-Review Exercises

2.1   Figure 2.19 shows a use case diagram for a modified version of our ATM system that also allows users to transfer money between accounts.

2.2   b.

2.3   d.

Fig. 2.19 | Use case diagram for a modified version of our ATM system that also allows users to transfer money between accounts.

2.9 Wrap-Up

You learned many important basic features of C++ in this chapter, including displaying data on the screen, inputting data from the keyboard and declaring variables of fundamental types. In particular, you learned to use the output stream object cout and the input stream object cin to build simple interactive programs. We explained how variables are stored in and retrieved from memory. You also learned how to use arithmetic operators to perform calculations. We discussed the order in which C++ applies operators (i.e., the rules of operator precedence), as well as the associativity of the operators. You also learned how C++'s if statement allows a program to make decisions. Finally, we introduced the equality and relational operators, which you use to form conditions in if statements.

The non-object-oriented applications presented here introduced you to basic programming concepts. As you'll see in Chapter 3, C++ applications typically contain just a few lines of code in function main—these statements normally create the objects that perform the work of the application, then the objects "take over from there." In Chapter 3, you'll learn how to implement your own classes and use objects of those classes in applications.

Summary

Section 2.2 First Program in C++: Printing a Line of Text
- Single-line comments begin with //. You insert comments to document your programs and improve their readability.
- Comments do not cause the computer to perform any action when the program is run—they are ignored by the C++ compiler and do not cause any machine-language object code to be generated.

- A preprocessor directive begins with # and is a message to the C++ preprocessor. Preprocessor directives are processed by the preprocessor before the program is compiled and don't end with a semicolon as C++ statements do.

- The line `#include <iostream>` tells the C++ preprocessor to include the contents of the input/output stream header file in the program. This file contains information necessary to compile programs that use `std::cin` and `std::cout` and operators `<<` and `>>`.

- White space (i.e., blank lines, space characters and tab characters) makes programs easier to read. White-space characters outside of literals are ignored by the compiler.

- C++ programs begin executing at `main`, even if `main` does not appear first in the program.

- The keyword `int` to the left of `main` indicates that `main` "returns" an integer value.

- A left brace, {, must begin the body of every function. A corresponding right brace, }, must end each function's body.

- A string in double quotes is sometimes referred to as a character string, message or string literal. White-space characters in strings are not ignored by the compiler.

- Every statement must end with a semicolon (also known as the statement terminator).

- Output and input in C++ are accomplished with streams of characters.

- The output stream object `std::cout`—normally connected to the screen—is used to output data. Multiple data items can be output by concatenating stream insertion (`<<`) operators.

- The input stream object `std::cin`—normally connected to the keyboard—is used to input data. Multiple data items can be input by concatenating stream extraction (`>>`) operators.

- The `std::cout` and `std::cin` stream objects facilitate interaction between the user and the computer. Because this interaction resembles a dialog, it is often called conversational computing or interactive computing.

- The notation `std::cout` specifies that we are using a name, in this case `cout`, that belongs to "namespace" `std`.

- When a backslash (i.e., an escape character) is encountered in a string of characters, the next character is combined with the backslash to form an escape sequence.

- The escape sequence `\n` means newline. It causes the cursor (i.e., the current screen-position indicator) to move to the beginning of the next line on the screen.

- A message that directs the user to take a specific action is known as a prompt.

- C++ keyword `return` is one of several means to exit a function.

Section 2.4 Another C++ Program: Adding Integers
- All variables in a C++ program must be declared before they can be used.

- A variable name in C++ is any valid identifier that is not a keyword. An identifier is a series of characters consisting of letters, digits and underscores (_). Identifiers cannot start with a digit. C++ identifiers can be any length; however, some systems and/or C++ implementations may impose some restrictions on the length of identifiers.

- C++ is case sensitive.

- Most calculations are performed in assignment statements.

- A variable is a location in the computer's memory where a value can be stored for use by a program.

- Variables of type `int` hold integer values, i.e., whole numbers such as 7, –11, 0, 31914.

Section 2.5 Memory Concepts
- Every variable stored in the computer's memory has a name, a value, a type and a size.

- Whenever a new value is placed in a memory location, the process is destructive; i.e., the new value replaces the previous value in that location. The previous value is lost.
- When a value is read from memory, the process is nondestructive; i.e., a copy of the value is read, leaving the original value undisturbed in the memory location.
- The std::endl stream manipulator outputs a newline, then "flushes the output buffer."

Section 2.6 Arithmetic
- C++ evaluates arithmetic expressions in a precise sequence determined by the rules of operator precedence and associativity.
- Parentheses may be used to group expressions.
- Integer division (i.e., both the numerator and the denominator are integers) yields an integer quotient. Any fractional part in integer division is truncated—no rounding occurs.
- The modulus operator, %, yields the remainder after integer division. The modulus operator can be used only with integer operands.

Section 2.7 Decision Making: Equality and Relational Operators
- The if statement allows a program to take alternative action based on whether a condition is met. The format for an if statement is

      if (*condition*)
          statement;

  If the condition is true, the statement in the body of the if is executed. If the condition is not met, i.e., the condition is false, the body statement is skipped.
- Conditions in if statements are commonly formed by using equality operators and relational operators. The result of using these operators is always the value true or false.
- The declaration

      using std::cout;

  is a using declaration that informs the compiler where to find cout (namespace std) and eliminates the need to repeat the std:: prefix. Once we include this using declaration, we can, for example, write cout instead of std::cout in the remainder of a program.

Terminology

/* ... */ comment (C-style comment)
// comment
arithmetic operator
assignment operator (=)
associativity of operators
binary operator
block
body of a function
cascading stream insertion operations
case sensitive
chaining stream insertion operations
character string
cin object
comma-separated list
comment (//)
compilation error

compiler error
compile-time error
compound statement
concatenating stream insertion operations
condition
cout object
cursor
data type
decision
declaration
destructive write
equality operators
    == "is equal to"
    != "is not equal to"
escape character (\)
escape sequence

exit a function	precedence
fatal error	preprocessor directive
function	prompt
identifier	redundant parentheses
`if` statement	relational operators
input/output stream header file `<iostream>`	< "is less than"
`int` data type	<= "is less than or equal to"
integer (`int`)	> "is greater than"
integer division	>= "is greater than or equal to"
left-to-right associativity	`return` statement
literal	rules of operator precedence
logic error	self-documenting program
`main` function	semicolon (;) statement terminator
memory	standard input stream object (`cin`)
memory location	standard output stream object (`cout`)
message	statement
modulus operator (%)	statement terminator (;)
multiplication operator (*)	stream
nested parentheses	stream extraction operator (>>)
newline character (\n)	stream insertion operator (<<)
nondestructive read	stream manipulator
nonfatal logic error	string
operand	string literal
operator	syntax error
operator associativity	`using` declaration
parentheses ()	variable
perform an action	white space

Self-Review Exercises

2.1   Fill in the blanks in each of the following.
a) Every C++ program begins execution at the function _____.
b) A _____ begins the body of every function and a _____ ends the body.
c) Every C++ statement ends with a(n) _____.
d) The escape sequence \n represents the _____ character, which causes the cursor to position to the beginning of the next line on the screen.
e) The _____ statement is used to make decisions.

2.2   State whether each of the following is *true* or *false*. If *false*, explain why. Assume the statement using `std::cout;` is used.
a) Comments cause the computer to print the text after the // on the screen when the program is executed.
b) The escape sequence \n, when output with `cout` and the stream insertion operator, causes the cursor to position to the beginning of the next line on the screen.
c) All variables must be declared before they are used.
d) All variables must be given a type when they are declared.
e) C++ considers the variables `number` and `NuMbEr` to be identical.
f) Declarations can appear almost anywhere in the body of a C++ function.
g) The modulus operator (%) can be used only with integer operands.
h) The arithmetic operators *, /, %, + and – all have the same level of precedence.
i) A C++ program that prints three lines of output must contain three statements using `cout` and the stream insertion operator.

2.3   Write a single C++ statement to accomplish each of the following (assume that using declarations have not been used):
  a) Declare the variables `c`, `thisIsAVariable`, `q76354` and `number` to be of type `int`.
  b) Prompt the user to enter an integer. End your prompting message with a colon (:) followed by a space and leave the cursor positioned after the space.
  c) Read an integer from the user at the keyboard and store it in integer variable `age`.
  d) If the variable `number` is not equal to 7, print `"The variable number is not equal to 7"`.
  e) Print the message `"This is a C++ program"` on one line.
  f) Print the message `"This is a C++ program"` on two lines. End the first line with `C++`.
  g) Print the message `"This is a C++ program"` with each word on a separate line.
  h) Print the message `"This is a C++ program"`. Separate each word from the next by a tab.

2.4   Write a statement (or comment) to accomplish each of the following (assume that using declarations have been used for `cin`, `cout` and `endl`):
  a) State that a program calculates the product of three integers.
  b) Declare the variables `x`, `y`, `z` and `result` to be of type `int` (in separate statements).
  c) Prompt the user to enter three integers.
  d) Read three integers from the keyboard and store them in the variables `x`, `y` and `z`.
  e) Compute the product of the three integers contained in variables `x`, `y` and `z`, and assign the result to the variable `result`.
  f) Print `"The product is "` followed by the value of the variable `result`.
  g) Return a value from `main` indicating that the program terminated successfully.

2.5   Using the statements you wrote in Exercise 2.4, write a complete program that calculates and displays the product of three integers. Add comments to the code where appropriate. [*Note:* You'll need to write the necessary using declarations.]

2.6   Identify and correct the errors in each of the following statements (assume that the statement using `std::cout;` is used):
  a) `if ( c < 7 );`
       `cout << "c is less than 7\n";`
  b) `if ( c => 7 )`
       `cout << "c is equal to or greater than 7\n";`

Answers to Self-Review Exercises

2.1   a) `main`.   b) left brace ({), right brace (}).   c) semicolon.   d) newline.   e) `if`.

2.2   a) False. Comments do not cause any action to be performed when the program is executed. They are used to document programs and improve their readability.
  b) True.
  c) True.
  d) True.
  e) False. C++ is case sensitive, so these variables are unique.
  f) True.
  g) True.
  h) False. The operators *, / and % have the same precedence, and the operators + and - have a lower precedence.
  i) False. One statement with cout and multiple \n escape sequences can print several lines.

2.3   a) `int c, thisIsAVariable, q76354, number;`
  b) `std::cout << "Enter an integer: ";`
  c) `std::cin >> age;`
  d) `if ( number != 7 )`
       `std::cout << "The variable number is not equal to 7\n";`

e) `std::cout << "This is a C++ program\n";`
f) `std::cout << "This is a C++\nprogram\n";`
g) `std::cout << "This\nis\na\nC++\nprogram\n";`
h) `std::cout << "This\tis\ta\tC++\tprogram\n";`

2.4 a) `// Calculate the product of three integers`
b) `int x;`
   `int y;`
   `int z;`
   `int result;`
c) `cout << "Enter three integers: ";`
d) `cin >> x >> y >> z;`
e) `result = x * y * z;`
f) `cout << "The product is " << result << endl;`
g) `return 0;`

2.5 (See program below.)

```
 1  // Calculate the product of three integers
 2  #include <iostream> // allows program to perform input and output
 3
 4  using std::cout; // program uses cout
 5  using std::cin; // program uses cin
 6  using std::endl; // program uses endl
 7
 8  // function main begins program execution
 9  int main()
10  {
11     int x; // first integer to multiply
12     int y; // second integer to multiply
13     int z; // third integer to multiply
14     int result; // the product of the three integers
15
16     cout << "Enter three integers: "; // prompt user for data
17     cin >> x >> y >> z; // read three integers from user
18     result = x * y * z; // multiply the three integers; store result
19     cout << "The product is " << result << endl; // print result; end line
20
21     return 0; // indicate program executed successfully
22  } // end function main
```

2.6 a) *Error:* Semicolon after the right parenthesis of the condition in the `if` statement.
Correction: Remove the semicolon after the right parenthesis. [*Note:* The result of this error is that the output statement will be executed whether or not the condition in the `if` statement is true.] The semicolon after the right parenthesis is a null (or empty) statement—a statement that does nothing. We'll learn more about the null statement in the next chapter.
b) *Error:* The relational operator =>.
Correction: Change => to >=, and you may want to change "equal to or greater than" to "greater than or equal to" as well.

Exercises

2.7 Discuss the meaning of each of the following objects:
a) `std::cin`
b) `std::cout`

2.8   Fill in the blanks in each of the following:
   a) _____ are used to document a program and improve its readability.
   b) The object used to print information on the screen is _____.
   c) A C++ statement that makes a decision is _____.
   d) Most calculations are normally performed by _____ statements.
   e) The _____ object inputs values from the keyboard.

2.9   Write a single C++ statement or line that accomplishes each of the following:
   a) Print the message "Enter two numbers".
   b) Assign the product of variables b and c to variable a.
   c) State that a program performs a payroll calculation (i.e., use text that helps to document a program).
   d) Input three integer values from the keyboard into integer variables a, b and c.

2.10   State which of the following are *true* and which are *false*. If *false*, explain your answers.
   a) C++ operators are evaluated from left to right.
   b) The following are all valid variable names: _under_bar_, m928134, t5, j7, her_sales, his_account_total, a, b, c, z, z2.
   c) The statement cout << "a = 5;"; is a typical example of an assignment statement.
   d) A valid C++ arithmetic expression with no parentheses is evaluated from left to right.
   e) The following are all invalid variable names: 3g, 87, 67h2, h22, 2h.

2.11   Fill in the blanks in each of the following:
   a) What arithmetic operations are on the same level of precedence as multiplication? _____.
   b) When parentheses are nested, which set of parentheses is evaluated first in an arithmetic expression? _____.
   c) A location in the computer's memory that may contain different values at various times throughout the execution of a program is called a _____.

2.12   What, if anything, prints when each of the following C++ statements is performed? If nothing prints, then answer "nothing." Assume x = 2 and y = 3.
   a) cout << x;
   b) cout << x + x;
   c) cout << "x=";
   d) cout << "x = " << x;
   e) cout << x + y << " = " << y + x;
   f) z = x + y;
   g) cin >> x >> y;
   h) // cout << "x + y = " << x + y;
   i) cout << "\n";

2.13   Which of the following C++ statements contain variables whose values are replaced?
   a) cin >> b >> c >> d >> e >> f;
   b) p = i + j + k + 7;
   c) cout << "variables whose values are replaced";
   d) cout << "a = 5";

2.14   Given the algebraic equation $y = ax^3 + 7$, which of the following, if any, are correct C++ statements for this equation?
   a) y = a * x * x * x + 7;
   b) y = a * x * x * (x + 7);
   c) y = (a * x) * x * (x + 7);
   d) y = (a * x) * x * x + 7;

e) `y = a * ( x * x * x ) + 7;`
f) `y = a * x * ( x * x + 7 );`

2.15 State the order of evaluation of the operators in each of the following C++ statements and show the value of x after each statement is performed.

a) `x = 7 + 3 * 6 / 2 - 1;`
b) `x = 2 % 2 + 2 * 2 - 2 / 2;`
c) `x = ( 3 * 9 * ( 3 + ( 9 * 3 / ( 3 ) ) ) );`

2.16 Write a program that asks the user to enter two numbers, obtains the two numbers from the user and prints the sum, product, difference, and quotient of the two numbers.

2.17 Write a program that prints the numbers 1 to 4 on the same line with each pair of adjacent numbers separated by one space. Do this several ways:

a) Using one statement with one stream insertion operator.
b) Using one statement with four stream insertion operators.
c) Using four statements.

2.18 Write a program that asks the user to enter two integers, obtains the numbers from the user, then prints the larger number followed by the words "is larger." If the numbers are equal, print the message "These numbers are equal."

2.19 Write a program that inputs three integers from the keyboard and prints the sum, average, product, smallest and largest of these numbers. The screen dialog should appear as follows:

```
Input three different integers: 13 27 14
Sum is 54
Average is 18
Product is 4914
Smallest is 13
Largest is 27
```

2.20 Write a program that reads in the radius of a circle as an integer and prints the circle's diameter, circumference and area. Use the constant value 3.14159 for π. Do all calculations in output statements. [*Note:* In this chapter, we have discussed only integer constants and variables. In Chapter 4 we discuss floating-point numbers, i.e., values that can have decimal points.]

2.21 Write a program that prints a box, an oval, an arrow and a diamond as follows:

```
*********        ***           *              *
*       *       *   *         ***            * *
*       *      *     *       *****          *   *
*       *      *     *         *           *     *
*       *      *     *         *          *       *
*       *      *     *         *           *     *
*       *      *     *         *            *   *
*       *       *   *          *             * *
*********        ***           *              *
```

2.22 What does the following code print?

```
cout << "*\n**\n***\n****\n*****" << endl;
```

2.23 Write a program that reads in five integers and determines and prints the largest and the smallest integers in the group. Use only the programming techniques you learned in this chapter.

2.24 Write a program that reads an integer and determines and prints whether it is odd or even. [*Hint:* Use the modulus operator. An even number is a multiple of two. Any multiple of two leaves a remainder of zero when divided by 2.]

2.25 Write a program that reads in two integers and determines and prints if the first is a multiple of the second. [*Hint:* Use the modulus operator.]

2.26 Display the following checkerboard pattern with eight output statements, then display the same pattern using as few statements as possible.

```
* * * * * * * *
 * * * * * * * *
* * * * * * * *
 * * * * * * * *
* * * * * * * *
 * * * * * * * *
* * * * * * * *
 * * * * * * * *
```

2.27 Here is a peek ahead. In this chapter you learned about integers and the type int. C++ can also represent uppercase letters, lowercase letters and a considerable variety of special symbols. C++ uses small integers internally to represent each different character. The set of characters a computer uses and the corresponding integer representations for those characters are called that computer's character set. You can print a character by enclosing that character in single quotes, as with

```
cout << 'A'; // print an uppercase A
```

You can print the integer equivalent of a character using static_cast as follows:

```
cout << static_cast< int >( 'A' ); // print 'A' as an integer
```

This is called a cast operation (we formally introduce casts in Chapter 4). When the preceding statement executes, it prints the value 65 (on systems that use the ASCII character set). Write a program that prints the integer equivalent of a character typed at the keyboard. Store the input in a variable of type char. Test your program several times using uppercase letters, lowercase letters, digits and special characters (like $).

2.28 Write a program that inputs a five-digit integer, separates the integer into its individual digits and prints the digits separated from one another by three spaces each. [*Hint:* Use the integer division and modulus operators.] For example, if the user types in 42339, the program should print:

```
4   2   3   3   9
```

2.29 Using only the techniques you learned in this chapter, write a program that calculates the squares and cubes of the integers from 0 to 10 and uses tabs to print the following neatly formatted table of values:

```
integer square cube
0        0      0
1        1      1
2        4      8
3        9      27
4        16     64
5        25     125
6        36     216
7        49     343
8        64     512
9        81     729
10       100    1000
```

3

Introduction to Classes and Objects

*Nothing can have value
without being an object of
utility.*
—Karl Marx

*Your public servants serve
you right.*
—Adlai E. Stevenson

*Knowing how to answer one
who speaks,
To reply to one who sends a
message.*
—Amenemope

*You'll see something new.
Two things. And I call them
Thing One and Thing Two.*
—Dr. Theodor Seuss Geisel

OBJECTIVES

In this chapter you'll learn:

- What classes, objects, member functions and data members are.

- How to define a class and use it to create an object.

- How to define member functions in a class to implement the class's behaviors.

- How to declare data members in a class to implement the class's attributes.

- How to call a member function of an object to make that member function perform its task.

- The differences between data members of a class and local variables of a function.

- How to use a constructor to ensure that an object's data is initialized when the object is created.

- How to engineer a class to separate its interface from its implementation and encourage reuse.

3.1 Introduction

In Chapter 2, you created simple programs that displayed messages to the user, obtained information from the user, performed calculations and made decisions. In this chapter, you'll begin writing programs that employ the basic concepts of object-oriented programming that we introduced in Section 1.21. One common feature of every program in Chapter 2 was that all the statements that performed tasks were located in function main. Typically, the programs you develop in this book will consist of function main and one or more classes, each containing data members and member functions. If you become part of a development team in industry, you might work on software systems that contain hundreds, or even thousands, of classes. In this chapter, we develop a simple, well-engineered framework for organizing object-oriented programs in C++.

First, we motivate the notion of classes with a real-world example. Then we present a carefully paced sequence of seven complete working programs to demonstrate creating and using your own classes. These examples begin our integrated case study on developing a grade-book class that instructors can use to maintain student test scores. This case study is enhanced over the next several chapters, culminating with the version presented in Chapter 7, Arrays and Vectors. We also introduce the C++ standard library class string in this chapter.

3.2 Classes, Objects, Member Functions and Data Members

Let's begin with a simple analogy to help you reinforce your understanding from Section 1.21 of classes and their contents. Suppose you want to drive a car and make it go faster by pressing down on its accelerator pedal. What must happen before you can do this? Well, before you can drive a car, someone has to design it and build it. A car typically begins as engineering drawings, similar to the blueprints used to design a house. These drawings include the design for an accelerator pedal that the driver will use to make the car go faster. In a sense, the pedal "hides" the complex mechanisms that actually make the car go faster, just as the brake pedal "hides" the mechanisms that slow the car, the steering wheel "hides" the mechanisms that turn the car and so on. This enables people with little or no knowledge of how cars are engineered to drive a car easily, simply by using the accelerator pedal, the brake pedal, the steering wheel, the transmission shifting mechanism and other such simple and user-friendly "interfaces" to the car's complex internal mechanisms.

Unfortunately, you cannot drive the engineering drawings of a car—before you can drive a car, it must be built from the engineering drawings that describe it. A completed car will have an actual accelerator pedal to make the car go faster. But even that's not enough—the car will not accelerate on its own, so the driver must press the accelerator pedal to tell the car to go faster.

Now let's use our car example to introduce the key object-oriented programming concepts of this section. Performing a task in a program requires a function (such as main, as described in Chapter 2). The function describes the mechanisms that actually perform its tasks. The function hides from its user the complex tasks that it performs, just as the accelerator pedal of a car hides from the driver the complex mechanisms of making the car go faster. In C++, we begin by creating a program unit called a class to house a function, just as a car's engineering drawings house the design of an accelerator pedal. Recall from Section 1.21 that a function belonging to a class is called a member function. In a class, you provide one or more member functions that are designed to perform the class's tasks. For example, a class that represents a bank account might contain one member function to deposit money into the account, another to withdraw money from the account and a third to inquire what the current account balance is.

Just as you cannot drive an engineering drawing of a car, you cannot "drive" a class. Just as someone has to build a car from its engineering drawings before you can actually drive the car, you must create an object of a class before you can get a program to perform the tasks the class describes. That is one reason C++ is known as an object-oriented programming language. Note also that just as *many* cars can be built from the same engineering drawing, *many* objects can be built from the same class.

When you drive a car, pressing its gas pedal sends a message to the car to perform a task—that is, make the car go faster. Similarly, you send messages to an object—each message is known as a member-function call and tells a member function of the object to perform its task. This is often called requesting a service from an object.

Thus far, we have used the car analogy to introduce classes, objects and member functions. In addition to the capabilities a car provides, it also has many attributes, such as its color, the number of doors, the amount of gas in its tank, its current speed and its total miles driven (i.e., its odometer reading). Like the car's capabilities, these attributes are represented as part of a car's design in its engineering diagrams. As you drive a car, these attributes are always associated with the car. Every car maintains its own attributes. For example, each car knows how much gas is in its own gas tank, but not how much is in the tanks of other cars. Similarly, an object has attributes that are carried with the object as it is used in a program. These attributes are specified as part of the object's class. For example, a bank account object has a balance attribute that represents the amount of money in the account. Each bank account object knows the balance in the account it represents, but not the balances of the other accounts in the bank. Attributes are specified by the class's data members.

3.3 Overview of the Chapter Examples

The remainder of this chapter presents seven simple examples that demonstrate the concepts we introduced in the context of the car analogy. These examples, summarized below, incrementally build a GradeBook class to demonstrate these concepts:

1. The first example presents a GradeBook class with one member function that simply displays a welcome message when it is called. We show how to create an object of that class and call the member function so that it displays the welcome message.

2. The second example modifies the first by allowing the member function to receive a course name as a so-called argument. Then, the member function displays the course name as part of the welcome message.

3. The third example shows how to store the course name in a GradeBook object. For this version of the class, we also show how to use member functions to set the course name in the object and get the course name from the object.

4. The fourth example demonstrates how the data in a GradeBook object can be initialized when the object is created—the initialization is performed by a special member function called the class's constructor. This example also demonstrates that each GradeBook object maintains its own course name data member.

5. The fifth example modifies the fourth by demonstrating how to place class GradeBook into a separate file to enable software reusability.

6. The sixth example modifies the fifth by demonstrating the good software-engineering principle of separating the interface of the class from its implementation. This makes the class easier to modify without affecting any clients of the class's objects—that is, any classes or functions that call the member functions of the class's objects from outside the objects.

7. The last example enhances class GradeBook by introducing data validation, which ensures that data in an object adheres to a particular format or is in a proper value range. For example, a Date object would require a month value in the range 1–12. In this GradeBook example, the member function that sets the course name for a GradeBook object ensures that the course name is 25 characters or fewer. If not, the member function uses only the first 25 characters of the course name and displays a warning message.

Note that the GradeBook examples in this chapter do not actually process or store grades. We begin processing grades with class GradeBook in Chapter 4 and we store grades in a GradeBook object in Chapter 7, Arrays and Vectors.

3.4 Defining a Class with a Member Function

We begin with an example (Fig. 3.1) that consists of class GradeBook (lines 9–17), which represents a grade book that an instructor can use to maintain student test scores, and a main function (lines 20–25) that creates a GradeBook object. Function main uses this object and its member function to display a message on the screen welcoming the instructor to the grade-book program.

First we describe how to define a class and a member function. Then we explain how an object is created and how to call a member function of an object. The first few examples

```
 1    // Fig. 3.1: fig03_01.cpp
 2    // Define class GradeBook with a member function displayMessage,
 3    // create a GradeBook object, and call its displayMessage function.
 4    #include <iostream>
 5    using std::cout;
 6    using std::endl;
 7
 8    // GradeBook class definition
 9    class GradeBook
10    {
11    public:
12       // function that displays a welcome message to the GradeBook user
13       void displayMessage()
14       {
15          cout << "Welcome to the Grade Book!" << endl;
16       } // end function displayMessage
17    }; // end class GradeBook
18
19    // function main begins program execution
20    int main()
21    {
22       GradeBook myGradeBook; // create a GradeBook object named myGradeBook
23       myGradeBook.displayMessage(); // call object's displayMessage function
24       return 0; // indicate successful termination
25    } // end main
```

```
Welcome to the Grade Book!
```

Fig. 3.1 | Define class GradeBook with a member function displayMessage, create a GradeBook object, and call its displayMessage function.

contain function main and the GradeBook class it uses in the same file. Later in the chapter, we introduce more sophisticated ways to structure your programs to achieve better software engineering.

Class *GradeBook*

Before function main (lines 20–25) can create an object of class GradeBook, we must tell the compiler what member functions and data members belong to the class. This is known as defining a class. The GradeBook class definition (lines 9–17) contains a member function called displayMessage (lines 13–16) that displays a message on the screen (line 15). Recall that a class is like a blueprint—so we need to make an object of class GradeBook (line 22) and call its displayMessage member function (line 23) to get line 15 to execute and display the welcome message. We'll soon explain lines 22–23 in detail.

The class definition begins in line 9 with the keyword class followed by the class name GradeBook. By convention, the name of a user-defined class begins with a capital letter, and for readability, each subsequent word in the class name begins with a capital letter. This capitalization style is often referred to as camel case, because the pattern of uppercase and lowercase letters resembles the silhouette of a camel.

Every class's body is enclosed in a pair of left and right braces ({ and }), as in lines 10 and 17. The class definition terminates with a semicolon (line 17).

Common Programming Error 3.1

Forgetting the semicolon at the end of a class definition is a syntax error.

Recall that the function main is always called automatically when you execute a program. Most functions do not get called automatically. As you'll soon see, you must call member function displayMessage explicitly to tell it to perform its task.

Line 11 contains the access-specifier label public:. The keyword public is an access specifier. Lines 13–16 define member function displayMessage. This member function appears after access specifier public: to indicate that the function is "available to the public"—that is, it can be called by other functions in the program (such as main), and by member functions of other classes (if there are any). Access specifiers are always followed by a colon (:). For the remainder of the text, when we refer to the access specifier public, we'll omit the colon as we did in this sentence. Section 3.6 introduces a second access specifier, private.

Each function in a program performs a task and may return a value when it completes its task—for example, a function might perform a calculation, then return the result of that calculation. When you define a function, you must specify a return type to indicate the type of the value returned by the function when it completes its task. In line 13, keyword void to the left of the function name displayMessage is the function's return type. Return type void indicates that displayMessage will not return (i.e., give back) any data to its calling function (in this example, main, as we'll see in a moment) when it completes its task. In Fig. 3.5, you'll see an example of a function that returns a value.

The name of the member function, displayMessage, follows the return type. By convention, function names begin with a lowercase first letter and all subsequent words in the name begin with a capital letter. The parentheses after the member function name indicate that this is a function. An empty set of parentheses, as shown in line 13, indicates that this member function does not require additional data to perform its task. You'll see an example of a member function that does require additional data in Section 3.5. Line 13 is commonly referred to as the function header. Every function's body is delimited by left and right braces ({ and }), as in lines 14 and 16.

The body of a function contains statements that perform the function's task. In this case, member function displayMessage contains one statement (line 15) that displays the message "Welcome to the Grade Book!". After this statement executes, the function has completed its task.

Common Programming Error 3.2

Returning a value from a function whose return type has been declared void is a compilation error.

Common Programming Error 3.3

Defining a function inside another function is a syntax error.

Testing Class GradeBook

Next, we'd like to use class GradeBook in a program. As you learned in Chapter 2, function main (lines 20–25) begins the execution of every program.

In this program, we'd like to call class GradeBook's displayMessage member function to display the welcome message. Typically, you cannot call a member function of a class until you create an object of that class. (As you'll learn in Section 10.7, static member functions are an exception.) Line 22 creates an object of class GradeBook called myGrade-Book. Note that the variable's type is GradeBook—the class we defined in lines 9–17. When we declare variables of type int, as we did in Chapter 2, the compiler knows what int is—it's a fundamental type. In line 22, however, the compiler does not automatically know what type GradeBook is—it's a user-defined type. We tell the compiler what GradeBook is by including the class definition (lines 9–17). If we omitted these lines, the compiler would issue an error message (such as "'GradeBook': undeclared identifier" in Microsoft Visual C++ or "'GradeBook': undeclared" in GNU C++). Each class you create becomes a new type that can be used to create objects. You can define new class types as needed; this is one reason why C++ is known as an extensible language.

Line 23 calls the member function displayMessage (defined in lines 13–16) using variable myGradeBook followed by the dot operator (.), the function name displayMessage and an empty set of parentheses. This call causes the displayMessage function to perform its task. At the beginning of line 23, "myGradeBook." indicates that main should use the GradeBook object that was created in line 22. The empty parentheses in line 13 indicate that member function displayMessage does not require additional data to perform its task. (In Section 3.5, you'll see how to pass data to a function.) When displayMessage completes its task, function main continues executing in line 24, which indicates that main performed its tasks successfully. This is the end of main, so the program terminates.

UML Class Diagram for Class *GradeBook*

Recall from Section 1.21 that the UML is a standardized graphical language used by programmers to represent their object-oriented systems. In the UML, each class is modeled in a UML class diagram as a rectangle with three compartments. Figure 3.2 presents a class diagram for class GradeBook (Fig. 3.1). The top compartment contains the class's name centered horizontally and in boldface type. The middle compartment contains the class's attributes, which correspond to data members in C++. This compartment is currently empty, because class GradeBook does not have any attributes. (Section 3.6 presents a version of class GradeBook with an attribute.) The bottom compartment contains the class's operations, which correspond to member functions in C++. The UML models operations by listing the operation name followed by a set of parentheses. Class GradeBook has only one member function, displayMessage, so the bottom compartment of Fig. 3.2 lists one operation with this name. Member function displayMessage does not require additional information to perform its tasks, so the parentheses following displayMessage in the class diagram are empty, just as they are in the member function's header in line 13

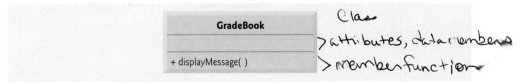

Fig. 3.2 | UML class diagram indicating that class GradeBook has a public displayMessage operation.

of Fig. 3.1. The plus sign (+) in front of the operation name indicates that `displayMessage` is a public operation in the UML (i.e., a `public` member function in C++).

3.5 Defining a Member Function with a Parameter

In our car analogy from Section 3.2, we mentioned that pressing a car's gas pedal sends a message to the car to perform a task—make the car go faster. But how fast should the car accelerate? As you know, the farther down you press the pedal, the faster the car accelerates. So the message to the car includes both the task to perform and additional information that helps the car perform the task. This additional information is known as a parameter—the value of the parameter helps the car determine how fast to accelerate. Similarly, a member function can require one or more parameters that represent additional data it needs to perform its task. A function call supplies values—called arguments—for each of the function's parameters. For example, to make a deposit into a bank account, suppose a `deposit` member function of an `Account` class specifies a parameter that represents the deposit amount. When the `deposit` member function is called, an argument value representing the deposit amount is copied to the member function's parameter. The member function then adds that amount to the account balance.

Defining and Testing Class GradeBook

Our next example (Fig. 3.3) redefines class `GradeBook` (lines 14–23) with a `displayMessage` member function (lines 18–22) that displays the course name as part of the welcome message. The new version of `displayMessage` requires a parameter (`courseName` in line 18) that represents the course name to output.

```
1   // Fig. 3.3: fig03_03.cpp
2   // Define class GradeBook with a member function that takes a parameter;
3   // Create a GradeBook object and call its displayMessage function.
4   #include <iostream>
5   using std::cout;
6   using std::cin;
7   using std::endl;
8
9   #include <string> // program uses C++ standard string class
10  using std::string;
11  using std::getline;
12
13  // GradeBook class definition
14  class GradeBook
15  {
16  public:
17     // function that displays a welcome message to the GradeBook user
18     void displayMessage( string courseName )          parameter
19     {
20        cout << "Welcome to the grade book for\n" << courseName << "!"
21           << endl;
22     } // end function displayMessage
23  }; // end class GradeBook
```

Fig. 3.3 | Define class `GradeBook` with a member function that takes a parameter, create a `GradeBook` object and call its `displayMessage` function. (Part 1 of 2.)

```
24
25   // function main begins program execution
26   int main()
27   {
28      string nameOfCourse; // string of characters to store the course name
29      GradeBook myGradeBook; // create a GradeBook object named myGradeBook
30
31      // prompt for and input course name
32      cout << "Please enter the course name:" << endl;
33      getline( cin, nameOfCourse ); // read a course name with blanks
34      cout << endl; // output a blank line
35
36      // call myGradeBook's displayMessage function
37      // and pass nameOfCourse as an argument
38      myGradeBook.displayMessage( nameOfCourse );
39      return 0; // indicate successful termination
40   } // end main
```

Handwritten annotations: cin.getline(nameOfCourse); ... arg ... getline(array, char, delimiter); — takes on 3 args

```
Please enter the course name:
CS101 Introduction to C++ Programming

Welcome to the grade book for
CS101 Introduction to C++ Programming!
```

Fig. 3.3 | Define class GradeBook with a member function that takes a parameter, create a GradeBook object and call its displayMessage function. (Part 2 of 2.)

Before discussing the new features of class GradeBook, let's see how the new class is used in main (lines 26–40). Line 28 creates a variable of type **string** called nameOfCourse that will be used to store the course name entered by the user. A variable of type string represents a string of characters such as "CS101 Introduction to C++ Programming". A string is actually an object of the C++ Standard Library class string. This class is defined in header file <string>, and the name string, like cout, belongs to namespace std. To enable line 28 to compile, line 9 includes the <string> header file. Note that the using declaration in line 10 allows us to simply write string in line 28 rather than std::string. For now, you can think of string variables like variables of other types such as int. You'll learn additional string capabilities in Section 3.10.

Line 29 creates an object of class GradeBook named myGradeBook. Line 32 prompts the user to enter a course name. Line 33 reads the name from the user and assigns it to the nameOfCourse variable, using the library function **getline** to perform the input. Before we explain this line of code, let's explain why we cannot simply write

```
cin >> nameOfCourse;
```

to obtain the course name. In our sample program execution, we use the course name "CS101 Introduction to C++ Programming," which contains multiple words. (Recall that we highlight user-supplied input in bold.) When cin is used with the stream extraction operator, it reads characters until the first white-space character is reached. Thus, only "CS101" would be read by the preceding statement. The rest of the course name would have to be read by subsequent input operations.

In this example, we'd like the user to type the complete course name and press *Enter* to submit it to the program, and we'd like to store the entire course name in the string variable nameOfCourse. The function call getline(cin, nameOfCourse) in line 33 reads characters (including the space characters that separate the words in the input) from the standard input stream object cin (i.e., the keyboard) until the newline character is encountered, places the characters in the string variable nameOfCourse and discards the newline character. Note that when you press *Enter* while typing program input, a newline is inserted in the input stream. Also note that the <string> header file must be included in the program to use function getline and that the name getline belongs to namespace std.

Line 38 calls myGradeBook's displayMessage member function. The nameOfCourse variable in parentheses is the argument that is passed to member function displayMessage so that it can perform its task. The value of variable nameOfCourse in main becomes the value of member function displayMessage's parameter courseName in line 18. When you execute this program, notice that member function displayMessage outputs as part of the welcome message the course name you type (in our sample execution, CS101 Introduction to C++ Programming).

More on Arguments and Parameters

To specify that a function requires data to perform its task, you place additional information in the function's parameter list, which is located in the parentheses following the function name. The parameter list may contain any number of parameters, including none at all (represented by empty parentheses as in Fig. 3.1, line 13) to indicate that a function does not require any parameters. Member function displayMessage's parameter list (Fig. 3.3, line 18) declares that the function requires one parameter. Each parameter must specify a type and an identifier. In this case, the type string and the identifier courseName indicate that member function displayMessage requires a string to perform its task. The member function body uses the parameter courseName to access the value that is passed to the function in the function call (line 38 in main). Lines 20–21 display parameter courseName's value as part of the welcome message. Note that the parameter variable's name (line 18) can be the same as or different from the argument variable's name (line 38)—you'll learn why in Chapter 6, Functions and an Introduction to Recursion.

A function can specify multiple parameters by separating each parameter from the next with a comma (we'll see an example in Figs. 6.4–6.5). The number and order of arguments in a function call must match the number and order of parameters in the parameter list of the called member function's header. Also, the argument types in the function call must be consistent with the types of the corresponding parameters in the function header. (As you'll learn in subsequent chapters, an argument's type and its corresponding parameter's type need not always be identical, but they must be "consistent.") In our example, the one string argument in the function call (i.e., nameOfCourse) exactly matches the one string parameter in the member-function definition (i.e., courseName).

Common Programming Error 3.4
Placing a semicolon after the right parenthesis enclosing the parameter list of a function definition is a syntax error.

Common Programming Error 3.5
Defining a function parameter again as a local variable in the function is a compilation error.

Good Programming Practice 3.1

To avoid ambiguity, do not use the same names for the arguments passed to a function and the corresponding parameters in the function definition.

Good Programming Practice 3.2

Choosing meaningful function names and meaningful parameter names makes programs more readable and helps avoid excessive use of comments.

Updated UML Class Diagram for Class GradeBook

The UML class diagram of Fig. 3.4 models class GradeBook of Fig. 3.3. Like the class GradeBook defined in Fig. 3.1, this GradeBook class contains public member function displayMessage. However, this version of displayMessage has a parameter. The UML models a parameter by listing the parameter name, followed by a colon and the parameter type in the parentheses following the operation name. The UML has its own data types similar to those of C++. The UML is language independent—it is used with many different programming languages—so its terminology does not exactly match that of C++. For example, the UML type String corresponds to the C++ type string. Member function displayMessage of class GradeBook (Fig. 3.3, lines 18–22) has a string parameter named courseName, so Fig. 3.4 lists courseName : String between the parentheses following the operation name displayMessage. Note that this version of the GradeBook class still does not have any data members.

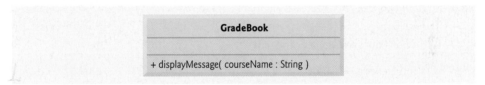

Fig. 3.4 | UML class diagram indicating that class GradeBook has a displayMessage operation with a courseName parameter of UML type String.

3.6 Data Members, *set* Functions and *get* Functions

In Chapter 2, we declared all of a program's variables in its main function. Variables declared in a function definition's body are known as local variables and can be used only from the line of their declaration in the function to the immediately following closing right brace (}). A local variable must be declared before it can be used in a function. A local variable cannot be accessed outside the function in which it is declared. When a function terminates, the values of its local variables are lost. (You'll see an exception to this in Chapter 6 when we discuss static local variables.) Recall from Section 3.2 that an object has attributes that are carried with it as it is used in a program. Such attributes exist throughout the life of the object.

A class normally consists of one or more member functions that manipulate the attributes that belong to a particular object of the class. Attributes are represented as variables in a class definition. Such variables are called data members and are declared inside a class definition but outside the bodies of the class's member-function definitions. Each object of a class maintains its own copy of its attributes in memory. The example in this section demonstrates a GradeBook class that contains a courseName data member to represent a particular GradeBook object's course name.

GradeBook Class with a Data Member, a set Function and a get Function

In our next example, class GradeBook (Fig. 3.5) maintains the course name as a data member so that it can be used or modified at any time during a program's execution. The class contains member functions setCourseName, getCourseName and displayMessage. Member function setCourseName stores a course name in a GradeBook data member. Member

```cpp
1   // Fig. 3.5: fig03_05.cpp
2   // Define class GradeBook that contains a courseName data member
3   // and member functions to set and get its value;
4   // Create and manipulate a GradeBook object with these functions.
5   #include <iostream>                    using namespace std;
6   using std::cout;
7   using std::cin;
8   using std::endl;
9
10  #include <string> // program uses C++ standard string class
11  using std::string;
12  using std::getline;
13
14  // GradeBook class definition
15  class GradeBook
16  {
17  public:
18     // function that sets the course name
19     void setCourseName( string name )
20     {
21        courseName = name; // store the course name in the object
22     } // end function setCourseName
23
24     // function that gets the course name
25     string getCourseName()
26     {
27        return courseName; // return the object's courseName
28     } // end function getCourseName
29
30     // function that displays a welcome message
31     void displayMessage()
32     {
33        // this statement calls getCourseName to get the
34        // name of the course this GradeBook represents
35        cout << "Welcome to the grade book for\n" << getCourseName() << "!"
36           << endl;
37     } // end function displayMessage
38  private:
39     string courseName; // course name for this GradeBook
40  }; // end class GradeBook
41
```

Fig. 3.5 | Defining and testing class GradeBook with a data member and *set* and *get* functions. (Part 1 of 2.)

```
42    // function main begins program execution
43    int main()
44    {
45       string nameOfCourse; // string of characters to store the course name
46       GradeBook myGradeBook; // create a GradeBook object named myGradeBook
47
48       // display initial value of courseName
49       cout << "Initial course name is: " << myGradeBook.getCourseName()
50          << endl;
51
52       // prompt for, input and set course name
53       cout << "\nPlease enter the course name:" << endl;
54       getline( cin, nameOfCourse ); // read a course name with blanks
55       myGradeBook.setCourseName( nameOfCourse ); // set the course name
56
57       cout << endl; // outputs a blank line
58       myGradeBook.displayMessage(); // display message with new course name
59       return 0; // indicate successful termination
60    } // end main
```

```
Initial course name is:

Please enter the course name:
CS101 Introduction to C++ Programming

Welcome to the grade book for
CS101 Introduction to C++ Programming!
```

Fig. 3.5 | Defining and testing class GradeBook with a data member and *set* and *get* functions.
(Part 2 of 2.)

function getCourseName obtains the course name from that data member. Member function displayMessage—which now specifies no parameters—still displays a welcome message that includes the course name. However, as you'll see, the function now obtains the course name by calling another function in the same class—getCourseName.

Good Programming Practice 3.3

Place a blank line between member-function definitions to enhance program readability.

A typical instructor teaches multiple courses, each with its own course name. Line 39 declares that courseName is a variable of type string. Because the variable is declared in the class definition (lines 15–40) but outside the bodies of the class's member-function definitions (lines 19–22, 25–28 and 31–37), the variable is a data member. Every instance (i.e., object) of class GradeBook contains one copy of each of the class's data members—if there are two GradeBook objects, each has its own copy of courseName (one per object), as you'll see in the example of Fig. 3.7. A benefit of making courseName a data member is that all the member functions of the class (in this case, class GradeBook) can manipulate any data members that appear in the class definition (in this case, courseName).

Access Specifiers public *and* private
Most data-member declarations appear after the access-specifier label private: (line 38). Like public, keyword private is an access specifier. Variables or functions declared after

access specifier `private` (and before the next access specifier) are accessible only to member functions of the class for which they are declared. Thus, data member `courseName` can be used only in member functions `setCourseName`, `getCourseName` and `displayMessage` of (every object of) class `GradeBook`. Data member `courseName`, because it is `private`, cannot be accessed by functions outside the class (such as `main`) or by member functions of other classes in the program. Attempting to access data member `courseName` in one of these program locations with an expression such as `myGradeBook.courseName` would result in a compilation error containing a message similar to

```
cannot access private member declared in class 'GradeBook'
```

Software Engineering Observation 3.1

As a rule of thumb, data members should be declared `private` and member functions should be declared `public`. (We'll see that it is appropriate to declare certain member functions `private`, if they are to be accessed only by other member functions of the class.)

Common Programming Error 3.6

An attempt by a function, which is not a member of a particular class (or a friend of that class, as we'll see in Chapter 10, Classes: A Deeper Look, Part 2), to access a `private` member of that class is a compilation error.

The default access for class members is `private` so all members after the class header and before the first access specifier are `private`. The access specifiers `public` and `private` may be repeated, but this is unnecessary and can be confusing.

Good Programming Practice 3.4

Despite the fact that the `public` and `private` access specifiers may be repeated and intermixed, list all the `public` members of a class first in one group and then list all the `private` members in another group. This focuses the client's attention on the class's `public` interface, rather than on the class's implementation.

Good Programming Practice 3.5

If you choose to list the `private` members first in a class definition, explicitly use the `private` access specifier despite the fact that `private` is assumed by default. This improves program clarity.

Declaring data members with access specifier `private` is known as data hiding. When a program creates (instantiates) a `GradeBook` object, data member `courseName` is encapsulated (hidden) in the object and can be accessed only by member functions of the object's class. In class `GradeBook`, member functions `setCourseName` and `getCourseName` manipulate the data member `courseName` directly (and `displayMessage` could do so if necessary).

Software Engineering Observation 3.2

You'll learn in Chapter 10 that functions and classes declared by a class to be friends can access the `private` members of the class.

Error-Prevention Tip 3.1

Making the data members of a class `private` and the member functions of the class `public` facilitates debugging because problems with data manipulations are localized to either the class's member functions or the friends of the class.

Member Functions *setCourseName and getCourseName*

Member function setCourseName (defined in lines 19–22) does not return any data when it completes its task, so its return type is void. The member function receives one parameter—name—which represents the course name that will be passed to it as an argument (as we'll see in line 55 of main). Line 21 assigns name to data member courseName. In this example, setCourseName does not attempt to validate the course name—i.e., the function does not check that the course name adheres to any particular format or follows any other rules regarding what a "valid" course name looks like. Suppose, for instance, that a university can print student transcripts containing course names of only 25 characters or fewer. In this case, we might want class GradeBook to ensure that its data member courseName never contains more than 25 characters. We discuss basic validation techniques in Section 3.10.

Member function getCourseName (defined in lines 25–28) returns a particular Grade-Book object's courseName. The member function has an empty parameter list, so it does not require additional data to perform its task. The function specifies that it returns a string. When a function that specifies a return type other than void is called and completes its task, the function returns a result to its calling function. For example, when you go to an automated teller machine (ATM) and request your account balance, you expect the ATM to give you back a value that represents your balance. Similarly, when a statement calls member function getCourseName on a GradeBook object, the statement expects to receive the GradeBook's course name (in this case, a string, as specified by the function's return type). If you have a function square that returns the square of its argument, the statement

```
result = square( 2 );
```

returns 4 from function square and assings to variable result the value 4. If you have a function maximum that returns the largest of three integer arguments, the statement

```
biggest = maximum( 27, 114, 51 );
```

returns 114 from function maximum and assigns to variable biggest the value 114.

 Common Programming Error 3.7

Forgetting to return a value from a function that is supposed to return a value is a compilation error.

Note that the statements in lines 21 and 27 each use variable courseName (line 39) even though it was not declared in any of the member functions. We can use courseName in the member functions of class GradeBook because courseName is a data member of the class. Also note that the order in which member functions are defined does not determine when they are called at execution time. So member function getCourseName could be defined before member function setCourseName.

Member Function *displayMessage*

Member function displayMessage (lines 31–37) does not return any data when it completes its task, so its return type is void. The function does not receive parameters, so its parameter list is empty. Lines 35–36 output a welcome message that includes the value of data member courseName. Line 35 calls member function getCourseName to obtain the value of courseName. Note that member function displayMessage could also access data member courseName directly, just as member functions setCourseName and getCourse-

Name do. We explain shortly why we choose to call member function getCourseName to obtain the value of courseName.

Testing Class GradeBook

The main function (lines 43–60) creates one object of class GradeBook and uses each of its member functions. Line 46 creates a GradeBook object named myGradeBook. Lines 49–50 display the initial course name by calling the object's getCourseName member function. Note that the first line of the output does not show a course name, because the object's courseName data member (i.e., a string) is initially empty—by default, the initial value of a string is the so-called empty string, i.e., a string that does not contain any characters. Nothing appears on the screen when an empty string is displayed.

Line 53 prompts the user to enter a course name. Local string variable nameOfCourse (declared in line 45) is set to the course name entered by the user, which is obtained by the call to the getline function (line 54). Line 55 calls object myGradeBook's setCourseName member function and supplies nameOfCourse as the function's argument. When the function is called, the argument's value is copied to parameter name (line 19) of member function setCourseName (lines 19–22). Then the parameter's value is assigned to data member courseName (line 21). Line 57 skips a line in the output; then line 58 calls object myGradeBook's displayMessage member function to display the welcome message containing the course name.

Software Engineering with Set and Get Functions

A class's private data members can be manipulated only by member functions of that class (and by "friends" of the class, as we'll see in Chapter 10). So a client of an object—that is, any class or function that calls the object's member functions from outside the object—calls the class's public member functions to request the class's services for particular objects of the class. This is why the statements in function main (Fig. 3.5, lines 43–60) call member functions setCourseName, getCourseName and displayMessage on a GradeBook object. Classes often provide public member functions to allow clients of the class to *set* (i.e., assign values to) or *get* (i.e., obtain the values of) private data members. The names of these member functions need not begin with set or get, but this naming convention is common. In this example, the member function that *sets* the courseName data member is called setCourseName, and the member function that *gets* the value of the courseName data member is called getCourseName. Note that *set* functions are also sometimes called mutators (because they mutate, or change, values), and *get* functions are also sometimes called accessors (because they access values).

Recall that declaring data members with access specifier private enforces data hiding. Providing public *set* and *get* functions allows clients of a class to access the hidden data, but only *indirectly*. The client knows that it is attempting to modify or obtain an object's data, but the client does not know how the object performs these operations. In some cases, a class may internally represent a piece of data one way, but expose that data to clients in a different way. For example, suppose a Clock class represents the time of day as a private int data member time that stores the number of seconds since midnight. However, when a client calls a Clock object's getTime member function, the object could return the time with hours, minutes and seconds in a string in the format "HH:MM:SS". Similarly, suppose the Clock class provides a *set* function named setTime that takes a string parameter in the "HH:MM:SS" format. Using string capabilities presented in

Chapter 18, the setTime function could convert this string to a number of seconds, which the function stores in its private data member. The *set* function could also check that the value it receives represents a valid time (e.g., "12:30:45" is valid but "42:85:70" is not). The *set* and *get* functions allow a client to interact with an object, but the object's private data remains safely encapsulated (i.e., hidden) in the object itself.

The *set* and *get* functions of a class also should be used by other member functions within the class to manipulate the class's private data, although these member functions *can* access the private data directly. In Fig. 3.5, member functions setCourseName and getCourseName are public member functions, so they are accessible to clients of the class, as well as to the class itself. Member function displayMessage calls member function get-CourseName to obtain the value of data member courseName for display purposes, even though displayMessage can access courseName directly—accessing a data member via its *get* function creates a better, more robust class (i.e., a class that is easier to maintain and less likely to stop working). If we decide to change the data member courseName in some way, the displayMessage definition will not require modification—only the bodies of the *get* and *set* functions that directly manipulate the data member will need to change. For example, suppose we decide that we want to represent the course name as two separate data members—courseNumber (e.g., "CS101") and courseTitle (e.g., "Introduction to C++ Programming"). Member function displayMessage can still issue a single call to member function getCourseName to obtain the full course name to display as part of the welcome message. In this case, getCourseName would need to build and return a string containing the courseNumber followed by the courseTitle. Member function displayMessage would continue to display the complete course title "CS101 Introduction to C++ Programming," because it is unaffected by the change to the class's data members. The benefits of calling a *set* function from another member function of a class will become clear when we discuss validation in Section 3.10.

Good Programming Practice 3.6

Always try to localize the effects of changes to a class's data members by accessing and manipulating the data members through their get *and* set *functions. Changes to the name of a data member or the data type used to store a data member then affect only the corresponding* get *and* set *functions, but not the callers of those functions.*

Software Engineering Observation 3.3

It is important to write programs that are understandable and easy to maintain. Change is the rule rather than the exception. You should anticipate that your code will be modified.

Software Engineering Observation 3.4

The class designer need not provide set *or* get *functions for each* private *data item; these capabilities should be provided only when appropriate. If a service is useful to the client code, that service should typically be provided in the class's* public *interface.*

GradeBook's UML Class Diagram with a Data Member and* set *and* get *Functions
Figure 3.6 contains an updated UML class diagram for the version of class GradeBook in Fig. 3.5. This diagram models GradeBook's data member courseName as an attribute in the middle compartment. The UML represents data members as attributes by listing the attribute name, followed by a colon and the attribute type. The UML type of attribute courseName is String, which corresponds to string in C++. Data member courseName is

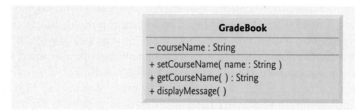

Fig. 3.6 | UML class diagram for class `GradeBook` with a private `courseName` attribute and public operations `setCourseName`, `getCourseName` and `displayMessage`.

`private` in C++, so the class diagram lists a minus sign (–) in front of the corresponding attribute's name. The minus sign in the UML is equivalent to the `private` access specifier in C++. Class `GradeBook` contains three `public` member functions, so the class diagram lists three operations in the third compartment. Recall that the plus (+) sign before each operation name indicates that the operation is `public` in C++. Operation `setCourseName` has a `String` parameter called `name`. The UML indicates the return type of an operation by placing a colon and the return type after the parentheses following the operation name. Member function `getCourseName` of class `GradeBook` (Fig. 3.5) has a `string` return type in C++, so the class diagram shows a `String` return type in the UML. Note that operations `setCourseName` and `displayMessage` do not return values (i.e., they return `void`), so the UML class diagram does not specify a return type after the parentheses of these operations. The UML does not use `void` as C++ does when a function does not return a value.

3.7 Initializing Objects with Constructors

As mentioned in Section 3.6, when an object of class `GradeBook` (Fig. 3.5) is created, its data member `courseName` is initialized to the empty string by default. What if you want to provide a course name when you create a `GradeBook` object? Each class you declare can provide a constructor that can be used to initialize an object of the class when the object is created. A constructor is a special member function that must be defined with the same name as the class, so that the compiler can distinguish it from the class's other member functions. An important difference between constructors and other functions is that constructors cannot return values, so they cannot specify a return type (not even `void`). Normally, constructors are declared `public`. The term "constructor" is often abbreviated as "ctor" in the literature—we generally avoid abbreviations.

C++ requires a constructor call for each object that is created, which helps ensure that each object is initialized before it is used in a program. The constructor call occurs implicitly when the object is created. If a class does not explicitly include a constructor, the compiler provides a default constructor—that is, a constructor with no parameters. For example, when line 46 of Fig. 3.5 creates a `GradeBook` object, the default constructor is called. The default constructor provided by the compiler creates a `GradeBook` object without giving any initial values to the object's fundamental type data members. [*Note:* For data members that are objects of other classes, the default constructor implicitly calls each data member's default constructor to ensure that the data member is initialized properly. This is why the `string` data member `courseName` (in Fig. 3.5) was initialized to the empty string—the default constructor for class `string` sets the `string`'s value to the empty string. You'll learn more about initializing data members that are objects of other classes in Section 10.3.]

In the example of Fig. 3.7, we specify a course name for a GradeBook object when the object is created (line 49). In this case, the argument "CS101 Introduction to C++ Programming" is passed to the GradeBook object's constructor (lines 17–20) and used to initialize the courseName. Figure 3.7 defines a modified GradeBook class containing a constructor with a string parameter that receives the initial course name.

```cpp
1   // Fig. 3.7: fig03_07.cpp
2   // Instantiating multiple objects of the GradeBook class and using
3   // the GradeBook constructor to specify the course name
4   // when each GradeBook object is created.
5   #include <iostream>
6   using std::cout;
7   using std::endl;
8
9   #include <string> // program uses C++ standard string class
10  using std::string;
11
12  // GradeBook class definition
13  class GradeBook
14  {
15  public:
16     // constructor initializes courseName with string supplied as argument
17     GradeBook( string name )
18     {
19        setCourseName( name ); // call set function to initialize courseName
20     } // end GradeBook constructor
21
22     // function to set the course name
23     void setCourseName( string name )
24     {
25        courseName = name; // store the course name in the object
26     } // end function setCourseName
27
28     // function to get the course name
29     string getCourseName()
30     {
31        return courseName; // return object's courseName
32     } // end function getCourseName
33
34     // display a welcome message to the GradeBook user
35     void displayMessage()
36     {
37        // call getCourseName to get the courseName
38        cout << "Welcome to the grade book for\n" << getCourseName()
39           << "!" << endl;
40     } // end function displayMessage
41  private:
42     string courseName; // course name for this GradeBook
43  }; // end class GradeBook
44
```

Fig. 3.7 | Instantiating multiple objects of the GradeBook class and using the GradeBook constructor to specify the course name when each GradeBook object is created. (Part 1 of 2.)

```
45   // function main begins program execution
46   int main()
47   {
48       // create two GradeBook objects
49       GradeBook gradeBook1( "CS101 Introduction to C++ Programming" );
50       GradeBook gradeBook2( "CS102 Data Structures in C++" );
51
52       // display initial value of courseName for each GradeBook
53       cout << "gradeBook1 created for course: " << gradeBook1.getCourseName()
54          << "\ngradeBook2 created for course: " << gradeBook2.getCourseName()
55          << endl;
56       return 0; // indicate successful termination
57   } // end main
```

```
gradeBook1 created for course: CS101 Introduction to C++ Programming
gradeBook2 created for course: CS102 Data Structures in C++
```

Fig. 3.7 | Instantiating multiple objects of the GradeBook class and using the GradeBook constructor to specify the course name when each GradeBook object is created. (Part 2 of 2.)

Defining a Constructor

Lines 17–20 of Fig. 3.7 define a constructor for class GradeBook. Notice that the constructor has the same name as its class, GradeBook. A constructor specifies in its parameter list the data it requires to perform its task. When you create a new object, you place this data in the parentheses that follow the object name (as we did in lines 49–50). Line 17 indicates that class GradeBook's constructor has a string parameter called name. Note that line 17 does not specify a return type, because constructors cannot return values (or even void).

Line 19 in the constructor's body passes the constructor's parameter name to member function setCourseName, which assigns a value to data member courseName. The set-CourseName member function (lines 23–26) simply assigns its parameter name to the data member courseName, so you might be wondering why we bother making the call to set-CourseName in line 19—the constructor certainly could perform the assignment courseName = name. In Section 3.10, we modify setCourseName to perform validation (ensuring that, in this case, the courseName is 25 or fewer characters in length). At that point the benefits of calling setCourseName from the constructor will become clear. Note that both the constructor (line 17) and the setCourseName function (line 23) use a parameter called name. You can use the same parameter names in different functions because the parameters are local to each function; they do not interfere with one another.

Testing Class GradeBook

Lines 46–57 of Fig. 3.7 define the main function that tests class GradeBook and demonstrates initializing GradeBook objects using a constructor. Line 49 in function main creates and initializes a GradeBook object called gradeBook1. When this line executes, the Grade-Book constructor (lines 17–20) is called (implicitly by C++) with the argument "CS101 Introduction to C++ Programming" to initialize gradeBook1's course name. Line 50 repeats this process for the GradeBook object called gradeBook2, this time passing the argument "CS102 Data Structures in C++" to initialize gradeBook2's course name. Lines 53–54 use each object's getCourseName member function to obtain the course names and show that they were indeed initialized when the objects were created. The output confirms that each GradeBook object maintains its own copy of data member courseName.

Two Ways to Provide a Default Constructor for a Class

Any constructor that takes no arguments is called a default constructor. A class gets a default constructor in one of two ways:

1. The compiler implicitly creates a default constructor in a class that does not define a constructor. Such a default constructor does not initialize the class's data members, but does call the default constructor for each data member that is an object of another class. [*Note:* An uninitialized variable typically contains a "garbage" value (e.g., an uninitialized int variable might contain -858993460, which is likely to be an incorrect value for that variable in most programs).]

2. You explicitly define a constructor that takes no arguments. Such a default constructor will perform the initialization specified by you and will call the default constructor for each data member that is an object of another class.

If you define a constructor with arguments, C++ will not implicitly create a default constructor for that class. Note that for each version of class GradeBook in Fig. 3.1, Fig. 3.3 and Fig. 3.5 the compiler implicitly defined a default constructor.

Error-Prevention Tip 3.2

Unless no initialization of your class's data members is necessary (almost never), provide a constructor to ensure that your class's data members are initialized with meaningful values when each new object of your class is created.

Software Engineering Observation 3.5

Data members can be initialized in a constructor of the class, or their values may be set later after the object is created. However, it is a good software engineering practice to ensure that an object is fully initialized before the client code invokes the object's member functions. In general, you should not rely on the client code to ensure that an object gets initialized properly.

Adding the Constructor to Class *GradeBook's* UML Class Diagram

The UML class diagram of Fig. 3.8 models class GradeBook of Fig. 3.7, which has a constructor with a name parameter of type string (represented by type String in the UML). Like operations, the UML models constructors in the third compartment of a class in a class diagram. To distinguish a constructor from a class's operations, the UML places the

GradeBook
– courseName : String
«constructor» + GradeBook(name : String) + setCourseName(name : String) + getCourseName( ) : String + displayMessage( )

Fig. 3.8 | UML class diagram indicating that class GradeBook has a constructor with a name parameter of UML type String.

word "constructor" between guillemets (« and ») before the constructor's name. It is customary to list the class's constructor before other operations in the third compartment.

3.8 Placing a Class in a Separate File for Reusability

We have developed class GradeBook as far as we need to for now from a programming perspective, so let's consider some software engineering issues. One of the benefits of creating class definitions is that, when packaged properly, our classes can be reused by programmers—potentially worldwide. For example, we can reuse C++ Standard Library type string in any C++ program by including the header file <string> in the program (and, as we'll see, by being able to link to the library's object code).

Unfortunately, programmers who wish to use our GradeBook class cannot simply include the file from Fig. 3.7 in another program. As you learned in Chapter 2, function main begins the execution of every program, and every program must have exactly one main function. If other programmers include the code from Fig. 3.7, they get extra baggage—our main function—and their programs will then have two main functions. When they attempt to compile their programs, the compiler will indicate an error. For example, attempting to compile a program with two main functions in Microsoft Visual C++ 2005 produces the error

```
error C2084: function 'int main(void)' already has a body
```

when the compiler tries to compile the second main function it encounters. Similarly, the GNU C++ compiler produces the error

```
redefinition of 'int main()'
```

These errors indicate that a program already has a main function. So, placing main in the same file with a class definition prevents that class from being reused by other programs. In this section, we demonstrate how to make class GradeBook reusable by separating it into another file from the main function.

Header Files

Each of the previous examples in the chapter consists of a single .cpp file, also known as a source-code file, that contains a GradeBook class definition and a main function. When building an object-oriented C++ program, it is customary to define reusable source code (such as a class) in a file that by convention has a .h filename extension—known as a header file. Programs use #include preprocessor directives to include header files and take advantage of reusable software components, such as type string provided in the C++ Standard Library and user-defined types like class GradeBook.

In our next example, we separate the code from Fig. 3.7 into two files—GradeBook.h (Fig. 3.9) and fig03_10.cpp (Fig. 3.10). As you look at the header file in Fig. 3.9, notice that it contains only the GradeBook class definition (lines 11–41) and lines 3–8, which allow class GradeBook to use cout, endl and type string. The main function that uses class GradeBook is defined in the source-code file fig03_10.cpp (Fig. 3.10) in lines 10–21. To help you prepare for the larger programs you'll encounter later in this book and in industry, we often use a separate source-code file containing function main to test our classes (this is called a driver program). You'll soon learn how a source-code file with main can use the class definition found in a header file to create objects of a class.

Including a Header File That Contains a User-Defined Class

A header file such as GradeBook.h (Fig. 3.9) cannot be used to begin program execution, because it does not contain a main function. If you try to compile and link GradeBook.h by itself to create an executable application, Microsoft Visual C++ 2005 produces the linker error message:

```
error LNK2019: unresolved external symbol _main referenced in
function _mainCRTStartup
```

To compile and link with GNU C++ on Linux, you must first include the header file in a .cpp source-code file, then GNU C++ produces a linker error message containing:

```
undefined reference to 'main'
```

This error indicates that the linker could not locate the program's main function. To test class GradeBook (defined in Fig. 3.9), you must write a separate source-code file containing a main function (such as Fig. 3.10) that instantiates and uses objects of the class.

```cpp
1   // Fig. 3.9: GradeBook.h
2   // GradeBook class definition in a separate file from main.
3   #include <iostream>
4   using std::cout;
5   using std::endl;
6
7   #include <string> // class GradeBook uses C++ standard string class
8   using std::string;
9
10  // GradeBook class definition
11  class GradeBook
12  {
13  public:
14     // constructor initializes courseName with string supplied as argument
15     GradeBook( string name )
16     {
17        setCourseName( name ); // call set function to initialize courseName
18     } // end GradeBook constructor
19
20     // function to set the course name
21     void setCourseName( string name )
22     {
23        courseName = name; // store the course name in the object
24     } // end function setCourseName
25
26     // function to get the course name
27     string getCourseName()
28     {
29        return courseName; // return object's courseName
30     } // end function getCourseName
31
32     // display a welcome message to the GradeBook user
33     void displayMessage()
34     {
```

Fig. 3.9 | GradeBook class definition. (Part 1 of 2.)

```
35              // call getCourseName to get the courseName
36         cout << "Welcome to the grade book for\n" << getCourseName()
37             << "!" << endl;
38       } // end function displayMessage
39    private:
40       string courseName; // course name for this GradeBook
41    }; // end class GradeBook
```

Fig. 3.9 | GradeBook class definition. (Part 2 of 2.)

```
 1    // Fig. 3.10: fig03_10.cpp
 2    // Including class GradeBook from file GradeBook.h for use in main.
 3    #include <iostream>
 4    using std::cout;
 5    using std::endl;
 6
 7    #include "GradeBook.h" // include definition of class GradeBook
 8
 9    // function main begins program execution
10    int main()
11    {
12       // create two GradeBook objects
13       GradeBook gradeBook1( "CS101 Introduction to C++ Programming" );
14       GradeBook gradeBook2( "CS102 Data Structures in C++" );
15
16       // display initial value of courseName for each GradeBook
17       cout << "gradeBook1 created for course: " << gradeBook1.getCourseName()
18          << "\ngradeBook2 created for course: " << gradeBook2.getCourseName()
19          << endl;
20       return 0; // indicate successful termination
21    } // end main
```

```
gradeBook1 created for course: CS101 Introduction to C++ Programming
gradeBook2 created for course: CS102 Data Structures in C++
```

Fig. 3.10 | Including class GradeBook from file GradeBook.h for use in main.

Recall from Section 3.4 that, while the compiler knows what fundamental data types like int are, the compiler does not know what a GradeBook is because it is a user-defined type. In fact, the compiler does not even know the classes in the C++ Standard Library. To help it understand how to use a class, we must explicitly provide the compiler with the class's definition—that's why, for example, to use type string, a program must include the <string> header file. This enables the compiler to determine the amount of memory that it must reserve for each object of the class and ensure that a program calls the class's member functions correctly.

To create GradeBook objects gradeBook1 and gradeBook2 in lines 13–14 of Fig. 3.10, the compiler must know the size of a GradeBook object. While objects conceptually contain data members and member functions, C++ objects contain only data. The compiler creates only one copy of the class's member functions and shares that copy among all the class's objects. Each object, of course, needs its own copy of the class's data members, because their contents can vary among objects (such as two different BankAccount objects having two different balance data members). The member-function code, however, is not modifiable, so it can be shared among all objects of the class. Therefore, the size of an object depends on the amount of memory required to store the class's data members. By including GradeBook.h in line 7, we give the compiler access to the information it needs (Fig. 3.9, line 40) to determine the size of a GradeBook object and to determine whether objects of the class are used correctly (in lines 13–14 and 17–18 of Fig. 3.10).

Line 7 instructs the C++ preprocessor to replace the directive with a copy of the contents of GradeBook.h (i.e., the GradeBook class definition) *before* the program is compiled. When the source-code file fig03_10.cpp is compiled, it now contains the GradeBook class definition (because of the #include), and the compiler is able to determine how to create GradeBook objects and see that their member functions are called correctly. Now that the class definition is in a header file (without a main function), we can include that header in *any* program that needs to reuse our GradeBook class.

How Header Files Are Located

Notice that the name of the GradeBook.h header file in line 7 of Fig. 3.10 is enclosed in quotes (" ") rather than angle brackets (< >). Normally, a program's source-code files and user-defined header files are placed in the same directory. When the preprocessor encounters a header file name in quotes (e.g., "GradeBook.h"), the preprocessor attempts to locate the header file in the same directory as the file in which the #include directive appears. If the preprocessor cannot find the header file in that directory, it searches for it in the same location(s) as the C++ Standard Library header files. When the preprocessor encounters a header file name in angle brackets (e.g., <iostream>), it assumes that the header is part of the C++ Standard Library and does not look in the directory of the program that is being preprocessed.

Error-Prevention Tip 3.3

To ensure that the preprocessor can locate header files correctly, #include preprocessor directives should place the names of user-defined header files in quotes (e.g., "GradeBook.h") and place the names of C++ Standard Library header files in angle brackets (e.g., <iostream>).

Additional Software Engineering Issues

Now that class GradeBook is defined in a header file, the class is reusable. Unfortunately, placing a class definition in a header file as in Fig. 3.9 still reveals the entire implementation of the class to the class's clients—GradeBook.h is simply a text file that anyone can open and read. Conventional software engineering wisdom says that to use an object of a class, the client code needs to know only what member functions to call, what arguments to provide to each member function and what return type to expect from each member function. The client code does not need to know how those functions are implemented.

If client code does know how a class is implemented, the client-code programmer might write client code based on the class's implementation details. Ideally, if that implementation changes, the class's clients should not have to change. Hiding the class's implementation details makes it easier to change the class's implementation while minimizing, and hopefully eliminating, changes to client code.

In Section 3.9, we show how to break up the GradeBook class into two files so that

1. the class is reusable,
2. the clients of the class know what member functions the class provides, how to call them and what return types to expect, and
3. the clients do not know how the class's member functions are implemented.

3.9 Separating Interface from Implementation

In the preceding section, we showed how to promote software reusability by separating a class definition from the client code (e.g., function main) that uses the class. We now introduce another fundamental principle of good software engineering—separating interface from implementation.

Interface of a Class

Interfaces define and standardize the ways in which things such as people and systems interact with one another. For example, a radio's controls serve as an interface between the radio's users and its internal components. The controls allow users to perform a limited set of operations (such as changing the station, adjusting the volume, and choosing between AM and FM stations). Various radios may implement these operations differently—some provide push buttons, some provide dials and some support voice commands. The interface specifies *what* operations a radio permits users to perform but does not specify *how* the operations are implemented inside the radio.

Similarly, the interface of a class describes *what* services a class's clients can use and how to *request* those services, but not *how* the class carries out the services. A class's interface consists of the class's public member functions (also known as the class's **public services**). For example, class GradeBook's interface (Fig. 3.9) contains a constructor and member functions setCourseName, getCourseName and displayMessage. GradeBook's clients (e.g., main in Fig. 3.10) use these functions to request the class's services. As you'll soon see, you can specify a class's interface by writing a class definition that lists only the member-function names, return types and parameter types.

Separating the Interface from the Implementation

In our prior examples, each class definition contained the complete definitions of the class's public member functions and the declarations of its private data members. However, it is better software engineering to define member functions outside the class definition, so that their implementation details can be hidden from the client code. This practice ensures that programmers do not write client code that depends on the class's implementation details. If they were to do so, the client code would be more likely to "break" if the class's implementation changed.

The program of Figs. 3.11–3.13 separates class GradeBook's interface from its implementation by splitting the class definition of Fig. 3.9 into two files—the header file GradeBook.h (Fig. 3.11) in which class GradeBook is defined, and the source-code file GradeBook.cpp (Fig. 3.12) in which GradeBook's member functions are defined. By convention, member-function definitions are placed in a source-code file of the same base name (e.g., GradeBook) as the class's header file but with a .cpp filename extension. The source-code file fig03_13.cpp (Fig. 3.13) defines function main (the client code). The code and output of Fig. 3.13 are identical to that of Fig. 3.10. Figure 3.14 shows how this three-file program is compiled from the perspectives of the GradeBook class programmer and the client-code programmer—we'll explain this figure in detail.

GradeBook.h: Defining a Class's Interface with Function Prototypes

Header file GradeBook.h (Fig. 3.11) contains another version of GradeBook's class definition (lines 9–18). This version is similar to the one in Fig. 3.9, but the function definitions in Fig. 3.9 are replaced here with function prototypes (lines 12–15) that describe the class's public interface without revealing the class's member-function implementations. A function prototype is a declaration of a function that tells the compiler the function's name, its return type and the types of its parameters. Note that the header file still specifies the class's private data member (line 17) as well. Again, the compiler must know the data members of the class to determine how much memory to reserve for each object of the class. Including the header file GradeBook.h in the client code (line 8 of Fig. 3.13) provides the compiler with the information it needs to ensure that the client code calls the member functions of class GradeBook correctly.

The function prototype in line 12 (Fig. 3.11) indicates that the constructor requires one string parameter. Recall that constructors do not have return types, so no return type appears in the function prototype. Member function setCourseName's function prototype (line 13) indicates that setCourseName requires a string parameter and does not return a value (i.e., its return type is void). Member function getCourseName's function prototype (line 14) indicates that the function does not require parameters and returns a string. Finally, member function displayMessage's function prototype (line 15) specifies that displayMessage does not require parameters and does not return a value. These function prototypes are the same as the corresponding function headers in Fig. 3.9, except that the parameter names (which are optional in prototypes) are not included and each function prototype must end with a semicolon.

```cpp
1   // Fig. 3.11: GradeBook.h
2   // GradeBook class definition. This file presents GradeBook's public
3   // interface without revealing the implementations of GradeBook's member
4   // functions, which are defined in GradeBook.cpp.
5   #include <string> // class GradeBook uses C++ standard string class
6   using std::string;
7
8   // GradeBook class definition
9   class GradeBook
10  {
11  public:
12     GradeBook( string ); // constructor that initializes courseName
13     void setCourseName( string ); // function that sets the course name
14     string getCourseName(); // function that gets the course name
15     void displayMessage(); // function that displays a welcome message
16  private:
17     string courseName; // course name for this GradeBook
18  }; // end class GradeBook
```

Fig. 3.11 | GradeBook class definition containing function prototypes that specify the interface of the class.

Common Programming Error 3.8

Forgetting the semicolon at the end of a function prototype is a syntax error.

Good Programming Practice 3.7

Although parameter names in function prototypes are optional (they are ignored by the compiler), many programmers use these names for documentation purposes.

Error-Prevention Tip 3.4

Parameter names in a function prototype (which, again, are ignored by the compiler) can be misleading if wrong or confusing names are used. For this reason, many programmers create function prototypes by copying the first line of the corresponding function definitions (when the source code for the functions is available), then appending a semicolon to the end of each prototype.

GradeBook.cpp: *Defining Member Functions in a Separate Source-Code File*

Source-code file GradeBook.cpp (Fig. 3.12) defines class GradeBook's member functions, which were declared in lines 12–15 of Fig. 3.11. The member-function definitions appear in lines 11–34 and are nearly identical to the member-function definitions in lines 15–38 of Fig. 3.9.

```cpp
 1   // Fig. 3.12: GradeBook.cpp
 2   // GradeBook member-function definitions. This file contains
 3   // implementations of the member functions prototyped in GradeBook.h.
 4   #include <iostream>
 5   using std::cout;
 6   using std::endl;
 7
 8   #include "GradeBook.h" // include definition of class GradeBook
 9
10   // constructor initializes courseName with string supplied as argument
11   GradeBook::GradeBook( string name )
12   {
13      setCourseName( name ); // call set function to initialize courseName
14   } // end GradeBook constructor
15
16   // function to set the course name
17   void GradeBook::setCourseName( string name )
18   {
19      courseName = name; // store the course name in the object
20   } // end function setCourseName
21
22   // function to get the course name
23   string GradeBook::getCourseName()
24   {
25      return courseName; // return object's courseName
26   } // end function getCourseName
27
```

Fig. 3.12 | GradeBook member-function definitions represent the implementation of class GradeBook. (Part 1 of 2.)

```
28   // display a welcome message to the GradeBook user
29   void GradeBook::displayMessage()
30   {
31      // call getCourseName to get the courseName
32      cout << "Welcome to the grade book for\n" << getCourseName()
33         << "!" << endl;
34   } // end function displayMessage
```

Fig. 3.12 | GradeBook member-function definitions represent the implementation of class GradeBook. (Part 2 of 2.)

Notice that each member-function name in the function headers (lines 11, 17, 23 and 29) is preceded by the class name and ::, which is known as the binary scope resolution operator. This "ties" each member function to the (now separate) GradeBook class definition (Fig. 3.11), which declares the class's member functions and data members. Without "GradeBook::" preceding each function name, these functions would not be recognized by the compiler as member functions of class GradeBook—the compiler would consider them "free" or "loose" functions, like main. Such functions cannot access GradeBook's private data or call the class's member functions, without specifying an object. So, the compiler would not be able to compile these functions. For example, lines 19 and 25 that access variable courseName would cause compilation errors because courseName is not declared as a local variable in each function—the compiler would not know that courseName is already declared as a data member of class GradeBook.

 Common Programming Error 3.9

When defining a class's member functions outside that class, omitting the class name and binary scope resolution operator (::) preceding the function names causes compilation errors.

To indicate that the member functions in GradeBook.cpp are part of class GradeBook, we must first include the GradeBook.h header file (line 8 of Fig. 3.12). This allows us to access the class name GradeBook in the GradeBook.cpp file. When compiling Grade-Book.cpp, the compiler uses the information in GradeBook.h to ensure that

1. the first line of each member function (lines 11, 17, 23 and 29) matches its prototype in the GradeBook.h file—for example, the compiler ensures that get-CourseName accepts no parameters and returns a string, and that

2. each member function knows about the class's data members and other member functions—for example, lines 19 and 25 can access variable courseName because it is declared in GradeBook.h as a data member of class GradeBook, and lines 13 and 32 can call functions setCourseName and getCourseName, respectively, be-cause each is declared as a member function of the class in GradeBook.h (and be-cause these calls conform with the corresponding prototypes).

*Testing Class **GradeBook***
Figure 3.13 performs the same GradeBook object manipulations as Fig. 3.10. Separating GradeBook's interface from the implementation of its member functions does not affect the way that this client code uses the class. It affects only how the program is compiled and linked, which we discuss in detail shortly.

```
 1   // Fig. 3.13: fig03_13.cpp
 2   // GradeBook class demonstration after separating
 3   // its interface from its implementation.
 4   #include <iostream>
 5   using std::cout;
 6   using std::endl;
 7
 8   #include "GradeBook.h" // include definition of class GradeBook
 9
10   // function main begins program execution
11   int main()
12   {
13      // create two GradeBook objects
14      GradeBook gradeBook1( "CS101 Introduction to C++ Programming" );
15      GradeBook gradeBook2( "CS102 Data Structures in C++" );
16
17      // display initial value of courseName for each GradeBook
18      cout << "gradeBook1 created for course: " << gradeBook1.getCourseName()
19         << "\ngradeBook2 created for course: " << gradeBook2.getCourseName()
20         << endl;
21      return 0; // indicate successful termination
22   } // end main
```

```
gradeBook1 created for course: CS101 Introduction to C++ Programming
gradeBook2 created for course: CS102 Data Structures in C++
```

Fig. 3.13 | GradeBook class demonstration after separating its interface from its implementation.

As in Fig. 3.10, line 8 of Fig. 3.13 includes the GradeBook.h header file so that the compiler can ensure that GradeBook objects are created and manipulated correctly in the client code. Before executing this program, the source-code files in Fig. 3.12 and Fig. 3.13 must both be compiled, then linked together—that is, the member-function calls in the client code need to be tied to the implementations of the class's member functions—a job performed by the linker.

The Compilation and Linking Process
The diagram in Fig. 3.14 shows the compilation and linking process that results in an executable GradeBook application that can be used by instructors. Often a class's interface and implementation will be created and compiled by one programmer and used by a separate programmer who implements the client code that uses the class. So, the diagram shows what is required by both the class-implementation programmer and the client-code programmer. The dashed lines in the diagram show the pieces required by the class-implementation programmer, the client-code programmer and the GradeBook application user, respectively. [*Note:* Figure 3.14 is not a UML diagram.]

A class-implementation programmer responsible for creating a reusable GradeBook class creates the header file GradeBook.h and the source-code file GradeBook.cpp that #includes the header file, then compiles the source-code file to create GradeBook's object code. To hide class GradeBook's member-function implementation details, the class-imple-

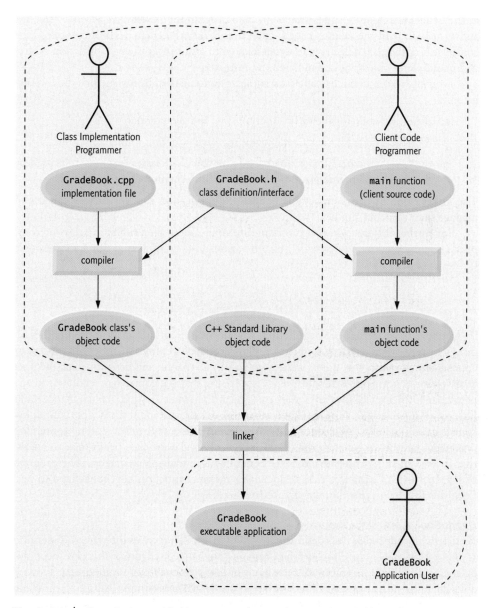

Fig. 3.14 | Compilation and linking process that produces an executable application.

mentation programmer would provide the client-code programmer with the header file `GradeBook.h` (which specifies the class's interface and data members) and the object code for class `GradeBook` (which contains the machine-language instructions that represent `GradeBook`'s member functions). The client-code programmer is not given `GradeBook.cpp`, so the client remains unaware of how `GradeBook`'s member functions are implemented.

The client code needs to know only `GradeBook`'s interface to use the class and must be able to link its object code. Since the interface of the class is part of the class definition in the GradeBook.h header file, the client-code programmer must have access to this file and #include it in the client's source-code file. When the client code is compiled, the compiler uses the class definition in GradeBook.h to ensure that the main function creates and manipulates objects of class GradeBook correctly.

To create the executable GradeBook application to be used by instructors, the last step is to link

1. the object code for the main function (i.e., the client code)

2. the object code for class GradeBook's member-function implementations

3. the C++ Standard Library object code for the C++ classes (e.g., string) used by the class-implementation programmer and the client-code programmer.

The linker's output is the executable GradeBook application that instructors can use to manage their students' grades.

For further information on compiling multiple-source-file programs, see your compiler's documentation. We provide links to various C++ compilers in our C++ Resource Center at www.deitel.com/cplusplus/.

3.10 Validating Data with *set* Functions

In Section 3.6, we introduced *set* functions for allowing clients of a class to modify the value of a private data member. In Fig. 3.5, class GradeBook defines member function set-CourseName to simply assign a value received in its parameter name to data member courseName. This member function does not ensure that the course name adheres to any particular format or follows any other rules regarding what a "valid" course name looks like. As we stated earlier, suppose that a university can print student transcripts containing course names of only 25 characters or less. If the university uses a system containing GradeBook objects to generate the transcripts, we might want class GradeBook to ensure that its data member courseName never contains more than 25 characters. The program of Figs. 3.15–3.17 enhances class GradeBook's member function setCourseName to perform this validation (also known as validity checking).

GradeBook *Class Definition*

Notice that GradeBook's class definition (Fig. 3.15)—and hence, its interface—is identical to that of Fig. 3.11. Since the interface remains unchanged, clients of this class need not be changed when the definition of member function setCourseName is modified. This enables clients to take advantage of the improved GradeBook class simply by linking the client code to the updated GradeBook's object code.

```
1   // Fig. 3.15: GradeBook.h
2   // GradeBook class definition presents the public interface of
3   // the class. Member-function definitions appear in GradeBook.cpp.
4   #include <string> // program uses C++ standard string class
5   using std::string;
6
```

Fig. 3.15 | GradeBook class definition. (Part 1 of 2.)

```
7   // GradeBook class definition
8   class GradeBook
9   {
10  public:
11     GradeBook( string ); // constructor that initializes a GradeBook object
12     void setCourseName( string ); // function that sets the course name
13     string getCourseName(); // function that gets the course name
14     void displayMessage(); // function that displays a welcome message
15  private:
16     string courseName; // course name for this GradeBook
17  }; // end class GradeBook
```

Fig. 3.15 | GradeBook class definition. (Part 2 of 2.)

Validating the Course Name with GradeBook Member Function setCourseName

The enhancement to class GradeBook is in the definition of setCourseName (Fig. 3.16, lines 18–31). The if statement in lines 20–21 determines whether parameter name contains a valid course name (i.e., a string of 25 or fewer characters). If the course name is valid, line 21 stores the course name in data member courseName. Note the expression name.length() in line 20. This is a member-function call just like myGradeBook.display-Message(). The C++ Standard Library's string class defines a member function length that returns the number of characters in a string object. Parameter name is a string object, so the call name.length() returns the number of characters in name. If this value is less than or equal to 25, name is valid and line 21 executes.

The if statement in lines 23–30 handles the case in which setCourseName receives an invalid course name (i.e., a name that is more than 25 characters long). Even if parameter name is too long, we still want to leave the GradeBook object in a consistent state—that is, a state in which the object's data member courseName contains a valid value (i.e., a string of 25 characters or less). Thus, we truncate (i.e., shorten) the specified course name and assign the first 25 characters of name to the courseName data member (unfortunately, this could truncate the course name awkwardly). Standard class string provides member function substr (short for "substring") that returns a new string object created by copying part of an existing string object. The call in line 26 (i.e., name.substr(0, 25)) passes two integers (0 and 25) to name's member function substr. These arguments indicate the portion of the string name that substr should return. The first argument specifies the starting position in the original string from which characters are copied—the first character in every string is considered to be at position 0. The second argument specifies the number of characters to copy. Therefore, the call in line 26 returns a 25-character substring of name starting at position 0 (i.e., the first 25 characters in name). For example, if name holds the value "CS101 Introduction to Programming in C++", substr returns "CS101 Introduction to Pro". After the call to substr, line 26 assigns the substring returned by substr to data member courseName. In this way, member function set-CourseName ensures that courseName is always assigned a string containing 25 or fewer characters. If the member function has to truncate the course name to make it valid, lines 28–29 display a warning message.

Note that the if statement in lines 23–30 contains two body statements—one to set the courseName to the first 25 characters of parameter name and one to print an accompanying message to the user. We want both of these statements to execute when name is too

```cpp
1   // Fig. 3.16: GradeBook.cpp
2   // Implementations of the GradeBook member-function definitions.
3   // The setCourseName function performs validation.
4   #include <iostream>
5   using std::cout;
6   using std::endl;
7
8   #include "GradeBook.h" // include definition of class GradeBook
9
10  // constructor initializes courseName with string supplied as argument
11  GradeBook::GradeBook( string name )
12  {
13     setCourseName( name ); // validate and store courseName
14  } // end GradeBook constructor
15
16  // function that sets the course name;
17  // ensures that the course name has at most 25 characters
18  void GradeBook::setCourseName( string name )
19  {
20     if ( name.length() <= 25 ) // if name has 25 or fewer characters
21        courseName = name; // store the course name in the object
22
23     if ( name.length() > 25 ) // if name has more than 25 characters
24     {
25        // set courseName to first 25 characters of parameter name
26        courseName = name.substr( 0, 25 ); // start at 0, length of 25
27
28        cout << "Name \"" << name << "\" exceeds maximum length (25).\n"
29           << "Limiting courseName to first 25 characters.\n" << endl;
30     } // end if
31  } // end function setCourseName
32
33  // function to get the course name
34  string GradeBook::getCourseName()
35  {
36     return courseName; // return object's courseName
37  } // end function getCourseName
38
39  // display a welcome message to the GradeBook user
40  void GradeBook::displayMessage()
41  {
42     // call getCourseName to get the courseName
43     cout << "Welcome to the grade book for\n" << getCourseName()
44        << "!" << endl;
45  } // end function displayMessage
```

Fig. 3.16 | Member-function definitions for class `GradeBook` with a *set* function that validates the length of data member `courseName`.

long, so we place them in a pair of braces, { }. Recall from Chapter 2 that this creates a block. You'll learn more about placing multiple statements in the body of a control statement in Chapter 4.

Note that the statement in lines 28–29 could also appear without a stream insertion operator at the start of the second line of the statement, as in:

```
cout << "Name \"" << name << "\" exceeds maximum length (25).\n"
        "Limiting courseName to first 25 characters.\n" << endl;
```

The C++ compiler combines adjacent string literals, even if they appear on separate lines of a program. Thus, in the statement above, the C++ compiler would combine the string literals "\" exceeds maximum length (25).\n" and "Limiting courseName to first 25 characters.\n" into a single string literal that produces output identical to that of lines 28–29 in Fig. 3.16. This behavior allows you to print lengthy strings by breaking them across lines in your program without including additional stream insertion operations.

Testing Class *GradeBook*

Figure 3.17 demonstrates the modified version of class GradeBook (Figs. 3.15–3.16) featuring validation. Line 14 creates a GradeBook object named gradeBook1. Recall that the

```
1   // Fig. 3.17: fig03_17.cpp
2   // Create and manipulate a GradeBook object; illustrate validation.
3   #include <iostream>
4   using std::cout;
5   using std::endl;
6
7   #include "GradeBook.h" // include definition of class GradeBook
8
9   // function main begins program execution
10  int main()
11  {
12     // create two GradeBook objects;
13     // initial course name of gradeBook1 is too long
14     GradeBook gradeBook1( "CS101 Introduction to Programming in C++" );
15     GradeBook gradeBook2( "CS102 C++ Data Structures" );
16
17     // display each GradeBook's courseName
18     cout << "gradeBook1's initial course name is: "
19        << gradeBook1.getCourseName()
20        << "\ngradeBook2's initial course name is: "
21        << gradeBook2.getCourseName() << endl;
22
23     // modify myGradeBook's courseName (with a valid-length string)
24     gradeBook1.setCourseName( "CS101 C++ Programming" );
25
26     // display each GradeBook's courseName
27     cout << "\ngradeBook1's course name is: "
28        << gradeBook1.getCourseName()
29        << "\ngradeBook2's course name is: "
30        << gradeBook2.getCourseName() << endl;
31     return 0; // indicate successful termination
32  } // end main
```

Fig. 3.17 | Creating and manipulating a GradeBook object in which the course name is limited to 25 characters in length. (Part 1 of 2.)

```
Name "CS101 Introduction to Programming in C++" exceeds maximum length (25).
Limiting courseName to first 25 characters.

gradeBook1's initial course name is: CS101 Introduction to Pro
gradeBook2's initial course name is: CS102 C++ Data Structures

gradeBook1's course name is: CS101 C++ Programming
gradeBook2's course name is: CS102 C++ Data Structures
```

Fig. 3.17 | Creating and manipulating a GradeBook object in which the course name is limited to 25 characters in length. (Part 2 of 2.)

GradeBook constructor calls setCourseName to initialize data member courseName. In previous versions of the class, the benefit of calling setCourseName in the constructor was not evident. Now, however, the constructor takes advantage of the validation provided by setCourseName. The constructor simply calls setCourseName, rather than duplicating its validation code. When line 14 of Fig. 3.17 passes an initial course name of "CS101 Introduction to Programming in C++" to the GradeBook constructor, the constructor passes this value to setCourseName, where the actual initialization occurs. Because this course name contains more than 25 characters, the body of the second if statement executes, causing courseName to be initialized to the truncated 25-character course name "CS101 Introduction to Pro" (the truncated part is highlighted in red in line 14). Notice that the output in Fig. 3.17 contains the warning message output by lines 28–29 of Fig. 3.16 in member function setCourseName. Line 15 creates another GradeBook object called gradeBook2—the valid course name passed to the constructor is exactly 25 characters.

Lines 18–21 of Fig. 3.17 display the truncated course name for gradeBook1 (we highlight this in red in the program output) and the course name for gradeBook2. Line 24 calls gradeBook1's setCourseName member function directly, to change the course name in the GradeBook object to a shorter name that does not need to be truncated. Then, lines 27–30 output the course names for the GradeBook objects again.

Additional Notes on Set *Functions*
A public *set* function such as setCourseName should carefully scrutinize any attempt to modify the value of a data member (e.g., courseName) to ensure that the new value is appropriate for that data item. For example, an attempt to *set* the day of the month to 37 should be rejected, an attempt to *set* a person's weight to zero or a negative value should be rejected, an attempt to *set* a grade on an exam to 185 (when the proper range is zero to 100) should be rejected, and so on

Software Engineering Observation 3.6

Making data members private and controlling access, especially write access, to those data members through public member functions helps ensure data integrity.

Error-Prevention Tip 3.5

The benefits of data integrity are not automatic simply because data members are made private—you must provide appropriate validity checking and report the errors.

> ### Software Engineering Observation 3.7
>
> *Member functions that set the values of* private *data should verify that the intended new values are proper; if they are not, the* set *functions should place the* private *data members into an appropriate state.*

A class's *set* functions can return values to the class's clients indicating that attempts were made to assign invalid data to objects of the class. A client of the class can test the return value of a *set* function to determine whether the client's attempt to modify the object was successful and to take appropriate action. In Chapter 16, we demonstrate how clients of a class can be notified via the exception-handling mechanism when an attempt is made to modify an object with an inappropriate value. To keep the program of Figs. 3.15–3.17 simple at this early point in the book, `setCourseName` in Fig. 3.16 just prints an appropriate message on the screen.

3.11 (Optional) Software Engineering Case Study: Identifying the Classes in the ATM Requirements Specification

Now we begin designing the ATM system that we introduced in Chapter 2. In this section, we identify the classes that are needed to build the ATM system by analyzing the nouns and noun phrases that appear in the requirements specification. We introduce UML class diagrams to model the relationships between these classes. This is an important first step in defining the structure of our system.

Identifying the Classes in a System

We begin our OOD process by identifying the classes required to build the ATM system. We'll eventually describe these classes using UML class diagrams and implement these classes in C++. First, we review the requirements specification of Section 2.8 and find key nouns and noun phrases to help us identify classes that comprise the ATM system. We may decide that some of these nouns and noun phrases are attributes of other classes in the system. We may also conclude that some of the nouns do not correspond to parts of the system and thus should not be modeled at all. Additional classes may become apparent to us as we proceed through the design process.

Figure 3.18 lists the nouns and noun phrases in the requirements specification. We list them from left to right in the order in which they appear in the requirements specification. We list only the singular form of each noun or noun phrase.

We create classes only for the nouns and noun phrases that have significance in the ATM system. We do not need to model "bank" as a class, because the bank is not a part of the ATM system—the bank simply wants us to build the ATM. "Customer" and "user" also represent entities outside of the system—they are important because they interact with our ATM system, but we do not need to model them as classes in the ATM software. Recall that we modeled an ATM user (i.e., a bank customer) as the actor in the use case diagram of Fig. 2.18.

We do not model "$20 bill" or "deposit envelope" as classes. These are physical objects in the real world, but they are not part of what is being automated. We can adequately represent the presence of bills in the system using an attribute of the class that models the cash dispenser. (We assign attributes to classes in Section 4.13.) For example, the cash dispenser maintains a count of the number of bills it contains. The requirements specification

Nouns and noun phrases in the requirements specification		
bank	money / fund	account number
ATM	screen	PIN
user	keypad	bank database
customer	cash dispenser	balance inquiry
transaction	$20 bill / cash	withdrawal
account	deposit slot	deposit
balance	deposit envelope	

Fig. 3.18 | Nouns and noun phrases in the requirements specification.

doesn't say anything about what the system should do with deposit envelopes after it receives them. We can assume that acknowledging the receipt of an envelope—an operation performed by the class that models the deposit slot—is sufficient to represent the presence of an envelope in the system. (We assign operations to classes in Section 6.22.)

In our simplified ATM system, representing various amounts of "money," including the "balance" of an account, as attributes of other classes seems most appropriate. Likewise, the nouns "account number" and "PIN" represent significant pieces of information in the ATM system. They are important attributes of a bank account. They do not, however, exhibit behaviors. Thus, we can most appropriately model them as attributes of an account class.

Though the requirements specification frequently describes a "transaction" in a general sense, we do not model the broad notion of a financial transaction at this time. Instead, we model the three types of transactions (i.e., "balance inquiry," "withdrawal" and "deposit") as individual classes. These classes possess specific attributes needed for executing the transactions they represent. For example, a withdrawal needs to know the amount of money the user wants to withdraw. A balance inquiry, however, does not require any additional data. Furthermore, the three transaction classes exhibit unique behaviors. A withdrawal includes dispensing cash to the user, whereas a deposit involves receiving deposit envelopes from the user. [*Note:* In Section 13.10, we "factor out" common features of all transactions into a general "transaction" class using the object-oriented concepts of abstract classes and inheritance.]

We determine the classes for our system based on the remaining nouns and noun phrases from Fig. 3.18. Each of these refers to one or more of the following:

- ATM
- screen
- keypad
- cash dispenser
- deposit slot
- account
- bank database
- balance inquiry

- withdrawal
- deposit

The elements of this list are likely to be classes we'll need to implement our system.

We can now model the classes in our system based on the list we have created. We capitalize class names in the design process—a UML convention—as we'll do when we write the actual C++ code that implements our design. If the name of a class contains more than one word, we run the words together and capitalize the first letter of each word (e.g., MultipleWordName). Using this convention, we create classes ATM, Screen, Keypad, Cash-Dispenser, DepositSlot, Account, BankDatabase, BalanceInquiry, Withdrawal and Deposit. We construct our system using all of these classes as building blocks. Before we begin building the system, however, we must gain a better understanding of how the classes relate to one another.

Modeling Classes

The UML enables us to model, via class diagrams, the classes in the ATM system and their interrelationships. Figure 3.19 represents class ATM. In the UML, each class is modeled as a rectangle with three compartments. The top compartment contains the name of the class, centered horizontally and in boldface. The middle compartment contains the class's attributes. (We discuss attributes in Section 4.13 and Section 5.11.) The bottom compartment contains the class's operations (discussed in Section 6.22). In Fig. 3.19 the middle and bottom compartments are empty, because we have not yet determined this class's attributes and operations.

Class diagrams also show the relationships among the classes of the system. Figure 3.20 shows how our classes ATM and Withdrawal relate to one another. For the moment, we choose to model only this subset of classes for simplicity; we present a more complete class diagram later in this section. Notice that the rectangles representing classes in this diagram are not subdivided into compartments. The UML allows the suppression of class attributes and operations in this manner, when appropriate, to create more readable diagrams. Such a diagram is said to be an elided diagram—one in which some information, such as the contents of the second and third compartments, is not modeled. We'll place information in these compartments in Section 4.13 and Section 6.22.

In Fig. 3.20, the solid line that connects the two classes represents an association—a relationship between classes. The numbers near each end of the line are multiplicity

Fig. 3.19 | Representing a class in the UML using a class diagram.

Fig. 3.20 | Class diagram showing an association among classes.

values, which indicate how many objects of each class participate in the association. In this case, following the line from one end to the other reveals that, at any given moment, one ATM object participates in an association with either zero or one Withdrawal objects—zero if the current user is not currently performing a transaction or has requested a different type of transaction, and one if the user has requested a withdrawal. The UML can model many types of multiplicity. Figure 3.21 lists and explains the multiplicity types.

An association can be named. For example, the word Executes above the line connecting classes ATM and Withdrawal in Fig. 3.20 indicates the name of that association. This part of the diagram reads "one object of class ATM executes zero or one objects of class Withdrawal." Note that association names are directional, as indicated by the filled arrowhead—so it would be improper, for example, to read the preceding association from right to left as "zero or one objects of class Withdrawal execute one object of class ATM."

The word currentTransaction at the Withdrawal end of the association line in Fig. 3.20 is a role name, which identifies the role the Withdrawal object plays in its relationship with the ATM. A role name adds meaning to an association between classes by identifying the role a class plays in the context of an association. A class can play several roles in the same system. For example, in a school personnel system, a person may play the role of "professor" when relating to students. The same person may take on the role of "colleague" when participating in a relationship with another professor, and "coach" when coaching student athletes. In Fig. 3.20, the role name currentTransaction indicates that the Withdrawal object participating in the Executes association with an object of class ATM represents the transaction currently being processed by the ATM. In other contexts, a Withdrawal object may take on other roles (e.g., the previous transaction). Notice that we do not specify a role name for the ATM end of the Executes association. Role names in class diagrams are often omitted when the meaning of an association is clear without them.

In addition to indicating simple relationships, associations can specify more complex relationships, such as objects of one class being composed of objects of other classes. Consider a real-world automated teller machine. What "pieces" does a manufacturer put together to build a working ATM? Our requirements specification tells us that the ATM is composed of a screen, a keypad, a cash dispenser and a deposit slot.

Symbol	Meaning
0	None
1	One
m	An integer value
0..1	Zero or one
m, n	m or n
$m..n$	At least m, but not more than n
*	Any nonnegative integer (zero or more)
0..*	Zero or more (identical to *)
1..*	One or more

Fig. 3.21 | Multiplicity types.

In Fig. 3.22, the solid diamonds attached to the association lines of class ATM indicate that class ATM has a composition relationship with classes Screen, Keypad, CashDispenser and DepositSlot. Composition implies a whole/part relationship. The class that has the composition symbol (the solid diamond) on its end of the association line is the whole (in this case, ATM), and the classes on the other end of the association lines are the parts—in this case, classes Screen, Keypad, CashDispenser and DepositSlot. The compositions in Fig. 3.22 indicate that an object of class ATM is formed from one object of class Screen, one object of class CashDispenser, one object of class Keypad and one object of class DepositSlot. The ATM "has a" screen, a keypad, a cash dispenser and a deposit slot. The "has-a" relationship defines composition. (We'll see in the Software Engineering Case Study section in Chapter 13 that the "is-a" relationship defines inheritance.)

According to the UML specification, composition relationships have the following properties:

1. Only one class in the relationship can represent the whole (i.e., the diamond can be placed on only one end of the association line). For example, either the screen is part of the ATM or the ATM is part of the screen, but the screen and the ATM cannot both represent the whole in the relationship.

2. The parts in the composition relationship exist only as long as the whole, and the whole is responsible for the creation and destruction of its parts. For example, the act of constructing an ATM includes manufacturing its parts. Furthermore, if the ATM is destroyed, its screen, keypad, cash dispenser and deposit slot are also destroyed.

3. A part may belong to only one whole at a time, although the part may be removed and attached to another whole, which then assumes responsibility for the part.

The solid diamonds in our class diagrams indicate composition relationships that fulfill these three properties. If a "has-a" relationship does not satisfy one or more of these criteria, the UML specifies that hollow diamonds be attached to the ends of association lines to indicate aggregation—a weaker form of composition. For example, a personal computer and a computer monitor participate in an aggregation relationship—the computer "has a" monitor,

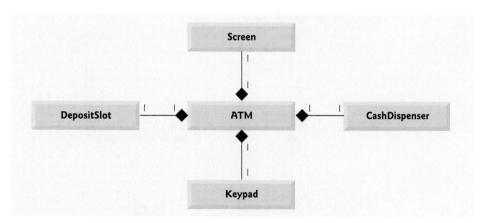

Fig. 3.22 | Class diagram showing composition relationships.

but the two parts can exist independently, and the same monitor can be attached to multiple computers at once, thus violating the second and third properties of composition.

Figure 3.23 shows a class diagram for the ATM system. This diagram models most of the classes that we identified earlier in this section, as well as the associations between them that we can infer from the requirements specification. [*Note:* Classes `BalanceInquiry` and `Deposit` participate in associations similar to those of class `Withdrawal`, so we have chosen to omit them from this diagram to keep it simple. In Chapter 13, we expand our class diagram to include all the classes in the ATM system.]

Figure 3.23 presents a graphical model of the structure of the ATM system. This class diagram includes classes `BankDatabase` and `Account` and several associations that were not present in either Fig. 3.20 or Fig. 3.22. The class diagram shows that class `ATM` has a *one-to-one relationship* with class `BankDatabase`—one ATM object authenticates users against one `BankDatabase` object. In Fig. 3.23, we also model the fact that the bank's database contains information about many accounts—one object of class `BankDatabase` participates in a composition relationship with zero or more objects of class `Account`. Recall from Fig. 3.21 that the multiplicity value 0..* at the `Account` end of the association between class `BankDatabase` and class `Account` indicates that zero or more objects of class `Account` take part in the association. Class `BankDatabase` has a *one-to-many relationship* with class `Account`—the `BankDatabase` contains many `Accounts`. Similarly, class `Account` has a *many-to-one relationship* with class `BankDatabase`—there can be many `Accounts` contained in the `BankDatabase`. [*Note:* Recall from Fig. 3.21 that the multiplicity value * is identical to 0..*. We include 0..* in our class diagrams for clarity.]

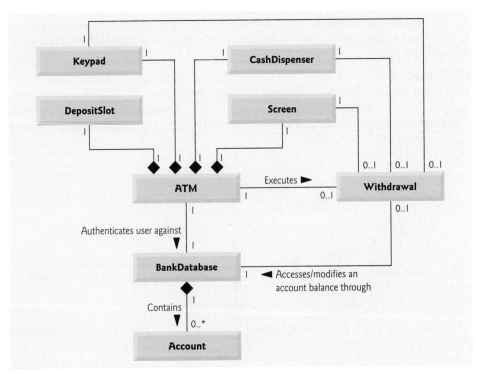

Fig. 3.23 | Class diagram for the ATM system model.

Figure 3.23 also indicates that if the user is performing a withdrawal, "one object of class `Withdrawal` accesses/modifies an account balance through one object of class `Bank-Database`." We could have created an association directly between class `Withdrawal` and class `Account`. The requirements specification, however, states that the "ATM must interact with the bank's account information database" to perform transactions. A bank account contains sensitive information, and systems engineers must always consider the security of personal data when designing a system. Thus, only the `BankDatabase` can access and manipulate an account directly. All other parts of the system must interact with the database to retrieve or update account information (e.g., an account balance).

The class diagram in Fig. 3.23 also models associations between class `Withdrawal` and classes `Screen`, `CashDispenser` and `Keypad`. A withdrawal transaction includes prompting the user to choose a withdrawal amount and receiving numeric input. These actions require the use of the screen and the keypad, respectively. Furthermore, dispensing cash to the user requires access to the cash dispenser.

Classes `BalanceInquiry` and `Deposit`, though not shown in Fig. 3.23, take part in several associations with the other classes of the ATM system. Like class `Withdrawal`, each of these classes associates with classes `ATM` and `BankDatabase`. An object of class `Balance-Inquiry` also associates with an object of class `Screen` to display the balance of an account to the user. Class `Deposit` associates with classes `Screen`, `Keypad` and `DepositSlot`. Like withdrawals, deposit transactions require use of the screen and the keypad to display prompts and receive input, respectively. To receive deposit envelopes, an object of class `Deposit` accesses the deposit slot.

We have now identified the classes in our ATM system (although we may discover others as we proceed with the design and implementation). In Section 4.13, we determine the attributes for each of these classes, and in Section 5.11, we use these attributes to examine how the system changes over time. In Section 6.22, we determine the operations of the classes in our system.

Software Engineering Case Study Self-Review Exercises

3.1 Suppose we have a class `Car` that represents a car. Think of some of the different pieces that a manufacturer would put together to produce a whole car. Create a class diagram (similar to Fig. 3.22) that models some of the composition relationships of class `Car`.

3.2 Suppose we have a class `File` that represents an electronic document in a stand-alone, non-networked computer represented by class `Computer`. What sort of association exists between class `Computer` and class `File`?

    a) Class `Computer` has a one-to-one relationship with class `File`.
    b) Class `Computer` has a many-to-one relationship with class `File`.
    c) Class `Computer` has a one-to-many relationship with class `File`.
    d) Class `Computer` has a many-to-many relationship with class `File`.

3.3 State whether the following statement is *true* or *false*, and if *false*, explain why: A UML diagram in which a class's second and third compartments are not modeled is said to be an elided diagram.

3.4 Modify the class diagram of Fig. 3.23 to include class `Deposit` instead of class `Withdrawal`.

Answers to Software Engineering Case Study Self-Review Exercises

3.1 [*Note:* Student answers may vary.] Figure 3.24 presents a class diagram that shows some of the composition relationships of a class `Car`.

3.2 c. [*Note:* In a computer network, this relationship could be many-to-many.]

3.3 True.

3.4 Figure 3.25 presents a class diagram for the ATM including class Deposit instead of class Withdrawal (as in Fig. 3.23). Note that Deposit does not access CashDispenser, but does access DepositSlot.

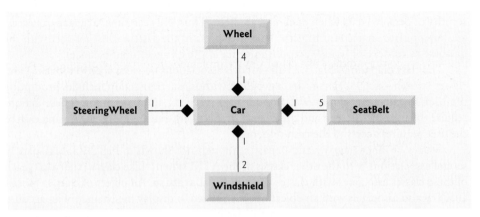

Fig. 3.24 | Class diagram showing composition relationships of a class Car.

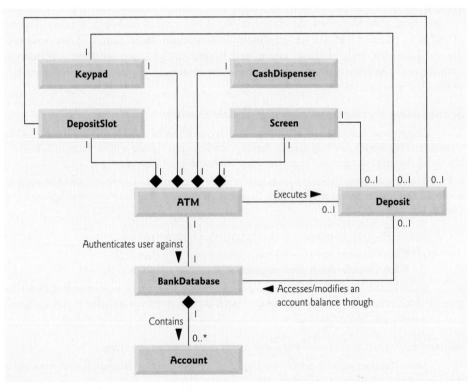

Fig. 3.25 | Class diagram for the ATM system model including class Deposit.

3.12 Wrap-Up

In this chapter, you learned how to create user-defined classes, and how to create and use objects of those classes. We declared data members of a class to maintain data for each object of the class. We also defined member functions that operate on that data. You learned how to call an object's member functions to request the services the object provides and how to pass data to those member functions as arguments. We discussed the difference between a local variable of a member function and a data member of a class. We also showed how to use a constructor to specify initial values for an object's data members. You learned how to separate the interface of a class from its implementation to promote good software engineering. We presented a diagram that shows the files that class-implementation programmers and client-code programmers need to compile the code they write. We demonstrated how *set* functions can be used to validate an object's data and ensure that objects are maintained in a consistent state. In addition, UML class diagrams were used to model classes and their constructors, member functions and data members. In the next chapter, we begin our introduction to control statements, which specify the order in which a function's actions are performed.

Summary

Section 3.2 Classes, Objects, Member Functions and Data Members
- Performing a task in a program requires a function. The function hides from its user the complex tasks that it performs.
- A function in a class is known as a member function and performs one of the class's tasks.
- You must create an object of a class before a program can perform the tasks the class describes. That is one reason C++ is known as an object-oriented programming language.
- Each message sent to an object is a member-function call that tells the object to perform a task.
- An object has attributes that are carried with the object as it is used in a program. These attributes are specified as data members in the object's class.

Section 3.4 Defining a Class with a Member Function
- A class definition contains the data members and member functions that define the class's attributes and behaviors, respectively.
- A class definition begins with the keyword class followed immediately by the class name.
- By convention, the name of a user-defined class begins with a capital letter and, for readability, each subsequent word in the class name begins with a capital letter.
- Every class's body is enclosed in a pair of braces ({ and }) and ends with a semicolon.
- Member functions that appear after access specifier public can be called by other functions in a program and by member functions of other classes.
- Access specifiers are always followed by a colon (:).
- Keyword void is a special return type which indicates that a function will perform a task but will not return any data to its calling function when it completes its task.
- By convention, function names begin with a lowercase first letter and all subsequent words in the name begin with a capital letter.
- An empty set of parentheses after a function name indicates that the function does not require additional data to perform its task.

- Every function's body is delimited by left and right braces ({ and }).
- Typically, you cannot call a member function until you create an object of its class.
- Each new class you create becomes a new type in C++ that can be used to declare variables and create objects. This is one reason why C++ is known as an extensible language.
- In the UML, each class is modeled in a class diagram as a rectangle with three compartments. The top compartment contains the class name, centered horizontally in boldface. The middle compartment contains the class's attributes (data members in C++). The bottom compartment contains the class's operations (member functions and constructors in C++).
- The UML models operations by listing the operation name followed by a set of parentheses. A plus sign (+) preceding the operation name indicates a public operation in the UML (i.e., a public member function in C++).

Section 3.5 Defining a Member Function with a Parameter
- A member function can require one or more parameters that represent additional data it needs to perform its task. A function call supplies arguments for each of the function's parameters.
- A member function is called by following the object name with a dot operator (.), the function name and a set of parentheses containing the function's arguments.
- A variable of C++ Standard Library class string represents a string of characters. This class is defined in header file <string>, and the name string belongs to namespace std.
- Function getline (from header <string>) reads characters from its first argument until a newline character is encountered, then places the characters (not including the newline) in the string variable specified as its second argument. The newline character is discarded.
- A parameter list may contain any number of parameters, including none at all (represented by empty parentheses) to indicate that a function does not require any parameters.
- The number of arguments in a function call must match the number of parameters in the parameter list of the called member function's header. Also, the argument types in the function call must be consistent with the types of the corresponding parameters in the function header.
- The UML models a parameter of an operation by listing the parameter name, followed by a colon and the parameter type between the parentheses following the operation name.
- The UML has its own data types. Not all the UML data types have the same names as the corresponding C++ types. The UML type String corresponds to the C++ type string.

Section 3.6 Data Members, set Functions and get Functions
- Variables declared in a function's body are local variables and can be used only from the point of their declaration in the function to the immediately following closing right brace (}). When a function terminates, the values of its local variables are lost.
- A local variable must be declared before it can be used in a function. A local variable cannot be accessed outside the function in which it is declared.
- Data members normally are private. Variables or functions declared private are accessible only to member functions of the class in which they are declared, or to friends of the class.
- When a program creates (instantiates) an object of a class, its private data members are encapsulated (hidden) in the object and can be accessed only by member functions of the object's class.
- When a function that specifies a return type other than void is called and completes its task, the function returns a result to its calling function.
- By default, the initial value of a string is the empty string—i.e., a string that does not contain any characters. Nothing appears on the screen when an empty string is displayed.

- Classes often provide public member functions to allow clients of the class to *set* or *get* private data members. The names of these member functions normally begin with *set* or *get*.

- *Set* and *get* functions allow clients of a class to indirectly access the hidden data. The client does not know how the object performs these operations.

- A class's *set* and *get* functions should be used by other member functions of the class to manipulate the class's private data. If the class's data representation is changed, member functions that access the data only via the *set* and *get* functions will not require modification.

- A public *set* function should carefully scrutinize any attempt to modify the value of a data member to ensure that the new value is appropriate for that data item.

- The UML represents data members as attributes by listing the attribute name, followed by a colon and the attribute type. Private attributes are preceded by a minus sign (–) in the UML.

- The UML indicates the return type of an operation by placing a colon and the return type after the parentheses following the operation name.

- UML class diagrams do not specify return types for operations that do not return values.

Section 3.7 Initializing Objects with Constructors
- Each class should provide a constructor to initialize an object of the class when the object is created. A constructor must be defined with the same name as the class.

- A difference between constructors and functions is that constructors cannot return values, so they cannot specify a return type (not even void). Normally, constructors are declared public.

- C++ requires a constructor call at the time each object is created, which helps ensure that every object is initialized before it is used in a program.

- A constructor with no parameters is a default constructor. If you do not provide a constructor, the compiler provides a default constructor. You can also define a default constructor explicitly. If you define a constructor for a class, C++ will not create a default constructor.

- The UML models constructors as operations in a class diagram's third compartment. To distinguish a constructor from a class's operations, the UML places the word "constructor" between guillemets (« and ») before the constructor's name.

Section 3.8 Placing a Class in a Separate File for Reusability
- Class definitions, when packaged properly, can be reused by programmers worldwide.

- It is customary to define a class in a header file that has a .h filename extension.

- If the class's implementation changes, the class's clients should not be required to change.

- Interfaces define and standardize the ways in which things such as people and systems interact.

- A class's interface describes the public member functions that are made available to the class's clients. The interface describes *what* services clients can use and how to *request* those services, but does not specify *how* the class carries out the services.

Section 3.9 Separating Interface from Implementation
- Separating interface from implementation makes programs easier to modify. Changes in the class's implementation do not affect the client as long as the class's interface remains unchanged.

- A function prototype contains a function's name, its return type and the number, types and order of the parameters the function expects to receive.

- Once a class is defined and its member functions are declared (via function prototypes), the member functions should be defined in a separate source-code file

- For each member function defined outside of its corresponding class definition, the function name must be preceded by the class name and the binary scope resolution operator (::).

Section 3.10 Validating Data with set Functions

- Class string's length member function returns the number of characters in a string object.

- Class string's member function substr returns a new string object containing a copy of part of an existing string object. The first argument specifies the starting position in the original string. The second argument specifies the number of characters to copy.

Terminology

access specifier
accessor
argument
attribute (UML)
binary scope resolution operator (::)
body of a class definition
calling function (caller)
camel case
class definition
class diagram (UML)
class-implementation programmer
client-code programmer
client of an object or class
compartment in a class diagram (UML)
consistent state
constructor
data hiding
data member
default constructor
defining a class
dot operator (.)
driver program
empty string
extensible language
function call
function header
function prototype
get function
getline function of <string> library
guillemets, « and » (UML)
.h filename extension
header file
implementation of a class

instance of a class
interface of a class
invoke a member function
length member function of class string
local variable
member function
member-function call
message (send to an object)
minus (-) sign (UML)
mutator
object code
operation (UML)
operation parameter (UML)
parameter
parameter list
plus (+) sign (UML)
private access specifier
public access specifier
public services of a class
request a service from an object
return type
separate interface from implementation
set function
software engineering
source-code file
string class
<string> header file
substr member function of class string
UML class diagram
user-defined type
validation
validity checking
void return type

Self-Review Exercises

3.1 Fill in the blanks in each of the following:
   a) A house is to a blueprint as a(n) _____ is to a class.
   b) Every class definition contains the keyword _____ followed immediately by the class's name.
   c) A class definition is typically stored in a file with the _____ filename extension.
   d) Each parameter in a function header must specify both a(n) _____ and a(n) _____.

    e) When each object of a class maintains its own copy of an attribute, the variable that represents the attribute is also known as a(n) _____.

    f) Keyword `public` is a(n) _____.

    g) Return type _____ indicates that a function will perform a task but will not return any information when it completes its task.

    h) Function _____ from the `<string>` library reads characters until a newline character is encountered, then copies those characters into the specified `string`.

    i) When a member function is defined outside the class definition, the function header must include the class name and the _____, followed by the function name to "tie" the member function to the class definition.

    j) The source-code file and any other files that use a class can include the class's header file via an _____ preprocessor directive.

3.2 State whether each of the following is *true* or *false*. If *false*, explain why.

    a) By convention, function names begin with a capital letter and all subsequent words in the name begin with a capital letter.

    b) Empty parentheses following a function name in a function prototype indicate that the function does not require any parameters to perform its task.

    c) Data members or member functions declared with access specifier `private` are accessible to member functions of the class in which they are declared.

    d) Variables declared in the body of a particular member function are known as data members and can be used in all member functions of the class.

    e) Every function's body is delimited by left and right braces ({ and }).

    f) Any source-code file that contains `int main()` can be used to execute a program.

    g) The types of arguments in a function call must be consistent with the types of the corresponding parameters in the function prototype's parameter list.

3.3 What is the difference between a local variable and a data member?

3.4 Explain the purpose of a function parameter. What is the difference between a parameter and an argument?

Answers to Self-Review Exercises

3.1 a) object. b) `class`. c) `.h` d) type, name. e) data member. f) access specifier. g) `void`. h) `getline`. i) binary scope resolution operator (`::`). j) `#include`.

3.2 a) False. Function names begin with a lowercase letter and all subsequent words in the name begin with a capital letter. b) True. c) True. d) False. Such variables are local variables and can be used only in the member function in which they are declared. e) True. f) True. g) True.

3.3 A local variable is declared in the body of a function and can be used only from the point at which it is declared to the immediately following closing brace. A data member is declared in a class, but not in the body of any of the class's member functions. Every object of a class has a separate copy of the class's data members. Data members are accessible to all member functions of the class.

3.4 A parameter represents additional information that a function requires to perform its task. Each parameter required by a function is specified in the function header. An argument is the value supplied in the function call. When the function is called, the argument value is passed into the function parameter so that the function can perform its task.

Exercises

3.5 Explain the difference between a function prototype and a function definition.

3.6 What is a default constructor? How are an object's data members initialized if a class has only an implicitly defined default constructor?

3.7 Explain the purpose of a data member.

3.8 What is a header file? What is a source-code file? Discuss the purpose of each.

3.9 Explain how a program could use class string without inserting a using declaration.

3.10 Explain why a class might provide a *set* function and a *get* function for a data member.

3.11 *(Modifying Class GradeBook)* Modify class GradeBook (Figs. 3.11–3.12) as follows:
  a) Include a second string data member that represents the course instructor's name.
  b) Provide a *set* function to change the instructor's name and a *get* function to retrieve it.
  c) Modify the constructor to specify course name and instructor name parameters.
  d) Modify function displayMessage to output the welcome message and course name, then the string "This course is presented by: " followed by the instructor's name.
Use your modified class in a test program that demonstrates the class's new capabilities.

3.12 *(Account Class)* Create an Account class that a bank might use to represent customers' bank accounts. Include a data member of type int to represent the account balance. [*Note:* In subsequent chapters, we'll use numbers that contain decimal points (e.g., 2.75)—called floating-point values—to represent dollar amounts.] Provide a constructor that receives an initial balance and uses it to initialize the data member. The constructor should validate the initial balance to ensure that it is greater than or equal to 0. If not, set the balance to 0 and display an error message indicating that the initial balance was invalid. Provide three member functions. Member function credit should add an amount to the current balance. Member function debit should withdraw money from the Account and ensure that the debit amount does not exceed the Account's balance. If it does, the balance should be left unchanged and the function should print a message indicating "Debit amount exceeded account balance." Member function getBalance should return the current balance. Create a program that creates two Account objects and tests the member functions of class Account.

3.13 *(Invoice Class)* Create a class called Invoice that a hardware store might use to represent an invoice for an item sold at the store. An Invoice should include four data members—a part number (type string), a part description (type string), a quantity of the item being purchased (type int) and a price per item (type int). [*Note:* In subsequent chapters, we'll use numbers that contain decimal points (e.g., 2.75)—called floating-point values—to represent dollar amounts.] Your class should have a constructor that initializes the four data members. Provide a *set* and a *get* function for each data member. In addition, provide a member function named getInvoiceAmount that calculates the invoice amount (i.e., multiplies the quantity by the price per item), then returns the amount as an int value. If the quantity is not positive, it should be set to 0. If the price per item is not positive, it should be set to 0. Write a test program that demonstrates class Invoice's capabilities.

3.14 *(Employee Class)* Create a class called Employee that includes three pieces of information as data members—a first name (type string), a last name (type string) and a monthly salary (type int). [*Note:* In subsequent chapters, we'll use numbers that contain decimal points (e.g., 2.75)—called floating-point values—to represent dollar amounts.] Your class should have a constructor that initializes the three data members. Provide a *set* and a *get* function for each data member. If the monthly salary is not positive, set it to 0. Write a test program that demonstrates class Employee's capabilities. Create two Employee objects and display each object's *yearly* salary. Then give each Employee a 10 percent raise and display each Employee's yearly salary again.

3.15 *(Date Class)* Create a class called Date that includes three pieces of information as data members—a month (type int), a day (type int) and a year (type int). Your class should have a constructor with three parameters that uses the parameters to initialize the three data members. For the purpose of this exercise, assume that the values provided for the year and day are correct, but ensure that the month value is in the range 1–12; if it is not, set the month to 1. Provide a *set* and a *get* function for each data member. Provide a member function displayDate that displays the month, day and year separated by forward slashes (/). Write a test program that demonstrates class Date's capabilities.

4

Control Statements: Part 1

Let's all move one place on.
—Lewis Carroll

The wheel is come full circle.
—William Shakespeare

How many apples fell on Newton's head before he took the hint!
—Robert Frost

All the evolution we know of proceeds from the vague to the definite.
—Charles Sanders Peirce

OBJECTIVES

In this chapter you'll learn:

- Basic problem-solving techniques.
- To develop algorithms through the process of top-down, stepwise refinement.
- To use the if and if...else selection statements to choose among alternative actions.
- To use the while repetition statement to execute statements in a program repeatedly.
- Counter-controlled repetition and sentinel-controlled repetition.
- To use the increment, decrement and assignment operators.

4.1 Introduction

Before writing a program to solve a problem, we must have a thorough understanding of the problem and a carefully planned approach to solving it. When writing a program, we must also understand the types of building blocks that are available and employ proven program construction techniques. In this chapter and in Chapter 5, Control Statements: Part 2, we discuss these issues as we present the theory and principles of structured programming. The concepts presented here are crucial to building effective classes and manipulating objects.

In this chapter, we introduce C++'s `if`, `if...else` and `while` statements, three of the building blocks that allow you to specify the logic required for member functions to perform their tasks. We devote a portion of this chapter (and Chapters 5 and 7) to further developing the `GradeBook` class introduced in Chapter 3. In particular, we add a member function to the `GradeBook` class that uses control statements to calculate the average of a set of student grades. Another example demonstrates additional ways to combine control statements to solve a similar problem. We introduce C++'s assignment operators and explore C++'s increment and decrement operators. These additional operators abbreviate and simplify many program statements.

4.2 Algorithms

Any solvable computing problem can be solved by the execution of a series of actions in a specific order. A procedure for solving a problem in terms of

1. the actions to execute and

2. the order in which the actions execute

is called an algorithm. The following example demonstrates that correctly specifying the order in which the actions execute is important.

Consider the "rise-and-shine algorithm" followed by one junior executive for getting out of bed and going to work: (1) Get out of bed, (2) take off pajamas, (3) take a shower, (4) get dressed, (5) eat breakfast, (6) carpool to work. This routine gets the executive to work well prepared to make critical decisions. Suppose that the same steps are performed in a slightly different order: (1) Get out of bed, (2) take off pajamas, (3) get dressed, (4) take a shower, (5) eat breakfast, (6) carpool to work. In this case, our junior executive shows up for work soaking wet. Specifying the order in which statements (actions) execute in a computer program is called program control. This chapter investigates program control using C++'s control statements.

4.3 Pseudocode

Pseudocode (or "fake" code) is an artificial and informal language that helps you develop algorithms without having to worry about the strict details of C++ language syntax. The pseudocode we present here is particularly useful for developing algorithms that will be converted to structured portions of C++ programs. Pseudocode is similar to everyday English; it is convenient and user friendly, although it is not an actual computer programming language.

Pseudocode does not execute on computers. Rather, it helps you "think out" a program before attempting to write it in a programming language, such as C++. This chapter provides several examples of how to use pseudocode to develop C++ programs.

The style of pseudocode we present consists purely of characters, so you can type pseudocode conveniently, using any editor program. The computer can produce a freshly printed copy of a pseudocode program on demand. A carefully prepared pseudocode program can easily be converted to a corresponding C++ program. In many cases, this simply requires replacing pseudocode statements with C++ equivalents.

Pseudocode normally describes only executable statements, which cause specific actions to occur after a programmer converts a program from pseudocode to C++ and the program is run on a computer. Declarations (that do not have initializers or do not involve constructor calls) are not executable statements. For example, the declaration

```
int i;
```

tells the compiler variable i's type and instructs the compiler to reserve space in memory for the variable. This declaration does not cause any action—such as input, output or a calculation—to occur when the program executes. We typically do not include variable declarations in our pseudocode. However, some programmers choose to list variables and mention their purposes at the beginning of pseudocode programs.

Let's look at an example of pseudocode that may be written to help a programmer create the addition program of Fig. 2.5. This pseudocode (Fig. 4.1) corresponds to the algorithm that inputs two integers from the user, adds these integers and displays their sum. Although we show the complete pseudocode listing here, we'll show how to create pseudocode from a problem statement later in the chapter.

Lines 1–2 correspond to the statements in lines 13–14 of Fig. 2.5. Notice that the pseudocode statements are simply English statements that convey what task is to be performed in C++. Likewise, lines 4–5 correspond to the statements in lines 16–17 of Fig. 2.5 and lines 7–8 correspond to the statements in lines 19 and 21 of Fig. 2.5.

1	*Prompt the user to enter the first integer*
2	*Input the first integer*
3	
4	*Prompt the user to enter the second integer*
5	*Input the second integer*
6	
7	*Add first integer and second integer, store result*
8	*Display result*

Fig. 4.1 | Pseudocode for the addition program of Fig. 2.5.

There are a few important aspects of the pseudocode in Fig. 4.1. Notice that the pseudocode corresponds to code only in function main. This occurs because pseudocode is normally used for algorithms, not complete programs. In this case, the pseudocode represents the algorithm. The function in which this code is placed is not important to the algorithm itself. For the same reason, line 23 of Fig. 2.5 (the return statement) is not included in the pseudocode—this return statement is placed at the end of every main function and is not important to the algorithm. Finally, lines 9–11 of Fig. 2.5 are not included in the pseudocode because these variable declarations are not executable statements.

4.4 Control Structures

Normally, statements in a program execute one after the other in the order in which they are written. This is called sequential execution. Various C++ statements we'll soon discuss enable you to specify that the next statement to execute may be other than the next one in sequence. This is called transfer of control.

During the 1960s, it became clear that the indiscriminate use of transfers of control was the root of much difficulty experienced by software development groups. The finger of blame was pointed at the goto statement, which allows you to specify a transfer of control to one of a wide range of possible destinations in a program (creating what is often called "spaghetti code"). The notion of so-called structured programming became almost synonymous with "goto elimination."

The research of Böhm and Jacopini[1] demonstrated that programs could be written without any goto statements. It became the challenge of the era for programmers to shift their styles to "goto-less programming." It was not until the 1970s that programmers started taking structured programming seriously. The results have been impressive, as software development groups have reported reduced development times, more frequent on-time delivery of systems and more frequent within-budget completion of software projects. The key to these successes is that structured programs are clearer, are easier to debug, test and modify and are more likely to be bug-free in the first place.

Böhm and Jacopini's work demonstrated that all programs could be written in terms of only three control structures, namely, the sequence structure, the selection structure

---

1. Böhm, C., and G. Jacopini, "Flow Diagrams, Turing Machines, and Languages with Only Two Formation Rules," *Communications of the ACM*, Vol. 9, No. 5, May 1966, pp. 366–371.

and the repetition structure. The term "control structures" comes from the field of computer science. When we introduce C++'s implementations of control structures, we'll refer to them in the terminology of the C++ standard document[2] as "control statements."

Sequence Structure in C++

The sequence structure is built into C++. Unless directed otherwise, the computer executes C++ statements one after the other in the order in which they are written—that is, in sequence. The Unified Modeling Language (UML) activity diagram of Fig. 4.2 illustrates a typical sequence structure in which two calculations are performed in order. C++ allows us to have as many actions as we want in a sequence structure. As we'll soon see, anywhere a single action may be placed, we may place several actions in sequence.

In this figure, the two statements involve adding a grade to a `total` variable and adding the value 1 to a `counter` variable. Such statements might appear in a program that takes the average of several student grades. To calculate an average, the total of the grades being averaged is divided by the number of grades. A counter variable would be used to keep track of the number of values being averaged. You'll see similar statements in the program of Section 4.8.

Activity diagrams are part of the UML. An activity diagram models the workflow (also called the activity) of a portion of a software system. Such workflows may include a portion of an algorithm, such as the sequence structure in Fig. 4.2. Activity diagrams are composed of special-purpose symbols, such as action state symbols (a rectangle with its left and right sides replaced with arcs curving outward), diamonds and small circles; these symbols are connected by transition arrows, which represent the flow of the activity.

Like pseudocode, activity diagrams help you develop and represent algorithms, although many programmers prefer pseudocode. Activity diagrams clearly show how control structures operate.

Consider the sequence-structure activity diagram of Fig. 4.2. It contains two action states that represent actions to perform. Each action state contains an action expression—e.g., "add grade to total" or "add 1 to counter"—that specifies a particular action to perform. Other actions might include calculations or input/output operations. The arrows

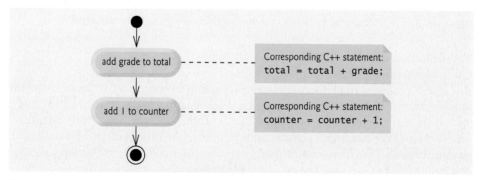

Fig. 4.2 | Sequence-structure activity diagram.

---

2. This document is more specifically known as *INCITS/ISO/IEC 14882-2003 Programming languages—C++* and is available for download (for a fee) at: webstore.ansi.org/ansidocstore/product.asp?sku=INCITS%2FISO%2FIEC+14882%2D2003.

in the activity diagram are called transition arrows. These arrows represent transitions, which indicate the order in which the actions represented by the action states occur—the program that implements the activities illustrated by the activity diagram in Fig. 4.2 first adds grade to total, then adds 1 to counter.

The solid circle located at the top of the activity diagram represents the activity's initial state—the beginning of the workflow before the program performs the modeled activities. The solid circle surrounded by a hollow circle that appears at the bottom of the activity diagram represents the final state—the end of the workflow after the program performs its activities.

Figure 4.2 also includes rectangles with the upper-right corners folded over. These are called notes in the UML. Notes are explanatory remarks that describe the purpose of symbols in the diagram. Notes can be used in any UML diagram—not just activity diagrams. Figure 4.2 uses UML notes to show the C++ code associated with each action state in the activity diagram. A dotted line connects each note with the element that the note describes. Activity diagrams normally do not show the C++ code that implements the activity. We use notes for this purpose here to illustrate how the diagram relates to C++ code. For more information on the UML, see our optional case study, which appears in the Software Engineering Case Study sections at the ends of Chapters 1–7, 9, 10, 12 and 13, or visit www.uml.org.

Selection Statements in C++

C++ provides three types of selection statements (discussed in this chapter and Chapter 5). The if selection statement either performs (selects) an action if a condition (predicate) is true or skips the action if the condition is false. The if...else selection statement performs an action if a condition is true or performs a different action if the condition is false. The switch selection statement (Chapter 5) performs one of many different actions, depending on the value of an integer expression.

The if selection statement is a single-selection statement because it selects or ignores a single action (or, as we'll soon see, a single group of actions). The if...else statement is called a double-selection statement because it selects between two different actions (or groups of actions). The switch selection statement is called a multiple-selection statement because it selects among many different actions (or groups of actions).

Repetition Statements in C++

C++ provides three types of repetition statements (also called looping statements or loops) that enable programs to perform statements repeatedly as long as a condition (called the loop-continuation condition) remains true. The repetition statements are the while, do...while and for statements. (Chapter 5 presents the do...while and for statements.) The while and for statements perform the action (or group of actions) in their bodies zero or more times—if the loop-continuation condition is initially false, the action (or group of actions) will not execute. The do...while statement performs the action (or group of actions) in its body at least once.

Each of the words if, else, switch, while, do and for is a C++ keyword. These words are reserved by the C++ programming language to implement various features, such as C++'s control statements. Keywords must not be used as identifiers, such as variable names. Figure 4.3 provides a complete list of C++ keywords.

C++ Keywords

Keywords common to the C and C++ programming languages

auto	break	case	char	const
continue	default	do	double	else
enum	extern	float	for	goto
if	int	long	register	return
short	signed	sizeof	static	struct
switch	typedef	union	unsigned	void
volatile	while			

C++-only keywords

and	and_eq	asm	bitand	bitor
bool	catch	class	compl	const_cast
delete	dynamic_cast	explicit	export	false
friend	inline	mutable	namespace	new
not	not_eq	operator	or	or_eq
private	protected	public	reinterpret_cast	static_cast
template	this	throw	true	try
typeid	typename	using	virtual	wchar_t
xor	xor_eq			

Fig. 4.3 | C++ keywords.

Common Programming Error 4.1

Using a keyword as an identifier is a syntax error.

Common Programming Error 4.2

Spelling a keyword with any uppercase letters is a syntax error. All of C++'s keywords contain only lowercase letters.

Summary of Control Statements in C++

C++ has only three kinds of control structures, which from this point forward we refer to as control statements: the sequence statement, selection statements (three types—if, if...else and switch) and repetition statements (three types—while, for and do...while). Each C++ program combines as many of these control statements as is appropriate for the algorithm the program implements. As with the sequence statement of Fig. 4.2, we can model each control statement as an activity diagram. Each diagram contains an initial state and a final state, which represent a control statement's entry point and exit point, respectively. These single-entry/single-exit control statements make it easy to build programs—the control statements are attached to one another by connecting the exit point of one to the entry point of the next. This is similar to the way a child stacks building blocks, so we call this control-statement stacking. We'll learn shortly that there is only one other way to connect control statements—called control-statement nesting, in which one control statement is contained inside another. Thus, algorithms in C++ programs are constructed from only three kinds of control statements, combined in only two ways. This is the essence of simplicity.

Software Engineering Observation 4.1

Any C++ program we'll ever build can be constructed from only seven different types of control statements (sequence, if, if...else, switch, while, do...while and for) combined in only two ways (control-statement stacking and control-statement nesting).

4.5   if Selection Statement

Programs use selection statements to choose among alternative courses of action. For example, suppose the passing grade on an exam is 60. The pseudocode statement

> *If student's grade is greater than or equal to 60*
>   *Print "Passed"*

determines whether the condition "student's grade is greater than or equal to 60" is true or false. If the condition is true, then "Passed" is printed and the next pseudocode statement in order is "performed" (remember that pseudocode is not a real programming language). If the condition is false, the print statement is ignored and the next pseudocode statement in order is performed. Note that the second line of this selection statement is indented. Such indentation is optional, but it is recommended because it emphasizes the inherent structure of structured programs. When you convert your pseudocode into C++ code, the C++ compiler ignores white-space characters (like blanks, tabs and newlines) used for indentation and vertical spacing.

Good Programming Practice 4.1

Consistently applying reasonable indentation conventions throughout your programs greatly improves program readability. We suggest three blanks per indent. Some people prefer using tabs, but these can vary across editors, causing a program written on one editor to align differently when used with another.

The preceding pseudocode *If* statement can be written in C++ as

```
if ( grade >= 60 )
   cout << "Passed";
```

Notice that the C++ code corresponds closely to the pseudocode. This is one of the properties of pseudocode that make it such a useful program development tool.

Figure 4.4 illustrates the single-selection if statement. It contains what is perhaps the most important symbol in an activity diagram—the diamond or decision symbol, which indicates that a decision is to be made. A decision symbol indicates that the workflow will continue along a path determined by the symbol's associated guard conditions, which can be true or false. Each transition arrow emerging from a decision symbol has a guard condition (specified in square brackets above or next to the transition arrow). If a particular guard condition is true, the workflow enters the action state to which that transition arrow points. In Fig. 4.4, if the grade is greater than or equal to 60, the program prints "Passed" to the screen, then transitions to the final state of this activity. If the grade is less than 60, the program immediately transitions to the final state without displaying a message.

Fig. 4.4 | if single-selection statement activity diagram.

We learned in Chapter 2 that decisions can be based on conditions containing relational or equality operators. Actually, in C++, a decision can be based on any expression—if the expression evaluates to zero, it is treated as false; if the expression evaluates to nonzero, it is treated as true. C++ provides the data type bool for variables that can hold only the values true and false—each of these is a C++ keyword.

Portability Tip 4.1

For compatibility with earlier versions of C, which used integers for Boolean values, the bool value true also can be represented by any nonzero value (compilers typically use 1) and the bool value false also can be represented as the value zero.

Note that the if statement is a single-entry/single-exit statement. We'll see that the activity diagrams for the remaining control statements also contain initial states, transition arrows, action states that indicate actions to perform, decision symbols (with associated guard conditions) that indicate decisions to be made and final states. This is consistent with the action/decision model of programming we have been emphasizing.

We can envision seven bins, each containing only empty UML activity diagrams of one of the seven types of control statements. Your task, then, is assembling a program from the activity diagrams of as many of each type of control statement as the algorithm demands, combining the activity diagrams in only two possible ways (stacking or nesting), then filling in the action states and decisions with action expressions and guard conditions in a manner appropriate to form a structured implementation for the algorithm. We'll discuss the variety of ways in which actions and decisions may be written.

4.6 if...else Double-Selection Statement

The if single-selection statement performs an indicated action only when the condition is true; otherwise the action is skipped. The if...else double-selection statement allows you to specify an action to perform when the condition is true and a different action to perform when the condition is false. For example, the pseudocode statement

If student's grade is greater than or equal to 60
    Print "Passed"
Else
    Print "Failed"

prints "Passed" if the student's grade is greater than or equal to 60, but prints "Failed" if the student's grade is less than 60. In either case, after printing occurs, the next pseudocode statement in sequence is "performed."

The preceding pseudocode *If...Else* statement can be written in C++ as

```
if ( grade >= 60 )
   cout << "Passed";
else
   cout << "Failed";
```

Note that the body of the else is also indented.

Good Programming Practice 4.2

Whatever indentation convention you choose should be applied consistently throughout your programs. It is difficult to read programs that do not obey uniform spacing conventions.

Good Programming Practice 4.3

Indent both body statements of an if...else statement.

Good Programming Practice 4.4

If there are several levels of indentation, each level should be indented the same additional amount of space to promote readability and maintainability.

Figure 4.5 illustrates the flow of control in the if...else statement. Once again, note that (besides the initial state, transition arrows and final state) the only other symbols in the activity diagram represent action states and decisions. We continue to emphasize this action/decision model of computing. Imagine again a deep bin of empty UML activity diagrams of double-selection statements—as many as you might need to stack and nest with the activity diagrams of other control statements to form a structured implementation of an algorithm. You fill in the action states and decision symbols with action expressions and guard conditions appropriate to the algorithm.

Conditional Operator (?:)

C++ provides the conditional operator (?:), which is closely related to the if...else statement. The conditional operator is C++'s only ternary operator—it takes three operands. The operands, together with the conditional operator, form a conditional expression. The

Fig. 4.5 | if...else double-selection statement activity diagram.

first operand is a condition, the second operand is the value for the entire conditional expression if the condition is `true` and the third operand is the value for the entire conditional expression if the condition is `false`. For example, the output statement

```
cout << ( grade >= 60 ? "Passed" : "Failed" );
```

contains a conditional expression, `grade >= 60 ? "Passed" : "Failed"`, that evaluates to the string `"Passed"` if the condition `grade >= 60` is `true`, but evaluates to the string `"Failed"` if the condition is `false`. Thus, the statement with the conditional operator performs essentially the same as the preceding `if...else` statement. As we'll see, the precedence of the conditional operator is low, so the parentheses in the preceding expression are required.

Error-Prevention Tip 4.1

To avoid precedence problems (and for clarity), place conditional expressions (that appear in larger expressions) in parentheses.

The values in a conditional expression also can be actions to execute. For example, the following conditional expression also prints `"Passed"` or `"Failed"`:

```
grade >= 60 ? cout << "Passed" : cout << "Failed";
```

The preceding conditional expression is read, "If `grade` is greater than or equal to 60, then `cout << "Passed"`; otherwise, `cout << "Failed"`." This, too, is comparable to the preceding `if...else` statement. Conditional expressions can appear in some program locations where `if...else` statements cannot.

Nested *if...else* Statements

Nested `if...else` statements test for multiple cases by placing `if...else` selection statements inside other `if...else` selection statements. For example, the following pseudocode `if...else` statement prints A for exam grades greater than or equal to 90, B for grades in the range 80 to 89, C for grades in the range 70 to 79, D for grades in the range 60 to 69 and F for all other grades:

> *If student's grade is greater than or equal to 90*
>   *Print "A"*
> *Else*
>   *If student's grade is greater than or equal to 80*
>   *Print "B"*
>   *Else*
>   *If student's grade is greater than or equal to 70*
>   *Print "C"*
>   *Else*
>   *If student's grade is greater than or equal to 60*
>   *Print "D"*
>   *Else*
>   *Print "F"*

This pseudocode can be written in C++ as

```
if ( studentGrade >= 90 ) // 90 and above gets "A"
   cout << "A";
else
   if ( studentGrade >= 80 ) // 80-89 gets "B"
      cout << "B";
   else
      if ( studentGrade >= 70 ) // 70-79 gets "C"
         cout << "C";
      else
         if ( studentGrade >= 60 ) // 60-69 gets "D"
            cout << "D";
         else // less than 60 gets "F"
            cout << "F";
```

If studentGrade is greater than or equal to 90, the first four conditions will be true, but only the output statement after the first test will execute. After that statement executes, the program skips the else-part of the "outermost" if...else statement. Most C++ programmers prefer to write the preceding if...else statement as

```
if ( studentGrade >= 90 ) // 90 and above gets "A"
   cout << "A";
else if ( studentGrade >= 80 ) // 80-89 gets "B"
   cout << "B";
else if ( studentGrade >= 70 ) // 70-79 gets "C"
   cout << "C";
else if ( studentGrade >= 60 ) // 60-69 gets "D"
   cout << "D";
else // less than 60 gets "F"
   cout << "F";
```

The two forms are identical except for the spacing and indentation, which the compiler ignores. The latter form is popular because it avoids deep indentation of the code to the right. Such indentation can leave little room on a line, forcing the line to be split and decreasing program readability.

Performance Tip 4.1

A nested if...else statement can perform much faster than a series of single-selection if statements because of the possibility of early exit after one of the conditions is satisfied.

Performance Tip 4.2

In a nested if...else statement, test the conditions that are more likely to be true at the beginning of the nested if...else statement. This will enable the nested if...else statement to run faster by exiting earlier than they would if infrequently occurring cases were testd first.

Dangling-else Problem

The C++ compiler always associates an else with the immediately preceding if unless told to do otherwise by the placement of braces ({ and }). This behavior can lead to what is referred to as the dangling-else problem. For example,

```
if ( x > 5 )
   if ( y > 5 )
      cout << "x and y are > 5";
else
   cout << "x is <= 5";
```

appears to indicate that if x is greater than 5, the nested if statement determines whether y is also greater than 5. If so, "x and y are > 5" is output. Otherwise, it appears that if x is not greater than 5, the else part of the if...else outputs "x is <= 5".

Beware! This nested if...else statement does not execute as it appears. The compiler actually interprets the statement as

```
if ( x > 5 )
   if ( y > 5 )
      cout << "x and y are > 5";
   else
      cout << "x is <= 5";
```

in which the body of the first if is a nested if...else. The outer if statement tests whether x is greater than 5. If so, execution continues by testing whether y is also greater than 5. If the second condition is true, the proper string—"x and y are > 5"—is displayed. However, if the second condition is false, the string "x is <= 5" is displayed, even though we know that x is greater than 5.

To force the nested if...else statement to execute as originally intended, we can write it as follows:

```
if ( x > 5 )
{
   if ( y > 5 )
      cout << "x and y are > 5";
}
else
   cout << "x is <= 5";
```

The braces ({}) indicate to the compiler that the second if statement is in the body of the first if and that the else is associated with the first if. Exercises 4.23–4.24 further investigate the dangling-else problem.

Blocks

The if selection statement expects only one statement in its body. Similarly, the if and else parts of an if...else statement each expect only one body statement. To include several statements in the body of an if or in either part of an if...else, enclose the statements in braces ({ and }). A set of statements contained within a pair of braces is called a compound statement or a block. We use the term "block" from this point forward.

 Software Engineering Observation 4.2

A block can be placed anywhere in a program that a single statement can be placed.

The following example includes a block in the else part of an if...else statement.

```
if ( studentGrade >= 60 )
   cout << "Passed.\n";
else
{
   cout << "Failed.\n";
   cout << "You must take this course again.\n";
}
```

In this case, if `studentGrade` is less than 60, the program executes both statements in the body of the `else` and prints

```
Failed.
You must take this course again.
```

Notice the braces surrounding the two statements in the `else` clause. These braces are important. Without the braces, the statement

```
cout << "You must take this course again.\n";
```

would be outside the body of the `else` part of the `if` and would execute regardless of whether the grade was less than 60. This is an example of a logic error.

Common Programming Error 4.3

Forgetting one or both of the braces that delimit a block can lead to syntax errors or logic errors in a program.

Good Programming Practice 4.5

Always putting the braces in an if...else statement (or any control statement) helps prevent their accidental omission, especially when adding statements to an if or else clause at a later time. To avoid omitting one or both of the braces, some programmers prefer to type the beginning and ending braces of blocks even before typing the individual statements within the braces.

Just as a block can be placed anywhere a single statement can be placed, it is also possible to have no statement at all—called a null statement (or an empty statement). The null statement is represented by placing a semicolon (`;`) where a statement would normally be.

Common Programming Error 4.4

Placing a semicolon after the condition in an if statement leads to a logic error in single-selection if statements and a syntax error in double-selection if...else statements (when the if part contains an actual body statement).

4.7 `while` Repetition Statement

A repetition statement (also called a looping statement or a loop) allows you to specify that a program should repeat an action while some condition remains true. The pseudocode statement

> *While there are more items on my shopping list*
> *Purchase next item and cross it off my list*

describes the repetition that occurs during a shopping trip. The condition, "there are more items on my shopping list" is either true or false. If it is true, then the action, "Purchase next item and cross it off my list" is performed. This action will be performed repeatedly while the condition remains true. The statement contained in the *While* repetition statement constitutes the body of the *While*, which can be a single statement or a block. Eventually, the condition will become false (when the last item on the shopping list has been purchased and crossed off the list). At this point, the repetition terminates, and the first pseudocode statement after the repetition statement executes.

As an example of C++'s while repetition statement, consider a program segment designed to find the first power of 3 larger than 100. Suppose the integer variable product has been initialized to 3. When the following while repetition statement finishes executing, product contains the result:

```
int product = 3;

while ( product <= 100 )
    product = 3 * product;
```

When the while statement begins execution, the value of product is 3. Each repetition of the while statement multiplies product by 3, so product takes on the values 9, 27, 81 and 243 successively. When product becomes 243, the while statement condition—product <= 100—becomes false. This terminates the repetition, so the final value of product is 243. At this point, program execution continues with the next statement after the while statement.

 Common Programming Error 4.5

Not providing, in the body of a while statement, an action that eventually causes the condition in the while to become false normally results in a logic error called an infinite loop, *in which the repetition statement never terminates. This can make a program appear to "hang" or "freeze" if the loop body does not contain statements that interact with the user.*

The UML activity diagram of Fig. 4.6 illustrates the flow of control that corresponds to the preceding while statement. Once again, the symbols in the diagram (besides the initial state, transition arrows, a final state and three notes) represent an action state and a decision. This diagram also introduces the UML's merge symbol, which joins two flows of activity into one flow of activity. The UML represents both the merge symbol and the decision symbol as diamonds. In this diagram, the merge symbol joins the transitions from the initial state and from the action state, so they both flow into the decision that determines whether the loop should begin (or continue) executing. The decision and merge symbols can be distinguished by the number of "incoming" and "outgoing" transition arrows. A decision symbol has one transition arrow pointing to the diamond and two or more transition arrows pointing out from the diamond to indicate possible transitions from that point. In addition, each transition arrow pointing out of a decision symbol has a guard condition next to it. A merge symbol has two or more transition arrows pointing to the diamond and only one transition arrow pointing from the diamond, to indicate multiple activity flows merging to continue the activity. Note that, unlike the decision symbol, the merge symbol does not have a counterpart in C++ code. None of the transition arrows associated with a merge symbol have guard conditions.

The diagram of Fig. 4.6 clearly shows the repetition of the while statement discussed earlier in this section. The transition arrow emerging from the action state points to the merge, which transitions back to the decision that is tested each time through the loop until the guard condition product > 100 becomes true. Then the while statement exits (reaches its final state) and control passes to the next statement in sequence in the program.

Imagine a deep bin of empty UML while repetition statement activity diagrams—as many as you might need to stack and nest with the activity diagrams of other control statements to form a structured implementation of an algorithm. You fill in the action states and decision symbols with action expressions and guard conditions appropriate to the algorithm.

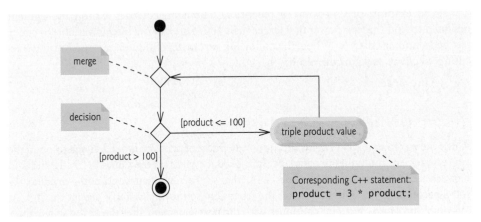

Fig. 4.6 | `while` repetition statement UML activity diagram.

> **Performance Tip 4.3**
>
> *Many of the* Performance Tips *we mention in this text result in only small improvements, so you might be tempted to ignore them. However, a small performance improvement for code that executes many times in a loop can result in substantial overall performance improvement.*

4.8 Formulating Algorithms: Counter-Controlled Repetition

To illustrate how programmers develop algorithms, this section and Section 4.9 solve two variations of a class average problem. Consider the following problem statement:

> *A class of ten students took a quiz. The grades (integers in the range 0 to 100) for this quiz are available to you. Calculate and display the total of all student grades and the class average on the quiz.*

The class average is equal to the sum of the grades divided by the number of students. The algorithm for solving this problem on a computer must input each of the grades, calculate the average and print the result.

Pseudocode Algorithm with Counter-Controlled Repetition

Let's use pseudocode to list the actions to execute and specify the order in which these actions should occur. We use counter-controlled repetition to input the grades one at a time. This technique uses a variable called a counter to control the number of times a group of statements will execute (also known as the number of iterations of the loop).

Counter-controlled repetition is often called definite repetition because the number of repetitions is known before the loop begins executing. In this example, repetition terminates when the counter exceeds 10. This section presents a fully developed pseudocode algorithm (Fig. 4.7) and a version of class GradeBook (Fig. 4.8–Fig. 4.9) that implements the algorithm in a C++ member function. The section then presents an application (Fig. 4.10) that demonstrates the algorithm in action. In Section 4.9 we demonstrate how to use pseudocode to develop such an algorithm from scratch.

Software Engineering Observation 4.3

Experience has shown that the most difficult part of solving a problem on a computer is developing the algorithm for the solution. Once a correct algorithm has been specified, the process of producing a working C++ program from the algorithm is normally straightforward.

Note the references in the pseudocode algorithm of Fig. 4.7 to a total and a counter. A total is a variable used to accumulate the sum of several values. A counter is a variable used to count—in this case, the grade counter indicates which of the 10 grades is about to be entered by the user. Variables used to store totals are normally initialized to zero before being used in a program; otherwise, the sum would include the previous value stored in the total's memory location.

```
 1   Set total to zero
 2   Set grade counter to one
 3
 4   While grade counter is less than or equal to ten
 5       Prompt the user to enter the next grade
 6       Input the next grade
 7       Add the grade into the total
 8       Add one to the grade counter
 9
10   Set the class average to the total divided by ten
11   Print the total of the grades for all students in the class
12   Print the class average
```

Fig. 4.7 | Pseudocode algorithm that uses counter-controlled repetition to solve the class average problem.

```cpp
 1   // Fig. 4.8: GradeBook.h
 2   // Definition of class GradeBook that determines a class average.
 3   // Member functions are defined in GradeBook.cpp
 4   #include <string> // program uses C++ standard string class
 5   using std::string;
 6
 7   // GradeBook class definition
 8   class GradeBook
 9   {
10   public:
11       GradeBook( string ); // constructor initializes course name
12       void setCourseName( string ); // function to set the course name
13       string getCourseName(); // function to retrieve the course name
14       void displayMessage(); // display a welcome message
15       void determineClassAverage(); // averages grades entered by the user
16   private:
17       string courseName; // course name for this GradeBook
18   }; // end class GradeBook
```

Fig. 4.8 | Class average problem using counter-controlled repetition: GradeBook header file.

```
1   // Fig. 4.9: GradeBook.cpp
2   // Member-function definitions for class GradeBook that solves the
3   // class average program with counter-controlled repetition.
4   #include <iostream>
5   using std::cout;
6   using std::cin;
7   using std::endl;
8
9   #include "GradeBook.h" // include definition of class GradeBook
10
11  // constructor initializes courseName with string supplied as argument
12  GradeBook::GradeBook( string name )
13  {
14     setCourseName( name ); // validate and store courseName
15  } // end GradeBook constructor
16
17  // function to set the course name;
18  // ensures that the course name has at most 25 characters
19  void GradeBook::setCourseName( string name )
20  {
21     if ( name.length() <= 25 ) // if name has 25 or fewer characters
22        courseName = name; // store the course name in the object
23     else // if name is longer than 25 characters
24     { // set courseName to first 25 characters of parameter name
25        courseName = name.substr( 0, 25 ); // select first 25 characters
26        cout << "Name \"" << name << "\" exceeds maximum length (25).\n"
27           << "Limiting courseName to first 25 characters.\n" << endl;
28     } // end if...else
29  } // end function setCourseName
30
31  // function to retrieve the course name
32  string GradeBook::getCourseName()
33  {
34     return courseName;
35  } // end function getCourseName
36
37  // display a welcome message to the GradeBook user
38  void GradeBook::displayMessage()
39  {
40     cout << "Welcome to the grade book for\n" << getCourseName() << "!\n"
41        << endl;
42  } // end function displayMessage
43
44  // determine class average based on 10 grades entered by user
45  void GradeBook::determineClassAverage()
46  {
47     int total; // sum of grades entered by user
48     int gradeCounter; // number of the grade to be entered next
49     int grade; // grade value entered by user
50     int average; // average of grades
51
```

Fig. 4.9 | Class average problem using counter-controlled repetition: GradeBook source code file. (Part I of 2.)

```
52      // initialization phase
53      total = 0; // initialize total
54      gradeCounter = 1; // initialize loop counter
55
56      // processing phase
57      while ( gradeCounter <= 10 ) // loop 10 times
58      {
59         cout << "Enter grade: "; // prompt for input
60         cin >> grade; // input next grade
61         total = total + grade; // add grade to total
62         gradeCounter = gradeCounter + 1; // increment counter by 1
63      } // end while
64
65      // termination phase
66      average = total / 10; // integer division yields integer result
67
68      // display total and average of grades
69      cout << "\nTotal of all 10 grades is " << total << endl;
70      cout << "Class average is " << average << endl;
71   } // end function determineClassAverage
```

Fig. 4.9 | Class average problem using counter-controlled repetition: GradeBook source code file. (Part 2 of 2.)

Enhancing GradeBook Validation

Before we discuss the class average algorithm's implementation, let's consider an enhancement we made to our GradeBook class. In Fig. 3.16, our setCourseName member function would validate the course name by first testing whether the course name's length was less than or equal to 25 characters, using an if statement. If this was true, the course name would be set. This code was then followed by another if statement that tested whether the course name's length was larger than 25 characters (in which case the course name would be shortened). Notice that the second if statement's condition is the exact opposite of the first if statement's condition. If one condition evaluates to true, the other must evaluate to false. Such a situation is ideal for an if...else statement, so we have modified our code, replacing the two if statements with one if...else statement (lines 21–28 of Fig. 4.9).

Implementing Counter-Controlled Repetition in Class GradeBook

Class GradeBook (Fig. 4.8–Fig. 4.9) contains a constructor (declared in line 11 of Fig. 4.8 and defined in lines 12–15 of Fig. 4.9) that assigns a value to the class's instance variable courseName (declared in line 17 of Fig. 4.8). Lines 19–29, 32–35 and 38–42 of Fig. 4.9 define member functions setCourseName, getCourseName and displayMessage, respectively. Lines 45–71 define member function determineClassAverage, which implements the class average algorithm described by the pseudocode in Fig. 4.7.

Lines 47–50 declare local variables total, gradeCounter, grade and average to be of type int. Variable grade stores the user input. Notice that the preceding declarations appear in the body of member function determineClassAverage.

In this chapter's versions of class GradeBook, we simply read and process a set of grades. The averaging calculation is performed in member function determineClassAverage using local variables—we do not preserve any information about student grades in the

```
1   // Fig. 4.10: fig04_10.cpp
2   // Create GradeBook object and invoke its determineClassAverage function.
3   #include "GradeBook.h" // include definition of class GradeBook
4
5   int main()
6   {
7      // create GradeBook object myGradeBook and
8      // pass course name to constructor
9      GradeBook myGradeBook( "CS101 C++ Programming" );
10
11     myGradeBook.displayMessage(); // display welcome message
12     myGradeBook.determineClassAverage(); // find average of 10 grades
13     return 0; // indicate successful termination
14  } // end main
```

```
Welcome to the grade book for
CS101 C++ Programming

Enter grade: 67
Enter grade: 78
Enter grade: 89
Enter grade: 67
Enter grade: 87
Enter grade: 98
Enter grade: 93
Enter grade: 85
Enter grade: 82
Enter grade: 100

Total of all 10 grades is 846
Class average is 84
```

Fig. 4.10 | Class average problem using counter-controlled repetition: Creating an object of class GradeBook (Fig. 4.8–Fig. 4.9) and invoking its determineClassAverage member function.

class's instance variables. In Chapter 7, Arrays and Vectors, we modify class GradeBook to maintain the grades in memory using an instance variable that refers to a data structure known as an array. This allows a GradeBook object to perform various calculations on the same set of grades without requiring the user to enter the grades multiple times.

 Good Programming Practice 4.6

Separate declarations from other statements in functions with a blank line for readability.

Lines 53–54 initialize total to 0 and gradeCounter to 1. Note that variables total and gradeCounter are initialized before they are used in a calculation. Counter variables normally are initialized to zero or one, depending on their use (we'll present examples showing each possibility). An uninitialized variable contains a "garbage" value (also called an undefined value)—the value last stored in the memory location reserved for that variable. Variables grade and average (for the user input and calculated average, respectively) need not be initialized here—their values will be assigned as they are input or calculated later in the function.

Common Programming Error 4.6

Not initializing counters and totals can lead to logic errors.

Error-Prevention Tip 4.2

Initialize each counter and total, either in its declaration or in an assignment statement. Totals are normally initialized to 0. Counters are normally initialized to 0 or 1, depending on how they are used (we'll show examples of when to use 0 and when to use 1).

Good Programming Practice 4.7

Declare each variable on a separate line with its own comment to make programs more readable.

Line 57 indicates that the `while` statement should continue looping (also called *iterating*) as long as `gradeCounter`'s value is less than or equal to 10. While this condition remains true, the `while` statement repeatedly executes the statements between the braces that delimit its body (lines 58–63).

Line 59 displays the prompt `"Enter grade: "`. This line corresponds to the pseudocode statement *"Prompt the user to enter the next grade."* Line 60 reads the grade entered by the user and assigns it to variable `grade`. This line corresponds to the pseudocode statement *"Input the next grade."* Recall that variable `grade` was not initialized earlier in the program, because the program obtains the value for `grade` from the user during each iteration of the loop. Line 61 adds the new grade entered by the user to the `total` and assigns the result to `total`, which replaces its previous value.

Line 62 adds 1 to `gradeCounter` to indicate that the program has processed a grade and is ready to input the next grade from the user. Incrementing `gradeCounter` eventually causes `gradeCounter` to exceed 10. At that point the `while` loop terminates because its condition (line 57) becomes false.

When the loop terminates, line 66 performs the averaging calculation and assigns its result to the variable `average`. Line 69 displays the text `"Total of all 10 grades is "` followed by variable `total`'s value. Line 70 then displays the text `"Class average is "` followed by variable `average`'s value. Member function `determineClassAverage` then returns control to the calling function (i.e., `main` in Fig. 4.10).

Demonstrating Class *GradeBook*

Figure 4.10 contains this application's `main` function, which creates an object of class `GradeBook` and demonstrates its capabilities. Line 9 of Fig. 4.10 creates a new `GradeBook` object called `myGradeBook`. The string in line 9 is passed to the `GradeBook` constructor (lines 12–15 of Fig. 4.9). Line 11 of Fig. 4.10 calls `myGradeBook`'s `displayMessage` member function to display a welcome message to the user. Line 12 then calls `myGradeBook`'s `determineClassAverage` member function to allow the user to enter 10 grades, for which the member function then calculates and prints the average—the member function performs the algorithm shown in the pseudocode of Fig. 4.7.

Notes on Integer Division and Truncation

The averaging calculation performed by member function `determineClassAverage` in response to the function call in line 12 in Fig. 4.10 produces an integer result. The program's output indicates that the sum of the grade values in the sample execution is 846, which, when divided by 10, should yield 84.6—a number with a decimal point. However, the result of the calculation `total / 10` (line 66 of Fig. 4.9) is the integer 84, because `total` and 10 are both integers. Dividing two integers results in integer division—any fractional part of the calculation is lost (i.e., *truncated*). We'll see how to obtain a result that includes a decimal point from the averaging calculation in the next section.

Common Programming Error 4.7

Assuming that integer division rounds (rather than truncates) can lead to incorrect results. For example, 7 ÷ 4, which yields 1.75 in conventional arithmetic, truncates to 1 in integer arithmetic, rather than rounding to 2.

In Fig. 4.9, if line 66 used `gradeCounter` rather than 10 for the calculation, the output for this program would display an incorrect value, 76. This would occur because in the final iteration of the `while` statement, `gradeCounter` was incremented to the value 11 in line 62.

Common Programming Error 4.8

Using a loop's counter-control variable in a calculation after the loop often causes a common logic error called an off-by-one error. In a counter-controlled loop that counts up by one each time through the loop, the loop terminates when the counter's value is one higher than its last legitimate value (i.e., 11 in the case of counting from 1 to 10).

4.9 Formulating Algorithms: Sentinel-Controlled Repetition

Let us generalize the class average problem. Consider the following problem:

> *Develop a class average program that processes grades for an arbitrary number of students each time it is run.*

In the previous class average example, the problem statement specified the number of students, so the number of grades (10) was known in advance. In this example, no indication is given of how many grades the user will enter during the program's execution. The program must process an arbitrary number of grades. How can the program determine when to stop the input of grades? How will it know when to calculate and print the class average?

One way to solve this problem is to use a special value called a sentinel value (also called a signal value, a dummy value or a flag value) to indicate "end of data entry." The user types grades in until all legitimate grades have been entered. The user then types the sentinel value to indicate that the last grade has been entered. Sentinel-controlled repetition is often called indefinite repetition because the number of repetitions is not known before the loop begins executing.

Clearly, the sentinel value must be chosen so that it cannot be confused with an acceptable input value. Grades on a quiz are normally nonnegative integers, so –1 is an acceptable sentinel value for this problem. Thus, a run of the class average program might process a stream of inputs such as 95, 96, 75, 74, 89 and –1. The program would then compute and print the class average for the grades 95, 96, 75, 74 and 89. Since –1 is the sentinel value, it should not enter into the averaging calculation.

Common Programming Error 4.9

Choosing a sentinel value that is also a legitimate data value is a logic error.

Developing the Pseudocode Algorithm with Top-Down, Stepwise Refinement: The Top and First Refinement

We approach the class average program with a technique called top-down, stepwise refinement, a technique that is essential to the development of well-structured programs. We begin with a pseudocode representation of the top—a single statement that conveys the overall function of the program:

> *Determine the class average for the quiz for an arbitrary number of students*

The top is, in effect, a *complete* representation of a program. Unfortunately, the top (as in this case) rarely conveys sufficient detail from which to write a program. So we now begin the refinement process. We divide the top into a series of smaller tasks and list these in the order in which they need to be performed. This results in the following first refinement.

> *Initialize variables*
> *Input, sum and count the quiz grades*
> *Calculate and print the total of all student grades and the class average*

This refinement uses only the sequence structure—the steps listed should execute in order, one after the other.

Software Engineering Observation 4.4

Each refinement, as well as the top itself, is a complete specification of the algorithm; only the level of detail varies.

Software Engineering Observation 4.5

Many programs can be divided logically into three phases: an initialization phase that initializes the program variables; a processing phase that inputs data values and adjusts program variables (such as counters and totals) accordingly; and a termination phase that calculates and outputs the final results.

Proceeding to the Second Refinement

The preceding *Software Engineering Observation* is often all you need for the first refinement in the top-down process. To proceed to the next level of refinement, i.e., the second refinement, we commit to specific variables. In this example, we need a running total of the numbers, a count of how many numbers have been processed, a variable to receive the value of each grade as it is input by the user and a variable to hold the calculated average. The pseudocode statement

> *Initialize variables*

can be refined as follows:

> *Initialize total to zero*
> *Initialize counter to zero*

Only the variables *total* and *counter* need to be initialized before they are used. The variables *average* and *grade* (for the calculated average and the user input, respectively) need not be initialized, because their values will be replaced as they are calculated or input.

The pseudocode statement

Input, sum and count the quiz grades

requires a repetition statement (i.e., a loop) that successively inputs each grade. We don't know in advance how many grades are to be processed, so we'll use sentinel-controlled repetition. The user enters legitimate grades one at a time. After entering the last legitimate grade, the user enters the sentinel value. The program tests for the sentinel value after each grade is input and terminates the loop when the user enters the sentinel value. The second refinement of the preceding pseudocode statement is then

Prompt the user to enter the first grade
Input the first grade (possibly the sentinel)

While the user has not yet entered the sentinel
    Add this grade into the running total
    Add one to the grade counter
    Prompt the user to enter the next grade
    Input the next grade (possibly the sentinel)

In pseudocode, we do not use braces around the statements that form the body of the *While* structure. We simply indent the statements under the *While* to show that they belong to the *While*. Again, pseudocode is only an informal program development aid.

The pseudocode statement

Calculate and print the total of all student grades and the class average

can be refined as follows:

If the counter is not equal to zero
    Set the average to the total divided by the counter
    Print the total of the grades for all students in the class
    Print the class average
else
    Print "No grades were entered"

We are careful here to test for the possibility of division by zero—normally a fatal logic error that, if undetected, would cause the program to fail (often called "bombing" or "crashing"). The complete second refinement of the pseudocode for the class average problem is shown in Fig. 4.11.

Common Programming Error 4.10

An attempt to divide by zero normally causes a fatal runtime error.

Error-Prevention Tip 4.3

When performing division by an expression whose value could be zero, explicitly test for this possibility and handle it appropriately in your program (such as by printing an error message) rather than allowing the fatal error to occur.

In Fig. 4.7 and Fig. 4.11, we include some blank lines and indentation in the pseudocode to make it more readable. The blank lines separate the pseudocode algorithms into their various phases, and the indentation emphasizes the control statement bodies.

1	*Initialize total to zero*
2	*Initialize counter to zero*
3	
4	*Prompt the user to enter the first grade*
5	*Input the first grade (possibly the sentinel)*
6	
7	*While the user has not yet entered the sentinel*
8	*Add this grade into the running total*
9	*Add one to the grade counter*
10	*Prompt the user to enter the next grade*
11	*Input the next grade (possibly the sentinel)*
12	
13	*If the counter is not equal to zero*
14	*Set the average to the total divided by the counter*
15	*Print the total of the grades for all students in the class*
16	*Print the class average*
17	*else*
18	*Print "No grades were entered"*

Fig. 4.11 | Class average problem pseudocode algorithm with sentinel-controlled repetition.

The pseudocode algorithm in Fig. 4.11 solves the more general class average problem. This algorithm was developed after only two levels of refinement. Sometimes more levels are necessary.

Software Engineering Observation 4.6

Terminate the top-down, stepwise refinement process when the pseudocode algorithm is specified in sufficient detail for you to be able to convert the pseudocode to C++. Normally, implementing the C++ program is then straightforward.

Software Engineering Observation 4.7

Many experienced programmers write programs without ever using program development tools like pseudocode. These programmers feel that their ultimate goal is to solve the problem on a computer and that writing pseudocode merely delays the production of final outputs. Although this method might work for simple and familiar problems, it can lead to serious difficulties in large, complex projects.

Implementing Sentinel-Controlled Repetition in Class GradeBook

Figures 4.12 and 4.13 show the C++ class GradeBook containing member function determineClassAverage that implements the pseudocode algorithm of Fig. 4.11 (this class is demonstrated in Fig. 4.14). Although each grade entered is an integer, the averaging calculation is likely to produce a number with a decimal point—in other words, a real number or floating-point number (e.g., 7.33, 0.0975 or 1000.12345). The type int cannot represent such a number, so this class must use another type to do so. C++ provides several data types for storing floating-point numbers in memory, including float and double. The primary difference between these types is that, compared to float variables, double variables can typically store numbers with larger magnitude and finer detail (i.e., more digits to the right of the decimal point—also known as the number's precision). This program introduces a special operator called a cast operator to force the averaging calculation to produce a floating-point numeric result. These features are explained in detail as we discuss the program.

In this example, we see that control statements can be stacked on top of one another (in sequence) just as a child stacks building blocks. The while statement (lines 67–75 of Fig. 4.13) is immediately followed by an if...else statement (lines 78–90) in sequence. Much of the code in this program is identical to the code in Fig. 4.9, so we concentrate on the new features and issues.

```
1   // Fig. 4.12: GradeBook.h
2   // Definition of class GradeBook that determines a class average.
3   // Member functions are defined in GradeBook.cpp
4   #include <string> // program uses C++ standard string class
5   using std::string;
6
7   // GradeBook class definition
8   class GradeBook
9   {
10  public:
11     GradeBook( string ); // constructor initializes course name
12     void setCourseName( string ); // function to set the course name
13     string getCourseName(); // function to retrieve the course name
14     void displayMessage(); // display a welcome message
15     void determineClassAverage(); // averages grades entered by the user
16  private:
17     string courseName; // course name for this GradeBook
18  }; // end class GradeBook
```

Fig. 4.12 | Class average problem using sentinel-controlled repetition: GradeBook header file.

```
1   // Fig. 4.13: GradeBook.cpp
2   // Member-function definitions for class GradeBook that solves the
3   // class average program with sentinel-controlled repetition.
4   #include <iostream>
5   using std::cout;
6   using std::cin;
7   using std::endl;
8   using std::fixed; // ensures that decimal point is displayed
9
10  #include <iomanip> // parameterized stream manipulators
11  using std::setprecision; // sets numeric output precision
12
13  // include definition of class GradeBook from GradeBook.h
14  #include "GradeBook.h"
15
```

Fig. 4.13 | Class average problem using sentinel-controlled repetition: GradeBook source code file. (Part 1 of 3.)

```cpp
16   // constructor initializes courseName with string supplied as argument
17   GradeBook::GradeBook( string name )
18   {
19      setCourseName( name ); // validate and store courseName
20   } // end GradeBook constructor
21
22   // function to set the course name;
23   // ensures that the course name has at most 25 characters
24   void GradeBook::setCourseName( string name )
25   {
26      if ( name.length() <= 25 ) // if name has 25 or fewer characters
27         courseName = name; // store the course name in the object
28      else // if name is longer than 25 characters
29      { // set courseName to first 25 characters of parameter name
30         courseName = name.substr( 0, 25 ); // select first 25 characters
31         cout << "Name \"" << name << "\" exceeds maximum length (25).\n"
32            << "Limiting courseName to first 25 characters.\n" << endl;
33      } // end if...else
34   } // end function setCourseName
35
36   // function to retrieve the course name
37   string GradeBook::getCourseName()
38   {
39      return courseName;
40   } // end function getCourseName
41
42   // display a welcome message to the GradeBook user
43   void GradeBook::displayMessage()
44   {
45      cout << "Welcome to the grade book for\n" << getCourseName() << "!\n"
46         << endl;
47   } // end function displayMessage
48
49   // determine class average based on 10 grades entered by user
50   void GradeBook::determineClassAverage()
51   {
52      int total; // sum of grades entered by user
53      int gradeCounter; // number of grades entered
54      int grade; // grade value
55      double average; // number with decimal point for average
56
57      // initialization phase
58      total = 0; // initialize total
59      gradeCounter = 0; // initialize loop counter
60
61      // processing phase
62      // prompt for input and read grade from user
63      cout << "Enter grade or -1 to quit: ";
64      cin >> grade; // input grade or sentinel value
65
```

Fig. 4.13 | Class average problem using sentinel-controlled repetition: GradeBook source code file. (Part 2 of 3.)

```
66      // loop until sentinel value read from user
67      while ( grade != -1 ) // while grade is not -1
68      {
69         total = total + grade; // add grade to total
70         gradeCounter = gradeCounter + 1; // increment counter
71
72         // prompt for input and read next grade from user
73         cout << "Enter grade or -1 to quit: ";
74         cin >> grade; // input grade or sentinel value
75      } // end while
76
77      // termination phase
78      if ( gradeCounter != 0 ) // if user entered at least one grade...
79      {
80         // calculate average of all grades entered
81         average = static_cast< double >( total ) / gradeCounter;
82
83         // display total and average (with two digits of precision)
84         cout << "\nTotal of all " << gradeCounter << " grades entered is "
85            << total << endl;
86         cout << "Class average is " << setprecision( 2 ) << fixed << average
87            << endl;
88      } // end if
89      else // no grades were entered, so output appropriate message
90         cout << "No grades were entered" << endl;
91   } // end function determineClassAverage
```

Fig. 4.13 | Class average problem using sentinel-controlled repetition: GradeBook source code file. (Part 3 of 3.)

```
1    // Fig. 4.14: fig04_14.cpp
2    // Create GradeBook object and invoke its determineClassAverage function.
3
4    // include definition of class GradeBook from GradeBook.h
5    #include "GradeBook.h"
6
7    int main()
8    {
9       // create GradeBook object myGradeBook and
10      // pass course name to constructor
11      GradeBook myGradeBook( "CS101 C++ Programming" );
12
13      myGradeBook.displayMessage(); // display welcome message
14      myGradeBook.determineClassAverage(); // find average of 10 grades
15      return 0; // indicate successful termination
16   } // end main
```

Fig. 4.14 | Class average problem using sentinel-controlled repetition: Creating an object of class GradeBook (Fig. 4.12–Fig. 4.13) and invoking its determineClassAverage member function. (Part 1 of 2.)

```
Welcome to the grade book for
CS101 C++ Programming

Enter grade or -1 to quit: 97
Enter grade or -1 to quit: 88
Enter grade or -1 to quit: 72
Enter grade or -1 to quit: -1

Total of all 3 grades entered is 257
Class average is 85.67
```

Fig. 4.14 | Class average problem using sentinel-controlled repetition: Creating an object of class GradeBook (Fig. 4.12–Fig. 4.13) and invoking its determineClassAverage member function. (Part 2 of 2.)

Line 55 declares the double variable average. Recall that we used an int variable in the preceding example to store the class average. Using type double in the current example allows us to store the class average calculation's result as a floating-point number. Line 59 initializes the variable gradeCounter to 0, because no grades have been entered yet. Remember that this program uses sentinel-controlled repetition. To keep an accurate record of the number of grades entered, the program increments variable gradeCounter only when the user enters a valid grade value (i.e., not the sentinel value) and the program completes the processing of the grade. Finally, notice that both input statements (lines 64 and 74) are preceded by an output statement that prompts the user for input.

Good Programming Practice 4.8

Prompt the user for each keyboard input. The prompt should indicate the form of the input and any special input values. For example, in a sentinel-controlled loop, the prompts requesting data entry should explicitly remind the user what the sentinel value is.

Program Logic for Sentinel-Controlled Repetition vs. Counter-Controlled Repetition

Compare the program logic for sentinel-controlled repetition in this application with that for counter-controlled repetition in Fig. 4.9. In counter-controlled repetition, each iteration of the while statement (lines 57–63 of Fig. 4.9) reads a value from the user, for the specified number of iterations. In sentinel-controlled repetition, the program reads the first value (lines 63–64 of Fig. 4.13) before reaching the while. This value determines whether the program's flow of control should enter the body of the while. If the condition of the while is false, the user entered the sentinel value, so the body of the while does not execute (i.e., no grades were entered). If, on the other hand, the condition is true, the body begins execution, and the loop adds the grade value to the total (line 69). Then lines 73–74 in the loop's body prompt for and input the next value from the user. Next, program control reaches the closing right brace (}) of the body in line 75, so execution continues with the test of the while's condition (line 67). The condition uses the most recent grade input by the user to determine whether the loop's body should execute again. Note that the value of variable grade is always input from the user immediately before the program tests the while condition. This allows the program to determine whether the value just input is the sentinel value *before* the program processes that value (i.e., adds it to the total and increments `gradeCounter`). If the sentinel value is input, the loop terminates, and the program does not add –1 to the `total`.

After the loop terminates, the `if...else` statement in lines 78–90 executes. The condition in line 78 determines whether any grades were entered. If none were, the `else` part (lines 89–90) of the `if...else` statement executes and displays the message `"No grades were entered"` and the member function returns control to the calling function.

Notice the block in the `while` loop in Fig. 4.13. Without the braces, the last three statements in the body of the loop would fall outside the loop, causing the computer to interpret this code incorrectly, as follows:

```
// loop until sentinel value read from user
while ( grade != -1 )
   total = total + grade; // add grade to total
gradeCounter = gradeCounter + 1; // increment counter

// prompt for input and read next grade from user
cout << "Enter grade or -1 to quit: ";
cin >> grade;
```

This would cause an infinite loop in the program if the user did not input –1 for the first grade (in line 64).

Common Programming Error 4.11

Omitting the braces that delimit a block can lead to logic errors, such as infinite loops. To prevent this problem, some programmers enclose the body of every control statement in braces, even if the body contains only a single statement.

Floating-Point Number Precision and Memory Requirements

Variables of type `float` represent single-precision floating-point numbers and have seven significant digits on most 32-bit systems. Variables of type `double` represent double-precision floating-point numbers. These require twice as much memory as `float` variables and provide 15 significant digits on most 32-bit systems—approximately double the precision of `float` variables. For the range of values required by most programs, variables of type `float` should suffice, but you can use `double` to "play it safe." In some programs, even variables of type `double` will be inadequate—such programs are beyond the scope of this book. Most programmers represent floating-point numbers with type `double`. In fact, C++ treats all floating-point numbers you type in a program's source code (such as 7.33 and 0.0975) as `double` values by default. Such values in the source code are known as floating-point constants. See Appendix C, Fundamental Types, for the ranges of values for `float`s and `double`s.

Floating-point numbers often arise as a result of division. In conventional arithmetic, when we divide 10 by 3, the result is 3.3333333…, with the sequence of 3s repeating infinitely. The computer allocates only a fixed amount of space to hold such a value, so clearly the stored floating-point value can be only an approximation.

Common Programming Error 4.12

Using floating-point numbers in a manner that assumes they are represented exactly (e.g., using them in comparisons for equality) can lead to incorrect results. Floating-point numbers are represented only approximately by most computers.

Although floating-point numbers are not always 100 percent precise, they have numerous applications. For example, when we speak of a "normal" body temperature of 98.6, we do not need to be precise to a large number of digits. When we read the temperature on a thermometer as 98.6, it may actually be 98.5999473210643. Calling this number simply 98.6 is fine for most applications involving body temperatures. Due to the imprecise nature of floating-point numbers, type `double` is preferred over type `float`, because `double` variables can represent floating-point numbers more accurately. For this reason, we use type `double` throughout the book.

Converting Between Fundamental Types Explicitly and Implicitly
The variable `average` is declared to be of type `double` (line 55 of Fig. 4.13) to capture the fractional result of our calculation. However, `total` and `gradeCounter` are both integer variables. Recall that dividing two integers results in integer division, in which any fractional part of the calculation is lost (i.e., truncated). In the following statement:

```
average = total / gradeCounter;
```

the division calculation is performed first, so the fractional part of the result is lost before it is assigned to `average`. To perform a floating-point calculation with integer values, we must create temporary values that are floating-point numbers for the calculation. C++ provides the unary cast operator to accomplish this task. Line 81 uses the cast operator `static_cast< double >( total )` to create a *temporary* floating-point copy of its operand in parentheses—`total`. Using a cast operator in this manner is called explicit conversion. The value stored in `total` is still an integer.

The calculation now consists of a floating-point value (the temporary `double` version of `total`) divided by the integer `gradeCounter`. The C++ compiler knows how to evaluate only expressions in which the data types of the operands are identical. To ensure that the operands are of the same type, the compiler performs an operation called promotion (also called implicit conversion) on selected operands. For example, in an expression containing values of data types `int` and `double`, C++ promotes `int` operands to `double` values. In our example, we are treating `total` as a `double` (by using the unary cast operator), so the compiler promotes `gradeCounter` to `double`, allowing the calculation to be performed—the result of the floating-point division is assigned to `average`. In Chapter 6, Functions and an Introduction to Recursion, we discuss all the fundamental data types and their order of promotion.

Common Programming Error 4.13

The cast operator can be used to convert between fundamental numeric types, such as `int` and `double`, and between related class types (as we discuss in Chapter 13, Object-Oriented Programming: Polymorphism). Casting to the wrong type may cause compilation errors or runtime errors.

Cast operators are available for use with every data type and with class types as well. The `static_cast` operator is formed by following keyword `static_cast` with angle brackets (< and >) around a data-type name. The cast operator is a unary operator—an operator that takes only one operand. In Chapter 2, we studied the binary arithmetic operators. C++ also supports unary versions of the plus (+) and minus (-) operators, so that you can write such expressions as -7 or +5. Cast operators have higher precedence than other unary operators, such as unary + and unary -. This precedence is higher than that of the multiplicative operators *, / and %, and lower than that of parentheses. We indicate the cast operator with the notation static_cast< *type* >() in our precedence charts (see, for example, Fig. 4.22).

Formatting for Floating-Point Numbers

The formatting capabilities in Fig. 4.13 are discussed here briefly and explained in depth in Chapter 15, Stream Input/Output. The call to setprecision in line 86 (with an argument of 2) indicates that double variable average should be printed with two digits of precision to the right of the decimal point (e.g., 92.37). This call is referred to as a parameterized stream manipulator (because of the 2 in parentheses). Programs that use these calls must contain the preprocessor directive (line 10)

```
#include <iomanip>
```

Line 11 specifies the name from the <iomanip> header file that is used in this program. Note that endl is a nonparameterized stream manipulator (because it is not followed by a value or expression in parentheses) and does not require the <iomanip> header file. If the precision is not specified, floating-point values are normally output with six digits of precision (i.e., the default precision on most 32-bit systems today), although we'll see an exception to this in a moment.

The stream manipulator fixed (line 86) indicates that floating-point values should be output in so-called fixed-point format, as opposed to scientific notation. Scientific notation is a way of displaying a number as a floating-point number between the values of 1.0 and 10.0, multiplied by a power of 10. For instance, the value 3,100.0 would be displayed in scientific notation as 3.1×10^3. Scientific notation is useful when displaying values that are very large or very small. Formatting using scientific notation is discussed further in Chapter 15. Fixed-point formatting, on the other hand, is used to force a floating-point number to display a specific number of digits. Specifying fixed-point formatting also forces the decimal point and trailing zeros to print, even if the value is a whole number amount, such as 88.00. Without the fixed-point formatting option, such a value prints in C++ as 88 without the trailing zeros and without the decimal point. When the stream manipulators fixed and setprecision are used in a program, the printed value is rounded to the number of decimal positions indicated by the value passed to setprecision (e.g., the value 2 in line 86), although the value in memory remains unaltered. For example, the values 87.946 and 67.543 are output as 87.95 and 67.54, respectively. Note that it also is possible to force a decimal point to appear by using stream manipulator showpoint. If showpoint is specified without fixed, then trailing zeros will not print. Like endl, stream manipulators fixed and showpoint are nonparameterized and do not require the <iomanip> header file. Both can be found in header <iostream>.

Lines 86 and 87 of Fig. 4.13 output the class average. In this example, we display the class average rounded to the nearest hundredth and output it with exactly two digits to the right of the decimal point. The parameterized stream manipulator (line 86) indicates that variable average's value should be displayed with two digits of precision to the right of the decimal point—indicated by setprecision(2). The three grades entered during the sample execution of the program in Fig. 4.14 total 257, which yields the average 85.666666.... The parameterized stream manipulator setprecision causes the value to be rounded to the specified number of digits. In this program, the average is rounded to the hundredths position and displayed as 85.67.

4.10 **Formulating Algorithms: Nested Control Statements**

For the next example, we once again formulate an algorithm by using pseudocode and top-down, stepwise refinement, and write a corresponding C++ program. We have seen that control statements can be stacked on top of one another (in sequence) just as a child stacks building blocks. In this case study, we examine the only other structured way control statements can be connected, namely, by nesting one control statement within another.

Consider the following problem statement:

A college offers a course that prepares students for the state licensing exam for real estate brokers. Last year, ten of the students who completed this course took the exam. The college wants to know how well its students did on the exam. You have been asked to write a program to summarize the results. You have been given a list of these 10 students. Next to each name is written a 1 if the student passed the exam or a 2 if the student failed.

Your program should analyze the results of the exam as follows:

1. Input each test result (i.e., a 1 or a 2). Display the prompting message "Enter result" each time the program requests another test result.

2. Count the number of test results of each type.

3. Display a summary of the test results indicating the number of students who passed and the number who failed.

4. If more than eight students passed the exam, print the message "Raise tuition."

After reading the problem statement carefully, we make the following observations:

1. The program must process test results for 10 students. A counter-controlled loop can be used because the number of test results is known in advance.

2. Each test result is a number—either a 1 or a 2. Each time the program reads a test result, the program must determine whether the number is a 1 or a 2. We test for a 1 in our algorithm. If the number is not a 1, we assume that it is a 2. (Exercise 4.20 considers the consequences of this assumption.)

3. Two counters are used to keep track of the exam results—one to count the number of students who passed the exam and one to count the number of students who failed the exam.

4. After the program has processed all the results, it must decide whether more than eight students passed the exam.

Let us proceed with top-down, stepwise refinement. We begin with a pseudocode representation of the top:

Analyze exam results and decide whether tuition should be raised

Once again, it is important to emphasize that the top is a *complete* representation of the program, but several refinements are likely to be needed before the pseudocode evolves naturally into a C++ program.

Our first refinement is

Initialize variables
Input the 10 exam results, and count passes and failures
Print a summary of the exam results and decide if tuition should be raised

Here, too, even though we have a complete representation of the entire program, further refinement is necessary. We now commit to specific variables. Counters are needed to record the passes and failures, a counter will be used to control the looping process and a variable is needed to store the user input. The last variable is not initialized, because its value is read from the user during each iteration of the loop.

The pseudocode statement

> *Initialize variables*

can be refined as follows:

> *Initialize passes to zero*
> *Initialize failures to zero*
> *Initialize student counter to one*

Notice that only the counters are initialized at the start of the algorithm.

The pseudocode statement

> *Input the 10 exam results, and count passes and failures*

requires a loop that successively inputs the result of each exam. Here it is known in advance that there are precisely 10 exam results, so counter-controlled looping is appropriate. Inside the loop (i.e., **nested** within the loop), an `if...else` statement will determine whether each exam result is a pass or a failure and will increment the appropriate counter. The refinement of the preceding pseudocode statement is then

> *While student counter is less than or equal to 10*
> *   Prompt the user to enter the next exam result*
> *   Input the next exam result*
>
> *   If the student passed*
> *   Add one to passes*
> *   Else*
> *   Add one to failures*
>
> *   Add one to student counter*

We use blank lines to isolate the *If...Else* control structure, which improves readability.

The pseudocode statement

> *Print a summary of the exam results and decide whether tuition should be raised*

can be refined as follows:

> *Print the number of passes*
> *Print the number of failures*
>
> *If more than eight students passed*
> *   Print "Raise tuition"*

The complete second refinement appears in Fig. 4.15. Notice that blank lines are also used to set off the *While* structure for program readability. This pseudocode is now sufficiently refined for conversion to C++.

Conversion to Class Analysis

The C++ class, `Analysis`, that implements the pseudocode algorithm is shown in Fig. 4.16–Fig. 4.17, and two sample executions appear in Fig. 4.18.

```
 1    Initialize passes to zero
 2    Initialize failures to zero
 3    Initialize student counter to one
 4
 5    While student counter is less than or equal to 10
 6        Prompt the user to enter the next exam result
 7        Input the next exam result
 8
 9        If the student passed
10            Add one to passes
11        Else
12            Add one to failures
13
14        Add one to student counter
15
16    Print the number of passes
17    Print the number of failures
18
19    If more than eight students passed
20        Print "Raise tuition"
```

Fig. 4.15 | Pseudocode for examination-results problem.

```
 1    // Fig. 4.16: Analysis.h
 2    // Definition of class Analysis that analyzes examination results.
 3    // Member function is defined in Analysis.cpp
 4
 5    // Analysis class definition
 6    class Analysis
 7    {
 8    public:
 9       void processExamResults(); // process 10 students' examination results
10    }; // end class Analysis
```

Fig. 4.16 | Examination-results problem: `Analysis` header file.

```
 1    // Fig. 4.17: Analysis.cpp
 2    // Member-function definitions for class Analysis that
 3    // analyzes examination results.
 4    #include <iostream>
 5    using std::cout;
 6    using std::cin;
 7    using std::endl;
```

Fig. 4.17 | Examination-results problem: Nested control statements in `Analysis` source code file. (Part 1 of 2.)

```
8
9    // include definition of class Analysis from Analysis.h
10   #include "Analysis.h"
11
12   // process the examination results of 10 students
13   void Analysis::processExamResults()
14   {
15      // initializing variables in declarations
16      int passes = 0; // number of passes
17      int failures = 0; // number of failures
18      int studentCounter = 1; // student counter
19      int result; // one exam result (1 = pass, 2 = fail)
20
21      // process 10 students using counter-controlled loop
22      while ( studentCounter <= 10 )
23      {
24         // prompt user for input and obtain value from user
25         cout << "Enter result (1 = pass, 2 = fail): ";
26         cin >> result; // input result
27
28         // if...else nested in while
29         if ( result == 1 )          // if result is 1,
30            passes = passes + 1;     // increment passes;
31         else                        // else result is not 1, so
32            failures = failures + 1; // increment failures
33
34         // increment studentCounter so loop eventually terminates
35         studentCounter = studentCounter + 1;
36      } // end while
37
38      // termination phase; display number of passes and failures
39      cout << "Passed " << passes << "\nFailed " << failures << endl;
40
41      // determine whether more than eight students passed
42      if ( passes > 8 )
43         cout << "Raise tuition " << endl;
44   } // end function processExamResults
```

Fig. 4.17 | Examination-results problem: Nested control statements in `Analysis` source code file. (Part 2 of 2.)

```
1    // Fig. 4.18: fig04_18.cpp
2    // Test program for class Analysis.
3    #include "Analysis.h" // include definition of class Analysis
4
5    int main()
6    {
7       Analysis application; // create Analysis object
8       application.processExamResults(); // call function to process results
9       return 0; // indicate successful termination
10   } // end main
```

Fig. 4.18 | Test program for class `Analysis`. (Part 1 of 2.)

```
Enter result (1 = pass, 2 = fail): 1
Enter result (1 = pass, 2 = fail): 1
Enter result (1 = pass, 2 = fail): 1
Enter result (1 = pass, 2 = fail): 1
Enter result (1 = pass, 2 = fail): 2
Enter result (1 = pass, 2 = fail): 1
Enter result (1 = pass, 2 = fail): 1
Enter result (1 = pass, 2 = fail): 1
Enter result (1 = pass, 2 = fail): 1
Enter result (1 = pass, 2 = fail): 1
Passed 9
Failed 1
Raise tuition
```

```
Enter result (1 = pass, 2 = fail): 1
Enter result (1 = pass, 2 = fail): 2
Enter result (1 = pass, 2 = fail): 2
Enter result (1 = pass, 2 = fail): 1
Enter result (1 = pass, 2 = fail): 1
Enter result (1 = pass, 2 = fail): 1
Enter result (1 = pass, 2 = fail): 2
Enter result (1 = pass, 2 = fail): 1
Enter result (1 = pass, 2 = fail): 1
Enter result (1 = pass, 2 = fail): 2
Passed 6
Failed 4
```

Fig. 4.18 | Test program for class Analysis. (Part 2 of 2.)

Lines 16–18 of Fig. 4.17 declare the variables that member function processExamResults of class Analysis uses to process the examination results. Note that we have taken advantage of a feature of C++ that allows variable initialization to be incorporated into declarations (passes is initialized to 0, failures is initialized to 0 and studentCounter is initialized to 1). Looping programs may require initialization at the beginning of each repetition; such reinitialization normally would be performed by assignment statements rather than in declarations or by moving the declarations inside the loop bodies.

The while statement (lines 22–36) loops 10 times. During each iteration, the loop inputs and processes one exam result. Notice that the if...else statement (lines 29–32) for processing each result is nested in the while statement. If the result is 1, the if...else statement increments passes; otherwise, it assumes the result is 2 and increments failures. Line 35 increments studentCounter before the loop condition is tested again in line 22. After 10 values have been input, the loop terminates and line 39 displays the number of passes and the number of failures. The if statement in lines 42–43 determines whether more than eight students passed the exam and, if so, outputs the message "Raise Tuition".

Demonstrating Class Analysis
Figure 4.18 creates an Analysis object (line 7) and invokes the object's processExamResults member function (line 8) to process a set of exam results entered by the user. Figure 4.18 shows the input and output from two sample executions of the program. At

the end of the first sample execution, the condition in line 42 of member function processExamResults in Fig. 4.17 is true—more than eight students passed the exam, so the
program outputs a message indicating that the tuition should be raised.

4.11 Assignment Operators

C++ provides several assignment operators for abbreviating assignment expressions. For
example, the statement

```
c = c + 3;
```

can be abbreviated with the addition assignment operator += as

```
c += 3;
```

The += operator adds the value of the expression on the right of the operator to the value
of the variable on the left of the operator and stores the result in the variable on the left of
the operator. Any statement of the form

variable = variable operator expression;

in which the same *variable* appears on both sides of the assignment operator and *operator*
is one of the binary operators +, -, *, /, or % (or others we'll discuss later in the text), can
be written in the form

variable operator= expression;

Thus the assignment c += 3 adds 3 to c. Figure 4.19 shows the arithmetic assignment operators, sample expressions using these operators and explanations.

Assignment operator	Sample expression	Explanation	Assigns
Assume: int c = 3, d = 5, e = 4, f = 6, g = 12;			
+=	c += 7	c = c + 7	10 to c
-=	d -= 4	d = d - 4	1 to d
*=	e *= 5	e = e * 5	20 to e
/=	f /= 3	f = f / 3	2 to f
%=	g %= 9	g = g % 9	3 to g

Fig. 4.19 | Arithmetic assignment operators.

4.12 Increment and Decrement Operators

In addition to the arithmetic assignment operators, C++ also provides two unary operators
for adding 1 to or subtracting 1 from the value of a numeric variable. These are the unary
increment operator, ++, and the unary decrement operator, --, which are summarized in
Fig. 4.20. A program can increment by 1 the value of a variable called c using the increment operator, ++, rather than the expression c = c + 1 or c += 1. An increment or decrement operator that is prefixed to (placed before) a variable is referred to as the prefix

Operator	Called	Sample expression	Explanation
++	preincrement	++a	Increment a by 1, then use the new value of a in the expression in which a resides.
++	postincrement	a++	Use the current value of a in the expression in which a resides, then increment a by 1.
--	predecrement	--b	Decrement b by 1, then use the new value of b in the expression in which b resides.
--	postdecrement	b--	Use the current value of b in the expression in which b resides, then decrement b by 1.

Fig. 4.20 | Increment and decrement operators.

increment or prefix decrement operator, respectively. An increment or decrement operator that is postfixed to (placed after) a variable is referred to as the postfix increment or postfix decrement operator, respectively.

Using the prefix increment (or decrement) operator to add (or subtract) 1 from a variable is known as preincrementing (or predecrementing) the variable. Preincrementing (or predecrementing) causes the variable to be incremented (decremented) by 1, then the new value of the variable is used in the expression in which it appears. Using the postfix increment (or decrement) operator to add (or subtract) 1 from a variable is known as postincrementing (or postdecrementing) the variable. Postincrementing (or postdecrementing) causes the current value of the variable to be used in the expression in which it appears, then the variable's value is incremented (decremented) by 1.

Good Programming Practice 4.9

Unlike binary operators, the unary increment and decrement operators should be placed next to their operands, with no intervening spaces.

Figure 4.21 demonstrates the difference between the prefix increment and postfix increment versions of the ++ increment operator. The decrement operator (--) works similarly. Note that this example does not contain a class, but just a source code file with function main performing all the application's work. In this chapter and in Chapter 3, you have seen examples consisting of one class (including the header and source code files for this class), as well as another source code file testing the class. This source code file contained function main, which created an object of the class and called its member functions. In this example, we simply want to show the mechanics of the ++ operator, so we use only one source code file with function main. Occasionally, when it does not make sense to try to create a reusable class to demonstrate a simple concept, we'll use a mechanical example contained entirely within the main function of a single source code file.

Line 12 initializes the variable c to 5, and line 13 outputs c's initial value. Line 14 outputs the value of the expression c++. This expression postincrements the variable c, so c's original value (5) is output, then c's value is incremented. Thus, line 14 outputs c's initial value (5) again. Line 15 outputs c's new value (6) to prove that the variable's value was indeed incremented in line 14.

```
1   // Fig. 4.21: fig04_21.cpp
2   // Preincrementing and postincrementing.
3   #include <iostream>
4   using std::cout;
5   using std::endl;
6
7   int main()
8   {
9      int c;
10
11     // demonstrate postincrement
12     c = 5; // assign 5 to c
13     cout << c << endl; // print 5
14     cout << c++ << endl; // print 5 then postincrement
15     cout << c << endl; // print 6
16
17     cout << endl; // skip a line
18
19     // demonstrate preincrement
20     c = 5; // assign 5 to c
21     cout << c << endl; // print 5
22     cout << ++c << endl; // preincrement then print 6
23     cout << c << endl; // print 6
24     return 0; // indicate successful termination
25  } // end main
```

```
5
5
6

5
6
6
```

Fig. 4.21 | Preincrementing and postincrementing.

Line 20 resets c's value to 5, and line 21 outputs that value. Line 22 outputs the value of the expression ++c. This expression preincrements c, so its value is incremented, then the new value (6) is output. Line 23 outputs c's value again to show that the value of c is still 6 after line 22 executes.

The arithmetic assignment operators and the increment and decrement operators can be used to simplify program statements. The three assignment statements in Fig. 4.17:

```
passes = passes + 1;
failures = failures + 1;
studentCounter = studentCounter + 1;
```

can be written more concisely with assignment operators as

```
passes += 1;
failures += 1;
studentCounter += 1;
```

with prefix increment operators as

```
++passes;
++failures;
++studentCounter;
```

or with postfix increment operators as

```
passes++;
failures++;
studentCounter++;
```

Note that, when incrementing (++) or decrementing (--) of a variable occurs in a statement by itself, the preincrement and postincrement forms have the same effect, and the predecrement and postdecrement forms have the same effect. It is only when a variable appears in the context of a larger expression that preincrementing the variable and postincrementing the variable have different effects (and similarly for predecrementing and postdecrementing).

Common Programming Error 4.14

Attempting to use the increment or decrement operator on an expression other than a modifiable variable name or reference, e.g., writing ++(x + 1), is a syntax error.

Figure 4.22 shows the precedence and associativity of the operators introduced to this point. The operators are shown top-to-bottom in decreasing order of precedence. The second column indicates the associativity of the operators at each level of precedence. Notice that the conditional operator (?:), the unary operators preincrement (++), predecrement (--), plus (+) and minus (-), and the assignment operators =, +=, -=, *=, /= and %= associate from right to left. All other operators in the operator precedence chart of Fig. 4.22 associate from left to right. The third column names the various groups of operators.

Operators						Associativity	Type
::						left to right	scope resolution
()						left to right	parentheses
++	--	static_cast< *type* >()				left to right	unary (postfix)
++	--	+	-			right to left	unary (prefix)
*	/	%				left to right	multiplicative
+	-					left to right	additive
<<	>>					left to right	insertion/extraction
<	<=	>	>=			left to right	relational
==	!=					left to right	equality
?:						right to left	conditional
=	+=	-=	*=	/=	%=	right to left	assignment

Fig. 4.22 | Operator precedence for the operators encountered so far in the text.

4.13 (Optional) Software Engineering Case Study: Identifying Class Attributes in the ATM System

In Section 3.11, we began the first stage of an object-oriented design (OOD) for our ATM system—analyzing the requirements specification and identifying the classes needed to implement the system. We listed the nouns and noun phrases in the requirements specification and identified a separate class for each one that plays a significant role in the ATM system. We then modeled the classes and their relationships in a UML class diagram (Fig. 3.23). Classes have attributes (data) and operations (behaviors). Class attributes are implemented in C++ programs as data members, and class operations are implemented as member functions. In this section, we determine many of the attributes needed in the ATM system. In Chapter 5, we examine how these attributes represent an object's state. In Chapter 6, we determine class operations.

Identifying Attributes

Consider the attributes of some real-world objects: A person's attributes include height, weight and whether the person is left-handed, right-handed or ambidextrous. A radio's attributes include its station setting, its volume setting and its AM or FM setting. A car's attributes include its speedometer and odometer readings, the amount of gas in its tank and what gear it is in. A personal computer's attributes include its manufacturer (e.g., Dell, Sun, Apple or IBM), type of screen (e.g., LCD or CRT), main memory size and hard disk size.

We can identify many attributes of the classes in our system by looking for descriptive words and phrases in the requirements specification. For each one we find that plays a significant role in the ATM system, we create an attribute and assign it to one or more of the classes identified in Section 3.11. We also create attributes to represent any additional data that a class may need, as such needs become apparent throughout the design process.

Figure 4.23 lists the words or phrases from the requirements specification that describe each class. We formed this list by reading the requirements specification and identifying any words or phrases that refer to characteristics of the classes in the system. For example, the requirements specification describes the steps taken to obtain a "withdrawal amount," so we list "amount" next to class `Withdrawal`.

Class	Descriptive words and phrases
`ATM`	user is authenticated
`BalanceInquiry`	account number
`Withdrawal`	account number amount
`Deposit`	account number amount
`BankDatabase`	[no descriptive words or phrases]

Fig. 4.23 | Descriptive words and phrases from the ATM requirements. (Part 1 of 2.)

Class	Descriptive words and phrases
Account	account number PIN balance
Screen	[no descriptive words or phrases]
Keypad	[no descriptive words or phrases]
CashDispenser	begins each day loaded with 500 $20 bills
DepositSlot	[no descriptive words or phrases]

Fig. 4.23 | Descriptive words and phrases from the
ATM requirements. (Part 2 of 2.)

Figure 4.23 leads us to create one attribute of class ATM. Class ATM maintains information about the state of the ATM. The phrase "user is authenticated" describes a state of the ATM (we introduce states in Section 5.11), so we include userAuthenticated as a Boolean attribute (i.e., an attribute that has a value of either true or false). The UML Boolean type is equivalent to the bool type in C++. This attribute indicates whether the ATM has successfully authenticated the current user—userAuthenticated must be true for the system to allow the user to perform transactions and access account information. This attribute helps ensure the security of the data in the system.

Classes BalanceInquiry, Withdrawal and Deposit share one attribute. Each transaction involves an "account number" that corresponds to the account of the user making the transaction. We assign an integer attribute accountNumber to each transaction class to identify the account to which an object of the class applies.

Descriptive words and phrases in the requirements specification also suggest some differences in the attributes required by each transaction class. The requirements specification indicates that to withdraw cash or deposit funds, users must enter a specific "amount" of money to be withdrawn or deposited, respectively. Thus, we assign to classes Withdrawal and Deposit an attribute amount to store the value supplied by the user. The amounts of money related to a withdrawal and a deposit are defining characteristics of these transactions that the system requires for them to take place. Class BalanceInquiry, however, needs no additional data to perform its task—it requires only an account number to indicate the account whose balance should be retrieved.

Class Account has several attributes. The requirements specification states that each bank account has an "account number" and "PIN," which the system uses for identifying accounts and authenticating users. We assign to class Account two integer attributes: accountNumber and pin. The requirements specification also specifies that an account maintains a "balance" of the amount of money in the account and that money the user deposits does not become available for a withdrawal until the bank verifies the amount of cash in the deposit envelope, and any checks in the envelope clear. An account must still record the amount of money that a user deposits, however. Therefore, we decide that an account should represent a balance using two attributes of UML type Double: availableBalance and totalBalance. Attribute availableBalance tracks the amount of money that a user can withdraw from the account. Attribute `totalBalance` refers to the total amount of money that the user has "on deposit" (i.e., the amount of money available, plus the amount waiting to be verified or cleared). For example, suppose an ATM user deposits $50.00 into an empty account. The `totalBalance` attribute would increase to $50.00 to record the deposit, but the `availableBalance` would remain at $0. [*Note:* We assume that the bank updates the `availableBalance` attribute of an `Account` soon after the ATM transaction occurs, in response to confirming that $50 worth of cash or checks was found in the deposit envelope. We assume that this update occurs through a transaction that a bank employee performs using some piece of bank software other than the ATM. Thus, we do not discuss this transaction in our case study.]

Class `CashDispenser` has one attribute. The requirements specification states that the cash dispenser "begins each day loaded with 500 $20 bills." The cash dispenser must keep track of the number of bills it contains to determine whether enough cash is on hand to satisfy withdrawal requests. We assign to class `CashDispenser` an integer attribute `count`, which is initially set to 500.

For real problems in industry, there is no guarantee that requirements specifications will be rich enough and precise enough for the object-oriented systems designer to determine all the attributes or even all the classes. The need for additional (or fewer) classes, attributes and behaviors may become clear as the design process proceeds. As we progress through this case study, we too will continue to add, modify and delete information about the classes in our system.

Modeling Attributes

The class diagram in Fig. 4.24 lists some of the attributes for the classes in our system—the descriptive words and phrases in Fig. 4.23 helped us identify these attributes. For simplicity, Fig. 4.24 does not show the associations among classes—we showed these in Fig. 3.23. This is a common practice of systems designers when designs are being developed. Recall from Section 3.11 that in the UML, a class's attributes are placed in the middle compartment of the class's rectangle. We list each attribute's name and type separated by a colon (:), followed in some cases by an equal sign (=) and an initial value.

Consider the `userAuthenticated` attribute of class `ATM`:

```
userAuthenticated : Boolean = false
```

This attribute declaration contains three pieces of information about the attribute. The *attribute name* is `userAuthenticated`. The *attribute type* is `Boolean`. In C++, an attribute can be represented by a fundamental type, such as `bool`, `int` or `double`, or a class type—as discussed in Chapter 3. We have chosen to model only primitive-type attributes in Fig. 4.24—we discuss the reasoning behind this decision shortly. [*Note:* Figure 4.24 lists UML data types for the attributes. When we implement the system, we'll associate the UML types `Boolean`, `Integer` and `Double` with the C++ fundamental types `bool`, `int` and `double`, respectively.]

We can also indicate an initial value for an attribute. The `userAuthenticated` attribute in class `ATM` has an initial value of `false`. This indicates that the system initially does not consider the user to be authenticated. If an attribute has no initial value specified, only its name and type (separated by a colon) are shown. For example, the `accountNumber` attribute of class `BalanceInquiry` is an `Integer`. Here we show no initial value, because

Fig. 4.24 | Classes with attributes.

the value of this attribute is a number that we do not yet know—it will be determined at execution time based on the account number entered by the current ATM user.

Figure 4.24 does not include any attributes for classes Screen, Keypad and DepositSlot. These are important components of our system, for which our design process simply has not yet revealed any attributes. We may still discover some, however, in the remaining design phases or when we implement these classes in C++. This is perfectly normal for the iterative process of software engineering.

Software Engineering Observation 4.8

At the early stages in the design process, classes often lack attributes (and operations). Such classes should not be eliminated, however, because attributes (and operations) may become evident in the later phases of design and implementation.

Note that Fig. 4.24 also does not include attributes for class BankDatabase. Recall from Chapter 3 that in C++, attributes can be represented by either fundamental types or class types. We have chosen to include only fundamental-type attributes in the class diagram in Fig. 4.24 (and in similar class diagrams throughout the case study). A class-type attribute is modeled more clearly as an association (in particular, a composition) between the class with the attribute and the class of the object of which the attribute is an instance. For example, the class diagram in Fig. 3.23 indicates that class BankDatabase participates in a composition relationship with zero or more `Account` objects. From this composition, we can determine that when we implement the ATM system in C++, we'll be required to create an attribute of class `BankDatabase` to hold zero or more `Account` objects. Similarly, we'll assign attributes to class `ATM` that correspond to its composition relationships with classes `Screen`, `Keypad`, `CashDispenser` and `DepositSlot`. These composition-based attributes would be redundant if modeled in Fig. 4.24, because the compositions modeled in Fig. 3.23 already convey the fact that the database contains information about zero or more accounts and that an ATM is composed of a screen, keypad, cash dispenser and deposit slot. Software developers typically model these whole/part relationships as compositions rather than as attributes required to implement the relationships.

The class diagram in Fig. 4.24 provides a solid basis for the structure of our model, but the diagram is not complete. In Section 5.11, we identify the states and activities of the objects in the model, and in Section 6.22 we identify the operations that the objects perform. As we present more of the UML and object-oriented design, we'll continue to strengthen the structure of our model.

Software Engineering Case Study Self-Review Exercises

4.1   We typically identify the attributes of the classes in our system by analyzing the _____ in the requirements specification.
a) nouns and noun phrases
b) descriptive words and phrases
c) verbs and verb phrases
d) All of the above.

4.2   Which of the following is not an attribute of an airplane?
a) length
b) wingspan
c) fly
d) number of seats

4.3   Describe the meaning of the following attribute declaration of class `CashDispenser` in the class diagram in Fig. 4.24:

```
count : Integer = 500
```

Answers to Software Engineering Case Study Self-Review Exercises

4.1   b.

4.2   c. Fly is an operation or behavior of an airplane, not an attribute.

4.3   This indicates that `count` is an `Integer` with an initial value of `500`. This attribute keeps track of the number of bills available in the `CashDispenser` at any given time.

4.14 Wrap-Up

This chapter presented basic problem-solving techniques that you use in building classes and developing member functions for these classes. We demonstrated how to construct an algorithm (i.e., an approach to solving a problem) in pseudocode, then how to refine the algorithm through several phases of pseudocode development, resulting in C++ code that can be executed as part of a function. You learned how to use top-down, stepwise refinement to plan out the specific actions that a function must perform and the order in which the function must perform them.

You learned that only three types of control structures—sequence, selection and repetition—are needed to develop any algorithm. We demonstrated two of C++'s selection statements—the if single-selection statement and the if...else double-selection statement. The if statement is used to execute a set of statements based on a condition—if the condition is true, the statements execute; if it is not, the statements are skipped. The if...else double-selection statement is used to execute one set of statements if a condition is true, and another set of statements if the condition is false. We then discussed the while repetition statement, where a set of statements are executed repeatedly as long as a condition is true. We used control-statement stacking to total and compute the average of a set of student grades with counter- and sentinel-controlled repetition, and we used control-statement nesting to analyze and make decisions based on a set of exam results. We introduced assignment operators, which can be used for abbreviating statements. We presented the increment and decrement operators, which can be used to add or subtract the value 1 from a variable. In Chapter 5, Control Statements: Part 2, we continue our discussion of control statements, introducing the for, do...while and switch statements.

Summary

Section 4.2 Algorithms
- An algorithm is a procedure for solving a problem in terms of the actions to execute and the order in which to execute them.
- Specifying the order in which statements (actions) execute in a program is called program control.

Section 4.3 Pseudocode
- Pseudocode helps a programmer think out a program before attempting to write it in a programming language.
- Activity diagrams are part of the Unified Modeling Language (UML)—an industry standard for modeling software systems.

Section 4.4 Control Structures
- An activity diagram models the workflow (also called the activity) of a software system.
- Activity diagrams are composed of special-purpose symbols, such as action state symbols, diamonds and small circles. These symbols are connected by transition arrows that represent the flow of the activity.
- Like pseudocode, activity diagrams help you develop and represent algorithms.
- An action state is represented as a rectangle with its left and right sides replaced with arcs curving outward. The action expression appears inside the action state.
- The arrows in an activity diagram represent transitions, which indicate the order in which the actions represented by action states occur.
- The solid circle located at the top of an activity diagram represents the initial state—the beginning of the workflow before the program performs the modeled actions.
- The solid circle surrounded by a hollow circle that appears at the bottom of the activity diagram represents the final state—the end of the workflow after the program performs its actions.
- Rectangles with the upper-right corners folded over are called notes in the UML. Notes are explanatory remarks that describe the purpose of symbols in the diagram. A dotted line connects each note with the element that the note describes.

- A diamond or decision symbol in an activity diagram indicates that a decision is to be made. The workflow will continue along a path determined by the symbol's associated guard conditions, which can be true or false. Each transition arrow emerging from a decision symbol has a guard condition (specified in square brackets next to the transition arrow). If a guard condition is true, the workflow enters the action state to which the transition arrow points.

- A diamond in an activity diagram also represents the merge symbol, which joins two flows of activity into one. A merge symbol has two or more transition arrows pointing to the diamond and only one transition arrow pointing from the diamond, to indicate multiple activity flows merging to continue the activity.

- Top-down, stepwise refinement is a process for refining pseudocode by maintaining a complete representation of the program during each refinement.

- There are three types of control structures—sequence, selection and repetition.

- The sequence structure is built into C++—by default, statements execute in the order they appear.

- A selection structure chooses among alternative courses of action.

Section 4.5 *if Selection Statement*
- The if single-selection statement either performs (selects) an action if a condition is true, or skips the action if the condition is false.

Section 4.6 *if...else Double-Selection Statement*
- The if...else double-selection statement performs (selects) an action if a condition is true and performs a different action if the condition is false.

- To include several statements in an if's body (or the body of an else for an if...else statement), enclose the statements in braces ({ and }). A set of statements contained within a pair of braces is called a block. A block can be placed anywhere in a program that a single statement can be placed.

- A null statement, indicating that no action is to be taken, is indicated by a semicolon (;).

Section 4.7 *while Repetition Statement*
- A repetition statement repeats an action while some condition remains true.

- A value that contains a fractional part is referred to as a floating-point number and is represented approximately by data types such as float and double.

Section 4.8 *Formulating Algorithms: Counter-Controlled Repetition*
- Counter-controlled repetition is used when the number of repetitions is known before a loop begins executing, i.e., when there is definite repetition.

- The unary cast operator static_cast can be used to create a temporary floating-point copy of its operand.

- Unary operators take only one operand; binary operators take two.

- The parameterized stream manipulator setprecision indicates the number of digits of precision that should be displayed to the right of the decimal point.

- The stream manipulator fixed indicates that floating-point values should be output in so-called fixed-point format, as opposed to scientific notation.

Section 4.9 *Formulating Algorithms: Sentinel-Controlled Repetition*
- Sentinel-controlled repetition is used when the number of repetitions is not known before a loop begins executing, i.e., when there is indefinite repetition.

Section 4.10 Formulating Algorithms: Nested Control Statements
- A nested control statement appears in the body of another control statement.

Section 4.11 Assignment Operators
- C++ provides the arithmetic assignment operators +=, -=, *=, /= and %= for abbreviating assignment expressions.

Section 4.12 Increment and Decrement Operators
- The increment operator, ++, and the decrement operator, --, increment or decrement a variable by 1, respectively. If the operator is prefixed to the variable, the variable is incremented or decremented by 1 first, then its new value is used in the expression in which it appears. If the operator is postfixed to the variable, the variable is first used in the expression in which it appears, then the variable's value is incremented or decremented by 1.

Terminology

action
action expression
action state
action state symbol
action/decision model of programming
activity diagram
addition assignment operator (+=)
algorithm
approximation of floating-point numbers
arithmetic assignment operators
arrow symbol
assignment operators
associate from left to right
associate from right to left
averaging calculation
binary arithmetic operator
block
"bombing"
bool fundamental type
cast operator
compound statement
conditional expression
conditional operator (?:)
control statement
control-statement nesting
control-statement stacking
counter
counter-controlled repetition
"crashing"
dangling-else problem
decision symbol
decrement operator (--)
default precision
definite repetition
diamond symbol
divide by zero

dotted line
double data type
double-precision floating-point number
double-selection statement
dummy value
empty statement
executable statement
explicit conversion
fatal logic error
final state
first refinement
fixed-point format
fixed stream manipulator
flag value
float data type
floating-point constant
floating-point number
"garbage" value
goto elimination
goto statement
if...else double-selection statement
implicit conversion
increment operator (++)
indefinite repetition
initial state
integer division
integer promotion
iterating
iterations of a loop
keywords
loop
loop-continuation condition
loop iterations
loop nested within a loop
looping statement
merge symbol

multiple-selection statement	sentinel value
nested control statement	sequence statement
nonparameterized stream manipulator	sequence-statement activity diagram
note in the UML	sequential execution
null statement	setprecision stream manipulator
object-oriented design (OOD)	showpoint stream manipulator
off-by-one error	signal value
operand	single-entry/single-exit control statement
operator precedence	single-selection if statement
order in which actions should execute	single-precision floating-point number
parameterized stream manipulator	small circle symbol
postdecrement	solid circle symbol
postfix decrement operator	static_cast operator
postfix increment operator	stream manipulator
postincrement	structured programming
precision	ternary operator
predecrement	top
prefix decrement operator	top-down, stepwise refinement
prefix increment operator	total
preincrement	transfer of control
procedure	transition
program control	transition arrow symbol
promotion	truncate
pseudocode	unary cast operator
repetition statement	unary minus (-) operator
rounding	unary operator
scientific notation	unary plus (+) operator
second refinement	undefined value
selection statement	while repetition statement
sentinel-controlled repetition	workflow of a portion of a software system

Self-Review Exercises

4.1   Answer each of the following questions.

a) All programs can be written in terms of three types of control structures: _____, _____ and _____.

b) The _____ selection statement is used to execute one action when a condition is true or a different action when that condition is false.

c) Repeating a set of instructions a specific number of times is called _____ repetition.

d) When it is not known in advance how many times a set of statements will be repeated, a(n) _____ value can be used to terminate the repetition.

4.2   Write four different C++ statements that each add 1 to integer variable x.

4.3   Write C++ statements to accomplish each of the following:

a) In one statement, assign the sum of the current value of x and y to z and postincrement the value of x.

b) Determine whether the value of the variable count is greater than 10. If it is, print "Count is greater than 10."

c) Predecrement the variable x by 1, then subtract it from the variable total.

d) Calculate the remainder after q is divided by divisor and assign the result to q. Write this statement two different ways.

4.4   Write C++ statements to accomplish each of the following tasks.
   a) Declare variables sum and x to be of type int.
   b) Set variable x to 1.
   c) Set variable sum to 0.
   d) Add variable x to variable sum and assign the result to variable sum.
   e) Print "The sum is: " followed by the value of variable sum.

4.5   Combine the statements that you wrote in Exercise 4.4 into a program that calculates and prints the sum of the integers from 1 to 10. Use the while statement to loop through the calculation and increment statements. The loop should terminate when the value of x becomes 11.

4.6   State the values of each variable after the calculation is performed. Assume that, when each statement begins executing, all variables have the integer value 5.
   a) product *= x++;
   b) quotient /= ++x;

4.7   Write single C++ statements or portions of statements that do the following:
   a) Input integer variable x with cin and >>.
   b) Input integer variable y with cin and >>.
   c) Set integer variable i to 1.
   d) Set integer variable power to 1.
   e) Multiply variable power by x and assign the result to power.
   f) Preincrement variable i by 1.
   g) Determine whether i is less than or equal to y.
   h) Output integer variable power with cout and <<.

4.8   Write a C++ program that uses the statements in Exercise 4.7 to calculate x raised to the y power. The program should have a while repetition statement.

4.9   Identify and correct the errors in each of the following:
   a) while (c <= 5)
        {
           product *= c;
           ++c;
   b) cin << value;
   c) if (gender == 1)
           cout << "Woman" << endl;
        else;
           cout << "Man" << endl;

4.10   What is wrong with the following while repetition statement?
        while (z >= 0)
           sum += z;

Answers to Self-Review Exercises

4.1   a) Sequence, selection and repetition. b) if...else. c) Counter-controlled or definite.
d) Sentinel, signal, flag or dummy.

4.2   x = x + 1;
        x += 1;
        ++x;
        x++;

4.3   a) z = x++ + y;
        b) if (count > 10)
               cout << "Count is greater than 10" << endl;

    c) total -= --x;
    d) q %= divisor;
        q = q % divisor;

4.4 a) int sum;
         int x;
     b) x = 1;
     c) sum = 0;
     d) sum += x;
         or
         sum = sum + x;
     e) cout << "The sum is: " << sum << endl;

4.5 See the following code:

```
1   // Exercise 4.5 Solution: ex04_05.cpp
2   // Calculate the sum of the integers from 1 to 10.
3   #include <iostream>
4   using std::cout;
5   using std::endl;
6
7   int main()
8   {
9      int sum; // stores sum of integers 1 to 10
10     int x; // counter
11
12     x = 1; // count from 1
13     sum = 0; // initialize sum
14
15     while ( x <= 10 ) // loop 10 times
16     {
17        sum += x; // add x to sum
18        ++x; // increment x
19     } // end while
20
21     cout << "The sum is: " << sum << endl;
22     return 0; // indicate successful termination
23  } // end main
```

```
The sum is: 55
```

4.6 a) product = 25, x = 6;
     b) quotient = 0, x = 6;

```
1   // Exercise 4.6 Solution: ex04_06.cpp
2   // Calculate the value of product and quotient.
3   #include <iostream>
4   using std::cout;
5   using std::endl;
6
7   int main()
8   {
9      int x = 5;
10     int product = 5;
11     int quotient = 5;
12
13     // part a
14     product *= x++; // part a statement
```

```
15        cout << "Value of product after calculation: " << product << endl;
16        cout << "Value of x after calculation: " << x << endl << endl;
17
18        // part b
19        x = 5; // reset value of x
20        quotient /= ++x; // part b statement
21        cout << "Value of quotient after calculation: " << quotient << endl;
22        cout << "Value of x after calculation: " << x << endl << endl;
23        return 0; // indicate successful termination
24    } // end main
```

```
Value of product after calculation: 25
Value of x after calculation: 6

Value of quotient after calculation: 0
Value of x after calculation: 6
```

4.7   a) cin >> x;
       b) cin >> y;
       c) i = 1;
       d) power = 1;
       e) power *= x;
           or
           power = power * x;
       f) ++i;
       g) if (i <= y)
       h) cout << power << endl;

4.8   See the following code:

```
1    // Exercise 4.8 Solution: ex04_08.cpp
2    // Raise x to the y power.
3    #include <iostream>
4    using std::cout;
5    using std::cin;
6    using std::endl;
7
8    int main()
9    {
10       int x; // base
11       int y; // exponent
12       int i; // counts from 1 to y
13       int power; // used to calculate x raised to power y
14
15       i = 1; // initialize i to begin counting from 1
16       power = 1; // initialize power
17
18       cout << "Enter base as an integer: ";  // prompt for base
19       cin >> x; // input base
20
21       cout << "Enter exponent as an integer: "; // prompt for exponent
22       cin >> y; // input exponent
23
24       // count from 1 to y and multiply power by x each time
25       while ( i <= y )
26       {
```

```
27          power *= x;
28          ++i;
29      } // end while
30
31      cout << power << endl; // display result
32      return 0; // indicate successful termination
33  } // end main
```

```
Enter base as an integer: 2
Enter exponent as an integer: 3
8
```

4.9   a) *Error:* Missing the closing right brace of the while body.
           Correction: Add closing right brace after the statement c++;.
       b) *Error:* Used stream insertion instead of stream extraction.
           Correction: Change << to >>.
       c) *Error:* Semicolon after else results in a logic error. The second output statement will
           always be executed.
           Correction: Remove the semicolon after else.

4.10   The value of the variable z is never changed in the while statement. Therefore, if the loop-
continuation condition (z >= 0) is initially true, an infinite loop is created. To prevent the infinite
loop, z must be decremented so that it eventually becomes less than 0.

Exercises

4.11   Identify and correct the error(s) in each of the following:

```
a)  if ( age >= 65 );
        cout << "Age is greater than or equal to 65" << endl;
    else
        cout << "Age is less than 65 << endl";
b)  if ( age >= 65 )
        cout << "Age is greater than or equal to 65" << endl;
    else;
        cout << "Age is less than 65 << endl";
c)  int x = 1, total;

    while ( x <= 10 )
    {
       total += x;
       ++x;
    }
d)  While ( x <= 100 )
        total += x;
        ++x;
e)  while ( y > 0 )
    {
        cout << y << endl;
        ++y;
    }
```

4.12   What does the following program print?

```
1   // Exercise 4.12: ex04_12.cpp
2   // What does this program print?
3   #include <iostream>
4   using std::cout;
5   using std::endl;
6
7   int main()
8   {
9       int y; // declare y
10      int x = 1; // initialize x
11      int total = 0; // initialize total
12
13      while ( x <= 10 ) // loop 10 times
14      {
15          y = x * x; // perform calculation
16          cout << y << endl; // output result
17          total += y; // add y to total
18          x++; // increment counter x
19      } // end while
20
21      cout << "Total is " << total << endl; // display result
22      return 0; // indicate successful termination
23  } // end main
```

For Exercises 4.13–4.16, perform each of these steps:

   a) Read the problem statement.
   b) Formulate the algorithm using pseudocode and top-down, stepwise refinement.
   c) Write a C++ program.
   d) Test, debug and execute the C++ program.

4.13   Drivers are concerned with the mileage obtained by their automobiles. One driver has kept track of several tankfuls of gasoline by recording miles driven and gallons used for each tankful. Develop a C++ program that uses a while statement to input the miles driven and gallons used for each tankful. The program should calculate and display the miles per gallon obtained for each tankful and print the combined miles per gallon obtained for all tankfuls up to this point.

```
Enter the miles used (-1 to quit): 287
Enter gallons: 13
MPG this tankful: 22.076923
Total MPG: 22.076923

Enter the miles used (-1 to quit): 200
Enter gallons: 10
MPG this tankful: 20.000000
Total MPG: 21.173913

Enter the miles used (-1 to quit): 120
Enter gallons: 5
MPG this tankful: 24.000000
Total MPG: 21.678571

Enter miles (-1 to quit): -1
```

4.14   Develop a C++ program that will determine whether a department-store customer has exceeded the credit limit on a charge account. For each customer, the following facts are available:
   a) Account number (an integer)
   b) Balance at the beginning of the month

c) Total of all items charged by this customer this month
d) Total of all credits applied to this customer's account this month
e) Allowed credit limit

The program should use a `while` statement to input each of these facts, calculate the new balance (= beginning balance + charges – credits) and determine whether the new balance exceeds the customer's credit limit. For those customers whose credit limit is exceeded, the program should display the customer's account number, credit limit, new balance and the message "Credit Limit Exceeded."

```
Enter account number (or -1 to quit): 100
Enter beginning balance: 5394.78
Enter total charges: 1000.00
Enter total credits: 500.00
Enter credit limit: 5500.00
New balance is 5894.78
Account:      100
Credit limit: 5500.00
Balance:      5894.78
Credit Limit Exceeded.

Enter Account Number (or -1 to quit): 200
Enter beginning balance: 1000.00
Enter total charges: 123.45
Enter total credits: 321.00
Enter credit limit: 1500.00
New balance is 802.45

Enter Account Number (or -1 to quit): 300
Enter beginning balance: 500.00
Enter total charges: 274.73
Enter total credits: 100.00
Enter credit limit: 800.00
New balance is 674.73

Enter Account Number (or -1 to quit): -1
```

4.15   One large chemical company pays its salespeople on a commission basis. The salespeople each receive $200 per week plus 9 percent of their gross sales for that week. For example, a salesperson who sells $5000 worth of chemicals in a week receives $200 plus 9 percent of $5000, or a total of $650. Develop a C++ program that uses a `while` statement to input each salesperson's gross sales for last week and calculates and displays that salesperson's earnings. Process one salesperson's figures at a time.

```
Enter sales in dollars (-1 to end): 5000.00
Salary is: $650.00

Enter sales in dollars (-1 to end): 6000.00
Salary is: $740.00

Enter sales in dollars (-1 to end): 7000.00
Salary is: $830.00

Enter sales in dollars (-1 to end): -1
```

4.16   Develop a C++ program that uses a `while` statement to determine the gross pay for each of several employees. The company pays "straight time" for the first 40 hours worked by each employee and pays "time-and-a-half" for all hours worked in excess of 40 hours. You are given a list of the employees of the company, the number of hours each employee worked last week and the hourly rate of each employee. Your program should input this information for each employee and should determine and display the employee's gross pay.

```
Enter hours worked (-1 to end): 39
Enter hourly rate of the employee ($00.00): 10.00
Salary is $390.00

Enter hours worked (-1 to end): 40
Enter hourly rate of the employee ($00.00): 10.00
Salary is $400.00

Enter hours worked (-1 to end): 41
Enter hourly rate of the employee ($00.00): 10.00
Salary is $415.00

Enter hours worked (-1 to end): -1
```

4.17 The process of finding the largest number (i.e., the maximum of a group of numbers) is used frequently in computer applications. For example, a program that determines the winner of a sales contest inputs the number of units sold by each salesperson. The salesperson who sells the most units wins the contest. Write a pseudocode program, then a C++ program that uses a while statement to determine and print the largest number of 10 numbers input by the user. Your program should use three variables, as follows:

counter: A counter to count to 10 (i.e., to keep track of how many numbers have been input and to determine when all 10 numbers have been processed).
number: The current number input to the program.
largest: The largest number found so far.

4.18 Write a C++ program that uses a while statement and the tab escape sequence \t to print the following table of values:

N	10*N	100*N	1000*N
1	10	100	1000
2	20	200	2000
3	30	300	3000
4	40	400	4000
5	50	500	5000

4.19 Using an approach similar to that in Exercise 4.17, find the *two* largest values among the 10 numbers. [*Note:* You must input each number only once.]

4.20 The examination-results program of Fig. 4.16–Fig. 4.18 assumes that any value input by the user that is not a 1 must be a 2. Modify the application to validate its inputs. On any input, if the value entered is other than 1 or 2, keep looping until the user enters a correct value.

4.21 What does the following program print?

```
1   // Exercise 4.21: ex04_21.cpp
2   // What does this program print?
3   #include <iostream>
4   using std::cout;
5   using std::endl;
6
7   int main()
8   {
9      int count = 1; // initialize count
10
11     while ( count <= 10 ) // loop 10 times
12     {
```

```
13        // output line of text
14        cout << ( count % 2 ? "*****" : "++++++++" ) << endl;
15        ++count; // increment count
16     } // end while
17
18     return 0; // indicate successful termination
19  } // end main
```

4.22   What does the following program print?

```
1   // Exercise 4.22: ex04_22.cpp
2   // What does this program print?
3   #include <iostream>
4   using std::cout;
5   using std::endl;
6
7   int main()
8   {
9      int row = 10; // initialize row
10     int column; // declare column
11
12     while ( row >= 1 ) // loop until row < 1
13     {
14        column = 1; // set column to 1 as iteration begins
15
16        while ( column <= 10 ) // loop 10 times
17        {
18           cout << ( row % 2 ? "<" : ">" ); // output
19           ++column; // increment column
20        } // end inner while
21
22        --row; // decrement row
23        cout << endl; // begin new output line
24     } // end outer while
25
26     return 0; // indicate successful termination
27  } // end main
```

4.23   *(Dangling-else Problem)* State the output for each of the following when x is 9 and y is 11 and when x is 11 and y is 9. Note that the compiler ignores the indentation in a C++ program. The C++ compiler always associates an else with the previous if unless told to do otherwise by the placement of braces {}. On first glance, you may not be sure which if and else match, so this is referred to as the "dangling-else" problem. We eliminated the indentation from the following code to make the problem more challenging. [*Hint:* Apply indentation conventions you have learned.]

   a) `if ( x < 10 )`
      `if ( y > 10 )`
      `cout << "*****" << endl;`
      `else`
      `cout << "#####" << endl;`
      `cout << "$$$$$" << endl;`

   b) `if ( x < 10 )`
      `{`
      `if ( y > 10 )`
      `cout << "*****" << endl;`
      `}`

```
else
{
cout << "#####" << endl;
cout << "$$$$$" << endl;
}
```

4.24   *(Another Dangling-else Problem)* Modify the following code to produce the output shown. Use proper indentation techniques. You must not make any changes other than inserting braces. The compiler ignores indentation in a C++ program. We eliminated the indentation from the following code to make the problem more challenging. [*Note:* It is possible that no modification is necessary.]

```
if ( y == 8 )
if ( x == 5 )
cout << "@@@@@" << endl;
else
cout << "#####" << endl;
cout << "$$$$$" << endl;
cout << "&&&&&" << endl;
```

a) Assuming x = 5 and y = 8, the following output is produced.

```
@@@@@
$$$$$
&&&&&
```

b) Assuming x = 5 and y = 8, the following output is produced.

```
@@@@@
```

c) Assuming x = 5 and y = 8, the following output is produced.

```
@@@@@
&&&&&
```

d) Assuming x = 5 and y = 7, the following output is produced. [*Note:* The last three output statements after the else are all part of a block.]

```
#####
$$$$$
&&&&&
```

4.25   Write a program that reads in the size of the side of a square then prints a hollow square of that size out of asterisks and blanks. Your program should work for squares of all side sizes between 1 and 20. For example, if your program reads a size of 5, it should print

```
*****
*   *
*   *
*   *
*****
```

4.26   A palindrome is a number or a text phrase that reads the same backward as forward. For example, each of the following five-digit integers is a palindrome: 12321, 55555, 45554 and 11611. Write a program that reads in a five-digit integer and determines whether it is a palindrome. [*Hint:* Use the division and modulus operators to separate the number into its individual digits.]

4.27   Input an integer containing only 0s and 1s (i.e., a "binary" integer) and print its decimal equivalent. Use the modulus and division operators to pick off the "binary" number's digits one at a time from right to left. Much as in the decimal number system, where the rightmost digit has a positional value of 1, the next digit left has a positional value of 10, then 100, then 1000, and so on, in the binary number system the rightmost digit has a positional value of 1, the next digit left has a positional value of 2, then 4, then 8, and so on. Thus the decimal number 234 can be interpreted as 2 * 100 + 3 * 10 + 4 * 1. The decimal equivalent of binary 1101 is 1 * 1 + 0 * 2 + 1 * 4 + 1 * 8 or 1 + 0 + 4 + 8, or 13. [*Note:* To learn more about binary numbers, refer to Appendix D.]

4.28   Write a program that displays the checkerboard pattern shown below. Your program must use only three output statements, one of each of the following forms:

```
cout << "* ";
cout << ' ';
cout << endl;
```

```
* * * * * * * *
 * * * * * * * *
* * * * * * * *
 * * * * * * * *
* * * * * * * *
 * * * * * * * *
* * * * * * * *
 * * * * * * * *
```

4.29   Write a program that prints the powers of the integer 2, namely 2, 4, 8, 16, 32, 64, etc. Your `while` loop should not terminate (i.e., you should create an infinite loop). To do this, simply use the keyword `true` as the expression for the `while` statement. What happens when you run this program?

4.30   Write a program that reads the radius of a circle (as a `double` value) and computes and prints the diameter, the circumference and the area. Use the value 3.14159 for π.

4.31   What is wrong with the following statement? Provide the correct statement to accomplish what the programmer was probably trying to do.

```
cout << ++( x + y );
```

4.32   Write a program that reads three nonzero `double` values and determines and prints whether they could represent the sides of a triangle.

4.33   Write a program that reads three nonzero integers and determines and prints whether they could be the sides of a right triangle.

4.34   *(Cryptography)* A company wants to transmit data over the telephone but is concerned that its phones could be tapped. All of the data is transmitted as four-digit integers. The company has asked you to write a program that encrypts the data so that it can be transmitted more securely. Your program should read a four-digit integer and encrypt it as follows: Replace each digit by *(the sum of that digit plus 7) modulus 10*. Then, swap the first digit with the third, swap the second digit with the fourth and print the encrypted integer. Write a separate program that inputs an encrypted four-digit integer and decrypts it to form the original number.

4.35   The factorial of a nonnegative integer n is written $n!$ (pronounced "n factorial") and is defined as follows:

$n! = n \cdot (n-1) \cdot (n-2) \cdot \ldots \cdot 1$ (for values of n greater than 1)

and

$n! = 1$ (for $n = 0$ or $n = 1$).

For example, $5! = 5 \cdot 4 \cdot 3 \cdot 2 \cdot 1$, which is 120. Use while statements in each of the following:

a) Write a program that reads a nonnegative integer and computes and prints its factorial.

b) Write a program that estimates the value of the mathematical constant e by using the formula:

$$e = 1 + \frac{1}{1!} + \frac{1}{2!} + \frac{1}{3!} + \ldots$$

Prompt the user for the desired accuracy of e (i.e., the number of terms in the summation).

c) Write a program that computes the value of e^x by using the formula

$$e^x = 1 + \frac{x}{1!} + \frac{x^2}{2!} + \frac{x^3}{3!} + \ldots$$

Prompt the user for the desired accuracy of e (i.e., the number of terms in the summation).

4.36   [*Note:* This exercise corresponds to Section 4.13, a portion of our Software Engineering Case Study.] Describe in 200 words or fewer what an automobile is and does. List the nouns and verbs separately. In the text, we stated that each noun might correspond to an object that will need to be built to implement a system, in this case a car. Pick five of the objects you listed, and, for each, list several attributes and several behaviors. Describe briefly how these objects interact with one another and other objects in your description. You have just performed several of the key steps in a typical object-oriented design.

5

Control Statements: Part 2

Not everything that can be counted counts, and not every thing that counts can be counted.
—Albert Einstein

Who can control his fate?
—William Shakespeare

The used key is always bright.
—Benjamin Franklin

Intelligence ... is the faculty of making artificial objects, especially tools to make tools.
—Henri Bergson

Every advantage in the past is judged in the light of the final issue.
—Demosthenes

OBJECTIVES

In this chapter you'll learn:

- The essentials of counter-controlled repetition.
- To use the `for` and `do...while` repetition statements to execute statements in a program repeatedly.
- To implement multiple selection using the `switch` selection statement.
- To use the `break` and `continue` program control statements to alter the flow of control.
- To use the logical operators to form complex conditional expressions in control statements.
- To avoid the consequences of confusing the equality and assignment operators.

5.1   Introduction

Chapter 4 began our introduction to the types of building blocks that are available for problem solving. We used those building blocks to employ proven program construction techniques. In this chapter, we continue our presentation of the theory and principles of structured programming by introducing C++'s remaining control statements. The control statements we study here and in Chapter 4 will help us in building and manipulating objects. We continue our early emphasis on object-oriented programming that began with a discussion of basic concepts in Chapter 1 and extensive object-oriented code examples and exercises in Chapters 3–4.

In this chapter, we demonstrate the for, do...while and switch statements. Through a series of short examples using while and for, we explore the essentials of counter-controlled repetition. We devote a portion of the chapter to expanding the GradeBook class presented in Chapters 3–4. In particular, we create a version of class GradeBook that uses a switch statement to count the number of A, B, C, D and F grades in a set of letter grades entered by the user. We introduce the break and continue program control statements. We discuss the logical operators, which enable you to use more powerful conditional expressions in control statements. We also examine the common error of confusing the equality (==) and assignment (=) operators, and how to avoid it. Finally, we summarize C++'s control statements and the proven problem-solving techniques presented in this chapter and Chapter 4.

5.2   Essentials of Counter-Controlled Repetition

This section uses the while repetition statement introduced in Chapter 4 to formalize the elements required to perform counter-controlled repetition. Counter-controlled repetition requires

1. the name of a control variable (or loop counter)
2. the initial value of the control variable

3. the loop-continuation condition that tests for the final value of the control variable (i.e., whether looping should continue)

4. the increment (or decrement) by which the control variable is modified each
time through the loop.

Consider the simple program in Fig. 5.1, which prints the numbers from 1 to 10. The
declaration in line 9 *names* the control variable (counter), declares it to be an integer,
reserves space for it in memory and sets it to an *initial value* of 1. Declarations that require
initialization are, in effect, executable statements. In C++, it is more precise to call a declaration that also reserves memory—as the preceding declaration does—a definition.
Because definitions are declarations, too, we'll use the term "declaration" except when the
distinction is important.

The declaration and initialization of counter (line 9) also could have been accomplished with the statements

```
int counter; // declare control variable
counter = 1; // initialize control variable to 1
```

We use both methods of initializing variables.

Line 14 *increments* the loop counter by 1 each time the loop's body is performed. The
loop-continuation condition (line 11) in the while statement determines whether the
value of the control variable is less than or equal to 10 (the final value for which the condition is true). Note that the body of this while executes even when the control variable
is 10. The loop terminates when the control variable is greater than 10 (i.e., when counter
becomes 11).

```
1   // Fig. 5.1: fig05_01.cpp
2   // Counter-controlled repetition.
3   #include <iostream>
4   using std::cout;
5   using std::endl;
6
7   int main()
8   {
9      int counter = 1; // declare and initialize control variable
10
11     while ( counter <= 10 ) // loop-continuation condition
12     {
13        cout << counter << " ";
14        counter++; // increment control variable by 1
15     } // end while
16
17     cout << endl; // output a newline
18     return 0; // successful termination
19  } // end main
```

```
1 2 3 4 5 6 7 8 9 10
```

Fig. 5.1 | Counter-controlled repetition.

Figure 5.1 can be made more concise by initializing counter to 0 and by replacing the while statement with

```
while ( ++counter <= 10 ) // loop-continuation condition
    cout << counter << " ";
```

This code saves a statement, because the incrementing is done directly in the while condition before the condition is tested. Also, the code eliminates the braces around the body of the while, because the while now contains only one statement. Coding in such a condensed fashion takes some practice and can lead to programs that are more difficult to read, debug, modify and maintain.

Common Programming Error 5.1

Floating-point values are approximate, so controlling counting loops with floating-point variables can result in imprecise counter values and inaccurate tests for termination.

Error-Prevention Tip 5.1

Control counting loops with integer values.

Good Programming Practice 5.1

Put a blank line before and after each control statement to make it stand out in the program.

Good Programming Practice 5.2

Too many levels of nesting can make a program difficult to understand. As a rule, try to avoid using more than three levels of indentation.

Good Programming Practice 5.3

Vertical spacing above and below control statements and indentation of the bodies of control statements within the control statement headers give programs a two-dimensional appearance that greatly improves readability.

5.3 for Repetition Statement

Section 5.2 presented the essentials of counter-controlled repetition. The while statement can be used to implement any counter-controlled loop. C++ also provides the for repetition statement, which specifies the counter-controlled repetition details in a single line of code. To illustrate the power of for, let us rewrite the program of Fig. 5.1. The result is shown in Fig. 5.2.

When the for statement (lines 11–12) begins executing, the control variable counter is declared and initialized to 1. Then, the loop-continuation condition (line 11 between the semicolons) counter <= 10 is checked. The initial value of counter is 1, so the condition is satisfied and the body statement (line 12) prints the value of counter, namely 1. Then, the expression counter++ increments control variable counter and the loop begins again with the loop-continuation test. The control variable is now equal to 2, so the final value is not exceeded and the program performs the body statement again. This process continues until the loop body has executed 10 times and the control variable counter is incremented to 11—this causes the loop-continuation test to fail and repetition to terminate. The program continues by performing the first statement after the for statement (in this case, the output statement in line 14).

```
 1   // Fig. 5.2: fig05_02.cpp
 2   // Counter-controlled repetition with the for statement.
 3   #include <iostream>
 4   using std::cout;
 5   using std::endl;
 6
 7   int main()
 8   {
 9      // for statement header includes initialization,
10      // loop-continuation condition and increment.
11      for ( int counter = 1; counter <= 10; counter++ )
12         cout << counter << " ";
13
14      cout << endl; // output a newline
15      return 0; // indicate successful termination
16   } // end main
```

```
1 2 3 4 5 6 7 8 9 10
```

Fig. 5.2 | Counter-controlled repetition with the for statement.

for Statement Header Components

Figure 5.3 takes a closer look at the for statement header (line 11) of Fig. 5.2. Notice that the for statement header "does it all"—it specifies each of the items needed for counter-controlled repetition with a control variable. If there is more than one statement in the body of the for, braces are required to enclose the body of the loop.

Notice that Fig. 5.2 uses the loop-continuation condition counter <= 10. If you incorrectly wrote counter < 10, then the loop would execute only 9 times. This is a common off-by-one error.

 Common Programming Error 5.2

Using an incorrect relational operator or using an incorrect final value of a loop counter in the condition of a while or for statement can cause off-by-one errors.

Fig. 5.3 | for statement header components.

Good Programming Practice 5.4

Using the final value in the condition of a while *or* for *statement and using the* <= *relational operator will help avoid off-by-one errors. For a loop used to print the values 1 to 10, for example, the loop-continuation condition should be* counter <= 10 *rather than* counter < 10 *(which is an off-by-one error) or* counter < 11 *(which is nevertheless correct). Many programmers prefer so-called zero-based counting, in which, to count 10 times through the loop,* counter *would be initialized to zero and the loop-continuation test would be* counter < 10.

The general form of the **for** statement is

```
for ( initialization; loopContinuationCondition; increment )
    statement
```

where the *initialization* expression initializes the loop's control variable, *loopContinuation-Condition* determines whether the loop should continue executing (this condition typically contains the final value of the control variable for which the condition is true) and *increment* increments the control variable. In most cases, the **for** statement can be represented by an equivalent **while** statement, as follows:

```
initialization;

while ( loopContinuationCondition )
{
    statement
    increment;
}
```

There is an exception to this rule, which we'll discuss in Section 5.7.

If the *initialization* expression in the **for** statement header declares the control variable (i.e., the control variable's type is specified before the variable name), the control variable can be used only in the body of the **for** statement—the control variable will be unknown outside the **for** statement. This restricted use of the control variable name is known as the variable's scope. The scope of a variable specifies where it can be used in a program. Scope is discussed in detail in Chapter 6, Functions and an Introduction to Recursion.

Common Programming Error 5.3

When the control variable of a for *statement is declared in the initialization section of the* for *statement header, using the control variable after the body of the statement is a compilation error.*

Portability Tip 5.1

In the C++ standard, the scope of the control variable declared in the initialization section of a for *statement differs from the scope in older C++ compilers. In prestandard compilers, the scope of the control variable does not terminate at the end of the block defining the body of the* for *statement; rather, the scope terminates at the end of the block that encloses the* for *statement. C++ code created with prestandard C++ compilers can break when compiled on standard-compliant compilers. If you are working with prestandard compilers and you want to be sure your code will work with standard-compliant compilers, there are two defensive programming strategies you can use: either declare control variables with different names in every* for *statement, or, if you prefer to use the same name for the control variable in several* for *statements, declare the control variable before the first* for *statement.*

As we'll see, the *initialization* and *increment* expressions can be comma-separated lists of expressions. The commas, as used in these expressions, are comma operators, which guarantee that lists of expressions evaluate from left to right. The comma operator has the lowest precedence of all C++ operators. The value and type of a comma-separated list of expressions is the value and type of the rightmost expression in the list. The comma operator is most often used in for statements. Its primary application is to enable you to use multiple initialization expressions and/or multiple increment expressions. For example, there may be several control variables in a single for statement that must be initialized and incremented.

Good Programming Practice 5.5

Place only expressions involving the control variables in the initialization and increment sections of a for statement. Manipulations of other variables should appear either before the loop (if they should execute only once, like initialization statements) or in the loop body (if they should execute once per repetition, like incrementing or decrementing statements).

The three expressions in the for statement header are optional (but the two semicolon separators are required). If the *loopContinuationCondition* is omitted, C++ assumes that the condition is true, thus creating an infinite loop. One might omit the *initialization* expression if the control variable is initialized earlier in the program. One might omit the *increment* expression if the increment is calculated by statements in the body of the for or if no increment is needed. The increment expression in the for statement acts as a stand-alone statement at the end of the body of the for. Therefore, the expressions

```
counter = counter + 1
counter += 1
++counter
counter++
```

are all equivalent in the incrementing portion of the for statement (when no other code appears there). Many programmers prefer the form counter++, because for loops evaluate the increment expression after the loop body executes. The postincrementing form therefore seems more natural. The variable being incremented here does not appear in a larger expression, so both preincrementing and postincrementing actually have the same effect.

Common Programming Error 5.4

Using commas instead of the two required semicolons in a for header is a syntax error.

Common Programming Error 5.5

Placing a semicolon immediately to the right of the right parenthesis of a for header makes the body of that for statement an empty statement. This is usually a logic error.

The initialization, loop-continuation condition and increment expressions of a for statement can contain arithmetic expressions. For example, if x = 2 and y = 10, and x and y are not modified in the loop body, the for header

```
for ( int j = x; j <= 4 * x * y; j += y / x )
```

is equivalent to

```
for ( int j = 2; j <= 80; j += 5 )
```

The "increment" of a for statement can be negative, in which case it is really a decrement and the loop actually counts downward (as shown in Section 5.4).

If the loop-continuation condition is initially false, the body of the for statement is not performed. Instead, execution proceeds with the statement following the for.

Frequently, the control variable is printed or used in calculations in the body of a for statement, but this is not required. It is common to use the control variable for controlling repetition while never mentioning it in the body of the for statement.

Error-Prevention Tip 5.2

Although the value of the control variable can be changed in the body of a for statement, avoid doing so, because this practice can lead to subtle logic errors.

for Statement UML Activity Diagram

The for statement's UML activity diagram is similar to that of the while statement (Fig. 4.6). Figure 5.4 shows the activity diagram of the for statement in Fig. 5.2. The diagram makes it clear that initialization occurs once before the loop-continuation test is evaluated the first time, and that incrementing occurs each time through the loop *after* the body statement executes. Note that (besides an initial state, transition arrows, a merge, a final state and several notes) the diagram contains only action states and a decision. Imagine, again, that you have a bin of empty for statement UML activity diagrams—as many as you might need to stack and nest with the activity diagrams of other control statements to form a structured implementation of an algorithm. You fill in the action states and decision symbols with action expressions and guard conditions appropriate to the algorithm.

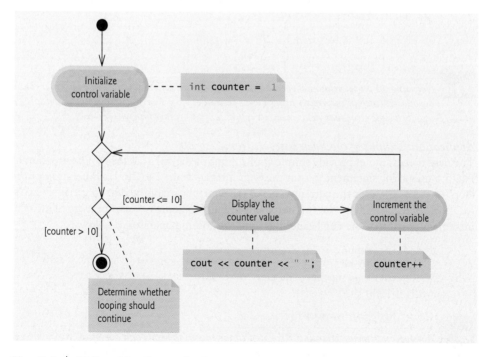

Fig. 5.4 | UML activity diagram for the for statement in Fig. 5.2.

5.4 Examples Using the for Statement

The following examples show methods of varying the control variable in a for statement. In each case, we write the appropriate for statement header. Note the change in the relational operator for loops that decrement the control variable.

a) Vary the control variable from 1 to 100 in increments of 1.

```
for ( int i = 1; i <= 100; i++ )
```

b) Vary the control variable from 100 down to 1 in increments of -1 (that is, decrements of 1).

```
for ( int i = 100; i >= 1; i-- )
```

c) Vary the control variable from 7 to 77 in steps of 7.

```
for ( int i = 7; i <= 77; i += 7 )
```

d) Vary the control variable from 20 down to 2 in steps of -2.

```
for ( int i = 20; i >= 2; i -= 2 )
```

e) Vary the control variable over the following sequence of values: 2, 5, 8, 11, 14, 17, 20.

```
for ( int i = 2; i <= 20; i += 3 )
```

f) Vary the control variable over the following sequence of values: 99, 88, 77, 66, 55, 44, 33, 22, 11, 0.

```
for ( int i = 99; i >= 0; i -= 11 )
```

 Common Programming Error 5.6

Not using the proper relational operator in the loop-continuation condition of a loop that counts downward (such as incorrectly using i <= 1 instead of i >= 1 in a loop counting down to 1) is usually a logic error that yields incorrect results when the program runs.

Application: Summing the Even Integers from 2 to 20

The next two examples provide simple applications of the for statement. The program of Fig. 5.5 uses a for statement to sum the even integers from 2 to 20. Each iteration of the loop (lines 12–13) adds the current value of the control variable number to variable total.

Note that the body of the for statement in Fig. 5.5 actually could be merged into the increment portion of the for header by using the comma operator as follows:

```
for ( int number = 2; // initialization
      number <= 20; // loop continuation condition
      total += number, number += 2 ) // total and increment
   ; // empty body
```

 Good Programming Practice 5.6

Although statements preceding a for and statements in the body of a for often can be merged into the for header, doing so can make the program more difficult to read, maintain, modify and debug.

```
 1   // Fig. 5.5: fig05_05.cpp
 2   // Summing integers with the for statement.
 3   #include <iostream>
 4   using std::cout;
 5   using std::endl;
 6
 7   int main()
 8   {
 9      int total = 0; // initialize total
10
11      // total even integers from 2 through 20
12      for ( int number = 2; number <= 20; number += 2 )
13         total += number;
14
15      cout << "Sum is " << total << endl; // display results
16      return 0; // successful termination
17   } // end main
```

```
Sum is 110
```

Fig. 5.5 | Summing integers with the for statement.

Good Programming Practice 5.7

Limit the size of control statement headers to a single line, if possible.

Application: Compound Interest Calculations

The next example computes compound interest using a for statement. Consider the following problem statement:

> A person invests $1000.00 in a savings account yielding 5 percent interest. Assuming that all interest is left on deposit in the account, calculate and print the amount of money in the account at the end of each year for 10 years. Use the following formula for determining these amounts:
>
> $a = p (1 + r)^n$
>
> where
>
> p *is the original amount invested (i.e., the principal)*,
> r *is the annual interest rate*,
> n *is the number of years and*
> a *is the amount on deposit at the end of the nth year.*

This problem involves a loop that performs the indicated calculation for each of the 10 years the money remains on deposit. The solution is shown in Fig. 5.6.

The for statement (lines 28–35) executes its body 10 times, varying a control variable from 1 to 10 in increments of 1. C++ does not include an exponentiation operator, so we use the standard library function pow (line 31) for this purpose. The function pow(x, y) calculates the value of x raised to the yth power. In this example, the algebraic expression $(1 + r)^n$ is written as pow(1.0 + rate, year), where variable rate represents *r* and variable year represents *n*. Function pow takes two arguments of type double and returns a double value.

```cpp
// Fig. 5.6: fig05_06.cpp
// Compound interest calculations with for.
#include <iostream>
using std::cout;
using std::endl;
using std::fixed;

#include <iomanip>
using std::setw; // enables program to set a field width
using std::setprecision;

#include <cmath> // standard C++ math library
using std::pow; // enables program to use function pow

int main()
{
   double amount; // amount on deposit at end of each year
   double principal = 1000.0; // initial amount before interest
   double rate = .05; // interest rate

   // display headers
   cout << "Year" << setw( 21 ) << "Amount on deposit" << endl;

   // set floating-point number format
   cout << fixed << setprecision( 2 );

   // calculate amount on deposit for each of ten years
   for ( int year = 1; year <= 10; year++ )
   {
      // calculate new amount for specified year
      amount = principal * pow( 1.0 + rate, year );

      // display the year and the amount
      cout << setw( 4 ) << year << setw( 21 ) << amount << endl;
   } // end for

   return 0; // indicate successful termination
} // end main
```

```
Year    Amount on deposit
   1          1050.00
   2          1102.50
   3          1157.63
   4          1215.51
   5          1276.28
   6          1340.10
   7          1407.10
   8          1477.46
   9          1551.33
  10          1628.89
```

Fig. 5.6 | Compound interest calculations with for.

This program will not compile without including header file <cmath> (line 12). Function pow requires two double arguments. Note that year is an integer. Header <cmath> includes information that tells the compiler to convert the value of year to a temporary double representation before calling the function. This information is contained in pow's function prototype. Chapter 6 summarizes other math library functions.

Common Programming Error 5.7

In general, forgetting to include the appropriate header file when using standard library functions (e.g., <cmath> in a program that uses math library functions) is a compilation error.

A Caution about Using Type **float** or **double** for Monetary Amounts

Notice that lines 17–19 declare the double variables amount, principal and rate. We did this for simplicity because we're dealing with fractional parts of dollars, and we need a type that allows decimal points in its values. Unfortunately, this can cause trouble. Here is a simple explanation of what can go wrong when using float or double to represent dollar amounts (assuming setprecision(2) is used to specify two digits of precision when printing): Two dollar amounts stored in the machine could be 14.234 (which prints as 14.23) and 18.673 (which prints as 18.67). When these amounts are added, they produce the internal sum 32.907, which prints as 32.91. Thus your printout could appear as

```
  14.23
+ 18.67
-------
  32.91
```

but a person adding the individual numbers as printed would expect the sum 32.90! You have been warned!

Good Programming Practice 5.8

Do not use variables of type float or double to perform monetary calculations. The imprecision of floating-point numbers can cause errors that result in incorrect monetary values. In the exercises, we explore the use of integers to perform monetary calculations. [Note: Some third-party vendors sell C++ class libraries that perform precise monetary calculations.]

Using Stream Manipulators to Format Numeric Output

The output statement in line 25 before the for loop and the output statement in line 34 in the for loop combine to print the values of the variables year and amount with the formatting specified by the parameterized stream manipulators setprecision and setw and the nonparameterized stream manipulator fixed. The stream manipulator setw(4) specifies that the next value output should appear in a field width of 4—i.e., cout prints the value with at least 4 character positions. If the value to be output is less than 4 character positions wide, the value is right justified in the field by default. If the value to be output is more than 4 character positions wide, the field width is extended to accommodate the entire value. To indicate that values should be output left justified, simply output nonparameterized stream manipulator left (found in header <iostream>). Right justification can be restored by outputting nonparameterized stream manipulator right.

The other formatting in the output statements indicates that variable amount is printed as a fixed-point value with a decimal point (specified in line 25 with the stream manipulator fixed) right justified in a field of 21 character positions (specified in line 34 with setw(21)) and two digits of precision to the right of the decimal point (specified in line 25 with manipulator setprecision(2)). We applied the stream manipulators fixed and setprecision to the output stream (i.e., cout) before the for loop because these format settings remain in effect until they are changed—such settings are called sticky settings and they do not need to be applied during each iteration of the loop. However, the field width specified with setw applies only to the next value output. We discuss C++'s powerful input/output formatting capabilities in Chapter 15, Stream Input/Output.

Note that the calculation 1.0 + rate, which appears as an argument to the pow function, is contained in the body of the for statement. In fact, this calculation produces the same result during each iteration of the loop, so repeating it is wasteful—it should be performed once before the loop.

Performance Tip 5.1

Avoid placing expressions whose values do not change inside loops—but, even if you do, many of today's sophisticated optimizing compilers will automatically place such expressions outside the loops in the generated machine-language code.

Performance Tip 5.2

Many compilers contain optimization features that improve the performance of the code you write, but it is still better to write good code from the start.

Be sure to try our Peter Minuit problem in Exercise 5.29. This problem demonstrates the wonders of compound interest.

5.5 do...while Repetition Statement

The do...while repetition statement is similar to the while statement. In the while statement, the loop-continuation condition test occurs at the beginning of the loop before the body of the loop executes. The do...while statement tests the loop-continuation condition *after* the loop body executes; therefore, the loop body always executes at least once. When a do...while terminates, execution continues with the statement after the while clause. Note that it is not necessary to use braces in the do...while statement if there is only one statement in the body; however, most programmers include the braces to avoid confusion between the while and do...while statements. For example,

```
while ( condition )
```

normally is regarded as the header of a while statement. A do...while with no braces around the single statement body appears as

```
do
    statement
while ( condition );
```

which can be confusing. You might misinterpret the last line—while(condition);—as a while statement containing as its body an empty statement. Thus, the do...while with one statement often is written as follows to avoid confusion:

```
do
{
    statement
} while ( condition );
```

Good Programming Practice 5.9

Always including braces in a do...while statement helps eliminate ambiguity between the while statement and the do...while statement containing one statement.

Figure 5.7 uses a do...while statement to print the numbers 1–10. Upon entering the do...while statement, line 13 outputs counter's value and line 14 increments counter. Then the program evaluates the loop-continuation test at the bottom of the loop (line 15). If the condition is true, the loop continues from the first body statement in the do...while (line 13). If the condition is false, the loop terminates and the program continues with the next statement after the loop (line 17).

```cpp
1   // Fig. 5.7: fig05_07.cpp
2   // do...while repetition statement.
3   #include <iostream>
4   using std::cout;
5   using std::endl;
6
7   int main()
8   {
9      int counter = 1; // initialize counter
10
11     do
12     {
13        cout << counter << " "; // display counter
14        counter++; // increment counter
15     } while ( counter <= 10 ); // end do...while
16
17     cout << endl; // output a newline
18     return 0; // indicate successful termination
19  } // end main
```

```
1 2 3 4 5 6 7 8 9 10
```

Fig. 5.7 | do...while repetition statement.

do...while *Statement UML Activity Diagram*

Figure 5.8 contains the UML activity diagram for the do...while statement. This diagram makes it clear that the loop-continuation condition is not evaluated until after the loop performs the loop-body action states at least once. Compare this activity diagram with that of the while statement (Fig. 4.6). Again, note that (besides an initial state, transition arrows, a merge, a final state and several notes) the diagram contains only action states and a decision. Imagine, again, that you have access to a bin of empty do...while statement UML activity diagrams—as many as you might need to stack and nest with the activity diagrams of other control statements to form a structured implementation of an algorithm. You fill in the action states and decision symbols with action expressions and guard conditions appropriate to the algorithm.

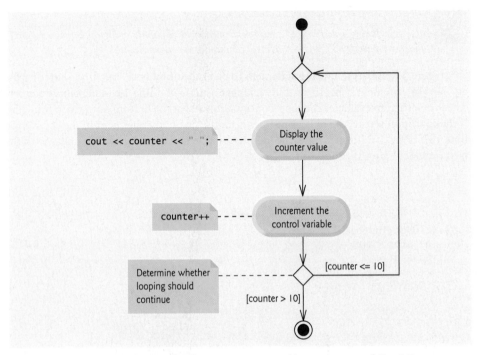

Fig. 5.8 | UML activity diagram for the do...while repetition statement of Fig. 5.7.

5.6 switch Multiple-Selection Statement

We discussed the if single-selection statement and the if...else double-selection statement in Chapter 4. C++ provides the switch multiple-selection statement to perform many different actions based on the possible values of a variable or expression. Each action is associated with the value of a constant integral expression (i.e., any combination of character constants and integer constants that evaluates to a constant integer value) to which the variable or expression may evaluate.

GradeBook* Class with switch *Statement to Count A, B, C, D and F Grades

We now present an enhanced version of the GradeBook class introduced in Chapter 3 and further developed in Chapter 4. The new version of the class asks the user to enter a set of letter grades, then displays a summary of the number of students who received each grade. The class uses a switch to determine whether each grade entered is an A, B, C, D or F and to increment the appropriate grade counter. Class GradeBook is defined in Fig. 5.9, and its member-function definitions appear in Fig. 5.10. Figure 5.11 shows sample inputs and outputs of the main program that uses class GradeBook to process a set of grades.

Like earlier versions of the class definition, the GradeBook class definition (Fig. 5.9) contains function prototypes for member functions setCourseName (line 13), getCourse-Name (line 14) and displayMessage (line 15), as well as the class's constructor (line 12). The class definition also declares private data member courseName (line 19).

Class GradeBook (Fig. 5.9) now contains five additional private data members (lines 20–24)—counter variables for each grade category (i.e., A, B, C, D and F). The class also

```
 1   // Fig. 5.9: GradeBook.h
 2   // Definition of class GradeBook that counts A, B, C, D and F grades.
 3   // Member functions are defined in GradeBook.cpp
 4
 5   #include <string> // program uses C++ standard string class
 6   using std::string;
 7
 8   // GradeBook class definition
 9   class GradeBook
10   {
11   public:
12      GradeBook( string ); // constructor initializes course name
13      void setCourseName( string ); // function to set the course name
14      string getCourseName(); // function to retrieve the course name
15      void displayMessage(); // display a welcome message
16      void inputGrades(); // input arbitrary number of grades from user
17      void displayGradeReport(); // display a report based on the grades
18   private:
19      string courseName; // course name for this GradeBook
20      int aCount; // count of A grades
21      int bCount; // count of B grades
22      int cCount; // count of C grades
23      int dCount; // count of D grades
24      int fCount; // count of F grades
25   }; // end class GradeBook
```

Fig. 5.9 | GradeBook class definition.

contains two additional public member functions—inputGrades and displayGradeReport. Member function inputGrades (declared in line 16) reads an arbitrary number of letter grades from the user using sentinel-controlled repetition and updates the appropriate grade counter for each grade entered. Member function displayGradeReport (declared in line 17) outputs a report containing the number of students who received each letter grade.

Source-code file GradeBook.cpp (Fig. 5.10) contains the member-function definitions for class GradeBook. Notice that lines 16–20 in the constructor initialize the five grade counters to 0—when a GradeBook object is first created, no grades have been entered yet. As you'll soon see, these counters are incremented in member function inputGrades as the user enters grades. The definitions of member functions setCourseName, getCourseName and displayMessage are identical to those found in the earlier versions of class GradeBook. Let's consider the new GradeBook member functions in detail.

```
 1   // Fig. 5.10: GradeBook.cpp
 2   // Member-function definitions for class GradeBook that
 3   // uses a switch statement to count A, B, C, D and F grades.
 4   #include <iostream>
 5   using std::cout;
 6   using std::cin;
 7   using std::endl;
```

Fig. 5.10 | GradeBook class uses switch statement to count letter grades A, B, C, D and F.
(Part 1 of 4.)

```
8
9   #include "GradeBook.h" // include definition of class GradeBook
10
11  // constructor initializes courseName with string supplied as argument;
12  // initializes counter data members to 0
13  GradeBook::GradeBook( string name )
14  {
15      setCourseName( name ); // validate and store courseName
16      aCount = 0; // initialize count of A grades to 0
17      bCount = 0; // initialize count of B grades to 0
18      cCount = 0; // initialize count of C grades to 0
19      dCount = 0; // initialize count of D grades to 0
20      fCount = 0; // initialize count of F grades to 0
21  } // end GradeBook constructor
22
23  // function to set the course name; limits name to 25 or fewer characters
24  void GradeBook::setCourseName( string name )
25  {
26      if ( name.length() <= 25 ) // if name has 25 or fewer characters
27          courseName = name; // store the course name in the object
28      else // if name is longer than 25 characters
29      { // set courseName to first 25 characters of parameter name
30          courseName = name.substr( 0, 25 ); // select first 25 characters
31          cout << "Name \"" << name << "\" exceeds maximum length (25).\n"
32              << "Limiting courseName to first 25 characters.\n" << endl;
33      } // end if...else
34  } // end function setCourseName
35
36  // function to retrieve the course name
37  string GradeBook::getCourseName()
38  {
39      return courseName;
40  } // end function getCourseName
41
42  // display a welcome message to the GradeBook user
43  void GradeBook::displayMessage()
44  {
45      // this statement calls getCourseName to get the
46      // name of the course this GradeBook represents
47      cout << "Welcome to the grade book for\n" << getCourseName() << "!\n"
48          << endl;
49  } // end function displayMessage
50
51  // input arbitrary number of grades from user; update grade counter
52  void GradeBook::inputGrades()
53  {
54      int grade; // grade entered by user
55
56      cout << "Enter the letter grades." << endl
57          << "Enter the EOF character to end input." << endl;
58
```

Fig. 5.10 | GradeBook class uses `switch` statement to count letter grades A, B, C, D and F. (Part 2 of 4.)

```
59      // loop until user types end-of-file key sequence
60      while ( ( grade = cin.get() ) != EOF )
61      {
62          // determine which grade was entered
63          switch ( grade ) // switch statement nested in while
64          {
65              case 'A': // grade was uppercase A
66              case 'a': // or lowercase a
67                  aCount++; // increment aCount
68                  break; // necessary to exit switch
69
70              case 'B': // grade was uppercase B
71              case 'b': // or lowercase b
72                  bCount++; // increment bCount
73                  break; // exit switch
74
75              case 'C': // grade was uppercase C
76              case 'c': // or lowercase c
77                  cCount++; // increment cCount
78                  break; // exit switch
79
80              case 'D': // grade was uppercase D
81              case 'd': // or lowercase d
82                  dCount++; // increment dCount
83                  break; // exit switch
84
85              case 'F': // grade was uppercase F
86              case 'f': // or lowercase f
87                  fCount++; // increment fCount
88                  break; // exit switch
89
90              case '\n': // ignore newlines,
91              case '\t': // tabs,
92              case ' ': // and spaces in input
93                  break; // exit switch
94
95              default: // catch all other characters
96                  cout << "Incorrect letter grade entered."
97                      << " Enter a new grade." << endl;
98                  break; // optional; will exit switch anyway
99          } // end switch
100     } // end while
101 } // end function inputGrades
102
103 // display a report based on the grades entered by user
104 void GradeBook::displayGradeReport()
105 {
106     // output summary of results
107     cout << "\n\nNumber of students who received each letter grade:"
108         << "\nA: " << aCount // display number of A grades
109         << "\nB: " << bCount // display number of B grades
```

Fig. 5.10 | GradeBook class uses switch statement to count letter grades A, B, C, D and F. (Part 3 of 4.)

```
110            << "\nC: " << cCount // display number of C grades
111            << "\nD: " << dCount // display number of D grades
112            << "\nF: " << fCount // display number of F grades
113            << endl;
114  } // end function displayGradeReport
```

Fig. 5.10 | GradeBook class uses switch statement to count letter grades A, B, C, D and F. (Part 4 of 4.)

Reading Character Input

The user enters letter grades for a course in member function inputGrades (lines 52–101). Inside the while header, in line 60, the parenthesized assignment (grade = cin.get()) executes first. The cin.get() function reads one character from the keyboard and stores that character in integer variable grade (declared in line 54). Characters normally are stored in variables of type char; however, characters can be stored in any integer data type, because types short, int and long are guaranteed to be at least as big as type char. Thus, we can treat a character either as an integer or as a character, depending on its use. For example, the statement

```
cout << "The character (" << 'a' << ") has the value "
   << static_cast< int > ( 'a' ) << endl;
```

prints the character a and its integer value as follows:

```
The character (a) has the value 97
```

The integer 97 is the character's numerical representation in the computer. Most computers today use the ASCII (American Standard Code for Information Interchange) character set, in which 97 represents the lowercase letter 'a'. A table of the ASCII characters and their decimal equivalents is presented in Appendix B, ASCII Character Set.

Assignment statements as a whole have the value that is assigned to the variable on the left side of the =. Thus, the value of the assignment expression grade = cin.get() is the same as the value returned by cin.get() and assigned to the variable grade.

The fact that assignment expressions have values can be useful for assigning the same value to several variables. For example,

```
a = b = c = 0;
```

first evaluates the assignment c = 0 (because the = operator associates from right to left). The variable b is then assigned the value of the assignment c = 0 (which is 0). Then, the variable a is assigned the value of the assignment b = (c = 0) (which is also 0). In the program, the value of the assignment grade = cin.get() is compared with the value of EOF (a symbol whose acronym stands for "end-of-file"). We use EOF (which normally has the value –1) as the sentinel value. *However, you do not type the value –1, nor do you type the letters EOF as the sentinel value.* Rather, you type a system-dependent keystroke combination that means "end-of-file" to indicate that you have no more data to enter. EOF is a symbolic integer constant defined in the <iostream> header file. If the value assigned to grade is equal to EOF, the while loop (lines 60–100) terminates. We have chosen to represent the characters entered into this program as ints, because EOF has type int.

On UNIX/Linux systems and many others, end-of-file is entered by typing

<Ctrl> d

on a line by itself. This notation means to press and hold down the *Ctrl* key, then press the *d* key. On other systems such as Microsoft Windows, end-of-file can be entered by typing

<Ctrl> z

[*Note:* In some cases, you must press *Enter* after the preceding key sequence. Also, the characters ^Z sometimes appear on the screen to represent end-of-file, as shown in Fig. 5.11.]

Portability Tip 5.2

The keystroke combinations for entering end-of-file are system dependent.

Portability Tip 5.3

Testing for the symbolic constant EOF rather than –1 makes programs more portable. The ANSI/ ISO C standard, from which C++ adopts the definition of EOF, states that EOF is a negative integral value (but not necessarily –1), so EOF could have different values on different systems.

In this program, the user enters grades at the keyboard. When the user presses the *Enter* (or *Return*) key, the characters are read by the cin.get() function, one character at a time. If the character entered is not end-of-file, the flow of control enters the switch statement (lines 63–99), which increments the appropriate letter-grade counter based on the grade entered.

switch *Statement Details*

The switch statement consists of a series of case labels and an optional default case. These are used in this example to determine which counter to increment, based on a grade. When the flow of control reaches the switch, the program evaluates the expression in the parentheses (i.e., grade) following keyword switch (line 63). This is called the controlling expression. The switch statement compares the value of the controlling expression with each case label. Assume the user enters the letter C as a grade. The program compares C to each case in the switch. If a match occurs (case 'C': in line 75), the program executes the statements for that case. For the letter C, line 77 increments cCount by 1. The break statement (line 78) causes program control to proceed with the first statement after the switch—in this program, control transfers to line 100. This line marks the end of the body of the while loop that inputs grades (lines 60–100), so control flows to the while's condition (line 60) to determine whether the loop should continue executing.

The cases in our switch explicitly test for the lowercase and uppercase versions of the letters A, B, C, D and F. Note the cases in lines 65–66 that test for the values 'A' and 'a' (both of which represent the grade A). Listing cases consecutively in this manner with no statements between them enables the cases to perform the same set of statements—when the controlling expression evaluates to either 'A' or 'a', the statements in lines 67–68 will execute. Note that each case can have multiple statements. The switch selection statement differs from other control statements in that it does not require braces around multiple statements in each case.

Without break statements, each time a match occurs in the switch, the statements for that case and subsequent cases execute until a break statement or the end of the `switch` is encountered. This is often referred to as "falling through" to the statements in subsequent `cases`. (This feature is perfect for writing a concise program that displays the iterative song "The Twelve Days of Christmas" in Exercise 5.28.)

Common Programming Error 5.8

Forgetting a `break` statement when one is needed in a `switch` statement is a logic error.

Common Programming Error 5.9

Omitting the space between the word `case` and the integral value being tested in a `switch` statement can cause a logic error. For example, writing `case3:` instead of `case 3:` simply creates an unused label. We'll say more about this in Appendix E, C Legacy Code Topics. In this situation, the `switch` statement will not perform the appropriate actions when the `switch`'s controlling expression has a value of 3.

Providing a `default` Case

If no match occurs between the controlling expression's value and a `case` label, the default case (lines 95–98) executes. We use the `default` case in this example to process all controlling-expression values that are neither valid grades nor newline, tab or space characters (we discuss how the program handles these white-space characters shortly). If no match occurs, the `default` case executes, and lines 96–97 print an error message indicating that an incorrect letter grade was entered. If no match occurs in a `switch` statement that does not contain a `default` case, program control simply continues with the first statement after the `switch`.

Good Programming Practice 5.10

Provide a `default` case in `switch` statements. Cases not explicitly tested in a `switch` statement without a `default` case are ignored. Including a `default` case focuses you on the need to process exceptional conditions. There are situations in which no `default` processing is needed. Although the `case` clauses and the `default` case clause in a `switch` statement can occur in any order, it is common practice to place the `default` clause last.

Good Programming Practice 5.11

The last `case` in a `switch` statement does not require a `break` statement. Some programmers include this `break` for clarity and for symmetry with other cases.

Ignoring Newline, Tab and Blank Characters in Input

Note that lines 90–93 in the `switch` statement of Fig. 5.10 cause the program to skip newline, tab and blank characters. Reading characters one at a time can cause some problems. To have the program read the characters, we must send them to the computer by pressing the *Enter* key on the keyboard. This places a newline character in the input after the character we wish to process. Often, this newline character must be specially processed to make the program work correctly. By including the preceding `cases` in our `switch` statement, we prevent the error message in the `default` case from being printed each time a newline, tab or space is encountered in the input.

Common Programming Error 5.10

Not processing newline and other white-space characters in the input when reading characters one at a time can cause logic errors.

Testing Class GradeBook

Figure 5.11 creates a GradeBook object (line 9). Line 11 invokes the its displayMessage member function to output a welcome message to the user. Line 12 invokes member function object's inputGrades to read a set of grades from the user and keep track of how many students received each grade. Note that the output window in Fig. 5.11 shows an error message displayed in response to entering an invalid grade (i.e., E). Line 13 invokes Grade-Book member function displayGradeReport (defined in lines 104–114 of Fig. 5.10), which outputs a report based on the grades entered (as in the output in Fig. 5.11).

```cpp
 1   // Fig. 5.11: fig05_11.cpp
 2   // Create GradeBook object, input grades and display grade report.
 3
 4   #include "GradeBook.h" // include definition of class GradeBook
 5
 6   int main()
 7   {
 8      // create GradeBook object
 9      GradeBook myGradeBook( "CS101 C++ Programming" );
10
11      myGradeBook.displayMessage(); // display welcome message
12      myGradeBook.inputGrades(); // read grades from user
13      myGradeBook.displayGradeReport(); // display report based on grades
14      return 0; // indicate successful termination
15   } // end main
```

```
Welcome to the grade book for
CS101 C++ Programming!

Enter the letter grades.
Enter the EOF character to end input.
a
B
c
C
A
d
f
C
E
Incorrect letter grade entered. Enter a new grade.
D
A
b
^Z


Number of students who received each letter grade:
A: 3
B: 2
C: 3
D: 2
F: 1
```

Fig. 5.11 | Creating a GradeBook object and calling its member functions.

switch Statement UML Activity Diagram

Figure 5.12 shows the UML activity diagram for the general switch multiple-selection statement. Most switch statements use a break in each case to terminate the switch statement after processing the case. Figure 5.12 emphasizes this by including break statements in the activity diagram. Without the break statement, control would not transfer to the first statement after the switch statement after a case is processed. Instead, control would transfer to the next case's actions.

The diagram makes it clear that the break statement at the end of a case causes control to exit the switch statement immediately. Again, note that (besides an initial state, transition arrows, a final state and several notes) the diagram contains action states and decisions. Also, note that the diagram uses merge symbols to merge the transitions from the break statements to the final state.

Imagine, again, that you have a bin of empty switch statement UML activity diagrams—as many as you might need to stack and nest with the activity diagrams of other control statements to form a structured implementation of an algorithm. You fill in the action states and decision symbols with action expressions and guard conditions appropriate to the algorithm. Note that, although nested control statements are common, it is rare to find nested switch statements in a program.

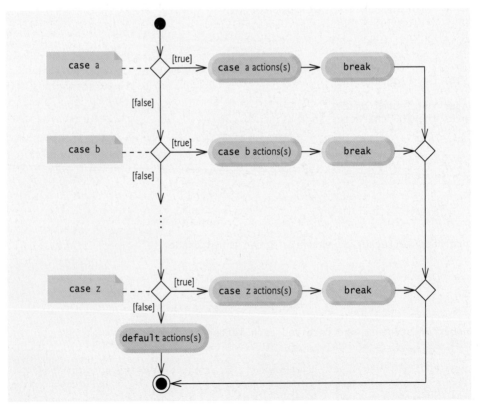

Fig. 5.12 | switch multiple-selection statement UML activity diagram with break statements.

When using the switch statement, remember that each case can be used to test only a *constant* integral expression—any combination of character constants and integer constants that evaluates to a constant integer value. A character constant is represented as the specific character in single quotes, such as 'A'. An integer constant is simply an integer value. Also, each case label can specify only one constant integral expression.

Common Programming Error 5.11

Specifying a nonconstant integral expression in a switch statement's case label is a syntax error.

Common Programming Error 5.12

Providing identical case labels in a switch statement is a compilation error. Providing case labels containing different expressions that evaluate to the same value also is a compilation error. For example, placing case 4 + 1: and case 3 + 2: in the same switch statement is a compilation error, because these are both equivalent to case 5:.

In Chapter 13, we present a more elegant way to implement switch logic. We'll use a technique called polymorphism to create programs that are often clearer, more concise, easier to maintain and easier to extend than programs that use switch logic.

Notes on Data Types

C++ has flexible data type sizes (see Appendix C, Fundamental Types). Different applications, for example, might need integers of different sizes. C++ provides several data types to represent integers. The range of integer values for each type depends on the particular computer's hardware. In addition to the types int and char, C++ provides the types short (an abbreviation of short int) and long (an abbreviation of long int). The minimum range of values for short integers is –32,768 to 32,767. For the vast majority of integer calculations, long integers are sufficient. The minimum range of values for long integers is –2,147,483,648 to 2,147,483,647. On most computers, ints are equivalent either to short or to long. The range of values for an int is at least the same as that for short integers and no larger than that for long integers. The data type char can be used to represent any of the characters in the computer's character set. It also can be used to represent small integers.

Portability Tip 5.4

Because ints can vary in size between systems, use long integers if you expect to process integers outside the range –32,768 to 32,767 and you would like to run the program on several different computer systems.

Performance Tip 5.3

If memory is at a premium, it might be desirable to use smaller integer sizes.

Performance Tip 5.4

Using smaller integer sizes can result in a slower program if the machine's instructions for manipulating them are not as efficient as those for the natural-size integers—i.e., integers whose size equals the machine's word size (e.g., 32 bits on a 32-bit machine, 64 bits on a 64-bit machine). Always test proposed efficiency "upgrades" to be sure they really improve performance.

5.7 break and continue Statements

In addition to the selection and repetition statements, C++ provides statements break and continue to alter the flow of control. The preceding section showed how break can be used to terminate a switch statement's execution. This section discusses how to use break in a repetition statement.

break *Statement*

The break statement, when executed in a while, for, do...while or switch statement, causes immediate exit from that statement. Program execution continues with the next statement. Common uses of the break statement are to escape early from a loop or to skip the remainder of a switch statement (as in Fig. 5.10). Figure 5.13 demonstrates the break statement (line 14) exiting a for repetition statement.

When the if statement detects that count is 5, the break statement executes. This terminates the for statement, and the program proceeds to line 19 (immediately after the for statement), which displays a message indicating the control variable value that terminated the loop. The for statement fully executes its body only four times instead of 10. Note that the control variable count is defined outside the for statement header, so that we can use the control variable both in the loop's body and after the loop completes its execution.

```cpp
1   // Fig. 5.13: fig05_13.cpp
2   // break statement exiting a for statement.
3   #include <iostream>
4   using std::cout;
5   using std::endl;
6
7   int main()
8   {
9      int count; // control variable also used after loop terminates
10
11     for ( count = 1; count <= 10; count++ ) // loop 10 times
12     {
13        if ( count == 5 )
14           break; // break loop only if x is 5
15
16        cout << count << " ";
17     } // end for
18
19     cout << "\nBroke out of loop at count = " << count << endl;
20     return 0; // indicate successful termination
21  } // end main
```

```
1 2 3 4
Broke out of loop at count = 5
```

Fig. 5.13 | break statement exiting a for statement.

continue *Statement*

The continue statement, when executed in a while, for or do...while statement, skips the remaining statements in the body of that statement and proceeds with the next iteration of the loop. In while and do...while statements, the loop-continuation test evaluates immediately after the continue statement executes. In the for statement, the increment expression executes, then the loop-continuation test evaluates.

Figure 5.14 uses the continue statement (line 12) in a for statement to skip the output statement (line 14) when the nested if (lines 11–12) determines that the value of count is 5. When the continue statement executes, program control continues with the increment of the control variable in the for header (line 9) and loops five more times.

In Section 5.3, we stated that the while statement could be used in most cases to represent the for statement. The one exception occurs when the increment expression in the while statement follows the continue statement. In this case, the increment does not execute before the program tests the loop-continuation condition, and the while does not execute in the same manner as the for.

Good Programming Practice 5.12

Some programmers feel that break and continue violate structured programming. The effects of these statements can be achieved by structured programming techniques we soon will learn, so these programmers do not use break and continue. Most programmers consider the use of break in switch statements acceptable.

Performance Tip 5.5

The break and continue statements, when used properly, perform faster than do the corresponding structured techniques.

Software Engineering Observation 5.1

There is a tension between achieving quality software engineering and achieving the best-performing software. Often, one of these goals is achieved at the expense of the other. For all but the most performance-intensive situations, apply the following rule of thumb: First, make your code simple and correct; then make it fast and small, but only if necessary.

```cpp
1  // Fig. 5.14: fig05_14.cpp
2  // continue statement terminating an iteration of a for statement.
3  #include <iostream>
4  using std::cout;
5  using std::endl;
6
7  int main()
8  {
9     for ( int count = 1; count <= 10; count++ ) // loop 10 times
10    {
11       if ( count == 5 ) // if count is 5,
12          continue;      // skip remaining code in loop
13
14       cout << count << " ";
15    } // end for
16
17    cout << "\nUsed continue to skip printing 5" << endl;
18    return 0; // indicate successful termination
19 } // end main
```

Fig. 5.14 | continue statement terminating a single iteration of a for statement. (Part 1 of 2.)

```
1 2 3 4 6 7 8 9 10
Used continue to skip printing 5
```

Fig. 5.14 | continue statement terminating a single iteration of a for statement. (Part 2 of 2.)

5.8 Logical Operators

So far we have studied only simple conditions, such as counter <= 10, total > 1000 and number != sentinelValue. We expressed these conditions in terms of the relational operators >, <, >= and <=, and the equality operators == and !=. Each decision tested precisely one condition. To test multiple conditions while making a decision, we performed these tests in separate statements or in nested if or if...else statements.

C++ provides logical operators that are used to form more complex conditions by combining simple conditions. The logical operators are && (logical AND), || (logical OR) and ! (logical NOT, also called logical negation).

Logical AND (&&) Operator

Suppose that we wish to ensure that two conditions are *both* true before we choose a certain path of execution. In this case, we can use the && (logical AND) operator, as follows:

```
if ( gender == 1 && age >= 65 )
    seniorFemales++;
```

This if statement contains two simple conditions. The condition gender == 1 is used here to determine whether a person is a female. The condition age >= 65 determines whether a person is a senior citizen. The simple condition to the left of the && operator evaluates first. If necessary, the simple condition to the right of the && operator evaluates next. As we'll discuss shortly, the right side of a logical AND expression is evaluated only if the left side is true. The if statement then considers the combined condition

```
gender == 1 && age >= 65
```

This condition is true if and only if both of the simple conditions are true. Finally, if this combined condition is indeed true, the statement in the if statement's body increments the count of seniorFemales. If either of the simple conditions is false (or both are), then the program skips the incrementing and proceeds to the statement following the if. The preceding combined condition can be made more readable by adding redundant parentheses:

```
( gender == 1 ) && ( age >= 65 )
```

 Common Programming Error 5.13

Although 3 < x < 7 is a mathematically correct condition, it does not evaluate as you might expect in C++. Use (3 < x && x < 7) to get the proper evaluation in C++.

Figure 5.15 summarizes the && operator. The table shows all four possible combinations of false and true values for *expression1* and *expression2*. Such tables are often called truth tables. C++ evaluates to false or true all expressions that include relational operators, equality operators and/or logical operators.

expression1	expression2	expression1 && expression2
false	false	false
false	true	false
true	false	false
true	true	true

Fig. 5.15 | && (logical AND) operator truth table.

Logical OR (||) Operator

Now let us consider the || (logical OR) operator. Suppose we wish to ensure at some point in a program that either *or* both of two conditions are true before we choose a certain path of execution. In this case, we use the || operator, as in the following program segment:

```
if ( ( semesterAverage >= 90 ) || ( finalExam >= 90 ) )
    cout << "Student grade is A" << endl;
```

This preceding condition also contains two simple conditions. The simple condition semesterAverage >= 90 evaluates to determine whether the student deserves an "A" in the course because of a solid performance throughout the semester. The simple condition finalExam >= 90 evaluates to determine whether the student deserves an "A" in the course because of an outstanding performance on the final exam. The if statement then considers the combined condition

```
( semesterAverage >= 90 ) || ( finalExam >= 90 )
```

and awards the student an "A" if either or both of the simple conditions are true. Note that the message "Student grade is A" prints unless both of the simple conditions are false. Figure 5.16 is a truth table for the logical OR operator (||).

The && operator has a higher precedence than the || operator. Both operators associate from left to right. An expression containing && or || operators evaluates only until the truth or falsehood of the expression is known. Thus, evaluation of the expression

```
( gender == 1 ) && ( age >= 65 )
```

stops immediately if gender is not equal to 1 (i.e., the entire expression is false) and continues if gender is equal to 1 (i.e., the entire expression could still be true if the condition age >= 65 is true). This performance feature for the evaluation of logical AND and logical OR expressions is called short-circuit evaluation.

expression1	expression2	expression1 || expression2
false	false	false
false	true	true
true	false	true
true	true	true

Fig. 5.16 | || (logical OR) operator truth table.

Performance Tip 5.6

In expressions using operator &&, if the separate conditions are independent of one another, make the condition most likely to be false the leftmost condition. In expressions using operator ||, make the condition most likely to be true the leftmost condition. This use of short-circuit evaluation can reduce a program's execution time.

Logical Negation (!) Operator

C++ provides the ! (logical NOT, also called logical negation) operator to enable a programmer to "reverse" the meaning of a condition. Unlike the && and || binary operators, which combine two conditions, the unary logical negation operator has only a single condition as an operand. The unary logical negation operator is placed before a condition when we are interested in choosing a path of execution if the original condition (without the logical negation operator) is false, such as in the following program segment:

```
if ( !( grade == sentinelValue ) )
   cout << "The next grade is " << grade << endl;
```

The parentheses around the condition grade == sentinelValue are needed because the logical negation operator has a higher precedence than the equality operator.

In most cases, you can avoid using logical negation by expressing the condition with an appropriate relational or equality operator. For example, the preceding if statement also can be written as follows:

```
if ( grade != sentinelValue )
   cout << "The next grade is " << grade << endl;
```

This flexibility often can help a programmer express a condition in a more "natural" or convenient manner. Figure 5.17 is a truth table for the logical negation operator (!).

expression	!expression
false	true
true	false

Fig. 5.17 | ! (logical negation) operator truth table.

Logical Operators Example

Figure 5.18 demonstrates the logical operators by producing their truth tables. The output shows each expression that is evaluated and its bool result. By default, bool values true and false are displayed by cout and the stream insertion operator as 1 and 0, respectively. We use stream manipulator boolalpha (a sticky manipulator) in line 11 to specify that the value of each bool expression should be displayed as either the word "true" or the word "false." For example, the result of the expression false && false in line 12 is false, so the second line of output includes the word "false." Lines 11–15 produce the truth table for &&. Lines 18–22 produce the truth table for ||. Lines 25–27 produce the truth table for !.

```
 1   // Fig. 5.18: fig05_18.cpp
 2   // Logical operators.
 3   #include <iostream>
 4   using std::cout;
 5   using std::endl;
 6   using std::boolalpha; // causes bool values to print as "true" or "false"
 7
 8   int main()
 9   {
10      // create truth table for && (logical AND) operator
11      cout << boolalpha << "Logical AND (&&)"
12         << "\nfalse && false: " << ( false && false )
13         << "\nfalse && true: " << ( false && true )
14         << "\ntrue && false: " << ( true && false )
15         << "\ntrue && true: " << ( true && true ) << "\n\n";
16
17      // create truth table for || (logical OR) operator
18      cout << "Logical OR (||)"
19         << "\nfalse || false: " << ( false || false )
20         << "\nfalse || true: " << ( false || true )
21         << "\ntrue || false: " << ( true || false )
22         << "\ntrue || true: " << ( true || true ) << "\n\n";
23
24      // create truth table for ! (logical negation) operator
25      cout << "Logical NOT (!)"
26         << "\n!false: " << ( !false )
27         << "\n!true: " << ( !true ) << endl;
28      return 0; // indicate successful termination
29   } // end main
```

```
Logical AND (&&)
false && false: false
false && true: false
true && false: false
true && true: true

Logical OR (||)
false || false: false
false || true: true
true || false: true
true || true: true

Logical NOT (!)
!false: true
!true: false
```

Fig. 5.18 | Logical operators.

Summary of Operator Precedence and Associativity
Figure 5.19 adds the logical operators to the operator precedence and associativity chart. The operators are shown from top to bottom, in decreasing order of precedence.

Operators						Associativity	Type
::						left to right	scope resolution
()						left to right	parentheses
++	--	static_cast< *type* >()				left to right	unary (postfix)
++	--	+	-	!		right to left	unary (prefix)
*	/	%				left to right	multiplicative
+	-					left to right	additive
<<	>>					left to right	insertion/extraction
<	<=	>	>=			left to right	relational
==	!=					left to right	equality
&&						left to right	logical AND
||						left to right	logical OR
?:						right to left	conditional
=	+=	-=	*=	/=	%=	right to left	assignment
,						left to right	comma

Fig. 5.19 | Operator precedence and associativity.

5.9 Confusing the Equality (==) and Assignment (=) Operators

There is one type of error that C++ programmers, no matter how experienced, tend to make so frequently that we feel it requires a separate section. That error is accidentally swapping the operators == (equality) and = (assignment). What makes these swaps so damaging is the fact that they ordinarily do not cause syntax errors. Rather, statements with these errors tend to compile correctly and the programs run to completion, often generating incorrect results through runtime logic errors. [*Note:* Some compilers issue a warning when = is used in a context where == normally is expected.]

Two aspects of C++ contribute to these problems. One is that any expression that produces a value can be used in the decision portion of any control statement. If the value of the expression is zero, it is treated as `false`, and if the value is nonzero, it is treated as `true`. The second is that assignments produce a value—namely, the value assigned to the variable on the left side of the assignment operator. For example, suppose we intend to write

```
if ( payCode == 4 )
    cout << "You get a bonus!" << endl;
```

but we accidentally write

```
if ( payCode = 4 )
    cout << "You get a bonus!" << endl;
```

The first `if` statement properly awards a bonus to the person whose `payCode` is equal to 4. The second `if` statement—the one with the error—evaluates the assignment expression in the `if` condition to the constant 4. Any nonzero value is interpreted as `true`, so the condition in this `if` statement is always `true` and the person always receives a bonus regardless of what the actual paycode is! Even worse, the paycode has been modified when it was only supposed to be examined!

Common Programming Error 5.14

Using operator == for assignment and using operator = for equality are logic errors.

Error-Prevention Tip 5.3

Programmers normally write conditions such as x == 7 with the variable name on the left and the constant on the right. By reversing these so that the constant is on the left and the variable name is on the right, as in 7 == x, you'll be protected by the compiler if you accidentally replace the == operator with = . The compiler treats this as a compilation error, because you can't change the value of a constant. This will prevent the potential devastation of a runtime logic error.

Variable names are said to be *lvalues* (for "left values") because they can be used on the left side of an assignment operator. Constants are said to be *rvalues* (for "right values") because they can be used on only the right side of an assignment operator. Note that *lvalues* can also be used as *rvalues*, but not vice versa.

There is another equally unpleasant situation. Suppose you want to assign a value to a variable with a simple statement like

    x = 1;

but instead write

    x == 1;

Here, too, this is not a syntax error. Rather, the compiler simply evaluates the conditional expression. If x is equal to 1, the condition is `true` and the expression evaluates to the value `true`. If x is not equal to 1, the condition is `false` and the expression evaluates to the value `false`. Regardless of the expression's value, there is no assignment operator, so the value simply is lost. The value of x remains unaltered, probably causing an execution-time logic error. Unfortunately, we do not have a handy trick available to help you with this problem!

Error-Prevention Tip 5.4

Use your text editor to search for all occurrences of = in your program and check that you have the correct assignment operator or logical operator in each place.

5.10 Structured Programming Summary

Just as architects design buildings by employing the collective wisdom of their profession, so should programmers design programs. Our field is younger than architecture is, and our collective wisdom is considerably sparser. We have learned that structured programming produces programs that are easier than unstructured programs to understand, test, debug, modify, and even prove correct in a mathematical sense.

Figure 5.20 uses activity diagrams to summarize C++'s control statements. The initial and final states indicate the single entry point and the single exit point of each control statement. Arbitrarily connecting individual symbols in an activity diagram can lead to unstructured programs. Therefore, the programming profession uses only a limited set of control statements that can be combined in only two simple ways to build structured programs.

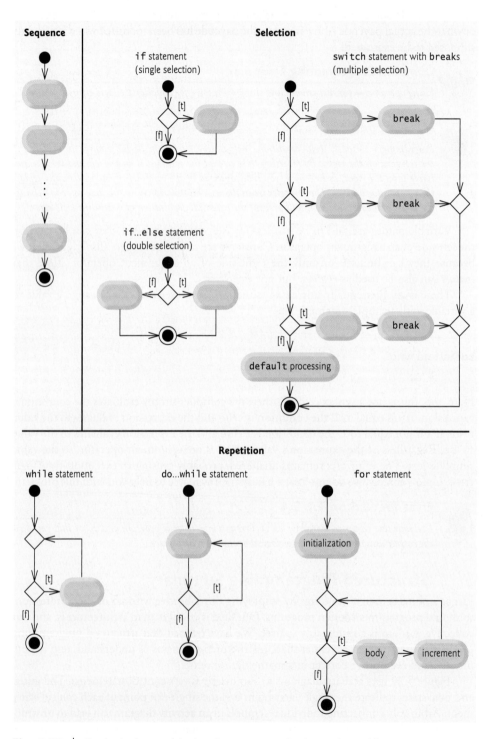

Fig. 5.20 | C++'s single-entry/single-exit sequence, selection and repetition statements.

For simplicity, only single-entry/single-exit control statements are used—there is only one way to enter and only one way to exit each control statement. Connecting control statements in sequence to form structured programs is simple—the final state of one control statement is connected to the initial state of the next—that is, they are placed one after another in a program. We have called this "control-statement stacking." The rules for forming structured programs also allow for control statements to be nested.

Figure 5.21 shows the rules for forming structured programs. The rules assume that action states may be used to indicate any action. The rules also assume that we begin with the so-called simplest activity diagram (Fig. 5.22), consisting of only an initial state, an action state, a final state and transition arrows.

Applying the rules of Fig. 5.21 always results in an activity diagram with a neat, building-block appearance. For example, repeatedly applying Rule 2 to the simplest activity diagram results in an activity diagram containing many action states in sequence (Fig. 5.23). Rule 2 generates a stack of control statements, so let us call Rule 2 the stacking rule. [*Note:* The vertical dashed lines in Fig. 5.23 are not part of the UML. We use them to separate the four activity diagrams that demonstrate Rule 2 of Fig. 5.21 being applied.]

Rule 3 is the nesting rule. Repeatedly applying Rule 3 to the simplest activity diagram results in one with neatly nested control statements. For example, in Fig. 5.24, the action state in the simplest activity diagram is replaced with a double-selection (if...else) statement. Then Rule 3 is applied again to the action states in the double-selection statement, replacing each with a double-selection statement. The dashed action-state symbols around each of the double-selection statements represent an action state that was replaced in the preceding activity diagram. [*Note:* The dashed arrows and dashed action state symbols shown in Fig. 5.24 are not part of the UML. They are used here as pedagogic devices to illustrate that any action state may be replaced with a control statement.]

Rule 4 generates larger, more involved and more deeply nested statements. The diagrams that emerge from applying the rules in Fig. 5.21 constitute the set of all possible activity diagrams and hence the set of all possible structured programs. The beauty of the structured approach is that we use only seven simple single-entry/single-exit control statements and assemble them in only two simple ways.

If the rules in Fig. 5.21 are followed, an activity diagram with illegal syntax (such as that in Fig. 5.25) cannot be created. If you are uncertain about whether a particular diagram is legal, apply the rules of Fig. 5.21 in reverse to reduce the diagram to the simplest activity diagram. If it is reducible to the simplest activity diagram, the original diagram is structured; otherwise, it is not.

Rules for forming structured programs
1) Begin with the "simplest activity diagram" (Fig. 5.22).
2) Any action state can be replaced by two action states in sequence.
3) Any action state can be replaced by any control statement (sequence, if, if...else, switch, while, do...while or for).
4) Rules 2 and 3 can be applied as often as you like and in any order.

Fig. 5.21 | Rules for forming structured programs.

Fig. 5.22 | Simplest activity diagram.

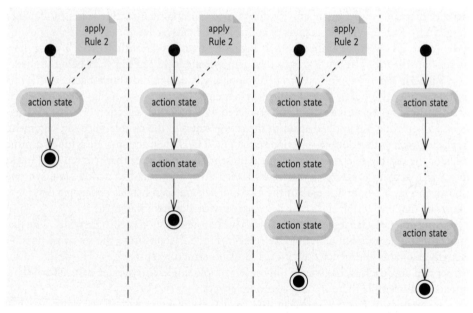

Fig. 5.23 | Repeatedly applying Rule 2 of Fig. 5.21 to the simplest activity diagram.

Structured programming promotes simplicity. Böhm and Jacopini have given us the result that only three forms of control are needed:

- Sequence
- Selection
- Repetition

The sequence structure is trivial. Simply list the statements to execute in the order in which they should execute.

Selection is implemented in one of three ways:

- `if` statement (single selection)
- `if...else` statement (double selection)
- `switch` statement (multiple selection)

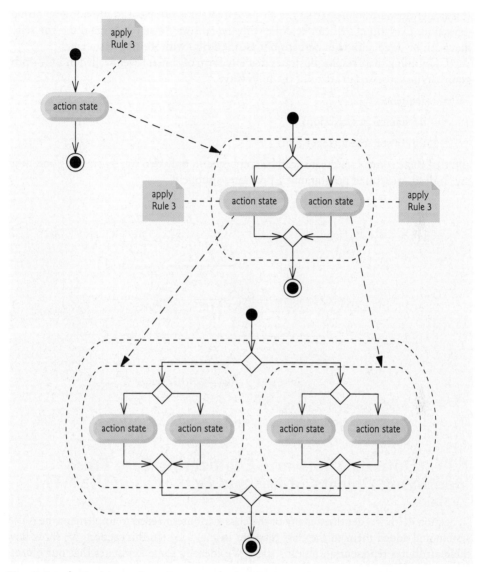

Fig. 5.24 | Applying Rule 3 of Fig. 5.21 to the simplest activity diagram several times.

It is straightforward to prove that the simple `if` statement is sufficient to provide any form of selection—everything that can be done with the `if...else` statement and the `switch` statement can be implemented (although perhaps not as clearly and efficiently) by combining `if` statements.

Repetition is implemented in one of three ways:

- `while` statement
- `do...while` statement
- `for` statement

It is straightforward to prove that the while statement is sufficient to provide any form of repetition. Everything that can be done with the do...while statement and the for statement can be done (although perhaps not as smoothly) with the while statement.

Combining these results illustrates that any form of control ever needed in a C++ program can be expressed in terms of the following:

- sequence
- if statement (selection)
- while statement (repetition)

and that these control statements can be combined in only two ways—stacking and nesting. Indeed, structured programming promotes simplicity.

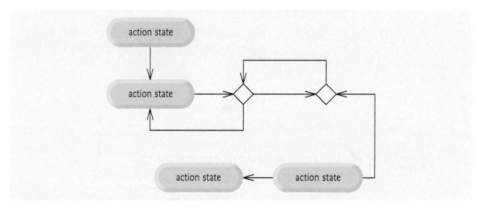

Fig. 5.25 | Activity diagram with illegal syntax.

5.11 (Optional) Software Engineering Case Study: Identifying Objects' States and Activities in the ATM System

In Section 4.13, we identified many of the class attributes needed to implement the ATM system and added them to the class diagram in Fig. 4.24. In this section, we show how these attributes represent an object's state. We identify some key states that our objects may occupy and discuss how objects change state in response to various events occurring in the system. We also discuss the workflow, or activities, that objects perform in the ATM system. We present the activities of BalanceInquiry and Withdrawal transaction objects in this section, as they represent two of the key activities in the ATM system.

State Machine Diagrams

Each object in a system goes through a series of discrete states. An object's current state is indicated by the values of the object's attributes at a given time. State machine diagrams (commonly called state diagrams) model key states of an object and show under what circumstances the object changes state. Unlike the class diagrams presented in earlier case study sections, which focused primarily on the structure of the system, state diagrams model some of the behavior of the system.

Figure 5.26 is a simple state diagram that models some of the states of an object of class ATM. The UML represents each state in a state diagram as a rounded rectangle with the name of the state placed inside it. A solid circle with an attached stick arrowhead designates the initial state. Recall that we modeled this state information as the Boolean attribute userAuthenticated in the class diagram of Fig. 4.24. This attribute is initialized to false, or the "User not authenticated" state, according to the state diagram.

The arrows with stick arrowheads indicate transitions between states. An object can transition from one state to another in response to various events that occur in the system. The name or description of the event that causes a transition is written near the line that corresponds to the transition. For example, the ATM object changes from the "User not authenticated" state to the "User authenticated" state after the database authenticates the user. Recall from the requirements specification that the database authenticates a user by comparing the account number and PIN entered by the user with those of the corresponding account in the database. If the database indicates that the user has entered a valid account number and the correct PIN, the ATM object transitions to the "User authenticated" state and changes its userAuthenticated attribute to a value of true. When the user exits the system by choosing the "exit" option from the main menu, the ATM object returns to the "User not authenticated" state in preparation for the next ATM user.

Software Engineering Observation 5.2

Software designers do not generally create state diagrams showing every possible state and state transition for all attributes—there are simply too many of them. State diagrams typically show only the most important or complex states and state transitions.

Fig. 5.26 | State diagram for the ATM object.

Activity Diagrams

Like a state diagram, an activity diagram models aspects of system behavior. Unlike a state diagram, an activity diagram models an object's workflow (sequence of events) during program execution. An activity diagram models the actions the object will perform and in what order. Recall that we used UML activity diagrams to illustrate the flow of control for the control statements presented in Chapter 4 and this chapter.

The activity diagram in Fig. 5.27 models the actions involved in executing a BalanceInquiry transaction. We assume that a BalanceInquiry object has already been initialized and assigned a valid account number (that of the current user), so the object knows which balance to retrieve. The diagram includes the actions that occur after the user selects a balance inquiry from the main menu and before the ATM returns the user to the main menu—a BalanceInquiry object does not perform or initiate these actions, so we do not model them here. The diagram begins with retrieving the available balance of the user's account from the database. Next, the BalanceInquiry retrieves the total balance of the account. Finally, the transaction displays the balances on the screen. This action completes the execution of the transaction.

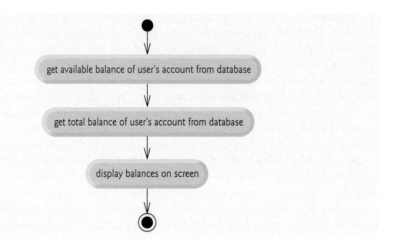

Fig. 5.27 | Activity diagram for a `BalanceInquiry` transaction.

The UML represents an action in an activity diagram as an action state modeled by a rectangle with its left and right sides replaced by arcs curving outward. Each action state contains an action expression—for example, "get available balance of user's account from database"—that specifies an action to be performed. An arrow with a stick arrowhead connects two action states, indicating the order in which the actions represented by the action states occur. The solid circle (at the top of Fig. 5.27) represents the activity's initial state—the beginning of the workflow before the object performs the modeled actions. In this case, the transaction first executes the "get available balance of user's account from database" action expression. Second, the transaction retrieves the total balance. Finally, the transaction displays both balances on the screen. The solid circle enclosed in an open circle (at the bottom of Fig. 5.27) represents the final state—the end of the workflow after the object performs the modeled actions.

Figure 5.28 shows an activity diagram for a `Withdrawal` transaction. We assume that a `Withdrawal` object has been assigned a valid account number. We do not model the user selecting a withdrawal from the main menu or the ATM returning the user to the main menu because these are not actions performed by a `Withdrawal` object. The transaction first displays a menu of standard withdrawal amounts (Fig. 2.17) and an option to cancel the transaction. The transaction then inputs a menu selection from the user. The activity flow now arrives at a decision symbol. This point determines the next action based on the associated guard conditions. If the user cancels the transaction, the system displays an appropriate message. Next, the cancellation flow reaches a merge symbol, where this activity flow joins the transaction's other possible activity flows (which we discuss shortly). Note that a merge can have any number of incoming transition arrows, but only one outgoing transition arrow. The decision at the bottom of the diagram determines whether the transaction should repeat from the beginning. When the user has canceled the transaction, the guard condition "cash dispensed or user canceled transaction" is true, so control transitions to the activity's final state.

If the user selects a withdrawal amount from the menu, the transaction sets `amount` (an attribute of class `Withdrawal` originally modeled in Fig. 4.24) to the value chosen by the user. The transaction next gets the available balance of the user's account (i.e., the

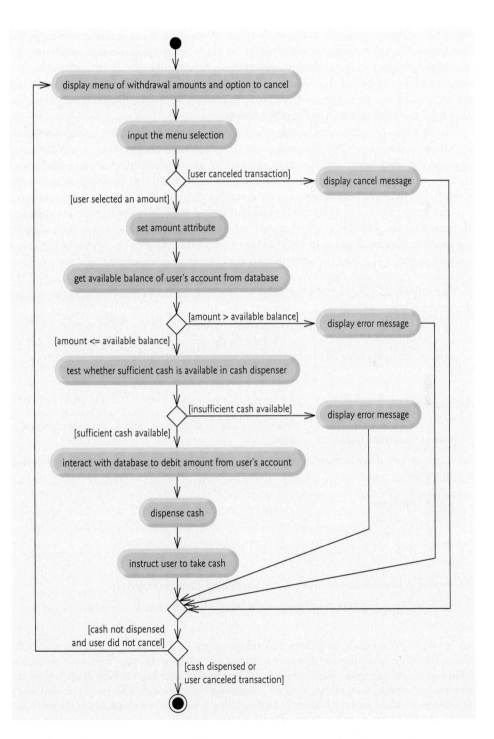

Fig. 5.28 | Activity diagram for a `Withdrawal` transaction.

availableBalance attribute of the user's Account object) from the database. The activity flow then arrives at another decision. If the requested withdrawal amount exceeds the user's available balance, the system displays an appropriate error message informing the user of the problem. Control then merges with the other activity flows before reaching the decision at the bottom of the diagram. The guard decision "cash not dispensed and user did not cancel" is true, so the activity flow returns to the top of the diagram, and the transaction prompts the user to input a new amount.

If the requested withdrawal amount is less than or equal to the user's available balance, the transaction tests whether the cash dispenser has enough cash to satisfy the withdrawal request. If it does not, the transaction displays an appropriate error message and passes through the merge before reaching the final decision. Cash was not dispensed, so the activity flow returns to the beginning of the activity diagram, and the transaction prompts the user to choose a new amount. If sufficient cash is available, the transaction interacts with the database to debit the withdrawal amount from the user's account (i.e., subtract the amount from both the availableBalance and totalBalance attributes of the user's Account object). The transaction then dispenses the desired amount of cash and instructs the user to take the cash that is dispensed. The main flow of activity next merges with the two error flows and the cancellation flow. In this case, cash was dispensed, so the activity flow reaches the final state.

We have taken the first steps in modeling the behavior of the ATM system and have shown how an object's attributes participate in the object's activities. In Section 6.22, we investigate the operations of our classes to create a more complete model of the system's behavior.

Software Engineering Case Study Self-Review Exercises

5.1   State whether the following statement is *true* or *false*, and if *false*, explain why: State diagrams model structural aspects of a system.

5.2   An activity diagram models the _____ that an object performs and the order in which it performs them.
  a) actions
  b) attributes
  c) states
  d) state transitions

5.3   Based on the requirements specification, create an activity diagram for a deposit transaction.

Answers to Software Engineering Case Study Self-Review Exercises

5.1   False. State diagrams model some of the behavior of a system.

5.2   a.

5.3   Figure 5.29 presents an activity diagram for a deposit transaction. The diagram models the actions that occur after the user chooses the deposit option from the main menu and before the ATM returns the user to the main menu. Recall that part of receiving a deposit amount from the user involves converting an integer number of cents to a dollar amount. Also recall that crediting a deposit amount to an account involves increasing only the totalBalance attribute of the user's Account object. The bank updates the availableBalance attribute of the user's Account object only after confirming the amount of cash in the deposit envelope and after the enclosed checks clear—this occurs independently of the ATM system.

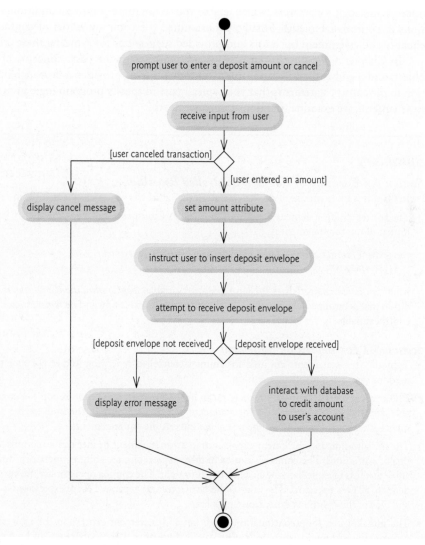

Fig. 5.29 | Activity diagram for a Deposit transaction.

5.12 Wrap-Up

In this chapter, we completed our introduction to C++'s control statements, which enable you to control the flow of execution in functions. Chapter 4 discussed the if, if...else and while statements. The current chapter demonstrated C++'s remaining control statements—for, do...while and switch. We have shown that any algorithm can be developed using combinations of the sequence structure (i.e., statements listed in the order in which they should execute), the three types of selection statements—if, if...else and switch—and the three types of repetition statements—while, do...while and for. In this chapter and Chapter 4, we have discussed how you can combine these building blocks to utilize proven program construction and problem-solving techniques. This chapter also introduced C++'s logical operators, which enable you to use more complex conditional expressions in control statements. Finally, we examined the common errors of confusing the equality and assignment operators and provided suggestions for avoiding these errors.

In Chapter 3, we introduced C++ programming with the basic concepts of classes, objects and member functions. Chapter 4 and this chapter provided a thorough introduction to the control statements that you typically use to specify program logic in functions. In Chapter 6, we examine functions in greater depth.

Summary

Section 5.2 Essentials of Counter-Controlled Repetition

- In C++, it is more precise to call a declaration that also reserves memory a definition.
- The for repetition statement handles all the details of counter-controlled repetition. The general format of the for statement is

  for (*initialization*; *loopContinuationCondition*; *increment*)
     statement

  where *initialization* initializes the loop's control variable, *loopContinuationCondition* is the condition that determines whether the loop should continue executing and *increment* increments the control variable.

Section 5.3 for Repetition Statement

- Typically, for statements are used for counter-controlled repetition and while statements are used for sentinel-controlled repetition.
- The scope of a variable specifies where it can be used in a program. For example, a control variable declared in the header of a for statement can be used only in the body of the for statement—the control variable will be unknown outside the for statement.
- The initialization and increment expressions in a for statement header can be comma-separated lists of expressions. The commas, as used in these expressions, are comma operators, which guarantee that lists of expressions evaluate from left to right. The comma operator has the lowest precedence of all C++ operators. The value and type of a comma-separated list of expressions is the value and type of the rightmost expression in the list.
- The initialization, loop-continuation condition and increment expressions of a for statement can contain arithmetic expressions. Also, the increment of a for statement can be negative, in which case it is really a decrement and the loop counts downward.
- If the loop-continuation condition in a for header is initially false, the body of the for statement is not performed. Instead, execution proceeds with the statement following the for.

Section 5.4 Examples Using the for Statement

- Standard library function pow(x, y) calculates the value of x raised to the yth power. Function pow takes two arguments of type double and returns a double value.
- Parameterized stream manipulator setw specifies the field width in which the next value output should appear. The value is right justified in the field by default. If the value to be output is larger than the field width, the field width is extended to accommodate the entire value. Nonparameterized stream manipulator left (found in header <iostream>) can be used to cause a value to be left justified in a field and right can be used to restore right justification.
- Sticky settings are those output-formatting settings that remain in effect until they are changed.

Section 5.5 do...while *Repetition Statement*

- The do...while repetition statement tests the loop-continuation condition at the end of the loop, so the body of the loop will be executed at least once. The format for the do...while statement is

```
do
{
    statement
} while ( condition );
```

Section 5.6 switch *Multiple-Selection Statement*

- The switch multiple-selection statement performs different actions based on the possible values of a variable or expression. Each action is associated with the value of a constant integral expression (i.e., any combination of character constants and integer constants that evaluates to a constant integer value) that the variable or expression on which the switch is based may assume.

- The switch statement consists of a series of case labels and an optional default case.

- The cin.get() function reads one character from the keyboard. Characters normally are stored in variables of type char; however, characters can be stored in any integer data type, because types short, int and long are guaranteed to be at least as big as type char. Thus, a character can be treated either as an integer or as a character, depending on its use.

- The end-of-file indicator is a system-dependent keystroke combination that specifies that there is no more data to input. EOF is a symbolic integer constant defined in the <iostream> header file that indicates "end-of-file."

- The expression in the parentheses following keyword switch is called the controlling expression of the switch. The switch statement compares the value of the controlling expression with each case label.

- Listing cases consecutively with no statements between them enables the cases to perform the same set of statements.

- Each case can have multiple statements. The switch selection statement differs from other control statements in that it does not require braces around multiple statements in each case.

- Each case can be used only to test only a constant integral expression. A character constant is represented as the specific character in single quotes, such as 'A'. An integer constant is simply an integer value. Also, each case label can specify only one constant integral expression.

- C++ provides several data types to represent integers—int, char, short and long. The range of integer values for each type depends on the particular computer's hardware.

Section 5.7 break *and* continue *Statements*

- The break statement, when executed in one of the repetition statements (for, while and do...while), causes immediate exit from the statement.

- The continue statement, when executed in one of the repetition statements (for, while and do...while), skips any remaining statements in the body of the repetition statement and proceeds with the next iteration of the loop. In a while or do...while statement, execution continues with the next evaluation of the condition. In a for statement, execution continues with the increment expression in the for statement header.

Section 5.8 *Logical Operators*

- Logical operators enable you to form complex conditions by combining simple conditions. The logical operators are && (logical AND), || (logical OR) and ! (logical negation).

- The && (logical AND) operator ensures that two conditions are *both* true before choosing a certain path of execution.

- The || (logical OR) operator ensures that either *or* both of two conditions are true before choosing a certain path of execution.

- An expression containing && or || operators evaluates only until the truth or falsehood of the expression is known. This performance feature for the evaluation of logical AND and logical OR expressions is called short-circuit evaluation.

- The ! (logical NOT, also called logical negation) operator enables a programmer to "reverse" the meaning of a condition. The unary logical negation operator is placed before a condition to choose a path of execution if the original condition (without the logical negation operator) is false. In most cases, you can avoid using logical negation by expressing the condition with an appropriate relational or equality operator.

- When used as a condition, any nonzero value implicitly converts to true; 0 (zero) implicitly converts to false.

- By default, bool values true and false are displayed by cout as 1 and 0, respectively. Stream manipulator boolalpha (a sticky manipulator) specifies that the value of each bool expression should be displayed as either the word "true" or the word "false."

Section 5.9 Confusing the Equality (==) and Assignment (=) Operators

- Any expression that produces a value can be used in the decision portion of any control statement. If the value of the expression is zero, it is treated as false, and if the value is nonzero, it is treated as true.

- An assignment produces a value—namely, the value assigned to the variable on the left side of the assignment operator.

Section 5.10 Structured Programming Summary

- Any form of control ever needed in a C++ program can be expressed in terms of sequence, selection and repetition statements, and these can be combined in only two ways—stacking and nesting.

Terminology

!, logical NOT operator
&&, logical AND operator
||, logical OR operator
ASCII character set
boolalpha stream manipulator
break statement
case label
char fundamental type
comma operator
constant integral expression
continue statement
controlling expression of a switch
decrement a control variable
default case in switch
definition
field width
final value of a control variable
for repetition statement
for header
increment a control variable

initial value of a control variable
left justification
left stream manipulator
logical AND (&&)
logical negation (!)
logical NOT (!)
logical operator
logical OR (||)
loop-continuation condition
lvalue ("left value")
name of a control variable
nesting rule
off-by-one error
right justification
right stream manipulator
rvalue ("right value")
scope of a variable
setw stream manipulator
short-circuit evaluation
simple condition

stacking rule
standard library function pow
sticky setting

switch multiple-selection statement
truth table
zero-based counting

Self-Review Exercises

5.1 State whether the following are *true* or *false*. If the answer is *false*, explain why.
  a) The default case is required in the switch selection statement.
  b) The break statement is required in the default case of a switch selection statement to exit the switch properly.
  c) The expression (x > y && a < b) is true if either the expression x > y is true or the expression a < b is true.
  d) An expression containing the || operator is true if either or both of its operands are true.

5.2 Write a C++ statement or a set of C++ statements to accomplish each of the following:
  a) Sum the odd integers between 1 and 99 using a for statement. Assume the integer variables sum and count have been declared.
  b) Print the value 333.546372 in a field width of 15 characters with precisions of 1, 2 and 3. Print each number on the same line. Left-justify each number in its field. What three values print?
  c) Calculate the value of 2.5 raised to the power 3 using function pow. Print the result with a precision of 2 in a field width of 10 positions. What prints?
  d) Print the integers from 1 to 20 using a while loop and the counter variable x. Assume that the variable x has been declared, but not initialized. Print only 5 integers per line. [*Hint:* Use the calculation x % 5. When the value of this is 0, print a newline character; otherwise, print a tab character.]
  e) Repeat Exercise 5.2(d) using a for statement.

5.3 Find the error(s), if any, in each of the following code segments and explain how to correct it (them).
  a)
```
x = 1;
while ( x <= 10 );
   x++;
}
```
  b)
```
for ( y = .1; y != 1.0; y += .1 )
   cout << y << endl;
```
  c)
```
switch ( n )
{
   case 1:
      cout << "The number is 1" << endl;
   case 2:
      cout << "The number is 2" << endl;
      break;
   default:
      cout << "The number is not 1 or 2" << endl;
      break;
}
```
  d) The following code should print the values 1 to 10.
```
n = 1;
while ( n < 10 )
   cout << n++ << endl;
```

Answers to Self-Review Exercises

5.1   a) False. The `default` case is optional. Nevertheless, it is considered good software engineering to always provide a `default` case.

   b) False. The `break` statement is used to exit the `switch` statement. The `break` statement is not required when the `default` case is the last case. Nor will the `break` statement be required if having control proceed with the next case makes sense.

   c) False. When using the `&&` operator, both of the relational expressions must be `true` for the entire expression to be `true`.

   d) True.

5.2   a)
```
sum = 0;
for ( count = 1; count <= 99; count += 2 )
   sum += count;
```

   b)
```
cout << fixed << left
   << setprecision( 1 ) << setw( 15 ) << 333.546372
   << setprecision( 2 ) << setw( 15 ) << 333.546372
   << setprecision( 3 ) << setw( 15 ) << 333.546372
   << endl;
```
Output is:
```
333.5          333.55         333.546
```

   c)
```
cout << fixed << setprecision( 2 )
   << setw( 10 ) << pow( 2.5, 3 )
   << endl;
```
Output is:
```
     15.63
```

   d)
```
x = 1;

while ( x <= 20 )
{
   cout << x;

   if ( x % 5 == 0 )
      cout << endl;
   else
      cout << '\t';

   x++;
}
```

   e)
```
for ( x = 1; x <= 20; x++ )
{
   cout << x;

   if ( x % 5 == 0 )
      cout << endl;
   else
      cout << '\t';
}
```

   or

```
for ( x = 1; x <= 20; x++ )
{
   if ( x % 5 == 0 )
      cout << x << endl;
   else
      cout << x << '\t';
}
```

5.3   a)   *Error:* The semicolon after the while header causes an infinite loop.
             Correction: Replace the semicolon by a {, or remove both the ; and the }.
       b)   *Error:* Using a floating-point number to control a for repetition statement.
             Correction: Use an integer and perform the proper calculation in order to get the values
             you desire.

```
for ( y = 1; y != 10; y++ )
   cout << ( static_cast< double >( y ) / 10 ) << endl;
```

       c)   *Error:* Missing break statement in the first case.
             Correction: Add a break statement at the end of the statements for the first case. Note
             that this is not an error if you want the statement of case 2: to execute every time the
             case 1: statement executes.
       d)   *Error:* Improper relational operator used in the while repetition-continuation condi-
             tion.
             Correction: Use <= rather than <, or change 10 to 11.

Exercises

5.4   Find the error(s), if any, in each of the following:
       a)   `For ( x = 100, x >= 1, x++ )`
             `   cout << x << endl;`
       b)   The following code should print whether integer value is odd or even:

```
switch ( value % 2 )
{
   case 0:
      cout << "Even integer" << endl;
   case 1:
      cout << "Odd integer" << endl;
}
```

       c)   The following code should output the odd integers from 19 to 1:

```
for ( x = 19; x >= 1; x += 2 )
   cout << x << endl;
```

       d)   The following code should output the even integers from 2 to 100:

```
counter = 2;

do
{
   cout << counter << endl;
   counter += 2;
} While ( counter < 100 );
```

5.5   Write a program that uses a for statement to sum a sequence of integers. Assume that the first integer read specifies the number of values remaining to be entered. Your program should read only one value per input statement. A typical input sequence might be

> 5 100 200 300 400 500

where the 5 indicates that the subsequent 5 values are to be summed.

5.6   Write a program that uses a for statement to calculate and print the average of several integers. Assume the last value read is the sentinel 9999. A typical input sequence might be

> 10 8 11 7 9 9999

indicating that the program should calculate the average of all the values preceding 9999.

5.7   What does the following program do?

```cpp
// Exercise 5.7: ex05_07.cpp
// What does this program print?
#include <iostream>
using std::cout;
using std::cin;
using std::endl;

int main()
{
   int x; // declare x
   int y; // declare y

   // prompt user for input
   cout << "Enter two integers in the range 1-20: ";
   cin >> x >> y;  // read values for x and y

   for ( int i = 1; i <= y; i++ ) // count from 1 to y
   {
      for ( int j = 1; j <= x; j++ ) // count from 1 to x
         cout << '@'; // output @

      cout << endl; // begin new line
   } // end outer for

   return 0; // indicate successful termination
} // end main
```

5.8   Write a program that uses a for statement to find the smallest of several integers. Assume that the first value read specifies the number of values remaining.

5.9   Write a program that uses a for statement to calculate and print the product of the odd integers from 1 to 15.

5.10   The factorial function is used frequently in probability problems. Using the definition of factorial in Exercise 4.35, write a program that uses a for statement to evaluate the factorials of the integers from 1 to 5. Print the results in tabular format. What difficulty might prevent you from calculating the factorial of 20?

5.11   Modify the compound interest program of Section 5.4 to repeat its steps for the interest rates 5 percent, 6 percent, 7 percent, 8 percent, 9 percent and 10 percent. Use a for statement to vary the interest rate.

5.12   Write a program that uses for statements to print the following patterns separately, one below the other. Use for loops to generate the patterns. All asterisks (*) should be printed by a single statement of the form cout << '*'; (this causes the asterisks to print side by side). [*Hint:* The last two patterns require that each line begin with an appropriate number of blanks. *Extra credit:* Combine your code from the four separate problems into a single program that prints all four patterns side by side by making clever use of nested for loops.]

```
(a)                    (b)                    (c)                    (d)
*                      **********             **********                      *
**                     *********              *********                      **
***                    ********               ********                      ***
****                   *******                *******                      ****
*****                  ******                 ******                      *****
******                 *****                  *****                      ******
*******                ****                   ****                      *******
********               ***                    ***                      ********
*********              **                     **                      *********
**********             *                      *                      **********
```

5.13   One interesting application of computers is drawing graphs and bar charts. Write a program that reads five numbers (each between 1 and 30). Assume that the user enters only valid values. For each number that is read, your program should print a line containing that number of adjacent asterisks. For example, if your program reads the number 7, it should print *******.

5.14   A mail order house sells five different products whose retail prices are: product 1 — $2.98, product 2—$4.50, product 3—$9.98, product 4—$4.49 and product 5—$6.87. Write a program that reads a series of pairs of numbers as follows:
a) product number
b) quantity sold
Your program should use a switch statement to determine the retail price for each product. Your program should calculate and display the total retail value of all products sold. Use a sentinel-controlled loop to determine when the program should stop looping and display the final results.

5.15   Modify the GradeBook program of Fig. 5.9–Fig. 5.11 so that it calculates the grade-point average for the set of grades. A grade of A is worth 4 points, B is worth 3 points, and so on.

5.16   Modify the program in Fig. 5.6 so it uses only integers to calculate the compound interest. [*Hint:* Treat all monetary amounts as integral numbers of pennies. Then "break" the result into its dollar portion and cents portion by using the division and modulus operations. Insert a period.]

5.17   Assume $i = 1$, $j = 2$, $k = 3$ and $m = 2$. What does each of the following statements print? Are the parentheses necessary in each case?
a) cout << (i == 1) << endl;
b) cout << (j == 3) << endl;
c) cout << (i >= 1 && j < 4) << endl;
d) cout << (m <= 99 && k < m) << endl;
e) cout << (j >= i || k == m) << endl;
f) cout << (k + m < j || 3 - j >= k) << endl;
g) cout << (!m) << endl;
h) cout << (!(j - m)) << endl;
i) cout << (!(k > m)) << endl;

5.18   Write a program that prints a table of the binary, octal and hexadecimal equivalents of the decimal numbers in the range 1 through 256. If you are not familiar with these number systems, read Appendix D, Number Systems, first.

5.19   Calculate the value of π from the infinite series

$$\pi = 4 - \frac{4}{3} + \frac{4}{5} - \frac{4}{7} + \frac{4}{9} - \frac{4}{11} + \cdots$$

Print a table that shows the approximate value of π after each of the first 1000 terms of this series.

5.20   *(Pythagorean Triples)* A right triangle can have sides that are all integers. A set of three integer values for the sides of a right triangle is called a Pythagorean triple. These three sides must satisfy the relationship that the sum of the squares of two of the sides is equal to the square of the hypotenuse. Find all Pythagorean triples for side1, side2 and hypotenuse all no larger than 500. Use a triple-nested for loop that tries all possibilities. This is an example of brute force computing. You'll learn in more advanced computer science courses that there are many interesting problems for which there is no known algorithmic approach other than sheer brute force.

5.21   A company pays its employees as managers (who receive a fixed weekly salary), hourly workers (who receive a fixed hourly wage for up to the first 40 hours they work and "time-and-a-half"— 1.5 times their hourly wage—for overtime hours worked), commission workers (who receive $250 plus 5.7 percent of their gross weekly sales), or pieceworkers (who receive a fixed amount of money per item for each of the items they produce—each pieceworker in this company works on only one type of item). Write a program to compute the weekly pay for each employee. You do not know the number of employees in advance. Each type of employee has its own pay code: Managers have code 1, hourly workers have code 2, commission workers have code 3 and pieceworkers have code 4. Use a switch to compute each employee's pay according to that employee's paycode. Within the switch, prompt the user (i.e., the payroll clerk) to enter the appropriate facts your program needs to calculate each employee's pay according to that employee's paycode.

5.22   *(De Morgan's Laws)* In this chapter, we discussed the logical operators &&, || and !. De Morgan's laws can sometimes make it more convenient for us to express a logical expression. These laws state that the expression !(*condition1* && *condition2*) is logically equivalent to the expression (!*condition1* || !*condition2*). Also, the expression !(*condition1* || *condition2*) is logically equivalent to the expression (!*condition1* && !*condition2*). Use De Morgan's laws to write equivalent expressions for each of the following, then write a program to show that the original expression and the new expression in each case are equivalent:

a) !(x < 5) && !(y >= 7)
b) !(a == b) || !(g != 5)
c) !((x <= 8) && (y > 4))
d) !((i > 4) || (j <= 6))

5.23   Write a program that prints the following diamond shape. You may use output statements that print either a single asterisk (*) or a single blank. Maximize your use of repetition (with nested for statements) and minimize the number of output statements.

```
    *
   ***
  *****
 *******
*********
 *******
  *****
   ***
    *
```

5.24   Modify the program you wrote in Exercise 5.23 to read an odd number in the range 1 to 19 to specify the number of rows in the diamond, then display a diamond of the appropriate size.

5.25 A criticism of the `break` and `continue` statements is that each is unstructured. Actually these statements can always be replaced by structured statements, although doing so can be awkward. Describe in general how you would remove any `break` statement from a loop in a program and replace it with some structured equivalent. [*Hint:* The break statement leaves a loop from within the body of the loop. Another way to leave is by failing the loop-continuation test. Consider using in the loop-continuation test a second test that indicates "early exit because of a 'break' condition."] Use the technique you developed here to remove the `break` statement from the program of Fig. 5.13.

5.26 What does the following program segment do?

```
1    for ( int i = 1; i <= 5; i++ )
2    {
3       for ( int j = 1; j <= 3; j++ )
4       {
5          for ( int k = 1; k <= 4; k++ )
6             cout << '*';
7
8          cout << endl;
9       } // end inner for
10
11      cout << endl;
12   } // end outer for
```

5.27 Describe in general how you would remove any `continue` statement from a loop in a program and replace it with some structured equivalent. Use the technique you developed here to remove the `continue` statement from the program of Fig. 5.14.

5.28 *("The Twelve Days of Christmas" Song)* Write a program that uses repetition and `switch` statements to print the song "The Twelve Days of Christmas." One `switch` statement should be used to print the day (i.e., "First," "Second," etc.). A separate `switch` statement should be used to print the remainder of each verse. Visit the website www.12days.com/library/carols/12daysofxmas.htm for the complete lyrics to the song.

5.29 *(Peter Minuit Problem)* Legend has it that, in 1626, Peter Minuit purchased Manhattan Island for $24.00 in barter. Did he make a good investment? To answer this question, modify the compound interest program of Fig. 5.6 to begin with a principal of $24.00 and to calculate the amount of interest on deposit if that money had been kept on deposit until this year (e.g., 381 years through 2007). Place the `for` loop that performs the compound interest calculation in an outer `for` loop that varies the interest rate from 5 percent to 10 percent to observe the wonders of compound interest.

6

Functions and an Introduction to Recursion

OBJECTIVES

In this chapter you'll learn:

- To construct programs modularly from functions.
- To use common math functions available in the C++ Standard Library.
- To create functions with multiple parameters.
- The mechanisms for passing information between functions and returning results.
- How the function call/return mechanism is supported by the function call stack and activation records.
- To use random number generation to implement game-playing applications.
- How the visibility of identifiers is limited to specific regions of programs.
- To write and use recursive functions, i.e., functions that call themselves.

6.1 Introduction

Most computer programs that solve real-world problems are much larger than the programs presented in the first few chapters of this book. Experience has shown that the best way to develop and maintain a large program is to construct it from small, simple pieces, or components. This technique is called divide and conquer. We introduced functions (as program pieces) in Chapter 3. In this chapter, we study functions in more depth. We emphasize how to declare and use functions to facilitate the design, implementation, operation and maintenance of large programs.

We'll overview a portion of the C++ Standard Library's math functions, showing several that require more than one parameter. Next, you'll learn how to declare a function with more than one parameter. We'll also present additional information about function prototypes and how the compiler uses them to convert the type of an argument in a function call to the type specified in a function's parameter list, if necessary.

Next, we'll take a brief diversion into simulation techniques with random number generation and develop a version of the casino dice game called craps that uses most of the programming techniques you have learned to this point in the book.

We then present C++'s storage classes and scope rules. These determine the period during which an object exists in memory and where its identifier can be referenced in a program. You'll also learn how C++ is able to keep track of which function is currently executing, how parameters and other local variables of functions are maintained in memory and how a function knows where to return after it completes execution. We discuss two topics that help improve program performance—inline functions that can eliminate the overhead of a function call and reference parameters that can be used to pass large data items to functions efficiently.

Many of the applications you develop will have more than one function of the same name. This technique, called function overloading, is used by programmers to implement functions that perform similar tasks for arguments of different types or possibly for different numbers of arguments. We consider function templates—a mechanism for defining a family of overloaded functions. The chapter concludes with a discussion of functions that call themselves, either directly, or indirectly (through another function)—a topic called recursion that is discussed at length in upper-level computer science courses.

6.2 Program Components in C++

C++ programs are typically written by combining new functions and classes you write with "prepackaged" functions and classes available in the C++ Standard Library. In this chapter, we concentrate on functions.

The C++ Standard Library provides a rich collection of functions for performing common mathematical calculations, string manipulations, character manipulations, input/output, error checking and many other useful operations. This makes your job easier, because these functions provide many of the capabilities programmers need. The C++ Standard Library functions are provided as part of the C++ programming environment.

Software Engineering Observation 6.1

Read the documentation for your compiler to familiarize yourself with the functions and classes in the C++ Standard Library.

Functions (called methods or procedures in other programming languages) allow you to modularize a program by separating its tasks into self-contained units. You have used functions in every program you have written. These functions are sometimes referred to as user-defined functions or programmer-defined functions. The statements in the function bodies are written only once, are reused from perhaps several locations in a program and are hidden from other functions.

There are several motivations for modularizing a program with functions. One is the divide-and-conquer approach, which makes program development more manageable by constructing programs from small, simple pieces. Another is software reuse—using existing functions as building blocks to create new programs. For example, in earlier programs, we did not have to define how to read a line of text from the keyboard—C++ provides this capability via the getline function of the <string> header file. A third motivation is to avoid repeating code. Also, dividing a program into meaningful functions makes the program easier to debug and maintain.

Software Engineering Observation 6.2

To promote software reusability, every function should be limited to performing a single, well-defined task, and the name of the function should express that task effectively. Such functions make programs easier to write, test, debug and maintain.

Error-Prevention Tip 6.1

A small function that performs one task is easier to test and debug than a larger function that performs many tasks.

Software Engineering Observation 6.3

If you cannot choose a concise name that expresses a function's task, your function might be attempting to perform too many diverse tasks. It is usually best to break such a function into several smaller functions.

As you know, a function is invoked by a function call, and when the called function completes its task, it either returns a result or simply returns control to the caller. An analogy to this program structure is the hierarchical form of management (Figure 6.1). A boss (similar to the calling function) asks a worker (similar to the called function) to perform a task and report back (i.e., return) the results after completing the task. The boss function does not know how the worker function performs its designated tasks. The worker may also call other worker functions, unbeknownst to the boss. This hiding of implementation details promotes good software engineering. Figure 6.1 shows the boss function communicating with several worker functions in a hierarchical manner. The boss function divides the responsibilities among the various worker functions. Note that worker1 acts as a "boss function" to worker4 and worker5.

6.3 Math Library Functions

As you know, a class can provide member functions that perform the services of the class. For example, in Chapters 3–5, you have called the member functions of various versions of a GradeBook object to display the GradeBook's welcome message, to set its course name, to obtain a set of grades and to calculate the average of those grades.

Sometimes functions are not members of a class. Such functions are called global functions. Like a class's member functions, the function prototypes for global functions

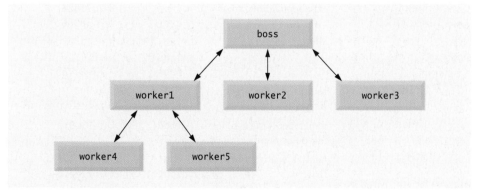

Fig. 6.1 | Hierarchical boss function/worker function relationship.

are placed in header files, so that the global functions can be reused in any program that includes the header file and that can link to the function's object code. For example, recall that we used function pow of the <cmath> header file to raise a value to a power in Figure 5.6. We introduce various functions from the <cmath> header file here to present the concept of global functions that do not belong to a particular class. In this chapter and in subsequent chapters, we use a combination of global functions (such as main) and classes with member functions to implement our example programs.

The <cmath> header file provides a collection of functions that enable you to perform common mathematical calculations. For example, you can calculate the square root of 900.0 with the function call

```
sqrt( 900.0 )
```

The preceding expression evaluates to 30.0. Function sqrt takes an argument of type double and returns a double result. Note that there is no need to create any objects before calling function sqrt. Also note that *all* functions in the <cmath> header file are global functions—therefore, each is called simply by specifying the name of the function followed by parentheses containing the function's arguments.

Function arguments may be constants, variables or more complex expressions. If c = 13.0, d = 3.0 and f = 4.0, then the statement

```
cout << sqrt( c + d * f ) << endl;
```

calculates and prints the square root of 13.0 + 3.0 * 4.0 = 25.0—namely, 5.0. Some math library functions are summarized in Fig. 6.2. In the figure, the variables x and y are of type double.

Function	Description	Example
ceil(x)	rounds x to the smallest integer not less than x	ceil(9.2) is 10.0 ceil(-9.8) is -9.0
cos(x)	trigonometric cosine of x (x in radians)	cos(0.0) is 1.0
exp(x)	exponential function e^x	exp(1.0) is 2.71828 exp(2.0) is 7.38906
fabs(x)	absolute value of x	fabs(5.1) is 5.1 fabs(0.0) is 0.0 fabs(-8.76) is 8.76
floor(x)	rounds x to the largest integer not greater than x	floor(9.2) is 9.0 floor(-9.8) is -10.0
fmod(x, y)	remainder of x/y as a floating-point number	fmod(2.6, 1.2) is 0.2
log(x)	natural logarithm of x (base e)	log(2.718282) is 1.0 log(7.389056) is 2.0

Fig. 6.2 | Math library functions. (Part 1 of 2.)

Function	Description	Example
log10(x)	logarithm of x (base 10)	log10(10.0) is 1.0 log10(100.0) is 2.0
pow(x, y)	x raised to power y (x^y)	pow(2, 7) is 128 pow(9, .5) is 3
sin(x)	trigonometric sine of x (x in radians)	sin(0.0) is 0
sqrt(x)	square root of x (where x is a nonnegative value)	sqrt(9.0) is 3.0
tan(x)	trigonometric tangent of x (x in radians)	tan(0.0) is 0

Fig. 6.2 | Math library functions. (Part 2 of 2.)

6.4 Function Definitions with Multiple Parameters

Chapters 3–5 presented classes containing simple functions that had at most one parameter. Functions often require more than one piece of information to perform their tasks. We now consider functions with multiple parameters.

The program in Figs. 6.3–6.5 modifies our GradeBook class by including a user-defined function called maximum that determines and returns the largest of three int values. When the application begins execution, the main function (lines 5–14 of Fig. 6.5) creates one object of class GradeBook (line 8) and calls the object's inputGrades member function (line 11) to read three integer grades from the user. In class GradeBook's implementation file (Fig. 6.4), lines 54–55 of member function inputGrades prompt the user to enter three integer values and read them from the user. Line 58 calls member function maximum (defined in lines 62–75). Function maximum determines the largest value, then the return statement (line 74) returns that value to the point at which function inputGrades invoked maximum (line 58). Member function inputGrades then stores maximum's return value in data member maximumGrade. This value is then output by calling function displayGradeReport (line 12 of Fig. 6.5). [*Note:* We named this function displayGradeReport because subsequent versions of class GradeBook will use this function to display a complete grade report, including the maximum and minimum grades.] In Chapter 7, Arrays and Vectors, we'll enhance the GradeBook to process an arbitrary number of grades.

```
1   // Fig. 6.3: GradeBook.h
2   // Definition of class GradeBook that finds the maximum of three grades.
3   // Member functions are defined in GradeBook.cpp
4   #include <string> // program uses C++ standard string class
5   using std::string;
6
```

Fig. 6.3 | GradeBook header file. (Part 1 of 2.)

```
7   // GradeBook class definition
8   class GradeBook
9   {
10  public:
11     GradeBook( string ); // constructor initializes course name
12     void setCourseName( string ); // function to set the course name
13     string getCourseName(); // function to retrieve the course name
14     void displayMessage(); // display a welcome message
15     void inputGrades(); // input three grades from user
16     void displayGradeReport(); // display a report based on the grades
17     int maximum( int, int, int ); // determine max of 3 values
18  private:
19     string courseName; // course name for this GradeBook
20     int maximumGrade; // maximum of three grades
21  }; // end class GradeBook
```

Fig. 6.3 | GradeBook header file. (Part 2 of 2.)

```
1   // Fig. 6.4: GradeBook.cpp
2   // Member-function definitions for class GradeBook that
3   // determines the maximum of three grades.
4   #include <iostream>
5   using std::cout;
6   using std::cin;
7   using std::endl;
8
9   #include "GradeBook.h" // include definition of class GradeBook
10
11  // constructor initializes courseName with string supplied as argument;
12  // initializes maximumGrade to 0
13  GradeBook::GradeBook( string name )
14  {
15     setCourseName( name ); // validate and store courseName
16     maximumGrade = 0; // this value will be replaced by the maximum grade
17  } // end GradeBook constructor
18
19  // function to set the course name; limits name to 25 or fewer characters
20  void GradeBook::setCourseName( string name )
21  {
22     if ( name.length() <= 25 ) // if name has 25 or fewer characters
23        courseName = name; // store the course name in the object
24     else // if name is longer than 25 characters
25     { // set courseName to first 25 characters of parameter name
26        courseName = name.substr( 0, 25 ); // select first 25 characters
27        cout << "Name \"" << name << "\" exceeds maximum length (25).\n"
28           << "Limiting courseName to first 25 characters.\n" << endl;
29     } // end if...else
30  } // end function setCourseName
31
```

Fig. 6.4 | GradeBook class defines function maximum. (Part 1 of 2.)

```
32    // function to retrieve the course name
33    string GradeBook::getCourseName()
34    {
35       return courseName;
36    } // end function getCourseName
37
38    // display a welcome message to the GradeBook user
39    void GradeBook::displayMessage()
40    {
41       // this statement calls getCourseName to get the
42       // name of the course this GradeBook represents
43       cout << "Welcome to the grade book for\n" << getCourseName() << "!\n"
44          << endl;
45    } // end function displayMessage
46
47    // input three grades from user; determine maximum
48    void GradeBook::inputGrades()
49    {
50       int grade1; // first grade entered by user
51       int grade2; // second grade entered by user
52       int grade3; // third grade entered by user
53
54       cout << "Enter three integer grades: ";
55       cin >> grade1 >> grade2 >> grade3;
56
57       // store maximum in member maximumGrade
58       maximumGrade = maximum( grade1, grade2, grade3 );
59    } // end function inputGrades
60
61    // returns the maximum of its three integer parameters
62    int GradeBook::maximum( int x, int y, int z )
63    {
64       int maximumValue = x; // assume x is the largest to start
65
66       // determine whether y is greater than maximumValue
67       if ( y > maximumValue )
68          maximumValue = y; // make y the new maximumValue
69
70       // determine whether z is greater than maximumValue
71       if ( z > maximumValue )
72          maximumValue = z; // make z the new maximumValue
73
74       return maximumValue;
75    } // end function maximum
76
77    // display a report based on the grades entered by user
78    void GradeBook::displayGradeReport()
79    {
80       // output maximum of grades entered
81       cout << "Maximum of grades entered: " << maximumGrade << endl;
82    } // end function displayGradeReport
```

Fig. 6.4 | GradeBook class defines function maximum. (Part 2 of 2.)

```
1   // Fig. 6.5: fig06_05.cpp
2   // Create GradeBook object, input grades and display grade report.
3   #include "GradeBook.h" // include definition of class GradeBook
4
5   int main()
6   {
7      // create GradeBook object
8      GradeBook myGradeBook( "CS101 C++ Programming" );
9
10     myGradeBook.displayMessage(); // display welcome message
11     myGradeBook.inputGrades(); // read grades from user
12     myGradeBook.displayGradeReport(); // display report based on grades
13     return 0; // indicate successful termination
14  } // end main
```

```
Welcome to the grade book for
CS101 C++ Programming!

Enter three integer grades: 86 67 75
Maximum of grades entered: 86
```

```
Welcome to the grade book for
CS101 C++ Programming!

Enter three integer grades: 67 86 75
Maximum of grades entered: 86
```

```
Welcome to the grade book for
CS101 C++ Programming!

Enter three integer grades: 67 75 86
Maximum of grades entered: 86
```

Fig. 6.5 | Demonstrating function maximum.

Software Engineering Observation 6.4

The commas used in line 58 of Fig. 6.4 to separate the arguments to function maximum are not comma operators as discussed in Section 5.3. The comma operator guarantees that its operands are evaluated left to right. The order of evaluation of a function's arguments, however, is not specified by the C++ standard. Thus, different compilers can evaluate function arguments in different orders. The C++ standard does guarantee that all arguments in a function call are evaluated before the called function executes.

Portability Tip 6.1

Sometimes when a function's arguments are more involved expressions, such as those with calls to other functions, the order in which the compiler evaluates the arguments could affect the values of one or more of the arguments. If the evaluation order changes between compilers, the argument values passed to the function could vary, causing subtle logic errors.

Error-Prevention Tip 6.2

If you have doubts about the order of evaluation of a function's arguments and whether the order would affect the values passed to the function, evaluate the arguments in separate assignment statements before the function call, assign the result of each expression to a local variable, then pass those variables as arguments to the function.

The prototype of member function `maximum` (Fig. 6.3, line 17) indicates that the function returns an integer value, that the function's name is `maximum` and that the function requires three integer parameters to accomplish its task. Function `maximum`'s header (Fig. 6.4, line 62) matches the function prototype and indicates that the parameter names are `x`, `y` and `z`. When `maximum` is called (Fig. 6.4, line 58), the parameter `x` is initialized with the value of the argument `grade1`, the parameter `y` is initialized with the value of the argument `grade2` and the parameter `z` is initialized with the value of the argument `grade3`. There must be one argument in the function call for each parameter (also called a *formal parameter*) in the function definition.

Notice that multiple parameters are specified in both the function prototype and the function header as a comma-separated list. The compiler refers to the function prototype to check that calls to `maximum` contain the correct number and types of arguments and that the types of the arguments are in the correct order. In addition, the compiler uses the prototype to ensure that the value returned by the function can be used correctly in the expression that called the function (e.g., a function call that returns `void` cannot be used as the right side of an assignment statement). Each argument must be consistent with the type of the corresponding parameter. For example, a parameter of type `double` can receive values like 7.35, 22 or –0.03456, but not a string like `"hello"`. If the arguments passed to a function do not match the types specified in the function's prototype, the compiler attempts to convert the arguments to those types. Section 6.5 discusses this conversion.

Common Programming Error 6.1

Declaring method parameters of the same type as `double x, y` instead of `double x, double y` is a syntax error—an explicit type is required for each parameter in the parameter list.

Common Programming Error 6.2

Compilation errors occur if the function prototype, function header and function calls do not all agree in the number, type and order of arguments and parameters, and in the return type.

Software Engineering Observation 6.5

A function that has many parameters may be performing too many tasks. Consider dividing the function into smaller functions that perform the separate tasks. Limit the function header to one line if possible.

To determine the maximum value (lines 62–75 of Fig. 6.4), we begin with the assumption that parameter `x` contains the largest value, so line 64 of function `maximum` declares local variable `maximumValue` and initializes it with the value of parameter `x`. Of course, it is possible that parameter `y` or `z` contains the actual largest value, so we must compare each of these values with `maximumValue`. The `if` statement in lines 67–68 determines whether `y` is greater than `maximumValue` and, if so, assigns `y` to `maximumValue`. The `if` statement in lines 71–72 determines whether `z` is greater than `maximumValue` and, if so, assigns z to maximumValue. At this point the largest of the three values is in maximumValue, so line 74 returns that value to the call in line 58. When program control returns to the point in the program where maximum was called, maximum's parameters x, y and z are no longer accessible to the program. We'll see why in the next section.

There are three ways to return control to the point at which a function was invoked. If the function does not return a result (i.e., the function has a void return type), control returns when the program reaches the function-ending right brace, or by execution of the statement

```
return;
```

If the function does return a result, the statement

```
return expression;
```

evaluates *expression* and returns the value of *expression* to the caller.

6.5 Function Prototypes and Argument Coercion

A function prototype (also called a function declaration) tells the compiler the name of a function, the type of data returned by the function, the number of parameters the function expects to receive, the types of those parameters and the order in which the parameters of those types are expected.

Software Engineering Observation 6.6

Function prototypes are required in C++. Use #include preprocessor directives to obtain function prototypes for the C++ Standard Library functions from the header files for the appropriate libraries (e.g., the prototype for math function sqrt is in header file <cmath>; a partial list of C++ Standard Library header files appears in Section 6.6). Also use #include to obtain header files containing function prototypes written by you or your group members.

Common Programming Error 6.3

If a function is defined before it is invoked, then the function's definition also serves as the function's prototype, so a separate prototype is unnecessary. If a function is invoked before it is defined, and that function does not have a function prototype, a compilation error occurs.

Software Engineering Observation 6.7

Always provide function prototypes, even though it is possible to omit them when functions are defined before they are used (in which case the function header acts as the function prototype as well). Providing the prototypes avoids tying the code to the order in which functions are defined (which can easily change as a program evolves).

Function Signatures

The portion of a function prototype that includes the name of the function and the types of its arguments is called the function signature or simply the signature. The function signature does not specify the function's return type. Functions in the same scope must have unique signatures. The scope of a function is the region of a program in which the function is known and accessible. We'll say more about scope in Section 6.10.

> **Common Programming Error 6.4**
>
> *It is a compilation error if two functions in the same scope have the same signature but different return types.*

In Fig. 6.3, if the function prototype in line 17 had been written

```
void maximum( int, int, int );
```

the compiler would report an error, because the void return type in the function prototype would differ from the int return type in the function header. Similarly, such a prototype would cause the statement

```
cout << maximum( 6, 7, 0 );
```

to generate a compilation error, because that statement depends on maximum to return a value to be displayed.

Argument Coercion

An important feature of function prototypes is argument coercion—i.e., forcing arguments to the appropriate types specified by the parameter declarations. For example, a program can call a function with an integer argument, even though the function prototype specifies a double argument—the function will still work correctly.

Argument Promotion Rules

Sometimes, argument values that do not correspond precisely to the parameter types in the function prototype can be converted by the compiler to the proper type before the function is called. These conversions occur as specified by C++'s promotion rules. The promotion rules indicate how to convert between types without losing data. An int can be converted to a double without changing its value. However, a double converted to an int truncates the fractional part of the double value. Keep in mind that double variables can hold numbers of much greater magnitude than int variables, so the loss of data may be considerable. Values may also be modified when converting large integer types to small integer types (e.g., long to short), signed to unsigned or unsigned to signed.

The promotion rules apply to expressions containing values of two or more data types; such expressions are also referred to as mixed-type expressions. The type of each value in a mixed-type expression is promoted to the "highest" type in the expression (actually a temporary version of each value is created and used for the expression—the original values remain unchanged). Promotion also occurs when the type of a function argument does not match the parameter type specified in the function definition or prototype. Figure 6.6 lists the fundamental data types in order from "highest type" to "lowest type."

Converting values to lower fundamental types can result in incorrect values. Therefore, a value can be converted to a lower fundamental type only by explicitly assigning the value to a variable of lower type (some compilers will issue a warning in this case) or by using a cast operator (see Section 4.9). Function argument values are converted to the parameter types in a function prototype as if they were being assigned directly to variables of those types. If a square function that uses an integer parameter is called with a floating-

Data types
long double
double
float
unsigned long int (synonymous with unsigned long)
long int (synonymous with long)
unsigned int (synonymous with unsigned)
int
unsigned short int (synonymous with unsigned short)
short int (synonymous with short)
unsigned char
char
bool

Fig. 6.6 | Promotion hierarchy for fundamental data types.

point argument, the argument is converted to int (a lower type), and square could return an incorrect value. For example, square(4.5) returns 16, not 20.25.

Common Programming Error 6.5

Converting from a higher data type in the promotion hierarchy to a lower type, or between signed and unsigned, can corrupt the data value, causing a loss of information.

Common Programming Error 6.6

It is a compilation error if the arguments in a function call do not match the number and types of the parameters declared in the corresponding function prototype. It is also an error if the number of arguments in the call matches, but the arguments cannot be implicitly converted to the expected types.

6.6 C++ Standard Library Header Files

The C++ Standard Library is divided into many portions, each with its own header file. The header files contain the function prototypes for the related functions that form each portion of the library. The header files also contain definitions of various class types and functions, as well as constants needed by those functions. A header file "instructs" the compiler on how to interface with library and user-written components.

Figure 6.7 lists some common C++ Standard Library header files, most of which are discussed later in the book. The term "macro" that is used several times in Fig. 6.7 is discussed in detail in Appendix F, Preprocessor. Header file names ending in .h are "old-style" header files that have been superseded by the C++ Standard Library header files. We use only the C++ Standard Library versions of each header file in this book to ensure that our examples will work on most standard C++ compilers.

C++ Standard Library header file	Explanation
`<iostream>`	Contains function prototypes for the C++ standard input and standard output functions, introduced in Chapter 2, and is covered in more detail in Chapter 15, Stream Input/Output. This header file replaces header file `<iostream.h>`.
`<iomanip>`	Contains function prototypes for stream manipulators that format streams of data. This header file is first used in Section 4.9 and is discussed in more detail in Chapter 15, Stream Input/Output. This header file replaces header file `<iomanip.h>`.
`<cmath>`	Contains function prototypes for math library functions (discussed in Section 6.3). This header file replaces header file `<math.h>`.
`<cstdlib>`	Contains function prototypes for conversions of numbers to text, text to numbers, memory allocation, random numbers and various other utility functions. Portions of the header file are covered in Section 6.7; Chapter 11, Operator Overloading; String and Array Objects; Chapter 16, Exception Handling; Chapter 21, Bits, Characters, C Strings and `structs`; and Appendix E, C Legacy Code Topics. This header file replaces header file `<stdlib.h>`.
`<ctime>`	Contains function prototypes and types for manipulating the time and date. This header file replaces header file `<time.h>`. This header file is used in Section 6.7.
`<vector>`, `<list>`, `<deque>`, `<queue>`, `<stack>`, `<map>`, `<set>`, `<bitset>`	These header files contain classes that implement the C++ Standard Library containers. Containers store data during a program's execution. The `<vector>` header is first introduced in Chapter 7, Arrays and Vectors. We discuss all these header files in Chapter 22, Standard Template Library (STL).
`<cctype>`	Contains function prototypes for functions that test characters for certain properties (such as whether the character is a digit or a punctuation), and function prototypes for functions that can be used to convert lowercase letters to uppercase letters and vice versa. This header file replaces header file `<ctype.h>`. These topics are discussed in Chapter 8, Pointers and Pointer-Based Strings, and Chapter 21, Bits, Characters, C Strings and `structs`.
`<cstring>`	Contains function prototypes for C-style string-processing functions. This header file replaces header file `<string.h>`. This header file is used in Chapter 11, Operator Overloading; String and Array Objects.
`<typeinfo>`	Contains classes for runtime type identification (determining data types at execution time). This header file is discussed in Section 13.8.
`<exception>`, `<stdexcept>`	These header files contain classes that are used for exception handling (discussed in Chapter 16, Exception Handling).

Fig. 6.7 | C++ Standard Library header files. (Part I of 2.)

C++ Standard Library header file	Explanation
`<memory>`	Contains classes and functions used by the C++ Standard Library to allocate memory to the C++ Standard Library containers. This header is used in Chapter 16, Exception Handling.
`<fstream>`	Contains function prototypes for functions that perform input from files on disk and output to files on disk (discussed in Chapter 17, File Processing). This header file replaces header file `<fstream.h>`.
`<string>`	Contains the definition of class `string` from the C++ Standard Library (discussed in Chapter 18, Class `string` and String Stream Processing).
`<sstream>`	Contains function prototypes for functions that perform input from strings in memory and output to strings in memory (discussed in Chapter 18, Class `string` and String Stream Processing).
`<functional>`	Contains classes and functions used by C++ Standard Library algorithms. This header file is used in Chapter 22.
`<iterator>`	Contains classes for accessing data in the C++ Standard Library containers. This header file is used in Chapter 22, Standard Template Library (STL).
`<algorithm>`	Contains functions for manipulating data in C++ Standard Library containers. This header file is used in Chapter 22.
`<cassert>`	Contains macros for adding diagnostics that aid program debugging. This replaces header file `<assert.h>` from pre-standard C++. This header file is used in Appendix F, Preprocessor.
`<cfloat>`	Contains the floating-point size limits of the system. This header file replaces header file `<float.h>`.
`<climits>`	Contains the integral size limits of the system. This header file replaces header file `<limits.h>`.
`<cstdio>`	Contains function prototypes for the C-style standard input/output library functions and information used by them. This header file replaces header file `<stdio.h>`.
`<locale>`	Contains classes and functions normally used by stream processing to process data in the natural form for different languages (e.g., monetary formats, sorting strings, character presentation, etc.).
`<limits>`	Contains classes for defining the numerical data type limits on each computer platform.
`<utility>`	Contains classes and functions that are used by many C++ Standard Library header files.

Fig. 6.7 | C++ Standard Library header files. (Part 2 of 2.)

6.7 Case Study: Random Number Generation

We now take a brief and hopefully entertaining diversion into a popular programming application, namely simulation and game playing. In this and the next section, we develop a game-playing program that includes multiple functions. The program uses many of the control statements and concepts discussed to this point.

The element of chance can be introduced into computer applications by using the C++ Standard Library function rand.

Consider the following statement:

```
i = rand();
```

The function rand generates an unsigned integer between 0 and RAND_MAX (a symbolic constant defined in the <cstdlib> header file). The value of RAND_MAX must be at least 32767—the maximum positive value for a two-byte (16-bit) integer. For GNU C++, the value of RAND_MAX is 2147483647; for Visual Studio, the value of RAND_MAX is 32767. If rand truly produces integers at random, every number between 0 and RAND_MAX has an equal *chance* (or probability) of being chosen each time rand is called.

The range of values produced directly by the function rand often is different than what a specific application requires. For example, a program that simulates coin tossing might require only 0 for "heads" and 1 for "tails." A program that simulates rolling a six-sided die would require random integers in the range 1 to 6. A program that randomly predicts the next type of spaceship (out of four possibilities) that will fly across the horizon in a video game might require random integers in the range 1 through 4.

Rolling a Six-Sided Die

To demonstrate rand, let us develop a program (Fig. 6.8) to simulate 20 rolls of a six-sided die and print the value of each roll. The function prototype for the rand function is in <cstdlib>. To produce integers in the range 0 to 5, we use the modulus operator (%) with rand as follows:

```
rand() % 6
```

This is called scaling. The number 6 is called the scaling factor. We then shift the range of numbers produced by adding 1 to our previous result. Figure 6.8 confirms that the results are in the range 1 to 6.

```cpp
1   // Fig. 6.8: fig06_08.cpp
2   // Shifted and scaled random integers.
3   #include <iostream>
4   using std::cout;
5   using std::endl;
6
7   #include <iomanip>
8   using std::setw;
9
10  #include <cstdlib> // contains function prototype for rand
11  using std::rand;
12
13  int main()
14  {
```

Fig. 6.8 | Shifted, scaled integers produced by 1 + rand() % 6. (Part 1 of 2.)

```
15    // loop 20 times
16    for ( int counter = 1; counter <= 20; counter++ )
17    {
18        // pick random number from 1 to 6 and output it
19        cout << setw( 10 ) << ( 1 + rand() % 6 );
20
21        // if counter is divisible by 5, start a new line of output
22        if ( counter % 5 == 0 )
23            cout << endl;
24    } // end for
25
26    return 0; // indicates successful termination
27 } // end main
```

6	6	5	5	6
5	1	1	5	3
6	6	2	4	2
6	2	3	4	1

Fig. 6.8 | Shifted, scaled integers produced by `1 + rand() % 6`. (Part 2 of 2.)

Rolling a Six-Sided Die 6,000,000 Times

To show that the numbers produced by function rand occur with approximately equal likelihood, Fig. 6.9 simulates 6,000,000 rolls of a die. Each integer in the range 1 to 6 should appear approximately 1,000,000 times. This is confirmed by the output window at the end of Fig. 6.9.

```
1    // Fig. 6.9: fig06_09.cpp
2    // Roll a six-sided die 6,000,000 times.
3    #include <iostream>
4    using std::cout;
5    using std::endl;
6
7    #include <iomanip>
8    using std::setw;
9
10   #include <cstdlib> // contains function prototype for rand
11   using std::rand;
12
13   int main()
14   {
15       int frequency1 = 0; // count of 1s rolled
16       int frequency2 = 0; // count of 2s rolled
17       int frequency3 = 0; // count of 3s rolled
18       int frequency4 = 0; // count of 4s rolled
19       int frequency5 = 0; // count of 5s rolled
20       int frequency6 = 0; // count of 6s rolled
21
22       int face; // stores most recently rolled value
23
```

Fig. 6.9 | Rolling a six-sided die 6,000,000 times. (Part 1 of 2.)

```
24    // summarize results of 6,000,000 rolls of a die
25    for ( int roll = 1; roll <= 6000000; roll++ )
26    {
27       face = 1 + rand() % 6; // random number from 1 to 6
28
29       // determine roll value 1-6 and increment appropriate counter
30       switch ( face )
31       {
32          case 1:
33             ++frequency1; // increment the 1s counter
34             break;
35          case 2:
36             ++frequency2; // increment the 2s counter
37             break;
38          case 3:
39             ++frequency3; // increment the 3s counter
40             break;
41          case 4:
42             ++frequency4; // increment the 4s counter
43             break;
44          case 5:
45             ++frequency5; // increment the 5s counter
46             break;
47          case 6:
48             ++frequency6; // increment the 6s counter
49             break;
50          default: // invalid value
51             cout << "Program should never get here!";
52       } // end switch
53    } // end for
54
55    cout << "Face" << setw( 13 ) << "Frequency" << endl; // output headers
56    cout << "   1" << setw( 13 ) << frequency1
57       << "\n   2" << setw( 13 ) << frequency2
58       << "\n   3" << setw( 13 ) << frequency3
59       << "\n   4" << setw( 13 ) << frequency4
60       << "\n   5" << setw( 13 ) << frequency5
61       << "\n   6" << setw( 13 ) << frequency6 << endl;
62    return 0; // indicates successful termination
63 } // end main
```

```
Face     Frequency
   1       999702
   2      1000823
   3       999378
   4       998898
   5      1000777
   6      1000422
```

Fig. 6.9 | Rolling a six-sided die 6,000,000 times. (Part 2 of 2.)

As the program output shows, we can simulate the rolling of a six-sided die by scaling and shifting the values produced by rand. Note that the program should never get to the default case (lines 50–51) provided in the switch structure, because the switch's controlling expression (face) always has values in the range 1–6; however, we provide the default case as a matter of good practice. After we study arrays in Chapter 7, we show how to replace the entire switch structure in Fig. 6.9 elegantly with a single-line statement.

Error-Prevention Tip 6.3

Provide a default case in a switch to catch errors even if you are absolutely, positively certain that you have no bugs!

Randomizing the Random Number Generator
Executing the program of Fig. 6.8 again produces

6	6	5	5	6
5	1	1	5	3
6	6	2	4	2
6	2	3	4	1

Notice that the program prints exactly the same sequence of values shown in Fig. 6.8. How can these be random numbers? Ironically, this repeatability is an important characteristic of function rand. When debugging a simulation program, this repeatability is essential for proving that corrections to the program work properly.

Function rand actually generates pseudorandom numbers. Repeatedly calling rand produces a sequence of numbers that appears to be random. However, the sequence repeats itself each time the program executes. Once a program has been thoroughly debugged, it can be conditioned to produce a different sequence of random numbers for each execution. This is called randomizing and is accomplished with the C++ Standard Library function srand. Function srand takes an unsigned integer argument and seeds the rand function to produce a different sequence of random numbers for each execution of the program.

Figure 6.10 demonstrates function srand. The program uses the data type unsigned, which is short for unsigned int. An int is stored in at least two bytes of memory (typically four bytes of memory on today's popular 32-bit systems) and can have positive and negative values. A variable of type unsigned int is also stored in at least two bytes of memory. A two-byte unsigned int can have only nonnegative values in the range 0–65535. A four-byte unsigned int can have only nonnegative values in the range 0–4294967295. Function srand takes an unsigned int value as an argument. The function prototype for the srand function is in header file <cstdlib>.

```
1  // Fig. 6.10: fig06_10.cpp
2  // Randomizing die-rolling program.
3  #include <iostream>
4  using std::cout;
5  using std::cin;
6  using std::endl;
7
```

Fig. 6.10 | Randomizing the die-rolling program. (Part 1 of 2.)

```
 8    #include <iomanip>
 9    using std::setw;
10
11    #include <cstdlib> // contains prototypes for functions srand and rand
12    using std::rand;
13    using std::srand;
14
15    int main()
16    {
17       unsigned seed; // stores the seed entered by the user
18
19       cout << "Enter seed: ";
20       cin >> seed;
21       srand( seed ); // seed random number generator
22
23       // loop 10 times
24       for ( int counter = 1; counter <= 10; counter++ )
25       {
26          // pick random number from 1 to 6 and output it
27          cout << setw( 10 ) << ( 1 + rand() % 6 );
28
29          // if counter is divisible by 5, start a new line of output
30          if ( counter % 5 == 0 )
31             cout << endl;
32       } // end for
33
34       return 0; // indicates successful termination
35    } // end main
```

```
Enter seed: 67
         6         1         4         6         2
         1         6         1         6         4
```

```
Enter seed: 432
         4         6         3         1         6
         3         1         5         4         2
```

```
Enter seed: 67
         6         1         4         6         2
         1         6         1         6         4
```

Fig. 6.10 | Randomizing the die-rolling program. (Part 2 of 2.)

Let us run the program several times and observe the results. Notice that the program produces a *different* sequence of random numbers each time it executes, provided that the user enters a different seed. We used the same seed in the first and third sample outputs, so the same series of 10 numbers is displayed in each of those outputs.

To randomize without having to enter a seed each time, we may use a statement like

```
srand( time( 0 ) );
```

This causes the computer to read its clock to obtain the value for the seed. Function time (with the argument 0 as written in the preceding statement) returns the current time as the number of seconds since January 1, 1970, at midnight Greenwich Mean Time (GMT). This value is converted to an unsigned integer and used as the seed to the random number generator. The function prototype for time is in <ctime>.

 Common Programming Error 6.7

Calling function srand more than once in a program restarts the pseudorandom number sequence and can affect the randomness of the numbers produced by rand.

Generalized Scaling and Shifting of Random Numbers

Previously, we demonstrated how to write a single statement to simulate the rolling of a six-sided die with the statement

```
face = 1 + rand() % 6;
```

which always assigns an integer (at random) to variable face in the range 1 ≤ face ≤ 6. Note that the width of this range (i.e., the number of consecutive integers in the range) is 6 and the starting number in the range is 1. Referring to the preceding statement, we see that the width of the range is determined by the number used to scale rand with the modulus operator (i.e., 6), and the starting number of the range is equal to the number (i.e., 1) that is added to the expression rand % 6. We can generalize this result as

number = *shiftingValue* + rand() % *scalingFactor*;

where *shiftingValue* is equal to the first number in the desired range of consecutive integers and *scalingFactor* is equal to the width of the desired range of consecutive integers. The exercises show that it is possible to choose integers at random from sets of values other than ranges of consecutive integers.

 Common Programming Error 6.8

Using srand in place of rand to attempt to generate random numbers is a compilation error— function srand does not return a value.

6.8 Case Study: Game of Chance; Introducing enum

One of the most popular games of chance is a dice game known as "craps," which is played in casinos and back alleys worldwide. The rules of the game are straightforward:

> *A player rolls two dice. Each die has six faces. These faces contain 1, 2, 3, 4, 5 and 6 spots. After the dice have come to rest, the sum of the spots on the two upward faces is calculated. If the sum is 7 or 11 on the first roll, the player wins. If the sum is 2, 3 or 12 on the first roll (called "craps"), the player loses (i.e., the "house" wins). If the sum is 4, 5, 6, 8, 9 or 10 on the first roll, then that sum becomes the player's "point." To win, you must continue rolling the dice until you "make your point." The player loses by rolling a 7 before making the point.*

The program in Fig. 6.11 simulates the game of craps.

In the rules of the game, notice that the player must roll two dice on the first roll and on all subsequent rolls. We define function rollDice (lines 71–83) to roll the dice and compute and print their sum. Function rollDice is defined once, but it is called from two places (lines 27 and 51) in the program. Interestingly, rollDice takes no arguments, so we have indicated an empty parameter list in the prototype (line 14) and in the function header (line 71). Function rollDice does return the sum of the two dice, so return type int is indicated in the function prototype and function header.

```cpp
// Fig. 6.11: fig06_11.cpp
// Craps simulation.
#include <iostream>
using std::cout;
using std::endl;

#include <cstdlib> // contains prototypes for functions srand and rand
using std::rand;
using std::srand;

#include <ctime> // contains prototype for function time
using std::time;

int rollDice(); // rolls dice, calculates amd displays sum

int main()
{
   // enumeration with constants that represent the game status
   enum Status { CONTINUE, WON, LOST }; // all caps in constants

   int myPoint; // point if no win or loss on first roll
   Status gameStatus; // can contain CONTINUE, WON or LOST

   // randomize random number generator using current time
   srand( time( 0 ) );

   int sumOfDice = rollDice(); // first roll of the dice

   // determine game status and point (if needed) based on first roll
   switch ( sumOfDice )
   {
      case 7: // win with 7 on first roll
      case 11: // win with 11 on first roll
         gameStatus = WON;
         break;
      case 2: // lose with 2 on first roll
      case 3: // lose with 3 on first roll
      case 12: // lose with 12 on first roll
         gameStatus = LOST;
         break;
      default: // did not win or lose, so remember point
         gameStatus = CONTINUE; // game is not over
         myPoint = sumOfDice; // remember the point
         cout << "Point is " << myPoint << endl;
         break; // optional at end of switch
   } // end switch

```

Fig. 6.11 | Craps simulation. (Part 1 of 3.)

```
48      // while game is not complete
49      while ( gameStatus == CONTINUE ) // not WON or LOST
50      {
51          sumOfDice = rollDice(); // roll dice again
52
53          // determine game status
54          if ( sumOfDice == myPoint ) // win by making point
55              gameStatus = WON;
56          else
57              if ( sumOfDice == 7 ) // lose by rolling 7 before point
58                  gameStatus = LOST;
59      } // end while
60
61      // display won or lost message
62      if ( gameStatus == WON )
63          cout << "Player wins" << endl;
64      else
65          cout << "Player loses" << endl;
66
67      return 0; // indicates successful termination
68  } // end main
69
70  // roll dice, calculate sum and display results
71  int rollDice()
72  {
73      // pick random die values
74      int die1 = 1 + rand() % 6; // first die roll
75      int die2 = 1 + rand() % 6; // second die roll
76
77      int sum = die1 + die2; // compute sum of die values
78
79      // display results of this roll
80      cout << "Player rolled " << die1 << " + " << die2
81          << " = " << sum << endl;
82      return sum; // end function rollDice
83  } // end function rollDice
```

```
Player rolled 2 + 5 = 7
Player wins
```

```
Player rolled 6 + 6 = 12
Player loses
```

```
Player rolled 3 + 3 = 6
Point is 6
Player rolled 5 + 3 = 8
Player rolled 4 + 5 = 9
Player rolled 2 + 1 = 3
Player rolled 1 + 5 = 6
Player wins
```

Fig. 6.11 | Craps simulation. (Part 2 of 3.)

```
Player rolled 1 + 3 = 4
Point is 4
Player rolled 4 + 6 = 10
Player rolled 2 + 4 = 6
Player rolled 6 + 4 = 10
Player rolled 2 + 3 = 5
Player rolled 2 + 4 = 6
Player rolled 1 + 1 = 2
Player rolled 4 + 4 = 8
Player rolled 4 + 3 = 7
Player loses
```

Fig. 6.11 | Craps simulation. (Part 3 of 3.)

The game is reasonably involved. The player may win or lose on the first roll or on any subsequent roll. The program uses variable gameStatus to keep track of this. Variable gameStatus is declared to be of new type Status. Line 19 declares a user-defined type called an enumeration. An enumeration, introduced by the keyword enum and followed by a type name (in this case, Status), is a set of integer constants represented by identifiers. The values of these enumeration constants start at 0, unless specified otherwise, and increment by 1. In the preceding enumeration, the constant CONTINUE has the value 0, WON has the value 1 and LOST has the value 2. The identifiers in an enum must be unique, but separate enumeration constants can have the same integer value (we show how to accomplish this momentarily).

Good Programming Practice 6.1

Capitalize the first letter of an identifier used as a user-defined type name.

Good Programming Practice 6.2

Use only uppercase letters in the names of enumeration constants. This makes these constants stand out in a program and reminds you that enumeration constants are not variables.

Variables of user-defined type Status can be assigned only one of the three values declared in the enumeration. When the game is won, the program sets variable gameStatus to WON (lines 34 and 55). When the game is lost, the program sets variable gameStatus to LOST (lines 39 and 58). Otherwise, the program sets variable gameStatus to CONTINUE (line 42) to indicate that the dice must be rolled again.

Another popular enumeration is

```
enum Months { JAN = 1, FEB, MAR, APR, MAY, JUN, JUL, AUG,
   SEP, OCT, NOV, DEC };
```

which creates user-defined type Months with enumeration constants representing the months of the year. The first value in the preceding enumeration is explicitly set to 1, so the remaining values increment from 1, resulting in the values 1 through 12. Any enumeration constant can be assigned an integer value in the enumeration definition, and subsequent enumeration constants each have a value 1 higher than the preceding constant in the list until the next explicit setting.

After the first roll, if the game is won or lost, the program skips the body of the `while` statement (lines 49–59) because `gameStatus` is not equal to `CONTINUE`. The program proceeds to the `if...else` statement in lines 62–65, which prints `"Player wins"` if `gameStatus` is equal to `WON` and `"Player loses"` if `gameStatus` is equal to `LOST`.

After the first roll, if the game is not over, the program saves the sum in `myPoint` (line 43). Execution proceeds with the `while` statement, because `gameStatus` is equal to `CON-TINUE`. During each iteration of the `while`, the program calls `rollDice` to produce a new sum. If `sum` matches `myPoint`, the program sets `gameStatus` to `WON` (line 55), the `while`-test fails, the `if...else` statement prints `"Player wins"` and execution terminates. If `sum` is equal to 7, the program sets `gameStatus` to `LOST` (line 58), the `while`-test fails, the `if...else` statement prints `"Player loses"` and execution terminates.

Note the interesting use of the various program control mechanisms we have discussed. The craps program uses two functions—`main` and `rollDice`—and the `switch`, `while`, `if...else`, nested `if...else` and nested `if` statements. In the exercises, we investigate various interesting characteristics of the game of craps.

Good Programming Practice 6.3

Using enumerations rather than integer constants can make programs clearer and more maintainable. You can set the value of an enumeration constant once in the enumeration declaration.

Common Programming Error 6.9

Assigning the integer equivalent of an enumeration constant (rather than the enumeration constant, itself) to a variable of the enumeration type is a compilation error.

Common Programming Error 6.10

After an enumeration constant has been defined, attempting to assign another value to the enumeration constant is a compilation error.

6.9 Storage Classes

The programs you have seen so far use identifiers for variable names. The attributes of variables include name, type, size and value. This chapter also uses identifiers as names for user-defined functions. Actually, each identifier in a program has other attributes, including storage class, scope and linkage.

C++ provides five storage-class specifiers: `auto`, `register`, `extern`, `mutable` and `static`. This section discusses storage-class specifiers `auto`, `register`, `extern` and `static`. Storage-class specifier `mutable` (discussed in detail in Chapter 25, Other Topics) is used exclusively with classes.

Storage Class, Scope and Linkage

An identifier's storage class determines the period during which that identifier exists in memory. Some identifiers exist briefly, some are repeatedly created and destroyed and others exist for the entire execution of a program. First we discuss the storage classes static and automatic.

An identifier's scope is where the identifier can be referenced in a program. Some identifiers can be referenced throughout a program; others can be referenced from only limited portions of a program. Section 6.10 discusses the scope of identifiers.

An identifier's linkage determines whether it is known only in the source file where it is declared or across multiple files that are compiled, then linked together. An identifier's storage-class specifier helps determine its storage class and linkage.

Storage Class Categories

The storage-class specifiers can be split into two storage classes: automatic storage class and static storage class. Keywords `auto` and `register` are used to declare variables of the automatic storage class. Such variables are created when program execution enters the block in which they are defined, they exist while the block is active and they are destroyed when the program exits the block.

Local Variables

Only local variables of a function can be of automatic storage class. A function's local variables and parameters normally are of automatic storage class. The storage class specifier `auto` explicitly declares variables of automatic storage class. For example, the following declaration indicates that `double` variable x is a local variable of automatic storage class—it exists only in the nearest enclosing pair of curly braces within the body of the function in which the definition appears:

```
auto double x;
```

Local variables are of automatic storage class by default, so keyword `auto` rarely is used. For the remainder of the text, we refer to variables of automatic storage class simply as automatic variables.

Performance Tip 6.1

Automatic storage is a means of conserving memory, because automatic storage class variables exist in memory only when the block in which they are defined is executing.

Software Engineering Observation 6.8

Automatic storage is an example of the principle of least privilege, which is fundamental to good software engineering. In the context of an application, the principle states that code should be granted only the amount of privilege and access that it needs to accomplish its designated task, but no more. Why should we have variables stored in memory and accessible when they are not needed?

Register Variables

Data in the machine-language version of a program is normally loaded into registers for calculations and other processing.

Performance Tip 6.2

The storage-class specifier `register` can be placed before an automatic variable declaration to suggest that the compiler maintain the variable in one of the computer's high-speed hardware registers rather than in memory. If intensely used variables such as counters or totals are maintained in hardware registers, the overhead of repeatedly loading the variables from memory into the registers and storing the results back into memory is eliminated.

Common Programming Error 6.11

Using multiple storage-class specifiers for an identifier is a syntax error. Only one storage class specifier can be applied to an identifier. For example, if you include register, do not also include auto.

The compiler might ignore register declarations. For example, there might not be a sufficient number of registers available for the compiler to use. The following definition *suggests* that the integer variable counter be placed in one of the computer's registers; regardless of whether the compiler does this, counter is initialized to 1:

```
register int counter = 1;
```

The register keyword can be used only with local variables and function parameters.

Performance Tip 6.3

Often, register is unnecessary. Optimizing compilers can recognize frequently used variables and may place them in registers without needing a register declaration.

Static Storage Class

Keywords extern and static declare identifiers for variables of the static storage class and for functions. Static-storage-class variables exist from the point at which the program begins execution and last for the duration of the program. A static-storage-class variable's storage is allocated when the program begins execution. Such a variable is initialized once when its declaration is encountered. For functions, the name of the function exists when the program begins execution, just as for all other functions. However, even though the variables and the function names exist from the start of program execution, this does not mean that these identifiers can be used throughout the program. Storage class and scope (where a name can be used) are separate issues, as we'll see in Section 6.10.

Identifiers with Static Storage Class

There are two types of identifiers with static storage class—external identifiers (such as global variables and global function names) and local variables declared with the storage-class specifier static. Global variables are created by placing variable declarations outside any class or function definition. Global variables retain their values throughout the execution of the program. Global variables and global functions can be referenced by any function that follows their declarations or definitions in the source file.

Software Engineering Observation 6.9

Declaring a variable as global rather than local allows unintended side effects to occur when a function that does not need access to the variable accidentally or maliciously modifies it. This is another example of the principle of least privilege. In general, except for truly global resources such as cin and cout, the use of global variables should be avoided except in certain situations with unique performance requirements.

Software Engineering Observation 6.10

Variables used only in a particular function should be declared as local variables in that function rather than as global variables.

Local variables declared with the keyword `static` are still known only in the function in which they are declared, but, unlike automatic variables, `static` local variables retain their values when the function returns to its caller. The next time the function is called, the `static` local variables contain the values they had when the function last completed execution. The following statement declares local variable `count` to be `static` and to be initialized to 1:

```
static int count = 1;
```

All numeric variables of the static storage class are initialized to zero if they are not explicitly initialized by you, but it is nevertheless a good practice to explicitly initialize all variables.

Storage-class specifiers `extern` and `static` have special meaning when they are applied explicitly to external identifiers such as global variables and global function names. In Appendix E, C Legacy Code Topics, we discuss using `extern` and `static` with external identifiers and multiple-source-file programs.

6.10 Scope Rules

The portion of the program where an identifier can be used is known as its scope. For example, when we declare a local variable in a block, it can be referenced only in that block and in blocks nested within that block. This section discusses four scopes for an identifier—function scope, file scope, block scope and function-prototype scope. Later we'll see two other scopes—class scope (Chapter 9) and namespace scope (Chapter 25).

An identifier declared outside any function or class has file scope. Such an identifier is "known" in all functions from the point at which it is declared until the end of the file. Global variables, function definitions and function prototypes placed outside a function all have file scope.

Labels (identifiers followed by a colon such as `start:`) are the only identifiers with function scope. Labels can be used anywhere in the function in which they appear, but cannot be referenced outside the function body. Labels are used in `goto` statements (Appendix E). Labels are implementation details that functions hide from one another.

Identifiers declared inside a block have block scope. Block scope begins at the identifier's declaration and ends at the terminating right brace (}) of the block in which the identifier is declared. Local variables have block scope, as do function parameters, which are also local variables of the function. Any block can contain variable declarations. When blocks are nested and an identifier in an outer block has the same name as an identifier in an inner block, the identifier in the outer block is "hidden" until the inner block terminates. While executing in the inner block, the inner block sees the value of its own local identifier and not the value of the identically named identifier in the enclosing block. Local variables declared `static` still have block scope, even though they exist from the time the program begins execution. Storage duration does not affect the scope of an identifier.

The only identifiers with function prototype scope are those used in the parameter list of a function prototype. As mentioned previously, function prototypes do not require names in the parameter list—only types are required. Names appearing in the parameter list of a function prototype are ignored by the compiler. Identifiers used in a function prototype can be reused elsewhere in the program without ambiguity. In a single prototype, a particular identifier can be used only once.

Common Programming Error 6.12

Accidentally using the same name for an identifier in an inner block that is used for an identifier in an outer block, when in fact you want the identifier in the outer block to be active for the duration of the inner block, is normally a logic error.

Good Programming Practice 6.4

Avoid variable names that hide names in outer scopes. This can be accomplished by avoiding the use of duplicate identifiers in a program.

The program of Fig. 6.12 demonstrates scoping issues with global variables, automatic local variables and `static` local variables.

```cpp
1   // Fig. 6.12: fig06_12.cpp
2   // A scoping example.
3   #include <iostream>
4   using std::cout;
5   using std::endl;
6
7   void useLocal(); // function prototype
8   void useStaticLocal(); // function prototype
9   void useGlobal(); // function prototype
10
11  int x = 1; // global variable
12
13  int main()
14  {
15     cout << "global x in main is " << x << endl;
16
17     int x = 5; // local variable to main
18
19     cout << "local x in main's outer scope is " << x << endl;
20
21     { // start new scope
22        int x = 7; // hides both x in outer scope and global x
23
24        cout << "local x in main's inner scope is " << x << endl;
25     } // end new scope
26
27     cout << "local x in main's outer scope is " << x << endl;
28
29     useLocal(); // useLocal has local x
30     useStaticLocal(); // useStaticLocal has static local x
31     useGlobal(); // useGlobal uses global x
32     useLocal(); // useLocal reinitializes its local x
33     useStaticLocal(); // static local x retains its prior value
34     useGlobal(); // global x also retains its prior value
35
36     cout << "\nlocal x in main is " << x << endl;
37     return 0; // indicates successful termination
38  } // end main
39
```

Fig. 6.12 | Scoping example. (Part 1 of 2.)

```
40   // useLocal reinitializes local variable x during each call
41   void useLocal()
42   {
43      int x = 25; // initialized each time useLocal is called
44
45      cout << "\nlocal x is " << x << " on entering useLocal" << endl;
46      x++;
47      cout << "local x is " << x << " on exiting useLocal" << endl;
48   } // end function useLocal
49
50   // useStaticLocal initializes static local variable x only the
51   // first time the function is called; value of x is saved
52   // between calls to this function
53   void useStaticLocal()
54   {
55      static int x = 50; // initialized first time useStaticLocal is called
56
57      cout << "\nlocal static x is " << x << " on entering useStaticLocal"
58         << endl;
59      x++;
60      cout << "local static x is " << x << " on exiting useStaticLocal"
61         << endl;
62   } // end function useStaticLocal
63
64   // useGlobal modifies global variable x during each call
65   void useGlobal()
66   {
67      cout << "\nglobal x is " << x << " on entering useGlobal" << endl;
68      x *= 10;
69      cout << "global x is " << x << " on exiting useGlobal" << endl;
70   } // end function useGlobal
```

```
global x in main is 1
local x in main's outer scope is 5
local x in main's inner scope is 7
local x in main's outer scope is 5

local x is 25 on entering useLocal
local x is 26 on exiting useLocal

local static x is 50 on entering useStaticLocal
local static x is 51 on exiting useStaticLocal

global x is 1 on entering useGlobal
global x is 10 on exiting useGlobal

local x is 25 on entering useLocal
local x is 26 on exiting useLocal

local static x is 51 on entering useStaticLocal
local static x is 52 on exiting useStaticLocal

global x is 10 on entering useGlobal
global x is 100 on exiting useGlobal

local x in main is 5
```

Fig. 6.12 | Scoping example. (Part 2 of 2.)

Line 11 declares and initializes global variable x to 1. This global variable is hidden in any block (or function) that declares a variable named x. In main, line 15 displays the value of global variable x. Line 17 declares a local variable x and initializes it to 5. Line 19 outputs this variable to show that the global x is hidden in main. Next, lines 21–25 define a new block in main in which another local variable x is initialized to 7 (line 22). Line 24 outputs this variable to show that it hides x in the outer block of main. When the block exits, the variable x with value 7 is destroyed automatically. Next, line 27 outputs the local variable x in the outer block of main to show that it is no longer hidden.

To demonstrate other scopes, the program defines three functions, each of which takes no arguments and returns nothing. Function useLocal (lines 41–48) declares automatic variable x (line 43) and initializes it to 25. When the program calls useLocal, the function prints the variable, increments it and prints it again before the function returns program control to its caller. Each time the program calls this function, the function recreates automatic variable x and reinitializes it to 25.

Function useStaticLocal (lines 53–62) declares static variable x and initializes it to 50. Local variables declared as static retain their values even when they are out of scope (i.e., the function in which they are declared is not executing). When the program calls useStaticLocal, the function prints x, increments it and prints it again before the function returns program control to its caller. In the next call to this function, static local variable x contains the value 51. The initialization in line 55 occurs only once—the first time useStaticLocal is called.

Function useGlobal (lines 65–70) does not declare any variables. Therefore, when it refers to variable x, the global x (line 11, preceding main) is used. When the program calls useGlobal, the function prints the global variable x, multiplies it by 10 and prints it again before the function returns program control to its caller. The next time the program calls useGlobal, the global variable has its modified value, 10. After executing functions use-Local, useStaticLocal and useGlobal twice each, the program prints the local variable x in main again to show that none of the function calls modified the value of x in main, because the functions all referred to variables in other scopes.

6.11 Function Call Stack and Activation Records

To understand how C++ performs function calls, we first need to consider a data structure (i.e., collection of related data items) known as a stack. Think of a stack as analogous to a pile of dishes. When a dish is placed on the pile, it is normally placed at the top (referred to as pushing the dish onto the stack). Similarly, when a dish is removed from the pile, it is normally removed from the top (referred to as popping the dish off the stack). Stacks are known as last-in, first-out (LIFO) data structures—the last item pushed (inserted) on the stack is the first item popped (removed) from the stack.

One of the most important mechanisms for computer science students to understand is the function call stack (sometimes referred to as the program execution stack). This data structure—working "behind the scenes"—supports the function call/return mechanism. It also supports the creation, maintenance and destruction of each called function's automatic variables. We explained the last-in, first-out (LIFO) behavior of stacks with our dish-stacking example. As we'll see in Figs. 6.14–6.16, this LIFO behavior is exactly what a function does when returning to the function that called it.

As each function is called, it may, in turn, call other functions, which may, in turn, call other functions—all before any of the functions returns. Each function eventually must return control to the function that called it. So, somehow, we must keep track of the return addresses that each function needs to return control to the function that called it. The function call stack is the perfect data structure for handling this information. Each time a function calls another function, an entry is pushed onto the stack. This entry, called a stack frame or an activation record, contains the return address that the called function needs in order to return to the calling function. It also contains some additional information we'll soon discuss. If the called function returns, instead of calling another function before returning, the stack frame for the function call is popped, and control transfers to the return address in the popped stack frame.

The beauty of the call stack is that each called function always finds the information it needs to return to its caller at the top of the call stack. And, if a function makes a call to another function, a stack frame for the new function call is simply pushed onto the call stack. Thus, the return address required by the newly called function to return to its caller is now located at the top of the stack.

The stack frames have another important responsibility. Most functions have automatic variables—parameters and any local variables the function declares. Automatic variables need to exist while a function is executing. They need to remain active if the function makes calls to other functions. But when a called function returns to its caller, the called function's automatic variables need to "go away." The called function's stack frame is a perfect place to reserve the memory for the called function's automatic variables. That stack frame exists as long as the called function is active. When that function returns—and no longer needs its local automatic variables—its stack frame is popped from the stack, and those local automatic variables are no longer known to the program.

Of course, the amount of memory in a computer is finite, so only a certain amount of memory can be used to store activation records on the function call stack. If more function calls occur than can have their activation records stored on the function call stack, an error known as stack overflow occurs.

Function Call Stack in Action

So, as we have seen, the call stack and activation records support the function call/return mechanism and the creation and destruction of automatic variables. Now let's consider how the call stack supports the operation of a square function called by main (lines 11–17 of Fig. 6.13). First the operating system calls main—this pushes an activation record onto the stack (shown in Fig. 6.14). The activation record tells main how to return to the

```
1   // Fig. 6.13: fig06_13.cpp
2   // square function used to demonstrate the function
3   // call stack and activation records.
4   #include <iostream>
5   using std::cin;
6   using std::cout;
7   using std::endl;
8
```

Fig. 6.13 | square function used to demonstrate the function call stack and activation records. (Part 1 of 2.)

```
 9   int square( int ); // prototype for function square
10
11   int main()
12   {
13      int a = 10; // value to square (local automatic variable in main)
14
15      cout << a << " squared: " << square( a ) << endl; // display a squared
16      return 0; // indicate successful termination
17   } // end main
18
19   // returns the square of an integer
20   int square( int x ) // x is a local variable
21   {
22      return x * x; // calculate square and return result
23   } // end function square
```

```
10 squared: 100
```

Fig. 6.13 | square function used to demonstrate the function call stack and activation records. (Part 2 of 2.)

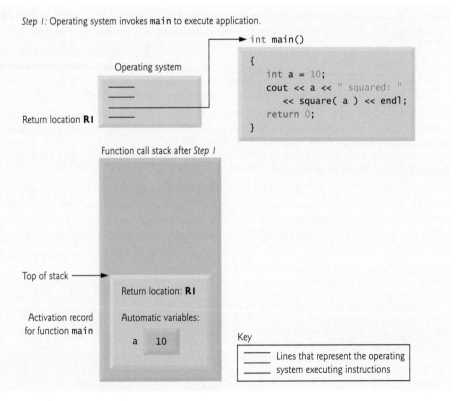

Fig. 6.14 | Function call stack after the operating system invokes main to execute the application.

operating system (i.e., transfer to return address R1) and contains the space for main's automatic variable (i.e., a, which is initialized to 10).

Function main—before returning to the operating system—now calls function square in line 15 of Fig. 6.13. This causes a stack frame for square (lines 20–23) to be pushed onto the function call stack (Fig. 6.15). This stack frame contains the return address that square needs to return to main (i.e., R2) and the memory for square's automatic variable (i.e., x).

After square calculates the square of its argument, it needs to return to main—and no longer needs the memory for its automatic variable x. So the stack is popped—giving square the return location in main (i.e., R2) and losing square's automatic variable. Figure 6.16 shows the function call stack after square's activation record has been popped.

Function main now displays the result of calling square (line 15), then executes the return statement (line 16). This causes the activation record for main to be popped from the stack. This gives main the address it needs to return to the operating system (i.e., R1 in Fig. 6.14) and causes the memory for main's automatic variable (i.e., a) to become unavailable.

You have now seen how valuable the notion of the stack data structure is in implementing a key mechanism that supports program execution. Data structures have many

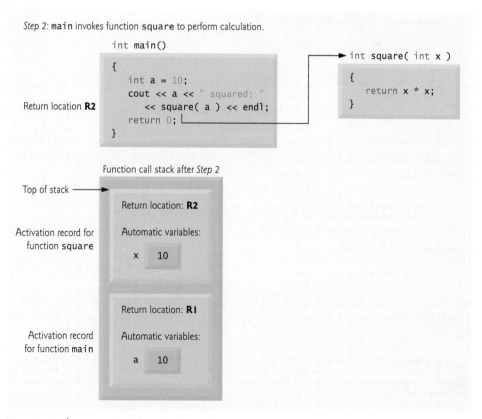

Fig. 6.15 | Function call stack after main invokes function square to perform the calculation.

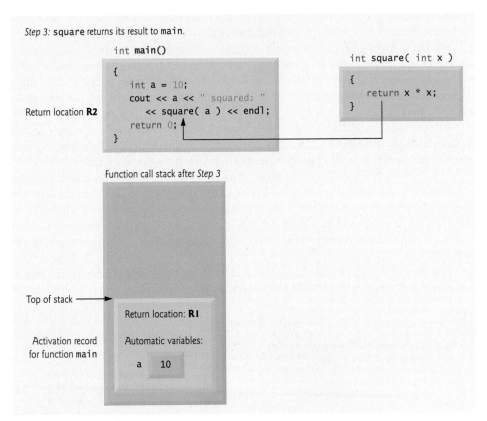

Fig. 6.16 | Function call stack after function `square` returns to `main`.

important applications in computer science. We discuss stacks, queues, lists, trees and other data structures in Chapter 20, Data Structures, and Chapter 22, Standard Template Library (STL).

6.12 Functions with Empty Parameter Lists

In C++, an empty parameter list is specified by writing either `void` or nothing at all in parentheses. The prototype

```
void print();
```

specifies that function `print` does not take arguments and does not return a value. Figure 6.17 demonstrates both ways to declare and use functions with empty parameter lists.

Portability Tip 6.2

The meaning of an empty function parameter list in C++ is dramatically different than in C. In C, it means all argument checking is disabled (i.e., the function call can pass any arguments it wants). In C++, it means that the function explicitly takes no arguments. Thus, C programs using this feature might cause compilation errors when compiled in C++.

```
1   // Fig. 6.17: fig06_17.cpp
2   // Functions that take no arguments.
3   #include <iostream>
4   using std::cout;
5   using std::endl;
6
7   void function1(); // function that takes no arguments
8   void function2( void ); // function that takes no arguments
9
10  int main()
11  {
12     function1(); // call function1 with no arguments
13     function2(); // call function2 with no arguments
14     return 0; // indicates successful termination
15  } // end main
16
17  // function1 uses an empty parameter list to specify that
18  // the function receives no arguments
19  void function1()
20  {
21     cout << "function1 takes no arguments" << endl;
22  } // end function1
23
24  // function2 uses a void parameter list to specify that
25  // the function receives no arguments
26  void function2( void )
27  {
28     cout << "function2 also takes no arguments" << endl;
29  } // end function2
```

```
function1 takes no arguments
function2 also takes no arguments
```

Fig. 6.17 | Functions that take no arguments.

 Common Programming Error 6.13

C++ programs do not compile unless function prototypes are provided for every function or each function is defined before it is called.

6.13 Inline Functions

Implementing a program as a set of functions is good from a software engineering stand-point, but function calls involve execution-time overhead. C++ provides inline functions to help reduce function call overhead—especially for small functions. Placing the qualifier inline before a function's return type in the function definition "advises" the compiler to generate a copy of the function's code in place (when appropriate) to avoid a function call. The trade-off is that multiple copies of the function code are inserted in the program (often making the program larger) rather than there being a single copy of the function to which control is passed each time the function is called. The compiler can ignore the inline qualifier and typically does so for all but the smallest functions.

Software Engineering Observation 6.11

Any change to an inline *function requires all clients of the function to be recompiled. This can be significant in some program development and maintenance situations.*

Good Programming Practice 6.5

The inline *qualifier should be used only with small, frequently used functions.*

Performance Tip 6.4

Using inline *functions can reduce execution time but may increase program size.*

Figure 6.18 uses inline function cube (lines 11–14) to calculate the volume of a cube of side side. Keyword const in the parameter list of function cube (line 11) tells the compiler that the function does not modify variable side. This ensures that the value of side is not changed by the function when the calculation is performed. (Keyword const is discussed in detail in Chapters 7, 8 and 10.) Notice that the complete definition of function cube appears before it is used in the program. This is required so that the compiler knows how to expand a cube function call into its inlined code. For this reason, reusable inline functions are typically placed in header files, so that their definitions can be included in each source file that uses them.

Software Engineering Observation 6.12

The const *qualifier should be used to enforce the principle of least privilege. Using the principle of least privilege to properly design software can greatly reduce debugging time and improper side effects and can make a program easier to modify and maintain.*

```
1   // Fig. 6.18: fig06_18.cpp
2   // Using an inline function to calculate the volume of a cube.
3   #include <iostream>
4   using std::cout;
5   using std::cin;
6   using std::endl;
7
8   // Definition of inline function cube. Definition of function appears
9   // before function is called, so a function prototype is not required.
10  // First line of function definition acts as the prototype.
11  inline double cube( const double side )
12  {
13      return side * side * side; // calculate cube
14  } // end function cube
15
16  int main()
17  {
18      double sideValue; // stores value entered by user
19      cout << "Enter the side length of your cube: ";
20      cin >> sideValue; // read value from user
21
```

Fig. 6.18 | inline function that calculates the volume of a cube. (Part 1 of 2.)

```
22      // calculate cube of sideValue and display result
23      cout << "Volume of cube with side "
24         << sideValue << " is " << cube( sideValue ) << endl;
25      return 0; // indicates successful termination
26   } // end main
```

```
Enter the side length of your cube: 3.5
Volume of cube with side 3.5 is 42.875
```

Fig. 6.18 | `inline` function that calculates the volume of a cube. (Part 2 of 2.)

6.14 References and Reference Parameters

Two ways to pass arguments to functions in many programming languages are pass-by-value and pass-by-reference. When an argument is passed by value, a *copy* of the argument's value is made and passed (on the function call stack) to the called function. Changes to the copy do not affect the original variable's value in the caller. This prevents the accidental side effects that so greatly hinder the development of correct and reliable software systems. Each argument that has been passed in the programs in this chapter so far has been passed by value.

Performance Tip 6.5

One disadvantage of pass-by-value is that, if a large data item is being passed, copying that data can take a considerable amount of execution time and memory space.

Reference Parameters

This section introduces reference parameters—the first of the two means C++ provides for performing pass-by-reference. With pass-by-reference, the caller gives the called function the ability to access the caller's data directly, and to modify that data if the called function chooses to do so.

Performance Tip 6.6

Pass-by-reference is good for performance reasons, because it can eliminate the pass-by-value overhead of copying large amounts of data.

Software Engineering Observation 6.13

Pass-by-reference can weaken security, because the called function can corrupt the caller's data.

Later, we'll show how to achieve the performance advantage of pass-by-reference while simultaneously achieving the software engineering advantage of protecting the caller's data from corruption.

A reference parameter is an alias for its corresponding argument in a function call. To indicate that a function parameter is passed by reference, simply follow the parameter's type in the function prototype by an ampersand (&); use the same convention when listing the parameter's type in the function header. For example, the following declaration in a function header

```
int &count
```

when read from right to left is pronounced "count is a reference to an int." In the function call, simply mention the variable by name to pass it by reference. Then, mentioning the variable by its parameter name in the body of the called function actually refers to the original variable in the calling function, and the original variable can be modified directly by the called function. As always, the function prototype and header must agree.

Passing Arguments by Value and by Reference

Figure 6.19 compares pass-by-value and pass-by-reference with reference parameters. The "styles" of the arguments in the calls to function squareByValue and function squareByReference are identical—both variables are simply mentioned by name in the function calls. Without checking the function prototypes or function definitions, it is not possible to tell from the calls alone whether either function can modify its arguments. Because function prototypes are mandatory, the compiler has no trouble resolving the ambiguity.

```cpp
1   // Fig. 6.19: fig06_19.cpp
2   // Comparing pass-by-value and pass-by-reference with references.
3   #include <iostream>
4   using std::cout;
5   using std::endl;
6
7   int squareByValue( int ); // function prototype (value pass)
8   void squareByReference( int & ); // function prototype (reference pass)
9
10  int main()
11  {
12     int x = 2; // value to square using squareByValue
13     int z = 4; // value to square using squareByReference
14
15     // demonstrate squareByValue
16     cout << "x = " << x << " before squareByValue\n";
17     cout << "Value returned by squareByValue: "
18        << squareByValue( x ) << endl;
19     cout << "x = " << x << " after squareByValue\n" << endl;
20
21     // demonstrate squareByReference
22     cout << "z = " << z << " before squareByReference" << endl;
23     squareByReference( z );
24     cout << "z = " << z << " after squareByReference" << endl;
25     return 0; // indicates successful termination
26  } // end main
27
28  // squareByValue multiplies number by itself, stores the
29  // result in number and returns the new value of number
30  int squareByValue( int number )
31  {
32     return number *= number; // caller's argument not modified
33  } // end function squareByValue
34
```

Fig. 6.19 | Passing arguments by value and by reference. (Part 1 of 2.)

```
35  // squareByReference multiplies numberRef by itself and stores the result
36  // in the variable to which numberRef refers in function main
37  void squareByReference( int &numberRef )
38  {
39     numberRef *= numberRef; // caller's argument modified
40  } // end function squareByReference
```

```
x = 2 before squareByValue
Value returned by squareByValue: 4
x = 2 after squareByValue

z = 4 before squareByReference
z = 16 after squareByReference
```

Fig. 6.19 | Passing arguments by value and by reference. (Part 2 of 2.)

Common Programming Error 6.14

Because reference parameters are mentioned only by name in the body of the called function, you might inadvertently treat reference parameters as pass-by-value parameters. This can cause unexpected side effects if the original copies of the variables are changed by the function.

Chapter 8 discusses pointers; pointers enable an alternate form of pass-by-reference in which the style of the call clearly indicates pass-by-reference (and the potential for modifying the caller's arguments).

Performance Tip 6.7

For passing large objects, use a constant reference parameter to simulate the appearance and security of pass-by-value and avoid the overhead of passing a copy of the large object.

Software Engineering Observation 6.14

Many programmers do not bother to declare parameters passed by value as const, *even though the called function should not be modifying the passed argument. Keyword* const *in this context would protect only a copy of the original argument, not the original argument itself, which when passed by value is safe from modification by the called function.*

To specify a reference to a constant, place the const qualifier before the type specifier in the parameter declaration.

Note the placement of & in function squareByReference's parameter list (line 37, Fig. 6.19). Some C++ programmers prefer to write the equivalent form int& numberRef.

Software Engineering Observation 6.15

For the combined reasons of clarity and performance, many C++ programmers prefer that modifiable arguments be passed to functions by using pointers (which we study in Chapter 8), small nonmodifiable arguments be passed by value and large nonmodifiable arguments be passed to functions by using references to constants.

References as Aliases within a Function

References can also be used as aliases for other variables within a function (although they typically are used with functions as shown in Fig. 6.19). For example, the code

```
int count = 1; // declare integer variable count
int &cRef = count; // create cRef as an alias for count
cRef++; // increment count (using its alias cRef)
```

increments variable count by using its alias cRef. Reference variables must be initialized in their declarations (see Fig. 6.20 and Fig. 6.21) and cannot be reassigned as aliases to other variables. Once a reference is declared as an alias for another variable, all operations supposedly performed on the alias (i.e., the reference) are actually performed on the original variable. The alias is simply another name for the original variable. Taking the address of a reference and comparing references do not cause syntax errors; rather, each operation actually occurs on the variable for which the reference is an alias. Unless it is a reference to a constant, a reference argument must be an *lvalue* (e.g., a variable name), not a constant or expression that returns an *rvalue* (e.g., the result of a calculation). See Section 5.9 for definitions of the terms *lvalue* and *rvalue*.

```
 1   // Fig. 6.20: fig06_20.cpp
 2   // References must be initialized.
 3   #include <iostream>
 4   using std::cout;
 5   using std::endl;
 6
 7   int main()
 8   {
 9      int x = 3;
10      int &y = x; // y refers to (is an alias for) x
11
12      cout << "x = " << x << endl << "y = " << y << endl;
13      y = 7; // actually modifies x
14      cout << "x = " << x << endl << "y = " << y << endl;
15      return 0; // indicates successful termination
16   } // end main
```

```
x = 3
y = 3
x = 7
y = 7
```

Fig. 6.20 | Initializing and using a reference.

```
 1   // Fig. 6.21: fig06_21.cpp
 2   // References must be initialized.
 3   #include <iostream>
 4   using std::cout;
 5   using std::endl;
 6
 7   int main()
 8   {
 9      int x = 3;
10      int &y; // Error: y must be initialized
```

Fig. 6.21 | Uninitialized reference causes a syntax error. (Part I of 2.)

```
11
12      cout << "x = " << x << endl << "y = " << y << endl;
13      y = 7;
14      cout << "x = " << x << endl << "y = " << y << endl;
15      return 0; // indicates successful termination
16   } // end main
```

Borland C++ command-line compiler error message:

```
Error E2304 C:\cpphtp6_examples\ch06\Fig06_21\fig06_21.cpp 10:
   Reference variable 'y' must be initialized in function main()
```

Microsoft Visual C++ compiler error message:

```
C:\cpphtp6_examples\ch06\Fig06_21\fig06_21.cpp(10) : error C2530: 'y' :
   references must be initialized
```

GNU C++ compiler error message:

```
fig06_21.cpp:10: error: 'y' declared as a reference but not initialized
```

Fig. 6.21 | Uninitialized reference causes a syntax error. (Part 2 of 2.)

Returning a Reference from a Function

Functions can return references, but this can be dangerous. When returning a reference to a variable declared in the called function, the variable should be declared `static` within that function. Otherwise, the reference refers to an automatic variable that is discarded when the function terminates; such a variable is said to be "undefined," and the program's behavior is unpredictable. References to undefined variables are called dangling references.

Common Programming Error 6.15

Not initializing a reference variable when it is declared is a compilation error, unless the declaration is part of a function's parameter list. Reference parameters are initialized when the function in which they are declared is called.

Common Programming Error 6.16

Attempting to reassign a previously declared reference to be an alias to another variable is a logic error. The value of the other variable is simply assigned to the variable for which the reference is already an alias.

Common Programming Error 6.17

Returning a reference to an automatic variable in a called function is a logic error. Some compilers issue a warning when this occurs.

Error Messages for Uninitialized References

The C++ standard does not specify the error messages that compilers use to indicate particular errors. For this reason, Fig. 6.21 shows the error messages produced by the Borland C++ command-line compiler, Microsoft Visual C++ 2005 compiler and GNU C++ compiler when a reference is not initialized.

6.15 Default Arguments

It is not uncommon for a program to invoke a function repeatedly with the same argument value for a particular parameter. In such cases, you can specify that such a parameter has a default argument, i.e., a default value to be passed to that parameter. When a program omits an argument for a parameter with a default argument in a function call, the compiler rewrites the function call and inserts the default value of that argument.

Default arguments must be the rightmost (trailing) arguments in a function's parameter list. When calling a function with two or more default arguments, if an omitted argument is not the rightmost argument in the argument list, then all arguments to the right of that argument also must be omitted. Default arguments must be specified with the first occurrence of the function name—typically, in the function prototype. If the function prototype is omitted because the function definition also serves as the prototype, then the default arguments should be specified in the function header. Default values can be any expression, including constants, global variables or function calls. Default arguments also can be used with `inline` functions.

Figure 6.22 demonstrates using default arguments in calculating the volume of a box. The function prototype for `boxVolume` (line 8) specifies that all three parameters have been given default values of 1. Note that we provided variable names in the function prototype for readability. As always, variable names are not required in function prototypes.

Common Programming Error 6.18

It is a compilation error to specify default arguments in both a function's prototype and header.

```
1    // Fig. 6.22: fig06_22.cpp
2    // Using default arguments.
3    #include <iostream>
4    using std::cout;
5    using std::endl;
6
7    // function prototype that specifies default arguments
8    int boxVolume( int length = 1, int width = 1, int height = 1 );
9
10   int main()
11   {
12      // no arguments--use default values for all dimensions
13      cout << "The default box volume is: " << boxVolume();
14
15      // specify length; default width and height
16      cout << "\n\nThe volume of a box with length 10,\n"
17         << "width 1 and height 1 is: " << boxVolume( 10 );
18
19      // specify length and width; default height
20      cout << "\n\nThe volume of a box with length 10,\n"
21         << "width 5 and height 1 is: " << boxVolume( 10, 5 );
22
```

Fig. 6.22 | Default arguments to a function. (Part 1 of 2.)

```
23      // specify all arguments
24      cout << "\n\nThe volume of a box with length 10,\n"
25          << "width 5 and height 2 is: " << boxVolume( 10, 5, 2 )
26          << endl;
27      return 0; // indicates successful termination
28   } // end main
29
30   // function boxVolume calculates the volume of a box
31   int boxVolume( int length, int width, int height )
32   {
33      return length * width * height;
34   } // end function boxVolume
```

```
The default box volume is: 1

The volume of a box with length 10,
width 1 and height 1 is: 10

The volume of a box with length 10,
width 5 and height 1 is: 50

The volume of a box with length 10,
width 5 and height 2 is: 100
```

Fig. 6.22 | Default arguments to a function. (Part 2 of 2.)

The first call to boxVolume (line 13) specifies no arguments, thus using all three default values of 1. The second call (line 17) passes only a length argument, thus using default values of 1 for the width and height arguments. The third call (line 21) passes arguments for only length and width, thus using a default value of 1 for the height argument. The last call (line 25) passes arguments for length, width and height, thus using no default values. Note that any arguments passed to the function explicitly are assigned to the function's parameters from left to right. Therefore, when boxVolume receives one argument, the function assigns the value of that argument to its length parameter (i.e., the leftmost parameter in the parameter list). When boxVolume receives two arguments, the function assigns the values of those arguments to its length and width parameters in that order. Finally, when boxVolume receives all three arguments, the function assigns the values of those arguments to its length, width and height parameters, respectively.

Good Programming Practice 6.6

Using default arguments can simplify writing function calls. However, some programmers feel that explicitly specifying all arguments is clearer.

Software Engineering Observation 6.16

If the default values for a function change, all client code using the function must be recompiled.

Common Programming Error 6.19

Specifying and attempting to use a default argument that is not a rightmost (trailing) argument (while not simultaneously defaulting all the rightmost arguments) is a syntax error.

6.16 Unary Scope Resolution Operator

It is possible to declare local and global variables of the same name. C++ provides the *unary scope resolution operator* (::) to access a global variable when a local variable of the same name is in scope. The unary scope resolution operator cannot be used to access a local variable of the same name in an outer block. A global variable can be accessed directly without the unary scope resolution operator if the name of the global variable is not the same as that of a local variable in scope.

Figure 6.23 demonstrates the unary scope resolution operator with local and global variables of the same name (lines 7 and 11). To emphasize that the local and global versions of variable `number` are distinct, the program declares one variable of type `int` and the other `double`.

Using the unary scope resolution operator (::) with a given variable name is optional when the only variable with that name is a global variable.

Common Programming Error 6.20

It is an error to attempt to use the unary scope resolution operator (::) to access a nonglobal variable in an outer block. If no global variable with that name exists, a compilation error occurs. If a global variable with that name exists, this is a logic error, because the program will refer to the global variable when you intended to access the nonglobal variable in the outer block.

Good Programming Practice 6.7

Always using the unary scope resolution operator (::) to refer to global variables makes programs easier to read and understand, because it makes it clear that you are intending to access a global variable rather than a nonglobal variable.

```cpp
1   // Fig. 6.23: fig06_23.cpp
2   // Using the unary scope resolution operator.
3   #include <iostream>
4   using std::cout;
5   using std::endl;
6
7   int number = 7; // global variable named number
8
9   int main()
10  {
11     double number = 10.5; // local variable named number
12
13     // display values of local and global variables
14     cout << "Local double value of number = " << number
15        << "\nGlobal int value of number = " << ::number << endl;
16     return 0; // indicates successful termination
17  } // end main
```

```
Local double value of number = 10.5
Global int value of number = 7
```

Fig. 6.23 | Unary scope resolution operator.

Software Engineering Observation 6.17

Always using the unary scope resolution operator (::) to refer to global variables makes programs easier to modify by reducing the risk of name collisions with nonglobal variables.

Error-Prevention Tip 6.4

Always using the unary scope resolution operator (::) to refer to a global variable eliminates possible logic errors that might occur if a nonglobal variable hides the global variable.

Error-Prevention Tip 6.5

Avoid using variables of the same name for different purposes in a program. Although this is allowed in various circumstances, it can lead to errors.

6.17 Function Overloading

C++ enables several functions of the same name to be defined, as long as these functions have different signatures. This capability is called function overloading. When an overloaded function is called, the C++ compiler selects the proper function by examining the number, types and order of the arguments in the call. Function overloading is commonly used to create several functions of the same name that perform similar tasks, but on different data types. For example, many functions in the math library are overloaded for different numeric data types—the C++ standard requires `float`, `double` and `long double` overloaded versions of the math library functions discussed in Section 6.3.

Good Programming Practice 6.8

Overloading functions that perform closely related tasks can make programs more readable and understandable.

Overloaded *square* Functions

Figure 6.24 uses overloaded `square` functions to calculate the square of an `int` (lines 8–12) and the square of a `double` (lines 15–19). Line 23 invokes the `int` version of function `square` by passing the literal value 7. C++ treats whole number literal values as type `int` by default. Similarly, line 25 invokes the `double` version of function `square` by passing the literal value 7.5, which C++ treats as a `double` value by default. In each case the compiler chooses the proper function to call, based on the type of the argument. The last two lines of the output window confirm that the proper function was called in each case.

```
1   // Fig. 6.24: fig06_24.cpp
2   // Overloaded functions.
3   #include <iostream>
4   using std::cout;
5   using std::endl;
6
7   // function square for int values
8   int square( int x )
9   {
```

Fig. 6.24 | Overloaded `square` functions. (Part 1 of 2.)

```
10      cout << "square of integer " << x << " is ";
11      return x * x;
12   } // end function square with int argument
13
14   // function square for double values
15   double square( double y )
16   {
17      cout << "square of double " << y << " is ";
18      return y * y;
19   } // end function square with double argument
20
21   int main()
22   {
23      cout << square( 7 ); // calls int version
24      cout << endl;
25      cout << square( 7.5 ); // calls double version
26      cout << endl;
27      return 0; // indicates successful termination
28   } // end main
```

```
square of integer 7 is 49
square of double 7.5 is 56.25
```

Fig. 6.24 | Overloaded square functions. (Part 2 of 2.)

How the Compiler Differentiates Overloaded Functions

Overloaded functions are distinguished by their signatures. A signature is a combination of a function's name and its parameter types (in order). The compiler encodes each function identifier with the number and types of its parameters (sometimes referred to as name mangling or name decoration) to enable type-safe linkage. Type-safe linkage ensures that the proper overloaded function is called and that the types of the arguments conform to the types of the parameters.

Figure 6.25 was compiled with the Borland C++ 5.6.4 command-line compiler. Rather than showing the execution output of the program (as we normally would), we show the mangled function names produced in assembly language by Borland C++. Each mangled name begins with @ followed by the function name. The function name is then separated from the mangled parameter list by $q. In the parameter list for function nothing2 (line 25; see the fourth output line), c represents a char, i represents an int, rf represents a float & (i.e., a reference to a float) and rd represents a double & (i.e., a reference to a double). In the parameter list for function nothing1, i represents an int, f represents a float, c represents a char and ri represents an int &. The two square functions are distinguished by their parameter lists; one specifies d for double and the other specifies i for int. The return types of the functions are not specified in the mangled names. Overloaded functions can have different return types, but if they do, they must also have different parameter lists. Again, you cannot have two functions with the same signature and different return types. Note that function name mangling is compiler specific. Also note that function main is not mangled, because it cannot be overloaded.

```
 1    // Fig. 6.25: fig06_25.cpp
 2    // Name mangling.
 3
 4    // function square for int values
 5    int square( int x )
 6    {
 7       return x * x;
 8    } // end function square
 9
10    // function square for double values
11    double square( double y )
12    {
13       return y * y;
14    } // end function square
15
16    // function that receives arguments of types
17    // int, float, char and int &
18    void nothing1( int a, float b, char c, int &d )
19    {
20       // empty function body
21    } // end function nothing1
22
23    // function that receives arguments of types
24    // char, int, float & and double &
25    int nothing2( char a, int b, float &c, double &d )
26    {
27       return 0;
28    } // end function nothing2
29
30    int main()
31    {
32       return 0; // indicates successful termination
33    } // end main
```

```
@square$qi
@square$qd
@nothing1$qifcri
@nothing2$qcirfrd
_main
```

Fig. 6.25 | Name mangling to enable type-safe linkage.

Common Programming Error 6.21

Creating overloaded functions with identical parameter lists and different return types is a compilation error.

The compiler uses only the parameter lists to distinguish between functions of the same name. Overloaded functions need not have the same number of parameters. You should use caution when overloading functions with default parameters, because this may cause ambiguity.

Common Programming Error 6.22

A function with default arguments omitted might be called identically to another overloaded function; this is a compilation error. For example, having in a program both a function that explicitly takes no arguments and a function of the same name that contains all default arguments results in a compilation error when an attempt is made to use that function name in a call passing no arguments. The compiler does not know which version of the function to choose.

Overloaded Operators

In Chapter 11, we discuss how to overload operators to define how they should operate on objects of user-defined data types. (In fact, we have been using many overloaded operators to this point, including the stream insertion operator << and the stream extraction operator >>, each of which is overloaded to be able to display data of all the fundamental types. We say more about overloading << and >> to be able to handle objects of user-defined types in Chapter 11.) Section 6.18 introduces function templates for automatically generating overloaded functions that perform identical tasks on different data types.

6.18 Function Templates

Overloaded functions are normally used to perform similar operations that involve different program logic on different data types. If the program logic and operations are identical for each data type, overloading may be performed more compactly and conveniently by using function templates. You write a single function template definition. Given the argument types provided in calls to this function, C++ automatically generates separate function template specializations to handle each type of call appropriately. Thus, defining a single function template essentially defines a whole family of overloaded functions.

Figure 6.26 contains the definition of a function template (lines 4–18) for a maximum function that determines the largest of three values. All function template definitions begin with the template keyword (line 4) followed by a template parameter list to the function template enclosed in angle brackets (< and >). Every parameter in the template

```
 1   // Fig. 6.26: maximum.h
 2   // Definition of function template maximum.
 3
 4   template < class T >   // or template< typename T >
 5   T maximum( T value1, T value2, T value3 )
 6   {
 7      T maximumValue = value1; // assume value1 is maximum
 8
 9      // determine whether value2 is greater than maximumValue
10      if ( value2 > maximumValue )
11         maximumValue = value2;
12
13      // determine whether value3 is greater than maximumValue
14      if ( value3 > maximumValue )
15         maximumValue = value3;
16
17      return maximumValue;
18   } // end function template maximum
```

Fig. 6.26 | Function template maximum header file.

parameter list (often referred to as a *formal type parameter*) is preceded by keyword type-name or keyword class (which are synonyms). The formal type parameters are place-holders for fundamental types or user-defined types. These placeholders are used to specify the types of the function's parameters (line 5), to specify the function's return type (line 5) and to declare variables within the body of the function definition (line 7). A function template is defined like any other function, but uses the formal type parameters as place-holders for actual data types.

The function template in Fig. 6.26 declares a single formal type parameter T (line 4) as a placeholder for the type of the data to be tested by function maximum. The name of a type parameter must be unique in the template parameter list for a particular template def-inition. When the compiler detects a maximum invocation in the program source code, the type of the data passed to maximum is substituted for T throughout the template definition, and C++ creates a complete function for determining the maximum of three values of the specified data type. Then the newly created function is compiled. Thus, templates are a means of code generation.

Common Programming Error 6.23

Not placing keyword class or keyword typename before every formal type parameter of a function template (e.g., writing < class S, T > instead of < class S, class T >) is a syntax error.

Figure 6.27 uses the maximum function template (lines 20, 30 and 40) to determine the largest of three int values, three double values and three char values, respectively.

```
1  // Fig. 6.27: fig06_27.cpp
2  // Function template maximum test program.
3  #include <iostream>
4  using std::cout;
5  using std::cin;
6  using std::endl;
7
8  #include "maximum.h" // include definition of function template maximum
9
10 int main()
11 {
12    // demonstrate maximum with int values
13    int int1, int2, int3;
14
15    cout << "Input three integer values: ";
16    cin >> int1 >> int2 >> int3;
17
18    // invoke int version of maximum
19    cout << "The maximum integer value is: "
20       << maximum( int1, int2, int3 );
21
22    // demonstrate maximum with double values
23    double double1, double2, double3;
24
25    cout << "\n\nInput three double values: ";
26    cin >> double1 >> double2 >> double3;
```

Fig. 6.27 | Demonstrating function template maximum. (Part 1 of 2.)

```
27
28     // invoke double version of maximum
29     cout << "The maximum double value is: "
30        << maximum( double1, double2, double3 );
31
32     // demonstrate maximum with char values
33     char char1, char2, char3;
34
35     cout << "\n\nInput three characters: ";
36     cin >> char1 >> char2 >> char3;
37
38     // invoke char version of maximum
39     cout << "The maximum character value is: "
40        << maximum( char1, char2, char3 ) << endl;
41     return 0; // indicates successful termination
42  } // end main
```

```
Input three integer values: 1 2 3
The maximum integer value is: 3

Input three double values: 3.3 2.2 1.1
The maximum double value is: 3.3

Input three characters: A C B
The maximum character value is: C
```

Fig. 6.27 | Demonstrating function template maximum. (Part 2 of 2.)

In Fig. 6.27, three functions are created as a result of the calls in lines 20, 30 and 40—expecting three int values, three double values and three char values, respectively. The function template specialization created for type int replaces each occurrence of T with int as follows:

```
int maximum( int value1, int value2, int value3 )
{
   int maximumValue = value1;

   // determine whether value2 is greater than maximumValue
   if ( value2 > maximumValue )
      maximumValue = value2;

   // determine whether value3 is greater than maximumValue
   if ( value3 > maximumValue )
      maximumValue = value3;

   return maximumValue;
} // end function template maximum
```

6.19 Recursion

The programs we have discussed are generally structured as functions that call one another in a disciplined, hierarchical manner. For some problems, it is useful to have functions call themselves. A **recursive function** is a function that calls itself, either directly, or indirectly (through another function). [*Note:* Although many compilers allow function `main` to call itself, Section 3.6.1, paragraph 3, and Section 5.2.2, paragraph 9, of the C++ standard document indicate that `main` should not be called within a program or recursively. Its sole purpose is to be the starting point for program execution.] Recursion is an important topic discussed at length in upper-level computer science courses. This section and the next present simple examples of recursion. This book contains an extensive treatment of recursion. Figure 6.33 (at the end of Section 6.21) summarizes the recursion examples and exercises in the book.

We first consider recursion conceptually, then examine two programs containing recursive functions. Recursive problem-solving approaches have a number of elements in common. A recursive function is called to solve a problem. The function actually knows how to solve only the simplest case(s), or so-called base case(s). If the function is called with a base case, the function simply returns a result. If the function is called with a more complex problem, it typically divides the problem into two conceptual pieces—a piece that the function knows how to do and a piece that it does not know how to do. To make recursion feasible, the latter piece must resemble the original problem, but be a slightly simpler or slightly smaller version. This new problem looks like the original problem, so the function launches (calls) a fresh copy of itself to work on the smaller problem—this is referred to as a recursive call and is also called the recursion step. The recursion step often includes the keyword `return`, because its result will be combined with the portion of the problem the function knew how to solve to form a result that will be passed back to the original caller, possibly `main`.

The recursion step executes while the original call to the function is still "open," i.e., it has not yet finished executing. The recursion step can result in many more such recursive calls, as the function keeps dividing each new subproblem with which the function is called into two conceptual pieces. In order for the recursion to eventually terminate, each time the function calls itself with a slightly simpler version of the original problem, this sequence of smaller and smaller problems must eventually converge on the base case. At that point, the function recognizes the base case and returns a result to the previous copy of the function, and a sequence of returns ensues all the way up the line until the original function call eventually returns the final result to `main`. All of this sounds quite exotic compared to the kind of "conventional" problem solving we have been using to this point. As an example of these concepts at work, let us write a recursive program to perform a popular mathematical calculation.

The factorial of a nonnegative integer n, written $n!$ (and pronounced "n factorial"), is the product

$$n \cdot (n-1) \cdot (n-2) \cdot \ldots \cdot 1$$

with 1! equal to 1, and 0! defined to be 1. For example, 5! is the product $5 \cdot 4 \cdot 3 \cdot 2 \cdot 1$, which is equal to 120.

The factorial of an integer, `number`, greater than or equal to 0, can be calculated iteratively (nonrecursively) by using a `for` statement as follows:

```
factorial = 1;

for ( int counter = number; counter >= 1; counter-- )
   factorial *= counter;
```

A recursive definition of the factorial function is arrived at by observing the following algebraic relationship:

$$n! = n \cdot (n-1)!$$

For example, 5! is clearly equal to 5 * 4! as is shown by the following:

$$5! = 5 \cdot 4 \cdot 3 \cdot 2 \cdot 1$$
$$5! = 5 \cdot (4 \cdot 3 \cdot 2 \cdot 1)$$
$$5! = 5 \cdot (4!)$$

The evaluation of 5! would proceed as shown in Fig. 6.28. Figure 6.28(a) shows how the succession of recursive calls proceeds until 1! is evaluated to be 1, which terminates the recursion. Figure 6.28(b) shows the values returned from each recursive call to its caller until the final value is calculated and returned.

The program of Fig. 6.29 uses recursion to calculate and print the factorials of the integers 0–10. (The choice of the data type unsigned long is explained momentarily.) The recursive function factorial (lines 23–29) first determines whether the terminating condition number <= 1 (line 25) is true. If number is less than or equal to 1, the factorial function returns 1 (line 26), no further recursion is necessary and the function terminates. If number is greater than 1, line 28 expresses the problem as the product of number and a recursive call to factorial evaluating the factorial of number - 1. Note that factorial(number - 1) is a slightly simpler problem than the original calculation factorial(number).

Function factorial has been declared to receive a parameter of type unsigned long and return a result of type unsigned long. This is shorthand notation for unsigned long

(a) Procession of recursive calls.   (b) Values returned from each recursive call.

Fig. 6.28 | Recursive evaluation of 5!.

```
1    // Fig. 6.29: fig06_29.cpp
2    // Demonstrating the recursive function factorial.
3    #include <iostream>
4    using std::cout;
5    using std::endl;
6
7    #include <iomanip>
8    using std::setw;
9
10   unsigned long factorial( unsigned long ); // function prototype
11
12   int main()
13   {
14      // calculate the factorials of 0 through 10
15      for ( int counter = 0; counter <= 10; counter++ )
16         cout << setw( 2 ) << counter << "! = " << factorial( counter )
17            << endl;
18
19      return 0; // indicates successful termination
20   } // end main
21
22   // recursive definition of function factorial
23   unsigned long factorial( unsigned long number )
24   {
25      if ( number <= 1 ) // test for base case
26         return 1; // base cases: 0! = 1 and 1! = 1
27      else // recursion step
28         return number * factorial( number - 1 );
29   } // end function factorial
```

```
 0! = 1
 1! = 1
 2! = 2
 3! = 6
 4! = 24
 5! = 120
 6! = 720
 7! = 5040
 8! = 40320
 9! = 362880
10! = 3628800
```

Fig. 6.29 | Demonstrating the recursive function `factorial`.

int. The C++ standard requires that a variable of type unsigned long int be at least as big as an int. Typically, an unsigned long int is stored in at least four bytes (32 bits); such a variable can hold a value in the range 0 to at least 4294967295. (The data type long int is also stored in at least four bytes and can hold a value at least in the range –2147483648 to 2147483647.) As can be seen in Fig. 6.29, factorial values become large quickly. We chose the data type unsigned long so that the program can calculate factorials greater than 7! on computers with small (such as two-byte) integers. Unfortunately, the function factorial produces large values so quickly that even unsigned long does not help us compute many factorial values before even the size of an unsigned long variable is exceeded.

The exercises explore using variables of data type double to calculate factorials of larger numbers. This points to a weakness in most programming languages, namely, that the languages are not easily extended to handle the unique requirements of various applications. As we'll see when we discuss object-oriented programming in more depth, C++ is an extensible language that allows us to create classes that can represent arbitrarily large integers if we wish. Such classes already are available in popular class libraries,[1] and we work on similar classes of our own in Exercise 9.14 and Exercise 11.14.

 Common Programming Error 6.24

Either omitting the base case, or writing the recursion step incorrectly so that it does not converge on the base case, causes "infinite" recursion, eventually exhausting memory. This is analogous to the problem of an infinite loop in an iterative (nonrecursive) solution.

6.20 Example Using Recursion: Fibonacci Series

The Fibonacci series

0, 1, 1, 2, 3, 5, 8, 13, 21, ...

begins with 0 and 1 and has the property that each subsequent Fibonacci number is the sum of the previous two Fibonacci numbers.

The series occurs in nature and, in particular, describes a form of spiral. The ratio of successive Fibonacci numbers converges on a constant value of 1.618.... This number, too, frequently occurs in nature and has been called the golden ratio or the golden mean. Humans tend to find the golden mean aesthetically pleasing. Architects often design windows, rooms and buildings whose length and width are in the ratio of the golden mean. Postcards are often designed with a golden mean length/width ratio.

The Fibonacci series can be defined recursively as follows:

fibonacci(0) = 0
fibonacci(1) = 1
fibonacci(n) = fibonacci($n - 1$) + fibonacci($n - 2$)

The program of Fig. 6.30 calculates the nth Fibonacci number recursively by using function fibonacci. Notice that Fibonacci numbers also tend to become large quickly, although slower than factorials do. Therefore, we chose the data type unsigned long for the parameter type and the return type in function fibonacci. Figure 6.30 shows the execution of the program, which displays the Fibonacci values for several numbers.

The application begins with a for statement that calculates and displays the Fibonacci values for the integers 0–10 and is followed by three calls to calculate the Fibonacci values of the integers 20, 30 and 35 (lines 18–20). The calls to fibonacci (lines 15, 18, 19 and 20) from main are not recursive calls, but the calls from line 30 of fibonacci are recursive. Each time the program invokes fibonacci (lines 25–31), the function immediately tests the base case to determine whether number is equal to 0 or 1 (line 27). If this is true, line 28 returns number. Interestingly, if number is greater than 1, the recursion step (line 30) generates *two* recursive calls, each for a slightly smaller problem than the original call to fibonacci. Figure 6.31 shows how function fibonacci would evaluate fibonacci(3).

---

1.   Such classes can be found at shoup.net/ntl, cliodhna.cop.uop.edu/~hetrick/c-sources.html and www.trumphurst.com/cpplibs/datapage.phtml?category='intro'.

```
1   // Fig. 6.30: fig06_30.cpp
2   // Testing the recursive fibonacci function.
3   #include <iostream>
4   using std::cout;
5   using std::cin;
6   using std::endl;
7
8   unsigned long fibonacci( unsigned long ); // function prototype
9
10  int main()
11  {
12     // calculate the fibonacci values of 0 through 10
13     for ( int counter = 0; counter <= 10; counter++ )
14        cout << "fibonacci( " << counter << " ) = "
15           << fibonacci( counter ) << endl;
16
17     // display higher fibonacci values
18     cout << "fibonacci( 20 ) = " << fibonacci( 20 ) << endl;
19     cout << "fibonacci( 30 ) = " << fibonacci( 30 ) << endl;
20     cout << "fibonacci( 35 ) = " << fibonacci( 35 ) << endl;
21     return 0; // indicates successful termination
22  } // end main
23
24  // recursive method fibonacci
25  unsigned long fibonacci( unsigned long number )
26  {
27     if ( ( number == 0 ) || ( number == 1 ) ) // base cases
28        return number;
29     else // recursion step
30        return fibonacci( number - 1 ) + fibonacci( number - 2 );
31  } // end function fibonacci
```

```
fibonacci( 0 ) = 0
fibonacci( 1 ) = 1
fibonacci( 2 ) = 1
fibonacci( 3 ) = 2
fibonacci( 4 ) = 3
fibonacci( 5 ) = 5
fibonacci( 6 ) = 8
fibonacci( 7 ) = 13
fibonacci( 8 ) = 21
fibonacci( 9 ) = 34
fibonacci( 10 ) = 55
fibonacci( 20 ) = 6765
fibonacci( 30 ) = 832040
fibonacci( 35 ) = 9227465
```

Fig. 6.30 | Demonstrating function `fibonacci`.

This figure raises some interesting issues about the order in which C++ compilers will evaluate the operands of operators. This is a separate issue from the order in which operators are applied to their operands, namely, the order dictated by the rules of operator precedence and associativity. Figure 6.31 shows that evaluating fibonacci(3) causes two

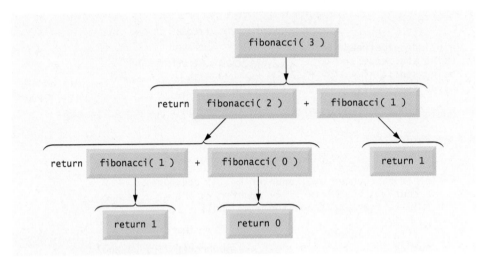

Fig. 6.31 | Set of recursive calls to function `fibonacci`.

recursive calls, namely, `fibonacci( 2 )` and `fibonacci( 1 )`. But in what order are these calls made?

Most programmers simply assume that the operands are evaluated left to right. C++ does not specify the order in which the operands of most operators (including +) are to be evaluated. Therefore, you must make no assumption about the order in which these calls execute. The calls could in fact execute `fibonacci( 2 )` first, then `fibonacci( 1 )`, or they could execute in the reverse order: `fibonacci( 1 )`, then `fibonacci( 2 )`. In this program and in most others, it turns out that the final result would be the same. However, in some programs the evaluation of an operand can have side effects (changes to data values) that could affect the final result of the expression.

C++ specifies the order of evaluation of the operands of only four operators—namely, `&&`, `||`, the comma (,) operator and `?:`. The first three are binary operators whose two operands are guaranteed to be evaluated left to right. The last operator is C++'s only ternary operator. Its leftmost operand is always evaluated first; if it evaluates to nonzero (true), the middle operand evaluates next and the last operand is ignored; if the leftmost operand evaluates to zero (false), the third operand evaluates next and the middle operand is ignored.

Common Programming Error 6.25

Writing programs that depend on the order of evaluation of the operands of operators other than `&&`, `||`, `?:` and the comma (,) operator can lead to logic errors.

Portability Tip 6.3

Programs that depend on the order of evaluation of the operands of operators other than `&&`, `||`, `?:` and the comma (,) operator can function differently on systems with different compilers.

A word of caution is in order about recursive programs like the one we use here to generate Fibonacci numbers. Each level of recursion in function `fibonacci` has a doubling effect on the number of function calls; i.e., the number of recursive calls that are required to calculate the *n*th Fibonacci number is on the order of 2^n. This rapidly gets out of hand. Calculating only the 20th Fibonacci number would require on the order of 2^{20} or about a million calls, calculating the 30th Fibonacci number would require on the order of 2^{30} or about a billion calls, and so on. Computer scientists refer to this as exponential complexity. Problems of this nature humble even the world's most powerful computers! Complexity issues in general, and exponential complexity in particular, are discussed in detail in the upper-level computer science course generally called "Algorithms."

Performance Tip 6.8

Avoid Fibonacci-style recursive programs that result in an exponential "explosion" of calls.

6.21 **Recursion vs. Iteration**

In the two previous sections, we studied two functions that easily can be implemented recursively or iteratively. This section compares the two approaches and discusses why you might choose one approach over the other in a particular situation.

Both iteration and recursion are based on a control statement: Iteration uses a repetition structure; recursion uses a selection structure. Both iteration and recursion involve repetition: Iteration explicitly uses a repetition structure; recursion achieves repetition through repeated function calls. Iteration and recursion both involve a termination test: Iteration terminates when the loop-continuation condition fails; recursion terminates when a base case is recognized. Iteration with counter-controlled repetition and recursion both gradually approach termination: Iteration modifies a counter until the counter assumes a value that makes the loop-continuation condition fail; recursion produces simpler versions of the original problem until the base case is reached. Both iteration and recursion can occur infinitely: An infinite loop occurs with iteration if the loop-continuation test never becomes false; infinite recursion occurs if the recursion step does not reduce the problem during each recursive call in a manner that converges on the base case.

To illustrate the differences between iteration and recursion, let us examine an iterative solution to the factorial problem (Fig. 6.32). Note that a repetition statement is used (lines 28–29 of Fig. 6.32) rather than the selection statement of the recursive solution (lines 24–27 of Fig. 6.29). Note that both solutions use a termination test. In the recursive solution, line 24 tests for the base case. In the iterative solution, line 28 tests the loop-continuation condition—if the test fails, the loop terminates. Finally, note that instead of producing simpler versions of the original problem, the iterative solution uses a counter that is modified until the loop-continuation condition becomes false.

```cpp
 1   // Fig. 6.32: fig06_32.cpp
 2   // Testing the iterative factorial function.
 3   #include <iostream>
 4   using std::cout;
 5   using std::endl;
 6
 7   #include <iomanip>
 8   using std::setw;
```

Fig. 6.32 | Iterative factorial solution. (Part 1 of 2.)

```
 9
10   unsigned long factorial( unsigned long ); // function prototype
11
12   int main()
13   {
14      // calculate the factorials of 0 through 10
15      for ( int counter = 0; counter <= 10; counter++ )
16         cout << setw( 2 ) << counter << "! = " << factorial( counter )
17            << endl;
18
19      return 0;
20   } // end main
21
22   // iterative function factorial
23   unsigned long factorial( unsigned long number )
24   {
25      unsigned long result = 1;
26
27      // iterative factorial calculation
28      for ( unsigned long i = number; i >= 1; i-- )
29         result *= i;
30
31      return result;
32   } // end function factorial
```

```
0! = 1
1! = 1
2! = 2
3! = 6
4! = 24
5! = 120
6! = 720
7! = 5040
8! = 40320
9! = 362880
10! = 3628800
```

Fig. 6.32 | Iterative factorial solution. (Part 2 of 2.)

Recursion has many negatives. It repeatedly invokes the mechanism, and consequently the overhead, of function calls. This can be expensive in both processor time and memory space. Each recursive call causes another copy of the function (actually only the function's variables) to be created; this can consume considerable memory. Iteration normally occurs within a function, so the overhead of repeated function calls and extra memory assignment is omitted. So why choose recursion?

Software Engineering Observation 6.18

Any problem that can be solved recursively can also be solved iteratively (nonrecursively). A recursive approach is normally chosen in preference to an iterative approach when the recursive approach more naturally mirrors the problem and results in a program that is easier to understand and debug. Another reason to choose a recursive solution is that an iterative solution is not apparent.

Performance Tip 6.9

Avoid using recursion in performance situations. Recursive calls take time and consume additional memory.

Common Programming Error 6.26

Accidentally having a nonrecursive function call itself, either directly or indirectly (through another function), is a logic error.

Most programming textbooks introduce recursion later than we have done here. We feel that recursion is a sufficiently rich and complex topic that it is better to introduce it earlier and spread the examples over the remainder of the text. Figure 6.33 summarizes the recursion examples and exercises in the text.

Location in text	Recursion examples and exercises
Chapter 6	
Section 6.19, Fig. 6.29	Factorial function
Section 6.20, Fig. 6.30	Fibonacci function
Exercise 6.40	Raising an integer to an integer power
Exercise 6.42	Towers of Hanoi
Exercise 6.44	Visualizing recursion
Exercise 6.45	Greatest common divisor
Exercise 6.50, Exercise 6.51	Mystery "What does this program do?" exercise
Chapter 7	
Exercise 7.18	Mystery "What does this program do?" exercise
Exercise 7.21	Mystery "What does this program do?" exercise
Exercise 7.31	Selection sort
Exercise 7.32	Determine whether a string is a palindrome
Exercise 7.33	Linear search
Exercise 7.34	Eight Queens
Exercise 7.35	Print an array
Exercise 7.36	Print a string backward
Exercise 7.37	Minimum value in an array
Chapter 8	
Exercise 8.24	Quicksort
Exercise 8.25	Maze traversal
Exercise 8.26	Generating mazes randomly
Exercise 8.27	Mazes of any size

Fig. 6.33 | Summary of recursion examples and exercises in the text. (Part 1 of 2.)

Location in text	Recursion examples and exercises
Chapter 19	
Section 19.3.3, Figs. 19.5–19.7	Mergesort
Exercise 19.8	Linear search
Exercise 19.9	Binary search
Exercise 19.10	Quicksort
Chapter 20	
Section 20.7, Figs. 20.20–20.22	Binary tree insert
Section 20.7, Figs. 20.20–20.22	Preorder traversal of a binary tree
Section 20.7, Figs. 20.20–20.22	Inorder traversal of a binary tree
Section 20.7, Figs. 20.20–20.22	Postorder traversal of a binary tree
Exercise 20.20	Print a linked list backward
Exercise 20.21	Search a linked list
Exercise 20.22	Binary tree delete
Exercise 20.23	Binary tree search
Exercise 20.24	Level order traversal of a binary tree
Exercise 20.25	Printing tree

Fig. 6.33 | Summary of recursion examples and exercises in the text. (Part 2 of 2.)

6.22 (Optional) Software Engineering Case Study: Identifying Class Operations in the ATM System

In the Software Engineering Case Study sections at the ends of Chapters 3, 4 and 5, we performed the first few steps in the object-oriented design of our ATM system. In Chapter 3, we identified the classes that we'll need to implement and we created our first class diagram. In Chapter 4, we described some attributes of our classes. In Chapter 5, we examined object states and modeled object state transitions and activities. Now, we determine some of the class operations (or behaviors) needed to implement the ATM system.

Identifying Operations

An operation is a service that objects of a class provide to clients of the class. Consider the operations of some real-world objects. A radio's operations include setting its station and volume (typically invoked by a person adjusting the radio's controls). A car's operations include accelerating (invoked by the driver pressing the accelerator pedal), decelerating (invoked by the driver pressing the brake pedal or releasing the gas pedal), turning and shifting gears. Software objects can offer operations as well—for example, a software graphics object might offer operations for drawing a circle, drawing a line, drawing a square and the like. A spreadsheet software object might offer operations like printing the spreadsheet, totaling the elements in a row or column and graphing information in the spreadsheet as a bar chart or pie chart.

We can derive many of the operations of each class by examining the key verbs and verb phrases in the requirements specification. We then relate each of these to particular classes in our system (Fig. 6.34). The verb phrases in Fig. 6.34 help us determine the operations of each class.

Modeling Operations

To identify operations, we examine the verb phrases listed for each class in Fig. 6.34. The "executes financial transactions" phrase associated with class ATM implies that class ATM instructs transactions to execute. Therefore, classes BalanceInquiry, Withdrawal and Deposit each need an operation to provide this service to the ATM. We place this operation (which we have named execute) in the third compartment of the three transaction classes in the updated class diagram of Fig. 6.35. During an ATM session, the ATM object will invoke the execute operation of each transaction object to tell it to execute.

The UML represents operations (which are implemented as member functions in C++) by listing the operation name, followed by a comma-separated list of parameters in parentheses, a colon and the return type:

operationName(parameter1, parameter2, ..., parameterN) : return type

Each parameter in the comma-separated parameter list consists of a parameter name, followed by a colon and the parameter type:

parameterName : parameterType

For the moment, we do not list the parameters of our operations—we'll identify and model the parameters of some of the operations shortly. For some, we do not yet know the return types, so we also omit them from the diagram. These omissions are perfectly normal at this point. As our design and implementation proceed, we'll add the remaining return types.

Class	Verbs and verb phrases
ATM	executes financial transactions
BalanceInquiry	[none in the requirements specification]
Withdrawal	[none in the requirements specification]
Deposit	[none in the requirements specification]
BankDatabase	authenticates a user, retrieves an account balance, credits a deposit amount to an account, debits a withdrawal amount from an account
Account	retrieves an account balance, credits a deposit amount to an account, debits a withdrawal amount from an account
Screen	displays a message to the user
Keypad	receives numeric input from the user
CashDispenser	dispenses cash, indicates whether it contains enough cash to satisfy a withdrawal request
DepositSlot	receives a deposit envelope

Fig. 6.34 | Verbs and verb phrases for each class in the ATM system.

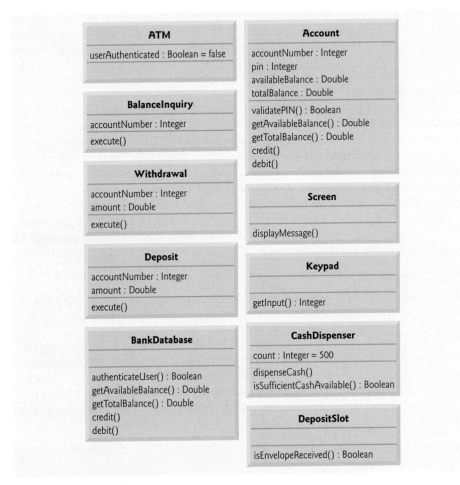

Fig. 6.35 | Classes in the ATM system with attributes and operations.

Operations of Class BankDatabase and Class Account

Figure 6.34 lists the phrase "authenticates a user" next to class BankDatabase—the database is the object that contains the account information necessary to determine whether the account number and PIN entered by a user match those of an account held at the bank. Therefore, class BankDatabase needs an operation that provides an authentication service to the ATM. We place the operation authenticateUser in the third compartment of class BankDatabase (Fig. 6.35). However, an object of class Account, not class BankDatabase, stores the account number and PIN that must be accessed to authenticate a user, so class Account must provide a service to validate a PIN obtained through user input against a PIN stored in an Account object. Therefore, we add a validatePIN operation to class Account. Note that we specify a return type of Boolean for the authenticateUser and validatePIN operations. Each operation returns a value indicating either that the operation was successful in performing its task (i.e., a return value of true) or that it was not (i.e., a return value of false).

Figure 6.34 lists several additional verb phrases for class BankDatabase: "retrieves an account balance," "credits a deposit amount to an account" and "debits a withdrawal amount from an account." Like "authenticates a user," these remaining phrases refer to services that the database must provide to the ATM, because the database holds all the account data used to authenticate a user and perform ATM transactions. However, objects of class Account actually perform the operations to which these phrases refer. Thus, we assign an operation to both class BankDatabase and class Account to correspond to each of these phrases. Recall from Section 3.11 that, because a bank account contains sensitive information, we do not allow the ATM to access accounts directly. The database acts as an intermediary between the ATM and the account data, thus preventing unauthorized access. As we'll see in Section 7.12, class ATM invokes the operations of class BankDatabase, each of which in turn invokes the operation with the same name in class Account.

The phrase "retrieves an account balance" suggests that classes BankDatabase and Account each need a getBalance operation. However, recall that we created two attributes in class Account to represent a balance—availableBalance and totalBalance. A balance inquiry requires access to both balance attributes so that it can display them to the user, but a withdrawal needs to check only the value of availableBalance. To allow objects in the system to obtain each balance attribute individually, we add operations getAvailableBalance and getTotalBalance to the third compartment of classes Bank-Database and Account (Fig. 6.35). We specify a return type of Double for each of these operations, because the balance attributes which they retrieve are of type Double.

The phrases "credits a deposit amount to an account" and "debits a withdrawal amount from an account" indicate that classes BankDatabase and Account must perform operations to update an account during a deposit and withdrawal, respectively. We there-fore assign credit and debit operations to classes BankDatabase and Account. You may recall that crediting an account (as in a deposit) adds an amount only to the totalBalance attribute. Debiting an account (as in a withdrawal), on the other hand, subtracts the amount from both balance attributes. We hide these implementation details inside class Account. This is a good example of encapsulation and information hiding.

If this were a real ATM system, classes BankDatabase and Account would also provide a set of operations to allow another banking system to update a user's account balance after either confirming or rejecting all or part of a deposit. Operation confirmDepositAmount, for example, would add an amount to the availableBalance attribute, thus making deposited funds available for withdrawal. Operation rejectDepositAmount would sub-tract an amount from the totalBalance attribute to indicate that a specified amount, which had recently been deposited through the ATM and added to the totalBalance, was not found in the deposit envelope. The bank would invoke this operation after deter-mining either that the user failed to include the correct amount of cash or that any checks did not clear (i.e, they "bounced"). While adding these operations would make our system more complete, we do not include them in our class diagrams or our implementation because they are beyond the scope of the case study.

Operations of Class *Screen*

Class Screen "displays a message to the user" at various times in an ATM session. All visual output occurs through the screen of the ATM. The requirements specification describes many types of messages (e.g., a welcome message, an error message, a thank you message) that the screen displays to the user. The requirements specification also indicates that the screen displays prompts and menus to the user. However, a prompt is really just a message describing what the user should input next, and a menu is essentially a type of prompt consisting of a series of messages (i.e., menu options) displayed consecutively. Therefore, rather than assign class Screen an individual operation to display each type of message, prompt and menu, we simply create one operation that can display any message specified by a parameter. We place this operation (displayMessage) in the third compartment of class Screen in our class diagram (Fig. 6.35). Note that we do not worry about the parameter of this operation at this time—we model the parameter later in this section.

Operations of Class *Keypad*

From the phrase "receives numeric input from the user" listed by class Keypad in Fig. 6.34, we conclude that class Keypad should perform a getInput operation. Because the ATM's keypad, unlike a computer keyboard, contains only the numbers 0–9, we specify that this operation returns an integer value. Recall from the requirements specification that in different situations the user may be required to enter a different type of number (e.g., an account number, a PIN, the number of a menu option, a deposit amount as a number of cents). Class Keypad simply obtains a numeric value for a client of the class—it does not determine whether the value meets any specific criteria. Any class that uses this operation must verify that the user enters appropriate numbers, and if not, display error messages via class Screen). [*Note:* When we implement the system, we simulate the ATM's keypad with a computer keyboard, and for simplicity we assume that the user does not enter nonnumeric input using keys on the computer keyboard that do not appear on the ATM's keypad. Later in the book, you'll learn how to examine inputs to determine if they are of particular types.]

Operations of Class *CashDispenser* and Class *DepositSlot*

Figure 6.34 lists "dispenses cash" for class CashDispenser. Therefore, we create operation dispenseCash and list it under class CashDispenser in Fig. 6.35. Class CashDispenser also "indicates whether it contains enough cash to satisfy a withdrawal request." Thus, we include isSufficientCashAvailable, an operation that returns a value of UML type Boolean, in class CashDispenser. Figure 6.34 also lists "receives a deposit envelope" for class DepositSlot. The deposit slot must indicate whether it received an envelope, so we place an operation isEnvelopeReceived, which returns a Boolean value, in the third compartment of class DepositSlot. [*Note:* A real hardware deposit slot would most likely send the ATM a signal to indicate that an envelope was received. We simulate this behavior, however, with an operation in class DepositSlot that class ATM can invoke to find out whether the deposit slot received an envelope.]

Operations of Class *ATM*

We do not list any operations for class ATM at this time. We are not yet aware of any services that class ATM provides to other classes in the system. When we implement the system with C++ code, however, operations of this class, and additional operations of the other classes in the system, may emerge.

Identifying and Modeling Operation Parameters

So far, we have not been concerned with the parameters of our operations—we have attempted to gain only a basic understanding of the operations of each class. Let's now take a closer look at some operation parameters. We identify an operation's parameters by examining what data the operation requires to perform its assigned task.

Consider the `authenticateUser` operation of class `BankDatabase`. To authenticate a user, this operation must know the account number and PIN supplied by the user. Thus we specify that operation `authenticateUser` takes integer parameters `userAccountNumber` and `userPIN`, which the operation must compare to the account number and PIN of an `Account` object in the database. We prefix these parameter names with "user" to avoid confusion between the operation's parameter names and the attribute names that belong to class `Account`. We list these parameters in the class diagram in Fig. 6.36 that models only class `BankDatabase`. [*Note:* It is perfectly normal to model only one class in a class diagram. In this case, we are most concerned with examining the parameters of this one class in particular, so we omit the other classes. In class diagrams later in the case study, in which parameters are no longer the focus of our attention, we omit the parameters to save space. Remember, however, that the operations listed in these diagrams still have parameters.]

Recall that the UML models each parameter in an operation's comma-separated parameter list by listing the parameter name, followed by a colon and the parameter type (in UML notation). Figure 6.36 thus specifies that operation `authenticateUser` takes two parameters—`userAccountNumber` and `userPIN`, both of type `Integer`. When we implement the system in C++, we'll represent these parameters with `int` values.

Class `BankDatabase` operations `getAvailableBalance`, `getTotalBalance`, `credit` and `debit` also each require a `userAccountNumber` parameter to identify the account to which the database must apply the operations, so we include these parameters in the class

BankDatabase
authenticateUser(userAccountNumber : Integer, userPIN : Integer) : Boolean getAvailableBalance(userAccountNumber : Integer) : Double getTotalBalance(userAccountNumber : Integer) : Double credit(userAccountNumber : Integer, amount : Double) debit(userAccountNumber : Integer, amount : Double)

Fig. 6.36 | Class `BankDatabase` with operation parameters.

Account
accountNumber : Integer pin : Integer availableBalance : Double totalBalance : Double
validatePIN(userPIN: Integer) : Boolean getAvailableBalance() : Double getTotalBalance() : Double credit(amount : Double) debit(amount : Double)

Fig. 6.37 | Class `Account` with operation parameters.

diagram of Fig. 6.36. In addition, operations `credit` and `debit` each require a `Double` parameter amount to specify the amount of money to be credited or debited, respectively.

The class diagram in Fig. 6.37 models the parameters of class `Account`'s operations. Operation `validatePIN` requires only a `userPIN` parameter, which contains the user-specified PIN to be compared with the PIN associated with the account. Like their counterparts in class `BankDatabase`, operations `credit` and `debit` in class `Account` each require a `Double` parameter amount that indicates the amount of money involved in the operation. Operations `getAvailableBalance` and `getTotalBalance` in class `Account` require no additional data to perform their tasks. Note that class `Account`'s operations do not require an account number parameter—each of these operations can be invoked only on a specific `Account` object, so including a parameter to specify an `Account` is unnecessary.

Figure 6.38 models class `Screen` with a parameter specified for operation `displayMessage`. This operation requires only a `String` parameter `message` that indicates the text to be displayed. Recall that the parameter types listed in our class diagrams are in UML notation, so the `String` type listed in Fig. 6.38 refers to the UML type. When we implement the system in C++, we'll in fact use a C++ `string` object to represent this parameter.

The class diagram in Fig. 6.39 specifies that operation `dispenseCash` of class `CashDispenser` takes a `Double` parameter amount to indicate the amount of cash (in dollars) to be dispensed. Operation `isSufficientCashAvailable` also takes a `Double` parameter amount to indicate the amount of cash in question.

Note that we do not discuss parameters for operation `execute` of classes `BalanceInquiry`, `Withdrawal` and `Deposit`, operation `getInput` of class `Keypad` and operation `isEnvelopeReceived` of class `DepositSlot`. At this point in our design process, we cannot determine whether these operations require additional data to perform their tasks, so we leave their parameter lists empty. As we progress through the case study, we may decide to add parameters to these operations.

In this section, we have determined many of the operations performed by the classes in the ATM system. We have identified the parameters and return types of some of the operations. As we continue our design process, the number of operations belonging to each class may vary—we might find that new operations are needed or that some current

Screen
displayMessage(message : String)

Fig. 6.38 | Class `Screen` with operation parameters.

CashDispenser
count : Integer = 500
dispenseCash(amount : Double) isSufficientCashAvailable(amount : Double) : Boolean

Fig. 6.39 | Class `CashDispenser` with operation parameters.

operations are unnecessary—and we might determine that some of our class operations need additional parameters and different return types.

Software Engineering Case Study Self-Review Exercises

6.1   Which of the following is not a behavior?
a) reading data from a file
b) printing output
c) text output
d) obtaining input from the user

6.2   If you were to add to the ATM system an operation that returns the amount attribute of class Withdrawal, how and where would you specify this operation in the class diagram of Fig. 6.35?

6.3   Describe the meaning of the following operation listing that might appear in a class diagram for an object-oriented design of a calculator:

```
add( x : Integer, y : Integer ) : Integer
```

Answers to Software Engineering Case Study Self-Review Exercises

6.1   c.

6.2   To specify an operation that retrieves the amount attribute of class Withdrawal, the following operation would be placed in the operation (i.e., third) compartment of class Withdrawal:

```
getAmount( ) : Double
```

6.3   This is an operation named add that takes integers x and y as parameters and returns an integer value.

6.23 Wrap-Up

In this chapter, you learned more about the details of function declarations. Functions have different pieces, such as the function prototype, function signature, function header and function body. You learned about argument coercion, or the forcing of arguments to the appropriate types specified by the parameter declarations of a function. We demonstrated how to use functions rand and srand to generate sets of random numbers that can be used for simulations. You also learned about the scope of variables, or the portion of a program where an identifier can be used. Two different ways to pass arguments to functions were covered—pass-by-value and pass-by-reference. For pass-by-reference, references are used as an alias to a variable. You learned that multiple functions in one class can be overloaded by providing functions with the same name and different signatures. Such functions can be used to perform the same or similar tasks, using different types or different numbers of parameters. We then demonstrated a simpler way of overloading functions using function templates, where a function is defined once but can be used for several different types. You were then introduced to the concept of recursion, where a function calls itself to solve a problem.

In Chapter 7, you'll learn how to maintain lists and tables of data in arrays. You'll see a more elegant array-based implementation of the dice-rolling application and two enhanced versions of our GradeBook case study that you studied in Chapters 3–5 that will use arrays to store the actual grades entered.

Summary

Section 6.1 Introduction

- Experience has shown that the best way to develop and maintain a large program is to construct it from small, simple pieces, or components. This technique is called divide and conquer.

Section 6.2 Program Components in C++

- C++ programs are typically written by combining new functions and classes you write with "pre-packaged" functions and classes available in the C++ Standard Library.
- Functions allow you to modularize a program by separating its tasks into self-contained units.
- The statements in the function bodies are written only once, are reused from perhaps several locations in a program and are hidden from other functions.

Section 6.3 Math Library Functions

- Sometimes functions are not members of a class. Such functions are called global functions.
- The function prototypes for global functions are placed in header files, so that the global functions can be reused in any program that includes the header file and that can link to the function's object code.

Section 6.4 Function Definitions with Multiple Parameters

- The compiler refers to the function prototype to check that calls to a method contain the correct number and types of arguments, that the types of the arguments are in the correct order and that the value returned by the function can be used correctly in the expression that called the function.
- There are three ways to return control to the point at which a function was invoked. If the function does not return a result, control returns when the program reaches the function-ending right brace, or by execution of the statement

  ```
  return;
  ```

  If the function does return a result, the statement

  ```
  return expression;
  ```

  evaluates *expression* and returns the value of *expression* to the caller.

Section 6.5 Function Prototypes and Argument Coercion

- A function prototype tells the compiler the name of a function, the type of data returned by that function, the number of parameters the function expects to receive, the types of those parameters and the order in which the parameters of those types are expected.
- The portion of a function prototype that includes the name of the function and the types of its arguments is called the function signature or simply the signature.
- An important feature of function prototypes is argument coercion—i.e., forcing arguments to the appropriate types specified by the parameter declarations.
- Argument values that do not correspond precisely to the parameter types in the function prototype can be converted by the compiler to the proper type as specified by C++'s promotion rules. The promotion rules indicate how to convert between types without losing data.

Section 6.6 C++ Standard Library Header Files

- The C++ Standard Library is divided into many portions, each with its own header file. The header files also contain definitions of various class types, functions and constants.
- A header file "instructs" the compiler on how to interface with library and user-written components.

Section 6.7 Case Study: Random Number Generation

- The element of chance can be introduced into computer applications by using the C++ Standard Library function rand.

- Function rand actually generates pseudorandom numbers. Calling rand repeatedly produces a sequence of numbers that appears to be random. However, the sequence repeats itself each time the program executes.

- Once a program has been thoroughly debugged, it can be conditioned to produce a different sequence of random numbers for each execution. This is called randomizing and is accomplished with the C++ Standard Library function srand.

- Function srand takes an unsigned integer argument and seeds the rand function to produce a different sequence of random numbers for each execution of the program.

- Random numbers in a range can be generated with

  number = shiftingValue + rand() % *scalingFactor*;

  where *shiftingValue* is equal to the first number in the desired range of consecutive integers and *scalingFactor* is equal to the width of the desired range of consecutive integers.

Section 6.8 Case Study: Game of Chance; Introducing **enum**

- An enumeration, introduced by the keyword enum and followed by a type name, is a set of integer constants represented by identifiers. The values of these enumeration constants start at 0, unless specified otherwise, and increment by 1.

Section 6.9 Storage Classes

- An identifier's storage class determines the period during which that identifier exists in memory.

- An identifier's scope is where the identifier can be referenced in a program.

- An identifier's linkage determines whether an identifier is known only in the source file where it is declared or across multiple files that are compiled, then linked together.

- Keywords auto and register are used to declare variables of the automatic storage class. Such variables are created when program execution enters the block in which they are defined, they exist while the block is active and they are destroyed when the program exits the block.

- Only local variables of a function can be of automatic storage class.

- The storage-class specifier auto explicitly declares variables of automatic storage class. Local variables are of automatic storage class by default, so keyword auto is rarely used.

- Keywords extern and static declare identifiers for variables of the static storage class and for functions. Static-storage-class variables exist from the point at which the program begins execution and last for the duration of the program.

- A static-storage-class variable's storage is allocated when the program begins execution. Such a variable is initialized once when its declaration is encountered. For functions, the name of the function exists when the program begins execution, just as for all other functions.

- There are two types of identifiers with static storage class—external identifiers (such as global variables and global function names) and local variables declared with the storage class-specifier static.

- Global variables are created by placing variable declarations outside any class or function definition. Global variables retain their values throughout the execution of the program. Global variables and global functions can be referenced by any function that follows their declarations or definitions in the source file.

Section 6.10 Scope Rules

- Local variables declared with the keyword static are still known only in the function in which they are declared, but, unlike automatic variables, static local variables retain their values when the function returns to its caller. The next time the function is called, the static local variables contain the values they had when the function last completed execution.

- An identifier declared outside any function or class has file scope.

- Labels are the only identifiers with function scope. Labels can be used anywhere in the function in which they appear, but cannot be referenced outside the function body.

- Identifiers declared inside a block have block scope. Block scope begins at the identifier's declaration and ends at the terminating right brace (}) of the block in which the identifier is declared.

- The only identifiers with function-prototype scope are those used in the parameter list of a function prototype.

Section 6.11 Function Call Stack and Activation Records

- Stacks are known as last-in, first-out (LIFO) data structures—the last item pushed (inserted) on the stack is the first item popped (removed) from the stack.

- One of the most important mechanisms for computer science students to understand is the function call stack (sometimes referred to as the program execution stack). This data structure supports the function call/return mechanism.

- The function call stack also supports the creation, maintenance and destruction of each called function's automatic variables.

- Each time a function calls another function, an entry is pushed onto the stack. This entry, called a stack frame or an activation record, contains the return address that the called function needs to return to the calling function, and the function call's automatic variables and parameters.

- The stack frame exists as long as the called function is active. When the called function returns—and no longer needs its local automatic variables—its stack frame is popped from the stack, and those local automatic variables are no longer known to the program.

Section 6.12 Functions with Empty Parameter Lists

- In C++, an empty parameter list is specified by writing either void or nothing in parentheses.

Section 6.13 Inline Functions

- C++ provides inline functions to help reduce function call overhead—especially for small functions. Placing the qualifier inline before a function's return type in the function definition "advises" the compiler to generate a copy of the function's code in place to avoid a function call.

Section 6.14 References and Reference Parameters

- Two ways to pass arguments to functions in many programming languages are pass-by-value and pass-by-reference.

- When an argument is passed by value, a *copy* of the argument's value is made and passed (on the function call stack) to the called function. Changes to the copy do not affect the original variable's value in the caller.

- With pass-by-reference, the caller gives the called function the ability to access the caller's data directly and to modify it if the called function chooses to do so.

- A reference parameter is an alias for its corresponding argument in a function call.

- To indicate that a function parameter is passed by reference, simply follow the parameter's type in the function prototype by an ampersand (&); use the same convention when listing the parameter's type in the function header.

- Once a reference is declared as an alias for another variable, all operations supposedly performed on the alias (i.e., the reference) are actually performed on the original variable. The alias is simply another name for the original variable.

Section 6.15 Default Arguments

- It is not uncommon for a program to invoke a function repeatedly with the same argument value for a particular parameter. In such cases, you can specify that such a parameter has a default argument, i.e., a default value to be passed to that parameter.

- When a program omits an argument for a parameter with a default argument, the compiler rewrites the function call and inserts the default value of that argument to be passed to the function call.

- Default arguments must be the rightmost (trailing) arguments in a function's parameter list.

- Default arguments should be specified with the first occurrence of the function name—typically, in the function prototype.

Section 6.16 Unary Scope Resolution Operator

- C++ provides the unary scope resolution operator (::) to access a global variable when a local variable of the same name is in scope.

Section 6.17 Function Overloading

- C++ enables several functions of the same name to be defined, as long as these functions have different sets of parameters. This capability is called function overloading.

- When an overloaded function is called, the C++ compiler selects the proper function by examining the number, types and order of the arguments in the call.

- Overloaded functions are distinguished by their signatures.

- The compiler encodes each function identifier with the number and types of its parameters to enable type-safe linkage. Type-safe linkage ensures that the proper overloaded function is called and that the types of the arguments conform to the types of the parameters.

Section 6.18 Function Templates

- Overloaded functions are normally used to perform similar operations that involve different program logic on different data types. If the program logic and operations are identical for each data type, overloading may be performed more compactly and conveniently using function templates.

- You write a single function template definition. Given the argument types provided in calls to this function, C++ automatically generates separate function template specializations to handle each type of call appropriately. Thus, defining a single function template essentially defines a family of overloaded functions.

- All function template definitions begin with the `template` keyword followed by a template parameter list to the function template enclosed in angle brackets (< and >).

- The formal type parameters are placeholders for fundamental types or user-defined types. These placeholders are used to specify the types of the function's parameters, to specify the function's return type and to declare variables within the body of the function definition.

Section 6.19 Recursion

- A recursive function is a function that calls itself, either directly or indirectly.

- A recursive function knows how to solve only the simplest case(s), or so-called base case(s). If the function is called with a base case, the function simply returns a result.

- If the function is called with a more complex problem, the function typically divides the problem into two conceptual pieces—a piece that the function knows how to do and a piece that it does not know how to do. To make recursion feasible, the latter piece must resemble the original problem, but be a slightly simpler or slightly smaller version of it.

- In order for the recursion to eventually terminate, each time the function calls itself with a slightly simpler version of the original problem, this sequence of smaller and smaller problems must eventually converge on the base case.

Section 6.20 Example Using Recursion: Fibonacci Series

- The ratio of successive Fibonacci numbers converges on a constant value of 1.618.... This number frequently occurs in nature and has been called the golden ratio or the golden mean.

Section 6.21 Recursion vs. Iteration

- Iteration and recursion have many similarities: both are based on a control statement, involve repetition, involve a termination test, gradually approach termination and can occur infinitely.

- Recursion has many negatives. It repeatedly invokes the mechanism, and consequently the overhead, of function calls. This can be expensive in both processor time and memory space. Each recursive call causes another copy of the function (actually only the function's variables) to be created; this can consume considerable memory.

Terminology

& to declare reference
activation record
alias
argument coercion
`auto` storage-class specifier
automatic local variable
automatic storage class
base case(s)
block scope
class scope
converge on a base case
dangling reference
default argument
divide-and-conquer approach
`enum` keyword
enumeration
enumeration constant
exponential complexity
`extern` storage-class specifier
factorial
Fibonacci series
file scope
formal parameter
formal type parameter
function call stack
function declaration
function definition
function name
function overloading
function prototype
function-prototype scope

function scope
function signature
function template
function template specialization
function call overhead
global function
global variable
golden mean
golden ratio
"highest" type
infinite loop
infinite recursion
initializing a reference
inline function
`inline` keyword
inner block
integral size limits
invoke a method
iteration
iterative solution
label
LIFO (last-in, first-out)
linkage
"lowest type"
mandatory function prototypes
mangled function name
methods
mixed-type expression
modularizing a program with functions
`mutable` storage-class specifier
name decoration

name mangling

name of a variable

namespace scope

nested blocks

numerical data type limits

optimizing compiler

out of scope

outer block

overloading

parameter

pass-by-reference

pass-by-value

pop off a stack

"prepackaged" functions

principle of least privilege

procedure

program execution stack

programmer-defined function

promotion rules

pseudorandom numbers

push onto a stack

rand function

RAND_MAX symbolic constant

random number

randomizing

recursion

recursion overhead

recursion step

recursive call

recursive evaluation

recursive function

recursive solution

reference parameter

reference to a constant

reference to an automatic variable

register storage-class specifier

repeatability of function rand

returning a reference from a function

rightmost (trailing) arguments

scaling

scaling factor

scope of an identifier

seed

sequence of random numbers

shift a range of numbers

shifted, scaled integers

shifting value

side effect of an expression

signature

software reuse

srand function

stack

stack frame

stack overflow

static keyword

static local variable

static storage class

static storage-class specifier

storage class

storage-class specifiers

template definition

template function

template keyword

template parameter list

terminating condition

terminating right brace (}) of a block

termination test

truncate fractional part of a double

type name (enumerations)

type of a variable

type parameter

type-safe linkage

unary scope resolution operator (::)

user-defined function

user-defined type

validate a function call

void return type

width of random number range

Self-Review Exercises

6.1 Answer each of the following:

a) Program components in C++ are called _____ and _____.

b) A function is invoked with a(n) _____.

c) A variable that is known only within the function in which it is defined is called a(n) _____.

d) The _____ statement in a called function passes the value of an expression back to the calling function.

e) The keyword _____ is used in a function header to indicate that a function does not return a value or to indicate that a function contains no parameters.

f) The _____ of an identifier is the portion of the program in which the identifier can be used.

g) The three ways to return control from a called function to a caller are _____, _____ and _____.

h) A(n) _____ allows the compiler to check the number, types and order of the arguments passed to a function.

i) Function _____ is used to produce random numbers.

j) Function _____ is used to set the random number seed to randomize a program.

k) The storage-class specifiers are `mutable`, _____, _____, _____ and _____.

l) Variables declared in a block or in the parameter list of a function are assumed to be of storage class _____ unless specified otherwise.

m) Storage-class specifier _____ is a recommendation to the compiler to store a variable in one of the computer's registers.

n) A variable declared outside any block or function is a(n) _____ variable.

o) For a local variable in a function to retain its value between calls to the function, it must be declared with the _____ storage-class specifier.

p) The six possible scopes of an identifier are _____, _____, _____, _____, _____ and _____.

q) A function that calls itself either directly or indirectly (i.e., through another function) is a(n) _____ function.

r) A recursive function typically has two components—one that provides a means for the recursion to terminate by testing for a(n) _____ case and one that expresses the problem as a recursive call for a slightly simpler problem than the original call.

s) It is possible to have various functions with the same name that operate on different types or numbers of arguments. This is called function _____.

t) The _____ enables access to a global variable with the same name as a variable in the current scope.

u) The _____ qualifier is used to declare read-only variables.

v) A function _____ enables a single function to be defined to perform a task on many different data types.

6.2   For the program in Fig. 6.40, state the scope (either function scope, file scope, block scope or function-prototype scope) of each of the following elements:

a) The variable x in `main`.

b) The variable y in `cube`.

c) The function `cube`.

d) The function `main`.

e) The function prototype for `cube`.

f) The identifier y in the function prototype for `cube`.

```
1   // Exercise 6.2: Ex06_02.cpp
2   #include <iostream>
3   using std::cout;
4   using std::endl;
5
6   int cube( int y ); // function prototype
7
8   int main()
9   {
10      int x;
```

Fig. 6.40 | Program for Exercise 6.2. (Part 1 of 2.)

```
11
12      for ( x = 1; x <= 10; x++ ) // loop 10 times
13         cout << cube( x ) << endl; // calculate cube of x and output results
14
15      return 0; // indicates successful termination
16   } // end main
17
18   // definition of function cube
19   int cube( int y )
20   {
21      return y * y * y;
22   } // end function cube
```

Fig. 6.40 | Program for Exercise 6.2. (Part 2 of 2.)

6.3 Write a program that tests whether the examples of the math library function calls shown in Fig. 6.2 actually produce the indicated results.

6.4 Give the function header for each of the following functions:
a) Function hypotenuse that takes two double-precision, floating-point arguments, side1 and side2, and returns a double-precision, floating-point result.
b) Function smallest that takes three integers, x, y and z, and returns an integer.
c) Function instructions that does not receive any arguments and does not return a value. [*Note:* Such functions are commonly used to display instructions to a user.]
d) Function intToDouble that takes an integer argument, number, and returns a double-precision, floating-point result.

6.5 Give the function prototype (without parameter names) for each of the following:
a) The function described in Exercise 6.4(a).
b) The function described in Exercise 6.4(b).
c) The function described in Exercise 6.4(c).
d) The function described in Exercise 6.4(d).

6.6 Write a declaration for each of the following:
a) Integer count that should be maintained in a register. Initialize count to 0.
b) Double-precision, floating-point variable lastVal that is to retain its value between calls to the function in which it is defined.

6.7 Find the error(s) in each of the following program segments, and explain how the error(s) can be corrected (see also Exercise 6.53):
a)
```
int g()
{
    cout << "Inside function g" << endl;
    int h()
    {
        cout << "Inside function h" << endl;
    }
}
```
b)
```
int sum( int x, int y )
{
    int result;

    result = x + y;
}
```

```
c) int sum( int n )
   {
      if ( n == 0 )
         return 0;
      else
         n + sum( n - 1 );
   }
d) void f( double a );
   {
      float a;
      cout << a << endl;
   }
e) void product()
   {
      int a;
      int b;
      int c;
      int result;
      cout << "Enter three integers: ";
      cin >> a >> b >> c;
      result = a * b * c;
      cout << "Result is " << result;
      return result;
   }
```

6.8   Why would a function prototype contain a parameter type declaration such as double &?

6.9   (True/False) All arguments to function calls in C++ are passed by value.

6.10   Write a complete program that prompts the user for the radius of a sphere, and calculates and prints the volume of that sphere. Use an inline function sphereVolume that returns the result of the following expression: (4.0 / 3.0) * 3.14159 * pow(radius, 3).

Answers to Self-Review Exercises

6.1   a) functions, classes. b) function call. c) local variable. d) return. e) void. f) scope. g) return;, return *expression*; or encounter the closing right brace of a function. h) function prototype. i) rand. j) srand. k) auto, register, extern, static. l) auto. m) register. n) global. o) static. p) function scope, file scope, block scope, function-prototype scope, class scope, namespace scope. q) recursive. r) base. s) overloading. t) unary scope resolution operator (::). u) const. v) template.

6.2   a) block scope. b) block scope. c) file scope. d) file scope. e) file scope. f) function-prototype scope.

6.3   See the following program:

```
1   // Exercise 6.3: Ex06_03.cpp
2   // Testing the math library functions.
3   #include <iostream>
4   using std::cout;
5   using std::endl;
6   using std::fixed;
7
8   #include <iomanip>
```

```cpp
 9    using std::setprecision;
10
11    #include <cmath>
12    using namespace std;
13
14    int main()
15    {
16       cout << fixed << setprecision( 1 );
17
18       cout << "sqrt(" << 900.0 << ") = " << sqrt( 900.0 )
19          << "\nsqrt(" << 9.0 << ") = " << sqrt( 9.0 );
20       cout << "\nexp(" << 1.0 << ") = " << setprecision( 6 )
21          << exp( 1.0 ) << "\nexp(" << setprecision( 1 ) << 2.0
22          << ") = " << setprecision( 6 ) << exp( 2.0 );
23       cout << "\nlog(" << 2.718282 << ") = " << setprecision( 1 )
24          << log( 2.718282 )
25          << "\nlog(" << setprecision( 6 ) << 7.389056 << ") = "
26          << setprecision( 1 ) << log( 7.389056 );
27       cout << "\nlog10(" << 1.0 << ") = " << log10( 1.0 )
28          << "\nlog10(" << 10.0 << ") = " << log10( 10.0 )
29          << "\nlog10(" << 100.0 << ") = " << log10( 100.0 ) ;
30       cout << "\nfabs(" << 13.5 << ") = " << fabs( 13.5 )
31          << "\nfabs(" << 0.0 << ") = " << fabs( 0.0 )
32          << "\nfabs(" << -13.5 << ") = " << fabs( -13.5 );
33       cout << "\nceil(" << 9.2 << ") = " << ceil( 9.2 )
34          << "\nceil(" << -9.8 << ") = " << ceil( -9.8 );
35       cout << "\nfloor(" << 9.2 << ") = " << floor( 9.2 )
36          << "\nfloor(" << -9.8 << ") = " << floor( -9.8 );
37       cout << "\npow(" << 2.0 << ", " << 7.0 << ") = "
38          << pow( 2.0, 7.0 ) << "\npow(" << 9.0 << ", "
39          << 0.5 << ") = " << pow( 9.0, 0.5 );
40       cout << setprecision(3) << "\nfmod("
41          << 13.675 << ", " << 2.333 << ") = "
42          << fmod( 13.675, 2.333 ) << setprecision( 1 );
43       cout << "\nsin(" << 0.0 << ") = " << sin( 0.0 );
44       cout << "\ncos(" << 0.0 << ") = " << cos( 0.0 );
45       cout << "\ntan(" << 0.0 << ") = " << tan( 0.0 ) << endl;
46       return 0; // indicates successful termination
47    } // end main
```

```
sqrt(900.0) = 30.0
sqrt(9.0) = 3.0
exp(1.0) = 2.718282
exp(2.0) = 7.389056
log(2.718282) = 1.0
log(7.389056) = 2.0
log10(1.0) = 0.0
log10(10.0) = 1.0
log10(100.0) = 2.0
fabs(13.5) = 13.5
fabs(0.0) = 0.0
fabs(-13.5) = 13.5
ceil(9.2) = 10.0
ceil(-9.8) = -9.0
floor(9.2) = 9.0
floor(-9.8) = -10.0
pow(2.0, 7.0) = 128.0
pow(9.0, 0.5) = 3.0
fmod(13.675, 2.333) = 2.010
sin(0.0) = 0.0
cos(0.0) = 1.0
tan(0.0) = 0.0
```

6.4 a) `double hypotenuse( double side1, double side2 )`
b) `int smallest( int x, int y, int z )`
c) `void instructions()`
d) `double intToDouble( int number )`

6.5 a) `double hypotenuse( double, double );`
b) `int smallest( int, int, int );`
c) `void instructions();`
d) `double intToDouble( int );`

6.6 a) `register int count = 0;`
b) `static double lastVal;`

6.7 a) *Error:* Function h is defined in function g.
Correction: Move the definition of h out of the definition of g.
b) *Error:* The function is supposed to return an integer, but does not.
Correction: Delete variable result and place the following statement in the function:

    return x + y;

c) *Error:* The result of n + sum(n - 1) is not returned; sum returns an improper result.
Correction: Rewrite the statement in the else clause as

    return n + sum(n - 1);

d) *Errors:* Semicolon after the right parenthesis that encloses the parameter list, and re-defining the parameter a in the function definition.
Corrections: Delete the semicolon after the right parenthesis of the parameter list, and delete the declaration float a;.
e) *Error:* The function returns a value when it is not supposed to.
Correction: Eliminate the return statement.

6.8 This creates a reference parameter of type "reference to double" that enables the function to modify the original variable in the calling function.

6.9 False. C++ enables pass-by-reference using reference parameters (and pointers, as we discuss in Chapter 8).

6.10 See the following program:

```
1   // Exercise 6.10 Solution: Ex06_10.cpp
2   // Inline function that calculates the volume of a sphere.
3   #include <iostream>
4   using std::cin;
5   using std::cout;
6   using std::endl;
7
8   #include <cmath>
9   using std::pow;
10
11  const double PI = 3.14159; // define global constant PI
12
13  // calculates volume of a sphere
14  inline double sphereVolume( const double radius )
15  {
16     return 4.0 / 3.0 * PI * pow( radius, 3 );
17  } // end inline function sphereVolume
18
19  int main()
20  {
```

```
21      double radiusValue;
22
23      // prompt user for radius
24      cout << "Enter the length of the radius of your sphere: ";
25      cin >> radiusValue; // input radius
26
27      // use radiusValue to calculate volume of sphere and display result
28      cout << "Volume of sphere with radius " << radiusValue
29         << " is " << sphereVolume( radiusValue ) << endl;
30      return 0; // indicates successful termination
31   } // end main
```

Exercises

6.11 Show the value of x after each of the following statements is performed:
   a) x = fabs(7.5)
   b) x = floor(7.5)
   c) x = fabs(0.0)
   d) x = ceil(0.0)
   e) x = fabs(-6.4)
   f) x = ceil(-6.4)
   g) x = ceil(-fabs(-8 + floor(-5.5)))

6.12 A parking garage charges a $2.00 minimum fee to park for up to three hours. The garage charges an additional $0.50 per hour for each hour *or part thereof* in excess of three hours. The maximum charge for any given 24-hour period is $10.00. Assume that no car parks for longer than 24 hours at a time. Write a program that calculates and prints the parking charges for each of three customers who parked their cars in this garage yesterday. You should enter the hours parked for each customer. Your program should print the results in a neat tabular format and should calculate and print the total of yesterday's receipts. The program should use the function calculateCharges to determine the charge for each customer. Your outputs should appear in the following format:

```
Car      Hours       Charge
1          1.5         2.00
2          4.0         2.50
3         24.0        10.00
TOTAL     29.5        14.50
```

6.13 An application of function floor is rounding a value to the nearest integer. The statement

```
y = floor( x + .5 );
```

rounds the number x to the nearest integer and assigns the result to y. Write a program that reads several numbers and uses the preceding statement to round each of these numbers to the nearest integer. For each number processed, print both the original number and the rounded number.

6.14 Function floor can be used to round a number to a specific decimal place. The statement

```
y = floor( x * 10 + .5 ) / 10;
```

rounds x to the tenths position (the first position to the right of the decimal point). The statement

```
y = floor( x * 100 + .5 ) / 100;
```

rounds x to the hundredths position (the second position to the right of the decimal point). Write a program that defines four functions to round a number x in various ways:

a) `roundToInteger( number )`
b) `roundToTenths( number )`
c) `roundToHundredths( number )`
d) `roundToThousandths( number )`

For each value read, your program should print the original value, the number rounded to the nearest integer, the number rounded to the nearest tenth, the number rounded to the nearest hundredth and the number rounded to the nearest thousandth.

6.15   Answer each of the following questions:
  a) What does it mean to choose numbers "at random?"
  b) Why is the rand function useful for simulating games of chance?
  c) Why would you randomize a program by using srand? Under what circumstances is it desirable not to randomize?
  d) Why is it often necessary to scale or shift the values produced by rand?
  e) Why is computerized simulation of real-world situations a useful technique?

6.16   Write statements that assign random integers to the variable n in the following ranges:
  a) $1 \leq n \leq 2$
  b) $1 \leq n \leq 100$
  c) $0 \leq n \leq 9$
  d) $1000 \leq n \leq 1112$
  e) $-1 \leq n \leq 1$
  f) $-3 \leq n \leq 11$

6.17   For each of the following sets of integers, write a single statement that prints a number at random from the set:
  a) 2, 4, 6, 8, 10.
  b) 3, 5, 7, 9, 11.
  c) 6, 10, 14, 18, 22.

6.18   Write a function `integerPower( base, exponent )` that returns the value of

$$base^{\,exponent}$$

For example, `integerPower( 3, 4 ) = 3 * 3 * 3 * 3`. Assume that *exponent* is a positive, non-zero integer and that *base* is an integer. The function `integerPower` should use for or while to control the calculation. Do not use any math library functions.

6.19   *(Hypotenuse)* Define a function hypotenuse that calculates the length of the hypotenuse of a right triangle when the other two sides are given. Use this function in a program to determine the length of the hypotenuse for each of the triangles shown below. The function should take two double arguments and return the hypotenuse as a double.

Triangle	Side 1	Side 2
1	3.0	4.0
2	5.0	12.0
3	8.0	15.0

6.20   Write a function `multiple` that determines for a pair of integers whether the second is a multiple of the first. The function should take two integer arguments and return true if the second is a multiple of the first, false otherwise. Use this function in a program that inputs a series of pairs of integers.

6.21 Write a program that inputs a series of integers and passes them one at a time to function even, which uses the modulus operator to determine whether an integer is even. The function should take an integer argument and return `true` if the integer is even and `false` otherwise.

6.22 Write a function that displays at the left margin of the screen a solid square of asterisks whose side is specified in integer parameter `side`. For example, if `side` is 4, the function displays the following:

```
****
****
****
****
```

6.23 Modify the function created in Exercise 6.22 to form the square out of whatever character is contained in character parameter `fillCharacter`. Thus, if `side` is 5 and `fillCharacter` is #, then this function should print the following:

```
#####
#####
#####
#####
#####
```

6.24 Use techniques similar to those developed in Exercise 6.22 and Exercise 6.23 to produce a program that graphs a wide range of shapes.

6.25 Write program segments that accomplish each of the following:
   a) Calculate the integer part of the quotient when integer a is divided by integer b.
   b) Calculate the integer remainder when integer a is divided by integer b.
   c) Use the program pieces developed in (a) and (b) to write a function that inputs an integer between 1 and 32767 and prints it as a series of digits, each pair of which is separated by two spaces. For example, the integer 4562 should print as follows:

```
4   5   6   2
```

6.26 Write a function that takes the time as three integer arguments (hours, minutes and seconds) and returns the number of seconds since the last time the clock "struck 12." Use this function to calculate the amount of time in seconds between two times, both of which are within one 12-hour cycle of the clock.

6.27 *(Celsius and Fahrenheit Temperatures)* Implement the following integer functions:
   a) Function `celsius` returns the Celsius equivalent of a Fahrenheit temperature.
   b) Function `fahrenheit` returns the Fahrenheit equivalent of a Celsius temperature.
   c) Use these functions to write a program that prints charts showing the Fahrenheit equivalents of all Celsius temperatures from 0 to 100 degrees, and the Celsius equivalents of all Fahrenheit temperatures from 32 to 212 degrees. Print the outputs in a neat tabular format that minimizes the number of lines of output while remaining readable.

6.28 Write a program that inputs three double-precision, floating-point numbers and passes them to a function that returns the smallest number.

6.29 *(Perfect Numbers)* An integer is said to be a *perfect number* if the sum of its divisors, including 1 (but not the number itself), is equal to the number. For example, 6 is a perfect number, because 6 = 1 + 2 + 3. Write a function perfect that determines whether parameter number is a perfect number. Use this function in a program that determines and prints all the perfect numbers between 1 and 1000. Print the divisors of each perfect number to confirm that the number is indeed perfect. Challenge the power of your computer by testing numbers much larger than 1000.

6.30 *(PrimeNumbers)* An integer is said to be *prime* if it is divisible by only 1 and itself. For example, 2, 3, 5 and 7 are prime, but 4, 6, 8 and 9 are not.

    a) Write a function that determines whether a number is prime.

    b) Use this function in a program that determines and prints all the prime numbers between 2 and 10,000. How many of these numbers do you really have to test before being sure that you have found all the primes?

    c) Initially, you might think that $n/2$ is the upper limit for which you must test to see whether a number is prime, but you need only go as high as the square root of n. Why? Rewrite the program, and run it both ways. Estimate the performance improvement.

6.31 *(Reverse Digits)* Write a function that takes an integer value and returns the number with its digits reversed. For example, given the number 7631, the function should return 1367.

6.32 The *greatest common divisor (GCD)* of two integers is the largest integer that evenly divides each of the numbers. Write a function gcd that returns the greatest common divisor of two integers.

6.33 Write a function qualityPoints that inputs a student's average and returns 4 if a student's average is 90–100, 3 if the average is 80–89, 2 if the average is 70–79, 1 if the average is 60–69 and 0 if the average is lower than 60.

6.34 Write a program that simulates coin tossing. For each toss of the coin, the program should print Heads or Tails. Let the program toss the coin 100 times and count the number of times each side of the coin appears. Print the results. The program should call a separate function flip that takes no arguments and returns 0 for tails and 1 for heads. [*Note:* If the program realistically simulates the coin tossing, then each side of the coin should appear approximately half the time.]

6.35 *(Computers in Education)* Computers are playing an increasing role in education. Write a program that helps an elementary school student learn multiplication. Use rand to produce two positive one-digit integers. It should then type a question such as

```
How much is 6 times 7?
```

The student then types the answer. Your program checks the student's answer. If it is correct, print "Very good!", then ask another multiplication question. If the answer is wrong, print "No. Please try again.", then let the student try the same question repeatedly until the student finally gets it right.

6.36 *(Computer Assisted Instruction)* The use of computers in education is referred to as *computer-assisted instruction* (CAI). One problem that develops in CAI environments is student fatigue. This can be eliminated by varying the computer's dialogue to hold the student's attention. Modify the program of Exercise 6.35 so the various comments are printed for each correct answer and each incorrect answer as follows:

Responses to a correct answer

```
Very good!
Excellent!
Nice work!
Keep up the good work!
```

Responses to an incorrect answer

```
No. Please try again.
Wrong. Try once more.
Don't give up!
No. Keep trying.
```

Use the random number generator to choose a number from 1 to 4 to select an appropriate response to each answer. Use a switch statement to issue the responses.

6.37 More sophisticated computer-aided instruction systems monitor the student's performance over a period of time. The decision to begin a new topic often is based on the student's success with previous topics. Modify the program of Exercise 6.36 to count the number of correct and incorrect responses typed by the student. After the student types 10 answers, your program should calculate the percentage of correct responses. If the percentage is lower than 75 percent, your program should print "Please ask your instructor for extra help" and terminate.

6.38 *(Guess-the-Number Game)* Write a program that plays the game of "guess the number" as follows: Your program chooses the number to be guessed by selecting an integer at random in the range 1 to 1000. The program then displays the following:

```
I have a number between 1 and 1000.
Can you guess my number?
Please type your first guess.
```

The player then types a first guess. The program responds with one of the following:

```
1. Excellent! You guessed the number!
   Would you like to play again (y or n)?
2. Too low. Try again.
3. Too high. Try again.
```

If the player's guess is incorrect, your program should loop until the player finally gets the number right. Your program should keep telling the player Too high or Too low to help the player "zero in" on the correct answer.

6.39 Modify the program of Exercise 6.38 to count the number of guesses the player makes. If the number is 10 or fewer, print "Either you know the secret or you got lucky!" If the player guesses the number in 10 tries, then print "Ahah! You know the secret!" If the player makes more than 10 guesses, then print "You should be able to do better!" Why should it take no more than 10 guesses? Well, with each "good guess" the player should be able to eliminate half of the numbers. Now show why any number from 1 to 1000 can be guessed in 10 or fewer tries.

6.40 Write a recursive function power(base, exponent) that, when invoked, returns

$base^{exponent}$

For example, power(3, 4) = 3 * 3 * 3 * 3. Assume that exponent is an integer greater than or equal to 1. *Hint:* The recursion step would use the relationship

$base^{exponent} = base \cdot base^{exponent - 1}$

and the terminating condition occurs when exponent is equal to 1, because

$base^1 = base$

6.41 *(Fibonacci Series)* The Fibonacci series

0, 1, 1, 2, 3, 5, 8, 13, 21, ...

begins with the terms 0 and 1 and has the property that each succeeding term is the sum of the two preceding terms. (a) Write a *nonrecursive* function fibonacci(n) that calculates the nth Fibonacci number. (b) Determine the largest int Fibonacci number that can be printed on your system. Modify the program of part (a) to use double instead of int to calculate and return Fibonacci numbers, and use this modified program to repeat part (b).

6.42 *(Towers of Hanoi)* In this chapter, you studied functions that can be easily implemented both recursively and iteratively. In this exercise, we present a problem whose recursive solution demonstrates the elegance of recursion, and whose iterative solution may not be as apparent.

The Towers of Hanoi is one of the most famous classic problems every budding computer scientist must grapple with. Legend has it that in a temple in the Far East, priests are attempting to move a stack of golden disks from one diamond peg to another (Fig. 6.41). The initial stack has 64 disks threaded onto one peg and arranged from bottom to top by decreasing size. The priests are attempting to move the stack from one peg to another under the constraints that exactly one disk is moved at a time and at no time may a larger disk be placed above a smaller disk. Three pegs are provided, one being used for temporarily holding disks. Supposedly, the world will end when the priests complete their task, so there is little incentive for us to facilitate their efforts.

Let us assume that the priests are attempting to move the disks from peg 1 to peg 3. We wish to develop an algorithm that prints the precise sequence of peg-to-peg disk transfers.

If we were to approach this problem with conventional methods, we would rapidly find ourselves hopelessly knotted up in managing the disks. Instead, attacking this problem with recursion in mind allows the steps to be simple. Moving *n* disks can be viewed in terms of moving only *n* – 1 disks (hence, the recursion), as follows:

a) Move *n* – 1 disks from peg 1 to peg 2, using peg 3 as a temporary holding area.
b) Move the last disk (the largest) from peg 1 to peg 3.
c) Move the *n* – 1 disks from peg 2 to peg 3, using peg 1 as a temporary holding area.

The process ends when the last task involves moving *n* = 1 disk (i.e., the base case). This task is accomplished by simply moving the disk, without the need for a temporary holding area.

Write a program to solve the Towers of Hanoi problem. Use a recursive function with four parameters:

a) The number of disks to be moved
b) The peg on which these disks are initially threaded
c) The peg to which this stack of disks is to be moved
d) The peg to be used as a temporary holding area

Fig. 6.41 | Towers of Hanoi for the case with four disks.

Your program should print the precise instructions it will take to move the disks from the starting peg to the destination peg. For example, to move a stack of three disks from peg 1 to peg 3, your program should print the following series of moves:

1 → 3 (This means move one disk from peg 1 to peg 3.)
1 → 2
3 → 2
1 → 3
2 → 1
2 → 3
1 → 3

6.43 Any program that can be implemented recursively can be implemented iteratively, although sometimes with more difficulty and less clarity. Try writing an iterative version of the Towers of Hanoi. If you succeed, compare your iterative version with the recursive version developed in Exercise 6.42. Investigate issues of performance, clarity and your ability to demonstrate the correctness of the programs.

6.44 *(Visualizing Recursion)* It is interesting to watch recursion "in action." Modify the factorial function of Fig. 6.29 to print its local variable and recursive call parameter. For each recursive call, display the outputs on a separate line and add a level of indentation. Do your utmost to make the outputs clear, interesting and meaningful. Your goal here is to design and implement an output format that helps a person understand recursion better. You may want to add such display capabilities to the many other recursion examples and exercises throughout the text.

6.45 *(Recursive Greatest Common Divisor)* The greatest common divisor of integers x and y is the largest integer that evenly divides both x and y. Write a recursive function gcd that returns the greatest common divisor of x and y, defined recursively as follows: If y is equal to 0, then gcd(x, y) is x; otherwise, gcd(x, y) is gcd(y, x % y), where % is the modulus operator. [*Note:* For this algorithm, x must be larger than y.]

6.46 Can main be called recursively on your system? Write a program containing a function main. Include static local variable count and initialize it to 1. Postincrement and print the value of count each time main is called. Compile your program. What happens?

6.47 Exercises 6.35—6.37 developed a computer-assisted instruction program to teach an elementary school student multiplication. This exercise suggests enhancements to that program.
   a) Modify the program to allow the user to enter a grade-level capability. A grade level of 1 means to use only single-digit numbers in the problems, a grade level of 2 means to use numbers as large as two digits, etc.
   b) Modify the program to allow the user to pick the type of arithmetic problems he or she wishes to study. An option of 1 means addition problems only, 2 means subtraction problems only, 3 means multiplication problems only, 4 means division problems only and 5 means a random mix of problems of all these types.

6.48 Write function distance that calculates the distance between two points *(x1, y1)* and *(x2, y2)*. All numbers and return values should be of type double.

6.49 What is wrong with the following program?

```
1  // Exercise 6.49: ex06_49.cpp
2  // What is wrong with this program?
3  #include <iostream>
4  using std::cin;
5  using std::cout;
```

```
6
7   int main()
8   {
9      int c;
10
11     if ( ( c = cin.get() ) != EOF )
12     {
13        main();
14        cout << c;
15     } // end if
16
17     return 0; // indicates successful termination
18  } // end main
```

6.50 What does the following program do?

```
1   // Exercise 6.50: ex06_50.cpp
2   // What does this program do?
3   #include <iostream>
4   using std::cout;
5   using std::cin;
6   using std::endl;
7
8   int mystery( int, int ); // function prototype
9
10  int main()
11  {
12     int x, y;
13
14     cout << "Enter two integers: ";
15     cin >> x >> y;
16     cout << "The result is " << mystery( x, y ) << endl;
17
18     return 0; // indicates successful termination
19  } // end main
20
21  // Parameter b must be a positive integer to prevent infinite recursion
22  int mystery( int a, int b )
23  {
24     if ( b == 1 ) // base case
25        return a;
26     else // recursion step
27        return a + mystery( a, b - 1 );
28  } // end function mystery
```

6.51 After you determine what the program of Exercise 6.50 does, modify the program to function properly after removing the restriction that the second argument be nonnegative.

6.52 Write a program that tests as many of the math library functions in Fig. 6.2 as you can. Exercise each of these functions by having your program print out tables of return values for a diversity of argument values.

6.53 Find the error in each of the following program segments and explain how to correct it:

a) float cube(float); // function prototype

```
cube( float number ) // function definition
{
   return number * number * number;
}
```

b) `register auto int x = 7;`
c) `int randomNumber = srand();`
d)
```
float y = 123.45678;
int x;

x = y;
cout << static_cast< float >( x ) << endl;
```
e)
```
double square( double number )
{
    double number;
    return number * number;
}
```
f)
```
int sum( int n )
{
    if ( n == 0 )
        return 0;
    else
        return n + sum( n );
}
```

6.54   Modify the craps program of Fig. 6.11 to allow wagering. Package as a function the portion of the program that runs one game of craps. Initialize variable `bankBalance` to 1000 dollars. Prompt the player to enter a wager. Use a `while` loop to check that `wager` is less than or equal to `bankBalance` and, if not, prompt the user to reenter `wager` until a valid `wager` is entered. After a correct `wager` is entered, run one game of craps. If the player wins, increase `bankBalance` by `wager` and print the new `bankBalance`. If the player loses, decrease `bankBalance` by `wager`, print the new `bankBalance`, check on whether `bankBalance` has become zero and, if so, print the message `"Sorry. You busted!"` As the game progresses, print various messages to create some "chatter" such as `"Oh, you're going for broke, huh?"`, `"Aw cmon, take a chance!"` or `"You're up big. Now's the time to cash in your chips!"`.

6.55   Write a C++ program that prompts the user for the radius of a circle, then calls `inline` function `circleArea` to calculate the area of that circle.

6.56   Write a complete C++ program with the two alternate functions specified below, of which each simply triples the variable `count` defined in `main`. Then compare and contrast the two approaches. These two functions are
    a) function `tripleByValue` that passes a copy of `count` by value, triples the copy and returns the new value and
    a) function `tripleByReference` that passes `count` by reference via a reference parameter and triples the original value of `count` through its alias (i.e., the reference parameter).

6.57   What is the purpose of the unary scope resolution operator?

6.58   Write a program that uses a function template called `min` to determine the smaller of two arguments. Test the program using integer, character and floating-point number arguments.

6.59   Write a program that uses a function template called `max` to determine the larger of two arguments. Test the program using integer, character and floating-point number arguments.

6.60   Determine whether the following program segments contain errors. For each error, explain how it can be corrected. [*Note:* For a particular program segment, it is possible that no errors are present in the segment.]

a) ```
template < class A >
int sum(int num1, int num2, int num3)
{
   return num1 + num2 + num3;
}
```

b) ```
void printResults( int x, int y )
{
   cout << "The sum is " << x + y << '\n';
   return x + y;
}
```

c) ```
template < A >
A product(A num1, A num2, A num3)
{
   return num1 * num2 * num3;
}
```

d) ```
double cube( int );
int cube( int );
```

Arrays and Vectors

*Now go, write it
before them in a table,
and note it in a book.*
—Isaiah 30:8

*Begin at the beginning, …
and go on till you come to
the end: then stop.*
—Lewis Carroll

*To go beyond is as
wrong as to fall short.*
—Confucius

OBJECTIVES

In this chapter you'll learn:

- To use the array data structure to represent a set of related data items.

- To use arrays to store, sort and search lists and tables of values.

- To declare arrays, initialize arrays and refer to the individual elements of arrays.

- To pass arrays to functions.

- Basic searching and sorting techniques.

- To declare and manipulate multidimensional arrays.

- To use C++ Standard Library class template `vector`.

7.1 Introduction

This chapter introduces the important topic of data structures—collections of related data items. Arrays are data structures consisting of related data items of the same type. You learned about classes in Chapter 3. In Chapter 21, we discuss the notion of structures. Structures and classes can each hold related data items of possibly different types. Arrays, structures and classes are "static" entities in that they remain the same size throughout program execution. (They may, of course, be of automatic storage class and hence be created and destroyed each time the blocks in which they are defined are entered and exited.)

After discussing how arrays are declared, created and initialized, we present a series of practical examples that demonstrate several common array manipulations. We then explain how character strings (represented until now by `string` objects) can also be represented by character arrays. We present an example of searching arrays to find particular elements. The chapter also introduces one of the most important computing applications—sorting data (i.e., putting the data in some particular order). Two sections of the chapter enhance the case study of class GradeBook in Chapters 3–6. In particular, we use arrays to enable the class to maintain a set of grades in memory and analyze student grades from multiple exams in a semester—two capabilities that were absent from previous versions of the GradeBook class. These and other chapter examples demonstrate the ways in which arrays allow programmers to organize and manipulate data.

The style of arrays we use throughout most of this chapter are C-style pointer-based arrays. (We'll study pointers in Chapter 8.) In the final section of this chapter, and in Chapter 22, Standard Template Library (STL), we'll cover arrays as full-fledged objects called vectors. We'll discover that these object-based arrays are safer and more versatile than the C-style, pointer-based arrays we discuss in the early part of this chapter.

7.2 Arrays

An array is a consecutive group of memory locations that all have the same type. To refer to a particular location or element in the array, we specify the name of the array and the position number of the particular element in the array.

Figure 7.1 shows an integer array called c. This array contains 12 elements. A program refers to any one of these elements by giving the name of the array followed by the position number of the particular element in square brackets ([]). The position number is more formally called a subscript or index (this number specifies the number of elements from the beginning of the array). The first element in every array has subscript 0 (zero) and is sometimes called the zeroth element. Thus, the elements of array c are c[0] (pronounced "c sub zero"), c[1], c[2] and so on. The highest subscript in array c is 11, which is 1 less than the number of elements in the array (12). Array names follow the same conventions as other variable names, i.e., they must be identifiers.

A subscript must be an integer or integer expression (using any integral type). If a program uses an expression as a subscript, then the program evaluates the expression to determine the subscript. For example, if we assume that variable a is equal to 5 and that variable b is equal to 6, then the statement

Fig. 7.1 | Array of 12 elements.

```
c[ a + b ] += 2;
```

adds 2 to array element c[11]. Note that a subscripted array name is an *lvalue*—it can be used on the left side of an assignment, just as nonarray variable names can.

Let us examine array c in Fig. 7.1 more closely. The name of the entire array is c. Its 12 elements are referred to as c[0] to c[11]. The value of c[0] is -45, the value of c[1] is 6, the value of c[2] is 0, the value of c[7] is 62, and the value of c[11] is 78. To print the sum of the values contained in the first three elements of array c, we'd write

```
cout << c[ 0 ] + c[ 1 ] + c[ 2 ] << endl;
```

To divide the value of c[6] by 2 and assign the result to the variable x, we would write

```
x = c[ 6 ] / 2;
```

Common Programming Error 7.1

Note the difference between the "seventh element of the array" and "array element 7." Array subscripts begin at 0, so the "seventh element of the array" has a subscript of 6, while "array element 7" has a subscript of 7 and is actually the eighth element of the array. Unfortunately, this distinction frequently is a source of off-by-one errors. To avoid such errors, we refer to specific array elements explicitly by their array name and subscript number (e.g., c[6] or c[7]).

The brackets used to enclose the subscript of an array are actually an operator. Brackets have the same level of precedence as parentheses. Figure 7.2 shows the precedence and associativity of the operators introduced so far. Note that brackets ([]) have been added to the first row of Fig. 7.2. The operators are shown top to bottom in decreasing order of precedence with their associativity and type.

Operators	Associativity	Type
::	left to right	scope resolution
() []	left to right	highest
++ -- static_cast< *type* >(*operand*)	left to right	unary (postfix)
++ -- + - !	right to left	unary (prefix)
* / %	left to right	multiplicative
+ -	left to right	additive
<< >>	left to right	insertion/extraction
< <= > >=	left to right	relational
== !=	left to right	equality
&&	left to right	logical AND
||	left to right	logical OR
?:	right to left	conditional
= += -= *= /= %=	right to left	assignment
,	left to right	comma

Fig. 7.2 | Operator precedence and associativity.

7.3 Declaring Arrays

Arrays occupy space in memory. To specify the type of the elements and the number of elements required by an array use a declaration of the form:

> *type arrayName*[*arraySize*];

The compiler reserves the appropriate amount of memory. (Recall that a declaration which reserves memory is more properly known as a definition in C++.) The *arraySize* must be an integer constant greater than zero. For example, to tell the compiler to reserve 12 elements for integer array c, use the declaration

```
int c[ 12 ]; // c is an array of 12 integers
```

Memory can be reserved for several arrays with a single declaration. The following declaration reserves 100 elements for the integer array b and 27 elements for the integer array x.

```
int b[ 100 ], // b is an array of 100 integers
    x[ 27 ]; // x is an array of 27 integers
```

Good Programming Practice 7.1

We declare one array per declaration for readability, modifiability and ease of commenting.

Arrays can be declared to contain values of any nonreference data type. For example, an array of type char can be used to store a character string. Until now, we have used string objects to store character strings. Section 7.4 introduces using character arrays to store strings. Character strings and their similarity to arrays (a relationship C++ inherited from C), and the relationship between pointers and arrays, are discussed in Chapter 8.

7.4 Examples Using Arrays

This section presents many examples that demonstrate how to declare arrays, how to initialize arrays and how to perform common array manipulations.

7.4.1 Declaring an Array and Using a Loop to Initialize the Array's Elements

The program in Fig. 7.3 declares 10-element integer array n (line 12). Lines 15–16 use a for statement to initialize the array elements to zeros. Like other automatic variables, automatic arrays are not implicitly initialized to zero although static arrays are. The first output statement (line 18) displays the column headings for the columns printed in the subsequent for statement (lines 21–22), which prints the array in tabular format. Remember that setw specifies the field width in which only the *next* value is to be output.

```
1   // Fig. 7.3: fig07_03.cpp
2   // Initializing an array.
3   #include <iostream>
4   using std::cout;
5   using std::endl;
```

Fig. 7.3 | Initializing an array's elements to zeros and printing the array. (Part 1 of 2.)

```
 6
 7   #include <iomanip>
 8   using std::setw;
 9
10   int main()
11   {
12      int n[ 10 ]; // n is an array of 10 integers
13
14      // initialize elements of array n to 0
15      for ( int i = 0; i < 10; i++ )
16         n[ i ] = 0; // set element at location i to 0
17
18      cout << "Element" << setw( 13 ) << "Value" << endl;
19
20      // output each array element's value
21      for ( int j = 0; j < 10; j++ )
22         cout << setw( 7 ) << j << setw( 13 ) << n[ j ] << endl;
23
24      return 0; // indicates successful termination
25   } // end main
```

```
Element        Value
      0            0
      1            0
      2            0
      3            0
      4            0
      5            0
      6            0
      7            0
      8            0
      9            0
```

Fig. 7.3 | Initializing an array's elements to zeros and printing the array. (Part 2 of 2.)

7.4.2 Initializing an Array in a Declaration with an Initializer List

The elements of an array also can be initialized in the array declaration by following the array name with an equals sign and a brace-delimited comma-separated list of initializers. The program in Fig. 7.4 uses an initializer list to initialize an integer array with 10 values (line 13) and prints the array in tabular format (lines 15–19).

```
 1   // Fig. 7.4: fig07_04.cpp
 2   // Initializing an array in a declaration.
 3   #include <iostream>
 4   using std::cout;
 5   using std::endl;
 6
 7   #include <iomanip>
 8   using std::setw;
 9
```

Fig. 7.4 | Initializing the elements of an array in its declaration. (Part 1 of 2.)

```
10   int main()
11   {
12      // use initializer list to initialize array n
13      int n[ 10 ] = { 32, 27, 64, 18, 95, 14, 90, 70, 60, 37 };
14
15      cout << "Element" << setw( 13 ) << "Value" << endl;
16
17      // output each array element's value
18      for ( int i = 0; i < 10; i++ )
19         cout << setw( 7 ) << i << setw( 13 ) << n[ i ] << endl;
20
21      return 0; // indicates successful termination
22   } // end main
```

```
Element        Value
    0             32
    1             27
    2             64
    3             18
    4             95
    5             14
    6             90
    7             70
    8             60
    9             37
```

Fig. 7.4 | Initializing the elements of an array in its declaration. (Part 2 of 2.)

If there are fewer initializers than elements in the array, the remaining array elements are initialized to zero. For example, the elements of array n in Fig. 7.3 could have been initialized to zero with the declaration

```
int n[ 10 ] = {}; // initialize elements of array n to 0
```

The declaration implicitly initializes the elements to zero, because there are fewer initializers (none in this case) than elements in the array. This technique can be used only in the array's declaration, whereas the initialization technique shown in Fig. 7.3 can be used repeatedly during program execution to "reinitialize" an array's elements.

If the array size is omitted from a declaration with an initializer list, the compiler determines the number of elements in the array by counting the number of elements in the initializer list. For example,

```
int n[] = { 1, 2, 3, 4, 5 };
```

creates a five-element array.

If the array size and an initializer list are specified in an array declaration, the number of initializers must be less than or equal to the array size. The array declaration

```
int n[ 5 ] = { 32, 27, 64, 18, 95, 14 };
```

causes a compilation error, because there are six initializers and only five array elements.

Common Programming Error 7.2

Providing more initializers in an array initializer list than there are elements in the array is a compilation error.

Common Programming Error 7.3

Forgetting to initialize the elements of an array whose elements should be initialized is a logic error.

7.4.3 Specifying an Array's Size with a Constant Variable and Setting Array Elements with Calculations

Figure 7.5 sets the elements of a 10-element array s to the even integers 2, 4, 6, ..., 20 (lines 17–18) and prints the array in tabular format (lines 20–24). These numbers are generated (line 18) by multiplying each successive value of the loop counter by 2 and adding 2.

Line 13 uses the const qualifier to declare a so-called constant variable arraySize with the value 10. Constant variables must be initialized with a constant expression when they are declared and cannot be modified thereafter (as shown in Fig. 7.6 and Fig. 7.7). Constant variables are also called named constants or read-only variables.

Common Programming Error 7.4

Not assigning a value to a constant variable when it is declared is a compilation error.

```
1   // Fig. 7.5: fig07_05.cpp
2   // Set array s to the even integers from 2 to 20.
3   #include <iostream>
4   using std::cout;
5   using std::endl;
6
7   #include <iomanip>
8   using std::setw;
9
10  int main()
11  {
12     // constant variable can be used to specify array size
13     const int arraySize = 10;
14
15     int s[ arraySize ]; // array s has 10 elements
16
17     for ( int i = 0; i < arraySize; i++ ) // set the values
18        s[ i ] = 2 + 2 * i;
19
20     cout << "Element" << setw( 13 ) << "Value" << endl;
21
22     // output contents of array s in tabular format
23     for ( int j = 0; j < arraySize; j++ )
24        cout << setw( 7 ) << j << setw( 13 ) << s[ j ] << endl;
25
26     return 0; // indicates successful termination
27  } // end main
```

Fig. 7.5 | Generating values to be placed into elements of an array. (Part 1 of 2.)

```
Element          Value
   0               2
   1               4
   2               6
   3               8
   4              10
   5              12
   6              14
   7              16
   8              18
   9              20
```

Fig. 7.5 | Generating values to be placed into elements of an array. (Part 2 of 2.)

```
 1   // Fig. 7.6: fig07_06.cpp
 2   // Using a properly initialized constant variable.
 3   #include <iostream>
 4   using std::cout;
 5   using std::endl;
 6
 7   int main()
 8   {
 9      const int x = 7; // initialized constant variable
10
11      cout << "The value of constant variable x is: " << x << endl;
12
13      return 0; // indicates successful termination
14   } // end main
```

```
The value of constant variable x is: 7
```

Fig. 7.6 | Initializing and using a constant variable.

```
 1   // Fig. 7.7: fig07_07.cpp
 2   // A const variable must be initialized.
 3
 4   int main()
 5   {
 6      const int x; // Error: x must be initialized
 7
 8      x = 7; // Error: cannot modify a const variable
 9
10      return 0; // indicates successful termination
11   } // end main
```

Borland C++ command-line compiler error message:

```
Error E2304 fig07_07.cpp 6: Constant variable 'x' must be initialized
   in function main()
Error E2024 fig07_07.cpp 8: Cannot modify a const object in function main()
```

Fig. 7.7 | const variables must be initialized. (Part I of 2.)

Microsoft Visual C++ 2005 compiler error message:

```
C:\cpphtp6_examples\ch07\fig07_07.cpp(6) : error C2734: 'x' : const object
    must be initialized if not extern
C:\cpphtp6_examples\ch07\fig07_07.cpp(8) : error C3892: 'x' : you cannot
    assign to a variable that is const
```

GNU C++ compiler error message:

```
fig07_07.cpp:6: error: uninitialized const 'x'
fig07_07.cpp:8: error: assignment of read-only variable 'x'
```

Fig. 7.7 | const variables must be initialized. (Part 2 of 2.)

Common Programming Error 7.5

Assigning a value to a constant variable in an executable statement is a compilation error.

In Fig. 7.7, note that the compilation errors produced by Borland C++ and Microsoft Visual C++ refer to the int variable x as a "const object." The ISO/IEC C++ standard defines an "object" as any "region of storage." Like objects of classes, fundamental-type variables also occupy space in memory, so they are often referred to as "objects."

Constant variables can be placed anywhere a constant expression is expected. In Fig. 7.5, constant variable arraySize specifies the size of array s in line 15.

Common Programming Error 7.6

Only constants can be used to declare the size of automatic and static arrays. Not using a constant for this purpose is a compilation error.

Using constant variables to specify array sizes makes programs more scalable. In Fig. 7.5, the first for statement could fill a 1000-element array by simply changing the value of arraySize in its declaration from 10 to 1000. If the constant variable arraySize had not been used, we would have to change lines 15, 17 and 23 of the program to scale the program to handle 1000 array elements. As programs get larger, this technique becomes more useful for writing clearer, easier-to-modify programs.

Software Engineering Observation 7.1

Defining the size of each array as a constant variable instead of a literal constant can make programs more scalable.

Good Programming Practice 7.2

Defining the size of an array as a constant variable instead of a literal constant makes programs clearer. This technique eliminates so-called magic numbers. For example, repeatedly mentioning the size 10 in array-processing code for a 10-element array gives the number 10 an artificial significance and can be confusing when the program includes other 10s that have nothing to do with the array size.

7.4.4 Summing the Elements of an Array

Often, the elements of an array represent a series of values to be used in a calculation. For example, if the elements of an array represent exam grades, a professor may wish to total the elements of the array and use that sum to calculate the class average for the exam. The examples using class GradeBook later in the chapter, namely Figs. 7.16–7.17 and Figs. 7.23–7.24, use this technique.

The program in Fig. 7.8 sums the values contained in the 10-element integer array a. The program declares, creates and initializes the array in line 10. The for statement (lines 14–15) performs the calculations. The values being supplied as initializers for array a also could be read into the program from the user at the keyboard, or from a file on disk (see Chapter 17, File Processing). For example, the for statement

```
for ( int j = 0; j < arraySize; j++ )
    cin >> a[ j ];
```

reads one value at a time from the keyboard and stores the value in element a[j].

```
1   // Fig. 7.8: fig07_08.cpp
2   // Compute the sum of the elements of the array.
3   #include <iostream>
4   using std::cout;
5   using std::endl;
6
7   int main()
8   {
9      const int arraySize = 10; // constant variable indicating size of array
10     int a[ arraySize ] = { 87, 68, 94, 100, 83, 78, 85, 91, 76, 87 };
11     int total = 0;
12
13     // sum contents of array a
14     for ( int i = 0; i < arraySize; i++ )
15        total += a[ i ];
16
17     cout << "Total of array elements: " << total << endl;
18
19     return 0; // indicates successful termination
20  } // end main
```

```
Total of array elements: 849
```

Fig. 7.8 | Computing the sum of the elements of an array.

7.4.5 Using Bar Charts to Display Array Data Graphically

Many programs present data to users in a graphical manner. For example, numeric values are often displayed as bars in a bar chart. In such a chart, longer bars represent proportionally larger numeric values. One simple way to display numeric data graphically is with a bar chart that shows each numeric value as a bar of asterisks (*).

Professors often like to examine the distribution of grades on an exam. A professor might graph the number of grades in each of several categories to visualize the grade distribution. Suppose the grades were 87, 68, 94, 100, 83, 78, 85, 91, 76 and 87. Note that there was one grade of 100, two grades in the 90s, four grades in the 80s, two grades in the 70s, one grade in the 60s and no grades below 60. Our next program (Fig. 7.9) stores this grade distribution data in an array of 11 elements, each corresponding to a category of

```cpp
1  // Fig. 7.9: fig07_09.cpp
2  // Bar chart printing program.
3  #include <iostream>
4  using std::cout;
5  using std::endl;
6
7  #include <iomanip>
8  using std::setw;
9
10 int main()
11 {
12    const int arraySize = 11;
13    int n[ arraySize ] = { 0, 0, 0, 0, 0, 0, 1, 2, 4, 2, 1 };
14
15    cout << "Grade distribution:" << endl;
16
17    // for each element of array n, output a bar of the chart
18    for ( int i = 0; i < arraySize; i++ )
19    {
20       // output bar labels ("0-9:", ..., "90-99:", "100:" )
21       if ( i == 0 )
22          cout << "  0-9: ";
23       else if ( i == 10 )
24          cout << "  100: ";
25       else
26          cout << i * 10 << "-" << ( i * 10 ) + 9 << ": ";
27
28       // print bar of asterisks
29       for ( int stars = 0; stars < n[ i ]; stars++ )
30          cout << '*';
31
32       cout << endl; // start a new line of output
33    } // end outer for
34
35    return 0; // indicates successful termination
36 } // end main
```

```
Grade distribution:
   0-9:
 10-19:
 20-29:
 30-39:
 40-49:
 50-59:
 60-69: *
 70-79: **
 80-89: ****
 90-99: **
   100: *
```

Fig. 7.9 | Bar chart printing program.

grades. For example, n[0] indicates the number of grades in the range 0–9, n[7] indicates the number of grades in the range 70–79 and n[10] indicates the number of grades of 100. The two versions of class GradeBook later in the chapter (Figs. 7.16–7.17 and

Figs. 7.23–7.24) contain code that calculates these grade frequencies based on a set of grades. For now, we manually create the array by looking at the set of grades.

The program reads the numbers from the array and graphs the information as a bar chart, displaying each grade range followed by a bar of asterisks indicating the number of grades in that range. To label each bar, lines 21–26 output a grade range (e.g., "70-79: ") based on the current value of counter variable i. The nested for statement (lines 29–30) outputs the bars. Note the loop-continuation condition in line 29 (stars < n[i]). Each time the program reaches the inner for, the loop counts from 0 up to n[i], thus using a value in array n to determine the number of asterisks to display. In this example, n[0]– n[5] contain zeros because no students received a grade below 60. Thus, the program displays no asterisks next to the first six grade ranges.

Common Programming Error 7.7

Although it is possible to use the same control variable in a for statement and in a second for statement nested inside, this is confusing and can lead to logic errors.

7.4.6 Using the Elements of an Array as Counters

Sometimes, programs use counter variables to summarize data, such as the results of a survey. In Fig. 6.9, we used separate counters in our die-rolling program to track the number of occurrences of each side of a die as the program rolled the die 6,000,000 times. An array version of this program is shown in Fig. 7.10.

```cpp
 1   // Fig. 7.10: fig07_10.cpp
 2   // Roll a six-sided die 6,000,000 times.
 3   #include <iostream>
 4   using std::cout;
 5   using std::endl;
 6
 7   #include <iomanip>
 8   using std::setw;
 9
10   #include <cstdlib>
11   using std::rand;
12   using std::srand;
13
14   #include <ctime>
15   using std::time;
16
17   int main()
18   {
19      const int arraySize = 7; // ignore element zero
20      int frequency[ arraySize ] = {}; // initialize elements to 0
21
22      srand( time( 0 ) ); // seed random number generator
23
24      // roll die 6,000,000 times; use die value as frequency index
25      for ( int roll = 1; roll <= 6000000; roll++ )
26         frequency[ 1 + rand() % 6 ]++;
27
```

Fig. 7.10 | Die-rolling program using an array instead of switch. (Part 1 of 2.)

```
28        cout << "Face" << setw( 13 ) << "Frequency" << endl;
29
30        // output each array element's value
31        for ( int face = 1; face < arraySize; face++ )
32           cout << setw( 4 ) << face << setw( 13 ) << frequency[ face ]
33              << endl;
34
35        return 0; // indicates successful termination
36  } // end main
```

Face	Frequency
1	1000167
2	1000149
3	1000152
4	998748
5	999626
6	1001158

Fig. 7.10 | Die-rolling program using an array instead of `switch`. (Part 2 of 2.)

Figure 7.10 uses the array `frequency` (line 20) to count the occurrences of each side of the die. *The single statement in line 26 of this program replaces the `switch` statement in lines 30–52 of Fig. 6.9.* Line 26 uses a random value to determine which `frequency` element to increment during each iteration of the loop. The calculation in line 26 produces a random subscript from 1 to 6, so array `frequency` must be large enough to store six counters. However, we use a seven-element array in which we ignore `frequency[ 0 ]`—it is more logical to have the die face value 1 increment `frequency[ 1 ]` than `frequency[ 0 ]`. Thus, each face value is used as a subscript for array `frequency`. We also replace lines 56–61 of Fig. 6.9 by looping through array `frequency` to output the results (lines 31–33).

7.4.7 Using Arrays to Summarize Survey Results

Our next example (Fig. 7.11) uses arrays to summarize the results of data collected in a survey. Consider the following problem statement:

> *Forty students were asked to rate the quality of the food in the student cafeteria on a scale of 1 to 10 (1 meaning awful and 10 meaning excellent). Place the 40 responses in an integer array and summarize the results of the poll.*

This is a typical array-processing application. We wish to summarize the number of responses of each type (i.e., 1 through 10). The array `responses` (lines 17–19) is a 40-element integer array of the students' responses to the survey. Note that array `responses` is declared `const`, as its values do not (and should not) change. We use an 11-element array `frequency` (line 22) to count the number of occurrences of each response. Each element of the array is used as a counter for one of the survey responses and is initialized to zero. As in Fig. 7.10, we ignore `frequency[ 0 ]`.

Software Engineering Observation 7.2

The `const` qualifier should be used to enforce the principle of least privilege. Using the principle of least privilege to properly design software can greatly reduce debugging time and improper side effects and can make a program easier to modify and maintain.

Good Programming Practice 7.3

Strive for program clarity. It is sometimes worthwhile to trade off the most efficient use of memory or processor time in favor of writing clearer programs.

Performance Tip 7.1

Sometimes performance considerations far outweigh clarity considerations.

The first for statement (lines 26–27) takes the responses one at a time from the array responses and increments one of the 10 counters in the frequency array (frequency[1] to frequency[10]). The key statement in the loop is line 27, which increments the appropriate frequency counter, depending on the value of responses[answer].

```
1    // Fig. 7.11: fig07_11.cpp
2    // Student poll program.
3    #include <iostream>
4    using std::cout;
5    using std::endl;
6
7    #include <iomanip>
8    using std::setw;
9
10   int main()
11   {
12      // define array sizes
13      const int responseSize = 40; // size of array responses
14      const int frequencySize = 11; // size of array frequency
15
16      // place survey responses in array responses
17      const int responses[ responseSize ] = { 1, 2, 6, 4, 8, 5, 9, 7, 8,
18         10, 1, 6, 3, 8, 6, 10, 3, 8, 2, 7, 6, 5, 7, 6, 8, 6, 7,
19         5, 6, 6, 5, 6, 7, 5, 6, 4, 8, 6, 8, 10 };
20
21      // initialize frequency counters to 0
22      int frequency[ frequencySize ] = {};
23
24      // for each answer, select responses element and use that value
25      // as frequency subscript to determine element to increment
26      for ( int answer = 0; answer < responseSize; answer++ )
27         frequency[ responses[ answer ] ]++;
28
29      cout << "Rating" << setw( 17 ) << "Frequency" << endl;
30
31      // output each array element's value
32      for ( int rating = 1; rating < frequencySize; rating++ )
33         cout << setw( 6 ) << rating << setw( 17 ) << frequency[ rating ]
34            << endl;
35
36      return 0; // indicates successful termination
37   } // end main
```

Fig. 7.11 | Poll analysis program. (Part 1 of 2.)

```
Rating         Frequency
   1               2
   2               2
   3               2
   4               2
   5               5
   6              11
   7               5
   8               7
   9               1
  10               3
```

Fig. 7.11 | Poll analysis program. (Part 2 of 2.)

Let's consider several iterations of the for loop. When control variable answer is 0, the value of responses[answer] is the value of responses[0] (i.e., 1 in line 17), so the program interprets frequency[responses[answer]]++ as

    frequency[1]++

which increments the value in array element 1. To evaluate the expression, start with the value in the innermost set of square brackets (answer). Once you know answer's value (which is the value of the loop control variable in line 26), plug it into the expression and evaluate the next outer set of square brackets (i.e., responses[answer], which is a value selected from the responses array in lines 17–19). Then use the resulting value as the subscript for the frequency array to specify which counter to increment.

When answer is 1, responses[answer] is the value of responses[1], which is 2, so the program interprets frequency[responses[answer]]++ as

    frequency[2]++

which increments array element 2.

When answer is 2, responses[answer] is the value of responses[2], which is 6, so the program interprets frequency[responses[answer]]++ as

    frequency[6]++

which increments array element 6, and so on. Regardless of the number of responses processed in the survey, the program requires only an 11-element array (ignoring element zero) to summarize the results, because all the response values are between 1 and 10 and the subscript values for an 11-element array are 0 through 10.

If the data in the responses array had contained an invalid value, such as 13, the program would have attempted to add 1 to frequency[13], which is outside the bounds of the array. *C++ has no array bounds checking to prevent the computer from referring to an element that does not exist.* Thus, an executing program can "walk off" either end of an array without warning. You should ensure that all array references remain within the bounds of the array.

Common Programming Error 7.8

Referring to an element outside the array bounds is an execution-time logic error. It is not a syntax error.

Error-Prevention Tip 7.1

When looping through an array, the array subscript should never go below 0 and should always be less than the total number of elements in the array (one less than the size of the array). Make sure that the loop-termination condition prevents accessing elements outside this range.

Portability Tip 7.1

The (normally serious) effects of referencing elements outside the array bounds are system dependent. Often this results in changes to the value of an unrelated variable or a fatal error that terminates program execution.

C++ is an extensible language. Section 7.11 presents C++ Standard Library class template `vector`, which enables programmers to perform many operations that are not available for C++'s built-in arrays. For example, we'll be able to compare `vector`s directly and assign one `vector` to another. In Chapter 11, we extend C++ further by implementing an array as a user-defined class of our own. This new array definition will enable us to input and output entire arrays with `cin` and `cout`, initialize arrays when they are created, prevent access to out-of-range array elements and change the range of subscripts (and even their subscript type) so that the first element of an array is not required to be element 0. We'll even be able to use noninteger subscripts.

Error-Prevention Tip 7.2

In Chapter 11, we'll see how to develop a class representing a "smart array," which checks that all subscript references are in bounds at runtime. Using such smart data types helps eliminate bugs.

7.4.8 Using Character Arrays to Store and Manipulate Strings

To this point, we have discussed only integer arrays. However, arrays may be of any type. We now introduce storing character strings in character arrays. Recall that, starting in Chapter 3, we have been using `string` objects to store character strings, such as the course name in our `GradeBook` class. A string such as `"hello"` is actually an array of characters. While `string` objects are convenient to use and reduce the potential for errors, character arrays that represent strings have several unique features, which we discuss in this section. As you continue your study of C++, you may encounter C++ capabilities that require you to use character arrays in preference to `string` objects. You may also be asked to update existing code using character arrays.

A character array can be initialized using a string literal. For example, the declaration

```
char string1[] = "first";
```

initializes the elements of array `string1` to the individual characters in the string literal `"first"`. The size of array `string1` in the preceding declaration is determined by the compiler based on the length of the string. It is important to note that the string `"first"` contains five characters *plus* a special string-termination character called the null character. Thus, array `string1` actually contains six elements. The character-constant that represents the null character is `'\0'` (backslash followed by zero). All strings represented by character arrays end with this character. A character array representing a string should always be declared large enough to hold the number of characters in the string and the terminating null character.

Character arrays also can be initialized with individual character constants in an initializer list. The preceding declaration is equivalent to the more tedious form

```
char string1[] = { 'f', 'i', 'r', 's', 't', '\0' };
```

Note the use of single quotes to delineate each character constant. Also, note that we explicitly provided the terminating null character as the last initializer value. Without it, this array would simply represent an array of characters, not a string. As we discuss in Chapter 8, not providing a terminating null character for a string can cause logic errors.

Because a string is an array of characters, we can access individual characters in a string directly with array subscript notation. For example, string1[0] is the character 'f', string1[3] is the character 's' and string1[5] is the null character.

We can input a string directly into a character array from the keyboard using cin and >>. For example, the declaration

```
char string2[ 20 ];
```

creates a character array capable of storing a string of up to 19 characters and a terminating null character. The statement

```
cin >> string2;
```

reads a string from the keyboard into string2 and appends the null character to the end of the string input by the user. Note that the preceding statement provides only the name of the array and no information about the size of the array. It is your responsibility to ensure that the array into which the string is read is capable of holding any string the user types at the keyboard. By default, cin reads characters from the keyboard until the first white-space character is encountered—regardless of the array size. Thus, inputting data with cin and >> can insert data beyond the end of the array (see Section 8.13 for information on preventing insertion beyond the end of a char array).

Common Programming Error 7.9

Not providing cin >> with a character array large enough to store a string typed at the keyboard can result in loss of data in a program and other serious runtime errors.

A character array representing a null-terminated string can be output with cout and <<. The statement

```
cout << string2;
```

prints the array string2. Note that cout <<, like cin >>, does not care how large the character array is. The characters of the string are output until a terminating null character is encountered; the null character is not printed. [*Note:* cin and cout assume that character arrays should be processed as strings terminated by null characters; cin and cout do not provide similar input and output processing capabilities for other array types.]

Figure 7.12 demonstrates initializing a character array with a string literal, reading a string into a character array, printing a character array as a string and accessing individual characters of a string.

Lines 23–24 of Fig. 7.12 use a for statement to loop through the string1 array and print its characters separated by spaces. The condition in the for statement, string1[i] != '\0', is true until the loop encounters the terminating null character of the string.

```
 1   // Fig. 7.12: fig07_12.cpp
 2   // Treating character arrays as strings.
 3   #include <iostream>
 4   using std::cout;
 5   using std::cin;
 6   using std::endl;
 7
 8   int main()
 9   {
10      char string1[ 20 ]; // reserves 20 characters
11      char string2[] = "string literal"; // reserves 15 characters
12
13      // read string from user into array string1
14      cout << "Enter the string \"hello there\": ";
15      cin >> string1; // reads "hello" [space terminates input]
16
17      // output strings
18      cout << "string1 is: " << string1 << "\nstring2 is: " << string2;
19
20      cout << "\nstring1 with spaces between characters is:\n";
21
22      // output characters until null character is reached
23      for ( int i = 0; string1[ i ] != '\0'; i++ )
24         cout << string1[ i ] << ' ';
25
26      cin >> string1; // reads "there"
27      cout << "\nstring1 is: " << string1 << endl;
28
29      return 0; // indicates successful termination
30   } // end main
```

```
Enter the string "hello there": hello there
string1 is: hello
string2 is: string literal
string1 with spaces between characters is:
h e l l o
string1 is: there
```

Fig. 7.12 | Character arrays processed as strings.

7.4.9 Static Local Arrays and Automatic Local Arrays

Chapter 6 discussed the storage-class specifier static. A static local variable in a function definition exists for the program's duration but is visible only in the function's body.

Performance Tip 7.2

We can apply static to a local array declaration so that the array is not created and initialized each time the program calls the function and is not destroyed each time the function terminates in the program. This can improve performance, especially when using large arrays.

A program initializes static local arrays when their declarations are first encountered. If a static array is not initialized explicitly by you, each element of that array is initialized to zero by the compiler when the array is created. Recall that C++ does not perform such default initialization for automatic variables.

Figure 7.13 demonstrates function `staticArrayInit` (lines 25–41) with a `static` local array (line 28) and function `automaticArrayInit` (lines 44–60) with an automatic local array (line 47).

```
 1   // Fig. 7.13: fig07_13.cpp
 2   // Static arrays are initialized to zero.
 3   #include <iostream>
 4   using std::cout;
 5   using std::endl;
 6
 7   void staticArrayInit( void ); // function prototype
 8   void automaticArrayInit( void ); // function prototype
 9
10   int main()
11   {
12      cout << "First call to each function:\n";
13      staticArrayInit();
14      automaticArrayInit();
15
16      cout << "\n\nSecond call to each function:\n";
17      staticArrayInit();
18      automaticArrayInit();
19      cout << endl;
20
21      return 0; // indicates successful termination
22   } // end main
23
24   // function to demonstrate a static local array
25   void staticArrayInit( void )
26   {
27      // initializes elements to 0 first time function is called
28      static int array1[ 3 ]; // static local array
29
30      cout << "\nValues on entering staticArrayInit:\n";
31
32      // output contents of array1
33      for ( int i = 0; i < 3; i++ )
34         cout << "array1[" << i << "] = " << array1[ i ] << "   ";
35
36      cout << "\nValues on exiting staticArrayInit:\n";
37
38      // modify and output contents of array1
39      for ( int j = 0; j < 3; j++ )
40         cout << "array1[" << j << "] = " << ( array1[ j ] += 5 ) << "   ";
41   } // end function staticArrayInit
42
43   // function to demonstrate an automatic local array
44   void automaticArrayInit( void )
45   {
46      // initializes elements each time function is called
47      int array2[ 3 ] = { 1, 2, 3 }; // automatic local array
48
```

Fig. 7.13 | `static` array initialization and automatic array initialization. (Part 1 of 2.)

```
49     cout << "\n\nValues on entering automaticArrayInit:\n";
50
51     // output contents of array2
52     for ( int i = 0; i < 3; i++ )
53        cout << "array2[" << i << "] = " << array2[ i ] << "   ";
54
55     cout << "\nValues on exiting automaticArrayInit:\n";
56
57     // modify and output contents of array2
58     for ( int j = 0; j < 3; j++ )
59        cout << "array2[" << j << "] = " << ( array2[ j ] += 5 ) << "   ";
60  } // end function automaticArrayInit
```

```
First call to each function:

Values on entering staticArrayInit:
array1[0] = 0  array1[1] = 0  array1[2] = 0
Values on exiting staticArrayInit:
array1[0] = 5  array1[1] = 5  array1[2] = 5

Values on entering automaticArrayInit:
array2[0] = 1  array2[1] = 2  array2[2] = 3
Values on exiting automaticArrayInit:
array2[0] = 6  array2[1] = 7  array2[2] = 8

Second call to each function:

Values on entering staticArrayInit:
array1[0] = 5  array1[1] = 5  array1[2] = 5
Values on exiting staticArrayInit:
array1[0] = 10  array1[1] = 10  array1[2] = 10

Values on entering automaticArrayInit:
array2[0] = 1  array2[1] = 2  array2[2] = 3
Values on exiting automaticArrayInit:
array2[0] = 6  array2[1] = 7  array2[2] = 8
```

Fig. 7.13 | `static` array initialization and automatic array initialization. (Part 2 of 2.)

Function `staticArrayInit` is called twice (lines 13 and 17). The `static` local array is initialized to zero by the compiler the first time the function is called. The function prints the array, adds 5 to each element and prints the array again. The second time the function is called, the `static` array contains the modified values stored during the first function call. Function `automaticArrayInit` also is called twice (lines 14 and 18). The elements of the automatic local array are initialized (line 47) with the values 1, 2 and 3. The function prints the array, adds 5 to each element and prints the array again. The second time the function is called, the array elements are reinitialized to 1, 2 and 3. The array has automatic storage class, so the array is recreated and reinitialized during each call to `automaticArrayInit`.

 Common Programming Error 7.10

Assuming that elements of a function's local `static` *array are initialized every time the function is called can lead to logic errors in a program.*

7.5 Passing Arrays to Functions

To pass an array argument to a function, specify the name of the array without any brackets. For example, if array `hourlyTemperatures` has been declared as

```
int hourlyTemperatures[ 24 ];
```

the function call

```
modifyArray( hourlyTemperatures, 24 );
```

passes array `hourlyTemperatures` and its size to function `modifyArray`. When passing an array to a function, the array size is normally passed as well, so the function can process the specific number of elements in the array. Otherwise, we would need to build this knowledge into the called function itself or, worse yet, place the array size in a global variable. In Section 7.11, when we present C++ Standard Library class template `vector` to represent a more robust type of array, you'll see that the size of a `vector` is built in—every `vector` object "knows" its own size, which can be obtained by invoking the `vector` object's `size` member function. Thus, when we pass a `vector` *object* into a function, we will not have to pass the size of the `vector` as an argument.

C++ passes arrays to functions by reference—the called functions can modify the element values in the callers' original arrays. The value of the name of the array is the address in the computer's memory of the first element of the array. Because the starting address of the array is passed, the called function knows precisely where the array is stored in memory. Therefore, when the called function modifies array elements in its function body, it is modifying the actual elements of the array in their original memory locations.

Performance Tip 7.3

Passing arrays by reference makes sense for performance reasons. If arrays were passed by value, a copy of each element would be passed. For large, frequently passed arrays, this would be time consuming and would require considerable storage for the copies of the array elements.

Software Engineering Observation 7.3

It is possible to pass an array by value (by using a simple trick we explain in Chapter 21)—however, this is rarely done.

Although entire arrays are passed by reference, individual array elements are passed by value exactly as simple variables are. Such simple single pieces of data are called scalars or scalar quantities. To pass an element of an array to a function, use the subscripted name of the array element as an argument in the function call. In Chapter 6, we showed how to pass scalars (i.e., individual variables and array elements) by reference with references. In Chapter 8, we show how to pass scalars by reference with pointers.

For a function to receive an array through a function call, the function's parameter list must specify that the function expects to receive an array. For example, the function header for function `modifyArray` might be written as

```
void modifyArray( int b[], int arraySize )
```

indicating that `modifyArray` expects to receive the address of an array of integers in parameter b and the number of array elements in parameter `arraySize`. The array's size is not required in the array brackets. If it is included, the compiler ignores it; thus, arrays of any size can be passed to the function. C++ passes arrays to functions by reference—when the called function uses the array name b, it refers to the actual array in the caller (i.e., array hourlyTemperatures discussed at the beginning of this section).

Note the strange appearance of the function prototype for modifyArray

```
void modifyArray( int [], int );
```

This prototype could have been written

```
void modifyArray( int anyArrayName[], int anyVariableName );
```

but, as we learned in Chapter 3, C++ compilers ignore variable names in prototypes. Remember, the prototype tells the compiler the number of arguments and the type of each argument (in the order in which the arguments are expected to appear).

The program in Fig. 7.14 demonstrates the difference between passing an entire array and passing an array element. Lines 22–23 print the five original elements of integer array a. Line 28 passes a and its size to function modifyArray (lines 45–50), which multiplies each of a's elements by 2 (through parameter b). Then, lines 32–33 print array a again in main. As the output shows, the elements of a are indeed modified by modifyArray. Next, line 36 prints the value of scalar a[3], then line 38 passes element a[3] to function modifyElement (lines 54–58), which multiplies its parameter by 2 and prints the new value. Note that when line 39 again prints a[3] in main, the value has not been modified, because individual array elements are passed by value.

```
1   // Fig. 7.14: fig07_14.cpp
2   // Passing arrays and individual array elements to functions.
3   #include <iostream>
4   using std::cout;
5   using std::endl;
6
7   #include <iomanip>
8   using std::setw;
9
10  void modifyArray( int [], int ); // appears strange; array and size
11  void modifyElement( int ); // receive array element value
12
13  int main()
14  {
15     const int arraySize = 5; // size of array a
16     int a[ arraySize ] = { 0, 1, 2, 3, 4 }; // initialize array a
17
18     cout << "Effects of passing entire array by reference:"
19        << "\n\nThe values of the original array are:\n";
20
21     // output original array elements
22     for ( int i = 0; i < arraySize; i++ )
23        cout << setw( 3 ) << a[ i ];
24
25     cout << endl;
26
27     // pass array a to modifyArray by reference
28     modifyArray( a, arraySize );
```

Fig. 7.14 | Passing arrays and individual array elements to functions. (Part 1 of 2.)

```
29       cout << "The values of the modified array are:\n";
30
31       // output modified array elements
32       for ( int j = 0; j < arraySize; j++ )
33          cout << setw( 3 ) << a[ j ];
34
35       cout << "\n\n\nEffects of passing array element by value:"
36          << "\n\na[3] before modifyElement: " << a[ 3 ] << endl;
37
38       modifyElement( a[ 3 ] ); // pass array element a[ 3 ] by value
39       cout << "a[3] after modifyElement: " << a[ 3 ] << endl;
40
41       return 0; // indicates successful termination
42    } // end main
43
44    // in function modifyArray, "b" points to the original array "a" in memory
45    void modifyArray( int b[], int sizeOfArray )
46    {
47       // multiply each array element by 2
48       for ( int k = 0; k < sizeOfArray; k++ )
49          b[ k ] *= 2;
50    } // end function modifyArray
51
52    // in function modifyElement, "e" is a local copy of
53    // array element a[ 3 ] passed from main
54    void modifyElement( int e )
55    {
56       // multiply parameter by 2
57       cout << "Value of element in modifyElement: " << ( e *= 2 ) << endl;
58    } // end function modifyElement
```

```
Effects of passing entire array by reference:

The values of the original array are:
   0  1  2  3  4
The values of the modified array are:
   0  2  4  6  8


Effects of passing array element by value:

a[3] before modifyElement: 6
Value of element in modifyElement: 12
a[3] after modifyElement: 6
```

Fig. 7.14 | Passing arrays and individual array elements to functions. (Part 2 of 2.)

There may be situations in your programs in which a function should not be allowed to modify array elements. C++ provides the type qualifier const that can be used to prevent modification of array values in the caller by code in a called function. When a function specifies an array parameter that is preceded by the const qualifier, the elements of the array become constant in the function body, and any attempt to modify an element of the array in the function body results in a compilation error. This enables you to prevent accidental modification of array elements in the function's body.

Figure 7.15 demonstrates the const qualifier. Function tryToModifyArray (lines 21–26) is defined with parameter const int b[], which specifies that array b is constant and cannot be modified. Each of the three attempts by the function to modify array b's elements (lines 23–25) results in a compilation error. The Borland C++ compiler, for example, produces the error "Cannot modify a const object." [*Note:* The C++ standard defines an "object" as any "region of storage," thus including variables or array elements of fundamental data types as well as instances of classes (what we've been calling objects).] This message indicates that using a const object (e.g., b[0]) as an *lvalue* is an error—you cannot assign a new value to a const object by placing it on the left of an assignment operator. Note that compiler error messages vary between compilers (as shown in Fig. 7.15). The const qualifier will be discussed again in Chapter 10.

Common Programming Error 7.11

Forgetting that arrays in the caller are passed by reference, and hence can be modified in called functions, may result in logic errors.

Software Engineering Observation 7.4

Applying the const type qualifier to an array parameter in a function definition to prevent the original array from being modified in the function body is another example of the principle of least privilege. Functions should not be given the capability to modify an array unless it is absolutely necessary.

```
1   // Fig. 7.15: fig07_15.cpp
2   // Demonstrating the const type qualifier.
3   #include <iostream>
4   using std::cout;
5   using std::endl;
6
7   void tryToModifyArray( const int [] ); // function prototype
8
9   int main()
10  {
11     int a[] = { 10, 20, 30 };
12
13     tryToModifyArray( a );
14     cout << a[ 0 ] << ' ' << a[ 1 ] << ' ' << a[ 2 ] << '\n';
15
16     return 0; // indicates successful termination
17  } // end main
18
19  // In function tryToModifyArray, "b" cannot be used
20  // to modify the original array "a" in main.
21  void tryToModifyArray( const int b[] )
22  {
23     b[ 0 ] /= 2; // compilation error
24     b[ 1 ] /= 2; // compilation error
25     b[ 2 ] /= 2; // compilation error
26  } // end function tryToModifyArray
```

Fig. 7.15 | const type qualifier applied to an array parameter. (Part I of 2.)

Borland C++ command-line compiler error message:

```
Error E2024 fig07_15.cpp 23: Cannot modify a const object
   in function tryToModifyArray(const int * const)
Error E2024 fig07_15.cpp 24: Cannot modify a const object
   in function tryToModifyArray(const int * const)
Error E2024 fig07_15.cpp 25: Cannot modify a const object
   in function tryToModifyArray(const int * const)
```

Microsoft Visual C++ 2005 compiler error message:

```
c:\cpphtp6_examples\ch07\fig07_15\fig07_15.cpp(23) : error C3892: 'b' : you
   cannot assign to a variable that is const
c:\cpphtp6_examples\ch07\fig07_15\fig07_15.cpp(24) : error C3892: 'b' : you
   cannot assign to a variable that is const
c:\cpphtp6_examples\ch07\fig07_15\fig07_15.cpp(25) : error C3892: 'b' : you
   cannot assign to a variable that is const
```

GNU C++ compiler error message:

```
fig07_15.cpp:23: error: assignment of read-only location
fig07_15.cpp:24: error: assignment of read-only location
fig07_15.cpp:25: error: assignment of read-only location
```

Fig. 7.15 | const type qualifier applied to an array parameter. (Part 2 of 2.)

7.6 Case Study: Class GradeBook Using an Array to Store Grades

This section further evolves class GradeBook, introduced in Chapter 3 and expanded in Chapters 4–6. Recall that this class represents a grade book used by a professor to store and analyze student grades. Previous versions of the class process grades entered by the user, but do not maintain the individual grade values in the class's data members. Thus, repeat calculations require the user to reenter the grades. One way to solve this problem would be to store each grade entered in an individual data member of the class. For example, we could create data members grade1, grade2, ..., grade10 in class GradeBook to store 10 student grades. However, the code to total the grades and determine the class average would be cumbersome. In this section, we solve this problem by storing grades in an array.

*Storing Student Grades in an Array in Class **GradeBook***
The version of class GradeBook (Figs. 7.16–7.17) presented here uses an array of integers to store the grades of several students on a single exam. This eliminates the need to repeatedly input the same set of grades. Array grades is declared as a data member in line 29 of Fig. 7.16—therefore, each GradeBook object maintains its own set of grades.

Note that the size of the array in line 29 of Fig. 7.16 is specified by public const static data member students (declared in line 13). This data member is public so that it is accessible to the clients of the class. We'll soon see an example of a client program using this constant. Declaring students with the const qualifier indicates that this data member is constant—its value cannot be changed after being initialized. Keyword static in this variable declaration indicates that the data member is shared by all objects of the

```
 1   // Fig. 7.16: GradeBook.h
 2   // Definition of class GradeBook that uses an array to store test grades.
 3   // Member functions are defined in GradeBook.cpp
 4
 5   #include <string> // program uses C++ Standard Library string class
 6   using std::string;
 7
 8   // GradeBook class definition
 9   class GradeBook
10   {
11   public:
12      // constant -- number of students who took the test
13      const static int students = 10; // note public data
14
15      // constructor initializes course name and array of grades
16      GradeBook( string, const int [] );
17
18      void setCourseName( string ); // function to set the course name
19      string getCourseName(); // function to retrieve the course name
20      void displayMessage(); // display a welcome message
21      void processGrades(); // perform various operations on the grade data
22      int getMinimum(); // find the minimum grade for the test
23      int getMaximum(); // find the maximum grade for the test
24      double getAverage(); // determine the average grade for the test
25      void outputBarChart(); // output bar chart of grade distribution
26      void outputGrades(); // output the contents of the grades array
27   private:
28      string courseName; // course name for this grade book
29      int grades[ students ]; // array of student grades
30   }; // end class GradeBook
```

Fig. 7.16 | Definition of class GradeBook using an array to store test grades.

```
 1   // Fig. 7.17: GradeBook.cpp
 2   // Member-function definitions for class GradeBook that
 3   // uses an array to store test grades.
 4   #include <iostream>
 5   using std::cout;
 6   using std::cin;
 7   using std::endl;
 8   using std::fixed;
 9
10   #include <iomanip>
11   using std::setprecision;
12   using std::setw;
13
14   #include "GradeBook.h" // GradeBook class definition
15
16   // constructor initializes courseName and grades array
17   GradeBook::GradeBook( string name, const int gradesArray[] )
18   {
19      setCourseName( name ); // initialize courseName
```

Fig. 7.17 | GradeBook class member functions manipulating an array of grades. (Part 1 of 4.)

```
20
21        // copy grades from gradesArray to grades data member
22        for ( int grade = 0; grade < students; grade++ )
23           grades[ grade ] = gradesArray[ grade ];
24     } // end GradeBook constructor
25
26     // function to set the course name
27     void GradeBook::setCourseName( string name )
28     {
29        courseName = name; // store the course name
30     } // end function setCourseName
31
32     // function to retrieve the course name
33     string GradeBook::getCourseName()
34     {
35        return courseName;
36     } // end function getCourseName
37
38     // display a welcome message to the GradeBook user
39     void GradeBook::displayMessage()
40     {
41        // this statement calls getCourseName to get the
42        // name of the course this GradeBook represents
43        cout << "Welcome to the grade book for\n" << getCourseName() << "!"
44           << endl;
45     } // end function displayMessage
46
47     // perform various operations on the data
48     void GradeBook::processGrades()
49     {
50        // output grades array
51        outputGrades();
52
53        // call function getAverage to calculate the average grade
54        cout << "\nClass average is " << setprecision( 2 ) << fixed <<
55           getAverage() << endl;
56
57        // call functions getMinimum and getMaximum
58        cout << "Lowest grade is " << getMinimum() << "\nHighest grade is "
59           << getMaximum() << endl;
60
61        // call function outputBarChart to print grade distribution chart
62        outputBarChart();
63     } // end function processGrades
64
65     // find minimum grade
66     int GradeBook::getMinimum()
67     {
68        int lowGrade = 100; // assume lowest grade is 100
69
70        // loop through grades array
71        for ( int grade = 0; grade < students; grade++ )
72        {
```

Fig. 7.17 | GradeBook class member functions manipulating an array of grades. (Part 2 of 4.)

```
73        // if current grade lower than lowGrade, assign it to lowGrade
74        if ( grades[ grade ] < lowGrade )
75           lowGrade = grades[ grade ]; // new lowest grade
76     } // end for
77
78     return lowGrade; // return lowest grade
79  } // end function getMinimum
80
81  // find maximum grade
82  int GradeBook::getMaximum()
83  {
84     int highGrade = 0; // assume highest grade is 0
85
86     // loop through grades array
87     for ( int grade = 0; grade < students; grade++ )
88     {
89        // if current grade higher than highGrade, assign it to highGrade
90        if ( grades[ grade ] > highGrade )
91           highGrade = grades[ grade ]; // new highest grade
92     } // end for
93
94     return highGrade; // return highest grade
95  } // end function getMaximum
96
97  // determine average grade for test
98  double GradeBook::getAverage()
99  {
100     int total = 0; // initialize total
101
102     // sum grades in array
103     for ( int grade = 0; grade < students; grade++ )
104        total += grades[ grade ];
105
106     // return average of grades
107     return static_cast< double >( total ) / students;
108  } // end function getAverage
109
110  // output bar chart displaying grade distribution
111  void GradeBook::outputBarChart()
112  {
113     cout << "\nGrade distribution:" << endl;
114
115     // stores frequency of grades in each range of 10 grades
116     const int frequencySize = 11;
117     int frequency[ frequencySize ] = {}; // initialize elements to 0
118
119     // for each grade, increment the appropriate frequency
120     for ( int grade = 0; grade < students; grade++ )
121        frequency[ grades[ grade ] / 10 ]++;
122
123     // for each grade frequency, print bar in chart
124     for ( int count = 0; count < frequencySize; count++ )
125     {
```

Fig. 7.17 | GradeBook class member functions manipulating an array of grades. (Part 3 of 4.)

```
126          // output bar labels ("0-9:", ..., "90-99:", "100:" )
127          if ( count == 0 )
128             cout << "  0-9: ";
129          else if ( count == 10 )
130             cout << "  100: ";
131          else
132             cout << count * 10 << "-" << ( count * 10 ) + 9 << ": ";
133
134          // print bar of asterisks
135          for ( int stars = 0; stars < frequency[ count ]; stars++ )
136             cout << '*';
137
138          cout << endl; // start a new line of output
139       } // end outer for
140    } // end function outputBarChart
141
142    // output the contents of the grades array
143    void GradeBook::outputGrades()
144    {
145       cout << "\nThe grades are:\n\n";
146
147       // output each student's grade
148       for ( int student = 0; student < students; student++ )
149          cout << "Student " << setw( 2 ) << student + 1 << ": " << setw( 3 )
150             << grades[ student ] << endl;
151    } // end function outputGrades
```

Fig. 7.17 | GradeBook class member functions manipulating an array of grades. (Part 4 of 4.)

class—all GradeBook objects store grades for the same number of students. Recall from Section 3.6 that when each object of a class maintains its own copy of an attribute, the variable that represents the attribute is known as a data member—each object (instance) of the class has a separate copy of the variable in memory. There are variables for which each object of a class does not have a separate copy. That is the case with static data members, which are also known as class variables. When objects of a class containing static data members are created, all the objects share one copy of the class's static data members. A static data member can be accessed within the class definition and the member-function definitions like any other data member. As you'll soon see, a public static data member can also be accessed outside of the class, even when no objects of the class exist, using the class name followed by the binary scope resolution operator (::) and the name of the data member. You'll learn more about static data members in Chapter 10.

The class's constructor (declared in line 16 of Fig. 7.16 and defined in lines 17–24 of Fig. 7.17) has two parameters—the course name and an array of grades. When a program creates a GradeBook object (e.g., line 13 of fig07_18.cpp), the program passes an existing int array to the constructor, which copies the array's values into the data member grades (lines 22–23 of Fig. 7.17). The grade values in the passed array could have been input from a user or read from a file on disk (as we discuss in Chapter 17, File Processing). In our test program, we simply initialize an array with a set of grade values (Fig. 7.18, lines 10–11). Once the grades are stored in data member grades of class GradeBook, all the class's member functions can access the grades array as needed to perform various calculations.

```cpp
1  // Fig. 7.18: fig07_18.cpp
2  // Creates GradeBook object using an array of grades.
3
4  #include "GradeBook.h" // GradeBook class definition
5
6  // function main begins program execution
7  int main()
8  {
9     // array of student grades
10    int gradesArray[ GradeBook::students ] =
11       { 87, 68, 94, 100, 83, 78, 85, 91, 76, 87 };
12
13    GradeBook myGradeBook(
14       "CS101 Introduction to C++ Programming", gradesArray );
15    myGradeBook.displayMessage();
16    myGradeBook.processGrades();
17    return 0;
18 } // end main
```

```
Welcome to the grade book for
CS101 Introduction to C++ Programming!

The grades are:

Student  1:  87
Student  2:  68
Student  3:  94
Student  4: 100
Student  5:  83
Student  6:  78
Student  7:  85
Student  8:  91
Student  9:  76
Student 10:  87

Class average is 84.90
Lowest grade is 68
Highest grade is 100

Grade distribution:
  0-9:
 10-19:
 20-29:
 30-39:
 40-49:
 50-59:
 60-69: *
 70-79: **
 80-89: ****
 90-99: **
   100: *
```

Fig. 7.18 | Creates a GradeBook object using an array of grades, then invokes member function processGrades to analyze them.

Member function processGrades (declared in line 21 of Fig. 7.16 and defined in lines 48–63 of Fig. 7.17) contains a series of member function calls that output a report summarizing the grades. Line 51 calls member function outputGrades to print the contents of the array grades. Lines 148–150 in member function outputGrades use a for statement to output each student's grade. Although array indices start at 0, a professor would typically number students starting at 1. Thus, lines 149–150 output student + 1 as the student number to produce grade labels "Student 1: ", "Student 2: ", and so on.

Member function processGrades next calls member function getAverage (lines 54–55) to obtain the average of the grades in the array. Member function getAverage (declared in line 24 of Fig. 7.16 and defined in lines 98–108 of Fig. 7.17) uses a for statement to total the values in array grades before calculating the average. Note that the averaging calculation in line 107 uses const static data member students to determine the number of grades being averaged.

Lines 58–59 in member function processGrades call member functions getMinimum and getMaximum to determine the lowest and highest grades of any student on the exam, respectively. Let's examine how member function getMinimum finds the *lowest* grade. Because the highest grade allowed is 100, we begin by assuming that 100 is the lowest grade (line 68). Then, we compare each of the elements in the array to the lowest grade, looking for smaller values. Lines 71–76 in member function getMinimum loop through the array, and lines 74–75 compare each grade to lowGrade. If a grade is less than lowGrade, lowGrade is set to that grade. When line 78 executes, lowGrade contains the lowest grade in the array. Member function getMaximum (lines 82–95) works similarly to member function getMinimum.

Finally, line 62 in member function processGrades calls member function output-BarChart to print a distribution chart of the grade data using a technique similar to that in Fig. 7.9. In that example, we manually calculated the number of grades in each category (i.e., 0–9, 10–19, …, 90–99 and 100) by simply looking at a set of grades. In this example, lines 120–121 use a technique similar to that in Fig. 7.10 and Fig. 7.11 to calculate the frequency of grades in each category. Line 117 declares and creates array frequency of 11 ints to store the frequency of grades in each grade category. For each grade in array grades, lines 120–121 increment the appropriate element of the frequency array. To determine which element to increment, line 121 divides the current grade by 10 using integer division. For example, if grade is 85, line 121 increments frequency[8] to update the count of grades in the range 80–89. Lines 124–139 next print the bar chart (see Fig. 7.18) based on the values in array frequency. Like lines 29–30 of Fig. 7.9, lines 135–136 of Fig. 7.17 use a value in array frequency to determine the number of asterisks to display in each bar.

Testing Class *GradeBook*

The program of Fig. 7.18 creates an object of class GradeBook (Figs. 7.16–7.17) using the int array gradesArray (declared and initialized in lines 10–11). Note that we use the binary scope resolution operator (::) in the expression "GradeBook::students" (line 10) to access class GradeBook's static constant students. We use this constant here to create an array that is the same size as array grades stored as a data member in class GradeBook. Lines 13–14 pass a course name and gradesArray to the GradeBook constructor. Line 15 displays a welcome message, and line 16 invokes the GradeBook object's processGrades member function. The output reveals the summary of the 10 grades in myGradeBook.

7.7 Searching Arrays with Linear Search

Often a programmer will be working with large amounts of data stored in arrays. It may be necessary to determine whether an array contains a value that matches a certain key value. The process of finding a particular element of an array is called searching. In this section we discuss the simple linear search. Exercise 7.33 at the end of this chapter asks you to implement a recursive version of the linear search. In Chapter 19, Searching and Sorting, we present the more complex, yet more efficient, binary search.

Linear Search

The linear search (Fig. 7.19, lines 37–44) compares each element of an array with a search key (line 40). Because the array is not in any particular order, it is just as likely that the value will be found in the first element as the last. On average, therefore, the program must compare the search key with half the elements of the array. To determine that a value is not in the array, the program must compare the search key to every element of the array.

The linear searching method works well for small arrays or for unsorted arrays (i.e., arrays whose elements are in no particular order). However, for large arrays, linear searching is inefficient. If the array is sorted (e.g., its elements are in ascending order), you can use the high-speed binary search technique that you'll learn about in Chapter 19, Searching and Sorting.

```cpp
1   // Fig. 7.19: fig07_19.cpp
2   // Linear search of an array.
3   #include <iostream>
4   using std::cout;
5   using std::cin;
6   using std::endl;
7
8   int linearSearch( const int [], int, int ); // prototype
9
10  int main()
11  {
12     const int arraySize = 100; // size of array a
13     int a[ arraySize ]; // create array a
14     int searchKey; // value to locate in array a
15
16     for ( int i = 0; i < arraySize; i++ )
17        a[ i ] = 2 * i; // create some data
18
19     cout << "Enter integer search key: ";
20     cin >> searchKey;
21
22     // attempt to locate searchKey in array a
23     int element = linearSearch( a, searchKey, arraySize );
24
25     // display results
26     if ( element != -1 )
27        cout << "Found value in element " << element << endl;
28     else
29        cout << "Value not found" << endl;
```

Fig. 7.19 | Linear search of an array. (Part 1 of 2.)

```
30
31      return 0; // indicates successful termination
32    } // end main
33
34    // compare key to every element of array until location is
35    // found or until end of array is reached; return subscript of
36    // element if key or -1 if key not found
37    int linearSearch( const int array[], int key, int sizeOfArray )
38    {
39       for ( int j = 0; j < sizeOfArray; j++ )
40          if ( array[ j ] == key ) // if found,
41             return j; // return location of key
42
43       return -1; // key not found
44    } // end function linearSearch
```

```
Enter integer search key: 36
Found value in element 18
```

```
Enter integer search key: 37
Value not found
```

Fig. 7.19 | Linear search of an array. (Part 2 of 2.)

7.8 Sorting Arrays with Insertion Sort

Sorting data (i.e., placing the data into some particular order such as ascending or descending) is one of the most important computing applications. A bank sorts all checks by account number so that it can prepare individual bank statements at the end of each month. Telephone companies sort their phone directories by last name and, within that, by first name to make it easy to find phone numbers. Virtually every organization must sort some data and, in many cases, massive amounts of it. Sorting data is an intriguing problem that has attracted some of the most intense research efforts in the field of computer science. In this chapter, we discuss a simple sorting scheme. In Chapter 19, Searching and Sorting, we investigate more complex schemes that yield superior performance, and we introduce Big O (pronounced "Big Oh") notation for characterizing how hard each scheme must work to accomplish its task.

 Performance Tip 7.4

Sometimes, simple algorithms perform poorly. Their virtue is that they are easy to write, test and debug. More complex algorithms are sometimes needed to realize optimal performance.

Insertion Sort

The program in Fig. 7.20 sorts the values of the 10-element array data into ascending order. The technique we use is called insertion sort—a simple, but inefficient, sorting algorithm. The first iteration of this algorithm takes the second element and, if it is less than the first element, swaps it with the first element (i.e., the program *inserts* the second element in front of the first element). The second iteration looks at the third element and inserts it into the correct position with respect to the first two elements, so all three elements are in order. At the ith iteration of this algorithm, the first i elements in the original array will be sorted.

Line 13 of Fig. 7.20 declares and initializes array data with the following values:

34   56   4   10   77   51   93   30   5   52

The program first looks at data[0] and data[1], whose values are 34 and 56, respectively. These two elements are already in order, so the program continues—if they were out of order, the program would swap them.

```cpp
1   // Fig. 7.20: fig07_20.cpp
2   // This program sorts an array's values into ascending order.
3   #include <iostream>
4   using std::cout;
5   using std::endl;
6
7   #include <iomanip>
8   using std::setw;
9
10  int main()
11  {
12     const int arraySize = 10; // size of array a
13     int data[ arraySize ] = { 34, 56, 4, 10, 77, 51, 93, 30, 5, 52 };
14     int insert; // temporary variable to hold element to insert
15
16     cout << "Unsorted array:\n";
17
18     // output original array
19     for ( int i = 0; i < arraySize; i++ )
20        cout << setw( 4 ) << data[ i ];
21
22     // insertion sort
23     // loop over the elements of the array
24     for ( int next = 1; next < arraySize; next++ )
25     {
26        insert = data[ next ]; // store the value in the current element
27
28        int moveItem = next; // initialize location to place element
29
30        // search for the location in which to put the current element
31        while ( ( moveItem > 0 ) && ( data[ moveItem - 1 ] > insert ) )
32        {
33           // shift element one slot to the right
34           data[ moveItem ] = data[ moveItem - 1 ];
35           moveItem--;
36        } // end while
37
38        data[ moveItem ] = insert; // place inserted element into the array
39     } // end for
40
41     cout << "\nSorted array:\n";
```

Fig. 7.20 | Sorting an array with insertion sort. (Part 1 of 2.)

```
42
43      // output sorted array
44      for ( int i = 0; i < arraySize; i++ )
45         cout << setw( 4 ) << data[ i ];
46
47      cout << endl;
48      return 0; // indicates successful termination
49   } // end main
```

```
Unsorted array:
   34  56   4  10  77  51  93  30   5  52
Sorted array:
    4   5  10  30  34  51  52  56  77  93
```

Fig. 7.20 | Sorting an array with insertion sort. (Part 2 of 2.)

In the second iteration, the program looks at the value of data[2], 4. This value is less than 56, so the program stores 4 in a temporary variable and moves 56 one element to the right. The program then checks and determines that 4 is less than 34, so it moves 34 one element to the right. The program has now reached the beginning of the array, so it places 4 in data[0]. The array now is

    4   34   56   10   77   51   93   30   5   52

In the third iteration, the program stores the value of data[3], 10, in a temporary variable. Then the program compares 10 to 56 and moves 56 one element to the right because it is larger than 10. The program then compares 10 to 34, moving 34 right one element. When the program compares 10 to 4, it observes that 10 is larger than 4 and places 10 in data[1]. The array now is

    4   10   34   56   77   51   93   30   5   52

Using this algorithm, at the ith iteration, the first i elements of the original array are sorted. They may not be in their final locations, however, because smaller values may be located later in the array.

The sorting is performed by the for statement in lines 24–39 that loops over the elements of the array. In each iteration, line 26 temporarily stores in variable insert (declared in line 14) the value of the element that will be inserted into the sorted portion of the array. Line 28 declares and initializes the variable moveItem, which keeps track of where to insert the element. Lines 31–36 loop to locate the correct position where the element should be inserted. The loop terminates either when the program reaches the front of the array or when it reaches an element that is less than the value to be inserted. Line 34 moves an element to the right, and line 35 decrements the position at which to insert the next element. After the while loop ends, line 38 inserts the element into place. When the for statement in lines 24–39 terminates, the elements of the array are sorted.

The chief virtue of the insertion sort is that it is easy to program; however, it runs slowly. This becomes apparent when sorting large arrays. In the exercises, we'll investigate some alternate algorithms for sorting an array. We investigate sorting and searching in greater depth in Chapter 19.

7.9 Multidimensional Arrays

Arrays with two or more dimensions are known as multidimensional arrays. Arrays with two dimensions often represent tables of values consisting of information arranged in rows and columns. To identify a particular table element, we must specify two subscripts. By convention, the first identifies the element's row and the second identifies the element's column. Arrays that require two subscripts to identify a particular element are called two-dimensional arrays or 2-D arrays. Note that multidimensional arrays can have more than two dimensions (i.e., subscripts). Figure 7.21 illustrates a two-dimensional array, a. The array contains three rows and four columns, so it is said to be a 3-by-4 array. In general, an array with m rows and n columns is called an m-by-n array.

Every element in array a is identified in Fig. 7.21 by an element name of the form a[i][j], where a is the name of the array, and i and j are the subscripts that uniquely identify each element in a. Notice that the names of the elements in row 0 all have a first subscript of 0; the names of the elements in column 3 all have a second subscript of 3.

 Common Programming Error 7.12

Referencing a two-dimensional array element a[x][y] incorrectly as a[x, y] is an error. Actually, a[x, y] is treated as a[y], because C++ evaluates the expression x, y (containing a comma operator) simply as y (the last of the comma-separated expressions).

A multidimensional array can be initialized in its declaration much like a one-dimensional array. For example, a two-dimensional array b with values 1 and 2 in its row 0 elements and values 3 and 4 in its row 1 elements could be declared and initialized with

```
int b[ 2 ][ 2 ] = { { 1, 2 }, { 3, 4 } };
```

The values are grouped by row in braces. So, 1 and 2 initialize b[0][0] and b[0][1], respectively, and 3 and 4 initialize b[1][0] and b[1][1], respectively. If there are not enough initializers for a given row, the remaining elements of that row are initialized to 0. Thus, the declaration

```
int b[ 2 ][ 2 ] = { { 1 }, { 3, 4 } };
```

initializes b[0][0] to 1, b[0][1] to 0, b[1][0] to 3 and b[1][1] to 4.

Figure 7.22 demonstrates initializing two-dimensional arrays in declarations. Lines 11–13 declare three arrays, each with two rows and three columns.

	Column 0	Column 1	Column 2	Column 3
Row 0	a[0][0]	a[0][1]	a[0][2]	a[0][3]
Row 1	a[1][0]	a[1][1]	a[1][2]	a[1][3]
Row 2	a[2][0]	a[2][1]	a[2][2]	a[2][3]

Column subscript
Row subscript
Array name

Fig. 7.21 | Two-dimensional array with three rows and four columns.

```
1   // Fig. 7.22: fig07_22.cpp
2   // Initializing multidimensional arrays.
3   #include <iostream>
4   using std::cout;
5   using std::endl;
6
7   void printArray( const int [][ 3 ] ); // prototype
8
9   int main()
10  {
11     int array1[ 2 ][ 3 ] = { { 1, 2, 3 }, { 4, 5, 6 } };
12     int array2[ 2 ][ 3 ] = { 1, 2, 3, 4, 5 };
13     int array3[ 2 ][ 3 ] = { { 1, 2 }, { 4 } };
14
15     cout << "Values in array1 by row are:" << endl;
16     printArray( array1 );
17
18     cout << "\nValues in array2 by row are:" << endl;
19     printArray( array2 );
20
21     cout << "\nValues in array3 by row are:" << endl;
22     printArray( array3 );
23     return 0; // indicates successful termination
24  } // end main
25
26  // output array with two rows and three columns
27  void printArray( const int a[][ 3 ] )
28  {
29     // loop through array's rows
30     for ( int i = 0; i < 2; i++ )
31     {
32        // loop through columns of current row
33        for ( int j = 0; j < 3; j++ )
34           cout << a[ i ][ j ] << ' ';
35
36        cout << endl; // start new line of output
37     } // end outer for
38  } // end function printArray
```

```
Values in array1 by row are:
1 2 3
4 5 6

Values in array2 by row are:
1 2 3
4 5 0

Values in array3 by row are:
1 2 0
4 0 0
```

Fig. 7.22 | Initializing multidimensional arrays.

The declaration of array1 (line 11) provides six initializers in two sublists. The first sublist initializes row 0 of the array to the values 1, 2 and 3; and the second sublist initializes row 1 of the array to the values 4, 5 and 6. If the braces around each sublist are removed from the `array1` initializer list, the compiler initializes the elements of row 0 followed by the elements of row 1, yielding the same result.

The declaration of `array2` (line 12) provides only five initializers. The initializers are assigned to row 0, then row 1. Any elements that do not have an explicit initializer are initialized to zero, so `array2[ 1 ][ 2 ]` is initialized to zero.

The declaration of `array3` (line 13) provides three initializers in two sublists. The sublist for row 0 explicitly initializes the first two elements of row 0 to 1 and 2; the third element is implicitly initialized to zero. The sublist for row 1 explicitly initializes the first element to 4 and implicitly initializes the last two elements to zero.

The program calls function `printArray` to output each array's elements. Notice that the function definition (lines 27–38) specifies the parameter `const int a[][ 3 ]`. When a function receives a one-dimensional array as an argument, the array brackets are empty in the function's parameter list. The size of the first dimension (i.e., the number of rows) of a two-dimensional array is not required either, but all subsequent dimension sizes are required. The compiler uses these sizes to determine the locations in memory of elements in multidimensional arrays. All array elements are stored consecutively in memory, regardless of the number of dimensions. In a two-dimensional array, row 0 is stored in memory followed by row 1. In a two-dimensional array, each row is a one-dimensional array. To locate an element in a particular row, the function must know exactly how many elements are in each row so it can skip the proper number of memory locations when accessing the array. Thus, when accessing `a[ 1 ][ 2 ]`, the function knows to skip row 0's three elements in memory to get to row 1. Then, the function accesses element 2 of that row.

Many common array manipulations use `for` repetition statements. For example, the following `for` statement sets all the elements in row 2 of array a in Fig. 7.21 to zero:

```
for ( column = 0; column < 4; column++ )
   a[ 2 ][ column ] = 0;
```

The `for` statement varies only the second subscript (i.e., the column subscript). The preceding `for` statement is equivalent to the following assignment statements:

```
a[ 2 ][ 0 ] = 0;
a[ 2 ][ 1 ] = 0;
a[ 2 ][ 2 ] = 0;
a[ 2 ][ 3 ] = 0;
```

The following nested `for` statement determines the total of all the elements in array a:

```
total = 0;

for ( row = 0; row < 3; row++ )

   for ( column = 0; column < 4; column++ )
      total += a[ row ][ column ];
```

The `for` statement totals the elements of the array one row at a time. The outer `for` statement begins by setting row (i.e., the row subscript) to 0, so the elements of row 0 may be totaled by the inner `for` statement. The outer `for` statement then increments row to 1, so the elements of row 1 can be totaled. Then, the outer `for` statement increments row to 2, so the elements of row 2 can be totaled. When the nested `for` statement terminates, `total` contains the sum of all the array elements.

7.10 Case Study: Class GradeBook Using a Two-Dimensional Array

In Section 7.6, we presented class GradeBook (Figs. 7.16–7.17), which used a one-dimensional array to store student grades on a single exam. In most semesters, students take several exams. Professors are likely to want to analyze grades across the entire semester, both for a single student and for the class as a whole.

Storing Student Grades in a Two-Dimensional Array in Class **GradeBook**
Figures 7.23–7.24 contain a version of class GradeBook that uses a two-dimensional array grades to store the grades of a number of students on multiple exams. Each row of the array represents a single student's grades for the entire course, and each column represents all the grades the students earned for one particular exam. A client program, such as fig07_25.cpp, passes the array as an argument to the GradeBook constructor. In this example, we use a ten-by-three array containing ten students' grades on three exams.

Five member functions (declared in lines 23–27 of Fig. 7.23) perform array manipulations to process the grades. Each of these member functions is similar to its counterpart in the earlier one-dimensional array version of class GradeBook (Figs. 7.16–7.17). Member function getMinimum (defined in lines 65–82 of Fig. 7.24) determines the lowest grade of any student for the semester. Member function getMaximum (defined in lines 85–102 of Fig. 7.24) determines the highest grade of any student for the semester. Member function getAverage (lines 105–115 of Fig. 7.24) determines a particular student's semester average. Member function outputBarChart (lines 118–149 of Fig. 7.24) outputs a bar chart of the distribution of all student grades for the semester. Member function output-Grades (lines 152–177 of Fig. 7.24) outputs the two-dimensional array in a tabular format, along with each student's semester average.

```
1   // Fig. 7.23: GradeBook.h
2   // Definition of class GradeBook that uses a
3   // two-dimensional array to store test grades.
4   // Member functions are defined in GradeBook.cpp
5   #include <string> // program uses C++ Standard Library string class
6   using std::string;
7
8   // GradeBook class definition
9   class GradeBook
10  {
11  public:
12     // constants
13     const static int students = 10; // number of students
14     const static int tests = 3; // number of tests
15
16     // constructor initializes course name and array of grades
17     GradeBook( string, const int [][ tests ] );
18
19     void setCourseName( string ); // function to set the course name
20     string getCourseName(); // function to retrieve the course name
```

Fig. 7.23 | Definition of class GradeBook with a two-dimensional array to store grades. (Part 1 of 2.)

```
21      void displayMessage(); // display a welcome message
22      void processGrades(); // perform various operations on the grade data
23      int getMinimum(); // find the minimum grade in the grade book
24      int getMaximum(); // find the maximum grade in the grade book
25      double getAverage( const int [], const int ); // get student's average
26      void outputBarChart(); // output bar chart of grade distribution
27      void outputGrades(); // output the contents of the grades array
28   private:
29      string courseName; // course name for this grade book
30      int grades[ students ][ tests ]; // two-dimensional array of grades
31   }; // end class GradeBook
```

Fig. 7.23 | Definition of class GradeBook with a two-dimensional array to store grades. (Part 2 of 2.)

```
1    // Fig. 7.24: GradeBook.cpp
2    // Member-function definitions for class GradeBook that
3    // uses a two-dimensional array to store grades.
4    #include <iostream>
5    using std::cout;
6    using std::cin;
7    using std::endl;
8    using std::fixed;
9
10   #include <iomanip> // parameterized stream manipulators
11   using std::setprecision; // sets numeric output precision
12   using std::setw; // sets field width
13
14   // include definition of class GradeBook from GradeBook.h
15   #include "GradeBook.h"
16
17   // two-argument constructor initializes courseName and grades array
18   GradeBook::GradeBook( string name, const int gradesArray[][ tests ] )
19   {
20      setCourseName( name ); // initialize courseName
21
22      // copy grades from gradeArray to grades
23      for ( int student = 0; student < students; student++ )
24
25         for ( int test = 0; test < tests; test++ )
26            grades[ student ][ test ] = gradesArray[ student ][ test ];
27   } // end two-argument GradeBook constructor
28
29   // function to set the course name
30   void GradeBook::setCourseName( string name )
31   {
32      courseName = name; // store the course name
33   } // end function setCourseName
```

Fig. 7.24 | GradeBook class member-function definitions manipulating a two-dimensional array of grades. (Part 1 of 4.)

```
34
35    // function to retrieve the course name
36    string GradeBook::getCourseName()
37    {
38       return courseName;
39    } // end function getCourseName
40
41    // display a welcome message to the GradeBook user
42    void GradeBook::displayMessage()
43    {
44       // this statement calls getCourseName to get the
45       // name of the course this GradeBook represents
46       cout << "Welcome to the grade book for\n" << getCourseName() << "!"
47          << endl;
48    } // end function displayMessage
49
50    // perform various operations on the data
51    void GradeBook::processGrades()
52    {
53       // output grades array
54       outputGrades();
55
56       // call functions getMinimum and getMaximum
57       cout << "\nLowest grade in the grade book is " << getMinimum()
58          << "\nHighest grade in the grade book is " << getMaximum() << endl;
59
60       // output grade distribution chart of all grades on all tests
61       outputBarChart();
62    } // end function processGrades
63
64    // find minimum grade in the entire gradebook
65    int GradeBook::getMinimum()
66    {
67       int lowGrade = 100; // assume lowest grade is 100
68
69       // loop through rows of grades array
70       for ( int student = 0; student < students; student++ )
71       {
72          // loop through columns of current row
73          for ( int test = 0; test < tests; test++ )
74          {
75             // if current grade less than lowGrade, assign it to lowGrade
76             if ( grades[ student ][ test ] < lowGrade )
77                lowGrade = grades[ student ][ test ]; // new lowest grade
78          } // end inner for
79       } // end outer for
80
81       return lowGrade; // return lowest grade
82    } // end function getMinimum
83
```

Fig. 7.24 | GradeBook class member-function definitions manipulating a two-dimensional array of grades. (Part 2 of 4.)

```
84   // find maximum grade in the entire gradebook
85   int GradeBook::getMaximum()
86   {
87      int highGrade = 0; // assume highest grade is 0
88
89      // loop through rows of grades array
90      for ( int student = 0; student < students; student++ )
91      {
92         // loop through columns of current row
93         for ( int test = 0; test < tests; test++ )
94         {
95            // if current grade greater than lowGrade, assign it to highGrade
96            if ( grades[ student ][ test ] > highGrade )
97               highGrade = grades[ student ][ test ]; // new highest grade
98         } // end inner for
99      } // end outer for
100
101      return highGrade; // return highest grade
102   } // end function getMaximum
103
104   // determine average grade for particular set of grades
105   double GradeBook::getAverage( const int setOfGrades[], const int grades )
106   {
107      int total = 0; // initialize total
108
109      // sum grades in array
110      for ( int grade = 0; grade < grades; grade++ )
111         total += setOfGrades[ grade ];
112
113      // return average of grades
114      return static_cast< double >( total ) / grades;
115   } // end function getAverage
116
117   // output bar chart displaying grade distribution
118   void GradeBook::outputBarChart()
119   {
120      cout << "\nOverall grade distribution:" << endl;
121
122      // stores frequency of grades in each range of 10 grades
123      const int frequencySize = 11;
124      int frequency[ frequencySize ] = {}; // initialize elements to 0
125
126      // for each grade, increment the appropriate frequency
127      for ( int student = 0; student < students; student++ )
128
129         for ( int test = 0; test < tests; test++ )
130            ++frequency[ grades[ student ][ test ] / 10 ];
131
132      // for each grade frequency, print bar in chart
133      for ( int count = 0; count < frequencySize; count++ )
134      {
```

Fig. 7.24 | GradeBook class member-function definitions manipulating a two-dimensional array of grades. (Part 3 of 4.)

```
135         // output bar label ("0-9:", ..., "90-99:", "100:" )
136         if ( count == 0 )
137             cout << "  0-9: ";
138         else if ( count == 10 )
139             cout << "  100: ";
140         else
141             cout << count * 10 << "-" << ( count * 10 ) + 9 << ": ";
142
143         // print bar of asterisks
144         for ( int stars = 0; stars < frequency[ count ]; stars++ )
145             cout << '*';
146
147         cout << endl; // start a new line of output
148     } // end outer for
149 } // end function outputBarChart
150
151 // output the contents of the grades array
152 void GradeBook::outputGrades()
153 {
154     cout << "\nThe grades are:\n\n";
155     cout << "              "; // align column heads
156
157     // create a column heading for each of the tests
158     for ( int test = 0; test < tests; test++ )
159         cout << "Test " << test + 1 << "  ";
160
161     cout << "Average" << endl; // student average column heading
162
163     // create rows/columns of text representing array grades
164     for ( int student = 0; student < students; student++ )
165     {
166         cout << "Student " << setw( 2 ) << student + 1;
167
168         // output student's grades
169         for ( int test = 0; test < tests; test++ )
170             cout << setw( 8 ) << grades[ student ][ test ];
171
172         // call member function getAverage to calculate student's average;
173         // pass row of grades and the value of tests as the arguments
174         double average = getAverage( grades[ student ], tests );
175         cout << setw( 9 ) << setprecision( 2 ) << fixed << average << endl;
176     } // end outer for
177 } // end function outputGrades
```

Fig. 7.24 | GradeBook class member-function definitions manipulating a two-dimensional array of grades. (Part 4 of 4.)

Member functions getMinimum, getMaximum, outputBarChart and outputGrades each loop through array grades by using nested for statements. For example, consider the nested for statement in member function getMinimum (lines 70–79). The outer for statement begins by setting student (i.e., the row subscript) to 0, so the elements of row 0 can be compared with variable lowGrade in the body of the inner for statement. The inner for statement loops through the grades of a particular row and compares each grade with lowGrade. If a grade is less than lowGrade, lowGrade is set to that grade. The outer for statement then increments the row subscript to 1. The elements of row 1 are compared with variable lowGrade. The outer for statement then increments the row subscript to 2, and the elements of row 2 are compared with variable lowGrade. This repeats until all rows of grades have been traversed. When execution of the nested statement is complete, low-Grade contains the smallest grade in the two-dimensional array. Member function get-Maximum works similarly to member function getMinimum.

Member function outputBarChart in Fig. 7.24 is nearly identical to the one in Fig. 7.17. However, to output the overall grade distribution for a whole semester, the member function uses a nested for statement (lines 127–130) to create the one-dimensional array frequency based on all the grades in the two-dimensional array. The rest of the code in each of the two outputBarChart member functions that displays the chart is identical.

Member function outputGrades (lines 152–177) also uses nested for statements to output values of the array grades, in addition to each student's semester average. The output in Fig. 7.25 shows the result, which resembles the tabular format of a professor's physical grade book. Lines 158–159 print the column headings for each test. We use a counter-controlled for statement so that we can identify each test with a number. Similarly, the for statement in lines 164–176 first outputs a row label using a counter variable to identify each student (line 166). Although array indices start at 0, note that lines 159 and 166 output

```
1   // Fig. 7.25: fig07_25.cpp
2   // Creates GradeBook object using a two-dimensional array of grades.
3
4   #include "GradeBook.h" // GradeBook class definition
5
6   // function main begins program execution
7   int main()
8   {
9      // two-dimensional array of student grades
10     int gradesArray[ GradeBook::students ][ GradeBook::tests ] =
11        { { 87, 96, 70 },
12          { 68, 87, 90 },
13          { 94, 100, 90 },
14          { 100, 81, 82 },
15          { 83, 65, 85 },
16          { 78, 87, 65 },
17          { 85, 75, 83 },
18          { 91, 94, 100 },
19          { 76, 72, 84 },
20          { 87, 93, 73 } };
21
22     GradeBook myGradeBook(
23        "CS101 Introduction to C++ Programming", gradesArray );
24     myGradeBook.displayMessage();
25     myGradeBook.processGrades();
26     return 0; // indicates successful termination
27  } // end main
```

Fig. 7.25 | Creates a GradeBook object using a two-dimensional array of grades, then invokes member function processGrades to analyze them. (Part 1 of 2.)

```
Welcome to the grade book for
CS101 Introduction to C++ Programming!

The grades are:

            Test 1  Test 2  Test 3  Average
Student  1    87      96      70     84.33
Student  2    68      87      90     81.67
Student  3    94     100      90     94.67
Student  4   100      81      82     87.67
Student  5    83      65      85     77.67
Student  6    78      87      65     76.67
Student  7    85      75      83     81.00
Student  8    91      94     100     95.00
Student  9    76      72      84     77.33
Student 10    87      93      73     84.33

Lowest grade in the grade book is 65
Highest grade in the grade book is 100

Overall grade distribution:
  0-9:
 10-19:
 20-29:
 30-39:
 40-49:
 50-59:
 60-69: ***
 70-79: ******
 80-89: ***********
 90-99: *******
   100: ***
```

Fig. 7.25 | Creates a GradeBook object using a two-dimensional array of grades, then invokes member function processGrades to analyze them. (Part 2 of 2.)

test + 1 and student + 1, respectively, to produce test and student numbers starting at 1 (see Fig. 7.25). The inner for statement in lines 169–170 uses the outer for statement's counter variable student to loop through a specific row of array grades and output each student's test grade. Finally, line 174 obtains each student's semester average by passing the current row of grades (i.e., grades[student]) to member function getAverage.

Member function getAverage (lines 105–115) takes two arguments—a one-dimensional array of test results for a particular student and the number of test results in the array. When line 174 calls getAverage, the first argument is grades[student], which specifies that a particular row of the two-dimensional array grades should be passed to getAverage. For example, based on the array created in Fig. 7.25, the argument grades[1] represents the three values (a one-dimensional array of grades) stored in row 1 of the two-dimensional array grades. A two-dimensional array can be considered an array whose elements are one-dimensional arrays. Member function getAverage calculates the sum of the array elements, divides the total by the number of test results and returns the floating-point result as a double value (line 114).

Testing Class GradeBook

The program in Fig. 7.25 creates an object of class GradeBook (Figs. 7.23–7.24) using the two-dimensional array of ints named gradesArray (declared and initialized in lines 10–20). Note that line 10 accesses class GradeBook's static constants students and tests to indicate the size of each dimension of array gradesArray. Lines 22–23 pass a course name and gradesArray to the GradeBook constructor. Lines 24–25 then invoke myGradeBook's displayMessage and processGrades member functions to display a welcome message and obtain a report summarizing the students' grades for the semester, respectively.

7.11 Introduction to C++ Standard Library Class Template vector

We now introduce C++ Standard Library class template vector, which represents a more robust type of array featuring many additional capabilities. As you'll see in later chapters, C-style pointer-based arrays (i.e., the type of arrays presented thus far) have great potential for errors. For example, as mentioned earlier, a program can easily "walk off" either end of an array, because C++ does not check whether subscripts fall outside the range of an array. Two arrays cannot be meaningfully compared with equality operators or relational operators. As you'll learn in Chapter 8, pointer variables (known more commonly as pointers) contain memory addresses as their values. Array names are simply pointers to where the arrays begin in memory, and, of course, two arrays will always be at different memory locations. When an array is passed to a general-purpose function designed to handle arrays of any size, the size of the array must be passed as an additional argument. Furthermore, one array cannot be assigned to another with the assignment operator(s)—array names are const pointers, and, as you'll learn in Chapter 8, a constant pointer cannot be used on the left side of an assignment operator. These and other capabilities certainly seem like "naturals" for dealing with arrays, but C++ does not provide such capabilities. However, the C++ Standard Library provides class template vector to allow programmers to create a more powerful and less error-prone alternative to arrays. In Chapter 11, Operator Overloading; String and Array Objects, we present the means to implement such array capabilities as those provided by vector. You'll learn how to customize operators for use with your own classes (a technique known as operator overloading).

The vector class template is available to anyone building applications with C++. The notations that the vector example uses might be unfamiliar to you, because vectors use template notation. Recall that Section 6.18 discussed function templates. In Chapter 14, we discuss class templates. For now, you should feel comfortable using class template vector by mimicking the syntax in the example we show in this section. You'll deepen your understanding as we study class templates in Chapter 14. Chapter 22 presents class template vector (and several other standard C++ container classes) in detail.

The program of Fig. 7.26 demonstrates capabilities provided by C++ Standard Library class template vector that are not available for C-style pointer-based arrays. Standard class template vector provides many of the same features as the Array class that we construct in Chapter 11, Operator Overloading; String and Array Objects. Standard class template vector is defined in header <vector> (line 11) and belongs to namespace std (line 12). Chapter 22 discusses the full functionality of standard class template vector.

Lines 19–20 create two vector objects that store values of type int—integers1 contains seven elements, and integers2 contains 10 elements. By default, all the elements of each vector object are set to 0. Note that vectors can be defined to store any data type, by replacing int in vector< int > with the appropriate data type. This notation, which specifies the type stored in the vector, is similar to the template notation that Section 6.18 introduced with function templates. Again, Chapter 14 discusses this syntax in detail.

```
1   // Fig. 7.26: fig07_26.cpp
2   // Demonstrating C++ Standard Library class template vector.
3   #include <iostream>
4   using std::cout;
5   using std::cin;
6   using std::endl;
7
8   #include <iomanip>
9   using std::setw;
10
11  #include <vector>
12  using std::vector;
13
14  void outputVector( const vector< int > & ); // display the vector
15  void inputVector( vector< int > & ); // input values into the vector
16
17  int main()
18  {
19     vector< int > integers1( 7 ); // 7-element vector< int >
20     vector< int > integers2( 10 ); // 10-element vector< int >
21
22     // print integers1 size and contents
23     cout << "Size of vector integers1 is " << integers1.size()
24        << "\nvector after initialization:" << endl;
25     outputVector( integers1 );
26
27     // print integers2 size and contents
28     cout << "\nSize of vector integers2 is " << integers2.size()
29        << "\nvector after initialization:" << endl;
30     outputVector( integers2 );
31
32     // input and print integers1 and integers2
33     cout << "\nEnter 17 integers:" << endl;
34     inputVector( integers1 );
35     inputVector( integers2 );
36
37     cout << "\nAfter input, the vectors contain:\n"
38        << "integers1:" << endl;
39     outputVector( integers1 );
40     cout << "integers2:" << endl;
41     outputVector( integers2 );
42
43     // use inequality (!=) operator with vector objects
44     cout << "\nEvaluating: integers1 != integers2" << endl;
45
46     if ( integers1 != integers2 )
47        cout << "integers1 and integers2 are not equal" << endl;
```

Fig. 7.26 | C++ Standard Library class template vector. (Part I of 4.)

```
48
49      // create vector integers3 using integers1 as an
50      // initializer; print size and contents
51      vector< int > integers3( integers1 ); // copy constructor
52
53      cout << "\nSize of vector integers3 is " << integers3.size()
54         << "\nvector after initialization:" << endl;
55      outputVector( integers3 );
56
57      // use overloaded assignment (=) operator
58      cout << "\nAssigning integers2 to integers1:" << endl;
59      integers1 = integers2; // assign integers2 to integers1
60
61      cout << "integers1:" << endl;
62      outputVector( integers1 );
63      cout << "integers2:" << endl;
64      outputVector( integers2 );
65
66      // use equality (==) operator with vector objects
67      cout << "\nEvaluating: integers1 == integers2" << endl;
68
69      if ( integers1 == integers2 )
70         cout << "integers1 and integers2 are equal" << endl;
71
72      // use square brackets to create rvalue
73      cout << "\nintegers1[5] is " << integers1[ 5 ];
74
75      // use square brackets to create lvalue
76      cout << "\n\nAssigning 1000 to integers1[5]" << endl;
77      integers1[ 5 ] = 1000;
78      cout << "integers1:" << endl;
79      outputVector( integers1 );
80
81      // attempt to use out-of-range subscript
82      cout << "\nAttempt to assign 1000 to integers1.at( 15 )" << endl;
83      integers1.at( 15 ) = 1000; // ERROR: out of range
84      return 0;
85   } // end main
86
87   // output vector contents
88   void outputVector( const vector< int > &array )
89   {
90      size_t i; // declare control variable
91
92      for ( i = 0; i < array.size(); i++ )
93      {
94         cout << setw( 12 ) << array[ i ];
95
96         if ( ( i + 1 ) % 4 == 0 ) // 4 numbers per row of output
97            cout << endl;
98      } // end for
99
```

Fig. 7.26 | C++ Standard Library class template vector. (Part 2 of 4.)

```
100      if ( i % 4 != 0 )
101         cout << endl;
102   } // end function outputVector
103
104   // input vector contents
105   void inputVector( vector< int > &array )
106   {
107      for ( size_t i = 0; i < array.size(); i++ )
108         cin >> array[ i ];
109   } // end function inputVector
```

```
Size of vector integers1 is 7
vector after initialization:
          0           0           0           0
          0           0           0

Size of vector integers2 is 10
vector after initialization:
          0           0           0           0
          0           0           0           0
          0           0

Enter 17 integers:
1 2 3 4 5 6 7 8 9 10 11 12 13 14 15 16 17

After input, the vectors contain:
integers1:
          1           2           3           4
          5           6           7
integers2:
          8           9          10          11
         12          13          14          15
         16          17

Evaluating: integers1 != integers2
integers1 and integers2 are not equal

Size of vector integers3 is 7
vector after initialization:
          1           2           3           4
          5           6           7

Assigning integers2 to integers1:
integers1:
          8           9          10          11
         12          13          14          15
         16          17
integers2:
          8           9          10          11
         12          13          14          15
         16          17

Evaluating: integers1 == integers2
integers1 and integers2 are equal
```

(continued ...)

Fig. 7.26 | C++ Standard Library class template `vector`. (Part 3 of 4.)

```
integers1[5] is 13

Assigning 1000 to integers1[5]
integers1:
            8           9          10          11
           12        1000          14          15
           16          17

Attempt to assign 1000 to integers1.at( 15 )

abnormal program termination
```

Fig. 7.26 | C++ Standard Library class template vector. (Part 4 of 4.)

Line 23 uses vector member function size to obtain the size (i.e., the number of elements) of integers1. Line 25 passes integers1 to function outputVector (lines 88–102), which uses square brackets, [] (line 94), to obtain the value in each element of the vector for output. Note the resemblance of this notation to that used to access the value of an array element. Lines 28 and 30 perform the same tasks for integers2.

Member function size of class template vector returns the number of elements in a vector as a value of type size_t (which represents the type unsigned int on many systems). As a result, line 90 declares the control variable i to be of type size_t, too. On some compilers, declaring i as an int causes the compiler to issue a warning message, since the loop-continuation condition (line 92) would compare a signed value (i.e., int i) and an unsigned value (i.e., a value of type size_t returned by function size).

Lines 34–35 pass integers1 and integers2 to function inputVector (lines 105–109) to read values for each vector's elements from the user. The function uses square brackets ([]) to form *lvalues* that are used to store the input values in each vector element.

Line 46 demonstrates that vector objects can be compared with one another using the != operator. If the contents of two vectors are not equal, the operator returns true; otherwise, it returns false.

The C++ Standard Library class template vector allows you to create a new vector object that is initialized with the contents of an existing vector. Line 51 creates a vector object integers3 and initializes it with a copy of integers1. This invokes vector's so-called copy constructor to perform the copy operation. You'll learn about copy constructors in detail in Chapter 11. Lines 53–55 output the size and contents of integers3 to demonstrate that it was initialized correctly.

Line 59 assigns integers2 to integers1, demonstrating that the assignment (=) operator can be used with vector objects. Lines 61–64 output the contents of both objects to show that they now contain identical values. Line 69 then compares integers1 to integers2 with the equality (==) operator to determine whether the contents of the two objects are equal after the assignment in line 59 (which they are).

Lines 73 and 77 demonstrate that a program can use square brackets ([]) to obtain a vector element as an *rvalue* and as an *lvalue*, respectively. Recall from Section 5.9 that an *rvalue* cannot be modified, but an *lvalue* can. As is the case with C-style pointer-based arrays, C++ does not perform any bounds checking when vector elements are accessed with square brackets. Therefore, you must ensure that operations using [] do not accidentally attempt to manipulate elements outside the bounds of the vector. Standard class template vector does, however, provide bounds checking in its member function at, which "throws an exception" (see Chapter 16, Exception Handling) if its argument is an invalid subscript. By default, this causes a C++ program to terminate. If the subscript is valid, function at returns the element at the specified location as a modifiable *lvalue* or an unmodifiable *lvalue*, depending on the context (non-const or const) in which the call appears. Line 83 demonstrates a call to function at with an invalid subscript. The resulting output varies by compiler.

In this section, we demonstrated the C++ Standard Library class template vector, a robust, reusable class that can replace C-style pointer-based arrays. In Chapter 11, you'll see that vector achieves many of its capabilities by "overloading" C++'s built-in operators, and you'll learn how to customize operators for use with your own classes in similar ways. For example, we create an Array class that, like class template vector, improves upon basic array capabilities. Our Array class also provides additional features, such as the ability to input and output entire arrays with operators >> and <<, respectively.

7.12 (Optional) Software Engineering Case Study: Collaboration Among Objects in the ATM System

In this section, we concentrate on the collaborations (interactions) among objects in our ATM system. When two objects communicate with each other to accomplish a task, they are said to collaborate—they do this by invoking one another's operations. A collaboration consists of an object of one class sending a message to an object of another class. Messages are sent in C++ via member-function calls.

In Section 6.22, we determined many of the operations of the classes in our system. In this section, we concentrate on the messages that invoke these operations. To identify the collaborations in the system, we return to the requirements specification in Section 2.8. Recall that this document specifies the range of activities that occur during an ATM session (e.g., authenticating a user, performing transactions). The steps used to describe how the system must perform each of these tasks are our first indication of the collaborations in our system. As we proceed through this and the remaining Software Engineering Case Study sections, we may discover additional collaborations.

Identifying the Collaborations in a System

We identify the collaborations in the system by carefully reading the requirements specification sections that specify what the ATM should do to authenticate a user and to perform each transaction type. For each action or step described, we decide which objects in our system must interact to achieve the desired result. We identify one object as the sending object (i.e., the object that sends the message) and another as the receiving object (i.e., the object that offers that operation to clients of the class). We then select one of the receiving object's operations (identified in Section 6.22) that must be invoked by the sending object to produce the proper behavior. For example, the ATM displays a welcome message when idle. We know that an object of class Screen displays a message to the user via its displayMessage operation. Thus, we decide that the system can display a welcome message by employing a collaboration between the ATM and the Screen in which the ATM sends a displayMessage message to the Screen by invoking the displayMessage operation of class Screen. [*Note:* To avoid repeating the phrase "an object of class...," we refer to each object simply by using its class name preceded by an article ("a," "an" or "the")— for example, "the ATM" refers to an object of class ATM.]

Figure 7.27 lists the collaborations that can be derived from the requirements specification. For each sending object, we list the collaborations in the order in which they are discussed in the requirements specification. We list each collaboration involving a unique sender, message and recipient only once, even though the collaboration may occur several times during an ATM session. For example, the first row in Fig. 7.27 indicates that the ATM collaborates with the Screen whenever the ATM needs to display a message to the user.

Let's consider the collaborations in Fig. 7.27. Before allowing a user to perform any transactions, the ATM must prompt the user to enter an account number, then to enter a PIN. It accomplishes each of these tasks by sending a displayMessage message to the Screen. Both of these actions refer to the same collaboration between the ATM and the Screen, which is already listed in Fig. 7.27. The ATM obtains input in response to a prompt by sending a getInput message to the Keypad. Next, the ATM must determine whether the user-specified account number and PIN match those of an account in the database. It does so by sending an authenticateUser message to the BankDatabase. Recall that the BankDatabase cannot authenticate a user directly—only the user's Account (i.e., the Account that contains the account number specified by the user) can access the user's PIN to authenticate the user. Figure 7.27 therefore lists a collaboration in which the BankDatabase sends a validatePIN message to an Account.

An object of class...	sends the message...	to an object of class...
ATM	displayMessage	Screen
	getInput	Keypad
	authenticateUser	BankDatabase
	execute	BalanceInquiry
	execute	Withdrawal
	execute	Deposit
BalanceInquiry	getAvailableBalance	BankDatabase
	getTotalBalance	BankDatabase
	displayMessage	Screen
Withdrawal	displayMessage	Screen
	getInput	Keypad
	getAvailableBalance	BankDatabase
	isSufficientCashAvailable	CashDispenser
	debit	BankDatabase
	dispenseCash	CashDispenser
Deposit	displayMessage	Screen
	getInput	Keypad
	isEnvelopeReceived	DepositSlot
	credit	BankDatabase
BankDatabase	validatePIN	Account
	getAvailableBalance	Account
	getTotalBalance	Account
	debit	Account
	credit	Account

Fig. 7.27 | Collaborations in the ATM system.

After the user is authenticated, the ATM displays the main menu by sending a series of displayMessage messages to the Screen and obtains input containing a menu selection by sending a getInput message to the Keypad. We have already accounted for these collaborations. After the user chooses a type of transaction to perform, the ATM executes the transaction by sending an execute message to an object of the appropriate transaction class (i.e., a BalanceInquiry, a Withdrawal or a Deposit). For example, if the user chooses to perform a balance inquiry, the ATM sends an execute message to a BalanceInquiry.

Further examination of the requirements specification reveals the collaborations involved in executing each transaction type. A BalanceInquiry retrieves the amount of money available in the user's account by sending a getAvailableBalance message to the BankDatabase, which responds by sending a getAvailableBalance message to the user's Account. Similarly, the BalanceInquiry retrieves the amount of money on deposit by sending a getTotalBalance message to the BankDatabase, which sends the same message to the user's Account. To display both measures of the user's balance at the same time, the BalanceInquiry sends a displayMessage message to the Screen.

A Withdrawal sends the Screen several displayMessage messages to display a menu of standard withdrawal amounts (i.e., $20, $40, $60, $100, $200). The Withdrawal sends the Keypad a getInput message to obtain the user's menu selection, then determines whether the requested withdrawal amount is less than or equal to the user's account balance. The Withdrawal can obtain the amount of money available in the account by sending the BankDatabase a getAvailableBalance message. The Withdrawal then tests whether the cash dispenser contains enough cash by sending the CashDispenser an isSufficientCashAvailable message. A Withdrawal sends the BankDatabase a debit message to decrease the user's account balance. The BankDatabase sends the same message to the appropriate Account. Recall that debiting funds from an Account decreases both the totalBalance and the availableBalance. To dispense the requested amount of cash, the Withdrawal sends the CashDispenser a dispenseCash message. Finally, the Withdrawal sends a displayMessage message to the Screen, instructing the user to take the cash.

A Deposit responds to an execute message first by sending a displayMessage message to the Screen to prompt the user for a deposit amount. The Deposit sends a getInput message to the Keypad to obtain the user's input. The Deposit then sends a displayMessage message to the Screen to tell the user to insert a deposit envelope. To determine whether the deposit slot received an incoming deposit envelope, the Deposit sends an isEnvelopeReceived message to the DepositSlot. The Deposit updates the user's account by sending a credit message to the BankDatabase, which subsequently sends a credit message to the user's Account. Recall that crediting funds to an Account increases the totalBalance but not the availableBalance.

Interaction Diagrams

Now that we have identified a set of possible collaborations between the objects in our ATM system, let us graphically model these interactions using the UML. The UML provides several types of interaction diagrams that model the behavior of a system by modeling how objects interact with one another. The communication diagram emphasizes which objects participate in collaborations. [*Note:* Communication diagrams were called collaboration diagrams in earlier versions of the UML.] Like the communication diagram, the sequence diagram shows collaborations among objects, but it emphasizes *when* messages are sent between objects *over time*.

Communication Diagrams

Figure 7.28 shows a communication diagram that models the ATM executing a BalanceInquiry. Objects are modeled in the UML as rectangles containing names in the form objectName : ClassName. In this example, which involves only one object of each type, we disregard the object name and list only a colon followed by the class name. [*Note:* Specifying the name of each object in a communication diagram is recommended when modeling multiple objects of the same type.] Communicating objects are connected with solid lines, and messages are passed between objects along these lines in the direction shown by arrows. The name of the message, which appears next to the arrow, is the name of an operation (i.e., a member function) belonging to the receiving object—think of the name as a service that the receiving object provides to sending objects (its "clients").

The solid filled arrow in Fig. 7.28 represents a message—or synchronous call—in the UML and a function call in C++. This arrow indicates that the flow of control is from the sending object (the ATM) to the receiving object (a BalanceInquiry). Since this is a synchronous call, the sending object may not send another message, or do anything at all, until the receiving object processes the message and returns control to the sending object—the sender just waits. For example, in Fig. 7.28, the ATM calls member function execute of a BalanceInquiry and may not send another message until execute has finished and returns control to the ATM. [*Note:* If this were an asynchronous call, represented by a stick arrowhead, the sending object would not have to wait for the receiving object to return control—it would continue sending additional messages immediately following the asynchronous call. Asynchronous calls often can be implemented in C++ using platform-specific libraries provided with your compiler. Such techniques are beyond the scope of this book.]

Fig. 7.28 | Communication diagram of the ATM executing a balance inquiry.

Sequence of Messages in a Communication Diagram

Figure 7.29 shows a communication diagram that models the interactions among objects in the system when an object of class BalanceInquiry executes. We assume that the object's accountNumber attribute contains the account number of the current user. The collaborations in Fig. 7.29 begin after the ATM sends an execute message to a BalanceInquiry (i.e., the interaction modeled in Fig. 7.28). The number to the left of a message name indicates the order in which the message is passed. The sequence of messages in a communication diagram progresses in numerical order from least to greatest. In this diagram, the numbering starts with message 1 and ends with message 3. The BalanceInquiry first sends a getAvailableBalance message to the BankDatabase (message 1), then sends a getTotal-Balance message to the BankDatabase (message 2). Within the parentheses following a message name, we can specify a comma-separated list of the names of the parameters sent with the message (i.e., arguments in a C++ function call)—the BalanceInquiry passes attribute accountNumber with its messages to the BankDatabase to indicate which Account's balance information to retrieve. Recall from Fig. 6.37 that operations getAvailableBalance and getTotalBalance of class BankDatabase each require a parameter to identify an account. The BalanceInquiry next displays the availableBalance and the totalBalance

Fig. 7.29 | Communication diagram for executing a balance inquiry.

to the user by passing a displayMessage message to the Screen (message 3) that includes a parameter indicating the message to be displayed.

Figure 7.29 models two additional messages passing from the BankDatabase to an Account (message 1.1 and message 2.1). To provide the ATM with the two balances of the user's Account (as requested by messages 1 and 2), the BankDatabase must pass a getAvailableBalance and a getTotalBalance message to the user's Account. Messages passed within the handling of another message are called nested messages. The UML recommends using a decimal numbering scheme to indicate nested messages. For example, message 1.1 is the first message nested in message 1—the BankDatabase passes a getAvailableBalance message while processing BankDatabase's message of the same name. [*Note:* If the BankDatabase needed to pass a second nested message while processing message 1, the second message would be numbered 1.2.] A message may be passed only when all the nested messages from the previous message have been passed—e.g., the BalanceInquiry passes message 3 only after messages 2 and 2.1 have been passed, in that order.

The nested numbering scheme used in communication diagrams helps clarify precisely when and in what context each message is passed. For example, if we numbered the messages in Fig. 7.29 using a flat numbering scheme (i.e., 1, 2, 3, 4, 5), someone looking at the diagram might not be able to determine that BankDatabase passes the getAvailableBalance message (message 1.1) to an Account *during* the BankDatabase's processing of message 1, as opposed to *after* completing the processing of message 1. The nested decimal numbers make it clear that the second getAvailableBalance message (message 1.1) is passed to an Account within the handling of the first getAvailableBalance message (message 1) by the BankDatabase.

Sequence Diagrams

Communication diagrams emphasize the participants in collaborations but model their timing a bit awkwardly. A sequence diagram helps model the timing of collaborations more clearly. Figure 7.30 shows a sequence diagram modeling the sequence of interactions that occur when a `Withdrawal` executes. The dotted line extending down from an object's rectangle is that object's lifeline, which represents the progression of time. Actions typically occur along an object's lifeline in chronological order from top to bottom—an action near the top typically happens before one near the bottom.

Message passing in sequence diagrams is similar to message passing in communication diagrams. A solid arrow with a filled arrowhead extending from the sending object to the receiving object represents a message between two objects. The arrowhead points to an activation on the receiving object's lifeline. An activation, shown as a thin vertical rectangle, indicates that an object is executing. When an object returns control, a return mes-

Fig. 7.30 | Sequence diagram that models a `Withdrawal` executing.

sage, represented as a dashed line with a stick arrowhead, extends from the activation of the object returning control to the activation of the object that initially sent the message. To eliminate clutter, we omit the return-message arrows—the UML allows this practice to make diagrams more readable. Like communication diagrams, sequence diagrams can indicate message parameters between the parentheses following a message name.

The sequence of messages in Fig. 7.30 begins when a Withdrawal prompts the user to choose a withdrawal amount by sending a displayMessage message to the Screen. The Withdrawal then sends a getInput message to the Keypad, which obtains input from the user. We have already modeled the control logic involved in a Withdrawal in the activity diagram of Fig. 5.28, so we do not show this logic in the sequence diagram of Fig. 7.30. Instead, we model the best-case scenario in which the balance of the user's account is greater than or equal to the chosen withdrawal amount, and the cash dispenser contains a sufficient amount of cash to satisfy the request. For information on how to model control logic in a sequence diagram, please refer to the web resources and recommended readings listed at the end of Section 2.8.

After obtaining a withdrawal amount, the Withdrawal sends a getAvailableBalance message to the BankDatabase, which in turn sends a getAvailableBalance message to the user's Account. Assuming that the user's account has enough money available to permit the transaction, the Withdrawal next sends an isSufficientCashAvailable message to the CashDispenser. Assuming that there is enough cash available, the Withdrawal decreases the balance of the user's account (i.e., both the totalBalance and the availableBalance) by sending a debit message to the BankDatabase. The BankDatabase responds by sending a debit message to the user's Account. Finally, the Withdrawal sends a dispenseCash message to the CashDispenser and a displayMessage message to the Screen, telling the user to remove the cash from the machine.

We have identified the collaborations among objects in the ATM system and modeled some of these collaborations using UML interaction diagrams—both communication diagrams and sequence diagrams. In the next Software Engineering Case Study section (Section 9.11), we enhance the structure of our model to complete a preliminary object-oriented design, then we begin implementing the ATM system.

Software Engineering Case Study Self-Review Exercises

7.1   A(n) _____ consists of an object of one class sending a message to an object of another class.
   a) association
   b) aggregation
   c) collaboration
   d) composition

7.2   Which form of interaction diagram emphasizes *what* collaborations occur? Which form emphasizes *when* collaborations occur?

7.3   Create a sequence diagram that models the interactions among objects in the ATM system that occur when a Deposit executes successfully, and explain the sequence of messages modeled by the diagram.

Answers to Software Engineering Case Study Self-Review Exercises

7.1   c.

7.2   Communication diagrams emphasize *what* collaborations occur. Sequence diagrams emphasize *when* collaborations occur.

7.3   Figure 7.31 presents a sequence diagram that models the interactions between objects in the ATM system that occur when a Deposit executes successfully. Figure 7.31 indicates that a Deposit first sends a displayMessage message to the Screen to ask the user to enter a deposit amount. Next the Deposit sends a getInput message to the Keypad to receive input from the user. The Deposit then instructs the user to enter a deposit envelope by sending a displayMessage message to the Screen. The Deposit next sends an isEnvelopeReceived message to the DepositSlot to confirm that the deposit envelope has been received by the ATM. Finally, the Deposit increases the totalBalance attribute (but not the availableBalance attribute) of the user's Account by sending a credit message to the BankDatabase. The BankDatabase responds by sending the same message to the user's Account.

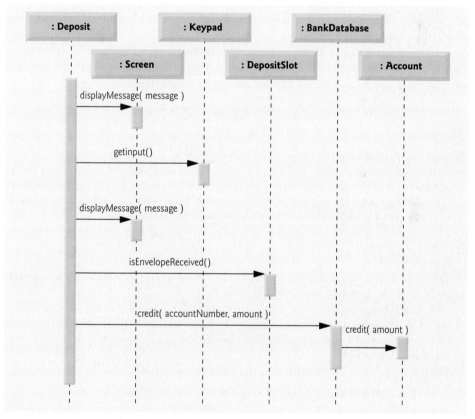

Fig. 7.31 | Sequence diagram that models a Deposit executing.

7.13 Wrap-Up

This chapter began our introduction to data structures, exploring the use of arrays and vectors to store data in and retrieve data from lists and tables of values. The chapter examples demonstrated how to declare an array, initialize an array and refer to individual elements of an array. We also illustrated how to pass arrays to functions and how to use the const qualifier to enforce the principle of least privilege. Chapter examples also presented basic searching and sorting techniques. You learned how to declare and manipulate multidimensional arrays. Finally, we demonstrated the capabilities of C++ Standard Library class template `vector`, which provides a more robust alternative to arrays.

We continue our coverage of data structures in Chapter 14, Templates, where we build a stack class template and in Chapter 20, Data Structures, which introduces other dynamic data structures, such as lists, queues, stacks and trees, that can grow and shrink as programs execute. Chapter 22, Standard Template Library (STL), introduces several of the C++ Standard Library's predefined data structures, which programmers can use instead of building their own. Chapter 22 presents the full functionality of class template `vector` and discusses many additional data structure classes, including `list` and `deque`, which are array-like data structures that can grow and shrink in response to a program's changing storage requirements.

We have now introduced the basic concepts of classes, objects, control statements, functions and arrays. In Chapter 8, we present one of C++'s most powerful features—the pointer. Pointers keep track of where data and functions are stored in memory, which allows us to manipulate those items in interesting ways. After introducing basic pointer concepts, we examine in detail the close relationship among arrays, pointers and strings.

Summary

Section 7.1 Introduction
- Data structures are collections of related data items. Arrays are data structures consisting of related data items of the same type. Arrays are "static" entities in that they remain the same size throughout program execution. (They may, of course, be of automatic storage class and hence be created and destroyed each time the blocks in which they are defined are entered and exited.)

Section 7.2 Arrays
- An array is a consecutive group of memory locations that share the same type.
- To refer to a particular location or element in an array, we specify the name of the array and the position number of the particular element in the array.
- A program refers to any one of an array's elements by giving the name of the array followed by the position number of the particular element in square brackets (`[]`). The position number is more formally called a subscript or index (this number specifies the number of elements from the beginning of the array).
- The first element in every array has subscript zero and is sometimes called the zeroth element.
- A subscript must be an integer or integer expression (using any integral type).
- The brackets used to enclose the subscript of an array are an operator in C++. Brackets have the same level of precedence as parentheses.

Section 7.3 Declaring Arrays
- Arrays occupy space in memory. You specify the type of each element and the number of elements required by an array as follows:

    type arrayName[*arraySize*];

    and the compiler reserves the appropriate amount of memory.

- Arrays can be declared to contain any data type. For example, an array of type `char` can be used to store a character string.

Section 7.4 Examples Using Arrays
- The elements of an array can be initialized in the array declaration by following the array name with an equals sign and an initializer list—a comma-separated list (enclosed in braces) of constant initializers. When initializing an array with an initializer list, if there are fewer initializers than elements in the array, the remaining elements are initialized to zero.
- If the array size is omitted from a declaration with an initializer list, the compiler determines the number of elements in the array by counting the number of elements in the initializer list.
- If the array size and an initializer list are specified in an array declaration, the number of initializers must be less than or equal to the array size. Providing more initializers in an array initializer list than there are elements in the array is a compilation error.
- Constants must be initialized with a constant expression when they are declared and cannot be modified thereafter. Constants can be placed anywhere a constant expression is expected.
- C++ has no array bounds checking to prevent the computer from referring to an element that does not exist. Thus, an executing program can "walk off" either end of an array without warning. You should ensure that all array references remain within the bounds of the array.
- A character array can be initialized using a string literal. The size of a character array is determined by the compiler based on the length of the string *plus* a special string-termination character called the null character (represented by the character constant `'\0'`).
- All strings represented by character arrays end with the null character. A character array representing a string should always be declared large enough to hold the number of characters in the string and the terminating null character.
- Character arrays also can be initialized with individual character constants in an initializer list.
- Individual characters in a string can be accessed directly with array subscript notation.
- A string can be input directly into a character array from the keyboard using `cin` and `>>`.
- A character array representing a null-terminated string can be output with `cout` and `<<`.
- A `static` local variable in a function definition exists for the duration of the program but is visible only in the function body.
- A program initializes `static` local arrays when their declarations are first encountered. If a `static` array is not initialized explicitly by you, each element of that array is initialized to zero by the compiler when the array is created.

Section 7.5 Passing Arrays to Functions
- To pass an array argument to a function, specify the name of the array without any brackets. To pass an element of an array to a function, use the subscripted name of the array element as an argument in the function call.
- Arrays are passed to functions by reference—the called functions can modify the element values in the callers' original arrays. The value of the name of the array is the address in the computer's memory of the first element of the array. Because the starting address of the array is passed, the called function knows precisely where the array is stored in memory.
- Individual array elements are passed by value exactly as simple variables are. Such simple single pieces of data are called scalars or scalar quantities.
- To receive an array argument, a function's parameter list must specify that the function expects to receive an array. The size of the array is not required between the array brackets.
- C++ provides the type qualifier `const` that can be used to prevent modification of array values in the caller by code in a called function. When an array parameter is preceded by the `const` quali-

fier, the elements of the array become constant in the function body, and any attempt to modify an element of the array in the function body results in a compilation error.

Section 7.6 Case Study: Class GradeBook Using an Array to Store Grades

- Class variables (static data members) are shared by all objects of the class in which the variables are declared.
- A static data member can be accessed within the class definition and the member-function definitions like any other data member.
- A public static data member can also be accessed outside of the class, even when no objects of the class exist, using the class name followed by the binary scope resolution operator (::) and the name of the data member.

Section 7.7 Searching Arrays with Linear Search

- The linear search compares each element of an array with a search key. Because the array is not in any particular order, it is just as likely that the value will be found in the first element as the last. On average, therefore, a program must compare the search key with half the elements of the array. To determine that a value is not in the array, the program must compare the search key to every element in the array. The linear searching method works well for small arrays and is acceptable for unsorted arrays.

Section 7.8 Sorting Arrays with Insertion Sort

- An array can be sorted using insertion sort. The first iteration of this algorithm takes the second element and, if it is less than the first element, swaps it with the first element (i.e., the program *inserts* the second element in front of the first element). The second iteration looks at the third element and inserts it into the correct position with respect to the first two elements, so all three elements are in order. At the ith iteration of this algorithm, the first i elements in the original array will be sorted. For small arrays, the insertion sort is acceptable, but for larger arrays it is inefficient compared to other more sophisticated sorting algorithms.

Section 7.9 Multidimensional Arrays

- Multidimensional arrays with two dimensions are often used to represent tables of values consisting of information arranged in rows and columns.
- Arrays that require two subscripts to identify a particular element are called two-dimensional arrays. An array with m rows and n columns is called an m-by-n array.

Section 7.11 Introduction to C++ Standard Library Class Template vector

- C++ Standard Library class template vector represents a more robust alternative to arrays featuring many capabilities that are not provided for C-style pointer-based arrays.
- By default, all the elements of an integer vector object are set to 0.
- A vector can be defined to store any data type using a declaration of the form

      vector< *type* > *name*(*size*);

- Member function size of class template vector returns the number of elements in the vector on which it is invoked.
- The value of an element of a vector can be accessed or modified using square brackets ([]).
- Objects of standard class template vector can be compared directly with the equality (==) and inequality (!=) operators. The assignment (=) operator can also be used with vector objects.
- An unmodifiable *lvalue* is an expression that identifies an object in memory (such as an element in a vector), but cannot be used to modify that object. A modifiable *lvalue* also identifies an object in memory, but can be used to modify the object.

- Standard class template vector provides bounds checking in its member function at, which "throws an exception" if its argument is an invalid subscript. By default, this causes a C++ program to terminate.

Terminology

2-D array

a[i]

a[i][j]

array

array initializer list

at member function of vector

bounds checking

column of a two-dimensional array

column subscript

const type qualifier

constant variable

data structure

declare an array

element of an array

index

index zero

initialize an array

initializer

initializer list

insertion sort

key value

linear search of an array

magic number

m-by-*n* array

modifiable *lvalue*

multidimensional array

name of an array

named constant

null character ('\0')

off-by-one error

one-dimensional array

pass-by-reference

passing arrays to functions

position number

read-only variables

row of a two-dimensional array

row subscript

scalability

scalar

scalar quantity

search an array

search key

size member function of vector

sort an array

square brackets []

static data member

string represented by a character array

subscript

table of values

tabular format

two-dimensional array

unmodifiable *lvalue*

value of an element

vector (C++ Standard Library class template)

"walk off" an array

zeroth element

Self-Review Exercises

7.1 Answer each of the following:
a) Lists and tables of values can be stored in _____ or _____.
b) The elements of an array are related by the fact that they have the same _____ and _____.
c) The number used to refer to a particular element of an array is called its _____.
d) A(n) _____ should be used to declare the size of an array, because it makes the program more scalable.
e) The process of placing the elements of an array in order is called _____ the array.
f) The process of determining if an array contains a particular key value is called _____ the array.
g) An array that uses two subscripts is referred to as a(n) _____ array.

7.2 State whether the following are *true* or *false*. If the answer is *false*, explain why.
a) An array can store many different types of values.
b) An array subscript should normally be of data type float.

c) If there are fewer initializers in an initializer list than the number of elements in the array, the remaining elements are initialized to the last value in the initializer list.

d) It is an error if an initializer list contains more initializers than there are elements in the array.

e) An individual array element that is passed to a function and modified in that function will contain the modified value when the called function completes execution.

7.3   Write one or more statements that perform the following tasks for and array called `fractions`:

a) Define a constant integer variable `arraySize` initialized to 10.

b) Declare an array with `arraySize` elements of type `double`, and initialize the elements to 0.

c) Name the fourth element of the array.

d) Refer to array element 4.

e) Assign the value `1.667` to array element 9.

f) Assign the value `3.333` to the seventh element of the array.

g) Print array elements 6 and 9 with two digits of precision to the right of the decimal point, and show the output that is actually displayed on the screen.

h) Print all the array elements using a `for` statement. Define the integer variable `i` as a control variable for the loop. Show the output.

7.4   Answer the following questions regarding an array called `table`:

a) Declare the array to be an integer array and to have 3 rows and 3 columns. Assume that the constant variable `arraySize` has been defined to be 3.

b) How many elements does the array contain?

c) Use a `for` statement to initialize each element of the array to the sum of its subscripts. Assume that the integer variables `i` and `j` are declared as control variables.

d) Write a program segment to print the values of each element of array `table` in tabular format with 3 rows and 3 columns. Assume that the array was initialized with the declaration

```
int table[ arraySize ][ arraySize ] = { { 1, 8 }, { 2, 4, 6 }, { 5 } };
```

and the integer variables `i` and `j` are declared as control variables. Show the output.

7.5   Find the error in each of the following program segments and correct the error:

a) `#include <iostream>;`

b) `arraySize = 10; // arraySize was declared const`

c) Assume that `int b[ 10 ] = {};`
```
for ( int i = 0; i <= 10; i++ )
    b[ i ] = 1;
```

d) Assume that `int a[ 2 ][ 2 ] = { { 1, 2 }, { 3, 4 } };`
```
a[ 1, 1 ] = 5;
```

Answers to Self-Review Exercises

7.1   a) arrays, vectors. b) array name, type. c) subscript or index. d) constant variable.
e) sorting. f) searching. g) two-dimensional.

7.2   a) False. An array can store only values of the same type.

b) False. An array subscript should be an integer or an integer expression.

c) False. The remaining elements are initialized to zero.

d) True.

e) False. Individual elements of an array are passed by value. If the entire array is passed to a function, then any modifications will be reflected in the original.

7.3   a)   `const int arraySize = 10;`
       b)   `double fractions[ arraySize ] = { 0.0 };`
       c)   `fractions[ 3 ]`
       d)   `fractions[ 4 ]`
       e)   `fractions[ 9 ] = 1.667;`
       f)   `fractions[ 6 ] = 3.333;`
       g)   `cout << fixed << setprecision( 2 );`
            `cout << fractions[ 6 ] << ' ' << fractions[ 9 ] << endl;`
            Output: 3.33 1.67.
       h)   `for ( int i = 0; i < arraySize; i++ )`
              `cout << "fractions[" << i << "] = " << fractions[ i ] << endl;`
            Output:

```
fractions[ 0 ] = 0.0
fractions[ 1 ] = 0.0
fractions[ 2 ] = 0.0
fractions[ 3 ] = 0.0
fractions[ 4 ] = 0.0
fractions[ 5 ] = 0.0
fractions[ 6 ] = 3.333
fractions[ 7 ] = 0.0
fractions[ 8 ] = 0.0
fractions[ 9 ] = 1.667
```

7.4   a)   `int table[ arraySize ][ arraySize ];`
       b)   Nine.
       c)   `for ( i = 0; i < arraySize; i++ )`

```
    for ( j = 0; j < arraySize; j++ )
        table[ i ][ j ] = i + j;
```
       d)   `cout << "    [0]  [1]  [2]" << endl;`

```
for ( int i = 0; i < arraySize; i++ ) {
    cout << '[' << i << "] ";

    for ( int j = 0; j < arraySize; j++ )
        cout << setw( 3 ) << table[ i ][ j ] << "  ";
    cout << endl;
}
```
            Output:

```
    [0]  [1]  [2]
[0]  1    8    0
[1]  2    4    6
[2]  5    0    0
```

7.5   a)   *Error:* Semicolon at end of `#include` preprocessor directive.
            Correction: Eliminate semicolon.
       b)   *Error:* Assigning a value to a constant variable using an assignment statement.
            Correction: Initialize the constant variable in a `const int arraySize` declaration.
       c)   *Error:* Referencing an array element outside the bounds of the array (`b[10]`).
            Correction: Change the final value of the control variable to 9.
       d)   *Error:* Array subscripting done incorrectly.
            Correction: Change the statement to `a[ 1 ][ 1 ] = 5;`

Exercises

7.6   Fill in the blanks in each of the following:
   a)   The names of the four elements of array p (int p[4];) are _____, _____, _____ and _____.
   b)   Naming an array, stating its type and specifying the number of elements in the array is called _____ the array.
   c)   By convention, the first subscript in a two-dimensional array identifies an element's _____ and the second subscript identifies an element's _____.
   d)   An *m*-by-*n* array contains _____ rows, _____ columns and _____ elements.
   e)   The name of the element in row 3 and column 5 of array d is _____.

7.7   Determine whether each of the following is *true* or *false*. If *false*, explain why.
   a)   To refer to a particular location or element within an array, we specify the name of the array and the value of the particular element.
   b)   An array definition reserves space for an array.
   c)   To indicate that 100 locations should be reserved for integer array p, you write the declaration

         p[100];

   d)   A for statement must be used to initialize the elements of a 15-element array to zero.
   e)   Nested for statements must be used to total the elements of a two-dimensional array.

7.8   Write C++ statements to accomplish each of the following:
   a)   Display the value of element 6 of character array f.
   b)   Input a value into element 4 of one-dimensional floating-point array b.
   c)   Initialize each of the 5 elements of one-dimensional integer array g to 8.
   d)   Total and print the elements of floating-point array c of 100 elements.
   e)   Copy array a into the first portion of array b. Assume double a[11], b[34];
   f)   Determine and print the smallest and largest values contained in 99-element floating-point array w.

7.9   Consider a 2-by-3 integer array t.
   a)   Write a declaration for t.
   b)   How many rows does t have?
   c)   How many columns does t have?
   d)   How many elements does t have?
   e)   Write the names of all the elements in row 1 of t.
   f)   Write the names of all the elements in column 2 of t.
   g)   Write a single statement that sets the element of t in the first row and second column to zero.
   h)   Write a series of statements that initialize each element of t to zero. Do not use a loop.
   i)   Write a nested for statement that initializes each element of t to zero.
   j)   Write a statement that inputs the values for the elements of t from the terminal.
   k)   Write a series of statements that determine and print the smallest value in array t.
   l)   Write a statement that displays the elements in row 0 of t.
   m)   Write a statement that totals the elements in column 3 of t.
   n)   Write a series of statements that prints the array t in neat, tabular format. List the column subscripts as headings across the top and list the row subscripts at the left of each row.

7.10   Use a one-dimensional array to solve the following problem. A company pays its salespeople on a commission basis. The salespeople each receive $200 per week plus 9 percent of their gross sales for that week. For example, a salesperson who grosses $5000 in sales in a week receives $200 plus 9 percent of $5000, or a total of $650. Write a program (using an array of counters) that determines how many of the salespeople earned salaries in each of the following ranges (assume that each salesperson's salary is truncated to an integer amount):

a) $200–299
b) $300–399
c) $400–499
d) $500–599
e) $600–699
f) $700–799
g) $800–899
h) $900–999
i) $1000 and over

7.11 *(Bubble Sort)* In the bubble sort algorithm, smaller values gradually "bubble" their way upward to the top of the array like air bubbles rising in water, while the larger values sink to the bottom. The bubble sort makes several passes through the array. On each pass, successive pairs of elements are compared. If a pair is in increasing order (or the values are identical), we leave the values as they are. If a pair is in decreasing order, their values are swapped in the array. Write a program that sorts an array of 10 integers using bubble sort.

7.12 The bubble sort described in Exercise 7.11 is inefficient for large arrays. Make the following simple modifications to improve the performance of the bubble sort:

a) After the first pass, the largest number is guaranteed to be in the highest-numbered element of the array; after the second pass, the two highest numbers are "in place," and so on. Instead of making nine comparisons on every pass, modify the bubble sort to make eight comparisons on the second pass, seven on the third pass, and so on.

b) The data in the array may already be in the proper order or near-proper order, so why make nine passes if fewer will suffice? Modify the sort to check at the end of each pass if any swaps have been made. If none have been made, then the data must already be in the proper order, so the program should terminate. If swaps have been made, then at least one more pass is needed.

7.13 Write single statements that perform the following one-dimensional array operations:

a) Initialize the 10 elements of integer array counts to zero.
b) Add 1 to each of the 15 elements of integer array bonus.
c) Read 12 values for double array monthlyTemperatures from the keyboard.
d) Print the 5 values of integer array bestScores in column format.

7.14 Find the error(s) in each of the following statements:

a) Assume that: char str[5];

```
cin >> str; // user types "hello"
```

b) Assume that: int a[3];

```
cout << a[ 1 ] << " " << a[ 2 ] << " " << a[ 3 ] << endl;
```

c) double f[3] = { 1.1, 10.01, 100.001, 1000.0001 };
d) Assume that: double d[2][10];

```
d[ 1, 9 ] = 2.345;
```

7.15 Use a one-dimensional array to solve the following problem. Read in 20 numbers, each of which is between 10 and 100, inclusive. As each number is read, validate it and store it in the array only if it is not a duplicate of a number already read. After reading all the values, display only the unique values that the user entered. Provide for the "worst case" in which all 20 numbers are different. Use the smallest possible array to solve this problem.

7.16   Label the elements of a 3-by-5 one-dimensional array `sales` to indicate the order in which they are set to zero by the following program segment:

```
for ( row = 0; row < 3; row++ )

    for ( column = 0; column < 5; column++ )
        sales[ row ][ column ] = 0;
```

7.17   Write a program that simulates the rolling of two dice. The program should use rand to roll the first die and should use rand again to roll the second die. The sum of the two values should then be calculated. [*Note:* Each die can show an integer value from 1 to 6, so the sum of the two values will vary from 2 to 12, with 7 being the most frequent sum and 2 and 12 being the least frequent sums.] Figure 7.32 shows the 36 possible combinations of the two dice. Your program should roll the two dice 36,000 times. Use a one-dimensional array to tally the numbers of times each possible sum appears. Print the results in a tabular format. Also, determine if the totals are reasonable (i.e., there are six ways to roll a 7, so approximately one-sixth of all the rolls should be 7).

	1	2	3	4	5	6
1	2	3	4	5	6	7
2	3	4	5	6	7	8
3	4	5	6	7	8	9
4	5	6	7	8	9	10
5	6	7	8	9	10	11
6	7	8	9	10	11	12

Fig. 7.32 | The 36 possible outcomes of rolling two dice.

7.18   What does the following program do?

```
1   // Ex. 7.18: Ex07_18.cpp
2   // What does this program do?
3   #include <iostream>
4   using std::cout;
5   using std::endl;
6
7   int whatIsThis( int [], int ); // function prototype
8
9   int main()
10  {
11      const int arraySize = 10;
12      int a[ arraySize ] = { 1, 2, 3, 4, 5, 6, 7, 8, 9, 10 };
13
14      int result = whatIsThis( a, arraySize );
15
16      cout << "Result is " << result << endl;
17      return 0; // indicates successful termination
18  } // end main
19
20  // What does this function do?
21  int whatIsThis( int b[], int size )
22  {
```

```
23      if ( size == 1 ) // base case
24          return b[ 0 ];
25      else // recursive step
26          return b[ size - 1 ] + whatIsThis( b, size - 1 );
27  } // end function whatIsThis
```

7.19 Modify the program of Fig. 6.11 to play 1000 games of craps. The program should keep track of the statistics and answer the following questions:

a) How many games are won on the 1st roll, 2nd roll, ..., 20th roll, and after the 20th roll?

b) How many games are lost on the 1st roll, 2nd roll, ..., 20th roll, and after the 20th roll?

c) What are the chances of winning at craps? [*Note:* You should discover that craps is one of the fairest casino games. What do you suppose this means?]

d) What is the average length of a game of craps?

e) Do the chances of winning improve with the length of the game?

7.20 (*Airline Reservations System*) A small airline has just purchased a computer for its new automated reservations system. You have been asked to program the new system. You are to write a program to assign seats on each flight of the airline's only plane (capacity: 10 seats).

Your program should display the following menu of alternatives—Please type 1 for "First Class" and Please type 2 for "Economy". If the person types 1, your program should assign a seat in the first class section (seats 1–5). If the person types 2, your program should assign a seat in the economy section (seats 6–10). Your program should print a boarding pass indicating the person's seat number and whether it is in the first class or economy section of the plane.

Use a one-dimensional array to represent the seating chart of the plane. Initialize all the elements of the array to 0 to indicate that all seats are empty. As each seat is assigned, set the corresponding elements of the array to 1 to indicate that the seat is no longer available.

Your program should, of course, never assign a seat that has already been assigned. When the first class section is full, your program should ask the person if it is acceptable to be placed in the economy section (and vice versa). If yes, then make the appropriate seat assignment. If no, then print the message "Next flight leaves in 3 hours."

7.21 What does the following program do?

```
1   // Ex. 7.21: Ex07_21.cpp
2   // What does this program do?
3   #include <iostream>
4   using std::cout;
5   using std::endl;
6
7   void someFunction( int [], int, int ); // function prototype
8
9   int main()
10  {
11      const int arraySize = 10;
12      int a[ arraySize ] = { 1, 2, 3, 4, 5, 6, 7, 8, 9, 10 };
13
14      cout << "The values in the array are:" << endl;
15      someFunction( a, 0, arraySize );
16      cout << endl;
17      return 0; // indicates successful termination
18  } // end main
19
```

```
20  // What does this function do?
21  void someFunction( int b[], int current, int size )
22  {
23     if ( current < size )
24     {
25        someFunction( b, current + 1, size );
26        cout << b[ current ] << "  ";
27     } // end if
28  } // end function someFunction
```

7.22   Use a two-dimensional array to solve the following problem. A company has four salespeople (1 to 4) who sell five different products (1 to 5). Once a day, each salesperson passes in a slip for
each different type of product sold. Each slip contains the following:
   a) The salesperson number
   b) The product number
   c) The total dollar value of that product sold that day

Thus, each salesperson passes in between 0 and 5 sales slips per day. Assume that the information
from all of the slips for last month is available. Write a program that will read all this information
for last month's sales and summarize the total sales by salesperson by product. All totals should be
stored in the two-dimensional array `sales`. After processing all the information for last month,
print the results in tabular format with each of the columns representing a particular salesperson
and each of the rows representing a particular product. Cross total each row to get the total sales of
each product for last month; cross total each column to get the total sales by salesperson for last
month. Your tabular printout should include these cross totals to the right of the totaled rows and
to the bottom of the totaled columns.

7.23   (*Turtle Graphics*) The Logo language, which is popular among elementary school children,
made the concept of *turtle graphics* famous. Imagine a mechanical turtle that walks around the room
under the control of a C++ program. The turtle holds a pen in one of two positions, up or down.
While the pen is down, the turtle traces out shapes as it moves; while the pen is up, the turtle moves
about freely without writing anything. In this problem, you'll simulate the operation of the turtle
and create a computerized sketchpad as well.

   Use a 20-by-20 array `floor` that is initialized to zeros. Read commands from an array that
contains them. Keep track of the current position of the turtle at all times and whether the pen is
currently up or down. Assume that the turtle always starts at position (0, 0) of the floor with its
pen up. The set of turtle commands your program must process are shown in Fig. 7.33.

   Suppose that the turtle is somewhere near the center of the floor. The following "program"
would draw and print a 12-by-12 square and end with the pen in the up position:

```
2
5,12
3
5,12
3
5,12
3
5,12
1
6
9
```

As the turtle moves with the pen down, set the appropriate elements of array `floor` to 1's. When
the 6 command (print) is given, wherever there is a 1 in the array, display an asterisk or some other
character you choose. Wherever there is a zero, display a blank. Write a program to implement the

Command	Meaning
1	Pen up
2	Pen down
3	Turn right
4	Turn left
5,10	Move forward 10 spaces (or a number other than 10)
6	Print the 20-by-20 array
9	End of data (sentinel)

Fig. 7.33 | Turtle graphics commands.

turtle graphics capabilities discussed here. Write several turtle graphics programs to draw interesting shapes. Add other commands to increase the power of your turtle graphics language.

7.24 (*Knight's Tour*) One of the more interesting puzzlers for chess buffs is the Knight's Tour problem. The question is this: Can the chess piece called the knight move around an empty chessboard and touch each of the 64 squares once and only once? We study this intriguing problem in depth in this exercise.

The knight makes L-shaped moves (over two in one direction and then over one in a perpendicular direction). Thus, from a square in the middle of an empty chessboard, the knight can make eight different moves (numbered 0 through 7) as shown in Fig. 7.34.

a) Draw an 8-by-8 chessboard on a sheet of paper and attempt a Knight's Tour by hand. Put a 1 in the first square you move to, a 2 in the second square, a 3 in the third, etc. Before starting the tour, estimate how far you think you'll get, remembering that a full tour consists of 64 moves. How far did you get? Was this close to your estimate?

b) Now let us develop a program that will move the knight around a chessboard. The board is represented by an 8-by-8 two-dimensional array board. Each of the squares is initialized to zero. We describe each of the eight possible moves in terms of both their horizontal and vertical components. For example, a move of type 0, as shown in Fig. 7.34, consists of moving two squares horizontally to the right and one square ver-

Fig. 7.34 | The eight possible moves of the knight.

tically upward. Move 2 consists of moving one square horizontally to the left and two squares vertically upward. Horizontal moves to the left and vertical moves upward are indicated with negative numbers. The eight moves may be described by two one-dimensional arrays, horizontal and vertical, as follows:

```
horizontal[ 0 ] = 2      vertical[ 0 ] = -1
horizontal[ 1 ] = 1      vertical[ 1 ] = -2
horizontal[ 2 ] = -1     vertical[ 2 ] = -2
horizontal[ 3 ] = -2     vertical[ 3 ] = -1
horizontal[ 4 ] = -2     vertical[ 4 ] = 1
horizontal[ 5 ] = -1     vertical[ 5 ] = 2
horizontal[ 6 ] = 1      vertical[ 6 ] = 2
horizontal[ 7 ] = 2      vertical[ 7 ] = 1
```

Let the variables currentRow and currentColumn indicate the row and column of the knight's current position. To make a move of type moveNumber, where moveNumber is between 0 and 7, your program uses the statements

```
currentRow += vertical[ moveNumber ];
currentColumn += horizontal[ moveNumber ];
```

Keep a counter that varies from 1 to 64. Record the latest count in each square the knight moves to. Remember to test each potential move to see if the knight has already visited that square, and, of course, test every potential move to make sure that the knight does not land off the chessboard. Now write a program to move the knight around the chessboard. Run the program. How many moves did the knight make?

c) After attempting to write and run a Knight's Tour program, you have probably developed some valuable insights. We'll use these to develop a heuristic (or strategy) for moving the knight. Heuristics do not guarantee success, but a carefully developed heuristic greatly improves the chance of success. You may have observed that the outer squares are more troublesome than the squares nearer the center of the board. In fact, the most troublesome, or inaccessible, squares are the four corners.

Intuition may suggest that you should attempt to move the knight to the most troublesome squares first and leave open those that are easiest to get to, so when the board gets congested near the end of the tour, there will be a greater chance of success.

We may develop an "accessibility heuristic" by classifying each square according to how accessible it is and then always moving the knight to the square (within the knight's L-shaped moves, of course) that is most inaccessible. We label a two-dimensional array accessibility with numbers indicating from how many squares each particular square is accessible. On a blank chessboard, each center square is rated as 8, each corner square is rated as 2 and the other squares have accessibility numbers of 3, 4 or 6 as follows:

```
2 3 4 4 4 4 3 2
3 4 6 6 6 6 4 3
4 6 8 8 8 8 6 4
4 6 8 8 8 8 6 4
4 6 8 8 8 8 6 4
4 6 8 8 8 8 6 4
3 4 6 6 6 6 4 3
2 3 4 4 4 4 3 2
```

Now write a version of the Knight's Tour program using the accessibility heuristic. At any time, the knight should move to the square with the lowest accessibility number. In case of a tie, the knight may move to any of the tied squares. Therefore, the tour may begin in any of the four corners. [*Note:* As the knight moves around the chessboard, your program should reduce the accessibility numbers as more and more squares become occupied. In this way, at any given time during the tour, each available square's accessibility number will remain equal to precisely the number of squares from which that square may be reached.] Run this version of your program. Did you get a full tour? Now modify the program to run 64 tours, one starting from each square of the chessboard. How many full tours did you get?

d) Write a version of the Knight's Tour program which, when encountering a tie between two or more squares, decides what square to choose by looking ahead to those squares reachable from the "tied" squares. Your program should move to the square for which the next move would arrive at a square with the lowest accessibility number.

7.25 (*Knight's Tour: Brute Force Approaches*) In Exercise 7.24, we developed a solution to the Knight's Tour problem. The approach used, called the "accessibility heuristic," generates many solutions and executes efficiently.

As computers continue increasing in power, we'll be able to solve more problems with sheer computer power and relatively unsophisticated algorithms. This is the "brute force" approach to problem solving.

a) Use random number generation to enable the knight to walk around the chessboard (in its legitimate L-shaped moves, of course) at random. Your program should run one tour and print the final chessboard. How far did the knight get?

b) Most likely, the preceding program produced a relatively short tour. Now modify your program to attempt 1000 tours. Use a one-dimensional array to keep track of the number of tours of each length. When your program finishes attempting the 1000 tours, it should print this information in neat tabular format. What was the best result?

c) Most likely, the preceding program gave you some "respectable" tours, but no full tours. Now "pull all the stops out" and simply let your program run until it produces a full tour. [*Caution:* This version of the program could run for hours on a powerful computer.] Once again, keep a table of the number of tours of each length, and print this table when the first full tour is found. How many tours did your program attempt before producing a full tour? How much time did it take?

d) Compare the brute force version of the Knight's Tour with the accessibility heuristic version. Which required a more careful study of the problem? Which algorithm was more difficult to develop? Which required more computer power? Could we be certain (in advance) of obtaining a full tour with the accessibility heuristic approach? Could we be certain (in advance) of obtaining a full tour with the brute force approach? Argue the pros and cons of brute force problem solving in general.

7.26 (*Eight Queens*) Another puzzler for chess buffs is the Eight Queens problem. Simply stated: Is it possible to place eight queens on an empty chessboard so that no queen is "attacking" any other, i.e., no two queens are in the same row, the same column, or along the same diagonal? Use the thinking developed in Exercise 7.24 to formulate a heuristic for solving the Eight Queens problem. Run your program. [*Hint:* It is possible to assign a value to each square of the chessboard indicating how many squares of an empty chessboard are "eliminated" if a queen is placed in that square. Each of the corners would be assigned the value 22, as in Fig. 7.35.] Once these "elimination numbers" are placed in all 64 squares, an appropriate heuristic might be: Place the next queen in the square with the smallest elimination number. Why is this strategy intuitively appealing?

7.27 (*Eight Queens: Brute Force Approaches*) In this exercise, you'll develop several brute-force approaches to solving the Eight Queens problem introduced in Exercise 7.26.

a) Solve the Eight Queens exercise, using the random brute force technique developed in Exercise 7.25.

b) Use an exhaustive technique, i.e., try all possible combinations of eight queens on the chessboard.

Fig. 7.35 | The 22 squares eliminated by placing a queen in the upper-left corner.

    c) Why do you suppose the exhaustive brute force approach may not be appropriate for solving the Knight's Tour problem?

    d) Compare and contrast the random brute force and exhaustive brute force approaches in general.

7.28 (*Knight's Tour: Closed-Tour Test*) In the Knight's Tour, a full tour occurs when the knight makes 64 moves touching each square of the chess board once and only once. A closed tour occurs when the 64th move is one move away from the location in which the knight started the tour. Modify the Knight's Tour program you wrote in Exercise 7.24 to test for a closed tour if a full tour has occurred.

7.29 (*The Sieve of Eratosthenes*) A prime integer is any integer that is evenly divisible only by itself and 1. The Sieve of Eratosthenes is a method of finding prime numbers. It operates as follows:

    a) Create an array with all elements initialized to 1 (true). Array elements with prime subscripts will remain 1. All other array elements will eventually be set to zero. You'll ignore elements 0 and 1 in this exercise.

    b) Starting with array subscript 2, every time an array element is found whose value is 1, loop through the remainder of the array and set to zero every element whose subscript is a multiple of the subscript for the element with value 1. For array subscript 2, all elements beyond 2 in the array that are multiples of 2 will be set to zero (subscripts 4, 6, 8, 10, etc.); for array subscript 3, all elements beyond 3 in the array that are multiples of 3 will be set to zero (subscripts 6, 9, 12, 15, etc.); and so on.

When this process is complete, the array elements that are still set to one indicate that the subscript is a prime number. These subscripts can then be printed. Write a program that uses an array of 1000 elements to determine and print the prime numbers between 2 and 999. Ignore element 0 of the array.

7.30 (*Bucket Sort*) A bucket sort begins with a one-dimensional array of positive integers to be sorted and a two-dimensional array of integers with rows subscripted from 0 to 9 and columns subscripted from 0 to $n - 1$, where n is the number of values in the array to be sorted. Each row of the two-dimensional array is referred to as a bucket. Write a function bucketSort that takes an integer array and the array size as arguments and performs as follows:

    a) Place each value of the one-dimensional array into a row of the bucket array based on the value's ones digit. For example, 97 is placed in row 7, 3 is placed in row 3 and 100 is placed in row 0. This is called a "distribution pass."

    b) Loop through the bucket array row by row, and copy the values back to the original array. This is called a "gathering pass." The new order of the preceding values in the one-dimensional array is 100, 3 and 97.

    c) Repeat this process for each subsequent digit position (tens, hundreds, thousands, etc.).

On the second pass, 100 is placed in row 0, 3 is placed in row 0 (because 3 has no tens digit) and 97 is placed in row 9. After the gathering pass, the order of the values in the one-dimensional array is 100, 3 and 97. On the third pass, 100 is placed in row 1, 3 is placed in row zero and 97 is placed in row zero (after the 3). After the last gathering pass, the original array is now in sorted order.

Note that the two-dimensional array of buckets is 10 times the size of the integer array being sorted. This sorting technique provides better performance than an insertion sort, but requires much more memory. The insertion sort requires space for only one additional element of data. This is an example of the space-time trade-off: The bucket sort uses more memory than the insertion sort, but performs better. This version of the bucket sort requires copying all the data back to the original array on each pass. Another possibility is to create a second two-dimensional bucket array and repeatedly swap the data between the two bucket arrays.

Recursion Exercises

7.31   (*Selection Sort*) A selection sort searches an array looking for the smallest element. Then, the smallest element is swapped with the first element of the array. The process is repeated for the subarray beginning with the second element of the array. Each pass of the array results in one element being placed in its proper location. This sort performs comparably to the insertion sort—for an array of n elements, $n-1$ passes must be made, and for each subarray, $n-1$ comparisons must be made to find the smallest value. When the subarray being processed contains one element, the array is sorted. Write recursive function selectionSort to perform this algorithm.

7.32   (*Palindromes*) A palindrome is a string that is spelled the same way forward and backward. Some examples of palindromes are "radar," "able was i ere i saw elba" and (if blanks are ignored) "a man a plan a canal panama." Write a recursive function testPalindrome that returns true if the string stored in the array is a palindrome, and false otherwise. The function should ignore spaces and punctuation in the string.

7.33   (*Linear Search)* Modify the program in Fig. 7.19 to use recursive function linearSearch to perform a linear search of the array. The function should receive an integer array and the size of the array as arguments. If the search key is found, return the array subscript; otherwise, return −1.

7.34   (*Eight Queens)* Modify the Eight Queens program you created in Exercise 7.26 to solve the problem recursively.

7.35   (*Print an Array*) Write a recursive function printArray that takes an array, a starting subscript and an ending subscript as arguments and returns nothing. The function should stop processing and return when the starting subscript equals the ending subscript.

7.36   (*Print a String Backward*) Write a recursive function stringReverse that takes a character array containing a string and a starting subscript as arguments, prints the string backward and returns nothing. The function should stop processing and return when the terminating null character is encountered.

7.37   (*Find the Minimum Value in an Array*) Write a recursive function recursiveMinimum that takes an integer array, a starting subscript and an ending subscript as arguments, and returns the smallest element of the array. The function should stop processing and return when the starting subscript equals the ending subscript.

vector Exercises

7.38   Use a vector of integers to solve the problem described in Exercise 7.10.

7.39   Modify the dice-rolling program you created in Exercise 7.17 to use a vector to store the numbers of times each possible sum of the two dice appears.

7.40   (*Find the Minimum Value in a vector*) Modify your solution to Exercise 7.37 to find the minimum value in a vector instead of an array.

8

Pointers and Pointer-Based Strings

OBJECTIVES

In this chapter you'll learn:

- What pointers are.
- The similarities and differences between pointers and references, and when to use each.
- To use pointers to pass arguments to functions by reference.
- To use pointer-based C-style strings.
- The close relationships among pointers, arrays and C-style strings.
- To use pointers to functions.
- To declare and use arrays of C-style strings.

8.1 Introduction

This chapter discusses one of the most powerful features of the C++ programming language, the pointer. In Chapter 6, we saw that references can be used to perform pass-by-reference. Pointers also enable pass-by-reference and can be used to create and manipulate dynamic data structures (i.e., data structures that can grow and shrink), such as linked lists, queues, stacks and trees. This chapter explains basic pointer concepts and reinforces the intimate relationship among arrays and pointers. The view of arrays as pointers derives from the C programming language. As we saw in Chapter 7, C++ Standard Library class vector provides an implementation of arrays as full-fledged objects.

Similarly, C++ actually offers two types of strings—string class objects (which we have been using since Chapter 3) and C-style, char * pointer-based strings. This chapter on pointers discusses char * strings to deepen your knowledge of pointers. In fact, the null-terminated strings that we introduced in Section 7.4 and used in Fig. 7.12 are char * pointer-based strings. This chapter also includes a substantial collection of string-processing exercises that use char *strings. C-style, char * pointer-based strings are widely used in legacy C and C++ systems. So, if you work with legacy C or C++ systems, you may be required to manipulate these char * pointer-based strings.

We'll examine the use of pointers with classes in Chapter 13, Object-Oriented Programming: Polymorphism, where we'll see that the so-called "polymorphic processing" of object-oriented programming is performed with pointers and references. Chapter 20, Data Structures, presents examples of creating and using dynamic data structures that are implemented with pointers.

8.2 **Pointer Variable Declarations and Initialization**

Pointer variables contain memory addresses as their values. Normally, a variable directly contains a specific value. However, a pointer contains the memory address of a variable that, in turn, contains a specific value. In this sense, a variable name directly references a value, and a pointer indirectly references a value (Fig. 8.1). Referencing a value through a pointer is often called indirection. Note that diagrams typically represent a pointer as an arrow from the variable that contains an address to the variable located at that address in memory.

Pointers, like any other variables, must be declared before they can be used. For example, for the pointer in Fig. 8.1, the declaration

```
int *countPtr, count;
```

declares the variable countPtr to be of type int * (i.e., a pointer to an int value) and is read, "countPtr is a pointer to int" or "countPtr points to an object of type int." Also, variable count in the preceding declaration is declared to be an int, not a pointer to an int. The * in the declaration applies only to countPtr. Each variable being declared as a pointer must be preceded by an asterisk (*). For example, the declaration

```
double *xPtr, *yPtr;
```

indicates that both xPtr and yPtr are pointers to double values. When * appears in a declaration, it is not an operator; rather, it indicates that the variable being declared is a pointer. Pointers can be declared to point to objects of any data type.

Common Programming Error 8.1

*Assuming that the * used to declare a pointer distributes to all variable names in a declaration's comma-separated list of variables can lead to errors. Each pointer must be declared with the * prefixed to the name (either with or without a space in between—the compiler ignores the space). Declaring only one variable per declaration helps avoid these types of errors and improves program readability.*

Good Programming Practice 8.1

Although it is not a requirement, including the letters Ptr in pointer variable names makes it clear that these variables are pointers and that they must be handled accordingly.

Pointers should be initialized either when they are declared or in an assignment. A pointer may be initialized to 0, NULL or an address of the corresponding type. A pointer

Fig. 8.1 | Directly and indirectly referencing a variable.

with the value 0 or NULL points to nothing and is known as a null pointer. Symbolic constant NULL is defined in header file <iostream> (and in several other standard library header files) to represent the value 0. Initializing a pointer to NULL is equivalent to initializing a pointer to 0, but in C++, 0 is used by convention. When 0 is assigned, it is converted to a pointer of the appropriate type. The value 0 is the only integer value that can be assigned directly to a pointer variable without first casting the integer to a pointer type. Assigning a variable's numeric address to a pointer is discussed in Section 8.3.

Error-Prevention Tip 8.1

Initialize pointers to prevent pointing to unknown or uninitialized areas of memory.

8.3 Pointer Operators

The address operator (&) is a unary operator that obtains the memory address of its operand. For example, assuming the declarations

```
int y = 5; // declare variable y
int *yPtr; // declare pointer variable yPtr
```

the statement

```
yPtr = &y; // assign address of y to yPtr
```

assigns the address of the variable y to pointer variable yPtr. Then variable yPtr is said to "point to" y. Now, yPtr indirectly references variable y's value. Note that the use of the & in the preceding statement is not the same as the use of the & in a reference variable declaration, which is always preceded by a data-type name. When declaring a reference, the & is part of the type. In an expression like &y, the & is an operator.

Figure 8.2 shows a schematic representation of memory after the preceding assignment. The "pointing relationship" is indicated by drawing an arrow from the box that represents the pointer yPtr in memory to the box that represents the variable y in memory.

Figure 8.3 shows another representation of the pointer in memory, assuming that integer variable y is stored at memory location 600000 and that pointer variable yPtr is stored at memory location 500000. The operand of the address operator must be an *lvalue* (i.e., something to which a value can be assigned, such as a variable name or a reference); the address operator cannot be applied to constants or to expressions that do not result in references.

The * operator, commonly referred to as the indirection operator or dereferencing operator, returns a synonym (i.e., an alias or a nickname) for the object to which its pointer operand points. For example (referring again to Fig. 8.2), the statement

```
cout << *yPtr << endl;
```

Fig. 8.2 | Graphical representation of a pointer pointing to a variable in memory.

Fig. 8.3 | Representation of y and yPtr in memory.

prints the value of variable y, namely, 5, just as the statement

```
cout << y << endl;
```

would. Using * in this manner is called dereferencing a pointer. Note that a dereferenced pointer may also be used on the left side of an assignment statement, as in

```
*yPtr = 9;
```

which would assign 9 to y in Fig. 8.3. The dereferenced pointer may also be used to receive an input value as in

```
cin >> *yPtr;
```

which places the input value in y. The dereferenced pointer is an *lvalue*.

Common Programming Error 8.2

Dereferencing a pointer that has not been properly initialized or that has not been assigned to point to a specific location in memory could cause a fatal execution-time error, or it could accidentally modify important data and allow the program to run to completion, possibly with incorrect results.

Common Programming Error 8.3

An attempt to dereference a variable that is not a pointer is a compilation error.

Common Programming Error 8.4

Dereferencing a null pointer is often a fatal execution-time error.

The program in Fig. 8.4 demonstrates the & and * pointer operators. Memory locations are output by << in this example as hexadecimal (i.e., base-16) integers. (See Appendix D, Number Systems, for more information on hexadecimal integers.) Note that the hexadecimal memory addresses output by this program are compiler and operating-system dependent, so you may get different results when you run the program.

Portability Tip 8.1

The format in which a pointer is output is compiler dependent. Some output pointer values as hexadecimal integers, some use decimal integers and some use other formats.

Notice that the address of a (line 15) and the value of aPtr (line 16) are identical in the output, confirming that the address of a is indeed assigned to the pointer variable aPtr. The & and * operators are inverses of one another—when they are both applied consecutively to aPtr in either order, they "cancel one another out" and the same result (the value in aPtr) is printed.

```
 1   // Fig. 8.4: fig08_04.cpp
 2   // Pointer operators & and *.
 3   #include <iostream>
 4   using std::cout;
 5   using std::endl;
 6
 7   int main()
 8   {
 9      int a; // a is an integer
10      int *aPtr; // aPtr is an int * -- pointer to an integer
11
12      a = 7; // assigned 7 to a
13      aPtr = &a; // assign the address of a to aPtr
14
15      cout << "The address of a is " << &a
16           << "\nThe value of aPtr is " << aPtr;
17      cout << "\n\nThe value of a is " << a
18           << "\nThe value of *aPtr is " << *aPtr;
19      cout << "\n\nShowing that * and & are inverses of "
20           << "each other.\n&*aPtr = " << &*aPtr
21           << "\n*&aPtr = " << *&aPtr << endl;
22      return 0; // indicates successful termination
23   } // end main
```

```
The address of a is 0012F580
The value of aPtr is 0012F580

The value of a is 7
The value of *aPtr is 7

Showing that * and & are inverses of each other.
&*aPtr = 0012F580
*&aPtr = 0012F580
```

Fig. 8.4 | Pointer operators & and *.

Figure 8.5 lists the precedence and associativity of the operators introduced to this point. Note that the address operator (&) and the dereferencing operator (*) are unary operators on the third level of precedence in the chart.

Operators	Associativity	Type
() []	left to right	highest
++ -- static_cast< *type* >(*operand*)	left to right	unary (postfix)
++ -- + - ! & *	right to left	unary (prefix)
* / %	left to right	multiplicative
+ -	left to right	additive

Fig. 8.5 | Operator precedence and associativity. (Part I of 2.)

Operators						Associativity	Type
<<	>>					left to right	insertion/extraction
<	<=	>	>=			left to right	relational
==	!=					left to right	equality
&&						left to right	logical AND
||						left to right	logical OR
?:						right to left	conditional
=	+=	-=	*=	/=	%=	right to left	assignment
,						left to right	comma

Fig. 8.5 | Operator precedence and associativity. (Part 2 of 2.)

8.4 Passing Arguments to Functions by Reference with Pointers

There are three ways in C++ to pass arguments to a function—pass-by-value, pass-by-reference with reference arguments and pass-by-reference with pointer arguments. Chapter 6 compared and contrasted pass-by-value and pass-by-reference with reference arguments. In this section, we explain pass-by-reference with pointer arguments.

As we saw in Chapter 6, return can be used to return one value from a called function to a caller (or to return control from a called function without passing back a value). We also saw that arguments can be passed to a function using reference arguments. Such arguments enable the called function to modify the original values of the arguments in the caller. Reference arguments also enable programs to pass large data objects to a function and avoid the overhead of passing the objects by value (which, of course, requires making a copy of the object). Pointers, like references, also can be used to modify one or more variables in the caller or to pass pointers to large data objects to avoid the overhead of passing the objects by value.

In C++, programmers can use pointers and the indirection operator (*) to accomplish pass-by-reference (exactly as pass-by-reference is done in C programs—C does not have references). When calling a function with an argument that should be modified, the address of the argument is passed. This is normally accomplished by applying the address operator (&) to the name of the variable whose value will be modified.

As we saw in Chapter 7, arrays are not passed using operator &, because the name of the array is the starting location in memory of the array (i.e., an array name is already a pointer). The name of an array, arrayName, is equivalent to &arrayName[0]. When the address of a variable is passed to a function, the indirection operator (*) can be used in the function to form a synonym for the name of the variable—this in turn can be used to modify the value of the variable at that location in the caller's memory.

Figure 8.6 and Fig. 8.7 present two versions of a function that cubes an integer—cubeByValue and cubeByReference. Figure 8.6 passes variable number by value to function cubeByValue (line 15). Function cubeByValue (lines 21–24) cubes its argument and passes the new value back to main using a return statement (line 23). The new value is

```
 1   // Fig. 8.6: fig08_06.cpp
 2   // Pass-by-value used to cube a variable's value.
 3   #include <iostream>
 4   using std::cout;
 5   using std::endl;
 6
 7   int cubeByValue( int ); // prototype
 8
 9   int main()
10   {
11      int number = 5;
12
13      cout << "The original value of number is " << number;
14
15      number = cubeByValue( number ); // pass number by value to cubeByValue
16      cout << "\nThe new value of number is " << number << endl;
17      return 0; // indicates successful termination
18   } // end main
19
20   // calculate and return cube of integer argument
21   int cubeByValue( int n )
22   {
23      return n * n * n; // cube local variable n and return result
24   } // end function cubeByValue
```

```
The original value of number is 5
The new value of number is 125
```

Fig. 8.6 | Pass-by-value used to cube a variable's value.

assigned to number (line 15) in main. Note that the calling function has the opportunity to examine the result of the function call before modifying variable number's value. For example, in this program, we could have stored the result of cubeByValue in another variable, examined its value and assigned the result to number only after determining that the returned value was reasonable.

Figure 8.7 passes the variable number to function cubeByReference using pass-by-reference with a pointer argument (line 16)—the address of number is passed to the function. Function cubeByReference (lines 23–26) specifies parameter nPtr (a pointer to int) to receive its argument. The function dereferences the pointer and cubes the value to which nPtr points (line 25). This directly changes the value of number in main.

Common Programming Error 8.5

Not dereferencing a pointer when it is necessary to do so to obtain the value to which the pointer points is an error.

A function receiving an address as an argument must define a pointer parameter to receive the address. For example, the header for function cubeByReference (line 23) specifies that cubeByReference receives the address of an int variable (i.e., a pointer to an int) as an argument, stores the address locally in nPtr and does not return a value.

The function prototype for cubeByReference (line 8) contains int * in parentheses. As with other variable types, it is not necessary to include names of pointer parameters in

```
1   // Fig. 8.7: fig08_07.cpp
2   // Pass-by-reference with a pointer argument used to cube a
3   // variable's value.
4   #include <iostream>
5   using std::cout;
6   using std::endl;
7
8   void cubeByReference( int * ); // prototype
9
10  int main()
11  {
12     int number = 5;
13
14     cout << "The original value of number is " << number;
15
16     cubeByReference( &number ); // pass number address to cubeByReference
17
18     cout << "\nThe new value of number is " << number << endl;
19     return 0; // indicates successful termination
20  } // end main
21
22  // calculate cube of *nPtr; modifies variable number in main
23  void cubeByReference( int *nPtr )
24  {
25     *nPtr = *nPtr * *nPtr * *nPtr; // cube *nPtr
26  } // end function cubeByReference
```

```
The original value of number is 5
The new value of number is 125
```

Fig. 8.7 | Pass-by-reference with a pointer argument used to cube a variable's value.

function prototypes. Parameter names included for documentation purposes are ignored by the compiler.

Figures 8.8–8.9 analyze graphically the execution of the programs in Fig. 8.6 and Fig. 8.7, respectively.

Software Engineering Observation 8.1

Use pass-by-value to pass arguments to a function unless the caller explicitly requires that the called function directly modify the value of the argument variable in the caller. This is another example of the principle of least privilege.

In the function header and in the prototype for a function that expects a one-dimensional array as an argument, the pointer notation in the parameter list of cubeByReference may be used. The compiler does not differentiate between a function that receives a pointer and a function that receives a one-dimensional array. This, of course, means that the function must "know" when it is receiving an array or simply a single variable which is being passed by reference. When the compiler encounters a function parameter for a one-dimensional array of the form int b[], the compiler converts the parameter to the pointer notation int *b (pronounced "b is a pointer to an integer"). Both forms of declaring a function parameter as a one-dimensional array are interchangeable.

Step 1: Before main calls cubeByValue:

```
int main()                          number
{
    int number = 5;                    5

    number = cubeByValue( number );
}
```

```
int cubeByValue( int n )
{
    return n * n * n;
}
                                    n

                            undefined
```

Step 2: After cubeByValue receives the call:

```
int main()                          number
{
    int number = 5;                    5

    number = cubeByValue( number );
}
```

```
int cubeByValue( int n )
{
    return n * n * n;
}
                                    n

                                    5
```

Step 3: After cubeByValue cubes parameter n and before cubeByValue returns to main:

```
int main()                          number
{
    int number = 5;                    5

    number = cubeByValue( number );
}
```

```
int cubeByValue( int n )
{                   125
    return n * n * n;
}
                                    n

                                    5
```

Step 4: After cubeByValue returns to main and before assigning the result to number:

```
int main()                          number
{
    int number = 5;                    5
                125
    number = cubeByValue( number );
}
```

```
int cubeByValue( int n )
{
    return n * n * n;
}
                                    n

                            undefined
```

Step 5: After main completes the assignment to number:

```
int main()                          number
{
    int number = 5;                   125
        125             125
    number = cubeByValue( number );
}
```

```
int cubeByValue( int n )
{
    return n * n * n;
}
                                    n

                            undefined
```

Fig. 8.8 | Pass-by-value analysis of the program of Fig. 8.6.

Step 1: Before `main` calls `cubeByReference`:

```
int main()                          number      void cubeByReference( int *nPtr )
{                                                {
   int number = 5;                    5             *nPtr = *nPtr * *nPtr * *nPtr;
                                                 }
   cubeByReference( &number );                                              nPtr
}
                                                                        undefined
```

Step 2: After `cubeByReference` receives the call and before `*nPtr` is cubed:

```
int main()                          number      void cubeByReference( int *nPtr )
{                                                {
   int number = 5;                    5             *nPtr = *nPtr * *nPtr * *nPtr;
                                                 }
   cubeByReference( &number );                                              nPtr
}
                                       call establishes this pointer
```

Step 3: After `*nPtr` is cubed and before program control returns to `main`:

```
int main()                          number      void cubeByReference( int *nPtr )
{                                                {            125
   int number = 5;                   125            *nPtr = *nPtr * *nPtr * *nPtr;
                                                 }
   cubeByReference( &number );          called function modifies caller's   nPtr
}                                       variable
```

Fig. 8.9 | Pass-by-reference analysis (with a pointer argument) of the program of Fig. 8.7.

8.5 Using const with Pointers

Recall that the const qualifier enables you to inform the compiler that the value of a particular variable should not be modified.

Over the years, a large base of legacy code was written in early versions of C that did not use const, because it was not available. For this reason, there are great opportunities for improvement in the software engineering of old (also called "legacy") C code. Also, many programmers currently using ANSI C and C++ do not use const in their programs, because they began programming in early versions of C. These programmers are missing many opportunities for good software engineering.

Many possibilities exist for using (or not using) const with function parameters. How do you choose the most appropriate of these possibilities? Let the principle of least privilege be your guide. Always award a function enough access to the data in its parameters to accomplish its specified task, but no more. This section discusses how to combine const with pointer declarations to enforce the principle of least privilege.

Chapter 6 explained that when a function is called using pass-by-value, a copy of the argument (or arguments) in the function call is made and passed to the function. If the copy is modified in the function, the original value is maintained in the caller without change. In many cases, a value passed to a function is modified so that the function can accomplish its task. However, in some instances, the value should not be altered in the called function, even though the called function manipulates only a copy of the original value.

For example, consider a function that takes a one-dimensional array and its size as arguments and subsequently prints the array. Such a function should loop through the array and output each array element individually. The size of the array is used in the function body to determine the highest subscript of the array so the loop can terminate when the printing completes. The size of the array does not change in the function body, so it should be declared const. Of course, because the array is only being printed, it, too, should be declared const. This is especially important because an entire array is *always* passed by reference and could easily be changed in the called function.

Software Engineering Observation 8.2

If a value does not (or should not) change in the body of a function to which it is passed, the parameter should be declared const to ensure that it is not accidentally modified.

If an attempt is made to modify a const value, a warning or an error is issued, depending on the particular compiler.

Error-Prevention Tip 8.2

Before using a function, check its function prototype to determine the parameters that it can modify.

There are four ways to pass a pointer to a function: a nonconstant pointer to nonconstant data (Fig. 8.10), a nonconstant pointer to constant data (Fig. 8.11 and Fig. 8.12), a constant pointer to nonconstant data (Fig. 8.13) and a constant pointer to constant data (Fig. 8.14). Each combination provides a different level of access privileges.

Nonconstant Pointer to Nonconstant Data

The highest access is granted by a nonconstant pointer to nonconstant data—the data can be modified through the dereferenced pointer, and the pointer can be modified to point to other data. The declaration for such a pointer does not include const. Such a pointer can be used to receive a null-terminated string in a function that changes the pointer value to process (and possibly modify) each character in the string. Recall from Section 7.4 that a null-terminated string can be placed in a character array that contains the characters of the string and a null character indicating where the string ends.

In Fig. 8.10, function convertToUppercase (lines 25–34) declares parameter sPtr (line 25) to be a nonconstant pointer to nonconstant data (again, const is not used). The function processes one character at a time from the null-terminated string stored in character array phrase (lines 27–33). Keep in mind that a character array's name is really equivalent to a const pointer to the first character of the array, so passing phrase as an argument to convertToUppercase is possible. Function islower (line 29) takes a character argument and returns true if the character is a lowercase letter and false otherwise. Characters in the range 'a' through 'z' are converted to their corresponding uppercase letters by function toupper (line 30); others remain unchanged—function toupper takes

```
1   // Fig. 8.10: fig08_10.cpp
2   // Converting lowercase letters to uppercase letters
3   // using a nonconstant pointer to nonconstant data.
4   #include <iostream>
5   using std::cout;
6   using std::endl;
7
8   #include <cctype> // prototypes for islower and toupper
9   using std::islower;
10  using std::toupper;
11
12  void convertToUppercase( char * );
13
14  int main()
15  {
16     char phrase[] = "characters and $32.98";
17
18     cout << "The phrase before conversion is: " << phrase;
19     convertToUppercase( phrase );
20     cout << "\nThe phrase after conversion is:  " << phrase << endl;
21     return 0; // indicates successful termination
22  } // end main
23
24  // convert string to uppercase letters
25  void convertToUppercase( char *sPtr )
26  {
27     while ( *sPtr != '\0' ) // loop while current character is not '\0'
28     {
29        if ( islower( *sPtr ) ) // if character is lowercase,
30           *sPtr = toupper( *sPtr ); // convert to uppercase
31
32        sPtr++; // move sPtr to next character in string
33     } // end while
34  } // end function convertToUppercase
```

```
The phrase before conversion is: characters and $32.98
The phrase after conversion is:  CHARACTERS AND $32.98
```

Fig. 8.10 | Converting a string to uppercase letters using a nonconstant pointer to nonconstant data.

one character as an argument. If the character is a lowercase letter, the corresponding uppercase letter is returned; otherwise, the original character is returned. Function toupper and function islower are part of the character-handling library <cctype> (see Chapter 21, Bits, Characters, C-Strings and structs). After processing one character, line 32 increments sPtr by 1 (this would not be possible if sPtr were declared const). When operator ++ is applied to a pointer that points to an array, the memory address stored in the pointer is modified to point to the next element of the array (in this case, the next character in the string). Adding one to a pointer is one valid operation in pointer arithmetic, which is covered in detail in Sections 8.8–8.9.

Nonconstant Pointer to Constant Data

A nonconstant pointer to constant data is a pointer that can be modified to point to any data item of the appropriate type, but the data to which it points cannot be modified through that pointer. Such a pointer might be used to receive an array argument to a function that will process each element of the array, but should not be allowed to modify the data. For example, function printCharacters (lines 22–26 of Fig. 8.11) declares parameter sPtr (line 22) to be of type const char *, so that it can receive a null-terminated pointer-based string. The declaration is read from right to left as "sPtr is a pointer to a character constant." The body of the function uses a for statement (lines 24–25) to output each character in the string until the null character is encountered. After each character is printed, pointer sPtr is incremented to point to the next character in the string (this works because the pointer is not const). Function main creates char array phrase to be passed to printCharacters. Again, we can pass the array phrase to printCharacters because the name of the array is really a pointer to the first character in the array.

Figure 8.12 demonstrates the compilation error messages produced when attempting to compile a function that receives a nonconstant pointer to constant data, then tries to use that pointer to modify the data. [*Note:* Recall that compiler error messages may vary among compilers.]

```cpp
1   // Fig. 8.11: fig08_11.cpp
2   // Printing a string one character at a time using
3   // a nonconstant pointer to constant data.
4   #include <iostream>
5   using std::cout;
6   using std::endl;
7
8   void printCharacters( const char * ); // print using pointer to const data
9
10  int main()
11  {
12     const char phrase[] = "print characters of a string";
13
14     cout << "The string is:\n";
15     printCharacters( phrase ); // print characters in phrase
16     cout << endl;
17     return 0; // indicates successful termination
18  } // end main
19
20  // sPtr can be modified, but it cannot modify the character to which
21  // it points, i.e., sPtr is a "read-only" pointer
22  void printCharacters( const char *sPtr )
23  {
24     for ( ; *sPtr != '\0'; sPtr++ ) // no initialization
25        cout << *sPtr; // display character without modification
26  } // end function printCharacters
```

```
The string is:
print characters of a string
```

Fig. 8.11 | Printing a string one character at a time using a nonconstant pointer to constant data.

```
 I   // Fig. 8.12: fig08_12.cpp
 2   // Attempting to modify data through a
 3   // nonconstant pointer to constant data.
 4
 5   void f( const int * ); // prototype
 6
 7   int main()
 8   {
 9      int y;
10
11      f( &y ); // f attempts illegal modification
12      return 0; // indicates successful termination
13   } // end main
14
15   // xPtr cannot modify the value of constant variable to which it points
16   void f( const int *xPtr )
17   {
18      *xPtr = 100; // error: cannot modify a const object
19   } // end function f
```

Borland C++ command-line compiler error message:

```
Error E2024 fig08_12.cpp 18:
   Cannot modify a const object in function f(const int *)
```

Microsoft Visual C++ compiler error message:

```
c:\cpphtp6_examples\ch08\Fig08_12\fig08_12.cpp(18) :
   error C3892: 'xPtr' : you cannot assign to a variable that is const
```

GNU C++ compiler error message:

```
fig08_12.cpp: In function `void f(const int*)':
fig08_12.cpp:18: error: assignment of read-only location
```

Fig. 8.12 | Attempting to modify data through a nonconstant pointer to constant data.

As we know, arrays are aggregate data types that store related data items of the same type under one name. When a function is called with an array as an argument, the array is passed to the function by reference. However, objects are always passed by value—a copy of the entire object is passed. This requires the execution-time overhead of making a copy of each data item in the object and storing it on the function call stack. When an object must be passed to a function, we can use a pointer to constant data (or a reference to constant data) to get the performance of pass-by-reference and the protection of pass-by-value. When a pointer to an object is passed, only a copy of the address of the object must be made—the object itself is not copied. On a machine with four-byte addresses, a copy of four bytes of memory is made rather than a copy of a possibly large object.

Performance Tip 8.1

If they do not need to be modified by the called function, pass large objects using pointers to constant data or references to constant data, to obtain the performance benefits of pass-by-reference.

> **Software Engineering Observation 8.3**
>
> *Pass large objects using pointers to constant data, or references to constant data, to obtain the security of pass-by-value.*

Constant Pointer to Nonconstant Data

A constant pointer to nonconstant data is a pointer that always points to the same memory location; the data at that location can be modified through the pointer. An example of such a pointer is an array name, which is a constant pointer to the beginning of the array. All data in the array can be accessed and changed by using the array name and array subscripting. A constant pointer to nonconstant data can be used to receive an array as an argument to a function that accesses array elements using array subscript notation. Pointers that are declared const must be initialized when they are declared. (If the pointer is a function parameter, it is initialized with a pointer that is passed to the function.) The program of Fig. 8.13 attempts to modify a constant pointer. Line 11 declares pointer ptr to be of type int * const. The declaration in the figure is read from right to left as "ptr is a constant pointer to a nonconstant integer." The pointer is initialized with the address of integer variable x. Line 14 attempts to assign the address of y to ptr, but the compiler generates an error message. Note that no error occurs when line 13 assigns the value 7 to

```cpp
 1   // Fig. 8.13: fig08_13.cpp
 2   // Attempting to modify a constant pointer to nonconstant data.
 3
 4   int main()
 5   {
 6      int x, y;
 7
 8      // ptr is a constant pointer to an integer that can
 9      // be modified through ptr, but ptr always points to the
10      // same memory location.
11      int * const ptr = &x; // const pointer must be initialized
12
13      *ptr = 7; // allowed: *ptr is not const
14      ptr = &y; // error: ptr is const; cannot assign to it a new address
15      return 0; // indicates successful termination
16   } // end main
```

Borland C++ command-line compiler error message:

```
Error E2024 fig08_13.cpp 14: Cannot modify a const object in function main()
```

Microsoft Visual C++ compiler error message:

```
c:\cpphtp5e_examples\ch08\Fig08_13\fig08_13.cpp(14) : error C3892: 'ptr' :
   you cannot assign to a variable that is const
```

GNU C++ compiler error message:

```
fig08_13.cpp: In function `int main()':
fig08_13.cpp:14: error: assignment of read-only variable `ptr'
```

Fig. 8.13 | Attempting to modify a constant pointer to nonconstant data.

*ptr—the nonconstant value to which ptr points can be modified using the dereferenced ptr, even though ptr itself has been declared const.

Common Programming Error 8.6

Not initializing a pointer that is declared const is a compilation error.

Constant Pointer to Constant Data

The least amount of access privilege is granted by a constant pointer to constant data. Such a pointer always points to the same memory location, and the data at that memory location cannot be modified using the pointer. This is how an array should be passed to a function that only reads the array, using array subscript notation, and does not modify the array. The program of Fig. 8.14 declares pointer variable ptr to be of type const int * const (line 14). This declaration is read from right to left as "ptr is a constant pointer to an integer constant." The figure shows the error messages generated when an attempt is

```
1   // Fig. 8.14: fig08_14.cpp
2   // Attempting to modify a constant pointer to constant data.
3   #include <iostream>
4   using std::cout;
5   using std::endl;
6
7   int main()
8   {
9      int x = 5, y;
10
11     // ptr is a constant pointer to a constant integer.
12     // ptr always points to the same location; the integer
13     // at that location cannot be modified.
14     const int *const ptr = &x;
15
16     cout << *ptr << endl;
17
18     *ptr = 7; // error: *ptr is const; cannot assign new value
19     ptr = &y; // error: ptr is const; cannot assign new address
20     return 0; // indicates successful termination
21  } // end main
```

Borland C++ command-line compiler error message:

```
Error E2024 fig08_14.cpp 18: Cannot modify a const object in function main()
Error E2024 fig08_14.cpp 19: Cannot modify a const object in function main()
```

Microsoft Visual C++ compiler error message:

```
c:\cpphtp5e_examples\ch08\Fig08_14\fig08_14.cpp(18) : error C3892: 'ptr' :
   you cannot assign to a variable that is const
c:\cpphtp5e_examples\ch08\Fig08_14\fig08_14.cpp(19) : error C3892: 'ptr' :
   you cannot assign to a variable that is const
```

Fig. 8.14 | Attempting to modify a constant pointer to constant data. (Part 1 of 2.)

GNU C++ compiler error message:

```
fig08_14.cpp: In function `int main()':
fig08_14.cpp:18: error: assignment of read-only location
fig08_14.cpp:19: error: assignment of read-only variable `ptr'
```

Fig. 8.14 | Attempting to modify a constant pointer to constant data. (Part 2 of 2.)

made to modify the data to which ptr points (line 18) and when an attempt is made to modify the address stored in the pointer variable (line 19). Note that no errors occur when the program attempts to dereference ptr, or when the program attempts to output the value to which ptr points (line 16), because neither the pointer nor the data it points to is being modified in this statement.

8.6 Selection Sort Using Pass-by-Reference

In this section, we define a sorting program to demonstrate passing arrays and individual array elements by reference. We use the selection sort algorithm, which is an easy-to-program, but unfortunately inefficient, sorting algorithm. The first iteration of the algorithm selects the smallest element in the array and swaps it with the first element. The second iteration selects the second-smallest element (which is the smallest element of the remaining elements) and swaps it with the second element. The algorithm continues until the last iteration selects the second-largest element and swaps it with the second-to-last index, leaving the largest element in the last index. After the ith iteration, the smallest i items of the array will be sorted into increasing order in the first i elements of the array.

As an example, consider the array

34 56 4 10 77 51 93 30 5 52

A program that implements the selection sort first determines the smallest value (4) in the array, which is contained in element 2. The program swaps the 4 with the value in element 0 (34), resulting in

4 56 **34** 10 77 51 93 30 5 52

[*Note:* We use bold to highlight the values that were swapped.] The program then determines the smallest value of the remaining elements (all elements except 4), which is 5, contained in element 8. The program swaps the 5 with the 56 in element 1, resulting in

4 **5** 34 10 77 51 93 30 **56** 52

On the third iteration, the program determines the next smallest value, 10, and swaps it with the value in element 2 (34).

4 5 **10** **34** 77 51 93 30 56 52

The process continues until the array is fully sorted.

4 5 10 30 34 51 52 56 77 93

Note that after the first iteration, the smallest element is in the first position. After the second iteration, the two smallest elements are in order in the first two positions. After the third iteration, the three smallest elements are in order in the first three positions.

Figure 8.15 implements selection sort using two functions—selectionSort and swap. Function selectionSort (lines 36–53) sorts the array. Line 38 declares the variable smallest, which will store the index of the smallest element in the remaining array. Lines 41–52 loop size - 1 times. Line 43 sets the index of the smallest element to the current index. Lines 46–49 loop over the remaining elements in the array. For each of these elements, line 48 compares its value to the value of the smallest element. If the current element is smaller than the smallest element, line 49 assigns the current element's index to smallest. When this loop finishes, smallest will contain the index of the smallest element in the remaining array. Line 51 calls function swap (lines 57–62) to place the smallest remaining element in the next spot in the array (i.e., exchange the array elements array[i] and array[smallest]).

Let us now look more closely at function swap. Remember that C++ enforces information hiding between functions, so swap does not have access to individual array elements in selectionSort. Because selectionSort *wants* swap to have access to the array elements to be swapped, selectionSort passes each of these elements to swap by refer-

```
 1   // Fig. 8.15: fig08_15.cpp
 2   // Selection sort with pass-by-reference. This program puts values into an
 3   // array, sorts them into ascending order and prints the resulting array.
 4   #include <iostream>
 5   using std::cout;
 6   using std::endl;
 7
 8   #include <iomanip>
 9   using std::setw;
10
11   void selectionSort( int * const, const int ); // prototype
12   void swap( int * const, int * const ); // prototype
13
14   int main()
15   {
16      const int arraySize = 10;
17      int a[ arraySize ] = { 2, 6, 4, 8, 10, 12, 89, 68, 45, 37 };
18
19      cout << "Data items in original order\n";
20
21      for ( int i = 0; i < arraySize; i++ )
22         cout << setw( 4 ) << a[ i ];
23
24      selectionSort( a, arraySize ); // sort the array
25
26      cout << "\nData items in ascending order\n";
27
28      for ( int j = 0; j < arraySize; j++ )
29         cout << setw( 4 ) << a[ j ];
30
31      cout << endl;
32      return 0; // indicates successful termination
33   } // end main
```

Fig. 8.15 | Selection sort with pass-by-reference. (Part 1 of 2.)

```
34
35   // function to sort an array
36   void selectionSort( int * const array, const int size )
37   {
38      int smallest; // index of smallest element
39
40      // loop over size - 1 elements
41      for ( int i = 0; i < size - 1; i++ )
42      {
43         smallest = i; // first index of remaining array
44
45         // loop to find index of smallest element
46         for ( int index = i + 1; index < size; index++ )
47
48            if ( array[ index ] < array[ smallest ] )
49               smallest = index;
50
51         swap( &array[ i ], &array[ smallest ] );
52      } // end if
53   } // end function selectionSort
54
55   // swap values at memory locations to which
56   // element1Ptr and element2Ptr point
57   void swap( int * const element1Ptr, int * const element2Ptr )
58   {
59      int hold = *element1Ptr;
60      *element1Ptr = *element2Ptr;
61      *element2Ptr = hold;
62   } // end function swap
```

```
Data items in original order
  2   6   4   8  10  12  89  68  45  37
Data items in ascending order
  2   4   6   8  10  12  37  45  68  89
```

Fig. 8.15 | Selection sort with pass-by-reference. (Part 2 of 2.)

ence—the address of each array element is passed explicitly. Although entire arrays are passed by reference, individual array elements are scalars and are ordinarily passed by value. Therefore, selectionSort uses the address operator (&) on each array element in the swap call (line 51) to effect pass-by-reference. Function swap (lines 57–62) receives &array[i] in pointer variable element1Ptr. Information hiding prevents swap from "knowing" the name array[i], but swap can use *element1Ptr as a synonym for array[i]. Thus, when swap references *element1Ptr, it is actually referencing array[i] in selectionSort. Similarly, when swap references *element2Ptr, it is actually referencing array[smallest] in selectionSort.

Even though swap is not allowed to use the statements

```
hold = array[ i ];
array[ i ] = array[ smallest ];
array[ smallest ] = hold;
```

precisely the same effect is achieved by

```
int hold = *element1Ptr;
*element1Ptr = *element2Ptr;
*element2Ptr = hold;
```

in the swap function of Fig. 8.15.

Several features of function selectionSort should be noted. The function header (line 36) declares array as int * const array, rather than int array[], to indicate that the function receives a one-dimensional array as an argument. Both parameter array's pointer and parameter size are declared const to enforce the principle of least privilege. Although parameter size receives a copy of a value in main and modifying the copy cannot change the value in main, selectionSort does not need to alter size to accomplish its task—the array size remains fixed during the execution of selectionSort. Therefore, size is declared const to ensure that it is not modified. If the size of the array were to be modified during the sorting process, the sorting algorithm would not run correctly.

Note that function selectionSort receives the size of the array as a parameter, because the function must have that information to sort the array. When an array is passed to a function, only the memory address of the first element of the array is received by the function; the array size must be passed separately to the function.

By defining function selectionSort to receive the array size as a parameter, we enable the function to be used by any program that sorts one-dimensional int arrays of arbitrary size. The size of the array could have been programmed directly into the function, but this would restrict the function to processing an array of a specific size and reduce the function's reusability—only programs processing one-dimensional int arrays of the specific size "hard coded" into the function could use the function.

Software Engineering Observation 8.4

When passing an array to a function, also pass the size of the array (rather than building into the function knowledge of the array size)—this makes the function more reusable.

8.7 sizeof Operator

C++ provides the unary operator sizeof to determine the size of an array (or of any other data type, variable or constant) in bytes during program compilation. When applied to the name of an array, as in Fig. 8.16 (line 14), the sizeof operator returns the total number of bytes in the array as a value of type size_t (an unsigned integer type that is at least as big as unsigned int). Note that this is different from the size of a vector< int >, for example, which is the number of integer elements in the vector. The computer we used to compile this program stores variables of type double in 8 bytes of memory, and array is declared to have 20 elements (line 12), so array uses 160 bytes in memory. When applied to a pointer parameter (line 24) in a function that receives an array as an argument, the sizeof operator returns the size of the pointer in bytes (4 on the system we used)—not the size of the array.

Common Programming Error 8.7

Using the sizeof operator in a function to find the size in bytes of an array parameter results in the size in bytes of a pointer, not the size in bytes of the array.

```
1    // Fig. 8.16: fig08_16.cpp
2    // Sizeof operator when used on an array name
3    // returns the number of bytes in the array.
4    #include <iostream>
5    using std::cout;
6    using std::endl;
7
8    size_t getSize( double * ); // prototype
9
10   int main()
11   {
12      double array[ 20 ]; // 20 doubles; occupies 160 bytes on our system
13
14      cout << "The number of bytes in the array is " << sizeof( array );
15
16      cout << "\nThe number of bytes returned by getSize is "
17         << getSize( array ) << endl;
18      return 0; // indicates successful termination
19   } // end main
20
21   // return size of ptr
22   size_t getSize( double *ptr )
23   {
24      return sizeof( ptr );
25   } // end function getSize
```

```
The number of bytes in the array is 160
The number of bytes returned by getSize is 4
```

Fig. 8.16 | sizeof operator when applied to an array name returns the number of bytes in the array.

[*Note:* When the Borland C++ compiler is used to compile Fig. 8.16, the compiler generates the warning message "Parameter 'ptr' is never used in function get-Size(double *)." This warning occurs because sizeof is actually a compile-time operator; thus, variable ptr is not used in the function's body at execution time. Many compilers issue warnings like this to let you know that a variable is not being used so that you can either remove it from your code or modify your code to use the variable properly. Similar messages occur in Fig. 8.17 with various compilers.]

The number of elements in an array also can be determined using the results of two sizeof operations. For example, consider the following array declaration:

```
double realArray[ 22 ];
```

If variables of data type double are stored in eight bytes of memory, array realArray contains a total of 176 bytes. To determine the number of elements in the array, the following expression (which is evaluated at compile time) can be used:

```
sizeof realArray / sizeof( double ) // calculate number of elements
```

The expression determines the number of bytes in array realArray (176) and divides that value by the number of bytes used in memory to store a double value (8)—the result is the number of elements in realArray (22).

Determining the Sizes of the Fundamental Types, an Array and a Pointer
Figure 8.17 uses sizeof to calculate the number of bytes used to store most of the standard data types. Notice that, in the output, the types double and long double have the same size. Types may have different sizes based on the platform running the program. On another system, for example, double and long double may be of different sizes.

```cpp
// Fig. 8.17: fig08_17.cpp
// Demonstrating the sizeof operator.
#include <iostream>
using std::cout;
using std::endl;

int main()
{
   char c; // variable of type char
   short s; // variable of type short
   int i; // variable of type int
   long l; // variable of type long
   float f; // variable of type float
   double d; // variable of type double
   long double ld; // variable of type long double
   int array[ 20 ]; // array of int
   int *ptr = array; // variable of type int *

   cout << "sizeof c = " << sizeof c
      << "\tsizeof(char) = " << sizeof( char )
      << "\nsizeof s = " << sizeof s
      << "\tsizeof(short) = " << sizeof( short )
      << "\nsizeof i = " << sizeof i
      << "\tsizeof(int) = " << sizeof( int )
      << "\nsizeof l = " << sizeof l
      << "\tsizeof(long) = " << sizeof( long )
      << "\nsizeof f = " << sizeof f
      << "\tsizeof(float) = " << sizeof( float )
      << "\nsizeof d = " << sizeof d
      << "\tsizeof(double) = " << sizeof( double )
      << "\nsizeof ld = " << sizeof ld
      << "\tsizeof(long double) = " << sizeof( long double )
      << "\nsizeof array = " << sizeof array
      << "\nsizeof ptr = " << sizeof ptr << endl;
   return 0; // indicates successful termination
} // end main
```

```
sizeof c = 1      sizeof(char) = 1
sizeof s = 2      sizeof(short) = 2
sizeof i = 4      sizeof(int) = 4
sizeof l = 4      sizeof(long) = 4
sizeof f = 4      sizeof(float) = 4
sizeof d = 8      sizeof(double) = 8
sizeof ld = 8     sizeof(long double) = 8
sizeof array = 80
sizeof ptr = 4
```

Fig. 8.17 | sizeof operator used to determine standard data type sizes.

Portability Tip 8.2

The number of bytes used to store a particular data type may vary among systems. When writing programs that depend on data type sizes, and that will run on several computer systems, use sizeof *to determine the number of bytes used to store the data types.*

Operator sizeof can be applied to any expression or type name. When sizeof is applied to a variable name (which is not an array name) or other expression, the number of bytes used to store the specific type of the expression's value is returned. Note that the parentheses used with sizeof are required only if a type name (e.g., int) is supplied as its operand. The parentheses used with sizeof are not required when sizeof's operand is an expression. Remember that sizeof is an operator, not a function, and that it has its effect at compile time, not execution time.

Common Programming Error 8.8

Omitting the parentheses in a sizeof *operation when the operand is a type name is a compilation error.*

Performance Tip 8.2

Because sizeof *is a compile-time unary operator, not an execution-time operator, using* sizeof *does not negatively impact execution performance.*

Error-Prevention Tip 8.3

To avoid errors associated with omitting the parentheses around the operand of operator sizeof, *many programmers include parentheses around every* sizeof *operand.*

8.8 Pointer Expressions and Pointer Arithmetic

Pointers are valid operands in arithmetic expressions, assignment expressions and comparison expressions. However, not all the operators normally used in these expressions are valid with pointer variables. This section describes the operators that can have pointers as operands and how these operators are used with pointers.

Several arithmetic operations may be performed on pointers. A pointer may be incremented (++) or decremented (--), an integer may be added to a pointer (+ or +=), an integer may be subtracted from a pointer (- or -=) or one pointer may be subtracted from another of the same type.

Assume that array int v[5] has been declared and that its first element is at memory location 3000. Assume that pointer vPtr has been initialized to point to v[0] (i.e., the value of vPtr is 3000). Figure 8.18 diagrams this situation for a machine with four-byte integers. Note that vPtr can be initialized to point to array v with either of the following statements (because the name of an array is equivalent to the address of its first element):

```
int *vPtr = v;
int *vPtr = &v[ 0 ];
```

Portability Tip 8.3

Most computers today have two-byte or four-byte integers. Some of the newer machines use eight-byte integers. Because the results of pointer arithmetic depend on the size of the objects a pointer points to, pointer arithmetic is machine dependent.

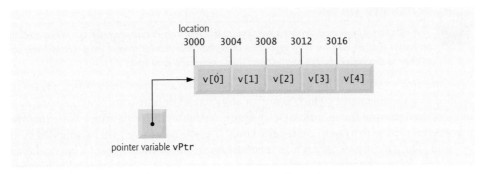

Fig. 8.18 | Array v and a pointer variable int *vPtr that points to v.

In conventional arithmetic, the addition 3000 + 2 yields the value 3002. This is normally not the case with pointer arithmetic. When an integer is added to, or subtracted from, a pointer, the pointer is not simply incremented or decremented by that integer, but by that integer times the size of the object to which the pointer refers. The number of bytes depends on the object's data type. For example, the statement

```
vPtr += 2;
```

would produce 3008 (3000 + 2 * 4), assuming that an int is stored in four bytes of memory. In the array v, vPtr would now point to v[2] (Fig. 8.19). If an integer is stored in two bytes of memory, then the preceding calculation would result in memory location 3004 (3000 + 2 * 2). If the array elements were of a different data type, the preceding statement would increment the pointer by twice the number of bytes it takes to store an object of that data type. When performing pointer arithmetic on a character array, the results will be consistent with regular arithmetic, because each character is one byte long.

If vPtr had been incremented to 3016, which points to v[4], the statement

```
vPtr -= 4;
```

would set vPtr back to 3000—the beginning of the array. If a pointer is being incremented or decremented by one, the increment (++) and decrement (--) operators can be used. Each of the statements

```
++vPtr;
vPtr++;
```

Fig. 8.19 | Pointer vPtr after pointer arithmetic.

increments the pointer to point to the next element of the array. Each of the statements

```
--vPtr;
vPtr--;
```

decrements the pointer to point to the previous element of the array.

Pointer variables pointing to the same array may be subtracted from one another. For example, if vPtr contains the address 3000 and v2Ptr contains the address 3008, the statement

```
x = v2Ptr - vPtr;
```

would assign to x the number of array elements from vPtr to v2Ptr—in this case, 2. Pointer arithmetic is meaningless unless performed on a pointer that points to an array. We cannot assume that two variables of the same type are stored contiguously in memory unless they are adjacent elements of an array.

Common Programming Error 8.9

Using pointer arithmetic on a pointer that does not refer to an array of values is a logic error.

Common Programming Error 8.10

Subtracting or comparing two pointers that do not refer to elements of the same array is a logic error.

Common Programming Error 8.11

Using pointer arithmetic to increment or decrement a pointer such that the pointer refers to an element outside the bounds of the array is normally a logic error.

A pointer can be assigned to another pointer if both pointers are of the same type. Otherwise, a cast operator must be used to convert the value of the pointer on the right of the assignment to the pointer type on the left of the assignment. The exception to this rule is the pointer to void (i.e., void *), which is a generic pointer capable of representing any pointer type. All pointer types can be assigned to a pointer of type void * without casting. However, a pointer of type void * cannot be assigned directly to a pointer of another type—the pointer of type void * must first be cast to the proper pointer type.

Software Engineering Observation 8.5

Nonconstant pointer arguments can be passed to constant pointer parameters. This is helpful when the body of a program uses a nonconstant pointer to access data, but does not want that data to be modified by a function called in the body of the program.

A void * pointer cannot be dereferenced. For example, the compiler "knows" that a pointer to int refers to four bytes of memory on a machine with four-byte integers, but a pointer to void simply contains a memory address for an unknown data type—the precise number of bytes to which the pointer refers and the type of the data are not known by the compiler. The compiler must know the data type to determine the number of bytes to be dereferenced for a particular pointer—for a pointer to void, this number of bytes cannot be determined from the type.

Common Programming Error 8.12

Assigning a pointer of one type to a pointer of another (other than void *) *without casting the first pointer to the type of the second pointer is a compilation error.*

Common Programming Error 8.13

All operations on a void * *pointer are compilation errors, except comparing* void * *pointers with other pointers, casting* void * *pointers to valid pointer types and assigning addresses to* void * *pointers.*

Pointers can be compared using equality and relational operators. Comparisons using relational operators are meaningless unless the pointers point to members of the same array. Pointer comparisons compare the addresses stored in the pointers. A comparison of two pointers pointing to the same array could show, for example, that one pointer points to a higher numbered element of the array than the other pointer does. A common use of pointer comparison is determining whether a pointer is 0 (i.e., the pointer is a null pointer—it does not point to anything).

8.9 Relationship Between Pointers and Arrays

Arrays and pointers are intimately related in C++ and may be used *almost* interchangeably. An array name can be thought of as a constant pointer. Pointers can be used to do any operation involving array subscripting.

Assume the following declarations:

```
int b[ 5 ]; // create 5-element int array b
int *bPtr; // create int pointer bPtr
```

Because the array name (without a subscript) is a (constant) pointer to the first element of the array, we can set bPtr to the address of the first element in array b with the statement

```
bPtr = b; // assign address of array b to bPtr
```

This is equivalent to assigning the address of the first element of the array as follows:

```
bPtr = &b[ 0 ]; // also assigns address of array b to bPtr
```

Array element b[3] can alternatively be referenced with the pointer expression

```
*( bPtr + 3 )
```

The 3 in the preceding expression is the offset to the pointer. When the pointer points to the beginning of an array, the offset indicates which element of the array should be referenced, and the offset value is identical to the array subscript. The preceding notation is referred to as pointer/offset notation. The parentheses are necessary, because the precedence of * is higher than the precedence of +. Without the parentheses, the above expression would add 3 to the value of *bPtr (i.e., 3 would be added to b[0], assuming that bPtr points to the beginning of the array). Just as the array element can be referenced with a pointer expression, the address

```
&b[ 3 ]
```

can be written with the pointer expression

```
bPtr + 3
```

The array name (which is implicitly const) can be treated as a pointer and used in pointer arithmetic. For example, the expression

```
*( b + 3 )
```

also refers to the array element b[3]. In general, all subscripted array expressions can be written with a pointer and an offset. In this case, pointer/offset notation was used with the name of the array as a pointer. Note that the preceding expression does not modify the array name in any way; b still points to the first element in the array.

Pointers can be subscripted exactly as arrays can. For example, the expression

```
bPtr[ 1 ]
```

refers to the array element b[1]; this expression uses pointer/subscript notation.

Remember that an array name is a constant pointer; it always points to the beginning of the array. Thus, the expression

```
b += 3
```

causes a compilation error, because it attempts to modify the value of the array name (a constant) with pointer arithmetic.

Common Programming Error 8.14

Although array names are pointers to the beginning of the array and pointers can be modified in arithmetic expressions, array names cannot be modified in arithmetic expressions, because array names are constant pointers.

Good Programming Practice 8.2

For clarity, use array notation instead of pointer notation when manipulating arrays.

Figure 8.20 uses the four notations discussed in this section for referring to array elements—array subscript notation, pointer/offset notation with the array name as a pointer, pointer subscript notation and pointer/offset notation with a pointer—to accomplish the same task, namely printing the four elements of the integer array b.

```cpp
1   // Fig. 8.20: fig08_20.cpp
2   // Using subscripting and pointer notations with arrays.
3   #include <iostream>
4   using std::cout;
5   using std::endl;
6
7   int main()
8   {
9       int b[] = { 10, 20, 30, 40 }; // create 4-element array b
10      int *bPtr = b; // set bPtr to point to array b
11
12      // output array b using array subscript notation
13      cout << "Array b printed with:\n\nArray subscript notation\n";
```

Fig. 8.20 | Referencing array elements with the array name and with pointers. (Part I of 2.)

```
14
15      for ( int i = 0; i < 4; i++ )
16         cout << "b[" << i << "] = " << b[ i ] << '\n';
17
18      // output array b using the array name and pointer/offset notation
19      cout << "\nPointer/offset notation where "
20         << "the pointer is the array name\n";
21
22      for ( int offset1 = 0; offset1 < 4; offset1++ )
23         cout << "*(b + " << offset1 << ") = " << *( b + offset1 ) << '\n';
24
25      // output array b using bPtr and array subscript notation
26      cout << "\nPointer subscript notation\n";
27
28      for ( int j = 0; j < 4; j++ )
29         cout << "bPtr[" << j << "] = " << bPtr[ j ] << '\n';
30
31      cout << "\nPointer/offset notation\n";
32
33      // output array b using bPtr and pointer/offset notation
34      for ( int offset2 = 0; offset2 < 4; offset2++ )
35         cout << "*(bPtr + " << offset2 << ") = "
36            << *( bPtr + offset2 ) << '\n';
37
38      return 0; // indicates successful termination
39   } // end main
```

```
Array b printed with:

Array subscript notation
b[0] = 10
b[1] = 20
b[2] = 30
b[3] = 40

Pointer/offset notation where the pointer is the array name
*(b + 0) = 10
*(b + 1) = 20
*(b + 2) = 30
*(b + 3) = 40

Pointer subscript notation
bPtr[0] = 10
bPtr[1] = 20
bPtr[2] = 30
bPtr[3] = 40

Pointer/offset notation
*(bPtr + 0) = 10
*(bPtr + 1) = 20
*(bPtr + 2) = 30
*(bPtr + 3) = 40
```

Fig. 8.20 | Referencing array elements with the array name and with pointers. (Part 2 of 2.)

To further illustrate the interchangeability of arrays and pointers, let us look at the two string-copying functions—copy1 and copy2—in the program of Fig. 8.21. Both functions copy a string into a character array. After a comparison of the function prototypes for copy1 and copy2, the functions appear identical (because of the interchangeability of arrays and pointers). These functions accomplish the same task, but they are implemented differently.

```cpp
1   // Fig. 8.21: fig08_21.cpp
2   // Copying a string using array notation and pointer notation.
3   #include <iostream>
4   using std::cout;
5   using std::endl;
6
7   void copy1( char *, const char * ); // prototype
8   void copy2( char *, const char * ); // prototype
9
10  int main()
11  {
12     char string1[ 10 ];
13     char *string2 = "Hello";
14     char string3[ 10 ];
15     char string4[] = "Good Bye";
16
17     copy1( string1, string2 ); // copy string2 into string1
18     cout << "string1 = " << string1 << endl;
19
20     copy2( string3, string4 ); // copy string4 into string3
21     cout << "string3 = " << string3 << endl;
22     return 0; // indicates successful termination
23  } // end main
24
25  // copy s2 to s1 using array notation
26  void copy1( char * s1, const char * s2 )
27  {
28     // copying occurs in the for header
29     for ( int i = 0; ( s1[ i ] = s2[ i ] ) != '\0'; i++ )
30        ; // do nothing in body
31  } // end function copy1
32
33  // copy s2 to s1 using pointer notation
34  void copy2( char *s1, const char *s2 )
35  {
36     // copying occurs in the for header
37     for ( ; ( *s1 = *s2 ) != '\0'; s1++, s2++ )
38        ; // do nothing in body
39  } // end function copy2
```

```
string1 = Hello
string3 = Good Bye
```

Fig. 8.21 | String copying using array notation and pointer notation.

Function `copy1` (lines 26–31) uses array subscript notation to copy the string in `s2` to the character array `s1`. The function declares an integer counter variable `i` to use as the array subscript. The `for` statement header (line 29) performs the entire copy operation—its body is the empty statement. The header specifies that `i` is initialized to zero and incremented by one on each iteration of the loop. The condition in the `for`, (`s1[ i ]` = `s2[ i ]`) != `'\0'`, performs the copy operation character by character from `s2` to `s1`. When the null character is encountered in `s2`, it is assigned to `s1`, and the loop terminates, because the null character is equal to `'\0'`. Remember that the value of an assignment statement is the value assigned to its left operand.

Function `copy2` (lines 34–39) uses pointers and pointer arithmetic to copy the string in `s2` to the character array `s1`. Again, the `for` statement header (line 37) performs the entire copy operation. The header does not include any variable initialization. As in function `copy1`, the condition (`*s1` = `*s2`) != `'\0'` performs the copy operation. Pointer `s2` is dereferenced, and the resulting character is assigned to the dereferenced pointer `s1`. After the assignment in the condition, the loop increments both pointers, so they point to the next element of array `s1` and the next character of string `s2`, respectively. When the loop encounters the null character in `s2`, the null character is assigned to the dereferenced pointer `s1` and the loop terminates. Note that the "increment portion" of this `for` statement has two increment expressions separated by a comma operator.

The first argument to both `copy1` and `copy2` must be an array large enough to hold the string in the second argument. Otherwise, an error may occur when an attempt is made to write into a memory location beyond the bounds of the array (recall that when using pointer-based arrays, there is no "built-in" bounds checking). Also, note that the second parameter of each function is declared as `const char *` (a pointer to a character constant—i.e., a constant string). In both functions, the second argument is copied into the first argument—characters are copied from the second argument one at a time, but the characters are never modified. Therefore, the second parameter is declared to point to a constant value to enforce the principle of least privilege—neither function needs to modify the second argument, so neither function is allowed to modify the second argument.

8.10 Arrays of Pointers

Arrays may contain pointers. A common use of such a data structure is to form an array of pointer-based strings, referred to simply as a string array. Each entry in the array is a string, but in C++ a string is essentially a pointer to its first character, so each entry in an array of strings is simply a pointer to the first character of a string. Consider the declaration of string array `suit` that might be useful in representing a deck of cards:

```
const char *suit[ 4 ] =
   { "Hearts", "Diamonds", "Clubs", "Spades" };
```

The `suit[4]` portion of the declaration indicates an array of four elements. The `const char *` portion of the declaration indicates that each element of array `suit` is of type "pointer to char constant data." The four values to be placed in the array are "Hearts", "Diamonds", "Clubs" and "Spades". Each is stored in memory as a null-terminated character string that is one character longer than the number of characters between quotes. The four strings are seven, nine, six and seven characters long (including their terminating null characters), respectively. Although it appears as though these strings are being placed in the suit array, only pointers are actually stored in the array, as shown in Fig. 8.22. Each pointer points to the first character of its corresponding string. Thus, even though the suit array is fixed in size, it provides access to character strings of any length. This flexibility is one example of C++'s powerful data-structuring capabilities.

The suit strings could be placed into a two-dimensional array, in which each row represents one suit and each column represents one of the letters of a suit name. Such a data structure must have a fixed number of columns per row, and that number must be as large as the largest string. Therefore, considerable memory is wasted when we store a large number of strings, of which most are shorter than the longest string. We use arrays of strings to help represent a deck of cards in the next section.

String arrays are commonly used with command-line arguments that are passed to function main when a program begins execution. Such arguments follow the program name when a program is executed from the command line. A typical use of command-line arguments is to pass options to a program. For example, from the command line on a Windows computer, the user can type

```
dir /p
```

to list the contents of the current directory and pause after each screen of information. When the dir command executes, the option /p is passed to dir as a command-line argument. Such arguments are placed in a string array that main receives as an argument. We discuss command-line arguments in Appendix E, C Legacy Code Topics.

8.11 Case Study: Card Shuffling and Dealing Simulation

This section uses random-number generation to develop a card shuffling and dealing simulation program. This program can then be used as a basis for implementing programs that play specific card games. To reveal some subtle performance problems, we have intentionally used suboptimal shuffling and dealing algorithms. In the exercises, we develop more efficient algorithms.

Using the top-down, stepwise-refinement approach, we develop a program that will shuffle a deck of 52 playing cards and then deal each of the 52 cards. The top-down approach is particularly useful in attacking larger, more complex problems than we have seen in the early chapters.

We use a 4-by-13 two-dimensional array deck to represent the deck of playing cards (Fig. 8.23). The rows correspond to the suits—row 0 corresponds to hearts, row 1 to diamonds, row 2 to clubs and row 3 to spades. The columns correspond to the face values of

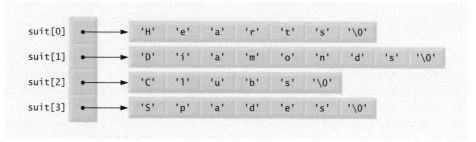

Fig. 8.22 | Graphical representation of the suit array.

Fig. 8.23 | Two-dimensional array representation of a deck of cards.

the cards—columns 0 through 9 correspond to the faces ace through 10, respectively, and columns 10 through 12 correspond to the jack, queen and king, respectively. We shall load the string array `suit` with character strings representing the four suits (as in Fig. 8.22) and the string array `face` with character strings representing the 13 face values.

This simulated deck of cards may be shuffled as follows. First the 52-element array `deck` is initialized to zeros. Then, a row (0–3) and a column (0–12) are each chosen at random. The number 1 is inserted in array element `deck[ row ][ column ]` to indicate that this card is going to be the first one dealt from the shuffled deck. This process continues with the numbers 2, 3, …, 52 being randomly inserted in the `deck` array to indicate which cards are to be placed second, third, …, and 52nd in the shuffled deck. As the `deck` array begins to fill with card numbers, it is possible that a card will be selected twice (i.e., `deck[ row ][ column ]` will be nonzero when it is selected). This selection is simply ignored, and other `row` and `column` combinations are repeatedly chosen at random until an unselected card is found. Eventually, the numbers 1 through 52 will occupy the 52 slots of the `deck` array. At this point, the deck of cards is fully shuffled.

This shuffling algorithm could execute for an indefinitely long period if cards that have already been shuffled are repeatedly selected at random. This phenomenon is known as indefinite postponement (also called starvation). In the exercises, we discuss a faster shuffling algorithm that also eliminates the possibility of indefinite postponement.

> **Performance Tip 8.3**
>
> *Sometimes algorithms that emerge in a "natural" way can contain subtle performance problems such as indefinite postponement. Seek algorithms that avoid indefinite postponement.*

To deal the first card, we search the array for the element `deck[ row ][ column ]` that matches 1. This is accomplished with nested `for` statements that vary `row` from 0 to 3 and `column` from 0 to 12. What card does that slot of the array correspond to? The `suit` array has been preloaded with the four suits, so to get the suit, we print the character string `suit[ row ]`. Similarly, to get the face value of the card, we print the character string `face[ column ]`. We also print the character string `" of "`. Printing this information in the proper order enables us to print each card in the form `"King of Clubs"`, `"Ace of Diamonds"` and so on.

Let us proceed with the top-down, stepwise-refinement process. The top is simply

Shuffle and deal 52 cards

Our first refinement yields

Initialize the suit array
Initialize the face array
Initialize the deck array
Shuffle the deck
Deal 52 cards

"Shuffle the deck" may be expanded as follows:

For each of the 52 cards
Place card number in randomly selected unoccupied slot of deck

"Deal 52 cards" may be expanded as follows:

For each of the 52 cards
Find card number in deck array and print face and suit of card

Incorporating these expansions yields our complete second refinement:

Initialize the suit array
Initialize the face array
Initialize the deck array

For each of the 52 cards
Place card number in randomly selected unoccupied slot of deck

For each of the 52 cards
Find card number in deck array and print face and suit of card

"Place card number in randomly selected unoccupied slot of deck" may be expanded as follows:

Choose slot of deck randomly

While chosen slot of deck has been previously chosen
Choose slot of deck randomly

Place card number in chosen slot of deck

"Find card number in deck array and print face and suit of card" may be expanded as follows:

For each slot of the deck array
If slot contains card number
Print the face and suit of the card

Incorporating these expansions yields our third refinement (Fig. 8.24).

This completes the refinement process. Figures 8.25–8.27 contain the card shuffling and dealing program and a sample execution. Lines 61–67 of function `deal` (Fig. 8.26) implement lines 1–2 of Fig. 8.24. The constructor (lines 22–35 of Fig. 8.26) implements lines 1–3 of Fig. 8.24. Function `shuffle` (lines 38–55 of Fig. 8.26) implements lines 5–11 of Fig. 8.24. Function `deal` (lines 58–88 of Fig. 8.26) implements lines 13–16 of Fig. 8.24. Note the output formatting used in function `deal` (lines 81–83 of Fig. 8.26).

```
 1   Initialize the suit array
 2   Initialize the face array
 3   Initialize the deck array
 4
 5   For each of the 52 cards
 6       Choose slot of deck randomly
 7
 8       While slot of deck has been previously chosen
 9           Choose slot of deck randomly
10
11       Place card number in chosen slot of deck
12
13   For each of the 52 cards
14
15       For each slot of deck array
16
17           If slot contains desired card number
18               Print the face and suit of the card
```

Fig. 8.24 | Pseudocode algorithm for card shuffling and dealing program.

```
 1   // Fig. 8.25: DeckOfCards.h
 2   // Definition of class DeckOfCards that
 3   // represents a deck of playing cards.
 4
 5   // DeckOfCards class definition
 6   class DeckOfCards
 7   {
 8   public:
 9      DeckOfCards(); // constructor initializes deck
10      void shuffle(); // shuffles cards in deck
11      void deal(); // deals cards in deck
12   private:
13      int deck[ 4 ][ 13 ]; // represents deck of cards
14   }; // end class DeckOfCards
```

Fig. 8.25 | DeckOfCards header file.

```
 1   // Fig. 8.26: DeckOfCards.cpp
 2   // Member-function definitions for class DeckOfCards that simulates
 3   // the shuffling and dealing of a deck of playing cards.
 4   #include <iostream>
 5   using std::cout;
 6   using std::left;
 7   using std::right;
 8
 9   #include <iomanip>
10   using std::setw;
```

Fig. 8.26 | Definitions of member functions for shuffling and dealing. (Part 1 of 3.)

```
11
12   #include <cstdlib> // prototypes for rand and srand
13   using std::rand;
14   using std::srand;
15
16   #include <ctime> // prototype for time
17   using std::time;
18
19   #include "DeckOfCards.h" // DeckOfCards class definition
20
21   // DeckOfCards default constructor initializes deck
22   DeckOfCards::DeckOfCards()
23   {
24      // loop through rows of deck
25      for ( int row = 0; row <= 3; row++ )
26      {
27         // loop through columns of deck for current row
28         for ( int column = 0; column <= 12; column++ )
29         {
30            deck[ row ][ column ] = 0; // initialize slot of deck to 0
31         } // end inner for
32      } // end outer for
33
34      srand( time( 0 ) ); // seed random number generator
35   } // end DeckOfCards default constructor
36
37   // shuffle cards in deck
38   void DeckOfCards::shuffle()
39   {
40      int row; // represents suit value of card
41      int column; // represents face value of card
42
43      // for each of the 52 cards, choose a slot of the deck randomly
44      for ( int card = 1; card <= 52; card++ )
45      {
46         do // choose a new random location until unoccupied slot is found
47         {
48            row = rand() % 4; // randomly select the row (0 to 3)
49            column = rand() % 13; // randomly select the column (0 to 12)
50         } while( deck[ row ][ column ] != 0 ); // end do...while
51
52         // place card number in chosen slot of deck
53         deck[ row ][ column ] = card;
54      } // end for
55   } // end function shuffle
56
57   // deal cards in deck
58   void DeckOfCards::deal()
59   {
60      // initialize suit array
61      static const char *suit[ 4 ] =
62         { "Hearts", "Diamonds", "Clubs", "Spades" };
63
```

Fig. 8.26 | Definitions of member functions for shuffling and dealing. (Part 2 of 3.)

```
64    // initialize face array
65    static const char *face[ 13 ] =
66       { "Ace", "Deuce", "Three", "Four", "Five", "Six", "Seven",
67       "Eight", "Nine", "Ten", "Jack", "Queen", "King" };
68
69    // for each of the 52 cards
70    for ( int card = 1; card <= 52; card++ )
71    {
72       // loop through rows of deck
73       for ( int row = 0; row <= 3; row++ )
74       {
75          // loop through columns of deck for current row
76          for ( int column = 0; column <= 12; column++ )
77          {
78             // if slot contains current card, display card
79             if ( deck[ row ][ column ] == card )
80             {
81                cout << setw( 5 ) << right << face[ column ]
82                   << " of " << setw( 8 ) << left << suit[ row ]
83                   << ( card % 2 == 0 ? '\n' : '\t' );
84             } // end if
85          } // end innermost for
86       } // end inner for
87    } // end outer for
88 } // end function deal
```

Fig. 8.26 | Definitions of member functions for shuffling and dealing. (Part 3 of 3.)

The output statement outputs the face right justified in a field of five characters and outputs the suit left justified in a field of eight characters (Fig. 8.27). The output is printed in two-column format—if the card being output is in the first column, a tab is output after the card to move to the second column (line 83); otherwise, a newline is output.

There is also a weakness in the dealing algorithm. Once a match is found, even if it is found on the first try, the two inner for statements continue searching the remaining elements of deck for a match. In the exercises, we correct this deficiency.

```
1    // Fig. 8.27: fig08_27.cpp
2    // Card shuffling and dealing program.
3    #include "DeckOfCards.h" // DeckOfCards class definition
4
5    int main()
6    {
7       DeckOfCards deckOfCards; // create DeckOfCards object
8
9       deckOfCards.shuffle(); // shuffle the cards in the deck
10      deckOfCards.deal(); // deal the cards in the deck
11      return 0; // indicates successful termination
12   } // end main
```

Fig. 8.27 | Card shuffling and dealing program. (Part 1 of 2.)

Nine of Spades	Seven of Clubs
Five of Spades	Eight of Clubs
Queen of Diamonds	Three of Hearts
Jack of Spades	Five of Diamonds
Jack of Diamonds	Three of Diamonds
Three of Clubs	Six of Clubs
Ten of Clubs	Nine of Diamonds
Ace of Hearts	Queen of Hearts
Seven of Spades	Deuce of Spades
Six of Hearts	Deuce of Clubs
Ace of Clubs	Deuce of Diamonds
Nine of Hearts	Seven of Diamonds
Six of Spades	Eight of Diamonds
Ten of Spades	King of Hearts
Four of Clubs	Ace of Spades
Ten of Hearts	Four of Spades
Eight of Hearts	Eight of Spades
Jack of Hearts	Ten of Diamonds
Four of Diamonds	King of Diamonds
Seven of Hearts	King of Spades
Queen of Spades	Four of Hearts
Nine of Clubs	Six of Diamonds
Deuce of Hearts	Jack of Clubs
King of Clubs	Three of Spades
Queen of Clubs	Five of Clubs
Five of Hearts	Ace of Diamonds

Fig. 8.27 | Card shuffling and dealing program. (Part 2 of 2.)

8.12 **Function Pointers**

A pointer to a function contains the address of the function in memory. In Chapter 7, we saw that the name of an array is actually the address in memory of the first element of the array. Similarly, the name of a function is actually the starting address in memory of the code that performs the function's task. Pointers to functions can be passed to functions, returned from functions, stored in arrays, assigned to other function pointers and used to call the underlying function.

Multipurpose Selection Sort Using Function Pointers

To illustrate the use of pointers to functions, Fig. 8.28 modifies the selection sort program of Fig. 8.15. Figure 8.28 consists of main (lines 17–55) and the functions selectionSort (lines 59–76), swap (lines 80–85), ascending (lines 89–92) and descending (lines 96–99). Function selectionSort receives a pointer to a function—either function ascending or function descending—as an argument in addition to the integer array to sort and the size of the array. Functions ascending and descending determine the sorting order. The program prompts the user to choose whether the array should be sorted in ascending order or in descending order (lines 24–26). If the user enters 1, a pointer to function ascending is passed to function selectionSort (line 37), causing the array to be sorted into increasing order. If the user enters 2, a pointer to function descending is passed to function selectionSort (line 45), causing the array to be sorted into decreasing order.

The following parameter appears in line 60 of selectionSort's function header:

```
bool ( *compare )( int, int )
```

This parameter specifies a pointer to a function. The keyword `bool` indicates that the function being pointed to returns a `bool` value. The text (`*compare`) indicates the name of the pointer to the function (the * indicates that parameter `compare` is a pointer). The text (`int, int`) indicates that the function pointed to by `compare` takes two integer arguments. Parentheses are needed around `*compare` to indicate that `compare` is a pointer to a function. If we had not included the parentheses, the declaration would have been

```
bool *compare( int, int )
```

which declares a function that receives two integers as parameters and returns a pointer to a `bool` value.

```cpp
1   // Fig. 8.28: fig08_28.cpp
2   // Multipurpose sorting program using function pointers.
3   #include <iostream>
4   using std::cout;
5   using std::cin;
6   using std::endl;
7
8   #include <iomanip>
9   using std::setw;
10
11  // prototypes
12  void selectionSort( int [], const int, bool (*)( int, int ) );
13  void swap( int * const, int * const );
14  bool ascending( int, int ); // implements ascending order
15  bool descending( int, int ); // implements descending order
16
17  int main()
18  {
19     const int arraySize = 10;
20     int order; // 1 = ascending, 2 = descending
21     int counter; // array index
22     int a[ arraySize ] = { 2, 6, 4, 8, 10, 12, 89, 68, 45, 37 };
23
24     cout << "Enter 1 to sort in ascending order,\n"
25        << "Enter 2 to sort in descending order: ";
26     cin >> order;
27     cout << "\nData items in original order\n";
28
29     // output original array
30     for ( counter = 0; counter < arraySize; counter++ )
31        cout << setw( 4 ) << a[ counter ];
32
33     // sort array in ascending order; pass function ascending
34     // as an argument to specify ascending sorting order
35     if ( order == 1 )
36     {
37        selectionSort( a, arraySize, ascending );
38        cout << "\nData items in ascending order\n";
39     } // end if
40
```

Fig. 8.28 | Multipurpose sorting program using function pointers. (Part 1 of 3.)

```
41      // sort array in descending order; pass function descending
42      // as an argument to specify descending sorting order
43      else
44      {
45          selectionSort( a, arraySize, descending );
46          cout << "\nData items in descending order\n";
47      } // end else part of if...else
48
49      // output sorted array
50      for ( counter = 0; counter < arraySize; counter++ )
51          cout << setw( 4 ) << a[ counter ];
52
53      cout << endl;
54      return 0; // indicates successful termination
55  } // end main
56
57  // multipurpose selection sort; the parameter compare is a pointer to
58  // the comparison function that determines the sorting order
59  void selectionSort( int work[], const int size,
60                      bool (*compare)( int, int ) )
61  {
62      int smallestOrLargest; // index of smallest (or largest) element
63
64      // loop over size - 1 elements
65      for ( int i = 0; i < size - 1; i++ )
66      {
67          smallestOrLargest = i; // first index of remaining vector
68
69          // loop to find index of smallest (or largest) element
70          for ( int index = i + 1; index < size; index++ )
71              if ( !(*compare)( work[ smallestOrLargest ], work[ index ] ) )
72                  smallestOrLargest = index;
73
74          swap( &work[ smallestOrLargest ], &work[ i ] );
75      } // end if
76  } // end function selectionSort
77
78  // swap values at memory locations to which
79  // element1Ptr and element2Ptr point
80  void swap( int * const element1Ptr, int * const element2Ptr )
81  {
82      int hold = *element1Ptr;
83      *element1Ptr = *element2Ptr;
84      *element2Ptr = hold;
85  } // end function swap
86
87  // determine whether element a is less than
88  // element b for an ascending order sort
89  bool ascending( int a, int b )
90  {
91      return a < b; // returns true if a is less than b
92  } // end function ascending
93
```

Fig. 8.28 | Multipurpose sorting program using function pointers. (Part 2 of 3.)

```
94   // determine whether element a is greater than
95   // element b for a descending order sort
96   bool descending( int a, int b )
97   {
98      return a > b; // returns true if a is greater than b
99   } // end function descending
```

```
Enter 1 to sort in ascending order,
Enter 2 to sort in descending order: 1

Data items in original order
   2   6   4   8  10  12  89  68  45  37
Data items in ascending order
   2   4   6   8  10  12  37  45  68  89
```

```
Enter 1 to sort in ascending order,
Enter 2 to sort in descending order: 2

Data items in original order
   2   6   4   8  10  12  89  68  45  37
Data items in descending order
  89  68  45  37  12  10   8   6   4   2
```

Fig. 8.28 | Multipurpose sorting program using function pointers. (Part 3 of 3.)

The corresponding parameter in the function prototype of selectionSort is

```
bool (*)( int, int )
```

Note that only types have been included. As always, for documentation purposes, you can include names that the compiler will ignore.

The function passed to selectionSort is called in line 71 as follows:

```
( *compare )( work[ smallestOrLargest ], work[ index ] )
```

Just as a pointer to a variable is dereferenced to access the value of the variable, a pointer to a function is dereferenced to execute the function. The parentheses around *compare are necessary—if they were left out, the * operator would attempt to dereference the value returned from the function call. The call to the function could have been made without dereferencing the pointer, as in

```
compare( work[ smallestOrLargest ], work[ index ] )
```

which uses the pointer directly as the function name. We prefer the first method of calling a function through a pointer, because it explicitly illustrates that compare is a pointer to a function that is dereferenced to call the function. The second method of calling a function through a pointer makes it appear as though compare is the name of an actual function in the program. This may be confusing to a user of the program who would like to see the definition of function compare and finds that it is not defined in the file.

Chapter 22, Standard Template Library (STL), presents many common uses of function pointers.

Arrays of Pointers to Functions

One use of function pointers is in menu-driven systems. For example, a program might prompt a user to select an option from a menu by entering an integer value. The user's choice can be used as a subscript into an array of function pointers, and the pointer in the array can be used to call the function.

Figure 8.29 provides a mechanical example that demonstrates declaring and using an array of pointers to functions. The program defines three functions—function0, function1 and function2—that each take an integer argument and do not return a value. Line 17 stores pointers to these three functions in array f. In this case, all the functions to which the array points must have the same return type and same parameter types. The declaration in line 17 is read beginning in the leftmost set of parentheses as, "f is an array of three pointers to functions that each take an int as an argument and return void." The

```cpp
1    // Fig. 8.29: fig08_29.cpp
2    // Demonstrating an array of pointers to functions.
3    #include <iostream>
4    using std::cout;
5    using std::cin;
6    using std::endl;
7
8    // function prototypes -- each function performs similar actions
9    void function0( int );
10   void function1( int );
11   void function2( int );
12
13   int main()
14   {
15      // initialize array of 3 pointers to functions that each
16      // take an int argument and return void
17      void (*f[ 3 ])( int ) = { function0, function1, function2 };
18
19      int choice;
20
21      cout << "Enter a number between 0 and 2, 3 to end: ";
22      cin >> choice;
23
24      // process user's choice
25      while ( ( choice >= 0 ) && ( choice < 3 ) )
26      {
27         // invoke the function at location choice in
28         // the array f and pass choice as an argument
29         (*f[ choice ])( choice );
30
31         cout << "Enter a number between 0 and 2, 3 to end: ";
32         cin >> choice;
33      } // end while
34
35      cout << "Program execution completed." << endl;
36      return 0; // indicates successful termination
37   } // end main
```

Fig. 8.29 | Array of pointers to functions. (Part 1 of 2.)

```
38
39   void function0( int a )
40   {
41      cout << "You entered " << a << " so function0 was called\n\n";
42   } // end function function0
43
44   void function1( int b )
45   {
46      cout << "You entered " << b << " so function1 was called\n\n";
47   } // end function function1
48
49   void function2( int c )
50   {
51      cout << "You entered " << c << " so function2 was called\n\n";
52   } // end function function2
```

```
Enter a number between 0 and 2, 3 to end: 0
You entered 0 so function0 was called

Enter a number between 0 and 2, 3 to end: 1
You entered 1 so function1 was called

Enter a number between 0 and 2, 3 to end: 2
You entered 2 so function2 was called

Enter a number between 0 and 2, 3 to end: 3
Program execution completed.
```

Fig. 8.29 | Array of pointers to functions. (Part 2 of 2.)

array is initialized with the names of the three functions (which, again, are pointers). The program prompts the user to enter a number between 0 and 2, or 3 to terminate. When the user enters a value between 0 and 2, the value is used as the subscript into the array of pointers to functions. Line 29 invokes one of the functions in array f. In the call, f[choice] selects the pointer at location choice in the array. The pointer is dereferenced to call the function, and choice is passed as the argument to the function. Each function prints its argument's value and its function name to indicate that the function is called correctly. In the exercises, you'll develop a menu-driven system. We'll see in Chapter 13, Object-Oriented Programming: Polymorphism, that arrays of pointers to functions are used by compiler developers to implement the mechanisms that support virtual functions—the key technology behind polymorphism.

8.13 Introduction to Pointer-Based String Processing

In this section, we introduce some common C++ Standard Library functions that facilitate string processing. The techniques discussed here are appropriate for developing text editors, word processors, page layout software, computerized typesetting systems and other kinds of text-processing software. We have already used the C++ Standard Library string class in several examples to represent strings as full-fledged objects. For example, the GradeBook class case study in Chapters 3–7 represents a course name using a string object. In Chapter 18 we present class string in detail. Although using string objects is usually straightforward, we use null-terminated, pointer-based strings in this section. Many C++ Standard Library functions operate only on null-terminated, pointer-based strings, which are more complicated to use than `string` objects. Also, if you work with legacy C++ programs, you may be required to manipulate these pointer-based strings.

8.13.1 Fundamentals of Characters and Pointer-Based Strings

Characters are the fundamental building blocks of C++ source programs. Every program is composed of a sequence of characters that—when grouped together meaningfully—is interpreted by the compiler as a series of instructions used to accomplish a task. A program may contain character constants. A character constant is an integer value represented as a character in single quotes. The value of a character constant is the integer value of the character in the machine's character set. For example, `'z'` represents the integer value of z (122 in the ASCII character set; see Appendix B), and `'\n'` represents the integer value of newline (10 in the ASCII character set).

A string is a series of characters treated as a single unit. A string may include letters, digits and various special characters such as +, -, *, /and $. String literals, or string constants, in C++ are written in double quotation marks as follows:

```
"John Q. Doe"             (a name)
"9999 Main Street"        (a street address)
"Maynard, Massachusetts"  (a city and state)
"(201) 555-1212"          (a telephone number)
```

A pointer-based string in C++ is an array of characters ending in the null character (`'\0'`), which marks where the string terminates in memory. A string is accessed via a pointer to its first character. The value of a string is the address of its first character, but the `sizeof` a string literal is the length of the string including the terminating null character. In this sense, strings are like arrays, because an array name is also a pointer to its first element.

A string literal may be used as an initializer in the declaration of either a character array or a variable of type char *. The declarations

```
char color[] = "blue";
const char *colorPtr = "blue";
```

each initialize a variable to the string "blue". The first declaration creates a five-element array color containing the characters `'b'`, `'l'`, `'u'`, `'e'` and `'\0'`. The second declaration creates pointer variable colorPtr that points to the letter b in the string "blue" (which ends in `'\0'`) somewhere in memory. String literals have `static` storage class (they exist for the duration of the program) and may or may not be shared if the same string literal is referenced from multiple locations in a program. According to the C++ standard (Section 2.13.4), the effect of attempting to modify a string literal is undefined; thus, you should always declare a pointer to a string literal as const char *.

The declaration char color[] = "blue"; could also be written

```
char color[] = { 'b', 'l', 'u', 'e', '\0' };
```

When declaring a character array to contain a string, the array must be large enough to store the string and its terminating null character. The preceding declaration determines the size of the array, based on the number of initializers provided in the initializer list.

Common Programming Error 8.15

Not allocating sufficient space in a character array to store the null character that terminates a string is an error.

Common Programming Error 8.16

Creating or using a C-style string that does not contain a terminating null character can lead to logic errors.

Error-Prevention Tip 8.4

When storing a string of characters in a character array, be sure that the array is large enough to hold the largest string that will be stored. C++ allows strings of any length to be stored. If a string is longer than the character array in which it is to be stored, characters beyond the end of the array will overwrite data in memory following the array, leading to logic errors.

A string can be read into a character array using stream extraction with cin. For example, the following statement can be used to read a string into character array word[20]:

```
cin >> word;
```

The string entered by the user is stored in word. The preceding statement reads characters until a white-space character or end-of-file indicator is encountered. Note that the string should be no longer than 19 characters to leave room for the terminating null character. The setw stream manipulator can be used to ensure that the string read into word does not exceed the size of the array. For example, the statement

```
cin >> setw( 20 ) >> word;
```

specifies that cin should read a maximum of 19 characters into array word and save the 20th location in the array to store the terminating null character for the string. The setw stream manipulator applies only to the next value being input. If more than 19 characters are entered, the remaining characters are not saved in word, but will be read in and can be stored in another variable.

In some cases, it is desirable to input an entire line of text into an array. For this purpose, C++ provides the function cin.getline in header file <iostream>. In Chapter 3 you were introduced to the similar function getline from header file <string>, which read input until a newline character was entered, and stored the input (without the newline character) into a string specified as an argument. The cin.getline function takes three arguments—a character array in which the line of text will be stored, a length and a delimiter character. For example, the program segment

```
char sentence[ 80 ];
cin.getline( sentence, 80, '\n' );
```

declares array sentence of 80 characters and reads a line of text from the keyboard into the array. The function stops reading characters when the delimiter character '\n' is encountered, when the end-of-file indicator is entered or when the number of characters read so far is one less than the length specified in the second argument. (The last character in the array is reserved for the terminating null character.) If the delimiter character is encountered, it is read and discarded. The third argument to cin.getline has '\n' as a default value, so the preceding function call could have been written as follows:

```
cin.getline( sentence, 80 );
```

Chapter 15, Stream Input/Output, provides a detailed discussion of cin.getline and other input/output functions.

Common Programming Error 8.17

Processing a single character as a char * string can lead to a fatal runtime error. A char * string is a pointer—probably a respectably large integer. However, a character is a small integer (ASCII values range 0–255). On many systems, dereferencing a char value causes an error, because low memory addresses are reserved for special purposes such as operating system interrupt handlers—so "memory access violations" occur.

Common Programming Error 8.18

Passing a string as an argument to a function when a character is expected is a compilation error.

8.13.2 String-Manipulation Functions of the String-Handling Library

The string-handling library provides many useful functions for manipulating string data, comparing strings, searching strings for characters and other strings, tokenizing strings (separating strings into logical pieces such as the separate words in a sentence) and determining the length of strings. This section presents some common string-manipulation functions of the string-handling library (from the C++ standard library). The functions are summarized in Fig. 8.30; then each is used in a live-code example. The prototypes for these functions are located in header file <cstring>.

Function prototype	Function description
`char *strcpy( char *s1, const char *s2 );`	
	Copies the string s2 into the character array s1. The value of s1 is returned.
`char *strncpy( char *s1, const char *s2, size_t n );`	
	Copies at most n characters of the string s2 into the character array s1. The value of s1 is returned.
`char *strcat( char *s1, const char *s2 );`	
	Appends the string s2 to s1. The first character of s2 overwrites the terminating null character of s1. The value of s1 is returned.
`char *strncat( char *s1, const char *s2, size_t n );`	
	Appends at most n characters of string s2 to string s1. The first character of s2 overwrites the terminating null character of s1. The value of s1 is returned.
`int strcmp( const char *s1, const char *s2 );`	
	Compares the string s1 with the string s2. The function returns a value of zero, less than zero or greater than zero if s1 is equal to, less than or greater than s2, respectively.

Fig. 8.30 | String-manipulation functions of the string-handling library. (Part 1 of 2.)

Function prototype	Function description
`int strncmp( const char *s1, const char *s2, size_t n );`	
	Compares up to n characters of the string s1 with the string s2. The function returns zero, less than zero or greater than zero if the n-character portion of s1 is equal to, less than or greater than the corresponding n-character portion of s2, respectively.
`char *strtok( char *s1, const char *s2 );`	
	A sequence of calls to `strtok` breaks string s1 into "tokens"—logical pieces such as words in a line of text. The string is broken up based on the characters contained in string s2. For instance, if we were to break the string `"this:is:a:string"` into tokens based on the character `':'`, the resulting tokens would be `"this"`, `"is"`, `"a"` and `"string"`. Function strtok returns only one token at a time—the first call contains s1 as the first argument, and subsequent calls to continue tokenizing the same string contain NULL as the first argument. A pointer to the current token is returned by each call. If there are no more tokens when the function is called, NULL is returned.
`size_t strlen( const char *s );`	
	Determines the length of string s. The number of characters preceding the terminating null character is returned.

Fig. 8.30 | String-manipulation functions of the string-handling library. (Part 2 of 2.)

Note that several functions in Fig. 8.30 contain parameters with data type `size_t`. This type is defined in the header file `<cstring>` to be an unsigned integral type such as unsigned `int` or unsigned `long`.

Common Programming Error 8.19

Forgetting to include the `<cstring>` header file when using functions from the string-handling library causes compilation errors.

Copying Strings with *strcpy and *strncpy

Function `strcpy` copies its second argument—a string—into its first argument—a character array that must be large enough to store the string and its terminating null character, (which is also copied). Function `strncpy` is much like strcpy, except that strncpy specifies the number of characters to be copied from the string into the array. Note that function strncpy does not necessarily copy the terminating null character of its second argument—a terminating null character is written only if the number of characters to be copied is at least one more than the length of the string. For example, if `"test"` is the second argument, a terminating null character is written only if the third argument to strncpy is at least 5 (four characters in `"test"` plus one terminating null character). If the third argument is larger than 5, null characters are appended to the array until the total number of characters specified by the third argument is written.

 **Common Programming Error 8.20**

When using strcpy, the terminating null character of the second argument (a char * string) will not be copied if the number of characters specified by strncpy's third argument is not greater than the second argument's length. In that case, a fatal error may occur if you do not manually terminate the resulting char * string with a null character.

Figure 8.31 uses strcpy (line 17) to copy the entire string in array x into array y and uses strncpy (line 23) to copy the first 14 characters of array x into array z. Line 24 appends a null character ('\0') to array z, because the call to strncpy in the program does not write a terminating null character. (The third argument is less than the string length of the second argument plus one.)

*Concatenating Strings with **strcat** and **strncat***

Function strcat appends its second argument (a string) to its first argument (a character array containing a string). The first character of the second argument replaces the null char-acter ('\0') that terminates the string in the first argument. You must ensure that the array used to store the first string is large enough to store the combination of the first string, the

```cpp
1  // Fig. 8.31: fig08_31.cpp
2  // Using strcpy and strncpy.
3  #include <iostream>
4  using std::cout;
5  using std::endl;
6
7  #include <cstring> // prototypes for strcpy and strncpy
8  using std::strcpy;
9  using std::strncpy;
10
11 int main()
12 {
13    char x[] = "Happy Birthday to You"; // string length 21
14    char y[ 25 ];
15    char z[ 15 ];
16
17    strcpy( y, x ); // copy contents of x into y
18
19    cout << "The string in array x is: " << x
20       << "\nThe string in array y is: " << y << '\n';
21
22    // copy first 14 characters of x into z
23    strncpy( z, x, 14 ); // does not copy null character
24    z[ 14 ] = '\0'; // append '\0' to z's contents
25
26    cout << "The string in array z is: " << z << endl;
27    return 0; // indicates successful termination
28 } // end main
```

```
The string in array x is: Happy Birthday to You
The string in array y is: Happy Birthday to You
The string in array z is: Happy Birthday
```

Fig. 8.31 | strcpy and strncpy.

second string and the terminating null character (copied from the second string). Function `strncat` appends a specified number of characters from the second string to the first string and appends a terminating null character to the result. The program of Fig. 8.32 demonstrates function `strcat` (lines 19 and 29) and function `strncat` (line 24).

```cpp
1   // Fig. 8.32: fig08_32.cpp
2   // Using strcat and strncat.
3   #include <iostream>
4   using std::cout;
5   using std::endl;
6
7   #include <cstring> // prototypes for strcat and strncat
8   using std::strcat;
9   using std::strncat;
10
11  int main()
12  {
13     char s1[ 20 ] = "Happy "; // length 6
14     char s2[] = "New Year "; // length 9
15     char s3[ 40 ] = "";
16
17     cout << "s1 = " << s1 << "\ns2 = " << s2;
18
19     strcat( s1, s2 ); // concatenate s2 to s1 (length 15)
20
21     cout << "\n\nAfter strcat(s1, s2):\ns1 = " << s1 << "\ns2 = " << s2;
22
23     // concatenate first 6 characters of s1 to s3
24     strncat( s3, s1, 6 ); // places '\0' after last character
25
26     cout << "\n\nAfter strncat(s3, s1, 6):\ns1 = " << s1
27        << "\ns3 = " << s3;
28
29     strcat( s3, s1 ); // concatenate s1 to s3
30     cout << "\n\nAfter strcat(s3, s1):\ns1 = " << s1
31        << "\ns3 = " << s3 << endl;
32     return 0; // indicates successful termination
33  } // end main
```

```
s1 = Happy
s2 = New Year

After strcat(s1, s2):
s1 = Happy New Year
s2 = New Year

After strncat(s3, s1, 6):
s1 = Happy New Year
s3 = Happy

After strcat(s3, s1):
s1 = Happy New Year
s3 = Happy Happy New Year
```

Fig. 8.32 | `strcat` and `strncat`.

Comparing Strings with *strcmp* and *strncmp*

Figure 8.33 compares three strings using `strcmp` (lines 21, 22 and 23) and `strncmp` (lines 26, 27 and 28). Function `strcmp` compares its first string argument with its second string argument character by character. The function returns zero if the strings are equal, a negative value if the first string is less than the second string and a positive value if the first string is greater than the second string. Function `strncmp` is equivalent to `strcmp`, except that `strncmp` compares up to a specified number of characters. Function `strncmp` stops comparing characters if it reaches the null character in one of its string arguments. The program prints the integer value returned by each function call.

 Common Programming Error 8.21

Assuming that strcmp and strncmp return one (a true value) when their arguments are equal is a logic error. Both functions return zero (C++'s false value) for equality. Therefore, when testing two strings for equality, the result of the strcmp or strncmp function should be compared with zero to determine whether the strings are equal.

To understand just what it means for one string to be "greater than" or "less than" another string, consider the process of alphabetizing a series of last names. You would, no doubt, place "Jones" before "Smith," because the first letter of "Jones" comes before the

```cpp
1  // Fig. 8.33: fig08_33.cpp
2  // Using strcmp and strncmp.
3  #include <iostream>
4  using std::cout;
5  using std::endl;
6
7  #include <iomanip>
8  using std::setw;
9
10 #include <cstring> // prototypes for strcmp and strncmp
11 using std::strcmp;
12 using std::strncmp;
13
14 int main()
15 {
16    char *s1 = "Happy New Year";
17    char *s2 = "Happy New Year";
18    char *s3 = "Happy Holidays";
19
20    cout << "s1 = " << s1 << "\ns2 = " << s2 << "\ns3 = " << s3
21       << "\n\nstrcmp(s1, s2) = " << setw( 2 ) << strcmp( s1, s2 )
22       << "\nstrcmp(s1, s3) = " << setw( 2 ) << strcmp( s1, s3 )
23       << "\nstrcmp(s3, s1) = " << setw( 2 ) << strcmp( s3, s1 );
24
25    cout << "\n\nstrncmp(s1, s3, 6) = " << setw( 2 )
26       << strncmp( s1, s3, 6 ) << "\nstrncmp(s1, s3, 7) = " << setw( 2 )
27       << strncmp( s1, s3, 7 ) << "\nstrncmp(s3, s1, 7) = " << setw( 2 )
28       << strncmp( s3, s1, 7 ) << endl;
29    return 0; // indicates successful termination
30 } // end main
```

Fig. 8.33 | strcmp and strncmp. (Part I of 2.)

```
s1 = Happy New Year
s2 = Happy New Year
s3 = Happy Holidays

strcmp(s1, s2) =  0
strcmp(s1, s3) =  1
strcmp(s3, s1) = -1

strncmp(s1, s3, 6) =  0
strncmp(s1, s3, 7) =  1
strncmp(s3, s1, 7) = -1
```

Fig. 8.33 | strcmp and strncmp. (Part 2 of 2.)

first letter of "Smith" in the alphabet. But the alphabet is more than just a list of 26 letters—it is an *ordered* list of characters. Each letter occurs in a specific position within the list. "Z" is more than just a letter of the alphabet; "Z" is specifically the 26th letter of the alphabet.

How does the computer know that one letter comes before another? All characters are represented inside the computer as numeric codes; when the computer compares two strings, it actually compares the numeric codes of the characters in the strings.

In an effort to standardize character representations, most computer manufacturers have designed their machines to utilize one of two popular coding schemes—ASCII or EBCDIC. Recall that ASCII stands for "American Standard Code for Information Interchange." EBCDIC stands for "Extended Binary Coded Decimal Interchange Code." There are other coding schemes as well.

ASCII and EBCDIC are called character codes, or character sets. Most readers of this book will be using desktop or notebook computers that use the ASCII character set. IBM mainframe computers use the EBCDIC character set. As Internet and World Wide Web usage becomes pervasive, the newer Unicode character set is growing in popularity (www.unicode.org). String and character manipulations actually involve the manipulation of the appropriate numeric codes and not the characters themselves. This explains the interchangeability of characters and small integers in C++. Since it is meaningful to say that one numeric code is greater than, less than or equal to another numeric code, it becomes possible to relate various characters or strings to one another by referring to the character codes. Appendix B contains the ASCII character codes.

Portability Tip 8.4

The internal numeric codes used to represent characters may be different on different computers that use different character sets.

Portability Tip 8.5

Do not explicitly test for ASCII codes, as in if (rating == 65); rather, use the corresponding character constant, as in if (rating == 'A').

[*Note:* With some compilers, functions strcmp and strncmp always return -1, 0 or 1, as in the sample output of Fig. 8.33. With other compilers, these functions return 0 or the difference between the numeric codes of the first characters that differ in the strings being compared. For example, when s1 and s3 are compared, the first characters that differ between them are the first character of the second word in each string—N (numeric code 78) in s1 and H (numeric code 72) in s3, respectively. In this case, the return value will be 6 (or -6 if s3 is compared to s1).]

Tokenizing a String with **strtok**

Function strtok breaks a string into a series of tokens. A token is a sequence of characters separated by delimiting characters (usually spaces or punctuation marks). For example, in a line of text, each word can be considered a token, and the spaces separating the words can be considered delimiters.

Multiple calls to strtok are required to break a string into tokens (assuming that the string contains more than one token). The first call to strtok contains two arguments, a string to be tokenized and a string containing characters that separate the tokens (i.e., delimiters). Line 19 in Fig. 8.34 assigns to tokenPtr a pointer to the first token in sentence. The second argument, " ", indicates that tokens in sentence are separated by spaces. Function strtok searches for the first character in sentence that is not a delimiting character (space). This begins the first token. The function then finds the next delimiting character in the string and replaces it with a null ('\0') character. This terminates the current token. Function strtok saves (in a static variable) a pointer to the next character following the token in sentence and returns a pointer to the current token.

```cpp
1   // Fig. 8.34: fig08_34.cpp
2   // Using strtok to tokenize a string.
3   #include <iostream>
4   using std::cout;
5   using std::endl;
6
7   #include <cstring> // prototype for strtok
8   using std::strtok;
9
10  int main()
11  {
12     char sentence[] = "This is a sentence with 7 tokens";
13     char *tokenPtr;
14
15     cout << "The string to be tokenized is:\n" << sentence
16        << "\n\nThe tokens are:\n\n";
17
18     // begin tokenization of sentence
19     tokenPtr = strtok( sentence, " " );
20
21     // continue tokenizing sentence until tokenPtr becomes NULL
22     while ( tokenPtr != NULL )
23     {
24        cout << tokenPtr << '\n';
25        tokenPtr = strtok( NULL, " " ); // get next token
26     } // end while
27
28     cout << "\nAfter strtok, sentence = " << sentence << endl;
29     return 0; // indicates successful termination
30  } // end main
```

Fig. 8.34 | Using strtok to tokenize a string. (Part 1 of 2.)

```
The string to be tokenized is:
This is a sentence with 7 tokens

The tokens are:

This
is
a
sentence
with
7
tokens

After strtok, sentence = This
```

Fig. 8.34 | Using strtok to tokenize a string. (Part 2 of 2.)

Subsequent calls to strtok to continue tokenizing sentence contain NULL as the first argument (line 25). The NULL argument indicates that the call to strtok should continue tokenizing from the location in sentence saved by the last call to strtok. Note that strtok maintains this saved information in a manner that is not visible to you. If no tokens remain when strtok is called, strtok returns NULL. The program of Fig. 8.34 uses strtok to tokenize the string "This is a sentence with 7 tokens". The program prints each token on a separate line. Line 28 outputs sentence after tokenization. Note that *strtok modifies the input string*; therefore, a copy of the string should be made if the program requires the original after the calls to strtok. When sentence is output after tokenization, note that only the word "This" prints, because strtok replaced each blank in sentence with a null character ('\0') during the tokenization process.

 Common Programming Error 8.22

Not realizing that strtok modifies the string being tokenized, then attempting to use that string as if it were the original unmodified string is a logic error.

Determining String Lengths

Function strlen takes a string as an argument and returns the number of characters in the string—the terminating null character is not included in the length. The length is also the index of the null character. The program of Fig. 8.35 demonstrates function strlen.

```
1   // Fig. 8.35: fig08_35.cpp
2   // Using strlen.
3   #include <iostream>
4   using std::cout;
5   using std::endl;
6
7   #include <cstring> // prototype for strlen
8   using std::strlen;
9
```

Fig. 8.35 | strlen returns the length of a char * string. (Part 1 of 2.)

```
10   int main()
11   {
12      char *string1 = "abcdefghijklmnopqrstuvwxyz";
13      char *string2 = "four";
14      char *string3 = "Boston";
15
16      cout << "The length of \"" << string1 << "\" is " << strlen( string1 )
17         << "\nThe length of \"" << string2 << "\" is " << strlen( string2 )
18         << "\nThe length of \"" << string3 << "\" is " << strlen( string3 )
19         << endl;
20      return 0; // indicates successful termination
21   } // end main
```

```
The length of "abcdefghijklmnopqrstuvwxyz" is 26
The length of "four" is 4
The length of "Boston" is 6
```

Fig. 8.35 | `strlen` returns the length of a `char *` string. (Part 2 of 2.)

8.14 Wrap-Up

In this chapter we provided a detailed introduction to pointers, or variables that contain memory addresses as their values. We began by demonstrating how to declare and initialize pointers. You saw how to use the address operator (&) to assign the address of a variable to a pointer and the indirection operator (*) to access the data stored in the variable indirectly referenced by a pointer. We discussed passing arguments by reference using both pointer arguments and reference arguments.

You learned how to use const with pointers to enforce the principle of least privilege. We demonstrated using nonconstant pointers to nonconstant data, nonconstant pointers to constant data, constant pointers to nonconstant data, and constant pointers to constant data. We then used selection sort to demonstrate passing arrays and individual array elements by reference. We discussed the sizeof operator, which can be used to determine the sizes of data types and variables in bytes during program compilation.

We demonstrated how to use pointers in arithmetic and comparison expressions. You saw that pointer arithmetic can be used to jump from one element of an array to another. You learned how to use arrays of pointers, and more specifically string arrays (arrays of strings). We discussed function pointers, which enable programmers to pass functions as parameters. We introduced several C++ functions that manipulate pointer-based strings. You learned string-processing capabilities such as copying strings, tokenizing strings and determining the length of strings.

In the next chapter, we begin our deeper treatment of classes. You'll learn about the scope of a class's members, and how to keep objects in a consistent state. You'll also learn about using special member functions called constructors and destructors, which execute when an object is created and destroyed, respectively, and we'll discuss when constructors and destructors are called. In addition, we'll demonstrate using default arguments with constructors and using default memberwise assignment to assign one object of a class to another object of the same class. We'll also discuss the danger of returning a reference to a private data member of a class.

Summary

Section 8.2 Pointer Variable Declarations and Initialization
- Pointers are variables that contain as their values memory addresses of other variables.
- The declaration

    ```
    int *ptr;
    ```

    declares ptr to be a pointer to a variable of type int and is read, "ptr is a pointer to int." The * as used here in a declaration indicates that the variable is a pointer.
- There are three values that can be used to initialize a pointer: 0, NULL or an address of an object of the same type. Initializing a pointer to 0 and initializing that same pointer to NULL are identical—0 is the convention in C++.
- The only integer that can be assigned to a pointer without casting is zero.

Section 8.3 Pointer Operators
- The & (address) operator obtains the memory address of its operand.
- The operand of the address operator must be a variable name (or another *lvalue*); the address operator cannot be applied to constants or to expressions that do not return a reference.
- The * operator, referred to as the indirection (or dereferencing) operator, returns a synonym, alias or nickname for the name of the object that its operand points to in memory. This is called dereferencing the pointer.

Section 8.4 Passing Arguments to Functions by Reference with Pointers
- When calling a function with an argument that the caller wants the called function to modify, the address of the argument may be passed. The called function then uses the indirection operator (*) to dereference the pointer and modify the value of the argument in the calling function.
- A function receiving an address as an argument must have a pointer as its corresponding parameter.

Section 8.5 Using const with Pointers
- The const qualifier enables you to inform the compiler that the value of a particular variable cannot be modified through the specified identifier. If an attempt is made to modify a const value, the compiler issues either a warning or an error, depending on the particular compiler.
- There are four ways to pass a pointer to a function—a nonconstant pointer to nonconstant data, a nonconstant pointer to constant data, a constant pointer to nonconstant data, and a constant pointer to constant data.
- The value of the array name is the address of the array's first element.
- To pass a single array element by reference using pointers, pass the address of the array element.

Section 8.6 Selection Sort Using Pass-by-Reference
- The selection sort algorithm is an easy-to-program, but inefficient, sorting algorithm. The first iteration of the algorithm selects the smallest element in the array and swaps it with the first element. The second iteration selects the second-smallest element (which is the smallest element of the remaining elements) and swaps it with the second element. The algorithm continues until the last iteration selects the second-largest element and swaps it with the second-to-last index, leaving the largest element in the last index. After the ith iteration, the smallest i items of the array will be sorted into increasing order in the first i elements of the array.

Section 8.7 sizeof Operator
- C++ provides unary operator sizeof to determine the size of an array (or of any other data type, variable or constant) in bytes at compile time.

- When applied to the name of an array, the sizeof operator returns the total number of bytes in the array as an integer.

Section 8.8 Pointer Expressions and Pointer Arithmetic
- The arithmetic operations that may be performed on pointers are incrementing (++) a pointer, decrementing (--) a pointer, adding (+ or +=) an integer to a pointer, subtracting (- or -=) an integer from a pointer and subtracting one pointer from another.
- When an integer is added or subtracted from a pointer, the pointer is incremented or decremented by that integer times the size of the object to which the pointer refers.
- Pointers can be assigned to one another if both pointers are of the same type. Otherwise, a cast must be used. The exception to this is a void * pointer, which is a generic pointer type that can hold pointer values of any type. Pointers to void can be assigned pointers of other types. A void * pointer can be assigned to a pointer of another type only with an explicit type cast.
- The only valid operations on a void * pointer are comparing void * pointers with other pointers, assigning addresses to void * pointers and casting void * pointers to valid pointer types.
- Pointers can be compared using the equality and relational operators. Comparisons using relational operators are meaningful only if the pointers point to members of the same array.

Section 8.9 Relationship Between Pointers and Arrays
- Pointers that point to arrays can be subscripted exactly as array names can.
- In pointer/offset notation, if the pointer points to the first element of the array, the offset is the same as an array subscript.
- All subscripted array expressions can be written with a pointer and an offset, using either the name of the array as a pointer or using a separate pointer that points to the array.

Section 8.10 Arrays of Pointers
- Arrays may contain pointers.
- Such a data structure can be used to form an array of pointer-based strings, referred to as a string array. Each entry in the array is a string, but in C++ a string is essentially a pointer to its first character, so each entry in an array of strings is simply a pointer to the first character of a string.
- String arrays are commonly used with command-line arguments that are passed to main when a program begins execution. Such arguments follow the program name when a program is executed from the command line.

Section 8.11 Case Study: Card Shuffling and Dealing Simulation
- Indefinite postponement (also called starvation) occurs when an algorithm can execute for an indefinitely long period of time.

Section 8.12 Function Pointers
- A pointer to a function is the address where the code for the function resides.
- Pointers to functions can be passed to functions, returned from functions, stored in arrays and assigned to other pointers.
- A common use of function pointers is in so-called menu-driven systems. The function pointers are used to select which function to call for a particular menu item.

Section 8.13 Introduction to Pointer-Based String Processing
- Function strcpy copies its second argument—a string—into its first argument—a character array. You must ensure that the target array is large enough to store the string and its terminating null character.

- Function strncpy is equivalent to strcpy, except that a call to strncpy specifies the number of characters to be copied from the string into the array. The terminating null character will be copied only if the number of characters to be copied is at least one more than the length of the string.

- Function strcat appends its second string argument—including the terminating null character—to its first string argument. The first character of the second string replaces the null ('\0') character of the first string. You must ensure that the target array used to store the first string is large enough to store both the first string and the second string.

- Function strncat is equivalent to strcat, except that a call to strncat appends a specified number of characters from the second string to the first string. A terminating null character is appended to the result.

- Function strcmp compares its first string argument with its second string argument character by character. The function returns zero if the strings are equal, a negative value if the first string is less than the second string and a positive value if the first string is greater than the second string.

- Function strncmp is equivalent to strcmp, except that strncmp compares a specified number of characters. If the number of characters in one of the strings is less than the number of characters specified, strncmp compares characters until the null character in the shorter string is encountered.

- A sequence of calls to strtok breaks a string into tokens that are separated by characters contained in a second string argument. The first call specifies the string to be tokenized as the first argument, and subsequent calls to continue tokenizing the same string specify NULL as the first argument. The function returns a pointer to the current token from each call. If there are no more tokens when strtok is called, NULL is returned.

- Function strlen takes a string as an argument and returns the number of characters in the string—the terminating null character is not included in the length of the string.

Terminology

& (address operator)
* (pointer dereference or indirection operator)
'\0' (null character)
address operator (&)
array of pointers to functions
ASCII (American Standard Code for Information Interchange)
calling functions by reference
character code
character constant
command-line arguments
comparing strings
concatenating strings
const with function parameters
constant pointer
constant pointer to constant data
constant pointer to nonconstant data
copying strings
decrement a pointer
delimiter character
dereference a 0 pointer
dereference a pointer
dereferencing operator (*)
directly reference a value

EBCDIC (Extended Binary Coded Decimal Interchange Code)
function pointer
getline function of cin
increment a pointer
indefinite postponement
indirection
indirection (*) operator
indirectly reference a value
interchangeability of arrays and pointers
islower function (<cctype>)
modify a constant pointer
modify address stored in pointer variable
nonconstant pointer to constant data
nonconstant pointer to nonconstant data
null character ('\0')
null pointer
null-terminated string
offset to a pointer
pass-by-reference with pointer arguments
pass-by-reference with reference arguments
pointer arithmetic
pointer-based strings
pointer dereference (*) operator

pointer subtraction
pointer to a function
reference to constant data
referencing array elements
selection sort algorithm
size_t type
sizeof operator
special characters
starvation
strcat function of header file <cstring>
strcmp function of header file <cstring>
strcpy function of header file <cstring>
string array

string being tokenized
string constant
string copying
strlen function of header file <cstring>
strncat function of header file <cstring>
strncmp function of header file <cstring>
strncpy function of header file <cstring>
strtok function of header file <cstring>
terminating null character
token
tokenizing strings
toupper function (<cctype>)
Unicode character set

Self-Review Exercises

8.1   Answer each of the following:

a) A pointer is a variable that contains as its value the _____ of another variable.

b) The three values that can be used to initialize a pointer are _____, _____ and _____.

c) The only integer that can be assigned directly to a pointer is _____.

8.2   State whether the following are *true* or *false*. If the answer is *false*, explain why.

a) The address operator & can be applied only to constants and to expressions.

b) A pointer that is declared to be of type void * can be dereferenced.

c) Pointers of different types can't be assigned to one another without a cast operation.

8.3   For each of the following, write C++ statements that perform the specified task. Assume that double-precision, floating-point numbers are stored in eight bytes and that the starting address of the array is at location 1002500 in memory. Each part of the exercise should use the results of previous parts where appropriate.

a) Declare an array of type double called numbers with 10 elements, and initialize the elements to the values 0.0, 1.1, 2.2, ..., 9.9. Assume that the symbolic constant SIZE has been defined as 10.

b) Declare a pointer nPtr that points to a variable of type double.

c) Use a for statement to print the elements of array numbers using array subscript notation. Print each number with one position of precision to the right of the decimal point.

d) Write two separate statements that each assign the starting address of array numbers to the pointer variable nPtr.

e) Use a for statement to print the elements of array numbers using pointer/offset notation with pointer nPtr.

f) Use a for statement to print the elements of array numbers using pointer/offset notation with the array name as the pointer.

g) Use a for statement to print the elements of array numbers using pointer/subscript notation with pointer nPtr.

h) Refer to the fourth element of array numbers using array subscript notation, pointer/offset notation with the array name as the pointer, pointer subscript notation with nPtr and pointer/offset notation with nPtr.

i) Assuming that nPtr points to the beginning of array numbers, what address is referenced by nPtr + 8? What value is stored at that location?

j) Assuming that nPtr points to numbers[5], what address is referenced by nPtr after nPtr -= 4 is executed? What is the value stored at that location?

8.4   For each of the following, write a single statement that performs the specified task. Assume that floating-point variables number1 and number2 have been declared and that number1 has been initialized to 7.3. Assume that variable ptr is of type char *. Assume that arrays s1 and s2 are each 100-element char arrays that are initialized with string literals.

  a) Declare the variable fPtr to be a pointer to an object of type double.
  b) Assign the address of variable number1 to pointer variable fPtr.
  c) Print the value of the object pointed to by fPtr.
  d) Assign the value of the object pointed to by fPtr to variable number2.
  e) Print the value of number2.
  f) Print the address of number1.
  g) Print the address stored in fPtr. Is the value printed the same as the address of number1?
  h) Copy the string stored in array s2 into array s1.
  i) Compare the string in s1 with the string in s2, and print the result.
  j) Append the first 10 characters from the string in s2 to the string in s1.
  k) Determine the length of the string in s1, and print the result.
  l) Assign to ptr the location of the first token in s2. The tokens delimiters are commas (,).

8.5   Perform the task specified by each of the following statements:

  a) Write the function header for a function called exchange that takes two pointers to double-precision, floating-point numbers x and y as parameters and does not return a value.
  b) Write the function prototype for the function in part (a).
  c) Write the function header for a function called evaluate that returns an integer and that takes as parameters integer x and a pointer to function poly. Function poly takes an integer parameter and returns an integer.
  d) Write the function prototype for the function in part (c).
  e) Write two statements that each initialize character array vowel with the string of vowels, "AEIOU".

8.6   Find the error in each of the following program segments. Assume the following declarations and statements:

```
int *zPtr;        // zPtr will reference array z
int *aPtr = 0;
void *sPtr = 0;
int number;
int z[ 5 ] = { 1, 2, 3, 4, 5 };
```

  a) ++zPtr;
  b) // use pointer to get first value of array
      number = zPtr;
  c) // assign array element 2 (the value 3) to number
      number = *zPtr[2];
  d) // print entire array z
      for (int i = 0; i <= 5; i++)
         cout << zPtr[i] << endl;
  e) // assign the value pointed to by sPtr to number
      number = *sPtr;
  f) ++z;
  g) char s[10];
      cout << strncpy(s, "hello", 5) << endl;
  h) char s[12];
      strcpy(s, "Welcome Home");
  i) if (strcmp(string1, string2))
         cout << "The strings are equal" << endl;
```
```

8.7   What (if anything) prints when each of the following statements is performed? If the statement contains an error, describe the error and indicate how to correct it. Assume the following variable declarations:

```
char s1[ 50 ] = "jack";
char s2[ 50 ] = "jill";
char s3[ 50 ];
```

a) `cout << strcpy( s3, s2 ) << endl;`
b) `cout << strcat( strcat( strcpy( s3, s1 ), " and " ), s2 )`
   `    << endl;`
c) `cout << strlen( s1 ) + strlen( s2 ) << endl;`
d) `cout << strlen( s3 ) << endl;`

Answers to Self-Review Exercises

8.1   a) address. b) 0, NULL, an address. c) 0.

8.2   a) False. The operand of the address operator must be an *lvalue*; the address operator cannot be applied to constants or to expressions that do not result in references.

b) False. A pointer to void cannot be dereferenced. Such a pointer does not have a type that enables the compiler to determine the number of bytes of memory to dereference and the type of the data to which the pointer points.

c) False. Pointers of any type can be assigned to void pointers. Pointers of type void can be assigned to pointers of other types only with an explicit type cast.

8.3   a) `double numbers[ SIZE ] = { 0.0, 1.1, 2.2, 3.3, 4.4, 5.5, 6.6, 7.7, 8.8, 9.9 };`
b) `double *nPtr;`
c) `cout << fixed << showpoint << setprecision( 1 );`
   `for ( int i = 0; i < SIZE; i++ )`
   `    cout << numbers[ i ] << ' ';`
d) `nPtr = numbers;`
   `nPtr = &numbers[ 0 ];`
e) `cout << fixed << showpoint << setprecision( 1 );`
   `for ( int j = 0; j < SIZE; j++ )`
   `    cout << *( nPtr + j ) << ' ';`
f) `cout << fixed << showpoint << setprecision( 1 );`
   `for ( int k = 0; k < SIZE; k++ )`
   `    cout << *( numbers + k ) << ' ';`
g) `cout << fixed << showpoint << setprecision( 1 );`
   `for ( int m = 0; m < SIZE; m++ )`
   `    cout << nPtr[ m ] << ' ';`
h) `numbers[ 3 ]`
   `*( numbers + 3 )`
   `nPtr[ 3 ]`
   `*( nPtr + 3 )`
i) The address is 1002500 + 8 * 8 = 1002564. The value is 8.8.
j) The address of numbers[5] is 1002500 + 5 * 8 = 1002540.
   The address of nPtr -= 4 is 1002540 - 4 * 8 = 1002508.
   The value at that location is 1.1.

8.4   a) `double *fPtr;`
b) `fPtr = &number1;`
c) `cout << "The value of *fPtr is " << *fPtr << endl;`

d) `number2 = *fPtr;`

e) `cout << "The value of number2 is " << number2 << endl;`

f) `cout << "The address of number1 is " << &number1 << endl;`

g) `cout << "The address stored in fPtr is " << fPtr << endl;`
Yes, the value is the same.

h) `strcpy( s1, s2 );`

i) `cout << "strcmp(s1, s2) = " << strcmp( s1, s2 ) << endl;`

j) `strncat( s1, s2, 10 );`

k) `cout << "strlen(s1) = " << strlen( s1 ) << endl;`

l) `ptr = strtok( s2, "," );`

8.5 a) `void exchange( double *x, double *y )`

b) `void exchange( double *, double * );`

c) `int evaluate( int x, int (*poly)( int ) )`

d) `int evaluate( int, int (*)( int ) );`

e) `char vowel[] = "AEIOU";`
`char vowel[] = { 'A', 'E', 'I', 'O', 'U', '\0' };`

8.6 a) *Error:* zPtr has not been initialized.
Correction: Initialize zPtr with zPtr = z;

b) *Error:* The pointer is not dereferenced.
Correction: Change the statement to number = *zPtr;

c) *Error:* zPtr[2] is not a pointer and should not be dereferenced.
Correction: Change *zPtr[2] to zPtr[2].

d) *Error:* Referring to an array element outside the array bounds with pointer subscripting.
Correction: To prevent this, change the relational operator in the for statement to <.

e) *Error:* Dereferencing a void pointer.
Correction: To dereference the void pointer, it must first be cast to an integer pointer.
Change the statement to number = *static_cast< int * >(sPtr);

f) *Error:* Trying to modify an array name with pointer arithmetic.
Correction: Use a pointer variable instead of the array name to accomplish pointer arithmetic, or subscript the array name to refer to a specific element.

g) *Error:* Function strncpy does not write a terminating null character to array s, because its third argument is equal to the length of the string "hello".
Correction: Make 6 the third argument of strncpy or assign '\0' to s[5] to ensure that the terminating null character is added to the string.

h) *Error:* Character array s is not large enough to store the terminating null character.
Correction: Declare the array with more elements.

i) *Error:* Function strcmp will return 0 if the strings are equal; therefore, the condition in the if statement will be false, and the output statement will not be executed.
Correction: Explicitly compare the strcmp result with 0 in the if statement's condition.

8.7 a) `jill`

b) `jack and jill`

c) `8`

d) `13`

Exercises

8.8 State whether the following are *true* or *false*. If *false*, explain why.

a) Two pointers that point to different arrays cannot be compared meaningfully.

b) Because the name of an array is a pointer to the first element of the array, array names can be manipulated in precisely the same manner as pointers.

8.9   For each of the following, write C++ statements that perform the specified task. Assume that unsigned integers are stored in two bytes and that the starting address of the array is at location 1002500 in memory.

a) Declare an array of type `unsigned int` called `values` with five elements, and initialize the elements to the even integers from 2 to 10. Assume that the symbolic constant `SIZE` has been defined as 5.

b) Declare a pointer `vPtr` that points to an object of type `unsigned int`.

c) Use a `for` statement to print the elements of array `values` using array subscript notation.

d) Write two separate statements that assign the starting address of array `values` to pointer variable `vPtr`.

e) Use a `for` statement to print the elements of array `values` using pointer/offset notation.

f) Use a `for` statement to print the elements of array `values` using pointer/offset notation with the array name as the pointer.

g) Use a `for` statement to print the elements of array `values` by subscripting the pointer to the array.

h) Refer to the fifth element of `values` using array subscript notation, pointer/offset notation with the array name as the pointer, pointer subscript notation and pointer/offset notation.

i) What address is referenced by `vPtr + 3`? What value is stored at that location?

j) Assuming that `vPtr` points to `values[ 4 ]`, what address is referenced by `vPtr -= 4`? What value is stored at that location?

8.10   For each of the following, write a single statement that performs the specified task. Assume that `long` variables `value1` and `value2` have been declared and `value1` has been initialized to 200000.

a) Declare the variable `longPtr` to be a pointer to an object of type `long`.

b) Assign the address of variable `value1` to pointer variable `longPtr`.

c) Print the value of the object pointed to by `longPtr`.

d) Assign the value of the object pointed to by `longPtr` to variable `value2`.

e) Print the value of `value2`.

f) Print the address of `value1`.

g) Print the address stored in `longPtr`. Is the value printed the same as `value1`'s address?

8.11   Perform the task specified by each of the following statements:

a) Write the function header for function `zero` that takes a long integer array parameter `bigIntegers` and does not return a value.

b) Write the function prototype for the function in part (a).

c) Write the function header for function `add1AndSum` that takes an integer array parameter `oneTooSmall` and returns an integer.

d) Write the function prototype for the function described in part (c).

Note: Exercise 8.12 through Exercise 8.15 are reasonably challenging. Once you have solved these problems, you ought to be able to implement many popular card games.

8.12   Modify the program in Fig. 8.27 so that the card dealing function deals a five-card poker hand. Then write functions to accomplish each of the following:

a) Determine whether the hand contains a pair.

b) Determine whether the hand contains two pairs.

c) Determine whether the hand contains three of a kind (e.g., three jacks).

d) Determine whether the hand contains four of a kind (e.g., four aces).

e) Determine whether the hand contains a flush (i.e., all five cards of the same suit).

f) Determine whether the contains a straight (i.e., five cards of consecutive face values).

8.13   Use the functions developed in Exercise 8.12 to write a program that deals two five-card poker hands, evaluates each hand and determines which is the better hand.

8.14 Modify the program developed in Exercise 8.13 so that it can simulate the dealer. The dealer's five-card hand is dealt "face down" so the player cannot see it. The program should then evaluate the dealer's hand, and, based on the quality of the hand, the dealer should draw one, two or three more cards to replace the corresponding number of unneeded cards in the original hand. The program should then reevaluate the dealer's hand. [*Caution:* This is a difficult problem!]

8.15 Modify the program developed in Exercise 8.14 so that it handles the dealer's hand, but the player is allowed to decide which cards of the player's hand to replace. The program should then evaluate both hands and determine who wins. Now use this new program to play 20 games against the computer. Who wins more games, you or the computer? Have one of your friends play 20 games against the computer. Who wins more games? Based on the results of these games, make appropriate modifications to refine your poker-playing program. [*Note:* This, too, is a difficult problem.] Play 20 more games. Does your modified program play a better game?

8.16 In the card shuffling and dealing program of Figs. 8.25–8.27, we intentionally used an inefficient shuffling algorithm that introduced the possibility of indefinite postponement. In this problem, you'll create a high-performance shuffling algorithm that avoids indefinite postponement.

Modify Figs. 8.25–8.27 as follows. Initialize the deck array as shown in Fig. 8.36. Modify the shuffle function to loop row by row and column by column through the array, touching every element once. Each element should be swapped with a randomly selected element of the array. Print the resulting array to determine whether the deck is satisfactorily shuffled (as in Fig. 8.37, for example). You may want your program to call the shuffle function several times to ensure a satisfactory shuffle.

Note that, although the approach in this problem improves the shuffling algorithm, the dealing algorithm still requires searching the deck array for card 1, then card 2, then card 3 and so on. Worse yet, even after the dealing algorithm locates and deals the card, the algorithm continues searching through the remainder of the deck. Modify the program of Figs. 8.25–8.27 so that once a card is dealt, no further attempts are made to match that card number, and the program immediately proceeds with dealing the next card.

Unshuffled deck array												
	0	1	2	3	4	5	6	7	8	9	10	11	12
0	1	2	3	4	5	6	7	8	9	10	11	12	13
1	14	15	16	17	18	19	20	21	22	23	24	25	26
2	27	28	29	30	31	32	33	34	35	36	37	38	39
3	40	41	42	43	44	45	46	47	48	49	50	51	52

Fig. 8.36 | Unshuffled deck array.

Sample shuffled deck array												
	0	1	2	3	4	5	6	7	8	9	10	11	12
0	19	40	27	25	36	46	10	34	35	41	18	2	44
1	13	28	14	16	21	30	8	11	31	17	24	7	1
2	12	33	15	42	43	23	45	3	29	32	4	47	26
3	50	38	52	39	48	51	9	5	37	49	22	6	20

Fig. 8.37 | Sample shuffled deck array.

8.17   (*Simulation: The Tortoise and the Hare*) In this exercise, you'll re-create the classic race of the tortoise and the hare. You'll use random number generation to develop a simulation of this memorable event.

Our contenders begin the race at "square 1" of 70 squares. Each square represents a possible position along the race course. The finish line is at square 70. The first contender to reach or pass square 70 is rewarded with a pail of fresh carrots and lettuce. The course weaves its way up the side of a slippery mountain, so occasionally the contenders lose ground.

There is a clock that ticks once per second. With each tick of the clock, your program should adjust the position of the animals according to the rules in Fig. 8.38.

Use variables to keep track of the positions of the animals (i.e., position numbers are 1–70). Start each animal at position 1 (i.e., the "starting gate"). If an animal slips left before square 1, move the animal back to square 1.

Generate the percentages in the preceding table by producing a random integer i in the range $1 \le i \le 10$. For the tortoise, perform a "fast plod" when $1 \le i \le 5$, a "slip" when $6 \le i \le 7$ or a "slow plod" when $8 \le i \le 10$. Use a similar technique to move the hare.

Begin the race by printing

```
BANG !!!!!
AND THEY'RE OFF !!!!!
```

For each tick of the clock (i.e., each repetition of a loop), print a 70-position line showing the letter T in the tortoise's position and the letter H in the hare's position. Occasionally, the contenders land on the same square. In this case, the tortoise bites the hare and your program should print OUCH!!! beginning at that position. All print positions other than the T, the H or the OUCH!!! (in case of a tie) should be blank.

After printing each line, test whether either animal has reached or passed square 70. If so, print the winner and terminate the simulation. If the tortoise wins, print TORTOISE WINS!!! YAY!!! If the hare wins, print Hare wins. Yuch. If both animals win on the same clock tick, you may want to favor the tortoise (the "underdog"), or you may want to print It's a tie. If neither animal wins, perform the loop again to simulate the next tick of the clock.

Animal	Move type	Percentage of the time	Actual move
Tortoise	Fast plod	50%	3 squares to the right
	Slip	20%	6 squares to the left
	Slow plod	30%	1 square to the right
Hare	Sleep	20%	No move at all
	Big hop	20%	9 squares to the right
	Big slip	10%	12 squares to the left
	Small hop	30%	1 square to the right
	Small slip	20%	2 squares to the left

Fig. 8.38 | Rules for moving the tortoise and the hare.

Special Section: Building Your Own Computer

In the next several problems, we take a temporary diversion away from the world of high-level-language programming. We "peel open" a computer and look at its internal structure. We introduce machine-language programming and write several machine-language programs. To make this an especially valuable experience, we then build a computer (using software-based *simulation*) on which you can execute your machine-language programs!

8.18 (*Machine-Language Programming*) Let us create a computer we'll call the Simpletron. As its name implies, it is a simple machine, but, as we'll soon see, it is a powerful one as well. The Simpletron runs programs written in the only language it directly understands, that is, Simpletron Machine Language, or SML for short.

The Simpletron contains an *accumulator*—a "special register" in which information is put before the Simpletron uses that information in calculations or examines it in various ways. All information in the Simpletron is handled in terms of *words*. A word is a signed four-digit decimal number, such as +3364, -1293, +0007, -0001, etc. The Simpletron is equipped with a 100-word memory, and these words are referenced by their location numbers 00, 01, ..., 99.

Before running an SML program, we must *load,* or place, the program into memory. The first instruction (or statement) of every SML program is always placed in location 00. The simulator will start executing at this location.

Each instruction written in SML occupies one word of the Simpletron's memory; thus, instructions are signed four-digit decimal numbers. Assume that the sign of an SML instruction is always plus, but the sign of a data word may be either plus or minus. Each location in the Simpletron's memory may contain an instruction, a data value used by a program or an unused (and hence undefined) area of memory. The first two digits of each SML instruction are the *operation code* that specifies the operation to be performed. SML operation codes are shown in Fig. 8.39.

Operation code	Meaning
Input/output operations	
const int READ = 10;	Read a word from the keyboard into a specific location in memory.
const int WRITE = 11;	Write a word from a specific location in memory to the screen.
Load and store operations	
const int LOAD = 20;	Load a word from a specific location in memory into the accumulator.
const int STORE = 21;	Store a word from the accumulator into a specific location in memory.
Arithmetic operations	
const int ADD = 30;	Add a word from a specific location in memory to the word in the accumulator (leave result in accumulator).
const int SUBTRACT = 31;	Subtract a word from a specific location in memory from the word in the accumulator (leave result in accumulator).
const int DIVIDE = 32;	Divide a word from a specific location in memory into the word in the accumulator (leave result in accumulator).

Fig. 8.39 | Simpletron Machine Language (SML) operation codes. (Part 1 of 2.)

Operation code	Meaning
const int MULTIPLY = 33;	Multiply a word from a specific location in memory by the word in the accumulator (leave result in accumulator).

Transfer-of-control operations

const int BRANCH = 40;	Branch to a specific location in memory.
const int BRANCHNEG = 41;	Branch to a specific location in memory if the accumulator is negative.
const int BRANCHZERO = 42;	Branch to a specific location in memory if the accumulator is zero.
const int HALT = 43;	Halt—the program has completed its task.

Fig. 8.39 | Simpletron Machine Language (SML) operation codes. (Part 2 of 2.)

The last two digits of an SML instruction are the *operand*—the address of the memory location containing the word to which the operation applies.

Now let us consider two simple SML programs. The first (Fig. 8.40) reads two numbers from the keyboard and computes and prints their sum. The instruction +1007 reads the first number from the keyboard and places it into location 07 (which has been initialized to zero). Instruction +1008 reads the next number into location 08. The *load* instruction, +2007, places (copies) the first number into the accumulator, and the *add* instruction, +3008, adds the second number to the number in the accumulator. *All SML arithmetic instructions leave their results in the accumulator.* The *store* instruction, +2109, places (copies) the result back into memory location 09. Then the *write* instruction, +1109, takes the number and prints it (as a signed four-digit decimal number). The *halt* instruction, +4300, terminates execution.

Location	Number	Instruction
00	+1007	(Read A)
01	+1008	(Read B)
02	+2007	(Load A)
03	+3008	(Add B)
04	+2109	(Store C)
05	+1109	(Write C)
06	+4300	(Halt)
07	+0000	(Variable A)
08	+0000	(Variable B)
09	+0000	(Result C)

Fig. 8.40 | SML Example 1.

The SML program in Fig. 8.41 reads two numbers from the keyboard, then determines and prints the larger value. Note the use of the instruction +4107 as a conditional transfer of control, much the same as C++'s if statement.

Location	Number	Instruction
00	+1009	(Read A)
01	+1010	(Read B)
02	+2009	(Load A)
03	+3110	(Subtract B)
04	+4107	(Branch negative to 07)
05	+1109	(Write A)
06	+4300	(Halt)
07	+1110	(Write B)
08	+4300	(Halt)
09	+0000	(Variable A)
10	+0000	(Variable B)

Fig. 8.41 | SML Example 2.

Now write SML programs to accomplish each of the following tasks:
a) Use a sentinel-controlled loop to read positive numbers and compute and print their sum. Terminate input when a negative number is entered.
b) Use a counter-controlled loop to read seven numbers, some positive and some negative, and compute and print their average.
c) Read a series of numbers, and determine and print the largest number. The first number read indicates how many numbers should be processed.

8.19 (*Computer Simulator*) It may at first seem outrageous, but in this problem you are going to build your own computer. No, you won't be soldering components together. Rather, you'll use the powerful technique of *software-based simulation* to create a *software model* of the Simpletron. You won't be disappointed. Your Simpletron simulator will turn the computer you are using into a Simpletron, and you actually will be able to run, test and debug the SML programs you wrote in Exercise 8.18.

When you run your Simpletron simulator, it should begin by printing

```
*** Welcome to Simpletron! ***

*** Please enter your program one instruction ***
*** (or data word) at a time. I will type the ***
*** location number and a question mark (?).  ***
*** You then type the word for that location. ***
*** Type the sentinel -99999 to stop entering ***
*** your program. ***
```

Your program should simulate the Simpletron's memory with a single-subscripted, 100-element array memory. Now assume that the simulator is running, and let us examine the dialog as we enter the program of Example 2 of Exercise 8.18:

```
00 ? +1009
01 ? +1010
02 ? +2009
03 ? +3110
04 ? +4107
05 ? +1109
06 ? +4300
07 ? +1110
08 ? +4300
09 ? +0000
10 ? +0000
11 ? -99999

*** Program loading completed ***
*** Program execution begins  ***
```

Note that the numbers to the right of each ? in the preceding dialog represent the SML program instructions input by the user.

The SML program has now been placed (or loaded) into array memory. Now the Simpletron executes your SML program. Execution begins with the instruction in location 00 and, like C++, continues sequentially, unless directed to some other part of the program by a transfer of control.

Use variable accumulator to represent the accumulator register. Use variable counter to keep track of the location in memory that contains the instruction being performed. Use variable operationCode to indicate the operation currently being performed (i.e., the left two digits of the instruction word). Use variable operand to indicate the memory location on which the current instruction operates. Thus, operand is the rightmost two digits of the instruction currently being performed. Do not execute instructions directly from memory. Rather, transfer the next instruction to be performed from memory to a variable called instructionRegister. Then "pick off" the left two digits and place them in operationCode, and "pick off" the right two digits and place them in operand. When Simpletron begins execution, the special registers are all initialized to zero.

Now let us "walk through" the execution of the first SML instruction, +1009 in memory location 00. This is called an *instruction execution cycle*.

The counter tells us the location of the next instruction to be performed. We *fetch* the contents of that location from memory by using the C++ statement

```
instructionRegister = memory[ counter ];
```

The operation code and operand are extracted from the instruction register by the statements

```
operationCode = instructionRegister / 100;
operand = instructionRegister % 100;
```

Now, the Simpletron must determine that the operation code is actually a *read* (versus a *write*, a *load*, etc.). A switch differentiates among the 12 operations of SML.

In the switch statement, the behavior of various SML instructions is simulated as shown in Fig. 8.42 (we leave the others to you).

read:	cin >> memory[operand];
load:	accumulator = memory[operand];
add:	accumulator += memory[operand];
branch:	We'll discuss the branch instructions shortly.
halt:	This instruction prints the message *** Simpletron execution terminated ***

Fig. 8.42 | Behavior of SML instructions.

The *halt* instruction also causes the Simpletron to print the name and contents of each register, as well as the complete contents of memory. Such a printout is often called a *register and memory dump*. To help you program your dump function, a sample dump format is shown in Fig. 8.43. Note that a dump after executing a Simpletron program would show the actual values of instructions and data values at the moment execution terminated. To format numbers with their sign as shown in the dump, use stream manipulator `showpos`. To disable the display of the sign, use stream manipulator `noshowpos`. For numbers that have fewer than four digits, you can format numbers with leading zeros between the sign and the value by using the following statement before outputting the value:

```
cout << setfill( '0' ) << internal;
```

Parameterized stream manipulator `setfill` (from header `<iomanip>`) specifies the fill character that will appear between the sign and the value when a number is displayed with a field width of five characters but does not have four digits. (One position in the field width is reserved for the sign.) Stream manipulator `internal` indicates that the fill characters should appear between the sign and the numeric value .

Let us proceed with the execution of our program's first instruction—+1009 in location 00. As we have indicated, the `switch` statement simulates this by performing the C++ statement

```
cin >> memory[ operand ];
```

A question mark (?) should be displayed on the screen before the `cin` statement executes to prompt the user for input. The Simpletron waits for the user to type a value and press the *Enter* key. The value is then read into location 09.

At this point, simulation of the first instruction is complete. All that remains is to prepare the Simpletron to execute the next instruction. The instruction just performed was not a transfer of control, so we need merely increment the instruction counter register as follows:

```
++counter;
```

This completes the simulated execution of the first instruction. The entire process (i.e., the instruction execution cycle) begins anew with the fetch of the next instruction to execute.

```
REGISTERS:
accumulator          +0000
counter                 00
instructionRegister  +0000
operationCode           00
operand                 00

MEMORY:
       0      1      2      3      4      5      6      7      8      9
 0 +0000 +0000 +0000 +0000 +0000 +0000 +0000 +0000 +0000 +0000
10 +0000 +0000 +0000 +0000 +0000 +0000 +0000 +0000 +0000 +0000
20 +0000 +0000 +0000 +0000 +0000 +0000 +0000 +0000 +0000 +0000
30 +0000 +0000 +0000 +0000 +0000 +0000 +0000 +0000 +0000 +0000
40 +0000 +0000 +0000 +0000 +0000 +0000 +0000 +0000 +0000 +0000
50 +0000 +0000 +0000 +0000 +0000 +0000 +0000 +0000 +0000 +0000
60 +0000 +0000 +0000 +0000 +0000 +0000 +0000 +0000 +0000 +0000
70 +0000 +0000 +0000 +0000 +0000 +0000 +0000 +0000 +0000 +0000
80 +0000 +0000 +0000 +0000 +0000 +0000 +0000 +0000 +0000 +0000
90 +0000 +0000 +0000 +0000 +0000 +0000 +0000 +0000 +0000 +0000
```

Fig. 8.43 | A sample register and memory dump.

Now let us consider how to simulate the branching instructions (i.e., the transfers of control). All we need to do is adjust the value in the instruction counter appropriately. Therefore, the unconditional branch instruction (40) is simulated in the `switch` as

```
counter = operand;
```

The conditional "branch if accumulator is zero" instruction is simulated as

```
if ( accumulator == 0 )
    counter = operand;
```

At this point, you should implement your Simpletron simulator and run each of the SML programs you wrote in Exercise 8.18. You may embellish SML with additional features and provide for these in your simulator.

Your simulator should check for various types of errors. During the program loading phase, for example, each number the user types into the Simpletron's memory must be in the range -9999 to +9999. Your simulator should use a `while` loop to test that each number entered is in this range and, if not, keep prompting the user to reenter the number until the user enters a correct number.

During the execution phase, your simulator should check for various serious errors, such as attempts to divide by zero, attempts to execute invalid operation codes, accumulator overflows (i.e., arithmetic operations resulting in values larger than +9999 or smaller than -9999) and the like. Such serious errors are called fatal errors. When a fatal error is detected, your simulator should print an error message such as

```
*** Attempt to divide by zero ***
*** Simpletron execution abnormally terminated ***
```

and should print a full register and memory dump in the format we have discussed previously. This will help the user locate the error in the program.

More Pointer Exercises

8.20   Modify the card shuffling and dealing program of Figs. 8.25–8.27 so the shuffling and dealing operations are performed by the same function (`shuffleAndDeal`). The function should contain one nested looping statement that is similar to function `shuffle` in Fig. 8.26.

8.21   What does this program do?

```
 1   // Ex. 8.21: ex08_21.cpp
 2   // What does this program do?
 3   #include <iostream>
 4   using std::cout;
 5   using std::cin;
 6   using std::endl;
 7
 8   void mystery1( char *, const char * ); // prototype
 9
10   int main()
11   {
12      char string1[ 80 ];
13      char string2[ 80 ];
14
15      cout << "Enter two strings: ";
16      cin >> string1 >> string2;
17      mystery1( string1, string2 );
18      cout << string1 << endl;
19      return 0; // indicates successful termination
20   } // end main
```

```
21
22    // What does this function do?
23    void mystery1( char *s1, const char *s2 )
24    {
25       while ( *s1 != '\0' )
26          s1++;
27
28       for ( ; *s1 = *s2; s1++, s2++ )
29          ; // empty statement
30    } // end function mystery1
```

8.22   What does this program do?

```
 1    // Ex. 8.22: ex08_22.cpp
 2    // What does this program do?
 3    #include <iostream>
 4    using std::cout;
 5    using std::cin;
 6    using std::endl;
 7
 8    int mystery2( const char * ); // prototype
 9
10    int main()
11    {
12       char string1[ 80 ];
13
14       cout << "Enter a string: ";
15       cin >> string1;
16       cout << mystery2( string1 ) << endl;
17       return 0; // indicates successful termination
18    } // end main
19
20    // What does this function do?
21    int mystery2( const char *s )
22    {
23       int x;
24
25       for ( x = 0; *s != '\0'; s++ )
26          x++;
27
28       return x;
29    } // end function mystery2
```

8.23   Find the error in each of the following segments. If the error can be corrected, explain how.

   a) `int *number;`
       `cout << number << endl;`
   b) `double *realPtr;`
       `long *integerPtr;`
       `integerPtr = realPtr;`
   c) `int * x, y;`
       `x = y;`
   d) `char s[] = "this is a character array";`
       `for ( ; *s != '\0'; s++)`
          `cout << *s << ' ';`
   e) `short *numPtr, result;`
       `void *genericPtr = numPtr;`
       `result = *genericPtr + 7;`

f) ```
    double x = 19.34;
    double xPtr = &;
    cout << xPtr << endl;
    ```
g)  ```
    char *s;
    cout << s << endl;
    ```

8.24 (*Quicksort*) You have previously seen the sorting techniques of the bucket sort and selection sort. We now present the recursive sorting technique called Quicksort. The basic algorithm for a single-subscripted array of values is as follows:

    a) *Partitioning Step:* Take the first element of the unsorted array and determine its final location in the sorted array (i.e., all values to the left of the element in the array are less than the element, and all values to the right of the element in the array are greater than the element). We now have one element in its proper location and two unsorted subarrays.

    b) *Recursive Step:* Perform *Step 1* on each unsorted subarray.

Each time *Step 1* is performed on a subarray, another element is placed in its final location of the sorted array, and two unsorted subarrays are created. When a subarray consists of one element, that subarray must be sorted; therefore, that element is in its final location.

    The basic algorithm seems simple enough, but how do we determine the final position of the first element of each subarray? As an example, consider the following set of values (the element in bold is the partitioning element—it will be placed in its final location in the sorted array):

        37 2 6 4 89 8 10 12 68 45

    a) Starting from the rightmost element of the array, compare each element with **37** until an element less than **37** is found. Then swap **37** and that element. The first element less than **37** is 12, so **37** and 12 are swapped. The values now reside in the array as follows:

        12 2 6 4 89 8 10 **37** 68 45

    Element 12 is in italics to indicate that it was just swapped with **37**.

    b) Starting from the left of the array, but beginning with the element after 12, compare each element with **37** until an element greater than **37** is found. Then swap **37** and that element. The first element greater than **37** is 89, so **37** and 89 are swapped. The values now reside in the array as follows:

        12 2 6 4 **37** 8 10 *89* 68 45

    c) Starting from the right, but beginning with the element before 89, compare each element with **37** until an element less than **37** is found. Then swap **37** and that element. The first element less than **37** is 10, so **37** and 10 are swapped. The values now reside in the array as follows:

        12 2 6 4 *10* 8 **37** 89 68 45

    d) Starting from the left, but beginning with the element after 10, compare each element with **37** until an element greater than **37** is found. Then swap **37** and that element. There are no more elements greater than **37**, so when we compare **37** with itself, we know that **37** has been placed in its final location of the sorted array.

Once the partition has been applied to the array, there are two unsorted subarrays. The subarray with values less than 37 contains 12, 2, 6, 4, 10 and 8. The subarray with values greater than 37 contains 89, 68 and 45. The sort continues with both subarrays being partitioned in the same manner as the original array.

    Based on the preceding discussion, write recursive function quickSort to sort a single-subscripted integer array. The function should receive as arguments an integer array, a starting subscript and an ending subscript. Function partition should be called by quickSort to perform the partitioning step.

8.25 (*Maze Traversal*) The grid of hashes (#) and dots (.) in Fig. 8.44 is a two-dimensional array representation of a maze. In the two-dimensional array, the hashes represent the walls of the maze and the dots represent squares in the possible paths through the maze. Moves can be made only to a location in the array that contains a dot.

There is a simple algorithm for walking through a maze that guarantees finding the exit (assuming that there is an exit). If there is not an exit, you'll arrive at the starting location again. Place your right hand on the wall to your right and begin walking forward. Never remove your hand from the wall. If the maze turns to the right, you follow the wall to the right. As long as you do not remove your hand from the wall, eventually you'll arrive at the exit of the maze. There may be a shorter path than the one you have taken, but you are guaranteed to get out of the maze if you follow the algorithm.

Write recursive function mazeTraverse to walk through the maze. The function should receive arguments that include a 12-by-12 character array representing the maze and the starting location of the maze. As mazeTraverse attempts to locate the exit from the maze, it should place the character X in each square in the path. The function should display the maze after each move, so the user can watch as the maze is solved.

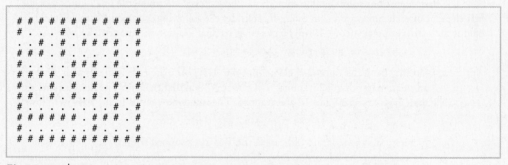

Fig. 8.44 | Two-dimensional array representation of a maze.

8.26 (*Generating Mazes Randomly*) Write a function mazeGenerator that takes as an argument a two-dimensional 12-by-12 character array and randomly produces a maze. The function should also provide the starting and ending locations of the maze. Try your function mazeTraverse from Exercise 8.25, using several randomly generated mazes.

8.27 (*Mazes of Any Size*) Generalize functions mazeTraverse and mazeGenerator of Exercise 8.25 and Exercise 8.26 to process mazes of any width and height.

8.28 (*Modifications to the Simpletron Simulator*) In Exercise 8.19, you wrote a software simulation of a computer that executes programs written in Simpletron Machine Language (SML). In this exercise, we propose several modifications and enhancements to the Simpletron Simulator. In Exercises 20.26–20.27, we propose building a compiler that converts programs written in a high-level programming language (a variation of BASIC) to SML. Some of the following modifications and enhancements may be required to execute the programs produced by the compiler. [*Note:* Some modifications may conflict with others and therefore must be done separately.]

    a) Extend the Simpletron Simulator's memory to contain 1000 memory locations to enable the Simpletron to handle larger programs.

    b) Allow the simulator to perform modulus calculations. This requires an additional Simpletron Machine Language instruction.

    c) Allow the simulator to perform exponentiation calculations. This requires an additional Simpletron Machine Language instruction.

d) Modify the simulator to use hexadecimal values rather than integer values to represent Simpletron Machine Language instructions.

e) Modify the simulator to allow output of a newline. This requires an additional Simpletron Machine Language instruction.

f) Modify the simulator to process floating-point values in addition to integer values.

g) Modify the simulator to handle string input. [*Hint:* Each Simpletron word can be divided into two groups, each holding a two-digit integer. Each two-digit integer represents the ASCII decimal equivalent of a character. Add a machine-language instruction that inputs a string and store the string beginning at a specific Simpletron memory location. The first half of the word at that location will be a count of the number of characters in the string (i.e., the length of the string). Each succeeding half-word contains one ASCII character expressed as two decimal digits. The machine-language instruction converts each character into its ASCII equivalent and assigns it to a half-word.]

h) Modify the simulator to handle output of strings stored in the format of part (g). [*Hint:* Add a machine-language instruction that will print a string beginning at a certain Simpletron memory location. The first half of the word at that location is a count of the number of characters in the string (i.e., the length of the string). Each succeeding half-word contains one ASCII character expressed as two decimal digits. The machine-language instruction checks the length and prints the string by translating each two-digit number into its equivalent character.]

i) Modify the simulator to include instruction SML_DEBUG that prints a memory dump after each instruction executes. Give SML_DEBUG an operation code of 44. The word +4401 turns on debug mode, and +4400 turns off debug mode.

8.29 What does this program do?

```cpp
// Ex. 8.29: ex08_29.cpp
// What does this program do?
#include <iostream>
using std::cout;
using std::cin;
using std::endl;

bool mystery3( const char *, const char * ); // prototype

int main()
{
   char string1[ 80 ], string2[ 80 ];

   cout << "Enter two strings: ";
   cin >> string1 >> string2;
   cout << "The result is " << mystery3( string1, string2 ) << endl;
   return 0; // indicates successful termination
} // end main

// What does this function do?
bool mystery3( const char *s1, const char *s2 )
{
   for ( ; *s1 != '\0' && *s2 != '\0'; s1++, s2++ )

      if ( *s1 != *s2 )
         return false;

   return true;
} // end function mystery3
```

String-Manipulation Exercises

[*Note:* The following exercises should be implemented using C-style, pointer-based strings.]

8.30 Write a program that uses function strcmp to compare two strings input by the user. The program should state whether the first string is less than, equal to or greater than the second string.

8.31 Write a program that uses function strncmp to compare two strings input by the user. The program should input the number of characters to compare. The program should state whether the first string is less than, equal to or greater than the second string.

8.32 Write a program that uses random number generation to create sentences. The program should use four arrays of pointers to char called article, noun, verb and preposition. The program should create a sentence by selecting a word at random from each array in the following order: article, noun, verb, preposition, article and noun. As each word is picked, it should be concatenated to the previous words in a character array that is large enough to hold the entire sentence. The words should be separated by spaces. When the final sentence is output, it should start with a capital letter and end with a period. The program should generate 20 such sentences.

The arrays should be filled as follows: The article array should contain the articles "the", "a", "one", "some" and "any"; the noun array should contain the nouns "boy", "girl", "dog", "town" and "car"; the verb array should contain the verbs "drove", "jumped", "ran", "walked" and "skipped"; the preposition array should contain the prepositions "to", "from", "over", "under" and "on".

After completing the program, modify it to produce a short story consisting of several of these sentences. (How about a random term-paper writer!)

8.33 *(Limericks)* A limerick is a humorous five-line verse in which the first and second lines rhyme with the fifth, and the third line rhymes with the fourth. Using techniques similar to those developed in Exercise 8.32, write a C++ program that produces random limericks. Polishing this program to produce good limericks is a challenging problem, but the result will be worth the effort!

8.34 Write a program that encodes English language phrases into pig Latin. Pig Latin is a form of coded language often used for amusement. Many variations exist in the methods used to form pig Latin phrases. For simplicity, use the following algorithm: To form a pig-Latin phrase from an English-language phrase, tokenize the phrase into words with function strtok. To translate each English word into a pig-Latin word, place the first letter of the English word at the end of the English word and add the letters "ay." Thus, the word "jump" becomes "umpjay," the word "the" becomes "hetay" and the word "computer" becomes "omputercay." Blanks between words remain as blanks. Assume that the English phrase consists of words separated by blanks, there are no punctuation marks and all words have two or more letters. Function printLatinWord should display each word. [*Hint:* Each time a token is found in a call to strtok, pass the token pointer to function printLatinWord and print the pig-Latin word.]

8.35 Write a program that inputs a telephone number as a string in the form (555) 555-5555. The program should use function strtok to extract the area code as a token, the first three digits of the phone number as a token, and the last four digits of the phone number as a token. The seven digits of the phone number should be concatenated into one string. Both the area code and the phone number should be printed.

8.36 Write a program that inputs a line of text, tokenizes the line with function strtok and outputs the tokens in reverse order.

8.37 Use the string-comparison functions discussed in Section 8.13.2 and the techniques for sorting arrays developed in Chapter 7 to write a program that alphabetizes a list of strings. Use the names of 10 towns in your area as data for your program.

8.38 Write two versions of each string-copy and string-concatenation function in Fig. 8.30. The first version should use array subscripting, and the second should use pointers and pointer arithmetic.

8.39 Write two versions of each string-comparison function in Fig. 8.30. The first version should use array subscripting, and the second should use pointers and pointer arithmetic.

8.40 Write two versions of function strlen in Fig. 8.30. The first version should use array subscripting, and the second should use pointers and pointer arithmetic.

Special Section: Advanced String-Manipulation Exercises

The preceding exercises are keyed to the text and designed to test your understanding of fundamental string-manipulation concepts. This section includes a collection of intermediate and advanced string-manipulation exercises. You should find these problems challenging, yet enjoyable. The problems vary considerably in difficulty. Some require an hour or two of program writing and implementation. Others are useful for lab assignments that might require two or three weeks of study and implementation. Some are challenging term projects.

8.41 *(Text Analysis)* The availability of computers with string-manipulation capabilities has resulted in some rather interesting approaches to analyzing the writings of great authors. Much attention has been focused on whether William Shakespeare ever lived. Some scholars believe there is substantial evidence that Francis Bacon, Christopher Marlowe or other authors actually penned the masterpieces attributed to Shakespeare. Researchers have used computers to find similarities in the writings of these authors. This exercise examines three methods for analyzing texts with a computer. Note that thousands of texts, including Shakespeare, are available online at www.gutenberg.org.

a) Write a program that reads several lines of text from the keyboard and prints a table indicating the number of occurrences of each letter of the alphabet in the text. For example, the phrase

```
To be, or not to be: that is the question:
```

contains one "a," two "b's," no "c's," etc.

b) Write a program that reads several lines of text and prints a table indicating the number of one-letter words, two-letter words, three-letter words, etc., appearing in the text. For example, the phrase

```
Whether 'tis nobler in the mind to suffer
```

contains the following word lengths and occurrences:

Word length	Occurrences
1	0
2	2
3	1
4	2 (including 'tis)
5	0
6	2
7	1

c) Write a program that reads several lines of text and prints a table indicating the number of occurrences of each different word in the text. The first version of your program should include the words in the table in the same order in which they appear in the text. For example, the lines

```
To be, or not to be: that is the question:
Whether 'tis nobler in the mind to suffer
```

contain the word "to" three times, the word "be" two times, the word "or" once, etc. A more interesting (and useful) printout should then be attempted in which the words are sorted alphabetically.

8.42 *(Word Processing)* One important function in word-processing systems is *type justification*—the alignment of words to both the left and right margins of a page. This generates a professional-looking document that gives the appearance of being set in type rather than prepared on a typewriter. Type justification can be accomplished on computer systems by inserting blank characters between the words in a line so that the rightmost word aligns with the right margin.

Write a program that reads several lines of text and prints this text in type-justified format. Assume that the text is to be printed on paper 8-1/2 inches wide and that one-inch margins are to be allowed on both the left and right sides. Assume that the computer prints 10 characters to the horizontal inch. Therefore, your program should print 6-1/2 inches of text, or 65 characters per line.

8.43 *(Printing Dates in Various Formats)* Dates are commonly printed in several different formats in business correspondence. Two of the more common formats are

```
07/21/1955
July 21, 1955
```

Write a program that reads a date in the first format and prints that date in the second format.

8.44 *(Check Protection)* Computers are frequently employed in check-writing systems such as payroll and accounts-payable applications. Many strange stories circulate regarding weekly paychecks being printed (by mistake) for amounts in excess of $1 million. Weird amounts are printed by computerized check-writing systems, because of human error or machine failure. Systems designers build controls into their systems to prevent such erroneous checks from being issued.

Another serious problem is the intentional alteration of a check amount by someone who intends to cash a check fraudulently. To prevent a dollar amount from being altered, most computerized check-writing systems employ a technique called *check protection*.

Checks designed for imprinting by computer contain a fixed number of spaces in which the computer may print an amount. Suppose that a paycheck contains eight blank spaces in which the computer is supposed to print the amount of a weekly paycheck. If the amount is large, then all eight of those spaces will be filled, for example,

```
1,230.60    (check amount)
--------
12345678    (position numbers)
```

On the other hand, if the amount is less than $1000, then several of the spaces would ordinarily be left blank. For example,

```
  99.87
--------
12345678
```

contains three blank spaces. If a check is printed with blank spaces, it is easier for someone to alter the amount of the check. To prevent a check from being altered, many check-writing systems insert *leading asterisks* to protect the amount as follows:

```
***99.87
--------
12345678
```

Write a program that inputs a dollar amount to be printed on a check and then prints the amount in check-protected format with leading asterisks if necessary. Assume that nine spaces are available for printing an amount.

8.45 *(Writing the Word Equivalent of a Check Amount)* Continuing the discussion of the previous example, we reiterate the importance of designing check-writing systems to prevent alteration of check amounts. One common security method requires that the check amount be both written in numbers and "spelled out" in words. Even if someone is able to alter the numerical amount of the check, it is extremely difficult to change the amount in words.

Write a program that inputs a numeric check amount and writes the word equivalent of the amount. Your program should be able to handle check amounts as large as $99.99. For example, the amount 112.43 should be written as

```
ONE HUNDRED TWELVE and 43/100
```

8.46 *(Morse Code)* Perhaps the most famous of all coding schemes is the Morse code, developed by Samuel Morse in 1832 for use with the telegraph system. The Morse code assigns a series of dots and dashes to each letter of the alphabet, each digit and a few special characters (such as period, comma, colon and semicolon). In sound-oriented systems, the dot represents a short sound, and the dash represents a long sound. Other representations of dots and dashes are used with light-oriented systems and signal-flag systems.

Separation between words is indicated by a space, or, quite simply, the absence of a dot or dash. In a sound-oriented system, a space is indicated by a short period of time during which no sound is transmitted. The international version of the Morse code appears in Fig. 8.45.

Write a program that reads an English-language phrase and encodes it into Morse code. Also write a program that reads a phrase in Morse code and converts it into the English-language equivalent. Use one blank between each Morse-coded letter and three blanks between each Morse-coded word.

Character	Code	Character	Code
A	.-	N	-.
B	-...	O	---
C	-.-.	P	.--.
D	-..	Q	--.-
E	.	R	.-.
F	..-.	S	...
G	--.	T	-
H	....	U	..-
I	..	V	...-
J	.---	W	.--
K	-.-	X	-..-
L	.-..	Y	-.--
M	--	Z	--..

Fig. 8.45 | Morse code alphabet. (Part 1 of 2.)

Character	Code	Character	Code
Digits			
1	. - - - -	6	- . . . .
2	. . - - -	7	- - . . .
3	. . . - -	8	- - - . .
4	. . . . -	9	- - - - .
5	. . . . .	0	- - - - -

Fig. 8.45 | Morse code alphabet. (Part 2 of 2.)

8.47 *(A Metric Conversion Program)* Write a program that will assist the user with metric conversions. Your program should allow the user to specify the names of the units as strings (i.e., centimeters, liters, grams, etc., for the metric system and inches, quarts, pounds, etc., for the English system) and should respond to simple questions such as

```
"How many inches are in 2 meters?"
"How many liters are in 10 quarts?"
```

Your program should recognize invalid conversions. For example, the question

```
"How many feet are in 5 kilograms?"
```

is not meaningful, because "feet" are units of length, while "kilograms" are units of weight.

A Challenging String-Manipulation Project

8.48 *(A Crossword Puzzle Generator)* Most people have worked a crossword puzzle, but few have ever attempted to generate one. Generating a crossword puzzle is a difficult problem. It is suggested here as a string-manipulation project requiring substantial sophistication and effort. There are many issues that you must resolve to get even the simplest crossword puzzle generator program working. For example, how does one represent the grid of a crossword puzzle inside the computer? Should one use a series of strings, or should two-dimensional arrays be used? You need a source of words (i.e., a computerized dictionary) that can be directly referenced by the program. In what form should these words be stored to facilitate the complex manipulations required by the program? The really ambitious reader will want to generate the "clues" portion of the puzzle, in which the brief hints for each "across" word and each "down" word are printed for the puzzle worker. Merely printing a version of the blank puzzle itself is not a simple problem.

Classes: A Deeper Look, Part I

My object all sublime
I shall achieve in time.
—W. S. Gilbert

Is it a world to hide virtues in?
—William Shakespeare

Don't be "consistent," but be simply true.
—Oliver Wendell Holmes, Jr.

This above all: to thine own self be true.
—William Shakespeare

OBJECTIVES

In this chapter you'll learn:

- How to use a preprocessor wrapper to prevent multiple definition errors caused by including more than one copy of a header file in a source-code file.

- To understand class scope and accessing class members via the name of an object, a reference to an object or a pointer to an object.

- To define constructors with default arguments.

- How destructors are used to perform "termination housekeeping" on an object before it is destroyed.

- When constructors and destructors are called and the order in which they are called.

- The logic errors that may occur when a **public** member function of a class returns a reference to **private** data.

- To assign the data members of one object to those of another object by default memberwise assignment.

9.1 Introduction

In the preceding chapters, we introduced many basic terms and concepts of C++ object-oriented programming. We also discussed our program development methodology: We selected appropriate attributes and behaviors for each class and specified the manner in which objects of our classes collaborated with objects of C++ Standard Library classes to accomplish each program's overall goals.

In this chapter, we take a deeper look at classes. We use an integrated Time class case study in both this chapter (three examples) and Chapter 10, Classes: A Deeper Look, Part 2 (two examples) to demonstrate several class construction capabilities. We begin with a Time class that reviews several of the features presented in the preceding chapters. The example also demonstrates an important C++ software engineering concept—using a "preprocessor wrapper" in header files to prevent the code in the header from being included into the same source code file more than once. Since a class can be defined only once, using such preprocessor directives prevents multiple definition errors.

Next, we discuss class scope and the relationships among members of a class. We also demonstrate how client code can access a class's public members via three types of "handles"—the name of an object, a reference to an object or a pointer to an object. As you'll see, object names and references can be used with the dot (.) member selection operator to access a public member, and pointers can be used with the arrow (->) member selection operator.

We discuss access functions that can read or display data in an object. A common use of access functions is to test the truth or falsity of conditions—such functions are known as predicate functions. We also demonstrate the notion of a utility function (also called a helper function)—a private member function that supports the operation of the class's public member functions, but is not intended for use by clients of the class.

In the second example of the Time class case study, we demonstrate how to pass arguments to constructors and show how default arguments can be used in a constructor to enable client code to initialize objects of a class using a variety of arguments. Next, we discuss a special member function called a destructor that is part of every class and is used to perform "termination housekeeping" on an object before the object is destroyed. We then demonstrate the order in which constructors and destructors are called, because your programs' correctness depends on using properly initialized objects that have not yet been destroyed.

Our last example of the Time class case study in this chapter shows a dangerous programming practice in which a member function returns a reference to private data. We discuss how this breaks the encapsulation of a class and allows client code to directly access an object's data. This last example shows that objects of the same class can be assigned to one another using default memberwise assignment, which copies the data members in the object on the right side of the assignment into the corresponding data members of the object on the left side of the assignment. The chapter concludes with a discussion of software reusability.

9.2 Time Class Case Study

Our first example (Figs. 9.1–9.3) creates class Time and a driver program that tests the class. You have already created many classes in this book. In this section, we review many of the concepts covered in Chapter 3 and demonstrate an important C++ software engineering concept—using a "preprocessor wrapper" in header files to prevent the code in the header from being included into the same source code file more than once. Since a class can be defined only once, using such preprocessor directives prevents multiple-definition errors.

```
1   // Fig. 9.1: Time.h
2   // Declaration of class Time.
3   // Member functions are defined in Time.cpp
4
5   // prevent multiple inclusions of header file
6   #ifndef TIME_H
7   #define TIME_H
8
9   // Time class definition
10  class Time
11  {
12  public:
13     Time(); // constructor
14     void setTime( int, int, int ); // set hour, minute and second
15     void printUniversal(); // print time in universal-time format
16     void printStandard(); // print time in standard-time format
17  private:
18     int hour; // 0 - 23 (24-hour clock format)
19     int minute; // 0 - 59
20     int second; // 0 - 59
21  }; // end class Time
22
23  #endif
```

Fig. 9.1 | Time class definition.

Time Class Definition

The class definition (Fig. 9.1) contains prototypes (lines 13–16) for member functions Time, setTime, printUniversal and printStandard. The class includes private integer members hour, minute and second (lines 18–20). Class Time's private data members can be accessed only by its four member functions. Chapter 12 introduces a third access specifier, protected, as we study inheritance and the part it plays in object-oriented programming.

Good Programming Practice 9.1

For clarity and readability, use each access specifier only once in a class definition. Place public members first, where they are easy to locate.

Software Engineering Observation 9.1

Each element of a class should have private visibility unless it can be proven that the element needs public visibility. This is another example of the principle of least privilege.

In Fig. 9.1, note that the class definition is enclosed in the following preprocessor wrapper (lines 6, 7 and 23):

```
// prevent multiple inclusions of header file
#ifndef TIME_H
#define TIME_H
   ...
#endif
```

When we build larger programs, other definitions and declarations will also be placed in header files. The preceding preprocessor wrapper prevents the code between #ifndef (which means "if not defined") and #endif from being included if the name TIME_H has been defined. If the header has not been included previously in a file, the name TIME_H is defined by the #define directive and the header file statements are included. If the header has been included previously, TIME_H is defined already and the header file is not included again. Attempts to include a header file multiple times (inadvertently) typically occur in large programs with many header files that may themselves include other header files. [*Note:* The commonly used convention for the symbolic constant name in the preprocessor directives is simply the header file name in upper case with the underscore character replacing the period.]

Error-Prevention Tip 9.1

Use #ifndef, #define and #endif preprocessor directives to form a preprocessor wrapper that prevents header files from being included more than once in a program.

Good Programming Practice 9.2

Use the name of the header file in upper case with the period replaced by an underscore in the #ifndef and #define preprocessor directives of a header file.

Time Class Member Functions

In Fig. 9.2, the Time constructor (lines 14–17) initializes the data members to 0 (i.e., the universal-time equivalent of 12 AM). This ensures that the object begins in a consistent state. Invalid values cannot be stored in the data members of a Time object, because the constructor is called when the Time object is created, and all subsequent attempts by a client to modify

```cpp
1   // Fig. 9.2: Time.cpp
2   // Member-function definitions for class Time.
3   #include <iostream>
4   using std::cout;
5
6   #include <iomanip>
7   using std::setfill;
8   using std::setw;
9
10  #include "Time.h" // include definition of class Time from Time.h
11
12  // Time constructor initializes each data member to zero.
13  // Ensures all Time objects start in a consistent state.
14  Time::Time()
15  {
16     hour = minute = second = 0;
17  } // end Time constructor
18
19  // set new Time value using universal time; ensure that
20  // the data remains consistent by setting invalid values to zero
21  void Time::setTime( int h, int m, int s )
22  {
23     hour = ( h >= 0 && h < 24 ) ? h : 0; // validate hour
24     minute = ( m >= 0 && m < 60 ) ? m : 0; // validate minute
25     second = ( s >= 0 && s < 60 ) ? s : 0; // validate second
26  } // end function setTime
27
28  // print Time in universal-time format (HH:MM:SS)
29  void Time::printUniversal()
30  {
31     cout << setfill( '0' ) << setw( 2 ) << hour << ":"
32        << setw( 2 ) << minute << ":" << setw( 2 ) << second;
33  } // end function printUniversal
34
35  // print Time in standard-time format (HH:MM:SS AM or PM)
36  void Time::printStandard()
37  {
38     cout << ( ( hour == 0 || hour == 12 ) ? 12 : hour % 12 ) << ":"
39        << setfill( '0' ) << setw( 2 ) << minute << ":" << setw( 2 )
40        << second << ( hour < 12 ? " AM" : " PM" );
41  } // end function printStandard
```

Fig. 9.2 | Time class member-function definitions.

the data members are scrutinized by function setTime (discussed shortly). Finally, it is important to note that you can define several overloaded constructors for a class.

The data members of a class cannot be initialized where they are declared in the class body. It is strongly recommended that these data members be initialized by the class's constructor (as there is no default initialization for fundamental-type data members). Data members can also be assigned values by Time's *set* functions. [*Note:* Chapter 10 demonstrates that only a class's static const data members of integral or enum types can be initialized in the class's body.]

Common Programming Error 9.1

Attempting to initialize a non-static data member of a class explicitly in the class definition is a syntax error.

Function `setTime` (lines 21–26) is a `public` function that declares three `int` parameters and uses them to set the time. A conditional expression tests each argument to determine whether the value is in a specified range. For example, the hour value (line 23) must be greater than or equal to 0 and less than 24, because the universal-time format represents hours as integers from 0 to 23 (e.g., 1 PM is hour 13 and 11 PM is hour 23; midnight is hour 0 and noon is hour 12). Similarly, both `minute` and `second` values (lines 24 and 25) must be greater than or equal to 0 and less than 60. Any values outside these ranges are set to zero to ensure that a `Time` object always contains consistent data—that is, the object's data values are always kept in range, even if the values provided as arguments to function `setTime` were incorrect. In this example, zero is a consistent value for `hour`, `minute` and `second`.

A value passed to `setTime` is a correct value if it is in the allowed range for the member it is initializing. So, any number in the range 0–23 would be a correct value for the `hour`. A correct value is always a consistent value. However, a consistent value is not necessarily a correct value. If `setTime` sets `hour` to 0 because the argument received was out of range, then `hour` is correct only if the current time is coincidentally midnight.

Function `printUniversal` (lines 29–33 of Fig. 9.2) takes no arguments and outputs the time in universal-time format, consisting of three colon-separated pairs of digits—for the hour, minute and second, respectively. For example, if the time were 1:30:07 PM, function `printUniversal` would return `13:30:07`. Note that line 31 uses parameterized stream manipulator `setfill` to specify the fill character that is displayed when an integer is output in a field wider than the number of digits in the value. By default, the fill characters appear to the left of the digits in the number. In this example, if the `minute` value is 2, it will be displayed as 02, because the fill character is set to zero (`'0'`). If the number being output fills the specified field, the fill character will not be displayed. Note that, once the fill character is specified with `setfill`, it applies for all subsequent values that are displayed in fields wider than the value being displayed (i.e., `setfill` is a "sticky" setting). This is in contrast to `setw`, which applies only to the next value displayed (`setw` is a "nonsticky" setting).

Error-Prevention Tip 9.2

Each sticky setting (such as a fill character or floating-point precision) should be restored to its previous setting when it is no longer needed. Failure to do so may result in incorrectly formatted output later in a program. Chapter 15, Stream Input/Output, discusses how to reset the fill character and precision.

Function `printStandard` (lines 36–41) takes no arguments and outputs the date in standard-time format, consisting of the `hour`, `minute` and `second` values separated by colons and followed by an AM or PM indicator (e.g., `1:27:06 PM`). Like function `printUniversal`, function `printStandard` uses `setfill( '0' )` to format the `minute` and `second` as two digit values with leading zeros if necessary. Line 38 uses the conditional operator (?:) to determine the value of `hour` to be displayed—if the hour is 0 or 12 (AM or PM), it appears as 12; otherwise, the `hour` appears as a value from 1 to 11. The conditional operator in line 40 determines whether AM or PM will be displayed.

Defining Member Functions Outside the Class Definition; Class Scope

Even though a member function declared in a class definition may be defined outside that class definition (and "tied" to the class via the binary scope resolution operator), that member function is still within that class's scope; i.e., its name is known only to other members of the class unless referred to via an object of the class, a reference to an object of the class, a pointer to an object of the class or the binary scope resolution operator. We'll say more about class scope shortly.

If a member function is defined in the body of a class definition, the compiler attempts to inline calls to the member function. Member functions defined outside a class definition can be inlined by explicitly using keyword `inline`. Remember that the compiler reserves the right not to inline any function.

Performance Tip 9.1

Defining a member function inside the class definition inlines the member function (if the compiler chooses to do so). This can improve performance.

Software Engineering Observation 9.2

Defining a small member function inside the class definition does not promote the best software engineering, because clients of the class will be able to see the implementation of the function, and the client code must be recompiled if the function definition changes.

Software Engineering Observation 9.3

Only the simplest and most stable member functions (i.e., whose implementations are unlikely to change) should be defined in the class header.

Member Functions vs. Global Functions

It is interesting that the `printUniversal` and `printStandard` member functions take no arguments. This is because these member functions implicitly know that they are to print the data members of the particular `Time` object for which they are invoked. This can make member function calls more concise than conventional function calls in procedural programming.

Software Engineering Observation 9.4

Using an object-oriented programming approach can often simplify function calls by reducing the number of parameters to be passed. This benefit of object-oriented programming derives from the fact that encapsulating data members and member functions within an object gives the member functions the right to access the data members.

Software Engineering Observation 9.5

Member functions are usually shorter than functions in non-object-oriented programs, because the data stored in data members have ideally been validated by a constructor or by member functions that store new data. Because the data is already in the object, the member-function calls often have no arguments or fewer arguments than typical function calls in non-object-oriented languages. Thus, the calls are shorter, the function definitions are shorter and the function prototypes are shorter. This improves many aspects of program development.

Error-Prevention Tip 9.3

The fact that member function calls generally take either no arguments or substantially fewer arguments than conventional function calls in non-object-oriented languages reduces the likelihood of passing the wrong arguments, the wrong types of arguments or the wrong number of arguments.

Using Class Time

Once class `Time` has been defined, it can be used as a type in object, array, pointer and reference declarations as follows:

```
Time sunset; // object of type Time
Time arrayOfTimes[ 5 ], // array of 5 Time objects
Time &dinnerTime = sunset; // reference to a Time object
Time *timePtr = &dinnerTime, // pointer to a Time object
```

Figure 9.3 uses class `Time`. Line 12 instantiates a single object of class `Time` called `t`. When the object is instantiated, the `Time` constructor is called to initialize each `private` data member to 0. Then, lines 16 and 18 print the time in universal and standard formats, respectively, to confirm that the members were initialized properly. Line 20 sets a new time by calling member function `setTime`, and lines 24 and 26 print the time again in both formats. Line 28 attempts to use `setTime` to set the data members to invalid values— function `setTime` recognizes this and sets the invalid values to 0 to maintain the object in a consistent state. Finally, lines 33 and 35 print the time again in both formats.

Looking Ahead to Composition and Inheritance

Often, classes do not have to be created "from scratch." Rather, they can include objects of other classes as members or they may be derived from other classes that provide attributes and behaviors the new classes can use. Such software reuse can greatly enhance programmer productivity and simplify code maintenance. Including class objects as members of other classes is called composition (or aggregation) and is discussed in Chapter 10. Deriving new classes from existing classes is called inheritance and is discussed in Chapter 12.

Object Size

People new to object-oriented programming often suppose that objects must be quite large because they contain data members and member functions. Logically, this is true—you may think of objects as containing data and functions (and our discussion has certainly encouraged this view); physically, however, this is not true.

Performance Tip 9.2

Objects contain only data, so objects are much smaller than if they also contained member functions. Applying operator `sizeof` to a class name or to an object of that class will report only the size of the class's data members. The compiler creates one copy (only) of the member functions separate from all objects of the class. All objects of the class share this one copy. Each object, of course, needs its own copy of the class's data, because the data can vary among the objects. The function code is nonmodifiable (also called reentrant code or pure procedure) and, hence, can be shared among all objects of one class.

9.3 Class Scope and Accessing Class Members

A class's data members (variables declared in the class definition) and member functions (functions declared in the class definition) belong to that class's scope. Nonmember functions are defined at file scope.

Within a class's scope, class members are immediately accessible by all of that class's member functions and can be referenced by name. Outside a class's scope, `public` class members are referenced through one of the handles on an object—an object name, a reference to an object or a pointer to an object. The type of the object, reference or pointer

```cpp
1   // Fig. 9.3: fig09_03.cpp
2   // Program to test class Time.
3   // NOTE: This file must be compiled with Time.cpp.
4   #include <iostream>
5   using std::cout;
6   using std::endl;
7
8   #include "Time.h" // include definition of class Time from Time.h
9
10  int main()
11  {
12     Time t; // instantiate object t of class Time
13
14     // output Time object t's initial values
15     cout << "The initial universal time is ";
16     t.printUniversal(); // 00:00:00
17     cout << "\nThe initial standard time is ";
18     t.printStandard(); // 12:00:00 AM
19
20     t.setTime( 13, 27, 6 ); // change time
21
22     // output Time object t's new values
23     cout << "\n\nUniversal time after setTime is ";
24     t.printUniversal(); // 13:27:06
25     cout << "\nStandard time after setTime is ";
26     t.printStandard(); // 1:27:06 PM
27
28     t.setTime( 99, 99, 99 ); // attempt invalid settings
29
30     // output t's values after specifying invalid values
31     cout << "\n\nAfter attempting invalid settings:"
32        << "\nUniversal time: ";
33     t.printUniversal(); // 00:00:00
34     cout << "\nStandard time: ";
35     t.printStandard(); // 12:00:00 AM
36     cout << endl;
37     return 0;
38  } // end main
```

```
The initial universal time is 00:00:00
The initial standard time is 12:00:00 AM

Universal time after setTime is 13:27:06
Standard time after setTime is 1:27:06 PM

After attempting invalid settings:
Universal time: 00:00:00
Standard time: 12:00:00 AM
```

Fig. 9.3 | Program to test class Time.

specifies the interface (i.e., the member functions) accessible to the client. [We'll see in Chapter 10 that an implicit handle is inserted by the compiler on every reference to a data member or member function from within an object.]

Member functions of a class can be overloaded, but only by other member functions of that class. To overload a member function, simply provide in the class definition a prototype for each version of the overloaded function, and provide a separate function definition for each version of the function.

Variables declared in a member function have block scope and are known only to that function. If a member function defines a variable with the same name as a variable with class scope, the class-scope variable is hidden by the block-scope variable in the block scope. Such a hidden variable can be accessed by preceding the variable name with the class name followed by the scope resolution operator (::). Hidden global variables can be accessed with the unary scope resolution operator (see Chapter 6).

The dot member selection operator (.) is preceded by an object's name or with a reference to an object to access the object's members. The arrow member selection operator (->) is preceded by a pointer to an object to access the object's members.

Figure 9.4 uses a simple class called Count (lines 8–25) with private data member x of type int (line 24), public member function setX (lines 12–15) and public member function print (lines 18–21) to illustrate accessing the members of a class with the member-selection operators. For simplicity, we have included this small class in the same file as the main function that uses it. Lines 29–31 create three variables related to type Count—counter (a Count object), counterPtr (a pointer to a Count object) and counterRef (a reference to a Count object). Variable counterRef refers to counter, and variable counterPtr points to counter. In lines 34–35 and 38–39, note that the program can invoke member functions setX and print by using the dot (.) member selection operator preceded by either the name of the object (counter) or a reference to the object (counterRef, which is an alias for counter). Similarly, lines 42–43 demonstrate that the program can invoke member functions setX and print by using a pointer (countPtr) and the arrow (->) member-selection operator.

9.4 Separating Interface from Implementation

In Chapter 3, we began by including a class's definition and member-function definitions in one file. We then demonstrated separating this code into two files—a header file for the class definition (i.e., the class's interface) and a source code file for the class's member-function definitions (i.e., the class's implementation). Recall that this makes it easier to modify programs—as far as clients of a class are concerned, changes in the class's implementation do not affect the client as long as the class's interface originally provided to the client remains unchanged.

Software Engineering Observation 9.6

Clients of a class do not need access to the class's source code in order to use the class. The clients do, however, need to be able to link to the class's object code (i.e., the compiled version of the class). This encourages independent software vendors (ISVs) to provide class libraries for sale or license. The ISVs provide in their products only the header files and the object modules. No proprietary information is revealed—as would be the case if source code were provided. The C++ user community benefits by having more ISV-produced class libraries available.

Actually, things are not quite this rosy. Header files do contain some portions of the implementation and hints about others. Inline member functions, for example, need to be in a header file, so that when the compiler compiles a client, the client can include the

```
1   // Fig. 9.4: fig09_04.cpp
2   // Demonstrating the class member access operators . and ->
3   #include <iostream>
4   using std::cout;
5   using std::endl;
6
7   // class Count definition
8   class Count
9   {
10  public: // public data is dangerous
11     // sets the value of private data member x
12     void setX( int value )
13     {
14        x = value;
15     } // end function setX
16
17     // prints the value of private data member x
18     void print()
19     {
20        cout << x << endl;
21     } // end function print
22
23  private:
24     int x;
25  }; // end class Count
26
27  int main()
28  {
29     Count counter; // create counter object
30     Count *counterPtr = &counter; // create pointer to counter
31     Count &counterRef = counter; // create reference to counter
32
33     cout << "Set x to 1 and print using the object's name: ";
34     counter.setX( 1 ); // set data member x to 1
35     counter.print(); // call member function print
36
37     cout << "Set x to 2 and print using a reference to an object: ";
38     counterRef.setX( 2 ); // set data member x to 2
39     counterRef.print(); // call member function print
40
41     cout << "Set x to 3 and print using a pointer to an object: ";
42     counterPtr->setX( 3 ); // set data member x to 3
43     counterPtr->print(); // call member function print
44     return 0;
45  } // end main
```

```
Set x to 1 and print using the object's name: 1
Set x to 2 and print using a reference to an object: 2
Set x to 3 and print using a pointer to an object: 3
```

Fig. 9.4 | Accessing an object's member functions through each type of object handle—the object's name, a reference to the object and a pointer to the object.

inline function definition in place. A class's `private` members are listed in the class definition in the header file, so these members are visible to clients even though the clients may not access the `private` members. In Chapter 10, we show how to use a "proxy class" to hide even the `private` data of a class from clients of the class.

> **Software Engineering Observation 9.7**
>
> *Information important to the interface of a class should be included in the header file. Information that will be used only internally in the class and will not be needed by clients of the class should be included in the unpublished source file. This is yet another example of the principle of least privilege.*

9.5 Access Functions and Utility Functions

Access functions can read or display data. Another common use for access functions is to test the truth or falsity of conditions—such functions are often called predicate functions. An example of a predicate function would be an `isEmpty` function for any container class—a class capable of holding many objects—such as a linked list, a stack or a queue. A program might test `isEmpty` before attempting to read another item from the container object. An `isFull` predicate function might test a container-class object to determine whether it has no additional room. Useful predicate functions for our `Time` class might be `isAM` and `isPM`.

The program of Figs. 9.5–9.7 demonstrates the notion of a utility function (also called a helper function). A utility function is not part of a class's `public` interface; rather, it is a `private` member function that supports the operation of the class's `public` member functions. Utility functions are not intended to be used by clients of a class (but can be used by friends of a class, as we'll see in Chapter 10).

Class `SalesPerson` (Fig. 9.5) declares an array of 12 monthly sales figures (line 16) and the prototypes for the class's constructor and member functions that manipulate the array.

In Fig. 9.6, the `SalesPerson` constructor (lines 15–19) initializes array `sales` to zero. The `public` member function `setSales` (lines 36–43) sets the sales figure for one month

```
1   // Fig. 9.5: SalesPerson.h
2   // SalesPerson class definition.
3   // Member functions defined in SalesPerson.cpp.
4   #ifndef SALESP_H
5   #define SALESP_H
6
7   class SalesPerson
8   {
9   public:
10     SalesPerson(); // constructor
11     void getSalesFromUser(); // input sales from keyboard
12     void setSales( int, double ); // set sales for a specific month
13     void printAnnualSales(); // summarize and print sales
14   private:
15     double totalAnnualSales(); // prototype for utility function
16     double sales[ 12 ]; // 12 monthly sales figures
17   }; // end class SalesPerson
18
19   #endif
```

Fig. 9.5 | `SalesPerson` class definition.

```cpp
1   // Fig. 9.6: SalesPerson.cpp
2   // SalesPerson class member-function definitions.
3   #include <iostream>
4   using std::cout;
5   using std::cin;
6   using std::endl;
7   using std::fixed;
8
9   #include <iomanip>
10  using std::setprecision;
11
12  #include "SalesPerson.h" // include SalesPerson class definition
13
14  // initialize elements of array sales to 0.0
15  SalesPerson::SalesPerson()
16  {
17     for ( int i = 0; i < 12; i++ )
18        sales[ i ] = 0.0;
19  } // end SalesPerson constructor
20
21  // get 12 sales figures from the user at the keyboard
22  void SalesPerson::getSalesFromUser()
23  {
24     double salesFigure;
25
26     for ( int i = 1; i <= 12; i++ )
27     {
28        cout << "Enter sales amount for month " << i << ": ";
29        cin >> salesFigure;
30        setSales( i, salesFigure );
31     } // end for
32  } // end function getSalesFromUser
33
34  // set one of the 12 monthly sales figures; function subtracts
35  // one from month value for proper subscript in sales array
36  void SalesPerson::setSales( int month, double amount )
37  {
38     // test for valid month and amount values
39     if ( month >= 1 && month <= 12 && amount > 0 )
40        sales[ month - 1 ] = amount; // adjust for subscripts 0-11
41     else // invalid month or amount value
42        cout << "Invalid month or sales figure" << endl;
43  } // end function setSales
44
45  // print total annual sales (with the help of utility function)
46  void SalesPerson::printAnnualSales()
47  {
48     cout << setprecision( 2 ) << fixed
49        << "\nThe total annual sales are: $"
50        << totalAnnualSales() << endl; // call utility function
51  } // end function printAnnualSales
52
```

Fig. 9.6 | SalesPerson class member-function definitions. (Part 1 of 2.)

```
53   // private utility function to total annual sales
54   double SalesPerson::totalAnnualSales()
55   {
56      double total = 0.0; // initialize total
57
58      for ( int i = 0; i < 12; i++ ) // summarize sales results
59         total += sales[ i ]; // add month i sales to total
60
61      return total;
62   } // end function totalAnnualSales
```

Fig. 9.6 | `SalesPerson` class member-function definitions. (Part 2 of 2.)

in array `sales`. The `public` member function `printAnnualSales` (lines 46–51) prints the total sales for the last 12 months. The `private` utility function `totalAnnualSales` (lines 54–62) totals the 12 monthly sales figures for the benefit of `printAnnualSales`. Member function `printAnnualSales` edits the sales figures into monetary format.

In Fig. 9.7, notice that the application's `main` function includes only a simple sequence of member-function calls—there are no control statements. The logic of manipulating the `sales` array is completely encapsulated in class `SalesPerson`'s member functions.

Software Engineering Observation 9.8

A phenomenon of object-oriented programming is that once a class is defined, creating and manipulating objects of that class often involve issuing only a simple sequence of member-function calls—few, if any, control statements are needed. By contrast, it is common to have control statements in the implementation of a class's member functions.

9.6 Time Class Case Study: Constructors with Default Arguments

The program of Figs. 9.8–9.10 enhances class `Time` to demonstrate how arguments are implicitly passed to a constructor. The constructor defined in Fig. 9.2 initialized hour,

```
1    // Fig. 9.7: fig09_07.cpp
2    // Utility function demonstration.
3    // Compile this program with SalesPerson.cpp
4
5    // include SalesPerson class definition from SalesPerson.h
6    #include "SalesPerson.h"
7
8    int main()
9    {
10      SalesPerson s; // create SalesPerson object s
11
12      s.getSalesFromUser(); // note simple sequential code; there are
13      s.printAnnualSales(); // no control statements in main
14      return 0;
15   } // end main
```

Fig. 9.7 | Utility function demonstration. (Part 1 of 2.)

```
Enter sales amount for month 1: 5314.76
Enter sales amount for month 2: 4292.38
Enter sales amount for month 3: 4589.83
Enter sales amount for month 4: 5534.03
Enter sales amount for month 5: 4376.34
Enter sales amount for month 6: 5698.45
Enter sales amount for month 7: 4439.22
Enter sales amount for month 8: 5893.57
Enter sales amount for month 9: 4909.67
Enter sales amount for month 10: 5123.45
Enter sales amount for month 11: 4024.97
Enter sales amount for month 12: 5923.92

The total annual sales are: $60120.59
```

Fig. 9.7 | Utility function demonstration. (Part 2 of 2.)

```cpp
1   // Fig. 9.8: Time.h
2   // Time class containing a constructor with default arguments.
3   // Member functions defined in Time.cpp.
4
5   // prevent multiple inclusions of header file
6   #ifndef TIME_H
7   #define TIME_H
8
9   // Time abstract data type definition
10  class Time
11  {
12  public:
13     Time( int = 0, int = 0, int = 0 ); // default constructor
14
15     // set functions
16     void setTime( int, int, int ); // set hour, minute, second
17     void setHour( int ); // set hour (after validation)
18     void setMinute( int ); // set minute (after validation)
19     void setSecond( int ); // set second (after validation)
20
21     // get functions
22     int getHour(); // return hour
23     int getMinute(); // return minute
24     int getSecond(); // return second
25
26     void printUniversal(); // output time in universal-time format
27     void printStandard(); // output time in standard-time format
28  private:
29     int hour; // 0 - 23 (24-hour clock format)
30     int minute; // 0 - 59
31     int second; // 0 - 59
32  }; // end class Time
33
34  #endif
```

Fig. 9.8 | Time class containing a constructor with default arguments.

minute and second to 0 (i.e., midnight in universal time). Like other functions, constructors can specify default arguments. Line 13 of Fig. 9.8 declares the Time constructor to include default arguments, specifying a default value of zero for each argument passed to the
constructor. In Fig. 9.9, lines 14–17 define the new version of the Time constructor that

```cpp
 1   // Fig. 9.9: Time.cpp
 2   // Member-function definitions for class Time.
 3   #include <iostream>
 4   using std::cout;
 5
 6   #include <iomanip>
 7   using std::setfill;
 8   using std::setw;
 9
10   #include "Time.h" // include definition of class Time from Time.h
11
12   // Time constructor initializes each data member to zero;
13   // ensures that Time objects start in a consistent state
14   Time::Time( int hr, int min, int sec )
15   {
16      setTime( hr, min, sec ); // validate and set time
17   } // end Time constructor
18
19   // set new Time value using universal time; ensure that
20   // the data remains consistent by setting invalid values to zero
21   void Time::setTime( int h, int m, int s )
22   {
23      setHour( h ); // set private field hour
24      setMinute( m ); // set private field minute
25      setSecond( s ); // set private field second
26   } // end function setTime
27
28   // set hour value
29   void Time::setHour( int h )
30   {
31      hour = ( h >= 0 && h < 24 ) ? h : 0; // validate hour
32   } // end function setHour
33
34   // set minute value
35   void Time::setMinute( int m )
36   {
37      minute = ( m >= 0 && m < 60 ) ? m : 0; // validate minute
38   } // end function setMinute
39
40   // set second value
41   void Time::setSecond( int s )
42   {
43      second = ( s >= 0 && s < 60 ) ? s : 0; // validate second
44   } // end function setSecond
45
```

Fig. 9.9 | Time class member-function definitions including a constructor that takes arguments.
(Part I of 2.)

```
46    // return hour value
47    int Time::getHour()
48    {
49       return hour;
50    } // end function getHour
51
52    // return minute value
53    int Time::getMinute()
54    {
55       return minute;
56    } // end function getMinute
57
58    // return second value
59    int Time::getSecond()
60    {
61       return second;
62    } // end function getSecond
63
64    // print Time in universal-time format (HH:MM:SS)
65    void Time::printUniversal()
66    {
67       cout << setfill( '0' ) << setw( 2 ) << getHour() << ":"
68          << setw( 2 ) << getMinute() << ":" << setw( 2 ) << getSecond();
69    } // end function printUniversal
70
71    // print Time in standard-time format (HH:MM:SS AM or PM)
72    void Time::printStandard()
73    {
74       cout << ( ( getHour() == 0 || getHour() == 12 ) ? 12 : getHour() % 12 )
75          << ":" << setfill( '0' ) << setw( 2 ) << getMinute()
76          << ":" << setw( 2 ) << getSecond() << ( hour < 12 ? " AM" : " PM" );
77    } // end function printStandard
```

Fig. 9.9 | Time class member-function definitions including a constructor that takes arguments. (Part 2 of 2.)

receives values for parameters hr, min and sec that will be used to initialize private data members hour, minute and second, respectively. Note that class Time provides *set* and *get* functions for each data member. The Time constructor now calls setTime, which calls the setHour, setMinute and setSecond functions to validate and assign values to the data members. The default arguments to the constructor ensure that, even if no values are provided in a constructor call, the constructor still initializes the data members to maintain the Time object in a consistent state. A constructor that defaults all its arguments is also a default constructor—i.e., a constructor that can be invoked with no arguments. There can be at most one default constructor per class.

In Fig. 9.9, line 16 of the constructor calls member function setTime with the values passed to the constructor (or the default values). Function setTime calls setHour to ensure that the value supplied for hour is in the range 0–23, then calls setMinute and setSecond to ensure that the values for minute and second are each in the range 0–59. If a value is out of range, that value is set to zero (to ensure that each data member remains in a consistent state). In Chapter 16, Exception Handling, we throw exceptions when a value is out of range, rather than simply assigning a default consistent value.

Note that the `Time` constructor could be written to include the same statements as member function `setTime`, or even the individual statements in the `setHour`, `setMinute` and `setSecond` functions. Calling `setHour`, `setMinute` and `setSecond` from the constructor may be slightly more efficient because the extra call to `setTime` would be eliminated. Similarly, copying the code from lines 31, 37 and 43 into constructor would eliminate the overhead of calling `setTime`, `setHour`, `setMinute` and `setSecond`. Coding the `Time` constructor or member function `setTime` as a copy of the code in lines 31, 37 and 43 would make maintenance of this class more difficult. If the implementations of `setHour`, `setMinute` and `setSecond` were to change, the implementation of any member function that duplicates lines 31, 37 and 43 would have to change accordingly. Having the `Time` constructor call `setTime` and having `setTime` call `setHour`, `setMinute` and `setSecond` enables us to limit the changes to code that validates the `hour`, `minute` or `second` to the corresponding *set* function. This reduces the likelihood of errors when altering the class's implementation. Also, the performance of the `Time` constructor and `setTime` can be enhanced by explicitly declaring them `inline` or by defining them in the class definition (which implicitly inlines the function definition).

 Software Engineering Observation 9.9

If a member function of a class already provides all or part of the functionality required by a constructor (or other member function) of the class, call that member function from the constructor (or other member function). This simplifies the maintenance of the code and reduces the likelihood of an error if the implementation of the code is modified. As a general rule: Avoid repeating code.

Software Engineering Observation 9.10

Any change to the default argument values of a function requires the client code to be recompiled (to ensure that the program still functions correctly).

Function `main` in Fig. 9.10 initializes five `Time` objects—one with all three arguments defaulted in the implicit constructor call (line 11), one with one argument specified (line

```
 1   // Fig. 9.10: fig09_10.cpp
 2   // Demonstrating a default constructor for class Time.
 3   #include <iostream>
 4   using std::cout;
 5   using std::endl;
 6
 7   #include "Time.h" // include definition of class Time from Time.h
 8
 9   int main()
10   {
11      Time t1; // all arguments defaulted
12      Time t2( 2 ); // hour specified; minute and second defaulted
13      Time t3( 21, 34 ); // hour and minute specified; second defaulted
14      Time t4( 12, 25, 42 ); // hour, minute and second specified
15      Time t5( 27, 74, 99 ); // all bad values specified
16
```

Fig. 9.10 | Constructor with default arguments. (Part 1 of 2.)

```
17        cout << "Constructed with:\n\nt1: all arguments defaulted\n   ";
18        t1.printUniversal(); // 00:00:00
19        cout << "\n   ";
20        t1.printStandard(); // 12:00:00 AM
21
22        cout << "\n\nt2: hour specified; minute and second defaulted\n   ";
23        t2.printUniversal(); // 02:00:00
24        cout << "\n   ";
25        t2.printStandard(); // 2:00:00 AM
26
27        cout << "\n\nt3: hour and minute specified; second defaulted\n   ";
28        t3.printUniversal(); // 21:34:00
29        cout << "\n   ";
30        t3.printStandard(); // 9:34:00 PM
31
32        cout << "\n\nt4: hour, minute and second specified\n   ";
33        t4.printUniversal(); // 12:25:42
34        cout << "\n   ";
35        t4.printStandard(); // 12:25:42 PM
36
37        cout << "\n\nt5: all invalid values specified\n   ";
38        t5.printUniversal(); // 00:00:00
39        cout << "\n   ";
40        t5.printStandard(); // 12:00:00 AM
41        cout << endl;
42        return 0;
43    } // end main
```

```
Constructed with:

t1: all arguments defaulted
   00:00:00
   12:00:00 AM

t2: hour specified; minute and second defaulted
   02:00:00
   2:00:00 AM

t3: hour and minute specified; second defaulted
   21:34:00
   9:34:00 PM

t4: hour, minute and second specified
   12:25:42
   12:25:42 PM

t5: all invalid values specified
   00:00:00
   12:00:00 AM
```

Fig. 9.10 | Constructor with default arguments. (Part 2 of 2.)

12), one with two arguments specified (line 13), one with three arguments specified (line 14) and one with three invalid arguments specified (line 15). Then the program displays each object in universal-time and standard-time formats.

Notes Regarding Class **Time***'s* Set *and* Get *Functions and Constructor*

Time's *set* and *get* functions are called throughout the class's body. In particular, function setTime (lines 21–26 of Fig. 9.9) calls functions setHour, setMinute and setSecond, and functions printUniversal and printStandard call functions getHour, getMinute and getSecond in line 67–68 and lines 74–76, respectively. In each case, these functions could have accessed the class's private data directly. However, consider changing the representation of the time from three int values (requiring 12 bytes of memory) to a single int value representing the total number of seconds that have elapsed since midnight (requiring only four bytes of memory). If we made such a change, only the bodies of the functions that access the private data directly would need to change—in particular, the individual *set* and *get* functions for the hour, minute and second. There would be no need to modify the bodies of functions setTime, printUniversal or printStandard, because they do not access the data directly. Designing the class in this manner reduces the likelihood of programming errors when altering the class's implementation.

Similarly, the Time constructor could be written to include a copy of the appropriate statements from function setTime. Doing so may be slightly more efficient, because the extra constructor call and call to setTime are eliminated. However, duplicating statements in multiple functions or constructors makes changing the class's internal data representation more difficult. Having the Time constructor call function setTime directly requires any changes to the implementation of setTime to be made only once.

Common Programming Error 9.2

A constructor can call other member functions of the class, such as set *or* get *functions, but because the constructor is initializing the object, the data members may not yet be in a consistent state. Using data members before they have been properly initialized can cause logic errors.*

9.7 Destructors

A destructor is another type of special member function. The name of the destructor for a class is the tilde character (~) followed by the class name. This naming convention has intuitive appeal, because as we'll see in a later chapter, the tilde operator is the bitwise complement operator, and, in a sense, the destructor is the complement of the constructor. Note that a destructor is often referred to with the abbreviation "dtor" in the literature. We prefer not to use this abbreviation.

A class's destructor is called implicitly when an object is destroyed. This occurs, for example, as an automatic object is destroyed when program execution leaves the scope in which that object was instantiated. *The destructor itself does not actually release the object's memory*—it performs termination housekeeping before the object's memory is reclaimed, so the memory may be reused to hold new objects.

A destructor receives no parameters and returns no value. A destructor may not specify a return type—not even void. A class may have only one destructor—destructor overloading is not allowed. A destructor must be public.

Common Programming Error 9.3

It is a syntax error to attempt to pass arguments to a destructor, to specify a return type for a destructor (even void *cannot be specified), to return values from a destructor or to overload a destructor.*

Even though destructors have not been provided for the classes presented so far, every class has a destructor. If you do not explicitly provide a destructor, the compiler creates an "empty" destructor. [*Note:* We'll see that such an implicitly created destructor does, in fact, perform important operations on objects that are created through composition (Chapter 10) and inheritance (Chapter 12).] In Chapter 11, we'll build destructors appropriate for classes whose objects contain dynamically allocated memory (e.g., for arrays and strings) or use other system resources (e.g., files on disk, which we study in Chapter 17). We discuss how to dynamically allocate and deallocate memory in Chapter 10.

Software Engineering Observation 9.11

As we'll see in the remainder of the book, constructors and destructors have much greater prominence in C++ and object-oriented programming than is possible to convey after only our brief introduction here.

9.8 When Constructors and Destructors Are Called

Constructors and destructors are called implicitly by the compiler. The order in which these function calls occur depends on the order in which execution enters and leaves the scopes where the objects are instantiated. Generally, destructor calls are made in the reverse order of the corresponding constructor calls, but as we'll see in Figs. 9.11–9.13, the storage classes of objects can alter the order in which destructors are called.

Constructors are called for objects defined in global scope before any other function (including `main`) in that file begins execution (although the order of execution of global object constructors between files is not guaranteed). The corresponding destructors are called when `main` terminates. Function `exit` forces a program to terminate immediately and does not execute the destructors of automatic objects. The function often is used to terminate a program when an error is detected in the input or if a file to be processed by the program cannot be opened. Function `abort` performs similarly to function `exit` but forces the program to terminate immediately, without allowing the destructors of any objects to be called. Function `abort` is usually used to indicate an abnormal termination of the program. (See Appendix E, for more information on functions `exit` and `abort`.)

The constructor for an automatic local object is called when execution reaches the point where that object is defined—the corresponding destructor is called when execution leaves the object's scope (i.e., the block in which that object is defined has finished executing). Constructors and destructors for automatic objects are called each time execution enters and leaves the scope of the object. Destructors are not called for automatic objects if the program terminates with a call to function `exit` or function `abort`.

The constructor for a `static` local object is called only once, when execution first reaches the point where the object is defined—the corresponding destructor is called when `main` terminates or the program calls function `exit`. Global and `static` objects are destroyed in the reverse order of their creation. Destructors are not called for `static` objects if the program terminates with a call to function `abort`.

The program of Figs. 9.11–9.13 demonstrates the order in which constructors and destructors are called for objects of class `CreateAndDestroy` (Fig. 9.11 and Fig. 9.12) of various storage classes in several scopes. Each object of class `CreateAndDestroy` contains an integer (`objectID`) and a `string` (`message`) that are used in the program's output to identify the object (Fig. 9.11 lines 16–17). This mechanical example is purely for pedagogic purposes. For this reason, line 23 of the destructor in Fig. 9.12 determines whether the object being destroyed has an `objectID` value 1 or 6 and, if so, outputs a newline character. This line makes the program's output easier to follow.

```
 1   // Fig. 9.11: CreateAndDestroy.h
 2   // CreateAndDestroy class definition.
 3   // Member functions defined in CreateAndDestroy.cpp.
 4   #include <string>
 5   using std::string;
 6
 7   #ifndef CREATE_H
 8   #define CREATE_H
 9
10   class CreateAndDestroy
11   {
12   public:
13      CreateAndDestroy( int, string ); // constructor
14      ~CreateAndDestroy(); // destructor
15   private:
16      int objectID; // ID number for object
17      string message; // message describing object
18   }; // end class CreateAndDestroy
19
20   #endif
```

Fig. 9.11 | CreateAndDestroy class definition.

```
 1   // Fig. 9.12: CreateAndDestroy.cpp
 2   // CreateAndDestroy class member-function definitions.
 3   #include <iostream>
 4   using std::cout;
 5   using std::endl;
 6
 7   #include "CreateAndDestroy.h"// include CreateAndDestroy class definition
 8
 9   // constructor
10   CreateAndDestroy::CreateAndDestroy( int ID, string messageString )
11   {
12      objectID = ID; // set object's ID number
13      message = messageString; // set object's descriptive message
14
15      cout << "Object " << objectID << "  constructor runs   "
16         << message << endl;
17   } // end CreateAndDestroy constructor
18
19   // destructor
20   CreateAndDestroy::~CreateAndDestroy()
21   {
22      // output newline for certain objects; helps readability
23      cout << ( objectID == 1 || objectID == 6 ? "\n" : "" );
24
25      cout << "Object " << objectID << "  destructor runs   "
26         << message << endl;
27   } // end ~CreateAndDestroy destructor
```

Fig. 9.12 | CreateAndDestroy class member-function definitions.

Figure 9.13 defines object first (line 12) in global scope. Its constructor is actually called before any statements in main execute and its destructor is called at program termination after the destructors for all other objects have run.

Function main (lines 14–26) declares three objects. Objects second (line 17) and fourth (line 23) are local automatic objects, and object third (line 18) is a static local object. The constructor for each of these objects is called when execution reaches the point where that object is declared. The destructors for objects fourth and then second are called (i.e., the reverse of the order in which their constructors were called) when execution reaches the end of main. Because object third is static, it exists until program termination. The destructor for object third is called before the destructor for global object first, but after all other objects are destroyed.

Function create (lines 29–36) declares three objects—fifth (line 32) and seventh (line 34) as local automatic objects, and sixth (line 33) as a static local object. The

```
1   // Fig. 9.13: fig09_13.cpp
2   // Demonstrating the order in which constructors and
3   // destructors are called.
4   #include <iostream>
5   using std::cout;
6   using std::endl;
7
8   #include "CreateAndDestroy.h" // include CreateAndDestroy class definition
9
10  void create( void ); // prototype
11
12  CreateAndDestroy first( 1, "(global before main)" ); // global object
13
14  int main()
15  {
16     cout << "\nMAIN FUNCTION: EXECUTION BEGINS" << endl;
17     CreateAndDestroy second( 2, "(local automatic in main)" );
18     static CreateAndDestroy third( 3, "(local static in main)" );
19
20     create(); // call function to create objects
21
22     cout << "\nMAIN FUNCTION: EXECUTION RESUMES" << endl;
23     CreateAndDestroy fourth( 4, "(local automatic in main)" );
24     cout << "\nMAIN FUNCTION: EXECUTION ENDS" << endl;
25     return 0;
26  } // end main
27
28  // function to create objects
29  void create( void )
30  {
31     cout << "\nCREATE FUNCTION: EXECUTION BEGINS" << endl;
32     CreateAndDestroy fifth( 5, "(local automatic in create)" );
33     static CreateAndDestroy sixth( 6, "(local static in create)" );
34     CreateAndDestroy seventh( 7, "(local automatic in create)" );
35     cout << "\nCREATE FUNCTION: EXECUTION ENDS" << endl;
36  } // end function create
```

Fig. 9.13 | Order in which constructors and destructors are called. (Part 1 of 2.)

```
Object 1   constructor runs   (global before main)

MAIN FUNCTION: EXECUTION BEGINS
Object 2   constructor runs   (local automatic in main)
Object 3   constructor runs   (local static in main)

CREATE FUNCTION: EXECUTION BEGINS
Object 5   constructor runs   (local automatic in create)
Object 6   constructor runs   (local static in create)
Object 7   constructor runs   (local automatic in create)

CREATE FUNCTION: EXECUTION ENDS
Object 7   destructor runs    (local automatic in create)
Object 5   destructor runs    (local automatic in create)

MAIN FUNCTION: EXECUTION RESUMES
Object 4   constructor runs   (local automatic in main)

MAIN FUNCTION: EXECUTION ENDS
Object 4   destructor runs    (local automatic in main)
Object 2   destructor runs    (local automatic in main)

Object 6   destructor runs    (local static in create)
Object 3   destructor runs    (local static in main)

Object 1   destructor runs    (global before main)
```

Fig. 9.13 | Order in which constructors and destructors are called. (Part 2 of 2.)

destructors for objects seventh and then fifth are called (i.e., the reverse of the order in which their constructors were called) when create terminates. Because sixth is static, it exists until program termination. The destructor for sixth is called before the destructors for third and first, but after all other objects are destroyed.

9.9 Time Class Case Study: A Subtle Trap—Returning a Reference to a private Data Member

A reference to an object is an alias for the name of the object and, hence, may be used on the left side of an assignment statement. In this context, the reference makes a perfectly acceptable *lvalue* that can receive a value. One way to use this capability (unfortunately!) is to have a public member function of a class return a reference to a private data member of that class. Note that if a function returns a const reference, that reference cannot be used as a modifiable *lvalue*.

The program of Figs. 9.14–9.16 uses a simplified Time class (Fig. 9.14 and Fig. 9.15) to demonstrate returning a reference to a private data member with member function badSetHour (declared in Fig. 9.14 in line 15 and defined in Fig. 9.15 in lines 29–33). Such a reference return actually makes a call to member function badSetHour an alias for private data member hour! The function call can be used in any way that the private data member can be used, including as an *lvalue* in an assignment statement, thus enabling clients of the class to clobber the class's private data at will! Note that the same problem would occur if a pointer to the private data were to be returned by the function.

```
 1    // Fig. 9.14: Time.h
 2    // Time class declaration.
 3    // Member functions defined in Time.cpp
 4
 5    // prevent multiple inclusions of header file
 6    #ifndef TIME_H
 7    #define TIME_H
 8
 9    class Time
10    {
11    public:
12       Time( int = 0, int = 0, int = 0 );
13       void setTime( int, int, int );
14       int getHour();
15       int &badSetHour( int ); // DANGEROUS reference return
16    private:
17       int hour;
18       int minute;
19       int second;
20    }; // end class Time
21
22    #endif
```

Fig. 9.14 | Time class declaration.

```
 1    // Fig. 9.15: Time.cpp
 2    // Time class member-function definitions.
 3    #include "Time.h" // include definition of class Time
 4
 5    // constructor function to initialize private data;
 6    // calls member function setTime to set variables;
 7    // default values are 0 (see class definition)
 8    Time::Time( int hr, int min, int sec )
 9    {
10       setTime( hr, min, sec );
11    } // end Time constructor
12
13    // set values of hour, minute and second
14    void Time::setTime( int h, int m, int s )
15    {
16       hour = ( h >= 0 && h < 24 ) ? h : 0; // validate hour
17       minute = ( m >= 0 && m < 60 ) ? m : 0; // validate minute
18       second = ( s >= 0 && s < 60 ) ? s : 0; // validate second
19    } // end function setTime
20
21    // return hour value
22    int Time::getHour()
23    {
24       return hour;
25    } // end function getHour
26
```

Fig. 9.15 | Time class member-function definitions. (Part 1 of 2.)

```
27   // POOR PROGRAMMING PRACTICE:
28   // Returning a reference to a private data member.
29   int &Time::badSetHour( int hh )
30   {
31      hour = ( hh >= 0 && hh < 24 ) ? hh : 0;
32      return hour; // DANGEROUS reference return
33   } // end function badSetHour
```

Fig. 9.15 | Time class member-function definitions. (Part 2 of 2.)

Figure 9.16 declares Time object t (line 12) and reference hourRef (line 15), which is initialized with the reference returned by the call t.badSetHour(20). Line 17 displays the value of the alias hourRef. This shows how hourRef breaks the encapsulation of the class—statements in main should not have access to the private data of the class. Next, line 18 uses the alias to set the value of hour to 30 (an invalid value) and line 19 displays the value returned by function getHour to show that assigning a value to hourRef actually modifies the private data in the Time object t. Finally, line 23 uses the badSetHour function call itself as an *lvalue* and assigns 74 (another invalid value) to the reference returned by the function.

```
 1   // Fig. 9.16: fig09_16.cpp
 2   // Demonstrating a public member function that
 3   // returns a reference to a private data member.
 4   #include <iostream>
 5   using std::cout;
 6   using std::endl;
 7
 8   #include "Time.h" // include definition of class Time
 9
10   int main()
11   {
12      Time t; // create Time object
13
14      // initialize hourRef with the reference returned by badSetHour
15      int &hourRef = t.badSetHour( 20 ); // 20 is a valid hour
16
17      cout << "Valid hour before modification: " << hourRef;
18      hourRef = 30; // use hourRef to set invalid value in Time object t
19      cout << "\nInvalid hour after modification: " << t.getHour();
20
21      // Dangerous: Function call that returns
22      // a reference can be used as an lvalue!
23      t.badSetHour( 12 ) = 74; // assign another invalid value to hour
24
25      cout << "\n\n********************************************************\n"
26         << "POOR PROGRAMMING PRACTICE!!!!!!!!\n"
27         << "t.badSetHour( 12 ) as an lvalue, invalid hour: "
28         << t.getHour()
29         << "\n********************************************************" << endl;
30      return 0;
31   } // end main
```

Fig. 9.16 | Returning a reference to a private data member. (Part 1 of 2.)

```
Valid hour before modification: 20
Invalid hour after modification: 30

****************************************************
POOR PROGRAMMING PRACTICE!!!!!!!!
t.badSetHour( 12 ) as an lvalue, invalid hour: 74
****************************************************
```

Fig. 9.16 | Returning a reference to a `private` data member. (Part 2 of 2.)

Line 28 again displays the value returned by function `getHour` to show that assigning a value to the result of the function call in line 23 modifies the `private` data in the `Time` object `t`.

Error-Prevention Tip 9.4

Returning a reference or a pointer to a private data member breaks the encapsulation of the class and makes the client code dependent on the representation of the class's data; this is a dangerous practice that should be avoided.

9.10 Default Memberwise Assignment

The assignment operator (=) can be used to assign an object to another object of the same type. By default, such assignment is performed by memberwise assignment—each data member of the object on the right of the assignment operator is assigned individually to the same data member in the object on the left of the assignment operator. Figures 9.17–9.18 define class `Date` for use in this example. Line 20 of Fig. 9.19 uses default memberwise assignment to assign the data members of `Date` object `date1` to the

```
1   // Fig. 9.17: Date.h
2   // Date class declaration.
3   // Member functions are defined in Date.cpp
4
5   // prevent multiple inclusions of header file
6   #ifndef DATE_H
7   #define DATE_H
8
9   // class Date definition
10  class Date
11  {
12  public:
13     Date( int = 1, int = 1, int = 2000 ); // default constructor
14     void print();
15  private:
16     int month;
17     int day;
18     int year;
19  }; // end class Date
20
21  #endif
```

Fig. 9.17 | Date class declaration.

```
1   // Fig. 9.18: Date.cpp
2   // Date class member-function definitions.
3   #include <iostream>
4   using std::cout;
5   using std::endl;
6
7   #include "Date.h" // include definition of class Date from Date.h
8
9   // Date constructor (should do range checking)
10  Date::Date( int m, int d, int y )
11  {
12     month = m;
13     day = d;
14     year = y;
15  } // end constructor Date
16
17  // print Date in the format mm/dd/yyyy
18  void Date::print()
19  {
20     cout << month << '/' << day << '/' << year;
21  } // end function print
```

Fig. 9.18 | Date class member-function definitions.

```
1   // Fig. 9.19: fig09_19.cpp
2   // Demonstrating that class objects can be assigned
3   // to each other using default memberwise assignment.
4   #include <iostream>
5   using std::cout;
6   using std::endl;
7
8   #include "Date.h" // include definition of class Date from Date.h
9
10  int main()
11  {
12     Date date1( 7, 4, 2004 );
13     Date date2; // date2 defaults to 1/1/2000
14
15     cout << "date1 = ";
16     date1.print();
17     cout << "\ndate2 = ";
18     date2.print();
19
20     date2 = date1; // default memberwise assignment
21
22     cout << "\n\nAfter default memberwise assignment, date2 = ";
23     date2.print();
24     cout << endl;
25     return 0;
26  } // end main
```

Fig. 9.19 | Default memberwise assignment. (Part I of 2.)

```
date1 = 7/4/2004
date2 = 1/1/2000

After default memberwise assignment, date2 = 7/4/2004
```

Fig. 9.19 | Default memberwise assignment. (Part 2 of 2.)

corresponding data members of Date object date2. In this case, the month member of date1 is assigned to the month member of date2, the day member of date1 is assigned to the day member of date2 and the year member of date1 is assigned to the year member of date2. [*Caution:* Memberwise assignment can cause serious problems when used with a class whose data members contain pointers to dynamically allocated memory; we discuss these problems in Chapter 11 and show how to deal with them.] Notice that the Date constructor does not contain any error checking; we leave this to the exercises.

Objects may be passed as function arguments and may be returned from functions. Such passing and returning is performed using pass-by-value by default—a copy of the object is passed or returned. In such cases, C++ creates a new object and uses a copy constructor to copy the original object's values into the new object. For each class, the compiler provides a default copy constructor that copies each member of the original object into the corresponding member of the new object. Like memberwise assignment, copy constructors can cause serious problems when used with a class whose data members contain pointers to dynamically allocated memory. Chapter 11 discusses how programmers can define customized copy constructors that properly copy objects containing pointers to dynamically allocated memory.

Performance Tip 9.3

Passing an object by value is good from a security standpoint, because the called function has no access to the original object in the caller, but pass-by-value can degrade performance when making a copy of a large object. An object can be passed by reference by passing either a pointer or a reference to the object. Pass-by-reference offers good performance but is weaker from a security standpoint, because the called function is given access to the original object. Pass-by-const-reference is a safe, good-performing alternative (this can be implemented with a const reference parameter or with a pointer-to-const-data parameter).

9.11 (Optional) Software Engineering Case Study: Starting to Program the Classes of the ATM System

In the Software Engineering Case Study sections in Chapters 1–7, we introduced the fundamentals of object orientation and developed an object-oriented design for our ATM system. Earlier in this chapter, we discussed many of the details of programming with C++ classes. We now begin implementing our object-oriented design in C++. At the end of this section, we show how to convert class diagrams to C++ header files. In the final Software Engineering Case Study section (Section 13.10), we modify the header files to incorporate the object-oriented concept of inheritance. We present the full C++ code implementation in Appendix G, ATM Case Study Code.

Visibility

We now apply access specifiers to the members of our classes. In Chapter 3, we introduced access specifiers `public` and `private`. Access specifiers determine the visibility or accessibility of an object's attributes and operations to other objects. Before we can begin implementing our design, we must consider which attributes and operations of our classes should be `public` and which should be `private`.

In Chapter 3, we observed that data members normally should be `private` and that member functions invoked by clients of a given class should be `public`. Member functions that are called only by other member functions of the class as "utility functions," however, normally should be `private`. The UML employs visibility markers for modeling the visibility of attributes and operations. Public visibility is indicated by placing a plus sign (+) before an operation or an attribute; a minus sign (–) indicates private visibility. Figure 9.20 shows our updated class diagram with visibility markers included. [*Note:* We do not include any operation parameters in Fig. 9.20. This is perfectly normal. Adding vis-

Fig. 9.20 | Class diagram with visibility markers.

ibility markers does not affect the parameters already modeled in the class diagrams of Figs. 6.36–6.39.]

Navigability

Before we begin implementing our design in C++, we introduce an additional UML notation. The class diagram in Fig. 9.21 further refines the relationships among classes in the ATM system by adding navigability arrows to the association lines. Navigability arrows (represented as arrows with stick arrowheads in the class diagram) indicate in which direction an association can be traversed and are based on the collaborations modeled in communication and sequence diagrams (see Section 7.12). When implementing a system designed using the UML, programmers use navigability arrows to help determine which objects need references or pointers to other objects. For example, the navigability arrow pointing from class ATM to class BankDatabase indicates that we can navigate from the former to the latter, thereby enabling the ATM to invoke the BankDatabase's operations. However, since Fig. 9.21 does not contain a navigability arrow pointing from class BankDatabase to class ATM, the BankDatabase cannot access the ATM's operations. Note that associations in a class diagram that have navigability arrows at both ends or do not have navigability arrows at all indicate bidirectional navigability—navigation can proceed in either direction across the association.

Like the class diagram of Fig. 3.23, the class diagram of Fig. 9.21 omits classes BalanceInquiry and Deposit to keep the diagram simple. The navigability of the associations in which these classes participate closely parallels the navigability of class Withdrawal's associations. Recall from Section 3.11 that BalanceInquiry has an association

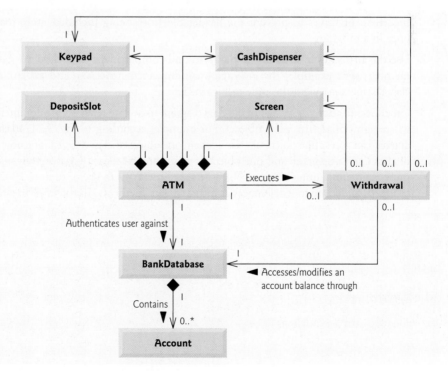

Fig. 9.21 | Class diagram with navigability arrows.

with class Screen. We can navigate from class BalanceInquiry to class Screen along this association, but we cannot navigate from class Screen to class BalanceInquiry. Thus, if we were to model class BalanceInquiry in Fig. 9.21, we would place a navigability arrow at class Screen's end of this association. Also recall that class Deposit associates with classes Screen, Keypad and DepositSlot. We can navigate from class Deposit to each of these classes, but not vice versa. We therefore would place navigability arrows at the Screen, Keypad and DepositSlot ends of these associations. [*Note:* We model these additional classes and associations in our final class diagram in Section 13.10, after we have simplified the structure of our system by incorporating the object-oriented concept of inheritance.]

Implementing the ATM System from Its UML Design

We are now ready to begin implementing the ATM system. We first convert the classes in the diagrams of Fig. 9.20 and Fig. 9.21 into C++ header files. This code will represent the "skeleton" of the system. In Chapter 13, we modify the header files to incorporate the object-oriented concept of inheritance. In Appendix G, we present the complete working C++ code for our model.

As an example, we begin to develop the header file for class Withdrawal from our design of class Withdrawal in Fig. 9.20. We use this figure to determine the attributes and operations of the class. We use the UML model in Fig. 9.21 to determine the associations among classes. We follow the following five guidelines for each class:

1. Use the name located in the first compartment of a class in a class diagram to define the class in a header file (Fig. 9.22). Use #ifndef, #define and #endif preprocessor directives to prevent the header file from being included more than once in a program.

2. Use the attributes located in the class's second compartment to declare the data members. For example, the private attributes accountNumber and amount of class Withdrawal yield the code in Fig. 9.23.

3. Use the associations described in the class diagram to declare references (or pointers, where appropriate) to other objects. For example, according to Fig. 9.21, Withdrawal can access one object of class Screen, one object of class Keypad, one object of class CashDispenser and one object of class BankDatabase. Class Withdrawal must maintain handles on these objects to send messages to them, so lines 19–22 of Fig. 9.24 declare four references as private data members. In the implementa-

```
1   // Fig. 9.22: Withdrawal.h
2   // Definition of class Withdrawal that represents a withdrawal transaction
3   #ifndef WITHDRAWAL_H
4   #define WITHDRAWAL_H
5
6   class Withdrawal
7   {
8   }; // end class Withdrawal
9
10  #endif // WITHDRAWAL_H
```

Fig. 9.22 | Definition of class Withdrawal enclosed in preprocessor wrappers.

```
1    // Fig. 9.23: Withdrawal.h
2    // Definition of class Withdrawal that represents a withdrawal transaction
3    #ifndef WITHDRAWAL_H
4    #define WITHDRAWAL_H
5
6    class Withdrawal
7    {
8    private:
9       // attributes
10      int accountNumber; // account to withdraw funds from
11      double amount; // amount to withdraw
12   }; // end class Withdrawal
13
14   #endif // WITHDRAWAL_H
```

Fig. 9.23 | Adding attributes to the `Withdrawal` class header file.

```
1    // Fig. 9.24: Withdrawal.h
2    // Definition of class Withdrawal that represents a withdrawal transaction
3    #ifndef WITHDRAWAL_H
4    #define WITHDRAWAL_H
5
6    #include "Screen.h" // include definition of class Screen
7    #include "Keypad.h" // include definition of class Keypad
8    #include "CashDispenser.h" // include definition of class CashDispenser
9    #include "BankDatabase.h" // include definition of class BankDatabase
10
11   class Withdrawal
12   {
13   private:
14      // attributes
15      int accountNumber; // account to withdraw funds from
16      double amount; // amount to withdraw
17
18      // references to associated objects
19      Screen &screen; // reference to ATM's screen
20      Keypad &keypad; // reference to ATM's keypad
21      CashDispenser &cashDispenser; // reference to ATM's cash dispenser
22      BankDatabase &bankDatabase; // reference to the account info database
23   }; // end class Withdrawal
24
25   #endif // WITHDRAWAL_H
```

Fig. 9.24 | Declaring references to objects associated with class `Withdrawal`.

tion of class `Withdrawal` in Appendix G, a constructor initializes these data members with references to actual objects. Note that lines 6–9 `#include` the header files containing the definitions of classes `Screen`, `Keypad`, `CashDispenser` and `BankDatabase` so that we can declare references to objects of these classes in lines 19–22.

4. It turns out that including the header files for classes `Screen`, `Keypad`, `CashDispenser` and `BankDatabase` in Fig. 9.24 does more than is necessary. Class `Withdrawal` contains *references* to objects of these classes—it does not contain actual

objects—and the amount of information required by the compiler to create a reference differs from that which is required to create an object. Recall that creating an object requires that you provide the compiler with a definition of the class that introduces the name of the class as a new user-defined type and indicates the data members that determine how much memory is required to store the object. Declaring a *reference* (or pointer) to an object, however, requires only that the compiler knows that the object's class exists—it does not need to know the size of the object. Any reference (or pointer), regardless of the class of the object to which it refers, contains only the memory address of the actual object. The amount of memory required to store an address is a physical characteristic of the computer's hardware. The compiler thus knows the size of any reference (or pointer). As a result, including a class's full header file when declaring only a reference to an object of that class is unnecessary—we need to introduce the name of the class, but we do not need to provide the data layout of the object, because the compiler already knows the size of all references. C++ provides a statement called a forward declaration that signifies that a header file contains references or pointers to a class, but that the class definition lies outside the header file. We can replace the #includes in the Withdrawal class definition of Fig. 9.24 with forward declarations of classes Screen, Keypad, CashDispenser and BankDatabase (lines 6–9 in Fig. 9.25). Rather than #include the entire header file for each of these classes, we place only a forward declaration of each class in the header file for class Withdrawal. Note that if class Withdrawal contained actual objects instead of refer-

```
1   // Fig. 9.25: Withdrawal.h
2   // Definition of class Withdrawal that represents a withdrawal transaction
3   #ifndef WITHDRAWAL_H
4   #define WITHDRAWAL_H
5
6   class Screen; // forward declaration of class Screen
7   class Keypad; // forward declaration of class Keypad
8   class CashDispenser; // forward declaration of class CashDispenser
9   class BankDatabase; // forward declaration of class BankDatabase
10
11  class Withdrawal
12  {
13  private:
14      // attributes
15      int accountNumber; // account to withdraw funds from
16      double amount; // amount to withdraw
17
18      // references to associated objects
19      Screen &screen; // reference to ATM's screen
20      Keypad &keypad; // reference to ATM's keypad
21      CashDispenser &cashDispenser; // reference to ATM's cash dispenser
22      BankDatabase &bankDatabase; // reference to the account info database
23  }; // end class Withdrawal
24
25  #endif // WITHDRAWAL_H
```

Fig. 9.25 | Using forward declarations in place of #include directives.

ences (i.e., if the ampersands in lines 19–22 were omitted), then we would indeed need to #include the full header files.

Note that using a forward declaration (where possible) instead of including a full header file helps avoid a preprocessor problem called a circular include. This problem occurs when the header file for a class A #includes the header file for a class B and vice versa. Some preprocessors are not be able to resolve such #include directives, causing a compilation error. If class A, for example, uses only a reference to an object of class B, then the #include in class A's header file can be replaced by a forward declaration of class B to prevent the circular include.

5. Use the operations located in the third compartment of Fig. 9.20 to write the function prototypes of the class's member functions. If we have not yet specified a return type for an operation, we declare the member function with return type void. Refer to the class diagrams of Figs. 6.22–6.25 to declare any necessary parameters. For example, adding the public operation execute in class Withdrawal, which has an empty parameter list, yields the prototype in line 15 of Fig. 9.26. [*Note:* We code the definitions of member functions in .cpp files when we implement the complete ATM system in Appendix G.]

Software Engineering Observation 9.12

Several UML modeling tools can convert UML-based designs into C++ code, considerably speeding the implementation process. For more information on these "automatic" code generators, refer to the Internet and web resources listed at the end of Section 2.8.

```
1   // Fig. 9.26: Withdrawal.h
2   // Definition of class Withdrawal that represents a withdrawal transaction
3   #ifndef WITHDRAWAL_H
4   #define WITHDRAWAL_H
5
6   class Screen; // forward declaration of class Screen
7   class Keypad; // forward declaration of class Keypad
8   class CashDispenser; // forward declaration of class CashDispenser
9   class BankDatabase; // forward declaration of class BankDatabase
10
11  class Withdrawal
12  {
13  public:
14     // operations
15     void execute(); // perform the transaction
16  private:
17     // attributes
18     int accountNumber; // account to withdraw funds from
19     double amount; // amount to withdraw
20
21     // references to associated objects
22     Screen &screen; // reference to ATM's screen
23     Keypad &keypad; // reference to ATM's keypad
24     CashDispenser &cashDispenser; // reference to ATM's cash dispenser
```

Fig. 9.26 | Adding operations to the Withdrawal class header file. (Part 1 of 2.)

```
25        BankDatabase &bankDatabase; // reference to the account info database
26   }; // end class Withdrawal
27
28   #endif // WITHDRAWAL_H
```

Fig. 9.26 | Adding operations to the Withdrawal class header file. (Part 2 of 2.)

This concludes our discussion of the basics of generating class header files from UML diagrams. In the final Software Engineering Case Study section (Section 13.10), we demonstrate how to modify the header files to incorporate the object-oriented concept of inheritance.

Software Engineering Case Study Self-Review Exercises

9.1   State whether the following statement is *true* or *false*, and if *false*, explain why: If an attribute of a class is marked with a minus sign (-) in a class diagram, the attribute is not directly accessible outside of the class.

9.2   In Fig. 9.21, the association between the ATM and the Screen indicates that:
   a) we can navigate from the Screen to the ATM
   b) we can navigate from the ATM to the Screen
   c) Both a and b; the association is bidirectional
   d) None of the above

9.3   Write C++ code to begin implementing the design for class Account.

Answers to Software Engineering Case Study Self-Review Exercises

9.1   True. The minus sign (-) indicates private visibility. We've mentioned "friendship" as an exception to private visibility. Friendship is discussed in Chapter 10.

9.2   b.

9.3   The design for class Account yields the header file in Fig. 9.27.

```
1    // Fig. 9.27: Account.h
2    // Account class definition. Represents a bank account.
3    #ifndef ACCOUNT_H
4    #define ACCOUNT_H
5
6    class Account
7    {
8    public:
9       bool validatePIN( int ); // is user-specified PIN correct?
10      double getAvailableBalance(); // returns available balance
11      double getTotalBalance(); // returns total balance
12      void credit( double ); // adds an amount to the Account
13      void debit( double ); // subtracts an amount from the Account
14   private:
15      int accountNumber; // account number
16      int pin; // PIN for authentication
17      double availableBalance; // funds available for withdrawal
```

Fig. 9.27 | Account class header file based on Fig. 9.20 and Fig. 9.21. (Part 1 of 2.)

```
18      double totalBalance; // funds available + funds waiting to clear
19    }; // end class Account
20
21    #endif // ACCOUNT_H
```

Fig. 9.27 | Account class header file based on Fig. 9.20 and Fig. 9.21. (Part 2 of 2.)

9.12 Wrap-Up

This chapter deepened our coverage of classes, using a rich Time class case study to introduce several new features of classes. You saw that member functions are usually shorter than global functions because member functions can directly access an object's data members, so the member functions can receive fewer arguments than functions in procedural programming languages. You learned how to use the arrow operator to access an object's members via a pointer of the object's class type.

You learned that member functions have class scope—i.e., the member function's name is known only to other members of the class unless referred to via an object of the class, a reference to an object of the class, a pointer to an object of the class or the binary scope resolution operator. We also discussed access functions (commonly used to retrieve the values of data members or to test the truth or falsity of conditions) and utility functions (private member functions that support the operation of the class's public member functions).

You learned that a constructor can specify default arguments that enable it to be called in a variety of ways. You also learned that any constructor that can be called with no arguments is a default constructor and that there can be at most one default constructor per class. We discussed destructors and their purpose of performing termination housekeeping on an object of a class before that object is destroyed. We also demonstrated the order in which an object's constructors and destructors are called.

We demonstrated the problems that can occur when a member function returns a reference to a private data member, which breaks the encapsulation of the class. We also showed that objects of the same type can be assigned to one another using default memberwise assignment. Finally, we discussed the benefits of using class libraries to enhance the speed with which code can be created and to increase the quality of software.

Chapter 10 presents additional class features. We'll demonstrate how const can be used to indicate that a member function does not modify an object of a class. You'll learn how to build classes with composition—the capability that allows a class to contain objects of other classes as members. We'll show how a class can allow so-called "friend" functions to access the class's non-public members. We'll also show how a class's non-static member functions can use a special pointer named this to access an object's members. Next, you'll learn how to use C++'s new and delete operators, which enable programmers to obtain and release memory as necessary during a program's execution.

Summary

Section 9.2 Time Class Case Study

- The preprocessor directives #ifndef (which means "if not defined") and #endif are used to prevent multiple inclusions of a header file. If the code between these directives has not previously been included in an application, `#define` defines a name that can be used to prevent future inclusions, and the code is included in the source code file.

- Data members of a class cannot be initialized where they are declared in the class body (except for a class's `static const` data members of integral or `enum` types, as you'll see in Chapter 10). It is strongly recommended that these data members be initialized by the class's constructor (as there is no default initialization for data members of fundamental types).

- Stream manipulator `setfill` specifies the fill character that is displayed when an integer is output in a field that is wider than the number of digits in the value.

- By default, the fill characters appear before the digits in the number.

- Stream manipulator `setfill` is a "sticky" setting, meaning that once the fill character is set, it applies for all subsequent fields being printed.

- Even though a member function declared in a class definition may be defined outside that class definition (and "tied" to the class via the binary scope resolution operator), that member function is still within that class's scope; i.e., its name is known only to other members of the class unless referred to via an object of the class, a reference to an object of the class or a pointer to an object of the class.

- If a member function is defined in the body of a class definition, the C++ compiler attempts to inline calls to the member function.

- Classes do not have to be created "from scratch." Rather, they can include objects of other classes as members or they may be derived from other classes that provide attributes and behaviors the new classes can use. Including class objects as members of other classes is called composition.

Section 9.3 Class Scope and Accessing Class Members
- A class's data members and member functions belong to that class's scope.
- Nonmember functions are defined at file scope.
- Within a class's scope, class members are immediately accessible by all of that class's member functions and can be referenced by name.
- Outside a class's scope, class members are referenced through one of the handles on an object—an object name, a reference to an object or a pointer to an object.
- Member functions of a class can be overloaded, but only by other member functions of that class.
- To overload a member function, provide in the class definition a prototype for each version of the overloaded function, and provide a separate definition for each version of the function.
- Variables declared in a member function have block scope and are known only to that function.
- If a member function defines a variable with the same name as a variable with class scope, the class-scope variable is hidden by the block-scope variable in the block scope.
- The dot member selection operator (`.`) is preceded by an object's name or by a reference to an object to access the object's `public` members.
- The arrow member selection operator (`->`) is preceded by a pointer to an object to access that object's `public` members.

Section 9.4 Separating Interface from Implementation
- Header files do contain some portions of the implementation and hints about others. Inline member functions, for example, need to be in a header file, so that when the compiler compiles a client, the client can include the `inline` function definition in place.
- A class's `private` members that are listed in the class definition in the header file are visible to clients, even though the clients may not access the `private` members.

Section 9.5 Access Functions and Utility Functions
- A utility function (also called a helper function) is a `private` member function that supports the operation of the class's `public` member functions. Utility functions are not intended to be used by clients of a class (but can be used by friends of a class).

Section 9.6 *Time* Class Case Study: Constructors with Default Arguments
- Like other functions, constructors can specify default arguments.

Section 9.7 Destructors
- A class's destructor is called implicitly when an object of the class is destroyed.
- The name of the destructor for a class is the tilde (~) character followed by the class name.
- A destructor does not release an object's storage—it performs termination housekeeping before the system reclaims an object's memory, so the memory may be reused to hold new objects.
- A destructor receives no parameters and returns no value. A class may have only one destructor.
- If you do not explicitly provide a destructor, the compiler creates an "empty" destructor, so every class has exactly one destructor.

Section 9.8 When Constructors and Destructors Are Called
- The order in which constructors and destructors are called depends on the order in which execution enters and leaves the scopes where the objects are instantiated.
- Generally, destructor calls are made in the reverse order of the corresponding constructor calls, but the storage classes of objects can alter the order in which destructors are called.

Section 9.9 *Time* Class Case Study: A Subtle Trap—Returning a Reference to a `private` Data Member
- A reference to an object is an alias for the name of the object and, hence, may be used on the left side of an assignment statement. In this context, the reference makes a perfectly acceptable *lvalue* that can receive a value. One way to use this capability (unfortunately!) is to have a `public` member function of a class return a reference to a `private` data member of that class. If the function returns a `const` reference, then the reference cannot be used as a modifiable *lvalue*.

Section 9.10 Default Memberwise Assignment
- The assignment operator (=) can be used to assign an object to another object of the same type. By default, such assignment is performed by memberwise assignment—each member of the object on the right of the assignment operator is assigned individually to the same member in the object on the left of the assignment operator.
- Objects may be passed as function arguments and may be returned from functions. Such passing and returning is performed using pass-by-value by default—a copy of the object is passed or returned. In such cases, C++ creates a new object and uses a copy constructor to copy the original object's values into the new object.
- For each class, the compiler provides a default copy constructor that copies each member of the original object into the corresponding member of the new object.

Terminology

abort function	arrow member selection operator (->)
access function	assigning class objects
aggregation	class libraries

class scope
composition
copy constructor
default arguments with constructors
default memberwise assignment
`#define` preprocessor directive
derive one class from another
destructor
`#endif` preprocessor directive
`exit` function
file scope
fill character
forward declaration
handle on an object
helper function
`#ifndef` preprocessor directive
implicit handle on an object
inheritance
initializer

memberwise assignment
name handle on an object
object handle
object leaves scope
order in which constructors and destructors are
    called
overloaded constructor
overloaded member function
pass an object by value
pointer handle on an object
predicate function
preprocessor wrapper
pure procedure
reentrant code
reference handle on an object
reusable componentry
`setfill` parameterized stream manipulator
termination housekeeping
tilde character (~) in a destructor name

Self-Review Exercises

9.1 Fill in the blanks in each of the following:

a) Class members are accessed via the _____ operator in conjunction with the name of
an object (or reference to an object) of the class or via the _____ operator in conjunction with a pointer to an object of the class.

b) Class members specified as _____ are accessible only to member functions of the
class and friends of the class.

c) Class members specified as _____ are accessible anywhere an object of the class is in
scope.

d) _____ can be used to assign an object of a class to another object of the same class.

9.2 Find the error(s) in each of the following and explain how to correct it (them):

a) Assume the following prototype is declared in class `Time`:

```
void ~Time( int );
```

b) The following is a partial definition of class `Time`:

```
class Time
{
public:
    // function prototypes
private:
    int hour = 0;
    int minute = 0;
    int second = 0;
}; // end class Time
```

c) Assume the following prototype is declared in class `Employee`:

```
int Employee( const char *, const char * );
```

Answers to Self-Review Exercises

9.1 a) dot (.), arrow (->). b) `private`. c) `public`. d) Default memberwise assignment (performed by the assignment operator).

9.2 a) *Error:* Destructors are not allowed to return values (or even specify a return type) or take arguments.

Correction: Remove the return type void and the parameter int from the declaration.

b) *Error:* Members cannot be explicitly initialized in the class definition.

Correction: Remove the explicit initialization from the class definition and initialize the data members in a constructor.

c) *Error:* Constructors are not allowed to return values.

Correction: Remove the return type int from the declaration.

Exercises

9.3 What is the purpose of the scope resolution operator?

9.4 *(Enhancing Class Time)* Provide a constructor that is capable of using the current time from the time() function—declared in the C++ Standard Library header <ctime>—to initialize an object of the Time class.

9.5 *(Complex Class)* Create a class called Complex for performing arithmetic with complex numbers. Write a program to test your class.

Complex numbers have the form

        realPart + imaginaryPart * i

where *i* is

$$\sqrt{-1}$$

Use double variables to represent the private data of the class. Provide a constructor that enables an object of this class to be initialized when it is declared. The constructor should contain default values in case no initializers are provided. Provide public member functions that perform the following tasks:

a) Adding two Complex numbers: The real parts are added together and the imaginary parts are added together.

b) Subtracting two Complex numbers: The real part of the right operand is subtracted from the real part of the left operand, and the imaginary part of the right operand is subtracted from the imaginary part of the left operand.

c) Printing Complex numbers in the form (a, b), where a is the real part and b is the imaginary part.

9.6 *(Rational Class)* Create a class called Rational for performing arithmetic with fractions. Write a program to test your class.

Use integer variables to represent the private data of the class—the numerator and the denominator. Provide a constructor that enables an object of this class to be initialized when it is declared. The constructor should contain default values in case no initializers are provided and should store the fraction in reduced form. For example, the fraction

$$\frac{2}{4}$$

would be stored in the object as 1 in the numerator and 2 in the denominator. Provide public member functions that perform each of the following tasks:

a) Adding two Rational numbers. The result should be stored in reduced form.

b) Subtracting two Rational numbers. The result should be stored in reduced form.

c) Multiplying two Rational numbers. The result should be stored in reduced form.

d) Dividing two Rational numbers. The result should be stored in reduced form.

e) Printing Rational numbers in the form a/b, where a is the numerator and b is the denominator.

f) Printing Rational numbers in floating-point format.

9.7   *(Enhancing Class Time)* Modify the Time class of Figs. 9.8–9.9 to include a tick member function that increments the time stored in a Time object by one second. The Time object should always remain in a consistent state. Write a program that tests the tick member function in a loop that prints the time in standard format during each iteration of the loop to illustrate that the tick member function works correctly. Be sure to test the following cases:

  a) Incrementing into the next minute.
  b) Incrementing into the next hour.
  c) Incrementing into the next day (i.e., 11:59:59 PM to 12:00:00 AM).

9.8   *(Enhancing Class Date)* Modify the Date class of Figs. 9.17–9.18 to perform error checking on the initializer values for data members month, day and year. Also, provide a member function nextDay to increment the day by one. The Date object should always remain in a consistent state. Write a program that tests function nextDay in a loop that prints the date during each iteration to illustrate that nextDay works correctly. Be sure to test the following cases:

  a) Incrementing into the next month.
  b) Incrementing into the next year.

9.9   *(Combining Class Time and Class Date)* Combine the modified Time class of Exercise 9.7 and the modified Date class of Exercise 9.8 into one class called DateAndTime. (In Chapter 12, we'll discuss inheritance, which will enable us to accomplish this task quickly without modifying the existing class definitions.) Modify the tick function to call the nextDay function if the time increments into the next day. Modify functions printStandard and printUniversal to output the date and time. Write a program to test the new class DateAndTime. Specifically, test incrementing the time into the next day.

9.10   *(Returning Error Indicators from Class Time's set Functions)* Modify the *set* functions in the Time class of Figs. 9.8–9.9 to return appropriate error values if an attempt is made to *set* a data member of an object of class Time to an invalid value. Write a program that tests your new version of class Time. Display error messages when *set* functions return error values.

9.11   *(Rectangle Class)* Create a class Rectangle with attributes length and width, each of which defaults to 1. Provide member functions that calculate the perimeter and the area of the rectangle. Also, provide *set* and *get* functions for the length and width attributes. The *set* functions should verify that length and width are each floating-point numbers larger than 0.0 and less than 20.0.

9.12   *(Enhancing Class Rectangle)* Create a more sophisticated Rectangle class than the one you created in Exercise 9.11. This class stores only the Cartesian coordinates of the four corners of the rectangle. The constructor calls a *set* function that accepts four sets of coordinates and verifies that each of these is in the first quadrant with no single *x*- or *y*-coordinate larger than 20.0. The *set* function also verifies that the supplied coordinates do, in fact, specify a rectangle. Provide member functions that calculate the length, width, perimeter and area. The length is the larger of the two dimensions. Include a predicate function square that determines whether the rectangle is a square.

9.13   *(Enhancing Class Rectangle)* Modify class Rectangle from Exercise 9.12 to include a draw function that displays the rectangle inside a 25-by-25 box enclosing the portion of the first quadrant in which the rectangle resides. Include a setFillCharacter function to specify the character out of which the body of the rectangle will be drawn. Include a setPerimeterCharacter function to specify the character that will be used to draw the border of the rectangle. If you feel ambitious, you might include functions to scale the size of the rectangle, rotate it, and move it around within the designated portion of the first quadrant.

9.14   *(HugeInteger Class)* Create a class HugeInteger that uses a 40-element array of digits to store integers as large as 40 digits each. Provide member functions input, output, add and subtract. For comparing HugeInteger objects, provide functions isEqualTo, isNotEqualTo, isGreaterThan, isLessThan, isGreaterThanOrEqualTo and isLessThanOrEqualTo—each of these is a "predicate" function that simply returns true if the relationship holds between the two HugeIntegers and returns false if the relationship does not hold. Also, provide a predicate function isZero. If you feel ambitious, provide member functions multiply, divide and modulus.

9.15 *(TicTacToe Class)* Create a class TicTacToe that will enable you to write a complete program to play the game of tic-tac-toe. The class contains as private data a 3-by-3 two-dimensional array of integers. The constructor should initialize the empty board to all zeros. Allow two human players. Wherever the first player moves, place a 1 in the specified square. Place a 2 wherever the second player moves. Each move must be to an empty square. After each move, determine whether the game has been won or is a draw. If you feel ambitious, modify your program so that the computer makes the moves for one of the players. Also, allow the player to specify whether he or she wants to go first or second. If you feel exceptionally ambitious, develop a program that will play three-dimensional tic-tac-toe on a 4-by-4-by-4 board. [*Caution:* This is an extremely challenging project that could take many weeks of effort!]

10

Classes:
A Deeper Look,
Part 2

*But what, to serve our
private ends,
Forbids the cheating of our
friends?*
—Charles Churchill

*Instead of this absurd
division into sexes they ought
to class people as static and
dynamic.*
—Evelyn Waugh

*Have no friends not equal to
yourself.*
—Confucius

OBJECTIVES

In this chapter you'll learn:

- To specify **const** (constant) objects and **const** member functions.
- To create objects composed of other objects.
- To use **friend** functions and **friend** classes.
- To use the **this** pointer.
- To create and destroy objects dynamically with operators **new** and **delete**, respectively.
- To use **static** data members and member functions.
- The concept of a container class.
- The notion of iterator classes that walk through the elements of container classes.
- To use proxy classes to hide implementation details from a class's clients.

10.1 Introduction

In this chapter, we continue our study of classes and data abstraction with several more advanced topics. We use `const` objects and `const` member functions to prevent modifications of objects and enforce the principle of least privilege. We discuss composition—a form of reuse in which a class can have objects of other classes as members. Next, we introduce friendship, which enables a class designer to specify nonmember functions that can access class's non-`public` members—a technique that is often used in operator overloading (Chapter 11) for performance reasons. We discuss a special pointer (called `this`), which is an implicit argument to each of a class's non-`static` member functions. It allows those member functions to access the correct object's data members and other non-`static` member functions. We then discuss dynamic memory management and show how to create and destroy objects dynamically with the `new` and `delete` operators. Next, we motivate the need for `static` class members and show how to use `static` data members and member functions in your own classes. Finally, we show how to create a proxy class to hide the implementation details of a class (including its `private` data members) from clients of the class.

Recall that Chapter 3 introduced C++ Standard Library class `string` to represent strings as full-fledged class objects. In this chapter, however, we use the pointer-based strings we introduced in Chapter 8 to help you master pointers and prepare for the professional world in which you'll see a great deal of C legacy code implemented over the last several decades. Thus, you'll become familiar with the two most prevalent methods of creating and manipulating strings in C++.

10.2 `const` (Constant) Objects and `const` Member Functions

We have emphasized the principle of least privilege as one of the most fundamental principles of good software engineering. Let us see how this principle applies to objects.

Some objects need to be modifiable and some do not. You may use keyword `const` to specify that an object is not modifiable and that any attempt to modify the object should result in a compilation error. The statement

```
const Time noon( 12, 0, 0 );
```

declares a `const` object `noon` of class `Time` and initializes it to 12 noon.

Software Engineering Observation 10.1

Declaring an object as `const` helps enforce the principle of least privilege. Attempts to modify the object are caught at compile time rather than causing execution-time errors. Using `const` properly is crucial to proper class design, program design and coding.

Performance Tip 10.1

Declaring variables and objects `const` can improve performance—today's sophisticated optimizing compilers can perform certain optimizations on constants that cannot be performed on variables.

C++ disallows member function calls for `const` objects unless the member functions themselves are also declared `const`. This is true even for *get* member functions that do not modify the object. In addition, the compiler does not allow member functions declared `const` to modify the object.

A function is specified as `const` *both* in its prototype (Fig. 10.1; lines 19–24) and in its definition (Fig. 10.2; lines 47, 53, 59 and 65) by inserting the keyword `const` after the function's parameter list and, in the case of the function definition, before the left brace that begins the function body.

Common Programming Error 10.1

Defining as `const` a member function that modifies a data member of an object is a compilation error.

Common Programming Error 10.2

Defining as `const` a member function that calls a non-`const` member function of the class on the same instance of the class is a compilation error.

Common Programming Error 10.3

Invoking a non-`const` member function on a `const` object is a compilation error.

Software Engineering Observation 10.2

A `const` member function can be overloaded with a non-`const` version. The compiler chooses which overloaded member function to use based on the object on which the function is invoked. If the object is `const`, the compiler uses the `const` version. If the object is not `const`, the compiler uses the non-`const` version.

An interesting problem arises for constructors and destructors, each of which typically modifies objects. The `const` declaration is not allowed for constructors and destructors. A constructor must be allowed to modify an object so that the object can be initialized properly. A destructor must be able to perform its termination housekeeping chores before an object's memory is reclaimed by the system.

Common Programming Error 10.4

Attempting to declare a constructor or destructor const *is a compilation error.*

Defining and Using **const** Member Functions

The program of Figs. 10.1–10.3 modifies class Time of Figs. 9.8–9.9 by making its *get* functions and printUniversal function const. In the header file Time.h (Fig. 10.1), lines 19–21 and 24 now include keyword const after each function's parameter list. The corresponding definition of each function in Fig. 10.2 (lines 47, 53, 59 and 65, respectively) also specifies keyword const after each function's parameter list.

Figure 10.3 instantiates two Time objects—non-const object wakeUp (line 7) and const object noon (line 8). The program attempts to invoke non-const member functions setHour (line 13) and printStandard (line 20) on the const object noon. In each case, the compiler generates an error message. The program also illustrates the three other member-function-call combinations on objects—a non-const member function on a non-const object (line 11), a const member function on a non-const object (line 15) and a const member function on a const object (lines 17–18). The error messages generated

```
 1   // Fig. 10.1: Time.h
 2   // Time class definition with const member functions.
 3   // Member functions defined in Time.cpp.
 4   #ifndef TIME_H
 5   #define TIME_H
 6
 7   class Time
 8   {
 9   public:
10      Time( int = 0, int = 0, int = 0 ); // default constructor
11
12      // set functions
13      void setTime( int, int, int ); // set time
14      void setHour( int ); // set hour
15      void setMinute( int ); // set minute
16      void setSecond( int ); // set second
17
18      // get functions (normally declared const)
19      int getHour() const; // return hour
20      int getMinute() const; // return minute
21      int getSecond() const; // return second
22
23      // print functions (normally declared const)
24      void printUniversal() const; // print universal time
25      void printStandard(); // print standard time (should be const)
26   private:
27      int hour; // 0 - 23 (24-hour clock format)
28      int minute; // 0 - 59
29      int second; // 0 - 59
30   }; // end class Time
31
32   #endif
```

Fig. 10.1 | Time class definition with const member functions.

for non-const member functions called on a const object are shown in the output window. Notice that, although some current compilers issue only warning messages for lines 13 and 20 (thus allowing this program to be executed), we consider these warnings to be errors—the ISO/IEC C++ standard disallows the invocation of a non-const member function on a const object.

```cpp
1   // Fig. 10.2: Time.cpp
2   // Time class member-function definitions.
3   #include <iostream>
4   using std::cout;
5
6   #include <iomanip>
7   using std::setfill;
8   using std::setw;
9
10  #include "Time.h" // include definition of class Time
11
12  // constructor function to initialize private data;
13  // calls member function setTime to set variables;
14  // default values are 0 (see class definition)
15  Time::Time( int hour, int minute, int second )
16  {
17      setTime( hour, minute, second );
18  } // end Time constructor
19
20  // set hour, minute and second values
21  void Time::setTime( int hour, int minute, int second )
22  {
23      setHour( hour );
24      setMinute( minute );
25      setSecond( second );
26  } // end function setTime
27
28  // set hour value
29  void Time::setHour( int h )
30  {
31      hour = ( h >= 0 && h < 24 ) ? h : 0; // validate hour
32  } // end function setHour
33
34  // set minute value
35  void Time::setMinute( int m )
36  {
37      minute = ( m >= 0 && m < 60 ) ? m : 0; // validate minute
38  } // end function setMinute
39
40  // set second value
41  void Time::setSecond( int s )
42  {
43      second = ( s >= 0 && s < 60 ) ? s : 0; // validate second
44  } // end function setSecond
45
```

Fig. 10.2 | Time class member-function definitions, including const member functions. (Part 1 of 2.)

```
46   // return hour value
47   int Time::getHour() const // get functions should be const
48   {
49      return hour;
50   } // end function getHour
51
52   // return minute value
53   int Time::getMinute() const
54   {
55      return minute;
56   } // end function getMinute
57
58   // return second value
59   int Time::getSecond() const
60   {
61      return second;
62   } // end function getSecond
63
64   // print Time in universal-time format (HH:MM:SS)
65   void Time::printUniversal() const
66   {
67      cout << setfill( '0' ) << setw( 2 ) << hour << ":"
68         << setw( 2 ) << minute << ":" << setw( 2 ) << second;
69   } // end function printUniversal
70
71   // print Time in standard-time format (HH:MM:SS AM or PM)
72   void Time::printStandard() // note lack of const declaration
73   {
74      cout << ( ( hour == 0 || hour == 12 ) ? 12 : hour % 12 )
75         << ":" << setfill( '0' ) << setw( 2 ) << minute
76         << ":" << setw( 2 ) << second << ( hour < 12 ? " AM" : " PM" );
77   } // end function printStandard
```

Fig. 10.2 | Time class member-function definitions, including const member functions. (Part 2 of 2.)

```
1    // Fig. 10.3: fig10_03.cpp
2    // Attempting to access a const object with non-const member functions.
3    #include "Time.h" // include Time class definition
4
5    int main()
6    {
7       Time wakeUp( 6, 45, 0 ); // non-constant object
8       const Time noon( 12, 0, 0 ); // constant object
9
10                                // OBJECT        MEMBER FUNCTION
11      wakeUp.setHour( 18 );     // non-const     non-const
12
13      noon.setHour( 12 );       // const         non-const
14
15      wakeUp.getHour();         // non-const     const
```

Fig. 10.3 | const objects and const member functions. (Part 1 of 2.)

```
16
17      noon.getMinute();        // const        const
18      noon.printUniversal();   // const        const
19
20      noon.printStandard();    // const        non-const
21      return 0;
22  } // end main
```

Borland C++ command-line compiler error messages:

```
Warning W8037 fig10_03.cpp 13: Non-const function Time::setHour(int)
   called for const object in function main()
Warning W8037 fig10_03.cpp 20: Non-const function Time::printStandard()
   called for const object in function main()
```

Microsoft Visual C++ 2005 compiler error messages:

```
C:\cpphtp6_examples\ch10\Fig10_01_03\fig10_03.cpp(13) : error C2662:
   'Time::setHour' : cannot convert 'this' pointer from 'const Time' to
   'Time &'
      Conversion loses qualifiers
C:\cpphtp6_examples\ch10\Fig10_01_03\fig10_03.cpp(20) : error C2662:
   'Time::printStandard' : cannot convert 'this' pointer from 'const Time' to
   'Time &'
      Conversion loses qualifiers
```

GNU C++ compiler error messages:

```
fig10_03.cpp:13: error: passing `const Time' as `this' argument of
   `void Time::setHour(int)' discards qualifiers
fig10_03.cpp:20: error: passing `const Time' as `this' argument of
   `void Time::printStandard()' discards qualifiers
```

Fig. 10.3 | const objects and const member functions. (Part 2 of 2.)

Notice that even though a constructor must be a non-const member function (Fig. 10.2, lines 15–18), it can still be used to initialize a const object (Fig. 10.3, line 8). The definition of the Time constructor (Fig. 10.2, lines 15–18) shows that it calls another non-const member function—setTime (lines 21–26)—to perform the initialization of a Time object. Invoking a non-const member function from the constructor call as part of the initialization of a const object is allowed. The "constness" of a const object is enforced from the time the constructor completes initialization of the object until that object's destructor is called.

Also notice that line 20 in Fig. 10.3 generates a compilation error even though member function printStandard of class Time does not modify the object on which it is invoked. The fact that a member function does not modify an object is not sufficient to indicate that the function is constant function—the function must explicitly be declared const.

Initializing a **const** Data Member with a Member Initializer
The program of Figs. 10.4–10.6 introduces using member initializer syntax. All data members *can* be initialized using member initializer syntax, but const data members and

```
1   // Fig. 10.4: Increment.h
2   // Definition of class Increment.
3   #ifndef INCREMENT_H
4   #define INCREMENT_H
5
6   class Increment
7   {
8   public:
9      Increment( int c = 0, int i = 1 ); // default constructor
10
11     // function addIncrement definition
12     void addIncrement()
13     {
14        count += increment;
15     } // end function addIncrement
16
17     void print() const; // prints count and increment
18  private:
19     int count;
20     const int increment; // const data member
21  }; // end class Increment
22
23  #endif
```

Fig. 10.4 | Increment class definition containing non-const data member count and const data member increment.

```
1   // Fig. 10.5: Increment.cpp
2   // Member-function definitions for class Increment demonstrate using a
3   // member initializer to initialize a constant of a built-in data type.
4   #include <iostream>
5   using std::cout;
6   using std::endl;
7
8   #include "Increment.h" // include definition of class Increment
9
10  // constructor
11  Increment::Increment( int c, int i )
12     : count( c ), // initializer for non-const member
13       increment( i ) // required initializer for const member
14  {
15     // empty body
16  } // end constructor Increment
17
18  // print count and increment values
19  void Increment::print() const
20  {
21     cout << "count = " << count << ", increment = " << increment << endl;
22  } // end function print
```

Fig. 10.5 | Member initializer used to initialize a constant of a built-in data type.

```
 1   // Fig. 10.6: fig10_06.cpp
 2   // Program to test class Increment.
 3   #include <iostream>
 4   using std::cout;
 5
 6   #include "Increment.h" // include definition of class Increment
 7
 8   int main()
 9   {
10      Increment value( 10, 5 );
11
12      cout << "Before incrementing: ";
13      value.print();
14
15      for ( int j = 1; j <= 3; j++ )
16      {
17         value.addIncrement();
18         cout << "After increment " << j << ": ";
19         value.print();
20      } // end for
21
22      return 0;
23   } // end main
```

```
Before incrementing: count = 10, increment = 5
After increment 1: count = 15, increment = 5
After increment 2: count = 20, increment = 5
After increment 3: count = 25, increment = 5
```

Fig. 10.6 | Invoking an `Increment` object's `print` and `addIncrement` member functions.

data members that are references *must* be initialized using member initializers. Later in this chapter, we'll see that member objects must be initialized this way as well. In Chapter 12, Object-Oriented Programming: Inheritance when we study inheritance, we'll see that base-class portions of derived classes also must be initialized this way.

The constructor definition (Fig. 10.5, lines 11–16) uses a member initializer list to initialize class `Increment`'s data members—non-const integer `count` and const integer `increment` (declared in lines 19–20 of Fig. 10.4). Member initializers appear between a constructor's parameter list and the left brace that begins the constructor's body. The member initializer list (Fig. 10.5, lines 12–13) is separated from the parameter list with a colon (:). Each member initializer consists of the data member name followed by parentheses containing the member's initial value. In this example, `count` is initialized with the value of constructor parameter `c` and `increment` is initialized with the value of constructor parameter `i`. Note that multiple member initializers are separated by commas. Also, note that the member initializer list executes before the body of the constructor executes.

Software Engineering Observation 10.3

A const object cannot be modified by assignment, so it must be initialized. When a data member of a class is declared const, a member initializer must be used to provide the constructor with the initial value of the data member for an object of the class. The same is true for references.

Erroneously Attempting to Initialize a* const *Data Member with an Assignment
The program of Figs. 10.7–10.9 illustrates the compilation errors caused by attempting to initialize const data member increment with an assignment statement (Fig. 10.8, line 14) in the Increment constructor's body rather than with a member initializer. Note that line 13 of Fig. 10.8 does not generate a compilation error, because count is not declared const.

Common Programming Error 10.5

Not providing a member initializer for a const *data member is a compilation error.*

Software Engineering Observation 10.4

Constant data members (const objects and const *variables) and data members declared as references must be initialized with member initializer syntax; assignments for these types of data in the constructor body are not allowed.*

Note that function print (Fig. 10.8, lines 18–21) is declared const. It might seem strange to label this function const, because a program probably will never have a const Increment object. However, it is possible that a program will have a const reference to an Increment object or a pointer to const that points to an Increment object. Typically, this occurs when objects of class Increment are passed to functions or returned from functions. In these cases, only class Increment's const member functions can be called through the reference or pointer. Thus, it is reasonable to declare function print as const—doing so prevents errors in these situations where an Increment object is treated as a const object.

```
1   // Fig. 10.7: Increment.h
2   // Definition of class Increment.
3   #ifndef INCREMENT_H
4   #define INCREMENT_H
5
6   class Increment
7   {
8   public:
9      Increment( int c = 0, int i = 1 ); // default constructor
10
11     // function addIncrement definition
12     void addIncrement()
13     {
14        count += increment;
15     } // end function addIncrement
16
17     void print() const; // prints count and increment
18   private:
19     int count;
20     const int increment; // const data member
21   }; // end class Increment
22
23   #endif
```

Fig. 10.7 | Increment class definition containing non-const data member count and const data member increment.

Error-Prevention Tip 10.1

Declare as const all of a class's member functions that do not modify the object in which they operate. Occasionally this may seem inappropriate, because you'll have no intention of creating const objects of that class or accessing objects of that class through const references or pointers to const. Declaring such member functions const does offer a benefit, though. If the member function is inadvertently written to modify the object, the compiler will issue an error message.

```
 1  // Fig. 10.8: Increment.cpp
 2  // Erroneous attempt to initialize a constant of a built-in data
 3  // type by assignment.
 4  #include <iostream>
 5  using std::cout;
 6  using std::endl;
 7
 8  #include "Increment.h" // include definition of class Increment
 9
10  // constructor; constant member 'increment' is not initialized
11  Increment::Increment( int c, int i )
12  {
13     count = c; // allowed because count is not constant
14     increment = i; // ERROR: Cannot modify a const object
15  } // end constructor Increment
16
17  // print count and increment values
18  void Increment::print() const
19  {
20     cout << "count = " << count << ", increment = " << increment << endl;
21  } // end function print
```

Fig. 10.8 | Erroneous attempt to initialize a constant of a built-in data type by assignment.

```
 1  // Fig. 10.9: fig10_09.cpp
 2  // Program to test class Increment.
 3  #include <iostream>
 4  using std::cout;
 5
 6  #include "Increment.h" // include definition of class Increment
 7
 8  int main()
 9  {
10     Increment value( 10, 5 );
11
12     cout << "Before incrementing: ";
13     value.print();
14
15     for ( int j = 1; j <= 3; j++ )
16     {
17        value.addIncrement();
18        cout << "After increment " << j << ": ";
19        value.print();
20     } // end for
```

Fig. 10.9 | Program to test class Increment generates compilation errors. (Part 1 of 2.)

```
21
22      return 0;
23   } // end main
```

Borland C++ command-line compiler error message:

```
Error E2024 Increment.cpp 14: Cannot modify a const object in function
    Increment::Increment(int,int)
```

Microsoft Visual C++ 2005 compiler error messages:

```
C:\cpphtp6_examples\ch10\Fig10_07_09\Increment.cpp(12) : error C2758:
    'Increment::increment' : must be initialized in constructor
    base/member initializer list
            C:\cpphtp6_examples\ch10\Fig10_07_09\Increment.h(20) :
                see declaration of 'Increment::increment'
C:\cpphtp6_examples\ch10\Fig10_07_09\Increment.cpp(14) : error C2166:
    l-value specifies const object
```

GNU C++ compiler error messages:

```
Increment.cpp:12: error: uninitialized member 'Increment::increment' with
    'const' type 'const int'
Increment.cpp:14: error: assignment of read-only data-member
    `Increment::increment'
```

Fig. 10.9 | Program to test class `Increment` generates compilation errors. (Part 2 of 2.)

10.3 Composition: Objects as Members of Classes

An `AlarmClock` object needs to know when it is supposed to sound its alarm, so why not include a `Time` object as a member of the `AlarmClock` class? Such a capability is called composition and is sometimes referred to as a *has-a* relationship—a class can have objects of other classes as members.

Software Engineering Observation 10.5

A common form of software reusability is composition, in which a class has objects of other classes as members.

When an object is created, its constructor is called automatically. Previously, we saw how to pass arguments to the constructor of an object we created in `main`. This section shows how an object's constructor can pass arguments to member-object constructors, which is accomplished via member initializers.

Software Engineering Observation 10.6

Member objects are constructed in the order in which they are declared in the class definition (not in the order they are listed in the constructor's member initializer list) and before their enclosing class objects (sometimes called host objects) are constructed.

The program of Figs. 10.10–10.14 uses class `Date` (Figs. 10.10–10.11) and class `Employee` (Figs. 10.12–10.13) to demonstrate objects as members of other objects. The definition of class `Employee` (Fig. 10.12) contains `private` data members `firstName`, `lastName`, `birthDate` and `hireDate`. Members `birthDate` and `hireDate` are `const` objects of class `Date`, which contains `private` data members `month`, `day` and `year`. The `Employee` constructor's header (Fig. 10.13, lines 18–21) specifies that the constructor has four parameters (`first`, `last`, `dateOfBirth` and `dateOfHire`). The first two parameters are used in the constructor's body to initialize the character arrays `firstName` and `lastName`. The last two parameters are passed via member initializers to the constructor for class `Date`. The colon (`:`) in the header separates the member initializers from the parameter list. The member initializers specify the `Employee` constructor parameters being passed to the constructors of the member `Date` objects. Parameter `dateOfBirth` is passed to object `birthDate`'s constructor (Fig. 10.13, line 20), and parameter `dateOfHire` is passed to object `hireDate`'s constructor (Fig. 10.13, line 21). Again, member initializers are separated by commas. As you study class `Date` (Fig. 10.10), notice that the class does not provide a constructor that receives a parameter of type `Date`. So, how is the member initializer list in class `Employee`'s constructor able to initialize the `birthDate` and `hireDate` objects by passing `Date` object's to their `Date` constructors? As we mentioned in Chapter 9, the compiler provides each class with a default copy constructor that copies each data member of the constructor's argument object into the corresponding member of the object being initialized. Chapter 11 discusses how you can define customized copy constructors.

Figure 10.14 creates two `Date` objects (lines 11–12) and passes them as arguments to the constructor of the `Employee` object created in line 13. Line 16 outputs the `Employee` object's data. When each `Date` object is created in lines 11–12, the `Date` constructor defined in lines 11–28 of Fig. 10.11 displays a line of output to show that the constructor was called (see the first two lines of the sample output). [*Note:* Line 13 of Fig. 10.14 causes two additional `Date` constructor calls that do not appear in the program's output. When each of the `Employee`'s `Date` member object's is initialized in the `Employee` con-

```
1   // Fig. 10.10: Date.h
2   // Date class definition; Member functions defined in Date.cpp
3   #ifndef DATE_H
4   #define DATE_H
5
6   class Date
7   {
8   public:
9      Date( int = 1, int = 1, int = 1900 ); // default constructor
10     void print() const; // print date in month/day/year format
11     ~Date(); // provided to confirm destruction order
12  private:
13     int month; // 1-12 (January-December)
14     int day; // 1-31 based on month
15     int year; // any year
16
17     // utility function to check if day is proper for month and year
18     int checkDay( int ) const;
19  }; // end class Date
20
21  #endif
```

Fig. 10.10 | Date class definition.

structor's member initializer list (Fig. 10.13, lines 21–21), the default copy constructor for class `Date` is called. This constructor is defined implicitly by the compiler and does not contain any output statements to demonstrate when it is called. We discuss copy constructors and default copy constructors in detail in Chapter 11.]

```cpp
1   // Fig. 10.11: Date.cpp
2   // Date class member-function definitions.
3   #include <iostream>
4   using std::cout;
5   using std::endl;
6
7   #include "Date.h" // include Date class definition
8
9   // constructor confirms proper value for month; calls
10  // utility function checkDay to confirm proper value for day
11  Date::Date( int mn, int dy, int yr )
12  {
13     if ( mn > 0 && mn <= 12 ) // validate the month
14        month = mn;
15     else
16     {
17        month = 1; // invalid month set to 1
18        cout << "Invalid month (" << mn << ") set to 1.\n";
19     } // end else
20
21     year = yr; // could validate yr
22     day = checkDay( dy ); // validate the day
23
24     // output Date object to show when its constructor is called
25     cout << "Date object constructor for date ";
26     print();
27     cout << endl;
28  } // end Date constructor
29
30  // print Date object in form month/day/year
31  void Date::print() const
32  {
33     cout << month << '/' << day << '/' << year;
34  } // end function print
35
36  // output Date object to show when its destructor is called
37  Date::~Date()
38  {
39     cout << "Date object destructor for date ";
40     print();
41     cout << endl;
42  } // end ~Date destructor
43
44  // utility function to confirm proper day value based on
45  // month and year; handles leap years, too
46  int Date::checkDay( int testDay ) const
47  {
```

Fig. 10.11 | `Date` class member-function definitions. (Part 1 of 2.)

```
48    static const int daysPerMonth[ 13 ] =
49       { 0, 31, 28, 31, 30, 31, 30, 31, 31, 30, 31, 30, 31 };
50
51    // determine whether testDay is valid for specified month
52    if ( testDay > 0 && testDay <= daysPerMonth[ month ] )
53       return testDay;
54
55    // February 29 check for leap year
56    if ( month == 2 && testDay == 29 && ( year % 400 == 0 ||
57       ( year % 4 == 0 && year % 100 != 0 ) ) )
58       return testDay;
59
60    cout << "Invalid day (" << testDay << ") set to 1.\n";
61    return 1; // leave object in consistent state if bad value
62 } // end function checkDay
```

Fig. 10.11 | Date class member-function definitions. (Part 2 of 2.)

```
1   // Fig. 10.12: Employee.h
2   // Employee class definition showing composition.
3   // Member functions defined in Employee.cpp.
4   #ifndef EMPLOYEE_H
5   #define EMPLOYEE_H
6
7   #include "Date.h" // include Date class definition
8
9   class Employee
10  {
11  public:
12     Employee( const char * const, const char * const,
13        const Date &, const Date & );
14     void print() const;
15     ~Employee(); // provided to confirm destruction order
16  private:
17     char firstName[ 25 ];
18     char lastName[ 25 ];
19     const Date birthDate; // composition: member object
20     const Date hireDate; // composition: member object
21  }; // end class Employee
22
23  #endif
```

Fig. 10.12 | Employee class definition showing composition.

Class Date and class Employee each include a destructor (lines 37–42 of Fig. 10.11 and lines 51–55 of Fig. 10.13, respectively) that prints a message when an object of its class is destructed. This enables us to confirm in the program output that objects are constructed from the inside out and destroyed in the reverse order, from the outside in (i.e., the Date member objects are destroyed after the Employee object that contains them). Notice the last four lines in the output of Fig. 10.14. The last two lines are the outputs of the Date destructor running on Date objects hire (line 12) and birth (line 11), respectively. These outputs confirm that the three objects created in main are destructed in the reverse of the order in which they were constructed. (The `Employee` destructor output is five lines from the bottom.) The fourth and third lines from the bottom of the output window show the destructors running for the `Employee`'s member objects `hireDate` (Fig. 10.12, line 20) and `birthDate` (Fig. 10.12, line 19). These outputs confirm that the `Employee` object is destructed from the outside in—i.e., the `Employee` destructor runs first (output shown five lines from the bottom of the output window), then the member objects are destructed in the reverse order from which they were constructed. Again, the outputs in Fig. 10.14 did not show the constructors running for these member objects, because these were the default copy constructors provided by the C++ compiler.

```
1   // Fig. 10.13: Employee.cpp
2   // Employee class member-function definitions.
3   #include <iostream>
4   using std::cout;
5   using std::endl;
6
7   #include <cstring> // strlen and strncpy prototypes
8   using std::strlen;
9   using std::strncpy;
10
11  #include "Employee.h" // Employee class definition
12  #include "Date.h" // Date class definition
13
14  // constructor uses member initializer list to pass initializer
15  // values to constructors of member objects birthDate and hireDate
16  // [Note: This invokes the so-called "default copy constructor" which the
17  // C++ compiler provides implicitly.]
18  Employee::Employee( const char * const first, const char * const last,
19     const Date &dateOfBirth, const Date &dateOfHire )
20     : birthDate( dateOfBirth ), // initialize birthDate
21       hireDate( dateOfHire ) // initialize hireDate
22  {
23     // copy first into firstName and be sure that it fits
24     int length = strlen( first );
25     length = ( length < 25 ? length : 24 );
26     strncpy( firstName, first, length );
27     firstName[ length ] = '\0';
28
29     // copy last into lastName and be sure that it fits
30     length = strlen( last );
31     length = ( length < 25 ? length : 24 );
32     strncpy( lastName, last, length );
33     lastName[ length ] = '\0';
34
35     // output Employee object to show when constructor is called
36     cout << "Employee object constructor: "
37        << firstName << ' ' << lastName << endl;
38  } // end Employee constructor
39
```

Fig. 10.13 | `Employee` class member-function definitions, including constructor with a member initializer list. (Part 1 of 2.)

```
40   // print Employee object
41   void Employee::print() const
42   {
43      cout << lastName << ", " << firstName << "  Hired: ";
44      hireDate.print();
45      cout << "  Birthday: ";
46      birthDate.print();
47      cout << endl;
48   } // end function print
49
50   // output Employee object to show when its destructor is called
51   Employee::~Employee()
52   {
53      cout << "Employee object destructor: "
54         << lastName << ", " << firstName << endl;
55   } // end ~Employee destructor
```

Fig. 10.13 | Employee class member-function definitions, including constructor with a member initializer list. (Part 2 of 2.)

A member object does not need to be initialized explicitly through a member initializer. If a member initializer is not provided, the member object's default constructor will be called implicitly. Values, if any, established by the default constructor can be overridden by *set* functions. However, for complex initialization, this approach may require significant additional work and time.

```
1    // Fig. 10.14: fig10_14.cpp
2    // Demonstrating composition--an object with member objects.
3    #include <iostream>
4    using std::cout;
5    using std::endl;
6
7    #include "Employee.h" // Employee class definition
8
9    int main()
10   {
11      Date birth( 7, 24, 1949 );
12      Date hire( 3, 12, 1988 );
13      Employee manager( "Bob", "Blue", birth, hire );
14
15      cout << endl;
16      manager.print();
17
18      cout << "\nTest Date constructor with invalid values:\n";
19      Date lastDayOff( 14, 35, 1994 ); // invalid month and day
20      cout << endl;
21      return 0;
22   } // end main
```

Fig. 10.14 | Demonstrating composition—an object with member objects. (Part 1 of 2.)

```
Date object constructor for date 7/24/1949
Date object constructor for date 3/12/1988
Employee object constructor: Bob Blue                        Note that there are actually three
                                                             constructor calls when an
Blue, Bob  Hired: 3/12/1988  Birthday: 7/24/1949             Employee is constructed—two
                                                             calls to the Date class's default
Test Date constructor with invalid values:                  copy constructor (called from lines
Invalid month (14) set to 1.                                 20–21 of Fig. 10.13) and the call to
Invalid day (35) set to 1.                                   the Employee class's constructor.
Date object constructor for date 1/1/1994

Date object destructor for date 1/1/1994
Employee object destructor: Blue, Bob
Date object destructor for date 3/12/1988
Date object destructor for date 7/24/1949
Date object destructor for date 3/12/1988
Date object destructor for date 7/24/1949
```

Fig. 10.14 | Demonstrating composition—an object with member objects. (Part 2 of 2.)

Common Programming Error 10.6

A compilation error occurs if a member object is not initialized with a member initializer and the member object's class does not provide a default constructor (i.e., the member object's class defines one or more constructors, but none is a default constructor).

Performance Tip 10.2

Initialize member objects explicitly through member initializers. This eliminates the overhead of "doubly initializing" member objects—once when the member object's default constructor is called and again when set functions are called in the constructor body (or later) to initialize the member object.

Software Engineering Observation 10.7

If a class member is an object of another class, making that member object public *does not violate the encapsulation and hiding of that member object's* private *members. However, it does violate the encapsulation and hiding of the containing class's implementation, so member objects of class types should still be* private, *like all other data members.*

In line 26 of Fig. 10.11, notice the call to Date member function print. Many member functions of classes in C++ require no arguments. This is because each member function contains an implicit handle (in the form of a pointer) to the object on which it operates. We discuss the implicit pointer, which is represented by keyword this, in Section 10.5.

Class Employee uses two 25-character arrays (Fig. 10.12, lines 17–18) to represent the first name and last name of the Employee. These arrays may waste space for names shorter than 24 characters. (Remember, one character in each array is for the terminating null character, '\0', of the string.) Also, names longer than 24 characters must be truncated to fit in these fixed-size character arrays. Section 10.7 presents another version of class Employee that dynamically creates the exact amount of space required to hold the first and the last name.

Note that the simplest way to represent an Employee's first and last name using the exact amount of space required is to use two string objects (C++ Standard Library class string was introduced in Chapter 3). If we did this, the `Employee` constructor would appear as follows

```
Employee::Employee( const string &first, const string &last,
   const Date &dateOfBirth, const Date &dateOfHire )
   : firstName( first), // initialize firstName
     lastName( last ), // initialize lastName
     birthDate( dateOfBirth ), // initialize birthDate
     hireDate( dateOfHire ) // initialize hireDate
{
   // output Employee object to show when constructor is called
   cout << "Employee object constructor: "
      << firstName << ' ' << lastName << endl;
} // end Employee constructor
```

Notice that data members `firstName` and `lastName` (now `string` objects) are initialized through member initializers. The `Employee` classes presented in Chapters 12–13 use `string` objects in this fashion. In this chapter, we use pointer-based strings to give you additional exposure to pointer manipulation.

10.4 friend Functions and friend Classes

A `friend` function of a class is defined outside that class's scope, yet has the right to access the non-`public` (and `public`) members of the class. Standalone functions or entire classes may be declared to be friends of another class.

Using `friend` functions can enhance performance. This section presents a mechanical example of how a `friend` function works. Later in the book, `friend` functions are used to overload operators for use with class objects (Chapter 11) and to create iterator classes (Chapter 20, Data Structures). Objects of an iterator class can successively select items or perform an operation on items in a container class object (see Section 10.9). Objects of container classes can store items. Using friends is often appropriate when a member function cannot be used for certain operations, as we'll see in Chapter 11.

To declare a function as a friend of a class, precede the function prototype in the class definition with keyword `friend`. To declare all member functions of class `ClassTwo` as friends of class `ClassOne`, place a declaration of the form

```
friend class ClassTwo;
```

in the definition of class `ClassOne`.

 Software Engineering Observation 10.8

Even though the prototypes for `friend` functions appear in the class definition, friends are not member functions.

 Software Engineering Observation 10.9

Member access notions of `private`, `protected` and `public` are not relevant to `friend` declarations, so `friend` declarations can be placed anywhere in a class definition.

 Good Programming Practice 10.1

Place all friendship declarations first inside the class definition's body and do not precede them with any access specifier.

Friendship is granted, not taken—i.e., for class B to be a friend of class A, class A must explicitly declare that class B is its friend. Also, the friendship relation is neither symmetric nor transitive; i.e., if class A is a friend of class B, and class B is a friend of class C, you cannot infer that class B is a friend of class A (again, friendship is not symmetric), that class C is a friend of class B (also because friendship is not symmetric), or that class A is a friend of class C (friendship is not transitive).

Software Engineering Observation 10.10

Some people in the OOP community feel that "friendship" corrupts information hiding and weakens the value of the object-oriented design approach. In this text, we identify several examples of the responsible use of friendship.

Modifying a Class's *private* Data with a Friend Function

Figure 10.15 is a mechanical example in which we define friend function setX to set the private data member x of class Count. Note that the friend declaration (line 10) appears

```cpp
1   // Fig. 10.15: fig10_15.cpp
2   // Friends can access private members of a class.
3   #include <iostream>
4   using std::cout;
5   using std::endl;
6
7   // Count class definition
8   class Count
9   {
10     friend void setX( Count &, int ); // friend declaration
11  public:
12     // constructor
13     Count()
14        : x( 0 ) // initialize x to 0
15     {
16        // empty body
17     } // end constructor Count
18
19     // output x
20     void print() const
21     {
22        cout << x << endl;
23     } // end function print
24  private:
25     int x; // data member
26  }; // end class Count
27
28  // function setX can modify private data of Count
29  // because setX is declared as a friend of Count (line 10)
30  void setX( Count &c, int val )
31  {
32     c.x = val; // allowed because setX is a friend of Count
33  } // end function setX
34
```

Fig. 10.15 | Friends can access private members of a class. (Part 1 of 2.)

```
35  int main()
36  {
37     Count counter; // create Count object
38
39     cout << "counter.x after instantiation: ";
40     counter.print();
41
42     setX( counter, 8 ); // set x using a friend function
43     cout << "counter.x after call to setX friend function: ";
44     counter.print();
45     return 0;
46  } // end main
```

```
counter.x after instantiation: 0
counter.x after call to setX friend function: 8
```

Fig. 10.15 | Friends can access `private` members of a class. (Part 2 of 2.)

first (by convention) in the class definition, even before `public` member functions are declared. Again, this `friend` declaration can appear anywhere in the class.

Function setX (lines 30–33) is a C-style, stand-alone function—it is not a member function of class Count. For this reason, when setX is invoked for object counter, line 42 passes counter as an argument to setX rather than using a handle (such as the name of the object) to call the function, as in

```
counter.setX( 8 );
```

As we mentioned, Fig. 10.15 is a mechanical example of using the `friend` construct. It would normally be appropriate to define function setX as a member function of class Count. It would also normally be appropriate to separate the program of Fig. 10.15 into three files:

1. A header file (e.g., Count.h) containing the Count class definition, which in turn contains the prototype of `friend` function setX

2. An implementation file (e.g., Count.cpp) containing the definitions of class Count's member functions and the definition of `friend` function setX

3. A test program (e.g., fig10_15.cpp) with main.

Erroneously Attempting to Modify a private Member with a Non-friend Function
Figure 10.16 demonstrates the error messages produced by the compiler when non-`friend` function cannotSetX (lines 29–32) is called to modify `private` data member x.

```
1  // Fig. 10.16: fig10_16.cpp
2  // Non-friend/non-member functions cannot access private data of a class.
3  #include <iostream>
4  using std::cout;
5  using std::endl;
6
```

Fig. 10.16 | Non-`friend`/nonmember functions cannot access `private` members. (Part 1 of 2.)

```
7   // Count class definition (note that there is no friendship declaration)
8   class Count
9   {
10  public:
11     // constructor
12     Count()
13        : x( 0 ) // initialize x to 0
14     {
15        // empty body
16     } // end constructor Count
17
18     // output x
19     void print() const
20     {
21        cout << x << endl;
22     } // end function print
23  private:
24     int x; // data member
25  }; // end class Count
26
27  // function cannotSetX tries to modify private data of Count,
28  // but cannot because the function is not a friend of Count
29  void cannotSetX( Count &c, int val )
30  {
31     c.x = val; // ERROR: cannot access private member in Count
32  } // end function cannotSetX
33
34  int main()
35  {
36     Count counter; // create Count object
37
38     cannotSetX( counter, 3 ); // cannotSetX is not a friend
39     return 0;
40  } // end main
```

Borland C++ command-line compiler error message:

```
Error E2247 Fig10_16/fig10_16.cpp 31: 'Count::x' is not accessible in
   function cannotSetX(Count &,int)
```

Microsoft Visual C++ 2005 compiler error messages:

```
C:\cpphtp6_examples\ch10\Fig10_16\fig10_16.cpp(31) : error C2248: 'Count::x'
   : cannot access private member declared in class 'Count'
        C:\cpphtp6_examples\ch10\Fig10_16\fig10_16.cpp(24) : see declaration
           of 'Count::x'
        C:\cpphtp6_examples\ch10\Fig10_16\fig10_16.cpp(9) : see declaration
           of 'Count'
```

GNU C++ compiler error messages:

```
fig10_16.cpp:24: error: `int Count::x' is private
fig10_16.cpp:31: error: within this context
```

Fig. 10.16 | Non-friend/nonmember functions cannot access private members. (Part 2 of 2.)

It is possible to specify overloaded functions as friends of a class. Each overloaded function intended to be a friend must be explicitly declared in the class definition as a friend of the class.

10.5 Using the this Pointer

We have seen that an object's member functions can manipulate the object's data. How do member functions know *which* object's data members to manipulate? Every object has access to its own address through a pointer called this (a C++ keyword). An object's this pointer is *not* part of the object itself—i.e., the size of the memory occupied by the this pointer is not reflected in the result of a sizeof operation on the object. Rather, the this pointer is passed (by the compiler) as an implicit argument to each of the object's non-static member functions. Section 10.7 introduces static class members and explains why the this pointer is *not* implicitly passed to static member functions.

Objects use the this pointer implicitly (as we have done to this point) or explicitly to reference their data members and member functions. The type of the this pointer depends on the type of the object and whether the member function in which this is used is declared const. For example, in a nonconstant member function of class Employee, the this pointer has type Employee * const (a constant pointer to a nonconstant Employee object). In a constant member function of the class Employee, the this pointer has the data type const Employee * const (a constant pointer to a constant Employee object).

The next example shows implicit and explicit use of the this pointer; later in this chapter and in Chapter 11, we show some substantial and subtle examples of using this.

*Implicitly and Explicitly Using the **this** Pointer to Access an Object's Data Members*
Figure 10.17 demonstrates the implicit and explicit use of the this pointer to enable a member function of class Test to print the private data x of a Test object.

```
1   // Fig. 10.17: fig10_17.cpp
2   // Using the this pointer to refer to object members.
3   #include <iostream>
4   using std::cout;
5   using std::endl;
6
7   class Test
8   {
9   public:
10      Test( int = 0 ); // default constructor
11      void print() const;
12   private:
13      int x;
14   }; // end class Test
15
16   // constructor
17   Test::Test( int value )
18      : x( value ) // initialize x to value
19   {
```

Fig. 10.17 | this pointer implicitly and explicitly accessing an object's members. (Part 1 of 2.)

```
20        // empty body
21   } // end constructor Test
22
23   // print x using implicit and explicit this pointers;
24   // the parentheses around *this are required
25   void Test::print() const
26   {
27        // implicitly use the this pointer to access the member x
28        cout << "        x = " << x;
29
30        // explicitly use the this pointer and the arrow operator
31        // to access the member x
32        cout << "\n   this->x = " << this->x;
33
34        // explicitly use the dereferenced this pointer and
35        // the dot operator to access the member x
36        cout << "\n(*this).x = " << ( *this ).x << endl;
37   } // end function print
38
39   int main()
40   {
41        Test testObject( 12 ); // instantiate and initialize testObject
42
43        testObject.print();
44        return 0;
45   } // end main
```

```
        x = 12
   this->x = 12
(*this).x = 12
```

Fig. 10.17 | this pointer implicitly and explicitly accessing an object's members. (Part 2 of 2.)

For illustration purposes, member function print (lines 25–37) first prints x by using the this pointer implicitly (line 28)—only the name of the data member is specified. Then print uses two different notations to access x through the this pointer—the arrow operator (->) off the this pointer (line 32) and the dot operator (.) off the dereferenced this pointer (line 36).

Note the parentheses around *this (line 36) when used with the dot member selection operator (.). The parentheses are required because the dot operator has higher precedence than the * operator. Without the parentheses, the expression *this.x would be evaluated as if it were parenthesized as *(this.x), which is a compilation error, because the dot operator cannot be used with a pointer.

 Common Programming Error 10.7

Attempting to use the member selection operator (.) with a pointer to an object is a compilation error—the dot member selection operator may be used only with an lvalue *such as an object's name, a reference to an object or a dereferenced pointer to an object.*

One interesting use of the this pointer is to prevent an object from being assigned to itself. As we'll see in Chapter 11, self-assignment can cause serious errors when the object contains pointers to dynamically allocated storage.

*Using the **this** Pointer to Enable Cascaded Function Calls*

Another use of the this pointer is to enable cascaded member-function calls—that is, invoking multiple functions in the same statement (as in line 14 of Fig. 10.20). The program of Figs. 10.18–10.20 modifies class Time's *set* functions setTime, setHour, setMinute and setSecond such that each returns a reference to a Time object to enable cascaded member-function calls. Notice in Fig. 10.19 that the last statement in the body of each of these member functions returns *this (lines 26, 33, 40 and 47) into a return type of Time &.

```
1   // Fig. 10.18: Time.h
2   // Cascading member function calls.
3
4   // Time class definition.
5   // Member functions defined in Time.cpp.
6   #ifndef TIME_H
7   #define TIME_H
8
9   class Time
10  {
11  public:
12     Time( int = 0, int = 0, int = 0 ); // default constructor
13
14     // set functions (the Time & return types enable cascading)
15     Time &setTime( int, int, int ); // set hour, minute, second
16     Time &setHour( int ); // set hour
17     Time &setMinute( int ); // set minute
18     Time &setSecond( int ); // set second
19
20     // get functions (normally declared const)
21     int getHour() const; // return hour
22     int getMinute() const; // return minute
23     int getSecond() const; // return second
24
25     // print functions (normally declared const)
26     void printUniversal() const; // print universal time
27     void printStandard() const; // print standard time
28  private:
29     int hour; // 0 - 23 (24-hour clock format)
30     int minute; // 0 - 59
31     int second; // 0 - 59
32  }; // end class Time
33
34  #endif
```

Fig. 10.18 | Time class definition modified to enable cascaded member-function calls.

```
1   // Fig. 10.19: Time.cpp
2   // Time class member-function definitions.
3   #include <iostream>
4   using std::cout;
```

Fig. 10.19 | Time class member-function definitions modified to enable cascaded member-function calls. (Part 1 of 3.)

```
5
6    #include <iomanip>
7    using std::setfill;
8    using std::setw;
9
10   #include "Time.h" // Time class definition
11
12   // constructor function to initialize private data;
13   // calls member function setTime to set variables;
14   // default values are 0 (see class definition)
15   Time::Time( int hr, int min, int sec )
16   {
17      setTime( hr, min, sec );
18   } // end Time constructor
19
20   // set values of hour, minute, and second
21   Time &Time::setTime( int h, int m, int s ) // note Time & return
22   {
23      setHour( h );
24      setMinute( m );
25      setSecond( s );
26      return *this; // enables cascading
27   } // end function setTime
28
29   // set hour value
30   Time &Time::setHour( int h ) // note Time & return
31   {
32      hour = ( h >= 0 && h < 24 ) ? h : 0; // validate hour
33      return *this; // enables cascading
34   } // end function setHour
35
36   // set minute value
37   Time &Time::setMinute( int m ) // note Time & return
38   {
39      minute = ( m >= 0 && m < 60 ) ? m : 0; // validate minute
40      return *this; // enables cascading
41   } // end function setMinute
42
43   // set second value
44   Time &Time::setSecond( int s ) // note Time & return
45   {
46      second = ( s >= 0 && s < 60 ) ? s : 0; // validate second
47      return *this; // enables cascading
48   } // end function setSecond
49
50   // get hour value
51   int Time::getHour() const
52   {
53      return hour;
54   } // end function getHour
55
```

Fig. 10.19 | Time class member-function definitions modified to enable cascaded member-function calls. (Part 2 of 3.)

```
56   // get minute value
57   int Time::getMinute() const
58   {
59      return minute;
60   } // end function getMinute
61
62   // get second value
63   int Time::getSecond() const
64   {
65      return second;
66   } // end function getSecond
67
68   // print Time in universal-time format (HH:MM:SS)
69   void Time::printUniversal() const
70   {
71      cout << setfill( '0' ) << setw( 2 ) << hour << ":"
72         << setw( 2 ) << minute << ":" << setw( 2 ) << second;
73   } // end function printUniversal
74
75   // print Time in standard-time format (HH:MM:SS AM or PM)
76   void Time::printStandard() const
77   {
78      cout << ( ( hour == 0 || hour == 12 ) ? 12 : hour % 12 )
79         << ":" << setfill( '0' ) << setw( 2 ) << minute
80         << ":" << setw( 2 ) << second << ( hour < 12 ? " AM" : " PM" );
81   } // end function printStandard
```

Fig. 10.19 | Time class member-function definitions modified to enable cascaded member-function calls. (Part 3 of 3.)

```
1    // Fig. 10.20: fig10_20.cpp
2    // Cascading member-function calls with the this pointer.
3    #include <iostream>
4    using std::cout;
5    using std::endl;
6
7    #include "Time.h" // Time class definition
8
9    int main()
10   {
11      Time t; // create Time object
12
13      // cascaded function calls
14      t.setHour( 18 ).setMinute( 30 ).setSecond( 22 );
15
16      // output time in universal and standard formats
17      cout << "Universal time: ";
18      t.printUniversal();
19
20      cout << "\nStandard time: ";
21      t.printStandard();
```

Fig. 10.20 | Cascading member-function calls with the this pointer. (Part 1 of 2.)

```
22
23        cout << "\n\nNew standard time: ";
24
25        // cascaded function calls
26        t.setTime( 20, 20, 20 ).printStandard();
27        cout << endl;
28        return 0;
29   } // end main
```

```
Universal time: 18:30:22
Standard time: 6:30:22 PM

New standard time: 8:20:20 PM
```

Fig. 10.20 | Cascading member-function calls with the this pointer. (Part 2 of 2.)

The program of Fig. 10.20 creates Time object t (line 11), then uses it in cascaded member-function calls (lines 14 and 26). Why does the technique of returning *this as a reference work? The dot operator (.) associates from left to right, so line 14 first evaluates t.setHour(18), then returns a reference to object t as the value of this function call. The remaining expression is then interpreted as

        t.setMinute(30).setSecond(22);

The t.setMinute(30) call executes and returns a reference to the object t. The remaining expression is interpreted as

        t.setSecond(22);

Line 26 also uses cascading. The calls must appear in the order shown in line 26, because printStandard as defined in the class does not return a reference to t. Placing the call to printStandard before the call to setTime in line 26 results in a compilation error. Chapter 11 presents several practical examples of using cascaded function calls. One such example uses multiple << operators with cout to output multiple values in a single statement.

10.6 Dynamic Memory Management with Operators new and delete

C++ enables programmers to control the allocation and deallocation of memory in a program for any built-in or user-defined type. This is known as dynamic memory management and is performed with operators new and delete. Recall that class Employee (Figs. 10.12–10.13) uses two 25-character arrays to represent the first and last name of an Employee. The Employee class definition (Fig. 10.12) must specify the number of elements in each of these arrays when it declares them as data members, because the size of the data members dictates the amount of memory required to store an Employee object. As we discussed earlier, these arrays may waste space for names shorter than 24 characters. Also, names longer than 24 characters must be truncated to fit in these fixed-size arrays.

Wouldn't it be nice if we could use arrays containing exactly the number of elements needed to store an Employee's first and last name? Dynamic memory management allows us to do exactly that. As you'll see in the example of Section 10.7, if we replace array data members `firstName` and `lastName` with pointers to `char`, we can use the `new` operator to dynamically allocate (i.e., reserve) the exact amount of memory required to hold each name at execution time. Dynamically allocating memory in this fashion causes an array (or any other built-in or user-defined type) to be created in the free store (sometimes called the heap)—a region of memory assigned to each program for storing dynamically allocated objects. Once the memory for an array is allocated in the free store, we can gain access to it by aiming a pointer at the first element of the array. When we no longer need the array, we can return the memory to the free store by using the `delete` operator to deallocate (i.e., release) the memory, which can then be reused by future `new` operations.

Again, we present the modified `Employee` class as described here in the example of Section 10.7. First, we present the details of using the `new` and `delete` operators to dynamically allocate memory to store objects, fundamental types and arrays.

Consider the following declaration and statement:

```
Time *timePtr;
timePtr = new Time;
```

The `new` operator allocates storage of the proper size for an object of type `Time`, calls the default constructor to initialize the object and returns a pointer to the type specified to the right of the `new` operator (i.e., a `Time *`). Note that `new` can be used to dynamically allocate any fundamental type (such as `int` or `double`) or class type. If `new` is unable to find sufficient space in memory for the object, it indicates that an error occurred by "throwing an exception." Chapter 16, Exception Handling, discusses how to deal with `new` failures in the context of the ISO/IEC C++ standard. In particular, we'll show how to "catch" the exception thrown by `new` and deal with it. When a program does not "catch" an exception, the program terminates immediately.

Portability Tip 10.1

On failure, the `new` operator returns a 0 pointer in versions of C++ prior to the ISO/IEC standard. We use the standard version of operator `new` throughout this book.

To destroy a dynamically allocated object and free the space for the object, use the `delete` operator as follows:

```
delete timePtr;
```

This statement first calls the destructor for the object to which `timePtr` points, then deallocates the memory associated with the object. After the preceding statement, the memory can be reused by the system to allocate other objects.

Common Programming Error 10.8

Not releasing dynamically allocated memory when it is no longer needed can cause the system to run out of memory prematurely. This is sometimes called a "memory leak."

You can provide an initializer for a newly created fundamental-type variable, as in

```
double *ptr = new double( 3.14159 );
```

which initializes a newly created `double` to `3.14159` and assigns the resulting pointer to `ptr`. The same syntax can be used to specify a comma-separated list of arguments to the constructor of an object. For example,

```
        Time *timePtr = new Time( 12, 45, 0 );
```

initializes a newly created Time object to 12:45 PM and assigns the resulting pointer to timePtr.

As discussed earlier, the new operator can be used to allocate arrays dynamically. For example, a 10-element integer array can be allocated and assigned to gradesArray as follows:

```
        int *gradesArray = new int[ 10 ];
```

which declares int pointer gradesArray and assigns it a pointer to the first element of a dynamically allocated 10-element array of ints. Recall that the size of an array created at compile time must be specified using a constant integral expression. However, the size of a dynamically allocated array can be specified using *any* non-negative integral expression that can be evaluated at execution time. Also note that, when allocating an array of objects dynamically, you cannot pass arguments to each object's constructor. Instead, each object in the array is initialized by its default constructor. To delete the dynamically allocated array to which gradesArray points, use the statement

```
        delete [] gradesArray;
```

The preceding statement deallocates the array to which gradesArray points. If the pointer in the preceding statement points to an array of objects, the statement first calls the destructor for every object in the array, then deallocates the memory. If the preceding statement did not include the square brackets ([]) and gradesArray pointed to an array of objects, the result is undefined. Some compilers call the detructor only for the first object in the array. Using delete on a null pointer (i.e., a pointer with the value 0) has no effect.

Common Programming Error 10.9

Using delete instead of delete [] for arrays of objects can lead to runtime logic errors. To ensure that every object in the array receives a destructor call, always delete memory allocated as an array with operator delete []. Similarly, always delete memory allocated as an individual element with operator delete; otherwise, the result of the operation is undefined.

10.7 static Class Members

There is an important exception to the rule that each object of a class has its own copy of all the data members of the class. In certain cases, only one copy of a variable should be shared by all objects of a class. A **static data member** is used for these and other reasons. Such a variable represents "class-wide" information (i.e., a property of the class shared by all instances, not a property of a specific object of the class). The declaration of a static member begins with keyword static. Recall that the versions of class GradeBook in Chapter 7 use static data members to store constants representing the number of grades that all GradeBook objects can hold.

Let us further motivate the need for static class-wide data with an example. Suppose that we have a video game with Martians and other space creatures. Each Martian tends to be brave and willing to attack other space creatures when the Martian is aware that there are at least five Martians present. If fewer than five are present, each Martian becomes cowardly. So each Martian needs to know the martianCount. We could endow each instance of class Martian with martianCount as a data member. If we do, every Martian will have a separate copy of the data member. Every time we create a new Martian, we'll have to update the data member martianCount in all Martian objects. Doing this would require every Martian object to have, or have access to, handles to all other Martian objects in memory. This wastes space with the redundant copies and wastes time in updating the separate copies. Instead, we declare martianCount to be static. This makes martian-Count class-wide data. Every Martian can access martianCount as if it were a data member of the Martian, but only one copy of the static variable martianCount is maintained by C++. This saves space. We save time by having the Martian constructor increment static variable martianCount and having the Martian destructor decrement martianCount. Because there is only one copy, we do not have to increment or decrement separate copies of martianCount for each Martian object.

> **Performance Tip 10.3**
>
> *Use static data members to save storage when a single copy of the data for all objects of a class will suffice.*

Although they may seem like global variables, a class's static data members have class scope. Also, static members can be declared public, private or protected. A fundamental-type static data member is initialized by default to 0. If you want a different initial value, a static data member can be initialized *once* (and only once). A const static data member of int or enum type can be initialized in its declaration in the class definition. However, all other static data members must be defined at file scope (i.e., outside the body of the class definition) and can be initialized only in those definitions. Note that static data members of class types (i.e., static member objects) that have default constructors need not be initialized because their default constructors will be called.

A class's private and protected static members are normally accessed through public member functions of the class or through friends of the class. (In Chapter 12, we'll see that a class's private and protected static members can also be accessed through protected member functions of the class.) A class's static members exist even when no objects of that class exist. To access a public static class member when no objects of the class exist, simply prefix the class name and the binary scope resolution operator (::) to the name of the data member. For example, if our preceding variable martian-Count is public, it can be accessed with the expression Martian::martianCount when there are no Martian objects. (Of course, using public data is discouraged.)

A class's public static class members can also be accessed through any object of that class using the object's name, the dot operator and the name of the member (e.g., myMartian.martianCount). To access a private or protected static class member when no objects of the class exist, provide a public static member function and call the function by prefixing its name with the class name and binary scope resolution operator. (As we'll see in Chapter 12, a protected static member function can serve this purpose, too.) A static member function is a service of the *class*, not of a specific object of the class.

> **Software Engineering Observation 10.11**
>
> *A class's static data members and static member functions exist and can be used even if no objects of that class have been instantiated.*

The program of Figs. 10.21–10.23 demonstrates a private static data member called count (Fig. 10.21, line 21) and a public static member function called getCount (Fig. 10.21, line 15). In Fig. 10.22, line 14 defines and initializes the data member count

```
 1   // Fig. 10.21: Employee.h
 2   // Employee class definition.
 3   #ifndef EMPLOYEE_H
 4   #define EMPLOYEE_H
 5
 6   class Employee
 7   {
 8   public:
 9      Employee( const char * const, const char * const ); // constructor
10      ~Employee(); // destructor
11      const char *getFirstName() const; // return first name
12      const char *getLastName() const; // return last name
13
14      // static member function
15      static int getCount(); // return number of objects instantiated
16   private:
17      char *firstName;
18      char *lastName;
19
20      // static data
21      static int count; // number of objects instantiated
22   }; // end class Employee
23
24   #endif
```

Fig. 10.21 | Employee class definition with a static data member to track the number of Employee objects in memory.

to zero *at file scope* and lines 18–21 define static member function getCount. Notice that neither line 14 nor line 18 includes keyword static, yet both lines refer to static class members. When static is applied to an item at file scope, that item becomes known only in that file. The static members of the class need to be available from any client code that accesses the file, so we cannot declare them static in the .cpp file—we declare them static only in the .h file. Data member count maintains a count of the number of objects of class Employee that have been instantiated. When objects of class Employee exist, member count can be referenced through any member function of an Employee object— in Fig. 10.22, count is referenced by both line 33 in the constructor and line 48 in the destructor. Also, note that since count is an int, it could have been initialized in the header file in line 21 of Fig. 10.21.

Common Programming Error 10.10

It is a compilation error to include keyword static in the definition of a static data members at file scope.

```
 1   // Fig. 10.22: Employee.cpp
 2   // Employee class member-function definitions.
 3   #include <iostream>
 4   using std::cout;
 5   using std::endl;
```

Fig. 10.22 | Employee class member-function definitions. (Part 1 of 3.)

```
6
7   #include <cstring> // strlen and strcpy prototypes
8   using std::strlen;
9   using std::strcpy;
10
11  #include "Employee.h" // Employee class definition
12
13  // define and initialize static data member at file scope
14  int Employee::count = 0; // cannot include keyword static
15
16  // define static member function that returns number of
17  // Employee objects instantiated (declared static in Employee.h)
18  int Employee::getCount()
19  {
20     return count;
21  } // end static function getCount
22
23  // constructor dynamically allocates space for first and last name and
24  // uses strcpy to copy first and last names into the object
25  Employee::Employee( const char * const first, const char * const last )
26  {
27     firstName = new char[ strlen( first ) + 1 ]; // create space
28     strcpy( firstName, first ); // copy first into object
29
30     lastName = new char[ strlen( last ) + 1 ]; // create space
31     strcpy( lastName, last ); // copy last into object
32
33     count++; // increment static count of employees
34
35     cout << "Employee constructor for " << firstName
36        << ' ' << lastName << " called." << endl;
37  } // end Employee constructor
38
39  // destructor deallocates dynamically allocated memory
40  Employee::~Employee()
41  {
42     cout << "~Employee() called for " << firstName
43        << ' ' << lastName << endl;
44
45     delete [] firstName; // release memory
46     delete [] lastName; // release memory
47
48     count--; // decrement static count of employees
49  } // end ~Employee destructor
50
51  // return first name of employee
52  const char *Employee::getFirstName() const
53  {
54     // const before return type prevents client from modifying
55     // private data; client should copy returned string before
56     // destructor deletes storage to prevent undefined pointer
57     return firstName;
58  } // end function getFirstName
```

Fig. 10.22 | Employee class member-function definitions. (Part 2 of 3.)

```
59
60   // return last name of employee
61   const char *Employee::getLastName() const
62   {
63      // const before return type prevents client from modifying
64      // private data; client should copy returned string before
65      // destructor deletes storage to prevent undefined pointer
66      return lastName;
67   } // end function getLastName
```

Fig. 10.22 | Employee class member-function definitions. (Part 3 of 3.)

In Fig. 10.22, note the use of the new operator (lines 27 and 30) in the Employee constructor to dynamically allocate the correct amount of memory for members firstName and lastName. If the new operator is unable to fulfill the request for memory for one or both of these character arrays, the program will terminate immediately. In Chapter 16, we'll provide a better mechanism for dealing with cases in which new is unable to allocate memory.

Also note in Fig. 10.22 that the implementations of functions getFirstName (lines 52–58) and getLastName (lines 61–67) return pointers to const character data. In this implementation, if the client wishes to retain a copy of the first name or last name, the client is responsible for copying the dynamically allocated memory in the Employee object after obtaining the pointer to const character data from the object. It is also possible to implement getFirstName and getLastName, so the client is required to pass a character array and the size of the array to each function. Then the functions could copy the first or last name into the character array provided by the client. Once again, note that we could have used class string here to return a copy of a string object to the caller rather than returning a pointer to the private data.

Figure 10.23 uses static member function getCount to determine the number of Employee objects currently instantiated. Note that when no objects are instantiated in the program, the Employee::getCount() function call is issued (lines 14 and 38). However, when objects are instantiated, function getCount can be called through either of the objects, as shown in the statement in lines 22–23, which uses pointer e1Ptr to invoke function getCount. Note that using e2Ptr->getCount() or Employee::getCount() in line 23 would produce the same result, because getCount always accesses the same static member count.

```
1   // Fig. 10.23: fig10_23.cpp
2   // static data member tracking the number of objects of a class.
3   #include <iostream>
4   using std::cout;
5   using std::endl;
6
7   #include "Employee.h" // Employee class definition
8
9   int main()
10  {
```

Fig. 10.23 | static data member tracking the number of objects of a class. (Part 1 of 2.)

```
11    // use class name and binary scope resolution operator to
12    // access static number function getCount
13    cout << "Number of employees before instantiation of any objects is "
14        << Employee::getCount() << endl; // use class name
15
16    // use new to dynamically create two new Employees
17    // operator new also calls the object's constructor
18    Employee *e1Ptr = new Employee( "Susan", "Baker" );
19    Employee *e2Ptr = new Employee( "Robert", "Jones" );
20
21    // call getCount on first Employee object
22    cout << "Number of employees after objects are instantiated is "
23        << e1Ptr->getCount();
24
25    cout << "\n\nEmployee 1: "
26        << e1Ptr->getFirstName() << " " << e1Ptr->getLastName()
27        << "\nEmployee 2: "
28        << e2Ptr->getFirstName() << " " << e2Ptr->getLastName() << "\n\n";
29
30    delete e1Ptr; // deallocate memory
31    e1Ptr = 0; // disconnect pointer from free-store space
32    delete e2Ptr; // deallocate memory
33    e2Ptr = 0; // disconnect pointer from free-store space
34
35    // no objects exist, so call static member function getCount again
36    // using the class name and the binary scope resolution operator
37    cout << "Number of employees after objects are deleted is "
38        << Employee::getCount() << endl;
39    return 0;
40 } // end main
```

```
Number of employees before instantiation of any objects is 0
Employee constructor for Susan Baker called.
Employee constructor for Robert Jones called.
Number of employees after objects are instantiated is 2

Employee 1: Susan Baker
Employee 2: Robert Jones

~Employee() called for Susan Baker
~Employee() called for Robert Jones
Number of employees after objects are deleted is 0
```

Fig. 10.23 | static data member tracking the number of objects of a class. (Part 2 of 2.)

Software Engineering Observation 10.12

Some organizations specify in their software engineering standards that all calls to static member functions be made using the class name rather than an object handle.

A member function should be declared static if it does not access non-static data members or non-static member functions of the class. Unlike non-static member functions, a static member function does not have a this pointer, because static data members and static member functions exist independently of any objects of a class. The this pointer must refer to a specific object of the class, and when a `static` member function is called, there might not be any objects of its class in memory.

Common Programming Error 10.11

Using the `this` pointer in a `static` member function is a compilation error.

Common Programming Error 10.12

Declaring a `static` member function `const` is a compilation error. The `const` qualifier indicates that a function cannot modify the contents of the object in which it operates, but `static` member functions exist and operate independently of any objects of the class.

Lines 18–19 of Fig. 10.23 use operator `new` to dynamically allocate two `Employee` objects. Remember that the program will terminate immediately if it is unable to allocate one or both of these objects. When each `Employee` object is allocated, its constructor is called. When `delete` is used in lines 30 and 32 to deallocate the `Employee` objects, each object's destructor is called.

Error-Prevention Tip 10.2

After deleting dynamically allocated memory, set the pointer that referred to that memory to 0. This disconnects the pointer from the previously allocated space on the free store. This space in memory could still contain information, despite having been deleted. By setting the pointer to 0, the program loses any access to that free-store space, which, in fact, could have already been reallocated for a different purpose. If you didn't set the pointer to 0, your code could inadvertently access this new information, causing extremely subtle, nonrepeatable logic errors.

10.8 Data Abstraction and Information Hiding

A class normally hides its implementation details from its clients. This is called information hiding. As an example of information hiding, let us consider the stack data structure introduced in Section 6.11.

Stacks can be implemented with arrays and with other data structures, such as linked lists. (We discuss stacks and linked lists in Chapter 14, Templates and Chapter 20.) A client of a stack class need not be concerned with the stack's implementation. The client knows only that when data items are placed in the stack, they will be recalled in last-in, first-out order. The client cares about *what* functionality a stack offers, not about *how* that functionality is implemented. This concept is referred to as data abstraction. Although programmers might know the details of a class's implementation, they should not write code that depends on these details. This enables a particular class (such as one that implements a stack and its operations, *push* and *pop*) to be replaced with another version without affecting the rest of the system. As long as the `public` services of the class do not change (i.e., every original `public` member function still has the same prototype in the new class definition), the rest of the system is not affected.

Many programming languages emphasize actions. In these languages, data exists to support the actions that programs must take. Data is "less interesting" than actions. Data is "crude." Only a few built-in data types exist, and it is difficult for programmers to create their own types. C++ and the object-oriented style of programming elevate the importance of data. The primary activities of object-oriented programming in C++ are the creation of types (i.e., classes) and the expression of the interactions among objects of those types. To create languages that emphasize data, the programming-languages community needed to formalize some notions about data. The formalization we consider here is the notion of abstract data types (ADTs), which improve the program development process.

What is an abstract data type? Consider the built-in type int, which most people would associate with an integer in mathematics. Rather, an int is an abstract representation of an integer. Unlike mathematical integers, computer ints are fixed in size. For example, type int on today's popular 32-bit machines is typically limited to the range –2,147,483,648 to +2,147,483,647. If the result of a calculation falls outside this range, an "overflow" error occurs and the computer responds in some machine-dependent manner. It might, for example, "quietly" produce an incorrect result, such as a value too large to fit in an int variable (commonly called arithmetic overflow). Mathematical integers do not have this problem. Therefore, the notion of a computer int is only an approximation of the notion of a real-world integer. The same is true with double.

Even char is an approximation; char values are normally eight-bit patterns of ones and zeros; these patterns look nothing like the characters they represent, such as a capital Z, a lowercase z, a dollar sign ($), a digit (5), and so on. Values of type char on most computers are quite limited compared with the range of real-world characters. The seven-bit ASCII character set (Appendix B) provides for 128 different character values. This is inadequate for representing languages such as Japanese and Chinese that require thousands of characters. As Internet and World Wide Web usage becomes pervasive, the newer Unicode character set is growing rapidly in popularity, owing to its ability to represent the characters of most languages. For more information on Unicode, visit www.unicode.org.

The point is that even the built-in data types provided with programming languages like C++ are really only approximations or imperfect models of real-world concepts and behaviors. We have taken int for granted until this point, but now you have a new perspective to consider. Types like int, double, char and others are all examples of abstract data types. They are essentially ways of representing real-world notions to some satisfactory level of precision within a computer system.

An abstract data type actually captures two notions—A data representation and the operations that can be performed on that data. For example, in C++, an int contains an integer value (data) and provides addition, subtraction, multiplication, division and modulus operations (among others)—division by zero is undefined. These allowed operations perform in a manner sensitive to machine parameters, such as the fixed word size of the underlying computer system. Another example is the notion of negative integers, whose operations and data representation are clear, but the operation of taking the square root of a negative integer is undefined. In C++, you can use classes to implement abstract data types and their services. For example, to implement a stack ADT, we create our own stack classes in Chapters 14 and 20, and we study the standard library stack class in Chapter 22, Standard Template Library (STL).

10.8.1 Example: Array Abstract Data Type

We discussed arrays in Chapter 7. As described there, an array is not much more than a pointer and some space in memory. This primitive capability is acceptable for performing array operations if you are cautious and undemanding. There are many operations that would be nice to perform with arrays, but that are not built into C++. With C++ classes, you can develop an array ADT that is preferable to "raw" arrays. The array class can provide many helpful new capabilities such as

- subscript range checking

- an arbitrary range of subscripts instead of having to start with 0

- array assignment

- array comparison

- array input/output

- arrays that know their sizes

- arrays that expand dynamically to accommodate more elements

- arrays that can print themselves in neat tabular format.

We create our own array class with many of these capabilities in Chapter 11. Recall that C++ Standard Library class template `vector` (introduced in Chapter 7) provides many of these capabilities as well. Chapter 22 explains class template `vector` in detail. C++ has a small set of built-in types. Classes extend the base programming language with new types.

Software Engineering Observation 10.13

You can create new types through the class mechanism. These new types can be designed to be used as conveniently as the built-in types. Thus, C++ is an extensible language. *Although the language is easy to extend with these new types, the base language itself cannot be changed.*

New classes created in C++ environments can be proprietary to an individual, to small groups or to companies. Classes can also be placed in standard class libraries intended for wide distribution. The C++ Standard includes a standard class library. Once you learn C++ and object-oriented programming, you'll be ready to take advantage of the new kinds of rapid, component-oriented software development made possible with increasingly abundant and rich libraries.

10.8.2 Example: String Abstract Data Type

C++ is an intentionally sparse language that provides programmers with only the raw capabilities needed to build a broad range of systems (consider it a tool for making tools). The language is designed to minimize performance burdens. C++ is appropriate for both applications programming and systems programming—the latter places extraordinary performance demands on programs. Certainly, it would have been possible to include a string data type among C++'s built-in data types. Instead, the language was designed to include mechanisms for creating and implementing string abstract data types through classes. We introduced the C++ Standard Library class `string` in Chapter 3, and in Chapter 11 we develop our own `String` ADT. We discuss class `string` in detail in Chapter 18.

10.8.3 Example: Queue Abstract Data Type

Each of us stands in line from time to time. A waiting line is also called a queue. We wait in line at the supermarket to check out, we wait in line to get gasoline, we wait in line to board a bus, we wait in line to pay a highway toll, and students know all too well about waiting in line during registration to get the courses they want. Computer systems use waiting lines internally, so we need to write programs that simulate what queues are and do.

A queue is another example of an abstract data type. Queues offer well-understood behavior to their clients. Clients put things in a queue one at a time—by invoking the queue's enqueue operation—and the clients get those things back one at a time on demand—by invoking the queue's dequeue operation. Conceptually, a queue can become infinitely long. A real queue, of course, is finite. Items are returned from a queue in first-in, first-out (FIFO) order—the first item inserted in the queue is the first item removed from the queue.

The queue hides an internal data representation that keeps track of the items currently waiting in line, and it offers a set of operations to its clients, namely, *enqueue* and *dequeue*. The clients are not concerned about the implementation of the queue. Clients merely want the queue to operate "as advertised." When a client enqueues a new item, the queue should accept that item and place it internally in some kind of first-in, first-out data structure. When the client wants the next item from the front of the queue, the queue should remove the item from its internal representation and deliver it to the outside world (i.e., to the client of the queue) in FIFO order (i.e., the item that has been in the queue the longest should be the next one returned by the next *dequeue* operation).

The queue ADT guarantees the integrity of its internal data structure. Clients may not manipulate this data structure directly. Only the queue member functions have access to its internal data. Clients may cause only allowable operations to be performed on the data representation; operations not provided in the ADT's public interface are rejected in some appropriate manner. This could mean issuing an error message, throwing an exception (see Chapter 16), terminating execution or simply ignoring the operation request.

We create our own queue class in Chapter 20, and we study the Standard Library queue class in Chapter 22.

10.9 Container Classes and Iterators

Among the most popular types of classes are container classes (also called collection classes), i.e., classes designed to hold collections of objects. Container classes commonly provide services such as insertion, deletion, searching, sorting, and testing an item to determine whether it is a member of the collection. Arrays, stacks, queues, trees and linked lists are examples of container classes; we studied arrays in Chapter 7 and will study each of these other data structures in Chapter 20, and Chapter 22.

It is common to associate iterator objects—or more simply iterators—with container classes. An iterator is an object that "walks through" a collection, returning the next item (or performing some action on the next item). Once an iterator for a class has been written, obtaining the next element from the class can be expressed simply. Just as a book being shared by several people could have several bookmarks in it at once, a container class can have several iterators operating on it at once. Each iterator maintains its own "position" information. We discuss containers and iterators in detail in Chapter 22.

10.10 Proxy Classes

Recall that two of the fundamental principles of good software engineering are separating interface from implementation and hiding implementation details. We strive to achieve these goals by defining a class in a header file and implementing its member functions in a separate implementation file. As we pointed out in Chapter 9, however, header files *do* contain a portion of a class's implementation and hints about others. For example, a class's `private` members are listed in the class definition in a header file, so these members are visible to clients, even though the clients may not access the `private` members. Revealing a class's `private` data in this manner potentially exposes proprietary information to clients of the class. We now introduce the notion of a proxy class that allows you to hide even the `private` data of a class from clients of the class. Providing clients of your class with a proxy class that knows only the `public` interface to your class enables the clients to use your class's services without giving the clients access to your class's implementation details.

Implementing a proxy class requires several steps, which we demonstrate in Figs. 10.24–10.27. First, we create the class definition for the class that contains the proprietary implementation we would like to hide. Our example class, called `Implementation`, is shown in Fig. 10.24. The proxy class `Interface` is shown in Figs. 10.25–10.26. The test program and sample output are shown in Fig. 10.27.

Class `Implementation` (Fig. 10.24) provides a single `private` data member called `value` (the data we would like to hide from the client), a constructor to initialize `value` and functions `setValue` and `getValue`.

We define a proxy class called `Interface` (Fig. 10.25) with an identical `public` interface (except for the constructor and destructor names) to that of class `Implementation`. The only `private` member of the proxy class is a pointer to an object of class `Implemen`-

```
1   // Fig. 10.24: Implementation.h
2   // Implementation class definition.
3
4   class Implementation
5   {
6   public:
7      // constructor
8      Implementation( int v )
9         : value( v ) // initialize value with v
10     {
11        // empty body
12     } // end constructor Implementation
13
14     // set value to v
15     void setValue( int v )
16     {
17        value = v; // should validate v
18     } // end function setValue
19
20     // return value
21     int getValue() const
22     {
23        return value;
24     } // end function getValue
25  private:
26     int value; // data that we would like to hide from the client
27  }; // end class Implementation
```

Fig. 10.24 | `Implementation` class definition.

```
 1    // Fig. 10.25: Interface.h
 2    // Proxy class Interface definition.
 3    // Client sees this source code, but the source code does not reveal
 4    // the data layout of class Implementation.
 5
 6    class Implementation; // forward class declaration required by line 17
 7
 8    class Interface
 9    {
10    public:
11       Interface( int ); // constructor
12       void setValue( int ); // same public interface as
13       int getValue() const; // class Implementation has
14       ~Interface(); // destructor
15    private:
16       // requires previous forward declaration (line 6)
17       Implementation *ptr;
18    }; // end class Interface
```

Fig. 10.25 | Proxy class `Interface` definition.

tation. Using a pointer in this manner allows us to hide the implementation details of class `Implementation` from the client. Notice that the only mentions in class `Interface` of the proprietary `Implementation` class are in the pointer declaration (line 17) and in line 6, a forward class declaration. When a class definition (such as class `Interface`) uses only a pointer or reference to an object of another class (such as to an object of class `Implementation`), the class header file for that other class (which would ordinarily reveal the `private` data of that class) is not required to be included with `#include`. This is because the compiler doesn't need to reserve space for an object of the class. The compiler does need to reserve space for the pointer or reference. The sizes of pointers and references are characteristics of the hardware platform on which the compiler runs, so the compiler already knows those sizes. You can simply declare that other class as a data type with a forward class declaration (line 6) before the type is used in the file.

The member-function implementation file for proxy class `Interface` (Fig. 10.26) is the only file that includes the header file `Implementation.h` (line 5) containing class `Implementation`. The file `Interface.cpp` (Fig. 10.26) is provided to the client as a precompiled object code file along with the header file `Interface.h` that includes the function prototypes of the services provided by the proxy class. Because file `Interface.cpp` is made available to the client only as object code, the client is not able to see the interactions between the proxy class and the proprietary class (lines 9, 17, 23 and 29). Notice that the proxy class imposes an extra "layer" of function calls as the "price to pay" for hiding the `private` data of class Implementation. Given the speed of today's computers and the fact that many compilers can inline simple function calls automatically, the effect of these extra function calls on performance is often negligible.

Figure 10.27 tests class `Interface`. Notice that only the header file for `Interface` is included in the client code (line 7)—there is no mention of the existence of a separate class called `Implementation`. Thus, the client never sees the `private` data of class `Implementation`, nor can the client code become dependent on the `Implementation` code.

```
1   // Fig. 10.26: Interface.cpp
2   // Implementation of class Interface--client receives this file only
3   // as precompiled object code, keeping the implementation hidden.
4   #include "Interface.h" // Interface class definition
5   #include "Implementation.h" // Implementation class definition
6
7   // constructor
8   Interface::Interface( int v )
9      : ptr ( new Implementation( v ) ) // initialize ptr to point to
10  {                                     // a new Implementation object
11     // empty body
12  } // end Interface constructor
13
14  // call Implementation's setValue function
15  void Interface::setValue( int v )
16  {
17     ptr->setValue( v );
18  } // end function setValue
19
20  // call Implementation's getValue function
21  int Interface::getValue() const
22  {
23     return ptr->getValue();
24  } // end function getValue
25
26  // destructor
27  Interface::~Interface()
28  {
29     delete ptr;
30  } // end ~Interface destructor
```

Fig. 10.26 | Interface class member-function definitions.

Software Engineering Observation 10.14

A proxy class insulates client code from implementation changes.

```
1   // Fig. 10.27: fig10_27.cpp
2   // Hiding a class's private data with a proxy class.
3   #include <iostream>
4   using std::cout;
5   using std::endl;
6
7   #include "Interface.h" // Interface class definition
8
9   int main()
10  {
11     Interface i( 5 ); // create Interface object
12
13     cout << "Interface contains: " << i.getValue()
14        << " before setValue" << endl;
```

Fig. 10.27 | Implementing a proxy class. (Part 1 of 2.)

```
15
16    i.setValue( 10 );
17
18    cout << "Interface contains: " << i.getValue()
19       << " after setValue" << endl;
20    return 0;
21  } // end main
```

```
Interface contains: 5 before setValue
Interface contains: 10 after setValue
```

Fig. 10.27 | Implementing a proxy class. (Part 2 of 2.)

10.11 Wrap-Up

In this chapter, we introduced several advanced topics related to classes and data abstraction. You learned how to specify const objects and const member functions to prevent modifications to objects, thus enforcing the principle of least privilege. You also learned that, through composition, a class can have objects of other classes as members. We introduced the topic of friendship and presented examples that demonstrate how to use friend functions.

You learned that the this pointer is passed as an implicit argument to each of a class's non-static member functions, allowing the functions to access the correct object's data members and other non-static member functions. You also saw explicit use of the this pointer to access the class's members and to enable cascaded member-function calls.

We introduced the concept of dynamic memory management. You learned that you can create and destroy objects dynamically with the new and delete operators, respectively. We motivated the need for static data members and demonstrated how to declare and use static data members and static member functions in your own classes.

You learned about data abstraction and information hiding—two of the fundamental concepts of object-oriented programming. We discussed abstract data types—ways of representing real-world or conceptual notions to some satisfactory level of precision within a computer system. You then learned about three example abstract data types—arrays, strings and queues. We introduced the concept of a container class that holds a collection of objects, as well as the notion of an iterator class that walks through the elements of a container class. Finally, you learned how to create a proxy class to hide the implementation details (including the private data members) of a class from clients of the class.

In Chapter 11, we continue our study of classes and objects by showing how to enable C++'s operators to work with objects—a process called operator overloading. For example, you'll see how to "overload" the << operator so it can be used to output a complete array without explicitly using a repetition statement.

Summary

Section 10.2 const (Constant) Objects and const Member Functions
- The keyword const can be used to specify that an object is not modifiable and that any attempt to modify the object should result in a compilation error.

- C++ compilers disallow non-const member function calls on const objects.
- An attempt by a const member function to modify an object of its class is a compilation error.
- A function is specified as const both in its prototype and in its definition.
- A const object must be initialized, not assigned to.
- Constructors and destructors cannot be declared const.
- const data member and reference data members *must* be initialized using member initializers.

Section 10.3 Composition: Objects as Members of Classes
- A class can have objects of other classes as members—this concept is called composition.
- Member objects are constructed in the order in which they are declared in the class definition and before their enclosing class objects are constructed.
- If a member initializer is not provided for a member object, the member object's default constructor will be called implicitly.

Section 10.4 **friend** Functions and **friend** Classes
- A friend function of a class is defined outside that class's scope, yet has the right to access the non-public (and public) members of the class. Stand-alone functions or entire classes may be declared to be friends of another class.
- A friend declaration can appear anywhere in the class. A friend is essentially a part of the public interface of the class.
- The friendship relation is neither symmetric nor transitive.

Section 10.5 Using the **this** Pointer
- Every object has access to its own address through the this pointer.
- An object's this pointer is not part of the object itself—i.e., the size of the memory occupied by the this pointer is not reflected in the result of a sizeof operation on the object.
- The this pointer is passed (by the compiler) as an implicit argument to each of the object's non-static member functions.
- Objects use the this pointer implicitly (as we have done to this point) or explicitly to reference their data members and member functions.
- The this pointer enables cascaded member-function calls in which multiple functions are invoked in the same statement.

Section 10.6 Dynamic Memory Management with Operators **new** and **delete**
- Dynamic memory management enables programmers to control the allocation and deallocation of memory in a program for any built-in or user-defined type.
- The free store (sometimes called the heap) is a region of memory assigned to each program for storing objects dynamically allocated at execution time.
- The new operator allocates storage of the proper size for an object, runs the object's constructor and returns a pointer of the correct type. The new operator can be used to dynamically allocate any fundamental type (such as int or double) or class type. If new is unable to find space in memory for the object, it indicates that an error occurred by "throwing" an "exception." This usually causes the program to terminate immediately, unless the exception is handled.
- To destroy a dynamically allocated object and free the space for the object, use the delete operator.

- An array of objects can be allocated dynamically with new as in

      int *ptr = new int[100];

which allocates an array of 100 integers and assigns the starting location of the array to ptr. The preceding array of integers is deleted with the statement

      delete [] ptr;

Section 10.7 static *Class Members*
- A static data member represents "class-wide" information (i.e., a property of the class shared by all instances, not a property of a specific object of the class).
- static data members have class scope and can be declared public, private or protected.
- A class's static members exist even when no objects of that class exist.
- To access a public static class member when no objects of the class exist, simply prefix the class name and the binary scope resolution operator (::) to the name of the data member.
- A class's public static class members can be accessed through any object of that class.
- A member function should be declared static if it does not access non-static data members or non-static member functions of the class. Unlike non-static member functions, a static member function does not have a this pointer, because static data members and static member functions exist independently of any objects of a class.

Section 10.8 *Data Abstraction and Information Hiding*
- Abstract data types are ways of representing real-world and conceptual notions to some satisfactory level of precision within a computer system.
- An abstract data type captures two notions: a data representation and the operations that can be performed on that data.
- C++ is an intentionally sparse language that provides programmers with only the raw capabilities needed to build a broad range of systems. C++ is designed to minimize performance burdens.
- Items are returned from a queue in first-in, first-out (FIFO) order—the first item inserted in the queue is the first item removed from the queue.

Section 10.9 *Container Classes and Iterators*
- Container classes (also called collection classes) are designed to hold collections of objects. Container classes commonly provide services such as insertion, deletion, searching, sorting, and testing an item to determine whether it is a member of the collection.
- It is common to associate iterators with container classes. An iterator is an object that "walks through" a collection, returning the next item (or performing some action on the next item).

Section 10.10 *Proxy Classes*
- Providing clients of your class with a proxy class that knows only the public interface to your class enables the clients to use your class's services without giving the clients access to your class's implementation details, such as its private data.
- When a class definition uses only a pointer or reference to an object of another class, the class header file for that other class (which would ordinarily reveal the private data of that class) is not required to be included with #include. You can simply declare that other class as a data type with a forward class declaration before the type is used in the file.

- The implementation file containing the member functions for a proxy class is the only file that includes the header file for the class whose `private` data we would like to hide.

- The implementation file containing the member functions for the proxy class is provided to the client as a precompiled object code file along with the header file that includes the function prototypes of the services provided by the proxy class.

Terminology

abstract data type (ADT)	`friend` class
allocate memory	`friend` function
arithmetic overflow	*has-a* relationship
cascaded member-function calls	heap
collection class	host object
composition	information hiding
const member function	iterator
const object	last-in, first-out (LIFO)
container class	member initializer
data abstraction	member initializer list
data representation	member object
deallocate memory	member object constructor
`delete` operator	memory leak
`delete[]` operator	`new []` operator
dequeue (queue operation)	`new` operator
dynamic memory management	operations in an ADT
dynamic objects	proxy class
enqueue (queue operation)	queue abstract data type
first-in, first-out (FIFO)	`static` data member
forward class declaration	`static` member function
free store	`this` pointer

Self-Review Exercises

10.1 Fill in the blanks in each of the following:
a) _____ must be used to initialize constant members of a class.
b) A nonmember function must be declared as a(n) _____ of a class to have access to that class's `private` data members.
c) The _____ operator dynamically allocates memory for an object of a specified type and returns a _____ to that type.
d) A constant object must be _____; it cannot be modified after it is created.
e) A(n) _____ data member represents class-wide information.
f) An object's non-`static` member functions have access to a "self pointer" to the object called the _____ pointer.
g) The keyword _____ specifies that an object or variable is not modifiable after it is initialized.
h) If a member initializer is not provided for a member object of a class, the object's _____ is called.
i) A member function should be declared `static` if it does not access _____ class members.
j) Member objects are constructed _____ their enclosing class object.
k) The _____ operator reclaims memory previously allocated by `new`.

10.2 Find the errors in the following class and explain how to correct them:

```
class Example
{
public:
   Example( int y = 10 )
      : data( y )
   {
      // empty body
   } // end Example constructor

   int getIncrementedData() const
   {
      return data++;
   } // end function getIncrementedData

   static int getCount()
   {
      cout << "Data is " << data << endl;
      return count;
   } // end function getCount
private:
   int data;
   static int count;
}; // end class Example
```

Answers to Self-Review Exercises

10.1 a) member initializers. b) `friend`. c) `new`, pointer. d) initialized. e) `static`. f) `this`. g) `const`. h) default constructor. i) non-`static`. j) before. k) `delete`.

10.2 *Error:* The class definition for `Example` has two errors. The first occurs in function `getIncrementedData`. The function is declared const, but it modifies the object.
Correction: To correct the first error, remove the const keyword from the definition of `getIncrementedData`.
Error: The second error occurs in function `getCount`. This function is declared `static`, so it is not allowed to access any non-`static` member (i.e., data) of the class.
Correction: To correct the second error, remove the output line from the `getCount` definition.

Exercises

10.3 Compare and contrast dynamic memory allocation and deallocation operators `new`, `new []`, `delete` and `delete []`.

10.4 Explain the notion of friendship. Explain the negative aspects of friendship as described in the text.

10.5 Can a correct `Time` class definition include both of the following constructors? If not, explain why not.

```
Time( int h = 0, int m = 0, int s = 0 );
Time();
```

10.6 What happens when a return type, even void, is specified for a constructor or destructor?

10.7 Modify class `Date` in Fig. 10.10 to have the following capabilities:
a) Output the date in multiple formats such as

```
DDD YYYY
MM/DD/YY
June 14, 1992
```

b) Use overloaded constructors to create Date objects initialized with dates of the formats in part (a).

c) Create a Date constructor that reads the system date using the standard library functions of the <ctime> header and sets the Date members. (See your compiler's reference documentation or www.cplusplus.com/ref/ctime/index.html for information on the functions in header <ctime>.)

In Chapter 11, we'll be able to create operators for testing the equality of two dates and for comparing dates to determine whether one date is prior to, or after, another.

10.8 Create a SavingsAccount class. Use a static data member annualInterestRate to store the annual interest rate for each of the savers. Each member of the class contains a private data member savingsBalance indicating the amount the saver currently has on deposit. Provide member function calculateMonthlyInterest that calculates the monthly interest by multiplying the balance by annualInterestRate divided by 12; this interest should be added to savingsBalance. Provide a static member function modifyInterestRate that sets the static annualInterestRate to a new value. Write a driver program to test class SavingsAccount. Instantiate two different objects of class SavingsAccount, saver1 and saver2, with balances of $2000.00 and $3000.00, respectively. Set the annualInterestRate to 3 percent. Then calculate the monthly interest and print the new balances for each of the savers. Then set the annualInterestRate to 4 percent, calculate the next month's interest and print the new balances for each of the savers.

10.9 Create class IntegerSet for which each object can hold integers in the range 0 through 100. A set is represented internally as an array of ones and zeros. Array element a[i] is 1 if integer i is in the set. Array element a[j] is 0 if integer j is not in the set. The default constructor initializes a set to the so-called "empty set," i.e., a set whose array representation contains all zeros.

Provide member functions for the common set operations. For example, provide a unionOfSets member function that creates a third set that is the set-theoretic union of two existing sets (i.e., an element of the third set's array is set to 1 if that element is 1 in either or both of the existing sets, and an element of the third set's array is set to 0 if that element is 0 in each of the existing sets).

Provide an intersectionOfSets member function which creates a third set which is the set-theoretic intersection of two existing sets (i.e., an element of the third set's array is set to 0 if that element is 0 in either or both of the existing sets, and an element of the third set's array is set to 1 if that element is 1 in each of the existing sets).

Provide an insertElement member function that inserts a new integer k into a set (by setting a[k] to 1). Provide a deleteElement member function that deletes integer m (by setting a[m] to 0).

Provide a printSet member function that prints a set as a list of numbers separated by spaces. Print only those elements that are present in the set (i.e., their position in the array has a value of 1). Print --- for an empty set.

Provide an isEqualTo member function that determines whether two sets are equal.

Provide an additional constructor that receives an array of integers and the size of that array and uses the array to initialize a set object.

Now write a driver program to test your IntegerSet class. Instantiate several IntegerSet objects. Test that all your member functions work properly.

10.10 It would be perfectly reasonable for the Time class of Figs. 10.18–10.19 to represent the time internally as the number of seconds since midnight rather than the three integer values hour, minute and second. Clients could use the same public methods and get the same results. Modify the Time class of Fig. 10.18 to implement the time as the number of seconds since midnight and show that there is no visible change in functionality to the clients of the class. [*Note:* This exercise nicely demonstrates the virtues of implementation hiding.]

11

Operator Overloading; String and Array Objects

OBJECTIVES

In this chapter you'll learn:

- What operator overloading is and how it can make programs more readable and programming more convenient.

- To redefine (overload) operators to work with objects of user-defined classes.

- The differences between overloading unary and binary operators.

- To convert objects from one class to another class.

- When to, and when not to, overload operators.

- To create PhoneNumber, Array, String and Date classes that demonstrate operator overloading.

- To use overloaded operators and other member functions of standard library class string.

- To use keyword explicit to prevent the compiler from using single-argument constructors to perform implicit conversions.

11.1 Introduction

Chapters 9–10 introduced the basics of C++ classes. Services were obtained from objects by sending messages (in the form of member-function calls) to the objects. This function call notation is cumbersome for certain kinds of classes (such as mathematical classes). Also, many common manipulations are performed with operators (e.g., input and output). We can use C++'s rich set of built-in operators to specify common object manipulations. This chapter shows how to enable C++'s operators to work with objects—a process called operator overloading. It is straightforward and natural to extend C++ with these new capabilities, but it must be done cautiously.

One example of an overloaded operator built into C++ is <<, which is used both as the stream insertion operator and as the bitwise left-shift operator (which is discussed in Chapter 21, Bits, Characters, Strings and structs). Similarly, >> is also overloaded; it is used both as the stream extraction operator and as the bitwise right-shift operator. Both of these operators are overloaded in the C++ Standard Library.

Although operator overloading sounds like an exotic capability, most programmers implicitly use overloaded operators regularly. For example, the C++ language itself overloads the addition operator (+) and the subtraction operator (-). These operators perform differently, depending on their context in integer arithmetic, floating-point arithmetic and pointer arithmetic.

C++ enables you to overload most operators to be sensitive to the context in which they are used—the compiler generates the appropriate code based on the context (in particular, the types of the operands). Some operators are overloaded frequently, especially the assignment, relational and various arithmetic operators such as + and -. The jobs performed by overloaded operators can also be performed by explicit function calls, but operator notation is often clearer and more familiar to programmers.

We discuss when to, and when not to, use operator overloading. We implement user-defined classes PhoneNumber, Array, String and Date to demonstrate how to overload operators, including the stream insertion, stream extraction, assignment, equality, relational, subscript, logical negation, parentheses and increment operators. The chapter ends with an example of C++'s Standard Library class string, which provides many overloaded operators that are similar to our String class that we present earlier in the chapter. In the exercises, we ask you to implement several classes with overloaded operators. The exercises also use classes Complex (for complex numbers) and HugeInt (for integers larger than a computer can represent with type long) to demonstrate overloaded arithmetic operators + and −, and ask you to enhance those classes by overloading other arithmetic operators.

11.2 Fundamentals of Operator Overloading

C++ programming is a type-sensitive and type-focused process. Programmers can use fundamental types and can define new types. The fundamental types can be used with C++'s rich collection of operators. Operators provide programmers with a concise notation for expressing manipulations of data of fundamental types.

Programmers can use operators with user-defined types as well. Although C++ does not allow new operators to be created, it does allow most existing operators to be overloaded so that, when these operators are used with objects, the operators have meaning appropriate to those objects. This is a powerful capability.

Software Engineering Observation 11.1

Operator overloading contributes to C++'s extensibility—one of the language's most appealing attributes.

Good Programming Practice 11.1

Use operator overloading when it makes a program clearer than accomplishing the same operations with function calls.

Good Programming Practice 11.2

Overloaded operators should mimic the functionality of their built-in counterparts—for example, the + operator should be overloaded to perform addition, not subtraction. Avoid excessive or inconsistent use of operator overloading, as this can make a program cryptic and difficult to read.

An operator is overloaded by writing a non-static member function definition or global function definition as you normally would, except that the function name now becomes the keyword operator followed by the symbol for the operator being overloaded. For example, the function name operator+ would be used to overload the addition operator (+). When operators are overloaded as member functions, they must be non-static, because they must be called on an object of the class and operate on that object.

To use an operator on class objects, that operator *must* be overloaded—with three exceptions. The assignment operator (=) may be used with every class to perform memberwise assignment of the data members of the class—each data member is assigned from the "source" object to the "target" object of the assignment. We'll soon see that such default memberwise assignment is dangerous for classes with pointer members; we'll explicitly overload the assignment operator for such classes. The address (&) and comma (,) operators may also be used with objects of any class without overloading. The address operator returns the address of the object in memory. The comma operator evaluates the expression to its left, then the expression to its right. Both of these operators can also be overloaded.

Overloading is especially appropriate for mathematical classes. These often require that a substantial set of operators be overloaded to ensure consistency with the way these mathematical classes are handled in the real world. For example, it would be unusual to overload only addition for a complex number class, because other arithmetic operators are also commonly used with complex numbers.

Operator overloading provides the same concise and familiar expressions for user-defined types that C++ provides with its rich collection of operators for fundamental types. Operator overloading is not automatic—you must write operator-overloading functions to perform the desired operations. Sometimes these functions are best made member functions; sometimes they are best as `friend` functions; occasionally they can be made global, non-`friend` functions. We present examples of these posibilities.

11.3 Restrictions on Operator Overloading

Most of C++'s operators can be overloaded. These are shown in Fig. 11.1. Figure 11.2 shows the operators that cannot be overloaded.

Common Programming Error 11.1

Attempting to overload a nonoverloadable operator is a syntax error.

Precedence, Associativity and Number of Operands

The precedence of an operator cannot be changed by overloading. This can lead to awkward situations in which an operator is overloaded in a manner for which its fixed precedence is inappropriate. However, parentheses can be used to force the order of evaluation of overloaded operators in an expression.

Operators that can be overloaded							
+	-	*	/	%	^	&	|
~	!	=	<	>	+=	-=	*=
/=	%=	^=	&=	|=	<<	>>	>>=
<<=	==	!=	<=	>=	&&	||	++
--	->*	,	->	[]	()	new	delete
new[]	delete[]						

Fig. 11.1 | Operators that can be overloaded.

Operators that cannot be overloaded			
.	.*	::	?:

Fig. 11.2 | Operators that cannot be overloaded.

The associativity of an operator (i.e., whether the operator is applied right-to-left or left-to-right) cannot be changed by overloading.

It is not possible to change the "arity" of an operator (i.e., the number of operands an operator takes): Overloaded unary operators remain unary operators; overloaded binary operators remain binary operators. C++'s only ternary operator (?:) cannot be overloaded. Operators &, *, + and - all have both unary and binary versions; these unary and binary versions can each be overloaded.

Common Programming Error 11.2

Attempting to change the "arity" of an operator via operator overloading is a compilation error.

Creating New Operators

It is not possible to create new operators; only existing operators can be overloaded. Unfortunately, this prevents you from using popular notations like the ** operator used in some other programming languages for exponentiation. [*Note:* You could overload an existing operator to perform exponentiation.]

Common Programming Error 11.3

Attempting to create new operators via operator overloading is a syntax error.

Operators for Fundamental Types

The meaning of how an operator works on objects of fundamental types cannot be changed by operator overloading. You cannot, for example, change the meaning of how + adds two integers. Operator overloading works only with objects of user-defined types or with a mixture of an object of a user-defined type and an object of a fundamental type.

Software Engineering Observation 11.2

At least one argument of an operator function must be an object or reference of a user-defined type. This prevents programmers from changing how operators work on fundamental types.

Common Programming Error 11.4

Attempting to modify how an operator works with objects of fundamental types is a compilation error.

Related Operators

Overloading an assignment operator and an addition operator to allow statements like

```
object2 = object2 + object1;
```

does not imply that the += operator is also overloaded to allow statements such as

```
object2 += object1;
```

Such behavior can be achieved only by explicitly overloading operator += for that class.

Common Programming Error 11.5

Assuming that overloading an operator such as + overloads related operators such as += or that overloading == overloads a related operator like != can lead to errors. Operators can be overloaded only explicitly; there is no implicit overloading.

11.4 **Operator Functions as Class Members vs. Global Functions**

Operator functions can be member functions or global functions; global functions are often made `friend`s for performance reasons. Member functions use the `this` pointer implicitly to obtain one of their class object arguments (the left operand for binary operators). Arguments for both operands of a binary operator must be explicitly listed in a global function call.

Operators That Must Be Overloaded as Member Functions
When overloading (), [], -> or any of the assignment operators, the operator overloading function must be declared as a class member. For the other operators, the operator overloading functions can be class members or global functions.

Operators as Member Functions and Global Functions
Whether an operator function is implemented as a member function or as a global function, the operator is still used the same way in expressions. So which implementation is best?

   When an operator function is implemented as a member function, the leftmost (or only) operand must be an object (or a reference to an object) of the operator's class. If the left operand must be an object of a different class or a fundamental type, this operator function must be implemented as a global function (as we'll do in Section 11.5 when overloading << and >> as the stream insertion and stream extraction operators, respectively). A global operator function can be made a `friend` of a class if that function must access `private` or `protected` members of that class directly.

   Operator member functions of a specific class are called (implicitly by the compiler) only when the left operand of a binary operator is specifically an object of that class, or when the single operand of a unary operator is an object of that class.

Why Overloaded Stream Insertion and Stream Extraction Operators Are Overloaded as Global Functions
The overloaded stream insertion operator (<<) is used in an expression in which the left operand has type `ostream &`, as in `cout << classObject`. To use the operator in this manner where the *right* operand is an object of a user-defined class, it must be overloaded as a global function. To be a member function, operator << would have to be a member of the `ostream` class. This is not possible for user-defined classes, since we are not allowed to modify C++ Standard Library classes. Similarly, the overloaded stream extraction operator (>>) is used in an expression in which the left operand has type `istream &`, as in `cin >> classObject`, and the *right* operand is an object of a user-defined class, so it, too, must be a global function. Also, each of these overloaded operator functions may require access to the `private` data members of the class object being output or input, so these overloaded operator functions can be made `friend` functions of the class for performance reasons.

> **Performance Tip 11.1**
>
> *It is possible to overload an operator as a global, non-`friend` function, but such a function requiring access to a class's `private` or `protected` data would need to use set or get functions provided in that class's `public` interface. The overhead of calling these functions could cause poor performance, so these functions can be inlined to improve performance.*

Commutative Operators

Another reason why one might choose a global function to overload an operator is to enable the operator to be commutative. For example, suppose we have an object, number, of type long int, and an object bigInteger1, of class HugeInteger (a class in which integers may be arbitrarily large rather than being limited by the machine word size of the underlying hardware; class HugeInteger is developed in the chapter exercises). The addition operator (+) produces a temporary HugeInteger object as the sum of a HugeInteger and a long int (as in the expression bigInteger1 + number), or as the sum of a long int and a HugeInteger (as in the expression number + bigInteger1). Thus, we require the addition operator to be commutative (exactly as it is with two fundamental-type operands). The problem is that the class object must appear on the *left* of the addition operator if that operator is to be overloaded as a member function. So, we overload the operator as a global function to allow the HugeInteger to appear on the *right* of the addition. The operator+ function, which deals with the HugeInteger on the left, can still be a member function. The global function simply swaps its arguments and calls the member function.

11.5 Overloading Stream Insertion and Stream Extraction Operators

C++ is able to input and output the fundamental types using the stream extraction operator >> and the stream insertion operator <<. The class libraries provided with C++ compilers overload these operators to process each fundamental type, including pointers and C-style char * strings. The stream insertion and stream extraction operators also can be overloaded to perform input and output for user-defined types. The program of Figs. 11.3–11.5 demonstrates overloading these operators to handle data of a user-defined telephone number class called PhoneNumber. This program assumes telephone numbers are input correctly.

```
1   // Fig. 11.3: PhoneNumber.h
2   // PhoneNumber class definition
3   #ifndef PHONENUMBER_H
4   #define PHONENUMBER_H
5
6   #include <iostream>
7   using std::ostream;
8   using std::istream;
9
10  #include <string>
11  using std::string;
12
13  class PhoneNumber
14  {
15     friend ostream &operator<<( ostream &, const PhoneNumber & );
16     friend istream &operator>>( istream &, PhoneNumber & );
17  private:
18     string areaCode; // 3-digit area code
19     string exchange; // 3-digit exchange
```

Fig. 11.3 | PhoneNumber class with overloaded stream insertion and stream extraction operators as friend functions. (Part 1 of 2.)

```
20      string line; // 4-digit line
21   }; // end class PhoneNumber
22
23   #endif
```

Fig. 11.3 | PhoneNumber class with overloaded stream insertion and stream extraction operators as friend functions. (Part 2 of 2.)

```
1   // Fig. 11.4: PhoneNumber.cpp
2   // Overloaded stream insertion and stream extraction operators
3   // for class PhoneNumber.
4   #include <iomanip>
5   using std::setw;
6
7   #include "PhoneNumber.h"
8
9   // overloaded stream insertion operator; cannot be
10  // a member function if we would like to invoke it with
11  // cout << somePhoneNumber;
12  ostream &operator<<( ostream &output, const PhoneNumber &number )
13  {
14     output << "(" << number.areaCode << ") "
15        << number.exchange << "-" << number.line;
16     return output; // enables cout << a << b << c;
17  } // end function operator<<
18
19  // overloaded stream extraction operator; cannot be
20  // a member function if we would like to invoke it with
21  // cin >> somePhoneNumber;
22  istream &operator>>( istream &input, PhoneNumber &number )
23  {
24     input.ignore(); // skip (
25     input >> setw( 3 ) >> number.areaCode; // input area code
26     input.ignore( 2 ); // skip ) and space
27     input >> setw( 3 ) >> number.exchange; // input exchange
28     input.ignore(); // skip dash (-)
29     input >> setw( 4 ) >> number.line; // input line
30     return input; // enables cin >> a >> b >> c;
31  } // end function operator>>
```

Fig. 11.4 | Overloaded stream insertion and stream extraction operators for class PhoneNumber.

```
1   // Fig. 11.5: fig11_05.cpp
2   // Demonstrating class PhoneNumber's overloaded stream insertion
3   // and stream extraction operators.
4   #include <iostream>
5   using std::cout;
6   using std::cin;
7   using std::endl;
```

Fig. 11.5 | Overloaded stream insertion and stream extraction operators. (Part 1 of 2.)

```
8
9    #include "PhoneNumber.h"
10
11   int main()
12   {
13       PhoneNumber phone; // create object phone
14
15       cout << "Enter phone number in the form (123) 456-7890:" << endl;
16
17       // cin >> phone invokes operator>> by implicitly issuing
18       // the global function call operator>>( cin, phone )
19       cin >> phone;
20
21       cout << "The phone number entered was: ";
22
23       // cout << phone invokes operator<< by implicitly issuing
24       // the global function call operator<<( cout, phone )
25       cout << phone << endl;
26       return 0;
27   } // end main
```

```
Enter phone number in the form (123) 456-7890:
(800) 555-1212
The phone number entered was: (800) 555-1212
```

Fig. 11.5 | Overloaded stream insertion and stream extraction operators. (Part 2 of 2.)

The stream extraction operator function operator>> (Fig. 11.4, lines 22–31) takes istream reference input and PhoneNumber reference num as arguments and returns an istream reference. Operator function operator>> inputs phone numbers of the form

        (800) 555-1212

into objects of class PhoneNumber. When the compiler sees the expression

        cin >> phone

in line 19 of Fig. 11.5, the compiler generates the global function call

        operator>>(cin, phone);

When this call executes, reference parameter input (Fig. 11.4, line 22) becomes an alias for cin and reference parameter number becomes an alias for phone. The operator function reads as strings the three parts of the telephone number into the areaCode (line 25), exchange (line 27) and line (line 29) members of the PhoneNumber object referenced by parameter number. Stream manipulator setw limits the number of characters read into each character array. When used with cin and strings, setw restricts the number of characters read to the number of characters specified by its argument (i.e., setw(3) allows three characters to be read). The parentheses, space and dash characters are skipped by calling istream member function ignore (Fig. 11.4, lines 24, 26 and 28), which discards the specified number of characters in the input stream (one character by default). Function operator>> returns istream reference input (i.e., cin). This enables input operations on

PhoneNumber objects to be cascaded with input operations on other PhoneNumber objects or on objects of other data types. For example, a program can input two PhoneNumber objects in one statement as follows:

```
cin >> phone1 >> phone2;
```

First, the expression `cin >> phone1` executes by making the global function call

```
operator>>( cin, phone1 );
```

This call then returns a reference to `cin` as the value of `cin >> phone1`, so the remaining portion of the expression is interpreted simply as `cin >> phone2`. This executes by making the global function call

```
operator>>( cin, phone2 );
```

The stream insertion operator function (Fig. 11.4, lines 12–17) takes an `ostream` reference (output) and a `const PhoneNumber` reference (number) as arguments and returns an `ostream` reference. Function `operator<<` displays objects of type `PhoneNumber`. When the compiler sees the expression

```
cout << phone
```

in line 25 of Fig. 11.5, the compiler generates the global function call

```
operator<<( cout, phone );
```

Function `operator<<` displays the parts of the telephone number as `strings`, because they are stored as `string` objects.

Error-Prevention Tip 11.1

Returning a reference from an overloaded << or >> operator function is typically successful because cout, cin *and most stream objects are global, or at least long-lived. Returning a reference to an automatic variable or other temporary object is dangerous—this can create "dangling references" to nonexisting objects.*

Note that the functions `operator>>` and `operator<<` are declared in `PhoneNumber` as global, `friend` functions (Fig. 11.3, lines 15–16). They are global functions because the object of class `PhoneNumber` appears in each case as the right operand of the operator. Remember, overloaded operator functions for binary operators can be member functions only when the left operand is an object of the class in which the function is a member. Overloaded input and output operators are declared as `friend`s if they need to access non-`public` class members directly for performance reasons or because the class may not offer appropriate *get* functions. Also note that the `PhoneNumber` reference in function `operator<<`'s parameter list (Fig. 11.4, line 12) is `const`, because the `PhoneNumber` will simply be output, and the `PhoneNumber` reference in function `operator>>`'s parameter list (line 22) is non-`const`, because the `PhoneNumber` object must be modified to store the input telephone number in the object.

Software Engineering Observation 11.3

New input/output capabilities for user-defined types are added to C++ without modifying standard input/output library classes. This is another example of C++'s extensibility.

11.6 Overloading Unary Operators

A unary operator for a class can be overloaded as a non-static member function with no arguments or as a global function with one argument; that argument must be either an object of the class or a reference to an object of the class. Member functions that implement overloaded operators must be non-static so that they can access the non-static data in each object of the class. Remember that static member functions can access only static members of the class.

Later in this chapter, we'll overload unary operator ! to test whether an object of the String class we create (Section 11.10) is empty and return a bool result. Consider the expression !s, in which s is an object of class String. When a unary operator such as ! is overloaded as a member function with no arguments and the compiler sees the expression !s, the compiler generates the function call s.operator!(). The operand s is the class object for which the String class member function operator! is being invoked. The function is declared in the class definition as follows:

```
class String
{
public:
    bool operator!() const;
    ...
}; // end class String
```

A unary operator such as ! may be overloaded as a global function with one parameter in two different ways—either with a parameter that is an object (this requires a copy of the object, so the side effects of the function are not applied to the original object), or with a parameter that is a reference to an object (no copy of the original object is made, so all side effects of this function are applied to the original object). If s is a String class object (or a reference to a String class object), then !s is treated as if the call operator!(s) had been written, invoking the global operator! function that is declared as follows:

```
bool operator!( const String & );
```

11.7 Overloading Binary Operators

A binary operator can be overloaded as a non-static member function with one parameter or as a global function with two parameters (one of those parameters must be either a class object or a reference to a class object).

Later in this chapter, we'll overload < to compare two String objects. When overloading binary operator < as a non-static member function of a String class with one argument, if y and z are String-class objects, then y < z is treated as if y.operator<(z) had been written, invoking the operator< member function declared below

```
class String

public:
    bool operator<( const String & ) const;
    ...
}; // end class String
```

If binary operator < is to be overloaded as a global function, it must take two arguments—one of which must be a class object or a reference to a class object. If y and z are

String-class objects or references to String-class objects, then y < z is treated as if the call operator<(y, z) had been written in the program, invoking global-function operator< declared as follows:

```
bool operator<( const String &, const String & );
```

11.8 Case Study: Array Class

Pointer-based arrays have a number of problems. For example, a program can easily "walk off" either end of an array, because C++ does not check whether subscripts fall outside the range of an array (you can still do this explicitly though). Arrays of size *n* must number their elements 0, …, *n* – 1; alternate subscript ranges are not allowed. An entire non-char array cannot be input or output at once; each array element must be read or written individually. Two arrays cannot be meaningfully compared with equality operators or relational operators (because the array names are simply pointers to where the arrays begin in memory and, of course, two arrays will always be at different memory locations). When an array is passed to a general-purpose function designed to handle arrays of any size, the size of the array must be passed as an additional argument. One array cannot be assigned to another with the assignment operator(s) (because array names are const pointers and a constant pointer cannot be used on the left side of an assignment operator). These and other capabilities certainly seem like "naturals" for dealing with arrays, but pointer-based arrays don't provide such capabilities. However, C++ does provide the means to implement such array capabilities through the use of classes and operator overloading.

In this example, we create a powerful array class that performs range checking to ensure that subscripts remain within the bounds of the Array. The class allows one array object to be assigned to another with the assignment operator. Objects of the Array class know their size, so the size does not need to be passed separately as an argument when passing an Array to a function. Entire Arrays can be input or output with the stream extraction and stream insertion operators, respectively. Array comparisons can be made with the equality operators == and !=.

This example will sharpen your appreciation of data abstraction. You'll probably want to suggest other enhancements to this Array class. Class development is an interesting, creative and intellectually challenging activity—always with the goal of "crafting valuable classes."

The program of Figs. 11.6–11.8 demonstrates class Array and its overloaded operators. First we walk through main (Fig. 11.8). Then we consider the class definition (Fig. 11.6) and each of the class's member-function and friend-function definitions (Fig. 11.7).

```
1   // Fig. 11.6: Array.h
2   // Array class definition with overloaded operators.
3   #ifndef ARRAY_H
4   #define ARRAY_H
5
```

Fig. 11.6 | Array class definition with overloaded operators. (Part 1 of 2.)

```
6   #include <iostream>
7   using std::ostream;
8   using std::istream;
9
10  class Array
11  {
12     friend ostream &operator<<( ostream &, const Array & );
13     friend istream &operator>>( istream &, Array & );
14  public:
15     Array( int = 10 ); // default constructor
16     Array( const Array & ); // copy constructor
17     ~Array(); // destructor
18     int getSize() const; // return size
19
20     const Array &operator=( const Array & ); // assignment operator
21     bool operator==( const Array & ) const; // equality operator
22
23     // inequality operator; returns opposite of == operator
24     bool operator!=( const Array &right ) const
25     {
26        return ! ( *this == right ); // invokes Array::operator==
27     } // end function operator!=
28
29     // subscript operator for non-const objects returns modifiable lvalue
30     int &operator[]( int );
31
32     // subscript operator for const objects returns rvalue
33     int operator[]( int ) const;
34  private:
35     int size; // pointer-based array size
36     int *ptr; // pointer to first element of pointer-based array
37  }; // end class Array
38
39  #endif
```

Fig. 11.6 | Array class definition with overloaded operators. (Part 2 of 2.)

```
1   // Fig 11.7: Array.cpp
2   // Array class member- and friend-function definitions.
3   #include <iostream>
4   using std::cerr;
5   using std::cout;
6   using std::cin;
7   using std::endl;
8
9   #include <iomanip>
10  using std::setw;
11
12  #include <cstdlib> // exit function prototype
13  using std::exit;
```

Fig. 11.7 | Array class member- and friend-function definitions. (Part 1 of 4.)

```
14
15   #include "Array.h" // Array class definition
16
17   // default constructor for class Array (default size 10)
18   Array::Array( int arraySize )
19   {
20      size = ( arraySize > 0 ? arraySize : 10 ); // validate arraySize
21      ptr = new int[ size ]; // create space for pointer-based array
22
23      for ( int i = 0; i < size; i++ )
24         ptr[ i ] = 0; // set pointer-based array element
25   } // end Array default constructor
26
27   // copy constructor for class Array;
28   // must receive a reference to prevent infinite recursion
29   Array::Array( const Array &arrayToCopy )
30      : size( arrayToCopy.size )
31   {
32      ptr = new int[ size ]; // create space for pointer-based array
33
34      for ( int i = 0; i < size; i++ )
35         ptr[ i ] = arrayToCopy.ptr[ i ]; // copy into object
36   } // end Array copy constructor
37
38   // destructor for class Array
39   Array::~Array()
40   {
41      delete [] ptr; // release pointer-based array space
42   } // end destructor
43
44   // return number of elements of Array
45   int Array::getSize() const
46   {
47      return size; // number of elements in Array
48   } // end function getSize
49
50   // overloaded assignment operator;
51   // const return avoids: ( a1 = a2 ) = a3
52   const Array &Array::operator=( const Array &right )
53   {
54      if ( &right != this ) // avoid self-assignment
55      {
56         // for Arrays of different sizes, deallocate original
57         // left-side array, then allocate new left-side array
58         if ( size != right.size )
59         {
60            delete [] ptr; // release space
61            size = right.size; // resize this object
62            ptr = new int[ size ]; // create space for array copy
63         } // end inner if
64
```

Fig. 11.7 | Array class member- and friend-function definitions. (Part 2 of 4.)

```
65          for ( int i = 0; i < size; i++ )
66              ptr[ i ] = right.ptr[ i ]; // copy array into object
67      } // end outer if
68
69      return *this; // enables x = y = z, for example
70  } // end function operator=
71
72  // determine if two Arrays are equal and
73  // return true, otherwise return false
74  bool Array::operator==( const Array &right ) const
75  {
76      if ( size != right.size )
77          return false; // arrays of different number of elements
78
79      for ( int i = 0; i < size; i++ )
80          if ( ptr[ i ] != right.ptr[ i ] )
81              return false; // Array contents are not equal
82
83      return true; // Arrays are equal
84  } // end function operator==
85
86  // overloaded subscript operator for non-const Arrays;
87  // reference return creates a modifiable lvalue
88  int &Array::operator[]( int subscript )
89  {
90      // check for subscript out-of-range error
91      if ( subscript < 0 || subscript >= size )
92      {
93          cerr << "\nError: Subscript " << subscript
94              << " out of range" << endl;
95          exit( 1 ); // terminate program; subscript out of range
96      } // end if
97
98      return ptr[ subscript ]; // reference return
99  } // end function operator[]
100
101 // overloaded subscript operator for const Arrays
102 // const reference return creates an rvalue
103 int Array::operator[]( int subscript ) const
104 {
105     // check for subscript out-of-range error
106     if ( subscript < 0 || subscript >= size )
107     {
108         cerr << "\nError: Subscript " << subscript
109             << " out of range" << endl;
110         exit( 1 ); // terminate program; subscript out of range
111     } // end if
112
113     return ptr[ subscript ]; // returns copy of this element
114 } // end function operator[]
115
```

Fig. 11.7 | Array class member- and friend-function definitions. (Part 3 of 4.)

```
116  // overloaded input operator for class Array;
117  // inputs values for entire Array
118  istream &operator>>( istream &input, Array &a )
119  {
120     for ( int i = 0; i < a.size; i++ )
121        input >> a.ptr[ i ];
122
123     return input; // enables cin >> x >> y;
124  } // end function
125
126  // overloaded output operator for class Array
127  ostream &operator<<( ostream &output, const Array &a )
128  {
129     int i;
130
131     // output private ptr-based array
132     for ( i = 0; i < a.size; i++ )
133     {
134        output << setw( 12 ) << a.ptr[ i ];
135
136        if ( ( i + 1 ) % 4 == 0 ) // 4 numbers per row of output
137           output << endl;
138     } // end for
139
140     if ( i % 4 != 0 ) // end last line of output
141        output << endl;
142
143     return output; // enables cout << x << y;
144  } // end function operator<<
```

Fig. 11.7 | Array class member- and friend-function definitions. (Part 4 of 4.)

```
1   // Fig. 11.8: fig11_08.cpp
2   // Array class test program.
3   #include <iostream>
4   using std::cout;
5   using std::cin;
6   using std::endl;
7
8   #include "Array.h"
9
10  int main()
11  {
12     Array integers1( 7 ); // seven-element Array
13     Array integers2; // 10-element Array by default
14
15     // print integers1 size and contents
16     cout << "Size of Array integers1 is "
17        << integers1.getSize()
18        << "\nArray after initialization:\n" << integers1;
19
```

Fig. 11.8 | Array class test program. (Part 1 of 3.)

```
20      // print integers2 size and contents
21      cout << "\nSize of Array integers2 is "
22         << integers2.getSize()
23         << "\nArray after initialization:\n" << integers2;
24
25      // input and print integers1 and integers2
26      cout << "\nEnter 17 integers:" << endl;
27      cin >> integers1 >> integers2;
28
29      cout << "\nAfter input, the Arrays contain:\n"
30         << "integers1:\n" << integers1
31         << "integers2:\n" << integers2;
32
33      // use overloaded inequality (!=) operator
34      cout << "\nEvaluating: integers1 != integers2" << endl;
35
36      if ( integers1 != integers2 )
37         cout << "integers1 and integers2 are not equal" << endl;
38
39      // create Array integers3 using integers1 as an
40      // initializer; print size and contents
41      Array integers3( integers1 ); // invokes copy constructor
42
43      cout << "\nSize of Array integers3 is "
44         << integers3.getSize()
45         << "\nArray after initialization:\n" << integers3;
46
47      // use overloaded assignment (=) operator
48      cout << "\nAssigning integers2 to integers1:" << endl;
49      integers1 = integers2; // note target Array is smaller
50
51      cout << "integers1:\n" << integers1
52         << "integers2:\n" << integers2;
53
54      // use overloaded equality (==) operator
55      cout << "\nEvaluating: integers1 == integers2" << endl;
56
57      if ( integers1 == integers2 )
58         cout << "integers1 and integers2 are equal" << endl;
59
60      // use overloaded subscript operator to create rvalue
61      cout << "\nintegers1[5] is " << integers1[ 5 ];
62
63      // use overloaded subscript operator to create lvalue
64      cout << "\n\nAssigning 1000 to integers1[5]" << endl;
65      integers1[ 5 ] = 1000;
66      cout << "integers1:\n" << integers1;
67
68      // attempt to use out-of-range subscript
69      cout << "\nAttempt to assign 1000 to integers1[15]" << endl;
70      integers1[ 15 ] = 1000; // ERROR: out of range
71      return 0;
72   } // end main
```

Fig. 11.8 | Array class test program. (Part 2 of 3.)

```
Size of Array integers1 is 7
Array after initialization:
           0            0            0            0
           0            0            0

Size of Array integers2 is 10
Array after initialization:
           0            0            0            0
           0            0            0            0
           0            0

Enter 17 integers:
1 2 3 4 5 6 7 8 9 10 11 12 13 14 15 16 17

After input, the Arrays contain:
integers1:
           1            2            3            4
           5            6            7
integers2:
           8            9           10           11
          12           13           14           15
          16           17

Evaluating: integers1 != integers2
integers1 and integers2 are not equal

Size of Array integers3 is 7
Array after initialization:
           1            2            3            4
           5            6            7

Assigning integers2 to integers1:
integers1:
           8            9           10           11
          12           13           14           15
          16           17
integers2:
           8            9           10           11
          12           13           14           15
          16           17

Evaluating: integers1 == integers2
integers1 and integers2 are equal

integers1[5] is 13

Assigning 1000 to integers1[5]
integers1:
           8            9           10           11
          12         1000           14           15
          16           17

Attempt to assign 1000 to integers1[15]

Error: Subscript 15 out of range
```

Fig. 11.8 | Array class test program. (Part 3 of 3.)

*Creating **Arrays**, Outputting Their Size and Displaying Their Contents*
The program begins by instantiating two objects of class Array—integers1 (Fig. 11.8, line 12) with seven elements, and integers2 (Fig. 11.8, line 13) with the default Array size—10 elements (specified by the Array default constructor's prototype in Fig. 11.6, line 15). Lines 16–18 use member function getSize to determine the size of integers1 and output integers1, using the Array overloaded stream insertion operator. The sample output confirms that the Array elements were set correctly to zeros by the constructor. Next, lines 21–23 output the size of Array integers2 and output integers2, using the Array overloaded stream insertion operator.

*Using the Overloaded Stream Insertion Operator to Fill an **Array***
Line 26 prompts the user to input 17 integers. Line 27 uses the Array overloaded stream extraction operator to read these values into both arrays. The first seven values are stored in integers1 and the remaining 10 values are stored in integers2. Lines 29–31 output the two arrays with the overloaded Array stream insertion operator to confirm that the input was performed correctly.

Using the Overloaded Inequality Operator
Line 36 tests the overloaded inequality operator by evaluating the condition

```
integers1 != integers2
```

The program output shows that the Arrays are not equal.

*Initializing a New **Array** with a Copy of an Existing **Array**'s Contents*
Line 41 instantiates a third Array called integers3 and initializes it with a copy of Array integers1. This invokes the Array copy constructor to copy the elements of integers1 into integers3. We discuss the details of the copy constructor shortly. Note that the copy constructor can also be invoked by writing line 41 as follows:

```
Array integers3 = integers1;
```

The equal sign in the preceding statement is *not* the assignment operator. When an equal sign appears in the declaration of an object, it invokes a constructor for that object. This form can be used to pass only a single argument to a constructor.

Lines 43–45 output the size of integers3 and output integers3, using the Array overloaded stream insertion operator to confirm that the Array elements were set correctly by the copy constructor.

Using the Overloaded Assignment Operator
Next, line 49 tests the overloaded assignment operator (=) by assigning integers2 to integers1. Lines 51–52 print both Array objects to confirm that the assignment was successful. Note that integers1 originally held 7 integers and was resized to hold a copy of the 10 elements in integers2. As we'll see, the overloaded assignment operator performs this resizing operation in a manner that is transparent to the client code.

Using the Overloaded Equality Operator
Next, line 57 uses the overloaded equality operator (==) to confirm that objects integers1 and integers2 are indeed identical after the assignment.

Using the Overloaded Subscript Operator
Line 61 uses the overloaded subscript operator to refer to integers1[5]—an in-range element of integers1. This subscripted name is used as an *rvalue* to print the value stored in integers1[5]. Line 65 uses integers1[5] as a modifiable *lvalue* on the left side of an assignment statement to assign a new value, 1000, to element 5 of integers1. We'll see that operator[] returns a reference to use as the modifiable *lvalue* after the operator confirms that 5 is a valid subscript for integers1.

Line 70 attempts to assign the value 1000 to integers1[15]—an out-of-range element. In this example, operator[] determines that the subscript is out of range, prints a message and terminates the program. Note that we highlighted line 70 of the program in red to emphasize that it is an error to access an element that is out of range. This is a runtime logic error.

Interestingly, the array subscript operator [] is not restricted for use only with arrays; it also can be used, for example, to select elements from other kinds of container classes, such as linked lists, strings and dictionaries. Also, when operator[] functions are defined, subscripts no longer have to be integers—characters, strings, floats or even objects of user-defined classes also could be used. In Chapter 22, Standard Template Library (STL), we discuss the STL map class that allows noninteger subscripts.

Array Class Definition
Now that we have seen how this program operates, let us walk through the class header (Fig. 11.6). As we refer to each member function in the header, we discuss that function's implementation in Fig. 11.7. In Fig. 11.6, lines 35–36 represent the private data members of class Array. Each Array object consists of a size member indicating the number of elements in the Array and an int pointer—ptr—that points to the dynamically allocated pointer-based array of integers managed by the Array object.

Overloading the Stream Insertion and Stream Extraction Operators as **friends**
Lines 12–13 of Fig. 11.6 declare the overloaded stream insertion operator and the overloaded stream extraction operator to be friends of class Array. When the compiler sees an expression like cout << arrayObject, it invokes global function operator<< with the call

```
operator<<( cout, arrayObject )
```

When the compiler sees an expression like cin >> arrayObject, it invokes global function operator>> with the call

```
operator>>( cin, arrayObject )
```

We note again that these stream insertion and stream extraction operator functions cannot be members of class Array, because the Array object is always mentioned on the right side of the stream insertion operator and the stream extraction operator. If these operator functions were to be members of class Array, the following awkward statements would have to be used to output and input an Array:

```
arrayObject << cout;
arrayObject >> cin;
```

Such statements would be confusing to most C++ programmers, who are familiar with cout and cin appearing as the left operands of << and >>, respectively.

Function operator<< (defined in Fig. 11.7, lines 127–144) prints the number of elements indicated by size from the integer array to which ptr points. Function operator>> (defined in Fig. 11.7, lines 118–124) inputs directly into the array to which ptr points. Each of these operator functions returns an appropriate reference to enable cascaded output or input statements, respectively. Note that each of these functions has access to an Array's private data because these functions are declared as friends of class Array. Also, note that class Array's getSize and operator[] functions could be used by operator<< and operator>>, in which case these operator functions would not need to be friends of class Array. However, the additional function calls might increase execution-time overhead.

Array Default Constructor

Line 15 of Fig. 11.6 declares the default constructor for the class and specifies a default size of 10 elements. When the compiler sees a declaration like line 13 in Fig. 11.8, it invokes class Array's default constructor (remember that the default constructor in this example actually receives a single int argument that has a default value of 10). The default constructor (defined in Fig. 11.7, lines 18–25) validates and assigns the argument to data member size, uses new to obtain the memory for the internal pointer-based representation of this array and assigns the pointer returned by new to data member ptr. Then the constructor uses a for statement to set all the elements of the array to zero. It is possible to have an Array class that does not initialize its members if, for example, these members are to be read at some later time; but this is considered to be a poor programming practice. Arrays, and objects in general, should be properly initialized and maintained in a consistent state.

Array Copy Constructor

Line 16 of Fig. 11.6 declares a copy constructor (defined in Fig. 11.7, lines 29–36) that initializes an Array by making a copy of an existing Array object. Such copying must be done carefully to avoid the pitfall of leaving both Array objects pointing to the same dynamically allocated memory. This is exactly the problem that would occur with default memberwise copying, if the compiler is allowed to define a default copy constructor for this class. Copy constructors are invoked whenever a copy of an object is needed, such as in passing an object by value to a function, returning an object by value from a function or initializing an object with a copy of another object of the same class. The copy constructor is called in a declaration when an object of class Array is instantiated and initialized with another object of class Array, as in the declaration in line 41 of Fig. 11.8.

 Software Engineering Observation 11.4

The argument to a copy constructor should be a const reference to allow a const object to be copied.

 Common Programming Error 11.6

Note that a copy constructor must receive its argument by reference, not by value. Otherwise, the copy constructor call results in infinite recursion (a fatal logic error) because receiving an object by value requires the copy constructor to make a copy of the argument object. Recall that any time a copy of an object is required, the class's copy constructor is called. If the copy constructor received its argument by value, the copy constructor would call itself recursively to make a copy of its argument!

The copy constructor for `Array` uses a member initializer (Fig. 11.7, line 30) to copy the `size` of the initializer `Array` into data member `size`, uses `new` (line 32) to obtain the memory for the internal pointer-based representation of this `Array` and assigns the pointer returned by `new` to data member `ptr`.[1] Then the copy constructor uses a `for` statement to copy all the elements of the initializer `Array` into the new `Array` object. Note that an object of a class can look at the `private` data of any other object of that class (using a handle that indicates which object to access).

Common Programming Error 11.7

If the copy constructor simply copied the pointer in the source object to the target object's pointer, then both objects would point to the same dynamically allocated memory. The first destructor to execute would then delete the dynamically allocated memory, and the other object's `ptr` would be undefined, a situation called a dangling pointer—this would likely result in a serious run-time error (such as early program termination) when the pointer was used.

Array Destructor

Line 17 of Fig. 11.6 declares the destructor for the class (defined in Fig. 11.7, lines 39–42). The destructor is invoked when an object of class `Array` goes out of scope. The destructor uses `delete []` to release the memory allocated dynamically by `new` in the constructor.

getSize Member Function

Line 18 of Fig. 11.6 declares function `getSize` (defined in Fig. 11.7, lines 45–48) that returns the number of elements in the `Array`.

Overloaded Assignment Operator

Line 20 of Fig. 11.6 declares the overloaded assignment operator function for the class. When the compiler sees the expression `integers1 = integers2` in line 49 of Fig. 11.8, the compiler invokes member function `operator=` with the call

```
integers1.operator=( integers2 )
```

The implementation of member function `operator=` (Fig. 11.7, lines 52–70) tests for self assignment (line 54) in which an object of class `Array` is being assigned to itself. When `this` is equal to the address of the `right` operand, a self-assignment is being attempted, so the assignment is skipped (i.e., the object already is itself; in a moment we'll see why self-assignment is dangerous). If it is not a self-assignment, then the member function determines whether the sizes of the two arrays are identical (line 58); in that case, the original array of integers in the left-side `Array` object is not reallocated. Otherwise, `operator=` uses `delete` (line 60) to release the memory originally allocated to the target array, copies the `size` of the source array to the `size` of the target array (line 61), uses `new` to allocate memory for the target array and places the pointer returned by `new` into the array's `ptr` member.[2] Then the `for` statement in lines 65–66 copies the array elements from the source array to the target array. Regardless of whether this is a self-assignment, the member function returns the current object (i.e., `*this` in line 69) as a constant reference; this enables cascaded `Array` assignments such as x = y = z. If self-assignment occurs, and function op-

---

1. Note that `new` could fail to obtain the needed memory. We deal with `new` failures in Chapter 16, Exception Handling.
2. Once again, `new` could fail. We discuss `new` failures in Chapter 16.

erator= did not test for this case, operator= would delete the dynamic memory associated with the Array object before the assignment was complete. This would leave ptr pointing to memory that had been deallocated, which could lead to fatal runtime errors.

Software Engineering Observation 11.5

A copy constructor, a destructor and an overloaded assignment operator are usually provided as a group for any class that uses dynamically allocated memory.

Common Programming Error 11.8

Not providing an overloaded assignment operator and a copy constructor for a class when objects of that class contain pointers to dynamically allocated memory is a logic error.

Software Engineering Observation 11.6

It is possible to prevent one object of a class from being assigned to another. This is done by declaring the assignment operator as a private member of the class.

Software Engineering Observation 11.7

It is possible to prevent class objects from being copied; to do this, simply make both the overloaded assignment operator and the copy constructor of that class private.

Overloaded Equality and Inequality Operators
Line 21 of Fig. 11.6 declares the overloaded equality operator (==) for the class. When the compiler sees the expression integers1 == integers2 in line 57 of Fig. 11.8, the compiler invokes member function operator== with the call

         integers1.operator==(integers2)

Member function operator== (defined in Fig. 11.7, lines 74–84) immediately returns false if the size members of the arrays are not equal. Otherwise, operator== compares each pair of elements. If they are all equal, the function returns true. The first pair of elements to differ causes the function to return false immediately.

   Lines 24–27 of the header file define the overloaded inequality operator (!=) for the class. Member function operator!= uses the overloaded operator== function to determine whether one Array is equal to another, then returns the opposite of that result. Writing operator!= in this manner enables you to reuse operator==, which reduces the amount of code that must be written in the class. Also, note that the full function definition for operator!= is in the Array header file. This allows the compiler to inline the definition of operator!= to eliminate the overhead of the extra function call.

Overloaded Subscript Operators
Lines 30 and 33 of Fig. 11.6 declare two overloaded subscript operators (defined in Fig. 11.7 in lines 88–99 and 103–114, respectively). When the compiler sees the expression integers1[5] (Fig. 11.8, line 61), the compiler invokes the appropriate overloaded operator[] member function by generating the call

         integers1.operator[](5)

The compiler creates a call to the const version of operator[] (Fig. 11.7, lines 103–114) when the subscript operator is used on a const Array object. For example, if const object z is instantiated with the statement

```
const Array z( 5 );
```

then the `const` version of `operator[]` is required to execute a statement such as

```
cout << z[ 3 ] << endl;
```

Remember, a program can invoke only the `const` member functions of a `const` object.

Each definition of `operator[]` determines whether the subscript it receives as an argument is in range. If it is not, each function prints an error message and terminates the program with a call to function `exit` (header `<cstdlib>`).[3] If the subscript is in range, the non-`const` version of `operator[]` returns the appropriate array element as a reference so that it may be used as a modifiable *lvalue* (e.g., on the left side of an assignment statement). If the subscript is in range, the `const` version of `operator[]` returns a copy of the appropriate element of the array. The returned character is an *rvalue*.

11.9 Converting between Types

Most programs process information of many types. Sometimes all the operations "stay within a type." For example, adding an `int` to an `int` produces an `int` (as long as the result is not too large to be represented as an `int`). It is often necessary, however, to convert data of one type to data of another type. This can happen in assignments, in calculations, in passing values to functions and in returning values from functions. The compiler knows how to perform certain conversions among fundamental types (as we discussed in Chapter 6). You can use cast operators to force conversions among fundamental types.

But what about user-defined types? The compiler cannot know in advance how to convert among user-defined types, and between user-defined types and fundamental types, so you must specify how to do this. Such conversions can be performed with conversion constructors—single-argument constructors that turn objects of other types (including fundamental types) into objects of a particular class. In Section 11.10, we use a conversion constructor to convert ordinary `char *` strings into `String` class objects.

A conversion operator (also called a cast operator) can be used to convert an object of one class into an object of another class or into an object of a fundamental type. Such a conversion operator must be a non-`static` member function. The function prototype

```
A::operator char *() const;
```

declares an overloaded cast operator function for converting an object of user-defined type `A` into a temporary `char *` object. The operator function is declared `const` because it does not modify the original object. An overloaded cast operator function does not specify a return type—the return type is the type to which the object is being converted. If `s` is a class object, when the compiler sees the expression `static_cast< char * >( s )`, the compiler generates the call

```
s.operator char *()
```

The operand `s` is the class object `s` for which the member function `operator char *` is being invoked.

---

3. Note that it is more appropriate when a subscript is out of range to "throw an exception" indicating the out-of-range subscript. Then the program can "catch" that exception, process it and possibly continue execution. See Chapter 16 for more information on exceptions.

Overloaded cast operator functions can be defined to convert objects of user-defined types into fundamental types or into objects of other user-defined types. The prototypes

```
A::operator int() const;
A::operator OtherClass() const;
```

declare overloaded cast operator functions that can convert an object of user-defined type A into an integer or into an object of user-defined type OtherClass, respectively.

One of the nice features of cast operators and conversion constructors is that, when necessary, the compiler can call these functions implicitly to create temporary objects. For example, if an object s of a user-defined String class appears in a program at a location where an ordinary char * is expected, such as

```
cout << s;
```

the compiler can call the overloaded cast-operator function operator char * to convert the object into a char * and use the resulting char * in the expression. With this cast operator provided for our String class, the stream insertion operator does not have to be overloaded to output a String using cout.

11.10 Case Study: String Class

As a capstone exercise to our study of overloading, we'll build our own String class to handle the creation and manipulation of strings (Figs. 11.9–11.11). The C++ standard library provides a similar, more robust class string as well. We present an example of the standard class string in Section 11.13 and study class string in detail in Chapter 18. For now, we'll make extensive use of operator overloading to craft our own class String.

First, we present the header file for class String. We discuss the private data used to represent String objects. Then we walk through the class's public interface, discussing each of the services the class provides. We discuss the member-function definitions for the class String. For each of the overloaded operator functions, we show the code in the program that invokes the overloaded operator function, and we provide an explanation of how the overloaded operator function works.

String Class Definition
Now let's walk through the String class header file in Fig. 11.9. We begin with the internal pointer-based representation of a String. Lines 55–56 declare the private data members of the class. Our String class has a length field, which represents the number of characters in the string, not including the null character at the end, and has a pointer sPtr that points to the dynamically allocated memory representing the character string.

```
1   // Fig. 11.9: String.h
2   // String class definition with operator overloading.
3   #ifndef STRING_H
4   #define STRING_H
5
6   #include <iostream>
7   using std::ostream;
8   using std::istream;
```

Fig. 11.9 | String class definition with operator overloading. (Part 1 of 2.)

```cpp
9
10   class String
11   {
12      friend ostream &operator<<( ostream &, const String & );
13      friend istream &operator>>( istream &, String & );
14   public:
15      String( const char * = "" ); // conversion/default constructor
16      String( const String & ); // copy constructor
17      ~String(); // destructor
18
19      const String &operator=( const String & ); // assignment operator
20      const String &operator+=( const String & ); // concatenation operator
21
22      bool operator!() const; // is String empty?
23      bool operator==( const String & ) const; // test s1 == s2
24      bool operator<( const String & ) const; // test s1 < s2
25
26      // test s1 != s2
27      bool operator!=( const String &right ) const
28      {
29         return !( *this == right );
30      } // end function operator!=
31
32      // test s1 > s2
33      bool operator>( const String &right ) const
34      {
35         return right < *this;
36      } // end function operator>
37
38      // test s1 <= s2
39      bool operator<=( const String &right ) const
40      {
41         return !( right < *this );
42      } // end function operator <=
43
44      // test s1 >= s2
45      bool operator>=( const String &right ) const
46      {
47         return !( *this < right );
48      } // end function operator>=
49
50      char &operator[]( int ); // subscript operator (modifiable lvalue)
51      char operator[]( int ) const; // subscript operator (rvalue)
52      String operator()( int, int = 0 ) const; // return a substring
53      int getLength() const; // return string length
54   private:
55      int length; // string length (not counting null terminator)
56      char *sPtr; // pointer to start of pointer-based string
57
58      void setString( const char * ); // utility function
59   }; // end class String
60
61   #endif
```

Fig. 11.9 | String class definition with operator overloading. (Part 2 of 2.)

```
 1    // Fig. 11.10: String.cpp
 2    // String class member-function and friend-function definitions.
 3    #include <iostream>
 4    using std::cerr;
 5    using std::cout;
 6    using std::endl;
 7
 8    #include <iomanip>
 9    using std::setw;
10
11    #include <cstring> // strcpy and strcat prototypes
12    using std::strcmp;
13    using std::strcpy;
14    using std::strcat;
15
16    #include <cstdlib> // exit prototype
17    using std::exit;
18
19    #include "String.h" // String class definition
20
21    // conversion (and default) constructor converts char * to String
22    String::String( const char *s )
23       : length( ( s != 0 ) ? strlen( s ) : 0 )
24    {
25       cout << "Conversion (and default) constructor: " << s << endl;
26       setString( s ); // call utility function
27    } // end String conversion constructor
28
29    // copy constructor
30    String::String( const String &copy )
31       : length( copy.length )
32    {
33       cout << "Copy constructor: " << copy.sPtr << endl;
34       setString( copy.sPtr ); // call utility function
35    } // end String copy constructor
36
37    // Destructor
38    String::~String()
39    {
40       cout << "Destructor: " << sPtr << endl;
41       delete [] sPtr; // release pointer-based string memory
42    } // end ~String destructor
43
44    // overloaded = operator; avoids self assignment
45    const String &String::operator=( const String &right )
46    {
47       cout << "operator= called" << endl;
48
49       if ( &right != this ) // avoid self assignment
50       {
51          delete [] sPtr; // prevents memory leak
52          length = right.length; // new String length
```

Fig. 11.10 | String class member-function and friend-function definitions. (Part 1 of 4.)

```
53            setString( right.sPtr ); // call utility function
54         } // end if
55         else
56            cout << "Attempted assignment of a String to itself" << endl;
57
58         return *this; // enables cascaded assignments
59      } // end function operator=
60
61      // concatenate right operand to this object and store in this object
62      const String &String::operator+=( const String &right )
63      {
64         size_t newLength = length + right.length; // new length
65         char *tempPtr = new char[ newLength + 1 ]; // create memory
66
67         strcpy( tempPtr, sPtr ); // copy sPtr
68         strcpy( tempPtr + length, right.sPtr ); // copy right.sPtr
69
70         delete [] sPtr; // reclaim old space
71         sPtr = tempPtr; // assign new array to sPtr
72         length = newLength; // assign new length to length
73         return *this; // enables cascaded calls
74      } // end function operator+=
75
76      // is this String empty?
77      bool String::operator!() const
78      {
79         return length == 0;
80      } // end function operator!
81
82      // Is this String equal to right String?
83      bool String::operator==( const String &right ) const
84      {
85         return strcmp( sPtr, right.sPtr ) == 0;
86      } // end function operator==
87
88      // Is this String less than right String?
89      bool String::operator<( const String &right ) const
90      {
91         return strcmp( sPtr, right.sPtr ) < 0;
92      } // end function operator<
93
94      // return reference to character in String as a modifiable lvalue
95      char &String::operator[]( int subscript )
96      {
97         // test for subscript out of range
98         if ( subscript < 0 || subscript >= length )
99         {
100           cerr << "Error: Subscript " << subscript
101              << " out of range" << endl;
102           exit( 1 ); // terminate program
103        } // end if
104
```

Fig. 11.10 | String class member-function and friend-function definitions. (Part 2 of 4.)

```
105       return sPtr[ subscript ]; // non-const return; modifiable lvalue
106    } // end function operator[]
107
108    // return reference to character in String as rvalue
109    char String::operator[]( int subscript ) const
110    {
111       // test for subscript out of range
112       if ( subscript < 0 || subscript >= length )
113       {
114          cerr << "Error: Subscript " << subscript
115             << " out of range" << endl;
116          exit( 1 ); // terminate program
117       } // end if
118
119       return sPtr[ subscript ]; // returns copy of this element
120    } // end function operator[]
121
122    // return a substring beginning at index and of length subLength
123    String String::operator()( int index, int subLength ) const
124    {
125       // if index is out of range or substring length < 0,
126       // return an empty String object
127       if ( index < 0 || index >= length || subLength < 0 )
128          return ""; // converted to a String object automatically
129
130       // determine length of substring
131       int len;
132
133       if ( ( subLength == 0 ) || ( index + subLength > length ) )
134          len = length - index;
135       else
136          len = subLength;
137
138       // allocate temporary array for substring and
139       // terminating null character
140       char *tempPtr = new char[ len + 1 ];
141
142       // copy substring into char array and terminate string
143       strncpy( tempPtr, &sPtr[ index ], len );
144       tempPtr[ len ] = '\0';
145
146       // create temporary String object containing the substring
147       String tempString( tempPtr );
148       delete [] tempPtr; // delete temporary array
149       return tempString; // return copy of the temporary String
150    } // end function operator()
151
152    // return string length
153    int String::getLength() const
154    {
155       return length;
156    } // end function getLength
```

Fig. 11.10 | `String` class member-function and `friend`-function definitions. (Part 3 of 4.)

```
157
158  // utility function called by constructors and operator=
159  void String::setString( const char *string2 )
160  {
161     sPtr = new char[ length + 1 ]; // allocate memory
162
163     if ( string2 != 0 ) // if string2 is not null pointer, copy contents
164        strcpy( sPtr, string2 ); // copy literal to object
165     else // if string2 is a null pointer, make this an empty string
166        sPtr[ 0 ] = '\0'; // empty string
167  } // end function setString
168
169  // overloaded output operator
170  ostream &operator<<( ostream &output, const String &s )
171  {
172     output << s.sPtr;
173     return output; // enables cascading
174  } // end function operator<<
175
176  // overloaded input operator
177  istream &operator>>( istream &input, String &s )
178  {
179     char temp[ 100 ]; // buffer to store input
180     input >> setw( 100 ) >> temp;
181     s = temp; // use String class assignment operator
182     return input; // enables cascading
183  } // end function operator>>
```

Fig. 11.10 | String class member-function and friend-function definitions. (Part 4 of 4.)

```
1   // Fig. 11.11: fig11_11.cpp
2   // String class test program.
3   #include <iostream>
4   using std::cout;
5   using std::endl;
6   using std::boolalpha;
7
8   #include "String.h"
9
10  int main()
11  {
12     String s1( "happy" );
13     String s2( " birthday" );
14     String s3;
15
16     // test overloaded equality and relational operators
17     cout << "s1 is \"" << s1 << "\"; s2 is \"" << s2
18        << "\"; s3 is \"" << s3 << "\""
19        << boolalpha << "\n\nThe results of comparing s2 and s1:"
20        << "\ns2 == s1 yields " << ( s2 == s1 )
21        << "\ns2 != s1 yields " << ( s2 != s1 )
```

Fig. 11.11 | String class test program. (Part 1 of 4.)

```
22          << "\ns2 >  s1 yields " << ( s2 >  s1 )
23          << "\ns2 <  s1 yields " << ( s2 <  s1 )
24          << "\ns2 >= s1 yields " << ( s2 >= s1 )
25          << "\ns2 <= s1 yields " << ( s2 <= s1 );
26
27
28       // test overloaded String empty (!) operator
29       cout << "\n\nTesting !s3:" << endl;
30
31       if ( !s3 )
32       {
33          cout << "s3 is empty; assigning s1 to s3;" << endl;
34          s3 = s1; // test overloaded assignment
35          cout << "s3 is \"" << s3 << "\"";
36       } // end if
37
38       // test overloaded String concatenation operator
39       cout << "\n\ns1 += s2 yields s1 = ";
40       s1 += s2; // test overloaded concatenation
41       cout << s1;
42
43       // test conversion constructor
44       cout << "\n\ns1 += \" to you\" yields" << endl;
45       s1 += " to you"; // test conversion constructor
46       cout << "s1 = " << s1 << "\n\n";
47
48       // test overloaded function call operator () for substring
49       cout << "The substring of s1 starting at\n"
50          << "location 0 for 14 characters, s1(0, 14), is:\n"
51          << s1( 0, 14 ) << "\n\n";
52
53       // test substring "to-end-of-String" option
54       cout << "The substring of s1 starting at\n"
55          << "location 15, s1(15), is: "
56          << s1( 15 ) << "\n\n";
57
58       // test copy constructor
59       String *s4Ptr = new String( s1 );
60       cout << "\n*s4Ptr = " << *s4Ptr << "\n\n";
61
62       // test assignment (=) operator with self-assignment
63       cout << "assigning *s4Ptr to *s4Ptr" << endl;
64       *s4Ptr = *s4Ptr; // test overloaded assignment
65       cout << "*s4Ptr = " << *s4Ptr << endl;
66
67       // test destructor
68       delete s4Ptr;
69
70       // test using subscript operator to create a modifiable lvalue
71       s1[ 0 ] = 'H';
72       s1[ 6 ] = 'B';
73       cout << "\ns1 after s1[0] = 'H' and s1[6] = 'B' is: "
74          << s1 << "\n\n";
```

Fig. 11.11 | String class test program. (Part 2 of 4.)

```
75
76     // test subscript out of range
77     cout << "Attempt to assign 'd' to s1[30] yields:" << endl;
78     s1[ 30 ] = 'd'; // ERROR: subscript out of range
79     return 0;
80  } // end main
```

```
Conversion (and default) constructor: happy
Conversion (and default) constructor:  birthday
Conversion (and default) constructor:
s1 is "happy"; s2 is " birthday"; s3 is ""

The results of comparing s2 and s1:
s2 == s1 yields false
s2 != s1 yields true
s2 >  s1 yields false
s2 <  s1 yields true
s2 >= s1 yields false
s2 <= s1 yields true

Testing !s3:
s3 is empty; assigning s1 to s3;
operator= called
s3 is "happy"

s1 += s2 yields s1 = happy birthday

s1 += " to you" yields
Conversion (and default) constructor:  to you
Destructor:  to you
s1 = happy birthday to you

Conversion (and default) constructor: happy birthday
Copy constructor: happy birthday
Destructor: happy birthday
The substring of s1 starting at
location 0 for 14 characters, s1(0, 14), is:
happy birthday

Destructor: happy birthday
Conversion (and default) constructor: to you
Copy constructor: to you
Destructor: to you
The substring of s1 starting at
location 15, s1(15), is: to you

Destructor: to you
Copy constructor: happy birthday to you

*s4Ptr = happy birthday to you

assigning *s4Ptr to *s4Ptr
operator= called
Attempted assignment of a String to itself
```

(continued ...)

Fig. 11.11 | String class test program. (Part 3 of 4.)

```
*s4Ptr = happy birthday to you
Destructor: happy birthday to you

s1 after s1[0] = 'H' and s1[6] = 'B' is: Happy Birthday to you

Attempt to assign 'd' to s1[30] yields:
Error: Subscript 30 out of range
```

Fig. 11.11 | String class test program. (Part 4 of 4.)

Overloading the Stream Insertion and Stream Extraction Operators as friends

Lines 12–13 (Fig. 11.9) declare the overloaded stream insertion operator function oper-ator<< (defined in Fig. 11.10, lines 170–174) and the overloaded stream extraction oper-ator function operator>> (defined in Fig. 11.10, lines 177–183) as friends of the class. The implementation of operator<< is straightforward. Note that operator>> restricts the total number of characters that can be read into array temp to 99 with setw (line 180); the 100th position is reserved for the string's terminating null character. [*Note:* We did not have this restriction for operator>> in class Array (Figs. 11.6–11.7), because that class's operator>> read one array element at a time and stopped reading values when the end of the array was reached. Object cin does not know how to do this by default for input of character arrays.] Also, note the use of operator= (line 181) to assign the C-style string temp to the String object to which s refers. This statement invokes the conversion con-structor to create a temporary String object containing the C-style string; the temporary String is then assigned to s. We could eliminate the overhead of creating the temporary String object here by providing another overloaded assignment operator that receives a parameter of type const char *.

String Conversion Constructor

Line 15 (Fig. 11.9) declares a conversion constructor. This constructor (defined in Fig. 11.10, lines 22–27) takes a const char * argument (that defaults to the empty string; Fig. 11.9, line 15) and initializes a String object containing that same character string. Any single-argument constructor can be thought of as a conversion constructor. As we'll see, such constructors are helpful when we are doing any String operation using char * arguments. The conversion constructor can convert a char * string into a String object, which can then be assigned to the target String object. The availability of this conversion constructor means that it is not necessary to supply an overloaded assignment operator for specifically assigning character strings to String objects. The compiler invokes the con-version constructor to create a temporary String object containing the character string; then the overloaded assignment operator is invoked to assign the temporary String object to another String object.

> **Software Engineering Observation 11.8**
>
> *When a conversion constructor is used to perform an implicit conversion, C++ can apply only one implicit constructor call (i.e., a single user-defined conversion) to try to match the needs of another overloaded operator. The compiler will not match an overloaded operator's needs by performing a series of implicit, user-defined conversions.*

The String conversion constructor could be invoked in such a declaration as String s1("happy"). The conversion constructor calculates the length of its character-string argument and assigns it to data member length in the member-initializer list. Then, line 26 calls utility function setString (defined in Fig. 11.10, lines 159–167), which uses new to allocate a sufficient amount of memory to private data member sPtr and uses strcpy to copy the character string into the memory to which sPtr points.[4]

String Copy Constructor
Line 16 in Fig. 11.9 declares a copy constructor (defined in Fig. 11.10, lines 30–35) that initializes a String object by making a copy of an existing String object. As with our class Array (Figs. 11.6–11.7), such copying must be done carefully to avoid the pitfall in which both String objects point to the same dynamically allocated memory. The copy constructor operates similarly to the conversion constructor, except that it simply copies the length member from the source String object to the target String object. Note that the copy constructor calls setString to create new space for the target object's internal character string. If it simply copied the sPtr in the source object to the target object's sPtr, then both objects would point to the same dynamically allocated memory. The first destructor to execute would then delete the dynamically allocated memory, and the other object's sPtr would be undefined (i.e., sPtr would be a dangling pointer), a situation likely to cause a serious runtime error.

String Destructor
Line 17 of Fig. 11.9 declares the String destructor (defined in Fig. 11.10, lines 38–42). The destructor uses delete [] to release the dynamic memory to which sPtr points.

Overloaded Assignment Operator
Line 19 (Fig. 11.9) declares the overloaded assignment operator function operator= (defined in Fig. 11.10, lines 45–59). When the compiler sees an expression like string1 = string2, the compiler generates the function call

```
string1.operator=( string2 );
```

The overloaded assignment operator function operator= tests for self-assignment. If this is a self-assignment, the function does not need to change the object. If this test were omitted, the function would immediately delete the space in the target object and thus lose the character string, such that the pointer would no longer be pointing to valid data—a classic example of a dangling pointer. If there is no self-assignment, the function deletes the memory and copies the length field of the source object to the target object. Then operator= calls setString to create new space for the target object and copy the character string from

---

4. There is a subtle issue in the implementation of this conversion constructor. As implemented, if a null pointer (i.e., 0) is passed to the constructor, the program will fail. The proper way to implement this constructor would be to detect whether the constructor argument is a null pointer, then "throw an exception." Chapter 16 discusses how we can make classes more robust in this manner. Also, note that a null pointer (0) is not the same as the empty string (""). A null pointer is a pointer that does not point to anything. An empty string is an actual string that contains only a null character ('\0').

the source object to the target object. Whether or not this is a self-assignment, `operator=` returns `*this` to enable cascaded assignments.

Overloaded Addition Assignment Operator

Line 20 of Fig. 11.9 declares the overloaded string-concatenation operator `+=` (defined in Fig. 11.10, lines 62–74). When the compiler sees the expression `s1 += s2` (line 40 of Fig. 11.11), the compiler generates the member-function call

```
s1.operator+=( s2 )
```

Function `operator+=` calculates the combined length of the concatenated string and stores it in local variable `newLength`, then creates a temporary pointer (`tempPtr`) and allocates a new character array in which the concatenated string will be stored. Next, `operator+=` uses `strcpy` to copy the original character strings from `sPtr` and `right.sPtr` into the memory to which `tempPtr` points. Note that the location into which `strcpy` will copy the first character of `right.sPtr` is determined by the pointer-arithmetic calculation `tempPtr + length`. This calculation indicates that the first character of `right.sPtr` should be placed at location `length` in the array to which `tempPtr` points. Next, `operator+=` uses `delete []` to release the space occupied by this object's original character string, assigns `tempPtr` to `sPtr` so that this `String` object points to the new character string, assigns `newLength` to `length` so that this `String` object contains the new string length and returns `*this` as a `const String &` to enable cascading of `+=` operators.

Do we need a second overloaded concatenation operator to allow concatenation of a `String` and a `char *`? No. The `const char *` conversion constructor converts a C-style string into a temporary `String` object, which then matches the existing overloaded concatenation operator. This is exactly what the compiler does when it encounters line 45 in Fig. 11.11. Again, C++ can perform such conversions only one level deep to facilitate a match. C++ can also perform an implicit compiler-defined conversion between fundamental types before it performs the conversion between a fundamental type and a class. Note that, when a temporary `String` object is created in this case, the conversion constructor and the destructor are called (see the output resulting from line 45, `s1 += " to you"`, in Fig. 11.11). This is an example of function-call overhead that is hidden from the client of the class when temporary class objects are created and destroyed during implicit conversions. Similar overhead is generated by copy constructors in call-by-value parameter passing and in returning class objects by value.

Performance Tip 11.2

Overloading the += concatenation operator with an additional version that takes a single argument of type const char * executes more efficiently than having only a version that takes a String argument. Without the const char * version of the += operator, a const char * argument would first be converted to a String object with class String's conversion constructor, then the += operator that receives a String argument would be called to perform the concatenation.

Software Engineering Observation 11.9

Using implicit conversions with overloaded operators, rather than overloading operators for many different operand types, often requires less code, which makes a class easier to modify, maintain and debug.

Overloaded Negation Operator

Line 22 of Fig. 11.9 declares the overloaded negation operator (defined in Fig. 11.10, lines 77–80). This operator determines whether an object of our String class is empty. For example, when the compiler sees the expression !string1, it generates the function call

```
string1.operator!()
```

This function simply returns the result of testing whether length is equal to zero.

Overloaded Equality and Relational Operators

Lines 23–24 of Fig. 11.9 declare the overloaded equality operator (defined in Fig. 11.10, lines 83–86) and the overloaded less-than operator (defined in Fig. 11.10, lines 89–92) for class String. These are similar, so let us discuss only one example, namely, overloading the == operator. When the compiler sees the expression string1 == string2, the compiler generates the member-function call

```
string1.operator==( string2 )
```

which returns true if string1 is equal to string2. Each of these operators uses function strcmp (from <cstring>) to compare the character strings in the String objects. Many C++ programmers advocate using some of the overloaded operator functions to implement others. So, the !=, >, <= and >= operators are implemented (Fig. 11.9, lines 27–48) in terms of operator== and operator<. For example, overloaded function operator>= (implemented in lines 45–48 in the header file) uses the overloaded < operator to determine whether one String object is greater than or equal to another. Note that the operator functions for !=, >, <= and >= are defined in the header file. The compiler inlines these definitions to eliminate the overhead of the extra function calls.

Software Engineering Observation 11.10

By implementing member functions using previously defined member functions, you reuse code to reduce the amount of code that must be written and maintained.

Overloaded Subscript Operators

Lines 50–51 in the header file declare two overloaded subscript operators (defined in Fig. 11.10, lines 95–106 and 109–120, respectively)—one for non-const Strings and one for const Strings. When the compiler sees an expression like string1[0], the compiler generates the member-function call

```
string1.operator[]( 0 )
```

(using the appropriate version of operator[] based on whether the String is const). Each implementation of operator[] first validates the subscript to ensure that it is in range. If the subscript is out of range, each function prints an error message and terminates the program with a call to exit.[5] If the subscript is in range, the non-const version of operator[] returns a char & to the appropriate character of the String object; this char & may be used as an *lvalue* to modify the designated character of the String object. The const version of operator[] returns the appropriate character of the String object; this can be used only as an *rvalue* to read the value of the character.

---

5. Again, it is more appropriate when a subscript is out of range to "throw an exception" indicating the out-of-range subscript.

Error-Prevention Tip 11.2

Returning a non-const char reference from an overloaded subscript operator in a String class is dangerous. For example, the client could use this reference to insert a null ('\0') anywhere in the string.

Overloaded Function Call Operator
Line 52 of Fig. 11.9 declares the overloaded function call operator (defined in Fig. 11.10, lines 123–150). We overload this operator to select a substring from a String. The two integer parameters specify the start location and the length of the substring being selected from the String. If the start location is out of range or the substring length is negative, the operator simply returns an empty String. If the substring length is 0, then the substring is selected to the end of the String object. For example, suppose string1 is a String object containing the string "AEIOU". For the expression string1(2, 2), the compiler generates the member-function call

```
string1.operator()( 2, 2 )
```

When this call executes, it produces a String object containing the string "IO" and returns a copy of that object.

Overloading the function call operator () is powerful, because functions can take arbitrarily long and complex parameter lists. So we can use this capability for many interesting purposes. One such use of the function call operator is an alternate array-subscripting notation: Instead of using C's awkward double-square-bracket notation for pointer-based two-dimensional arrays, such as in a[b][c], some programmers prefer to overload the function call operator to enable the notation a(b, c). The overloaded function call operator must be a non-static member function. This operator is used only when the "function name" is an object of class String.

String Member Function getLength
Line 53 in Fig. 11.9 declares function getLength (defined in Fig. 11.10, lines 153–156), which returns the length of a String.

Notes on Our String Class
At this point, you should step through the code in main, examine the output window and check each use of an overloaded operator. As you study the output, pay special attention to the implicit constructor calls that are generated to create temporary String objects throughout the program. Many of these calls introduce additional overhead into the program that can be avoided if the class provides overloaded operators that take char * arguments. However, additional operator functions can make the class harder to maintain, modify and debug.

11.11 Overloading ++ and --

The prefix and postfix versions of the increment and decrement operators can all be overloaded. We'll see how the compiler distinguishes between the prefix version and the postfix version of an increment or decrement operator.

To overload the increment operator to allow both prefix and postfix increment usage, each overloaded operator function must have a distinct signature, so that the compiler will be able to determine which version of ++ is intended. The prefix versions are overloaded exactly as any other prefix unary operator would be.

Overloading the Prefix Increment Operator
Suppose, for example, that we want to add 1 to the day in Date object d1. When the compiler sees the preincrementing expression ++d1, the compiler generates the member-function call

```
d1.operator++()
```

The prototype for this operator function would be

```
Date &operator++();
```

If the prefix increment operator is implemented as a global function, then, when the compiler sees the expression ++d1, the compiler generates the function call

```
operator++( d1 )
```

The prototype for this operator function would be declared in the Date class as

```
Date &operator++( Date & );
```

Overloading the Postfix Increment Operator
Overloading the postfix increment operator presents a challenge, because the compiler must be able to distinguish between the signatures of the overloaded prefix and postfix increment operator functions. The convention that has been adopted in C++ is that, when the compiler sees the postincrementing expression d1++, it generates the member-function call

```
d1.operator++( 0 )
```

The prototype for this function is

```
Date operator++( int )
```

The argument 0 is strictly a "dummy value" that enables the compiler to distinguish between the prefix and postfix increment operator functions.

If the postfix increment is implemented as a global function, then, when the compiler sees the expression d1++, the compiler generates the function call

```
operator++( d1, 0 )
```

The prototype for this function would be

```
Date operator++( Date &, int );
```

Once again, the 0 argument is used by the compiler to distinguish between the prefix and postfix increment operators implemented as global functions. Note that the postfix increment operator returns Date objects by value, whereas the prefix increment operator returns Date objects by reference, because the postfix increment operator typically returns a temporary object that contains the original value of the object before the increment occurred. C++ treats such objects as *rvalues*, which cannot be used on the left side of an assignment. The prefix increment operator returns the actual incremented object with its new value. Such an object can be used as an *lvalue* in a continuing expression.

Performance Tip 11.3

The extra object that is created by the postfix increment (or decrement) operator can result in a significant performance problem—especially when the operator is used in a loop. For this reason, you should use the postfix increment (or decrement) operator only when the logic of the program requires postincrementing (or postdecrementing).

Everything stated in this section for overloading prefix and postfix increment operators applies to overloading predecrement and postdecrement operators. Next, we examine a Date class with overloaded prefix and postfix increment operators.

11.12 Case Study: A Date Class

The program of Figs. 11.12–11.14 demonstrates a Date class. The class uses overloaded prefix and postfix increment operators to add 1 to the day in a Date object, while causing appropriate increments to the month and year if necessary. The Date header file (Fig. 11.12) specifies that Date's public interface includes an overloaded stream insertion operator (line 11), a default constructor (line 13), a setDate function (line 14), an overloaded prefix increment operator (line 15), an overloaded postfix increment operator (line 16), an overloaded += addition assignment operator (line 17), a function to test for leap years (line 18) and a function to determine whether a day is the last day of the month (line 19).

```
1   // Fig. 11.12: Date.h
2   // Date class definition with overloaded increment operators.
3   #ifndef DATE_H
4   #define DATE_H
5
6   #include <iostream>
7   using std::ostream;
8
9   class Date
10  {
11     friend ostream &operator<<( ostream &, const Date & );
12  public:
13     Date( int m = 1, int d = 1, int y = 1900 ); // default constructor
14     void setDate( int, int, int ); // set month, day, year
15     Date &operator++(); // prefix increment operator
16     Date operator++( int ); // postfix increment operator
17     const Date &operator+=( int ); // add days, modify object
18     bool leapYear( int ) const; // is date in a leap year?
19     bool endOfMonth( int ) const; // is date at the end of month?
20  private:
21     int month;
22     int day;
23     int year;
24
25     static const int days[]; // array of days per month
26     void helpIncrement(); // utility function for incrementing date
27  }; // end class Date
28
29  #endif
```

Fig. 11.12 | Date class definition with overloaded increment operators.

```
1   // Fig. 11.13: Date.cpp
2   // Date class member- and friend-function definitions.
3   #include <iostream>
4   #include "Date.h"
5
6   // initialize static member at file scope; one classwide copy
7   const int Date::days[] =
8      { 0, 31, 28, 31, 30, 31, 30, 31, 31, 30, 31, 30, 31 };
9
10  // Date constructor
11  Date::Date( int m, int d, int y )
12  {
13     setDate( m, d, y );
14  } // end Date constructor
15
16  // set month, day and year
17  void Date::setDate( int mm, int dd, int yy )
18  {
19     month = ( mm >= 1 && mm <= 12 ) ? mm : 1;
20     year = ( yy >= 1900 && yy <= 2100 ) ? yy : 1900;
21
22     // test for a leap year
23     if ( month == 2 && leapYear( year ) )
24        day = ( dd >= 1 && dd <= 29 ) ? dd : 1;
25     else
26        day = ( dd >= 1 && dd <= days[ month ] ) ? dd : 1;
27  } // end function setDate
28
29  // overloaded prefix increment operator
30  Date &Date::operator++()
31  {
32     helpIncrement(); // increment date
33     return *this; // reference return to create an lvalue
34  } // end function operator++
35
36  // overloaded postfix increment operator; note that the
37  // dummy integer parameter does not have a parameter name
38  Date Date::operator++( int )
39  {
40     Date temp = *this; // hold current state of object
41     helpIncrement();
42
43     // return unincremented, saved, temporary object
44     return temp; // value return; not a reference return
45  } // end function operator++
46
47  // add specified number of days to date
48  const Date &Date::operator+=( int additionalDays )
49  {
50     for ( int i = 0; i < additionalDays; i++ )
51        helpIncrement();
52
```

Fig. 11.13 | Date class member- and friend-function definitions. (Part 1 of 2.)

```
53       return *this; // enables cascading
54    } // end function operator+=
55
56    // if the year is a leap year, return true; otherwise, return false
57    bool Date::leapYear( int testYear ) const
58    {
59       if ( testYear % 400 == 0 ||
60          ( testYear % 100 != 0 && testYear % 4 == 0 ) )
61          return true; // a leap year
62       else
63          return false; // not a leap year
64    } // end function leapYear
65
66    // determine whether the day is the last day of the month
67    bool Date::endOfMonth( int testDay ) const
68    {
69       if ( month == 2 && leapYear( year ) )
70          return testDay == 29; // last day of Feb. in leap year
71       else
72          return testDay == days[ month ];
73    } // end function endOfMonth
74
75    // function to help increment the date
76    void Date::helpIncrement()
77    {
78       // day is not end of month
79       if ( !endOfMonth( day ) )
80          day++; // increment day
81       else
82          if ( month < 12 ) // day is end of month and month < 12
83          {
84             month++; // increment month
85             day = 1; // first day of new month
86          } // end if
87          else // last day of year
88          {
89             year++; // increment year
90             month = 1; // first month of new year
91             day = 1; // first day of new month
92          } // end else
93    } // end function helpIncrement
94
95    // overloaded output operator
96    ostream &operator<<( ostream &output, const Date &d )
97    {
98       static char *monthName[ 13 ] = { "", "January", "February",
99          "March", "April", "May", "June", "July", "August",
100         "September", "October", "November", "December" };
101      output << monthName[ d.month ] << ' ' << d.day << ", " << d.year;
102      return output; // enables cascading
103   } // end function operator<<
```

Fig. 11.13 | Date class member- and friend-function definitions. (Part 2 of 2.)

```
1   // Fig. 11.14: fig11_14.cpp
2   // Date class test program.
3   #include <iostream>
4   using std::cout;
5   using std::endl;
6
7   #include "Date.h" // Date class definition
8
9   int main()
10  {
11     Date d1; // defaults to January 1, 1900
12     Date d2( 12, 27, 1992 ); // December 27, 1992
13     Date d3( 0, 99, 8045 ); // invalid date
14
15     cout << "d1 is " << d1 << "\nd2 is " << d2 << "\nd3 is " << d3;
16     cout << "\n\nd2 += 7 is " << ( d2 += 7 );
17
18     d3.setDate( 2, 28, 1992 );
19     cout << "\n\n  d3 is " << d3;
20     cout << "\n++d3 is " << ++d3 << " (leap year allows 29th)";
21
22     Date d4( 7, 13, 2002 );
23
24     cout << "\n\nTesting the prefix increment operator:\n"
25        << "  d4 is " << d4 << endl;
26     cout << "++d4 is " << ++d4 << endl;
27     cout << "  d4 is " << d4;
28
29     cout << "\n\nTesting the postfix increment operator:\n"
30        << "  d4 is " << d4 << endl;
31     cout << "d4++ is " << d4++ << endl;
32     cout << "  d4 is " << d4 << endl;
33     return 0;
34  } // end main
```

```
d1 is January 1, 1900
d2 is December 27, 1992
d3 is January 1, 1900

d2 += 7 is January 3, 1993

  d3 is February 28, 1992
++d3 is February 29, 1992 (leap year allows 29th)

Testing the prefix increment operator:
  d4 is July 13, 2002
++d4 is July 14, 2002
  d4 is July 14, 2002

Testing the postfix increment operator:
  d4 is July 14, 2002
d4++ is July 14, 2002
  d4 is July 15, 2002
```

Fig. 11.14 | Date class test program.

Function `main` (Fig. 11.14) creates three `Date` objects (lines 11–13)—`d1` is initialized by default to January 1, 1900; `d2` is initialized to December 27, 1992; and `d3` is initialized to an invalid date. The `Date` constructor (defined in Fig. 11.13, lines 11–14) calls `setDate` to validate the month, day and year specified. An invalid month is set to 1, an invalid year is set to 1900 and an invalid day is set to 1.

Lines 15–16 of `main` output each of the constructed `Date` objects, using the overloaded stream insertion operator (defined in Fig. 11.13, lines 96–103). Line 16 of `main` uses the overloaded operator `+=` to add seven days to `d2`. Line 18 uses function `setDate` to set `d3` to February 28, 1992, which is a leap year. Then, line 20 preincrements `d3` to show that the date increments properly to February 29. Next, line 22 creates a `Date` object, `d4`, which is initialized with the date July 13, 2002. Then line 26 increments `d4` by 1 with the overloaded prefix increment operator. Lines 24–27 output `d4` before and after the preincrement operation to confirm that it worked correctly. Finally, line 31 increments `d4` with the overloaded postfix increment operator. Lines 29–32 output `d4` before and after the postincrement operation to confirm that it worked correctly.

Overloading the prefix increment operator is straightforward. The prefix increment operator (defined in Fig. 11.13, lines 30–34) calls utility function `helpIncrement` (defined in Fig. 11.13, lines 76–93) to increment the date. This function deals with "wraparounds" or "carries" that occur when we increment the last day of the month. These carries require incrementing the month. If the month is already 12, then the year must also be incremented and the month must be set to 1. Function `helpIncrement` uses function `endOfMonth` to increment the day correctly.

The overloaded prefix increment operator returns a reference to the current `Date` object (i.e., the one that was just incremented). This occurs because the current object, `*this`, is returned as a `Date &`. This enables a preincremented `Date` object to be used as an *lvalue*, which is how the built-in prefix increment operator works for fundamental types.

Overloading the postfix increment operator (defined in Fig. 11.13, lines 38–45) is trickier. To emulate the effect of the postincrement, we must return an unincremented copy of the `Date` object. For example, if `int` variable x has the value 7, the statement

```
cout << x++ << endl;
```

outputs the original value of variable x. So we'd like our postfix increment operator to operate the same way on a `Date` object. On entry to `operator++`, we save the current object (`*this`) in `temp` (line 40). Next, we call `helpIncrement` to increment the current `Date` object. Then, line 44 returns the unincremented copy of the object previously stored in `temp`. Note that this function cannot return a reference to the local `Date` object `temp`, because a local variable is destroyed when the function in which it is declared exits. Thus, declaring the return type to this function as `Date &` would return a reference to an object that no longer exists. Returning a reference (or a pointer) to a local variable is a common error for which most compilers will issue a warning.

11.13 Standard Library Class `string`

In this chapter, you learned that you can build a `String` class (Figs. 11.9–11.11) that is better than the C-style, `char *` strings that C++ absorbed from C. You also learned that you can build an `Array` class (Figs. 11.6–11.8) that is better than the C-style, pointer-based arrays that C++ absorbed from C.

Building useful, reusable classes such as `String` and `Array` takes work. However, once such classes are tested and debugged, they can be reused by you, your colleagues, your company, many companies, an entire industry or even many industries (if they are placed in public or for-sale libraries). The designers of C++ did exactly that, building class `string` (which we have been using since Chapter 3) and class template `vector` (which we introduced in Chapter 7) into standard C++. These classes are available to anyone building applications with C++. As you'll see in Chapter 22, the C++ Standard Library provides several predefined class templates for use in your programs.

To close this chapter, we redo our `String` (Figs. 11.9–11.11) example, using the standard C++ `string` class. We rework our example to demonstrate similar functionality provided by standard class `string`. We also demonstrate three member functions of standard class `string`—empty, substr and at—that were not part of our `String` example. Function empty determines whether a `string` is empty, function substr returns a `string` that represents a portion of an existing `string` and function at returns the character at a specific index in a `string` (after checking that the index is in range). Chapter 18 presents class `string` in detail.

Standard Library Class *string*

The program of Fig. 11.15 reimplements the program of Fig. 11.11, using standard class `string`. As you'll see in this example, class `string` provides all the functionality of our class `String` presented in Figs. 11.9–11.10. Class `string` is defined in header `<string>` (line 7) and belongs to namespace `std` (line 8).

```
1   // Fig. 11.15: fig11_15.cpp
2   // Standard Library string class test program.
3   #include <iostream>
4   using std::cout;
5   using std::endl;
6
7   #include <string>
8   using std::string;
9
10  int main()
11  {
12     string s1( "happy" );
13     string s2( " birthday" );
14     string s3;
15
16     // test overloaded equality and relational operators
17     cout << "s1 is \"" << s1 << "\"; s2 is \"" << s2
18        << "\"; s3 is \"" << s3 << '\"'
19        << "\n\nThe results of comparing s2 and s1:"
20        << "\ns2 == s1 yields " << ( s2 == s1 ? "true" : "false" )
21        << "\ns2 != s1 yields " << ( s2 != s1 ? "true" : "false" )
22        << "\ns2 >  s1 yields " << ( s2 > s1 ? "true" : "false" )
23        << "\ns2 <  s1 yields " << ( s2 < s1 ? "true" : "false" )
24        << "\ns2 >= s1 yields " << ( s2 >= s1 ? "true" : "false" )
25        << "\ns2 <= s1 yields " << ( s2 <= s1 ? "true" : "false" );
26
```

Fig. 11.15 | Standard Library class `string`. (Part 1 of 3.)

```
27        // test string member-function empty
28        cout << "\n\nTesting s3.empty():" << endl;
29
30        if ( s3.empty() )
31        {
32           cout << "s3 is empty; assigning s1 to s3;" << endl;
33           s3 = s1; // assign s1 to s3
34           cout << "s3 is \"" << s3 << "\"";
35        } // end if
36
37        // test overloaded string concatenation operator
38        cout << "\n\ns1 += s2 yields s1 = ";
39        s1 += s2; // test overloaded concatenation
40        cout << s1;
41
42        // test overloaded string concatenation operator with C-style string
43        cout << "\n\ns1 += \" to you\" yields" << endl;
44        s1 += " to you";
45        cout << "s1 = " << s1 << "\n\n";
46
47        // test string member function substr
48        cout << "The substring of s1 starting at location 0 for\n"
49           << "14 characters, s1.substr(0, 14), is:\n"
50           << s1.substr( 0, 14 ) << "\n\n";
51
52        // test substr "to-end-of-string" option
53        cout << "The substring of s1 starting at\n"
54           << "location 15, s1.substr(15), is:\n"
55           << s1.substr( 15 ) << endl;
56
57        // test copy constructor
58        string *s4Ptr = new string( s1 );
59        cout << "\n*s4Ptr = " << *s4Ptr << "\n\n";
60
61        // test assignment (=) operator with self-assignment
62        cout << "assigning *s4Ptr to *s4Ptr" << endl;
63        *s4Ptr = *s4Ptr;
64        cout << "*s4Ptr = " << *s4Ptr << endl;
65
66        // test destructor
67        delete s4Ptr;
68
69        // test using subscript operator to create lvalue
70        s1[ 0 ] = 'H';
71        s1[ 6 ] = 'B';
72        cout << "\ns1 after s1[0] = 'H' and s1[6] = 'B' is: "
73           << s1 << "\n\n";
74
75        // test subscript out of range with string member function "at"
76        cout << "Attempt to assign 'd' to s1.at( 30 ) yields:" << endl;
77        s1.at( 30 ) = 'd'; // ERROR: subscript out of range
78        return 0;
79     } // end main
```

Fig. 11.15 | Standard Library class `string`. (Part 2 of 3.)

```
s1 is "happy"; s2 is " birthday"; s3 is ""

The results of comparing s2 and s1:
s2 == s1 yields false
s2 != s1 yields true
s2 >  s1 yields false
s2 <  s1 yields true
s2 >= s1 yields false
s2 <= s1 yields true

Testing s3.empty():
s3 is empty; assigning s1 to s3;
s3 is "happy"

s1 += s2 yields s1 = happy birthday

s1 += " to you" yields
s1 = happy birthday to you

The substring of s1 starting at location 0 for
14 characters, s1.substr(0, 14), is:
happy birthday

The substring of s1 starting at
location 15, s1.substr(15), is:
to you

*s4Ptr = happy birthday to you

assigning *s4Ptr to *s4Ptr
*s4Ptr = happy birthday to you

s1 after s1[0] = 'H' and s1[6] = 'B' is: Happy Birthday to you

Attempt to assign 'd' to s1.at( 30 ) yields:

abnormal program termination
```

Fig. 11.15 | Standard Library class string. (Part 3 of 3.)

Lines 12–14 create three string objects—s1 is initialized with the literal "happy", s2 is initialized with the literal " birthday" and s3 uses the default string constructor to create an empty string. Lines 17–18 output these three objects, using cout and operator <<, which the string class designers overloaded to handle string objects. Then lines 19–25 show the results of comparing s2 to s1 by using class string's overloaded equality and relational operators.

Our class String (Figs. 11.9–11.10) provided an overloaded operator! that tested a String to determine whether it was empty. Standard class string does not provide this functionality as an overloaded operator; instead, it provides member function empty, which we demonstrate in line 30. Member function empty returns true if the string is empty; otherwise, it returns false.

Line 33 demonstrates class string's overloaded assignment operator by assigning s1 to s3. Line 34 outputs s3 to demonstrate that the assignment worked correctly.

Line 39 demonstrates class `string`'s overloaded += operator for string concatenation. In this case, the contents of `s2` are appended to `s1`. Then line 40 outputs the resulting string that is stored in `s1`. Line 44 demonstrates that a C-style string literal can be appended to a `string` object by using operator +=. Line 45 displays the result.

Our class `String` (Figs. 11.9–11.10) provided overloaded `operator()` to obtain substrings. Standard class `string` does not provide this functionality as an overloaded operator; instead, it provides member function `substr` (lines 50 and 55). The call to `substr` in line 50 obtains a 14-character substring (specified by the second argument) of `s1` starting at position 0 (specified by the first argument). The call to `substr` in line 55 obtains a substring starting from position 15 of `s1`. When the second argument is not specified, `substr` returns the remainder of the `string` on which it is called.

Line 58 dynamically allocates a `string` object and initializes it with a copy of `s1`. This results in a call to class `string`'s copy constructor. Line 63 uses class `string`'s overloaded = operator to demonstrate that it handles self-assignment properly.

Lines 70–71 used class `string`'s overloaded [] operator to create *lvalues* that enable new characters to replace existing characters in `s1`. Line 73 outputs the new value of `s1`. In our class `String` (Figs. 11.9–11.10), the overloaded [] operator performed bounds checking to determine whether the subscript it received as an argument was a valid subscript in the string. If the subscript was invalid, the operator printed an error message and terminated the program. Standard class `string`'s overloaded [] operator does not perform any bounds checking. Therefore, you must ensure that operations using standard class `string`'s overloaded [] operator do not accidentally manipulate elements outside the bounds of the `string`. Standard class `string` does provide bounds checking in its member function `at`, which "throws an exception" if its argument is an invalid subscript. By default, this causes a C++ program to terminate.[6] If the subscript is valid, function `at` returns the character at the specified location as a modifiable *lvalue* or an unmodifiable *lvalue* (i.e., a `const` reference), depending on the context in which the call appears. Line 77 demonstrates a call to function `at` with an invalid subscript.

11.14 explicit Constructors

In Section 11.8 and Section 11.9, we discussed that any single-argument constructor can be used by the compiler to perform an implicit conversion—the type received by the constructor is converted to an object of the class in which the constructor is defined. The conversion is automatic and you need not use a cast operator. In some situations, implicit conversions are undesirable or error-prone. For example, our `Array` class in Fig. 11.6 defines a constructor that takes a single `int` argument. The intent of this constructor is to create an `Array` object containing the number of elements specified by the `int` argument. However, this constructor can be misused by the compiler to perform an implicit conversion.

Common Programming Error 11.9

Unfortunately, the compiler might use implicit conversions in cases that you do not expect, resulting in ambiguous expressions that generate compilation errors or resulting in execution-time logic errors.

---

6.   Again, Chapter 16, Exception Handling, demonstrates how to "catch" and handle such exceptions.

Accidentally Using a Single-Argument Constructor as a Conversion Constructor
The program (Fig. 11.16) uses the Array class of Figs. 11.6–11.7 to demonstrate an improper implicit conversion.

Line 13 in main instantiates Array object integers1 and calls the single argument constructor with the int value 7 to specify the number of elements in the Array. Recall from Fig. 11.7 that the Array constructor that receives an int argument initializes all the array elements to 0. Line 14 calls function outputArray (defined in lines 20–24), which receives as its argument a const Array & to an Array. The function outputs the number of elements in its Array argument and the contents of the Array. In this case, the size of the Array is 7, so seven 0s are output.

Line 15 calls function outputArray with the int value 3 as an argument. However, this program does not contain a function called outputArray that takes an int argument. So, the compiler determines whether class Array provides a conversion constructor that can convert an int into an Array. Since any constructor that receives a single argument is considered to be a conversion constructor, the compiler assumes the Array constructor that receives a single int is a conversion constructor and uses it to convert the argument 3 into a temporary Array object that contains three elements. Then, the compiler passes the

```
 1   // Fig. 11.16: Fig11_16.cpp
 2   // Driver for simple class Array.
 3   #include <iostream>
 4   using std::cout;
 5   using std::endl;
 6
 7   #include "Array.h"
 8
 9   void outputArray( const Array & ); // prototype
10
11   int main()
12   {
13      Array integers1( 7 ); // 7-element array
14      outputArray( integers1 ); // output Array integers1
15      outputArray( 3 ); // convert 3 to an Array and output Array's contents
16      return 0;
17   } // end main
18
19   // print Array contents
20   void outputArray( const Array &arrayToOutput )
21   {
22      cout << "The Array received has " << arrayToOutput.getSize()
23         << " elements. The contents are:\n" << arrayToOutput << endl;
24   } // end outputArray
```

```
The Array received has 7 elements. The contents are:
        0           0           0           0
        0           0           0

The Array received has 3 elements. The contents are:
        0           0           0
```

Fig. 11.16 | Single-argument constructors and implicit conversions.

temporary `Array` object to function `outputArray` to output the `Array`'s contents. Thus, even though we do not explicitly provide an `outputArray` function that receives an `int` argument, the compiler is able to compile line 15. The output shows the contents of the three-element `Array` containing 0s.

Preventing Accidental Use of a Single-Argument Constructor as a Conversion Constructor

C++ provides the keyword `explicit` to suppress implicit conversions via conversion constructors when such conversions should not be allowed. A constructor that is declared explicit cannot be used in an implicit conversion. Figure 11.17 declares an `explicit` constructor in class `Array`. The only modification to `Array.h` was the addition of the key-

```
1   // Fig. 11.17: Array.h
2   // Array class for storing arrays of integers.
3   #ifndef ARRAY_H
4   #define ARRAY_H
5
6   #include <iostream>
7   using std::ostream;
8   using std::istream;
9
10  class Array
11  {
12     friend ostream &operator<<( ostream &, const Array & );
13     friend istream &operator>>( istream &, Array & );
14  public:
15     explicit Array( int = 10 ); // default constructor
16     Array( const Array & ); // copy constructor
17     ~Array(); // destructor
18     int getSize() const; // return size
19
20     const Array &operator=( const Array & ); // assignment operator
21     bool operator==( const Array & ) const; // equality operator
22
23     // inequality operator; returns opposite of == operator
24     bool operator!=( const Array &right ) const
25     {
26        return ! ( *this == right ); // invokes Array::operator==
27     } // end function operator!=
28
29     // subscript operator for non-const objects returns lvalue
30     int &operator[]( int );
31
32     // subscript operator for const objects returns rvalue
33     const int &operator[]( int ) const;
34  private:
35     int size; // pointer-based array size
36     int *ptr; // pointer to first element of pointer-based array
37  }; // end class Array
38
39  #endif
```

Fig. 11.17 | `Array` class definition with `explicit` constructor.

word explicit to the declaration of the single-argument constructor in line 15. No modifications are required to the source-code file containing class Array's member-function definitions.

Figure 11.18 presents a slightly modified version of the program in Fig. 11.16. When this program is compiled, the compiler produces an error message indicating that the integer value passed to outputArray in line 15 cannot be converted to a const Array &. The compiler error message is shown in the output window. Line 16 demonstrates how the explicit constructor can be used to create a temporary Array of 3 elements and pass it to function outputArray.

Common Programming Error 11.10

Attempting to invoke an explicit constructor for an implicit conversion is a compilation error.

Common Programming Error 11.11

Using the explicit keyword on data members or member functions other than a single-argument constructor is a compilation error.

```cpp
1   // Fig. 11.18: Fig11_18.cpp
2   // Driver for simple class Array.
3   #include <iostream>
4   using std::cout;
5   using std::endl;
6
7   #include "Array.h"
8
9   void outputArray( const Array & ); // prototype
10
11  int main()
12  {
13     Array integers1( 7 ); // 7-element array
14     outputArray( integers1 ); // output Array integers1
15     outputArray( 3 ); // convert 3 to an Array and output Array's contents
16     outputArray( Array( 3 ) ); // explicit single-argument constructor call
17     return 0;
18  } // end main
19
20  // print array contents
21  void outputArray( const Array &arrayToOutput )
22  {
23     cout << "The Array received has " << arrayToOutput.getSize()
24        << " elements. The contents are:\n" << arrayToOutput << endl;
25  } // end outputArray
```

```
c:\cpphtp6_examples\ch11\Fig11_17_18\Fig11_18.cpp(15) : error C2664:
   'outputArray' : cannot convert parameter 1 from 'int' to 'const Array &'
      Reason: cannot convert from 'int' to 'const Array'
      Constructor for class 'Array' is declared 'explicit'
```

Fig. 11.18 | Demonstrating an explicit constructor.

Error-Prevention Tip 11.3

Use the explicit *keyword on single-argument constructors that should not be used by the compiler to perform implicit conversions.*

11.15 Wrap-Up

In this chapter, you learned how to build more robust classes by defining overloaded operators that enable programmers to treat objects of your classes as if they were fundamental C++ data types. We presented basic operator overloading concepts, as well as several restrictions that the C++ standard places on overloaded operators. You learned reasons for implementing overloaded operators as member functions or as global functions. We discussed the differences between overloading unary and binary operators as member functions and global functions. With global functions, we showed how to input and output objects of our classes using the overloaded stream extraction and stream insertion operators, respectively. We showed a special syntax that is required to differentiate between the prefix and postfix versions of the increment (++) operator. We also demonstrated standard C++ class string, which makes extensive use of overloaded operators to create a robust, reusable class that can replace C-style, pointer-based strings. Finally, you learned how to use keyword explicit to prevent the compiler from using a single-argument constructor to perform implicit conversions. In the next chapter, we continue our discussion of classes by introducing a form of software reuse called inheritance. We'll see that when classes share common attributes and behaviors, it is possible to define those attributes and behaviors in a common "base" class and "inherit" those capabilities into new class definitions.

Summary

Section 11.1 Introduction

- C++ enables you to overload most operators to be sensitive to the context in which they are used—the compiler generates the appropriate code based on the context (in particular, the types of the operands).

- Many of C++'s operators can be overloaded to work with user-defined types.

- One example of an overloaded operator built into C++ is operator <<, which is used both as the stream insertion operator and as the bitwise left-shift operator. Similarly, >> is also overloaded; it is used both as the stream extraction operator and as the bitwise right-shift operator. Both of these operators are overloaded in the C++ Standard Library.

- The C++ language itself overloads + and -. These operators perform differently, depending on their context in integer arithmetic, floating-point arithmetic and pointer arithmetic.

- The jobs performed by overloaded operators can also be performed by function calls, but operator notation is often clearer and more familiar to programmers.

Section 11.2 Fundamentals of Operator Overloading

- An operator is overloaded by writing a non-static member-function definition or global function definition in which the function name is the keyword operator followed by the symbol for the operator being overloaded.

- When operators are overloaded as member functions, they must be non-static, because they must be called on an object of the class and operate on that object.

- To use an operator on class objects, that operator *must* be overloaded, with three exceptions— the assignment operator (=), the address operator (&) and the comma operator (,).

Section 11.3 Restrictions on Operator Overloading
- You cannot change the precedence and associativity of an operator by overloading.
- You cannot change the "arity" of an operator (i.e., the number of operands an operator takes).
- You cannot create new operators—only existing operators can be overloaded.
- You cannot change the meaning of how an operator works on objects of fundamental types.
- Overloading an assignment operator and an addition operator for a class does not imply that the += operator is also overloaded. Such behavior can be achieved only by explicitly overloading operator += for that class.

Section 11.4 Operator Functions as Class Members vs. Global Functions
- Operator functions can be member functions or global functions—global functions are often made `friend`s for performance reasons. Member functions use the `this` pointer implicitly to obtain one of their class object arguments (the left operand for binary operators). Arguments for both operands of a binary operator must be explicitly listed in a global function call.
- When overloading (), [], -> or any of the assignment operators, the operator overloading function must be declared as a class member. For the other operators, the operator overloading functions can be class members or global functions.
- When an operator function is implemented as a member function, the leftmost (or only) operand must be an object (or a reference to an object) of the operator's class.
- If the left operand must be an object of a different class or a fundamental type, this operator function must be implemented as a global function.
- A global operator function can be made a `friend` of a class if that function must access `private` or `protected` members of that class directly.

Section 11.5 Overloading Stream Insertion and Stream Extraction Operators
- The overloaded stream insertion operator (<<) is used in an expression in which the left operand has type `ostream &`. For this reason, it must be overloaded as a global function. To be a member function, operator << would have to be a member of the `ostream` class, but this is not possible, since we are not allowed to modify C++ Standard Library classes. Similarly, the overloaded stream extraction operator (>>) must be a global function.
- Another reason to choose a global function to overload an operator is to enable the operator to be commutative.
- When used with `cin` and `strings`, `setw` restricts the number of characters read to the number of characters specified by its argument.
- `istream` member function `ignore` discards the specified number of characters in the input stream (one character by default).
- Overloaded input and output operators are declared as `friend`s if they need to access non-`public` class members directly for performance reasons.

Section 11.6 Overloading Unary Operators
- A unary operator for a class can be overloaded as a non-`static` member function with no arguments or as a global function with one argument; that argument must be either an object of the class or a reference to an object of the class.
- Member functions that implement overloaded operators must be non-`static` so that they can access the non-`static` data in each object of the class.

Section 11.7 Overloading Binary Operators

- A binary operator can be overloaded as a non-static member function with one argument or as a global function with two arguments (one of those arguments must be either a class object or a reference to a class object).

Section 11.8 Case Study: Array Class

- A copy constructor initializes a new object of a class by copying the members of an existing object of that class. When objects of a class contain dynamically allocated memory, the class should provide a copy constructor to ensure that each copy of an object has its own separate copy of the dynamically allocated memory. Typically, such a class would also provide a destructor and an overloaded assignment operator.

- The implementation of member function operator= should test for self-assignment, in which an object is being assigned to itself.

- The compiler calls the const version of operator[] when the subscript operator is used on a const object and calls the non-const version of the operator when it is used on a non-const object.

- The array subscript operator ([]) is not restricted for use with arrays. It can be used to select elements from other types of container classes. Also, with overloading, the index values no longer need to be integers—characters or strings could be used, for example.

Section 11.9 Converting between Types

- The compiler cannot know in advance how to convert among user-defined types, and between user-defined types and fundamental types, so you must specify how to do this. Such conversions can be performed with conversion constructors—single-argument constructors that turn objects of other types (including fundamental types) into objects of a particular class.

- A conversion operator (also called a cast operator) can be used to convert an object of one class into an object of another class or into an object of a fundamental type. Such a conversion operator must be a non-static member function. Overloaded cast-operator functions can be defined for converting objects of user-defined types into fundamental types or into objects of other user-defined types.

- An overloaded cast operator function does not specify a return type—the return type is the type to which the object is being converted.

- One of the nice features of cast operators and conversion constructors is that, when necessary, the compiler can call these functions implicitly to create temporary objects.

Section 11.10 Case Study: String Class

- Any single-argument constructor can be thought of as a conversion constructor.

- Overloading the function call operator () is powerful, because functions can take arbitrarily long and complex parameter lists.

Section 11.11 Overloading ++ and --

- The prefix and postfix increment and decrement operator can all be overloaded.

- To overload the increment operator to allow both preincrement and postincrement usage, each overloaded operator function must have a distinct signature, so that the compiler will be able to determine which version of ++ is intended. The prefix versions are overloaded exactly as any other prefix unary operator would be. Providing a unique signature to the postfix increment operator is accomplished by providing a second argument, which must be of type int. This argument is not supplied in the client code. It is used implicitly by the compiler to distinguish between the prefix and postfix versions of the increment operator.

Section 11.13 Standard Library Class `string`

- Standard class `string` is defined in header `<string>` and belongs to namespace `std`.

- Class `string` provides many overloaded operators, including equality, relational, assignment, addition assignment (for concatenation) and subscript operators.

- Class `string` provides member function `empty`, which returns `true` if the `string` is empty; otherwise, it returns `false`.

- Standard class `string` member function `substr` obtains a substring of a length specified by the second argument, starting at the position specified by the first argument. When the second argument is not specified, `substr` returns the remainder of the `string` on which it is called.

- Class `string`'s overloaded `[]` operator does not perform any bounds checking. Therefore, you must ensure that operations using standard class `string`'s overloaded `[]` operator do not accidentally manipulate elements outside the bounds of the `string`.

- Standard class `string` provides bounds checking with member function `at`, which "throws an exception" if its argument is an invalid subscript. By default, this causes the program to terminate. If the subscript is valid, function `at` returns the character at the specified location as an *lvalue* or an *rvalue*, depending on the context in which the call appears.

Section 11.14 `explicit` Constructors

- C++ provides the keyword `explicit` to suppress implicit conversions via conversion constructors when such conversions should not be allowed. A constructor that is declared `explicit` cannot be used in an implicit conversion.

Terminology

"arity" of an operator
Array class
assignment-operator functions
associativity not changed by overloading
cast operator function
commutative operation
const version of `operator[]`
conversion between fundamental and class types
conversion constructor
conversion operator
copy constructor
empty member function of `string`
explicit constructor
function call operator ()
global function to overload an operator
`ignore` member function of `istream`
implicit user-defined conversions
lvalue ("left value")
operator function
operator keyword
operator overloading
`operator!`
`operator!=`
`operator()`
`operator+`

`operator++`
`operator++( int )`
`operator<`
`operator<<`
`operator=`
`operator==`
`operator>=`
`operator>>`
`operator[]`
overloadable operators
overloaded ! operator
overloaded != operator
overloaded () operator
overloaded + operator
overloaded ++ operator
overloaded ++(int) operator
overloaded += operator
overloaded < operator
overloaded << operator
overloaded <= operator
overloaded == operator
overloaded > operator
overloaded >= operator
overloaded >> operator
overloaded assignment (=) operator

overloaded [] operator
overloaded stream insertion operator
overloaded stream extraction operators
overloading a binary operator
overloading a unary operator
self-assignment

string (standard C++ class)
string concatenation
substr member function of string
substring
user-defined conversion
user-defined type

Self-Review Exercises

11.1 Fill in the blanks in each of the following:
   a) Suppose a and b are integer variables and we form the sum a + b. Now suppose c and d are floating-point variables and we form the sum c + d. The two + operators here are clearly being used for different purposes. This is an example of _____.
   b) Keyword _____ introduces an overloaded-operator function definition.
   c) To use operators on class objects, they must be overloaded, with the exception of operators _____, _____ and _____.
   d) The _____, _____ and _____ of an operator cannot be changed by overloading the operator.

11.2 Explain the multiple meanings of the operators << and >>.

11.3 In what context might the name operator/ be used?

11.4 (True/False) Only existing operators can be overloaded.

11.5 How does the precedence of an overloaded operator compare with the precedence of the original operator?

Answers to Self-Review Exercises

11.1 a) operator overloading. b) operator. c) assignment (=), address (&), comma (,). d) precedence, associativity, "arity."

11.2 Operator >> is both the right-shift operator and the stream extraction operator, depending on its context. Operator << is both the left-shift operator and the stream insertion operator, depending on its context.

11.3 For operator overloading: It would be the name of a function that would provide an overloaded version of the / operator for a specific class.

11.4 True.

11.5 The precedence is identical.

Exercises

11.6 Give as many examples as you can of operator overloading implicit in C++. Give a reasonable example of a situation in which you might want to overload an operator explicitly in C++.

11.7 The operators that cannot be overloaded are _____, _____, _____ and _____.

11.8 String concatenation requires two operands—the two strings that are to be concatenated. In the text, we showed how to implement an overloaded concatenation operator that concatenates the second String object to the right of the first String object, thus modifying the first String object. In some applications, it is desirable to produce a concatenated String object without modifying the String arguments. Implement operator+ to allow operations such as

```
string1 = string2 + string3;
```

11.9 *(Ultimate Operator Overloading Exercise)* To appreciate the care that should go into selecting operators for overloading, list each of the overloadable operators, and for each, list a possible meaning (or several, if appropriate) for each of several classes you have studied in this text. We suggest you try:

a) Array
b) Stack
c) String

After doing this, comment on which operators seem to have meaning for a wide variety of classes. Which operators seem to be of little value for overloading? Which operators seem ambiguous?

11.10 Now work the process described in Exercise 11.9 in reverse. List each of C++'s overloadable operators. For each, list what you feel is perhaps the "ultimate operation" the operator should be used to represent. If there are several excellent operations, list them all.

11.11 One nice example of overloading the function call operator () is to allow another form of double-array subscripting popular in some programming languages. Instead of saying

```
chessBoard[ row ][ column ]
```

for an array of objects, overload the function call operator to allow the alternate form

```
chessBoard( row, column )
```

Create a class DoubleSubscriptedArray that has similar features to class Array in Figs. 11.6–11.7. At construction time, the class should be able to create an array of any number of rows and any number of columns. The class should supply operator() to perform double-subscripting operations. For example, in a 3-by-5 DoubleSubscriptedArray called a, the user could write a(1, 3) to access the element at row 1 and column 3. Remember that operator() can receive any number of arguments (see class String in Figs. 11.9–11.10 for an example of operator()). The underlying representation of the double-subscripted array should be a single-subscripted array of integers with *rows* * *columns* number of elements. Function operator() should perform the proper pointer arithmetic to access each element of the array. There should be two versions of operator()—one that returns int & (so that an element of a DoubleSubscriptedArray can be used as an *lvalue*) and one that returns const int & (so that an element of a const DoubleSubscriptedArray can be used only as an *rvalue*). The class should also provide the following operators: ==, !=, =, << (for outputting the array in row and column format) and >> (for inputting the entire array contents).

11.12 Overload the subscript operator to return the largest element of a collection, the second largest, the third largest, and so on.

11.13 Consider class Complex shown in Figs. 11.19–11.21. The class enables operations on so-called *complex numbers*. These are numbers of the form realPart + imaginaryPart * *i*, where *i* has the value

$$\sqrt{-1}$$

a) Modify the class to enable input and output of complex numbers through the overloaded >> and << operators, respectively (you should remove the print function from the class).
b) Overload the multiplication operator to enable multiplication of two complex numbers as in algebra.
c) Overload the == and != operators to allow comparisons of complex numbers.

```
1   // Fig. 11.19: Complex.h
2   // Complex class definition.
3   #ifndef COMPLEX_H
4   #define COMPLEX_H
5
6   class Complex
7   {
8   public:
9      Complex( double = 0.0, double = 0.0 ); // constructor
10     Complex operator+( const Complex & ) const; // addition
11     Complex operator-( const Complex & ) const; // subtraction
12     void print() const; // output
13  private:
14     double real; // real part
15     double imaginary; // imaginary part
16  }; // end class Complex
17
18  #endif
```

Fig. 11.19 | Complex class definition.

```
1   // Fig. 11.20: Complex.cpp
2   // Complex class member-function definitions.
3   #include <iostream>
4   using std::cout;
5
6   #include "Complex.h" // Complex class definition
7
8   // Constructor
9   Complex::Complex( double realPart, double imaginaryPart )
10     : real( realPart ),
11       imaginary( imaginaryPart )
12  {
13     // empty body
14  } // end Complex constructor
15
16  // addition operator
17  Complex Complex::operator+( const Complex &operand2 ) const
18  {
19     return Complex( real + operand2.real,
20        imaginary + operand2.imaginary );
21  } // end function operator+
22
23  // subtraction operator
24  Complex Complex::operator-( const Complex &operand2 ) const
25  {
26     return Complex( real - operand2.real,
27        imaginary - operand2.imaginary );
28  } // end function operator-
29
30  // display a Complex object in the form: (a, b)
31  void Complex::print() const
32  {
33     cout << '(' << real << ", " << imaginary << ')';
34  } // end function print
```

Fig. 11.20 | Complex class member-function definitions.

```
1    // Fig. 11.21: fig11_21.cpp
2    // Complex class test program.
3    #include <iostream>
4    using std::cout;
5    using std::endl;
6
7    #include "Complex.h"
8
9    int main()
10   {
11      Complex x;
12      Complex y( 4.3, 8.2 );
13      Complex z( 3.3, 1.1 );
14
15      cout << "x: ";
16      x.print();
17      cout << "\ny: ";
18      y.print();
19      cout << "\nz: ";
20      z.print();
21
22      x = y + z;
23      cout << "\n\nx = y + z:" << endl;
24      x.print();
25      cout << " = ";
26      y.print();
27      cout << " + ";
28      z.print();
29
30      x = y - z;
31      cout << "\n\nx = y - z:" << endl;
32      x.print();
33      cout << " = ";
34      y.print();
35      cout << " - ";
36      z.print();
37      cout << endl;
38      return 0;
39   } // end main
```

```
x: (0, 0)
y: (4.3, 8.2)
z: (3.3, 1.1)

x = y + z:
(7.6, 9.3) = (4.3, 8.2) + (3.3, 1.1)

x = y - z:
(1, 7.1) = (4.3, 8.2) - (3.3, 1.1)
```

Fig. 11.21 | Complex numbers.

11.14 A machine with 32-bit integers can represent integers in the range of approximately –2 billion to +2 billion. This fixed-size restriction is rarely troublesome, but there are applications in which we would like to be able to use a much wider range of integers. This is what C++ was built to do, namely, create powerful new data types. Consider class HugeInt of Figs. 11.22–11.24. Study the class carefully, then answer the following:

    a) Describe precisely how it operates.

    b) What restrictions does the class have?

c) Overload the * multiplication operator.
d) Overload the / division operator.
e) Overload all the relational and equality operators.

[*Note:* We do not show an assignment operator or copy constructor for class `HugeInteger`, because the assignment operator and copy constructor provided by the compiler are capable of copying the entire array data member properly.]

```
1   // Fig. 11.22: Hugeint.h
2   // HugeInt class definition.
3   #ifndef HUGEINT_H
4   #define HUGEINT_H
5
6   #include <iostream>
7   using std::ostream;
8
9   class HugeInt
10  {
11     friend ostream &operator<<( ostream &, const HugeInt & );
12  public:
13     HugeInt( long = 0 ); // conversion/default constructor
14     HugeInt( const char * ); // conversion constructor
15
16     // addition operator; HugeInt + HugeInt
17     HugeInt operator+( const HugeInt & ) const;
18
19     // addition operator; HugeInt + int
20     HugeInt operator+( int ) const;
21
22     // addition operator;
23     // HugeInt + string that represents large integer value
24     HugeInt operator+( const char * ) const;
25  private:
26     short integer[ 30 ];
27  }; // end class HugetInt
28
29  #endif
```

Fig. 11.22 | HugeInt class definition.

```
1   // Fig. 11.23: Hugeint.cpp
2   // HugeInt member-function and friend-function definitions.
3   #include <cctype> // isdigit function prototype
4   #include <cstring> // strlen function prototype
5   #include "Hugeint.h" // HugeInt class definition
6
7   // default constructor; conversion constructor that converts
8   // a long integer into a HugeInt object
9   HugeInt::HugeInt( long value )
10  {
11     // initialize array to zero
12     for ( int i = 0; i <= 29; i++ )
13        integer[ i ] = 0;
14
15     // place digits of argument into array
16     for ( int j = 29; value != 0 && j >= 0; j-- )
17     {
```

Fig. 11.23 | HugeInt class member-function and `friend`-function definitions. (Part 1 of 3.)

```
18              integer[ j ] = value % 10;
19              value /= 10;
20         } // end for
21    } // end HugeInt default/conversion constructor
22
23    // conversion constructor that converts a character string
24    // representing a large integer into a HugeInt object
25    HugeInt::HugeInt( const char *string )
26    {
27       // initialize array to zero
28       for ( int i = 0; i <= 29; i++ )
29          integer[ i ] = 0;
30
31       // place digits of argument into array
32       int length = strlen( string );
33
34       for ( int j = 30 - length, k = 0; j <= 29; j++, k++ )
35
36          if ( isdigit( string[ k ] ) )
37             integer[ j ] = string[ k ] - '0';
38    } // end HugeInt conversion constructor
39
40    // addition operator; HugeInt + HugeInt
41    HugeInt HugeInt::operator+( const HugeInt &op2 ) const
42    {
43       HugeInt temp; // temporary result
44       int carry = 0;
45
46       for ( int i = 29; i >= 0; i-- )
47       {
48          temp.integer[ i ] =
49             integer[ i ] + op2.integer[ i ] + carry;
50
51          // determine whether to carry a 1
52          if ( temp.integer[ i ] > 9 )
53          {
54             temp.integer[ i ] %= 10;  // reduce to 0-9
55             carry = 1;
56          } // end if
57          else // no carry
58             carry = 0;
59       } // end for
60
61       return temp; // return copy of temporary object
62    } // end function operator+
63
64    // addition operator; HugeInt + int
65    HugeInt HugeInt::operator+( int op2 ) const
66    {
67       // convert op2 to a HugeInt, then invoke
68       // operator+ for two HugeInt objects
69       return *this + HugeInt( op2 );
70    } // end function operator+
71
72    // addition operator;
73    // HugeInt + string that represents large integer value
74    HugeInt HugeInt::operator+( const char *op2 ) const
75    {
```

Fig. 11.23 | HugeInt class member-function and friend-function definitions. (Part 2 of 3.)

```
76      // convert op2 to a HugeInt, then invoke
77      // operator+ for two HugeInt objects
78      return *this + HugeInt( op2 );
79   } // end operator+
80
81   // overloaded output operator
82   ostream& operator<<( ostream &output, const HugeInt &num )
83   {
84      int i;
85
86      for ( i = 0; ( num.integer[ i ] == 0 ) && ( i <= 29 ); i++ )
87         ; // skip leading zeros
88
89      if ( i == 30 )
90         output << 0;
91      else
92
93         for ( ; i <= 29; i++ )
94            output << num.integer[ i ];
95
96      return output;
97   } // end function operator<<
```

Fig. 11.23 | `HugeInt` class member-function and `friend`-function definitions. (Part 3 of 3.)

```
1    // Fig. 11.24: fig11_24.cpp
2    // HugeInt test program.
3    #include <iostream>
4    using std::cout;
5    using std::endl;
6
7    #include "Hugeint.h"
8
9    int main()
10   {
11      HugeInt n1( 7654321 );
12      HugeInt n2( 7891234 );
13      HugeInt n3( "99999999999999999999999999999" );
14      HugeInt n4( "1" );
15      HugeInt n5;
16
17      cout << "n1 is " << n1 << "\nn2 is " << n2
18         << "\nn3 is " << n3 << "\nn4 is " << n4
19         << "\nn5 is " << n5 << "\n\n";
20
21      n5 = n1 + n2;
22      cout << n1 << " + " << n2 << " = " << n5 << "\n\n";
23
24      cout << n3 << " + " << n4 << "\n= " << ( n3 + n4 ) << "\n\n";
25
26      n5 = n1 + 9;
27      cout << n1 << " + " << 9 << " = " << n5 << "\n\n";
28
29      n5 = n2 + "10000";
30      cout << n2 << " + " << "10000" << " = " << n5 << endl;
31      return 0;
32   } // end main
```

Fig. 11.24 | Huge integers. (Part 1 of 2.)

```
n1 is 7654321
n2 is 7891234
n3 is 99999999999999999999999999999
n4 is 1
n5 is 0

7654321 + 7891234 = 15545555

99999999999999999999999999999 + 1
= 100000000000000000000000000000

7654321 + 9 = 7654330

7891234 + 10000 = 7901234
```

Fig. 11.24 | Huge integers. (Part 2 of 2.)

11.15 Create a class `RationalNumber` (fractions) with the following capabilities:
  a) Create a constructor that prevents a 0 denominator in a fraction, reduces or simplifies fractions that are not in reduced form and avoids negative denominators.
  b) Overload the addition, subtraction, multiplication and division operators for this class.
  c) Overload the relational and equality operators for this class.

11.16 Study the C string-handling library functions (www.cplusplus.com/reference/clibrary/cstring/) and implement each of the functions as part of class `String` (Figs. 11.9–11.10). Then, use these functions to perform text manipulations.

11.17 Develop class `Polynomial`. The internal representation of a `Polynomial` is an array of terms. Each term contains a coefficient and an exponent, e.g., the term

$$2x^4$$

has the coefficient 2 and the exponent 4. Develop a complete class containing proper constructor and destructor functions as well as *set* and *get* functions. The class should also provide the following overloaded operator capabilities:
  a) Overload the addition operator (+) to add two `Polynomial`s.
  b) Overload the subtraction operator (-) to subtract two `Polynomial`s.
  c) Overload the assignment operator to assign one `Polynomial` to another.
  d) Overload the multiplication operator (*) to multiply two `Polynomial`s.
  e) Overload the addition assignment operator (+=), subtraction assignment operator (-=), and multiplication assignment operator (*=).

11.18 In the program of Figs. 11.3–11.5, Fig. 11.4 contains the comment "overloaded stream insertion operator; cannot be a member function if we would like to invoke it with cout << somePhoneNumber;." Actually, the stream insertion operator could be a `PhoneNumber` class member function if we were willing to invoke it either as somePhoneNumber.operator<<(cout); or as somePhoneNumber << cout;. Rewrite the program of Fig. 11.5 with the overloaded stream insertion operator<< as a member function and try the two preceding statements in the program to demonstrate that they work.

12

Object-Oriented Programming: Inheritance

OBJECTIVES

In this chapter you'll learn:

■ To create classes by inheriting from existing classes.

■ How inheritance promotes software reuse.

■ The notions of base classes and derived classes and the relationships between them.

■ The **protected** member access specifier.

■ The use of constructors and destructors in inheritance hierarchies.

■ The order in which constructors and destructors are called in inheritance hierarchies.

■ The differences between **public**, **protected** and **private** inheritance.

■ The use of inheritance to customize existing software.

12.1 Introduction

This chapter continues our discussion of object-oriented programming (OOP) by introducing another of its key features—inheritance. Inheritance is a form of software reuse in which you create a class that absorbs an existing class's data and behaviors and enhances them with new capabilities. Software reusability saves time during program development. It also encourages the reuse of proven, debugged, high-quality software, which increases the likelihood that a system will be implemented effectively.

When creating a class, instead of writing completely new data members and member functions, you can designate that the new class should inherit the members of an existing class. This existing class is called the base class, and the new class is referred to as the derived class. (Other programming languages, such as Java, refer to the base class as the superclass and the derived class as the subclass.) A derived class represents a more specialized group of objects. Typically, a derived class contains behaviors inherited from its base class plus additional behaviors. As we'll see, a derived class can also customize behaviors inherited from the base class. A direct base class is the base class from which a derived class explicitly inherits. An indirect base class is inherited from two or more levels up in the class hierarchy. In the case of single inheritance, a class is derived from one base class. C++ also supports multiple inheritance, in which a derived class inherits from multiple (possibly unrelated) base classes. Single inheritance is straightforward—we show several examples that should enable you to become proficient quickly. Multiple inheritance can be complex and error prone. We discuss multiple inheritance in Chapter 25, Other Topics.

C++ offers `public`, `protected` and `private` inheritance. In this chapter, we concentrate on `public` inheritance and briefly explain the other two. In Chapter 20, Data Structures, we show how `private` inheritance can be used as an alternative to composition. The third form, `protected` inheritance, is rarely used. With `public` inheritance, every object of a derived class is also an object of that derived class's base class. However, base-class objects are not objects of their derived classes. For example, if we have vehicle as a base class and car as a derived class, then all cars are vehicles, but not all vehicles are cars. As we continue our study of object-oriented programming in this chapter and Chapter 13, we take advantage of this relationship to perform some interesting manipulations.

Experience in building software systems indicates that significant amounts of code deal with closely related special cases. When you are preoccupied with special cases, the details can obscure the big picture. With object-oriented programming, you focus on the commonalities among objects in the system rather than on the special cases.

We distinguish between the *is-a* relationship and the *has-a* relationship. The *is-a* relationship represents inheritance. In an *is-a* relationship, an object of a derived class also can be treated as an object of its base class—for example, a car *is a* vehicle, so any attributes and behaviors of a vehicle are also attributes and behaviors of a car. By contrast, the *has-a* relationship represents composition. (Composition was discussed in Chapter 10.) In a *has-a* relationship, an object contains one or more objects of other classes as members. For example, a car includes many components—it *has a* steering wheel, *has a* brake pedal, *has a* transmission and *has* many other components.

Derived-class member functions might require access to base-class data members and member functions. A derived class can access the non-`private` members of its base class. Base-class members that should not be accessible to the member functions of derived classes should be declared `private` in the base class. A derived class *can* effect state changes in `private` base-class members, but only through non-`private` member functions provided in the base class and inherited into the derived class.

Software Engineering Observation 12.1

Member functions of a derived class cannot directly access `private` members of the base class.

Software Engineering Observation 12.2

If a derived class could access its base class's `private` members, classes that inherit from that derived class could access that data as well. This would propagate access to what should be `private` data, and the benefits of information hiding would be lost.

One problem with inheritance is that a derived class can inherit data members and member functions it does not need or should not have. It is the class designer's responsibility to ensure that the capabilities provided by a class are appropriate for future derived classes. Even when a base-class member function is appropriate for a derived class, the derived class often requires that the member function behave in a manner specific to the derived class. In such cases, the base-class member function can be redefined in the derived class with an appropriate implementation.

12.2 Base Classes and Derived Classes

Often, an object of one class *is an* object of another class, as well. For example, in geometry, a rectangle *is a* quadrilateral (as are squares, parallelograms and trapezoids). Thus, in C++, class `Rectangle` can be said to *inherit* from class `Quadrilateral`. In this context, class `Quadrilateral` is a base class, and class `Rectangle` is a derived class. A rectangle *is a* specific type of quadrilateral, but it is incorrect to claim that a quadrilateral *is a* rectangle—the quadrilateral could be a parallelogram or some other shape. Figure 12.1 lists several simple examples of base classes and derived classes.

Because every derived-class object *is an* object of its base class, and one base class can have many derived classes, the set of objects represented by a base class typically is larger than the set of objects represented by any of its derived classes. For example, the base class Vehicle represents all vehicles, including cars, trucks, boats, airplanes, bicycles and so on. By contrast, derived class Car represents a smaller, more specific subset of all vehicles.

Inheritance relationships form treelike hierarchical structures. A base class exists in a hierarchical relationship with its derived classes. Although classes can exist independently, once they are employed in inheritance relationships, they become affiliated with other classes. A class becomes either a base class—supplying members to other classes, a derived class—inheriting its members from other classes, or both.

Let us develop a simple inheritance hierarchy with five levels (represented by the UML class diagram in Fig. 12.2). A university community has thousands of members.

Base class	Derived classes
Student	GraduateStudent, UndergraduateStudent
Shape	Circle, Triangle, Rectangle, Sphere, Cube
Loan	CarLoan, HomeImprovementLoan, MortgageLoan
Employee	Faculty, Staff
Account	CheckingAccount, SavingsAccount

Fig. 12.1 | Inheritance examples.

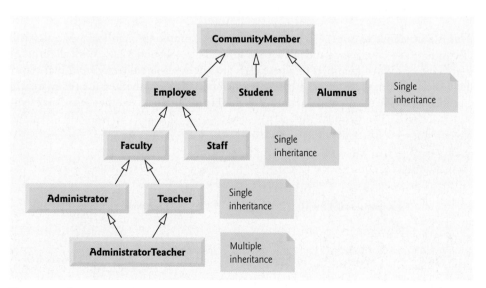

Fig. 12.2 | Inheritance hierarchy for university CommunityMembers.

These members consist of employees, students and alumni. Employees are either faculty members or staff members. Faculty members are either administrators (such as deans and department chairpersons) or teachers. Some administrators, however, also teach classes. Note that we have used multiple inheritance to form class AdministratorTeacher. Also note that this inheritance hierarchy could contain many other classes. For example, students can be graduate or undergraduate students. Undergraduate students can be freshmen, sophomores, juniors and seniors.

Each arrow in the hierarchy (Fig. 12.2) represents an *is-a* relationship. For example, as we follow the arrows in this class hierarchy, we can state "an Employee *is a* Community-Member" and "a Teacher *is a* Faculty member." CommunityMember is the direct base class of Employee, Student and Alumnus. In addition, CommunityMember is an indirect base class of all the other classes in the diagram. Starting from the bottom of the diagram, you can follow the arrows and apply the *is-a* relationship to the topmost base class. For example, an AdministratorTeacher *is an* Administrator, *is a* Faculty member, *is an* Employee and *is a* CommunityMember.

Now consider the Shape inheritance hierarchy in Fig. 12.3. This hierarchy begins with base class Shape. Classes TwoDimensionalShape and ThreeDimensionalShape derive from base class Shape—Shapes are either TwoDimensionalShapes or ThreeDimensional-Shapes. The third level of this hierarchy contains some more specific types of TwoDimensionalShapes and ThreeDimensionalShapes. As in Fig. 12.2, we can follow the arrows from the bottom of the diagram to the topmost base class in this class hierarchy to identify several *is-a* relationships. For instance, a Triangle *is a* TwoDimensionalShape and *is a* Shape, while a Sphere *is a* ThreeDimensionalShape and *is a* Shape. Note that this hierarchy could contain many other classes, such as Rectangles, Ellipses and Trapezoids, which are all TwoDimensionalShapes.

To specify that class TwoDimensionalShape (Fig. 12.3) is derived from (or inherits from) class Shape, class TwoDimensionalShape's definition could begin as follows:

```
class TwoDimensionalShape : public Shape
```

This is an example of **public inheritance**, the most commonly used form. We also will discuss **private** inheritance and **protected** inheritance (Section 12.6). With all forms of inheritance, private members of a base class are not accessible directly from that class's derived classes, but these private base-class members are still inherited (i.e., they are still considered parts of the derived classes). With public inheritance, all other base-class mem-

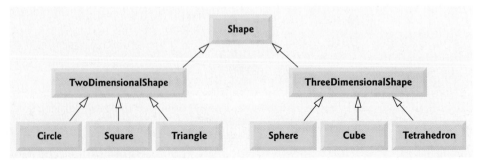

Fig. 12.3 | Inheritance hierarchy for Shapes.

bers retain their original member access when they become members of the derived class (e.g., public members of the base class become public members of the derived class, and, as we'll soon see, protected members of the base class become protected members of the derived class). Through these inherited base-class members, the derived class can manipulate private members of the base class (if these inherited members provide such functionality in the base class). Note that friend functions are not inherited.

Inheritance is not appropriate for every class relationship. In Chapter 10, we discussed the *has-a* relationship, in which classes have members that are objects of other classes. Such relationships create classes by composition of existing classes. For example, given the classes Employee, BirthDate and TelephoneNumber, it is improper to say that an Employee *is a* BirthDate or that an Employee *is a* TelephoneNumber. However, it is appropriate to say that an Employee *has a* BirthDate and that an Employee *has a* TelephoneNumber.

It is possible to treat base-class objects and derived-class objects similarly; their commonalities are expressed in the members of the base class. Objects of all classes derived from a common base class can be treated as objects of that base class (i.e., such objects have an *is-a* relationship with the base class). In Chapter 13, we consider many examples that take advantage of this relationship.

12.3 protected Members

Chapter 3 introduced access specifiers public and private. A base class's public members are accessible within the body of that base class and anywhere that the program has a handle (i.e., a name, reference or pointer) to an object of that base class or one of its derived classes. A base class's private members are accessible only within the body of that base class and the friends of that base class. In this section, we introduce an additional access specifier: protected.

Using protected access offers an intermediate level of protection between public and private access. A base class's protected members can be accessed within the body of that base class, by members and friends of that base class, and by members and friends of any classes derived from that base class.

Derived-class member functions can refer to public and protected members of the base class simply by using the member names. When a derived-class member function redefines a base-class member function, the base-class member can be accessed from the derived class by preceding the base-class member name with the base-class name and the binary scope resolution operator (::). We discuss accessing redefined members of the base class in Section 12.4 and using protected data in Section 12.4.4.

12.4 Relationship between Base Classes and Derived Classes

In this section, we use an inheritance hierarchy containing types of employees in a company's payroll application to discuss the relationship between a base class and a derived class. Commission employees (who will be represented as objects of a base class) are paid a percentage of their sales, while base-salaried commission employees (who will be represented as objects of a derived class) receive a base salary plus a percentage of their sales. We divide our discussion of the relationship between commission employees and base-salaried commission employees into a carefully paced series of five examples:

1. In the first example, we create class CommissionEmployee, which contains as private data members a first name, last name, social security number, commission rate (percentage) and gross (i.e., total) sales amount.

2. The second example defines class BasePlusCommissionEmployee, which contains as private data members a first name, last name, social security number, commission rate, gross sales amount and base salary. We create the latter class by writing every line of code the class requires—we'll soon see that it is much more efficient to create this class simply by inheriting from class CommissionEmployee.

3. The third example defines a new version of class BasePlusCommissionEmployee class that inherits directly from class CommissionEmployee (i.e., a BasePlusCommissionEmployee *is a* CommissionEmployee who also has a base salary) and attempts to access class CommissionEmployee's private members—this results in compilation errors, because the derived class does not have access to the base class's private data.

4. The fourth example shows that if CommissionEmployee's data is declared as protected, a new version of class BasePlusCommissionEmployee that inherits from class CommissionEmployee *can* access that data directly. For this purpose, we define a new version of class CommissionEmployee with protected data. Both the inherited and noninherited BasePlusCommissionEmployee classes contain identical functionality, but we show how the version of BasePlusCommissionEmployee that inherits from class CommissionEmployee is easier to create and manage.

5. After we discuss the convenience of using protected data, we create the fifth example, which sets the CommissionEmployee data members back to private to enforce good software engineering. This example demonstrates that derived class BasePlusCommissionEmployee can use base class CommissionEmployee's public member functions to manipulate CommissionEmployee's private data.

12.4.1 Creating and Using a CommissionEmployee Class

Let's examine CommissionEmployee's class definition (Figs. 12.4–12.5). The CommissionEmployee header file (Fig. 12.4) specifies class CommissionEmployee's public services, which include a constructor (lines 12–13) and member functions earnings (line 30) and print (line 31). Lines 15–28 declare public *get* and *set* functions that manipulate the class's data members (declared in lines 33–37) firstName, lastName, socialSecurityNumber, grossSales and commissionRate. The CommissionEmployee header file specifies that these data members are private, so objects of other classes cannot directly access this data. Declaring data members as private and providing non-private *get* and *set* functions to manipulate and validate the data members helps enforce good software engineering. Member functions setGrossSales (defined in lines 57–60 of Fig. 12.5) and setCommissionRate (defined in lines 69–72 of Fig. 12.5), for example, validate their arguments before assigning the values to data members grossSales and commissionRate, respectively.

The CommissionEmployee constructor definition purposely does not use member-initializer syntax in the first several examples of this section, so that we can demonstrate how private and protected specifiers affect member access in derived classes. As shown in Fig. 12.5, lines 13–15, we assign values to data members firstName, lastName and

```
 1   // Fig. 12.4: CommissionEmployee.h
 2   // CommissionEmployee class definition represents a commission employee.
 3   #ifndef COMMISSION_H
 4   #define COMMISSION_H
 5
 6   #include <string> // C++ standard string class
 7   using std::string;
 8
 9   class CommissionEmployee
10   {
11   public:
12      CommissionEmployee( const string &, const string &, const string &,
13         double = 0.0, double = 0.0 );
14
15      void setFirstName( const string & ); // set first name
16      string getFirstName() const; // return first name
17
18      void setLastName( const string & ); // set last name
19      string getLastName() const; // return last name
20
21      void setSocialSecurityNumber( const string & ); // set SSN
22      string getSocialSecurityNumber() const; // return SSN
23
24      void setGrossSales( double ); // set gross sales amount
25      double getGrossSales() const; // return gross sales amount
26
27      void setCommissionRate( double ); // set commission rate (percentage)
28      double getCommissionRate() const; // return commission rate
29
30      double earnings() const; // calculate earnings
31      void print() const; // print CommissionEmployee object
32   private:
33      string firstName;
34      string lastName;
35      string socialSecurityNumber;
36      double grossSales; // gross weekly sales
37      double commissionRate; // commission percentage
38   }; // end class CommissionEmployee
39
40   #endif
```

Fig. 12.4 | `CommissionEmployee` class header file.

```
 1   // Fig. 12.5: CommissionEmployee.cpp
 2   // Class CommissionEmployee member-function definitions.
 3   #include <iostream>
 4   using std::cout;
 5
 6   #include "CommissionEmployee.h" // CommissionEmployee class definition
 7
```

Fig. 12.5 | Implementation file for `CommissionEmployee` class that represents an employee who is paid a percentage of gross sales. (Part 1 of 3.)

```
 8    // constructor
 9    CommissionEmployee::CommissionEmployee(
10       const string &first, const string &last, const string &ssn,
11       double sales, double rate )
12    {
13       firstName = first; // should validate
14       lastName = last;   // should validate
15       socialSecurityNumber = ssn; // should validate
16       setGrossSales( sales ); // validate and store gross sales
17       setCommissionRate( rate ); // validate and store commission rate
18    } // end CommissionEmployee constructor
19
20    // set first name
21    void CommissionEmployee::setFirstName( const string &first )
22    {
23       firstName = first; // should validate
24    } // end function setFirstName
25
26    // return first name
27    string CommissionEmployee::getFirstName() const
28    {
29       return firstName;
30    } // end function getFirstName
31
32    // set last name
33    void CommissionEmployee::setLastName( const string &last )
34    {
35       lastName = last; // should validate
36    } // end function setLastName
37
38    // return last name
39    string CommissionEmployee::getLastName() const
40    {
41       return lastName;
42    } // end function getLastName
43
44    // set social security number
45    void CommissionEmployee::setSocialSecurityNumber( const string &ssn )
46    {
47       socialSecurityNumber = ssn; // should validate
48    } // end function setSocialSecurityNumber
49
50    // return social security number
51    string CommissionEmployee::getSocialSecurityNumber() const
52    {
53       return socialSecurityNumber;
54    } // end function getSocialSecurityNumber
55
56    // set gross sales amount
57    void CommissionEmployee::setGrossSales( double sales )
58    {
```

Fig. 12.5 | Implementation file for CommissionEmployee class that represents an employee who is paid a percentage of gross sales. (Part 2 of 3.)

```
59         grossSales = ( sales < 0.0 ) ? 0.0 : sales;
60      } // end function setGrossSales
61
62      // return gross sales amount
63      double CommissionEmployee::getGrossSales() const
64      {
65         return grossSales;
66      } // end function getGrossSales
67
68      // set commission rate
69      void CommissionEmployee::setCommissionRate( double rate )
70      {
71         commissionRate = ( rate > 0.0 && rate < 1.0 ) ? rate : 0.0;
72      } // end function setCommissionRate
73
74      // return commission rate
75      double CommissionEmployee::getCommissionRate() const
76      {
77         return commissionRate;
78      } // end function getCommissionRate
79
80      // calculate earnings
81      double CommissionEmployee::earnings() const
82      {
83         return commissionRate * grossSales;
84      } // end function earnings
85
86      // print CommissionEmployee object
87      void CommissionEmployee::print() const
88      {
89         cout << "commission employee: " << firstName << ' ' << lastName
90            << "\nsocial security number: " << socialSecurityNumber
91            << "\ngross sales: " << grossSales
92            << "\ncommission rate: " << commissionRate;
93      } // end function print
```

Fig. 12.5 | Implementation file for CommissionEmployee class that represents an employee who is paid a percentage of gross sales. (Part 3 of 3.)

socialSecurityNumber in the constructor body. Later in this section, we'll return to using member-initializer lists in the constructors.

Note that we do not validate the values of the constructor's arguments first, last and ssn before assigning them to the corresponding data members. We certainly could validate the first and last names—perhaps by ensuring that they are of a reasonable length. Similarly, a social security number could be validated to ensure that it contains nine digits, with or without dashes (e.g., 123-45-6789 or 123456789).

Member function earnings (lines 81–84) calculates a CommissionEmployee's earnings. Line 83 multiplies the commissionRate by the grossSales and returns the result. Member function print (lines 87–93) displays the values of a CommissionEmployee object's data members.

Figure 12.6 tests class CommissionEmployee. Lines 16–17 instantiate object employee of class CommissionEmployee and invoke CommissionEmployee's constructor to initialize the object with "Sue" as the first name, "Jones" as the last name, "222-22-2222" as the social security number, 10000 as the gross sales amount and .06 as the commission rate. Lines 23–29 use employee's *get* functions to display the values of its data members. Lines 31–32 invoke the object's member functions setGrossSales and setCommissionRate to change the values of data members grossSales and commissionRate, respectively. Line 36 then calls employee's print member function to output the updated CommissionEmployee information. Finally, line 39 displays the CommissionEmployee's earnings, calculated by the object's earnings member function using the updated values of data members gross-Sales and commissionRate.

```cpp
1   // Fig. 12.6: fig12_06.cpp
2   // Testing class CommissionEmployee.
3   #include <iostream>
4   using std::cout;
5   using std::endl;
6   using std::fixed;
7
8   #include <iomanip>
9   using std::setprecision;
10
11  #include "CommissionEmployee.h" // CommissionEmployee class definition
12
13  int main()
14  {
15     // instantiate a CommissionEmployee object
16     CommissionEmployee employee(
17        "Sue", "Jones", "222-22-2222", 10000, .06 );
18
19     // set floating-point output formatting
20     cout << fixed << setprecision( 2 );
21
22     // get commission employee data
23     cout << "Employee information obtained by get functions: \n"
24        << "\nFirst name is " << employee.getFirstName()
25        << "\nLast name is " << employee.getLastName()
26        << "\nSocial security number is "
27        << employee.getSocialSecurityNumber()
28        << "\nGross sales is " << employee.getGrossSales()
29        << "\nCommission rate is " << employee.getCommissionRate() << endl;
30
31     employee.setGrossSales( 8000 ); // set gross sales
32     employee.setCommissionRate( .1 ); // set commission rate
33
34     cout << "\nUpdated employee information output by print function: \n"
35        << endl;
36     employee.print(); // display the new employee information
37
38     // display the employee's earnings
39     cout << "\n\nEmployee's earnings: $" << employee.earnings() << endl;
40
41     return 0;
42  } // end main
```

Fig. 12.6 | CommissionEmployee class test program. (Part 1 of 2.)

```
Employee information obtained by get functions:

First name is Sue
Last name is Jones
Social security number is 222-22-2222
Gross sales is 10000.00
Commission rate is 0.06

Updated employee information output by print function:

commission employee: Sue Jones
social security number: 222-22-2222
gross sales: 8000.00
commission rate: 0.10

Employee's earnings: $800.00
```

Fig. 12.6 | CommissionEmployee class test program. (Part 2 of 2.)

12.4.2 Creating a BasePlusCommissionEmployee Class Without Using Inheritance

We now discuss the second part of our introduction to inheritance by creating and testing (a completely new and independent) class BasePlusCommissionEmployee (Figs. 12.7–12.8), which contains a first name, last name, social security number, gross sales amount, commission rate *and* base salary.

Defining Class BasePlusCommissionEmployee
The BasePlusCommissionEmployee header file (Fig. 12.7) specifies class BasePlusCommissionEmployee's public services, which include the BasePlusCommissionEmployee constructor (lines 13–14) and member functions earnings (line 34) and print (line 35).

```cpp
1   // Fig. 12.7: BasePlusCommissionEmployee.h
2   // BasePlusCommissionEmployee class definition represents an employee
3   // that receives a base salary in addition to commission.
4   #ifndef BASEPLUS_H
5   #define BASEPLUS_H
6
7   #include <string> // C++ standard string class
8   using std::string;
9
10  class BasePlusCommissionEmployee
11  {
12  public:
13     BasePlusCommissionEmployee( const string &, const string &,
14        const string &, double = 0.0, double = 0.0, double = 0.0 );
15
16     void setFirstName( const string & ); // set first name
17     string getFirstName() const; // return first name
18
```

Fig. 12.7 | BasePlusCommissionEmployee class header file. (Part 1 of 2.)

```
19      void setLastName( const string & ); // set last name
20      string getLastName() const; // return last name
21
22      void setSocialSecurityNumber( const string & ); // set SSN
23      string getSocialSecurityNumber() const; // return SSN
24
25      void setGrossSales( double ); // set gross sales amount
26      double getGrossSales() const; // return gross sales amount
27
28      void setCommissionRate( double ); // set commission rate
29      double getCommissionRate() const; // return commission rate
30
31      void setBaseSalary( double ); // set base salary
32      double getBaseSalary() const; // return base salary
33
34      double earnings() const; // calculate earnings
35      void print() const; // print BasePlusCommissionEmployee object
36   private:
37      string firstName;
38      string lastName;
39      string socialSecurityNumber;
40      double grossSales; // gross weekly sales
41      double commissionRate; // commission percentage
42      double baseSalary; // base salary
43   }; // end class BasePlusCommissionEmployee
44
45   #endif
```

Fig. 12.7 | BasePlusCommissionEmployee class header file. (Part 2 of 2.)

Lines 16–32 declare public *get* and *set* functions for the class's private data members (declared in lines 37–42) firstName, lastName, socialSecurityNumber, grossSales, commissionRate and baseSalary. These variables and member functions encapsulate all the necessary features of a base-salaried commission employee. Note the similarity between this class and class CommissionEmployee (Figs. 12.4–12.5)—in this example, we will not yet exploit that similarity.

Class BasePlusCommissionEmployee's earnings member function (defined in lines 96–99 of Fig. 12.8) computes the earnings of a base-salaried commission employee. Line 98 returns the result of adding the employee's base salary to the product of the commission rate and the employee's gross sales.

*Testing Class **BasePlusCommissionEmployee***
Figure 12.9 tests class BasePlusCommissionEmployee. Lines 17–18 instantiate object employee of class BasePlusCommissionEmployee, passing "Bob", "Lewis", "333-33-3333", 5000, .04 and 300 to the constructor as the first name, last name, social security number, gross sales, commission rate and base salary, respectively. Lines 24–31 use BasePlus-CommissionEmployee's *get* functions to retrieve the values of the object's data members for output. Line 33 invokes the object's setBaseSalary member function to change the base salary. Member function setBaseSalary (Fig. 12.8, lines 84–87) ensures that data member baseSalary is not assigned a negative value, because an employee's base salary cannot be negative. Line 37 of Fig. 12.9 invokes the object's print member function to output

the updated BasePlusCommissionEmployee's information, and line 40 calls member function earnings to display the BasePlusCommissionEmployee's earnings.

```cpp
 1   // Fig. 12.8: BasePlusCommissionEmployee.cpp
 2   // Class BasePlusCommissionEmployee member-function definitions.
 3   #include <iostream>
 4   using std::cout;
 5
 6   // BasePlusCommissionEmployee class definition
 7   #include "BasePlusCommissionEmployee.h"
 8
 9   // constructor
10   BasePlusCommissionEmployee::BasePlusCommissionEmployee(
11      const string &first, const string &last, const string &ssn,
12      double sales, double rate, double salary )
13   {
14      firstName = first; // should validate
15      lastName = last; // should validate
16      socialSecurityNumber = ssn; // should validate
17      setGrossSales( sales ); // validate and store gross sales
18      setCommissionRate( rate ); // validate and store commission rate
19      setBaseSalary( salary ); // validate and store base salary
20   } // end BasePlusCommissionEmployee constructor
21
22   // set first name
23   void BasePlusCommissionEmployee::setFirstName( const string &first )
24   {
25      firstName = first; // should validate
26   } // end function setFirstName
27
28   // return first name
29   string BasePlusCommissionEmployee::getFirstName() const
30   {
31      return firstName;
32   } // end function getFirstName
33
34   // set last name
35   void BasePlusCommissionEmployee::setLastName( const string &last )
36   {
37      lastName = last; // should validate
38   } // end function setLastName
39
40   // return last name
41   string BasePlusCommissionEmployee::getLastName() const
42   {
43      return lastName;
44   } // end function getLastName
45
46   // set social security number
47   void BasePlusCommissionEmployee::setSocialSecurityNumber(
48      const string &ssn )
49   {
```

Fig. 12.8 | BasePlusCommissionEmployee class represents an employee who receives a base salary in addition to a commission. (Part 1 of 3.)

```
50        socialSecurityNumber = ssn; // should validate
51     } // end function setSocialSecurityNumber
52
53     // return social security number
54     string BasePlusCommissionEmployee::getSocialSecurityNumber() const
55     {
56        return socialSecurityNumber;
57     } // end function getSocialSecurityNumber
58
59     // set gross sales amount
60     void BasePlusCommissionEmployee::setGrossSales( double sales )
61     {
62        grossSales = ( sales < 0.0 ) ? 0.0 : sales;
63     } // end function setGrossSales
64
65     // return gross sales amount
66     double BasePlusCommissionEmployee::getGrossSales() const
67     {
68        return grossSales;
69     } // end function getGrossSales
70
71     // set commission rate
72     void BasePlusCommissionEmployee::setCommissionRate( double rate )
73     {
74        commissionRate = ( rate > 0.0 && rate < 1.0 ) ? rate : 0.0;
75     } // end function setCommissionRate
76
77     // return commission rate
78     double BasePlusCommissionEmployee::getCommissionRate() const
79     {
80        return commissionRate;
81     } // end function getCommissionRate
82
83     // set base salary
84     void BasePlusCommissionEmployee::setBaseSalary( double salary )
85     {
86        baseSalary = ( salary < 0.0 ) ? 0.0 : salary;
87     } // end function setBaseSalary
88
89     // return base salary
90     double BasePlusCommissionEmployee::getBaseSalary() const
91     {
92        return baseSalary;
93     } // end function getBaseSalary
94
95     // calculate earnings
96     double BasePlusCommissionEmployee::earnings() const
97     {
98        return baseSalary + ( commissionRate * grossSales );
99     } // end function earnings
100
```

Fig. 12.8 | BasePlusCommissionEmployee class represents an employee who receives a base salary in addition to a commission. (Part 2 of 3.)

```
101   // print BasePlusCommissionEmployee object
102   void BasePlusCommissionEmployee::print() const
103   {
104      cout << "base-salaried commission employee: " << firstName << ' '
105         << lastName << "\nsocial security number: " << socialSecurityNumber
106         << "\ngross sales: " << grossSales
107         << "\ncommission rate: " << commissionRate
108         << "\nbase salary: " << baseSalary;
109   } // end function print
```

Fig. 12.8 | BasePlusCommissionEmployee class represents an employee who receives a base salary in addition to a commission. (Part 3 of 3.)

```
 1   // Fig. 12.9: fig12_09.cpp
 2   // Testing class BasePlusCommissionEmployee.
 3   #include <iostream>
 4   using std::cout;
 5   using std::endl;
 6   using std::fixed;
 7
 8   #include <iomanip>
 9   using std::setprecision;
10
11   // BasePlusCommissionEmployee class definition
12   #include "BasePlusCommissionEmployee.h"
13
14   int main()
15   {
16      // instantiate BasePlusCommissionEmployee object
17      BasePlusCommissionEmployee
18         employee( "Bob", "Lewis", "333-33-3333", 5000, .04, 300 );
19
20      // set floating-point output formatting
21      cout << fixed << setprecision( 2 );
22
23      // get commission employee data
24      cout << "Employee information obtained by get functions: \n"
25         << "\nFirst name is " << employee.getFirstName()
26         << "\nLast name is " << employee.getLastName()
27         << "\nSocial security number is "
28         << employee.getSocialSecurityNumber()
29         << "\nGross sales is " << employee.getGrossSales()
30         << "\nCommission rate is " << employee.getCommissionRate()
31         << "\nBase salary is " << employee.getBaseSalary() << endl;
32
33      employee.setBaseSalary( 1000 ); // set base salary
34
35      cout << "\nUpdated employee information output by print function: \n"
36         << endl;
37      employee.print(); // display the new employee information
38
```

Fig. 12.9 | BasePlusCommissionEmployee class test program. (Part 1 of 2.)

```
39      // display the employee's earnings
40      cout << "\n\nEmployee's earnings: $" << employee.earnings() << endl;
41
42      return 0;
43   } // end main
```

```
Employee information obtained by get functions:

First name is Bob
Last name is Lewis
Social security number is 333-33-3333
Gross sales is 5000.00
Commission rate is 0.04
Base salary is 300.00

Updated employee information output by print function:

base-salaried commission employee: Bob Lewis
social security number: 333-33-3333
gross sales: 5000.00
commission rate: 0.04
base salary: 1000.00

Employee's earnings: $1200.00
```

Fig. 12.9 | BasePlusCommissionEmployee class test program. (Part 2 of 2.)

Exploring the Similarities Between Class *BasePlusCommissionEmployee* and Class *CommissionEmployee*

Note that most of the code for class BasePlusCommissionEmployee (Figs. 12.7–12.8) is similar, if not identical, to the code for class CommissionEmployee (Figs. 12.4–12.5). For example, in class BasePlusCommissionEmployee, private data members firstName and lastName and member functions setFirstName, getFirstName, setLastName and get-LastName are identical to those of class CommissionEmployee. Classes CommissionEmployee and BasePlusCommissionEmployee also both contain private data members socialSecurityNumber, commissionRate and grossSales, as well as *get* and *set* functions to manipulate these members. In addition, the BasePlusCommissionEmployee constructor is almost identical to that of class CommissionEmployee, except that BasePlusCommissionEmployee's constructor also sets the baseSalary. The other additions to class BasePlusCommissionEmployee are private data member baseSalary and member functions setBaseSalary and getBaseSalary. Class BasePlusCommissionEmployee's print member function is nearly identical to that of class CommissionEmployee, except that BasePlusCommissionEmployee's print also outputs the value of data member baseSalary.

We literally copied code from class CommissionEmployee and pasted it into class BasePlusCommissionEmployee, then modified class BasePlusCommissionEmployee to include a base salary and member functions that manipulate the base salary. This "copy-and-paste" approach is error prone and time consuming. Worse yet, it can spread many physical copies of the same code throughout a system, creating a code-maintenance nightmare. Is there a way to "absorb" the data members and member functions of a class in a way that makes them part of another class without duplicating code? In the next several examples, we do exactly this, using inheritance.

Software Engineering Observation 12.3

Copying and pasting code from one class to another can spread errors across multiple source code files. To avoid duplicating code (and possibly errors), use inheritance, rather than the "copy-and-paste" approach, in situations where you want one class to "absorb" the data members and member functions of another class.

Software Engineering Observation 12.4

With inheritance, the common data members and member functions of all the classes in the hierarchy are declared in a base class. When changes are required for these common features, you need to make the changes only in the base class—derived classes then inherit the changes. Without inheritance, changes would need to be made to all the source code files that contain a copy of the code in question.

12.4.3 Creating a CommissionEmployee-BasePlusCommissionEmployee Inheritance Hierarchy

Now we create and test a new BasePlusCommissionEmployee class (Figs. 12.10–12.11) that derives from class CommissionEmployee (Figs. 12.4–12.5). In this example, a BasePlusCommissionEmployee object *is a* CommissionEmployee (because inheritance passes on the capabilities of class CommissionEmployee), but class BasePlusCommission-

```
1   // Fig. 12.10: BasePlusCommissionEmployee.h
2   // BasePlusCommissionEmployee class derived from class
3   // CommissionEmployee.
4   #ifndef BASEPLUS_H
5   #define BASEPLUS_H
6
7   #include <string> // C++ standard string class
8   using std::string;
9
10  #include "CommissionEmployee.h" // CommissionEmployee class declaration
11
12  class BasePlusCommissionEmployee : public CommissionEmployee
13  {
14  public:
15     BasePlusCommissionEmployee( const string &, const string &,
16        const string &, double = 0.0, double = 0.0, double = 0.0 );
17
18     void setBaseSalary( double ); // set base salary
19     double getBaseSalary() const; // return base salary
20
21     double earnings() const; // calculate earnings
22     void print() const; // print BasePlusCommissionEmployee object
23  private:
24     double baseSalary; // base salary
25  }; // end class BasePlusCommissionEmployee
26
27  #endif
```

Fig. 12.10 | BasePlusCommissionEmployee class definition indicating inheritance relationship with class CommissionEmployee.

Employee also has data member baseSalary (Fig. 12.10, line 24). The colon (:) in line 12 of the class definition indicates inheritance. Keyword public indicates the type of inheritance. As a derived class (formed with public inheritance), BasePlusCommissionEmployee inherits all the members of class CommissionEmployee, except for the constructor—each class provides its own constructors that are specific to the class. [Note that destructors, too, are not inherited.] Thus, the public services of BasePlusCommissionEmployee include its constructor (lines 15–16) and the public member functions inherited from class CommissionEmployee—although we cannot see these inherited member functions in BasePlusCommissionEmployee's source code, they are nevertheless a part of derived class BasePlusCommissionEmployee. The derived class's public services also include member functions setBaseSalary, getBaseSalary, earnings and print (lines 18–22).

Figure 12.11 shows BasePlusCommissionEmployee's member-function implementations. The constructor (lines 10–17) introduces base-class initializer syntax (line 14), which uses a member initializer to pass arguments to the base-class (CommissionEmployee) constructor. C++ requires that a derived-class constructor call its base-class constructor to initialize the base-class data members that are inherited into the derived class. Line 14 accomplishes this task by invoking the CommissionEmployee constructor by name, passing the constructor's parameters first, last, ssn, sales and rate as arguments to initialize base-class data members firstName, lastName, socialSecurityNumber, grossSales and commissionRate. If BasePlusCommissionEmployee's constructor did not invoke class CommissionEmployee's constructor explicitly, C++ would attempt to invoke class CommissionEmployee's default constructor—but the class does not have such a constructor, so the compiler would issue an error. Recall from Chapter 3 that the compiler provides a default constructor with no parameters in any class that does not explicitly include a constructor. However, CommissionEmployee *does* explicitly include a constructor, so a default constructor is not provided, and any attempts to implicitly call CommissionEmployee's default constructor would result in compilation errors.

```cpp
1  // Fig. 12.11: BasePlusCommissionEmployee.cpp
2  // Class BasePlusCommissionEmployee member-function definitions.
3  #include <iostream>
4  using std::cout;
5
6  // BasePlusCommissionEmployee class definition
7  #include "BasePlusCommissionEmployee.h"
8
9  // constructor
10 BasePlusCommissionEmployee::BasePlusCommissionEmployee(
11    const string &first, const string &last, const string &ssn,
12    double sales, double rate, double salary )
13    // explicitly call base-class constructor
14    : CommissionEmployee( first, last, ssn, sales, rate )
15 {
16    setBaseSalary( salary ); // validate and store base salary
17 } // end BasePlusCommissionEmployee constructor
18
```

Fig. 12.11 | BasePlusCommissionEmployee implementation file: private base-class data cannot be accessed from derived class. (Part 1 of 3.)

```
19   // set base salary
20   void BasePlusCommissionEmployee::setBaseSalary( double salary )
21   {
22      baseSalary = ( salary < 0.0 ) ? 0.0 : salary;
23   } // end function setBaseSalary
24
25   // return base salary
26   double BasePlusCommissionEmployee::getBaseSalary() const
27   {
28      return baseSalary;
29   } // end function getBaseSalary
30
31   // calculate earnings
32   double BasePlusCommissionEmployee::earnings() const
33   {
34      // derived class cannot access the base class's private data
35      return baseSalary + ( commissionRate * grossSales );
36   } // end function earnings
37
38   // print BasePlusCommissionEmployee object
39   void BasePlusCommissionEmployee::print() const
40   {
41      // derived class cannot access the base class's private data
42      cout << "base-salaried commission employee: " << firstName << ' '
43         << lastName << "\nsocial security number: " << socialSecurityNumber
44         << "\ngross sales: " << grossSales
45         << "\ncommission rate: " << commissionRate
46         << "\nbase salary: " << baseSalary;
47   } // end function print
```

```
C:\cpphtp6_examples\ch12\Fig12_10_11\BasePlusCommissionEmployee.cpp(35) :
    error C2248: 'CommissionEmployee::commissionRate' :
    cannot access private member declared in class 'CommissionEmployee'
        C:\cpphtp6_examples\ch12\Fig12_10_11\CommissionEmployee.h(37) :
        see declaration of 'CommissionEmployee::commissionRate'
        C:\cpphtp5e_examples\ch12\Fig12_10_11\CommissionEmployee.h(10) :
        see declaration of 'CommissionEmployee'

C:\cpphtp6_examples\ch12\Fig12_10_11\BasePlusCommissionEmployee.cpp(35) :
    error C2248: 'CommissionEmployee::grossSales' :
    cannot access private member declared in class 'CommissionEmployee'
        C:\cpphtp6_examples\ch12\Fig12_10_11\CommissionEmployee.h(36) :
        see declaration of 'CommissionEmployee::grossSales'
        C:\cpphtp6_examples\ch12\Fig12_10_11\CommissionEmployee.h(10) :
        see declaration of 'CommissionEmployee'

C:\cpphtp6_examples\ch12\Fig12_10_11\BasePlusCommissionEmployee.cpp(42) :
    error C2248: 'CommissionEmployee::firstName' :
    cannot access private member declared in class 'CommissionEmployee'
        C:\cpphtp6_examples\ch12\Fig12_10_11\CommissionEmployee.h(33) :
        see declaration of 'CommissionEmployee::firstName'
        C:\cpphtp6_examples\ch12\Fig12_10_11\CommissionEmployee.h(10) :
        see declaration of 'CommissionEmployee'
```

Fig. 12.11 | BasePlusCommissionEmployee implementation file: private base-class data cannot be accessed from derived class. (Part 2 of 3.)

```
C:\cpphtp6_examples\ch12\Fig12_10_11\BasePlusCommissionEmployee.cpp(43) :
   error C2248: 'CommissionEmployee::lastName' :
   cannot access private member declared in class 'CommissionEmployee'
      C:\cpphtp6_examples\ch12\Fig12_10_11\CommissionEmployee.h(34) :
         see declaration of 'CommissionEmployee::lastName'
      C:\cpphtp6_examples\ch12\Fig12_10_11\CommissionEmployee.h(10) :
         see declaration of 'CommissionEmployee'

C:\cpphtp6_examples\ch12\Fig12_10_11\BasePlusCommissionEmployee.cpp(43) :
   error C2248: 'CommissionEmployee::socialSecurityNumber' :
   cannot access private member declared in class 'CommissionEmployee'
      C:\cpphtp6_examples\ch12\Fig12_10_11\CommissionEmployee.h(35) :
         see declaration of 'CommissionEmployee::socialSecurityNumber'
      C:\cpphtp6_examples\ch12\Fig12_10_11\CommissionEmployee.h(10) :
         see declaration of 'CommissionEmployee'

C:\cpphtp6_examples\ch12\Fig12_10_11\BasePlusCommissionEmployee.cpp(44) :
   error C2248: 'CommissionEmployee::grossSales' :
   cannot access private member declared in class 'CommissionEmployee'
      C:\cpphtp6_examples\ch12\Fig12_10_11\CommissionEmployee.h(36) :
         see declaration of 'CommissionEmployee::grossSales'
      C:\cpphtp6_examples\ch12\Fig12_10_11\CommissionEmployee.h(10) :
         see declaration of 'CommissionEmployee'

C:\cpphtp6_examples\ch12\Fig12_10_11\BasePlusCommissionEmployee.cpp(45) :
   error C2248: 'CommissionEmployee::commissionRate' :
   cannot access private member declared in class 'CommissionEmployee'
      C:\cpphtp6_examples\ch12\Fig12_10_11\CommissionEmployee.h(37) :
         see declaration of 'CommissionEmployee::commissionRate'
      C:\cpphtp6_examples\ch12\Fig12_10_11\CommissionEmployee.h(10) :
         see declaration of 'CommissionEmployee'
```

Fig. 12.11 | BasePlusCommissionEmployee implementation file: private base-class data cannot be accessed from derived class. (Part 3 of 3.)

Common Programming Error 12.1

A compilation error occurs if a derived-class constructor calls one of its base-class constructors with arguments that are inconsistent with the number and types of parameters specified in one of the base-class constructor definitions.

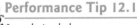

Performance Tip 12.1

In a derived-class constructor, initializing member objects and invoking base-class constructors explicitly in the member initializer list prevents duplicate initialization in which a default constructor is called, then data members are modified again in the derived-class constructor's body.

The compiler generates errors for line 35 of Fig. 12.11 because base class Commission-Employee's data members commissionRate and grossSales are private—derived class BasePlusCommissionEmployee's member functions are not allowed to access base class CommissionEmployee's private data. Note that we used red text in Fig. 12.11 to indicate erroneous code. The compiler issues additional errors in lines 42–45 of BasePlus-CommissionEmployee's print member function for the same reason. As you can see, C++ rigidly enforces restrictions on accessing private data members, so that even a derived class (which is intimately related to its base class) cannot access the base class's private data. [*Note:* To save space, we show only the error messages from Visual C++ 2005 in this example. The error messages produced by your compiler may differ from those shown here. Also notice that we highlight key portions of the lengthy error messages in bold.]

We purposely included the erroneous code in Fig. 12.11 to emphasize that a derived class's member functions cannot access its base class's private data. The errors in Base-PlusCommissionEmployee could have been prevented by using the *get* member functions inherited from class CommissionEmployee. For example, line 35 could have invoked get-CommissionRate and getGrossSales to access CommissionEmployee's private data members commissionRate and grossSales, respectively. Similarly, lines 42–45 could have used appropriate *get* member functions to retrieve the values of the base class's data members. In the next example, we show how using protected data also allows us to avoid the errors encountered in this example.

Including the Base-Class Header File in the Derived-Class Header File with `#include`

Notice that we #include the base class's header file in the derived class's header file (line 10 of Fig. 12.10). This is necessary for three reasons. First, for the derived class to use the base class's name in line 12, we must tell the compiler that the base class exists—the class definition in CommissionEmployee.h does exactly that.

The second reason is that the compiler uses a class definition to determine the size of an object of that class (as we discussed in Section 3.8). A client program that creates an object of a class must #include the class definition to enable the compiler to reserve the proper amount of memory for the object. When using inheritance, a derived-class object's size depends on the data members declared explicitly in its class definition *and* the data members inherited from its direct and indirect base classes. Including the base class's definition in line 10 allows the compiler to determine the memory requirements for the base class's data members that become part of a derived-class object and thus contribute to the total size of the derived-class object.

The last reason for line 10 is to allow the compiler to determine whether the derived class uses the base class's inherited members properly. For example, in the program of Figs. 12.10–12.11, the compiler uses the base-class header file to determine that the data members being accessed by the derived class are private in the base class. Since these are inaccessible to the derived class, the compiler generates errors. The compiler also uses the base class's function prototypes to validate function calls made by the derived class to the inherited base-class functions—you'll see an example of such a function call in Fig. 12.16.

Linking Process in an Inheritance Hierarchy

In Section 3.9, we discussed the linking process for creating an executable GradeBook application. In that example, you saw that the client's object code was linked with the object code for class GradeBook, as well as the object code for any C++ Standard Library classes used in either the client code or in class GradeBook.

The linking process is similar for a program that uses classes in an inheritance hierarchy. The process requires the object code for all classes used in the program and the object code for the direct and indirect base classes of any derived classes used by the program. Suppose a client wants to create an application that uses class BasePlusCommission-Employee, which is a derived class of CommissionEmployee (we'll see an example of this in Section 12.4.4). When compiling the client application, the client's object code must be linked with the object code for classes BasePlusCommissionEmployee and CommissionEmployee, because BasePlusCommissionEmployee inherits member functions from its base class CommissionEmployee. The code is also linked with the object code for any C++ Standard Library classes used in class CommissionEmployee, class BasePlusCommissionEmployee or the client code. This provides the program with access to the implementations of all of the functionality that the program may use.

12.4.4 CommissionEmployee–BasePlusCommissionEmployee Inheritance Hierarchy Using protected Data

To enable class BasePlusCommissionEmployee to directly access CommissionEmployee data members firstName, lastName, socialSecurityNumber, grossSales and commissionRate, we can declare those members as protected in the base class. As we discussed in Section 12.3, a base class's protected members can be accessed by members and friends of the base class and by members and friends of any classes derived from that base class.

 Good Programming Practice 12.1

Declare public members first, protected members second and private members last.

Defining Base Class CommissionEmployee with protected Data

Class CommissionEmployee (Figs. 12.12–12.13) now declares data members firstName, lastName, socialSecurityNumber, grossSales and commissionRate as protected (Fig. 12.12, lines 33–37) rather than private. The member-function implementations in Fig. 12.13 are identical to those in Fig. 12.5.

```
 1   // Fig. 12.12: CommissionEmployee.h
 2   // CommissionEmployee class definition with protected data.
 3   #ifndef COMMISSION_H
 4   #define COMMISSION_H
 5
 6   #include <string> // C++ standard string class
 7   using std::string;
 8
 9   class CommissionEmployee
10   {
11   public:
12      CommissionEmployee( const string &, const string &, const string &,
13         double = 0.0, double = 0.0 );
14
15      void setFirstName( const string & ); // set first name
16      string getFirstName() const; // return first name
17
18      void setLastName( const string & ); // set last name
19      string getLastName() const; // return last name
20
21      void setSocialSecurityNumber( const string & ); // set SSN
22      string getSocialSecurityNumber() const; // return SSN
23
```

Fig. 12.12 | CommissionEmployee class definition that declares protected data to allow access by derived classes. (Part 1 of 2.)

```
24      void setGrossSales( double ); // set gross sales amount
25      double getGrossSales() const; // return gross sales amount
26
27      void setCommissionRate( double ); // set commission rate
28      double getCommissionRate() const; // return commission rate
29
30      double earnings() const; // calculate earnings
31      void print() const; // print CommissionEmployee object
32  protected:
33      string firstName;
34      string lastName;
35      string socialSecurityNumber;
36      double grossSales; // gross weekly sales
37      double commissionRate; // commission percentage
38  }; // end class CommissionEmployee
39
40  #endif
```

Fig. 12.12 | CommissionEmployee class definition that declares protected data to allow access by derived classes. (Part 2 of 2.)

```
1   // Fig. 12.13: CommissionEmployee.cpp
2   // Class CommissionEmployee member-function definitions.
3   #include <iostream>
4   using std::cout;
5
6   #include "CommissionEmployee.h" // CommissionEmployee class definition
7
8   // constructor
9   CommissionEmployee::CommissionEmployee(
10      const string &first, const string &last, const string &ssn,
11      double sales, double rate )
12  {
13      firstName = first; // should validate
14      lastName = last; // should validate
15      socialSecurityNumber = ssn; // should validate
16      setGrossSales( sales ); // validate and store gross sales
17      setCommissionRate( rate ); // validate and store commission rate
18  } // end CommissionEmployee constructor
19
20  // set first name
21  void CommissionEmployee::setFirstName( const string &first )
22  {
23      firstName = first; // should validate
24  } // end function setFirstName
25
26  // return first name
27  string CommissionEmployee::getFirstName() const
28  {
29      return firstName;
30  } // end function getFirstName
31
```

Fig. 12.13 | CommissionEmployee class with protected data. (Part 1 of 3.)

```
32   // set last name
33   void CommissionEmployee::setLastName( const string &last )
34   {
35      lastName = last; // should validate
36   } // end function setLastName
37
38   // return last name
39   string CommissionEmployee::getLastName() const
40   {
41      return lastName;
42   } // end function getLastName
43
44   // set social security number
45   void CommissionEmployee::setSocialSecurityNumber( const string &ssn )
46   {
47      socialSecurityNumber = ssn; // should validate
48   } // end function setSocialSecurityNumber
49
50   // return social security number
51   string CommissionEmployee::getSocialSecurityNumber() const
52   {
53      return socialSecurityNumber;
54   } // end function getSocialSecurityNumber
55
56   // set gross sales amount
57   void CommissionEmployee::setGrossSales( double sales )
58   {
59      grossSales = ( sales < 0.0 ) ? 0.0 : sales;
60   } // end function setGrossSales
61
62   // return gross sales amount
63   double CommissionEmployee::getGrossSales() const
64   {
65      return grossSales;
66   } // end function getGrossSales
67
68   // set commission rate
69   void CommissionEmployee::setCommissionRate( double rate )
70   {
71      commissionRate = ( rate > 0.0 && rate < 1.0 ) ? rate : 0.0;
72   } // end function setCommissionRate
73
74   // return commission rate
75   double CommissionEmployee::getCommissionRate() const
76   {
77      return commissionRate;
78   } // end function getCommissionRate
79
80   // calculate earnings
81   double CommissionEmployee::earnings() const
82   {
83      return commissionRate * grossSales;
84   } // end function earnings
```

Fig. 12.13 | CommissionEmployee class with protected data. (Part 2 of 3.)

```
85
86   // print CommissionEmployee object
87   void CommissionEmployee::print() const
88   {
89      cout << "commission employee: " << firstName << ' ' << lastName
90         << "\nsocial security number: " << socialSecurityNumber
91         << "\ngross sales: " << grossSales
92         << "\ncommission rate: " << commissionRate;
93   } // end function print
```

Fig. 12.13 | CommissionEmployee class with protected data. (Part 3 of 3.)

Modifying Derived Class BasePlusCommissionEmployee

We now modify class BasePlusCommissionEmployee (Figs. 12.14–12.15) so that it inherits from the class CommissionEmployee in Figs. 12.12–12.13. Because class BasePlusCommissionEmployee inherits from this version of class CommissionEmployee, objects of class BasePlusCommissionEmployee can access inherited data members that are declared protected in class CommissionEmployee (i.e., data members firstName, lastName, socialSecurityNumber, grossSales and commissionRate). As a result, the compiler does not generate errors when compiling the BasePlusCommissionEmployee earnings and print member-function definitions in Fig. 12.15 (lines 32–36 and 39–47, respectively). This

```
1   // Fig. 12.14: BasePlusCommissionEmployee.h
2   // BasePlusCommissionEmployee class derived from class
3   // CommissionEmployee.
4   #ifndef BASEPLUS_H
5   #define BASEPLUS_H
6
7   #include <string> // C++ standard string class
8   using std::string;
9
10  #include "CommissionEmployee.h" // CommissionEmployee class declaration
11
12  class BasePlusCommissionEmployee : public CommissionEmployee
13  {
14  public:
15     BasePlusCommissionEmployee( const string &, const string &,
16        const string &, double = 0.0, double = 0.0, double = 0.0 );
17
18     void setBaseSalary( double ); // set base salary
19     double getBaseSalary() const; // return base salary
20
21     double earnings() const; // calculate earnings
22     void print() const; // print BasePlusCommissionEmployee object
23  private:
24     double baseSalary; // base salary
25  }; // end class BasePlusCommissionEmployee
26
27  #endif
```

Fig. 12.14 | BasePlusCommissionEmployee class header file.

```cpp
1   // Fig. 12.15: BasePlusCommissionEmployee.cpp
2   // Class BasePlusCommissionEmployee member-function definitions.
3   #include <iostream>
4   using std::cout;
5
6   // BasePlusCommissionEmployee class definition
7   #include "BasePlusCommissionEmployee.h"
8
9   // constructor
10  BasePlusCommissionEmployee::BasePlusCommissionEmployee(
11     const string &first, const string &last, const string &ssn,
12     double sales, double rate, double salary )
13     // explicitly call base-class constructor
14     : CommissionEmployee( first, last, ssn, sales, rate )
15  {
16     setBaseSalary( salary ); // validate and store base salary
17  } // end BasePlusCommissionEmployee constructor
18
19  // set base salary
20  void BasePlusCommissionEmployee::setBaseSalary( double salary )
21  {
22     baseSalary = ( salary < 0.0 ) ? 0.0 : salary;
23  } // end function setBaseSalary
24
25  // return base salary
26  double BasePlusCommissionEmployee::getBaseSalary() const
27  {
28     return baseSalary;
29  } // end function getBaseSalary
30
31  // calculate earnings
32  double BasePlusCommissionEmployee::earnings() const
33  {
34     // can access protected data of base class
35     return baseSalary + ( commissionRate * grossSales );
36  } // end function earnings
37
38  // print BasePlusCommissionEmployee object
39  void BasePlusCommissionEmployee::print() const
40  {
41     // can access protected data of base class
42     cout << "base-salaried commission employee: " << firstName << ' '
43        << lastName << "\nsocial security number: " << socialSecurityNumber
44        << "\ngross sales: " << grossSales
45        << "\ncommission rate: " << commissionRate
46        << "\nbase salary: " << baseSalary;
47  } // end function print
```

Fig. 12.15 | BasePlusCommissionEmployee implementation file for
BasePlusCommissionEmployee class that inherits protected data from CommissionEmployee.

shows the special privileges that a derived class is granted to access protected base-class
data members. Objects of a derived class also can access protected members in any of that
derived class's indirect base classes.

Class `BasePlusCommissionEmployee` does not inherit class `CommissionEmployee`'s constructor. However, class `BasePlusCommissionEmployee`'s constructor (Fig. 12.15, lines 10–17) calls class `CommissionEmployee`'s constructor explicitly with member initializer syntax (line 14). Recall that `BasePlusCommissionEmployee`'s constructor must explicitly call the constructor of class `CommissionEmployee`, because `CommissionEmployee` does not contain a default constructor that could be invoked implicitly.

Testing the Modified *BasePlusCommissionEmployee* Class

Figure 12.16 uses a `BasePlusCommissionEmployee` object to perform the same tasks that Fig. 12.9 performed on an object of the first version of class `BasePlusCommissionEmployee` (Figs. 12.7–12.8). Note that the outputs of the two programs are identical. We created the first class `BasePlusCommissionEmployee` without using inheritance and created this version of `BasePlusCommissionEmployee` using inheritance; however, both classes provide the same functionality. Note that the code for class `BasePlusCommissionEmployee` (i.e., the header and implementation files), which is 74 lines, is considerably shorter than the

```
1   // Fig. 12.16: fig12_16.cpp
2   // Testing class BasePlusCommissionEmployee.
3   #include <iostream>
4   using std::cout;
5   using std::endl;
6   using std::fixed;
7
8   #include <iomanip>
9   using std::setprecision;
10
11  // BasePlusCommissionEmployee class definition
12  #include "BasePlusCommissionEmployee.h"
13
14  int main()
15  {
16     // instantiate BasePlusCommissionEmployee object
17     BasePlusCommissionEmployee
18        employee( "Bob", "Lewis", "333-33-3333", 5000, .04, 300 );
19
20     // set floating-point output formatting
21     cout << fixed << setprecision( 2 );
22
23     // get commission employee data
24     cout << "Employee information obtained by get functions: \n"
25        << "\nFirst name is " << employee.getFirstName()
26        << "\nLast name is " << employee.getLastName()
27        << "\nSocial security number is "
28        << employee.getSocialSecurityNumber()
29        << "\nGross sales is " << employee.getGrossSales()
30        << "\nCommission rate is " << employee.getCommissionRate()
31        << "\nBase salary is " << employee.getBaseSalary() << endl;
32
33     employee.setBaseSalary( 1000 ); // set base salary
34
```

Fig. 12.16 | `protected` base-class data can be accessed from derived class. (Part 1 of 2.)

```
35      cout << "\nUpdated employee information output by print function: \n"
36         << endl;
37      employee.print(); // display the new employee information
38
39      // display the employee's earnings
40      cout << "\n\nEmployee's earnings: $" << employee.earnings() << endl;
41
42      return 0;
43   } // end main
```

```
Employee information obtained by get functions:

First name is Bob
Last name is Lewis
Social security number is 333-33-3333
Gross sales is 5000.00
Commission rate is 0.04
Base salary is 300.00

Updated employee information output by print function:

base-salaried commission employee: Bob Lewis
social security number: 333-33-3333
gross sales: 5000.00
commission rate: 0.04
base salary: 1000.00

Employee's earnings: $1200.00
```

Fig. 12.16 | protected base-class data can be accessed from derived class. (Part 2 of 2.)

code for the noninherited version of the class, which is 154 lines, because the inherited version absorbs part of its functionality from CommissionEmployee, whereas the noninherited version does not absorb any functionality. Also, there is now only one copy of the CommissionEmployee functionality declared and defined in class CommissionEmployee. This makes the source code easier to maintain, modify and debug, because the source code related to a CommissionEmployee exists only in the files of Figs. 12.12–12.13.

Notes on Using *protected* Data
In this example, we declared base-class data members as protected, so derived classes can modify the data directly. Inheriting protected data members slightly increases performance, because we can directly access the members without incurring the overhead of calls to *set* or *get* member functions. In most cases, however, it is better to use private data members to encourage proper software engineering, and leave code optimization issues to the compiler. Your code will be easier to maintain, modify and debug.

Using protected data members creates two serious problems. First, the derived-class object does not have to use a member function to set the value of the base class's protected data member. Therefore, a derived-class object easily can assign an invalid value to the protected data member, thus leaving the object in an inconsistent state. For example, with CommissionEmployee's data member grossSales declared as protected, a derived-class (e.g., BasePlusCommissionEmployee) object can assign a negative value to gross-Sales. The second problem with using protected data members is that derived-class member functions are more likely to be written so that they depend on the base-class implementation. In practice, derived classes should depend only on the base-class services (i.e., non-private member functions) and not on the base-class implementation. With protected data members in the base class, if the base-class implementation changes, we may need to modify all derived classes of that base class. For example, if for some reason we were to change the names of data members firstName and lastName to first and last, then we would have to do so for all occurrences in which a derived class references these base-class data members directly. In such a case, the software is said to be fragile or brittle, because a small change in the base class can "break" derived-class implementation. You should be able to change the base-class implementation while still providing the same services to derived classes. (Of course, if the base-class services change, we must reimplement our derived classes—good object-oriented design attempts to prevent this.)

Software Engineering Observation 12.5

It is appropriate to use the protected *access specifier when a base class should provide a service (i.e., a member function) only to its derived classes (and* friends*), not to other clients.*

Software Engineering Observation 12.6

Declaring base-class data members private *(as opposed to declaring them* protected*) enables programmers to change the base-class implementation without having to change derived-class implementations.*

Error-Prevention Tip 12.1

When possible, avoid including protected *data members in a base class. Rather, include non-private member functions that access* private *data members, ensuring that the object maintains a consistent state.*

12.4.5 CommissionEmployee–BasePlusCommissionEmployee Inheritance Hierarchy Using private Data

We now reexamine our hierarchy once more, this time using the best software engineering practices. Class CommissionEmployee (Figs. 12.17–12.18) now declares data members firstName, lastName, socialSecurityNumber, grossSales and commissionRate as private (Fig. 12.17, lines 33–37) and provides public member functions setFirstName, getFirstName, setLastName, getLastName, setSocialSecurityNumber, getSocialSecurityNumber, setGrossSales, getGrossSales, setCommissionRate, getCommissionRate, earnings and print for manipulating these values. If we decide to change the data member names, the earnings and print definitions will not require modification—only the definitions of the *get* and *set* member functions that directly manipulate the data members will need to change. Note that these changes occur solely within the base class—no changes to the derived class are needed. Localizing the effects of changes like this is a good software engineering practice. Derived class BasePlusCommissionEmployee (Figs. 12.19–12.20) inherits CommissionEmployee's non-private member functions and can access the private base-class members via those member functions.

```
1   // Fig. 12.17: CommissionEmployee.h
2   // CommissionEmployee class definition with good software engineering.
3   #ifndef COMMISSION_H
4   #define COMMISSION_H
5
6   #include <string> // C++ standard string class
7   using std::string;
8
9   class CommissionEmployee
10  {
11  public:
12     CommissionEmployee( const string &, const string &, const string &,
13        double = 0.0, double = 0.0 );
14
15     void setFirstName( const string & ); // set first name
16     string getFirstName() const; // return first name
17
18     void setLastName( const string & ); // set last name
19     string getLastName() const; // return last name
20
21     void setSocialSecurityNumber( const string & ); // set SSN
22     string getSocialSecurityNumber() const; // return SSN
23
24     void setGrossSales( double ); // set gross sales amount
25     double getGrossSales() const; // return gross sales amount
26
27     void setCommissionRate( double ); // set commission rate
28     double getCommissionRate() const; // return commission rate
29
30     double earnings() const; // calculate earnings
31     void print() const; // print CommissionEmployee object
32  private:
33     string firstName;
34     string lastName;
35     string socialSecurityNumber;
36     double grossSales; // gross weekly sales
37     double commissionRate; // commission percentage
38  }; // end class CommissionEmployee
39
40  #endif
```

Fig. 12.17 | CommissionEmployee class defined using good software engineering practices.

```
1   // Fig. 12.18: CommissionEmployee.cpp
2   // Class CommissionEmployee member-function definitions.
3   #include <iostream>
4   using std::cout;
5
6   #include "CommissionEmployee.h" // CommissionEmployee class definition
7
```

Fig. 12.18 | CommissionEmployee class implementation file: CommissionEmployee class uses member functions to manipulate its private data. (Part 1 of 3.)

```
 8   // constructor
 9   CommissionEmployee::CommissionEmployee(
10      const string &first, const string &last, const string &ssn,
11      double sales, double rate )
12      : firstName( first ), lastName( last ), socialSecurityNumber( ssn )
13   {
14      setGrossSales( sales ); // validate and store gross sales
15      setCommissionRate( rate ); // validate and store commission rate
16   } // end CommissionEmployee constructor
17
18   // set first name
19   void CommissionEmployee::setFirstName( const string &first )
20   {
21      firstName = first; // should validate
22   } // end function setFirstName
23
24   // return first name
25   string CommissionEmployee::getFirstName() const
26   {
27      return firstName;
28   } // end function getFirstName
29
30   // set last name
31   void CommissionEmployee::setLastName( const string &last )
32   {
33      lastName = last; // should validate
34   } // end function setLastName
35
36   // return last name
37   string CommissionEmployee::getLastName() const
38   {
39      return lastName;
40   } // end function getLastName
41
42   // set social security number
43   void CommissionEmployee::setSocialSecurityNumber( const string &ssn )
44   {
45      socialSecurityNumber = ssn; // should validate
46   } // end function setSocialSecurityNumber
47
48   // return social security number
49   string CommissionEmployee::getSocialSecurityNumber() const
50   {
51      return socialSecurityNumber;
52   } // end function getSocialSecurityNumber
53
54   // set gross sales amount
55   void CommissionEmployee::setGrossSales( double sales )
56   {
57      grossSales = ( sales < 0.0 ) ? 0.0 : sales;
58   } // end function setGrossSales
```

Fig. 12.18 | CommissionEmployee class implementation file: CommissionEmployee class uses member functions to manipulate its private data. (Part 2 of 3.)

```
59
60   // return gross sales amount
61   double CommissionEmployee::getGrossSales() const
62   {
63      return grossSales;
64   } // end function getGrossSales
65
66   // set commission rate
67   void CommissionEmployee::setCommissionRate( double rate )
68   {
69      commissionRate = ( rate > 0.0 && rate < 1.0 ) ? rate : 0.0;
70   } // end function setCommissionRate
71
72   // return commission rate
73   double CommissionEmployee::getCommissionRate() const
74   {
75      return commissionRate;
76   } // end function getCommissionRate
77
78   // calculate earnings
79   double CommissionEmployee::earnings() const
80   {
81      return getCommissionRate() * getGrossSales();
82   } // end function earnings
83
84   // print CommissionEmployee object
85   void CommissionEmployee::print() const
86   {
87      cout << "commission employee: "
88         << getFirstName() << ' ' << getLastName()
89         << "\nsocial security number: " << getSocialSecurityNumber()
90         << "\ngross sales: " << getGrossSales()
91         << "\ncommission rate: " << getCommissionRate();
92   } // end function print
```

Fig. 12.18 | CommissionEmployee class implementation file: CommissionEmployee class uses member functions to manipulate its private data. (Part 3 of 3.)

In the CommissionEmployee constructor implementation (Fig. 12.18, lines 9–16), note that we use member initializers (line 12) to set the values of members firstName, lastName and socialSecurityNumber. We show how derived-class BasePlusCommissionEmployee (Figs. 12.19–12.20) can invoke non-private base-class member functions (setFirstName, getFirstName, setLastName, getLastName, setSocialSecurityNumber and getSocialSecurityNumber) to manipulate these data members.

Performance Tip 12.2

Using a member function to access a data member's value can be slightly slower than accessing the data directly. However, today's optimizing compilers are carefully designed to perform many optimizations implicitly (such as inlining set and get member-function calls). As a result, programmers should write code that adheres to proper software engineering principles, and leave optimization issues to the compiler. A good rule is, "Do not second-guess the compiler."

Class BasePlusCommissionEmployee (Figs. 12.19–12.20) has several changes to its member-function implementations (Fig. 12.20) that distinguish it from the previous version of the class (Figs. 12.14–12.15). Member functions earnings (Fig. 12.20, lines 32–35) and

```
1   // Fig. 12.19: BasePlusCommissionEmployee.h
2   // BasePlusCommissionEmployee class derived from class
3   // CommissionEmployee.
4   #ifndef BASEPLUS_H
5   #define BASEPLUS_H
6
7   #include <string> // C++ standard string class
8   using std::string;
9
10  #include "CommissionEmployee.h" // CommissionEmployee class declaration
11
12  class BasePlusCommissionEmployee : public CommissionEmployee
13  {
14  public:
15     BasePlusCommissionEmployee( const string &, const string &,
16        const string &, double = 0.0, double = 0.0, double = 0.0 );
17
18     void setBaseSalary( double ); // set base salary
19     double getBaseSalary() const; // return base salary
20
21     double earnings() const; // calculate earnings
22     void print() const; // print BasePlusCommissionEmployee object
23  private:
24     double baseSalary; // base salary
25  }; // end class BasePlusCommissionEmployee
26
27  #endif
```

Fig. 12.19 | BasePlusCommissionEmployee class header file.

```
1   // Fig. 12.20: BasePlusCommissionEmployee.cpp
2   // Class BasePlusCommissionEmployee member-function definitions.
3   #include <iostream>
4   using std::cout;
5
6   // BasePlusCommissionEmployee class definition
7   #include "BasePlusCommissionEmployee.h"
8
9   // constructor
10  BasePlusCommissionEmployee::BasePlusCommissionEmployee(
11     const string &first, const string &last, const string &ssn,
12     double sales, double rate, double salary )
13     // explicitly call base-class constructor
14     : CommissionEmployee( first, last, ssn, sales, rate )
15  {
```

Fig. 12.20 | BasePlusCommissionEmployee class that inherits from class CommissionEmployee but cannot directly access the class's private data. (Part 1 of 2.)

```
16        setBaseSalary( salary ); // validate and store base salary
17    } // end BasePlusCommissionEmployee constructor
18
19    // set base salary
20    void BasePlusCommissionEmployee::setBaseSalary( double salary )
21    {
22        baseSalary = ( salary < 0.0 ) ? 0.0 : salary;
23    } // end function setBaseSalary
24
25    // return base salary
26    double BasePlusCommissionEmployee::getBaseSalary() const
27    {
28        return baseSalary;
29    } // end function getBaseSalary
30
31    // calculate earnings
32    double BasePlusCommissionEmployee::earnings() const
33    {
34        return getBaseSalary() + CommissionEmployee::earnings();
35    } // end function earnings
36
37    // print BasePlusCommissionEmployee object
38    void BasePlusCommissionEmployee::print() const
39    {
40        cout << "base-salaried ";
41
42        // invoke CommissionEmployee's print function
43        CommissionEmployee::print();
44
45        cout << "\nbase salary: " << getBaseSalary();
46    } // end function print
```

Fig. 12.20 | BasePlusCommissionEmployee class that inherits from class
CommissionEmployee but cannot directly access the class's private data. (Part 2 of 2.)

print (lines 38–46) each invoke member function getBaseSalary to obtain the base salary value, rather than accessing baseSalary directly. This insulates earnings and print from potential changes to the implementation of data member baseSalary. For example, if we decide to rename data member baseSalary or change its type, only member functions set-BaseSalary and getBaseSalary will need to change.

Class BasePlusCommissionEmployee's earnings function (Fig. 12.20, lines 32–35) redefines class CommissionEmployee's earnings member function (Fig. 12.18, lines 79–82) to calculate the earnings of a base-salaried commission employee. Class BasePlusCommissionEmployee's version of earnings obtains the portion of the employee's earnings based on commission alone by calling base-class CommissionEmployee's earnings function with the expression CommissionEmployee::earnings() (Fig. 12.20, line 34). BasePlusCommissionEmployee's earnings function then adds the base salary to this value to calculate the total earnings of the employee. Note the syntax used to invoke a redefined base-class member function from a derived class—place the base-class name and the binary scope resolution operator (::) before the base-class member-function name. This member-function invocation is a good software engineering practice: Recall from *Software Engi-*

neering Observation 9.9 that, if an object's member function performs the actions needed by another object, we should call that member function rather than duplicating its code body. By having BasePlusCommissionEmployee's earnings function invoke Commission-Employee's earnings function to calculate part of a BasePlusCommissionEmployee object's earnings, we avoid duplicating the code and reduce code-maintenance problems.

Common Programming Error 12.2

When a base-class member function is redefined in a derived class, the derived-class version often calls the base-class version to do additional work. Failure to use the :: operator prefixed with the name of the base class when referencing the base class's member function causes infinite recursion, because the derived-class member function would then call itself.

Common Programming Error 12.3

Including a base-class member function with a different signature in the derived class hides the base-class version of the function. Attempts to call the base-class version through the public interface of a derived-class object result in compilation errors.

Similarly, BasePlusCommissionEmployee's print function (Fig. 12.20, lines 38–46) redefines class CommissionEmployee's print member function (Fig. 12.18, lines 85–92) to output information that is appropriate for a base-salaried commission employee. Class BasePlusCommissionEmployee's version displays part of a BasePlusCommissionEmployee object's information (i.e., the string "commission employee" and the values of class CommissionEmployee's private data members) by calling CommissionEmployee's print member function with the qualified name CommissionEmployee::print() (Fig. 12.20, line 43). BasePlusCommissionEmployee's print function then outputs the remainder of a BasePlusCommissionEmployee object's information (i.e., the value of class BasePlus-CommissionEmployee's base salary).

Figure 12.21 performs the same manipulations on a BasePlusCommissionEmployee object as did Fig. 12.9 and Fig. 12.16 on objects of classes CommissionEmployee and BasePlusCommissionEmployee, respectively. Although each "base-salaried commission employee" class behaves identically, class BasePlusCommissionEmployee is the best engineered. By using inheritance and by calling member functions that hide the data and ensure consistency, we have efficiently and effectively constructed a well-engineered class.

```cpp
1   // Fig. 12.21: fig12_21.cpp
2   // Testing class BasePlusCommissionEmployee.
3   #include <iostream>
4   using std::cout;
5   using std::endl;
6   using std::fixed;
7
8   #include <iomanip>
9   using std::setprecision;
10
11  // BasePlusCommissionEmployee class definition
12  #include "BasePlusCommissionEmployee.h"
```

Fig. 12.21 | Base-class private data is accessible to a derived class via public or protected member function inherited by the derived class. (Part 1 of 2.)

```
13
14  int main()
15  {
16      // instantiate BasePlusCommissionEmployee object
17      BasePlusCommissionEmployee
18          employee( "Bob", "Lewis", "333-33-3333", 5000, .04, 300 );
19
20      // set floating-point output formatting
21      cout << fixed << setprecision( 2 );
22
23      // get commission employee data
24      cout << "Employee information obtained by get functions: \n"
25          << "\nFirst name is " << employee.getFirstName()
26          << "\nLast name is " << employee.getLastName()
27          << "\nSocial security number is "
28          << employee.getSocialSecurityNumber()
29          << "\nGross sales is " << employee.getGrossSales()
30          << "\nCommission rate is " << employee.getCommissionRate()
31          << "\nBase salary is " << employee.getBaseSalary() << endl;
32
33      employee.setBaseSalary( 1000 ); // set base salary
34
35      cout << "\nUpdated employee information output by print function: \n"
36          << endl;
37      employee.print(); // display the new employee information
38
39      // display the employee's earnings
40      cout << "\n\nEmployee's earnings: $" << employee.earnings() << endl;
41
42      return 0;
43  } // end main
```

```
Employee information obtained by get functions:

First name is Bob
Last name is Lewis
Social security number is 333-33-3333
Gross sales is 5000.00
Commission rate is 0.04
Base salary is 300.00

Updated employee information output by print function:

base-salaried commission employee: Bob Lewis
social security number: 333-33-3333
gross sales: 5000.00
commission rate: 0.04
base salary: 1000.00

Employee's earnings: $1200.00
```

Fig. 12.21 | Base-class `private` data is accessible to a derived class via `public` or `protected` member function inherited by the derived class. (Part 2 of 2.)

In this section, you saw an evolutionary set of examples that was carefully designed to teach key capabilities for good software engineering with inheritance. You learned how to create a derived class using inheritance, how to use `protected` base-class members to enable a derived class to access inherited base-class data members and how to redefine base-class functions to provide versions that are more appropriate for derived-class objects. In addition, you learned how to apply software engineering techniques from Chapters 9–10 and this chapter to create classes that are easy to maintain, modify and debug.

12.5 Constructors and Destructors in Derived Classes

As we explained in the preceding section, instantiating a derived-class object begins a chain of constructor calls in which the derived-class constructor, before performing its own tasks, invokes its direct base class's constructor either explicitly (via a base-class member initializer) or implicitly (calling the base class's default constructor). Similarly, if the base class is derived from another class, the base-class constructor is required to invoke the constructor of the next class up in the hierarchy, and so on. The last constructor called in this chain is the constructor of the class at the base of the hierarchy, whose body actually finishes executing first. The original derived-class constructor's body finishes executing last. Each base-class constructor initializes the base-class data members that the derived-class object inherits. For example, consider the `CommissionEmployee/BasePlusCommissionEmployee` hierarchy from Figs. 12.17–12.20. When a program creates an object of class `BasePlusCommissionEmployee`, the `CommissionEmployee` constructor is called. Since class `CommissionEmployee` is at the base of the hierarchy, its constructor executes, initializing the `private` data members of `CommissionEmployee` that are part of the `BasePlusCommissionEmployee` object. When `CommissionEmployee`'s constructor completes execution, it returns control to `BasePlusCommissionEmployee`'s constructor, which initializes the `BasePlusCommissionEmployee` object's `baseSalary`.

Software Engineering Observation 12.7

When a program creates a derived-class object, the derived-class constructor immediately calls the base-class constructor, the base-class constructor's body executes, then the derived class's member initializers execute and finally the derived-class constructor's body executes. This process cascades up the hierarchy if it contains more than two levels.

When a derived-class object is destroyed, the program calls that object's destructor. This begins a chain (or cascade) of destructor calls in which the derived-class destructor and the destructors of the direct and indirect base classes and the classes' members execute in reverse of the order in which the constructors executed. When a derived-class object's destructor is called, the destructor performs its task, then invokes the destructor of the next base class up the hierarchy. This process repeats until the destructor of the final base class at the top of the hierarchy is called. Then the object is removed from memory.

Software Engineering Observation 12.8

Suppose that we create an object of a derived class where both the base class and the derived class contain (via composition) objects of other classes. When an object of that derived class is created, first the constructors for the base class's member objects execute, then the base-class constructor executes, then the constructors for the derived class's member objects execute, then the derived class's constructor executes. Destructors for derived-class objects are called in the reverse of the order in which their corresponding constructors are called.

Base-class constructors, destructors and overloaded assignment operators (see Chapter 11, Operator Overloading; String and Array Objects) are not inherited by derived classes. Derived-class constructors, destructors and overloaded assignment operators, however, can call base-class constructors, destructors and overloaded assignment operators.

Our next example defines class CommissionEmployee (Figs. 12.22–12.23) and class BasePlusCommissionEmployee (Figs. 12.24–12.25) with constructors and destructors that each print a message when invoked. As you'll see in the output in Fig. 12.26, these messages demonstrate the order in which the constructors and destructors are called for objects in an inheritance hierarchy.

```
1   // Fig. 12.22: CommissionEmployee.h
2   // CommissionEmployee class definition represents a commission employee.
3   #ifndef COMMISSION_H
4   #define COMMISSION_H
5
6   #include <string> // C++ standard string class
7   using std::string;
8
9   class CommissionEmployee
10  {
11  public:
12     CommissionEmployee( const string &, const string &, const string &,
13        double = 0.0, double = 0.0 );
14     ~CommissionEmployee(); // destructor
15
16     void setFirstName( const string & ); // set first name
17     string getFirstName() const; // return first name
18
19     void setLastName( const string & ); // set last name
20     string getLastName() const; // return last name
21
22     void setSocialSecurityNumber( const string & ); // set SSN
23     string getSocialSecurityNumber() const; // return SSN
24
25     void setGrossSales( double ); // set gross sales amount
26     double getGrossSales() const; // return gross sales amount
27
28     void setCommissionRate( double ); // set commission rate
29     double getCommissionRate() const; // return commission rate
30
31     double earnings() const; // calculate earnings
32     void print() const; // print CommissionEmployee object
33  private:
34     string firstName;
35     string lastName;
36     string socialSecurityNumber;
37     double grossSales; // gross weekly sales
38     double commissionRate; // commission percentage
39  }; // end class CommissionEmployee
40
41  #endif
```

Fig. 12.22 | CommissionEmployee class header file.

In this example, we modified the CommissionEmployee constructor (lines 10–21 of Fig. 12.23) and included a CommissionEmployee destructor (lines 24–29), each of which outputs a line of text upon its invocation. We also modified the BasePlusCommissionEmployee constructor (lines 11–22 of Fig. 12.25) and included a BasePlusCommissionEmployee destructor (lines 25–30), each of which outputs a line of text upon its invocation.

```cpp
1   // Fig. 12.23: CommissionEmployee.cpp
2   // Class CommissionEmployee member-function definitions.
3   #include <iostream>
4   using std::cout;
5   using std::endl;
6
7   #include "CommissionEmployee.h" // CommissionEmployee class definition
8
9   // constructor
10  CommissionEmployee::CommissionEmployee(
11     const string &first, const string &last, const string &ssn,
12     double sales, double rate )
13     : firstName( first ), lastName( last ), socialSecurityNumber( ssn )
14  {
15     setGrossSales( sales ); // validate and store gross sales
16     setCommissionRate( rate ); // validate and store commission rate
17
18     cout << "CommissionEmployee constructor: " << endl;
19     print();
20     cout << "\n\n";
21  } // end CommissionEmployee constructor
22
23  // destructor
24  CommissionEmployee::~CommissionEmployee()
25  {
26     cout << "CommissionEmployee destructor: " << endl;
27     print();
28     cout << "\n\n";
29  } // end CommissionEmployee destructor
30
31  // set first name
32  void CommissionEmployee::setFirstName( const string &first )
33  {
34     firstName = first; // should validate
35  } // end function setFirstName
36
37  // return first name
38  string CommissionEmployee::getFirstName() const
39  {
40     return firstName;
41  } // end function getFirstName
42
43  // set last name
44  void CommissionEmployee::setLastName( const string &last )
45  {
```

Fig. 12.23 | CommissionEmployee's constructor outputs text. (Part 1 of 3.)

```
46       lastName = last; // should validate
47    } // end function setLastName
48
49    // return last name
50    string CommissionEmployee::getLastName() const
51    {
52       return lastName;
53    } // end function getLastName
54
55    // set social security number
56    void CommissionEmployee::setSocialSecurityNumber( const string &ssn )
57    {
58       socialSecurityNumber = ssn; // should validate
59    } // end function setSocialSecurityNumber
60
61    // return social security number
62    string CommissionEmployee::getSocialSecurityNumber() const
63    {
64       return socialSecurityNumber;
65    } // end function getSocialSecurityNumber
66
67    // set gross sales amount
68    void CommissionEmployee::setGrossSales( double sales )
69    {
70       grossSales = ( sales < 0.0 ) ? 0.0 : sales;
71    } // end function setGrossSales
72
73    // return gross sales amount
74    double CommissionEmployee::getGrossSales() const
75    {
76       return grossSales;
77    } // end function getGrossSales
78
79    // set commission rate
80    void CommissionEmployee::setCommissionRate( double rate )
81    {
82       commissionRate = ( rate > 0.0 && rate < 1.0 ) ? rate : 0.0;
83    } // end function setCommissionRate
84
85    // return commission rate
86    double CommissionEmployee::getCommissionRate() const
87    {
88       return commissionRate;
89    } // end function getCommissionRate
90
91    // calculate earnings
92    double CommissionEmployee::earnings() const
93    {
94       return getCommissionRate() * getGrossSales();
95    } // end function earnings
96
```

Fig. 12.23 | CommissionEmployee's constructor outputs text. (Part 2 of 3.)

```
97   // print CommissionEmployee object
98   void CommissionEmployee::print() const
99   {
100     cout << "commission employee: "
101        << getFirstName() << ' ' << getLastName()
102        << "\nsocial security number: " << getSocialSecurityNumber()
103        << "\ngross sales: " << getGrossSales()
104        << "\ncommission rate: " << getCommissionRate();
105  } // end function print
```

Fig. 12.23 | CommissionEmployee's constructor outputs text. (Part 3 of 3.)

```
1    // Fig. 12.24: BasePlusCommissionEmployee.h
2    // BasePlusCommissionEmployee class derived from class
3    // CommissionEmployee.
4    #ifndef BASEPLUS_H
5    #define BASEPLUS_H
6
7    #include <string> // C++ standard string class
8    using std::string;
9
10   #include "CommissionEmployee.h" // CommissionEmployee class declaration
11
12   class BasePlusCommissionEmployee : public CommissionEmployee
13   {
14   public:
15      BasePlusCommissionEmployee( const string &, const string &,
16         const string &, double = 0.0, double = 0.0, double = 0.0 );
17      ~BasePlusCommissionEmployee(); // destructor
18
19      void setBaseSalary( double ); // set base salary
20      double getBaseSalary() const; // return base salary
21
22      double earnings() const; // calculate earnings
23      void print() const; // print BasePlusCommissionEmployee object
24   private:
25      double baseSalary; // base salary
26   }; // end class BasePlusCommissionEmployee
27
28   #endif
```

Fig. 12.24 | BasePlusCommissionEmployee class header file.

```
1    // Fig. 12.25: BasePlusCommissionEmployee.cpp
2    // Class BasePlusCommissionEmployee member-function definitions.
3    #include <iostream>
4    using std::cout;
5    using std::endl;
6
7    // BasePlusCommissionEmployee class definition
8    #include "BasePlusCommissionEmployee.h"
```

Fig. 12.25 | BasePlusCommissionEmployee's constructor outputs text. (Part 1 of 2.)

```
9
10   // constructor
11   BasePlusCommissionEmployee::BasePlusCommissionEmployee(
12      const string &first, const string &last, const string &ssn,
13      double sales, double rate, double salary )
14      // explicitly call base-class constructor
15      : CommissionEmployee( first, last, ssn, sales, rate )
16   {
17      setBaseSalary( salary ); // validate and store base salary
18
19      cout << "BasePlusCommissionEmployee constructor: " << endl;
20      print();
21      cout << "\n\n";
22   } // end BasePlusCommissionEmployee constructor
23
24   // destructor
25   BasePlusCommissionEmployee::~BasePlusCommissionEmployee()
26   {
27      cout << "BasePlusCommissionEmployee destructor: " << endl;
28      print();
29      cout << "\n\n";
30   } // end BasePlusCommissionEmployee destructor
31
32   // set base salary
33   void BasePlusCommissionEmployee::setBaseSalary( double salary )
34   {
35      baseSalary = ( salary < 0.0 ) ? 0.0 : salary;
36   } // end function setBaseSalary
37
38   // return base salary
39   double BasePlusCommissionEmployee::getBaseSalary() const
40   {
41      return baseSalary;
42   } // end function getBaseSalary
43
44   // calculate earnings
45   double BasePlusCommissionEmployee::earnings() const
46   {
47      return getBaseSalary() + CommissionEmployee::earnings();
48   } // end function earnings
49
50   // print BasePlusCommissionEmployee object
51   void BasePlusCommissionEmployee::print() const
52   {
53      cout << "base-salaried ";
54
55      // invoke CommissionEmployee's print function
56      CommissionEmployee::print();
57
58      cout << "\nbase salary: " << getBaseSalary();
59   } // end function print
```

Fig. 12.25 | BasePlusCommissionEmployee's constructor outputs text. (Part 2 of 2.)

Figure 12.26 demonstrates the order in which constructors and destructors are called for objects of classes that are part of an inheritance hierarchy. Function main (lines 15–34) begins by instantiating CommissionEmployee object employee1 (lines 21–22) in a separate block inside main (lines 20–23). The object goes in and out of scope immediately (the end of the block is reached immediately after the object is created), so both the Commission-Employee constructor and destructor are called. Next, lines 26–27 instantiate BasePlus-CommissionEmployee object employee2. This invokes the CommissionEmployee constructor to display outputs with values passed from the BasePlusCommissionEmployee constructor, then the output specified in the BasePlusCommissionEmployee constructor is performed. Lines 30–31 then instantiate BasePlusCommissionEmployee object employee3. Again, the CommissionEmployee and BasePlusCommissionEmployee constructors are both called. Note that, in each case, the body of the CommissionEmployee constructor is executed before the body of the BasePlusCommissionEmployee constructor executes. When the end of main is reached, the destructors are called for objects employee2 and employee3. But, because destructors are called in the reverse order of their corresponding constructors, the BasePlusCommissionEmployee destructor and CommissionEmployee destructor are called (in that order) for object employee3, then the BasePlusCommissionEmployee and CommissionEmployee destructors are called (in that order) for object employee2.

```cpp
// Fig. 12.26: fig12_26.cpp
// Display order in which base-class and derived-class constructors
// and destructors are called.
#include <iostream>
using std::cout;
using std::endl;
using std::fixed;

#include <iomanip>
using std::setprecision;

// BasePlusCommissionEmployee class definition
#include "BasePlusCommissionEmployee.h"

int main()
{
   // set floating-point output formatting
   cout << fixed << setprecision( 2 );

   { // begin new scope
      CommissionEmployee employee1(
         "Bob", "Lewis", "333-33-3333", 5000, .04 );
   } // end scope

   cout << endl;
   BasePlusCommissionEmployee
      employee2( "Lisa", "Jones", "555-55-5555", 2000, .06, 800 );

```

Fig. 12.26 | Constructor and destructor call order. (Part 1 of 3.)

```
29      cout << endl;
30      BasePlusCommissionEmployee
31         employee3( "Mark", "Sands", "888-88-8888", 8000, .15, 2000 );
32      cout << endl;
33      return 0;
34   } // end main
```

```
CommissionEmployee constructor:
commission employee: Bob Lewis
social security number: 333-33-3333
gross sales: 5000.00
commission rate: 0.04

CommissionEmployee destructor:
commission employee: Bob Lewis
social security number: 333-33-3333
gross sales: 5000.00
commission rate: 0.04


CommissionEmployee constructor:
commission employee: Lisa Jones
social security number: 555-55-5555
gross sales: 2000.00
commission rate: 0.06

BasePlusCommissionEmployee constructor:
base-salaried commission employee: Lisa Jones
social security number: 555-55-5555
gross sales: 2000.00
commission rate: 0.06
base salary: 800.00


CommissionEmployee constructor:
commission employee: Mark Sands
social security number: 888-88-8888
gross sales: 8000.00
commission rate: 0.15

BasePlusCommissionEmployee constructor:
base-salaried commission employee: Mark Sands
social security number: 888-88-8888
gross sales: 8000.00
commission rate: 0.15
base salary: 2000.00


BasePlusCommissionEmployee destructor:
base-salaried commission employee: Mark Sands
social security number: 888-88-8888
gross sales: 8000.00
commission rate: 0.15
base salary: 2000.00
```
                                          (continued ...)

Fig. 12.26 | Constructor and destructor call order. (Part 2 of 3.)

```
CommissionEmployee destructor:
commission employee: Mark Sands
social security number: 888-88-8888
gross sales: 8000.00
commission rate: 0.15

BasePlusCommissionEmployee destructor:
base-salaried commission employee: Lisa Jones
social security number: 555-55-5555
gross sales: 2000.00
commission rate: 0.06
base salary: 800.00

CommissionEmployee destructor:
commission employee: Lisa Jones
social security number: 555-55-5555
gross sales: 2000.00
commission rate: 0.06
```

Fig. 12.26 | Constructor and destructor call order. (Part 3 of 3.)

12.6 public, protected and private Inheritance

When deriving a class from a base class, the base class may be inherited through public, protected or private inheritance. Use of protected and private inheritance is rare, and each should be used only with great care; we normally use public inheritance in this book. (Chapter 20 demonstrates private inheritance as an alternative to composition.) Figure 12.27 summarizes for each type of inheritance the accessibility of base-class members in a derived class. The first column contains the base-class access specifiers.

When deriving a class from a public base class, public members of the base class become public members of the derived class, and protected members of the base class become protected members of the derived class. A base class's private members are never accessible directly from a derived class, but can be accessed through calls to the public and protected members of the base class.

When deriving from a protected base class, public and protected members of the base class become protected members of the derived class. When deriving from a private base class, public and protected members of the base class become private members (e.g., the functions become utility functions) of the derived class. Private and protected inheritance are not *is-a* relationships.

12.7 Software Engineering with Inheritance

In this section, we discuss the use of inheritance to customize existing software. When we use inheritance to create a new class from an existing one, the new class inherits the data members and member functions of the existing class, as described in Fig. 12.27. We can customize the new class to meet our needs by including additional members and by redefining base-class members. The derived-class programmer does this in C++ without accessing the base class's source code. The derived class must be able to link to the base class's

Base-class member-access specifier	Type of inheritance		
	public inheritance	**protected** inheritance	**private** inheritance
public	**public** in derived class. Can be accessed directly by member functions, **friend** functions and nonmember functions.	**protected** in derived class. Can be accessed directly by member functions and **friend** functions.	**private** in derived class. Can be accessed directly by member functions and **friend** functions.
protected	**protected** in derived class. Can be accessed directly by member functions and **friend** functions.	**protected** in derived class. Can be accessed directly by member functions and **friend** functions.	**private** in derived class. Can be accessed directly by member functions and **friend** functions.
private	Hidden in derived class. Can be accessed by member functions and **friend** functions through **public** or **protected** member functions of the base class.	Hidden in derived class. Can be accessed by member functions and **friend** functions through **public** or **protected** member functions of the base class.	Hidden in derived class. Can be accessed by member functions and **friend** functions through **public** or **protected** member functions of the base class.

Fig. 12.27 | Summary of base-class member accessibility in a derived class.

object code. This powerful capability is attractive to independent software vendors (ISVs). ISVs can develop proprietary classes for sale or license and make these classes available to users in object-code format. Users then can derive new classes from these library classes rapidly and without accessing the ISVs' proprietary source code. All the ISVs need to supply with the object code are the header files.

Sometimes it is difficult for students to appreciate the scope of problems faced by designers who work on large-scale software projects in industry. People experienced with such projects say that effective software reuse improves the software development process. Object-oriented programming facilitates software reuse, thus shortening development times and enhancing software quality.

The availability of substantial and useful class libraries delivers the maximum benefits of software reuse through inheritance. Just as shrink-wrapped software produced by independent software vendors became an explosive-growth industry with the arrival of the personal computer, interest in the creation and sale of class libraries is growing exponentially. Application designers build their applications with these libraries, and library designers are rewarded by having their libraries included with the applications. The standard C++ libraries that are shipped with C++ compilers tend to be rather general purpose and limited in scope. However, there is massive worldwide commitment to the development of class libraries for a huge variety of applications arenas.

Software Engineering Observation 12.9

At the design stage in an object-oriented system, the designer often determines that certain classes are closely related. The designer should "factor out" common attributes and behaviors and place these in a base class, then use inheritance to form derived classes, endowing them with capabilities beyond those inherited from the base class.

Software Engineering Observation 12.10

The creation of a derived class does not affect its base class's source code. Inheritance preserves the integrity of a base class.

Software Engineering Observation 12.11

Just as designers of non-object-oriented systems should avoid proliferation of functions, designers of object-oriented systems should avoid proliferation of classes. Proliferation of classes creates management problems and can hinder software reusability, because it becomes difficult for a client to locate the most appropriate class of a huge class library. The alternative is to create fewer classes that provide more substantial functionality, but such classes might provide too much functionality.

Performance Tip 12.3

If classes produced through inheritance are larger than they need to be (i.e., contain too much functionality), memory and processing resources might be wasted. Inherit from the class whose functionality is "closest" to what is needed.

Reading derived-class definitions can be confusing, because inherited members are not shown physically in the derived classes, but nevertheless are present. A similar problem exists when documenting derived-class members.

12.8 Wrap-Up

This chapter introduced inheritance—the ability to create a class by absorbing an existing class's data members and member functions and embellishing them with new capabilities. Through a series of examples using an employee inheritance hierarchy, you learned the notions of base classes and derived classes and used `public` inheritance to create a derived class that inherits members from a base class. The chapter introduced the access specifier `protected`—derived-class member functions can access `protected` base-class members. You learned how to access redefined base-class members by qualifying their names with the base-class name and binary scope resolution operator (`::`). You also saw the order in which constructors and destructors are called for objects of classes that are part of an inheritance hierarchy. Finally, we explained the three types of inheritance—`public`, `protected` and `private`—and the accessibility of base-class members in a derived class when using each type.

In Chapter 13, Object-Oriented Programming: Polymorphism, we build on our discussion of inheritance by introducing polymorphism—an object-oriented concept that enables us to write programs that handle, in a more general manner, objects of a wide variety of classes related by inheritance. After studying Chapter 13, you'll be familiar with classes, objects, encapsulation, inheritance and polymorphism—the essential concepts of object-oriented programming.

Summary

Section 12.1 Introduction
- Software reuse reduces program development time and cost.

Section 12.2 Base Classes and Derived Classes
- Inheritance is a form of software reuse in which you create a class that absorbs an existing class's data and behaviors and enhances them with new capabilities. The existing class is called the base class, and the new class is referred to as the derived class.
- A direct base class is the one from which a derived class explicitly inherits (specified by the class name to the right of the : in the first line of a class definition). An indirect base class is inherited from two or more levels up the class hierarchy.
- With single inheritance, a class is derived from one base class. With multiple inheritance, a class inherits from multiple (possibly unrelated) base classes.
- A derived class represents a more specialized group of objects. Typically, a derived class contains behaviors inherited from its base class plus additional behaviors. A derived class can also customize behaviors inherited from the base class.
- Every object of a derived class is also an object of that class's base class. However, a base-class object is not an object of that class's derived classes.
- The *is-a* relationship represents inheritance. In an *is-a* relationship, an object of a derived class also can be treated as an object of its base class.
- The *has-a* relationship represents composition—an object contains one or more objects of other classes as members, but does not disclose their behavior directly in its interface.
- A derived class cannot access the `private` members of its base class directly; allowing this would violate the encapsulation of the base class. A derived class can, however, access the `public` and `protected` members of its base class directly.
- A derived class can effect state changes in `private` base-class members, but only through non-`private` member functions provided in the base class and inherited into the derived class.
- When a base-class member function is inappropriate for a derived class, that member function can be redefined in the derived class with an appropriate implementation.
- Single-inheritance relationships form treelike hierarchical structures—a base class exists in a hierarchical relationship with its derived classes.
- It is possible to treat base-class objects and derived-class objects similarly; the commonality shared between the object types is expressed in the data members and member functions of the base class.

Section 12.3 `protected` Members
- A base class's `public` members are accessible anywhere that the program has a handle to an object of that base class or to an object of one of that base class's derived classes—or, when using the binary scope resolution operator, whenever the class's name is in scope.
- A base class's `private` members are accessible only within the definition of that base class or from friends of that class.
- A base class's `protected` members have an intermediate level of protection between `public` and `private` access. A base class's `protected` members can be accessed by members and `friends` of that base class and by members and `friends` of any classes derived from that base class.
- Unfortunately, `protected` data members often present two major problems. First, the derived-class object does not have to use a *set* function to change the value of the base-class's `protected` data. Second, derived-class member functions are more likely to depend on base-class implementation details.

- When a derived-class member function redefines a base-class member function, the base-class member function can be accessed from the derived class by qualifying the base-class member function name with the base-class name and the binary scope resolution operator (::).

Section 12.5 Constructors and Destructors in Derived Classes
- When an object of a derived class is instantiated, the base class's constructor is called immediately (either explicitly or implicitly) to initialize the base-class data members in the derived-class object (before the derived-class data members are initialized).

Section 12.6 `public`, `protected` and `private` Inheritance
- Declaring data members `private`, while providing non-`private` member functions to manipulate and perform validity checking on this data, enforces good software engineering.

- When a derived-class object is destroyed, the destructors are called in the reverse order of the constructors—first the derived-class destructor is called, then the base-class destructor is called.

- When deriving a class from a base class, the base class may be declared as either `public`, `protected` or `private`.

- When deriving a class from a `public` base class, `public` members of the base class become `public` members of the derived class, and `protected` members of the base class become `protected` members of the derived class.

- When deriving a class from a `protected` base class, `public` and `protected` members of the base class become `protected` members of the derived class.

- When deriving a class from a `private` base class, `public` and `protected` members of the base class become `private` members of the derived class.

Terminology

base class	indirect base class
base-class constructor	inherit the members of an existing class
base-class default constructor	inheritance
base-class destructor	*is-a* relationship
base-class initializer	multiple inheritance
brittle software	private base class
class hierarchy	private inheritance
composition	protected base class
customize software	protected inheritance
derived class	protected keyword
derived-class constructor	protected member of a class
derived-class destructor	public base class
direct base class	public inheritance
fragile software	qualified name
friend of a base class	redefine a base-class member function
friend of a derived class	single inheritance
has-a relationship	subclass
hierarchical relationship	superclass

Self-Review Exercises

12.1   Fill in the blanks in each of the following statements:
   a) _____ is a form of software reuse in which new classes absorb the data and behaviors of existing classes and embellish these classes with new capabilities.

b) A base class's _____ members can be accessed only in the base-class definition or in derived-class definitions.

c) In a(n) _____ relationship, an object of a derived class also can be treated as an object of its base class.

d) In a(n) _____ relationship, a class object has one or more objects of other classes as members.

e) In single inheritance, a class exists in a(n) _____ relationship with its derived classes.

f) A base class's _____ members are accessible within that base class and anywhere that the program has a handle to an object of that base class or to an object of one of its derived classes.

g) A base class's `protected` access members have a level of protection between those of `public` and _____ access.

h) C++ provides for _____, which allows a derived class to inherit from many base classes, even if the base classes are unrelated.

i) When an object of a derived class is instantiated, the base class's _____ is called implicitly or explicitly to do any necessary initialization of the base-class data members in the derived-class object.

j) When deriving a class from a base class with `public` inheritance, `public` members of the base class become _____ members of the derived class, and `protected` members of the base class become _____ members of the derived class.

k) When deriving a class from a base class with `protected` inheritance, `public` members of the base class become _____ members of the derived class, and `protected` members of the base class become _____ members of the derived class.

12.2 State whether each of the following is *true* or *false*. If *false*, explain why.

a) Base-class constructors are not inherited by derived classes.

b) A *has-a* relationship is implemented via inheritance.

c) A `Car` class has an *is-a* relationship with the `SteeringWheel` and `Brakes` classes.

d) Inheritance encourages the reuse of proven high-quality software.

e) When a derived-class object is destroyed, the destructors are called in the reverse order of the constructors.

Answers to Self-Review Exercises

12.1 a) Inheritance. b) `protected`. c) *is-a* or inheritance. d) *has-a* or composition or aggregation. e) hierarchical. f) `public`. g) `private`. h) multiple inheritance. i) constructor. j) `public`, `protected`. k) `protected`, `protected`.

12.2 a) True. b) False. A *has-a* relationship is implemented via composition. An *is-a* relationship is implemented via inheritance. c) False. This is an example of a *has-a* relationship. Class `Car` has an *is-a* relationship with class `Vehicle`. d) True. e) True.

Exercises

12.3 Many programs written with inheritance could be written with composition instead, and vice versa. Rewrite class `BasePlusCommissionEmployee` of the `CommissionEmployee`–`BasePlusCommissionEmployee` hierarchy to use composition rather than inheritance. After you do this, assess the relative merits of the two approaches for designing classes `CommissionEmployee` and `BasePlusCommissionEmployee`, as well as for object-oriented programs in general. Which approach is more natural? Why?

12.4 Discuss the ways in which inheritance promotes software reuse, saves time during program development and helps prevent errors.

12.5 Some programmers prefer not to use `protected` access because they believe it breaks the encapsulation of the base class. Discuss the relative merits of using `protected` access vs. using `private` access in base classes.

12.6 Draw an inheritance hierarchy for students at a university similar to the hierarchy shown in Fig. 12.2. Use `Student` as the base class of the hierarchy, then include classes `UndergraduateStudent` and `GraduateStudent` that derive from `Student`. Continue to extend the hierarchy as deep (i.e., as many levels) as possible. For example, `Freshman`, `Sophomore`, `Junior` and `Senior` might derive from `UndergraduateStudent`, and `DoctoralStudent` and `MastersStudent` might derive from `Graduate-Student`. After drawing the hierarchy, discuss the relationships that exist between the classes. [*Note:* You do not need to write any code for this exercise.]

12.7 The world of shapes is much richer than the shapes included in the inheritance hierarchy of Fig. 12.3. Write down all the shapes you can think of—both two-dimensional and three-dimensional—and form them into a more complete `Shape` hierarchy with as many levels as possible. Your hierarchy should have the base class `Shape` from which class `TwoDimensionalShape` and class `Three-DimensionalShape` are derived. [*Note:* You do not need to write any code for this exercise.] We'll use this hierarchy in the exercises of Chapter 13 to process a set of distinct shapes as objects of base-class `Shape`. (This technique, called polymorphism, is the subject of Chapter 13.)

12.8 Draw an inheritance hierarchy for classes `Quadrilateral`, `Trapezoid`, `Parallelogram`, `Rectangle` and `Square`. Use `Quadrilateral` as the base class of the hierarchy. Make the hierarchy as deep as possible.

12.9 (*Package Inheritance Hierarchy*) Package-delivery services, such as FedEx®, DHL® and UPS®, offer a number of different shipping options, each with specific costs associated. Create an inheritance hierarchy to represent various types of packages. Use `Package` as the base class of the hierarchy, then include classes `TwoDayPackage` and `OvernightPackage` that derive from `Package`. Base class `Package` should include data members representing the name, address, city, state and ZIP code for both the sender and the recipient of the package, in addition to data members that store the weight (in ounces) and cost per ounce to ship the package. `Package`'s constructor should initialize these data members. Ensure that the weight and cost per ounce contain positive values. `Package` should provide a `public` member function `calculateCost` that returns a `double` indicating the cost associated with shipping the package. `Package`'s `calculateCost` function should determine the cost by multiplying the weight by the cost per ounce. Derived class `TwoDayPackage` should inherit the functionality of base class `Package`, but also include a data member that represents a flat fee that the shipping company charges for two-day-delivery service. `TwoDayPackage`'s constructor should receive a value to initialize this data member. `TwoDayPackage` should redefine member function `calculate-Cost` so that it computes the shipping cost by adding the flat fee to the weight-based cost calculated by base class `Package`'s `calculateCost` function. Class `OvernightPackage` should inherit directly from class `Package` and contain an additional data member representing an additional fee per ounce charged for overnight-delivery service. `OvernightPackage` should redefine member function `calculateCost` so that it adds the additional fee per ounce to the standard cost per ounce before calculating the shipping cost. Write a test program that creates objects of each type of `Package` and tests member function `calculateCost`.

12.10 (*Account Inheritance Hierarchy*) Create an inheritance hierarchy that a bank might use to represent customers' bank accounts. All customers at this bank can deposit (i.e., credit) money into their accounts and withdraw (i.e., debit) money from their accounts. More specific types of accounts also exist. Savings accounts, for instance, earn interest on the money they hold. Checking accounts, on the other hand, charge a fee per transaction (i.e., credit or debit).

Create an inheritance hierarchy containing base class `Account` and derived classes `Savings-Account` and `CheckingAccount` that inherit from class `Account`. Base class `Account` should include one data member of type `double` to represent the account balance. The class should provide a constructor that receives an initial balance and uses it to initialize the data member. The constructor should validate the initial balance to ensure that it is greater than or equal to 0.0. If not, the balance should be set to 0.0 and the constructor should display an error message, indicating that the initial balance was invalid. The class should provide three member functions. Member function credit should add an amount to the current balance. Member function debit should withdraw money from the Account and ensure that the debit amount does not exceed the Account's balance. If it does, the balance should be left unchanged and the function should print the message "Debit amount exceeded account balance." Member function getBalance should return the current balance.

Derived class SavingsAccount should inherit the functionality of an Account, but also include a data member of type double indicating the interest rate (percentage) assigned to the Account. SavingsAccount's constructor should receive the initial balance, as well as an initial value for the SavingsAccount's interest rate. SavingsAccount should provide a public member function calculateInterest that returns a double indicating the amount of interest earned by an account. Member function calculateInterest should determine this amount by multiplying the interest rate by the account balance. [*Note:* SavingsAccount should inherit member functions credit and debit as is without redefining them.]

Derived class CheckingAccount should inherit from base class Account and include an additional data member of type double that represents the fee charged per transaction. CheckingAccount's constructor should receive the initial balance, as well as a parameter indicating a fee amount. Class CheckingAccount should redefine member functions credit and debit so that they subtract the fee from the account balance whenever either transaction is performed successfully. CheckingAccount's versions of these functions should invoke the base-class Account version to perform the updates to an account balance. CheckingAccount's debit function should charge a fee only if money is actually withdrawn (i.e., the debit amount does not exceed the account balance). [*Hint:* Define Account's debit function so that it returns a bool indicating whether money was withdrawn. Then use the return value to determine whether a fee should be charged.]

After defining the classes in this hierarchy, write a program that creates objects of each class and tests their member functions. Add interest to the SavingsAccount object by first invoking its calculateInterest function, then passing the returned interest amount to the object's credit function.

13

Object-Oriented Programming: Polymorphism

OBJECTIVES

In this chapter you'll learn:

- What polymorphism is, how it makes programming more convenient and how it makes systems more extensible and maintainable.

- To declare and use `virtual` functions to effect polymorphism.

- The distinction between abstract and concrete classes.

- To declare pure `virtual` functions to create abstract classes.

- How to use runtime type information (RTTI) with downcasting, `dynamic_cast`, `typeid` and `type_info`.

- How C++ implements `virtual` functions and dynamic binding "under the hood."

- How to use `virtual` destructors to ensure that all appropriate destructors run on an object.

13.1 Introduction

In Chapters 9–12, we discussed key object-oriented programming technologies including classes, objects, encapsulation, operator overloading and inheritance. We now continue our study of OOP by explaining and demonstrating polymorphism with inheritance hierarchies. Polymorphism enables us to "program in the general" rather than "program in the specific." In particular, polymorphism enables us to write programs that process objects of classes that are part of the same class hierarchy as if they were all objects of the hierarchy's base class. As we'll soon see, polymorphism works off base-class pointer handles and base-class reference handles, but not off name handles.

Consider the following example of polymorphism. Suppose we create a program that simulates the movement of several types of animals for a biological study. Classes `Fish`, `Frog` and `Bird` represent the three types of animals under investigation. Imagine that each of these classes inherits from base class `Animal`, which contains a function move and maintains an animal's current location. Each derived class implements function move. Our program maintains a `vector` of pointers to objects of the various `Animal` derived classes. To simulate the animals' movements, the program sends each object the same message once per second—namely, move. However, each specific type of `Animal` responds to a move message in its own unique way—a `Fish` might swim two feet, a `Frog` might jump three feet and a `Bird` might fly ten feet. The program issues the same message (i.e., move) to each animal object generically, but each object knows how to modify its location appropriately for its specific type of movement. Relying on each object to know how to "do the right thing" (i.e., do what is appropriate for that type of object) in response to the same function call is the key concept of polymorphism. The same message (in this case, move) sent to a variety of objects has "many forms" of results—hence the term polymorphism.

With polymorphism, we can design and implement systems that are easily extensible—new classes can be added with little or no modification to the general portions of the program, as long as the new classes are part of the inheritance hierarchy that the program processes generically. The only parts of a program that must be altered to accommodate new classes are those that require direct knowledge of the new classes that you add to the hierarchy. For example, if we create class `Tortoise` that inherits from class `Animal` (which might respond to a move message by crawling one inch), we need to write only the `Tortoise` class and the part of the simulation that instantiates a `Tortoise` object. The portions of the simulation that process each `Animal` generically can remain the same.

We begin with a sequence of small, focused examples that lead up to an understanding of `virtual` functions and dynamic binding—polymorphism's two underlying technologies. We then present a case study that revisits Chapter 12's `Employee` hierarchy. In the case study, we define a common "interface" (i.e., set of functionality) for all the classes in the hierarchy. This common functionality among employees is defined in a so-called abstract base class, `Employee`, from which classes `SalariedEmployee`, `HourlyEmployee` and `CommissionEmployee` inherit directly and class `BaseCommissionEmployee` inherits indirectly. We'll soon see what makes a class "abstract" or its opposite—"concrete."

In this hierarchy, every employee has an `earnings` function to calculate the employee's weekly pay. These `earnings` functions vary by employee type—for instance, `Salaried-Employees` are paid a fixed weekly salary regardless of the number of hours worked, while `HourlyEmployees` are paid by the hour and receive overtime pay. We show how to process each employee "in the general"—that is, using base-class pointers to call the `earnings` function of several derived-class objects. This way, you need to be concerned with only one type of function call, which can be used to execute several different functions based on the objects referred to by the base-class pointers.

A key feature of this chapter is its (optional) detailed discussion of polymorphism, `virtual` functions and dynamic binding "under the hood," which uses a detailed diagram to explain how polymorphism can be implemented in C++.

Occasionally, when performing polymorphic processing, we need to program "in the specific," meaning that operations need to be performed on a specific type of object in a hierarchy—the operation cannot be generally applied to several types of objects. We reuse our `Employee` hierarchy to demonstrate the powerful capabilities of runtime type information (RTTI) and dynamic casting, which enable a program to determine the type of an object at execution time and act on that object accordingly. We use these capabilities to determine whether a particular employee object is a `BasePlusCommissionEmployee`, then give that employee a 10 percent bonus on his or her base salary.

13.2 Polymorphism Examples

In this section, we discuss several polymorphism examples. With polymorphism, one function can cause different actions to occur, depending on the type of the object on which the function is invoked. This gives you tremendous expressive capability. If class Rectangle is derived from class Quadrilateral, then a Rectangle object is a more specific version of a Quadrilateral object. Therefore, any operation (such as calculating the perimeter or the area) that can be performed on an object of class Quadrilateral also can be performed on an object of class Rectangle. Such operations also can be performed on other kinds of Quadrilaterals, such as Squares, Parallelograms and Trapezoids. The polymorphism occurs when a program invokes a virtual function through a base-class (i.e., Quadrilateral) pointer or reference—C++ dynamically (i.e., at execution time) chooses the correct function for the class from which the object was instantiated. You'll see a code example that illustrates this process in Section 13.3.

As another example, suppose that we design a video game that manipulates objects of many different types, including objects of classes Martian, Venutian, Plutonian, SpaceShip and LaserBeam. Imagine that each of these classes inherits from the common base class SpaceObject, which contains member function draw. Each derived class implements this function in a manner appropriate for that class. A screen-manager program maintains a container (e.g., a vector) that holds SpaceObject pointers to objects of the various classes. To refresh the screen, the screen manager periodically sends each object the same message—namely, draw. Each type of object responds in a unique way. For example, a Martian object might draw itself in red with the appropriate number of antennae. A SpaceShip object might draw itself as a silver flying saucer. A LaserBeam object might draw itself as a bright red beam across the screen. Again, the same message (in this case, draw) sent to a variety of objects has "many forms" of results.

A polymorphic screen manager facilitates adding new classes to a system with minimal modifications to its code. Suppose that we want to add objects of class Mercurian to our video game. To do so, we must build a class Mercurian that inherits from SpaceObject, but provides its own definition of member function draw. Then, when pointers to objects of class Mercurian appear in the container, you do not need to modify the code for the screen manager. The screen manager invokes member function draw on every object in the container, regardless of the object's type, so the new Mercurian objects simply "plug right in." Thus, without modifying the system (other than to build and include the classes themselves), programmers can use polymorphism to accommodate additional classes, including ones that were not even envisioned when the system was created.

Software Engineering Observation 13.1

With virtual functions and polymorphism, you can deal in generalities and let the execution-time environment concern itself with the specifics. You can direct a variety of objects to behave in manners appropriate to those objects without even knowing their types (as long as those objects belong to the same inheritance hierarchy and are being accessed off a common base-class pointer).

Software Engineering Observation 13.2

Polymorphism promotes extensibility: Software written to invoke polymorphic behavior is written independently of the types of the objects to which messages are sent. Thus, new types of objects that can respond to existing messages can be incorporated into such a system without modifying the base system. Only client code that instantiates new objects must be modified to accommodate new types.

13.3 Relationships Among Objects in an Inheritance Hierarchy

Section 12.4 created an employee class hierarchy, in which class BasePlusCommission-Employee inherited from class CommissionEmployee. The Chapter 12 examples manipulated CommissionEmployee and BasePlusCommissionEmployee objects by using the objects' names to invoke their member functions. We now examine the relationships among classes in a hierarchy more closely. The next several sections present a series of examples that demonstrate how base-class and derived-class pointers can be aimed at base-class and derived-class objects, and how those pointers can be used to invoke member functions that manipulate those objects. In Section 13.3.4, we demonstrate how to get polymorphic behavior from base-class pointers aimed at derived-class objects.

In Section 13.3.1, we assign the address of a derived-class object to a base-class pointer, then show that invoking a function via the base-class pointer invokes the base-class functionality—i.e., the type of the handle determines which function is called. In Section 13.3.2, we assign the address of a base-class object to a derived-class pointer, which results in a compilation error. We discuss the error message and investigate why the compiler does not allow such an assignment. In Section 13.3.3, we assign the address of a derived-class object to a base-class pointer, then examine how the base-class pointer can be used to invoke only the base-class functionality—when we attempt to invoke derived-class member functions through the base-class pointer, compilation errors occur. Finally, in Section 13.3.4, we introduce virtual functions and polymorphism by declaring a base-class function as virtual. We then assign the address of a derived-class object to the base-class pointer and use that pointer to invoke derived-class functionality—precisely the capability we need to achieve polymorphic behavior.

A key concept in these examples is to demonstrate that an object of a derived class can be treated as an object of its base class. This enables various interesting manipulations. For example, a program can create an array of base-class pointers that point to objects of many derived-class types. Despite the fact that the derived-class objects are of different types, the compiler allows this because each derived-class object *is an* object of its base class. However, we cannot treat a base-class object as an object of any of its derived classes. For example, a CommissionEmployee is not a BasePlusCommissionEmployee in the hierarchy defined in Chapter 12—a CommissionEmployee does not have a baseSalary data member and does not have member functions setBaseSalary and getBaseSalary. The *is-a* relationship applies only from a derived class to its direct and indirect base classes.

13.3.1 Invoking Base-Class Functions from Derived-Class Objects

The example in Figs. 13.1–13.5 demonstrates three ways to aim base-class pointers and derived-class pointers at base-class objects and derived-class objects. The first two are straightforward—we aim a base-class pointer at a base-class object (and invoke base-class functionality), and we aim a derived-class pointer at a derived-class object (and invoke derived-class functionality). Then, we demonstrate the relationship between derived classes and base classes (i.e., the *is-a* relationship of inheritance) by aiming a base-class pointer at a derived-class object (and showing that the base-class functionality is indeed available in the derived-class object).

Class CommissionEmployee (Figs. 13.1–13.2), which we discussed in Chapter 12, is used to represent employees who are paid a percentage of their sales. Class BasePlusCom-

```
1   // Fig. 13.1: CommissionEmployee.h
2   // CommissionEmployee class definition represents a commission employee.
3   #ifndef COMMISSION_H
4   #define COMMISSION_H
5
6   #include <string> // C++ standard string class
7   using std::string;
8
9   class CommissionEmployee
10  {
11  public:
12     CommissionEmployee( const string &, const string &, const string &,
13        double = 0.0, double = 0.0 );
14
15     void setFirstName( const string & ); // set first name
16     string getFirstName() const; // return first name
17
18     void setLastName( const string & ); // set last name
19     string getLastName() const; // return last name
20
21     void setSocialSecurityNumber( const string & ); // set SSN
22     string getSocialSecurityNumber() const; // return SSN
23
24     void setGrossSales( double ); // set gross sales amount
25     double getGrossSales() const; // return gross sales amount
26
27     void setCommissionRate( double ); // set commission rate
28     double getCommissionRate() const; // return commission rate
29
30     double earnings() const; // calculate earnings
31     void print() const; // print CommissionEmployee object
32  private:
33     string firstName;
34     string lastName;
35     string socialSecurityNumber;
36     double grossSales; // gross weekly sales
37     double commissionRate; // commission percentage
38  }; // end class CommissionEmployee
39
40  #endif
```

Fig. 13.1 | CommissionEmployee class header file.

missionEmployee (Figs. 13.3–13.4), which we also discussed in Chapter 12, is used to represent employees who receive a base salary plus a percentage of their sales. Each Base-PlusCommissionEmployee object *is a* CommissionEmployee that also has a base salary. Class BasePlusCommissionEmployee's earnings member function (lines 32–35 of Fig. 13.4) redefines class CommissionEmployee's earnings member function (lines 79–82 of Fig. 13.2) to include the object's base salary. Class BasePlusCommissionEmployee's print member function (lines 38–46 of Fig. 13.4) redefines class CommissionEmployee's print member function (lines 85–92 of Fig. 13.2) to display the same information as the print function in class CommissionEmployee, as well as the employee's base salary.

```
 1   // Fig. 13.2: CommissionEmployee.cpp
 2   // Class CommissionEmployee member-function definitions.
 3   #include <iostream>
 4   using std::cout;
 5
 6   #include "CommissionEmployee.h" // CommissionEmployee class definition
 7
 8   // constructor
 9   CommissionEmployee::CommissionEmployee(
10      const string &first, const string &last, const string &ssn,
11      double sales, double rate )
12      : firstName( first ), lastName( last ), socialSecurityNumber( ssn )
13   {
14      setGrossSales( sales ); // validate and store gross sales
15      setCommissionRate( rate ); // validate and store commission rate
16   } // end CommissionEmployee constructor
17
18   // set first name
19   void CommissionEmployee::setFirstName( const string &first )
20   {
21      firstName = first; // should validate
22   } // end function setFirstName
23
24   // return first name
25   string CommissionEmployee::getFirstName() const
26   {
27      return firstName;
28   } // end function getFirstName
29
30   // set last name
31   void CommissionEmployee::setLastName( const string &last )
32   {
33      lastName = last;   // should validate
34   } // end function setLastName
35
36   // return last name
37   string CommissionEmployee::getLastName() const
38   {
39      return lastName;
40   } // end function getLastName
41
42   // set social security number
43   void CommissionEmployee::setSocialSecurityNumber( const string &ssn )
44   {
45      socialSecurityNumber = ssn; // should validate
46   } // end function setSocialSecurityNumber
47
48   // return social security number
49   string CommissionEmployee::getSocialSecurityNumber() const
50   {
51      return socialSecurityNumber;
52   } // end function getSocialSecurityNumber
53
```

Fig. 13.2 | CommissionEmployee class implementation file. (Part 1 of 2.)

```
54   // set gross sales amount
55   void CommissionEmployee::setGrossSales( double sales )
56   {
57      grossSales = ( sales < 0.0 ) ? 0.0 : sales;
58   } // end function setGrossSales
59
60   // return gross sales amount
61   double CommissionEmployee::getGrossSales() const
62   {
63      return grossSales;
64   } // end function getGrossSales
65
66   // set commission rate
67   void CommissionEmployee::setCommissionRate( double rate )
68   {
69      commissionRate = ( rate > 0.0 && rate < 1.0 ) ? rate : 0.0;
70   } // end function setCommissionRate
71
72   // return commission rate
73   double CommissionEmployee::getCommissionRate() const
74   {
75      return commissionRate;
76   } // end function getCommissionRate
77
78   // calculate earnings
79   double CommissionEmployee::earnings() const
80   {
81      return getCommissionRate() * getGrossSales();
82   } // end function earnings
83
84   // print CommissionEmployee object
85   void CommissionEmployee::print() const
86   {
87      cout << "commission employee: "
88         << getFirstName() << ' ' << getLastName()
89         << "\nsocial security number: " << getSocialSecurityNumber()
90         << "\ngross sales: " << getGrossSales()
91         << "\ncommission rate: " << getCommissionRate();
92   } // end function print
```

Fig. 13.2 | CommissionEmployee class implementation file. (Part 2 of 2.)

```
1    // Fig. 13.3: BasePlusCommissionEmployee.h
2    // BasePlusCommissionEmployee class derived from class
3    // CommissionEmployee.
4    #ifndef BASEPLUS_H
5    #define BASEPLUS_H
6
7    #include <string> // C++ standard string class
8    using std::string;
9
```

Fig. 13.3 | BasePlusCommissionEmployee class header file. (Part 1 of 2.)

```
10  #include "CommissionEmployee.h" // CommissionEmployee class declaration
11
12  class BasePlusCommissionEmployee : public CommissionEmployee
13  {
14  public:
15     BasePlusCommissionEmployee( const string &, const string &,
16        const string &, double = 0.0, double = 0.0, double = 0.0 );
17
18     void setBaseSalary( double ); // set base salary
19     double getBaseSalary() const; // return base salary
20
21     double earnings() const; // calculate earnings
22     void print() const; // print BasePlusCommissionEmployee object
23  private:
24     double baseSalary; // base salary
25  }; // end class BasePlusCommissionEmployee
26
27  #endif
```

Fig. 13.3 | BasePlusCommissionEmployee class header file. (Part 2 of 2.)

```
1   // Fig. 13.4: BasePlusCommissionEmployee.cpp
2   // Class BasePlusCommissionEmployee member-function definitions.
3   #include <iostream>
4   using std::cout;
5
6   // BasePlusCommissionEmployee class definition
7   #include "BasePlusCommissionEmployee.h"
8
9   // constructor
10  BasePlusCommissionEmployee::BasePlusCommissionEmployee(
11     const string &first, const string &last, const string &ssn,
12     double sales, double rate, double salary )
13     // explicitly call base-class constructor
14     : CommissionEmployee( first, last, ssn, sales, rate )
15  {
16     setBaseSalary( salary ); // validate and store base salary
17  } // end BasePlusCommissionEmployee constructor
18
19  // set base salary
20  void BasePlusCommissionEmployee::setBaseSalary( double salary )
21  {
22     baseSalary = ( salary < 0.0 ) ? 0.0 : salary;
23  } // end function setBaseSalary
24
25  // return base salary
26  double BasePlusCommissionEmployee::getBaseSalary() const
27  {
28     return baseSalary;
29  } // end function getBaseSalary
30
```

Fig. 13.4 | BasePlusCommissionEmployee class implementation file. (Part 1 of 2.)

```
31   // calculate earnings
32   double BasePlusCommissionEmployee::earnings() const
33   {
34      return getBaseSalary() + CommissionEmployee::earnings();
35   } // end function earnings
36
37   // print BasePlusCommissionEmployee object
38   void BasePlusCommissionEmployee::print() const
39   {
40      cout << "base-salaried ";
41
42      // invoke CommissionEmployee's print function
43      CommissionEmployee::print();
44
45      cout << "\nbase salary: " << getBaseSalary();
46   } // end function print
```

Fig. 13.4 | BasePlusCommissionEmployee class implementation file. (Part 2 of 2.)

In Fig. 13.5, lines 19–20 create a CommissionEmployee object and line 23 creates a pointer to a CommissionEmployee object; lines 26–27 create a BasePlusCommission-Employee object and line 30 creates a pointer to a BasePlusCommissionEmployee object. Lines 37 and 39 use each object's name (commissionEmployee and basePlusCommis-sionEmployee, respectively) to invoke each object's print member function. Line 42 assigns the address of base-class object commissionEmployee to base-class pointer commissionEmployeePtr, which line 45 uses to invoke member function print on that CommissionEmployee object. This invokes the version of print defined in base class Com-missionEmployee. Similarly, line 48 assigns the address of derived-class object basePlus-CommissionEmployee to derived-class pointer basePlusCommissionEmployeePtr, which line 52 uses to invoke member function print on that BasePlusCommissionEmployee object. This invokes the version of print defined in derived class BasePlusCommission-Employee. Line 55 then assigns the address of derived-class object basePlusCommission-Employee to base-class pointer commissionEmployeePtr, which line 59 uses to invoke member function print. This "crossover" is allowed because an object of a derived class *is an* object of its base class. Note that despite the fact that the base class Commission-

```
1    // Fig. 13.5: fig13_05.cpp
2    // Aiming base-class and derived-class pointers at base-class
3    // and derived-class objects, respectively.
4    #include <iostream>
5    using std::cout;
6    using std::endl;
7    using std::fixed;
8
9    #include <iomanip>
10   using std::setprecision;
11
```

Fig. 13.5 | Assigning addresses of base-class and derived-class objects to base-class and derived-class pointers. (Part 1 of 3.)

```
12   // include class definitions
13   #include "CommissionEmployee.h"
14   #include "BasePlusCommissionEmployee.h"
15
16   int main()
17   {
18      // create base-class object
19      CommissionEmployee commissionEmployee(
20         "Sue", "Jones", "222-22-2222", 10000, .06 );
21
22      // create base-class pointer
23      CommissionEmployee *commissionEmployeePtr = 0;
24
25      // create derived-class object
26      BasePlusCommissionEmployee basePlusCommissionEmployee(
27         "Bob", "Lewis", "333-33-3333", 5000, .04, 300 );
28
29      // create derived-class pointer
30      BasePlusCommissionEmployee *basePlusCommissionEmployeePtr = 0;
31
32      // set floating-point output formatting
33      cout << fixed << setprecision( 2 );
34
35      // output objects commissionEmployee and basePlusCommissionEmployee
36      cout << "Print base-class and derived-class objects:\n\n";
37      commissionEmployee.print(); // invokes base-class print
38      cout << "\n\n";
39      basePlusCommissionEmployee.print(); // invokes derived-class print
40
41      // aim base-class pointer at base-class object and print
42      commissionEmployeePtr = &commissionEmployee; // perfectly natural
43      cout << "\n\n\nCalling print with base-class pointer to "
44         << "\nbase-class object invokes base-class print function:\n\n";
45      commissionEmployeePtr->print(); // invokes base-class print
46
47      // aim derived-class pointer at derived-class object and print
48      basePlusCommissionEmployeePtr = &basePlusCommissionEmployee; // natural
49      cout << "\n\n\nCalling print with derived-class pointer to "
50         << "\nderived-class object invokes derived-class "
51         << "print function:\n\n";
52      basePlusCommissionEmployeePtr->print(); // invokes derived-class print
53
54      // aim base-class pointer at derived-class object and print
55      commissionEmployeePtr = &basePlusCommissionEmployee;
56      cout << "\n\n\nCalling print with base-class pointer to "
57         << "derived-class object\ninvokes base-class print "
58         << "function on that derived-class object:\n\n";
59      commissionEmployeePtr->print(); // invokes base-class print
60      cout << endl;
61      return 0;
62   } // end main
```

Fig. 13.5 | Assigning addresses of base-class and derived-class objects to base-class and derived-class pointers. (Part 2 of 3.)

```
Print base-class and derived-class objects:

commission employee: Sue Jones
social security number: 222-22-2222
gross sales: 10000.00
commission rate: 0.06

base-salaried commission employee: Bob Lewis
social security number: 333-33-3333
gross sales: 5000.00
commission rate: 0.04
base salary: 300.00


Calling print with base-class pointer to
base-class object invokes base-class print function:

commission employee: Sue Jones
social security number: 222-22-2222
gross sales: 10000.00
commission rate: 0.06


Calling print with derived-class pointer to
derived-class object invokes derived-class print function:

base-salaried commission employee: Bob Lewis
social security number: 333-33-3333
gross sales: 5000.00
commission rate: 0.04
base salary: 300.00


Calling print with base-class pointer to derived-class object
invokes base-class print function on that derived-class object:

commission employee: Bob Lewis
social security number: 333-33-3333
gross sales: 5000.00
commission rate: 0.04
```

Fig. 13.5 | Assigning addresses of base-class and derived-class objects to base-class and derived-class pointers. (Part 3 of 3.)

Employee pointer points to a derived class BasePlusCommissionEmployee object, the base class CommissionEmployee's print member function is invoked (rather than BasePlus-CommissionEmployee's print function). The output of each print member-function invocation in this program reveals that *the invoked functionality depends on the type of the handle (i.e., the pointer or reference type) used to invoke the function, not the type of the object to which the handle points.* In Section 13.3.4, when we introduce virtual functions, we demonstrate that it is possible to invoke the object type's functionality, rather than invoke the handle type's functionality. We'll see that this is crucial to implementing polymorphic behavior—the key topic of this chapter.

13.3.2 Aiming Derived-Class Pointers at Base-Class Objects

In Section 13.3.1, we assigned the address of a derived-class object to a base-class pointer and explained that the C++ compiler allows this assignment, because a derived-class object *is a* base-class object. We take the opposite approach in Fig. 13.6, as we aim a derived-class pointer at a base-class object. [*Note:* This program uses classes CommissionEmployee and BasePlusCommissionEmployee of Figs. 13.1–13.4.] Lines 8–9 of Fig. 13.6 create a CommissionEmployee object, and line 10 creates a BasePlusCommissionEmployee pointer. Line 14 attempts to assign the address of base-class object commissionEmployee to derived-class pointer basePlusCommissionEmployeePtr, but the C++ compiler generates an error. The compiler prevents this assignment, because a CommissionEmployee is not a BasePlusCommissionEmployee. Consider the consequences if the compiler were to allow this assignment. Through a BasePlusCommissionEmployee pointer, we can invoke every BasePlusCommissionEmployee member function, including setBaseSalary, for the object to which the pointer points (i.e., the base-class object commissionEmployee). However, the CommissionEmployee object does not provide a setBaseSalary member function, nor does it provide a baseSalary data member to set. This could lead to problems, because member function setBaseSalary would assume that there is a baseSalary data member to set at its "usual location" in a BasePlusCommissionEmployee object. This memory does not belong to the CommissionEmployee object, so member function setBaseSalary might overwrite other important data in memory, possibly data that belongs to a different object.

```cpp
1   // Fig. 13.6: fig13_06.cpp
2   // Aiming a derived-class pointer at a base-class object.
3   #include "CommissionEmployee.h"
4   #include "BasePlusCommissionEmployee.h"
5
6   int main()
7   {
8      CommissionEmployee commissionEmployee(
9         "Sue", "Jones", "222-22-2222", 10000, .06 );
10     BasePlusCommissionEmployee *basePlusCommissionEmployeePtr = 0;
11
12     // aim derived-class pointer at base-class object
13     // Error: a CommissionEmployee is not a BasePlusCommissionEmployee
14     basePlusCommissionEmployeePtr = &commissionEmployee;
15     return 0;
16  } // end main
```

Borland C++ command-line compiler error messages:

```
Error E2034 Fig13_06\fig13_06.cpp 14: Cannot convert 'CommissionEmployee *'
   to 'BasePlusCommissionEmployee *' in function main()
```

GNU C++ compiler error messages:

```
fig13_06.cpp:14: error: invalid conversion from `CommissionEmployee*' to
   `BasePlusCommissionEmployee*'
```

Fig. 13.6 | Aiming a derived-class pointer at a base-class object. (Part 1 of 2.)

Microsoft Visual C++ 2005 compiler error messages:

```
C:\cpphtp6_examples\ch13\Fig13_06\fig13_06.cpp(14) : error C2440:
   '=' : cannot convert from 'CommissionEmployee *__w64 ' to
   'BasePlusCommissionEmployee *'
        Cast from base to derived requires dynamic_cast or static_cast
```

Fig. 13.6 | Aiming a derived-class pointer at a base-class object. (Part 2 of 2.)

13.3.3 Derived-Class Member-Function Calls via Base-Class Pointers

Off a base-class pointer, the compiler allows us to invoke only base-class member functions. Thus, if a base-class pointer is aimed at a derived-class object, and an attempt is made to access a *derived-class-only member function*, a compilation error will occur.

Figure 13.7 shows the consequences of attempting to invoke a derived-class member function off a base-class pointer. [*Note:* We are again using classes CommissionEmployee and BasePlusCommissionEmployee of Figs. 13.1–13.4.] Line 9 creates commissionEmployeePtr—a pointer to a CommissionEmployee object—and lines 10–11 create a BasePlusCommissionEmployee object. Line 14 aims commissionEmployeePtr at derived-class object basePlusCommissionEmployee. Recall from Section 13.3.1 that this is allowed,

```
1   // Fig. 13.7: fig13_07.cpp
2   // Attempting to invoke derived-class-only member functions
3   // through a base-class pointer.
4   #include "CommissionEmployee.h"
5   #include "BasePlusCommissionEmployee.h"
6
7   int main()
8   {
9      CommissionEmployee *commissionEmployeePtr = 0; // base class
10     BasePlusCommissionEmployee basePlusCommissionEmployee(
11        "Bob", "Lewis", "333-33-3333", 5000, .04, 300 ); // derived class
12
13     // aim base-class pointer at derived-class object
14     commissionEmployeePtr = &basePlusCommissionEmployee;
15
16     // invoke base-class member functions on derived-class
17     // object through base-class pointer (allowed)
18     string firstName = commissionEmployeePtr->getFirstName();
19     string lastName = commissionEmployeePtr->getLastName();
20     string ssn = commissionEmployeePtr->getSocialSecurityNumber();
21     double grossSales = commissionEmployeePtr->getGrossSales();
22     double commissionRate = commissionEmployeePtr->getCommissionRate();
23
24     // attempt to invoke derived-class-only member functions
25     // on derived-class object through base-class pointer (disallowed)
26     double baseSalary = commissionEmployeePtr->getBaseSalary();
27     commissionEmployeePtr->setBaseSalary( 500 );
28     return 0;
29  } // end main
```

Fig. 13.7 | Attempting to invoke derived-class-only functions via a base-class pointer. (Part 1 of 2.)

Borland C++ command-line compiler error messages:

```
Error E2316 Fig13_07\fig13_07.cpp 26: 'getBaseSalary' is not a member of
    'CommissionEmployee' in function main()
Error E2316 Fig13_07\fig13_07.cpp 27: 'setBaseSalary' is not a member of
    'CommissionEmployee' in function main()
```

Microsoft Visual C++ 2005 compiler error messages:

```
C:\cpphtp6_examples\ch13\Fig13_07\fig13_07.cpp(26) : error C2039:
    'getBaseSalary' : is not a member of 'CommissionEmployee'
        C:\cpphtp6_examples\ch13\Fig13_07\CommissionEmployee.h(10) :
            see declaration of 'CommissionEmployee'
C:\cpphtp6_examples\ch13\Fig13_07\fig13_07.cpp(27) : error C2039:
    'setBaseSalary' : is not a member of 'CommissionEmployee'
        C:\cpphtp6_examples\ch13\Fig13_07\CommissionEmployee.h(10) :
            see declaration of 'CommissionEmployee'
```

GNU C++ compiler error messages:

```
fig13_07.cpp:26: error: `getBaseSalary' undeclared (first use this function)
fig13_07.cpp:26: error: (Each undeclared identifier is reported only once for
    each function it appears in.)
fig13_07.cpp:27: error: `setBaseSalary' undeclared (first use this function)
```

Fig. 13.7 | Attempting to invoke derived-class-only functions via a base-class pointer. (Part 2 of 2.)

because a BasePlusCommissionEmployee *is a* CommissionEmployee (in the sense that a BasePlusCommissionEmployee object contains all the functionality of a CommissionEmployee object). Lines 18–22 invoke base-class member functions getFirstName, getLastName, getSocialSecurityNumber, getGrossSales and getCommissionRate off the base-class pointer. All of these calls are legitimate, because BasePlusCommissionEmployee inherits these member functions from CommissionEmployee. We know that commissionEmployeePtr is aimed at a BasePlusCommissionEmployee object, so in lines 26–27 we attempt to invoke BasePlusCommissionEmployee member functions getBaseSalary and setBaseSalary. The compiler generates errors on both of these calls, because they are not made to member functions of base-class CommissionEmployee. The handle can be used to invoke only those functions that are members of that handle's associated class type. (In this case, off a CommissionEmployee *, we can invoke only CommissionEmployee member functions setFirstName, getFirstName, setLastName, getLastName, setSocialSecurityNumber, getSocialSecurityNumber, setGrossSales, getGrossSales, setCommissionRate, getCommissionRate, earnings and print.)

The compiler does allow access to derived-class-only members from a base-class pointer that is aimed at a derived-class object if we explicitly cast the base-class pointer to a derived-class pointer—a technique known as downcasting. As you learned in Section 13.3.1, it is possible to aim a base-class pointer at a derived-class object. However, as we demonstrated in Fig. 13.7, a base-class pointer can be used to invoke only the functions declared in the base class. Downcasting allows a derived-class-specific operation on a derived-class object pointed to by a base-class pointer. After a downcast, the program can invoke derived-class functions that are not in the base class. We'll show you a concrete example of downcasting in Section 13.8.

Software Engineering Observation 13.3

If the address of a derived-class object has been assigned to a pointer of one of its direct or indirect base classes, it is acceptable to cast that base-class pointer back to a pointer of the derived-class type. In fact, this must be done to send that derived-class object messages that do not appear in the base class.

13.3.4 Virtual Functions

In Section 13.3.1, we aimed a base-class `CommissionEmployee` pointer at a derived-class `BasePlusCommissionEmployee` object, then invoked member function `print` through that pointer. Recall that the type of the handle determines which class's functionality to invoke. In that case, the `CommissionEmployee` pointer invoked the `CommissionEmployee` member function `print` on the `BasePlusCommissionEmployee` object, even though the pointer was aimed at a `BasePlusCommissionEmployee` object that has its own customized `print` function. *With virtual functions, the type of the object being pointed to, not the type of the handle, determines which version of a virtual function to invoke.*

First, we consider why `virtual` functions are useful. Suppose that a set of shape classes such as `Circle`, `Triangle`, `Rectangle` and `Square` are all derived from base class `Shape`. Each of these classes might be endowed with the ability to draw itself via a member function `draw`. Although each class has its own `draw` function, the function for each shape is quite different. In a program that draws a set of shapes, it would be useful to be able to treat all the shapes generically as objects of the base class `Shape`. Then, to draw any shape, we could simply use a base-class `Shape` pointer to invoke function `draw` and let the program determine dynamically (i.e., at runtime) which derived-class `draw` function to use, based on the type of the object to which the base-class `Shape` pointer points at any given time.

To enable this kind of behavior, we declare `draw` in the base class as a **virtual function**, and we **override** `draw` in each of the derived classes to draw the appropriate shape. From an implementation perspective, overriding a function is no different than redefining one (which is the approach we have been using until now). An overridden function in a derived class has the same signature and return type (i.e., prototype) as the function it overrides in its base class. If we do not declare the base-class function as `virtual`, we can redefine that function. By contrast, if we declare the base-class function as `virtual`, we can override that function to enable polymorphic behavior. We declare a `virtual` function by preceding the function's prototype with the keyword `virtual` in the base class. For example,

```
virtual void draw() const;
```

would appear in base class `Shape`. The preceding prototype declares that function `draw` is a `virtual` function that takes no arguments and returns nothing. This function is declared `const` because a `draw` function typically would not make changes to the `Shape` object on which it is invoked—virtual functions do not have to be `const` functions.

Software Engineering Observation 13.4

Once a function is declared virtual, it remains virtual all the way down the inheritance hierarchy from that point, even if that function is not explicitly declared virtual when a derived class overrides it.

Good Programming Practice 13.1

Even though certain functions are implicitly virtual *because of a declaration made higher in the class hierarchy, explicitly declare these functions* virtual *at every level of the hierarchy to promote program clarity.*

Error-Prevention Tip 13.1

When a programmer browses a class hierarchy to locate a class to reuse, it is possible that a function in that class will exhibit virtual *function behavior even though it is not explicitly declared* virtual. *This happens when the class inherits a* virtual *function from its base class, and it can lead to subtle logic errors. Such errors can be avoided by explicitly declaring all* virtual *functions* virtual *throughout the inheritance hierarchy.*

Software Engineering Observation 13.5

When a derived class chooses not to override a virtual *function from its base class, the derived class simply inherits its base class's* virtual *function implementation.*

If a program invokes a virtual function through a base-class pointer to a derived-class object (e.g., shapePtr->draw()), the program will choose the correct derived-class draw function dynamically (i.e., at execution time) based on the object type—not the pointer type. Choosing the appropriate function to call at execution time (rather than at compile time) is known as dynamic binding or late binding.

When a virtual function is called by referencing a specific object by name and using the dot member-selection operator (e.g., squareObject.draw()), the function invocation is resolved at compile time (this is called static binding) and the virtual function that is called is the one defined for (or inherited by) the class of that particular object—this is not polymorphic behavior. Thus, dynamic binding with virtual functions occurs only off pointer (and, as we'll soon see, reference) handles.

Now let's see how virtual functions can enable polymorphic behavior in our employee hierarchy. Figures 13.8–13.9 are the header files for classes CommissionEmployee and BasePlusCommissionEmployee, respectively. Note that the only difference between these files and those of Fig. 13.1 and Fig. 13.3 is that we specify each class's earnings and print member functions as virtual (lines 30–31 of Fig. 13.8 and lines 21–22 of Fig. 13.9). Because functions earnings and print are virtual in class CommissionEmployee, class BasePlusCommissionEmployee's earnings and print functions override class CommissionEmployee's. Now, if we aim a base-class CommissionEmployee pointer at a derived-class BasePlusCommissionEmployee object, and the program uses that pointer to call either function earnings or print, the BasePlusCommissionEmployee object's corresponding function will be invoked. There were no changes to the member-function implementations of classes CommissionEmployee and BasePlusCommissionEmployee, so we reuse the versions of Fig. 13.2 and Fig. 13.4.

We modified Fig. 13.5 to create the program of Fig. 13.10. Lines 46–57 demonstrate again that a CommissionEmployee pointer aimed at a CommissionEmployee object can be used to invoke CommissionEmployee functionality, and a BasePlusCommissionEmployee pointer aimed at a BasePlusCommissionEmployee object can be used to invoke BasePlusCommissionEmployee functionality. Line 60 aims base-class pointer commissionEmployeePtr at derived-class object basePlusCommissionEmployee. Note that when line 67 invokes member function print off the base-class pointer, the derived-class BasePlusCommissionEmployee's print member function is invoked, so line 67 outputs different text than line 59 does in Fig. 13.5 (when member function print was not declared virtual).

```
1  // Fig. 13.8: CommissionEmployee.h
2  // CommissionEmployee class definition represents a commission employee.
3  #ifndef COMMISSION_H
4  #define COMMISSION_H
5
6  #include <string> // C++ standard string class
7  using std::string;
8
9  class CommissionEmployee
10 {
11 public:
12    CommissionEmployee( const string &, const string &, const string &,
13       double = 0.0, double = 0.0 );
14
15    void setFirstName( const string & ); // set first name
16    string getFirstName() const; // return first name
17
18    void setLastName( const string & ); // set last name
19    string getLastName() const; // return last name
20
21    void setSocialSecurityNumber( const string & ); // set SSN
22    string getSocialSecurityNumber() const; // return SSN
23
24    void setGrossSales( double ); // set gross sales amount
25    double getGrossSales() const; // return gross sales amount
26
27    void setCommissionRate( double ); // set commission rate
28    double getCommissionRate() const; // return commission rate
29
30    virtual double earnings() const; // calculate earnings
31    virtual void print() const; // print CommissionEmployee object
32 private:
33    string firstName;
34    string lastName;
35    string socialSecurityNumber;
36    double grossSales; // gross weekly sales
37    double commissionRate; // commission percentage
38 }; // end class CommissionEmployee
39
40 #endif
```

Fig. 13.8 | CommissionEmployee class header file declares earnings and print functions as virtual.

```
1  // Fig. 13.9: BasePlusCommissionEmployee.h
2  // BasePlusCommissionEmployee class derived from class
3  // CommissionEmployee.
4  #ifndef BASEPLUS_H
5  #define BASEPLUS_H
6
```

Fig. 13.9 | BasePlusCommissionEmployee class header file declares earnings and print functions as virtual. (Part 1 of 2.)

```
 7   #include <string> // C++ standard string class
 8   using std::string;
 9
10   #include "CommissionEmployee.h" // CommissionEmployee class declaration
11
12   class BasePlusCommissionEmployee : public CommissionEmployee
13   {
14   public:
15      BasePlusCommissionEmployee( const string &, const string &,
16         const string &, double = 0.0, double = 0.0, double = 0.0 );
17
18      void setBaseSalary( double ); // set base salary
19      double getBaseSalary() const; // return base salary
20
21      virtual double earnings() const; // calculate earnings
22      virtual void print() const; // print BasePlusCommissionEmployee object
23   private:
24      double baseSalary; // base salary
25   }; // end class BasePlusCommissionEmployee
26
27   #endif
```

Fig. 13.9 | BasePlusCommissionEmployee class header file declares earnings and print functions as virtual. (Part 2 of 2.)

We see that declaring a member function virtual causes the program to dynamically determine which function to invoke based on the type of object to which the handle points, rather than on the type of the handle. Note again that when commissionEmployeePtr points to a CommissionEmployee object (line 46), class CommissionEmployee's print function is invoked, and when CommissionEmployeePtr points to a BasePlusCommissionEmployee object, class BasePlusCommissionEmployee's print function is invoked. Thus, the same message—print, in this case—sent (off a base-class pointer) to a variety of objects related by inheritance to that base class, takes on many forms—this is polymorphic behavior.

```
 1   // Fig. 13.10: fig13_10.cpp
 2   // Introducing polymorphism, virtual functions and dynamic binding.
 3   #include <iostream>
 4   using std::cout;
 5   using std::endl;
 6   using std::fixed;
 7
 8   #include <iomanip>
 9   using std::setprecision;
10
11   // include class definitions
12   #include "CommissionEmployee.h"
13   #include "BasePlusCommissionEmployee.h"
```

Fig. 13.10 | Demonstrating polymorphism by invoking a derived-class virtual function via a base-class pointer to a derived-class object. (Part 1 of 3.)

```
14
15   int main()
16   {
17      // create base-class object
18      CommissionEmployee commissionEmployee(
19         "Sue", "Jones", "222-22-2222", 10000, .06 );
20
21      // create base-class pointer
22      CommissionEmployee *commissionEmployeePtr = 0;
23
24      // create derived-class object
25      BasePlusCommissionEmployee basePlusCommissionEmployee(
26         "Bob", "Lewis", "333-33-3333", 5000, .04, 300 );
27
28      // create derived-class pointer
29      BasePlusCommissionEmployee *basePlusCommissionEmployeePtr = 0;
30
31      // set floating-point output formatting
32      cout << fixed << setprecision( 2 );
33
34      // output objects using static binding
35      cout << "Invoking print function on base-class and derived-class "
36         << "\nobjects with static binding\n\n";
37      commissionEmployee.print(); // static binding
38      cout << "\n\n";
39      basePlusCommissionEmployee.print(); // static binding
40
41      // output objects using dynamic binding
42      cout << "\n\n\nInvoking print function on base-class and "
43         << "derived-class \nobjects with dynamic binding";
44
45      // aim base-class pointer at base-class object and print
46      commissionEmployeePtr = &commissionEmployee;
47      cout << "\n\nCalling virtual function print with base-class pointer"
48         << "\nto base-class object invokes base-class "
49         << "print function:\n\n";
50      commissionEmployeePtr->print(); // invokes base-class print
51
52      // aim derived-class pointer at derived-class object and print
53      basePlusCommissionEmployeePtr = &basePlusCommissionEmployee;
54      cout << "\n\nCalling virtual function print with derived-class "
55         << "pointer\nto derived-class object invokes derived-class "
56         << "print function:\n\n";
57      basePlusCommissionEmployeePtr->print(); // invokes derived-class print
58
59      // aim base-class pointer at derived-class object and print
60      commissionEmployeePtr = &basePlusCommissionEmployee;
61      cout << "\n\nCalling virtual function print with base-class pointer"
62         << "\nto derived-class object invokes derived-class "
63         << "print function:\n\n";
64
```

Fig. 13.10 | Demonstrating polymorphism by invoking a derived-class virtual function via a base-class pointer to a derived-class object. (Part 2 of 3.)

```
65      // polymorphism; invokes BasePlusCommissionEmployee's print;
66      // base-class pointer to derived-class object
67      commissionEmployeePtr->print();
68      cout << endl;
69      return 0;
70   } // end main
```

```
Invoking print function on base-class and derived-class
objects with static binding

commission employee: Sue Jones
social security number: 222-22-2222
gross sales: 10000.00
commission rate: 0.06

base-salaried commission employee: Bob Lewis
social security number: 333-33-3333
gross sales: 5000.00
commission rate: 0.04
base salary: 300.00


Invoking print function on base-class and derived-class
objects with dynamic binding

Calling virtual function print with base-class pointer
to base-class object invokes base-class print function:

commission employee: Sue Jones
social security number: 222-22-2222
gross sales: 10000.00
commission rate: 0.06

Calling virtual function print with derived-class pointer
to derived-class object invokes derived-class print function:

base-salaried commission employee: Bob Lewis
social security number: 333-33-3333
gross sales: 5000.00
commission rate: 0.04
base salary: 300.00

Calling virtual function print with base-class pointer
to derived-class object invokes derived-class print function:

base-salaried commission employee: Bob Lewis
social security number: 333-33-3333
gross sales: 5000.00
commission rate: 0.04
base salary: 300.00
```

Fig. 13.10 | Demonstrating polymorphism by invoking a derived-class `virtual` function via a base-class pointer to a derived-class object. (Part 3 of 3.)

13.3.5 Summary of the Allowed Assignments Between Base-Class and Derived-Class Objects and Pointers

Now that you have seen a complete application that processes diverse objects polymorphically, we summarize what you can and cannot do with base-class and derived-class objects and pointers. Although a derived-class object also *is a* base-class object, the two objects are nevertheless different. As discussed previously, derived-class objects can be treated as if they were base-class objects. This is a logical relationship, because the derived class contains all the members of the base class. However, base-class objects cannot be treated as if they were derived-class objects—the derived class can have additional derived-class-only members. For this reason, aiming a derived-class pointer at a base-class object is not allowed without an explicit cast—such an assignment would leave the derived-class-only members undefined on the base-class object. The cast relieves the compiler of the responsibility of issuing an error message. In a sense, by using the cast you are saying, "I know that what I'm doing is dangerous and I take full responsibility for my actions."

In the current section and in Chapter 12, we have discussed four ways to aim base-class pointers and derived-class pointers at base-class objects and derived-class objects:

1. Aiming a base-class pointer at a base-class object is straightforward—calls made off the base-class pointer simply invoke base-class functionality.

2. Aiming a derived-class pointer at a derived-class object is straightforward—calls made off the derived-class pointer simply invoke derived-class functionality.

3. Aiming a base-class pointer at a derived-class object is safe, because the derived-class object *is an* object of its base class. However, this pointer can be used to invoke only base-class member functions. If you attempt to refer to a derived-class-only member through the base-class pointer, the compiler reports an error. To avoid this error, you must cast the base-class pointer to a derived-class pointer. The derived-class pointer can then be used to invoke the derived-class object's complete functionality. This technique, called downcasting, is a potentially dangerous operation—Section 13.8 demonstrates how to safely use downcasting. If a virtual function is defined in the base and derived classes (either by inheritance or overriding), and if that function is invoked on a derived-class object via a base-class pointer, then the derived-class version of that function is called. This is an example of the polymorphic behavior that occurs only with virtual functions.

4. Aiming a derived-class pointer at a base-class object generates a compilation error. The *is-a* relationship applies only from a derived class to its direct and indirect base classes, and not vice versa. A base-class object does not contain the derived-class-only members that can be invoked off a derived-class pointer.

Common Programming Error 13.1

After aiming a base-class pointer at a derived-class object, attempting to reference derived-class-only members with the base-class pointer is a compilation error.

Common Programming Error 13.2

Treating a base-class object as a derived-class object can cause errors.

13.4 Type Fields and switch Statements

One way to determine the type of an object that is incorporated in a larger program is to use a switch statement. This allows us to distinguish among object types, then invoke an appropriate action for a particular object. For example, in a hierarchy of shapes in which each shape object has a shapeType attribute, a switch statement could check the object's shapeType to determine which print function to call.

Using switch logic exposes programs to a variety of potential problems. For example, you might forget to include a type test when one is warranted, or might forget to test all possible cases in a switch statement. When modifying a switch-based system by adding new types, you might forget to insert the new cases in all relevant switch statements. Every addition or deletion of a class requires the modification of every switch statement in the system; tracking these statements down can be time consuming and error prone.

Software Engineering Observation 13.6

Polymorphic programming can eliminate the need for switch logic. By using the polymorphism mechanism to perform the equivalent logic, programmers can avoid the kinds of errors typically associated with switch logic.

Software Engineering Observation 13.7

An interesting consequence of using polymorphism is that programs take on a simplified appearance. They contain less branching logic and simpler sequential code. This simplification facilitates testing, debugging and program maintenance.

13.5 Abstract Classes and Pure virtual Functions

When we think of a class as a type, we assume that programs will create objects of that type. However, there are cases in which it is useful to define classes from which you never intend to instantiate any objects. Such classes are called abstract classes. Because these classes normally are used as base classes in inheritance hierarchies, we refer to them as abstract base classes. These classes cannot be used to instantiate objects, because, as we'll soon see, abstract classes are incomplete—derived classes must define the "missing pieces." We build programs with abstract classes in Section 13.6.

The purpose of an abstract class is to provide an appropriate base class from which other classes can inherit. Classes that can be used to instantiate objects are called concrete classes. Such classes provide implementations of every member function they define. We could have an abstract base class TwoDimensionalShape and derive such concrete classes as Square, Circle and Triangle. We could also have an abstract base class ThreeDimensionalShape and derive such concrete classes as Cube, Sphere and Cylinder. Abstract base classes are too generic to define real objects; we need to be more specific before we can think of instantiating objects. For example, if someone tells you to "draw the two-dimensional shape," what shape would you draw? Concrete classes provide the specifics that make it reasonable to instantiate objects.

An inheritance hierarchy does not need to contain any abstract classes, but, as we'll see, many object-oriented systems have class hierarchies headed by abstract base classes. In some cases, abstract classes constitute the top few levels of the hierarchy. A good example of this is the shape hierarchy in Fig. 12.3, which begins with abstract base class Shape. On the next level of the hierarchy we have two more abstract base classes, namely, TwoDimensionalShape and ThreeDimensionalShape. The next level of the hierarchy defines concrete classes for two-dimensional shapes (namely, Circle, Square and Triangle) and for three-dimensional shapes (namely, Sphere, Cube and Tetrahedron).

A class is made abstract by declaring one or more of its virtual functions to be "pure." A pure virtual function is specified by placing "= 0" in its declaration, as in

```
virtual void draw() const = 0; // pure virtual function
```

The "= 0" is known as a pure specifier. Pure virtual functions do not provide implementations. Every concrete derived class *must* override all base-class pure virtual functions with concrete implementations of those functions. The difference between a virtual function and a pure virtual function is that a virtual function has an implementation and gives the derived class the *option* of overriding the function; by contrast, a pure virtual function does not provide an implementation and *requires* the derived class to override the function for that derived class to be concrete; otherwise the derived class remains abstract.

Pure virtual functions are used when it does not make sense for the base class to have an implementation of a function, but you want all concrete derived classes to implement the function. Returning to our earlier example of space objects, it does not make sense for the base class SpaceObject to have an implementation for function draw (as there is no way to draw a generic space object without having more information about what type of space object is being drawn). An example of a function that would be defined as virtual (and not pure virtual) would be one that returns a name for the object. We can name a generic SpaceObject (for instance, as "space object"), so a default implementation for this function can be provided, and the function does not need to be pure virtual. The function is still declared virtual, however, because it is expected that derived classes will override this function to provide more specific names for the derived-class objects.

Software Engineering Observation 13.8

An abstract class defines a common public interface for the various classes in a class hierarchy. An abstract class contains one or more pure virtual functions that concrete derived classes must override.

Common Programming Error 13.3

Attempting to instantiate an object of an abstract class causes a compilation error.

Common Programming Error 13.4

Failure to override a pure virtual function in a derived class, then attempting to instantiate objects of that class, is a compilation error.

Software Engineering Observation 13.9

An abstract class has at least one pure virtual function. An abstract class also can have data members and concrete functions (including constructors and destructors), which are subject to the normal rules of inheritance by derived classes.

Although we cannot instantiate objects of an abstract base class, we *can* use the abstract base class to declare pointers and references that can refer to objects of any concrete classes derived from the abstract class. Programs typically use such pointers and references to manipulate derived-class objects polymorphically.

Consider another application of polymorphism. A screen manager needs to display a variety of objects, including new types of objects that you'll add to the system after writing the screen manager. The system might need to display various shapes, such as Circles, Triangles or Rectangles, which are derived from abstract base class Shape. The screen manager uses Shape pointers to manage the objects that are displayed. To draw any object (regardless of the level at which that object's class appears in the inheritance hierarchy), the screen manager uses a base-class pointer to the object to invoke the object's draw function, which is a pure virtual function in base class Shape; therefore, each concrete derived class must implement function draw. Each Shape object in the inheritance hierarchy knows how to draw itself. The screen manager does not have to worry about the type of each object or whether the screen manager has ever encountered objects of that type.

Polymorphism is particularly effective for implementing layered software systems. In operating systems, for example, each type of physical device could operate quite differently from the others. Even so, commands to *read* or *write* data from and to devices may have a certain uniformity. The *write* message sent to a device-driver object needs to be interpreted specifically in the context of that device driver and how that device driver manipulates devices of a specific type. However, the *write* call itself really is no different from the *write* to any other device in the system—place some number of bytes from memory onto that device. An object-oriented operating system might use an abstract base class to provide an interface appropriate for all device drivers. Then, through inheritance from that abstract base class, derived classes are formed that all operate similarly. The capabilities (i.e., the public functions) offered by the device drivers are provided as pure virtual functions in the abstract base class. The implementations of these pure virtual functions are provided in the derived classes that correspond to the specific types of device drivers. This architecture also allows new devices to be added to a system easily, even after the operating system has been defined. The user can just plug in the device and install its new device driver. The operating system "talks" to this new device through its device driver, which has the same public member functions as all other device drivers—those defined in the device driver abstract base class.

It is common in object-oriented programming to define an iterator class that can traverse all the objects in a container (such as an array). For example, a program can print a list of objects in a vector by creating an iterator object, then using the iterator to obtain the next element of the list each time the iterator is called. Iterators often are used in polymorphic programming to traverse an array or a linked list of pointers to objects from various levels of a hierarchy. The pointers in such a list are all base-class pointers. (Chapter 22, Standard Template Library (STL), presents a thorough treatment of iterators.) A list of pointers to objects of base class TwoDimensionalShape could contain pointers to objects of classes Square, Circle, Triangle and so on. Using polymorphism to send a draw message, off a TwoDimensionalShape * pointer, to each object in the list would draw each object correctly on the screen.

13.6 Case Study: Payroll System Using Polymorphism

This section reexamines the CommissionEmployee-BasePlusCommissionEmployee hierarchy that we explored throughout Section 12.4. In this example, we use an abstract class and polymorphism to perform payroll calculations based on the type of employee. We create an enhanced employee hierarchy to solve the following problem:

A company pays its employees weekly. The employees are of four types: Salaried employees are paid a fixed weekly salary regardless of the number of hours worked, hourly employees are paid by the hour and receive overtime pay for all hours worked in excess of 40 hours, commission employees are paid a percentage of their sales and base-salary-plus-commission employees receive a base salary plus a percentage of their sales. For the current pay period, the company has decided to reward base-salary-plus-commission employees by adding 10 percent to their base salaries. The company wants to implement a C++ program that performs its payroll calculations polymorphically.

We use abstract class `Employee` to represent the general concept of an employee. The classes that derive directly from `Employee` are `SalariedEmployee`, `CommissionEmployee` and `HourlyEmployee`. Class `BasePlusCommissionEmployee`—derived from `Commission-Employee`—represents the last employee type. The UML class diagram in Fig. 13.11 shows the inheritance hierarchy for our polymorphic employee payroll application. Note that the abstract class name `Employee` is italicized, as per the convention of the UML.

Abstract base class `Employee` declares the "interface" to the hierarchy—that is, the set of member functions that a program can invoke on all `Employee` objects. Each employee, regardless of the way his or her earnings are calculated, has a first name, a last name and a social security number, so `private` data members `firstName`, `lastName` and `socialSecurityNumber` appear in abstract base class `Employee`.

Software Engineering Observation 13.10

A derived class can inherit interface or implementation from a base class. Hierarchies designed for implementation inheritance tend to have their functionality high in the hierarchy—each new derived class inherits one or more member functions that were defined in a base class, and the derived class uses the base-class definitions. Hierarchies designed for interface inheritance tend to have their functionality lower in the hierarchy—a base class specifies one or more functions that should be defined for each class in the hierarchy (i.e., they have the same prototype), but the individual derived classes provide their own implementations of the function(s).

The following sections implement the `Employee` class hierarchy. The first five each implement one of the abstract or concrete classes. The last section implements a test program that builds objects of all these classes and processes the objects polymorphically.

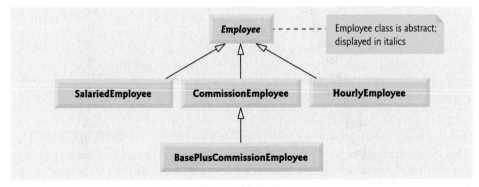

Fig. 13.11 | `Employee` hierarchy UML class diagram.

13.6.1 Creating Abstract Base Class Employee

Class Employee (Figs. 13.13–13.14, discussed in further detail shortly) provides functions earnings and print, in addition to various *get* and *set* functions that manipulate Employee's data members. An earnings function certainly applies generically to all employees, but each earnings calculation depends on the employee's class. So we declare earnings as pure virtual in base class Employee because a default implementation does not make sense for that function—there is not enough information to determine what amount earnings should return. Each derived class overrides earnings with an appropriate implementation. To calculate an employee's earnings, the program assigns the address of an employee's object to a base class Employee pointer, then invokes the earnings function on that object. We maintain a vector of Employee pointers, each of which points to an Employee object (of course, there cannot be Employee objects, because Employee is an abstract class—because of inheritance, however, all objects of all derived classes of Employee may nevertheless be thought of as Employee objects). The program iterates through the vector and calls function earnings for each Employee object. C++ processes these function calls polymorphically. Including earnings as a pure virtual function in Employee forces every direct derived class of Employee that wishes to be a concrete class to override earnings. This enables the designer of the class hierarchy to demand that each derived class provide an appropriate pay calculation, if indeed that derived class is to be concrete.

Function print in class Employee displays the first name, last name and social security number of the employee. As we'll see, each derived class of Employee overrides function print to output the employee's type (e.g., "salaried employee:") followed by the rest of the employee's information.

The diagram in Fig. 13.12 shows each of the five classes in the hierarchy down the left side and functions earnings and print across the top. For each class, the diagram shows the desired results of each function. Note that class Employee specifies "= 0" for function earnings to indicate that this is a pure virtual function. Each derived class overrides this function to provide an appropriate implementation. We do not list base class Employee's *get* and *set* functions because they are not overridden in any of the derived classes—each of these functions is inherited and used "as is" by each of the derived classes.

Let us consider class Employee's header file (Fig. 13.13). The public member functions include a constructor that takes the first name, last name and social security number as arguments (line 12); *set* functions that set the first name, last name and social security number (lines 14, 17 and 20, respectively); *get* functions that return the first name, last name and social security number (lines 15, 18 and 21, respectively); pure virtual function earnings (line 24) and virtual function print (line 25).

Recall that we declared earnings as a pure virtual function because first we must know the specific Employee type to determine the appropriate earnings calculations. Declaring this function as pure virtual indicates that each concrete derived class *must* provide an appropriate earnings implementation and that a program can use base-class Employee pointers to invoke function earnings polymorphically for any type of Employee.

Figure 13.14 contains the member-function implementations for class Employee. No implementation is provided for virtual function earnings. Note that the Employee constructor (lines 10–15) does not validate the social security number. Normally, such validation should be provided. An exercise in Chapter 12 asks you to validate a social security number to ensure that it is in the form ###-##-####, where each # represents a digit.

	earnings	print
Employee	= 0	*firstName lastName* social security number: *SSN*
Salaried- Employee	weeklySalary	salaried employee: *firstName lastName* social security number: *SSN* weekly salary: *weeklysalary*

Hourly-
Employee
	If hours <= 40
	  wage * hours
	If hours > 40
	  (40 * wage) +
	  ((hours - 40)
	  * wage * 1.5)
		hourly employee: *firstName lastName*
		social security number: *SSN*
		hourly wage: *wage*; hours worked: *hours*

Commission- Employee	commissionRate * grossSales	commission employee: *firstName lastName* social security number: *SSN* gross sales: *grossSales*; commission rate: *commissionRate*
BasePlus- Commission- Employee	baseSalary + (commissionRate * grossSales)	base salaried commission employee: *firstName lastName* social security number: *SSN* gross sales: *grossSales*; commission rate: *commissionRate*; base salary: *baseSalary*

Fig. 13.12 | Polymorphic interface for the `Employee` hierarchy classes.

```
 1  // Fig. 13.13: Employee.h
 2  // Employee abstract base class.
 3  #ifndef EMPLOYEE_H
 4  #define EMPLOYEE_H
 5
 6  #include <string> // C++ standard string class
 7  using std::string;
 8
 9  class Employee
10  {
11  public:
12     Employee( const string &, const string &, const string & );
13
14     void setFirstName( const string & ); // set first name
15     string getFirstName() const; // return first name
16
17     void setLastName( const string & ); // set last name
18     string getLastName() const; // return last name
19
```

Fig. 13.13 | `Employee` class header file. (Part 1 of 2.)

```
20      void setSocialSecurityNumber( const string & ); // set SSN
21      string getSocialSecurityNumber() const; // return SSN
22
23      // pure virtual function makes Employee abstract base class
24      virtual double earnings() const = 0; // pure virtual
25      virtual void print() const; // virtual
26  private:
27      string firstName;
28      string lastName;
29      string socialSecurityNumber;
30  }; // end class Employee
31
32  #endif // EMPLOYEE_H
```

Fig. 13.13 | Employee class header file. (Part 2 of 2.)

```
1   // Fig. 13.14: Employee.cpp
2   // Abstract-base-class Employee member-function definitions.
3   // Note: No definitions are given for pure virtual functions.
4   #include <iostream>
5   using std::cout;
6
7   #include "Employee.h" // Employee class definition
8
9   // constructor
10  Employee::Employee( const string &first, const string &last,
11     const string &ssn )
12     : firstName( first ), lastName( last ), socialSecurityNumber( ssn )
13  {
14     // empty body
15  } // end Employee constructor
16
17  // set first name
18  void Employee::setFirstName( const string &first )
19  {
20     firstName = first;
21  } // end function setFirstName
22
23  // return first name
24  string Employee::getFirstName() const
25  {
26     return firstName;
27  } // end function getFirstName
28
29  // set last name
30  void Employee::setLastName( const string &last )
31  {
32     lastName = last;
33  } // end function setLastName
34
```

Fig. 13.14 | Employee class implementation file. (Part 1 of 2.)

```
35   // return last name
36   string Employee::getLastName() const
37   {
38       return lastName;
39   } // end function getLastName
40
41   // set social security number
42   void Employee::setSocialSecurityNumber( const string &ssn )
43   {
44       socialSecurityNumber = ssn; // should validate
45   } // end function setSocialSecurityNumber
46
47   // return social security number
48   string Employee::getSocialSecurityNumber() const
49   {
50       return socialSecurityNumber;
51   } // end function getSocialSecurityNumber
52
53   // print Employee's information (virtual, but not pure virtual)
54   void Employee::print() const
55   {
56       cout << getFirstName() << ' ' << getLastName()
57           << "\nsocial security number: " << getSocialSecurityNumber();
58   } // end function print
```

Fig. 13.14 | `Employee` class implementation file. (Part 2 of 2.)

Note that `virtual` function `print` (Fig. 13.14, lines 54–58) provides an implementation that will be overridden in each of the derived classes. Each of these functions will, however, use the abstract class's version of `print` to print information common to all classes in the `Employee` hierarchy.

13.6.2 Creating Concrete Derived Class `SalariedEmployee`

Class `SalariedEmployee` (Figs. 13.15–13.16) derives from class `Employee` (line 8 of Fig. 13.15). The `public` member functions include a constructor that takes a first name, a last name, a social security number and a weekly salary as arguments (lines 11–12); a *set* function to assign a new nonnegative value to data member `weeklySalary` (lines 14); a *get* function to return `weeklySalary`'s value (line 15); a `virtual` function `earnings` that calculates a `SalariedEmployee`'s earnings (line 18) and a `virtual` function `print` (line 19) that outputs the employee's type, namely, `"salaried employee: "` followed by employee-specific information produced by base class `Employee`'s `print` function and `SalariedEmployee`'s `getWeeklySalary` function.

Figure 13.16 contains the member-function implementations for `SalariedEmployee`. The class's constructor passes the first name, last name and social security number to the `Employee` constructor (line 11) to initialize the `private` data members that are inherited from the base class, but not accessible in the derived class. Function `earnings` (line 30–33) overrides pure `virtual` function `earnings` in `Employee` to provide a concrete implementation that returns the `SalariedEmployee`'s weekly salary. If we did not implement `earnings`, class `SalariedEmployee` would be an abstract class, and any attempt to instantiate an object of the class would result in a compilation error (and, of course, we

```
 1   // Fig. 13.15: SalariedEmployee.h
 2   // SalariedEmployee class derived from Employee.
 3   #ifndef SALARIED_H
 4   #define SALARIED_H
 5
 6   #include "Employee.h" // Employee class definition
 7
 8   class SalariedEmployee : public Employee
 9   {
10   public:
11      SalariedEmployee( const string &, const string &,
12         const string &, double = 0.0 );
13
14      void setWeeklySalary( double ); // set weekly salary
15      double getWeeklySalary() const; // return weekly salary
16
17      // keyword virtual signals intent to override
18      virtual double earnings() const; // calculate earnings
19      virtual void print() const; // print SalariedEmployee object
20   private:
21      double weeklySalary; // salary per week
22   }; // end class SalariedEmployee
23
24   #endif // SALARIED_H
```

Fig. 13.15 | `SalariedEmployee` class header file.

```
 1   // Fig. 13.16: SalariedEmployee.cpp
 2   // SalariedEmployee class member-function definitions.
 3   #include <iostream>
 4   using std::cout;
 5
 6   #include "SalariedEmployee.h" // SalariedEmployee class definition
 7
 8   // constructor
 9   SalariedEmployee::SalariedEmployee( const string &first,
10      const string &last, const string &ssn, double salary )
11      : Employee( first, last, ssn )
12   {
13      setWeeklySalary( salary );
14   } // end SalariedEmployee constructor
15
16   // set salary
17   void SalariedEmployee::setWeeklySalary( double salary )
18   {
19      weeklySalary = ( salary < 0.0 ) ? 0.0 : salary;
20   } // end function setWeeklySalary
21
22   // return salary
23   double SalariedEmployee::getWeeklySalary() const
24   {
```

Fig. 13.16 | `SalariedEmployee` class implementation file. (Part I of 2.)

```
25        return weeklySalary;
26    } // end function getWeeklySalary
27
28    // calculate earnings;
29    // override pure virtual function earnings in Employee
30    double SalariedEmployee::earnings() const
31    {
32        return getWeeklySalary();
33    } // end function earnings
34
35    // print SalariedEmployee's information
36    void SalariedEmployee::print() const
37    {
38        cout << "salaried employee: ";
39        Employee::print(); // reuse abstract base-class print function
40        cout << "\nweekly salary: " << getWeeklySalary();
41    } // end function print
```

Fig. 13.16 | `SalariedEmployee` class implementation file. (Part 2 of 2.)

want `SalariedEmployee` here to be a concrete class). Note that in class `SalariedEmployee`'s header file, we declared member functions `earnings` and `print` as `virtual` (lines 18–19 of Fig. 13.15)—actually, placing the `virtual` keyword before these member functions is redundant. We defined them as `virtual` in base class `Employee`, so they remain `virtual` functions throughout the class hierarchy. Recall from *Good Programming Practice 13.1* that explicitly declaring such functions `virtual` at every level of the hierarchy can promote program clarity.

Function `print` of class `SalariedEmployee` (lines 36–41 of Fig. 13.16) overrides `Employee` function `print`. If class `SalariedEmployee` did not override `print`, `SalariedEmployee` would inherit the `Employee` version of `print`. In that case, `SalariedEmployee`'s `print` function would simply return the employee's full name and social security number, which does not adequately represent a `SalariedEmployee`. To print a `SalariedEmployee`'s complete information, the derived class's `print` function outputs `"salaried employee: "` followed by the base-class `Employee`-specific information (i.e., first name, last name and social security number) printed by invoking the base class's `print` function using the scope resolution operator (line 39)—this is a nice example of code reuse. The output produced by `SalariedEmployee`'s `print` function contains the employee's weekly salary obtained by invoking the class's `getWeeklySalary` function.

13.6.3 Creating Concrete Derived Class `HourlyEmployee`

Class `HourlyEmployee` (Figs. 13.17–13.18) also derives from class `Employee` (line 8 of Fig. 13.17). The `public` member functions include a constructor (lines 11–12) that takes as arguments a first name, a last name, a social security number, an hourly wage and the number of hours worked; *set* functions that assign new values to data members `wage` and `hours`, respectively (lines 14 and 17); *get* functions to return the values of `wage` and `hours`, respectively (lines 15 and 18); a `virtual` function `earnings` that calculates an `HourlyEmployee`'s earnings (line 21) and a `virtual` function `print` that outputs the employee's type, namely, `"hourly employee: "` and employee-specific information (line 22).

```
 1   // Fig. 13.17: HourlyEmployee.h
 2   // HourlyEmployee class definition.
 3   #ifndef HOURLY_H
 4   #define HOURLY_H
 5
 6   #include "Employee.h" // Employee class definition
 7
 8   class HourlyEmployee : public Employee
 9   {
10   public:
11      HourlyEmployee( const string &, const string &,
12         const string &, double = 0.0, double = 0.0 );
13
14      void setWage( double ); // set hourly wage
15      double getWage() const; // return hourly wage
16
17      void setHours( double ); // set hours worked
18      double getHours() const; // return hours worked
19
20      // keyword virtual signals intent to override
21      virtual double earnings() const; // calculate earnings
22      virtual void print() const; // print HourlyEmployee object
23   private:
24      double wage; // wage per hour
25      double hours; // hours worked for week
26   }; // end class HourlyEmployee
27
28   #endif // HOURLY_H
```

Fig. 13.17 | HourlyEmployee class header file.

```
 1   // Fig. 13.18: HourlyEmployee.cpp
 2   // HourlyEmployee class member-function definitions.
 3   #include <iostream>
 4   using std::cout;
 5
 6   #include "HourlyEmployee.h" // HourlyEmployee class definition
 7
 8   // constructor
 9   HourlyEmployee::HourlyEmployee( const string &first, const string &last,
10      const string &ssn, double hourlyWage, double hoursWorked )
11      : Employee( first, last, ssn )
12   {
13      setWage( hourlyWage ); // validate hourly wage
14      setHours( hoursWorked ); // validate hours worked
15   } // end HourlyEmployee constructor
16
17   // set wage
18   void HourlyEmployee::setWage( double hourlyWage )
19   {
20      wage = ( hourlyWage < 0.0 ? 0.0 : hourlyWage );
21   } // end function setWage
```

Fig. 13.18 | HourlyEmployee class implementation file. (Part 1 of 2.)

```
22
23   // return wage
24   double HourlyEmployee::getWage() const
25   {
26      return wage;
27   } // end function getWage
28
29   // set hours worked
30   void HourlyEmployee::setHours( double hoursWorked )
31   {
32      hours = ( ( ( hoursWorked >= 0.0 ) && ( hoursWorked <= 168.0 ) ) ?
33         hoursWorked : 0.0 );
34   } // end function setHours
35
36   // return hours worked
37   double HourlyEmployee::getHours() const
38   {
39      return hours;
40   } // end function getHours
41
42   // calculate earnings;
43   // override pure virtual function earnings in Employee
44   double HourlyEmployee::earnings() const
45   {
46      if ( getHours() <= 40 ) // no overtime
47         return getWage() * getHours();
48      else
49         return 40 * getWage() + ( ( getHours() - 40 ) * getWage() * 1.5 );
50   } // end function earnings
51
52   // print HourlyEmployee's information
53   void HourlyEmployee::print() const
54   {
55      cout << "hourly employee: ";
56      Employee::print(); // code reuse
57      cout << "\nhourly wage: " << getWage() <<
58         "; hours worked: " << getHours();
59   } // end function print
```

Fig. 13.18 | HourlyEmployee class implementation file. (Part 2 of 2.)

Figure 13.18 contains the member-function implementations for class HourlyEmployee. Lines 18–21 and 30–34 define *set* functions that assign new values to data members wage and hours, respectively. Function setWage (lines 18–21) ensures that wage is non-negative, and function setHours (lines 30–34) ensures that data member hours is between 0 and 168 (the total number of hours in a week). Class HourlyEmployee's *get* functions are implemented in lines 24–27 and 37–40. We do not declare these functions virtual, so classes derived from class HourlyEmployee cannot override them (although derived classes certainly can redefine them). Note that the HourlyEmployee constructor, like the SalariedEmployee constructor, passes the first name, last name and social security number to the base class Employee constructor (line 11) to initialize the inherited private data members declared in the base class. In addition, HourlyEmployee's print function calls base-class function `print` (line 56) to output the `Employee`-specific information (i.e., first name, last name and social security number)—this is another nice example of code reuse.

13.6.4 Creating Concrete Derived Class CommissionEmployee

Class `CommissionEmployee` (Figs. 13.19–13.20) derives from class `Employee` (line 8 of Fig. 13.19). The member-function implementations (Fig. 13.20) include a constructor (lines 9–15) that takes a first name, a last name, a social security number, a sales amount and a commission rate; *set* functions (lines 18–21 and 30–33) to assign new values to data members `commissionRate` and `grossSales`, respectively; *get* functions (lines 24–27 and 36–39) that retrieve the values of these data members; function `earnings` (lines 43–46) to calculate a `CommissionEmployee`'s earnings; and function `print` (lines 49–55), which outputs the employee's type, namely, `"commission employee: "` and employee-specific information. The `CommissionEmployee`'s constructor also passes the first name, last name and social security number to the `Employee` constructor (line 11) to initialize `Employee`'s pri-

```cpp
1   // Fig. 13.19: CommissionEmployee.h
2   // CommissionEmployee class derived from Employee.
3   #ifndef COMMISSION_H
4   #define COMMISSION_H
5
6   #include "Employee.h" // Employee class definition
7
8   class CommissionEmployee : public Employee
9   {
10  public:
11     CommissionEmployee( const string &, const string &,
12        const string &, double = 0.0, double = 0.0 );
13
14     void setCommissionRate( double ); // set commission rate
15     double getCommissionRate() const; // return commission rate
16
17     void setGrossSales( double ); // set gross sales amount
18     double getGrossSales() const; // return gross sales amount
19
20     // keyword virtual signals intent to override
21     virtual double earnings() const; // calculate earnings
22     virtual void print() const; // print CommissionEmployee object
23  private:
24     double grossSales; // gross weekly sales
25     double commissionRate; // commission percentage
26  }; // end class CommissionEmployee
27
28  #endif // COMMISSION_H
```

Fig. 13.19 | `CommissionEmployee` class header file.

```cpp
1   // Fig. 13.20: CommissionEmployee.cpp
2   // CommissionEmployee class member-function definitions.
3   #include <iostream>
```

Fig. 13.20 | `CommissionEmployee` class implementation file. (Part 1 of 2.)

```cpp
4    using std::cout;
5
6    #include "CommissionEmployee.h" // CommissionEmployee class definition
7
8    // constructor
9    CommissionEmployee::CommissionEmployee( const string &first,
10       const string &last, const string &ssn, double sales, double rate )
11       : Employee( first, last, ssn )
12   {
13      setGrossSales( sales );
14      setCommissionRate( rate );
15   } // end CommissionEmployee constructor
16
17   // set commission rate
18   void CommissionEmployee::setCommissionRate( double rate )
19   {
20      commissionRate = ( ( rate > 0.0 && rate < 1.0 ) ? rate : 0.0 );
21   } // end function setCommissionRate
22
23   // return commission rate
24   double CommissionEmployee::getCommissionRate() const
25   {
26       return commissionRate;
27   } // end function getCommissionRate
28
29   // set gross sales amount
30   void CommissionEmployee::setGrossSales( double sales )
31   {
32      grossSales = ( ( sales < 0.0 ) ? 0.0 : sales );
33   } // end function setGrossSales
34
35   // return gross sales amount
36   double CommissionEmployee::getGrossSales() const
37   {
38       return grossSales;
39   } // end function getGrossSales
40
41   // calculate earnings;
42   // override pure virtual function earnings in Employee
43   double CommissionEmployee::earnings() const
44   {
45       return getCommissionRate() * getGrossSales();
46   } // end function earnings
47
48   // print CommissionEmployee's information
49   void CommissionEmployee::print() const
50   {
51      cout << "commission employee: ";
52      Employee::print(); // code reuse
53      cout << "\ngross sales: " << getGrossSales()
54         << "; commission rate: " << getCommissionRate();
55   } // end function print
```

Fig. 13.20 | CommissionEmployee class implementation file. (Part 2 of 2.)

vate data members. Function print calls base-class function print (line 52) to display the Employee-specific information (i.e., first name, last name and social security number).

13.6.5 Creating Indirect Concrete Derived Class BasePlusCommissionEmployee

Class BasePlusCommissionEmployee (Figs. 13.21–13.22) directly inherits from class CommissionEmployee (line 8 of Fig. 13.21) and therefore is an *indirect* derived class of class Employee. Class BasePlusCommissionEmployee's member-function implementations include a constructor (lines 10–16 of Fig. 13.22) that takes as arguments a first name, a last name, a social security number, a sales amount, a commission rate and a base salary. It then passes the first name, last name, social security number, sales amount and commission rate to the CommissionEmployee constructor (line 13) to initialize the inherited members. BasePlusCommissionEmployee also contains a *set* function (lines 19–22) to assign a new value to data member baseSalary and a *get* function (lines 25–28) to return baseSalary's value. Function earnings (lines 32–35) calculates a BasePlusCommissionEmployee's earnings. Note that line 34 in function earnings calls base-class CommissionEmployee's earnings function to calculate the commission-based portion of the employee's earnings. This is a nice example of code reuse. BasePlusCommissionEmployee's print function (lines 38–43) outputs "base-salaried", followed by the output of base-class CommissionEmployee's print function (another example of code reuse), then the base salary. The resulting output begins with "base-salaried commission employee: " followed by the rest of the Base-

```
1   // Fig. 13.21: BasePlusCommissionEmployee.h
2   // BasePlusCommissionEmployee class derived from Employee.
3   #ifndef BASEPLUS_H
4   #define BASEPLUS_H
5
6   #include "CommissionEmployee.h" // CommissionEmployee class definition
7
8   class BasePlusCommissionEmployee : public CommissionEmployee
9   {
10  public:
11     BasePlusCommissionEmployee( const string &, const string &,
12        const string &, double = 0.0, double = 0.0, double = 0.0 );
13
14     void setBaseSalary( double ); // set base salary
15     double getBaseSalary() const; // return base salary
16
17     // keyword virtual signals intent to override
18     virtual double earnings() const; // calculate earnings
19     virtual void print() const; // print BasePlusCommissionEmployee object
20  private:
21     double baseSalary; // base salary per week
22  }; // end class BasePlusCommissionEmployee
23
24  #endif // BASEPLUS_H
```

Fig. 13.21 | BasePlusCommissionEmployee class header file.

```cpp
1   // Fig. 13.22: BasePlusCommissionEmployee.cpp
2   // BasePlusCommissionEmployee member-function definitions.
3   #include <iostream>
4   using std::cout;
5
6   // BasePlusCommissionEmployee class definition
7   #include "BasePlusCommissionEmployee.h"
8
9   // constructor
10  BasePlusCommissionEmployee::BasePlusCommissionEmployee(
11     const string &first, const string &last, const string &ssn,
12     double sales, double rate, double salary )
13     : CommissionEmployee( first, last, ssn, sales, rate )
14  {
15     setBaseSalary( salary ); // validate and store base salary
16  } // end BasePlusCommissionEmployee constructor
17
18  // set base salary
19  void BasePlusCommissionEmployee::setBaseSalary( double salary )
20  {
21     baseSalary = ( ( salary < 0.0 ) ? 0.0 : salary );
22  } // end function setBaseSalary
23
24  // return base salary
25  double BasePlusCommissionEmployee::getBaseSalary() const
26  {
27      return baseSalary;
28  } // end function getBaseSalary
29
30  // calculate earnings;
31  // override pure virtual function earnings in Employee
32  double BasePlusCommissionEmployee::earnings() const
33  {
34      return getBaseSalary() + CommissionEmployee::earnings();
35  } // end function earnings
36
37  // print BasePlusCommissionEmployee's information
38  void BasePlusCommissionEmployee::print() const
39  {
40     cout << "base-salaried ";
41     CommissionEmployee::print(); // code reuse
42     cout << "; base salary: " << getBaseSalary();
43  } // end function print
```

Fig. 13.22 | BasePlusCommissionEmployee class implementation file.

PlusCommissionEmployee's information. Recall that CommissionEmployee's print displays the employee's first name, last name and social security number by invoking the print function of its base class (i.e., Employee)—yet another example of code reuse. Note that BasePlusCommissionEmployee's print initiates a chain of functions calls that spans all three levels of the Employee hierarchy.

13.6.6 Demonstrating Polymorphic Processing

To test our Employee hierarchy, the program in Fig. 13.23 creates an object of each of the four concrete classes SalariedEmployee, HourlyEmployee, CommissionEmployee and BasePlusCommissionEmployee. The program manipulates these objects, first with static binding, then polymorphically, using a vector of Employee pointers. Lines 31–38 create objects of each of the four concrete Employee derived classes. Lines 43–51 output each Employee's information and earnings. Each member-function invocation in lines 43–51 is

```cpp
 1   // Fig. 13.23: fig13_23.cpp
 2   // Processing Employee derived-class objects individually
 3   // and polymorphically using dynamic binding.
 4   #include <iostream>
 5   using std::cout;
 6   using std::endl;
 7   using std::fixed;
 8
 9   #include <iomanip>
10   using std::setprecision;
11
12   #include <vector>
13   using std::vector;
14
15   // include definitions of classes in Employee hierarchy
16   #include "Employee.h"
17   #include "SalariedEmployee.h"
18   #include "HourlyEmployee.h"
19   #include "CommissionEmployee.h"
20   #include "BasePlusCommissionEmployee.h"
21
22   void virtualViaPointer( const Employee * const ); // prototype
23   void virtualViaReference( const Employee & ); // prototype
24
25   int main()
26   {
27      // set floating-point output formatting
28      cout << fixed << setprecision( 2 );
29
30      // create derived-class objects
31      SalariedEmployee salariedEmployee(
32         "John", "Smith", "111-11-1111", 800 );
33      HourlyEmployee hourlyEmployee(
34         "Karen", "Price", "222-22-2222", 16.75, 40 );
35      CommissionEmployee commissionEmployee(
36         "Sue", "Jones", "333-33-3333", 10000, .06 );
37      BasePlusCommissionEmployee basePlusCommissionEmployee(
38         "Bob", "Lewis", "444-44-4444", 5000, .04, 300 );
39
40      cout << "Employees processed individually using static binding:\n\n";
41
42      // output each Employee's information and earnings using static binding
43      salariedEmployee.print();
```

Fig. 13.23 | Employee class hierarchy driver program. (Part 1 of 4.)

```cpp
44     cout << "\nearned $" << salariedEmployee.earnings() << "\n\n";
45     hourlyEmployee.print();
46     cout << "\nearned $" << hourlyEmployee.earnings() << "\n\n";
47     commissionEmployee.print();
48     cout << "\nearned $" << commissionEmployee.earnings() << "\n\n";
49     basePlusCommissionEmployee.print();
50     cout << "\nearned $" << basePlusCommissionEmployee.earnings()
51        << "\n\n";
52
53     // create vector of four base-class pointers
54     vector < Employee * > employees( 4 );
55
56     // initialize vector with Employees
57     employees[ 0 ] = &salariedEmployee;
58     employees[ 1 ] = &hourlyEmployee;
59     employees[ 2 ] = &commissionEmployee;
60     employees[ 3 ] = &basePlusCommissionEmployee;
61
62     cout << "Employees processed polymorphically via dynamic binding:\n\n";
63
64     // call virtualViaPointer to print each Employee's information
65     // and earnings using dynamic binding
66     cout << "Virtual function calls made off base-class pointers:\n\n";
67
68     for ( size_t i = 0; i < employees.size(); i++ )
69        virtualViaPointer( employees[ i ] );
70
71     // call virtualViaReference to print each Employee's information
72     // and earnings using dynamic binding
73     cout << "Virtual function calls made off base-class references:\n\n";
74
75     for ( size_t i = 0; i < employees.size(); i++ )
76        virtualViaReference( *employees[ i ] ); // note dereferencing
77
78     return 0;
79  } // end main
80
81  // call Employee virtual functions print and earnings off a
82  // base-class pointer using dynamic binding
83  void virtualViaPointer( const Employee * const baseClassPtr )
84  {
85     baseClassPtr->print();
86     cout << "\nearned $" << baseClassPtr->earnings() << "\n\n";
87  } // end function virtualViaPointer
88
89  // call Employee virtual functions print and earnings off a
90  // base-class reference using dynamic binding
91  void virtualViaReference( const Employee &baseClassRef )
92  {
93     baseClassRef.print();
94     cout << "\nearned $" << baseClassRef.earnings() << "\n\n";
95  } // end function virtualViaReference
```

Fig. 13.23 | Employee class hierarchy driver program. (Part 2 of 4.)

```
Employees processed individually using static binding:

salaried employee: John Smith
social security number: 111-11-1111
weekly salary: 800.00
earned $800.00

hourly employee: Karen Price
social security number: 222-22-2222
hourly wage: 16.75; hours worked: 40.00
earned $670.00

commission employee: Sue Jones
social security number: 333-33-3333
gross sales: 10000.00; commission rate: 0.06
earned $600.00

base-salaried commission employee: Bob Lewis
social security number: 444-44-4444
gross sales: 5000.00; commission rate: 0.04; base salary: 300.00
earned $500.00

Employees processed polymorphically using dynamic binding:

Virtual function calls made off base-class pointers:

salaried employee: John Smith
social security number: 111-11-1111
weekly salary: 800.00
earned $800.00

hourly employee: Karen Price
social security number: 222-22-2222
hourly wage: 16.75; hours worked: 40.00
earned $670.00

commission employee: Sue Jones
social security number: 333-33-3333
gross sales: 10000.00; commission rate: 0.06
earned $600.00

base-salaried commission employee: Bob Lewis
social security number: 444-44-4444
gross sales: 5000.00; commission rate: 0.04; base salary: 300.00
earned $500.00

Virtual function calls made off base-class references:

salaried employee: John Smith
social security number: 111-11-1111
weekly salary: 800.00
earned $800.00

hourly employee: Karen Price
social security number: 222-22-2222
hourly wage: 16.75; hours worked: 40.00
earned $670.00
```

(continued ...)

Fig. 13.23 | Employee class hierarchy driver program. (Part 3 of 4.)

```
commission employee: Sue Jones
social security number: 333-33-3333
gross sales: 10000.00; commission rate: 0.06
earned $600.00

base-salaried commission employee: Bob Lewis
social security number: 444-44-4444
gross sales: 5000.00; commission rate: 0.04; base salary: 300.00
earned $500.00
```

Fig. 13.23 | Employee class hierarchy driver program. (Part 4 of 4.)

an example of static binding—at compile time, because we are using name handles (not pointers or references that could be set at execution time), the compiler can identify each object's type to determine which print and earnings functions are called.

Line 54 allocates vector employees, which contains four Employee pointers. Line 57 aims employees[0] at object salariedEmployee. Line 58 aims employees[1] at object hourlyEmployee. Line 59 aims employees[2] at object commissionEmployee. Line 60 aims employee[3] at object basePlusCommissionEmployee. The compiler allows these assignments, because a SalariedEmployee *is an* Employee, an HourlyEmployee *is an* Employee, a CommissionEmployee *is an* Employee and a BasePlusCommissionEmployee *is an* Employee. Therefore, we can assign the addresses of SalariedEmployee, HourlyEmployee, CommissionEmployee and BasePlusCommissionEmployee objects to base-class Employee pointers (even though Employee is an abstract class).

The loop in lines 68–69 traverses vector employees and invokes function virtual-ViaPointer (lines 83–87) for each element in employees. Function virtualViaPointer receives in parameter baseClassPtr (of type const Employee * const) the address stored in an employees element. Each call to virtualViaPointer uses baseClassPtr to invoke virtual functions print (line 85) and earnings (line 86). Note that function virtual-ViaPointer does not contain any SalariedEmployee, HourlyEmployee, CommissionEmployee or BasePlusCommissionEmployee type information. The function knows only about base-class type Employee. Therefore, at compile time, the compiler cannot know which concrete class's functions to call through baseClassPtr. Yet at execution time, each virtual-function invocation calls the function on the object to which baseClassPtr points at that moment. The output illustrates that the appropriate functions for each class are indeed invoked and that each object's proper information is displayed. For instance, the weekly salary is displayed for the SalariedEmployee, and the gross sales are displayed for the CommissionEmployee and BasePlusCommissionEmployee. Also note that obtaining the earnings of each Employee polymorphically in line 86 produces the same results as obtaining these employees' earnings via static binding in lines 44, 46, 48 and 50. All virtual function calls to print and earnings are resolved at runtime with dynamic binding.

Finally, another for statement (lines 75–76) traverses employees and invokes function virtualViaReference (lines 91–95) for each element in the vector. Function virtualViaReference receives in its parameter baseClassRef (of type const Employee &) a reference formed by dereferencing the pointer stored in each employees element (line 76). Each call to virtualViaReference invokes virtual functions print (line 93) and earnings (line 94) via reference baseClassRef to demonstrate that polymorphic processing occurs with base-class references as well. Each virtual-function invocation calls the function on the object to which baseClassRef refers at runtime. This is another example of dynamic binding. The output produced using base-class references is identical to the output produced using base-class pointers.

13.7 (Optional) Polymorphism, Virtual Functions and Dynamic Binding "Under the Hood"

C++ makes polymorphism easy to program. It is certainly possible to program for polymorphism in non-object-oriented languages such as C, but doing so requires complex and potentially dangerous pointer manipulations. This section discusses how C++ can implement polymorphism, virtual functions and dynamic binding internally. This will give you a solid understanding of how these capabilities really work. More importantly, it will help you appreciate the overhead of polymorphism—in terms of additional memory consumption and processor time. This will help you determine when to use polymorphism and when to avoid it. As you'll see in Chapter 22, the STL components were implemented without polymorphism and virtual functions—this was done to avoid the associated execution-time overhead and achieve optimal performance to meet the unique requirements of the STL.

First, we'll explain the data structures that the C++ compiler builds at compile time to support polymorphism at execution time. You'll see that polymorphism is accomplished through three levels of pointers (i.e., "triple indirection"). Then we'll show how an executing program uses these data structures to execute virtual functions and achieve the dynamic binding associated with polymorphism. Note that our discussion explains one possible implementation; this is not a language requirement.

When C++ compiles a class that has one or more virtual functions, it builds a *virtual function table* (*vtable*) for that class. An executing program uses the *vtable* to select the proper function implementation each time a virtual function of that class is called. The leftmost column of Fig. 13.24 illustrates the *vtables* for classes Employee, SalariedEmployee, HourlyEmployee, CommissionEmployee and BasePlusCommissionEmployee.

In the *vtable* for class Employee, the first function pointer is set to 0 (i.e., the null pointer). This is done because function earnings is a pure virtual function and therefore lacks an implementation. The second function pointer points to function print, which displays the employee's full name and social security number. [*Note:* We have abbreviated the output of each print function in this figure to conserve space.] Any class that has one or more null pointers in its *vtable* is an abstract class. Classes without any null *vtable* pointers (such as SalariedEmployee, HourlyEmployee, CommissionEmployee and BasePlusCommissionEmployee) are concrete classes.

Class SalariedEmployee overrides function earnings to return the employee's weekly salary, so the function pointer points to the earnings function of class SalariedEmployee. SalariedEmployee also overrides print, so the corresponding function pointer points to the SalariedEmployee member function that prints "salaried employee: " followed by the employee's name, social security number and weekly salary.

The earnings function pointer in the *vtable* for class HourlyEmployee points to HourlyEmployee's earnings function that returns the employee's wage multiplied by the number of hours worked. Note that to conserve space, we have omitted the fact that hourly employees receive time-and-a-half pay for overtime hours worked. The print func-

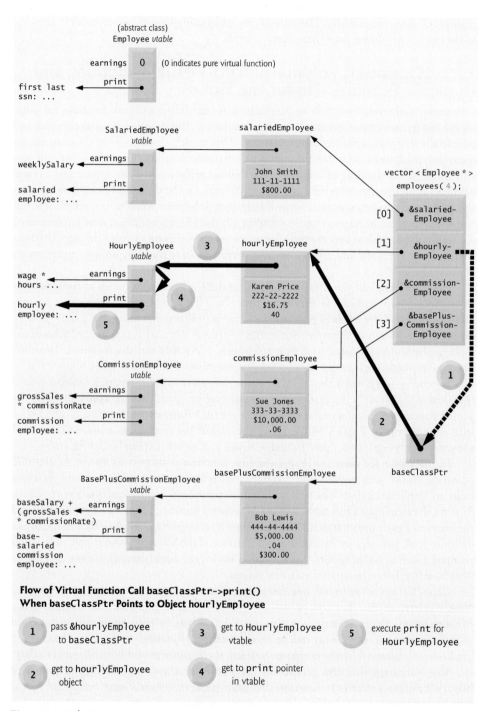

Fig. 13.24 | How virtual function calls work.

tion pointer points to the HourlyEmployee version of the function, which prints "hourly employee: ", the employee's name, social security number, hourly wage and hours worked. Both functions override the functions in class Employee.

The earnings function pointer in the *vtable* for class CommissionEmployee points to CommissionEmployee's earnings function that returns the employee's gross sales multiplied by the commission rate. The print function pointer points to the CommissionEmployee version of the function, which prints the employee's type, name, social security number, commission rate and gross sales. As in class HourlyEmployee, both functions override the functions in class Employee.

The earnings function pointer in the *vtable* for class BasePlusCommissionEmployee points to the BasePlusCommissionEmployee's earnings function, which returns the employee's base salary plus gross sales multiplied by commission rate. The print function pointer points to the BasePlusCommissionEmployee version of the function, which prints the employee's base salary plus the type, name, social security number, commission rate and gross sales. Both functions override the functions in class CommissionEmployee.

Notice that in our Employee case study, each concrete class provides its own implementation for virtual functions earnings and print. You've learned that each class which inherits directly from abstract base class Employee must implement earnings in order to be a concrete class, because earnings is a pure virtual function. These classes do not need to implement function print, however, to be considered concrete—print is not a pure virtual function and derived classes can inherit class Employee's implementation of print. Furthermore, class BasePlusCommissionEmployee does not have to implement either function print or earnings—both function implementations can be inherited from class CommissionEmployee. If a class in our hierarchy were to inherit function implementations in this manner, the *vtable* pointers for these functions would simply point to the function implementation that was being inherited. For example, if BasePlusCommissionEmployee did not override earnings, the earnings function pointer in the *vtable* for class BasePlusCommissionEmployee would point to the same earnings function as the *vtable* for class CommissionEmployee points to.

Polymorphism is accomplished through an elegant data structure involving three levels of pointers. We have discussed one level—the function pointers in the *vtable*. These point to the actual functions that execute when a virtual function is invoked.

Now we consider the second level of pointers. Whenever an object of a class with one or more virtual functions is instantiated, the compiler attaches to the object a pointer to the *vtable* for that class. This pointer is normally at the front of the object, but it is not required to be implemented that way. In Fig. 13.24, these pointers are associated with the objects created in Fig. 13.23 (one object for each of the types SalariedEmployee, HourlyEmployee, CommissionEmployee and BasePlusCommissionEmployee). Notice that the diagram displays each of the object's data member values. For example, the salariedEmployee object contains a pointer to the SalariedEmployee *vtable*; the object also contains the values John Smith, 111-11-1111 and $800.00.

The third level of pointers simply contains the handles to the objects that receive the virtual function calls. The handles in this level may also be references. Note that Fig. 13.24 depicts the vector employees that contains Employee pointers.

Now let us see how a typical virtual function call executes. Consider the call baseClassPtr->print() in function virtualViaPointer (line 85 of Fig. 13.23). Assume that `baseClassPtr` contains `employees[ 1 ]` (i.e., the address of object `hourlyEmployee` in `employees`). When the compiler compiles this statement, it determines that the call is indeed being made via a base-class pointer and that `print` is a `virtual` function.

The compiler determines that `print` is the *second* entry in each of the *vtables*. To locate this entry, the compiler notes that it will need to skip the first entry. Thus, the compiler compiles an offset or displacement of four bytes (four bytes for each pointer on today's popular 32-bit machines, and only one pointer needs to be skipped) into the table of machine-language object-code pointers to find the code that will execute the `virtual` function call.

The compiler generates code that performs the following operations [*Note:* The numbers in the list correspond to the circled numbers in Fig. 13.24]:

1. Select the ith entry of `employees` (in this case, the address of object `hourlyEmployee`), and pass it as an argument to function `virtualViaPointer`. This sets parameter `baseClassPtr` to point to `hourlyEmployee`.

2. Dereference that pointer to get to the `hourlyEmployee` object—which, as you recall, begins with a pointer to the `HourlyEmployee` *vtable*.

3. Dereference `hourlyEmployee`'s *vtable* pointer to get to the `HourlyEmployee` *vtable*.

4. Skip the offset of four bytes to select the `print` function pointer.

5. Dereference the `print` function pointer to form the "name" of the actual function to execute, and use the function call operator `()` to execute the appropriate `print` function, which in this case prints the employee's type, name, social security number, hourly wage and hours worked.

The data structures of Fig. 13.24 may appear to be complex, but this complexity is managed by the compiler and hidden from you, making polymorphic programming straightforward. The pointer dereferencing operations and memory accesses that occur on every `virtual` function call require some additional execution time. The *vtables* and the *vtable* pointers added to the objects require some additional memory. You now have enough information to determine whether `virtual` functions are appropriate for your programs.

Performance Tip 13.1

Polymorphism, as typically implemented with `virtual` *functions and dynamic binding in C++, is efficient. Programmers may use these capabilities with nominal impact on performance.*

Performance Tip 13.2

Virtual functions and dynamic binding enable polymorphic programming as an alternative to `switch` *logic programming. Optimizing compilers normally generate polymorphic code that runs as efficiently as hand-coded* `switch`*-based logic. The overhead of polymorphism is acceptable for most applications. But in some situations—real-time applications with stringent performance requirements, for example—the overhead of polymorphism may be too high.*

Software Engineering Observation 13.11

Dynamic binding enables independent software vendors (ISVs) to distribute software without revealing proprietary secrets. Software distributions can consist of only header files and object files—no source code needs to be revealed. Software developers can then use inheritance to derive new classes from those provided by the ISVs. Other software that worked with the classes the ISVs provided will still work with the derived classes and will use the overridden `virtual` *functions provided in these classes (via dynamic binding).*

13.8 Case Study: Payroll System Using Polymorphism and Runtime Type Information with Downcasting, dynamic_cast, typeid and type_info

Recall from the problem statement at the beginning of Section 13.6 that, for the current pay period, our fictitious company has decided to reward BasePlusCommissionEmployees by adding 10 percent to their base salaries. When processing Employee objects polymorphically in Section 13.6.6, we did not need to worry about the "specifics." Now, however, to adjust the base salaries of BasePlusCommissionEmployees, we have to determine the specific type of each Employee object at execution time, then act appropriately. This section demonstrates the powerful capabilities of runtime type information (RTTI) and dynamic casting, which enable a program to determine the type of an object at execution time and act on that object accordingly.

[*Note:* Some compilers require that RTTI be enabled before it can be used in a program. Consult your compiler's documentation to determine whether your compiler has similar requirements. In Visual C++ 2005, this option is enabled by default.]

Figure 13.25 uses the Employee hierarchy developed in Section 13.6 and increases by 10 percent the base salary of each BasePlusCommissionEmployee. Line 31 declares four-element vector employees that stores pointers to Employee objects. Lines 34–41 populate the vector with the addresses of dynamically allocated objects of classes SalariedEmployee (Figs. 13.15–13.16), HourlyEmployee (Figs. 13.17–13.18), CommissionEmployee (Figs. 13.19–13.20) and BasePlusCommissionEmployee (Figs. 13.21–13.22).

```
 1   // Fig. 13.25: fig13_25.cpp
 2   // Demonstrating downcasting and runtime type information.
 3   // NOTE: You may need to enable RTTI on your compiler
 4   // before you can execute this application.
 5   #include <iostream>
 6   using std::cout;
 7   using std::endl;
 8   using std::fixed;
 9
10   #include <iomanip>
11   using std::setprecision;
12
13   #include <vector>
14   using std::vector;
15
16   #include <typeinfo>
17
18   // include definitions of classes in Employee hierarchy
19   #include "Employee.h"
20   #include "SalariedEmployee.h"
21   #include "HourlyEmployee.h"
22   #include "CommissionEmployee.h"
23   #include "BasePlusCommissionEmployee.h"
24
25   int main()
26   {
```

Fig. 13.25 | Demonstrating downcasting and runtime type information. (Part 1 of 3.)

```
27      // set floating-point output formatting
28      cout << fixed << setprecision( 2 );
29
30      // create vector of four base-class pointers
31      vector < Employee * > employees( 4 );
32
33      // initialize vector with various kinds of Employees
34      employees[ 0 ] = new SalariedEmployee(
35         "John", "Smith", "111-11-1111", 800 );
36      employees[ 1 ] = new HourlyEmployee(
37         "Karen", "Price", "222-22-2222", 16.75, 40 );
38      employees[ 2 ] = new CommissionEmployee(
39         "Sue", "Jones", "333-33-3333", 10000, .06 );
40      employees[ 3 ] = new BasePlusCommissionEmployee(
41         "Bob", "Lewis", "444-44-4444", 5000, .04, 300 );
42
43      // polymorphically process each element in vector employees
44      for ( size_t i = 0; i < employees.size(); i++ )
45      {
46         employees[ i ]->print(); // output employee information
47         cout << endl;
48
49         // downcast pointer
50         BasePlusCommissionEmployee *derivedPtr =
51            dynamic_cast < BasePlusCommissionEmployee * >
52               ( employees[ i ] );
53
54         // determine whether element points to base-salaried
55         // commission employee
56         if ( derivedPtr != 0 ) // 0 if not a BasePlusCommissionEmployee
57         {
58            double oldBaseSalary = derivedPtr->getBaseSalary();
59            cout << "old base salary: $" << oldBaseSalary << endl;
60            derivedPtr->setBaseSalary( 1.10 * oldBaseSalary );
61            cout << "new base salary with 10% increase is: $"
62               << derivedPtr->getBaseSalary() << endl;
63         } // end if
64
65         cout << "earned $" << employees[ i ]->earnings() << "\n\n";
66      } // end for
67
68      // release objects pointed to by vector's elements
69      for ( size_t j = 0; j < employees.size(); j++ )
70      {
71         // output class name
72         cout << "deleting object of "
73            << typeid( *employees[ j ] ).name() << endl;
74
75         delete employees[ j ];
76      } // end for
77
78      return 0;
79   } // end main
```

Fig. 13.25 | Demonstrating downcasting and runtime type information. (Part 2 of 3.)

```
salaried employee: John Smith
social security number: 111-11-1111
weekly salary: 800.00
earned $800.00

hourly employee: Karen Price
social security number: 222-22-2222
hourly wage: 16.75; hours worked: 40.00
earned $670.00

commission employee: Sue Jones
social security number: 333-33-3333
gross sales: 10000.00; commission rate: 0.06
earned $600.00

base-salaried commission employee: Bob Lewis
social security number: 444-44-4444
gross sales: 5000.00; commission rate: 0.04; base salary: 300.00
old base salary: $300.00
new base salary with 10% increase is: $330.00
earned $530.00

deleting object of class SalariedEmployee
deleting object of class HourlyEmployee
deleting object of class CommissionEmployee
deleting object of class BasePlusCommissionEmployee
```

Fig. 13.25 | Demonstrating downcasting and runtime type information. (Part 3 of 3.)

The for statement in lines 44–66 iterates through the employees vector and displays each Employee's information by invoking member function print (line 46). Recall that because print is declared virtual in base class Employee, the system invokes the appropriate derived-class object's print function.

In this example, as we encounter BasePlusCommissionEmployee objects, we wish to increase their base salary by 10 percent. Since we process the employees generically (i.e., polymorphically), we cannot (with the techniques we've learned) be certain as to which type of Employee is being manipulated at any given time. This creates a problem, because BasePlusCommissionEmployee employees must be identified when we encounter them so they can receive the 10 percent salary increase. To accomplish this, we use operator dynamic_cast (line 51) to determine whether the type of each object is BasePlusCommissionEmployee. This is the downcast operation we referred to in Section 13.3.3. Lines 50–52 dynamically downcast employees[i] from type Employee * to type BasePlusCommissionEmployee *. If the vector element points to an object that *is a* BasePlusCommissionEmployee object, then that object's address is assigned to commissionPtr; otherwise, 0 is assigned to derived-class pointer derivedPtr.

If the value returned by the dynamic_cast operator in lines 50–52 is not 0, the object is the correct type, and the if statement (lines 56–63) performs the special processing required for the BasePlusCommissionEmployee object. Lines 58, 60 and 62 invoke BasePlusCommissionEmployee functions getBaseSalary and setBaseSalary to retrieve and update the employee's salary.

Line 65 invokes member function `earnings` on the object to which `employees[ i ]` points. Recall that `earnings` is declared `virtual` in the base class, so the program invokes the derived-class object's `earnings` function—another example of dynamic binding.

Lines 69–76 display each employee's object type and uses the `delete` operator to deallocate the dynamic memory to which each `vector` element points. Operator `typeid` (line 73) returns a reference to an object of class `type_info` that contains the information about the type of its operand, including the name of that type. When invoked, `type_info` member function `name` (line 73) returns a pointer-based string that contains the type name (e.g., `"class BasePlusCommissionEmployee"`) of the argument passed to `typeid`. To use `typeid`, the program must include header file `<typeinfo>` (line 16).

Portability Tip 13.1

The string returned by `type_info` member function `name` may vary by compiler.

Note that we avoid several compilation errors in this example by downcasting an `Employee` pointer to a `BasePlusCommissionEmployee` pointer (lines 50–52). If we remove the `dynamic_cast` from line 51 and attempt to assign the current `Employee` pointer directly to `BasePlusCommissionEmployee` pointer `derivedPtr`, we'll receive a compilation error. C++ does not allow a program to assign a base-class pointer to a derived-class pointer because the *is-a* relationship does not apply—a `CommissionEmployee` is *not* a `BasePlusCommissionEmployee`. The *is-a* relationship applies only between the derived class and its base classes, not vice versa.

Similarly, if lines 58, 60 and 62 used the current base-class pointer from `employees`, rather than derived-class pointer `derivedPtr`, to invoke derived-class-only functions `getBaseSalary` and `setBaseSalary`, we would receive a compilation error at each of these lines. As you learned in Section 13.3.3, attempting to invoke derived-class-only functions through a base-class pointer is not allowed. Although lines 58, 60 and 62 execute only if `commissionPtr` is not 0 (i.e., if the cast can be performed), we cannot attempt to invoke derived-class `BasePlusCommissionEmployee` functions `getBaseSalary` and `setBaseSalary` on the base-class `Employee` pointer. Recall that, using a base class `Employee` pointer, we can invoke only functions found in base class `Employee`—`earnings`, `print` and `Employee`'s *get* and *set* functions.

13.9 Virtual Destructors

A problem can occur when using polymorphism to process dynamically allocated objects of a class hierarchy. So far you have seen nonvirtual destructors—destructors that are not declared with keyword `virtual`. If a derived-class object with a nonvirtual destructor is destroyed explicitly by applying the `delete` operator to a base-class pointer to the object, the C++ standard specifies that the behavior is undefined.

The simple solution to this problem is to create a virtual destructor (i.e., a destructor that is declared with keyword `virtual`) in the base class. This makes all derived-class destructors `virtual` *even though they do not have the same name as the base-class destructor*. Now, if an object in the hierarchy is destroyed explicitly by applying the `delete` operator to a base-class pointer, the destructor for the appropriate class is called based on the object to which the base-class pointer points. Remember, when a derived-class object is destroyed, the base-class part of the derived-class object is also destroyed, so it is important for the destructors of both the derived class and base class to execute. The base-class destructor automatically executes after the derived-class destructor.

Error-Prevention Tip 13.2

If a class has virtual *functions, provide a* virtual *destructor, even if one is not required for the class. This ensures that a custom derived-class destructor (if there is one) will be invoked when a derived-class object is deleted via a base class pointer.*

Common Programming Error 13.5

Constructors cannot be virtual. *Declaring a constructor* virtual *is a compilation error.*

13.10 (Optional) Software Engineering Case Study: Incorporating Inheritance into the ATM System

We now revisit our ATM system design to see how it might benefit from inheritance. To apply inheritance, we first look for commonality among classes in the system. We create an inheritance hierarchy to model similar (yet not identical) classes in a more efficient and elegant manner that enables us to process objects of these classes polymorphically. We then modify our class diagram to incorporate the new inheritance relationships. Finally, we demonstrate how our updated design is translated into C++ header files.

In Section 3.11, we encountered the problem of representing a financial transaction in the system. Rather than create one class to represent all transaction types, we decided to create three individual transaction classes—BalanceInquiry, Withdrawal and Deposit—to represent the transactions that the ATM system can perform. Figure 13.26 shows the attributes and operations of these classes. Note that they have one attribute (account-Number) and one operation (execute) in common. Each class requires attribute account-Number to specify the account to which the transaction applies. Each class contains operation execute, which the ATM invokes to perform the transaction. Clearly, Balance-Inquiry, Withdrawal and Deposit represent *types of* transactions. Figure 13.26 reveals commonality among the transaction classes, so using inheritance to factor out the common features seems appropriate for designing these classes. We place the common functionality in base class Transaction and derive classes BalanceInquiry, Withdrawal and Deposit from Transaction (Fig. 13.27).

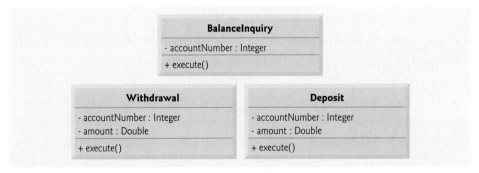

Fig. 13.26 | Attributes and operations of classes BalanceInquiry, Withdrawal and Deposit.

The UML specifies a relationship called a generalization to model inheritance. Figure 13.27 is the class diagram that models the inheritance relationship between base class Transaction and its three derived classes. The arrows with triangular hollow arrowheads indicate that classes BalanceInquiry, Withdrawal and Deposit are derived from class Transaction. Class Transaction is said to be a generalization of its derived classes. The derived classes are said to be specializations of class Transaction.

Classes BalanceInquiry, Withdrawal and Deposit share integer attribute accountNumber, so we factor out this common attribute and place it in base class Transaction. We no longer list accountNumber in the second compartment of each derived class, because the three derived classes inherit this attribute from Transaction. Recall, however, that derived classes cannot access private attributes of a base class. We therefore include public member function getAccountNumber in class Transaction. Each derived class inherits this member function, enabling the derived class to access its accountNumber as needed to execute a transaction.

According to Fig. 13.26, classes BalanceInquiry, Withdrawal and Deposit also share operation execute, so base class Transaction should contain public member function execute. However, it does not make sense to implement execute in class Transaction, because the functionality that this member function provides depends on the specific type of the actual transaction. We therefore declare member function execute as a pure virtual function in base class Transaction. This makes Transaction an abstract class and forces any class derived from Transaction that must be a concrete class (i.e., BalanceInquiry, Withdrawal and Deposit) to implement pure virtual member function execute to make the derived class concrete. The UML requires that we place abstract class names (and pure virtual functions—abstract operations in the UML) in italics, so Transaction and its member function execute appear in italics in Fig. 13.27. Note that operation execute is not italicized in derived classes BalanceInquiry, Withdrawal and Deposit. Each derived class overrides base class Transaction's execute member function with an appropriate implementation. Note that Fig. 13.27 includes operation execute in the third compartment of classes BalanceInquiry, Withdrawal and Deposit, because each class has a different concrete implementation of the overridden member function.

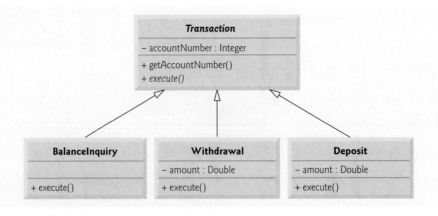

Fig. 13.27 | Class diagram modeling generalization relationship between base class Transaction and derived classes BalanceInquiry, Withdrawal and Deposit.

As you learned in this chapter, a derived class can inherit interface or implementation from a base class. Compared to a hierarchy designed for implementation inheritance, one designed for interface inheritance tends to have its functionality lower in the hierarchy— a base class signifies one or more functions that should be defined by each class in the hierarchy, but the individual derived classes provide their own implementations of the function(s). The inheritance hierarchy designed for the ATM system takes advantage of this type of inheritance, which provides the ATM with an elegant way to execute all transactions "in the general." Each class derived from Transaction inherits some implementation details (e.g., data member accountNumber), but the primary benefit of incorporating inheritance into our system is that the derived classes share a common interface (e.g., pure virtual member function execute). The ATM can aim a Transaction pointer at any transaction, and when the ATM invokes execute through this pointer, the version of execute appropriate to that transaction (i.e., the version implemented in that derived class's .cpp file) runs automatically. For example, suppose a user chooses to perform a balance inquiry. The ATM aims a Transaction pointer at a new object of class BalanceInquiry; the compiler allows this because a BalanceInquiry *is a* Transaction. When the ATM uses this pointer to invoke execute, BalanceInquiry's version of execute is called.

This polymorphic approach also makes the system easily extensible. Should we wish to create a new transaction type (e.g., funds transfer or bill payment), we would just create an additional Transaction derived class that overrides the execute member function with a version appropriate for the new transaction type. We would need to make only minimal changes to the system code to allow users to choose the new transaction type from the main menu and for the ATM to instantiate and execute objects of the new derived class. The ATM could execute transactions of the new type using the current code, because it executes all transactions identically.

As you learned earlier in the chapter, an abstract class like Transaction is one for which you never intend to instantiate objects. An abstract class simply declares common attributes and behaviors for its derived classes in an inheritance hierarchy. Class Transaction defines the concept of what it means to be a transaction that has an account number and executes. You may wonder why we bother to include pure virtual member function execute in class Transaction if execute lacks a concrete implementation. Conceptually, we include this member function because it is the defining behavior of all transactions—executing. Technically, we must include member function execute in base class Transaction so that the ATM (or any other class) can polymorphically invoke each derived class's overridden version of this function through a Transaction pointer or reference.

Derived classes BalanceInquiry, Withdrawal and Deposit inherit attribute accountNumber from base class Transaction, but classes Withdrawal and Deposit contain the additional attribute amount that distinguishes them from class BalanceInquiry. Classes Withdrawal and Deposit require this additional attribute to store the amount of money that the user wishes to withdraw or deposit. Class BalanceInquiry has no need for such an attribute and requires only an account number to execute. Even though two of the three Transaction derived classes share this attribute, we do not place it in base class Transaction—we place only features common to *all* the derived classes in the base class, so derived classes do not inherit unnecessary attributes (and operations).

Figure 13.28 presents an updated class diagram of our model that incorporates inheritance and introduces class Transaction. We model an association between class ATM and class

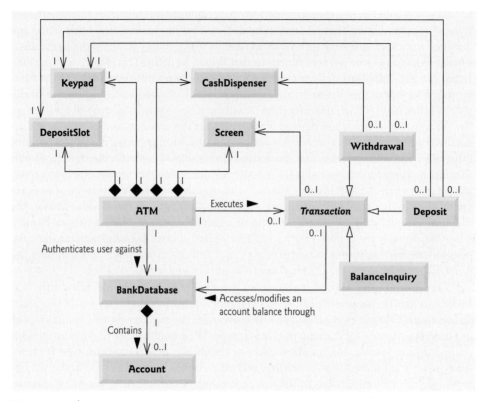

Fig. 13.28 | Class diagram of the ATM system (incorporating inheritance). Note that abstract class name Transaction appears in italics.

Transaction to show that the ATM, at any given moment, either is executing a transaction or is not (i.e., zero or one objects of type Transaction exist in the system at a time). Because a Withdrawal is a type of Transaction, we no longer draw an association line directly between class ATM and class Withdrawal—derived class Withdrawal inherits base class Transaction's association with class ATM. Derived classes BalanceInquiry and Deposit also inherit this association, which replaces the previously omitted associations between classes BalanceInquiry and Deposit and class ATM. Note again the use of triangular hollow arrowheads to indicate the specializations of class Transaction, as indicated in Fig. 13.27.

We also add an association between class Transaction and the BankDatabase (Fig. 13.28). All Transactions require a reference to the BankDatabase so they can access and modify account information. Each Transaction derived class inherits this reference, so we no longer model the association between class Withdrawal and the BankDatabase. Note that the association between class Transaction and the BankDatabase replaces the previously omitted associations between classes BalanceInquiry and Deposit and the BankDatabase.

We include an association between class Transaction and the Screen because all Transactions display output to the user via the Screen. Each derived class inherits this association. Therefore, we no longer include the association previously modeled between Withdrawal and the Screen. Class Withdrawal still participates in associations with the CashDispenser and the Keypad. We do not move these associations to base class Transaction, because the association with the Keypad applies only to classes Withdrawal and Deposit, and the association with the CashDispenser applies only to class Withdrawal.

Our class diagram incorporating inheritance (Fig. 13.28) also models Deposit and BalanceInquiry. We show associations between Deposit and both the DepositSlot and the Keypad. Note that class BalanceInquiry takes part in no associations other than those inherited from class Transaction—a BalanceInquiry interacts only with the BankDatabase and the Screen.

The class diagram of Fig. 9.20 showed attributes and operations with visibility markers. Now we present a modified class diagram in Fig. 13.29 that includes abstract base class Transaction. This abbreviated diagram does not show inheritance relationships (these appear in Fig. 13.28), but instead shows the attributes and operations after we have employed inheritance in our system. Note that abstract class name Transaction and abstract operation name execute in class Transaction appear in italics. To save space, as

Fig. 13.29 | Class diagram after incorporating inheritance into the system.

we did in Fig. 4.24, we do not include those attributes shown by associations in Fig. 13.28—we do, however, include them in the C++ implementation in Appendix G. We also omit all operation parameters, as we did in Fig. 9.20—incorporating inheritance does not affect the parameters already modeled in Figs. 6.36–6.39.

Software Engineering Observation 13.12

A complete class diagram shows all the associations among classes and all the attributes and operations for each class. When the number of class attributes, operations and associations is substantial (as in Fig. 13.28 and Fig. 13.29), a good practice that promotes readability is to divide this information between two class diagrams—one focusing on associations and the other on attributes and operations. However, when examining classes modeled in this fashion, it is crucial to consider both class diagrams to get a complete view of the classes. For example, one must refer to Fig. 13.28 to observe the inheritance relationship between Transaction and its derived classes that is omitted from Fig. 13.29.

Implementing the ATM System Design Incorporating Inheritance

In Section 9.11, we began implementing the ATM system design in C++ code. We now modify our implementation to incorporate inheritance, using class Withdrawal as an example.

1. If a class A is a generalization of class B, then class B is derived from (and is a specialization of) class A. For example, abstract base class Transaction is a generalization of class Withdrawal. Thus, class Withdrawal is derived from (and is a specialization of) class Transaction. Figure 13.30 contains a portion of class Withdrawal's header file, in which the class definition indicates the inheritance relationship between Withdrawal and Transaction (line 9).

2. If class A is an abstract class and class B is derived from class A, then class B must implement the pure virtual functions of class A if class B is to be a concrete class. For example, class Transaction contains pure virtual function execute, so class Withdrawal must implement this member function if we want to instantiate a Withdrawal object. Figure 13.31 contains the C++ header file for class Withdrawal from Fig. 13.28 and Fig. 13.29. Class Withdrawal inherits data member accountNumber from base class Transaction, so Withdrawal does not declare this data member. Class Withdrawal also inherits references to the Screen and the BankDatabase from its base class Transaction, so we do not include these references in our code. Figure 13.29 specifies attribute amount and operation execute for class Withdrawal. Line 19 of Fig. 13.31 declares a data member for attribute amount. Line 16 contains the function prototype for operation execute. Recall that, to be a concrete class, derived class Withdrawal must provide a concrete implementation of the pure virtual function execute in base class Transaction. The prototype in line 16 signals your intent to override the base class pure virtual function. You must provide this prototype if you will provide an implementation in the .cpp file. We present this implementation in Appendix G. The keypad and cashDispenser references (lines 20–21) are data members derived from Withdrawal's associations in Fig. 13.28. In the implementation of this class in Appendix G, a constructor initializes these references to actual objects. Once again, to be able to compile the declarations of the references in lines 20–21, we include the forward declarations in lines 8–9.

```
I    // Fig. 13.30: Withdrawal.h
2    // Definition of class Withdrawal that represents a withdrawal transaction
3    #ifndef WITHDRAWAL_H
4    #define WITHDRAWAL_H
5
6    #include "Transaction.h" // Transaction class definition
7
8    // class Withdrawal derives from base class Transaction
9    class Withdrawal : public Transaction
10   {
11   }; // end class Withdrawal
12
13   #endif // WITHDRAWAL_H
```

Fig. 13.30 | Withdrawal class definition that derives from Transaction.

```
I    // Fig. 13.31: Withdrawal.h
2    // Definition of class Withdrawal that represents a withdrawal transaction
3    #ifndef WITHDRAWAL_H
4    #define WITHDRAWAL_H
5
6    #include "Transaction.h" // Transaction class definition
7
8    class Keypad; // forward declaration of class Keypad
9    class CashDispenser; // forward declaration of class CashDispenser
10
11   // class Withdrawal derives from base class Transaction
12   class Withdrawal : public Transaction
13   {
14   public:
15      // member function overriding execute in base class Transaction
16      virtual void execute(); // perform the transaction
17   private:
18      // attributes
19      double amount; // amount to withdraw
20      Keypad &keypad; // reference to ATM's keypad
21      CashDispenser &cashDispenser; // reference to ATM's cash dispenser
22   }; // end class Withdrawal
23
24   #endif // WITHDRAWAL_H
```

Fig. 13.31 | Withdrawal class header file based on Fig. 13.28 and Fig. 13.29.

ATM Case Study Wrap-Up

This concludes our object-oriented design of the ATM system. A complete C++ implementation of the ATM system in 877 lines of code appears in Appendix G. This working implementation uses key programming notions, including classes, objects, encapsulation, visibility, composition, inheritance and polymorphism. The code is abundantly commented and conforms to the coding practices you've learned. Mastering this code is a wonderful capstone experience for you after studying Chapters 1–13.

Software Engineering Case Study Self-Review Exercises

13.1 The UML uses an arrow with a _____ to indicate a generalization relationship.
a) solid filled arrowhead
b) triangular hollow arrowhead
c) diamond-shaped hollow arrowhead
d) stick arrowhead

13.2 State whether the following statement is *true* or *false*, and if *false*, explain why: The UML requires that we underline abstract class names and operation names.

13.3 Write a C++ header file to begin implementing the design for class Transaction specified in Fig. 13.28 and Fig. 13.29. Be sure to include private references based on class Transaction's associations. Also be sure to include public *get* functions for any of the private data members that the derived classes must access to perform their tasks.

Answers to Software Engineering Case Study Self-Review Exercises

13.1 b.

13.2 False. The UML requires that we italicize abstract class names and operation names.

13.3 The design for class Transaction yields the header file in Fig. 13.32. In the implementation in Appendix G, a constructor initializes private reference attributes screen and bankDatabase to actual objects, and member functions getScreen and getBankDatabase access these attributes. These member functions allow classes derived from Transaction to access the ATM's screen and interact with the bank's database.

```cpp
1   // Fig. 13.32: Transaction.h
2   // Transaction abstract base class definition.
3   #ifndef TRANSACTION_H
4   #define TRANSACTION_H
5
6   class Screen; // forward declaration of class Screen
7   class BankDatabase; // forward declaration of class BankDatabase
8
9   class Transaction
10  {
11  public:
12     int getAccountNumber(); // return account number
13     Screen &getScreen(); // return reference to screen
14     BankDatabase &getBankDatabase(); // return reference to bank database
15
16     // pure virtual function to perform the transaction
17     virtual void execute() = 0; // overridden in derived classes
18  private:
19     int accountNumber; // indicates account involved
20     Screen &screen; // reference to the screen of the ATM
21     BankDatabase &bankDatabase; // reference to the account info database
22  }; // end class Transaction
23
24  #endif // TRANSACTION_H
```

Fig. 13.32 | Transaction class header file based on Fig. 13.28 and Fig. 13.29.

13.11 Wrap-Up

In this chapter we discussed polymorphism, which enables us to "program in the general" rather than "program in the specific," and we showed how this makes programs more extensible. We began with an example of how polymorphism would allow a screen manager to display several "space" objects. We then demonstrated how base-class and derived-class pointers can be aimed at base-class and derived-class objects. We said that aiming base-class pointers at base-class objects is natural, as is aiming derived-class pointers at derived-class objects. Aiming base-class pointers at derived-class objects is also natural because a derived-class object *is an* object of its base class. You learned why aiming derived-class pointers at base-class objects is dangerous and why the compiler disallows such assignments. We introduced virtual functions, which enable the proper functions to be called when objects at various levels of an inheritance hierarchy are referenced (at execution time) via base-class pointers. This is known as dynamic or late binding. We then discussed pure virtual functions (virtual functions that do not provide an implementation) and abstract classes (classes with one or more pure virtual functions). You learned that abstract classes cannot be used to instantiate objects, while concrete classes can. We then demonstrated using abstract classes in an inheritance hierarchy. You learned how polymorphism works "under the hood" with *vtables* that are created by the compiler. We discussed downcasting base-class pointers to derived-class pointers to enable a program to call derived-class-only member functions. The chapter concluded with a discussion of virtual destructors, and how they ensure that all appropriate destructors in an inheritance hierarchy run on a derived-class object when that object is deleted via a base-class pointer.

In the next chapter, we discuss templates, a sophisticated feature of C++ that enables programmers to define a family of related classes or functions with a single code segment.

Summary

Section 13.1 Introduction

- Polymorphism enables us to "program in the general" rather than "program in the specific."
- Polymorphism enables us to write programs that process objects of classes that are part of the same class hierarchy as if they were all objects of the hierarchy's base class.
- With polymorphism, we can design and implement systems that are easily extensible—new classes can be added with little or no modification to the general portions of the program, as long as the new classes are part of the inheritance hierarchy that the program processes generically. The only parts of a program that must be altered to accommodate new classes are those that require direct knowledge of the new classes that you add to the hierarchy.
- Runtime type information (RTTI) and dynamic casting enable a program to determine the type of an object at execution time and act on that object accordingly.

Section 13.2 Polymorphism Examples

- With polymorphism, one function can cause different actions to occur, depending on the type of the object on which the function is invoked.
- With virtual functions and polymorphism, it becomes possible to design and implement systems that are more easily extensible. Programs can be written to process objects of types that may not exist when the program is under development.

Section 13.3 Relationships Among Objects in an Inheritance Hierarchy

- C++ enables polymorphism—the ability for objects of different classes related by inheritance to respond differently to the same member-function call.

- Polymorphism is implemented via `virtual` functions and dynamic binding.

- When a request is made through a base-class pointer or reference to use a `virtual` function, C++ chooses the correct overridden function in the appropriate derived class associated with the object.

- If a `virtual` function is called by referencing a specific object by name and using the dot member-selection operator, the reference is resolved at compile time (this is called static binding); the `virtual` function that is called is the one defined for the class of that particular object.

- Derived classes can provide their own implementations of a base-class `virtual` function if necessary, but if they do not, the base class's implementation is used.

Section 13.4 Type Fields and `switch` *Statements*

- Polymorphic programming with `virtual` functions can eliminate the need for `switch` logic. You can use the `virtual` function mechanism to perform the equivalent logic automatically, thus avoiding the kinds of errors typically associated with `switch` logic.

Section 13.5 Abstract Classes and Pure `virtual` *Functions*

- In many situations it is useful to define abstract classes for which you never intend to create objects. Because these are used only as base classes, we refer to them as abstract base classes. No objects of an abstract class may be instantiated.

- Classes from which objects can be instantiated are called concrete classes.

- A class is made abstract by declaring one or more of its `virtual` functions to be pure. A pure `virtual` function is one with a pure specifier (= 0) in its declaration.

- If a class is derived from a class with a pure `virtual` function and that derived class does not supply a definition for that pure `virtual` function, then that `virtual` function remains pure in the derived class. Consequently, the derived class is also an abstract class.

- Although we cannot instantiate objects of abstract base classes, we can declare pointers and references to objects of abstract base classes. Such pointers and references can be used to enable polymorphic manipulations of derived-class objects instantiated from concrete derived classes.

Section 13.7 (Optional) Polymorphism, Virtual Functions and Dynamic Binding "Under the Hood"

- Dynamic binding requires that at runtime, the call to a virtual member function be routed to the `virtual` function version appropriate for the class. A `virtual` function table called the *vtable* is implemented as an array containing function pointers. Each class with `virtual` functions has a *vtable*. For each `virtual` function in the class, the *vtable* has an entry containing a function pointer to the version of the `virtual` function to use for an object of that class. The `virtual` function to use for a particular class could be the function defined in that class, or it could be a function inherited either directly or indirectly from a base class higher in the hierarchy.

- When a base class provides a `virtual` member function, derived classes can override the `virtual` function, but they do not have to override it. Thus, a derived class can use a base class's version of a `virtual` function.

- Each object of a class with `virtual` functions contains a pointer to the *vtable* for that class. When a function call is made from a base-class pointer to a derived-class object, the appropriate function pointer in the *vtable* is obtained and dereferenced to complete the call at execution time. This *vtable* lookup and pointer dereferencing require nominal runtime overhead.

- Any class that has one or more 0 pointers in its *vtable* is an abstract class. Classes without any 0 *vtable* pointers are concrete classes.

- New kinds of classes are regularly added to systems. New classes are accommodated by dynamic binding (also called late binding). The type of an object need not be known at compile time for a virtual-function call to be compiled. At runtime, the appropriate member function will be called for the object to which the pointer points.

Section 13.8 Case Study: Payroll System Using Polymorphism and Runtime Type Information with Downcasting, `dynamic_cast`, `typeid` and `type_info`

- Operator `dynamic_cast` checks the type of the object to which the pointer points, then determines whether this type has an *is-a* relationship with the type to which the pointer is being converted. If there is an *is-a* relationship, `dynamic_cast` returns the object's address. If not, `dynamic_cast` returns 0.

- Operator `typeid` returns a reference to an object of class `type_info` that contains information about the type of its operand, including the name of the type. To use `typeid`, the program must include header file `<typeinfo>`.

- When invoked, `type_info` member function `name` returns a pointer-based string that contains the name of the type that the `type_info` object represents.

- Operators `dynamic_cast` and `typeid` are part of C++'s runtime type information (RTTI) feature, which allows a program to determine an object's type at runtime.

Section 13.9 Virtual Destructors

- Declare the base-class destructor `virtual` if the class contains `virtual` functions. This makes all derived-class destructors virtual, even though they do not have the same name as the base-class destructor. If an object in the hierarchy is destroyed explicitly by applying the `delete` operator to a base-class pointer to a derived-class object, the destructor for the appropriate class is called. After a derived-class destructor runs, the destructors for all of that class's base classes run all the way up the hierarchy—the root class's destructor runs last.

Terminology

abstract base class
abstract class
base-class pointer to a base-class object
base-class pointer to a derived-class object
concrete class
dangerous pointer manipulation
derived-class pointer to a base-class object
derived-class pointer to a derived-class object
downcasting
dynamic binding
dynamic casting
`dynamic_cast`
dynamically determine function to execute
flow of control of a `virtual` function call
implementation inheritance
interface inheritance
iterator class
late binding
`name` function of class `type_info`

nonvirtual destructor
object's *vtable* pointer
offset into a *vtable*
override a function
polymorphic programming
polymorphism
polymorphism as an alternative to `switch` logic
programming in the general
programming in the specific
pure specifier (with virtual functions)
pure `virtual` function
RTTI (runtime type information)
static binding
`switch` logic
`type_info` class
`typeid` operator
`<typeinfo>` header file
`virtual` destructor

virtual function
virtual function table (*vtable*)
virtual keyword

vtable
vtable pointer

Self-Review Exercises

13.1   Fill in the blanks in each of the following statements:
   a) Treating a base-class object as a(n) _____ can cause errors.
   b) Polymorphism helps eliminate _____ logic.
   c) If a class contains at least one pure virtual function, it is a(n) _____ class.
   d) Classes from which objects can be instantiated are called _____ classes.
   e) Operator _____ can be used to downcast base-class pointers safely.
   f) Operator typeid returns a reference to a(n) _____ object.
   g) _____ involves using a base-class pointer or reference to invoke virtual functions on base-class and derived-class objects.
   h) Overridable functions are declared using keyword _____.
   i) Casting a base-class pointer to a derived-class pointer is called _____.

13.2   State whether each of the following is *true* or *false*. If *false*, explain why.
   a) All virtual functions in an abstract base class must be declared as pure virtual functions.
   b) Referring to a derived-class object with a base-class handle is dangerous.
   c) A class is made abstract by declaring that class virtual.
   d) If a base class declares a pure virtual function, a derived class must implement that function to become a concrete class.
   e) Polymorphic programming can eliminate the need for switch logic.

Answers to Self-Review Exercises

13.1   a) derived-class object. b) switch. c) abstract. d) concrete. e) dynamic_cast. f) type_info. g) Polymorphism. h) virtual. i) downcasting.

13.2   a) False. An abstract base class can include virtual functions with implementations. b) False. Referring to a base-class object with a derived-class handle is dangerous. c) False. Classes are never declared virtual. Rather, a class is made abstract by including at least one pure virtual function in the class. d) True. e) True.

Exercises

13.3   How is it that polymorphism enables you to program "in the general" rather than "in the specific"? Discuss the key advantages of programming "in the general."

13.4   Discuss the problems of programming with switch logic. Explain why polymorphism can be an effective alternative to using switch logic.

13.5   Distinguish between inheriting interface and inheriting implementation. How do inheritance hierarchies designed for inheriting interface differ from those designed for inheriting implementation?

13.6   What are virtual functions? Describe a circumstance in which virtual functions would be appropriate.

13.7   Distinguish between static binding and dynamic binding. Explain the use of virtual functions and the *vtable* in dynamic binding.

13.8   Distinguish between virtual functions and pure virtual functions.

13.9 Suggest one or more levels of abstract base classes for the Shape hierarchy discussed in this chapter and shown in Fig. 12.3. (The first level is Shape, and the second level consists of the classes TwoDimensionalShape and ThreeDimensionalShape.)

13.10 How does polymorphism promote extensibility?

13.11 You have been asked to develop a flight simulator that will have elaborate graphical outputs. Explain why polymorphic programming could be especially effective for a problem of this nature.

13.12 *(Payroll System Modification)* Modify the payroll system of Figs. 13.13–13.23 to include private data member birthDate in class Employee. Use class Date from Figs. 11.12–11.13 to represent an employee's birthday. Assume that payroll is processed once per month. Create a vector of Employee references to store the various employee objects. In a loop, calculate the payroll for each Employee (polymorphically), and add a $100.00 bonus to the person's payroll amount if the current month is the month in which the Employee's birthday occurs.

13.13 *(Shape Hierarchy)* Implement the Shape hierarchy designed in Exercise 12.7 (which is based on the hierarchy in Fig. 12.3). Each TwoDimensionalShape should contain function getArea to calculate the area of the two-dimensional shape. Each ThreeDimensionalShape should have member functions getArea and getVolume to calculate the surface area and volume, respectively, of the three-dimensional shape. Create a program that uses a vector of Shape pointers to objects of each concrete class in the hierarchy. The program should print the object to which each vector element points. Also, in the loop that processes all the shapes in the vector, determine whether each shape is a TwoDimensionalShape or a ThreeDimensionalShape. If a shape is a TwoDimensionalShape, display its area. If a shape is a ThreeDimensionalShape, display its area and volume.

13.14 *(Polymorphic Screen Manager Using Shape Hierarchy)* Develop a basic graphics package. Use the Shape hierarchy implemented in Exercise 13.13. Limit yourself to two-dimensional shapes such as squares, rectangles, triangles and circles. Interact with the user. Let the user specify the position, size, shape and fill characters to be used in drawing each shape. The user can specify more than one of the same shape. As you create each shape, place a Shape * pointer to each new Shape object into an array. Each Shape class should now have its own draw member function. Write a polymorphic screen manager that walks through the array, sending draw messages to each object in the array to form a screen image. Redraw the screen image each time the user specifies an additional shape.

13.15 *(Package Inheritance Hierarchy)* Use the Package inheritance hierarchy created in Exercise 12.9 to create a program that displays the address information and calculates the shipping costs for several Packages. The program should contain a vector of Package pointers to objects of classes TwoDayPackage and OvernightPackage. Loop through the vector to process the Packages polymorphically. For each Package, invoke *get* functions to obtain the address information of the sender and the recipient, then print the two addresses as they would appear on mailing labels. Also, call each Package's calculateCost member function and print the result. Keep track of the total shipping cost for all Packages in the vector, and display this total when the loop terminates.

13.16 *(Polymorphic Banking Program Using Account Hierarchy)* Develop a polymorphic banking program using the Account hierarchy created in Exercise 12.10. Create a vector of Account pointers to SavingsAccount and CheckingAccount objects. For each Account in the vector, allow the user to specify an amount of money to withdraw from the Account using member function debit and an amount of money to deposit into the Account using member function credit. As you process each Account, determine its type. If an Account is a SavingsAccount, calculate the amount of interest owed to the Account using member function calculateInterest, then add the interest to the account balance using member function credit. After processing an Account, print the updated account balance obtained by invoking base-class member function getBalance.

14

Templates

OBJECTIVES

In this chapter you'll learn:

- To use function templates to conveniently create a group of related (overloaded) functions.

- To distinguish between function templates and function-template specializations.

- To use class templates to create a group of related types.

- To distinguish between class templates and class-template specializations.

- To overload function templates.

- To understand the relationships among templates, friends, inheritance and static members.

14.1 Introduction

In this chapter, we discuss one of C++'s more powerful software reuse features, namely templates. Function templates and class templates enable programmers to specify, with a single code segment, an entire range of related (overloaded) functions—called function-template specializations—or an entire range of related classes—called class-template specializations. This technique is called generic programming.

We might write a single function template for an array-sort function, then have C++ generate separate function-template specializations that will sort `int` arrays, `float` arrays, `string` arrays and so on. We introduced function templates in Chapter 6. We present an additional discussion and example in this chapter.

We might write a single class template for a stack class, then have C++ generate separate class-template specializations, such as a stack-of-`int` class, a stack-of-`float` class, a stack-of-`string` class and so on.

Note the distinction between templates and template specializations: Function templates and class templates are like stencils out of which we trace shapes; function-template specializations and class-template specializations are like the separate tracings that all have the same shape, but could, for example, be drawn in different colors.

In this chapter, we present a function template and a class template. We also consider the relationships between templates and other C++ features, such as overloading, inheritance, friends and `static` members. The design and details of the template mechanisms discussed here are based on the work of Bjarne Stroustrup as presented in his paper, *Parameterized Types for C++*, and as published in the *Proceedings of the USENIX C++ Conference* held in Denver, Colorado, in October 1988.

This chapter is only an introduction to templates. Chapter 22, Standard Template Library (STL), presents an in-depth treatment of the template container classes, iterators and algorithms of the STL. Chapter 22 contains dozens of live-code template-based examples illustrating more sophisticated template-programming techniques than those used here.

Software Engineering Observation 14.1

Most C++ compilers require the complete definition of a template to appear in the client source-code file that uses the template. For this reason and for reusability, templates are often defined in header files, which are then #included into the appropriate client source-code files. For class templates, this means that the member functions are also defined in the header file.

14.2 Function Templates

Overloaded functions normally perform *similar* or *identical* operations on different types of data. If the operations are *identical* for each type, they can be expressed more compactly and conveniently using function templates. Initially, you write a single function-template definition. Based on the argument types provided explicitly or inferred from calls to this function, the compiler generates separate source-code functions (i.e., function-template specializations) to handle each function call appropriately. In C, this task can be performed using macros created with the preprocessor directive #define (see Appendix F, Preprocessor). However, macros can have serious side effects and do not enable the compiler to perform type checking. Function templates provide a compact solution, like macros, but enable full type checking.

Error-Prevention Tip 14.1

Function templates, like macros, enable software reuse. Unlike macros, function templates help eliminate many types of errors through the scrutiny of full C++ type checking.

All function-template definitions begin with keyword `template` followed by a list of template parameters to the function template enclosed in angle brackets (< and >); each template parameter that represents a type must be preceded by either of the interchangeable keywords `class` or `typename`, as in

        template< typename T >

or

        template< class ElementType >

or

        template< typename BorderType, typename FillType >

The type template parameters of a function-template definition are used to specify the types of the arguments to the function, to specify the return type of the function and to declare variables within the function. The function definition follows and appears like any other function definition. Note that keywords `typename` and `class` used to specify function-template parameters actually mean "any built-in type or user-defined type."

Common Programming Error 14.1

Not placing keyword class or keyword typename before each type template parameter of a function template is a syntax error.

Example: Function Template `printArray`

Let us examine function template `printArray` in Fig. 14.1, lines 8–15. Function template `printArray` declares (line 8) a single template parameter T (T can be any valid identifier) for the type of the array to be printed by function `printArray`; T is referred to as a type template parameter, or type parameter. You'll see nontype template parameters in Section 14.5.

When the compiler detects a `printArray` function invocation in the client program (e.g., lines 30, 35 and 40), the compiler uses its overload resolution capabilities to find a definition of function `printArray` that best matches the function call. In this case, the only `printArray` function with the appropriate number of parameters is the `printArray` function template (lines 8–15). Consider the function call at line 30. The compiler compares the type of printArray's first argument (int * at line 30) to the printArray function template's first parameter (const T * const at line 9) and deduces that replacing the type parameter T with int would make the argument consistent with the parameter. Then, the compiler substitutes int for T throughout the template definition and compiles a printArray specialization that can display an array of int values. In Fig. 14.1, the compiler creates three printArray specializations—one that expects an int array, one that expects a double array and one that expects a char array. For example, the function-template specialization for type int is

```
void printArray( const int * const array, int count )
{
   for ( int i = 0; i < count; i++ )
      cout << array[ i ] << " ";

   cout << endl;
} // end function printArray
```

The name of a template parameter can be declared only once in the template parameter list of a template header but can be used repeatedly in the function's header and body. Template parameter names among function templates need not be unique.

```
 1   // Fig. 14.1: fig14_01.cpp
 2   // Using template functions.
 3   #include <iostream>
 4   using std::cout;
 5   using std::endl;
 6
 7   // function template printArray definition
 8   template< typename T >
 9   void printArray( const T * const array, int count )
10   {
11      for ( int i = 0; i < count; i++ )
12         cout << array[ i ] << " ";
13
14      cout << endl;
15   } // end function template printArray
16
17   int main()
18   {
19      const int ACOUNT = 5; // size of array a
20      const int BCOUNT = 7; // size of array b
21      const int CCOUNT = 6; // size of array c
22
23      int a[ ACOUNT ] = { 1, 2, 3, 4, 5 };
24      double b[ BCOUNT ] = { 1.1, 2.2, 3.3, 4.4, 5.5, 6.6, 7.7 };
25      char c[ CCOUNT ] = "HELLO"; // 6th position for null
26
27      cout << "Array a contains:" << endl;
28
```

Fig. 14.1 | Function-template specializations of function template printArray. (Part 1 of 2.)

```
29        // call integer function-template specialization
30        printArray( a, ACOUNT );
31
32        cout << "Array b contains:" << endl;
33
34        // call double function-template specialization
35        printArray( b, BCOUNT );
36
37        cout << "Array c contains:" << endl;
38
39        // call character function-template specialization
40        printArray( c, CCOUNT );
41        return 0;
42   } // end main
```

```
Array a contains:
1 2 3 4 5
Array b contains:
1.1 2.2 3.3 4.4 5.5 6.6 7.7
Array c contains:
H E L L O
```

Fig. 14.1 | Function-template specializations of function template `printArray`. (Part 2 of 2.)

Figure 14.1 demonstrates function template `printArray` (lines 8–15). The program begins by declaring five-element `int` array a, seven-element `double` array b and six-element `char` array c (lines 23–25, respectively). Then, the program outputs each array by calling `printArray`—once with a first argument a of type `int *` (line 30), once with a first argument b of type `double *` (line 35) and once with a first argument c of type `char *` (line 40). The call in line 30, for example, causes the compiler to infer that T is `int` and to instantiate a `printArray` function-template specialization, for which type parameter T is `int`. The call in line 35 causes the compiler to infer that T is `double` and to instantiate a second `printArray` function-template specialization, for which type parameter T is `double`. The call in line 40 causes the compiler to infer that T is `char` and to instantiate a third `printArray` function-template specialization, for which type parameter T is char. It is important to note that if T (line 8) represents a user-defined type (which it does not in Fig. 14.1), there must be an overloaded stream insertion operator for that type; otherwise, the first stream insertion operator in line 12 will not compile.

Common Programming Error 14.2

If a template is invoked with a user-defined type, and if that template uses functions or operators (e.g., ==, +, <=) with objects of that class type, then those functions and operators must be overloaded for the user-defined type. Forgetting to overload such operators causes compilation errors.

In this example, the template mechanism saves you from having to write three separate overloaded functions with prototypes

```
void printArray( const int *, int );
void printArray( const double *, int );
void printArray( const char *, int );
```

that all use the same code, except for type T (as used in line 9).

Performance Tip 14.1

Although templates offer software-reusability benefits, remember that multiple function-template specializations and class-template specializations are instantiated in a program (at compile time), despite the fact that the templates are written only once. These copies can consume considerable memory. This is not normally an issue, though, because the code generated by the template is the same size as the code you would have written to produce the separate overloaded functions.

14.3 Overloading Function Templates

Function templates and overloading are intimately related. The function-template specializations generated from a function template all have the same name, so the compiler uses overloading resolution to invoke the proper function.

A function template may be overloaded in several ways. We can provide other function templates that specify the same function name but different function parameters. For example, function template printArray of Fig. 14.1 could be overloaded with another printArray function template with additional parameters lowSubscript and highSubscript to specify the portion of the array to output (see Exercise 14.4).

A function template also can be overloaded by providing nontemplate functions with the same function name but different function arguments. For example, function template printArray of Fig. 14.1 could be overloaded with a nontemplate version that specifically prints an array of character strings in neat, tabular format (see Exercise 14.5).

The compiler performs a matching process to determine what function to call when a function is invoked. First, the compiler finds all function templates that match the function named in the function call and creates specializations based on the arguments in the function call. Then, the compiler finds all the ordinary functions that match the function named in the function call. If one of the ordinary functions or function-template specializations is the best match for the function call, that ordinary function or specialization is used. If an ordinary function and a specialization are equally good matches for the function call, then the ordinary function is used. Otherwise, if there are multiple matches for the function call, the compiler considers the call to be ambiguous and the compiler generates an error message.

Common Programming Error 14.3

A compilation error occurs if no matching function definition can be found for a particular function call or of there are multiple matches that the compiler considers ambigous.

14.4 Class Templates

It is possible to understand the concept of a "stack" (a data structure into which we insert items at the top and retrieve those items in last-in, first-out order) independent of the type of the items being placed in the stack. However, to instantiate a stack, a data type must be specified. This creates a wonderful opportunity for software reusability. We need the means for describing the notion of a stack generically and instantiating classes that are type-specific versions of this generic stack class. C++ provides this capability through class templates.

Software Engineering Observation 14.2

Class templates encourage software reusability by enabling type-specific versions of generic classes to be instantiated.

Class templates are called parameterized types, because they require one or more type parameters to specify how to customize a "generic class" template to form a class-template specialization.

To produce a variety of class-template specializations you write only one class-template definition. Each time an additional class-template specialization is needed, you use a concise, simple notation, and the compiler writes the source code for the specialization you require. One Stack class template, for example, could thus become the basis for creating many Stack classes (such as "Stack of double," "Stack of int," "Stack of char," "Stack of Employee," etc.) used in a program.

Creating Class Template Stack< T >

Note the Stack class-template definition in Fig. 14.2. It looks like a conventional class definition, except that it is preceded by the header (line 6)

```
template< typename T >
```

to specify a class-template definition with type parameter T which acts as a placeholder for the type of the Stack class to be created. You need not specifically use identifier T—any valid identifier can be used. The type of element to be stored on this Stack is mentioned generically as T throughout the Stack class header and member-function definitions. In a moment, we show how T becomes associated with a specific type, such as double or int. Due to the way this class template is designed, there are two constraints for nonfundamental data types used with this Stack—they must have a default constructor (for use in line 44 to create the array that stores the stack elements), and they must support the assignment operator (lines 56 and 70).

The member-function definitions of a class template are function templates. The member-function definitions that appear outside the class template definition each begin with the header

```
template< typename T >
```

(lines 40, 51 and 65). Thus, each definition resembles a conventional function definition, except that the Stack element type always is listed generically as type parameter T. The binary scope resolution operator is used with the class-template name Stack< T > (lines 41, 52 and 66) to tie each member-function definition to the class template's scope. In this case, the generic class name is Stack< T >. When doubleStack is instantiated as type Stack< double >, the Stack constructor function-template specialization uses new to create an array of elements of type double to represent the stack (line 44). The statement

```
stackPtr = new T[ size ];
```

in the Stack class-template definition is generated by the compiler in the class-template specialization Stack< double > as

```
stackPtr = new double[ size ];
```

```cpp
 1   // Fig. 14.2: Stack.h
 2   // Stack class template.
 3   #ifndef STACK_H
 4   #define STACK_H
 5
 6   template< typename T >
 7   class Stack
 8   {
 9   public:
10      Stack( int = 10 ); // default constructor (Stack size 10)
11
12      // destructor
13      ~Stack()
14      {
15         delete [] stackPtr; // deallocate internal space for Stack
16      } // end ~Stack destructor
17
18      bool push( const T & ); // push an element onto the Stack
19      bool pop( T & ); // pop an element off the Stack
20
21      // determine whether Stack is empty
22      bool isEmpty() const
23      {
24         return top == -1;
25      } // end function isEmpty
26
27      // determine whether Stack is full
28      bool isFull() const
29      {
30         return top == size - 1;
31      } // end function isFull
32
33   private:
34      int size; // # of elements in the Stack
35      int top; // location of the top element (-1 means empty)
36      T *stackPtr; // pointer to internal representation of the Stack
37   }; // end class template Stack
38
39   // constructor template
40   template< typename T >
41   Stack< T >::Stack( int s )
42      : size( s > 0 ? s : 10 ), // validate size
43        top( -1 ), // Stack initially empty
44        stackPtr( new T[ size ] ) // allocate memory for elements
45   {
46      // empty body
47   } // end Stack constructor template
48
49   // push element onto Stack;
50   // if successful, return true; otherwise, return false
51   template< typename T >
52   bool Stack< T >::push( const T &pushValue )
53   {
```

Fig. 14.2 | Class template Stack. (Part 1 of 2.)

```
54        if ( !isFull() )
55        {
56            stackPtr[ ++top ] = pushValue; // place item on Stack
57            return true; // push successful
58        } // end if
59
60        return false; // push unsuccessful
61    } // end function template push
62
63    // pop element off Stack;
64    // if successful, return true; otherwise, return false
65    template< typename T >
66    bool Stack< T >::pop( T &popValue )
67    {
68        if ( !isEmpty() )
69        {
70            popValue = stackPtr[ top-- ]; // remove item from Stack
71            return true; // pop successful
72        } // end if
73
74        return false; // pop unsuccessful
75    } // end function template pop
76
77    #endif
```

Fig. 14.2 | Class template Stack. (Part 2 of 2.)

Creating a Driver to Test Class Template Stack< T >

Now, let us consider the driver (Fig. 14.3) that exercises the Stack class template. The driver begins by instantiating object doubleStack of size 5 (line 11). This object is declared to be of class Stack< double > (pronounced "Stack of double"). The compiler associates type double with type parameter T in the class template to produce the source code for a Stack class of type double. Although templates offer software-reusability benefits, remember that multiple class-template specializations are instantiated in a program (at compile time), even though the template is written only once.

Lines 17–21 invoke push to place the double values 1.1, 2.2, 3.3, 4.4 and 5.5 onto doubleStack. The while loop terminates when the driver attempts to push a sixth value onto doubleStack (which is full, because it holds a maximum of five elements). Note that function push returns false when it is unable to push a value onto the stack.[1]

Lines 27–28 invoke pop in a while loop to remove the five values from the stack (note, in the output of Fig. 14.3, that the values do pop off in last-in, first-out order). When the driver attempts to pop a sixth value, the doubleStack is empty, so the pop loop terminates.

---

1. Class Stack (Fig. 14.2) provides the function isFull, which you can use to determine whether the stack is full before attempting a push operation. This would avoid the potential error of pushing onto a full stack. In Chapter 16, Exception Handling, if the operation cannot be completed, function push would "throw an exception." You can write code to "catch" that exception, then decide how to handle it appropriately for the application. The same technique can be used with function pop when an attempt is made to pop an element from an empty stack.

```cpp
 1   // Fig. 14.3: fig14_03.cpp
 2   // Stack class template test program.
 3   #include <iostream>
 4   using std::cout;
 5   using std::endl;
 6
 7   #include "Stack.h" // Stack class template definition
 8
 9   int main()
10   {
11      Stack< double > doubleStack( 5 ); // size 5
12      double doubleValue = 1.1;
13
14      cout << "Pushing elements onto doubleStack\n";
15
16      // push 5 doubles onto doubleStack
17      while ( doubleStack.push( doubleValue ) )
18      {
19         cout << doubleValue << ' ';
20         doubleValue += 1.1;
21      } // end while
22
23      cout << "\nStack is full. Cannot push " << doubleValue
24         << "\n\nPopping elements from doubleStack\n";
25
26      // pop elements from doubleStack
27      while ( doubleStack.pop( doubleValue ) )
28         cout << doubleValue << ' ';
29
30      cout << "\nStack is empty. Cannot pop\n";
31
32      Stack< int > intStack; // default size 10
33      int intValue = 1;
34      cout << "\nPushing elements onto intStack\n";
35
36      // push 10 integers onto intStack
37      while ( intStack.push( intValue ) )
38      {
39         cout << intValue++ << ' ';
40      } // end while
41
42      cout << "\nStack is full. Cannot push " << intValue
43         << "\n\nPopping elements from intStack\n";
44
45      // pop elements from intStack
46      while ( intStack.pop( intValue ) )
47         cout << intValue << ' ';
48
49      cout << "\nStack is empty. Cannot pop" << endl;
50      return 0;
51   } // end main
```

Fig. 14.3 | Class template Stack test program. (Part 1 of 2.)

```
Pushing elements onto doubleStack
1.1 2.2 3.3 4.4 5.5
Stack is full. Cannot push 6.6

Popping elements from doubleStack
5.5 4.4 3.3 2.2 1.1
Stack is empty. Cannot pop

Pushing elements onto intStack
1 2 3 4 5 6 7 8 9 10
Stack is full. Cannot push 11

Popping elements from intStack
10 9 8 7 6 5 4 3 2 1
Stack is empty. Cannot pop
```

Fig. 14.3 | Class template Stack test program. (Part 2 of 2.)

Line 32 instantiates integer stack intStack with the declaration

```
Stack< int > intStack;
```

(pronounced "intStack is a Stack of int"). Because no size is specified, the size defaults to 10 as specified in the default constructor (Fig. 14.2, line 10). Lines 37–40 loop and invoke push to place values onto intStack until it is full, then lines 46–47 loop and invoke pop to remove values from intStack until it is empty. Once again, notice in the output that the values pop off in last-in, first-out order.

Creating Function Templates to Test Class Template Stack< T >

Notice that the code in function main of Fig. 14.3 is almost identical for both the double-Stack manipulations in lines 11–30 and the intStack manipulations in lines 32–50. This presents another opportunity to use a function template. Figure 14.4 defines function template testStack (lines 14–38) to perform the same tasks as main in Fig. 14.3—push a series of values onto a Stack< T > and pop the values off a Stack< T >. Function template testStack uses template parameter T (specified at line 14) to represent the data type stored in the Stack< T >. The function template takes four arguments (lines 16–19)—a reference

```
 1   // Fig. 14.4: fig14_04.cpp
 2   // Stack class template test program. Function main uses a
 3   // function template to manipulate objects of type Stack< T >.
 4   #include <iostream>
 5   using std::cout;
 6   using std::endl;
 7
 8   #include <string>
 9   using std::string;
10
11   #include "Stack.h" // Stack class template definition
12
```

Fig. 14.4 | Passing a Stack template object to a function template. (Part 1 of 2.)

```
13   // function template to manipulate Stack< T >
14   template< typename T >
15   void testStack(
16      Stack< T > &theStack, // reference to Stack< T >
17      T value, // initial value to push
18      T increment, // increment for subsequent values
19      const string stackName ) // name of the Stack< T > object
20   {
21      cout << "\nPushing elements onto " << stackName << '\n';
22
23      // push element onto Stack
24      while ( theStack.push( value ) )
25      {
26         cout << value << ' ';
27         value += increment;
28      } // end while
29
30      cout << "\nStack is full. Cannot push " << value
31         << "\n\nPopping elements from " << stackName << '\n';
32
33      // pop elements from Stack
34      while ( theStack.pop( value ) )
35         cout << value << ' ';
36
37      cout << "\nStack is empty. Cannot pop" << endl;
38   } // end function template testStack
39
40   int main()
41   {
42      Stack< double > doubleStack( 5 ); // size 5
43      Stack< int > intStack; // default size 10
44
45      testStack( doubleStack, 1.1, 1.1, "doubleStack" );
46      testStack( intStack, 1, 1, "intStack" );
47
48      return 0;
49   } // end main
```

```
Pushing elements onto doubleStack
1.1 2.2 3.3 4.4 5.5
Stack is full. Cannot push 6.6

Popping elements from doubleStack
5.5 4.4 3.3 2.2 1.1
Stack is empty. Cannot pop

Pushing elements onto intStack
1 2 3 4 5 6 7 8 9 10
Stack is full. Cannot push 11

Popping elements from intStack
10 9 8 7 6 5 4 3 2 1
Stack is empty. Cannot pop
```

Fig. 14.4 | Passing a Stack template object to a function template. (Part 2 of 2.)

to an object of type Stack< T >, a value of type T that will be the first value pushed onto the Stack< T >, a value of type T used to increment the values pushed onto the Stack< T > and a string that represents the name of the Stack< T > object for output purposes. Function main (lines 40–49) instantiates an object of type Stack< double > called doubleStack (line 42) and an object of type Stack< int > called intStack (line 43) and uses these objects in lines 45 and 46. The compiler infers the type of T for testStack from the type used to instantiate the function's first argument (i.e., the type used to instantiate double-Stack or intStack). The output of Fig. 14.4 precisely matches the output of Fig. 14.3.

14.5 Nontype Parameters and Default Types for Class Templates

Class template Stack of Section 14.4 used only a type parameter in the template header (Fig. 14.2, line 6). It is also possible to use nontype template parameters or nontype parameters, which can have default arguments and are treated as consts. For example, the template header could be modified to take an int elements parameter as follows:

```
template< typename T, int elements > // nontype parameter elements
```

Then, a declaration such as

```
Stack< double, 100 > mostRecentSalesFigures;
```

could be used to instantiate (at compile time) a 100-element Stack class-template specialization of double values named mostRecentSalesFigures; this class-template specialization would be of type Stack< double, 100 >. The class header then might contain a private data member with an array declaration such as

```
T stackHolder[ elements ]; // array to hold Stack contents
```

In addition, a type parameter can specify a default type. For example,

```
template< typename T = string > // defaults to type string
```

might specify that a Stack contains string objects by default. Then, a declaration such as

```
Stack<> jobDescriptions;
```

could be used to instantiate a Stack class-template specialization of strings named job-Descriptions; this class-template specialization would be of type Stack< string >. Default type parameters must be the rightmost (trailing) parameters in a template's type-parameter list. When one is instantiating a class with two or more default types, if an omitted type is not the rightmost type parameter in the type-parameter list, then all type parameters to the right of that type also must be omitted.

> **Performance Tip 14.2**
>
> *When appropriate, specify the size of a container class (such as an array class or a stack class) at compile time (possibly through a nontype template parameter). This eliminates the execution-time overhead of using new to create the space dynamically.*

> **Software Engineering Observation 14.3**
>
> *Specifying the size of a container at compile time avoids the potentially fatal execution-time error if new is unable to obtain the needed memory.*

In the exercises, you'll be asked to use a nontype parameter to create a template for our class `Array` developed in Chapter 11. This template will enable `Array` objects to be instantiated with a specified number of elements of a specified type at compile time, rather than creating space for the `Array` objects at execution time.

In some cases, it may not be possible to use a particular type with a class template. For example, the `Stack` template of Fig. 14.2 requires that user-defined types that will be stored in a `Stack` must provide a default constructor and an assignment operator. If a particular user-defined type will not work with our `Stack` template or requires customized processing, you can define an explicit specialization of the class template for a particular type. Let's assume we want to create an explicit specialization `Stack` for `Employee` objects. To do this, form a new class with the name `Stack< Employee >` as follows:

```
template<>
class Stack< Employee >
{
    // body of class definition
};
```

Note that the `Stack< Employee >` explicit specialization is a complete replacement for the `Stack` class template that is specific to type `Employee`—it does not use anything from the original class template and can even have different members.

14.6 Notes on Templates and Inheritance

Templates and inheritance relate in several ways:

- A class template can be derived from a class-template specialization.
- A class template can be derived from a nontemplate class.
- A class-template specialization can be derived from a class-template specialization.
- A nontemplate class can be derived from a class-template specialization.

14.7 Notes on Templates and Friends

We have seen that functions and entire classes can be declared as `friend`s of nontemplate classes. With class templates, friendship can be established between a class template and a global function, a member function of another class (possibly a class-template specialization), or even an entire class (possibly a class-template specialization).

Throughout this section, we assume that we have defined a class template for a class named `X` with a single type parameter `T`, as in:

```
template< typename T > class X
```

Under this assumption, it is possible to make a function `f1` a friend of every class-template specialization instantiated from the class template for class `X`. To do so, use a friendship declaration of the form

```
friend void f1();
```

For example, function f1 is a friend of X< double >, X< string > and X< Employee >, etc.

It is also possible to make a function f2 a friend of only a class-template specialization with the same type argument. To do so, use a friendship declaration of the form

```
friend void f2( X< T > & );
```

For example, if T is a float, function f2(X< float > &) is a friend of class-template specialization X< float > but not a friend of class-template specification X< string >.

You can declare that a member function of another class is a friend of any class-template specialization generated from the class template. To do so, the friend declaration must qualify the name of the other class's member function using the class name and the binary scope resolution operator, as in:

```
friend void A::f3();
```

The declaration makes member function f3 of class A a friend of every class-template specialization instantiated from the preceding class template. For example, function f3 of class A is a friend of X< double >, X< string > and X< Employee >, etc.

As with a global function, another class's member function can be a friend of only a class-template specialization with the same type argument. A friendship declaration of the form

```
friend void C< T >::f4( X< T > & );
```

for a particular type T such as float makes member function

```
C< float >::f4( X< float > & )
```

a friend function of *only* class-template specialization X< float >.

In some cases, it is desirable to make an entire class's set of member functions friends of a class template. In this case, a friend declaration of the form

```
friend class Y;
```

makes every member function of class Y a friend of every class-template specialization produced from the class template X.

Finally, it is possible to make all member functions of one class-template specialization friends of another class-template specialization with the same type argument. For example, a friend declaration of the form:

```
friend class Z< T >;
```

indicates that when a class-template specialization is instantiated with a particular type for T (such as float), all members of class Z< float > become friends of class-template specialization X< float >. We use this particular relationship in several examples of Chapter 20, Data Structures.

14.8 Notes on Templates and static Members

What about static data members? Recall that, with a nontemplate class, one copy of each static data member is shared among all objects of the class, and the static data member must be initialized at file scope.

Each class-template specialization instantiated from a class template has its own copy of each `static` data member of the class template; all objects of that specialization share that one `static` data member. In addition, as with `static` data members of nontemplate classes, `static` data members of class-template specializations must be defined and, if necessary, initialized at file scope. Each class-template specialization gets its own copy of the class template's `static` member functions.

14.9 Wrap-Up

This chapter introduced one of C++'s most powerful features—templates. You learned how to use function templates to enable the compiler to produce a set of function-template specializations that represent a group of related overloaded functions. We also discussed how to overload a function template to create a specialized version of a function that handles a particular data type's processing in a manner that differs from the other function-template specializations. Next, you learned about class templates and class-template specializations. You saw examples of how to use a class template to create a group of related types that each perform identical processing on different data types. Finally, you learned about some of the relationships among templates, friends, inheritance and `static` members.

In the next chapter, we discuss many of C++'s I/O capabilities and demonstrate several stream manipulators that perform various formatting tasks.

Summary

Section 14.1 Introduction
- Templates enable us to specify a range of related (overloaded) functions—called function-template specializations—or a range of related classes—called class-template specializations.

Section 14.2 Function Templates
- To use function-template specializations, you write a single function-template definition. Based on the argument types provided in calls to this function, C++ generates separate specializations to handle each type of call appropriately. These are compiled along with the rest of a program's source code.
- All function-template definitions begin with the keyword `template` followed by template parameters to the function template enclosed in angle brackets (< and >); each template parameter that represents a type must be preceded by keyword `class` or `typename`. Keywords `typename` and `class` used to specify function-template parameters mean "any built-in type or user-defined type."
- Template-definition template parameters are used to specify the kinds of arguments to the function, the return type of the function and to declare variables in the function.
- The name of a template parameter can be declared only once in the type-parameter list of a template header. Formal type-parameter names among function templates need not be unique.

Section 14.3 Overloading Function Templates
- A function template may be overloaded in several ways. We can provide other function templates that specify the same function name but different function parameters. A function template can also be overloaded by providing other nontemplate functions with the same function name, but different function parameters.

Section 14.4 Class Templates

- Class templates provide the means for describing a class generically and for instantiating classes that are type-specific versions of this generic class.
- Class templates are called parameterized types; they require type parameters to specify how to customize a generic class template to form a specific class-template specialization.
- To use class-template specializations you write one class template. When you need a new type-specific class, you use a concise notation, and the compiler writes the source code for the class-template specialization.
- A class-template definition looks like a conventional class definition, except that it is preceded by `template< typename T >` (or `template< class T >`) to indicate this is a class-template definition with type parameter `T` which acts as a placeholder for the type of the class to create. The type `T` is mentioned throughout the class header and member-function definitions as a generic type name.
- Member-function definitions outside a class template each begin with `template< typename T >` (or `template< class T >`). Then, each function definition resembles a conventional function definition, except that the generic data in the class always is listed generically as type parameter `T`. The binary scope-resolution operator is used with the class-template name to tie each member-function definition to the class template's scope.

Section 14.5 Nontype Parameters and Default Types for Class Templates

- It is possible to use nontype parameters in the header of a class or function template.
- An explicit specialization of a class template can be provided to override a class template for a specific type.

Section 14.6 Notes on Templates and Inheritance

- A class template can be derived from a class-template specialization. A class template can be derived from a nontemplate class. A class-template specialization can be derived from a class-template specialization. A nontemplate class can be derived from a class-template specialization.

Section 14.7 Notes on Templates and Friends

- Functions and entire classes can be declared as friends of nontemplate classes. With class templates, friendship arrangements can be declared. Friendship can be established between a class template and a global function, a member function of another class (possibly a class-template specialization) or even an entire class (possibly a class-template specialization).

Section 14.8 Notes on Templates and `static` *Members*

- Each class-template specialization instantiated from a class template has its own copy of each `static` data member of the class template; all objects of that specialization share that `static` data member. And as with `static` data members of nontemplate classes, `static` data members of class-template specializations must be defined and, if necessary, initialized at file scope.
- Each class-template specialization gets a copy of the class template's `static` member functions.

Terminology

angle brackets (< and >)	friend of a template
class template	function template
class-template definition	function-template definition
class-template specialization	function-template specialization
explicit specialization	generic programming

keyword class in a template type parameter
keyword template
keyword typename
macro
member function of a class-template
    specialization
nontype parameter
nontype template parameter
overloading a function template
parameterized type
class-template specialization
static data member of a class template

static data member of a class-template
    specialization
static member function of a class template
static member function of a class-template
    specialization
template parameter
template< class T >
template< typename T >
typename
type parameter
type template parameter

Self-Review Exercises

14.1 State which of the following statements are *true* and which are *false*. If a statement is *false*, explain why.

    a) The template parameters of a function-template definition are used to specify the types of the arguments to the function, to specify the return type of the function and to declare variables within the function.

    b) Keywords typename and class as used with a template type parameter specifically mean "any user-defined class type."

    c) A function template can be overloaded by another function template with the same function name.

    d) Template parameter names among template definitions must be unique.

    e) Each member-function definition outside a class template must begin with a template header.

    f) A friend function of a class template must be a function-template specialization.

    g) If several class-template specializations are generated from a single class template with a single static data member, each of the class-template specializations shares a single copy of the class template's static data member.

14.2 Fill in the blanks in each of the following:

    a) Templates enable us to specify, with a single code segment, an entire range of related functions called _____, or an entire range of related classes called _____.

    b) All function-template definitions begin with the keyword _____, followed by a list of template parameters to the function template enclosed in _____.

    c) The related functions generated from a function template all have the same name, so the compiler uses _____ resolution to invoke the proper function.

    d) Class templates also are called _____ types.

    e) The _____ operator is used with a class-template name to tie each member-function definition to the class template's scope.

    f) As with static data members of nontemplate classes, static data members of class-template specializations must also be defined and, if necessary, initialized at _____ scope.

Answers to Self-Review Exercises

14.1 a) True. b) False. Keywords typename and class in this context also allow for a type parameter of a fundamental type. c) True. d) False. Template parameter names among function templates need not be unique. e) True. f) False. It could be a nontemplate function. g) False. Each class-template specialization will have its own copy of the static data member.

14.2   a) function-template specializations, class-template specializations. b) `template`, angle brackets (`<` and `>`). c) overloading. d) parameterized. e) binary scope resolution. f) file.

Exercises

14.3   Write a function template `selectionSort` based on the sort program of Fig. 8.15. Write a driver program that inputs, sorts and outputs an `int` array and a `float` array.

14.4   Overload function template `printArray` of Fig. 14.1 so that it takes two additional integer arguments, namely `int lowSubscript` and `int highSubscript`. A call to this function will print only the designated portion of the array. Validate `lowSubscript` and `highSubscript`; if either is out of range or if `highSubscript` is less than or equal to `lowSubscript`, the overloaded `printArray` function should return 0; otherwise, `printArray` should return the number of elements printed. Then modify `main` to exercise both versions of `printArray` on arrays a, b and c (lines 23–25 of Fig. 14.1). Be sure to test all capabilities of both versions of `printArray`.

14.5   Overload function template `printArray` of Fig. 14.1 with a nontemplate version that specifically prints an array of character strings in neat, tabular, column format.

14.6   Write a simple function template for predicate function `isEqualTo` that compares its two arguments of the same type with the equality operator (`==`) and returns `true` if they are equal and `false` if they are not equal. Use this function template in a program that calls `isEqualTo` only with a variety of built-in types. Now write a separate version of the program that calls `isEqualTo` with a user-defined class type, but does not overload the equality operator. What happens when you attempt to run this program? Now overload the equality operator (with the operator function) `operator==`. Now what happens when you attempt to run this program?

14.7   Use an `int` template nontype parameter `numberOfElements` and a type parameter `elementType` to help create a template for the `Array` class (Figs. 11.6–11.7) we developed in Chapter 11. This template will enable `Array` objects to be instantiated with a specified number of elements of a specified element type at compile time.

14.8   Write a program with class template `Array`. The template can instantiate an `Array` of any element type. Override the template with a specific definition for an `Array` of `float` elements (`class Array< float >`). The driver should demonstrate the instantiation of an `Array` of `int` through the template and should show that an attempt to instantiate an `Array` of `float` uses the definition provided in `class Array< float >`.

14.9   Distinguish between the terms "function template" and "function-template specialization."

14.10   Which is more like a stencil—a class template or a class-template specialization? Explain your answer.

14.11   What is the relationship between function templates and overloading?

14.12   Why might you choose to use a function template instead of a macro?

14.13   What performance problem can result from using function templates and class templates?

14.14   The compiler performs a matching process to determine which function-template specialization to call when a function is invoked. Under what circumstances does an attempt to make a match result in a compile error?

14.15   Why is it appropriate to refer to a class template as a parameterized type?

14.16   Explain why a C++ program would use the statement

```
Array< Employee > workerList( 100 );
```

14.17 Review your answer to Exercise 14.16. Why might a C++ program use the statement

```
Array< Employee > workerList;
```

14.18 Explain the use of the following notation in a C++ program:

```
template< typename T > Array< T >::Array( int s )
```

14.19 Why might you use a nontype parameter with a class template for a container such as an array or stack?

14.20 Suppose that a class template has the header

```
template< typename T > class Ct1
```

Describe the friendship relationships established by placing each of the following friend declarations inside this class template. Identifiers beginning with "f" are functions, identifiers beginning with "C" are classes, identifiers beginning with "Ct" are class templates and T is a template type parameter (i.e., T can represent any fundamental or class type).
  a) `friend void f1();`
  b) `friend void f2( Ct1< T > & );`
  c) `friend void C2::f3();`
  d) `friend void Ct3< T >::f4( Ct1< T > & );`
  e) `friend class C4;`
  f) `friend class Ct5< T >;`

14.21 Suppose that class template Employee has a static data member count. Suppose that three class-template specializations are instantiated from the class template. How many copies of the static data member will exist? How will the use of each be constrained (if at all)?

15

Stream
Input/Output

Consciousness ... does not appear to itself chopped up in bits ... A "river" or a "stream" are the metaphors by which it is most naturally described.
—William James

All the news that's fit to print.
—Adolph S. Ochs

Remove not the landmark on the boundary of the fields.
—Amenehope

OBJECTIVES

In this chapter you'll learn:

- To use C++ object-oriented stream input/output.
- To format input and output.
- The stream-I/O class hierarchy.
- To use stream manipulators.
- To control justification and padding.
- To determine the success or failure of input/output operations.
- To tie output streams to input streams.

15.1 **Introduction**

The C++ standard libraries provide an extensive set of input/output capabilities. This chapter discusses a range of capabilities sufficient for performing most common I/O operations and overviews the remaining capabilities. We discussed some of these features earlier in the text; now we provide a more complete treatment. Many of the I/O features that we'll discuss are object oriented. This style of I/O makes use of other C++ features, such as references, function overloading and operator overloading.

C++ uses type-safe I/O. Each I/O operation is executed in a manner sensitive to the data type. If an I/O member function has been defined to handle a particular data type, then that member function is called to handle that data type. If there is no match between the type of the actual data and a function for handling that data type, the compiler generates an error. Thus, improper data cannot "sneak" through the system (as can occur in C, allowing for some subtle and bizarre errors).

Users can specify how to perform I/O for objects of user-defined types by overloading the stream insertion operator (<<) and the stream extraction operator (>>). This extensibility is one of C++'s most valuable features.

Software Engineering Observation 15.1

Use the C++-style I/O exclusively in C++ programs, even though C-style I/O is available to C++ programmers.

Error-Prevention Tip 15.1

C++ I/O is type safe.

Software Engineering Observation 15.2

C++ enables a common treatment of I/O for predefined types and user-defined types. This commonality facilitates software development and reuse.

15.2 Streams

C++ I/O occurs in streams, which are sequences of bytes. In input operations, the bytes flow from a device (e.g., a keyboard, a disk drive, a network connection, etc.) to main memory. In output operations, bytes flow from main memory to a device (e.g., a display screen, a printer, a disk drive, a network connection, etc.).

An application associates meaning with bytes. The bytes could represent characters, raw data, graphics images, digital speech, digital video or any other information an application may require.

The system I/O mechanisms should transfer bytes from devices to memory (and vice versa) consistently and reliably. Such transfers often involve some mechanical motion, such as the rotation of a disk or a tape, or the typing of keystrokes at a keyboard. The time these transfers take is typically much greater than the time the processor requires to manipulate data internally. Thus, I/O operations require careful planning and tuning to ensure optimal performance.

C++ provides both "low-level" and "high-level" I/O capabilities. Low-level I/O capabilities (i.e., unformatted I/O) specify that some number of bytes should be transferred device-to-memory or memory-to-device. In such transfers, the individual byte is the item of interest. Such low-level capabilities provide high-speed, high-volume transfers but are not particularly convenient for programmers.

Programmers generally prefer a higher-level view of I/O (i.e., formatted I/O), in which bytes are grouped into meaningful units, such as integers, floating-point numbers, characters, strings and user-defined types. These type-oriented capabilities are satisfactory for most I/O other than high-volume file processing.

Performance Tip 15.1

Use unformatted I/O for the best performance in high-volume file processing.

Portability Tip 15.1

Using unformatted I/O can lead to portability problems, because unformatted data is not portable across all platforms.

15.2.1 Classic Streams vs. Standard Streams

In the past, the C++ classic stream libraries enabled input and output of chars. Because a char normally occupies one byte, it can represent only a limited set of characters (such as those in the ASCII character set). However, many languages use alphabets that contain more characters than a single-byte char can represent. The ASCII character set does not provide these characters; the Unicode® character set does. Unicode is an extensive international character set that represents the majority of the world's "commercially viable" languages, mathematical symbols and much more. For more information on Unicode, visit www.unicode.org.

C++ includes the standard stream libraries, which enable developers to build systems capable of performing I/O operations with Unicode characters. For this purpose, C++ includes an additional character type called wchar_t, which can store 2-byte Unicode characters. The C++ standard also redesigned the classic C++ stream classes, which processed only chars, as class templates with separate specializations for processing characters of types char and wchar_t, respectively. We use the char type of class templates throughout this book.

15.2.2 iostream Library Header Files

The C++ iostream library provides hundreds of I/O capabilities. Several header files contain portions of the library interface.

Most C++ programs include the <iostream> header file, which declares basic services required for all stream-I/O operations. The <iostream> header file defines the cin, cout, cerr and clog objects, which correspond to the standard input stream, the standard output stream, the unbuffered standard error stream and the buffered standard error stream, respectively. (cerr and clog are discussed in Section 15.2.3.) Both unformatted- and formatted-I/O services are provided.

The <iomanip> header declares services useful for performing formatted I/O with so-called parameterized stream manipulators, such as setw and setprecision.

The <fstream> header declares services for user-controlled file processing. We use this header in the file-processing programs of Chapter 17, File Processing.

C++ implementations generally contain other I/O-related libraries that provide system-specific capabilities, such as the controlling of special-purpose devices for audio and video I/O.

15.2.3 Stream Input/Output Classes and Objects

The iostream library provides many templates for handling common I/O operations. For example, class template basic_istream supports stream-input operations, class template basic_ostream supports stream-output operations, and class template basic_iostream supports both stream-input and stream-output operations. Each template has a predefined template specialization that enables char I/O. In addition, the iostream library provides a set of typedefs that provide aliases for these template specializations. The **typedef** specifier declares synonyms (aliases) for previously defined data types. Programmers sometimes use typedef to create shorter or more readable type names. For example, the statement

```
typedef Card *CardPtr;
```

defines an additional type name, CardPtr, as a synonym for type Card *. Note that creating a name using typedef does not create a data type; typedef creates only a type name that may be used in the program. Section 21.5 discusses typedef in detail. The typedef istream represents a specialization of basic_istream that enables char input. Similarly, the typedef ostream represents a specialization of basic_ostream that enables char output. Also, the typedef iostream represents a specialization of basic_iostream that enables both char input and output. We use these typedefs throughout this chapter.

Stream-I/O Template Hierarchy and Operator Overloading

Templates basic_istream and basic_ostream both derive through single inheritance from base template basic_ios.[1] Template basic_iostream derives through multiple inheritance[2] from templates basic_istream and basic_ostream. The UML class diagram of Fig. 15.1 summarizes these inheritance relationships.

Operator overloading provides a convenient notation for performing input/output. The left-shift operator (<<) is overloaded to designate stream output and is referred to as the stream insertion operator. The right-shift operator (>>) is overloaded to designate stream input and is referred to as the stream extraction operator. These operators are used with the standard stream objects cin, cout, cerr and clog and, commonly, with user-defined stream objects.

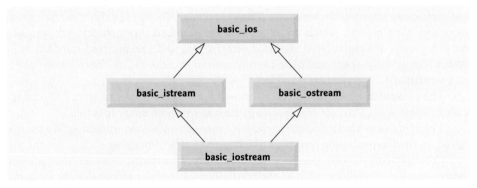

Fig. 15.1 | Stream-I/O template hierarchy portion.

---

1. In this chapter, we discuss templates only in the context of the template specializations that enable char I/O. These specializations are classes and thus can inherit from each other.
2. Multiple inheritance is discussed in Chapter 25, Other Topics.

Standard Stream Objects *cin, cout, cerr and* `clog`

The predefined object `cin` is an `istream` instance and is said to be "connected to" (or attached to) the standard input device, which usually is the keyboard. The stream extraction operator (>>) as used in the following statement causes a value for integer variable `grade` (assuming that `grade` has been declared as an `int` variable) to be input from `cin` to memory:

```
cin >> grade; // data "flows" in the direction of the arrows
```

Note that the compiler determines the data type of `grade` and selects the appropriate overloaded stream extraction operator. Assuming that `grade` has been declared properly, the stream extraction operator does not require additional type information (as is the case, for example, in C-style I/O). The >> operator is overloaded to input data items of built-in types, strings and pointer values.

The predefined object `cout` is an `ostream` instance and is said to be "connected to" the standard output device, which usually is the display screen. The stream insertion operator (<<), as used in the following statement, causes the value of variable `grade` to be output from memory to the standard output device:

```
cout << grade; // data "flows" in the direction of the arrows
```

Note that the compiler also determines the data type of `grade` (assuming `grade` has been declared properly) and selects the appropriate stream insertion operator, so the stream insertion operator does not require additional type information. The << operator is overloaded to output data items of built-in types, strings and pointer values.

The predefined object `cerr` is an `ostream` instance and is said to be "connected to" the standard error device. Outputs to object `cerr` are unbuffered, implying that each stream insertion to `cerr` causes its output to appear immediately—this is appropriate for notifying a user promptly about errors.

The predefined object `clog` is an instance of the `ostream` class and is said to be "connected to" the standard error device. Outputs to `clog` are buffered. This means that each insertion to `clog` could cause its output to be held in a buffer until the buffer is filled or until the buffer is flushed. Buffering is an I/O performance-enhancement technique discussed in operating-systems courses.

File-Processing Templates

C++ file processing uses class templates `basic_ifstream` (for file input), `basic_ofstream` (for file output) and `basic_fstream` (for file input and output). Each class template has a predefined template specialization that enables char I/O. C++ provides a set of `typedefs` that provide aliases for these template specializations. For example, the typedef `ifstream` represents a specialization of `basic_ifstream` that enables char input from a file. Similarly, typedef `ofstream` represents a specialization of `basic_ofstream` that enables char output to a file. Also, typedef `fstream` represents a specialization of `basic_fstream` that enables char input from, and output to, a file. Template `basic_ifstream` inherits from `basic_istream`, `basic_ofstream` inherits from `basic_ostream` and `basic_fstream` inherits from `basic_iostream`. The UML class diagram of Fig. 15.2 summarizes the various inheritance relationships of the I/O-related classes. The full stream-I/O class hierarchy provides most of the capabilities that programmers need. Consult the class-library reference for your C++ system for additional file-processing information.

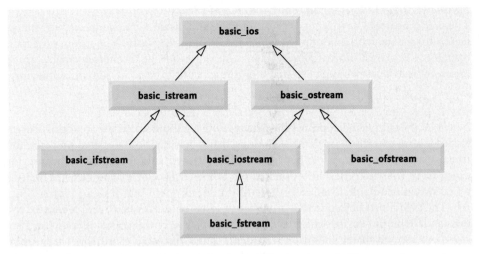

Fig. 15.2 | Stream-I/O template hierarchy portion showing the main file-processing templates.

15.3 Stream Output

Formatted and unformatted output capabilities are provided by ostream. Capabilities for output include output of standard data types with the stream insertion operator (<<); output of characters via the put member function; unformatted output via the write member function (Section 15.5); output of integers in decimal, octal and hexadecimal formats (Section 15.6.1); output of floating-point values with various precision (Section 15.6.2), with forced decimal points (Section 15.7.1), in scientific notation and in fixed notation (Section 15.7.5); output of data justified in fields of designated widths (Section 15.7.2); output of data in fields padded with specified characters (Section 15.7.3); and output of uppercase letters in scientific notation and hexadecimal notation (Section 15.7.6).

15.3.1 Output of char * Variables

C++ determines data types automatically, an improvement over C. This feature sometimes "gets in the way." For example, suppose we want to print the value of a char * to a character string (i.e., the memory address of the first character of that string). However, the << operator has been overloaded to print data of type char * as a null-terminated string. The solution is to cast the char * to a void * (in fact, this should be done to any pointer variable you wish to output as an address). Figure 15.3 demonstrates printing a char * variable in both string and address formats. Note that the address prints as a hexadecimal (base-16) number. [*Note:* To learn more about hexadecimal numbers, read Appendix D, Number Systems.] We say more about controlling the bases of numbers in Section 15.6.1, Section 15.7.4, Section 15.7.5 and Section 15.7.7. [*Note:* The memory address shown in the output of the program in Fig. 15.3 may differ among compilers.]

15.3.2 Character Output Using Member Function put

We can use the put member function to output characters. For example, the statement

```
cout.put( 'A' );
```

```
 1   // Fig. 15.3: Fig15_03.cpp
 2   // Printing the address stored in a char * variable.
 3   #include <iostream>
 4   using std::cout;
 5   using std::endl;
 6
 7   int main()
 8   {
 9      char *word = "again";
10
11      // display value of char *, then display value of char *
12      // static_cast to void *
13      cout << "Value of word is: " << word << endl
14         << "Value of static_cast< void * >( word ) is: "
15         << static_cast< void * >( word ) << endl;
16      return 0;
17   } // end main
```

```
Value of word is: again
Value of static_cast< void * >( word ) is: 00428300
```

Fig. 15.3 | Printing the address stored in a `char *` variable.

displays a single character A. Calls to put may be cascaded, as in the statement

```
cout.put( 'A' ).put( '\n' );
```

which outputs the letter A followed by a newline character. As with <<, the preceding statement executes in this manner, because the dot operator (.) associates from left to right, and the put member function returns a reference to the ostream object (cout) that received the put call. The put function also may be called with a numeric expression that represents an ASCII value, as in the following statement

```
cout.put( 65 );
```

which also outputs A.

15.4 Stream Input

Now let us consider stream input. Formatted and unformatted input capabilities are provided by istream. The stream extraction operator (i.e., the overloaded >> operator) normally skips white-space characters (such as blanks, tabs and newlines) in the input stream; later we'll see how to change this behavior. After each input, the stream extraction operator returns a reference to the stream object that received the extraction message (e.g., cin in the expression cin >> grade). If that reference is used as a condition (e.g., in a while statement's loop-continuation condition), the stream's overloaded void * cast operator function is implicitly invoked to convert the reference into a non-null pointer value or the null pointer based on the success or failure of the last input operation. A non-null pointer converts to the bool value true to indicate success and the null pointer converts to the bool value false to indicate failure. When an attempt is made to read past the end of a stream, the stream's overloaded void * cast operator returns the null pointer to indicate end-of-file.

Each stream object contains a set of state bits used to control the state of the stream (i.e., formatting, setting error states, etc.). These bits are used by the stream's overloaded void * cast operator to determine whether to return a non-null pointer or the null pointer. Stream extraction causes the stream's `failbit` to be set if data of the wrong type is input and causes the stream's `badbit` to be set if the operation fails. Section 15.7 and Section 15.8 discuss stream state bits in detail, then show how to test these bits after an I/O operation.

15.4.1 get and getline Member Functions

The `get` member function with no arguments inputs one character from the designated stream (including white-space characters and other nongraphic characters, such as the key sequence that represents end-of-file) and returns it as the value of the function call. This version of get returns EOF when end-of-file is encountered on the stream.

Using Member Functions *eof, get and put*

Figure 15.4 demonstrates the use of member functions eof and get on input stream cin and member function put on output stream cout. The program first prints the value of cin.eof()—i.e., false (0 on the output)—to show that end-of-file has not occurred on cin. The user enters a line of text and presses *Enter* followed by end-of-file (*<Ctrl>-z* on Microsoft Windows systems, *<Ctrl>-d* on UNIX and Macintosh systems). Line 17 reads each character, which line 18 outputs to cout using member function put. When end-of-file is encountered, the while statement ends, and line 22 displays the value of cin.eof(), which is now true (1 on the output), to show that end-of-file has been set on cin. Note that this program uses the version of istream member function get that takes no argu-

```cpp
1   // Fig. 15.4: Fig15_04.cpp
2   // Using member functions get, put and eof.
3   #include <iostream>
4   using std::cin;
5   using std::cout;
6   using std::endl;
7
8   int main()
9   {
10      int character; // use int, because char cannot represent EOF
11
12      // prompt user to enter line of text
13      cout << "Before input, cin.eof() is " << cin.eof() << endl
14         << "Enter a sentence followed by end-of-file:" << endl;
15
16      // use get to read each character; use put to display it
17      while ( ( character = cin.get() ) != EOF )
18         cout.put( character );
19
20      // display end-of-file character
21      cout << "\nEOF in this system is: " << character << endl;
22      cout << "After input of EOF, cin.eof() is " << cin.eof() << endl;
23      return 0;
24   } // end main
```

Fig. 15.4 | get, put and eof member functions. (Part 1 of 2.)

```
Before input, cin.eof() is 0
Enter a sentence followed by end-of-file:
Testing the get and put member functions
Testing the get and put member functions
^Z

EOF in this system is: -1
After input of EOF, cin.eof() is 1
```

Fig. 15.4 | get, put and eof member functions. (Part 2 of 2.)

ments and returns the character being input (line 17). Function eof returns true only after the program attempts to read past the last character in the stream.

The get member function with a character-reference argument inputs the next character from the input stream (even if this is a white-space character) and stores it in the character argument. This version of get returns a reference to the istream object for which the get member function is being invoked.

A third version of get takes three arguments—a character array, a size limit and a delimiter (with default value '\n'). This version reads characters from the input stream. It either reads one fewer than the specified maximum number of characters and terminates or terminates as soon as the delimiter is read. A null character is inserted to terminate the input string in the character array used as a buffer by the program. The delimiter is not placed in the character array but does remain in the input stream (the delimiter will be the next character read). Thus, the result of a second consecutive get is an empty line, unless the delimiter character is removed from the input stream (possibly with cin.ignore()).

Comparing cin and cin.get
Figure 15.5 compares input using stream extraction with cin (which reads characters until a white-space character is encountered) and input using cin.get. Note that the call to cin.get (line 24) does not specify a delimiter, so the default '\n' character is used.

```
1   // Fig. 15.5: Fig15_05.cpp
2   // Contrasting input of a string via cin and cin.get.
3   #include <iostream>
4   using std::cin;
5   using std::cout;
6   using std::endl;
7
8   int main()
9   {
10      // create two char arrays, each with 80 elements
11      const int SIZE = 80;
12      char buffer1[ SIZE ];
13      char buffer2[ SIZE ];
14
```

Fig. 15.5 | Input of a string using cin with stream extraction contrasted with input using cin.get. (Part 1 of 2.)

```
15        // use cin to input characters into buffer1
16        cout << "Enter a sentence:" << endl;
17        cin >> buffer1;
18
19        // display buffer1 contents
20        cout << "\nThe string read with cin was:" << endl
21            << buffer1 << endl << endl;
22
23        // use cin.get to input characters into buffer2
24        cin.get( buffer2, SIZE );
25
26        // display buffer2 contents
27        cout << "The string read with cin.get was:" << endl
28            << buffer2 << endl;
29        return 0;
30    } // end main
```

```
Enter a sentence:
Contrasting string input with cin and cin.get

The string read with cin was:
Contrasting

The string read with cin.get was:
 string input with cin and cin.get
```

Fig. 15.5 | Input of a string using cin with stream extraction contrasted with input using cin.get. (Part 2 of 2.)

Using Member Function getline
Member function getline operates similarly to the third version of the get member function and inserts a null character after the line in the character array. The getline function removes the delimiter from the stream (i.e., reads the character and discards it), but does not store it in the character array. The program of Fig. 15.6 demonstrates the use of the getline member function to input a line of text (line 15).

```
1   // Fig. 15.6: Fig15_06.cpp
2   // Inputting characters using cin member function getline.
3   #include <iostream>
4   using std::cin;
5   using std::cout;
6   using std::endl;
7
8   int main()
9   {
10      const int SIZE = 80;
11      char buffer[ SIZE ]; // create array of 80 characters
12
```

Fig. 15.6 | Inputting character data with cin member function getline. (Part 1 of 2.)

```
13        // input characters in buffer via cin function getline
14        cout << "Enter a sentence:" << endl;
15        cin.getline( buffer, SIZE );
16
17        // display buffer contents
18        cout << "\nThe sentence entered is:" << endl << buffer << endl;
19        return 0;
20    } // end main
```

```
Enter a sentence:
Using the getline member function

The sentence entered is:
Using the getline member function
```

Fig. 15.6 | Inputting character data with `cin` member function `getline`. (Part 2 of 2.)

15.4.2 `istream` Member Functions `peek`, `putback` and `ignore`

The `ignore` member function of `istream` either reads and discards a designated number of characters (the default is one character) or terminates upon encountering a designated delimiter (the default delimiter is EOF, which causes `ignore` to skip to the end of the file when reading from a file).

The `putback` member function places the previous character obtained by a `get` from an input stream back into that stream. This function is useful for applications that scan an input stream looking for a field beginning with a specific character. When that character is input, the application returns the character to the stream, so the character can be included in the input data.

The `peek` member function returns the next character from an input stream but does not remove the character from the stream.

15.4.3 Type-Safe I/O

C++ offers type-safe I/O. The << and >> operators are overloaded to accept data items of specific types. If unexpected data is processed, various error bits are set, which the user may test to determine whether an I/O operation succeeded or failed. If operator << has not been overloaded for a user-defined type and you attempt to input into or output the contents of an object of that user-defined type, the compiler reports an error. This enables the program to "stay in control." We discuss these error states in Section 15.8.

15.5 Unformatted I/O Using `read`, `write` and `gcount`

Unformatted input/output is performed using the `read` and `write` member functions of `istream` and `ostream`, respectively. Member function `read` inputs some number of bytes to a character array in memory; member function `write` outputs bytes from a character array. These bytes are not formatted in any way. They are input or output as raw bytes. For example, the call

```
char buffer[] = "HAPPY BIRTHDAY";
cout.write( buffer, 10 );
```

outputs the first 10 bytes of buffer (including null characters, if any, that would cause output with cout and << to terminate). The call

```
cout.write( "ABCDEFGHIJKLMNOPQRSTUVWXYZ", 10 );
```

displays the first 10 characters of the alphabet.

The read member function inputs a designated number of characters into a character array. If fewer than the designated number of characters are read, failbit is set. Section 15.8 shows how to determine whether failbit has been set. Member function gcount reports the number of characters read by the last input operation.

Figure 15.7 demonstrates istream member functions read and gcount, and ostream member function write. The program inputs 20 characters (from a longer input sequence) into the array buffer with read (line 15), determines the number of characters input with gcount (line 19) and outputs the characters in buffer with write (line 19).

```
1   // Fig. 15.7: Fig15_07.cpp
2   // Unformatted I/O using read, gcount and write.
3   #include <iostream>
4   using std::cin;
5   using std::cout;
6   using std::endl;
7
8   int main()
9   {
10      const int SIZE = 80;
11      char buffer[ SIZE ]; // create array of 80 characters
12
13      // use function read to input characters into buffer
14      cout << "Enter a sentence:" << endl;
15      cin.read( buffer, 20 );
16
17      // use functions write and gcount to display buffer characters
18      cout << endl << "The sentence entered was:" << endl;
19      cout.write( buffer, cin.gcount() );
20      cout << endl;
21      return 0;
22   } // end main
```

```
Enter a sentence:
Using the read, write, and gcount member functions
The sentence entered was:
Using the read, writ
```

Fig. 15.7 | Unformatted I/O using the read, gcount and write member functions.

15.6 Introduction to Stream Manipulators

C++ provides various **stream manipulators** that perform formatting tasks. The stream manipulators provide capabilities such as setting field widths, setting precision, setting and unsetting format state, setting the fill character in fields, flushing streams, inserting a newline into the output stream (and flushing the stream), inserting a null character into the output stream and skipping white space in the input stream. These features are described in the following sections.

15.6.1 Integral Stream Base: dec, oct, hex and setbase

Integers are interpreted normally as decimal (base-10) values. To change the base in which integers are interpreted on a stream, insert the hex manipulator to set the base to hexadecimal (base 16) or insert the oct manipulator to set the base to octal (base 8). Insert the dec manipulator to reset the stream base to decimal. These are all sticky manipulators.

The base of a stream also may be changed by the setbase stream manipulator, which takes one integer argument of 10, 8, or 16 to set the base to decimal, octal or hexadecimal, respectively. Because setbase takes an argument, it is called a parameterized stream manipulator. Using setbase (or any other parameterized manipulator) requires the inclusion of the <iomanip> header file. The stream base value remains the same until changed explicitly; setbase settings are "sticky." Figure 15.8 demonstrates stream manipulators hex, oct, dec and setbase.

```cpp
1   // Fig. 15.8: Fig15_08.cpp
2   // Using stream manipulators hex, oct, dec and setbase.
3   #include <iostream>
4   using std::cin;
5   using std::cout;
6   using std::dec;
7   using std::endl;
8   using std::hex;
9   using std::oct;
10
11  #include <iomanip>
12  using std::setbase;
13
14  int main()
15  {
16     int number;
17
18     cout << "Enter a decimal number: ";
19     cin >> number; // input number
20
21     // use hex stream manipulator to show hexadecimal number
22     cout << number << " in hexadecimal is: " << hex
23        << number << endl;
24
25     // use oct stream manipulator to show octal number
26     cout << dec << number << " in octal is: "
27        << oct << number << endl;
28
29     // use setbase stream manipulator to show decimal number
30     cout << setbase( 10 ) << number << " in decimal is: "
31        << number << endl;
32     return 0;
33  } // end main
```

Fig. 15.8 | Stream manipulators hex, oct, dec and setbase. (Part 1 of 2.)

```
Enter a decimal number: 20
20 in hexadecimal is: 14
20 in octal is: 24
20 in decimal is: 20
```

Fig. 15.8 | Stream manipulators hex, oct, dec and setbase. (Part 2 of 2.)

15.6.2 Floating-Point Precision (precision, setprecision)

We can control the precision of floating-point numbers (i.e., the number of digits to the right of the decimal point) by using either the setprecision stream manipulator or the precision member function of ios_base. A call to either of these sets the precision for all subsequent output operations until the next precision-setting call. A call to member function precision with no argument returns the current precision setting (this is what you need to use so that you can restore the original precision eventually after a "sticky" setting is no longer needed). The program of Fig. 15.9 uses both member function precision (line 28) and the setprecision manipulator (line 37) to print a table that shows the square root of 2, with precision varying from 0–9.

```cpp
1   // Fig. 15.9: Fig15_09.cpp
2   // Controlling precision of floating-point values.
3   #include <iostream>
4   using std::cout;
5   using std::endl;
6   using std::fixed;
7
8   #include <iomanip>
9   using std::setprecision;
10
11  #include <cmath>
12  using std::sqrt; // sqrt prototype
13
14  int main()
15  {
16     double root2 = sqrt( 2.0 ); // calculate square root of 2
17     int places; // precision, vary from 0-9
18
19     cout << "Square root of 2 with precisions 0-9." << endl
20        << "Precision set by ios_base member function "
21        << "precision:" << endl;
22
23     cout << fixed; // use fixed-point notation
24
25     // display square root using ios_base function precision
26     for ( places = 0; places <= 9; places++ )
27     {
28        cout.precision( places );
29        cout << root2 << endl;
30     } // end for
31
```

Fig. 15.9 | Precision of floating-point values. (Part 1 of 2.)

```
32      cout << "\nPrecision set by stream manipulator "
33         << "setprecision:" << endl;
34
35      // set precision for each digit, then display square root
36      for ( places = 0; places <= 9; places++ )
37         cout << setprecision( places ) << root2 << endl;
38
39      return 0;
40   } // end main
```

```
Square root of 2 with precisions 0-9.
Precision set by ios_base member function precision:
1
1.4
1.41
1.414
1.4142
1.41421
1.414214
1.4142136
1.41421356
1.414213562

Precision set by stream manipulator setprecision:
1
1.4
1.41
1.414
1.4142
1.41421
1.414214
1.4142136
1.41421356
1.414213562
```

Fig. 15.9 | Precision of floating-point values. (Part 2 of 2.)

15.6.3 Field Width (`width`, `setw`)

The `width` member function (of base class `ios_base`) sets the field width (i.e., the number of character positions in which a value should be output or the maximum number of characters that should be input) and returns the previous width. If values output are narrower than the field width, fill characters are inserted as padding. A value wider than the designated width will not be truncated—the full number will be printed. The `width` function with no argument returns the current setting.

 Common Programming Error 15.1

The width setting applies only for the next insertion or extraction (i.e., the width setting is not "sticky"); afterward, the width is set implicitly to 0 (i.e., input and output will be performed with default settings). Assuming that the width setting applies to all subsequent outputs is a logic error.

Common Programming Error 15.2

When a field is not sufficiently wide to handle outputs, the outputs print as wide as necessary, which can yield confusing outputs.

Figure 15.10 demonstrates the use of the width member function on both input and output. Note that, on input into a char array, a maximum of one fewer characters than the width will be read, because provision is made for the null character to be placed in the input string. Remember that stream extraction terminates when nonleading white space is encountered. The setw stream manipulator also may be used to set the field width.

```cpp
1   // Fig. 15.10: Fig15_10.cpp
2   // Demonstrating member function width.
3   #include <iostream>
4   using std::cin;
5   using std::cout;
6   using std::endl;
7
8   int main()
9   {
10      int widthValue = 4;
11      char sentence[ 10 ];
12
13      cout << "Enter a sentence:" << endl;
14      cin.width( 5 ); // input only 5 characters from sentence
15
16      // set field width, then display characters based on that width
17      while ( cin >> sentence )
18      {
19         cout.width( widthValue++ );
20         cout << sentence << endl;
21         cin.width( 5 ); // input 5 more characters from sentence
22      } // end while
23
24      return 0;
25   } // end main
```

```
Enter a sentence:
This is a test of the width member function
This
   is
     a
  test
     of
    the
   widt
       h
     memb
        er
     func
      tion
```

Fig. 15.10 | width member function of class ios_base.

[*Note:* When prompted for input in Fig. 15.10, the user should enter a line of text and press *Enter* followed by end-of-file (*<Ctrl>-z* on Microsoft Windows systems, *<Ctrl>-d* on UNIX and Macintosh systems).]

15.6.4 User-Defined Output Stream Manipulators

You can create your own stream manipulators.[3] Figure 15.11 shows the creation and use of new nonparameterized stream manipulators bell (lines 10–13), carriageReturn (lines 16–19), tab (lines 22–25) and endLine (lines 29–32). For output stream manipulators, the return type and parameter must be of type ostream &. When line 37 inserts the end-Line manipulator in the output stream, function endLine is called and line 31 outputs the escape sequence \n and the flush manipulator to the standard output stream cout. Similarly, when lines 37–46 insert the manipulators tab, bell and carriageReturn in the

```cpp
1   // Fig. 15.11: Fig15_11.cpp
2   // Creating and testing user-defined, nonparameterized
3   // stream manipulators.
4   #include <iostream>
5   using std::cout;
6   using std::flush;
7   using std::ostream;
8
9   // bell manipulator (using escape sequence \a)
10  ostream& bell( ostream& output )
11  {
12     return output << '\a'; // issue system beep
13  } // end bell manipulator
14
15  // carriageReturn manipulator (using escape sequence \r)
16  ostream& carriageReturn( ostream& output )
17  {
18     return output << '\r'; // issue carriage return
19  } // end carriageReturn manipulator
20
21  // tab manipulator (using escape sequence \t)
22  ostream& tab( ostream& output )
23  {
24     return output << '\t'; // issue tab
25  } // end tab manipulator
26
27  // endLine manipulator (using escape sequence \n and member
28  // function flush)
29  ostream& endLine( ostream& output )
30  {
31     return output << '\n' << flush; // issue endl-like end of line
32  } // end endLine manipulator
33
```

Fig. 15.11 | User-defined, nonparameterized stream manipulators. (Part 1 of 2.)

---

3. You also may create your own parameterized stream manipulators. This concept is beyond the scope of this book.

```
34   int main()
35   {
36      // use tab and endLine manipulators
37      cout << "Testing the tab manipulator:" << endLine
38         << 'a' << tab << 'b' << tab << 'c' << endLine;
39
40      cout << "Testing the carriageReturn and bell manipulators:"
41         << endLine << "..........";
42
43      cout << bell; // use bell manipulator
44
45      // use carriageReturn and endLine manipulators
46      cout << carriageReturn << "-----" << endLine;
47      return 0;
48   } // end main
```

```
Testing the tab manipulator:
a       b       c
Testing the carriageReturn and bell manipulators:
-----.....
```

Fig. 15.11 | User-defined, nonparameterized stream manipulators. (Part 2 of 2.)

output stream, their corresponding functions—tab (line 22), bell (line 10) and carriageReturn (line 16) are called, which in turn output various escape sequences.

15.7 Stream Format States and Stream Manipulators

Various stream manipulators can be used to specify the kinds of formatting to be performed during stream-I/O operations. Stream manipulators control the output's format settings. Figure 15.12 lists each stream manipulator that controls a given stream's format state. All these manipulators belong to class ios_base. We show examples of most of these stream manipulators in the next several sections.

Stream manipulator	Description
skipws	Skip white-space characters on an input stream. This setting is reset with stream manipulator noskipws.
left	Left justify output in a field. Padding characters appear to the right if necessary.
right	Right justify output in a field. Padding characters appear to the left if necessary.
internal	Indicate that a number's sign should be left justified in a field and a number's magnitude should be right justified in that same field (i.e., padding characters appear between the sign and the number).
dec	Specify that integers should be treated as decimal (base 10) values.

Fig. 15.12 | Format state stream manipulators from `<iostream>`. (Part 1 of 2.)

Stream manipulator	Description
oct	Specify that integers should be treated as octal (base 8) values.
hex	Specify that integers should be treated as hexadecimal (base 16) values.
showbase	Specify that the base of a number is to be output ahead of the number (a leading 0 for octals; a leading 0x or 0X for hexadecimals). This setting is reset with stream manipulator noshowbase.
showpoint	Specify that floating-point numbers should be output with a decimal point. This is used normally with fixed to guarantee a certain number of digits to the right of the decimal point, even if they are zeros. This setting is reset with stream manipulator noshowpoint.
uppercase	Specify that uppercase letters (i.e., X and A through F) should be used in a hexadecimal integer and that uppercase E should be used when representing a floating-point value in scientific notation. This setting is reset with stream manipulator nouppercase.
showpos	Specify that positive numbers should be preceded by a plus sign (+). This setting is reset with stream manipulator noshowpos.
scientific	Specify output of a floating-point value in scientific notation.
fixed	Specify output of a floating-point value in fixed-point notation with a specific number of digits to the right of the decimal point.

Fig. 15.12 | Format state stream manipulators from `<iostream>`. (Part 2 of 2.)

15.7.1 Trailing Zeros and Decimal Points (showpoint)

Stream manipulator showpoint forces a floating-point number to be output with its decimal point and trailing zeros. For example, the floating-point value 79.0 prints as 79 without using showpoint and prints as 79.000000 (or as many trailing zeros as are specified by the current precision) using showpoint. To reset the showpoint setting, output the stream manipulator noshowpoint. The program in Fig. 15.13 shows how to use stream manipulator showpoint to control the printing of trailing zeros and decimal points for floating-point values. Recall that the default precision of a floating-point number is 6. When neither the fixed nor the scientific stream manipulator is used, the precision represents the number of significant digits to display (i.e., the total number of digits to display), not the number of digits to display after decimal point.

```
1   // Fig. 15.13: Fig15_13.cpp
2   // Using showpoint to control the printing of
3   // trailing zeros and decimal points for doubles.
4   #include <iostream>
5   using std::cout;
6   using std::endl;
7   using std::showpoint;
```

Fig. 15.13 | Controlling the printing of trailing zeros and decimal points in floating-point values. (Part 1 of 2.)

```
8
9   int main()
10  {
11      // display double values with default stream format
12      cout << "Before using showpoint" << endl
13          << "9.9900 prints as: " << 9.9900 << endl
14          << "9.9000 prints as: " << 9.9000 << endl
15          << "9.0000 prints as: " << 9.0000 << endl << endl;
16
17      // display double value after showpoint
18      cout << showpoint
19          << "After using showpoint" << endl
20          << "9.9900 prints as: " << 9.9900 << endl
21          << "9.9000 prints as: " << 9.9000 << endl
22          << "9.0000 prints as: " << 9.0000 << endl;
23      return 0;
24  } // end main
```

```
Before using showpoint
9.9900 prints as: 9.99
9.9000 prints as: 9.9
9.0000 prints as: 9

After using showpoint
9.9900 prints as: 9.99000
9.9000 prints as: 9.90000
9.0000 prints as: 9.00000
```

Fig. 15.13 | Controlling the printing of trailing zeros and decimal points in floating-point values. (Part 2 of 2.)

15.7.2 Justification (left, right and internal)

Stream manipulators left and right enable fields to be left justified with padding characters to the right or right justified with padding characters to the left, respectively. The padding character is specified by the fill member function or the setfill parameterized stream manipulator (which we discuss in Section 15.7.3). Figure 15.14 uses the setw, left and right manipulators to left justify and right justify integer data in a field.

```
1   // Fig. 15.14: Fig15_14.cpp
2   // Demonstrating left justification and right justification.
3   #include <iostream>
4   using std::cout;
5   using std::endl;
6   using std::left;
7   using std::right;
8
9   #include <iomanip>
10  using std::setw;
```

Fig. 15.14 | Left justification and right justification with stream manipulators left and right. (Part 1 of 2.)

```
11
12   int main()
13   {
14       int x = 12345;
15
16       // display x right justified (default)
17       cout << "Default is right justified:" << endl
18           << setw( 10 ) << x;
19
20       // use left manipulator to display x left justified
21       cout << "\n\nUse std::left to left justify x:\n"
22           << left << setw( 10 ) << x;
23
24       // use right manipulator to display x right justified
25       cout << "\n\nUse std::right to right justify x:\n"
26           << right << setw( 10 ) << x << endl;
27       return 0;
28   } // end main
```

```
Default is right justified:
     12345

Use std::left to left justify x:
12345

Use std::right to right justify x:
     12345
```

Fig. 15.14 | Left justification and right justification with stream manipulators `left` and `right`. (Part 2 of 2.)

Stream manipulator `internal` indicates that a number's sign (or base when using stream manipulator `showbase`) should be left justified within a field, that the number's magnitude should be right justified and that intervening spaces should be padded with the fill character. Figure 15.15 shows the `internal` stream manipulator specifying internal spacing (line 15). Note that `showpos` forces the plus sign to print (line 15). To reset the showpos setting, output the stream manipulator `noshowpos`.

```
1    // Fig. 15.15: Fig15_15.cpp
2    // Printing an integer with internal spacing and plus sign.
3    #include <iostream>
4    using std::cout;
5    using std::endl;
6    using std::internal;
7    using std::showpos;
8
9    #include <iomanip>
10   using std::setw;
11
```

Fig. 15.15 | Printing an integer with internal spacing and plus sign. (Part 1 of 2.)

```
12   int main()
13   {
14       // display value with internal spacing and plus sign
15       cout << internal << showpos << setw( 10 ) << 123 << endl;
16       return 0;
17   } // end main
```

```
+        123
```

Fig. 15.15 | Printing an integer with internal spacing and plus sign. (Part 2 of 2.)

15.7.3 Padding (fill, setfill)

The fill member function specifies the fill character to be used with justified fields; if no value is specified, spaces are used for padding. The fill function returns the prior padding character. The setfill manipulator also sets the padding character. Figure 15.16 demonstrates using member function fill (line 40) and stream manipulator setfill (lines 44 and 47) to set the fill character.

```
1    // Fig. 15.16: Fig15_16.cpp
2    // Using member function fill and stream manipulator setfill to change
3    // the padding character for fields larger than the printed value.
4    #include <iostream>
5    using std::cout;
6    using std::dec;
7    using std::endl;
8    using std::hex;
9    using std::internal;
10   using std::left;
11   using std::right;
12   using std::showbase;
13
14   #include <iomanip>
15   using std::setfill;
16   using std::setw;
17
18   int main()
19   {
20       int x = 10000;
21
22       // display x
23       cout << x << " printed as int right and left justified\n"
24           << "and as hex with internal justification.\n"
25           << "Using the default pad character (space):" << endl;
26
27       // display x with base
28       cout << showbase << setw( 10 ) << x << endl;
29
```

Fig. 15.16 | Using member function fill and stream manipulator setfill to change the padding character for fields larger than the values being printed. (Part 1 of 2.)

```
30      // display x with left justification
31      cout << left << setw( 10 ) << x << endl;
32
33      // display x as hex with internal justification
34      cout << internal << setw( 10 ) << hex << x << endl << endl;
35
36      cout << "Using various padding characters:" << endl;
37
38      // display x using padded characters (right justification)
39      cout << right;
40      cout.fill( '*' );
41      cout << setw( 10 ) << dec << x << endl;
42
43      // display x using padded characters (left justification)
44      cout << left << setw( 10 ) << setfill( '%' ) << x << endl;
45
46      // display x using padded characters (internal justification)
47      cout << internal << setw( 10 ) << setfill( '^' ) << hex
48          << x << endl;
49      return 0;
50  } // end main
```

```
10000 printed as int right and left justified
and as hex with internal justification.
Using the default pad character (space):
     10000
10000
0x    2710

Using various padding characters:
*****10000
10000%%%%%
0x^^^^2710
```

Fig. 15.16 | Using member function `fill` and stream manipulator `setfill` to change the padding character for fields larger than the values being printed. (Part 2 of 2.)

15.7.4 Integral Stream Base (dec, oct, hex, showbase)

C++ provides stream manipulators `dec`, `hex` and `oct` to specify that integers are to be displayed as decimal, hexadecimal and octal values, respectively. Stream insertions default to decimal if none of these manipulators is used. With stream extraction, integers prefixed with 0 (zero) are treated as octal values, integers prefixed with 0x or 0X are treated as hexadecimal values, and all other integers are treated as decimal values. Once a particular base is specified for a stream, all integers on that stream are processed using that base until a different base is specified or until the program terminates.

Stream manipulator `showbase` forces the base of an integral value to be output. Decimal numbers are output by default, octal numbers are output with a leading 0, and hexadecimal numbers are output with either a leading 0x or a leading 0X (as we discuss in Section 15.7.6, stream manipulator `uppercase` determines which option is chosen). Figure 15.17 demonstrates the use of stream manipulator `showbase` to force an integer to

```
1   // Fig. 15.17: Fig15_17.cpp
2   // Using stream manipulator showbase.
3   #include <iostream>
4   using std::cout;
5   using std::endl;
6   using std::hex;
7   using std::oct;
8   using std::showbase;
9
10  int main()
11  {
12     int x = 100;
13
14     // use showbase to show number base
15     cout << "Printing integers preceded by their base:" << endl
16        << showbase;
17
18     cout << x << endl; // print decimal value
19     cout << oct << x << endl; // print octal value
20     cout << hex << x << endl; // print hexadecimal value
21     return 0;
22  } // end main
```

```
Printing integers preceded by their base:
100
0144
0x64
```

Fig. 15.17 | Stream manipulator showbase.

print in decimal, octal and hexadecimal formats. To reset the showbase setting, output the stream manipulator noshowbase.

15.7.5 Floating-Point Numbers; Scientific and Fixed Notation (scientific, fixed)

Stream manipulators scientific and fixed control the output format of floating-point numbers. Stream manipulator scientific forces the output of a floating-point number to display in scientific format. Stream manipulator fixed forces a floating-point number to display a specific number of digits (as specified by member function precision or stream manipulator setprecision) to the right of the decimal point. Without using another manipulator, the floating-point-number value determines the output format.

Figure 15.18 demonstrates displaying floating-point numbers in fixed and scientific formats using stream manipulators scientific (line 21) and fixed (line 25). The exponent format in scientific notation might differ across different compilers.

15.7.6 Uppercase/Lowercase Control (uppercase)

Stream manipulator uppercase outputs an uppercase X or E with hexadecimal-integer values or with scientific notation floating-point values, respectively (Fig. 15.19). Using stream manipulator uppercase also causes all letters in a hexadecimal value to be upper-

```
1   // Fig. 15.18: Fig15_18.cpp
2   // Displaying floating-point values in system default,
3   // scientific and fixed formats.
4   #include <iostream>
5   using std::cout;
6   using std::endl;
7   using std::fixed;
8   using std::scientific;
9
10  int main()
11  {
12     double x = 0.001234567;
13     double y = 1.946e9;
14
15     // display x and y in default format
16     cout << "Displayed in default format:" << endl
17        << x << '\t' << y << endl;
18
19     // display x and y in scientific format
20     cout << "\nDisplayed in scientific format:" << endl
21        << scientific << x << '\t' << y << endl;
22
23     // display x and y in fixed format
24     cout << "\nDisplayed in fixed format:" << endl
25        << fixed << x << '\t' << y << endl;
26     return 0;
27  } // end main
```

```
Displayed in default format:
0.00123457      1.946e+009

Displayed in scientific format:
1.234567e-003   1.946000e+009

Displayed in fixed format:
0.001235        1946000000.000000
```

Fig. 15.18 | Floating-point values displayed in default, scientific and fixed formats.

case. By default, the letters for hexadecimal values and the exponents in scientific notation floating-point values appear in lowercase. To reset the uppercase setting, output the stream manipulator **nouppercase**.

```
1   // Fig. 15.19: Fig15_19.cpp
2   // Stream manipulator uppercase.
3   #include <iostream>
4   using std::cout;
5   using std::endl;
6   using std::hex;
7   using std::showbase;
8   using std::uppercase;
```

Fig. 15.19 | Stream manipulator uppercase. (Part 1 of 2.)

```
 9
10   int main()
11   {
12      cout << "Printing uppercase letters in scientific" << endl
13         << "notation exponents and hexadecimal values:" << endl;
14
15      // use std:uppercase to display uppercase letters; use std::hex and
16      // std::showbase to display hexadecimal value and its base
17      cout << uppercase << 4.345e10 << endl
18         << hex << showbase << 123456789 << endl;
19      return 0;
20   } // end main
```

```
Printing uppercase letters in scientific
notation exponents and hexadecimal values:
4.345E+010
0X75BCD15
```

Fig. 15.19 | Stream manipulator `uppercase`. (Part 2 of 2.)

15.7.7 Specifying Boolean Format (`boolalpha`)

C++ provides data type `bool`, whose values may be `false` or `true`, as a preferred alternative to the old style of using 0 to indicate `false` and nonzero to indicate `true`. A `bool` variable outputs as 0 or 1 by default. However, we can use stream manipulator `boolalpha` to set the output stream to display `bool` values as the strings `"true"` and `"false"`. Use stream manipulator `noboolalpha` to set the output stream to display `bool` values as integers (i.e., the default setting). The program of Fig. 15.20 demonstrates these stream manipulators. Line 14 displays the `bool` value, which line 11 sets to `true`, as an integer. Line 18 uses manipulator `boolalpha` to display the `bool` value as a string. Lines 21–22 then change the `bool`'s value and use manipulator `noboolalpha`, so line 25 can display the `bool` value as an integer. Line 29 uses manipulator `boolalpha` to display the `bool` value as a string. Both `boolalpha` and `noboolalpha` are "sticky" settings.

Good Programming Practice 15.1

Displaying bool values as true or false, rather than nonzero or 0, respectively, makes program outputs clearer.

```
 1   // Fig. 15.20: Fig15_20.cpp
 2   // Demonstrating stream manipulators boolalpha and noboolalpha.
 3   #include <iostream>
 4   using std::boolalpha;
 5   using std::cout;
 6   using std::endl;
 7   using std::noboolalpha;
 8
 9   int main()
10   {
11      bool booleanValue = true;
```

Fig. 15.20 | Stream manipulators `boolalpha` and `noboolalpha`. (Part 1 of 2.)

```
12
13      // display default true booleanValue
14      cout << "booleanValue is " << booleanValue << endl;
15
16      // display booleanValue after using boolalpha
17      cout << "booleanValue (after using boolalpha) is "
18         << boolalpha << booleanValue << endl << endl;
19
20      cout << "switch booleanValue and use noboolalpha" << endl;
21      booleanValue = false; // change booleanValue
22      cout << noboolalpha << endl; // use noboolalpha
23
24      // display default false booleanValue after using noboolalpha
25      cout << "booleanValue is " << booleanValue << endl;
26
27      // display booleanValue after using boolalpha again
28      cout << "booleanValue (after using boolalpha) is "
29         << boolalpha << booleanValue << endl;
30      return 0;
31   } // end main
```

```
booleanValue is 1
booleanValue (after using boolalpha) is true

switch booleanValue and use noboolalpha

booleanValue is 0
booleanValue (after using boolalpha) is false
```

Fig. 15.20 | Stream manipulators `boolalpha` and `noboolalpha`. (Part 2 of 2.)

15.7.8 Setting and Resetting the Format State via Member Function `flags`

Throughout Section 15.7, we have been using stream manipulators to change output format characteristics. We now discuss how to return an output stream's format to its default state after having applied several manipulations. Member function `flags` without an argument returns the current format settings as a `fmtflags` data type (of class ios_base), which represents the format state. Member function `flags` with a `fmtflags` argument sets the format state as specified by the argument and returns the prior state settings. The initial settings of the value that `flags` returns might differ across several systems. The program of Fig. 15.21 uses member function `flags` to save the stream's original format state (line 22), then restore the original format settings (line 30).

```
1   // Fig. 15.21: Fig15_21.cpp
2   // Demonstrating the flags member function.
3   #include <iostream>
4   using std::cout;
5   using std::endl;
6   using std::ios_base;
```

Fig. 15.21 | `flags` member function. (Part 1 of 2.)

```
7    using std::oct;
8    using std::scientific;
9    using std::showbase;
10
11   int main()
12   {
13      int integerValue = 1000;
14      double doubleValue = 0.0947628;
15
16      // display flags value, int and double values (original format)
17      cout << "The value of the flags variable is: " << cout.flags()
18         << "\nPrint int and double in original format:\n"
19         << integerValue << '\t' << doubleValue << endl << endl;
20
21      // use cout flags function to save original format
22      ios_base::fmtflags originalFormat = cout.flags();
23      cout << showbase << oct << scientific; // change format
24
25      // display flags value, int and double values (new format)
26      cout << "The value of the flags variable is: " << cout.flags()
27         << "\nPrint int and double in a new format:\n"
28         << integerValue << '\t' << doubleValue << endl << endl;
29
30      cout.flags( originalFormat ); // restore format
31
32      // display flags value, int and double values (original format)
33      cout << "The restored value of the flags variable is: "
34         << cout.flags()
35         << "\nPrint values in original format again:\n"
36         << integerValue << '\t' << doubleValue << endl;
37      return 0;
38   } // end main
```

```
The value of the flags variable is: 513
Print int and double in original format:
1000    0.0947628

The value of the flags variable is: 012011
Print int and double in a new format:
01750   9.476280e-002

The restored value of the flags variable is: 513
Print values in original format again:
1000    0.0947628
```

Fig. 15.21 | flags member function. (Part 2 of 2.)

15.8 Stream Error States

The state of a stream may be tested through bits in class ios_base. In a moment, we show how to test these bits, in the example of Fig. 15.22.

The **eofbit** is set for an input stream after end-of-file is encountered. A program can use member function eof to determine whether end-of-file has been encountered on a stream after an attempt to extract data beyond the end of the stream. The call

```
cin.eof()
```

returns true if end-of-file has been encountered on cin and false otherwise.

The failbit is set for a stream when a format error occurs on the stream, such as when the program is inputting integers and a nondigit character is encountered in the input stream. When such an error occurs, the characters are not lost. The fail member function reports whether a stream operation has failed. Usually, recovering from such errors is possible.

The badbit is set for a stream when an error occurs that results in the loss of data. The bad member function reports whether a stream operation failed. Generally, such serious failures are nonrecoverable.

```
 1   // Fig. 15.22: Fig15_22.cpp
 2   // Testing error states.
 3   #include <iostream>
 4   using std::cin;
 5   using std::cout;
 6   using std::endl;
 7
 8   int main()
 9   {
10      int integerValue;
11
12      // display results of cin functions
13      cout << "Before a bad input operation:"
14         << "\ncin.rdstate(): " << cin.rdstate()
15         << "\n    cin.eof(): " << cin.eof()
16         << "\n   cin.fail(): " << cin.fail()
17         << "\n    cin.bad(): " << cin.bad()
18         << "\n   cin.good(): " << cin.good()
19         << "\n\nExpects an integer, but enter a character: ";
20
21      cin >> integerValue; // enter character value
22      cout << endl;
23
24      // display results of cin functions after bad input
25      cout << "After a bad input operation:"
26         << "\ncin.rdstate(): " << cin.rdstate()
27         << "\n    cin.eof(): " << cin.eof()
28         << "\n   cin.fail(): " << cin.fail()
29         << "\n    cin.bad(): " << cin.bad()
30         << "\n   cin.good(): " << cin.good() << endl << endl;
31
32      cin.clear(); // clear stream
33
34      // display results of cin functions after clearing cin
35      cout << "After cin.clear()" << "\ncin.fail(): " << cin.fail()
36         << "\ncin.good(): " << cin.good() << endl;
37      return 0;
38   } // end main
```

Fig. 15.22 | Testing error states. (Part 1 of 2.)

```
Before a bad input operation:
cin.rdstate(): 0
   cin.eof(): 0
  cin.fail(): 0
   cin.bad(): 0
  cin.good(): 1

Expects an integer, but enter a character: A

After a bad input operation:
cin.rdstate(): 2
   cin.eof(): 0
  cin.fail(): 1
   cin.bad(): 0
  cin.good(): 0

After cin.clear()
cin.fail(): 0
cin.good(): 1
```

Fig. 15.22 | Testing error states. (Part 2 of 2.)

The goodbit is set for a stream if none of the bits eofbit, failbit or badbit is set for the stream.

The good member function returns true if the bad, fail and eof functions would all return false. I/O operations should be performed only on "good" streams.

The rdstate member function returns the error state of the stream. A call to cout.rdstate, for example, would return the state of the stream, which then could be tested by a switch statement that examines eofbit, badbit, failbit and goodbit. The preferred means of testing the state of a stream is to use member functions eof, bad, fail and good—using these functions does not require you to be familiar with particular status bits.

The clear member function is used to restore a stream's state to "good," so that I/O may proceed on that stream. The default argument for clear is goodbit, so the statement

    cin.clear();

clears cin and sets goodbit for the stream. The statement

    cin.clear(ios::failbit)

sets the failbit. You might want to do this when performing input on cin with a user-defined type and encountering a problem. The name clear might seem inappropriate in this context, but it is correct.

The program of Fig. 15.22 demonstrates member functions rdstate, eof, fail, bad, good and clear. [*Note:* The actual values output may differ across different compilers.]

The operator! member function of basic_ios returns true if the badbit is set, the failbit is set or both are set. The operator void * member function returns false (0) if the badbit is set, the failbit is set or both are set. These functions are useful in file processing when a true/false condition is being tested under the control of a selection statement or repetition statement.

15.9 Tying an Output Stream to an Input Stream

Interactive applications generally involve an istream for input and an ostream for output. When a prompting message appears on the screen, the user responds by entering the appropriate data. Obviously, the prompt needs to appear before the input operation proceeds. With output buffering, outputs appear only when the buffer fills, when outputs are flushed explicitly by the program or automatically at the end of the program. C++ provides member function tie to synchronize (i.e., "tie together") the operation of an istream and an ostream to ensure that outputs appear before their subsequent inputs. The call

```
cin.tie( &cout );
```

ties cout (an ostream) to cin (an istream). Actually, this particular call is redundant, because C++ performs this operation automatically to create a user's standard input/output environment. However, the user would tie other istream/ostream pairs explicitly. To untie an input stream, inputStream, from an output stream, use the call

```
inputStream.tie( 0 );
```

15.10 Wrap-Up

This chapter summarized how C++ performs input/output using streams. You learned about the stream-I/O classes and objects, as well as the stream I/O template class hierarchy. We discussed ostream's formatted and unformatted output capabilities performed by the put and write functions. You saw examples using istream's formatted and unformatted input capabilities performed by the eof, get, getline, peek, putback, ignore and read functions. Next, we discussed stream manipulators and member functions that perform formatting tasks—dec, oct, hex and setbase for displaying integers; precision and setprecision for controlling floating-point precision; and width and setw for setting field width. You also learned additional formatting iostream manipulators and member functions—showpoint for displaying decimal point and trailing zeros; left, right and internal for justification; fill and setfill for padding; scientific and fixed for displaying floating-point numbers in scientific and fixed notation; uppercase for uppercase/lowercase control; boolalpha for specifying boolean format; and flags and fmtflags for resetting the format state.

In the next chapter, we introduce exception handling, which allows programmers to deal with certain problems that may occur during a program's execution. We demonstrate basic exception-handling techniques that often permit a program to continue executing as if no problem had been encountered. We also present several classes that the C++ Standard Library provides for handling exceptions.

Summary

Section 15.1 Introduction
- I/O operations are performed in a manner sensitive to the type of the data.

Section 15.2 Streams
- C++ I/O occurs in streams. A stream is a sequence of bytes.

- I/O mechanisms of the system move bytes from devices to memory and vice versa efficiently and reliably.
- C++ provides "low-level" and "high-level" I/O capabilities. Low-level I/O-capabilities specify that some number of bytes should be transferred device-to-memory or memory-to-device. High-level I/O is performed with bytes grouped into such meaningful units as integers, floats, characters, strings and user-defined types.
- C++ provides both unformatted-I/O and formatted-I/O operations. Unformatted-I/O transfers are fast, but process raw data that is difficult for people to use. Formatted I/O processes data in meaningful units, but requires extra processing time that can degrade the performance of high-volume data transfers.
- The `<iostream>` header file declares all stream-I/O operations.
- Header `<iomanip>` declares the parameterized stream manipulators.
- The `<fstream>` header declares file-processing operations.
- The `basic_istream` template supports stream-input operations.
- The `basic_ostream` template supports stream-output operations.
- The `basic_iostream` template supports both stream-input and stream-output operations.
- The `basic_istream` template and the `basic_ostream` template are each derived through single inheritance from the `basic_ios` template.
- The `basic_iostream` template is derived through multiple inheritance from both the `basic_istream` template and the `basic_ostream` template.
- The left-shift operator (`<<`) is overloaded to designate stream output and is referred to as the stream insertion operator.
- The right-shift operator (`>>`) is overloaded to designate stream input and is referred to as the stream extraction operator.
- The `istream` object `cin` is tied to the standard input device, normally the keyboard.
- The `ostream` object `cout` is tied to the standard output device, normally the screen.
- The `ostream` object `cerr` is tied to the standard error device. Outputs to `cerr` are unbuffered; each insertion to `cerr` appears immediately.
- The C++ compiler determines data types automatically for input and output.

Section 15.3 Stream Output
- Addresses are displayed in hexadecimal format by default.
- To print the address in a pointer variable, cast the pointer to `void *`.
- Member function `put` outputs one character. Calls to `put` may be cascaded.

Section 15.4 Stream Input
- Stream input is performed with the stream extraction operator `>>`. This operator automatically skips white-space characters in the input stream.
- The `>>` operator returns `false` after end-of-file is encountered on a stream.
- Stream extraction causes `failbit` to be set for improper input and `badbit` to be set if the operation fails.
- A series of values can be input using the stream extraction operation in a `while` loop header. The extraction returns 0 when end-of-file is encountered.
- The `get` member function with no arguments inputs one character and returns the character; `EOF` is returned if end-of-file is encountered on the stream.

- Member function get with a character-reference argument inputs the next character from the input stream and stores it in the character argument. This version of get returns a reference to the istream object for which the get member function is being invoked.

- Member function get with three arguments—a character array, a size limit and a delimiter (with default value newline)—reads characters from the input stream up to a maximum of limit – 1 characters, or until the delimiter is read. The input string is terminated with a null character. The delimiter is not placed in the character array but remains in the input stream.

- The getline member function operates like the three-argument get member function. The get-line function removes the delimiter from the input stream but does not store it in the string.

- Member function ignore skips the specified number of characters (the default is 1) in the input stream; it terminates if the specified delimiter is encountered (the default delimiter is EOF).

- The putback member function places the previous character obtained by a get on a stream back onto that stream.

- The peek member function returns the next character from an input stream but does not extract (remove) the character from the stream.

- C++ offers type-safe I/O. If unexpected data is processed by the << and >> operators, various error bits are set, which the user may test to determine whether an I/O operation succeeded or failed. If operator << has not been overloaded for a user-defined type, a compiler error is reported.

Section 15.5 Unformatted I/O Using read, write and gcount

- Unformatted I/O is performed with member functions read and write. These input or output some number of bytes to or from memory, beginning at a designated memory address. They are input or output as raw bytes with no formatting.

- The gcount member function returns the number of characters input by the previous read operation on that stream.

- Member function read inputs a specified number of characters into a character array. failbit is set if fewer than the specified number of characters are read.

Section 15.6 Introduction to Stream Manipulators

- To change the base in which integers output, use the manipulator hex to set the base to hexadecimal (base 16) or oct to set the base to octal (base 8). Use manipulator dec to reset the base to decimal. The base remains the same until changed explicitly.

- The parameterized stream manipulator setbase also sets the base for integer output. setbase takes one integer argument of 10, 8 or 16 to set the base.

- Floating-point precision can be controlled using either the setprecision stream manipulator or the precision member function. Both set the precision for all subsequent output operations until the next precision-setting call. The precision member function with no argument returns the current precision value.

- Parameterized manipulators require the inclusion of the <iomanip> header file.

- Member function width sets the field width and returns the previous width. Values narrower than the field are padded with fill characters. The field-width setting applies only for the next insertion or extraction; the field width is set to 0 implicitly (subsequent values will be output as large as necessary). Values wider than a field are printed in their entirety. Function width with no argument returns the current width setting. Manipulator setw also sets the width.

- For input, the setw stream manipulator establishes a maximum string size; if a larger string is entered, the larger line is broken into pieces no larger than the designated size.

- Programmers may create their own stream manipulators.

Section 15.7 Stream Format States and Stream Manipulators

- Stream manipulator showpoint forces a floating-point number to be output with a decimal point and with the number of significant digits specified by the precision.

- Stream manipulators left and right cause fields to be left justified with padding characters to the right or right justified with padding characters to the left.

- Stream manipulator internal indicates that a number's sign (or base when using stream manipulator showbase) should be left justified within a field, its magnitude should be right justified and intervening spaces should be padded with the fill character.

- Member function fill specifies the fill character to be used with stream manipulators left, right and internal (space is the default); the prior padding character is returned. Stream manipulator setfill also sets the fill character.

- Stream manipulators oct, hex and dec specify that integers are to be treated as octal, hexadecimal or decimal values, respectively. Integer output defaults to decimal if none of these bits is set; stream extractions process the data in the form the data is supplied.

- Stream manipulator showbase forces the base of an integral value to be output.

- Stream manipulator scientific is used to output a floating-point number in scientific format. Stream manipulator fixed is used to output a floating-point number with the precision specified by the precision member function.

- Stream manipulator uppercase outputs an uppercase X or E for hexadecimal integers and scientific notation floating-point values, respectively. Hexadecimal values appear in all uppercase.

- Member function flags with no argument returns the long value of the current format state settings. Function flags with a long argument sets the format state specified by the argument.

Section 15.8 Stream Error States

- The state of a stream may be tested through bits in class ios_base.

- The eofbit is set for an input stream after end-of-file is encountered during an input operation. The eof member function reports whether the eofbit has been set.

- A stream's failbit is set when a format error occurs. The fail member function reports whether a stream operation has failed; it is normally possible to recover from such errors.

- A stream's badbit is set when an error occurs that results in data loss. Member function bad reports whether such a stream operation failed. Such serious failures are normally nonrecoverable.

- The good member function returns true if the bad, fail and eof functions would all return false. I/O operations should be performed only on "good" streams.

- The rdstate member function returns the error state of the stream.

- Member function clear restores a stream's state to "good," so that I/O may proceed.

Section 15.9 Tying an Output Stream to an Input Stream

- C++ provides the tie member function to synchronize istream and ostream operations to ensure that outputs appear before subsequent inputs.

Terminology

bad member function of basic_ios
badbit
basic_fstream class template
basic_ifstream class template
basic_ios class template

basic_iostream class template
basic_istream class template
basic_ofstream class template
basic_ostream class template
boolalpha stream manipulator

clear member function of basic_ios

dec stream manipulator

default fill character (space)

default precision

end-of-file

eof member function of basic_ios

eofbit

fail member function of basic_ios

failbit

field width

fill character

fill member function of basic_ios

fixed stream manipulator

flags member function of ios_base

fmtflags

format states

formatted I/O

fstream

gcount member function of basic_istream

get member function of basic_istream

getline member function of basic_istream

good member function of basic_ios

hex stream manipulator

ifstream

ignore member function of basic_istream

internal stream manipulator

<iomanip> header file

ios_base class

iostream

istream

leading 0 (octal)

leading 0x or 0X (hexadecimal)

left stream manipulator

noboolalpha stream manipulator

noshowbase stream manipulator

noshowpoint stream manipulator

noshowpos stream manipulator

noskipws stream manipulator

nouppercase stream manipulator

oct stream manipulator

ofstream

operator void* member function of basic_ios

operator! member function of basic_ios

ostream

output buffering

padding

parameterized stream manipulator

peek member function of basic_istream

precision member function of ios_base

predefined streams

put member function of basic_ostream

putback member function of basic_istream

rdstate member function of basic_ios

read member function of basic_istream

right stream manipulator

scientific stream manipulator

setbase stream manipulator

setfill stream manipulator

setprecision stream manipulator

setw stream manipulator

showbase stream manipulator

showpoint stream manipulator

showpos stream manipulator

skipws stream manipulator

stream extraction operator (>>)

stream input

stream insertion operator (<<)

stream manipulator

stream output

tie member function of basic_ios

typedef

type-safe I/O

unbuffered output

unformatted I/O

uppercase stream manipulator

width stream manipulator

write member function of basic_ostream

Self-Review Exercises

15.1 Answer each of the following:
a) Input/output in C++ occurs as _____ of bytes.
b) The stream manipulators that format justification are _____, _____ and _____.
c) Member function _____ can be used to set and reset format state.
d) Most C++ programs that do I/O should include the _____ header file that contains the declarations required for all stream-I/O operations.
e) When using parameterized manipulators, the header file _____ must be included.
f) Header file _____ contains the declarations required for file processing.

g) The ostream member function _____ is used to perform unformatted output.

h) Input operations are supported by class _____.

i) Standard error stream outputs are directed to the stream objects _____ or _____.

j) Output operations are supported by class _____.

k) The symbol for the stream insertion operator is _____.

l) The four objects that correspond to the standard devices on the system include _____, _____, _____ and _____.

m) The symbol for the stream extraction operator is _____.

n) The stream manipulators _____, _____ and _____ specify that integers should be displayed in octal, hexadecimal and decimal formats, respectively.

o) The _____ stream manipulator causes positive numbers to display with a plus sign.

15.2 State whether the following are *true* or *false*. If the answer is *false*, explain why.

a) The stream member function flags with a long argument sets the flags state variable to its argument and returns its previous value.

b) The stream insertion operator << and the stream extraction operator >> are overloaded to handle all standard data types—including strings and memory addresses (stream insertion only)—and all user-defined data types.

c) The stream member function flags with no arguments resets the stream's format state.

d) The stream extraction operator >> can be overloaded with an operator function that takes an istream reference and a reference to a user-defined type as arguments and returns an istream reference.

e) The stream insertion operator << can be overloaded with an operator function that takes an istream reference and a reference to a user-defined type as arguments and returns an istream reference.

f) Input with the stream extraction operator >> always skips leading white-space characters in the input stream, by default.

g) The stream member function rdstate returns the current state of the stream.

h) The cout stream normally is connected to the display screen.

i) The stream member function good returns true if the bad, fail and eof member functions all return false.

j) The cin stream normally is connected to the display screen.

k) If a nonrecoverable error occurs during a stream operation, the bad member function will return true.

l) Output to cerr is unbuffered and output to clog is buffered.

m) Stream manipulator showpoint forces floating-point values to print with the default six digits of precision unless the precision value has been changed, in which case floating-point values print with the specified precision.

n) The ostream member function put outputs the specified number of characters.

o) The stream manipulators dec, oct and hex affect only the next integer output operation.

p) By default, memory addresses are displayed as long integers.

15.3 For each of the following, write a single statement that performs the indicated task.

a) Output the string "Enter your name: ".

b) Use a stream manipulator that causes the exponent in scientific notation and the letters in hexadecimal values to print in capital letters.

c) Output the address of the variable myString of type char *.

d) Use a stream manipulator to ensure that floating-point values print in scientific notation.

e) Output the address in variable integerPtr of type int *.

f) Use a stream manipulator such that, when integer values are output, the integer base for octal and hexadecimal values is displayed.

g) Output the value pointed to by floatPtr of type float *.

h) Use a stream member function to set the fill character to `'*'` for printing in field widths larger than the values being output. Repeat this statement with a stream manipulator.
i) Output the characters `'O'` and `'K'` in one statement with `ostream` function `put`.
j) Get the value of the next character to input without extracting it from the stream.
k) Input a single character into variable `charValue` of type `char`, using the `istream` member function `get` in two different ways.
l) Input and discard the next six characters in the input stream.
m) Use `istream` member function `read` to input 50 characters into `char` array `line`.
n) Read 10 characters into character array `name`. Stop reading characters if the `'.'` delimiter is encountered. Do not remove the delimiter from the input stream. Write another statement that performs this task and removes the delimiter from the input.
o) Use the `istream` member function `gcount` to determine the number of characters input into character array `line` by the last call to `istream` member function `read`, and output that number of characters, using `ostream` member function `write`.
p) Output 124, 18.376, `'Z'`, 1000000 and `"String"`, separated by spaces.
q) Print the current precision setting, using a member function of object `cout`.
r) Input an integer value into `int` variable `months` and a floating-point value into `float` variable `percentageRate`.
s) Print 1.92, 1.925 and 1.9258 separated by tabs and with 3 digits of precision, using a stream manipulator.
t) Print integer 100 in octal, hexadecimal and decimal, using stream manipulators and separated by tabs.
u) Print integer 100 in decimal, octal and hexadecimal separated by tabs, using a stream manipulator to change the base.
v) Print 1234 right justified in a 10-digit field.
w) Read characters into character array `line` until the character `'z'` is encountered, up to a limit of 20 characters (including a terminating null character). Do not extract the delimiter character from the stream.
x) Use integer variables `x` and `y` to specify the field width and precision used to display the `double` value 87.4573, and display the value.

15.4 Identify the error in each of the following statements and explain how to correct it.
a) `cout << "Value of x <= y is: " << x <= y;`
b) The following statement should print the integer value of `'c'`.
`cout << 'c';`
c) `cout << ""A string in quotes"";`

15.5 For each of the following, show the output.
a) `cout << "12345" << endl;`
`cout.width( 5 );`
`cout.fill( '*' );`
`cout << 123 << endl << 123;`
b) `cout << setw( 10 ) << setfill( '$' ) << 10000;`
c) `cout << setw( 8 ) << setprecision( 3 ) << 1024.987654;`
d) `cout << showbase << oct << 99 << endl << hex << 99;`
e) `cout << 100000 << endl << showpos << 100000;`
f) `cout << setw( 10 ) << setprecision( 2 ) << scientific << 444.93738;`

Answers to Self-Review Exercises

15.1 a) streams. b) `left`, `right` and `internal`. c) flags. d) `<iostream>`. e) `<iomanip>`. f) `<fstream>`. g) `write`. h) `istream`. i) `cerr` or `clog`. j) `ostream`. k) `<<`. l) `cin`, `cout`, `cerr` and `clog`. m) `>>`. n) `oct`, `hex` and `dec`. o) `showpos`.

15.2 a) False. The stream member function `flags` with a `fmtflags` argument sets the `flags` state variable to its argument and returns the prior state settings. b) False. The stream insertion and stream extraction operators are not overloaded for all user-defined types. The programmer of a class must specifically provide the overloaded operator functions to overload the stream operators for use with each user-defined type. c) False. The stream member function `flags` with no arguments returns the current format settings as a `fmtflags` data type, which represents the format state. d) True. e) False. To overload the stream insertion operator `<<`, the overloaded operator function must take an `ostream` reference and a reference to a user-defined type as arguments and return an `ostream` reference. f) True. g) True. h) True. i) True. j) False. The `cin` stream is connected to the standard input of the computer, which normally is the keyboard. k) True. l) True. m) True. n) False. The `ostream` member function `put` outputs its single-character argument. o) False. The stream manipulators `dec`, `oct` and `hex` set the output format state for integers to the specified base until the base is changed again or the program terminates. p) False. Memory addresses are displayed in hexadecimal format by default. To display addresses as `long` integers, the address must be cast to a `long` value.

15.3
a) `cout << "Enter your name: ";`
b) `cout << uppercase;`
c) `cout << static_cast< void * >( myString );`
d) `cout << scientific;`
e) `cout << integerPtr;`
f) `cout << showbase;`
g) `cout << *floatPtr;`
h) `cout.fill( '*' );`
   `cout << setfill( '*' );`
i) `cout.put( 'O' ).put( 'K' );`
j) `cin.peek();`
k) `charValue = cin.get();`
   `cin.get( charValue );`
l) `cin.ignore( 6 );`
m) `cin.read( line, 50 );`
n) `cin.get( name, 10, '.' );`
   `cin.getline( name, 10, '.' );`
o) `cout.write( line, cin.gcount() );`
p) `cout << 124 << ' ' << 18.376 << ' ' << "Z " << 1000000 << " String";`
q) `cout << cout.precision();`
r) `cin >> months >> percentageRate;`
s) `cout << setprecision( 3 ) << 1.92 << '\t' << 1.925 << '\t' << 1.9258;`
t) `cout << oct << 100 << '\t' << hex << 100 << '\t' << dec << 100;`
u) `cout << 100 << '\t' << setbase( 8 ) << 100 << '\t' << setbase( 16 ) << 100;`
v) `cout << setw( 10 ) << 1234;`
w) `cin.get( line, 20, 'z' );`
x) `cout << setw( x ) << setprecision( y ) << 87.4573;`

15.4
a) *Error:* The precedence of the `<<` operator is higher than that of `<=`, which causes the statement to be evaluated improperly and also causes a compiler error.
   Correction: Place parentheses around the expression x `<=` y.
b) *Error:* In C++, characters are not treated as small integers, as they are in C.
   Correction: To print the numerical value for a character in the computer's character set, the character must be cast to an integer value, as in the following:
   `cout << static_cast< int >( 'c' );`

c) *Error:* Quote characters cannot be printed in a string unless an escape sequence is used.
   Correction: Print the string in one of the following ways:

```
cout << "\"A string in quotes\"";
```

15.5 a) 12345
         **123
         123
      b) $$$$$10000
      c) 1024.988
      d) 0143
         0x63
      e) 100000
         +100000
      f)   4.45e+002

Exercises

15.6 Write a statement for each of the following:
   a) Print integer 40000 left justified in a 15-digit field.
   b) Read a string into character array variable state.
   c) Print 200 with and without a sign.
   d) Print the decimal value 100 in hexadecimal form preceded by 0x.
   e) Read characters into array charArray until the character 'p' is encountered, up to a limit of 10 characters (including the terminating null character). Extract the delimiter from the input stream, and discard it.
   f) Print 1.234 in a 9-digit field with preceding zeros.

15.7 Write a program to test the inputting of integer values in decimal, octal and hexadecimal formats. Output each integer read by the program in all three formats. Test the program with the following input data: 10, 010, 0x10.

15.8 Write a program that prints pointer values, using casts to all the integer data types. Which ones print strange values? Which ones cause errors?

15.9 Write a program to test the results of printing the integer value 12345 and the floating-point value 1.2345 in various-sized fields. What happens when the values are printed in fields containing fewer digits than the values?

15.10 Write a program that prints the value 100.453627 rounded to the nearest digit, tenth, hundredth, thousandth and ten-thousandth.

15.11 Write a program that inputs a string from the keyboard and determines the length of the string. Print the string in a field width that is twice the length of the string.

15.12 Write a program that converts integer Fahrenheit temperatures from 0 to 212 degrees to floating-point Celsius temperatures with 3 digits of precision. Use the formula

```
celsius = 5.0 / 9.0 * ( fahrenheit - 32 );
```

to perform the calculation. The output should be printed in two right-justified columns and the Celsius temperatures should be preceded by a sign for both positive and negative values.

15.13 In some programming languages, strings are entered surrounded by either single or double quotation marks. Write a program that reads the three strings suzy, "suzy" and 'suzy'. Are the single and double quotes ignored or read as part of the string?

15.14 In Fig. 11.5, the stream extraction and stream insertion operators were overloaded for input and output of objects of the PhoneNumber class. Rewrite the stream extraction operator to perform the following error checking on input. The operator>> function will need to be reimplemented.

a) Input the entire phone number into an array. Test that the proper number of characters has been entered. There should be a total of 14 characters read for a phone number of the form (800) 555-1212. Use ios_base-member-function clear to set failbit for improper input.

b) The area code and exchange do not begin with 0 or 1. Test the first digit of the area-code and exchange portions of the phone number to be sure that neither begins with 0 or 1. Use ios_base-member-function clear to set failbit for improper input.

c) The middle digit of an area code used to be limited to 0 or 1 (although this has changed recently). Test the middle digit for a value of 0 or 1. Use the ios_base-member-function clear to set failbit for improper input. If none of the above operations results in failbit being set for improper input, copy the three parts of the telephone number into the areaCode, exchange and line members of the PhoneNumber object. If failbit has been set on the input, have the program print an error message and end, rather than print the phone number.

15.15   Write a program that accomplishes each of the following:

a) Create a user-defined class Point that contains the private integer data members xCoordinate and yCoordinate and declares stream insertion and stream extraction overloaded operator functions as friends of the class.

b) Define the stream insertion and stream extraction operator functions. The stream extraction operator function should determine whether the data entered is valid, and, if not, it should set the failbit to indicate improper input. The stream insertion operator should not be able to display the point after an input error occurred.

c) Write a main function that tests input and output of user-defined class Point, using the overloaded stream extraction and stream insertion operators.

15.16   Write a program that accomplishes each of the following:

a) Create a user-defined class Complex that contains the private integer data members real and imaginary and declares stream insertion and stream extraction overloaded operator functions as friends of the class.

b) Define the stream insertion and stream extraction operator functions. The stream extraction operator function should determine whether the data entered is valid, and, if not, it should set failbit to indicate improper input. The input should be of the form

3 + 8i

c) The values can be negative or positive, and it is possible that one of the two values is not provided, in which case the appropriate data member should be set to 0. The stream insertion operator should not be able to display the point if an input error occurred. For negative imaginary values, a minus sign should be printed rather than a plus sign.

d) Write a main function that tests input and output of user-defined class Complex, using the overloaded stream extraction and stream insertion operators.

15.17   Write a program that uses a for statement to print a table of ASCII values for the characters in the ASCII character set from 33 to 126. The program should print the decimal value, octal value, hexadecimal value and character value for each character. Use the stream manipulators dec, oct and hex to print the integer values.

15.18   Write a program to show that the getline and three-argument get istream member functions both end the input string with a string-terminating null character. Also, show that get leaves the delimiter character on the input stream, whereas getline extracts the delimiter character and discards it. What happens to the unread characters in the stream?

16

Exception Handling

OBJECTIVES

In this chapter you'll learn:

- What exceptions are and when to use them.
- To use **try**, **catch** and **throw** to detect, handle and indicate exceptions, respectively.
- To process uncaught and unexpected exceptions.
- To declare new exception classes.
- How stack unwinding enables exceptions not caught in one scope to be caught in another scope.
- To handle **new** failures.
- To use **auto_ptr** to prevent memory leaks.
- To understand the standard exception hierarchy.

16.1 Introduction

In this chapter, we introduce exception handling. An exception is an indication of a problem that occurs during a program's execution. The name "exception" implies that the problem occurs infrequently—if the "rule" is that a statement normally executes correctly, then the "exception to the rule" is that a problem occurs. Exception handling enables programmers to create applications that can resolve (or handle) exceptions. In many cases, handling an exception allows a program to continue executing as if no problem had been encountered. A more severe problem could prevent a program from continuing normal execution, instead requiring the program to notify the user of the problem before terminating in a controlled manner. The features presented in this chapter enable programmers to write robust and fault-tolerant programs that are able to deal with problems that may arise and continue executing or terminate gracefully. The style and details of C++ exception handling are based in part on the work of Andrew Koenig and Bjarne Stroustrup, as presented in their paper, "Exception Handling for C++ (revised)."[1]

 Error-Prevention Tip 16.1

Exception handling helps improve a program's fault tolerance.

 Software Engineering Observation 16.1

Exception handling provides a standard mechanism for processing errors. This is especially important when working on a project with a large team of programmers.

---

1. Koenig, A., and B. Stroustrup, "Exception Handling for C++ (revised)," *Proceedings of the Usenix C++ Conference*, pp. 149–176, San Francisco, April 1990.

The chapter begins with an overview of exception-handling concepts, then demonstrates basic exception-handling techniques. We show these techniques via an example that demonstrates handling an exception that occurs when a function attempts to divide by zero. We then discuss additional exception-handling issues, such as how to handle exceptions that occur in a constructor or destructor and how to handle exceptions that occur if operator new fails to allocate memory for an object. We conclude the chapter by introducing several classes that the C++ Standard Library provides for handling exceptions.

16.2 Exception-Handling Overview

Program logic frequently tests conditions that determine how program execution proceeds. Consider the following pseudocode:

> *Perform a task*
>
> *If the preceding task did not execute correctly*
> *Perform error processing*
>
> *Perform next task*
>
> *If the preceding task did not execute correctly*
> *Perform error processing*
>
> *...*

In this pseudocode, we begin by performing a task. We then test whether that task executed correctly. If not, we perform error processing. Otherwise, we continue with the next task. Although this form of error handling works, intermixing program logic with error-handling logic can make the program difficult to read, modify, maintain and debug—especially in large applications.

Performance Tip 16.1

If the potential problems occur infrequently, intermixing program logic and error-handling logic can degrade a program's performance, because the program must (potentially frequently) perform tests to determine whether the task executed correctly and the next task can be performed.

Exception handling enables you to remove error-handling code from the "main line" of the program's execution, which improves program clarity and enhances modifiability. Programmers can decide to handle any exceptions they choose—all exceptions, all exceptions of a certain type or all exceptions of a group of related types (e.g., exception types that belong to an inheritance hierarchy). Such flexibility reduces the likelihood that errors will be overlooked and thereby makes a program more robust.

With programming languages that do not support exception handling, programmers often delay writing error-processing code or sometimes forget to include it. This results in less robust software products. C++ enables you to deal with exception handling easily from the inception of a project.

16.3 Example: Handling an Attempt to Divide by Zero

Let us consider a simple example of exception handling (Figs. 16.1–16.2). The purpose of this example is to show how to prevent a common arithmetic problem—division by zero.

In C++, division by zero using integer arithmetic typically causes a program to terminate prematurely. In floating-point arithmetic, some C++ implementations allow division by zero, in which case positive or negative infinity is displayed as INF or -INF, respectively.

In this example, we define a function named quotient that receives two integers input by the user and divides its first int parameter by its second int parameter. Before performing the division, the function casts the first int parameter's value to type double. Then, the second int parameter's value is promoted to type double for the calculation. So function quotient actually performs the division using two double values and returns a double result.

Although division by zero is allowed in floating-point arithmetic, for the purpose of this example we treat any attempt to divide by zero as an error. Thus, function quotient tests its second parameter to ensure that it is not zero before allowing the division to proceed. If the second parameter is zero, the function uses an exception to indicate to the caller that a problem occurred. The caller (main in this example) can then process the exception and allow the user to type two new values before calling function quotient again. In this way, the program can continue to execute even after an improper value is entered, thus making the program more robust.

The example consists of two files. DivideByZeroException.h (Fig. 16.1) defines an exception class that represents the type of the problem that might occur in the example, and fig16_02.cpp (Fig. 16.2) defines the quotient function and the main function that calls it. Function main contains the code that demonstrates exception handling.

Defining an Exception Class to Represent the Type of Problem That Might Occur
Figure 16.1 defines class DivideByZeroException as a derived class of Standard Library class runtime_error (defined in header file <stdexcept>). Class runtime_error—a derived class of Standard Library class exception (defined in header file <exception>)—is the C++ standard base class for representing runtime errors. Class exception is the standard C++ base class for all exceptions. (Section 16.13 discusses class exception and its derived classes in detail.) A typical exception class that derives from the runtime_error class defines only a constructor (e.g., lines 12–13) that passes an error-message string to the base-class runtime_error constructor. Every exception class that derives directly or indirectly

```
 1   // Fig. 16.1: DivideByZeroException.h
 2   // Class DivideByZeroException definition.
 3   #include <stdexcept> // stdexcept header file contains runtime_error
 4   using std::runtime_error; // standard C++ library class runtime_error
 5
 6   // DivideByZeroException objects should be thrown by functions
 7   // upon detecting division-by-zero exceptions
 8   class DivideByZeroException : public runtime_error
 9   {
10   public:
11      // constructor specifies default error message
12      DivideByZeroException()
13         : runtime_error( "attempted to divide by zero" ) {}
14   }; // end class DivideByZeroException
```

Fig. 16.1 | Class DivideByZeroException definition.

```cpp
1   // Fig. 16.2: Fig16_02.cpp
2   // A simple exception-handling example that checks for
3   // divide-by-zero exceptions.
4   #include <iostream>
5   using std::cin;
6   using std::cout;
7   using std::endl;
8
9   #include "DivideByZeroException.h" // DivideByZeroException class
10
11  // perform division and throw DivideByZeroException object if
12  // divide-by-zero exception occurs
13  double quotient( int numerator, int denominator )
14  {
15     // throw DivideByZeroException if trying to divide by zero
16     if ( denominator == 0 )
17        throw DivideByZeroException(); // terminate function
18
19     // return division result
20     return static_cast< double >( numerator ) / denominator;
21  } // end function quotient
22
23  int main()
24  {
25     int number1; // user-specified numerator
26     int number2; // user-specified denominator
27     double result; // result of division
28
29     cout << "Enter two integers (end-of-file to end): ";
30
31     // enable user to enter two integers to divide
32     while ( cin >> number1 >> number2 )
33     {
34        // try block contains code that might throw exception
35        // and code that should not execute if an exception occurs
36        try
37        {
38           result = quotient( number1, number2 );
39           cout << "The quotient is: " << result << endl;
40        } // end try
41
42        // exception handler handles a divide-by-zero exception
43        catch ( DivideByZeroException &divideByZeroException )
44        {
45           cout << "Exception occurred: "
46              << divideByZeroException.what() << endl;
47        } // end catch
48
49        cout << "\nEnter two integers (end-of-file to end): ";
50     } // end while
51
```

Fig. 16.2 | Exception-handling example that throws exceptions on attempts to divide by zero. (Part 1 of 2.)

```
52      cout << endl;
53      return 0; // terminate normally
54   } // end main
```

```
Enter two integers (end-of-file to end): 100 7
The quotient is: 14.2857

Enter two integers (end-of-file to end): 100 0
Exception occurred: attempted to divide by zero

Enter two integers (end-of-file to end): ^Z
```

Fig. 16.2 | Exception-handling example that throws exceptions on attempts to divide by zero. (Part 2 of 2.)

from exception contains the virtual function what, which returns an exception object's error message. Note that you are not required to derive a custom exception class, such as DivideByZeroException, from the standard exception classes provided by C++. However, doing so allows programmers to use the virtual function what to obtain an appropriate error message. We use an object of this DivideByZeroException class in Fig. 16.2 to indicate when an attempt is made to divide by zero.

Demonstrating Exception Handling

The program in Fig. 16.2 uses exception handling to wrap code that might throw a "divide-by-zero" exception and to handle that exception, should one occur. The application enables the user to enter two integers, which are passed as arguments to function quotient (lines 13–21). This function divides its first parameter (numerator) by its second parameter (denominator). Assuming that the user does not specify 0 as the denominator for the division, function quotient returns the division result. However, if the user inputs 0 for the denominator, function quotient throws an exception. In the sample output, the first two lines show a successful calculation, and the next two lines show a failed calculation due to an attempt to divide by zero. When the exception occurs, the program informs the user of the mistake and prompts the user to input two new integers. After we discuss the code, we'll consider the user inputs and flow of program control that yield these outputs.

Enclosing Code in a *try* Block

The program begins by prompting the user to enter two integers. The integers are input in the condition of the while loop (line 32). After the user inputs values that represent the numerator and denominator, program control proceeds into the loop's body (lines 33–50). Line 38 passes these values to function quotient (lines 13–21), which either divides the integers and returns a result, or throws an exception (i.e., indicates that an error occurred) on an attempt to divide by zero. Exception handling is geared to situations in which the function that detects an error is unable to handle it.

C++ provides try blocks to enable exception handling. A try block consists of keyword try followed by braces ({}) that define a block of code in which exceptions might occur. The try block encloses statements that might cause exceptions and statements that should be skipped if an exception occurs.

Note that a try block (lines 36–40) encloses the invocation of function quotient and the statement that displays the division result. In this example, because the invocation of function quotient (line 38) can throw an exception, we enclose this function invocation in a try block. Enclosing the output statement (line 39) in the try block ensures that the output will occur only if function quotient returns a result.

Software Engineering Observation 16.2

Exceptions may surface through explicitly mentioned code in a try block, through calls to other functions and through deeply nested function calls initiated by code in a try block.

Defining a catch *Handler to Process a* DivideByZeroException

Exceptions are processed by catch handlers (also called exception handlers), which catch and handle exceptions. At least one catch handler (lines 43–47) must immediately follow each try block. Each catch handler begins with the keyword catch and specifies in parentheses an exception parameter that represents the type of exception the catch handler can process (DivideByZeroException in this case). When an exception occurs in a try block, the catch handler that executes is the one whose type matches the type of the exception that occurred (i.e., the type in the catch block matches the thrown exception type exactly or is a base class of it). If an exception parameter includes an optional parameter name, the catch handler can use that parameter name to interact with the caught exception in the body of the catch handler, which is delimited by braces ({ and }). A catch handler typically reports the error to the user, logs it to a file, terminates the program gracefully or tries an alternate strategy to accomplish the failed task. In this example, the catch handler simply reports that the user attempted to divide by zero. Then the program prompts the user to enter two new integer values.

Common Programming Error 16.1

It is a syntax error to place code between a try block and its corresponding catch handlers or between its catch handlers.

Common Programming Error 16.2

Each catch handler can have only a single parameter—specifying a comma-separated list of exception parameters is a syntax error.

Common Programming Error 16.3

It is a logic error to catch the same type in two different catch handlers following a single try block.

Termination Model of Exception Handling

If an exception occurs as the result of a statement in a try block, the try block expires (i.e., terminates immediately). Next, the program searches for the first catch handler that can process the type of exception that occurred. The program locates the matching catch by comparing the thrown exception's type to each catch's exception-parameter type until the program finds a match. A match occurs if the types are identical or if the thrown exception's type is a derived class of the exception-parameter type. When a match occurs, the code contained in the matching catch handler executes. When a catch handler finishes processing by reaching its closing right brace (}), the exception is considered handled and the local variables defined within the catch handler (including the catch parameter) go out of scope. Program control does not return to the point at which the exception occurred (known as the throw point), because the `try` block has expired. Rather, control resumes with the first statement (line 49) after the last `catch` handler following the `try` block. This is known as the termination model of exception handling. [*Note:* Some languages use the resumption model of exception handling, in which, after an exception is handled, control resumes just after the throw point.] As with any other block of code, when a `try` block terminates, local variables defined in the block go out of scope.

Common Programming Error 16.4

Logic errors can occur if you assume that after an exception is handled, control will return to the first statement after the throw point.

Error-Prevention Tip 16.2

With exception handling, a program can continue executing (rather than terminating) after dealing with a problem. This helps ensure the kind of robust applications that contribute to what is called mission-critical computing or business-critical computing.

If the `try` block completes its execution successfully (i.e., no exceptions occur in the `try` block), then the program ignores the `catch` handlers and program control continues with the first statement after the last `catch` following that `try` block. If no exceptions occur in a `try` block, the program ignores the `catch` handler(s) for that block.

If an exception that occurs in a `try` block has no matching `catch` handler, or if an exception occurs in a statement that is not in a `try` block, the function that contains the statement terminates immediately, and the program attempts to locate an enclosing `try` block in the calling function. This process is called stack unwinding and is discussed in Section 16.8.

Flow of Program Control When the User Enters a Nonzero Denominator

Consider the flow of control when the user inputs the numerator 100 and the denominator 7 (i.e., the first two lines of output in Fig. 16.2). In line 16, function `quotient` determines that the `denominator` does not equal zero, so line 20 performs the division and returns the result (14.2857) to line 38 as a `double` (the `static_cast< double >` in line 20 ensures the proper return value type). Program control then continues sequentially from line 38, so line 39 displays the division result—line 40 ends the `try` block. Because the `try` block completed successfully and did not throw an exception, the program does not execute the statements contained in the `catch` handler (lines 43–47), and control continues to line 49 (the first line of code after the `catch` handler), which prompts the user to enter two more integers.

Flow of Program Control When the User Enters a Denominator of Zero

Now let us consider a more interesting case in which the user inputs the numerator 100 and the denominator 0 (i.e., the third and fourth lines of output in Fig. 16.2). In line 16, `quotient` determines that the `denominator` equals zero, which indicates an attempt to divide by zero. Line 17 throws an exception, which we represent as an object of class `DivideByZeroException` (Fig. 16.1).

To throw an exception, line 17 uses keyword **throw** followed by an operand that represents the type of exception to throw. Normally, a `throw` statement specifies one operand. (In Section 16.5, we discuss how to use a `throw` statement with no operand.) The operand of a `throw` can be of any type. If the operand is an object, we call it an exception object—in this example, the exception object is an object of type `DivideByZeroException`. However, a `throw` operand also can assume other values, such as the value of an expression that does not result in an object (e.g., `throw x > 5`) or the value of an `int` (e.g., `throw 5`). The examples in this chapter focus exclusively on throwing exception objects.

Common Programming Error 16.5

Use caution when `throwing` the result of a conditional expression (?:)—promotion rules could cause the value to be of a type different from the one expected. For example, when throwing an `int` or a `double` from the same conditional expression, the `int` is promoted to a `double`. So, a `catch` handler that catches an `int` would never execute based on such a conditional expression.

As part of throwing an exception, the `throw` operand is created and used to initialize the parameter in the `catch` handler, which we discuss momentarily. In this example, the `throw` statement in line 17 creates an object of class `DivideByZeroException`. When line 17 throws the exception, function `quotient` exits immediately. Therefore, line 17 throws the exception before function `quotient` can perform the division in line 20. This is a central characteristic of exception handling: A function should throw an exception *before* the error has an opportunity to occur.

Because we decided to enclose the invocation of function `quotient` (line 38) in a `try` block, program control enters the `catch` handler (lines 43–47) that immediately follows the `try` block. This `catch` handler serves as the exception handler for the divide-by-zero exception. In general, when an exception is thrown within a `try` block, the exception is caught by a `catch` handler that specifies the type matching the thrown exception. In this program, the `catch` handler specifies that it catches `DivideByZeroException` objects—this type matches the object type thrown in function `quotient`. Actually, the `catch` handler catches a reference to the `DivideByZeroException` object created by function `quotient`'s `throw` statement (line 17). The exception object is maintained by the exception-handling mechanism.

Performance Tip 16.2

Catching an exception object by reference eliminates the overhead of copying the object that represents the thrown exception.

Good Programming Practice 16.1

Associating each type of runtime error with an appropriately named exception object improves program clarity.

The `catch` handler's body (lines 45–46) prints the associated error message returned by calling function `what` of base-class `runtime_error`. This function returns the string that the `DivideByZeroException` constructor (lines 12–13 in Fig. 16.1) passed to the `runtime_error` base-class constructor.

16.4 When to Use Exception Handling

Exception handling is designed to process synchronous errors, which occur when a statement executes. Common examples of these errors are out-of-range array subscripts, arithmetic overflow (i.e., a value outside the representable range of values), division by zero, invalid function parameters and unsuccessful memory allocation (due to lack of memory).

Exception handling is not designed to process errors associated with asynchronous events (e.g., disk I/O completions, network message arrivals, mouse clicks and keystrokes), which occur in parallel with, and independent of, the program's flow of control.

Software Engineering Observation 16.3

Incorporate your exception-handling strategy into your system from the design process's inception. Including effective exception handling after a system has been implemented can be difficult.

Software Engineering Observation 16.4

Exception handling provides a single, uniform technique for processing problems. This helps programmers working on large projects understand each other's error-processing code.

Software Engineering Observation 16.5

Avoid using exception handling as an alternate form of flow of control. These "additional" exceptions can "get in the way" of genuine error-type exceptions.

Software Engineering Observation 16.6

Exception handling simplifies combining software components and enables them to work together effectively by enabling predefined components to communicate problems to application-specific components, which can then process the problems in an application-specific manner.

The exception-handling mechanism also is useful for processing problems that occur when a program interacts with software elements, such as member functions, constructors, destructors and classes. Rather than handling problems internally, such software elements often use exceptions to notify programs when problems occur. This enables programmers to implement customized error handling for each application.

Performance Tip 16.3

When no exceptions occur, exception-handling code incurs little or no performance penalty. Thus, programs that implement exception handling operate more efficiently than do programs that intermix error-handling code with program logic.

Software Engineering Observation 16.7

Functions with common error conditions should return 0 or NULL (or other appropriate values) rather than throw exceptions. A program calling such a function can check the return value to determine success or failure of the function call.

Complex applications normally consist of predefined software components and application-specific components that use the predefined components. When a predefined component encounters a problem, that component needs a mechanism to communicate the problem to the application-specific component—the predefined component cannot know in advance how each application processes a problem that occurs.

16.5 Rethrowing an Exception

It is possible that an exception handler, upon receiving an exception, might decide either that it cannot process that exception or that it can process the exception only partially. In such cases, the exception handler can defer the exception handling (or perhaps a portion of it) to another exception handler. In either case, you achieve this by rethrowing the exception via the statement

```
throw;
```

Regardless of whether a handler can process (even partially) an exception, the handler can rethrow the exception for further processing outside the handler. The next enclosing try block detects the rethrown exception, which a catch handler listed after that enclosing try block attempts to handle.

 Common Programming Error 16.6

Executing an empty throw statement that is situated outside a catch handler causes a call to function terminate, which abandons exception processing and terminates the program immediately.

The program of Fig. 16.3 demonstrates rethrowing an exception. In main's try block (lines 32–37), line 35 calls function throwException (lines 11–27). The throwException function also contains a try block (lines 14–18), from which the throw statement in line 17 throws an instance of standard-library-class exception. Function throwException's catch handler (lines 19–24) catches this exception, prints an error message (lines 21–22) and rethrows the exception (line 23). This terminates function throwException and returns control to line 35 in the try...catch block in main. The try block terminates (so line 36 does not execute), and the catch handler in main (lines 38–41) catches this exception and prints an error message (line 40). [*Note:* Since we do not use the exception parameters in the catch handlers of this example, we omit the exception parameter names and specify only the type of exception to catch (lines 19 and 38).]

```
1   // Fig. 16.3: Fig16_03.cpp
2   // Demonstrating exception rethrowing.
3   #include <iostream>
4   using std::cout;
5   using std::endl;
6
7   #include <exception>
8   using std::exception;
9
10  // throw, catch and rethrow exception
11  void throwException()
12  {
13     // throw exception and catch it immediately
14     try
15     {
16        cout << " Function throwException throws an exception\n";
17        throw exception(); // generate exception
18     } // end try
19     catch ( exception & ) // handle exception
20     {
21        cout << " Exception handled in function throwException"
22           << "\n Function throwException rethrows exception";
```

Fig. 16.3 | Rethrowing an exception. (Part 1 of 2.)

```
23              throw; // rethrow exception for further processing
24         } // end catch
25
26         cout << "This also should not print\n";
27    } // end function throwException
28
29    int main()
30    {
31         // throw exception
32         try
33         {
34              cout << "\nmain invokes function throwException\n";
35              throwException();
36              cout << "This should not print\n";
37         } // end try
38         catch ( exception & ) // handle exception
39         {
40              cout << "\n\nException handled in main\n";
41         } // end catch
42
43         cout << "Program control continues after catch in main\n";
44         return 0;
45    } // end main
```

```
main invokes function throwException
   Function throwException throws an exception
   Exception handled in function throwException
   Function throwException rethrows exception

Exception handled in main
Program control continues after catch in main
```

Fig. 16.3 | Rethrowing an exception. (Part 2 of 2.)

16.6 Exception Specifications

An optional exception specification (also called a throw list) enumerates a list of exceptions that a function can throw. For example, consider the function declaration

```
int someFunction( double value )
   throw ( ExceptionA, ExceptionB, ExceptionC )
{
   // function body
}
```

In this definition, the exception specification, which begins with keyword throw immediately following the closing parenthesis of the function's parameter list, indicates that function someFunction can throw exceptions of types ExceptionA, ExceptionB and ExceptionC. A function can throw only exceptions of the types indicated by the specification or exceptions of any type derived from these types. If the function throws an exception that does not belong to a specified type, the exception-handling mechanism calls function unexpected, which terminates the program.

A function that does not provide an exception specification can `throw` any exception. Placing `throw()`—an *empty exception specification*—after a function's parameter list states that the function does not `throw` exceptions. If the function attempts to `throw` an exception, function `unexpected` is invoked. Section 16.7 shows how function `unexpected` can be customized by calling function `set_unexpected`.

Common Programming Error 16.7

Throwing an exception that has not been declared in a function's exception specification causes a call to function `unexpected`.

Error-Prevention Tip 16.3

The compiler will not generate a compilation error if a function contains a `throw` expression for an exception not listed in the function's exception specification. An error occurs only when that function attempts to throw that exception at execution time. To avoid surprises at execution time, carefully check your code to ensure that functions do not throw exceptions not listed in their exception specifications.

16.7 Processing Unexpected Exceptions

Function `unexpected` calls the function registered with function `set_unexpected` (defined in header file `<exception>`). If no function has been registered in this manner, function `terminate` is called by default. Cases in which function `terminate` is called include:

1. the exception mechanism cannot find a matching `catch` for a thrown exception

2. a destructor attempts to `throw` an exception during stack unwinding

3. an attempt is made to rethrow an exception when there is no exception currently being handled

4. a call to function `unexpected` defaults to calling function `terminate`

(Section 15.5.1 of the C++ Standard Document discusses several additional cases.) Function `set_terminate` can specify the function to invoke when `terminate` is called. Otherwise, `terminate` calls `abort`, which terminates the program without calling the destructors of any remaining objects of automatic or static storage class. This could lead to resource leaks when a program terminates prematurely.

Function `set_terminate` and function `set_unexpected` each return a pointer to the last function called by `terminate` and `unexpected`, respectively (0, the first time each is called). This enables you to save the function pointer so it can be restored later. Functions `set_terminate` and `set_unexpected` take as arguments pointers to functions with `void` return types and no arguments.

If the last action of a programmer-defined termination function is not to exit a program, function `abort` will be called to end program execution after the other statements of the programmer-defined termination function are executed.

16.8 Stack Unwinding

When an exception is thrown but not caught in a particular scope, the function call stack is "unwound," and an attempt is made to `catch` the exception in the next outer `try...catch` block. Unwinding the function call stack means that the function in which the exception was not caught terminates, all local variables in that function are destroyed and control returns to the statement that originally invoked that function. If a `try` block encloses that statement, an attempt is made to `catch` the exception. If a `try` block does not enclose that statement, stack unwinding occurs again. If no `catch` handler ever catches this exception, function `terminate` is called to terminate the program. The program of Fig. 16.4 demonstrates stack unwinding.

```cpp
1   // Fig. 16.4: Fig16_04.cpp
2   // Demonstrating stack unwinding.
3   #include <iostream>
4   using std::cout;
5   using std::endl;
6
7   #include <stdexcept>
8   using std::runtime_error;
9
10  // function3 throws runtime error
11  void function3() throw ( runtime_error )
12  {
13     cout << "In function 3" << endl;
14
15     // no try block, stack unwinding occurs, return control to function2
16     throw runtime_error( "runtime_error in function3" ); // no print
17  } // end function3
18
19  // function2 invokes function3
20  void function2() throw ( runtime_error )
21  {
22     cout << "function3 is called inside function2" << endl;
23     function3(); // stack unwinding occurs, return control to function1
24  } // end function2
25
26  // function1 invokes function2
27  void function1() throw ( runtime_error )
28  {
29     cout << "function2 is called inside function1" << endl;
30     function2(); // stack unwinding occurs, return control to main
31  } // end function1
32
33  // demonstrate stack unwinding
34  int main()
35  {
36     // invoke function1
37     try
38     {
39        cout << "function1 is called inside main" << endl;
40        function1(); // call function1 which throws runtime_error
41     } // end try
42     catch ( runtime_error &error ) // handle runtime error
43     {
44        cout << "Exception occurred: " << error.what() << endl;
```

Fig. 16.4 | Stack unwinding. (Part I of 2.)

```
45              cout << "Exception handled in main" << endl;
46          } // end catch
47
48          return 0;
49      } // end main
```

```
function1 is called inside main
function2 is called inside function1
function3 is called inside function2
In function 3
Exception occurred: runtime_error in function3
Exception handled in main
```

Fig. 16.4 | Stack unwinding. (Part 2 of 2.)

In main, the try block (lines 37–41) calls function1 (lines 27–31). Next, function1 calls function2 (lines 20–24), which in turn calls function3 (lines 11–17). Line 16 of function3 throws a runtime_error object. However, because no try block encloses the throw statement in line 16, stack unwinding occurs—function3 terminates in line 16, then returns control to the statement in function2 that invoked function3 (i.e., line 23). Because no try block encloses line 23, stack unwinding occurs again—function2 terminates in line 23 and returns control to the statement in function1 that invoked function2 (i.e., line 30). Because no try block encloses line 30, stack unwinding occurs one more time—function1 terminates in line 30 and returns control to the statement in main that invoked function1 (i.e., line 40). The try block of lines 37–41 encloses this statement, so the first matching catch handler located after this try block (line 42–46) catches and processes the exception. Line 44 uses function what to display the exception message. Recall that function what is a virtual function of class exception that can be overridden by a derived class to return an appropriate error message.

16.9 Constructors, Destructors and Exception Handling

First, let's discuss an issue that we have mentioned but not yet resolved satisfactorily: What happens when an error is detected in a constructor? For example, how should an object's constructor respond when new fails because it was unable to allocate required memory for storing that object's internal representation? Because the constructor cannot return a value to indicate an error, we must choose an alternative means of indicating that the object has not been constructed properly. One scheme is to return the improperly constructed object and hope that anyone using it would make appropriate tests to determine that it is in an inconsistent state. Another scheme is to set some variable outside the constructor. The preferred alternative is to require the constructor to throw an exception that contains the error information, thus offering an opportunity for the program to handle the failure.

Before an exception is thrown by a constructor, destructors are called for any member objects built as part of the object being constructed. Destructors are called for every automatic object constructed in a try block before an exception is thrown. Stack unwinding is guaranteed to have been completed at the point that an exception handler begins executing. If a destructor invoked as a result of stack unwinding throws an exception, terminate is called.

If an object has member objects, and if an exception is thrown before the outer object is fully constructed, then destructors will be executed for the member objects that have been constructed prior to the occurrence of the exception. If an array of objects has been partially constructed when an exception occurs, only the destructors for the constructed objects in the array will be called.

An exception could preclude the operation of code that would normally release a resource, thus causing a resource leak. One technique to resolve this problem is to initialize a local object to acquire the resource. When an exception occurs, the destructor for that object will be invoked and can free the resource.

Error-Prevention Tip 16.4

When an exception is thrown from the constructor for an object that is created in a new expression, the dynamically allocated memory for that object is released.

16.10 Exceptions and Inheritance

Various exception classes can be derived from a common base class, as we discussed in Section 16.3, when we created class `DivideByZeroException` as a derived class of class `exception`. If a `catch` handler catches a pointer or reference to an exception object of a base-class type, it also can `catch` a pointer or reference to all objects of classes publicly derived from that base class—this allows for polymorphic processing of related errors.

Error-Prevention Tip 16.5

Using inheritance with exceptions enables an exception handler to catch related errors with concise notation. One approach is to catch each type of pointer or reference to a derived-class exception object individually, but a more concise approach is to catch pointers or references to base-class exception objects instead. Also, catching pointers or references to derived-class exception objects individually is error prone, especially if you forget to test explicitly for one or more of the derived-class pointer or reference types.

16.11 Processing new Failures

The C++ standard specifies that, when operator new fails, it throws a `bad_alloc` exception (defined in header file <new>). However, some compilers are not compliant with the C++ standard and therefore use the version of new that returns 0 on failure. For example, the Microsoft Visual C++ 2005 throws a `bad_alloc` exception when new fails, while the Microsoft Visual C++ 6.0 returns 0 on new failure.

Compilers vary in their support for new-failure handling. Many older C++ compilers return 0 by default when new fails. Some compilers support new throwing an exception if header file <new> (or <new.h>) is included. Other compilers throw bad_alloc by default, regardless of whether header file <new> is included. Consult the compiler documentation to determine the compiler's support for new-failure handling.

In this section, we present three examples of new failing. The first example returns 0 when new fails. The second example uses the version of new that `throws` a bad_alloc exception when new fails. The third example uses function `set_new_handler` to handle new failures. [*Note:* The examples in Figs. 16.5–16.7 allocate large amounts of dynamic memory, which could cause your computer to become sluggish.]

new *Returning 0 on Failure*

Figure 16.5 demonstrates new returning 0 on failure to allocate the requested amount of memory. The for statement in lines 13–24 should loop 50 times and, on each pass, allocate an array of 50,000,000 double values (i.e., 400,000,000 bytes, because a double is normally 8 bytes). The if statement in line 17 tests the result of each new operation to determine whether new allocated the memory successfully. If new fails and returns 0, line 19 prints an error message, and the loop terminates. [*Note:* We used Microsoft Visual C++ 6.0 to run this example, because Microsoft Visual C++ 2005 throws a bad_alloc exception on new failure instead of returning 0.]

The output shows that the program performed only three iterations before new failed, and the loop terminated. Your output might differ based on the physical memory, disk space available for virtual memory on your system and the compiler you are using.

```cpp
1   // Fig. 16.5: Fig16_05.cpp
2   // Demonstrating pre-standard new returning 0 when memory
3   // allocation fails.
4   #include <iostream>
5   using std::cerr;
6   using std::cout;
7
8   int main()
9   {
10     double *ptr[ 50 ];
11
12     // aim each ptr[i] at a big block of memory
13     for ( int i = 0; i < 50; i++ )
14     {
15        ptr[ i ] = new double[ 50000000 ]; // allocate big block
16
17        if ( ptr[ i ] == 0 ) // did new fail to allocate memory
18        {
19           cerr << "Memory allocation failed for ptr[" << i << "]\n";
20           break;
21        } // end if
22        else // successful memory allocation
23           cout << "ptr[" << i << "] points to 50,000,000 new doubles\n";
24     } // end for
25
26     return 0;
27  } // end main
```

```
ptr[0] points to 50,000,000 new doubles
ptr[1] points to 50,000,000 new doubles
ptr[2] points to 50,000,000 new doubles
Memory allocation failed for ptr[3]
```

Fig. 16.5 | Demonstrating pre-standard new returning 0 when memory allocation fails.

new *Throwing* bad_alloc *on Failure*

Figure 16.6 demonstrates new throwing bad_alloc on failure to allocate the requested memory. The for statement (lines 20–24) inside the try block should loop 50 times and, on each pass, allocate an array of 50,000,000 double values. If new fails and throws a bad_alloc exception, the loop terminates, and the program continues in line 28, where the catch handler catches and processes the exception. Lines 30–31 print the message "Exception occurred:" followed by the message returned from the base-class-exception version of function what (i.e., an implementation-defined exception-specific message, such as "Allocation Failure" in Microsoft Visual C++ 2005). The output shows that the program performed only three iterations of the loop before new failed and threw the bad_alloc exception. Your output might differ based on the physical memory, disk space available for virtual memory on your system and the compiler you are using.

```cpp
1   // Fig. 16.6: Fig16_06.cpp
2   // Demonstrating standard new throwing bad_alloc when memory
3   // cannot be allocated.
4   #include <iostream>
5   using std::cerr;
6   using std::cout;
7   using std::endl;
8
9   #include <new> // standard operator new
10  using std::bad_alloc;
11
12  int main()
13  {
14     double *ptr[ 50 ];
15
16     // aim each ptr[i] at a big block of memory
17     try
18     {
19        // allocate memory for ptr[ i ]; new throws bad_alloc on failure
20        for ( int i = 0; i < 50; i++ )
21        {
22           ptr[ i ] = new double[ 50000000 ]; // may throw exception
23           cout << "ptr[" << i << "] points to 50,000,000 new doubles\n";
24        } // end for
25     } // end try
26
27     // handle bad_alloc exception
28     catch ( bad_alloc &memoryAllocationException )
29     {
30        cerr << "Exception occurred: "
31           << memoryAllocationException.what() << endl;
32     } // end catch
33
34     return 0;
35  } // end main
```

```
ptr[0] points to 50,000,000 new doubles
ptr[1] points to 50,000,000 new doubles
ptr[2] points to 50,000,000 new doubles
Exception occurred: bad allocation
```

Fig. 16.6 | new throwing bad_alloc on failure.

The C++ standard specifies that standard-compliant compilers can continue to use a version of new that returns 0 upon failure. For this purpose, header file <new> defines object nothrow (of type nothrow_t), which is used as follows:

```
double *ptr = new( nothrow ) double[ 50000000 ];
```

The preceding statement uses the version of new that does not throw bad_alloc exceptions (i.e., nothrow) to allocate an array of 50,000,000 doubles.

Software Engineering Observation 16.8

To make programs more robust, use the version of new that throws bad_alloc exceptions on failure.

Handling new Failures Using Function set_new_handler

An additional feature for handling new failures is function set_new_handler (prototyped in standard header file <new>). This function takes as its argument a pointer to a function that takes no arguments and returns void. This pointer points to the function that will be called if new fails. This provides you with a uniform approach to handling all new failures, regardless of where a failure occurs in the program. Once set_new_handler registers a new handler in the program, operator new does not throw bad_alloc on failure; rather, it defers the error handling to the new-handler function.

If new allocates memory successfully, it returns a pointer to that memory. If new fails to allocate memory and set_new_handler did not register a new-handler function, new throws a bad_alloc exception. If new fails to allocate memory and a new-handler function has been registered, the new-handler function is called. The C++ standard specifies that the new-handler function should perform one of the following tasks:

1. Make more memory available by deleting other dynamically allocated memory (or telling the user to close other applications) and return to operator new to attempt to allocate memory again.

2. Throw an exception of type bad_alloc.

3. Call function abort or exit (both found in header file <cstdlib>) to terminate the program.

Figure 16.7 demonstrates set_new_handler. Function customNewHandler (lines 14–18) prints an error message (line 16), then terminates the program via a call to abort (line 17). The output shows that the program performed only three iterations of the loop before new failed and invoked function customNewHandler. Your output might differ based on the physical memory, disk space available for virtual memory on your system and the compiler you use to compile the program.

```
1   // Fig. 16.7: Fig16_07.cpp
2   // Demonstrating set_new_handler.
3   #include <iostream>
4   using std::cerr;
5   using std::cout;
6
```

Fig. 16.7 | set_new_handler specifying the function to call when new fails. (Part 1 of 2.)

```
 7   #include <new> // standard operator new and set_new_handler
 8   using std::set_new_handler;
 9
10   #include <cstdlib> // abort function prototype
11   using std::abort;
12
13   // handle memory allocation failure
14   void customNewHandler()
15   {
16      cerr << "customNewHandler was called";
17      abort();
18   } // end function customNewHandler
19
20   // using set_new_handler to handle failed memory allocation
21   int main()
22   {
23      double *ptr[ 50 ];
24
25      // specify that customNewHandler should be called on
26      // memory allocation failure
27      set_new_handler( customNewHandler );
28
29      // aim each ptr[i] at a big block of memory; customNewHandler will be
30      // called on failed memory allocation
31      for ( int i = 0; i < 50; i++ )
32      {
33         ptr[ i ] = new double[ 50000000 ]; // may throw exception
34         cout << "ptr[" << i << "] points to 50,000,000 new doubles\n";
35      } // end for
36
37      return 0;
38   } // end main
```

```
ptr[0] points to 50,000,000 new doubles
ptr[1] points to 50,000,000 new doubles
ptr[2] points to 50,000,000 new doubles
customNewHandler was called
```

Fig. 16.7 | set_new_handler specifying the function to call when new fails. (Part 2 of 2.)

16.12 Class auto_ptr and Dynamic Memory Allocation

A common programming practice is to allocate dynamic memory, assign the address of that memory to a pointer, use the pointer to manipulate the memory and deallocate the memory with delete when the memory is no longer needed. If an exception occurs after successful memory allocation but before the delete statement executes, a memory leak could occur. The C++ standard provides class template auto_ptr in header file <memory> to deal with this situation.

An object of class auto_ptr maintains a pointer to dynamically allocated memory. When an auto_ptr object destructor is called (for example, when an auto_ptr object goes out of scope), it performs a delete operation on its pointer data member. Class template auto_ptr provides overloaded operators * and -> so that an auto_ptr object can be used just as a regular pointer variable is. Figure 16.10 demonstrates an auto_ptr object that points to a dynamically allocated object of class Integer (Figs. 16.8–16.9).

```
1   // Fig. 16.8: Integer.h
2   // Integer class definition.
3
4   class Integer
5   {
6   public:
7      Integer( int i = 0 ); // Integer default constructor
8      ~Integer(); // Integer destructor
9      void setInteger( int i ); // functions to set Integer
10     int getInteger() const; // function to return Integer
11  private:
12     int value;
13  }; // end class Integer
```

Fig. 16.8 | Integer class definition.

```
1   // Fig. 16.9: Integer.cpp
2   // Integer member function definitions.
3   #include <iostream>
4   using std::cout;
5   using std::endl;
6
7   #include "Integer.h"
8
9   // Integer default constructor
10  Integer::Integer( int i )
11     : value( i )
12  {
13     cout << "Constructor for Integer " << value << endl;
14  } // end Integer constructor
15
16  // Integer destructor
17  Integer::~Integer()
18  {
19     cout << "Destructor for Integer " << value << endl;
20  } // end Integer destructor
21
22  // set Integer value
23  void Integer::setInteger( int i )
24  {
25     value = i;
26  } // end function setInteger
27
28  // return Integer value
29  int Integer::getInteger() const
30  {
31     return value;
32  } // end function getInteger
```

Fig. 16.9 | Member function definitions of class Integer.

Line 18 of Fig. 16.10 creates auto_ptr object ptrToInteger and initializes it with a pointer to a dynamically allocated Integer object that contains the value 7. Line 21 uses the auto_ptr overloaded -> operator to invoke function setInteger on the Integer object that ptrToInteger manages. Line 24 uses the auto_ptr overloaded * operator to dereference ptrToInteger, then uses the dot (.) operator to invoke function getInteger on the Integer object. Like a regular pointer, an auto_ptr's -> and * overloaded operators can be used to access the object to which the auto_ptr points.

Because ptrToInteger is a local automatic variable in main, ptrToInteger is destroyed when main terminates. The auto_ptr destructor forces a delete of the Integer object pointed to by ptrToInteger, which in turn calls the Integer class destructor. The memory that Integer occupies is released, regardless of how control leaves the block (e.g., by a return statement or by an exception). Most importantly, using this technique can prevent memory leaks. For example, suppose a function returns a pointer aimed at some object. Unfortunately, the function caller that receives this pointer might not delete the object, thus resulting in a memory leak. However, if the function returns an auto_ptr to

```cpp
1   // Fig. 16.10: Fig16_10.cpp
2   // Demonstrating auto_ptr.
3   #include <iostream>
4   using std::cout;
5   using std::endl;
6
7   #include <memory>
8   using std::auto_ptr; // auto_ptr class definition
9
10  #include "Integer.h"
11
12  // use auto_ptr to manipulate Integer object
13  int main()
14  {
15     cout << "Creating an auto_ptr object that points to an Integer\n";
16
17     // "aim" auto_ptr at Integer object
18     auto_ptr< Integer > ptrToInteger( new Integer( 7 ) );
19
20     cout << "\nUsing the auto_ptr to manipulate the Integer\n";
21     ptrToInteger->setInteger( 99 ); // use auto_ptr to set Integer value
22
23     // use auto_ptr to get Integer value
24     cout << "Integer after setInteger: " << ( *ptrToInteger ).getInteger()
25     return 0;
26  } // end main
```

```
Creating an auto_ptr object that points to an Integer
Constructor for Integer 7

Using the auto_ptr to manipulate the Integer
Integer after setInteger: 99

Destructor for Integer 99
```

Fig. 16.10 | auto_ptr object manages dynamically allocated memory.

the object, the object will be deleted automatically when the `auto_ptr` object's destructor gets called.

Only one `auto_ptr` at a time can own a dynamically allocated object and the object cannot be an array. By using its overloaded assignment operator or copy constructor, an `auto_ptr` can transfer ownership of the dynamic memory it manages. The last `auto_ptr` object that maintains the pointer to the dynamic memory will delete the memory. This makes `auto_ptr` an ideal mechanism for returning dynamically allocated memory to client code. When the `auto_ptr` goes out of scope in the client code, the `auto_ptr`'s destructor deletes the dynamic memory.

16.13 Standard Library Exception Hierarchy

Experience has shown that exceptions fall nicely into a number of categories. The C++ Standard Library includes a hierarchy of exception classes (Fig. 16.11). As we first discussed in Section 16.3, this hierarchy is headed by base-class `exception` (defined in header file `<exception>`), which contains `virtual` function `what`, which derived classes can override to issue appropriate error messages.

Immediate derived classes of base-class `exception` include `runtime_error` and `logic_error` (both defined in header `<stdexcept>`), each of which has several derived classes. Also derived from `exception` are the exceptions thrown by C++ operators—for example, `bad_alloc` is thrown by `new` (Section 16.11), `bad_cast` is thrown by `dynamic_cast` (Chapter 13) and `bad_typeid` is thrown by `typeid` (Chapter 13). Including `bad_exception` in the `throw` list of a function means that, if an unexpected exception occurs, function `unexpected` can throw `bad_exception` rather than terminating the program's execution (by default) or calling another function specified by `set_unexpected`.

Common Programming Error 16.8

Placing a catch handler that catches a base-class object before a catch that catches an object of a class derived from that base class is a logic error. The base-class catch catches all objects of classes derived from that base class, so the derived-class catch will never execute.

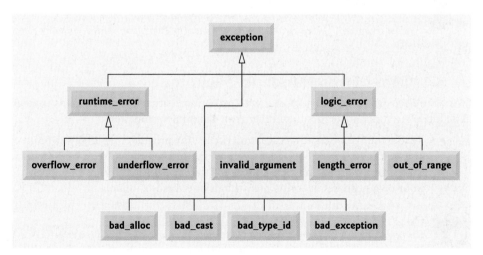

Fig. 16.11 | Standard Library exception classes.

Class `logic_error` is the base class of several standard exception classes that indicate errors in program logic. For example, class `invalid_argument` indicates that an invalid argument was passed to a function. (Proper coding can, of course, prevent invalid arguments from reaching a function.) Class `length_error` indicates that a length larger than the maximum size allowed for the object being manipulated was used for that object. Class `out_of_range` indicates that a value, such as a subscript into an array, exceeded its allowed range of values.

Class `runtime_error`, which we used briefly in Section 16.8, is the base class of several other standard exception classes that indicate execution-time errors. For example, class `overflow_error` describes an arithmetic overflow error (i.e., the result of an arithmetic operation is larger than the largest number that can be stored in the computer) and class `underflow_error` describes an arithmetic underflow error (i.e., the result of an arithmetic operation is smaller than the smallest number that can be stored in the computer).

Common Programming Error 16.9

Programmer-defined exception classes need not be derived from class `exception`*. Thus, writing* `catch( exception anyException )` *is not guaranteed to* `catch` *all exceptions a program could encounter.*

Error-Prevention Tip 16.6

To `catch` *all exceptions potentially thrown in a* `try` *block, use* `catch(...)`*. One weakness with catching exceptions in this way is that the type of the caught exception is unknown at compile time. Another weakness is that, without a named parameter, there is no way to refer to the exception object inside the exception handler.*

Software Engineering Observation 16.9

The standard `exception` *hierarchy is a good starting point for creating exceptions. Programmers can build programs that can* `throw` *standard exceptions,* `throw` *exceptions derived from the standard exceptions or* `throw` *their own exceptions not derived from the standard exceptions.*

Software Engineering Observation 16.10

Use `catch(...)` *to perform recovery that does not depend on the exception type (e.g., releasing common resources). The exception can be rethrown to alert more specific enclosing* `catch` *handlers.*

16.14 Other Error-Handling Techniques

We have discussed several ways to deal with exceptional situations prior to this chapter. The following summarizes these and other error-handling techniques:

- Ignore the exception. If an exception occurs, the program might fail as a result of the uncaught exception. This is devastating for commercial software products and special-purpose mission-critical software, but, for software developed for your own purposes, ignoring many kinds of errors is common.

Common Programming Error 16.10

Aborting a program component due to an uncaught exception could leave a resource—such as a file stream or an I/O device—in a state in which other programs are unable to acquire the resource. This is known as a resource leak.

- Abort the program. This, of course, prevents a program from running to completion and producing incorrect results. For many types of errors, this is appropriate, especially for nonfatal errors that enable a program to run to completion (potentially misleading you to think that the program functioned correctly). This strategy is inappropriate for mission-critical applications. Resource issues also are important here—if a program obtains a resource, the program should release that resource before program termination.

- Set error indicators. The problem with this approach is that programs might not check these error indicators at all points at which the errors could be troublesome. Another problem is that the program, after processing the problem, might not clear the error indicators.

- Test for the error condition, issue an error message and call exit (in <cstdlib>) to pass an appropriate error code to the program's environment.

- Use functions setjump and longjump. These <csetjmp> library functions enable you to specify an immediate jump from a deeply nested function call to an error handler. Without using setjump or longjump, a program must execute several returns to exit the deeply nested function calls. Functions setjump and longjump are dangerous, because they unwind the stack without calling destructors for automatic objects. This can lead to serious problems.

- Certain kinds of errors have dedicated capabilities for handling them. For example, when operator new fails to allocate memory, a new_handler function can be called to handle the error. This function can be customized by supplying a function name as the argument to set_new_handler, as we discuss in Section 16.11.

16.15 Wrap-Up

In this chapter, you learned how to use exception handling to deal with errors in a program. You learned that exception handling enables programmers to remove error-handling code from the "main line" of the program's execution. We demonstrated exception handling in the context of a divide-by-zero example. We also showed how to use try blocks to enclose code that may throw an exception, and how to use catch handlers to deal with exceptions that may arise. You learned how to throw and rethrow exceptions, and how to handle the exceptions that occur in constructors. The chapter continued with discussions of processing new failures, dynamic memory allocation with class auto_ptr and the standard library exception hierarchy. In the next chapter, you'll learn about file processing, including how persistent data is stored and how to manipulate it.

Summary

Section 16.1 Introduction
- An exception is an indication of a problem that occurs during a program's execution.
- Exception handling enables you to create programs that can resolve problems that occur at execution time—often allowing programs to continue executing as if no problems had been encountered. More severe problems may require a program to notify the user of the problem before terminating in a controlled manner.

Section 16.2 Exception-Handling Overview

- Exception handling enables you to remove error-handling code from the "main line" of the program's execution, which improves program clarity and enhances modifiability.

Section 16.3 Example: Handling an Attempt to Divide by Zero

- Class exception is the standard C++ base class for exceptions. Class exception provides virtual function what that returns an appropriate error message and can be overridden in derived classes.
- Class runtime_error (defined in header <stdexcept>) is the C++ standard base class for representing runtime errors.
- C++ uses the termination model of exception handling.
- A try block consists of keyword try followed by braces ({}) that define a block of code in which exceptions might occur. The try block encloses statements that might cause exceptions and statements that should not execute if exceptions occur.
- At least one catch handler must immediately follow a try block. Each catch handler specifies an exception parameter that represents the type of exception the catch handler can process.
- If an exception parameter includes an optional parameter name, the catch handler can use that parameter name to interact with a caught exception object.
- The point in the program at which an exception occurs is called the throw point.
- If an exception occurs in a try block, the try block expires and program control transfers to the first catch in which the exception parameter's type matches that of the thrown exception.
- When a try block terminates, local variables defined in the block go out of scope.
- When a try block terminates due to an exception, the program searches for the first catch handler that can process the type of exception that occurred. The program locates the matching catch by comparing the thrown exception's type to each catch's exception-parameter type until the program finds a match. A match occurs if the types are identical or if the thrown exception's type is a derived class of the exception-parameter type. When a match occurs, the code contained within the matching catch handler executes.
- When a catch handler finishes processing, the catch parameter and local variables defined within the catch handler go out of scope. Any remaining catch handlers that correspond to the try block are ignored, and execution resumes at the first line of code after the try...catch sequence.
- If no exceptions occur in a try block, the program ignores the catch handler(s) for that block. Program execution resumes with the next statement after the try...catch sequence.
- If an exception that occurs in a try block has no matching catch handler, or if an exception occurs in a statement that is not in a try block, the function that contains the statement terminates immediately, and the program attempts to locate an enclosing try block in the calling function. This process is called stack unwinding.
- To throw an exception, use keyword throw followed by an operand that represents the type of exception to throw. The operand of a throw can be of any type.

Section 16.4 When to Use Exception Handling

- Exception handling is for synchronous errors, which occur when a statement executes.
- Exception handling is not designed to process errors associated with asynchronous events, which occur in parallel with, and independent of, the program's flow of control.

Section 16.5 Rethrowing an Exception

- The exception handler can defer the exception handling (or perhaps a portion of it) to another exception handler. In either case, the handler achieves this by rethrowing the exception.

- Common examples of exceptions are out-of-range array subscripts, arithmetic overflow, division by zero, invalid function parameters and unsuccessful memory allocations.

Section 16.6 Exception Specifications
- An optional exception specification enumerates a list of exceptions that a function can throw. A function can throw only exceptions of the types indicated by the exception specification or exceptions of any type derived from these types. If the function throws an exception that does not belong to a specified type, function unexpected is called and the program terminates.
- A function with no exception specification can throw any exception. The empty exception specification throw() indicates that a function does not throw exceptions. If a function with an empty exception specification attempts to throw an exception, function unexpected is invoked.

Section 16.7 Processing Unexpected Exceptions
- Function unexpected calls the function registered with function set_unexpected. If no function has been registered in this manner, function terminate is called by default.
- Function set_terminate can specify the function to invoke when terminate is called. Otherwise, terminate calls abort, which terminates the program without calling the destructors of objects that are declared static and auto.
- Functions set_terminate and set_unexpected each return a pointer to the last function called by terminate and unexpected, respectively (0, the first time each is called). This enables you to save the function pointer so it can be restored later.
- Functions set_terminate and set_unexpected take as arguments pointers to functions with void return types and no arguments.
- If a programmer-defined termination function does not exit a program, function abort will be called after the programmer-defined termination function completes execution.

Section 16.8 Stack Unwinding
- Unwinding the function call stack means that the function in which the exception was not caught terminates, all local variables in that function are destroyed and control returns to the statement that originally invoked that function.

Section 16.9 Constructors, Destructors and Exception Handling
- Exceptions thrown by a constructor cause destructors to be called for any objects built as part of the object being constructed before the exception is thrown.
- Each automatic object constructed in a try block is destructed before an exception is thrown.
- Stack unwinding completes before an exception handler begins executing.
- If a destructor invoked as a result of stack unwinding throws an exception, terminate is called.
- If an object has member objects, and if an exception is thrown before the outer object is fully constructed, then destructors will be executed for the member objects that have been constructed before the exception occurs.
- If an array of objects has been partially constructed when an exception occurs, only the destructors for the constructed array element objects will be called.
- When an exception is thrown from the constructor for an object that is created in a new expression, the dynamically allocated memory for that object is released.

Section 16.10 Exceptions and Inheritance
- If a catch handler catches a pointer or reference to an exception object of a base-class type, it also can catch a pointer or reference to all objects of classes derived publicly from that base class— this allows for polymorphic processing of related errors.

Section 16.11 Processing **new** Failures

- The C++ standard document specifies that, when operator new fails, it throws a bad_alloc exception (defined in header file <new>).

- Function set_new_handler takes as its argument a pointer to a function that takes no arguments and returns void. This pointer points to the function that will be called if new fails.

- Once set_new_handler registers a new handler in the program, operator new does not throw bad_alloc on failure; rather, it defers the error handling to the new-handler function.

- If new allocates memory successfully, it returns a pointer to that memory.

- If an exception occurs after successful memory allocation but before the delete statement executes, a memory leak could occur.

Section 16.12 Class **auto_ptr** and Dynamic Memory Allocation

- The C++ Standard Library provides class template auto_ptr to deal with memory leaks.

- An object of class auto_ptr maintains a pointer to dynamically allocated memory. An auto_ptr object's destructor performs a delete operation on the auto_ptr's pointer data member.

- Class template auto_ptr provides overloaded operators * and -> so that an auto_ptr object can be used just as a regular pointer variable is. An auto_ptr also transfers ownership of the dynamic memory it manages via its copy constructor and overloaded assignment operator.

Section 16.13 Standard Library Exception Hierarchy

- The C++ Standard Library includes a hierarchy of exception classes. This hierarchy is headed by base-class exception.

- Immediate derived classes of base class exception include runtime_error and logic_error (both defined in header <stdexcept>), each of which has several derived classes.

- Several operators throw standard exceptions—operator new throws bad_alloc, operator dynamic_cast throws bad_cast and operator typeid throws bad_typeid.

- Including bad_exception in the throw list of a function means that, if an unexpected exception occurs, function unexpected can throw bad_exception rather than terminating the program's execution or calling another function specified by set_unexpected.

Terminology

abort function	exception handler
arithmetic overflow error	exception handling
arithmetic underflow error	<exception> header file
asynchronous event	exception object
auto_ptr class template	exception parameter
bad_alloc exception	exception specification
bad_cast exception	fault-tolerant programs
bad_exception exception	handle an exception
bad_typeid exception	invalid_argument exception
catch(...)	length_error exception
catch all exceptions	logic_error exception
catch an exception	<memory> header file
catch handler	new failure handler
catch keyword	nothrow object
empty exception specification	out_of_range exception
exception	overflow_error exception
exception class	resumption model of exception handling

rethrow an exception
robust application
`runtime_error` exception
`set_new_handler` function
`set_terminate` function
`set_unexpected` function
stack unwinding
`<stdexcept>` header file
synchronous errors
`terminate` function
termination model of exception handling

throw an exception
throw an unexpected exception
`throw` keyword
throw list
`throw` without arguments
throw point
`try` block
`try` keyword
`underflow_error` exception
`unexpected` function
`what` virtual function of class `exception`

Self-Review Exercises

16.1   List five common examples of exceptions.

16.2   Give several reasons why exception-handling techniques should not be used for conventional program control.

16.3   Why are exceptions appropriate for dealing with errors produced by library functions?

16.4   What is a "resource leak"?

16.5   If no exceptions are thrown in a `try` block, where does control proceed to after the `try` block completes execution?

16.6   What happens if an exception is thrown outside a `try` block?

16.7   Give a key advantage and a key disadvantage of using `catch(...)`.

16.8   What happens if no `catch` handler matches the type of a thrown object?

16.9   What happens if several handlers match the type of the thrown object?

16.10   Why would a programmer specify a base-class type as the type of a `catch` handler, then throw objects of derived-class types?

16.11   Suppose a `catch` handler with a precise match to an exception object type is available. Under what circumstances might a different handler be executed for exception objects of that type?

16.12   Must throwing an exception cause program termination?

16.13   What happens when a `catch` handler `throws` an exception?

16.14   What does the statement `throw;` do?

16.15   How do you restrict the exception types that a function can throw?

16.16   What happens if a function `throws` an exception of a type not allowed by the exception specification for the function?

16.17   What happens to the automatic objects that have been constructed in a `try` block when that block `throws` an exception?

Answers to Self-Review Exercises

16.1   Insufficient memory to satisfy a `new` request, array subscript out of bounds, arithmetic overflow, division by zero, invalid function parameters.

16.2   (a) Exception handling is designed to handle infrequently occurring situations that often result in program termination, so compiler writers are not required to implement exception handling to perform optimally. (b) Flow of control with conventional control structures generally is clearer and more efficient than with exceptions. (c) Problems can occur because the stack is unwound when an exception occurs and resources allocated prior to the exception might not be freed. (d) The "additional" exceptions make it more difficult for you to handle the larger number of exception cases.

16.3   It is unlikely that a library function will perform error processing that will meet the unique needs of all users.

16.4   A program that terminates abruptly could leave a resource in a state in which other programs would not be able to acquire the resource, or the program itself might not be able to reacquire a "leaked" resource.

16.5   The exception handlers (in the catch handlers) for that try block are skipped, and the program resumes execution after the last catch handler.

16.6   An exception thrown outside a try block causes a call to terminate.

16.7   The form catch(...) catches any type of exception thrown in a try block. An advantage is that all possible exceptions will be caught. A disadvantage is that the catch has no parameter, so it cannot reference information in the thrown object and cannot know the cause of the exception.

16.8   This causes the search for a match to continue in the next enclosing try block if there is one. As this process continues, it might eventually be determined that there is no handler in the program that matches the type of the thrown object; in this case, terminate is called, which by default calls abort. An alternative terminate function can be provided as an argument to set_terminate.

16.9   The first matching exception handler after the try block is executed.

16.10   This is a nice way to catch related types of exceptions.

16.11   A base-class handler would catch objects of all derived-class types.

16.12   No, but it does terminate the block in which the exception is thrown.

16.13   The exception will be processed by a catch handler (if one exists) associated with the try block (if one exists) enclosing the catch handler that caused the exception.

16.14   It rethrows the exception if it appears in a catch handler; otherwise, function unexpected is called.

16.15   Provide an exception specification listing the exception types that the function can throw.

16.16   Function unexpected is called.

16.17   The try block expires, causing destructors to be called for each of these objects.

Exercises

16.18   List various exceptional conditions that have occurred throughout this text. List as many additional exceptional conditions as you can. For each of these exceptions, describe briefly how a program typically would handle the exception, using the exception-handling techniques discussed in this chapter. Some typical exceptions are division by zero, arithmetic overflow, array subscript out of bounds, exhaustion of the free store, etc.

16.19   Under what circumstances would you not provide a parameter name when defining the type of the object that will be caught by a handler?

16.20   A program contains the statement

```
throw;
```

Where would you normally expect to find such a statement? What if that statement appeared in a different part of the program?

16.21 Compare and contrast exception handling with the various other error-processing schemes discussed in the text.

16.22 Why should exceptions not be used as an alternate form of program control?

16.23 Describe a technique for handling related exceptions.

16.24 Until this chapter, we have found that dealing with errors detected by constructors can be awkward. Exception handling gives us a better means of handling such errors. Consider a constructor for a String class. The constructor uses new to obtain space from the free store. Suppose new fails. Show how you would deal with this without exception handling. Discuss the key issues. Show how you would deal with such memory exhaustion with exception handling. Explain why the exception-handling approach is superior.

16.25 Suppose a program throws an exception and the appropriate exception handler begins executing. Now suppose that the exception handler itself throws the same exception. Does this create infinite recursion? Write a program to check your observation.

16.26 Use inheritance to create various derived classes of runtime_error. Then show that a catch handler specifying the base class can catch derived-class exceptions.

16.27 Write a conditional expression that returns either a double or an int. Provide an int catch handler and a double catch handler. Show that only the double catch handler executes, regardless of whether the int or the double is returned.

16.28 Write a program that generates and handles a memory-exhaustion exception. Your program should loop on a request to create dynamic memory through operator new.

16.29 Write a program illustrating that all destructors for objects constructed in a block are called before an exception is thrown from that block.

16.30 Write a program illustrating that member object destructors are called for only those member objects that were constructed before an exception occurred.

16.31 Write a program that demonstrates several exception types being caught with the catch(...) exception handler.

16.32 Write a program illustrating that the order of exception handlers is important. The first matching handler is the one that executes. Attempt to compile and run your program two different ways to show that two different handlers execute with two different effects.

16.33 Write a program that shows a constructor passing information about constructor failure to an exception handler after a try block.

16.34 Write a program that illustrates rethrowing an exception.

16.35 Write a program that illustrates that a function with its own try block does not have to catch every possible error generated within the try. Some exceptions can slip through to, and be handled in, outer scopes.

16.36 Write a program that throws an exception from a deeply nested function and still has the catch handler following the try block enclosing the call chain catch the exception.

17

File Processing

OBJECTIVES

In this chapter you'll learn:

- To create, read, write and update files.
- Sequential file processing.
- Random-access file processing.
- To use high-performance unformatted I/O operations.
- The differences between formatted-data and raw-data file processing.
- To build a transaction-processing program using random-access file processing.

17.1 Introduction

Storage of data in variables and arrays is temporary. Files are used for data persistence—permanent retention data. Computers store files on secondary storage devices, such as hard disks, CDs, DVDs, flash drives and tapes. In this chapter, we explain how to build C++ programs that create, update and process data files. We consider both sequential files and random-access files. We compare formatted-data file processing and raw-data file processing. We examine techniques for input of data from, and output of data to, string streams rather than files in Chapter 18, Class string and String Stream Processing.

17.2 Data Hierarchy

Ultimately, all data items that digital computers process are reduced to combinations of zeros and ones. This occurs because it is simple and economical to build electronic devices that can assume two stable states—one state represents 0 and the other represents 1. It is remarkable that the impressive functions performed by computers ultimately involve only the most fundamental manipulations of 0s and 1s.

The smallest data item that computers support is called a bit (short for "binary digit"—a digit that can assume one of two values). Each data item, or bit, can assume either the value 0 or the value 1. Computer circuitry performs various simple bit manipulations, such as examining the value of a bit, setting the value of a bit and reversing a bit (from 1 to 0 or from 0 to 1).

Programming with data in the low-level form of bits is cumbersome. It is preferable to program with data in forms such as decimal digits (0–9), letters (A–Z and a–z) and special symbols (e.g., $, @, %, &, * and many others). Digits, letters and special symbols are referred to as characters. The set of all characters used to write programs and represent data items on a particular computer is called that computer's character set. Because computers can process only 1s and 0s, every character in a computer's character set is represented as a pattern of 1s and 0s. Bytes are composed of eight bits. Programmers create programs and data items with characters; computers manipulate and process these characters as patterns of bits. For example, C++ provides data type char. Each char typically occupies one byt. C++ also provides data type wchar_t, which can occupy more than one byte (to support larger character sets, such as the Unicode® character set; for more information on Unicode®, visit www.unicode.org).

Just as characters are composed of bits, fields are composed of characters. A field is a group of characters that conveys some meaning. For example, a field consisting of upper-case and lowercase letters can represent a person's name.

Data items processed by computers form a data hierarchy (Fig. 17.1), in which data items become larger and more complex in structure as we progress from bits, to characters, to fields and to larger data aggregates.

Typically, a record (which can be represented as a class in C++) is composed of several fields (called data members in C++). In a payroll system, for example, a record for a particular employee might include the following fields:

1. Employee identification number

2. Name

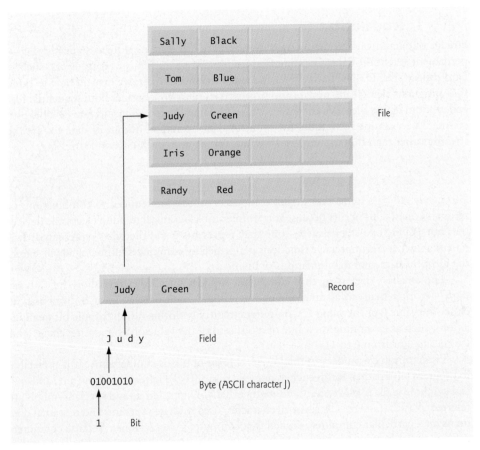

Fig. 17.1 | Data hierarchy.

3. Address

4. Hourly pay rate

5. Number of exemptions claimed

6. Year-to-date earnings

7. Amount of taxes withheld

Thus, a record is a group of related fields. In the preceding example, each field is associated with the same employee. A file is a group of related records.[1] A company's payroll file normally contains one record for each employee. Thus, a payroll file for a small company might contain only 22 records, whereas one for a large company might contain 100,000 records. It is not unusual for a company to have many files, some containing millions, billions, trillions or more characters of information.

To facilitate retrieving specific records from a file, at least one field in each record is chosen as a record key. A record key identifies a record as belonging to a particular person or entity and distinguishes that record from all others. In the payroll record described previously, the employee identification number normally would be chosen as the record key.

There are many ways of organizing records in a file. A common type of organization is called a sequential file, in which records typically are stored in order by a record-key field. In a payroll file, records usually are placed in order by employee identification number. The first employee record in the file contains the lowest employee identification number, and subsequent records contain increasingly higher ones.

Most businesses use many different files to store data. For example, a company might have payroll files, accounts-receivable files (listing money due from clients), accounts-payable files (listing money due to suppliers), inventory files (listing facts about all the items handled by the business) and many other types of files. A group of related files often are stored in a database. A collection of programs designed to create and manage databases is called a database management system (DBMS).

17.3 Files and Streams

C++ views each file as a sequence of bytes (Fig. 17.2). Each file ends either with an end-of-file marker or at a specific byte number recorded in a system-maintained, administrative data structure. When a file is *opened*, an object is created, and a stream is associated with the object. In Chapter 15, we saw that objects cin, cout, cerr and clog are created when

Fig. 17.2 | C++'s view of a file of *n* bytes.

---

1. Generally, a file can contain arbitrary data in arbitrary formats. In some operating systems, a file is viewed as nothing more than a collection of bytes. In such an operating system, any organization of the bytes in a file (such as organizing the data into records) is a view created by the application programmer.

<iostream> is included. The streams associated with these objects provide communication channels between a program and a particular file or device. For example, the cin object (standard input stream object) enables a program to input data from the keyboard or from other devices, the cout object (standard output stream object) enables a program to output data to the screen or other devices, and the cerr and clog objects (standard error stream objects) enable a program to output error messages to the screen or other devices.

To perform file processing in C++, header files <iostream> and <fstream> must be included. Header <fstream> includes the definitions for the stream class templates basic_ifstream (for file input), basic_ofstream (for file output) and basic_fstream (for file input and output). Each class template has a predefined template specialization that enables char I/O. In addition, the <fstream> library provides typedef aliases for these template specializations. For example, the typedef ifstream represents a specialization of basic_ifstream that enables char input from a file. Similarly, typedef ofstream represents a specialization of basic_ofstream that enables char output to files. Also, typedef fstream represents a specialization of basic_fstream that enables char input from, and output to, files.

Files are opened by creating objects of these stream template specializations. These templates "derive" from class templates basic_istream, basic_ostream and basic_iostream, respectively. Thus, all member functions, operators and manipulators that belong to these templates (which we described in Chapter 15) also can be applied to file streams. Figure 17.3 summarizes the inheritance relationships of the I/O classes that we have discussed to this point.

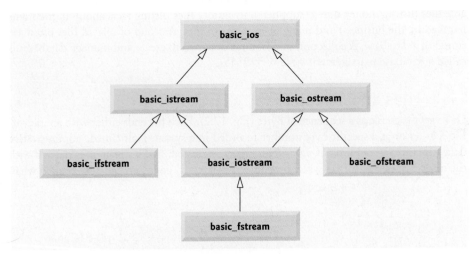

Fig. 17.3 | Portion of stream I/O template hierarchy.

17.4 Creating a Sequential File

C++ imposes no structure on a file. Thus, a concept like that of a "record" does not exist in a C++ file. Therefore, you must structure files to meet the application's requirements. In the following example, we see how you can impose a simple record structure on a file.

Figure 17.4 creates a sequential file that might be used in an accounts-receivable system to help manage the money owed by a company's credit clients. For each client, the program obtains the client's account number, name and balance (i.e., the amount the client owes the company for goods and services received in the past). The data obtained for each client constitutes a record for that client. The account number serves as the record key; that is, the program creates and maintains the file in account number order. This program assumes the user enters the records in account number order. In a comprehensive

```cpp
1   // Fig. 17.4: Fig17_04.cpp
2   // Create a sequential file.
3   #include <iostream>
4   using std::cerr;
5   using std::cin;
6   using std::cout;
7   using std::endl;
8   using std::ios;
9
10  #include <fstream> // file stream
11  using std::ofstream; // output file stream
12
13  #include <cstdlib>
14  using std::exit; // exit function prototype
15
16  int main()
17  {
18     // ofstream constructor opens file
19     ofstream outClientFile( "clients.dat", ios::out );
20
21     // exit program if unable to create file
22     if ( !outClientFile ) // overloaded ! operator
23     {
24        cerr << "File could not be opened" << endl;
25        exit( 1 );
26     } // end if
27
28     cout << "Enter the account, name, and balance." << endl
29        << "Enter end-of-file to end input.\n? ";
30
31     int account;
32     char name[ 30 ];
33     double balance;
34
35     // read account, name and balance from cin, then place in file
36     while ( cin >> account >> name >> balance )
37     {
38        outClientFile << account << ' ' << name << ' ' << balance << endl;
39        cout << "? ";
40     } // end while
41
42     return 0; // ofstream destructor closes file
43  } // end main
```

Fig. 17.4 | Creating a sequential file. (Part 1 of 2.)

```
Enter the account, name, and balance.
Enter end-of-file to end input.
? 100 Jones 24.98
? 200 Doe 345.67
? 300 White 0.00
? 400 Stone -42.16
? 500 Rich 224.62
? ^Z
```

Fig. 17.4 | Creating a sequential file. (Part 2 of 2.)

accounts receivable system, a sorting capability would be provided for the user to enter records in any order—the records then would be sorted and written to the file.

Let us examine this program. As stated previously, files are opened by creating ifstream, ofstream or fstream objects. In Fig. 17.4, the file is to be opened for output, so an ofstream object is created. Two arguments are passed to the object's constructor— the filename and the file-open mode (line 19). For an ofstream object, the file-open mode can be either ios::out to output data to a file or ios::app to append data to the end of a file (without modifying any data already in the file). Existing files opened with mode ios::out are truncated—all data in the file is discarded. If the specified file does not yet exist, then the ofstream object creates the file, using that filename.

Line 19 creates an ofstream object named outClientFile associated with the file clients.dat that is opened for output. The arguments "clients.dat" and ios::out are passed to the ofstream constructor, which opens the file—this establishes a "line of communication" with the file. By default, ofstream objects are opened for output, so line 19 could have used the alternate statement

```
ofstream outClientFile( "clients.dat" );
```

to open clients.dat for output. Figure 17.5 lists the file-open modes.

Common Programming Error 17.1

Use caution when opening an existing file for output (ios::out), especially when you want to preserve the file's contents, which will be discarded without warning.

Mode	Description
ios::app	Append all output to the end of the file.
ios::ate	Open a file for output and move to the end of the file (normally used to append data to a file). Data can be written anywhere in the file.
ios::in	Open a file for input.
ios::out	Open a file for output.
ios::trunc	Discard the file's contents if they exist (this also is the default action for ios::out).
ios::binary	Open a file for binary (i.e., nontext) input or output.

Fig. 17.5 | File open modes.

An ofstream object can be created without opening a specific file—a file can be attached to the object later. For example, the statement

```
ofstream outClientFile;
```

creates an ofstream object named outClientFile. The ofstream member function open opens a file and attaches it to an existing ofstream object as follows:

```
outClientFile.open( "clients.dat", ios::out );
```

Common Programming Error 17.2

Not opening a file before attempting to reference it in a program will result in an error.

After creating an ofstream object and attempting to open it, the program tests whether the open operation was successful. The if statement in lines 22–26 uses the overloaded ios operator member function operator! to determine whether the open operation succeeded. The condition returns a true value if either the failbit or the badbit is set for the stream on the open operation. Some possible errors are attempting to open a nonexistent file for reading, attempting to open a file for reading or writing without permission, and opening a file for writing when no disk space is available.

If the condition indicates an unsuccessful attempt to open the file, line 24 outputs the error message "File could not be opened", and line 25 invokes function exit to terminate the program. The argument to exit is returned to the environment from which the program was invoked. Argument 0 indicates that the program terminated normally; any other value indicates that the program terminated due to an error. The calling environment (most likely the operating system) uses the value returned by exit to respond appropriately to the error.

Another overloaded ios operator member function—operator void *—converts the stream to a pointer, so it can be tested as 0 (i.e., the null pointer) or nonzero (i.e., any other pointer value). When a pointer value is used as a condition, C++ converts a null pointer to the bool value false and converts a non-null pointer to the bool value true. If the failbit or badbit (see Chapter 15) has been set for the stream, 0 (false) is returned. The condition in the while statement of lines 36–40 invokes the operator void * member function on cin implicitly. The condition remains true as long as neither the failbit nor the badbit has been set for cin. Entering the end-of-file indicator sets the failbit for cin. The operator void * function can be used to test an input object for end-of-file instead of calling the eof member function explicitly on the input object.

If line 19 opened the file successfully, the program begins processing data. Lines 28–29 prompt the user to enter either the various fields for each record or the end-of-file indicator when data entry is complete. Figure 17.6 lists the keyboard combinations for entering end-of-file for various computer systems.

Line 36 extracts each set of data and determines whether end-of-file has been entered. When end-of-file is encountered or bad data is entered, operator void * returns the null pointer (which converts to the bool value false) and the while statement terminates. The user enters end-of-file to inform the program to process no additional data. The end-of-file indicator is set when the user enters the end-of-file key combination. The while statement loops until the end-of-file indicator is set.

Computer system	Keyboard combination
UNIX/Linux/Mac OS X	*<Ctrl-d>* (on a line by itself)
Microsoft Windows	*<Ctrl-z>* (sometimes followed by pressing *Enter*)
VAX (VMS)	*<Ctrl-z>*

Fig. 17.6 | End-of-file key combinations for various popular computer systems.

Line 38 writes a set of data to the file `clients.dat`, using the stream insertion operator `<<` and the `outClientFile` object associated with the file at the beginning of the program. The data may be retrieved by a program designed to read the file (see Section 17.5). Note that, because the file created in Fig. 17.4 is simply a text file, it can be viewed by any text editor.

Once the user enters the end-of-file indicator, `main` terminates. This implicitly invokes the `outClientFile` object's destructor function, which closes the `clients.dat` file. You also can close the `ofstream` object explicitly, using member function `close` in the statement

```
outClientFile.close();
```

Performance Tip 17.1

Closing files explicitly when the program no longer needs to reference them can reduce resource usage (especially if the program continues execution after closing the files).

In the sample execution for the program of Fig. 17.4, the user enters information for five accounts, then signals that data entry is complete by entering end-of-file (^Z is displayed for Microsoft Windows). This dialog window does not show how the data records appear in the file. To verify that the program created the file successfully, the next section shows how to create a program that reads this file and prints its contents.

17.5 Reading Data from a Sequential File

Files store data so it may be retrieved for processing when needed. The previous section demonstrated how to create a file for sequential access. In this section, we discuss how to read data sequentially from a file.

Figure 17.7 reads records from the `clients.dat` file that we created using the program of Fig. 17.4 and displays the contents of these records. Creating an `ifstream` object opens a file for input. The `ifstream` constructor can receive the filename and the file open mode as arguments. Line 31 creates an `ifstream` object called `inClientFile` and associates it with the `clients.dat` file. The arguments in parentheses are passed to the `ifstream` constructor function, which opens the file and establishes a "line of communication" with the file.

Good Programming Practice 17.1

Open a file for input only (using `ios::in`) if the file's contents should not be modified. This prevents unintentional modification of the file's contents and is an example of the principle of least privilege.

```cpp
 1   // Fig. 17.7: Fig17_07.cpp
 2   // Reading and printing a sequential file.
 3   #include <iostream>
 4   using std::cerr;
 5   using std::cout;
 6   using std::endl;
 7   using std::fixed;
 8   using std::ios;
 9   using std::left;
10   using std::right;
11   using std::showpoint;
12
13   #include <fstream> // file stream
14   using std::ifstream; // input file stream
15
16   #include <iomanip>
17   using std::setw;
18   using std::setprecision;
19
20   #include <string>
21   using std::string;
22
23   #include <cstdlib>
24   using std::exit; // exit function prototype
25
26   void outputLine( int, const string, double ); // prototype
27
28   int main()
29   {
30      // ifstream constructor opens the file
31      ifstream inClientFile( "clients.dat", ios::in );
32
33      // exit program if ifstream could not open file
34      if ( !inClientFile )
35      {
36         cerr << "File could not be opened" << endl;
37         exit( 1 );
38      } // end if
39
40      int account;
41      char name[ 30 ];
42      double balance;
43
44      cout << left << setw( 10 ) << "Account" << setw( 13 )
45         << "Name" << "Balance" << endl << fixed << showpoint;
46
47      // display each record in file
48      while ( inClientFile >> account >> name >> balance )
49         outputLine( account, name, balance );
50
51      return 0; // ifstream destructor closes the file
52   } // end main
53
```

Fig. 17.7 | Reading and printing a sequential file. (Part 1 of 2.)

```
54   // display single record from file
55   void outputLine( int account, const string name, double balance )
56   {
57      cout << left << setw( 10 ) << account << setw( 13 ) << name
58         << setw( 7 ) << setprecision( 2 ) << right << balance << endl;
59   } // end function outputLine
```

```
Account    Name          Balance
100        Jones           24.98
200        Doe            345.67
300        White            0.00
400        Stone          -42.16
500        Rich           224.62
```

Fig. 17.7 | Reading and printing a sequential file. (Part 2 of 2.)

Objects of class ifstream are opened for input by default. We could have used the statement

```
ifstream inClientFile( "clients.dat" );
```

to open clients.dat for input. Just as with an ofstream object, an ifstream object can be created without opening a specific file, because a file can be attached to it later.

The program uses the condition !inClientFile to determine whether the file was opened successfully before attempting to retrieve data from the file. Line 48 reads a set of data (i.e., a record) from the file. After the preceding line is executed the first time, account has the value 100, name has the value "Jones" and balance has the value 24.98. Each time line 48 executes, it reads another record from the file into the variables account, name and balance. Line 49 displays the records, using function outputLine (lines 55–59), which uses parameterized stream manipulators to format the data for display. When the end of file has been reached, the implicit call to operator void * in the while condition returns the null pointer (which converts to the bool value false), the ifstream destructor function closes the file and the program terminates.

To retrieve data sequentially from a file, programs normally start reading from the beginning of the file and read all the data consecutively until the desired data is found. It might be necessary to process the file sequentially several times (from the beginning of the file) during the execution of a program. Both istream and ostream provide member functions for repositioning the file-position pointer (the byte number of the next byte in the file to be read or written). These member functions are seekg ("seek get") for istream and seekp ("seek put") for ostream. Each istream object has a "get pointer," which indicates the byte number in the file from which the next input is to occur, and each ostream object has a "put pointer," which indicates the byte number in the file at which the next output should be placed. The statement

```
inClientFile.seekg( 0 );
```

repositions the file-position pointer to the beginning of the file (location 0) attached to inClientFile. The argument to seekg normally is a long integer. A second argument can be specified to indicate the seek direction, which can be ios::beg (the default) for positioning relative to the beginning of a stream, ios::cur for positioning relative to the current position in a stream or `ios::end` for positioning relative to the end of a stream. The file-position pointer is an integer value that specifies the location in the file as a number of bytes from the file's starting location (this is also referred to as the offset from the beginning of the file). Some examples of positioning the "get" file-position pointer are

```
// position to the nth byte of fileObject (assumes ios::beg)
fileObject.seekg( n );

// position n bytes forward in fileObject
fileObject.seekg( n, ios::cur );

// position n bytes back from end of fileObject
fileObject.seekg( n, ios::end );

// position at end of fileObject
fileObject.seekg( 0, ios::end );
```

The same operations can be performed using `ostream` member function `seekp`. Member functions `tellg` and `tellp` are provided to return the current locations of the "get" and "put" pointers, respectively. The following statement assigns the "get" file-position pointer value to variable `location` of type `long`:

```
location = fileObject.tellg();
```

Figure 17.8 enables a credit manager to display the account information for those customers with zero balances (i.e., customers who do not owe the company any money), credit (negative) balances (i.e., customers to whom the company owes money), and debit (positive) balances (i.e., customers who owe the company money for goods and services received in the past). The program displays a menu and allows the credit manager to enter one of three options to obtain credit information. Option 1 produces a list of accounts with zero balances. Option 2 produces a list of accounts with credit balances. Option 3 produces a list of accounts with debit balances. Option 4 terminates program execution. Entering an invalid option displays the prompt to enter another choice.

```
 1  // Fig. 17.8: Fig17_08.cpp
 2  // Credit inquiry program.
 3  #include <iostream>
 4  using std::cerr;
 5  using std::cin;
 6  using std::cout;
 7  using std::endl;
 8  using std::fixed;
 9  using std::ios;
10  using std::left;
11  using std::right;
12  using std::showpoint;
13
14  #include <fstream>
15  using std::ifstream;
16
```

Fig. 17.8 | Credit inquiry program. (Part 1 of 4.)

```
17   #include <iomanip>
18   using std::setw;
19   using std::setprecision;
20
21   #include <string>
22   using std::string;
23
24   #include <cstdlib>
25   using std::exit; // exit function prototype
26
27   enum RequestType { ZERO_BALANCE = 1, CREDIT_BALANCE, DEBIT_BALANCE, END };
28   int getRequest();
29   bool shouldDisplay( int, double );
30   void outputLine( int, const string, double );
31
32   int main()
33   {
34      // ifstream constructor opens the file
35      ifstream inClientFile( "clients.dat", ios::in );
36
37      // exit program if ifstream could not open file
38      if ( !inClientFile )
39      {
40         cerr << "File could not be opened" << endl;
41         exit( 1 );
42      } // end if
43
44      int request;
45      int account;
46      char name[ 30 ];
47      double balance;
48
49      // get user's request (e.g., zero, credit or debit balance)
50      request = getRequest();
51
52      // process user's request
53      while ( request != END )
54      {
55         switch ( request )
56         {
57            case ZERO_BALANCE:
58               cout << "\nAccounts with zero balances:\n";
59               break;
60            case CREDIT_BALANCE:
61               cout << "\nAccounts with credit balances:\n";
62               break;
63            case DEBIT_BALANCE:
64               cout << "\nAccounts with debit balances:\n";
65               break;
66         } // end switch
67
68         // read account, name and balance from file
69         inClientFile >> account >> name >> balance;
```

Fig. 17.8 | Credit inquiry program. (Part 2 of 4.)

```
70
71          // display file contents (until eof)
72          while ( !inClientFile.eof() )
73          {
74             // display record
75             if ( shouldDisplay( request, balance ) )
76                outputLine( account, name, balance );
77
78             // read account, name and balance from file
79             inClientFile >> account >> name >> balance;
80          } // end inner while
81
82          inClientFile.clear(); // reset eof for next input
83          inClientFile.seekg( 0 ); // reposition to beginning of file
84          request = getRequest(); // get additional request from user
85       } // end outer while
86
87       cout << "End of run." << endl;
88       return 0; // ifstream destructor closes the file
89    } // end main
90
91    // obtain request from user
92    int getRequest()
93    {
94       int request; // request from user
95
96       // display request options
97       cout << "\nEnter request" << endl
98          << " 1 - List accounts with zero balances" << endl
99          << " 2 - List accounts with credit balances" << endl
100         << " 3 - List accounts with debit balances" << endl
101         << " 4 - End of run" << fixed << showpoint;
102
103      do // input user request
104      {
105         cout << "\n? ";
106         cin >> request;
107      } while ( request < ZERO_BALANCE && request > END );
108
109      return request;
110   } // end function getRequest
111
112   // determine whether to display given record
113   bool shouldDisplay( int type, double balance )
114   {
115      // determine whether to display zero balances
116      if ( type == ZERO_BALANCE && balance == 0 )
117         return true;
118
119      // determine whether to display credit balances
120      if ( type == CREDIT_BALANCE && balance < 0 )
121         return true;
122
```

Fig. 17.8 | Credit inquiry program. (Part 3 of 4.)

```
123     // determine whether to display debit balances
124     if ( type == DEBIT_BALANCE && balance > 0 )
125        return true;
126
127     return false;
128  } // end function shouldDisplay
129
130  // display single record from file
131  void outputLine( int account, const string name, double balance )
132  {
133     cout << left << setw( 10 ) << account << setw( 13 ) << name
134        << setw( 7 ) << setprecision( 2 ) << right << balance << endl;
135  } // end function outputLine
```

```
Enter request
 1 - List accounts with zero balances
 2 - List accounts with credit balances
 3 - List accounts with debit balances
 4 - End of run
? 1

Accounts with zero balances:
300       White              0.00

Enter request
 1 - List accounts with zero balances
 2 - List accounts with credit balances
 3 - List accounts with debit balances
 4 - End of run
? 2

Accounts with credit balances:
400       Stone            -42.16

Enter request
 1 - List accounts with zero balances
 2 - List accounts with credit balances
 3 - List accounts with debit balances
 4 - End of run
? 3

Accounts with debit balances:
100       Jones             24.98
200       Doe              345.67
500       Rich             224.62

Enter request
 1 - List accounts with zero balances
 2 - List accounts with credit balances
 3 - List accounts with debit balances
 4 - End of run
? 4
End of run.
```

Fig. 17.8 | Credit inquiry program. (Part 4 of 4.)

17.6 **Updating Sequential Files**

Data that is formatted and written to a sequential file as shown in Section 17.4 cannot be modified without the risk of destroying other data in the file. For example, if the name "White" needs to be changed to "Worthington," the old name cannot be overwritten without corrupting the file. The record for White was written to the file as

```
300 White 0.00
```

If this record were rewritten beginning at the same location in the file using the longer name, the record would be

```
300 Worthington 0.00
```

The new record contains six more characters than the original record. Therefore, the characters beyond the second "o" in "Worthington" would overwrite the beginning of the next sequential record in the file. The problem is that, in the formatted input/output model using the stream insertion operator << and the stream extraction operator >>, fields—and hence records—can vary in size. For example, values 7, 14, –117, 2074, and 27383 are all ints, which store the same number of "raw data" bytes internally (typically four bytes on today's popular 32-bit machines). However, these integers become different-sized fields when output as formatted text (character sequences). Therefore, the formatted input/output model usually is not used to update records in place.

Such updating can be done awkwardly. For example, to make the preceding name change, the records before 300 White 0.00 in a sequential file could be copied to a new file, the updated record then written to the new file, and the records after 300 White 0.00 copied to the new file. This requires processing every record in the file to update one record. If many records are being updated in one pass of the file, though, this technique can be acceptable.

17.7 **Random-Access Files**

So far, we have seen how to create sequential files and search them to locate information. Sequential files are inappropriate for instant-access applications, in which a particular record must be located immediately. Common instant-access applications are airline reservation systems, banking systems, point-of-sale systems, automated teller machines and other kinds of transaction-processing systems that require rapid access to specific data. A bank might have hundreds of thousands (or even millions) of other customers, yet, when a customer uses an automated teller machine, the program checks that customer's account in a few seconds or less for sufficient funds. This kind of instant access is made possible with random-access files. Individual records of a random-access file can be accessed directly (and quickly) without having to search other records.

As we have said, C++ does not impose structure on a file. So the application that wants to use random-access files must create them. A variety of techniques can be used. Perhaps the easiest method is to require that all records in a file be of the same fixed length. Using same-size, fixed-length records makes it easy for a program to calculate (as a function of the record size and the record key) the exact location of any record relative to the beginning of the file. We soon will see how this facilitates immediate access to specific records, even in large files.

Figure 17.9 illustrates C++'s view of a random-access file composed of fixed-length records (each record, in this case, is 100 bytes long). A random-access file is like a railroad train with many same-size cars—some empty and some with contents.

Data can be inserted into a random-access file without destroying other data in the file. Data stored previously also can be updated or deleted without rewriting the entire file. In the following sections, we explain how to create a random-access file, enter data into the file, read the data both sequentially and randomly, update the data and delete data that is no longer needed.

17.8 Creating a Random-Access File

The `ostream` member function `write` outputs a fixed number of bytes, beginning at a specific location in memory, to the specified stream. When the stream is associated with a file, function `write` writes the data at the location in the file specified by the "put" file-position pointer. The `istream` member function `read` inputs a fixed number of bytes from the specified stream to an area in memory beginning at a specified address. If the stream is associated with a file, function `read` inputs bytes at the location in the file specified by the "get" file-position pointer.

Writing Bytes with `ostream` *Member Function* `write`
When writing the integer `number` to a file, instead of using the statement

```
outFile << number;
```

which for a four-byte integer could print as few digits as one or as many as 11 (10 digits plus a sign, each requiring a single byte of storage), we can use the statement

```
outFile.write( reinterpret_cast< const char * >( &number ),
   sizeof( number ) );
```

which always writes the binary version of the integer's four bytes (on a machine with four-byte integers). Function `write` treats its first argument as a group of bytes by viewing the object in memory as a `const char *`, which is a pointer to a byte. Starting from that location, function `write` outputs the number of bytes specified by its second argument—an integer of type `size_t`. As we'll see, `istream` function `read` can subsequently be used to read the four bytes back into integer variable `number`.

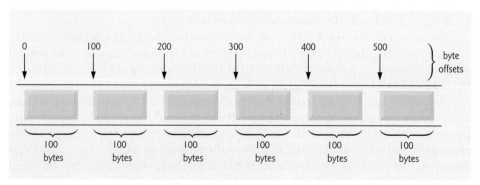

Fig. 17.9 | C++ view of a random-access file.

Converting Between Pointer Types with the `reinterpret_cast` *Operator*
Unfortunately, most pointers that we pass to function `write` as the first argument are not of type `const char *`. To output objects of other types, we must convert the pointers to those objects to type `const char *`; otherwise, the compiler will not compile calls to function `write`. C++ provides the `reinterpret_cast` operator for cases like this in which a pointer of one type must be cast to an unrelated pointer type. You can also use this cast operator to convert between pointer and integer types, and vice versa. Without a `reinterpret_cast`, the `write` statement that outputs the integer `number` will not compile because the compiler does not allow a pointer of type `int *` (the type returned by the expression `&number`) to be passed to a function that expects an argument of type `const char *`—as far as the compiler is concerned, these types are incompatible.

A `reinterpret_cast` is performed at compile time and does not change the value of the object to which its operand points. Instead, it requests that the compiler reinterpret the operand as the target type (specified in the angle brackets following the keyword `reinterpret_cast`). In Fig. 17.12, we use `reinterpret_cast` to convert a `ClientData` pointer to a `const char *`, which reinterprets a `ClientData` object as bytes to be output to a file. Random-access file-processing programs rarely write a single field to a file. Normally, they write one object of a class at a time, as we show in the following examples.

Error-Prevention Tip 17.1

It is easy to use `reinterpret_cast` *to perform dangerous manipulations that could lead to serious execution-time errors.*

Portability Tip 17.1

Using `reinterpret_cast` *is compiler dependent and can cause programs to behave differently on different platforms. The* `reinterpret_cast` *operator should not be used unless absolute necessary.*

Portability Tip 17.2

A program that reads unformatted data (written by `write`*) must be compiled and executed on a system compatible with the program that wrote the data, because different systems may represent internal data differently.*

Credit Processing Program
Consider the following problem statement:

> *Create a credit-processing program capable of storing at most 100 fixed-length records for a company that can have up to 100 customers. Each record should consist of an account number that acts as the record key, a last name, a first name and a balance. The program should be able to update an account, insert a new account, delete an account and insert all the account records into a formatted text file for printing.*

The next several sections introduce the techniques for creating this credit-processing program. Figure 17.12 illustrates opening a random-access file, defining the record format using an object of class `ClientData` (Figs. 17.10–17.11) and writing data to the disk in binary format. This program initializes all 100 records of the file `credit.dat` with empty objects, using function `write`. Each empty object contains 0 for the account number, the null string (represented by empty quotation marks) for the last and first name and 0.0 for the balance. Each record is initialized with the amount of empty space in which the account data will be stored.

```
1   // Fig. 17.10: ClientData.h
2   // Class ClientData definition used in Fig. 17.12-Fig. 17.15.
3   #ifndef CLIENTDATA_H
4   #define CLIENTDATA_H
5
6   #include <string>
7   using std::string;
8
9   class ClientData
10  {
11  public:
12     // default ClientData constructor
13     ClientData( int = 0, string = "", string = "", double = 0.0 );
14
15     // accessor functions for accountNumber
16     void setAccountNumber( int );
17     int getAccountNumber() const;
18
19     // accessor functions for lastName
20     void setLastName( string );
21     string getLastName() const;
22
23     // accessor functions for firstName
24     void setFirstName( string );
25     string getFirstName() const;
26
27     // accessor functions for balance
28     void setBalance( double );
29     double getBalance() const;
30  private:
31     int accountNumber;
32     char lastName[ 15 ];
33     char firstName[ 10 ];
34     double balance;
35  }; // end class ClientData
36
37  #endif
```

Fig. 17.10 | ClientData class header file.

Objects of class string do not have uniform size, rather they use dynamically allocated memory to accommodate strings of various lengths. This program must maintain fixed-length records, so class ClientData stores the client's first and last name in fixed-length char arrays. Member functions setLastName (Fig. 17.11, lines 37–45) and setFirstName (Fig. 17.11, lines 54–62) each copy the characters of a string object into the corresponding char array. Consider function setLastName. Line 40 initializes the const char * lastName-Value with the result of a call to string member function data, which returns an array containing the characters of the string. [*Note:* This array is not guaranteed to be null terminated.] Line 41 invokes string member function size to get the length of lastName-String. Line 42 ensures that length is fewer than 15 characters, then line 43 copies length characters from lastNameValue into the char array lastName. Member function setFirst-Name performs the same steps for the first name.

```cpp
1   // Fig. 17.11: ClientData.cpp
2   // Class ClientData stores customer's credit information.
3   #include <string>
4   using std::string;
5
6   #include "ClientData.h"
7
8   // default ClientData constructor
9   ClientData::ClientData( int accountNumberValue,
10     string lastNameValue, string firstNameValue, double balanceValue )
11  {
12     setAccountNumber( accountNumberValue );
13     setLastName( lastNameValue );
14     setFirstName( firstNameValue );
15     setBalance( balanceValue );
16  } // end ClientData constructor
17
18  // get account-number value
19  int ClientData::getAccountNumber() const
20  {
21     return accountNumber;
22  } // end function getAccountNumber
23
24  // set account-number value
25  void ClientData::setAccountNumber( int accountNumberValue )
26  {
27     accountNumber = accountNumberValue; // should validate
28  } // end function setAccountNumber
29
30  // get last-name value
31  string ClientData::getLastName() const
32  {
33     return lastName;
34  } // end function getLastName
35
36  // set last-name value
37  void ClientData::setLastName( string lastNameString )
38  {
39     // copy at most 15 characters from string to lastName
40     const char *lastNameValue = lastNameString.data();
41     int length = lastNameString.size();
42     length = ( length < 15 ? length : 14 );
43     strncpy( lastName, lastNameValue, length );
44     lastName[ length ] = '\0'; // append null character to lastName
45  } // end function setLastName
46
47  // get first-name value
48  string ClientData::getFirstName() const
49  {
50     return firstName;
51  } // end function getFirstName
52
```

Fig. 17.11 | ClientData class represents a customer's credit information. (Part 1 of 2.)

```
53   // set first-name value
54   void ClientData::setFirstName( string firstNameString )
55   {
56      // copy at most 10 characters from string to firstName
57      const char *firstNameValue = firstNameString.data();
58      int length = firstNameString.size();
59      length = ( length < 10 ? length : 9 );
60      strncpy( firstName, firstNameValue, length );
61      firstName[ length ] = '\0'; // append null character to firstName
62   } // end function setFirstName
63
64   // get balance value
65   double ClientData::getBalance() const
66   {
67      return balance;
68   } // end function getBalance
69
70   // set balance value
71   void ClientData::setBalance( double balanceValue )
72   {
73      balance = balanceValue;
74   } // end function setBalance
```

Fig. 17.11 | ClientData class represents a customer's credit information. (Part 2 of 2.)

In Fig. 17.12, line 18 creates an ofstream object for the file credit.dat. The second argument to the constructor—ios::out | ios::binary—indicates that we are opening the file for output in binary mode, which is required if we are to write fixed-length records. Lines 31–32 cause the blankClient to be written to the credit.dat file associated with ofstream object outCredit. Remember that operator sizeof returns the size in bytes of the object contained in parentheses (see Chapter 8). The first argument to function write at line 31 must be of type const char *. However, the data type of &blankClient is ClientData *. To convert &blankClient to const char *, line 31 uses the cast operator reinterpret_cast, so the call to write compiles without issuing a compilation error.

```
1    // Fig. 17.12: Fig17_12.cpp
2    // Creating a randomly accessed file.
3    #include <iostream>
4    using std::cerr;
5    using std::endl;
6    using std::ios;
7
8    #include <fstream>
9    using std::ofstream;
10
11   #include <cstdlib>
12   using std::exit; // exit function prototype
13
14   #include "ClientData.h" // ClientData class definition
15
```

Fig. 17.12 | Creating a random-access file with 100 blank records sequentially. (Part 1 of 2.)

```
16   int main()
17   {
18      ofstream outCredit( "credit.dat", ios::out | ios::binary );
19
20      // exit program if ofstream could not open file
21      if ( !outCredit )
22      {
23         cerr << "File could not be opened." << endl;
24         exit( 1 );
25      } // end if
26
27      ClientData blankClient; // constructor zeros out each data member
28
29      // output 100 blank records to file
30      for ( int i = 0; i < 100; i++ )
31         outCredit.write( reinterpret_cast< const char * >( &blankClient ),
32            sizeof( ClientData ) );
33
34      return 0;
35   } // end main
```

Fig. 17.12 | Creating a random-access file with 100 blank records sequentially. (Part 2 of 2.)

17.9 **Writing Data Randomly to a Random-Access File**

Figure 17.13 writes data to the file credit.dat and uses the combination of fstream functions seekp and write to store data at exact locations in the file. Function seekp sets the "put" file-position pointer to a specific position in the file, then write outputs the data. Note that line 19 includes the header file ClientData.h defined in Fig. 17.10, so the program can use ClientData objects.

```
1    // Fig. 17.13: Fig17_13.cpp
2    // Writing to a random-access file.
3    #include <iostream>
4    using std::cerr;
5    using std::cin;
6    using std::cout;
7    using std::endl;
8    using std::ios;
9
10   #include <iomanip>
11   using std::setw;
12
13   #include <fstream>
14   using std::fstream;
15
16   #include <cstdlib>
17   using std::exit; // exit function prototype
18
19   #include "ClientData.h" // ClientData class definition
20
```

Fig. 17.13 | Writing to a random-access file. (Part 1 of 3.)

```
21   int main()
22   {
23      int accountNumber;
24      char lastName[ 15 ];
25      char firstName[ 10 ];
26      double balance;
27
28      fstream outCredit( "credit.dat", ios::in | ios::out | ios::binary );
29
30      // exit program if fstream cannot open file
31      if ( !outCredit )
32      {
33         cerr << "File could not be opened." << endl;
34         exit( 1 );
35      } // end if
36
37      cout << "Enter account number (1 to 100, 0 to end input)\n? ";
38
39      // require user to specify account number
40      ClientData client;
41      cin >> accountNumber;
42
43      // user enters information, which is copied into file
44      while ( accountNumber > 0 && accountNumber <= 100 )
45      {
46         // user enters last name, first name and balance
47         cout << "Enter lastname, firstname, balance\n? ";
48         cin >> setw( 15 ) >> lastName;
49         cin >> setw( 10 ) >> firstName;
50         cin >> balance;
51
52         // set record accountNumber, lastName, firstName and balance values
53         client.setAccountNumber( accountNumber );
54         client.setLastName( lastName );
55         client.setFirstName( firstName );
56         client.setBalance( balance );
57
58         // seek position in file of user-specified record
59         outCredit.seekp( ( client.getAccountNumber() - 1 ) *
60            sizeof( ClientData ) );
61
62         // write user-specified information in file
63         outCredit.write( reinterpret_cast< const char * >( &client ),
64            sizeof( ClientData ) );
65
66         // enable user to enter another account
67         cout << "Enter account number\n? ";
68         cin >> accountNumber;
69      } // end while
70
71      return 0;
72   } // end main
```

Fig. 17.13 | Writing to a random-access file. (Part 2 of 3.)

```
Enter account number (1 to 100, 0 to end input)
? 37
Enter lastname, firstname, balance
? Barker Doug 0.00
Enter account number
? 29
Enter lastname, firstname, balance
? Brown Nancy -24.54
Enter account number
? 96
Enter lastname, firstname, balance
? Stone Sam 34.98
Enter account number
? 88
Enter lastname, firstname, balance
? Smith Dave 258.34
Enter account number
? 33
Enter lastname, firstname, balance
? Dunn Stacey 314.33
Enter account number
? 0
```

Fig. 17.13 | Writing to a random-access file. (Part 3 of 3.)

Lines 59–60 position the "put" file-position pointer for object outCredit to the byte location calculated by

```
( client.getAccountNumber() - 1 ) * sizeof( ClientData )
```

Because the account number is between 1 and 100, 1 is subtracted from the account number when calculating the byte location of the record. Thus, for record 1, the file-position pointer is set to byte 0 of the file. Note that line 28 uses the fstream object outCredit to open the existing credit.dat file. The file is opened for input and output in binary mode by combining the file-open modes ios::in, ios::out and ios::binary. Multiple file-open modes are combined by separating each open mode from the next with the bitwise inclusive OR operator (|). Opening the existing credit.dat file in this manner ensures that this program can manipulate the records written to the file by the program of Fig. 17.12, rather than creating the file from scratch. Chapter 21, Bits, Characters, C Strings and structs discusses the bitwise inclusive OR operator in detail.

17.10 Reading from a Random-Access File Sequentially

In the previous sections, we created a random-access file and wrote data to that file. In this section, we develop a program that reads the file sequentially and prints only those records that contain data. These programs produce an additional benefit. See if you can determine what it is; we'll reveal it at the end of this section.

The istream function read inputs a specified number of bytes from the current position in the specified stream into an object. For example, lines 57–58 from Fig. 17.14 read the number of bytes specified by sizeof(ClientData) from the file associated with ifstream object inCredit and store the data in the client record. Note that function read requires a first argument of type char *. Since &client is of type ClientData *,

&client must be cast to char * using the cast operator reinterpret_cast. Note that line 24 includes the header file clientData.h defined in Fig. 17.10, so the program can use ClientData objects.

Figure 17.14 reads every record in the credit.dat file sequentially, checks each record to determine whether it contains data, and displays formatted outputs for records containing data. The condition in line 50 uses the ios member function eof to determine when the end of file is reached and causes execution of the while statement to terminate. Also, if an error occurs when reading from the file, the loop terminates, because inCredit evaluates to false. The data input from the file is output by function outputLine (lines 65–72), which takes two arguments—an ostream object and a clientData structure to be output. The ostream parameter type is interesting, because any ostream object (such as cout) or any object of a derived class of ostream (such as an object of type ofstream) can

```
 1   // Fig. 17.14: Fig17_14.cpp
 2   // Reading a random-access file sequentially.
 3   #include <iostream>
 4   using std::cerr;
 5   using std::cout;
 6   using std::endl;
 7   using std::fixed;
 8   using std::ios;
 9   using std::left;
10   using std::right;
11   using std::showpoint;
12
13   #include <iomanip>
14   using std::setprecision;
15   using std::setw;
16
17   #include <fstream>
18   using std::ifstream;
19   using std::ostream;
20
21   #include <cstdlib>
22   using std::exit; // exit function prototype
23
24   #include "ClientData.h" // ClientData class definition
25
26   void outputLine( ostream&, const ClientData & ); // prototype
27
28   int main()
29   {
30      ifstream inCredit( "credit.dat", ios::in | ios::binary );
31
32      // exit program if ifstream cannot open file
33      if ( !inCredit )
34      {
35         cerr << "File could not be opened." << endl;
36         exit( 1 );
37      } // end if
```

Fig. 17.14 | Reading a random-access file sequentially. (Part 1 of 2.)

```
38
39      cout << left << setw( 10 ) << "Account" << setw( 16 )
40         << "Last Name" << setw( 11 ) << "First Name" << left
41         << setw( 10 ) << right << "Balance" << endl;
42
43      ClientData client; // create record
44
45      // read first record from file
46      inCredit.read( reinterpret_cast< char * >( &client ),
47         sizeof( ClientData ) );
48
49      // read all records from file
50      while ( inCredit && !inCredit.eof() )
51      {
52         // display record
53         if ( client.getAccountNumber() != 0 )
54            outputLine( cout, client );
55
56         // read next from file
57         inCredit.read( reinterpret_cast< char * >( &client ),
58            sizeof( ClientData ) );
59      } // end while
60
61      return 0;
62   } // end main
63
64   // display single record
65   void outputLine( ostream &output, const ClientData &record )
66   {
67      output << left << setw( 10 ) << record.getAccountNumber()
68         << setw( 16 ) << record.getLastName()
69         << setw( 11 ) << record.getFirstName()
70         << setw( 10 ) << setprecision( 2 ) << right << fixed
71         << showpoint << record.getBalance() << endl;
72   } // end function outputLine
```

Account	Last Name	First Name	Balance
29	Brown	Nancy	-24.54
33	Dunn	Stacey	314.33
37	Barker	Doug	0.00
88	Smith	Dave	258.34
96	Stone	Sam	34.98

Fig. 17.14 | Reading a random-access file sequentially. (Part 2 of 2.)

be supplied as the argument. This means that the same function can be used, for example, to perform output to the standard-output stream and to a file stream without writing separate functions.

What about that additional benefit we promised? If you examine the output window, you'll notice that the records are listed in sorted order (by account number). This is a consequence of how we stored these records in the file, using direct-access techniques. Compared to the insertion sort we used in Chapter 7, sorting using direct-access techniques is relatively fast. The speed is achieved by making the file large enough to hold every possible record that might be created. This, of course, means that the file could be occupied sparsely most of the time, resulting in a waste of storage. This is another example of the space-time trade-off: By using large amounts of space, we are able to develop a much faster sorting algorithm. Fortunately, the continuous reduction in price of storage units has made this less of an issue.

17.11 Case Study: A Transaction-Processing Program

We now present a substantial transaction-processing program (Fig. 17.15) using a random-access file to achieve "instant" -access processing. The program maintains a bank's account information. The program updates existing accounts, adds new accounts, deletes accounts and stores a formatted listing of all current accounts in a text file. We assume that the program of Fig. 17.12 has been executed to create the file credit.dat and that the program of Fig. 17.13 has been executed to insert the initial data.

```
 1   // Fig. 17.15: Fig17_15.cpp
 2   // This program reads a random-access file sequentially, updates
 3   // data previously written to the file, creates data to be placed
 4   // in the file, and deletes data previously stored in the file.
 5   #include <iostream>
 6   using std::cerr;
 7   using std::cin;
 8   using std::cout;
 9   using std::endl;
10   using std::fixed;
11   using std::ios;
12   using std::left;
13   using std::right;
14   using std::showpoint;
15
16   #include <fstream>
17   using std::ofstream;
18   using std::ostream;
19   using std::fstream;
20
21   #include <iomanip>
22   using std::setw;
23   using std::setprecision;
24
25   #include <cstdlib>
26   using std::exit; // exit function prototype
27
28   #include "ClientData.h" // ClientData class definition
29
30   int enterChoice();
31   void createTextFile( fstream& );
32   void updateRecord( fstream& );
33   void newRecord( fstream& );
34   void deleteRecord( fstream& );
```

Fig. 17.15 | Bank account program. (Part 1 of 6.)

```
35   void outputLine( ostream&, const ClientData & );
36   int getAccount( const char * const );
37
38   enum Choices { PRINT = 1, UPDATE, NEW, DELETE, END };
39
40   int main()
41   {
42      // open file for reading and writing
43      fstream inOutCredit( "credit.dat", ios::in | ios::out | ios::binary );
44
45      // exit program if fstream cannot open file
46      if ( !inOutCredit )
47      {
48         cerr << "File could not be opened." << endl;
49         exit ( 1 );
50      } // end if
51
52      int choice; // store user choice
53
54      // enable user to specify action
55      while ( ( choice = enterChoice() ) != END )
56      {
57         switch ( choice )
58         {
59            case PRINT: // create text file from record file
60               createTextFile( inOutCredit );
61               break;
62            case UPDATE: // update record
63               updateRecord( inOutCredit );
64               break;
65            case NEW: // create record
66               newRecord( inOutCredit );
67               break;
68            case DELETE: // delete existing record
69               deleteRecord( inOutCredit );
70               break;
71            default: // display error if user does not select valid choice
72               cerr << "Incorrect choice" << endl;
73               break;
74         } // end switch
75
76         inOutCredit.clear(); // reset end-of-file indicator
77      } // end while
78
79      return 0;
80   } // end main
81
82   // enable user to input menu choice
83   int enterChoice()
84   {
85      // display available options
86      cout << "\nEnter your choice" << endl
87           << "1 - store a formatted text file of accounts" << endl
```

Fig. 17.15 | Bank account program. (Part 2 of 6.)

```
88          << "    called \"print.txt\" for printing" << endl
89          << "2 - update an account" << endl
90          << "3 - add a new account" << endl
91          << "4 - delete an account" << endl
92          << "5 - end program\n? ";
93
94      int menuChoice;
95      cin >> menuChoice; // input menu selection from user
96      return menuChoice;
97   } // end function enterChoice
98
99   // create formatted text file for printing
100  void createTextFile( fstream &readFromFile )
101  {
102      // create text file
103      ofstream outPrintFile( "print.txt", ios::out );
104
105      // exit program if ofstream cannot create file
106      if ( !outPrintFile )
107      {
108         cerr << "File could not be created." << endl;
109         exit( 1 );
110      } // end if
111
112      outPrintFile << left << setw( 10 ) << "Account" << setw( 16 )
113         << "Last Name" << setw( 11 ) << "First Name" << right
114         << setw( 10 ) << "Balance" << endl;
115
116      // set file-position pointer to beginning of readFromFile
117      readFromFile.seekg( 0 );
118
119      // read first record from record file
120      ClientData client;
121      readFromFile.read( reinterpret_cast< char * >( &client ),
122         sizeof( ClientData ) );
123
124      // copy all records from record file into text file
125      while ( !readFromFile.eof() )
126      {
127         // write single record to text file
128         if ( client.getAccountNumber() != 0 ) // skip empty records
129            outputLine( outPrintFile, client );
130
131         // read next record from record file
132         readFromFile.read( reinterpret_cast< char * >( &client ),
133            sizeof( ClientData ) );
134      } // end while
135  } // end function createTextFile
136
137  // update balance in record
138  void updateRecord( fstream &updateFile )
139  {
```

Fig. 17.15 | Bank account program. (Part 3 of 6.)

```
140    // obtain number of account to update
141    int accountNumber = getAccount( "Enter account to update" );
142
143    // move file-position pointer to correct record in file
144    updateFile.seekg( ( accountNumber - 1 ) * sizeof( ClientData ) );
145
146    // read first record from file
147    ClientData client;
148    updateFile.read( reinterpret_cast< char * >( &client ),
149       sizeof( ClientData ) );
150
151    // update record
152    if ( client.getAccountNumber() != 0 )
153    {
154       outputLine( cout, client ); // display the record
155
156       // request user to specify transaction
157       cout << "\nEnter charge (+) or payment (-): ";
158       double transaction; // charge or payment
159       cin >> transaction;
160
161       // update record balance
162       double oldBalance = client.getBalance();
163       client.setBalance( oldBalance + transaction );
164       outputLine( cout, client ); // display the record
165
166       // move file-position pointer to correct record in file
167       updateFile.seekp( ( accountNumber - 1 ) * sizeof( ClientData ) );
168
169       // write updated record over old record in file
170       updateFile.write( reinterpret_cast< const char * >( &client ),
171          sizeof( ClientData ) );
172    } // end if
173    else // display error if account does not exist
174       cerr << "Account #" << accountNumber
175          << " has no information." << endl;
176 } // end function updateRecord
177
178 // create and insert record
179 void newRecord( fstream &insertInFile )
180 {
181    // obtain number of account to create
182    int accountNumber = getAccount( "Enter new account number" );
183
184    // move file-position pointer to correct record in file
185    insertInFile.seekg( ( accountNumber - 1 ) * sizeof( ClientData ) );
186
187    // read record from file
188    ClientData client;
189    insertInFile.read( reinterpret_cast< char * >( &client ),
190       sizeof( ClientData ) );
191
```

Fig. 17.15 | Bank account program. (Part 4 of 6.)

```
192    // create record, if record does not previously exist
193    if ( client.getAccountNumber() == 0 )
194    {
195       char lastName[ 15 ];
196       char firstName[ 10 ];
197       double balance;
198
199       // user enters last name, first name and balance
200       cout << "Enter lastname, firstname, balance\n? ";
201       cin >> setw( 15 ) >> lastName;
202       cin >> setw( 10 ) >> firstName;
203       cin >> balance;
204
205       // use values to populate account values
206       client.setLastName( lastName );
207       client.setFirstName( firstName );
208       client.setBalance( balance );
209       client.setAccountNumber( accountNumber );
210
211       // move file-position pointer to correct record in file
212       insertInFile.seekp( ( accountNumber - 1 ) * sizeof( ClientData ) );
213
214       // insert record in file
215       insertInFile.write( reinterpret_cast< const char * >( &client ),
216          sizeof( ClientData ) );
217    } // end if
218    else // display error if account already exists
219       cerr << "Account #" << accountNumber
220          << " already contains information." << endl;
221 } // end function newRecord
222
223 // delete an existing record
224 void deleteRecord( fstream &deleteFromFile )
225 {
226    // obtain number of account to delete
227    int accountNumber = getAccount( "Enter account to delete" );
228
229    // move file-position pointer to correct record in file
230    deleteFromFile.seekg( ( accountNumber - 1 ) * sizeof( ClientData ) );
231
232    // read record from file
233    ClientData client;
234    deleteFromFile.read( reinterpret_cast< char * >( &client ),
235       sizeof( ClientData ) );
236
237    // delete record, if record exists in file
238    if ( client.getAccountNumber() != 0 )
239    {
240       ClientData blankClient; // create blank record
241
242       // move file-position pointer to correct record in file
243       deleteFromFile.seekp( ( accountNumber - 1 ) *
244          sizeof( ClientData ) );
```

Fig. 17.15 | Bank account program. (Part 5 of 6.)

```
245
246          // replace existing record with blank record
247          deleteFromFile.write(
248             reinterpret_cast< const char * >( &blankClient ),
249             sizeof( ClientData ) );
250
251          cout << "Account #" << accountNumber << " deleted.\n";
252       } // end if
253       else // display error if record does not exist
254          cerr << "Account #" << accountNumber << " is empty.\n";
255    } // end deleteRecord
256
257    // display single record
258    void outputLine( ostream &output, const ClientData &record )
259    {
260       output << left << setw( 10 ) << record.getAccountNumber()
261          << setw( 16 ) << record.getLastName()
262          << setw( 11 ) << record.getFirstName()
263          << setw( 10 ) << setprecision( 2 ) << right << fixed
264          << showpoint << record.getBalance() << endl;
265    } // end function outputLine
266
267    // obtain account-number value from user
268    int getAccount( const char * const prompt )
269    {
270       int accountNumber;
271
272       // obtain account-number value
273       do
274       {
275          cout << prompt << " (1 - 100): ";
276          cin >> accountNumber;
277       } while ( accountNumber < 1 || accountNumber > 100 );
278
279       return accountNumber;
280    } // end function getAccount
```

Fig. 17.15 | Bank account program. (Part 6 of 6.)

The program has five options (Option 5 is for terminating the program). Option 1 calls function createTextFile to store a formatted list of all the account information in a text file called print.txt that may be printed. Function createTextFile (lines 100–135) takes an fstream object as an argument to be used to input data from the credit.dat file. Function createTextFile invokes istream member function read (lines 132–133) and uses the sequential-file-access techniques of Fig. 17.14 to input data from credit.dat. Function outputLine, discussed in Section 17.10, is used to output the data to file print.txt. Note that createTextFile uses istream member function seekg (line 117) to ensure that the file-position pointer is at the beginning of the file. After choosing Option 1, the print.txt file contains

```
Account   Last Name   First Name   Balance
29        Brown       Nancy         -24.54
33        Dunn        Stacey        314.33
37        Barker      Doug            0.00
88        Smith       Dave          258.34
96        Stone       Sam            34.98
```

Option 2 calls updateRecord (lines 138–176) to update an account. This function updates only an existing record, so the function first determines whether the specified record is empty. Lines 148–149 read data into object client, using istream member function read. Then line 152 compares the value returned by getAccountNumber of the client structure to zero to determine whether the record contains information. If this value is zero, lines 174–175 print an error message indicating that the record is empty. If the record contains information, line 154 displays the record, using function outputLine, line 159 inputs the transaction amount and lines 162–171 calculate the new balance and rewrite the record to the file. A typical output for Option 2 is

```
Enter account to update (1 - 100): 37
37          Barker         Doug            0.00

Enter charge (+) or payment (-): +87.99
37          Barker         Doug            87.99
```

Option 3 calls function newRecord (lines 179–221) to add a new account to the file. If the user enters an account number for an existing account, newRecord displays an error message indicating that the account exists (lines 219–220). This function adds a new account in the same manner as the program of Fig. 17.12. A typical output for Option 3 is

```
Enter new account number (1 - 100): 22
Enter lastname, firstname, balance
? Johnston Sarah 247.45
```

Option 4 calls function deleteRecord (lines 224–255) to delete a record from the file. Line 227 prompts the user to enter the account number. Only an existing record may be deleted, so, if the specified account is empty, line 254 displays an error message. If the account exists, lines 247–249 reinitialize that account by copying an empty record (blankClient) to the file. Line 251 displays a message to inform the user that the record has been deleted. A typical output for Option 4 is

```
Enter account to delete (1 - 100): 29
Account #29 deleted.
```

Note that line 43 opens the credit.dat file by creating an fstream object for both reading and writing, using modes ios::in and ios::out "or-ed" together.

17.12 Overview of Object Serialization

This chapter and Chapter 15 introduced the object-oriented style of input/output. However, our examples concentrated on I/O of fundamental types rather than objects of user-defined types. In Chapter 11, we showed how to input and output objects using operator overloading. We accomplished object input by overloading the stream extraction operator, >>, for the appropriate istream. We accomplished object output by overloading the stream insertion operator, <<, for the appropriate ostream. In both cases, only an object's data members were input or output, and, in each case, they were in a format meaningful only for objects of that particular type. An object's member functions are not input or output with the object's data; rather, one copy of the class's member functions remains available internally and is shared by all objects of the class.

When object data members are output to a disk file, we lose the object's type information. We store only the values of the object's attributes, not type information, on the disk. If the program that reads this data knows the object type to which the data corresponds, the program can read the data into an object of that type as we did in our random-access file examples.

An interesting problem occurs when we store objects of different types in the same file. How can we distinguish them (or their collections of data members) as we read them into a program? The problem is that objects typically do not have type fields (we discussed this issue in Chapter 13).

One approach used by several programming languages is called object serialization. A so-called serialized object is an object represented as a sequence of bytes that includes the object's data as well as information about the object's type and the types of data stored in the object. After a serialized object has been written to a file, it can be read from the file and deserialized—that is, the type information and bytes that represent the object and its data can be used to recreate the object in memory. C++ does not provide a built-in serialization mechanism; however, there are third party and open source C++ libraries that support object serialization. The open source Boost C++ Libraries (www.boost.org) provide support for serializing objects in text, binary and extensible markup language (XML) formats (www.boost.org/libs/serialization/doc/index.html). We overview the Boost C++ Libraries in Chapter 24.

17.13 Wrap-Up

In this chapter, we presented various file-processing techniques to manipulate persistent data. You learned that data is stored in computers in the form of 0s and 1s, and that combinations of these values form bytes, fields, records and eventually files. You were introduced to the differences between character-based and byte-based streams, and to several file-processing class templates in header file <fstream>. Then, you learned how to use sequential file processing to manipulate records stored in order, by the record-key field. You also learned how to use random-access files to instantly retrieve and manipulate fixed-length records. We presented a substantial transaction-processing case study using a random-access file to achieve "instant" -access processing. Finally, we discussed the basic concepts of object serialization. In the next chapter, we discuss typical string-manipulation operations provided by class template basic_string. We also introduce string stream-processing capabilities that allow strings to be input from and output to memory.

Summary

Section 17.1 Introduction
- Files are used for data persistence—permanent retention of data.
- Computers store files on secondary storage devices, such as hard disks, CDs, DVDs, flash memory and tapes.

Section 17.2 Data Hierarchy
- The smallest data item that computers support is called a bit (short for "binary digit"—a digit that can assume one of two values, 0 or 1).
- Digits, letters and special symbols are referred to as characters.
- The set of all characters used to write programs and represent data items on a particular computer is called that computer's character set.
- Bytes are composed of eight bits.
- Just as characters are composed of bits, fields are composed of characters. A field is a group of characters that conveys some meaning.
- Typically, a record (i.e., a class in C++) is composed of several fields (i.e., data members in C++).
- At least one field in a record is chosen as a record key to identify a record as belonging to a particular person or entity that is distinct from all other records in the file.
- In a sequential file, records typically are stored in order by a record-key field.
- A group of related files often is stored in a database.
- A collection of programs designed to create and manage databases is called a database management system (DBMS).

Section 17.3 Files and Streams
- C++ views each file as a sequence of bytes.
- Each file ends either with an end-of-file marker or at a specific byte number recorded in a system-maintained, administrative data structure.
- When a file is opened, an object is created, and a stream is associated with the object.
- To perform file processing in C++, header files <iostream> and <fstream> must be included.
- Header <fstream> includes the definitions for the stream class templates basic_ifstream (for file input), basic_ofstream (for file output) and basic_fstream (for file input and output).
- Each class template has a predefined template specialization that enables char I/O. The <fstream> library provides typedef aliases for these template specializations. The typedef ifstream represents a specialization of basic_ifstream that enables char input from a file. The typedef ofstream represents a specialization of basic_ofstream that enables char output to files. The typedef fstream represents a specialization of basic_fstream that enables char input from, and output to, files.
- The file-processing templates derive from class templates basic_istream, basic_ostream and basic_iostream, respectively. Thus, all member functions, operators and manipulators that belong to these templates also can be applied to file streams.

Section 17.4 Creating a Sequential File
- C++ imposes no structure on a file, so you must structure files to meet the application's requirements.
- A file can be opened for output when an ofstream object is created. Two arguments are passed to the object's constructor—the filename and the file-open mode.

- For an `ofstream` object, the file-open mode can be either `ios::out` to output data to a file or `ios::app` to append data to the end of a file. Existing files opened with mode `ios::out` are truncated—all data in the file is discarded. If the specified file does not yet exist, then the `ofstream` object creates the file, using that filename.

- By default, `ofstream` objects are opened for output, so the second constructor argument is not required.

- An `ofstream` object can be created without opening a specific file—a file can be attached to the object later with member function `open`.

- The `ios` operator member function `operator!` determines whether a stream was opened correctly. This operator can be used in a condition that returns a true value if either the `failbit` or the `badbit` is set for the stream on the open operation. Some possible errors that yield a true result are attempting to open a nonexistent file for reading, attempting to open a file for reading or writing without permission, and opening a file for writing when no disk space is available.

- Another overloaded `ios` operator member function—`operator void *`—converts the stream to a pointer, so it can be tested as 0 or nonzero. When a pointer value is used as a condition, a null pointer represents the `bool` value `false` and a non-null pointer represents the `bool` value `true`. If the `failbit` or `badbit` has been set for the stream, 0 (`false`) is returned.

- Entering the end-of-file indicator sets the `failbit` for `cin`.

- The `operator void *` function can be used to test an input object for end-of-file instead of calling the `eof` member function explicitly on the input object.

- When a stream object's destructor is called, the corresponding stream is closed. You also can close the stream object explicitly, using the stream's `close` member function.

- Closing files explicitly when they are no longer needed can reduce a program's resource usage.

Section 17.5 Reading Data from a Sequential File
- Files store data so it may be retrieved for processing when needed.

- Creating an `ifstream` object opens a file for input. The `ifstream` constructor can receive the filename and the file open mode as arguments.

- Open a file for input only (using `ios::in`) if the file's contents should not be modified. This prevents unintentional modification of the file's contents and is an example of the principle of least privilege.

- Objects of class `ifstream` are opened for input by default, so the second constructor argument is not required.

- Just as with an ofstream object, an ifstream object can be created without opening a specific file, because a file can be attached to it later.

- To retrieve data sequentially from a file, programs normally start reading from the beginning of the file and read all the data consecutively until the desired data is found.

- Both `istream` and `ostream` provide member functions for repositioning the file-position pointer (the byte number of the next byte in the file to be read or written). These member functions are `seekg` ("seek get") for `istream` and `seekp` ("seek put") for `ostream`. Each `istream` object has a "get pointer," which indicates the byte number in the file from which the next input is to occur, and each `ostream` object has a "put pointer," which indicates the byte number in the file at which the next output should be placed.

- The argument to `seekg` normally is a long integer. A second argument can be specified to indicate the seek direction, which can be `ios::beg` (the default) for positioning relative to the beginning of a stream, `ios::cur` for positioning relative to the current position in a stream or `ios::end` for positioning relative to the end of a stream.

- The file-position pointer is an integer value that specifies the location in the file as a number of bytes from the file's starting location (i.e., the offset from the beginning of the file).

- Member functions `tellg` and `tellp` are provided to return the current locations of the "get" and "put" pointers, respectively.

Section 17.6 Updating Sequential Files

- Data that is formatted and written to a sequential file cannot be modified without the risk of destroying other data in the file. The problem is that records can vary in size.

- Updating can be done awkwardly. Records before the one to update could be copied to a new file, the updated record then would be written to the new file, then subsequent records after the modified one would be copied to the new file. This requires processing every record in the file to update one record. If many records are being updated in one pass of the file, though, this technique can be acceptable.

Section 17.7 Random-Access Files

- Sequential files are inappropriate for instant-access applications, in which a particular record must be located immediately.

- Common instant-access applications are airline reservation systems, banking systems, point-of-sale systems, automated teller machines and other kinds of transaction-processing systems that require rapid access to specific data.

- Instant access is made possible with random-access files. Individual records of a random-access file can be accessed directly (and quickly) without having to search other records.

- The easiest method to format files for random access is to require that all records in a file be of the same fixed length. Using same-size, fixed-length records makes it easy for a program to calculate (as a function of the record size and the record key) the exact location of any record relative to the beginning of the file.

- Data can be inserted into a random-access file without destroying other data in the file.

- Data stored previously can be updated or deleted without rewriting the entire file.

Section 17.8 Creating a Random-Access File

- The `ostream` member function `write` outputs a fixed number of bytes, beginning at a specific location in memory, to the specified stream. Function `write` writes the data at the location in the file specified by the "put" file-position pointer.

- The `istream` member function read inputs a fixed number of bytes from the specified stream to an area in memory beginning at a specified address. If the stream is associated with a file, function read inputs bytes at the location in the file specified by the "get" file-position pointer.

- Function `write` treats its first argument as a group of bytes by viewing the object in memory as a `const char *`, which is a pointer to a byte (remember that a char is one byte). Starting from that location, function `write` outputs the number of bytes specified by its second argument. The `istream` function read can subsequently be used to read the bytes back into memory.

- C++ provides the `reinterpret_cast` operator to convert a pointer of one type to an unrelated pointer type. You can also use this cast operator to convert between pointer and integer types, and vice versa.

- A `reinterpret_cast` is performed at compile time and does not change the value of the object to which its operand points.

- A program that reads unformatted data (written by `write`) must be compiled and executed on a system compatible with the program that wrote the data, because different systems may represent internal data differently.

- Objects of class `string` do not have uniform size, rather they use dynamically allocated memory to accommodate strings of various lengths.
- The `string` member function `data` returns an array containing the characters of the `string`. This array is not guaranteed to be null terminated.
- The string member function `size` gets the length of a `string`.
- The file open mode `ios::binary` indicates that a file should be opened in binary mode.

Section 17.9 Writing Data Randomly to a Random-Access File
- Multiple file-open modes are combined by separating each open mode from the next with the bitwise inclusive OR operator (|).

Section 17.10 Reading from a Random-Access File Sequentially
- The `istream` function `read` inputs a specified number of bytes from the current position in the specified stream into an object.
- A function that receives an `ostream` parameter can receive any `ostream` object (such as `cout`) or any object of a derived class of `ostream` (such as an object of type `ofstream`) as an argument. This means that the same function can be used, for example, to perform output to the standard-output stream and to a file stream without writing separate functions.

Section 17.12 Overview of Object Serialization
- When object data members are output to a disk file, we lose the object's type information. We store only the values of the object's attributes, not type information, on the disk. If the program that reads this data knows the object type to which the data corresponds, the program can read the data into an object of that type.
- Several programming languages support object serialization. A so-called serialized object is an object represented as a sequence of bytes that includes the object's data as well as information about the object's type and the types of data stored in the object. After a serialized object has been written to a file, it can be read from the file and deserialized—that is, the type information and bytes that represent the object and its data can be used to recreate the object in memory.
- C++ does not provide a built-in serialization mechanism, however; there are third party and open source C++ libraries that support object serialization.
- The open source Boost C++ Libraries provide support for serializing objects in text, binary and extensible markup language (XML) formats (`www.boost.org/libs/serialization/doc/index.html`).

Terminology

append data to a file binary digit
bit
byte
character field
character set
`clog` (standard error buffered)
`close` member function of `ofstream`
database
database management system (DBMS)
data member function of `string`
data hierarchy
data persistence
decimal digit

end-of-file
field
file
file name
file open modes
file-position pointer
`fstream`
`<fstream>` header file
`ifstream`
instant-access application
`ios::app` file open mode
`ios::ate` file open mode
`ios::beg` seek starting point

ios::binary file open mode
ios::cur seek starting point
ios::end seek starting point
ios::in file open mode
ios::out file open mode
ios::trunc file open mode
object input/output
offset from the beginning of a file
ofstream
open a file
open member function of ofstream
operator void *
random-access file
read member function of istream

record
record key
secondary storage device
seek direction
seekg istream member function
seekp ostream member function
sequential file
size function of string
special symbol
tellg istream member function
tellp ostream member function
transaction-processing system
truncate an existing file

Self-Review Exercises

17.1   Fill in the blanks in each of the following:
  a) Ultimately, all data items processed by a computer are reduced to combinations of _____ and _____.
  b) The smallest data item a computer can process is called a(n) _____.
  c) A(n) _____ is a group of related records.
  d) Digits, letters and special symbols are referred to as _____.
  e) A group of related files is called a(n) _____.
  f) Member function _____ of the file streams fstream, ifstream and ofstream closes a file.
  g) The istream member function _____ reads a character from the specified stream.
  h) Member function _____ of the file streams fstream, ifstream and ofstream opens a file.
  i) The istream member function _____ is normally used when reading data from a file in random-access applications.
  j) Member functions _____ and _____ of istream and ostream set the file-position pointer to a specific location in an input or output stream, respectively.

17.2   State which of the following are *true* and which are *false*. If *false*, explain why.
  a) Member function read cannot be used to read data from the input object cin.
  b) You must create the cin, cout, cerr and clog objects explicitly.
  c) A program must call function close explicitly to close a file associated with an ifstream, ofstream or fstream object.
  d) If the file-position pointer points to a location in a sequential file other than the beginning of the file, the file must be closed and reopened to read from the beginning of the file.
  e) The ostream member function write can write to standard-output stream cout.
  f) Data in sequential files always is updated without overwriting nearby data.
  g) Searching all records in a random-access file to find a specific record is unnecessary.
  h) Records in random-access files must be of uniform length.
  i) Member functions seekp and seekg must seek relative to the beginning of a file.

17.3   Assume that each of the following statements applies to the same program.
  a) Write a statement that opens file oldmast.dat for input; use an ifstream object called inOldMaster.

b) Write a statement that opens file `trans.dat` for input; use an `ifstream` object called `inTransaction`.

c) Write a statement that opens file `newmast.dat` for output (and creation); use `ofstream` object `outNewMaster`.

d) Write a statement that reads a record from the file `oldmast.dat`. The record consists of integer `accountNumber`, string `name` and floating-point `currentBalance`; use `ifstream` object `inOldMaster`.

e) Write a statement that reads a record from the file `trans.dat`. The record consists of integer `accountNum` and floating-point `dollarAmount`; use `ifstream` object `inTransaction`.

f) Write a statement that writes a record to the file `newmast.dat`. The record consists of integer `accountNum`, string `name`, and floating-point `currentBalance`; use `ofstream` object `outNewMaster`.

17.4 Find the error(s) and show how to correct it (them) in each of the following.

a) File `payables.dat` referred to by `ofstream` object `outPayable` has not been opened.

```
outPayable << account << company << amount << endl;
```

b) The following statement should read a record from the file `payables.dat`. The `ifstream` object `inPayable` refers to this file, and `istream` object `inReceivable` refers to the file `receivables.dat`.

```
inReceivable >> account >> company >> amount;
```

c) The file `tools.dat` should be opened to add data to the file without discarding the current data.

```
ofstream outTools( "tools.dat", ios::out );
```

Answers to Self-Review Exercises

17.1 a) 1s, 0s. b) bit. c) file. d) characters. e) database. f) `close`. g) `get`. h) `open`. i) `read`. j) `seekg`, `seekp`.

17.2 a) False. Function `read` can read from any input stream object derived from `istream`.

b) False. These four streams are created automatically for you. The `<iostream>` header must be included in a file to use them. This header includes declarations for each stream object.

c) False. The files will be closed when destructors for `ifstream`, `ofstream` or `fstream` objects execute when the stream objects go out of scope or before program execution terminates, but it is a good programming practice to close all files explicitly with `close` once they are no longer needed.

d) False. Member function `seekp` or `seekg` can be used to reposition the "put" or "get" file-position pointer to the beginning of the file.

e) True.

f) False. In most cases, sequential file records are not of uniform length. Therefore, it is possible that updating a record will cause other data to be overwritten.

g) True.

h) False. Records in a random-access file normally are of uniform length.

i) False. It is possible to seek from the beginning of the file, from the end of the file and from the current position in the file.

17.3 a) `ifstream inOldMaster( "oldmast.dat", ios::in );`

b) `ifstream inTransaction( "trans.dat", ios::in );`

c) `ofstream outNewMaster( "newmast.dat", ios::out );`

d) `inOldMaster >> accountNumber >> name >> currentBalance;`

e) `inTransaction >> accountNum >> dollarAmount;`

f) `outNewMaster << accountNum << name << currentBalance;`

17.4 a) *Error:* The file `payables.dat` has not been opened before the attempt is made to output data to the stream.
Correction: Use `ostream` function `open` to open `payables.dat` for output.

b) *Error:* The incorrect `istream` object is being used to read a record from the file named `payables.dat`.
Correction: Use `istream` object `inPayable` to refer to `payables.dat`.

c) *Error:* The file's contents are discarded because the file is opened for output (`ios::out`).
Correction: To add data to the file, open the file either for updating (`ios::ate`) or for appending (`ios::app`).

Exercises

17.5 Fill in the blanks in each of the following:

a) Computers store large amounts of data on secondary storage devices as _____.

b) A(n) _____ is composed of several fields.

c) To facilitate the retrieval of specific records from a file, one field in each record is chosen as a(n) _____.

d) The vast majority of information stored in computer systems is stored in _____ files.

e) A group of related characters that conveys meaning is called a(n) _____.

f) The standard stream objects declared by header <iostream> are _____, _____, _____ and _____.

g) `ostream` member function _____ outputs a character to the specified stream.

h) `ostream` member function _____ is generally used to write data to a randomly accessed file.

i) `istream` member function _____ repositions the file-position pointer in a file.

17.6 State which of the following are *true* and which are *false*. If *false*, explain why.

a) The impressive functions performed by computers essentially involve the manipulation of zeros and ones.

b) People prefer to manipulate bits instead of characters and fields because bits are more compact.

c) People specify programs and data items as characters; computers then manipulate and process these characters as groups of zeros and ones.

d) A person's 5-digit zip code is an example of a numeric field.

e) A person's street address is generally considered to be an alphabetic field in computer applications.

f) Data items represented in computers form a data hierarchy in which data items become larger and more complex as we progress from fields to characters to bits, etc.

g) A record key identifies a record as belonging to a particular field.

h) Most organizations store all information in a single file to facilitate computer processing.

i) When a program creates a file, the file is automatically retained by the computer for future reference; i.e., files are said to be persistent.

17.7 Exercise 17.3 asked you to write a series of single statements. Actually, these statements form the core of an important type of file-processing program, namely, a file-matching program. In commercial data processing, it is common to have several files in each application system. In an accounts receivable system, for example, there is generally a master file containing detailed information about each customer, such as the customer's name, address, telephone number, outstanding balance, credit limit, discount terms, contract arrangements and, possibly, a condensed history of recent purchases and cash payments.

As transactions occur (e.g., sales are made and cash payments arrive), they are entered into a file. At the end of each business period (a month for some companies, a week for others and a day in some cases), the file of transactions (called `trans.dat` in Exercise 17.3) is applied to the master file (called `oldmast.dat` in Exercise 17.3), thus updating each account's record of purchases and payments. During an updating run, the master file is rewritten as a new file (`newmast.dat`), which is then used at the end of the next business period to begin the updating process again.

File-matching programs must deal with certain problems that do not exist in single-file programs. For example, a match does not always occur. A customer on the master file might not have made any purchases or cash payments in the current business period, and therefore no record for this customer will appear on the transaction file. Similarly, a customer who did make some purchases or cash payments may have just moved to this community, and the company may not have had a chance to create a master record for this customer.

Use the statements from Exercise 17.3 as a basis for writing a complete file-matching accounts receivable program. Use the account number on each file as the record key for matching purposes. Assume that each file is a sequential file with records stored in increasing order by account number.

When a match occurs (i.e., records with the same account number appear on both the master and transaction files), add the dollar amount on the transaction file to the current balance on the master file, and write the `newmast.dat` record. (Assume purchases are indicated by positive amounts on the transaction file and payments are indicated by negative amounts.) When there is a master record for a particular account but no corresponding transaction record, merely write the master record to `newmast.dat`. When there is a transaction record but no corresponding master record, print the error message "Unmatched transaction record for account number ..." (fill in the account number from the transaction record).

17.8 After writing the program of Exercise 17.7, write a simple program to create some test data for checking out the program. Use the following sample account data:

Master file Account number	Name	Balance
100	Alan Jones	348.17
300	Mary Smith	27.19
500	Sam Sharp	0.00
700	Suzy Green	−14.22

Transaction file Account number	Transaction amount
100	27.14
300	62.11
400	100.56
900	82.17

17.9   Run the program of Exercise 17.7, using the files of test data created in Exercise 17.8. Print the new master file. Check that the accounts have been updated correctly.

17.10   It is possible (actually common) to have several transaction records with the same record key. This occurs because a particular customer might make several purchases and cash payments during a business period. Rewrite your accounts receivable file-matching program of Exercise 17.7 to provide for the possibility of handling several transaction records with the same record key. Modify the test data of Exercise 17.8 to include the following additional transaction records:

Account number	Dollar amount
300	83.89
700	80.78
700	1.53

17.11   Write a series of statements that accomplish each of the following. Assume that we have defined class `Person` that contains the `private` data members

```
char lastName[ 15 ];
char firstName[ 15 ];
char age[ 4 ];
```

and `public` member functions

```
// accessor functions for lastName
void setLastName( string );
string getLastName() const;

// accessor functions for firstName
void setFirstName( string );
string getFirstName() const;

// accessor functions for age
void setAge( string );
string getAge() const;
```

Also assume that any random-access files have been opened properly.
a) Initialize the file nameage.dat with 100 records that store values lastName = "unassigned", firstName = "" and age = "0".
b) Input 10 last names, first names and ages, and write them to the file.
c) Update a record that already contains information. If the record does not contain information, inform the user "No info".
d) Delete a record that contains information by reinitializing that particular record.

17.12   You are the owner of a hardware store and need to keep an inventory that can tell you what different tools you have, how many of each you have on hand and the cost of each one. Write a program that initializes the random-access file hardware.dat to 100 empty records, lets you input the data concerning each tool, enables you to list all your tools, lets you delete a record for a tool that you no longer have and lets you update *any* information in the file. The tool identification number should be the record number. Use the following information to start your file:

Record #	Tool name	Quantity	Cost
3	Electric sander	7	57.98
17	Hammer	76	11.99
24	Jig saw	21	11.00
39	Lawn mower	3	79.50
56	Power saw	18	99.99
68	Screwdriver	106	6.99
77	Sledge hammer	11	21.50
83	Wrench	34	7.50

17.13 (*Telephone Number Word Generator*) Standard telephone keypads contain the digits 0 through 9. The numbers 2 through 9 each have three letters associated with them, as is indicated by the following table:

Digit	Letter
2	A B C
3	D E F
4	G H I
5	J K L
6	M N O
7	P R S
8	T U V
9	W X Y

Many people find it difficult to memorize phone numbers, so they use the correspondence between digits and letters to develop seven-letter words that correspond to their phone numbers. For example, a person whose telephone number is 686-2377 might use the correspondence indicated in the above table to develop the seven-letter word "NUMBERS."

Businesses frequently attempt to get telephone numbers that are easy for their clients to remember. If a business can advertise a simple word for its customers to dial, then no doubt the business will receive a few more calls.

Each seven-letter word corresponds to exactly one seven-digit telephone number. The restaurant wishing to increase its take-home business could surely do so with the number 825-3688 (i.e., "TAKEOUT").

Each seven-digit phone number corresponds to many separate seven-letter words. Unfortunately, most of these represent unrecognizable juxtapositions of letters. It is possible, however, that the owner of a barber shop would be pleased to know that the shop's telephone number, 424-7288, corresponds to "HAIRCUT." A veterinarian with the phone number 738-2273 would be pleased to know that the number corresponds to "PETCARE."

Write a program that, given a seven-digit number, writes to a file every possible seven-letter word corresponding to that number. There are 2187 (3 to the seventh power) such words. Avoid phone numbers with the digits 0 and 1.

17.14   Write a program that uses the `sizeof` operator to determine the sizes in bytes of the various data types on your computer system. Write the results to the file `datasize.dat`, so that you may print the results later. The results should be displayed in two-column format with the type name in the left column and the size of the type in right column, as in:

```
char                    1
unsigned char           1
short int               2
unsigned short int      2
int                     4
unsigned int            4
long int                4
unsigned long int       4
float                   4
double                  8
long double            10
```

[*Note:* The sizes of the built-in data types on your computer might differ from those listed above.]

Class **string**
and String
Stream
Processing

OBJECTIVES

In this chapter you'll learn:

- To use class **string** from the C++ Standard Library to treat **string**s as full-fledged objects.

- To assign, concatenate, compare, search and swap **string**s.

- To determine **string** characteristics.

- To find, replace and insert characters in **string**s.

- To convert **string**s to C-style strings and vice versa.

- To use **string** iterators.

- To perform input from and output to **string**s in memory.

18.1 Introduction

The class template `basic_string` provides typical string-manipulation operations such as copying, searching, etc. The template definition and all support facilities are defined in namespace std; these include the `typedef` statement

```
typedef basic_string< char > string;
```

that creates the alias type `string` for `basic_string< char >`. A `typedef` also is provided for the `wchar_t` type. Type `wchar_t`[1] stores characters (e.g., two-byte characters, four-byte characters, etc.) for supporting other character sets. We use `string` exclusively throughout this chapter. To use `strings`, include header file `<string>`.

A `string` object can be initialized with a constructor argument such as

```
string text( "Hello" ); // creates a string from a const char *
```

which creates a `string` containing the characters in `"Hello"`, or with two constructor arguments as in

```
string name( 8, 'x' ); // string of 8 'x' characters
```

which creates a `string` containing eight `'x'` characters. Class `string` also provides a default constructor (which creates an empty string) and a copy constructor. An empty `string` is a `string` that does not contain any characters.

A `string` also can be initialized via the alternate constructor syntax in the definition of a `string` as in

```
string month = "March"; // same as: string month( "March" );
```

---

1. Type `wchar_t` commonly is used to represent Unicode®, which does have 16-bit characters, but the size of `wchar_t` is not fixed by the standard. The Unicode Standard outlines a specification to produce consistent encoding of the world's characters and symbols. To learn more about the Unicode Standard, visit www.unicode.org.

Remember that operator = in the preceding declaration is not an assignment; rather it is an implicit call to the string class constructor, which does the conversion.

Note that class string provides no conversions from int or char to string in a string definition. For example, the definitions

```
string error1 = 'c';
string error2( 'u' );
string error3 = 22;
string error4( 8 );
```

result in syntax errors. Note that assigning a single character to a string object is permitted in an assignment statement as in

```
string1 = 'n';
```

Common Programming Error 18.1

Attempting to convert an int or char to a string via an initialization in a declaration or via a constructor argument is a compilation error.

Unlike C-style char * strings, strings are not necessarily null terminated. [*Note:* The C++ standard document provides only a description of the interface for class string— implementation is platform dependent.] The length of a string can be retrieved with member function **length** and with member function **size**. The subscript operator, [], can be used with strings to access and modify individual characters. Like C-style strings, strings have a first subscript of 0 and a last subscript of length() − 1.

Most string member functions take as arguments a starting subscript location and the number of characters on which to operate.

The stream extraction operator (>>) is overloaded to support strings. The statements

```
string stringObject;
cin >> stringObject;
```

declare a string object and read a string from the standard input device. Input is delimited by white-space characters. When a delimiter is encountered, the input operation is terminated. Function **getline** also is overloaded for strings. Assuming string1 is a string, the statement

```
getline( cin, string1 );
```

reads a string from the keyboard into string1. Input is delimited by a newline ('\n'), so getLine can read a line of text into a string object.

18.2 string Assignment and Concatenation

Figure 18.1 demonstrates string assignment and concatenation. Line 7 includes header <string> for class string. The strings string1, string2 and string3 are created in lines 12–14. Line 16 assigns the value of string1 to string2. After the assignment takes place, string2 is a copy of string1. Line 17 uses member function **assign** to copy string1 into string3. A separate copy is made (i.e., string1 and string3 are independent objects). Class string also provides an overloaded version of member function assign that copies a specified number of characters, as in

```
targetString.assign( sourceString, start, numberOfCharacters );
```

where `sourceString` is the `string` to be copied, `start` is the starting subscript and num-berOfCharacters is the number of characters to copy.

Line 22 uses the subscript operator to assign `'r'` to `string3[ 2 ]` (forming `"car"`) and to assign `'r'` to `string2[ 0 ]` (forming `"rat"`). The `string`s are then output.

```cpp
 1   // Fig. 18.1: Fig18_01.cpp
 2   // Demonstrating string assignment and concatenation.
 3   #include <iostream>
 4   using std::cout;
 5   using std::endl;
 6
 7   #include <string>
 8   using std::string;
 9
10   int main()
11   {
12      string string1( "cat" );
13      string string2; // initialized to the empty string
14      string string3; // initialized to the empty string
15
16      string2 = string1; // assign string1 to string2
17      string3.assign( string1 ); // assign string1 to string3
18      cout << "string1: " << string1 << "\nstring2: " << string2
19         << "\nstring3: " << string3 << "\n\n";
20
21      // modify string2 and string3
22      string2[ 0 ] = string3[ 2 ] = 'r';
23
24      cout << "After modification of string2 and string3:\n" << "string1: "
25         << string1 << "\nstring2: " << string2 << "\nstring3: ";
26
27      // demonstrating member function at
28      for ( int i = 0; i < string3.length(); i++ )
29         cout << string3.at( i );
30
31      // declare string4 and string5
32      string string4( string1 + "apult" ); // concatenation
33      string string5;
34
35      // overloaded +=
36      string3 += "pet"; // create "carpet"
37      string1.append( "acomb" ); // create "catacomb"
38
39      // append subscript locations 4 through end of string1 to
40      // create string "comb" (string5 was initially empty)
41      string5.append( string1, 4, string1.length() - 4 );
42
43      cout << "\n\nAfter concatenation:\nstring1: " << string1
44         << "\nstring2: " << string2 << "\nstring3: " << string3
45         << "\nstring4: " << string4 << "\nstring5: " << string5 << endl;
46      return 0;
47   } // end main
```

Fig. 18.1 | Demonstrating `string` assignment and concatenation. (Part 1 of 2.)

```
string1: cat
string2: cat
string3: cat

After modification of string2 and string3:
string1: cat
string2: rat
string3: car

After concatenation:
string1: catacomb
string2: rat
string3: carpet
string4: catapult
string5: comb
```

Fig. 18.1 | Demonstrating `string` assignment and concatenation. (Part 2 of 2.)

Lines 28–29 output the contents of `string3` one character at a time using member function **at**. Member function at provides checked access (or range checking); i.e., going past the end of the `string` throws an `out_of_range` exception. (See Chapter 16 for a detailed discussion of exception handling.) Note that the subscript operator, `[]`, does not provide checked access. This is consistent with its use on arrays.

Common Programming Error 18.2

Accessing a `string` subscript outside the bounds of the `string` using function at is a logic error that causes an `out_of_range` exception.

Common Programming Error 18.3

Accessing an element beyond the size of the `string` using the subscript operator is an unreported logic error.

String `string4` is declared (line 32) and initialized to the result of concatenating `string1` and `"apult"` using the overloaded + operator, which for class `string` denotes concatenation. Line 36 uses the addition assignment operator, `+=`, to concatenate `string3` and `"pet"`. Line 37 uses member function **append** to concatenate `string1` and `"acomb"`.

Line 41 appends the string `"comb"` to empty `string string5`. This member function is passed the `string` (`string1`) to retrieve characters from, the starting subscript in the string (4) and the number of characters to append (the value returned by `string1.length() - 4`).

18.3 Comparing strings

Class `string` provides member functions for comparing `strings`. Figure 18.2 demonstrates class `string`'s comparison capabilities.

The program declares four `strings` (lines 12–15) and outputs each `string` (lines 17–18). The condition in line 21 tests `string1` against `string4` for equality using the overloaded equality operator. If the condition is `true`, `"string1 == string4"` is output. If the condition is `false`, the condition in line 25 is tested. All the `string` class overloaded operator functions demonstrated here as well as those not demonstrated here (!=, <, >= and <=) return bool values.

```
1   // Fig. 18.2: Fig18_02.cpp
2   // Demonstrating string comparison capabilities.
3   #include <iostream>
4   using std::cout;
5   using std::endl;
6
7   #include <string>
8   using std::string;
9
10  int main()
11  {
12     string string1( "Testing the comparison functions." );
13     string string2( "Hello" );
14     string string3( "stinger" );
15     string string4( string2 );
16
17     cout << "string1: " << string1 << "\nstring2: " << string2
18        << "\nstring3: " << string3 << "\nstring4: " << string4 << "\n\n";
19
20     // comparing string1 and string4
21     if ( string1 == string4 )
22        cout << "string1 == string4\n";
23     else // string1 != string4
24     {
25        if ( string1 > string4 )
26           cout << "string1 > string4\n";
27        else // string1 < string4
28           cout << "string1 < string4\n";
29     } // end else
30
31     // comparing string1 and string2
32     int result = string1.compare( string2 );
33
34     if ( result == 0 )
35        cout << "string1.compare( string2 ) == 0\n";
36     else // result != 0
37     {
38        if ( result > 0 )
39           cout << "string1.compare( string2 ) > 0\n";
40        else // result < 0
41           cout << "string1.compare( string2 ) < 0\n";
42     } // end else
43
44     // comparing string1 (elements 2-5) and string3 (elements 0-5)
45     result = string1.compare( 2, 5, string3, 0, 5 );
46
47     if ( result == 0 )
48        cout << "string1.compare( 2, 5, string3, 0, 5 ) == 0\n";
49     else // result != 0
50     {
```

Fig. 18.2 | Comparing `strings`. (Part 1 of 2.)

```
51        if ( result > 0 )
52            cout << "string1.compare( 2, 5, string3, 0, 5 ) > 0\n";
53        else // result < 0
54            cout << "string1.compare( 2, 5, string3, 0, 5 ) < 0\n";
55     } // end else
56
57     // comparing string2 and string4
58     result = string4.compare( 0, string2.length(), string2 );
59
60     if ( result == 0 )
61         cout << "string4.compare( 0, string2.length(), "
62             << "string2 ) == 0" << endl;
63     else // result != 0
64     {
65         if ( result > 0 )
66             cout << "string4.compare( 0, string2.length(), "
67                 << "string2 ) > 0" << endl;
68         else // result < 0
69             cout << "string4.compare( 0, string2.length(), "
70                 << "string2 ) < 0" << endl;
71     } // end else
72
73     // comparing string2 and string4
74     result = string2.compare( 0, 3, string4 );
75
76     if ( result == 0 )
77         cout << "string2.compare( 0, 3, string4 ) == 0" << endl;
78     else // result != 0
79     {
80         if ( result > 0 )
81             cout << "string2.compare( 0, 3, string4 ) > 0" << endl;
82         else // result < 0
83             cout << "string2.compare( 0, 3, string4 ) < 0" << endl;
84     } // end else
85
86     return 0;
87  } // end main
```

```
string1: Testing the comparison functions.
string2: Hello
string3: stinger
string4: Hello

string1 > string4
string1.compare( string2 ) > 0
string1.compare( 2, 5, string3, 0, 5 ) == 0
string4.compare( 0, string2.length(), string2 ) == 0
string2.compare( 0, 3, string4 ) < 0
```

Fig. 18.2 | Comparing strings. (Part 2 of 2.)

Line 32 uses string member function compare to compare string1 to string2. Variable result is assigned 0 if the strings are equivalent, a positive number if string1 is lexicographically greater than string2 or a negative number if string1 is lexicographically less than `string2`. Because a `string` starting with `'T'` is considered lexicographically greater than a `string` starting with `'H'`, `result` is assigned a value greater than 0, as confirmed by the output. A lexicon is a dictionary. When we say that a `string` is lexicographically less than another, we mean that the `compare` method uses the numerical values of the characters (see Appendix B, ASCII Character Set) in each `string` to determine that the first `string` is less than the second.

Line 45 uses an overloaded version of member function `compare` to compare portions of `string1` and `string3`. The first two arguments (2 and 5) specify the starting subscript and length of the portion of `string1` ("sting") to compare with `string3`. The third argument is the comparison `string`. The last two arguments (0 and 5) are the starting subscript and length of the portion of the comparison `string` being compared (also "sting"). The value assigned to `result` is 0 for equality, a positive number if `string1` is lexicographically greater than `string3` or a negative number if `string1` is lexicographically less than `string3`. Because the two pieces of `strings` being compared here are identical, `result` is assigned 0.

Line 58 uses another overloaded version of function `compare` to compare `string4` and `string2`. The first two arguments are the same—the starting subscript and length. The last argument is the comparison `string`. The value returned is also the same—0 for equality, a positive number if `string4` is lexicographically greater than `string2` or a negative number if `string4` is lexicographically less than `string2`. Because the two pieces of `strings` being compared here are identical, `result` is assigned 0.

Line 74 calls member function `compare` to compare the first 3 characters in `string2` to `string4`. Because "Hel" is less than "Hello", a value less than zero is returned.

18.4 Substrings

Class `string` provides member function `substr` for retrieving a substring from a `string`. The result is a new `string` object that is copied from the source `string`. Figure 18.3 demonstrates `substr`.

```
1   // Fig. 18.3: Fig18_03.cpp
2   // Demonstrating string member function substr.
3   #include <iostream>
4   using std::cout;
5   using std::endl;
6
7   #include <string>
8   using std::string;
9
10  int main()
11  {
12     string string1( "The airplane landed on time." );
13
14     // retrieve substring "plane" which
15     // begins at subscript 7 and consists of 5 characters
16     cout << string1.substr( 7, 5 ) << endl;
17     return 0;
18  } // end main
```

Fig. 18.3 | Demonstrating `string` member function `substr`. (Part 1 of 2.)

plane

Fig. 18.3 | Demonstrating `string` member function `substr`. (Part 2 of 2.)

The program declares and initializes a `string` at line 12. Line 16 uses member function `substr` to retrieve a substring from `string1`. The first argument specifies the beginning subscript of the desired substring; the second argument specifies the substring's length.

18.5 **Swapping strings**

Class `string` provides member function `swap` for swapping `strings`. Figure 18.4 swaps two `strings`. Lines 12–13 declare and initialize `strings` `first` and `second`. Each `string` is then output. Line 18 uses `string` member function `swap` to swap the values of `first` and `second`. The two `strings` are printed again to confirm that they were indeed swapped. The `string` member function `swap` is useful for implementing programs that sort strings.

```cpp
1   // Fig. 18.4: Fig18_04.cpp
2   // Using the swap function to swap two strings.
3   #include <iostream>
4   using std::cout;
5   using std::endl;
6
7   #include <string>
8   using std::string;
9
10  int main()
11  {
12     string first( "one" );
13     string second( "two" );
14
15     // output strings
16     cout << "Before swap:\n first: " << first << "\nsecond: " << second;
17
18     first.swap( second ); // swap strings
19
20     cout << "\n\nAfter swap:\n first: " << first
21        << "\nsecond: " << second << endl;
22     return 0;
23  } // end main
```

```
Before swap:
 first: one
second: two

After swap:
 first: two
second: one
```

Fig. 18.4 | Using function `swap` to swap two `strings`.

18.6 `string` Characteristics

Class `string` provides member functions for gathering information about a `string`'s size, length, capacity, maximum length and other characteristics. A `string`'s size or length is the number of characters currently stored in the `string`. A `string`'s capacity is the number of characters that can be stored in the `string` without allocating more memory. The capacity of a `string` must be at least equal to the current size of the `string`, though it can be greater. The exact capacity of a `string` depends on the implementation. The maximum size is the largest possible size a `string` can have. If this value is exceeded, a `length_error` exception is thrown. Figure 18.5 demonstrates `string` class member functions for determining various characteristics of `string`s.

```cpp
1   // Fig. 18.5: Fig18_05.cpp
2   // Demonstrating member functions related to size and capacity.
3   #include <iostream>
4   using std::cout;
5   using std::endl;
6   using std::cin;
7   using std::boolalpha;
8
9   #include <string>
10  using std::string;
11
12  void printStatistics( const string & );
13
14  int main()
15  {
16     string string1; // empty string
17
18     cout << "Statistics before input:\n" << boolalpha;
19     printStatistics( string1 );
20
21     // read in only "tomato" from "tomato soup"
22     cout << "\n\nEnter a string: ";
23     cin >> string1; // delimited by whitespace
24     cout << "The string entered was: " << string1;
25
26     cout << "\nStatistics after input:\n";
27     printStatistics( string1 );
28
29     // read in "soup"
30     cin >> string1; // delimited by whitespace
31     cout << "\n\nThe remaining string is: " << string1 << endl;
32     printStatistics( string1 );
33
34     // append 46 characters to string1
35     string1 += "1234567890abcdefghijklmnopqrstuvwxyz1234567890";
36     cout << "\n\nstring1 is now: " << string1 << endl;
37     printStatistics( string1 );
38
```

Fig. 18.5 | Printing `string` characteristics. (Part 1 of 2.)

```
39      // add 10 elements to string1
40      string1.resize( string1.length() + 10 );
41      cout << "\n\nStats after resizing by (length + 10):\n";
42      printStatistics( string1 );
43
44      cout << endl;
45      return 0;
46   } // end main
47
48   // display string statistics
49   void printStatistics( const string &stringRef )
50   {
51      cout << "capacity: " << stringRef.capacity() << "\nmax size: "
52         << stringRef.max_size() << "\nsize: " << stringRef.size()
53         << "\nlength: " << stringRef.length()
54         << "\nempty: " << stringRef.empty();
55   } // end printStatistics
```

```
Statistics before input:
capacity: 0
max size: 4294967293
size: 0
length: 0
empty: true

Enter a string: tomato soup
The string entered was: tomato
Statistics after input:
capacity: 15
max size: 4294967293
size: 6
length: 6
empty: false

The remaining string is: soup
capacity: 15
max size: 4294967293
size: 4
length: 4
empty: false

string1 is now: soup1234567890abcdefghijklmnopqrstuvwxyz1234567890
capacity: 63
max size: 4294967293
size: 50
length: 50
empty: false

Stats after resizing by (length + 10):
capacity: 63
max size: 4294967293
size: 60
length: 60
empty: false
```

Fig. 18.5 | Printing string characteristics. (Part 2 of 2.)

The program declares empty `string` `string1` (line 16) and passes it to function `printStatistics` (line 19). Function `printStatistics` (lines 49–55) takes a reference to a `const` `string` as an argument and outputs the capacity (using member function `capacity`), maximum size (using member function `max_size`), size (using member function `size`), length (using member function `length`) and whether the `string` is empty (using member function `empty`). The initial call to `printStatistics` indicates that the initial values for the capacity, size and length of `string1` are 0.

The size and length of 0 indicate that there are no characters stored in `string`. Because the initial capacity is 0, when characters are placed in `string1`, memory is allocated to accommodate the new characters. Recall that the size and length are always identical. In this implementation, the maximum size is 4294967293. Object `string1` is an empty `string`, so function `empty` returns `true`.

Line 23 inputs a string. In this example, `"tomato soup"` is input. Because a space character is a delimiter, only `"tomato"` is stored in `string1`; however, `"soup"` remains in the input buffer. Line 27 calls function `printStatistics` to output statistics for `string1`. Notice in the output that the length is 6 and the capacity is 15.

> **Performance Tip 18.1**
>
> *To minimize the number of times memory is allocated and deallocated, some `string` class implementations provide a default capacity that is larger than the length of the `string`.*

Line 30 reads `"soup"` from the input buffer and stores it in `string1`, thereby replacing `"tomato"`. Line 32 passes `string1` to `printStatistics`.

Line 35 uses the overloaded `+=` operator to concatenate a 46-character-long string to `string1`. Line 37 passes `string1` to `printStatistics`. Notice that the capacity has increased to 63 elements and the length is now 50.

Line 40 uses member function `resize` to increase the length of `string1` by 10 characters. The additional elements are set to null characters. Notice that in the output the capacity has not changed and the length is now 60.

18.7 Finding Substrings and Characters in a `string`

Class `string` provides `const` member functions for finding substrings and characters in a `string`. Figure 18.6 demonstrates the find functions.

```cpp
1   // Fig. 18.6: Fig18_06.cpp
2   // Demonstrating the string find member functions.
3   #include <iostream>
4   using std::cout;
5   using std::endl;
6
7   #include <string>
8   using std::string;
9
10  int main()
11  {
12     string string1( "noon is 12 pm; midnight is not." );
13     int location;
```

Fig. 18.6 | Demonstrating the `string` find functions. (Part 1 of 2.)

```
14
15     // find "is" at location 5 and 24
16     cout << "Original string:\n" << string1
17        << "\n\n(find) \"is\" was found at: " << string1.find( "is" )
18        << "\n(rfind) \"is\" was found at: " << string1.rfind( "is" );
19
20     // find 'o' at location 1
21     location = string1.find_first_of( "misop" );
22     cout << "\n\n(find_first_of) found '" << string1[ location ]
23        << "' from the group \"misop\" at: " << location;
24
25     // find 'o' at location 29
26     location = string1.find_last_of( "misop" );
27     cout << "\n\n(find_last_of) found '" << string1[ location ]
28        << "' from the group \"misop\" at: " << location;
29
30     // find '1' at location 8
31     location = string1.find_first_not_of( "noi spm" );
32     cout << "\n\n(find_first_not_of) '" << string1[ location ]
33        << "' is not contained in \"noi spm\" and was found at: "
34        << location;
35
36     // find '.' at location 12
37     location = string1.find_first_not_of( "12noi spm" );
38     cout << "\n\n(find_first_not_of) '" << string1[ location ]
39        << "' is not contained in \"12noi spm\" and was "
40        << "found at: " << location << endl;
41
42     // search for characters not in string1
43     location = string1.find_first_not_of(
44        "noon is 12 pm; midnight is not." );
45     cout << "\nfind_first_not_of(\"noon is 12 pm; midnight is not.\")"
46        << " returned: " << location << endl;
47     return 0;
48  } // end main
```

```
Original string:
noon is 12 pm; midnight is not.

(find) "is" was found at: 5
(rfind) "is" was found at: 24

(find_first_of) found 'o' from the group "misop" at: 1

(find_last_of) found 'o' from the group "misop" at: 29

(find_first_not_of) '1' is not contained in "noi spm" and was found at: 8

(find_first_not_of) '.' is not contained in "12noi spm" and was found at: 12

find_first_not_of("noon is 12 pm; midnight is not.") returned: -1
```

Fig. 18.6 | Demonstrating the `string find` functions. (Part 2 of 2.)

String `string1` is declared and initialized in line 12. Line 17 attempts to find `"is"` in `string1` using function `find`. If `"is"` is found, the subscript of the starting location of that string is returned. If the `string` is not found, the value `string::npos` (a `public static` constant defined in class `string`) is returned. This value is returned by the `string` find-related functions to indicate that a substring or character was not found in the `string`.

Line 18 uses member function `rfind` to search `string1` backward (i.e., right-to-left). If `"is"` is found, the subscript location is returned. If the string is not found, `string::npos` is returned. [*Note:* The rest of the find functions presented in this section return the same type unless otherwise noted.]

Line 21 uses member function `find_first_of` to locate the first occurrence in `string1` of any character in `"misop"`. The searching is done from the beginning of `string1`. The character `'o'` is found in element 1.

Line 26 uses member function `find_last_of` to find the last occurrence in `string1` of any character in `"misop"`. The searching is done from the end of `string1`. The character `'o'` is found in element 29.

Line 31 uses member function `find_first_not_of` to find the first character in `string1` not contained in `"noi spm"`. The character `'1'` is found in element 8. Searching is done from the beginning of `string1`.

Line 37 uses member function `find_first_not_of` to find the first character not contained in `"12noi spm"`. The character `'.'` is found in element 12. Searching is done from the end of `string1`.

Lines 43–44 use member function `find_first_not_of` to find the first character not contained in `"noon is 12 pm; midnight is not."`. In this case, the `string` being searched contains every character specified in the string argument. Because a character was not found, `string::npos` (which has the value –1 in this case) is returned.

18.8 Replacing Characters in a `string`

Figure 18.7 demonstrates `string` member functions for replacing and erasing characters. Lines 13–17 declare and initialize `string string1`. Line 23 uses `string` member function `erase` to erase everything from (and including) the character in position 62 to the end of `string1`. [*Note:* Each newline character occupies one element in the `string`.]

Lines 29–36 use `find` to locate each occurrence of the space character. Each space is then replaced with a period by a call to `string` member function `replace`. Function `replace` takes three arguments: the subscript of the character in the `string` at which replacement should begin, the number of characters to replace and the replacement string. Member function `find` returns `string::npos` when the search character is not found. In line 35, 1 is added to `position` to continue searching at the location of the next character.

Lines 40–48 use function `find` to find every period and another overloaded function `replace` to replace every period and its following character with two semicolons. The arguments passed to this version of `replace` are the subscript of the element where the replace operation begins, the number of characters to replace, a replacement character string from which a substring is selected to use as replacement characters, the element in the character string where the replacement substring begins and the number of characters in the replacement character string to use.

```cpp
1   // Fig. 18.7: Fig18_07.cpp
2   // Demonstrating string member functions erase and replace.
3   #include <iostream>
4   using std::cout;
5   using std::endl;
6
7   #include <string>
8   using std::string;
9
10  int main()
11  {
12     // compiler concatenates all parts into one string
13     string string1( "The values in any left subtree"
14        "\nare less than the value in the"
15        "\nparent node and the values in"
16        "\nany right subtree are greater"
17        "\nthan the value in the parent node" );
18
19     cout << "Original string:\n" << string1 << endl << endl;
20
21     // remove all characters from (and including) location 62
22     // through the end of string1
23     string1.erase( 62 );
24
25     // output new string
26     cout << "Original string after erase:\n" << string1
27        << "\n\nAfter first replacement:\n";
28
29     int position = string1.find( " " ); // find first space
30
31     // replace all spaces with period
32     while ( position != string::npos )
33     {
34        string1.replace( position, 1, "." );
35        position = string1.find( " ", position + 1 );
36     } // end while
37
38     cout << string1 << "\n\nAfter second replacement:\n";
39
40     position = string1.find( "." ); // find first period
41
42     // replace all periods with two semicolons
43     // NOTE: this will overwrite characters
44     while ( position != string::npos )
45     {
46        string1.replace( position, 2, "xxxxx;;yyy", 5, 2 );
47        position = string1.find( ".", position + 1 );
48     } // end while
49
50     cout << string1 << endl;
51     return 0;
52  } // end main
```

Fig. 18.7 | Demonstrating functions `erase` and `replace`. (Part 1 of 2.)

```
Original string:
The values in any left subtree
are less than the value in the
parent node and the values in
any right subtree are greater
than the value in the parent node

Original string after erase:
The values in any left subtree
are less than the value in the


After first replacement:
The.values.in.any.left.subtree
are.less.than.the.value.in.the


After second replacement:
The;;alues;;n;;ny;;eft;;ubtree
are;;ess;;han;;he;;alue;;n;;he
```

Fig. 18.7 | Demonstrating functions **erase** and **replace**. (Part 2 of 2.)

18.9 Inserting Characters into a string

Class string provides member functions for inserting characters into a string. Figure 18.8 demonstrates the string insert capabilities.

The program declares, initializes and then outputs strings string1, string2, string3 and string4. Line 22 uses string member function **insert** to insert string2's content before element 10 of string1.

Line 25 uses insert to insert string4 before string3's element 3. The last two arguments specify the starting and last element of string4 that should be inserted. Using string::npos causes the entire string to be inserted.

```cpp
1   // Fig. 18.8: Fig18_08.cpp
2   // Demonstrating class string insert member functions.
3   #include <iostream>
4   using std::cout;
5   using std::endl;
6
7   #include <string>
8   using std::string;
9
10  int main()
11  {
12     string string1( "beginning end" );
13     string string2( "middle " );
14     string string3( "12345678" );
15     string string4( "xx" );
16
```

Fig. 18.8 | Demonstrating the **string insert** member functions. (Part 1 of 2.)

```
17        cout << "Initial strings:\nstring1: " << string1
18           << "\nstring2: " << string2 << "\nstring3: " << string3
19           << "\nstring4: " << string4 << "\n\n";
20
21        // insert "middle" at location 10 in string1
22        string1.insert( 10, string2 );
23
24        // insert "xx" at location 3 in string3
25        string3.insert( 3, string4, 0, string::npos );
26
27        cout << "Strings after insert:\nstring1: " << string1
28           << "\nstring2: " << string2 << "\nstring3: " << string3
29           << "\nstring4: " << string4 << endl;
30        return 0;
31   } // end main
```

```
Initial strings:
string1: beginning end
string2: middle
string3: 12345678
string4: xx

Strings after insert:
string1: beginning middle end
string2: middle
string3: 123xx45678
string4: xx
```

Fig. 18.8 | Demonstrating the `string insert` member functions. (Part 2 of 2.)

18.10 Conversion to C-Style Pointer-Based char * Strings

Class `string` provides member functions for converting `string` class objects to C-style pointer-based strings. As mentioned earlier, unlike pointer-based strings, `string`s are not necessarily null terminated. These conversion functions are useful when a given function takes a pointer-based string as an argument. Figure 18.9 demonstrates conversion of `string`s to pointer-based strings.

The program declares a `string`, an `int` and two `char` pointers (lines 12–15). The `string` `string1` is initialized to `"STRINGS"`, `ptr1` is initialized to 0 and `length` is initialized to the length of `string1`. Memory of sufficient size to hold a pointer-based string equivalent of `string` `string1` is allocated dynamically and attached to `char` pointer `ptr2`.

Line 18 uses `string` member function `copy` to copy object `string1` into the `char` array pointed to by `ptr2`. Line 19 manually places a terminating null character in the array pointed to by `ptr2`.

Line 23 uses function `c_str` to obtain a `const char *` that points to a null terminated C-style string with the same content as `string1`. The pointer is passed to the stream insertion operator for output.

Line 29 assigns the `const char *` `ptr1` a pointer returned by class `string` member function `data`. This member function returns a non-null-terminated C-style character array. Note that we do not modify `string` `string1` in this example. If `string1` were to be

```
1   // Fig. 18.9: Fig18_09.cpp
2   // Converting to C-style strings.
3   #include <iostream>
4   using std::cout;
5   using std::endl;
6
7   #include <string>
8   using std::string;
9
10  int main()
11  {
12     string string1( "STRINGS" ); // string constructor with char* arg
13     const char *ptr1 = 0; // initialize *ptr1
14     int length = string1.length();
15     char *ptr2 = new char[ length + 1 ]; // including null
16
17     // copy characters from string1 into allocated memory
18     string1.copy( ptr2, length, 0 ); // copy string1 to ptr2 char*
19     ptr2[ length ] = '\0'; // add null terminator
20
21     cout << "string string1 is " << string1
22        << "\nstring1 converted to a C-Style string is "
23        << string1.c_str()   << "\nptr1 is ";
24
25     // Assign to pointer ptr1 the const char * returned by
26     // function data(). NOTE: this is a potentially dangerous
27     // assignment. If string1 is modified, pointer ptr1 can
28     // become invalid.
29     ptr1 = string1.data();
30
31     // output each character using pointer
32     for ( int i = 0; i < length; i++ )
33        cout << *( ptr1 + i ); // use pointer arithmetic
34
35     cout << "\nptr2 is " << ptr2 << endl;
36     delete [] ptr2; // reclaim dynamically allocated memory
37     return 0;
38  } // end main
```

```
string string1 is STRINGS
string1 converted to a C-Style string is STRINGS
ptr1 is STRINGS
ptr2 is STRINGS
```

Fig. 18.9 | Converting `strings` to C-style strings and character arrays.

modified (e.g., the `string`'s dynamic memory changes its address due to a member function call such as `string1.insert( 0, "abcd" );`), `ptr1` could become invalid—which could lead to unpredictable results.

Lines 32–33 use pointer arithmetic to output the character array pointed to by `ptr1`. In lines 35–36, the C-style string pointed to by `ptr2` is output and the memory allocated for `ptr2` is deleted to avoid a memory leak.

Common Programming Error 18.4

Not terminating the character array returned by data *with a null character can lead to execution-time errors.*

Good Programming Practice 18.1

Whenever possible, use the more robust string *class objects rather than C-style pointer-based strings.*

18.11 Iterators

Class `string` provides iterators for forward and backward traversal of `string`s. Iterators provide access to individual characters with syntax that is similar to pointer operations. Iterators are not range checked. Note that in this section we provide "mechanical examples" to demonstrate the use of iterators. We discuss more robust uses of iterators in Chapter 22. Figure 18.10 demonstrates iterators.

```
1  // Fig. 18.10: Fig18_10.cpp
2  // Using an iterator to output a string.
3  #include <iostream>
4  using std::cout;
5  using std::endl;
6
7  #include <string>
8  using std::string;
9
10 int main()
11 {
12    string string1( "Testing iterators" );
13    string::const_iterator iterator1 = string1.begin();
14
15    cout << "string1 = " << string1
16       << "\n(Using iterator iterator1) string1 is: ";
17
18    // iterate through string
19    while ( iterator1 != string1.end() )
20    {
21       cout << *iterator1; // dereference iterator to get char
22       iterator1++; // advance iterator to next char
23    } // end while
24
25    cout << endl;
26    return 0;
27 } // end main
```

```
string1 = Testing iterators
(Using iterator iterator1) string1 is: Testing iterators
```

Fig. 18.10 | Using an iterator to output a `string`.

Lines 12–13 declare `string string1` and `string::const_iterator iterator1`. A `const_iterator` is an iterator that cannot modify the `string`—in this case the `string` through which it is iterating. Iterator `iterator1` is initialized to the beginning of `string1` with the `string` class member function `begin`. Two versions of `begin` exist—one that returns an `iterator` for iterating through a non-`const` `string` and a `const` version that returns a `const_iterator` for iterating through a `const` `string`. Line 15 outputs `string1`.

Lines 19–23 use iterator `iterator1` to "walk through" `string1`. Class `string` member function `end` returns an `iterator` (or a `const_iterator`) for the position past the last element of `string1`. Each element is printed by dereferencing the iterator much as you would dereference a pointer, and the iterator is advanced one position using operator `++`.

Class `string` provides member functions `rend` and `rbegin` for accessing individual `string` characters in reverse from the end of a `string` toward the beginning. Member functions `rend` and `rbegin` return `reverse_iterators` or `const_reverse_iterators` (based on whether the `string` is non-`const` or `const`). In the exercises, we ask you to write a program that demonstrates these capabilities. We'll use iterators and reverse iterators more in Chapter 22.

Error-Prevention Tip 18.1

Use `string` member function `at` (rather than iterators) when you want the benefit of range checking.

Good Programming Practice 18.2

When the operations involving the iterator should not modify the data being processed, use a `const_iterator`. This is another example of employing the principle of least privilege.

18.12 String Stream Processing

In addition to standard stream I/O and file stream I/O, C++ stream I/O includes capabilities for inputting from, and outputting to, `strings` in memory. These capabilities often are referred to as in-memory I/O or string stream processing.

Input from a `string` is supported by class `istringstream`. Output to a `string` is supported by class `ostringstream`. The class names `istringstream` and `ostringstream` are actually aliases defined by the `typedef`s

```
typedef basic_istringstream< char > istringstream;
typedef basic_ostringstream< char > ostringstream;
```

Class templates `basic_istringstream` and `basic_ostringstream` provide the same functionality as classes `istream` and `ostream` plus other member functions specific to in-memory formatting. Programs that use in-memory formatting must include the `<sstream>` and `<iostream>` header files.

One application of these techniques is data validation. A program can read an entire line at a time from the input stream into a `string`. Next, a validation routine can scrutinize the contents of the `string` and correct (or repair) the data, if necessary. Then the program can proceed to input from the `string`, knowing that the input data is in the proper format.

Outputting to a `string` is a nice way to take advantage of the powerful output formatting capabilities of C++ streams. Data can be prepared in a `string` to mimic the edited screen format. That `string` could be written to a disk file to preserve the screen image.

An ostringstream object uses a string object to store the output data. The str member function of class ostringstream returns a copy of that string.

Figure 18.11 demonstrates an ostringstream object. The program creates ostringstream object outputString (line 15) and uses the stream insertion operator to output a series of strings and numerical values to the object.

Lines 27–28 output string string1, string string2, string string3, double double1, string string4, int integer, string string5 and the address of int integer—all to outputString in memory. Line 31 uses the stream insertion operator and the call outputString.str() to display a copy of the string created in lines 27–28. Line 34 demonstrates that more data can be appended to the string in memory by simply issuing another stream insertion operation to outputString. Lines 35–36 display string outputString after appending additional characters.

```cpp
 1   // Fig. 18.11: Fig18_11.cpp
 2   // Using a dynamically allocated ostringstream object.
 3   #include <iostream>
 4   using std::cout;
 5   using std::endl;
 6
 7   #include <string>
 8   using std::string;
 9
10   #include <sstream> // header file for string stream processing
11   using std::ostringstream; // stream insertion operators
12
13   int main()
14   {
15      ostringstream outputString; // create ostringstream instance
16
17      string string1( "Output of several data types " );
18      string string2( "to an ostringstream object:" );
19      string string3( "\n        double: " );
20      string string4( "\n           int: " );
21      string string5( "\naddress of int: " );
22
23      double double1 = 123.4567;
24      int integer = 22;
25
26      // output strings, double and int to ostringstream outputString
27      outputString << string1 << string2 << string3 << double1
28         << string4 << integer << string5 << &integer;
29
30      // call str to obtain string contents of the ostringstream
31      cout << "outputString contains:\n" << outputString.str();
32
33      // add additional characters and call str to output string
34      outputString << "\nmore characters added";
35      cout << "\n\nafter additional stream insertions,\n"
36         << "outputString contains:\n" << outputString.str() << endl;
37      return 0;
38   } // end main
```

Fig. 18.11 | Using a dynamically allocated ostringstream object. (Part 1 of 2.)

```
outputString contains:
Output of several data types to an ostringstream object:
        double: 123.457
           int: 22
address of int: 0012F540

after additional stream insertions,
outputString contains:
Output of several data types to an ostringstream object:
        double: 123.457
           int: 22
address of int: 0012F540
more characters added
```

Fig. 18.11 | Using a dynamically allocated `ostringstream` object. (Part 2 of 2.)

An `istringstream` object inputs data from a `string` in memory to program variables. Data is stored in an `istringstream` object as characters. Input from the `istringstream` object works identically to input from any file. The end of the `string` is interpreted by the `istringstream` object as end-of-file.

Figure 18.12 demonstrates input from an `istringstream` object. Lines 15–16 create `string input` containing the data and `istringstream` object `inputString` constructed to contain the data in `string input`. The `string input` contains the data

```
Input test 123 4.7 A
```

which, when read as input to the program, consist of two strings (`"Input"` and `"test"`), an int (`123`), a double (`4.7`) and a char (`'A'`). These characters are extracted to variables `string1`, `string2`, `integer`, `double1` and `character` in line 23.

```cpp
1   // Fig. 18.12: Fig18_12.cpp
2   // Demonstrating input from an istringstream object.
3   #include <iostream>
4   using std::cout;
5   using std::endl;
6
7   #include <string>
8   using std::string;
9
10  #include <sstream>
11  using std::istringstream;
12
13  int main()
14  {
15     string input( "Input test 123 4.7 A" );
16     istringstream inputString( input );
17     string string1;
18     string string2;
19     int integer;
20     double double1;
21     char character;
```

Fig. 18.12 | Demonstrating input from an `istringstream` object. (Part 1 of 2.)

```
22
23      inputString >> string1 >> string2 >> integer >> double1 >> character;
24
25      cout << "The following items were extracted\n"
26         << "from the istringstream object:" << "\nstring: " << string1
27         << "\nstring: " << string2 << "\n   int: " << integer
28         << "\ndouble: " << double1 << "\n  char: " << character;
29
30      // attempt to read from empty stream
31      long value;
32      inputString >> value;
33
34      // test stream results
35      if ( inputString.good() )
36         cout << "\n\nlong value is: " << value << endl;
37      else
38         cout << "\n\ninputString is empty" << endl;
39
40      return 0;
41   } // end main
```

```
The following items were extracted
from the istringstream object:
string: Input
string: test
   int: 123
double: 4.7
  char: A

inputString is empty
```

Fig. 18.12 | Demonstrating input from an istringstream object. (Part 2 of 2.)

The data is then output in lines 25–28. The program attempts to read from input-String again in line 32. The if condition in line 35 uses function good (Section 15.8) to test if any data remains. Because no data remains, the function returns false and the else part of the if...else statement is executed.

18.13 Wrap-Up

This chapter introduced the class string from the C++ Standard Library, which allows programs to treat strings as full-fledged objects. We discussed assigning, concatenating, comparing, searching and swapping strings. We also introduced a number of methods to determine string characteristics, to find, replace and insert characters in a string, and to convert strings to C-style strings and vice versa. You also learned about string iterators and performing input from and output to strings in memory. In Chapter 19, Searching and Sorting, we discuss the binary search algorithm and the merge sort algorithm. We also use Big O notation to analyze and compare the efficiency of various searching and sorting algorithms.

Summary

Section 18.1 Introduction
- C++ class template `basic_string` provides typical string-manipulation operations such as copying, searching, etc.
- The `typedef` statement

      typedef basic_string< char > string;

  creates the alias type `string` for `basic_string< char >`. A `typedef` also is provided for the `wchar_t` type. Type `wchar_t` normally stores two-byte (16-bit) characters for supporting other character sets. The size of `wchar_t` is not fixed by the standard.
- To use strings, include C++ Standard Library header file `<string>`.
- Class `string` provides no constructors that convert from `int` or `char` to `string`.
- Assigning a single character to a `string` object is permitted in an assignment statement.
- `string`s are not necessarily null terminated.
- Most `string` member functions take as arguments a starting subscript location and the number of characters on which to operate.

Section 18.2 `string` Assignment and Concatenation
- Class `string` provides overloaded `operator=` and member function `assign` for `string` assignments.
- The subscript operator, `[]`, provides read/write access to any element of a `string`.
- `string` member function `at` provides checked access—going past either end of the `string` throws an `out_of_range` exception. The subscript operator, `[]`, does not provide checked access.
- Class `string` provides the overloaded `+` and `+=` operators and member function `append` to perform `string` concatenation.

Section 18.3 Comparing **string**s
- Class `string` provides overloaded `==`, `!=`, `<`, `>`, `<=` and `>=` operators for `string` comparisons.
- `string` member function `compare` compares two `string`s (or substrings) and returns 0 if the `string`s are equal, a positive number if the first `string` is lexicographically greater than the second or a negative number if the first string is lexicographically less than the second.

Section 18.4 Substrings
- `string` member function `substr` retrieves a substring from a `string`.

Section 18.5 Swapping **string**s
- `string` member function `swap` swaps the contents of two `string`s.

Section 18.6 `string` Characteristics
- `string` member functions `size` and `length` return the size or length of a `string` (i.e., the number of characters currently stored in the `string`).
- `string` member function `capacity` returns the total number of characters that can be stored in the `string` without increasing the amount of memory allocated to the `string`.
- `string` member function `max_size` returns the maximum size a `string` can have.
- `string` member function `resize` changes the length of a `string`.

Section 18.7 Finding Substrings and Characters in a `string`
- Class `string` find functions `find`, `rfind`, `find_first_of`, `find_last_of` and `find_first_not_of` locate substrings or characters in a `string`.

Section 18.8 Replacing Characters in a `string`
- `string` member function `erase` deletes elements of a `string`.x
- `string` member function `replace` replaces characters in a `string`.

Section 18.9 Inserting Characters into a `string`
- `string` member function `insert` inserts characters in a `string`.

Section 18.10 Conversion to C-Style Pointer-Based `char *` Strings
- `string` member function `c_str` returns a `const char *` pointing to a null-terminated C-style character string that contains all the characters in a `string`.
- `string` member function `data` returns a `const char *` pointing to a non-null-terminated C-style character array that contains all the characters in a `string`.

Section 18.11 Iterators
- Class `string` provides member functions `end` and `begin` to iterate through individual elements.
- Class `string` provides member functions `rend` and `rbegin` for accessing individual `string` characters in reverse from the end of a `string` toward the beginning.

Section 18.12 String Stream Processing
- Input from a `string` is supported by type `istringstream`. Output to a `string` is supported by type `ostringstream`.
- `ostringstream` member function `str` returns a `string` copy of a `string`.

Terminology

size member function of class string
<sstream> header file
str member function of class ostringstream
string::npos constant

string stream processing
substr member function of class string
swap member function of class string
wchar_t type

Self-Review Exercises

18.1 Fill in the blanks in each of the following:
 a) Header _____ must be included for class string.
 b) Class string belongs to the _____ namespace.
 c) Function _____ deletes characters from a string.
 d) Function _____ finds the first occurrence of any character from a string.

18.2 State which of the following statements are *true* and which are *false*. If a statement is *false*, explain why.
 a) Concatenation of string objects can be performed with the addition assignment operator, +=.
 b) Characters within a string begin at index 0.
 c) The assignment operator, =, copies a string.
 d) A C-style string is a string object.

18.3 Find the error(s) in each of the following, and explain how to correct it (them):
 a)
```
string string1( 28 ); // construct string1
string string2( 'z' ); // construct string2
```
 b)
```
// assume std namespace is known
const char *ptr = name.data(); // name is "joe bob"
ptr[ 3 ] = '-';
cout << ptr << endl;
```

Answers to Self-Review Exercises

18.1 a) <string>. b) std. c) erase. d) find_first_of.

18.2 a) True.
 b) True.
 c) True.
 d) False. A string is an object that provides many different services. A C-style string does not provide any services. C-style strings are null terminated; strings are not necessarily null terminated. C-style strings are pointers and strings are objects.

18.3 a) Constructors for class string do not exist for integer and character arguments. Other valid constructors should be used—converting the arguments to strings if need be.
 b) Function data does not add a null terminator. Also, the code attempts to modify a const char. Replace all of the lines with the code:
```
cout << name.substr( 0, 3 ) + "-" + name.substr( 4 ) << endl;
```

Exercises

18.4 Fill in the blanks in each of the following:
 a) Class string member functions _____ and _____ convert strings to C-style strings.
 b) Class string member function _____ is used for assignment.
 c) _____ is the return type of function rbegin.
 d) Class string member function _____ is used to retrieve a substring.

18.5   State which of the following statements are *true* and which are *false*. If a statement is *false*, explain why.

    a) `strings` are always null terminated.

    b) Class `string` member function `max_size` returns the maximum size for a `string`.

    c) Class `string` member function `at` can throw an `out_of_range` exception.

    d) Class `string` member function `begin` returns an `iterator`.

18.6   Find any errors in the following and explain how to correct them:

    a) `std::cout << s.data() << std::endl; // s is "hello"`

    b) `erase( s.rfind( "x" ), 1 ); // s is "xenon"`

    c)
```
string& foo()
{
    string s( "Hello" );
    ...    // other statements
    return;
} // end function foo
```

18.7   (*Simple Encryption*) Some information on the Internet may be encrypted with a simple algorithm known as "rot13," which rotates each character by 13 positions in the alphabet. Thus, `'a'` corresponds to `'n'`, and `'x'` corresponds to `'k'`. rot13 is an example of symmetric key encryption. With symmetric key encryption, both the encrypter and decrypter use the same key.

    a) Write a program that encrypts a message using rot13.

    b) Write a program that decrypts the scrambled message using 13 as the key.

    c) After writing the programs of part (a) and part (b), briefly answer the following question: If you did not know the key for part (b), how difficult do you think it would be to break the code? What if you had access to substantial computing power (e.g., supercomputers)? In Exercise 18.26 we ask you to write a program to accomplish this.

18.8   Write a program using iterators that demonstrates the use of functions `rbegin` and `rend`.

18.9   Write a program that reads in several `strings` and prints only those ending in "r" or "ay". Only lowercase letters should be considered.

18.10   Write a program that demonstrates passing a `string` both by reference and by value.

18.11   Write a program that separately inputs a first name and a last name and concatenates the two into a new `string`.

18.12   Write a program that plays the game of Hangman. The program should pick a word (which is either coded directly into the program or read from a text file) and display the following:

```
Guess the word:    XXXXXX
```

Each X represents a letter. The user tries to guess the letters in the word. The appropriate response yes or no should be displayed after each guess. After each incorrect guess, display the diagram with another body part filled. After seven incorrect guesses, the user should be hanged. The display should look as follows:

```
     0
    /|\
     |
    / \
```

After each guess, display all user guesses. If the user guesses the word correctly, the program should display

```
Congratulations!!! You guessed my word. Play again? yes/no
```

18.13   Write a program that inputs a `string` and prints the `string` backward. Convert all upper-case characters to lowercase and all lowercase characters to uppercase.

18.14   Write a program that uses the comparison capabilities introduced in this chapter to alpha-betize a series of animal names. Only uppercase letters should be used for the comparisons.

18.15   Write a program that creates a cryptogram out of a `string`. A cryptogram is a message or word in which each letter is replaced with another letter. For example the `string`

        The bird was named squawk

might be scrambled to form

        cin vrjs otz ethns zxqtop

Note that spaces are not scrambled. In this particular case, `'T'` was replaced with `'x'`, each `'a'` was replaced with `'h'`, etc. Uppercase letters become lowercase letters in the cryptogram. Use tech-niques similar to those in Exercise 18.7.

18.16   Modify Exercise 18.15 to allow the user to solve the cryptogram. The user should input two characters at a time: The first character specifies a letter in the cryptogram, and the second letter specifies the replacement letter. If the replacement letter is correct, replace the letter in the crypto-gram with the replacement letter in uppercase.

18.17   Write a program that inputs a sentence and counts the number of palindromes in it. A pal-indrome is a word that reads the same backward and forward. For example, "tree" is not a palin-drome, but "noon" is.

18.18   Write a program that counts the total number of vowels in a sentence. Output the frequen-cy of each vowel.

18.19   Write a program that inserts the characters "******" in the exact middle of a `string`.

18.20   Write a program that erases the sequences "by" and "BY" from a `string`.

18.21   Write a program that inputs a line of text, replaces all punctuation marks with spaces and uses the C-string library function `strtok` to tokenize the `string` into individual words.

18.22   Write a program that inputs a line of text and prints the text backward. Use iterators in your solution.

18.23   Write a recursive version of Exercise 18.22.

18.24   Write a program that demonstrates the use of the erase functions that take `iterator` argu-ments.

18.25   Write a program that generates the following from the `string` `"abcdefghijklmnopqrstu-vwxyz{"`:

```
                   a
                  bcb
                 cdedc
                defgfed
               efghihgfe
              fghijkjihgf
             ghijklmlkjihg
            hijklmnonmlkjih
           ijklmnopqponmlkji
          jklmnopqrsrqponmlkj
         klmnopqrstutsrqponmlk
        lmnopqrstuvwvutsrqponml
       mnopqrstuvwxyxwvutsrqponm
      nopqrstuvwxyz{zyxwvutsrqpon
```

18.26 In Exercise 18.7, we asked you to write a simple encryption algorithm. Write a program that will attempt to decrypt a "rot13" message using simple frequency substitution. (Assume that you do not know the key.) The most frequent letters in the encrypted phrase should be replaced with the most commonly used English letters (a, e, i, o, u, s, t, r, etc.). Write the possibilities to a file. What made the code breaking easy? How can the encryption mechanism be improved?

18.27 Write a version of the selection sort routine (Fig. 8.28) that sorts strings. Use function swap in your solution.

18.28 Modify class Employee in Figs. 13.6–13.7 by adding a private utility function called isValidSocialSecurityNumber. This member function should validate the format of a social security number (e.g., ###-##-####, where # is a digit). If the format is valid, return true; otherwise return false.

19

Searching and Sorting

OBJECTIVES

In this chapter you'll learn:

- To search for a given value in a vector using binary search.

- To use Big O notation to express the efficiency of an algorithm and to compare the performance of algorithms.

- To review the efficiency of the selection sort and insertion sort algorithms.

- To sort a vector using the recursive merge sort algorithm.

- To determine the efficiency of various searching and sorting algorithms.

- To enumerate the searching and sorting algorithms discussed in this text.

- To understand the nature of algorithms of constant, linear and quadratic runtime.

19.1 Introduction

Searching data involves determining whether a value (referred to as the search key) is present in the data and, if so, finding the value's location. Two popular search algorithms are the simple linear search (introduced in Section 7.7) and the faster but more complex binary search, which is introduced in this chapter.

Sorting places data in order, typically ascending or descending, based on one or more sort keys. A list of names could be sorted alphabetically, bank accounts could be sorted by account number, employee payroll records could be sorted by social security number, and so on. Previously, you learned about insertion sort (Section 7.8) and selection sort (Section 8.6). This chapter introduces the more efficient, but more complex merge sort. Figure 19.1 summarizes the searching and sorting algorithms discussed in the examples and exercises of this book. This chapter also introduces Big O notation, which is used to estimate the worst-case runtime for an algorithm—that is, how hard an algorithm may have to work to solve a problem.

19.2 Searching Algorithms

Looking up a phone number, accessing a website and checking the definition of a word in a dictionary all involve searching large amounts of data. Searching algorithms all accomplish the same goal—finding an element that matches a given search key, if such an element does, in fact, exist. There are, however, a number of things that differentiate search algorithms from one another. The major difference is the amount of effort they require to complete the search. One way to describe this effort is with Big O notation. For searching and sorting algorithms, this is particularly dependent on the number of data elements.

In Chapter 7, we discussed the linear search algorithm, which is a simple and easy-to-implement searching algorithm. We'll now discuss the efficiency of the linear search algorithm as measured by Big O notation. Then, we'll introduce a searching algorithm that is relatively efficient but more complex and difficult to implement.

19.2.1 Efficiency of Linear Search

Suppose an algorithm simply tests whether the first element of a vector is equal to the second element of the vector. If the vector has 10 elements, this algorithm requires only one comparison. If the vector has 1000 elements, the algorithm still requires only one comparison. In fact, the algorithm is independent of the number of vector elements. This algo-

Chapter	Algorithm	Location
Searching Algorithms		
7	Linear search	Section 7.7
20	Binary search	Section 19.2.2
	Recursive linear search	Exercise 19.8
	Recursive binary search	Exercise 19.9
21	Binary tree search	Section 20.7
	Linear search of a linked list	Exercise 20.21
23	binary_search standard library function	Section 22.5.6
Sorting Algorithms		
7	Insertion sort	Section 7.8
8	Selection sort	Section 8.6
19	Recursive merge sort	Section 19.3.3
	Bubble sort	Exercises 19.5 and 19.6
	Bucket sort	Exercise 19.7
	Recursive quicksort	Exercise 19.10
20	Binary tree sort	Section 20.7
22	sort standard library function	Section 22.5.6
	Heap sort	Section 22.5.12

Fig. 19.1 | Searching and sorting algorithms in this text.

rithm is said to have a **constant runtime**, which is represented in Big O notation as $O(1)$. An algorithm that is $O(1)$ does not necessarily require only one comparison. $O(1)$ just means that the number of comparisons is *constant*—it does not grow as the size of the vector increases. An algorithm that tests whether the first element of a vector is equal to any of the next three elements will always require three comparisons, but in Big O notation it is still considered $O(1)$. $O(1)$ is often pronounced "on the order of 1" or more simply "order 1."

An algorithm that tests whether the first element of a vector is equal to *any* of the other elements of the vector requires at most $n - 1$ comparisons, where n is the number of elements in the vector. If the vector has 10 elements, the algorithm requires up to nine comparisons. If the vector has 1000 elements, the algorithm requires up to 999 comparisons. As n grows larger, the n part of the expression "dominates," and subtracting one becomes inconsequential. Big O is designed to highlight these dominant terms and ignore terms that become unimportant as n grows. For this reason, an algorithm that requires a total of $n - 1$ comparisons (such as the one we described in this paragraph) is said to be $O(n)$. An $O(n)$ algorithm is referred to as having a **linear runtime**. $O(n)$ is often pronounced "on the order of n" or more simply "order n."

Now suppose you have an algorithm that tests whether *any* element of a vector is duplicated elsewhere in the vector. The first element must be compared with every other element in the vector. The second element must be compared with every other element except the first (it was already compared to the first). The third element must be compared with every other element except the first two. In the end, this algorithm will end up making $(n - 1) + (n - 2) + \ldots + 2 + 1$ or $n^2/2 - n/2$ comparisons. As n increases, the n^2 term dominates and the n term becomes inconsequential. Again, Big O notation highlights the n^2 term, leaving $n^2/2$. As we'll soon see, however, constant factors are omitted in Big O notation.

Big O is concerned with how an algorithm's runtime grows in relation to the number of items processed. Suppose an algorithm requires n^2 comparisons. With four elements, the algorithm will require 16 comparisons; with eight elements, 64 comparisons. With this algorithm, doubling the number of elements quadruples the number of comparisons. Consider a similar algorithm requiring $n^2/2$ comparisons. With four elements, the algorithm will require eight comparisons; with eight elements, 32 comparisons. Again, doubling the number of elements quadruples the number of comparisons. Both of these algorithms grow as the square of n, so Big O ignores the constant, and both algorithms are considered to be $O(n^2)$, which is referred to as quadratic runtime and pronounced "on the order of n-squared" or more simply "order n-squared."

When n is small, $O(n^2)$ algorithms (running on today's billion-operation-per-second personal computers) will not noticeably affect performance. But as n grows, you'll start to notice the performance degradation. An $O(n^2)$ algorithm running on a million-element vector would require a trillion "operations" (where each could actually require several machine instructions to execute). This could require a few hours to execute. A billion-element vector would require a quintillion operations, a number so large that the algorithm could take decades! Unfortunately, $O(n^2)$ algorithms tend to be easier to write. In this chapter, you'll see algorithms with more favorable Big O measures. These efficient algorithms often take a bit more cleverness and effort to create, but their superior performance can be worth the extra effort, especially as n gets large and as algorithms are compounded into larger programs.

The linear search algorithm runs in $O(n)$ time. The worst case in this algorithm is that every element must be checked to determine whether the search key exists in the vector. If the size of the vector is doubled, the number of comparisons that the algorithm must perform is also doubled. Note that linear search can provide outstanding performance if the element matching the search key happens to be at or near the front of the vector. But we seek algorithms that perform well, on average, across all searches, including those where the element matching the search key is near the end of the vector.

Linear search is the easiest search algorithm to implement, but it can be slow compared to other search algorithms. If a program needs to perform many searches on large vectors, it may be better to implement a different, more efficient algorithm, such as the binary search which we present in the next section.

Performance Tip 19.1

Sometimes the simplest algorithms perform poorly. Their virtue is that they are easy to program, test and debug. Sometimes more complex algorithms are required to realize maximum performance.

19.2.2 Binary Search

The binary search algorithm is more efficient than the linear search algorithm, but it requires that the vector first be sorted. This is only worthwhile when the vector, once sorted, will be searched a great many times—or when the searching application has stringent performance requirements. The first iteration of this algorithm tests the middle element in the vector. If this matches the search key, the algorithm ends. Assuming the vector is sorted in ascending order, then if the search key is less than the middle element, the search key cannot match any element in the second half of the vector and the algorithm continues with only the first half of the vector (i.e., the first element up to, but not including, the middle element). If the search key is greater than the middle element, the search key cannot match any element in the first half of the vector and the algorithm continues with only the second half of the vector (i.e., the element after the middle element through the last element). Each iteration tests the middle value of the remaining portion of the vector. If the element does not match the search key, the algorithm eliminates half of the remaining elements. The algorithm ends either by finding an element that matches the search key or by reducing the subvector to zero size.

As an example, consider the sorted 15-element vector

2   3   5   10   27   30   34   51   56   65   77   81   82   93   99

and the search key 65. A binary search would first check whether 51 is the search key (because 51 is the middle element of the vector). The search key (65) is larger than 51, so 51 is eliminated from consideration along with the first half of the vector (all elements smaller than 51.) Next, the algorithm checks whether 81 (the middle element of the remainder of the vector) matches the search key. The search key (65) is smaller than 81, so 81 is eliminated from consideration along with the elements larger than 81. After just two tests, the algorithm has narrowed the number of elements to check to three (56, 65 and 77). The algorithm then checks 65 (which matches the search key), and returns the index (9) of the vector element containing 65. In this case, the algorithm required just three comparisons to determine whether a vector element matched the search key. Using a linear search algorithm would have required 10 comparisons. [*Note:* In this example, we have chosen to use a vector with 15 elements, so that there will always be an obvious middle element in the vector. With an even number of elements, the middle of the vector lies between two elements. We implement the algorithm to choose the larger of those two elements.]

Figures 19.2–19.3 define class BinarySearch and its member functions, respectively. Class BinarySearch is similar to LinearSearch (Section 7.7)—it has a constructor, a search function (binarySearch), a displayElements function, two private data members and a private utility function (displaySubElements). Lines 18–28 of Fig. 19.3 define the constructor. After initializing the vector with random ints from 10–99 (lines 24–25), line 27 calls the Standard Library function sort on the vector data. Recall that the binary search algorithm will work only on a sorted vector. Function sort requires two arguments that specify the range of elements to sort. These arguments are specified with iterators (dicussed briefly in Section 10.9 and in detail in Chapter 22). The vector member functions begin and end return iterators that can be used with function sort to indicate that all the elements from the beginning to the end should be sorted.

Lines 31–61 define function binarySearch. The search key is passed into parameter searchElement (line 31). Lines 33–35 calculate the low end index, high end index and middle index of the portion of the vector that the program is currently searching. At the beginning of the function, the low end is 0, the high end is the size of the vector minus 1 and the middle is the average of these two values. Line 36 initializes the location of the found element to -1—the value that will be returned if the search key is not found. Lines

```
1   // Fig 19.2: BinarySearch.h
2   // Class that contains a vector of random integers and a function
3   // that uses binary search to find an integer.
4   #include <vector>
5   using std::vector;
6
7   class BinarySearch
8   {
9   public:
10      BinarySearch( int ); // constructor initializes vector
11      int binarySearch( int ) const; // perform a binary search on vector
12      void displayElements() const; // display vector elements
13   private:
14      int size; // vector size
15      vector< int > data; // vector of ints
16      void displaySubElements( int, int ) const; // display range of values
17   }; // end class BinarySearch
```

Fig. 19.2 | BinarySearch class definition.

```
1   // Fig 19.3: BinarySearch.cpp
2   // BinarySearch class member-function definition.
3   #include <iostream>
4   using std::cout;
5   using std::endl;
6
7   #include <cstdlib> // prototypes for functions srand and rand
8   using std::rand;
9   using std::srand;
10
11  #include <ctime> // prototype for function time
12  using std::time;
13
14  #include <algorithm> // prototype for sort function
15  #include "BinarySearch.h" // class BinarySearch definition
16
17  // constructor initializes vector with random ints and sorts the vector
18  BinarySearch::BinarySearch( int vectorSize )
19  {
20     size = ( vectorSize > 0 ? vectorSize : 10 ); // validate vectorSize
21     srand( time( 0 ) ); // seed using current time
22
23     // fill vector with random ints in range 10-99
24     for ( int i = 0; i < size; i++ )
25        data.push_back( 10 + rand() % 90 ); // 10-99
26
27     std::sort( data.begin(), data.end() ); // sort the data
28  } // end BinarySearch constructor
29
30  // perform a binary search on the data
31  int BinarySearch::binarySearch( int searchElement ) const
32  {
```

Fig. 19.3 | BinarySearch class member-function definition. (Part 1 of 2.)

```
33    int low = 0; // low end of the search area
34    int high = size - 1; // high end of the search area
35    int middle = ( low + high + 1 ) / 2; // middle element
36    int location = -1; // return value; -1 if not found
37
38    do // loop to search for element
39    {
40        // print remaining elements of vector to be searched
41        displaySubElements( low, high );
42
43        // output spaces for alignment
44        for ( int i = 0; i < middle; i++ )
45            cout << "   ";
46
47        cout << " * " << endl; // indicate current middle
48
49        // if the element is found at the middle
50        if ( searchElement == data[ middle ] )
51            location = middle; // location is the current middle
52        else if ( searchElement < data[ middle ] ) // middle is too high
53            high = middle - 1; // eliminate the higher half
54        else // middle element is too low
55            low = middle + 1; // eliminate the lower half
56
57        middle = ( low + high + 1 ) / 2; // recalculate the middle
58    } while ( ( low <= high ) && ( location == -1 ) );
59
60    return location; // return location of search key
61 } // end function binarySearch
62
63 // display values in vector
64 void BinarySearch::displayElements() const
65 {
66     displaySubElements( 0, size - 1 );
67 } // end function displayElements
68
69 // display certain values in vector
70 void BinarySearch::displaySubElements( int low, int high ) const
71 {
72     for ( int i = 0; i < low; i++ ) // output spaces for alignment
73         cout << "   ";
74
75     for ( int i = low; i <= high; i++ ) // output elements left in vector
76         cout << data[ i ] << " ";
77
78     cout << endl;
79 } // end function displaySubElements
```

Fig. 19.3 | BinarySearch class member-function definition. (Part 2 of 2.)

38–58 loop until low is greater than high (this occurs when the element is not found) or location does not equal -1 (indicating that the search key was found). Line 50 tests whether the value in the middle element is equal to searchElement. If this is true, line 51 assigns middle to location. Then the loop terminates and location is returned to the caller. Each iteration of the loop tests a single value (line 50) and eliminates half of the remaining values in the vector (line 53 or 55).

Lines 25–41 of Fig. 19.4 loop until the user enters the value -1. For each other number the user enters, the program performs a binary search on the data to determine whether it matches an element in the vector. The first line of output from this program is the vector of ints, in increasing order. When the user instructs the program to search for 38, the program first tests the middle element, which is 67 (as indicated by *). The search key is less than 67, so the program eliminates the second half of the vector and tests the middle element from the first half of the vector. The search key equals 38, so the program returns the index 3.

```cpp
1   // Fig 19.4: Fig19_04.cpp
2   // BinarySearch test program.
3   #include <iostream>
4   using std::cin;
5   using std::cout;
6   using std::endl;
7
8   #include "BinarySearch.h" // class BinarySearch definition
9
10  int main()
11  {
12     int searchInt; // search key
13     int position; // location of search key in vector
14
15     // create vector and output it
16     BinarySearch searchVector ( 15 );
17     searchVector.displayElements();
18
19     // get input from user
20     cout << "\nPlease enter an integer value (-1 to quit): ";
21     cin >> searchInt; // read an int from user
22     cout << endl;
23
24     // repeatedly input an integer; -1 terminates the program
25     while ( searchInt != -1 )
26     {
27        // use binary search to try to find integer
28        position = searchVector.binarySearch( searchInt );
29
30        // return value of -1 indicates integer was not found
31        if ( position == -1 )
32           cout << "The integer " << searchInt << " was not found.\n";
33        else
34           cout << "The integer " << searchInt
35              << " was found in position " << position << ".\n";
36
37        // get input from user
38        cout << "\n\nPlease enter an integer value (-1 to quit): ";
39        cin >> searchInt; // read an int from user
```

Fig. 19.4 | BinarySearch test program. (Part 1 of 2.)

```
40          cout << endl;
41       } // end while
42
43       return 0;
44  } // end main
```

```
26 31 33 38 47 49 49 67 73 74 82 89 90 91 95

Please enter an integer value (-1 to quit): 38

26 31 33 38 47 49 49 67 73 74 82 89 90 91 95
                *
26 31 33 38 47 49 49
          *
The integer 38 was found in position 3.


Please enter an integer value (-1 to quit): 91

26 31 33 38 47 49 49 67 73 74 82 89 90 91 95
                *
                        73 74 82 89 90 91 95
                                *
                                   90 91 95
                                      *
The integer 91 was found in position 13.


Please enter an integer value (-1 to quit): 25

26 31 33 38 47 49 49 67 73 74 82 89 90 91 95
                *
26 31 33 38 47 49 49
          *
26 31 33
    *
26
*
The integer 25 was not found.


Please enter an integer value (-1 to quit): -1
```

Fig. 19.4 | BinarySearch test program. (Part 2 of 2.)

Efficiency of Binary Search

In the worst-case scenario, searching a sorted vector of 1023 elements will take only 10 comparisons when using a binary search. Repeatedly dividing 1023 by 2 (because, after each comparison, we are able to eliminate from consideration half of the vector) and rounding down (because we also remove the middle element) yields the values 511, 255, 127, 63, 31, 15, 7, 3, 1 and 0. The number 1023 ($2^{10} - 1$) is divided by 2 only 10 times to get the value 0, which indicates that there are no more elements to test. Dividing by 2 is equivalent to one comparison in the binary search algorithm. Thus, a vector of 1,048,575 ($2^{20} - 1$) elements takes a maximum of 20 comparisons to find the key, and a vector of about one billion elements takes a maximum of 30 comparisons to find the key. This is a tremendous improvement in performance over the linear search. For a one-billion-element vector, this is a difference between an average of 500 million comparisons for the linear search and a maximum of only 30 comparisons for the binary search! The maximum number of comparisons needed for the binary search of any sorted vector is the exponent of the first power of 2 greater than the number of elements in the vector, which is represented as $\log_2 n$. All logarithms grow at roughly the same rate, so in Big O notation the base can be omitted. This results in a Big O of $O(\log n)$ for a binary search, which is also known as logarithmic runtime and pronounced "on the order of log n" or more simply "order log n."

19.3 Sorting Algorithms

Sorting data (i.e., placing the data into some particular order, such as ascending or descending) is one of the most important computing applications. A bank sorts all of its checks by account number so that it can prepare individual bank statements at the end of each month. Telephone companies sort their lists of accounts by last name and, further, by first name to make it easy to find phone numbers. Virtually every organization must sort some data, and often, massive amounts of it. Sorting data is an intriguing, computer-intensive problem that has attracted intense research efforts.

An important point to understand about sorting is that the end result—the sorted vector—will be the same no matter which algorithm you use to sort the vector. The choice of algorithm affects only the runtime and memory use of the program. In previous chapters, we introduced the selection sort and insertion sort—simple algorithms to implement, but inefficient. The next section examines the efficiency of these two algorithms using Big O notation. The last algorithm—merge sort, which we introduce in this chapter—is much faster but is more difficult to implement.

19.3.1 Efficiency of Selection Sort

Selection sort is an easy-to-implement, but inefficient, sorting algorithm. The first iteration of the algorithm selects the smallest element in the vector and swaps it with the first element. The second iteration selects the second-smallest element (which is the smallest element of the remaining elements) and swaps it with the second element. The algorithm continues until the last iteration selects the second-largest element and swaps it with the second-to-last element, leaving the largest element in the last index. After the ith iteration, the smallest i elements of the vector will be sorted into increasing order in the first i elements of the vector.

The selection sort algorithm iterates $n - 1$ times, each time swapping the smallest remaining element into its sorted position. Locating the smallest remaining element requires $n - 1$ comparisons during the first iteration, $n - 2$ during the second iteration, then $n - 3, \ldots, 3, 2, 1$. This results in a total of $n(n - 1)/2$ or $(n^2 - n)/2$ comparisons. In Big O notation, smaller terms drop out and constants are ignored, leaving a final Big O of $O(n^2)$.

19.3.2 Efficiency of Insertion Sort

Insertion sort is another simple, but inefficient, sorting algorithm. The first iteration of this algorithm takes the second element in the vector and, if it is less than the first element, swaps it with the first element. The second iteration looks at the third element and inserts it into the correct position with respect to the first two elements, so all three elements are in order. At the ith iteration of this algorithm, the first i elements in the original vector will be sorted.

Insertion sort iterates $n - 1$ times, inserting an element into the appropriate position in the elements sorted so far. For each iteration, determining where to insert the element can require comparing the element to each of the preceding elements in the vector. In the worst case, this will require $n - 1$ comparisons. Each individual repetition statement runs in $O(n)$ time. For determining Big O notation, nested statements mean that you must multiply the number of comparisons. For each iteration of an outer loop, there will be a certain number of iterations of the inner loop. In this algorithm, for each $O(n)$ iteration of the outer loop, there will be $O(n)$ iterations of the inner loop, resulting in a Big O of $O(n * n)$ or $O(n^2)$.

19.3.3 Merge Sort (A Recursive Implementation)

Merge sort is an efficient sorting algorithm but is conceptually more complex than selection sort and insertion sort. The merge sort algorithm sorts a vector by splitting it into two equal-sized subvectors, sorting each subvector and then merging them into one larger vector. With an odd number of elements, the algorithm creates the two subvectors such that one has one more element than the other.

The implementation of merge sort in this example is recursive. The base case is a vector with one element. A one-element vector is, of course, sorted, so merge sort immediately returns when it is called with a one-element vector. The recursion step splits a vector of two or more elements into two equal-sized subvectors, recursively sorts each subvector, then merges them into one larger, sorted vector. [Again, if there is an odd number of elements, one subvector is one element larger than the other.]

Suppose the algorithm has already merged smaller vectors to create sorted vectors A:

    4   10   34   56   77

and B:

    5   30   51   52   93

Merge sort combines these two vectors into one larger, sorted vector. The smallest value in A is 4 (located in the zeroth element of A). The smallest value in B is 5 (located in the zeroth element of B). In order to determine the smallest element in the larger vector, the algorithm compares 4 and 5. The value from A is smaller, so 4 becomes the value of the first element in the merged vector. The algorithm continues by comparing 10 (the value of the second element in A) to 5 (the value of the first element in B). The value from B is smaller, so 5 becomes the value of the second element in the larger vector. The algorithm continues by comparing 10 to 30, with 10 becoming the value of the third element in the vector, and so on.

Figure 19.5 defines class `MergeSort`, and lines 31–34 of Fig. 19.6 define the `sort` function. Line 33 calls function `sortSubVector` with 0 and `size - 1` as the arguments. These arguments correspond to the beginning and ending indices of the vector to be sorted, causing `sortSubVector` to operate on the entire vector. Function `sortSubVector` is defined in lines 37–61. Line 40 tests the base case. If the size of the vector is 1, the vector

```
 1   // Fig 19.5: MergeSort.h
 2   // Class that creates a vector filled with random integers.
 3   // Provides a function to sort the vector with merge sort.
 4   #include <vector>
 5   using std::vector;
 6
 7   // MergeSort class definition
 8   class MergeSort
 9   {
10   public:
11      MergeSort( int ); // constructor initializes vector
12      void sort(); // sort vector using merge sort
13      void displayElements() const; // display vector elements
14   private:
15      int size; // vector size
16      vector< int > data; // vector of ints
17      void sortSubVector( int, int ); // sort subvector
18      void merge( int, int, int, int ); // merge two sorted vectors
19      void displaySubVector( int, int ) const; // display subvector
20   }; // end class SelectionSort
```

Fig. 19.5 | MergeSort class definition.

```
 1   // Fig 19.6: MergeSort.cpp
 2   // Class MergeSort member-function definition.
 3   #include <iostream>
 4   using std::cout;
 5   using std::endl;
 6
 7   #include <vector>
 8   using std::vector;
 9
10   #include <cstdlib> // prototypes for functions srand and rand
11   using std::rand;
12   using std::srand;
13
14   #include <ctime> // prototype for function time
15   using std::time;
16
17   #include "MergeSort.h" // class MergeSort definition
18
19   // constructor fill vector with random integers
20   MergeSort::MergeSort( int vectorSize )
21   {
22      size = ( vectorSize > 0 ? vectorSize : 10 ); // validate vectorSize
23      srand( time( 0 ) ); // seed random number generator using current time
24
25      // fill vector with random ints in range 10-99
26      for ( int i = 0; i < size; i++ )
27         data.push_back( 10 + rand() % 90 );
28   } // end MergeSort constructor
```

Fig. 19.6 | MergeSort class member-function definition. (Part 1 of 3.)

```
29
30    // split vector, sort subvectors and merge subvectors into sorted vector
31    void MergeSort::sort()
32    {
33       sortSubVector( 0, size - 1 ); // recursively sort entire vector
34    } // end function sort
35
36    // recursive function to sort subvectors
37    void MergeSort::sortSubVector( int low, int high )
38    {
39       // test base case; size of vector equals 1
40       if ( ( high - low ) >= 1 ) // if not base case
41       {
42          int middle1 = ( low + high ) / 2; // calculate middle of vector
43          int middle2 = middle1 + 1; // calculate next element over
44
45          // output split step
46          cout << "split:   ";
47          displaySubVector( low, high );
48          cout << endl << "           ";
49          displaySubVector( low, middle1 );
50          cout << endl << "           ";
51          displaySubVector( middle2, high );
52          cout << endl << endl;
53
54          // split vector in half; sort each half (recursive calls)
55          sortSubVector( low, middle1 ); // first half of vector
56          sortSubVector( middle2, high ); // second half of vector
57
58          // merge two sorted vectors after split calls return
59          merge( low, middle1, middle2, high );
60       } // end if
61    } // end function sortSubVector
62
63    // merge two sorted subvectors into one sorted subvector
64    void MergeSort::merge( int left, int middle1, int middle2, int right )
65    {
66       int leftIndex = left; // index into left subvector
67       int rightIndex = middle2; // index into right subvector
68       int combinedIndex = left; // index into temporary working vector
69       vector< int > combined( size ); // working vector
70
71       // output two subvectors before merging
72       cout << "merge:   ";
73       displaySubVector( left, middle1 );
74       cout << endl << "           ";
75       displaySubVector( middle2, right );
76       cout << endl;
77
78       // merge vectors until reaching end of either
79       while ( leftIndex <= middle1 && rightIndex <= right )
80       {
```

Fig. 19.6 | MergeSort class member-function definition. (Part 2 of 3.)

```
81          // place smaller of two current elements into result
82          // and move to next space in vector
83          if ( data[ leftIndex ] <= data[ rightIndex ] )
84              combined[ combinedIndex++ ] = data[ leftIndex++ ];
85          else
86              combined[ combinedIndex++ ] = data[ rightIndex++ ];
87      } // end while
88
89      if ( leftIndex == middle2 ) // if at end of left vector
90      {
91          while ( rightIndex <= right ) // copy in rest of right vector
92              combined[ combinedIndex++ ] = data[ rightIndex++ ];
93      } // end if
94      else // at end of right vector
95      {
96          while ( leftIndex <= middle1 ) // copy in rest of left vector
97              combined[ combinedIndex++ ] = data[ leftIndex++ ];
98      } // end else
99
100         // copy values back into original vector
101         for ( int i = left; i <= right; i++ )
102             data[ i ] = combined[ i ];
103
104         // output merged vector
105         cout << "              ";
106         displaySubVector( left, right );
107         cout << endl << endl;
108     } // end function merge
109
110     // display elements in vector
111     void MergeSort::displayElements() const
112     {
113         displaySubVector( 0, size - 1 );
114     } // end function displayElements
115
116     // display certain values in vector
117     void MergeSort::displaySubVector( int low, int high ) const
118     {
119         // output spaces for alignment
120         for ( int i = 0; i < low; i++ )
121             cout << "   ";
122
123         // output elements left in vector
124         for ( int i = low; i <= high; i++ )
125             cout << " " << data[ i ];
126     } // end function displaySubVector
```

Fig. 19.6 | MergeSort class member-function definition. (Part 3 of 3.)

is already sorted, so the function simply returns immediately. If the size of the vector is greater than 1, the function splits the vector in two, recursively calls function sortSub-Vector to sort the two subvectors, then merges them. Line 55 recursively calls function sortSubVector on the first half of the vector, and line 56 recursively calls function sort-SubVector on the second half of the vector. When these two function calls return, each half of the vector has been sorted. Line 59 calls function merge (lines 64–108) on the two halves of the vector to combine the two sorted vectors into one larger sorted vector.

Lines 79–87 in function merge loop until the program reaches the end of either subvector. Line 83 tests which element at the beginning of the vectors is smaller. If the element in the left vector is smaller, line 84 places it in position in the combined vector. If the element in the right vector is smaller, line 86 places it in position in the combined vector. When the while loop has completed (line 87), one entire subvector is placed in the combined vector, but the other subvector still contains data. Line 89 tests whether the left vector has reached the end. If so, lines 91–92 fill the combined vector with the elements of the right vector. If the left vector has not reached the end, then the right vector must have reached the end, and lines 96–97 fill the combined vector with the elements of the left vector. Finally, lines 101–102 copy the combined vector into the original vector. Figure 19.7 creates and uses a MergeSort object. The output from this program displays the splits and merges performed by merge sort, showing the progress of the sort at each step of the algorithm.

Efficiency of Merge Sort

Merge sort is a far more efficient algorithm than either insertion sort or selection sort (although that may be difficult to believe when looking at the rather busy output in Fig. 19.7). Consider the first (nonrecursive) call to function sortSubVector. This results in two recursive calls to function sortSubVector with subvectors each approximately half the size of the original vector, and a single call to function merge. This call to function merge requires, at worst, $n - 1$ comparisons to fill the original vector, which is $O(n)$.

```
 1   // Fig 19.7: Fig19_07.cpp
 2   // MergeSort test program.
 3   #include <iostream>
 4   using std::cout;
 5   using std::endl;
 6
 7   #include "MergeSort.h" // class MergeSort definition
 8
 9   int main()
10   {
11      // create object to perform merge sort
12      MergeSort sortVector( 10 );
13
14      cout << "Unsorted vector:" << endl;
15      sortVector.displayElements(); // print unsorted vector
16      cout << endl << endl;
17
18      sortVector.sort(); // sort vector
19
20      cout << "Sorted vector:" << endl;
21      sortVector.displayElements(); // print sorted vector
22      cout << endl;
23      return 0;
24   } // end main
```

Fig. 19.7 | MergeSort test program. (Part 1 of 3.)

```
Unsorted vector:
 30 47 22 67 79 18 60 78 26 54

split:      30 47 22 67 79 18 60 78 26 54
            30 47 22 67 79
                           18 60 78 26 54

split:      30 47 22 67 79
            30 47 22
                    67 79

split:      30 47 22
            30 47
                  22

split:      30 47
            30
               47

merge:      30
               47
            30 47

merge:      30 47
                  22
            22 30 47

split:                 67 79
                       67
                          79

merge:                 67
                          79
                       67 79

merge:      22 30 47
                       67 79
            22 30 47 67 79

split:                     18 60 78 26 54
                           18 60 78
                                    26 54

split:                     18 60 78
                           18 60
                                 78

split:                     18 60
                           18
                              60

merge:                     18
                              60
                           18 60
```

(continued …)

Fig. 19.7 | MergeSort test program. (Part 2 of 3.)

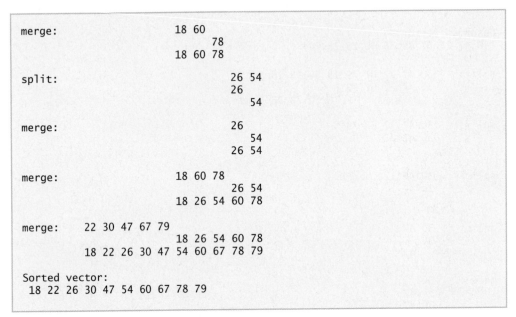

```
merge:                    18 60
                                78
                          18 60 78

split:                          26 54
                                26
                                     54

merge:                          26
                                     54
                                26 54

merge:                    18 60 78
                                     26 54
                          18 26 54 60 78

merge:        22 30 47 67 79
                          18 26 54 60 78
              18 22 26 30 47 54 60 67 78 79

Sorted vector:
 18 22 26 30 47 54 60 67 78 79
```

Fig. 19.7 | MergeSort test program. (Part 3 of 3.)

(Recall that each vector element is chosen by comparing one element from each of the sub-vectors.) The two calls to function sortSubVector result in four more recursive calls to function sortSubVector—each with a subvector approximately one-quarter the size of the original vector—and two calls to function merge. These two calls to function merge each require, at worst, $n/2 - 1$ comparisons, for a total number of comparisons of $O(n)$. This process continues, each call to sortSubVector generating two additional calls to sortSubVector and a call to merge, until the algorithm has split the vector into one-element subvectors. At each level, $O(n)$ comparisons are required to merge the subvectors. Each level splits the size of the vectors in half, so doubling the size of the vector requires one more level. Quadrupling the size of the vector requires two more levels. This pattern is logarithmic and results in $\log_2 n$ levels. This results in a total efficiency of $O(n \log n)$. Figure 19.8 summarizes many of the searching and sorting algorithms covered in this book and lists the Big O for each of them. Figure 19.9 lists the Big O values we have covered in this chapter along with a number of values for n to highlight the differences in the growth rates.

Algorithm	Location	Big O
Searching Algorithms		
Linear search	Section 7.7	$O(n)$
Binary search	Section 19.2.2	$O(\log n)$
Recursive linear search	Exercise 19.8	$O(n)$
Recursive binary search	Exercise 19.9	$O(\log n)$

Fig. 19.8 | Searching and sorting algorithms with Big O values. (Part 1 of 2.)

Algorithm	Location	Big O
Sorting Algorithms		
Insertion sort	Section 7.8	$O(n^2)$
Selection sort	Section 8.6	$O(n^2)$
Merge sort	Section 19.3.3	$O(n \log n)$
Bubble sort	Exercises 16.3 and 16.4	$O(n^2)$
Quicksort	Exercise 19.10	Worst case: $O(n^2)$ Average case: $O(n \log n)$

Fig. 19.8 | Searching and sorting algorithms with Big O values. (Part 2 of 2.)

n	Approximate decimal value	$O(\log n)$	$O(n)$	$O(n \log n)$	$O(n^2)$
2^{10}	1000	10	2^{10}	$10 \cdot 2^{10}$	2^{20}
2^{20}	1,000,000	20	2^{20}	$20 \cdot 2^{20}$	2^{40}
2^{30}	1,000,000,000	30	2^{30}	$30 \cdot 2^{30}$	2^{60}

Fig. 19.9 | Approximate number of comparisons for common Big O notations.

19.4 Wrap-Up

This chapter discussed searching and sorting data. We discussed the binary search algorithm, which is faster but more complex than linear search (Section 7.7). The binary search algorithm will work only on a sorted array, but each iteration of binary search eliminates from consideration half of the elements in the array. You also learned the merge sort algorithm, which is more efficient than either insertion sort (Section 7.8) or selection sort (Section 8.6). We also introduced Big O notation, which helps you express the efficiency of an algorithm. Big O notation measures the worst-case runtime for an algorithm. The Big O value is useful for comparing algorithms to choose the most efficient one. In the next chapter, you'll learn about dynamic data structures that can grow or shrink at execution time.

Summary

Section 19.1 Introduction
- Searching data involves determining whether a search key is present in the data and, if so, finding its location.
- Sorting involves arranging data into order.
- One way to describe the efficiency of an algorithm is with Big O notation (*O*), which indicates how hard an algorithm may have to work to solve a problem.

Section 19.2 Searching Algorithms
- A major difference among searching algorithms is the amount of effort they require in order to return a result.

Section 19.2.1 Efficiency of Linear Search
- For searching and sorting algorithms, Big O describes how the amount of effort of a particular algorithm varies depending on how many elements are in the data.
- An algorithm that is $O(1)$ is said to have a constant runtime. This does not mean that the algorithm requires only one comparison—it just means that the number of comparisons does not grow as the size of the vector increases.
- An $O(n)$ algorithm is referred to as having a linear runtime.
- Big O highlights dominant factors and ignores terms that are unimportant with high values of n.
- Big O notation represents the growth rate of algorithm runtimes, so constants are ignored.
- The linear search algorithm runs in $O(n)$ time.
- In the worst case for linear search every element must be checked to determine whether the search element exists. This occurs if the search key is the last element in the vector or is not present.

Section 19.2.2 Binary Search
- The binary search algorithm is more efficient than the linear search algorithm, but it requires that the vector first be sorted. This is worthwhile only when the vector, once sorted, will be searched a great many times—or when the searching application has stringent performance requirements.
- The first iteration of binary search tests the middle element in the vector. If this is the search key, the algorithm returns its location. If the search key is less than the middle element, binary search continues with the first half of the vector. If the search key is greater than the middle element, binary search continues with the second half of the vector. Each iteration of binary search tests the middle value of the remaining vector and, if the element is not found, eliminates from consideration half of the remaining elements.
- Binary search is more efficient than linear search, because with each comparison it eliminates from consideration half of the elements in the vector.
- Binary search runs in $O(\log n)$ time because each step removes half of the remaining elements from consideration.
- If the size of the vector is doubled, binary search requires only one extra comparison to complete successfully.

Section 19.3.1 Efficiency of Selection Sort
- Selection sort is a simple, but inefficient, sorting algorithm.
- The first iteration of selection sort selects the smallest element in the vector and swaps it with the first element. The second iteration of selection sort selects the second-smallest element (which is the smallest remaining element) and swaps it with the second element. Selection sort continues until the last iteration selects the second-largest element and swaps it with the second-to-last index, leaving the largest element in the last index. At the ith iteration of selection sort, the smallest i elements of the whole vector are sorted into the first i elements.

Section 19.3.2 Efficiency of Insertion Sort
- The selection sort algorithm runs in $O(n^2)$ time.
- The first iteration of insertion sort takes the second element value in the vector and, if it is less than the first element value, swaps it with the first element value. The second iteration of insertion sort looks at the third element value and inserts it in the correct position with respect to the

first two element values. After the ith iteration of insertion sort, the first i element values in the original vector are sorted. Only $n - 1$ iterations are required.

- The insertion sort algorithm runs in $O(n^2)$ time.

Section 19.3.3 Merge Sort (A Recursive Implementation)

- Merge sort is a sorting algorithm that is faster, but more complex to implement, than selection sort and insertion sort.

- The merge sort algorithm sorts a vector by splitting the vector into two equal-sized subvectors, sorting each subvector and merging the subvectors into one larger vector.

- Merge sort's base case is a vector with one element. A one-element vector is already sorted, so merge sort immediately returns when it is called with a one-element vector. The merge part of merge sort takes two sorted vectors (these could be one-element vectors) and combines them into one larger sorted vector.

- Merge sort performs the merge by looking at the first element in each vector, which is also the smallest element in the vector. Merge sort takes the smallest of these and places it in the first element of the larger, sorted vector. If there are still elements in the subvector, merge sort looks at the second element in that subvector (which is now the smallest element remaining) and compares it to the first element in the other subvector. Merge sort continues this process until the larger vector is filled.

- In the worst case, the first call to merge sort has to make $O(n)$ comparisons to fill the n slots in the final vector.

- The merging portion of the merge sort algorithm is performed on two subvectors, each of approximately size $n/2$. Creating each of these subvectors requires $n/2 - 1$ comparisons for each subvector, or $O(n)$ comparisons total. This pattern continues, as each level works on twice as many vectors, but each is half the size of the previous vector.

- Similar to binary search, this halving results in $\log n$ levels, each level requiring $O(n)$ comparisons, for a total efficiency of $O(n \log n)$.

Terminology

Big O notation	$O(\log n)$
binary search	$O(n \log n)$
bubble sort (exercise)	$O(n)$
constant runtime	$O(n^2)$
efficiency of binary search	order 1
efficiency of insertion sort	order $\log n$
efficiency of linear search	order n
efficiency of merge sort	order n-squared
efficiency of selection sort	quadratic runtime
efficient searching algorithms	quick sort
efficient sorting algorithms	random-access iterator
inefficient searching algorithms	search key
inefficient sorting algorithms	searching data
linear runtime	selection sort
linear search	sort key
logarithmic runtime	sort standard library function
merge sort (recursive implementation)	sorting data
merge two vectors	split the vector in merge sort
$O(1)$	worst-case runtime for an algorithm

Self-Review Exercises

19.1 Fill in the blanks in each of the following statements:
a) A selection sort application would take approximately _____ times as long to run on a 128-element vector as on a 32-element vector.
b) The efficiency of merge sort is _____.

19.2 What key aspect of both the binary search and the merge sort accounts for the logarithmic portion of their respective Big Os?

19.3 In what sense is the insertion sort superior to the merge sort? In what sense is the merge sort superior to the insertion sort?

19.4 In the text, we say that after the merge sort splits the vector into two subvectors, it then sorts these two subvectors and merges them. Why might someone be puzzled by our statement that "it then sorts these two subvectors"?

Answers to Self-Review Exercises

19.1 a) 16, because an $O(n^2)$ algorithm takes 16 times as long to sort four times as much information. b) $O(n \log n)$.

19.2 Both of these algorithms incorporate "halving"—somehow reducing something by half. The binary search eliminates from consideration half of the vector after each comparison. The merge sort splits the vector in half each time it is called.

19.3 The insertion sort is easier to understand and to implement than the merge sort. The merge sort is far more efficient ($O(n \log n)$) than the insertion sort ($O(n^2)$).

19.4 In a sense, it does not really sort these two subvectors. It simply keeps splitting the original vector in half until it provides a one-element subvector, which is, of course, sorted. It then builds up the original two subvectors by merging these one-element vectors to form larger subvectors, which are then merged, and so on.

Exercises

[*Note:* Most of the exercises shown here are duplicates of exercises from Chapters 7–8. We include the exercises again here as a convenience for readers studying searching and sorting in this chapter.]

19.5 (*Bubble Sort*) Implement bubble sort—another simple yet inefficient sorting technique. It is called bubble sort or sinking sort because smaller values gradually "bubble" their way to the top of the vector (i.e., toward the first element) like air bubbles rising in water, while the larger values sink to the bottom (end) of the vector. The technique uses nested loops to make several passes through the vector. Each pass compares successive pairs of elements. If a pair is in increasing order (or the values are equal), the bubble sort leaves the values as they are. If a pair is in decreasing order, the bubble sort swaps their values in the vector.

The first pass compares the first two element values of the vector and swaps them if necessary. It then compares the second and third element values in the vector. The end of this pass compares the last two element values in the vector and swaps them if necessary. After one pass, the largest value will be in the last element. After two passes, the largest two values will be in the last two elements. Explain why bubble sort is an $O(n^2)$ algorithm.

19.6 (*Enhanced Bubble Sort*) Make the following simple modifications to improve the performance of the bubble sort you developed in Exercise 19.5:
a) After the first pass, the largest value is guaranteed to be in the highest-numbered element of the vector; after the second pass, the two highest values are "in place"; and so on. Instead of making nine comparisons (for a 10-element vector) on every pass, modify

the bubble sort to make only the eight necessary comparisons on the second pass, seven on the third pass, and so on.

b) The data in the vector may already be in the proper order or near-proper order, so why make nine passes (of a 10-element vector) if fewer will suffice? Modify the sort to check at the end of each pass whether any swaps have been made. If none have been made, the data must already be in the proper order, so the program should terminate. If swaps have been made, at least one more pass is needed.

19.7 (*Bucket Sort*) A bucket sort begins with a one-dimensional vector of positive integers to be sorted and a two-dimensional vector of integers with rows indexed from 0 to 9 and columns indexed from 0 to $n - 1$, where n is the number of values to be sorted. Each row of the two-dimensional vector is referred to as a *bucket*. Write a class named BucketSort containing a function called sort that operates as follows:

a) Place each value of the one-dimensional vector into a row of the bucket vector, based on the value's "ones" (rightmost) digit. For example, 97 is placed in row 7, 3 is placed in row 3 and 100 is placed in row 0. This procedure is called a *distribution pass*.

b) Loop through the bucket vector row by row, and copy the values back to the original vector. This procedure is called a *gathering pass*. The new order of the preceding values in the one-dimensional vector is 100, 3 and 97.

c) Repeat this process for each subsequent digit position (tens, hundreds, thousands, etc.).

   On the second (tens digit) pass, 100 is placed in row 0, 3 is placed in row 0 (because 3 has no tens digit) and 97 is placed in row 9. After the gathering pass, the order of the values in the one-dimensional vector is 100, 3 and 97. On the third (hundreds digit) pass, 100 is placed in row 1, 3 is placed in row 0 and 97 is placed in row 0 (after the 3). After this last gathering pass, the original vector is in sorted order.

   Note that the two-dimensional vector of buckets is 10 times the length of the integer vector being sorted. This sorting technique provides better performance than a bubble sort, but requires much more memory—the bubble sort requires space for only one additional element of data. This comparison is an example of the space–time trade-off: The bucket sort uses more memory than the bubble sort, but performs better. This version of the bucket sort requires copying all the data back to the original vector on each pass. Another possibility is to create a second two-dimensional bucket vector and repeatedly swap the data between the two bucket vectors.

19.8 (*Recursive Linear Search*) Modify Exercise 7.33 to use recursive function recursiveLinearSearch to perform a linear search of the vector. The function should receive the search key and starting index as arguments. If the search key is found, return its index in the vector; otherwise, return –1. Each call to the recursive function should check one element value in the vector.

19.9 (*Recursive Binary Search*) Modify Fig. 19.3 to use recursive function recursiveBinarySearch to perform a binary search of the vector. The function should receive the search key, starting index and ending index as arguments. If the search key is found, return its index in the vector. If the search key is not found, return –1.

19.10 (*Quicksort*) The recursive sorting technique called quicksort uses the following basic algorithm for a one-dimensional vector of values:

a) *Partitioning Step*: Take the first element of the unsorted vector and determine its final location in the sorted vector (i.e., all values to the left of the element in the vector are less than the element's value, and all values to the right of the element in the vector are greater than the element's value—we show how to do this below). We now have one value in its proper location and two unsorted subvectors.

b) *Recursion Step*: Perform the *Partitioning Step* on each unsorted subvector. Each time the *Partitioning Step* is performed on a subvector, another value is placed in its final location of the sorted vector, and two unsorted subvectors are created. When a subvector consists of one element, that element's value is in its final location (because a one-element vector is already sorted).

The basic algorithm seems simple enough, but how do we determine the final position of the first element value of each subvector? As an example, consider the following set of values (the value in bold is for the partitioning element—it will be placed in its final location in the sorted vector):

37   2   6   4   89   8   10   12   68   45

Starting from the rightmost element of the vector, compare each element value with 37 until an element value less than 37 is found; then swap 37 and that element's value. The first element value less than 37 is 12, so 37 and 12 are swapped. The new vector is

12   2   6   4   89   8   10   **37**   68   45

Element value 12 is in italics to indicate that it was just swapped with 37.

Starting from the left of the vector, but beginning with the element value after 12, compare each element value with 37 until an element value greater than 37 is found—then swap 37 and that element value. The first element value greater than 37 is 89, so 37 and 89 are swapped. The new vector is

12   2   6   4   **37**   8   10   *89*   68   45

Starting from the right, but beginning with the element value before 89, compare each element value with 37 until an element value less than 37 is found—then swap 37 and that element value. The first element value less than 37 is 10, so 37 and 10 are swapped. The new vector is

12   2   6   4   *10*   8   **37**   89   68   45

Starting from the left, but beginning with the element value after 10, compare each element value with 37 until an element value greater than 37 is found—then swap 37 and that element value. There are no more element values greater than 37, so when we compare 37 with itself, we know that 37 has been placed in its final location of the sorted vector. Every value to the left of 37 is smaller than it, and every value to the right of 37 is larger than it.

Once the partition has been applied on the previous vector, there are two unsorted subvectors. The subvector with values less than 37 contains 12, 2, 6, 4, 10 and 8. The subvector with values greater than 37 contains 89, 68 and 45. The sort continues recursively, with both subvectors being partitioned in the same manner as the original vector.

Based on the preceding discussion, write recursive function `quickSortHelper` to sort a one-dimensional integer vector. The function should receive as arguments a starting index and an ending index on the original vector being sorted.

20

Data Structures

OBJECTIVES

In this chapter you'll learn:

- To form linked data structures using pointers, self-referential classes and recursion.

- To create and manipulate dynamic data structures such as linked lists, queues, stacks and binary trees.

- To use binary search trees for high-speed searching and sorting.

- To understand various important applications of linked data structures.

- To understand how to create reusable data structures with class templates, inheritance and composition.

20.1 Introduction

We've studied fixed-size data structures such as one-dimensional arrays and two-dimensional arrays. This chapter introduces dynamic data structures that grow and shrink during execution. Linked lists are collections of data items logically "lined up in a row"—insertions and removals are made anywhere in a linked list. Stacks are important in compilers and operating systems: Insertions and removals are made only at one end of a stack—its top. Queues represent waiting lines; insertions are made at the back (also referred to as the tail) of a queue and removals are made from the front (also referred to as the head) of a queue. Binary trees facilitate high-speed searching and sorting of data, efficient elimination of duplicate data items, representation of file-system directories and compilation of expressions into machine language. These data structures have many other interesting applications.

We discuss several popular and important data structures and implement programs that create and manipulate them. We use classes, class templates, inheritance and composition to create and package these data structures for reusability and maintainability.

Studying this chapter is solid preparation for Chapter 22, Standard Template Library (STL). The STL is a major portion of the C++ Standard Library. The STL provides containers, iterators for traversing those containers and algorithms for processing the elements of those containers. You'll see that the STL has taken each of the data structures we discuss in this chapter and packaged them into templatized classes. The STL code is carefully written to be portable, efficient and extensible. Once you understand the principles and construction of data structures as presented in this chapter, you'll be able to make the best use of the prepackaged data structures, iterators and algorithms in the STL, a world-class set of reusable components.

The chapter examples are practical programs that you'll be able to use in more advanced courses and in industry applications. The programs employ extensive pointer manipulation. The exercises include a rich collection of useful applications.

We encourage you to attempt the major project described in the special section Building Your Own Compiler. You have been using a C++ compiler to translate your programs to machine language so that you could execute these programs on your computer. In this project, you'll actually build your own compiler. It will read a file of statements written in a simple, yet powerful, high-level language similar to early versions of the popular language BASIC. Your compiler will translate these statements into a file of Simpletron Machine Language (SML) instructions—SML is the language you learned in the

Chapter 8 special section, Building Your Own Computer. Your Simpletron Simulator program will then execute the SML program produced by your compiler! Implementing this project using an object-oriented approach will give you a wonderful opportunity to exercise most of what you have learned in this book. The special section carefully walks you through the specifications of the high-level language and describes the algorithms you'll need to convert each type of high-level language statement into machine-language instructions. If you enjoy being challenged, you might attempt the many enhancements to both the compiler and the Simpletron Simulator suggested in this chapter's exercises.

20.2 Self-Referential Classes

A self-referential class contains a pointer member that points to a class object of the same class type. For example, the definition

```
class Node
{
public:
    Node( int ); // constructor
    void setData( int ); // set data member
    int getData() const; // get data member
    void setNextPtr( Node * ); // set pointer to next Node
    Node *getNextPtr() const; // get pointer to next Node
private:
    int data; // data stored in this Node
    Node *nextPtr; // pointer to another object of same type
}; // end class Node
```

defines a type, Node. Type Node has two private data members—integer member data and pointer member nextPtr. Member nextPtr points to an object of type Node—another object of the same type as the one being declared here, hence the term "self-referential class." Member nextPtr is referred to as a link—i.e., nextPtr can "tie" an object of type Node to another object of the same type. Type Node also has five member functions—a constructor that receives an integer to initialize member data, a setData function to set the value of member data, a getData function to return the value of member data, a setNextPtr function to set the value of member nextPtr and a getNextPtr function to return the value of member nextPtr.

Self-referential class objects can be linked together to form useful data structures such as lists, queues, stacks and trees. Figure 20.1 illustrates two self-referential class objects linked together to form a list. Note that a slash—representing a null (0) pointer—is placed in the link member of the second self-referential class object to indicate that the link does not point to another object. The slash is only for illustration purposes; it does not correspond to the backslash character in C++. A null pointer normally indicates the end of a data structure just as the null character ('\0') indicates the end of a string.

Fig. 20.1 | Two self-referential class objects linked together.

Common Programming Error 20.1

Not setting the link in the last node of a linked data structure to null (0) is a (possibly fatal) logic error.

20.3 Dynamic Memory Allocation and Data Structures

Creating and maintaining dynamic data structures requires dynamic memory allocation, which enables a program to obtain more memory at execution time to hold new nodes. When that memory is no longer needed by the program, the memory can be released so that it can be reused to allocate other objects in the future. The limit for dynamic memory allocation can be as large as the amount of available physical memory in the computer or the amount of available virtual memory in a virtual memory system. Often, the limits are much smaller, because available memory must be shared among many programs.

The new operator takes as an argument the type of the object being dynamically allocated and returns a pointer to an object of that type. For example, the statement

```
Node *newPtr = new Node( 10 ); // create Node with data 10
```

allocates `sizeof( Node )` bytes, runs the Node constructor and assigns the new Node's address to newPtr. If no memory is available, new throws a bad_alloc exception. The value 10 is passed to the Node constructor which initializes the Node's data member to 10.

The delete operator runs the Node destructor and deallocates memory allocated with new—the memory is returned to the system so that the memory can be reallocated in the future. To free memory dynamically allocated by the preceding new, use the statement

```
delete newPtr;
```

Note that newPtr itself is not deleted; rather the space newPtr points to is deleted. If pointer newPtr has the null pointer value 0, the preceding statement has no effect. It is not an error to delete a null pointer.

The following sections discuss lists, stacks, queues and trees. The data structures presented in this chapter are created and maintained with dynamic memory allocation, self-referential classes, class templates and function templates.

20.4 Linked Lists

A linked list is a linear collection of self-referential class objects, called nodes, connected by pointer links—hence, the term "linked" list. A linked list is accessed via a pointer to the list's first node. Each subsequent node is accessed via the link-pointer member stored in the previous node. By convention, the link pointer in the last node of a list is set to null (0) to mark the end of the list. Data is stored in a linked list dynamically—each node is created as necessary. A node can contain data of any type, including objects of other classes. If nodes contain base-class pointers to base-class and derived-class objects related by inheritance, we can have a linked list of such nodes and process them polymorphically using virtual function calls. Stacks and queues are also linear data structures and, as we'll see, can be viewed as constrained versions of linked lists. Trees are nonlinear data structures.

Lists of data can be stored in arrays, but linked lists provide several advantages. A linked list is appropriate when the number of data elements to be represented at one time is unpredictable. Linked lists are dynamic, so the length of a list can increase or decrease as necessary. The size of a "conventional" C++ array, however, cannot be altered, because the array size is fixed at compile time. "Conventional" arrays can become full. Linked lists become full only when the system has insufficient memory to satisfy dynamic storage allocation requests.

Performance Tip 20.1

An array can be declared to contain more elements than the number of items expected, but this can waste memory. Linked lists can provide better memory utilization in these situations. Linked lists allow the program to adapt at runtime. Note that class template vector *(introduced in Section 7.11) implements a dynamically resizable array-based data structure.*

Linked lists can be maintained in sorted order by inserting each new element at the proper point in the list. Existing list elements do not need to be moved.

Performance Tip 20.2

Insertion and deletion in a sorted array can be time consuming—all the elements following the inserted or deleted element must be shifted appropriately. A linked list allows efficient insertion operations anywhere in the list.

Performance Tip 20.3

The elements of an array are stored contiguously in memory. This allows immediate access to any array element, because the address of any element can be calculated directly based on its position relative to the beginning of the array. Linked lists do not afford such immediate "direct access" to their elements. So accessing individual elements in a linked list can be considerably more expensive than accessing individual elements in an array. The selection of a data structure is typically based on the performance of specific operations used by a program and the order in which the data items are maintained in the data structure. For example, it is typically more efficient to insert an item in a sorted linked list than a sorted array.

Linked-list nodes are normally not stored contiguously in memory. Logically, however, the nodes of a linked list appear to be contiguous. Figure 20.2 illustrates a linked list with several nodes.

Performance Tip 20.4

Using dynamic memory allocation (instead of fixed-size arrays) for data structures that grow and shrink at execution time can save memory. Keep in mind, however, that pointers occupy space and that dynamic memory allocation incurs the overhead of function calls.

Fig. 20.2 | A graphical representation of a list.

Linked List Implementation

The program of Figs. 20.3–20.5 uses a List class template (see Chapter 14 for information on class templates) to manipulate a list of integer values and a list of floating-point values. The driver program (Fig. 20.5) provides five options: 1) Insert a value at the beginning of the list, 2) insert a value at the end of the list, 3) delete a value from the beginning of the list, 4) delete a value from the end of the list and 5) end the list processing. A detailed discussion of the program follows. Exercise 20.20 asks you to implement a recursive function that prints a linked list backward, and Exercise 20.21 asks you to implement a recursive function that searches a linked list for a particular data item.

The program uses class templates ListNode (Fig. 20.3) and List (Fig. 20.4). Encapsulated in each List object is a linked list of ListNode objects. Class template ListNode (Fig. 20.3) contains private members data and nextPtr (lines 19–20), a constructor to initialize these members and function getData to return the data in a node. Member data stores a value of type NODETYPE, the type parameter passed to the class template. Member nextPtr stores a pointer to the next ListNode object in the linked list. Note that line 13 of the ListNode class template definition declares class List< NODETYPE > as a friend. This makes all member functions of a given specialization of class template List friends of the corresponding specialization of class template ListNode, so they can access the private members of ListNode objects of that type. Because the ListNode template parameter

```
 1    // Fig. 20.3: ListNode.h
 2    // Template ListNode class definition.
 3    #ifndef LISTNODE_H
 4    #define LISTNODE_H
 5
 6    // forward declaration of class List required to announce that class
 7    // List exists so it can be used in the friend declaration at line 13
 8    template< typename NODETYPE > class List;
 9
10    template< typename NODETYPE>
11    class ListNode
12    {
13       friend class List< NODETYPE >; // make List a friend
14
15    public:
16       ListNode( const NODETYPE & ); // constructor
17       NODETYPE getData() const; // return data in node
18    private:
19       NODETYPE data; // data
20       ListNode< NODETYPE > *nextPtr; // next node in list
21    }; // end class ListNode
22
23    // constructor
24    template< typename NODETYPE>
25    ListNode< NODETYPE >::ListNode( const NODETYPE &info )
26       : data( info ), nextPtr( 0 )
27    {
28       // empty body
29    } // end ListNode constructor
```

Fig. 20.3 | ListNode class-template definition. (Part 1 of 2.)

```
30
31  // return copy of data in node
32  template< typename NODETYPE >
33  NODETYPE ListNode< NODETYPE >::getData() const
34  {
35      return data;
36  } // end function getData
37
38  #endif
```

Fig. 20.3 | ListNode class-template definition. (Part 2 of 2.)

```
1   // Fig. 20.4: List.h
2   // Template List class definition.
3   #ifndef LIST_H
4   #define LIST_H
5
6   #include <iostream>
7   using std::cout;
8
9   #include "listnode.h" // ListNode class definition
10
11  template< typename NODETYPE >
12  class List
13  {
14  public:
15      List(); // constructor
16      ~List(); // destructor
17      void insertAtFront( const NODETYPE & );
18      void insertAtBack( const NODETYPE & );
19      bool removeFromFront( NODETYPE & );
20      bool removeFromBack( NODETYPE & );
21      bool isEmpty() const;
22      void print() const;
23  private:
24      ListNode< NODETYPE > *firstPtr; // pointer to first node
25      ListNode< NODETYPE > *lastPtr; // pointer to last node
26
27      // utility function to allocate new node
28      ListNode< NODETYPE > *getNewNode( const NODETYPE & );
29  }; // end class List
30
31  // default constructor
32  template< typename NODETYPE >
33  List< NODETYPE >::List()
34      : firstPtr( 0 ), lastPtr( 0 )
35  {
36      // empty body
37  } // end List constructor
38
```

Fig. 20.4 | List class-template definition. (Part 1 of 4.)

```
39   // destructor
40   template< typename NODETYPE >
41   List< NODETYPE >::~List()
42   {
43      if ( !isEmpty() ) // List is not empty
44      {
45         cout << "Destroying nodes ...\n";
46
47         ListNode< NODETYPE > *currentPtr = firstPtr;
48         ListNode< NODETYPE > *tempPtr;
49
50         while ( currentPtr != 0 ) // delete remaining nodes
51         {
52            tempPtr = currentPtr;
53            cout << tempPtr->data << '\n';
54            currentPtr = currentPtr->nextPtr;
55            delete tempPtr;
56         } // end while
57      } // end if
58
59      cout << "All nodes destroyed\n\n";
60   } // end List destructor
61
62   // insert node at front of list
63   template< typename NODETYPE >
64   void List< NODETYPE >::insertAtFront( const NODETYPE &value )
65   {
66      ListNode< NODETYPE > *newPtr = getNewNode( value ); // new node
67
68      if ( isEmpty() ) // List is empty
69         firstPtr = lastPtr = newPtr; // new list has only one node
70      else // List is not empty
71      {
72         newPtr->nextPtr = firstPtr; // point new node to previous 1st node
73         firstPtr = newPtr; // aim firstPtr at new node
74      } // end else
75   } // end function insertAtFront
76
77   // insert node at back of list
78   template< typename NODETYPE >
79   void List< NODETYPE >::insertAtBack( const NODETYPE &value )
80   {
81      ListNode< NODETYPE > *newPtr = getNewNode( value ); // new node
82
83      if ( isEmpty() ) // List is empty
84         firstPtr = lastPtr = newPtr; // new list has only one node
85      else // List is not empty
86      {
87         lastPtr->nextPtr = newPtr; // update previous last node
88         lastPtr = newPtr; // new last node
89      } // end else
90   } // end function insertAtBack
91
```

Fig. 20.4 | List class-template definition. (Part 2 of 4.)

```
 92   // delete node from front of list
 93   template< typename NODETYPE >
 94   bool List< NODETYPE >::removeFromFront( NODETYPE &value )
 95   {
 96      if ( isEmpty() ) // List is empty
 97         return false; // delete unsuccessful
 98      else
 99      {
100         ListNode< NODETYPE > *tempPtr = firstPtr; // hold tempPtr to delete
101
102         if ( firstPtr == lastPtr )
103            firstPtr = lastPtr = 0; // no nodes remain after removal
104         else
105            firstPtr = firstPtr->nextPtr; // point to previous 2nd node
106
107         value = tempPtr->data; // return data being removed
108         delete tempPtr; // reclaim previous front node
109         return true; // delete successful
110      } // end else
111   } // end function removeFromFront
112
113   // delete node from back of list
114   template< typename NODETYPE >
115   bool List< NODETYPE >::removeFromBack( NODETYPE &value )
116   {
117      if ( isEmpty() ) // List is empty
118         return false; // delete unsuccessful
119      else
120      {
121         ListNode< NODETYPE > *tempPtr = lastPtr; // hold tempPtr to delete
122
123         if ( firstPtr == lastPtr ) // List has one element
124            firstPtr = lastPtr = 0; // no nodes remain after removal
125         else
126         {
127            ListNode< NODETYPE > *currentPtr = firstPtr;
128
129            // locate second-to-last element
130            while ( currentPtr->nextPtr != lastPtr )
131               currentPtr = currentPtr->nextPtr; // move to next node
132
133            lastPtr = currentPtr; // remove last node
134            currentPtr->nextPtr = 0; // this is now the last node
135         } // end else
136
137         value = tempPtr->data; // return value from old last node
138         delete tempPtr; // reclaim former last node
139         return true; // delete successful
140      } // end else
141   } // end function removeFromBack
142
```

Fig. 20.4 | List class-template definition. (Part 3 of 4.)

```
143  // is List empty?
144  template< typename NODETYPE >
145  bool List< NODETYPE >::isEmpty() const
146  {
147     return firstPtr == 0;
148  } // end function isEmpty
149
150  // return pointer to newly allocated node
151  template< typename NODETYPE >
152  ListNode< NODETYPE > *List< NODETYPE >::getNewNode(
153     const NODETYPE &value )
154  {
155     return new ListNode< NODETYPE >( value );
156  } // end function getNewNode
157
158  // display contents of List
159  template< typename NODETYPE >
160  void List< NODETYPE >::print() const
161  {
162     if ( isEmpty() ) // List is empty
163     {
164        cout << "The list is empty\n\n";
165        return;
166     } // end if
167
168     ListNode< NODETYPE > *currentPtr = firstPtr;
169
170     cout << "The list is: ";
171
172     while ( currentPtr != 0 ) // get element data
173     {
174        cout << currentPtr->data << ' ';
175        currentPtr = currentPtr->nextPtr;
176     } // end while
177
178     cout << "\n\n";
179  } // end function print
180
181  #endif
```

Fig. 20.4 | List class-template definition. (Part 4 of 4.)

```
1  // Fig. 20.5: Fig21_05.cpp
2  // List class test program.
3  #include <iostream>
4  using std::cin;
5  using std::cout;
6  using std::endl;
7
```

Fig. 20.5 | Manipulating a linked list. (Part 1 of 4.)

```
 8   #include <string>
 9   using std::string;
10
11   #include "List.h" // List class definition
12
13   // function to test a List
14   template< typename T >
15   void testList( List< T > &listObject, const string &typeName )
16   {
17      cout << "Testing a List of " << typeName << " values\n";
18      instructions(); // display instructions
19
20      int choice; // store user choice
21      T value; // store input value
22
23      do // perform user-selected actions
24      {
25         cout << "? ";
26         cin >> choice;
27
28         switch ( choice )
29         {
30            case 1: // insert at beginning
31               cout << "Enter " << typeName << ": ";
32               cin >> value;
33               listObject.insertAtFront( value );
34               listObject.print();
35               break;
36            case 2: // insert at end
37               cout << "Enter " << typeName << ": ";
38               cin >> value;
39               listObject.insertAtBack( value );
40               listObject.print();
41               break;
42            case 3: // remove from beginning
43               if ( listObject.removeFromFront( value ) )
44                  cout << value << " removed from list\n";
45
46               listObject.print();
47               break;
48            case 4: // remove from end
49               if ( listObject.removeFromBack( value ) )
50                  cout << value << " removed from list\n";
51
52               listObject.print();
53               break;
54         } // end switch
55      } while ( choice != 5 ); // end do...while
56
57      cout << "End list test\n\n";
58   } // end function testList
59
```

Fig. 20.5 | Manipulating a linked list. (Part 2 of 4.)

```
60   // display program instructions to user
61   void instructions()
62   {
63      cout << "Enter one of the following:\n"
64         << "  1 to insert at beginning of list\n"
65         << "  2 to insert at end of list\n"
66         << "  3 to delete from beginning of list\n"
67         << "  4 to delete from end of list\n"
68         << "  5 to end list processing\n";
69   } // end function instructions
70
71   int main()
72   {
73      // test List of int values
74      List< int > integerList;
75      testList( integerList, "integer" );
76
77      // test List of double values
78      List< double > doubleList;
79      testList( doubleList, "double" );
80      return 0;
81   } // end main
```

```
Testing a List of integer values
Enter one of the following:
  1 to insert at beginning of list
  2 to insert at end of list
  3 to delete from beginning of list
  4 to delete from end of list
  5 to end list processing
? 1
Enter integer: 1
The list is: 1

? 1
Enter integer: 2
The list is: 2 1

? 2
Enter integer: 3
The list is: 2 1 3

? 2
Enter integer: 4
The list is: 2 1 3 4

? 3
2 removed from list
The list is: 1 3 4

? 3
1 removed from list
The list is: 3 4
```

(continued ...)

Fig. 20.5 | Manipulating a linked list. (Part 3 of 4.)

```
? 4
4 removed from list
The list is: 3

? 4
3 removed from list
The list is empty

? 5
End list test

Testing a List of double values
Enter one of the following:
   1 to insert at beginning of list
   2 to insert at end of list
   3 to delete from beginning of list
   4 to delete from end of list
   5 to end list processing
? 1
Enter double: 1.1
The list is: 1.1

? 1
Enter double: 2.2
The list is: 2.2 1.1

? 2
Enter double: 3.3
The list is: 2.2 1.1 3.3

? 2
Enter double: 4.4
The list is: 2.2 1.1 3.3 4.4

? 3
2.2 removed from list
The list is: 1.1 3.3 4.4

? 3
1.1 removed from list
The list is: 3.3 4.4

? 4
4.4 removed from list
The list is: 3.3

? 4
3.3 removed from list
The list is empty

? 5
End list test

All nodes destroyed

All nodes destroyed
```

Fig. 20.5 | Manipulating a linked list. (Part 4 of 4.)

NODETYPE is used as the template argument for List in the friend declaration, ListNodes specialized with a particular type can be processed only by a List specialized with the same type (e.g., a List of int values manages ListNode objects that store int values).

Lines 24–25 of the List class template (Fig. 20.4) declare private data members firstPtr (a pointer to the first ListNode in a List) and lastPtr (a pointer to the last ListNode in a List). The default constructor (lines 32–37) initializes both pointers to 0 (null). The destructor (lines 40–60) ensures that all ListNode objects in a List object are destroyed when that List object is destroyed. The primary List functions are insertAtFront (lines 63–75), insertAtBack (lines 78–90), removeFromFront (lines 93–111) and removeFromBack (lines 114–141).

Function isEmpty (lines 144–148) is called a predicate function—it does not alter the List; rather, it determines whether the List is empty (i.e., the pointer to the first node of the List is null). If the List is empty, true is returned; otherwise, false is returned. Function print (lines 159–179) displays the List's contents. Utility function getNewNode (lines 151–156) returns a dynamically allocated ListNode object. This function is called from functions insertAtFront and insertAtBack.

Error-Prevention Tip 20.1

Assign null (0) to the link member of a new node. Pointers must be initialized before they are used.

The driver program (Fig. 20.5) uses function template testList to enable the user to manipulate objects of class List. Lines 74 and 78 create List objects for types int and double, respectively. Lines 75 and 79 invoke the testList function template with these List objects.

Member Function *insertAtFront*

Over the next several pages, we discuss each of the member functions of class List in detail. Function insertAtFront (Fig. 20.4, lines 63–75) places a new node at the front of the list. The function consists of several steps:

1. Call function getNewNode (line 66), passing it value, which is a constant reference to the node value to be inserted.

2. Function getNewNode (lines 151–156) uses operator new to create a new list node and return a pointer to this newly allocated node, which is assigned to newPtr in insertAtFront (line 66).

3. If the list is empty (line 68), then both firstPtr and lastPtr are set to newPtr (line 69).

4. If the list is not empty (line 70), then the node pointed to by newPtr is threaded into the list by copying firstPtr to newPtr->nextPtr (line 72), so that the new node points to what used to be the first node of the list, and copying newPtr to firstPtr (line 73), so that firstPtr now points to the new first node of the list.

Figure 20.6 illustrates function insertAtFront. Part (a) of the figure shows the list and the new node before the insertAtFront operation. The dashed arrows in part (b) illustrate *Step 4* of the insertAtFront operation that enables the node containing 12 to become the new list front.

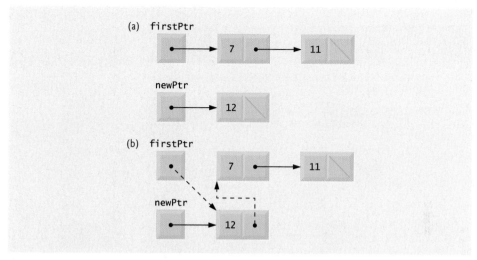

Fig. 20.6 | Operation `insertAtFront` represented graphically.

Member Function `insertAtBack`

Function `insertAtBack` (Fig. 20.4, lines 78–90) places a new node at the back of the list. The function consists of several steps:

1. Call function `getNewNode` (line 81), passing it `value`, which is a constant reference to the node value to be inserted.

2. Function `getNewNode` (lines 151–156) uses operator `new` to create a new list node and return a pointer to this newly allocated node, which is assigned to `newPtr` in `insertAtBack` (line 81).

3. If the list is empty (line 83), then both `firstPtr` and `lastPtr` are set to `newPtr` (line 84).

4. If the list is not empty (line 85), then the node pointed to by `newPtr` is threaded into the list by copying `newPtr` into `lastPtr->nextPtr` (line 87), so that the new node is pointed to by what used to be the last node of the list, and copying `newPtr` to `lastPtr` (line 88), so that `lastPtr` now points to the new last node of the list.

Figure 20.7 illustrates an `insertAtBack` operation. Part (a) of the figure shows the list and the new node before the operation. The dashed arrows in part (b) illustrate *Step 4* of function `insertAtBack` that enables a new node to be added to the end of a list that is not empty.

Member Function `removeFromFront`

Function `removeFromFront` (Fig. 20.4, lines 93–111) removes the front node of the list and copies the node value to the reference parameter. The function returns `false` if an attempt is made to remove a node from an empty list (lines 96–97) and returns `true` if the removal is successful. The function consists of several steps:

1. Assign `tempPtr` the address to which `firstPtr` points (line 100). Eventually, `tempPtr` will be used to delete the node being removed.

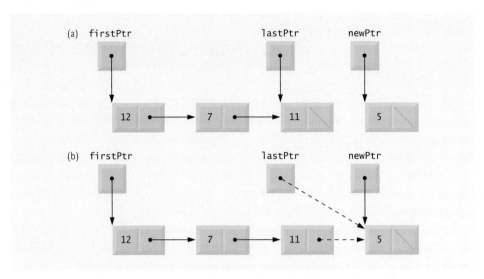

Fig. 20.7 | Operation insertAtBack represented graphically.

2. If firstPtr is equal to lastPtr (line 102), i.e., if the list has only one element prior to the removal attempt, then set firstPtr and lastPtr to zero (line 103) to dethread that node from the list (leaving the list empty).

3. If the list has more than one node prior to removal, then leave lastPtr as is and set firstPtr to firstPtr->nextPtr (line 105); i.e., modify firstPtr to point to what was the second node prior to removal (and is now the new first node).

4. After all these pointer manipulations are complete, copy to reference parameter value the data member of the node being removed (line 107).

5. Now delete the node pointed to by tempPtr (line 108).

6. Return true, indicating successful removal (line 109).

Figure 20.8 illustrates function removeFromFront. Part (a) illustrates the list before the removal operation. Part (b) shows the actual pointer manipulations for removing the front node from a nonempty list.

Member Function *removeFromBack*
Function removeFromBack (Fig. 20.4, lines 114–141) removes the back node of the list and copies the node value to the reference parameter. The function returns false if an attempt is made to remove a node from an empty list (lines 117–118) and returns true if the removal is successful. The function consists of several steps:

1. Assign to tempPtr the address to which lastPtr points (line 121). Eventually, tempPtr will be used to delete the node being removed.

2. If firstPtr is equal to lastPtr (line 123), i.e., if the list has only one element prior to the removal attempt, then set firstPtr and lastPtr to zero (line 124) to dethread that node from the list (leaving the list empty).

3. If the list has more than one node prior to removal, then assign currentPtr the address to which firstPtr points (line 127) to prepare to "walk the list."

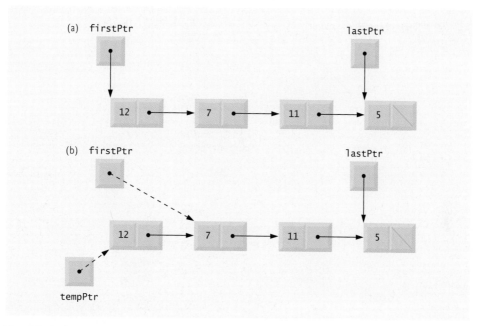

Fig. 20.8 | Operation removeFromFront represented graphically.

4. Now "walk the list" with currentPtr until it points to the node before the last node. This node will become the last node after the remove operation completes. This is done with a while loop (lines 130–131) that keeps replacing currentPtr by currentPtr->nextPtr, while currentPtr->nextPtr is not lastPtr.

5. Assign lastPtr to the address to which currentPtr points (line 133) to dethread the back node from the list.

6. Set currentPtr->nextPtr to zero (line 134) in the new last node of the list.

7. After all the pointer manipulations are complete, copy to reference parameter value the data member of the node being removed (line 137).

8. Now delete the node pointed to by tempPtr (line 138).

9. Return true (line 139), indicating successful removal.

Figure 20.9 illustrates removeFromBack. Part (a) of the figure illustrates the list before the removal operation. Part (b) of the figure shows the actual pointer manipulations.

Member Function print

Function print (lines 159–179) first determines whether the list is empty (line 162). If so, it prints "The list is empty" and returns (lines 164–165). Otherwise, it iterates through the list and outputs the value in each node. The function initializes currentPtr as a copy of firstPtr (line 168), then prints the string "The list is: " (line 170). While currentPtr is not null (line 172), currentPtr->data is printed (line 174) and currentPtr is assigned the value of currentPtr->nextPtr (line 175). Note that if the link in the last node of the list is not null, the printing algorithm will erroneously attempt to print past the end

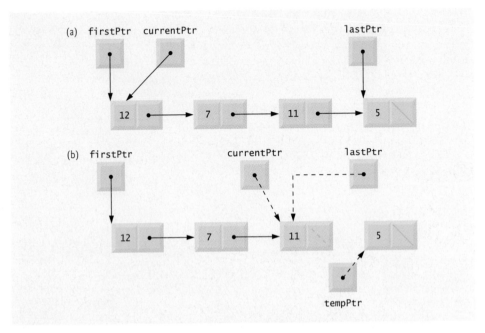

Fig. 20.9 | Operation removeFromBack represented graphically.

of the list. The printing algorithm is identical for linked lists, stacks and queues (because we base each of these data structures on the same linked list infrastructure).

Linear and Circular Singly Linked and Doubly Linked Lists

The kind of linked list we have been discussing is a singly linked list—the list begins with a pointer to the first node, and each node contains a pointer to the next node "in sequence." This list terminates with a node whose pointer member has the value 0. A singly linked list may be traversed in only one direction.

A circular, singly linked list (Fig. 20.10) begins with a pointer to the first node, and each node contains a pointer to the next node. The "last node" does not contain a 0 pointer; rather, the pointer in the last node points back to the first node, thus closing the "circle."

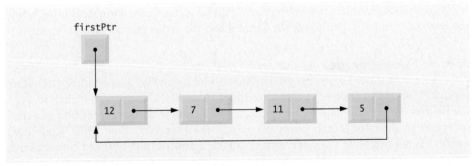

Fig. 20.10 | Circular, singly linked list.

A doubly linked list (Fig. 20.11) allows traversals both forward and backward. Such a list is often implemented with two "start pointers"—one that points to the first element of the list to allow front-to-back traversal of the list and one that points to the last element to allow back-to-front traversal. Each node has both a forward pointer to the next node in the list in the forward direction and a backward pointer to the next node in the list in the backward direction. If your list contains an alphabetized telephone directory, for example, a search for someone whose name begins with a letter near the front of the alphabet might begin from the front of the list. Searching for someone whose name begins with a letter near the end of the alphabet might begin from the back of the list.

In a circular, doubly linked list (Fig. 20.12), the forward pointer of the last node points to the first node, and the backward pointer of the first node points to the last node, thus closing the "circle."

20.5 Stacks

Chapter 14, Templates, explained the notion of a stack class template with an underlying array implementation. In this section, we use an underlying pointer-based linked-list implementation. We also discuss stacks in Chapter 22, Standard Template Library (STL).

A stack data structure allows nodes to be added to the stack and removed from the stack only at the top. For this reason, a stack is referred to as a last-in, first-out (LIFO) data structure. One way to implement a stack is as a constrained version of a linked list. In such an implementation, the link member in the last node of the stack is set to null (zero) to indicate the bottom of the stack.

Fig. 20.11 | Doubly linked list.

Fig. 20.12 | Circular, doubly linked list.

The primary member functions used to manipulate a stack are push and pop. Function push inserts a new node at the top of the stack. Function pop removes a node from the top of the stack, stores the popped value in a reference variable that is passed to the calling function and returns true if the pop operation was successful (false otherwise).

Stacks have many interesting applications. For example, when a function call is made, the called function must know how to return to its caller, so the return address is pushed onto a stack. If a series of function calls occurs, the successive return values are pushed onto the stack in last-in, first-out order, so that each function can return to its caller. Stacks support recursive function calls in the same manner as conventional nonrecursive calls. Section 6.11 discusses the function call stack in detail.

Stacks provide the memory for, and store the values of, automatic variables on each invocation of a function. When the function returns to its caller or throws an exception, the destructor (if any) for each local object is called, the space for that function's automatic variables is popped off the stack and those variables are no longer known to the program.

Stacks are used by compilers in the process of evaluating expressions and generating machine-language code. The exercises explore several applications of stacks, including using them to develop your own complete working compiler.

We'll take advantage of the close relationship between lists and stacks to implement a stack class primarily by reusing a list class. First, we implement the stack class through private inheritance of the list class. Then we implement an identically performing stack class through composition by including a list object as a private member of a stack class. Of course, all of the data structures in this chapter, including these two stack classes, are implemented as templates to encourage further reusability.

The program of Figs. 20.13–20.14 creates a Stack class template (Fig. 20.13) primarily through private inheritance (line 9) of the List class template of Fig. 20.4. We want the Stack to have member functions push (lines 13–16), pop (lines 19–22), isStackEmpty (lines 25–28) and printStack (lines 31–34). Note that these are essentially the insertAtFront, removeFromFront, isEmpty and print functions of the List class template. Of course, the List class template contains other member functions (i.e., insertAtBack and

```
 1   // Fig. 20.13: Stack.h
 2   // Template Stack class definition derived from class List.
 3   #ifndef STACK_H
 4   #define STACK_H
 5
 6   #include "List.h" // List class definition
 7
 8   template< typename STACKTYPE >
 9   class Stack : private List< STACKTYPE >
10   {
11   public:
12      // push calls the List function insertAtFront
13      void push( const STACKTYPE &data )
14      {
15         insertAtFront( data );
16      } // end function push
17
```

Fig. 20.13 | Stack class-template definition. (Part 1 of 2.)

```
18      // pop calls the List function removeFromFront
19      bool pop( STACKTYPE &data )
20      {
21         return removeFromFront( data );
22      } // end function pop
23
24      // isStackEmpty calls the List function isEmpty
25      bool isStackEmpty() const
26      {
27         return isEmpty();
28      } // end function isStackEmpty
29
30      // printStack calls the List function print
31      void printStack() const
32      {
33         print();
34      } // end function print
35   }; // end class Stack
36
37   #endif
```

Fig. 20.13 | Stack class-template definition. (Part 2 of 2.)

removeFromBack) that we would not want to make accessible through the public interface to the Stack class. So when we indicate that the Stack class template is to inherit from the List class template, we specify private inheritance. This makes all the List class template's member functions private in the Stack class template. When we implement the Stack's member functions, we then have each of these call the appropriate member function of the List class—push calls insertAtFront (line 15), pop calls removeFromFront (line 21), isStackEmpty calls isEmpty (line 27) and printStack calls print (line 33)—this is referred to as delegation.

The stack class template is used in main (Fig. 20.14) to instantiate integer stack intStack of type Stack< int > (line 11). Integers 0 through 2 are pushed onto intStack (lines 16–20), then popped off intStack (lines 25–30). The program uses the Stack class template to create doubleStack of type Stack< double > (line 32). Values 1.1, 2.2 and 3.3 are pushed onto doubleStack (lines 38–43), then popped off doubleStack (lines 48–53).

```
1    // Fig. 20.14: Fig21_14.cpp
2    // Template Stack class test program.
3    #include <iostream>
4    using std::cout;
5    using std::endl;
6
7    #include "Stack.h" // Stack class definition
8
9    int main()
10   {
11      Stack< int > intStack; // create Stack of ints
12
```

Fig. 20.14 | A simple stack program. (Part 1 of 3.)

```
13        cout << "processing an integer Stack" << endl;
14
15        // push integers onto intStack
16        for ( int i = 0; i < 3; i++ )
17        {
18            intStack.push( i );
19            intStack.printStack();
20        } // end for
21
22        int popInteger; // store int popped from stack
23
24        // pop integers from intStack
25        while ( !intStack.isStackEmpty() )
26        {
27            intStack.pop( popInteger );
28            cout << popInteger << " popped from stack" << endl;
29            intStack.printStack();
30        } // end while
31
32        Stack< double > doubleStack; // create Stack of doubles
33        double value = 1.1;
34
35        cout << "processing a double Stack" << endl;
36
37        // push floating-point values onto doubleStack
38        for ( int j = 0; j < 3; j++ )
39        {
40            doubleStack.push( value );
41            doubleStack.printStack();
42            value += 1.1;
43        } // end for
44
45        double popDouble; // store double popped from stack
46
47        // pop floating-point values from doubleStack
48        while ( !doubleStack.isStackEmpty() )
49        {
50            doubleStack.pop( popDouble );
51            cout << popDouble << " popped from stack" << endl;
52            doubleStack.printStack();
53        } // end while
54
55        return 0;
56    } // end main
```

```
processing an integer Stack
The list is: 0

The list is: 1 0

The list is: 2 1 0
```

(continued ...)

Fig. 20.14 | A simple stack program. (Part 2 of 3.)

```
2 popped from stack
The list is: 1 0

1 popped from stack
The list is: 0

0 popped from stack
The list is empty

processing a double Stack
The list is: 1.1

The list is: 2.2 1.1

The list is: 3.3 2.2 1.1

3.3 popped from stack
The list is: 2.2 1.1

2.2 popped from stack
The list is: 1.1

1.1 popped from stack
The list is empty

All nodes destroyed

All nodes destroyed
```

Fig. 20.14 | A simple stack program. (Part 3 of 3.)

Another way to implement a Stack class template is by reusing the List class template through composition. Figure 20.15 is a new implementation of the Stack class template that contains a List< STACKTYPE > object called stackList (line 38). This version of the Stack class template uses class List from Fig. 20.4. To test this class, use the driver program in Fig. 20.14, but include the new header file—Stackcomposition.h in line 6 of that file. The output of the program is identical for both versions of class Stack.

```
1  // Fig. 20.15: Stackcomposition.h
2  // Template Stack class definition with composed List object.
3  #ifndef STACKCOMPOSITION_H
4  #define STACKCOMPOSITION_H
5
6  #include "List.h" // List class definition
7
8  template< typename STACKTYPE >
9  class Stack
10 {
11 public:
12    // no constructor; List constructor does initialization
```

Fig. 20.15 | Stack class template with a composed List object. (Part 1 of 2.)

```
13
14      // push calls stackList object's insertAtFront member function
15      void push( const STACKTYPE &data )
16      {
17         stackList.insertAtFront( data );
18      } // end function push
19
20      // pop calls stackList object's removeFromFront member function
21      bool pop( STACKTYPE &data )
22      {
23         return stackList.removeFromFront( data );
24      } // end function pop
25
26      // isStackEmpty calls stackList object's isEmpty member function
27      bool isStackEmpty() const
28      {
29         return stackList.isEmpty();
30      } // end function isStackEmpty
31
32      // printStack calls stackList object's print member function
33      void printStack() const
34      {
35         stackList.print();
36      } // end function printStack
37   private:
38      List< STACKTYPE > stackList; // composed List object
39   }; // end class Stack
40
41   #endif
```

Fig. 20.15 | Stack class template with a composed List object. (Part 2 of 2.)

20.6 Queues

A queue is similar to a supermarket checkout line—the first person in line is serviced first, and other customers enter the line at the end and wait to be serviced. Queue nodes are removed only from the head of the queue and are inserted only at the tail of the queue. For this reason, a queue is referred to as a first-in, first-out (FIFO) data structure. The insert and remove operations are known as enqueue and dequeue.

Queues have many applications in computer systems. Computers that have a single processor can service only one user at a time. Entries for the other users are placed in a queue. Each entry gradually advances to the front of the queue as users receive service. The entry at the front of the queue is the next to receive service.

Queues are also used to support print spooling. For example, a single printer might be shared by all users of a network. Many users can send print jobs to the printer, even when the printer is already busy. These print jobs are placed in a queue until the printer becomes available. A program called a spooler managers the queue to ensure that, as each print job completes, the next print job is sent to the printer.

Information packets also wait in queues in computer networks. Each time a packet arrives at a network node, it must be routed to the next node on the network along the path to the packet's final destination. The routing node routes one packet at a time, so additional packets are enqueued until the router can route them.

A file server in a computer network handles file access requests from many clients throughout the network. Servers have a limited capacity to service requests from clients. When that capacity is exceeded, client requests wait in queues.

The program of Figs. 20.16–20.17 creates a Queue class template (Fig. 20.16) through private inheritance (line 9) of the List class template of Fig. 20.4. We want the Queue to have member functions enqueue (lines 13–16), dequeue (lines 19–22), isQueue-Empty (lines 25–28) and printQueue (lines 31–34). Note that these are essentially the insertAtBack, removeFromFront, isEmpty and print functions of the List class template. Of course, the List class template contains other member functions (i.e., insertAt-Front and removeFromBack) that we would not want to make accessible through the

```cpp
1   // Fig. 20.16: Queue.h
2   // Template Queue class definition derived from class List.
3   #ifndef QUEUE_H
4   #define QUEUE_H
5
6   #include "List.h" // List class definition
7
8   template< typename QUEUETYPE >
9   class Queue : private List< QUEUETYPE >
10  {
11  public:
12     // enqueue calls List member function insertAtBack
13     void enqueue( const QUEUETYPE &data )
14     {
15        insertAtBack( data );
16     } // end function enqueue
17
18     // dequeue calls List member function removeFromFront
19     bool dequeue( QUEUETYPE &data )
20     {
21        return removeFromFront( data );
22     } // end function dequeue
23
24     // isQueueEmpty calls List member function isEmpty
25     bool isQueueEmpty() const
26     {
27        return isEmpty();
28     } // end function isQueueEmpty
29
30     // printQueue calls List member function print
31     void printQueue() const
32     {
33        print();
34     } // end function printQueue
35  }; // end class Queue
36
37  #endif
```

Fig. 20.16 | Queue class-template definition.

public interface to the Queue class. So when we indicate that the Queue class template is to inherit the List class template, we specify private inheritance. This makes all the List class template's member functions private in the Queue class template. When we implement the Queue's member functions, we have each of these call the appropriate member function of the list class—enqueue calls insertAtBack (line 15), dequeue calls remove-FromFront (line 21), isQueueEmpty calls isEmpty (line 27) and printQueue calls print (line 33). Again, this is called delegation.

Figure 20.17 uses the Queue class template to instantiate integer queue intQueue of type Queue< int > (line 11). Integers 0 through 2 are enqueued to intQueue (lines 16–20), then dequeued from intQueue in first-in, first-out order (lines 25–30). Next, the program instantiates queue doubleQueue of type Queue< double > (line 32). Values 1.1, 2.2 and 3.3 are enqueued to doubleQueue (lines 38–43), then dequeued from doubleQueue in first-in, first-out order (lines 48–53).

```cpp
 1   // Fig. 20.17: Fig21_17.cpp
 2   // Template Queue class test program.
 3   #include <iostream>
 4   using std::cout;
 5   using std::endl;
 6
 7   #include "Queue.h" // Queue class definition
 8
 9   int main()
10   {
11      Queue< int > intQueue; // create Queue of integers
12
13      cout << "processing an integer Queue" << endl;
14
15      // enqueue integers onto intQueue
16      for ( int i = 0; i < 3; i++ )
17      {
18         intQueue.enqueue( i );
19         intQueue.printQueue();
20      } // end for
21
22      int dequeueInteger; // store dequeued integer
23
24      // dequeue integers from intQueue
25      while ( !intQueue.isQueueEmpty() )
26      {
27         intQueue.dequeue( dequeueInteger );
28         cout << dequeueInteger << " dequeued" << endl;
29         intQueue.printQueue();
30      } // end while
31
32      Queue< double > doubleQueue; // create Queue of doubles
33      double value = 1.1;
34
35      cout << "processing a double Queue" << endl;
36
```

Fig. 20.17 | Queue-processing program. (Part 1 of 2.)

```
37      // enqueue floating-point values onto doubleQueue
38      for ( int j = 0; j < 3; j++ )
39      {
40         doubleQueue.enqueue( value );
41         doubleQueue.printQueue();
42         value += 1.1;
43      } // end for
44
45      double dequeueDouble; // store dequeued double
46
47      // dequeue floating-point values from doubleQueue
48      while ( !doubleQueue.isQueueEmpty() )
49      {
50         doubleQueue.dequeue( dequeueDouble );
51         cout << dequeueDouble << " dequeued" << endl;
52         doubleQueue.printQueue();
53      } // end while
54
55      return 0;
56   } // end main
```

```
processing an integer Queue
The list is: 0

The list is: 0 1

The list is: 0 1 2

0 dequeued
The list is: 1 2

1 dequeued
The list is: 2

2 dequeued
The list is empty

processing a double Queue
The list is: 1.1

The list is: 1.1 2.2

The list is: 1.1 2.2 3.3

1.1 dequeued
The list is: 2.2 3.3

2.2 dequeued
The list is: 3.3

3.3 dequeued
The list is empty

All nodes destroyed

All nodes destroyed
```

Fig. 20.17 | Queue-processing program. (Part 2 of 2.)

20.7 Trees

Linked lists, stacks and queues are linear data structures. A tree is a nonlinear, two-dimensional data structure. Tree nodes contain two or more links. This section discusses binary trees (Fig. 20.18)—trees whose nodes all contain two links (none, one or both of which may be null).

Basic Terminology

For this discussion, refer to nodes A, B, C and D in Fig. 20.18. The root node (node B) is the first node in a tree. Each link in the root node refers to a child (nodes A and D). The left child (node A) is the root node of the left subtree (which contains only node A), and the right child (node D) is the root node of the right subtree (which contains nodes D and C). The children of a given node are called siblings (e.g., nodes A and D are siblings). A node with no children is a leaf node (e.g., nodes A and C are leaf nodes). Computer scientists normally draw trees from the root node down—the opposite of how trees grow in nature.

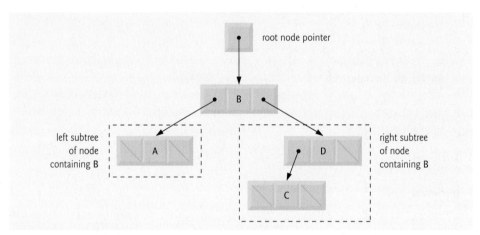

Fig. 20.18 | A graphical representation of a binary tree.

Binary Search Trees

A binary search tree (with no duplicate node values) has the characteristic that the values in any left subtree are less than the value in its parent node, and the values in any right subtree are greater than the value in its parent node. Figure 20.19 illustrates a binary search tree with 9 values. Note that the shape of the binary search tree that corresponds to a set of data can vary, depending on the order in which the values are inserted into the tree.

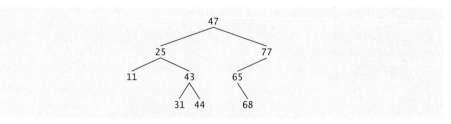

Fig. 20.19 | A binary search tree.

Implementing the Binary Search Tree Program

The program of Figs. 20.20–20.22 creates a binary search tree and traverses it (i.e., walks through all its nodes) three ways—using recursive inorder, preorder and postorder traversals. We explain these traversal algorithms shortly.

We begin our discussion with the driver program (Fig. 20.22), then continue with the implementations of classes TreeNode (Fig. 20.20) and Tree (Fig. 20.21). Function main (Fig. 20.22) begins by instantiating integer tree intTree of type Tree< int > (line 15). The program prompts for 10 integers, each of which is inserted in the binary tree by calling insertNode (line 24). The program then performs preorder, inorder and postorder traversals (these are explained shortly) of intTree (lines 28, 31 and 34, respectively). The program then instantiates floating-point tree doubleTree of type Tree< double > (line 36). The program prompts for 10 double values, each of which is inserted in the binary tree by calling insertNode (line 46). The program then performs preorder, inorder and postorder traversals of doubleTree (lines 50, 53 and 56, respectively).

```
1   // Fig. 20.20: TreeNode.h
2   // Template TreeNode class definition.
3   #ifndef TREENODE_H
4   #define TREENODE_H
5
6   // forward declaration of class Tree
7   template< typename NODETYPE > class Tree;
8
9   // TreeNode class-template definition
10  template< typename NODETYPE >
11  class TreeNode
12  {
13     friend class Tree< NODETYPE >;
14  public:
15     // constructor
16     TreeNode( const NODETYPE &d )
17        : leftPtr( 0 ), // pointer to left subtree
18          data( d ), // tree node data
19          rightPtr( 0 ) // pointer to right substree
20     {
21        // empty body
22     } // end TreeNode constructor
23
24     // return copy of node's data
25     NODETYPE getData() const
26     {
27        return data;
28     } // end getData function
29  private:
30     TreeNode< NODETYPE > *leftPtr; // pointer to left subtree
31     NODETYPE data;
32     TreeNode< NODETYPE > *rightPtr; // pointer to right subtree
33  }; // end class TreeNode
34
35  #endif
```

Fig. 20.20 | TreeNode class-template definition.

```
 1   // Fig. 20.21: Tree.h
 2   // Template Tree class definition.
 3   #ifndef TREE_H
 4   #define TREE_H
 5
 6   #include <iostream>
 7   using std::cout;
 8   using std::endl;
 9
10   #include "TreeNode.h"
11
12   // Tree class-template definition
13   template< typename NODETYPE > class Tree
14   {
15   public:
16      Tree(); // constructor
17      void insertNode( const NODETYPE & );
18      void preOrderTraversal() const;
19      void inOrderTraversal() const;
20      void postOrderTraversal() const;
21   private:
22      TreeNode< NODETYPE > *rootPtr;
23
24      // utility functions
25      void insertNodeHelper( TreeNode< NODETYPE > **, const NODETYPE & );
26      void preOrderHelper( TreeNode< NODETYPE > * ) const;
27      void inOrderHelper( TreeNode< NODETYPE > * ) const;
28      void postOrderHelper( TreeNode< NODETYPE > * ) const;
29   }; // end class Tree
30
31   // constructor
32   template< typename NODETYPE >
33   Tree< NODETYPE >::Tree()
34   {
35      rootPtr = 0; // indicate tree is initially empty
36   } // end Tree constructor
37
38   // insert node in Tree
39   template< typename NODETYPE >
40   void Tree< NODETYPE >::insertNode( const NODETYPE &value )
41   {
42      insertNodeHelper( &rootPtr, value );
43   } // end function insertNode
44
45   // utility function called by insertNode; receives a pointer
46   // to a pointer so that the function can modify pointer's value
47   template< typename NODETYPE >
48   void Tree< NODETYPE >::insertNodeHelper(
49      TreeNode< NODETYPE > **ptr, const NODETYPE &value )
50   {
51      // subtree is empty; create new TreeNode containing value
52      if ( *ptr == 0 )
53         *ptr = new TreeNode< NODETYPE >( value );
```

Fig. 20.21 | Tree class-template definition. (Part 1 of 3.)

```
54      else // subtree is not empty
55      {
56          // data to insert is less than data in current node
57          if ( value < ( *ptr )->data )
58              insertNodeHelper( &( ( *ptr )->leftPtr ), value );
59          else
60          {
61              // data to insert is greater than data in current node
62              if ( value > ( *ptr )->data )
63                  insertNodeHelper( &( ( *ptr )->rightPtr ), value );
64              else // duplicate data value ignored
65                  cout << value << " dup" << endl;
66          } // end else
67      } // end else
68  } // end function insertNodeHelper
69
70  // begin preorder traversal of Tree
71  template< typename NODETYPE >
72  void Tree< NODETYPE >::preOrderTraversal() const
73  {
74      preOrderHelper( rootPtr );
75  } // end function preOrderTraversal
76
77  // utility function to perform preorder traversal of Tree
78  template< typename NODETYPE >
79  void Tree< NODETYPE >::preOrderHelper( TreeNode< NODETYPE > *ptr ) const
80  {
81      if ( ptr != 0 )
82      {
83          cout << ptr->data << ' '; // process node
84          preOrderHelper( ptr->leftPtr ); // traverse left subtree
85          preOrderHelper( ptr->rightPtr ); // traverse right subtree
86      } // end if
87  } // end function preOrderHelper
88
89  // begin inorder traversal of Tree
90  template< typename NODETYPE >
91  void Tree< NODETYPE >::inOrderTraversal() const
92  {
93      inOrderHelper( rootPtr );
94  } // end function inOrderTraversal
95
96  // utility function to perform inorder traversal of Tree
97  template< typename NODETYPE >
98  void Tree< NODETYPE >::inOrderHelper( TreeNode< NODETYPE > *ptr ) const
99  {
100     if ( ptr != 0 )
101     {
102         inOrderHelper( ptr->leftPtr ); // traverse left subtree
103         cout << ptr->data << ' '; // process node
104         inOrderHelper( ptr->rightPtr ); // traverse right subtree
105     } // end if
106 } // end function inOrderHelper
```

Fig. 20.21 | Tree class-template definition. (Part 2 of 3.)

```
107
108   // begin postorder traversal of Tree
109   template< typename NODETYPE >
110   void Tree< NODETYPE >::postOrderTraversal() const
111   {
112      postOrderHelper( rootPtr );
113   } // end function postOrderTraversal
114
115   // utility function to perform postorder traversal of Tree
116   template< typename NODETYPE >
117   void Tree< NODETYPE >::postOrderHelper(
118      TreeNode< NODETYPE > *ptr ) const
119   {
120      if ( ptr != 0 )
121      {
122         postOrderHelper( ptr->leftPtr ); // traverse left subtree
123         postOrderHelper( ptr->rightPtr ); // traverse right subtree
124         cout << ptr->data << ' '; // process node
125      } // end if
126   } // end function postOrderHelper
127
128   #endif
```

Fig. 20.21 | Tree class-template definition. (Part 3 of 3.)

Now we discuss the class-template definitions. We begin with the TreeNode class template (Fig. 20.20) definition that declares Tree< NODETYPE > as its friend (line 13). This makes all member functions of a given specialization of class template Tree (Fig. 20.21) friends of the corresponding specialization of class template TreeNode, so they can access the private members of TreeNode objects of that type. Because the TreeNode template parameter NODETYPE is used as the template argument for Tree in the friend declaration, TreeNodes specialized with a particular type can be processed only by a Tree specialized with the same type (e.g., a Tree of int values manages TreeNode objects that store int values).

Lines 30–32 declare a TreeNode's private data—the node's data value, and pointers leftPtr (to the node's left subtree) and rightPtr (to the node's right subtree). The constructor (lines 16–22) sets data to the value supplied as a constructor argument and sets pointers leftPtr and rightPtr to zero (thus initializing this node to be a leaf node). Member function getData (lines 25–28) returns the data value.

```
1   // Fig. 20.22: Fig21_22.cpp
2   // Tree class test program.
3   #include <iostream>
4   using std::cout;
5   using std::cin;
6   using std::fixed;
7
```

Fig. 20.22 | Creating and traversing a binary tree. (Part 1 of 3.)

```
 8   #include <iomanip>
 9   using std::setprecision;
10
11   #include "Tree.h" // Tree class definition
12
13   int main()
14   {
15      Tree< int > intTree; // create Tree of int values
16      int intValue;
17
18      cout << "Enter 10 integer values:\n";
19
20      // insert 10 integers to intTree
21      for ( int i = 0; i < 10; i++ )
22      {
23         cin >> intValue;
24         intTree.insertNode( intValue );
25      } // end for
26
27      cout << "\nPreorder traversal\n";
28      intTree.preOrderTraversal();
29
30      cout << "\nInorder traversal\n";
31      intTree.inOrderTraversal();
32
33      cout << "\nPostorder traversal\n";
34      intTree.postOrderTraversal();
35
36      Tree< double > doubleTree; // create Tree of double values
37      double doubleValue;
38
39      cout << fixed << setprecision( 1 )
40         << "\n\n\nEnter 10 double values:\n";
41
42      // insert 10 doubles to doubleTree
43      for ( int j = 0; j < 10; j++ )
44      {
45         cin >> doubleValue;
46         doubleTree.insertNode( doubleValue );
47      } // end for
48
49      cout << "\nPreorder traversal\n";
50      doubleTree.preOrderTraversal();
51
52      cout << "\nInorder traversal\n";
53      doubleTree.inOrderTraversal();
54
55      cout << "\nPostorder traversal\n";
56      doubleTree.postOrderTraversal();
57
58      cout << endl;
59      return 0;
60   } // end main
```

Fig. 20.22 | Creating and traversing a binary tree. (Part 2 of 3.)

```
Enter 10 integer values:
50 25 75 12 33 67 88 6 13 68

Preorder traversal
50 25 12 6 13 33 75 67 68 88
Inorder traversal
6 12 13 25 33 50 67 68 75 88
Postorder traversal
6 13 12 33 25 68 67 88 75 50


Enter 10 double values:
39.2 16.5 82.7 3.3 65.2 90.8 1.1 4.4 89.5 92.5

Preorder traversal
39.2 16.5 3.3 1.1 4.4 82.7 65.2 90.8 89.5 92.5
Inorder traversal
1.1 3.3 4.4 16.5 39.2 65.2 82.7 89.5 90.8 92.5
Postorder traversal
1.1 4.4 3.3 16.5 65.2 89.5 92.5 90.8 82.7 39.2
```

Fig. 20.22 | Creating and traversing a binary tree. (Part 3 of 3.)

The Tree class template (Fig. 20.21) has as private data rootPtr (line 22), a pointer to the root node of the tree. Lines 17–20 of the class template declare the public member functions insertNode (that inserts a new node in the tree) and preOrderTraversal, inOrderTraversal and postOrderTraversal, each of which walks the tree in the designated manner. Each of these member functions calls its own separate recursive utility function to perform the appropriate operations on the internal representation of the tree, so the program is not required to access the underlying private data to perform these functions. Remember that the recursion requires us to pass in a pointer that represents the next subtree to process. The Tree constructor initializes rootPtr to zero to indicate that the tree is initially empty.

The Tree class's utility function insertNodeHelper (lines 47–68) is called by insertNode (lines 39–43) to recursively insert a node into the tree. *A node can only be inserted as a leaf node in a binary search tree.* If the tree is empty, a new TreeNode is created, initialized and inserted in the tree (lines 53–54).

If the tree is not empty, the program compares the value to be inserted with the data value in the root node. If the insert value is smaller (line 57), the program recursively calls insertNodeHelper (line 58) to insert the value in the left subtree. If the insert value is larger (line 62), the program recursively calls insertNodeHelper (line 64) to insert the value in the right subtree. If the value to be inserted is identical to the data value in the root node, the program prints the message " dup" (line 65) and returns without inserting the duplicate value into the tree. Note that insertNode passes the address of rootPtr to insertNodeHelper (line 42) so it can modify the value stored in rootPtr (i.e., the address of the root node). To receive a pointer to rootPtr (which is also a pointer), insertNodeHelper's first argument is declared as a pointer to a pointer to a TreeNode.

Each of the member functions inOrderTraversal (lines 90–94), preOrderTraversal (lines 71–75) and postOrderTraversal (lines 109–113) traverses the tree and prints the node values. For the purpose of the following discussion, we use the binary search tree in Fig. 20.23.

Fig. 20.23 | A binary search tree.

Inorder Traversal Algorithm

Function `inOrderTraversal` invokes utility function `inOrderHelper` to perform the inorder traversal of the binary tree. The steps for an inorder traversal are:

1. Traverse the left subtree with an inorder traversal. (This is performed by the call to `inOrderHelper` at line 102.)

2. Process the value in the node—i.e., print the node value (line 103).

3. Traverse the right subtree with an inorder traversal. (This is performed by the call to `inOrderHelper` at line 104.)

The value in a node is not processed until the values in its left subtree are processed, because each call to `inOrderHelper` immediately calls `inOrderHelper` again with the pointer to the left subtree. The inorder traversal of the tree in Fig. 20.23 is

        6 13 17 27 33 42 48

Note that the inorder traversal of a binary search tree prints the node values in ascending order. The process of creating a binary search tree actually sorts the data—thus, this process is called the binary tree sort.

Preorder Traversal Algorithm

Function `preOrderTraversal` invokes utility function `preOrderHelper` to perform the preorder traversal of the binary tree. The steps for an preorder traversal are:

1. Process the value in the node (line 83).

2. Traverse the left subtree with a preorder traversal. (This is performed by the call to `preOrderHelper` at line 84.)

3. Traverse the right subtree with a preorder traversal. (This is performed by the call to `preOrderHelper` at line 85.)

The value in each node is processed as the node is visited. After the value in a given node is processed, the values in the left subtree are processed. Then the values in the right subtree are processed. The preorder traversal of the tree in Fig. 20.23 is

        27 13 6 17 42 33 48

Postorder Traversal Algorithm

Function `postOrderTraversal` invokes utility function `postOrderHelper` to perform the postorder traversal of the binary tree. The steps for a postorder traversal are:

1. Traverse the left subtree with a postorder traversal. (This is performed by the call to `postOrderHelper` at line 122.)

2. Traverse the right subtree with a postorder traversal. (This is performed by the call to postOrderHelper at line 123.)

3. Process the value in the node (line 124).

The value in each node is not printed until the values of its children are printed. The post-OrderTraversal of the tree in Fig. 20.23 is

        6 17 13 33 48 42 27

Duplicate Elimination
The binary search tree facilitates duplicate elimination. As the tree is being created, an attempt to insert a duplicate value will be recognized, because a duplicate will follow the same "go left" or "go right" decisions on each comparison as the original value did when it was inserted in the tree. Thus, the duplicate will eventually be compared with a node containing the same value. The duplicate value may be discarded at this point.

Searching a binary tree for a value that matches a key value is also fast. If the tree is balanced, then each branch contains about half the number of nodes in the tree. Each comparison of a node to the search key eliminates half the nodes. This is called an $O(\log n)$ algorithm (Big O notation is discussed in Chapter 19). So a binary search tree with n elements would require a maximum of $\log_2 n$ comparisons either to find a match or to determine that no match exists. This means, for example, that when searching a (balanced) 1000-element binary search tree, no more than 10 comparisons need to be made, because $2^{10} > 1000$. When searching a (balanced) 1,000,000-element binary search tree, no more than 20 comparisons need to be made, because $2^{20} > 1,000,000$.

Overview of the Binary Tree Exercises
In the exercises, algorithms are presented for several other binary tree operations such as deleting an item from a binary tree, printing a binary tree in a two-dimensional tree format and performing a level-order traversal of a binary tree. The level-order traversal of a binary tree visits the nodes of the tree row by row, starting at the root node level. On each level of the tree, the nodes are visited from left to right. Other binary tree exercises include allowing a binary search tree to contain duplicate values, inserting string values in a binary tree and determining how many levels are contained in a binary tree.

20.8 Wrap-Up

In this chapter, you learned that linked lists are collections of data items that are "linked up in a chain." You also learned that a program can perform insertions and deletions anywhere in a linked list (though our implementation only performed insertions and deletions at the ends of the list). We demonstrated that the stack and queue data structures are constrained versions of lists. For stacks, you saw that insertions and deletions are made only at the top. For queues that represent waiting lines, you saw that insertions are made at the tail and deletions are made from the head. We also presented the binary tree data structure. You saw a binary search tree that facilitated high-speed searching and sorting of data and efficient duplicate elimination. Throughout the chapter, you learned how to create these data structures for reusability (as templates) and maintainability. In the next chapter, we introduce structs, which are similar to classes, and discuss the manipulation of bits, characters and C-style strings.

Summary

Section 20.1 Introduction
- Dynamic data structures grow and shrink during execution.
- Linked lists are collections of data items "lined up in a row"—insertions and removals are made anywhere in a linked list.
- Stacks are important in compilers and operating systems: Insertions and removals are made only at one end of a stack—its top.
- Queues represent waiting lines; insertions are made at the back (also referred to as the tail) of a queue and removals are made from the front (also referred to as the head).
- Binary trees facilitate high-speed searching and sorting of data, efficient elimination of duplicate data items, representation of file-system directories and compilation of expressions into machine language.

Section 20.2 Self-Referential Classes
- A self-referential class contains a pointer member that points to a class object of the same class type.
- Self-referential class objects can be linked together to form useful data structures such as lists, queues, stacks and trees.

Section 20.3 Dynamic Memory Allocation and Data Structures
- The limit for dynamic memory allocation can be as large as the amount of available physical memory in the computer or the amount of available virtual memory in a virtual memory system.

Section 20.4 Linked Lists
- A linked list is a linear collection of self-referential class objects, called nodes, connected by pointer links—hence, the term "linked" list.
- A linked list is accessed via a pointer to the first node of the list. Each subsequent node is accessed via the link-pointer member stored in the previous node.
- Linked lists, stacks and queues are linear data structures. Trees are nonlinear data structures.
- A linked list is appropriate when the number of data elements to be represented at one time is unpredictable.
- Linked lists are dynamic, so the length of a list can increase or decrease as necessary.
- A singly linked list begins with a pointer to the first node, and each node contains a pointer to the next node "in sequence."
- A circular, singly linked list begins with a pointer to the first node, and each node contains a pointer to the next node. The "last node" does not contain a null pointer; rather, the pointer in the last node points back to the first node, thus closing the "circle."
- A doubly linked list allows traversals both forward and backward.
- A doubly linked list is often implemented with two "start pointers"—one that points to the first element of the list to allow front-to-back traversal of the list and one that points to the last element to allow back-to-front traversal. Each node has both a forward pointer to the next node in the list in the forward direction and a backward pointer to the next node in the backward direction.
- In a circular, doubly linked list, the forward pointer of the last node points to the first node, and the backward pointer of the first node points to the last node, thus closing the "circle."

Section 20.5 Stacks
- A stack data structure allows nodes to be added to and removed from the stack only at the top.
- A stack is referred to as a last-in, first-out (LIFO) data structure.

- The primary member functions used to manipulate a stack are push and pop. Function push inserts a new node at the top of the stack. Function pop removes a node from the top of the stack.

Section 20.6 Queues

- A queue is similar to a supermarket checkout line—the first person in line is serviced first, and other customers enter the line at the end and wait to be serviced.
- Queue nodes are removed only from a queue's head and are inserted only at its tail.
- A queue is referred to as a first-in, first-out (FIFO) data structure. The insert and remove operations are known as enqueue and dequeue.

Section 20.7 Trees

- Binary trees are trees whose nodes all contain two links (none, one or both of which may be null).
- The root node is the first node in a tree.
- Each link in the root node refers to a child. The left child is the root node of the left subtree, and the right child is the root node of the right subtree.
- The children of a single node are called siblings. A node with no children is called a leaf node.
- A binary search tree (with no duplicate node values) has the characteristic that the values in any left subtree are less than the value in its parent node, and the values in any right subtree are greater than the value in its parent node.
- A node can only be inserted as a leaf node in a binary search tree.
- An inorder traversal of a binary tree traverses the left subtree inorder, processes the value in the root node and then traverses the right subtree inorder. The value in a node is not processed until the values in its left subtree are processed.
- A preorder traversal processes the value in the root node, traverses the left subtree preorder, then traverses the right subtree preorder. The value in each node is processed as the node is encountered.
- A postorder traversal traverses the left subtree postorder, traverses the right subtree postorder, then processes the value in the root node. The value in each node is not processed until the values in both its subtrees are processed.
- The binary search tree helps eliminate duplicate data. As the tree is being created, an attempt to insert a duplicate value will be recognized and the duplicate value may be discarded.
- The level-order traversal of a binary tree visits the nodes of the tree row by row, starting at the root node level. On each level of the tree, the nodes are visited from left to right.

Terminology

binary search tree	first-in, first-out (FIFO)
binary tree	head of a queue
binary tree sort	inorder traversal of a binary tree
child node	inserting a node
circular, doubly linked list	last-in, first-out (LIFO)
circular, singly linked list	leaf node
data structure	left child
delegation	left subtree
dequeue	level-order traversal
doubly linked list	linear data structure
duplicate elimination	link
dynamic data structures	linked list
enqueue	node

nonlinear data structure
parent node
pointer link
pop
postorder traversal of a binary tree
preorder traversal of a binary tree
print spooling
push
queue
right child

right subtree
root node
self-referential structure
siblings
singly linked list
spooler
stack
tail of a queue
top of a stack

Self-Review Exercises

20.1 Fill in the blanks in each of the following:
   a) A self-_____ class is used to form dynamic data structures that can grow and shrink at execution time
   b) The _____ operator is used to dynamically allocate memory and construct an object; this operator returns a pointer to the object.
   c) A(n) _____ is a constrained version of a linked list in which nodes can be inserted and deleted only from the start of the list and node values are returned in last-in, first-out order.
   d) A function that does not alter a linked list, but looks at the list to determine whether it is empty, is an example of a(n) _____ function.
   e) A queue is referred to as a(n) _____ data structure, because the first nodes inserted are the first nodes removed.
   f) The pointer to the next node in a linked list is referred to as a(n) _____.
   g) The _____ operator is used to destroy an object and release dynamically allocated memory.
   h) A(n) _____ is a constrained version of a linked list in which nodes can be inserted only at the end of the list and deleted only from the start of the list.
   i) A(n) _____ is a nonlinear, two-dimensional data structure that contains nodes with two or more links.
   j) A stack is referred to as a(n) _____ data structure, because the last node inserted is the first node removed.
   k) The nodes of a(n) _____ tree contain two link members.
   l) The first node of a tree is the _____ node.
   m) Each link in a tree node points to a(n) _____ or _____ of that node.
   n) A tree node that has no children is called a(n) _____ node.
   o) The four traversal algorithms we mentioned in the text for binary search trees are _____, _____, _____ and _____.

20.2 What are the differences between a linked list and a stack?

20.3 What are the differences between a stack and a queue?

20.4 Perhaps a more appropriate title for this chapter would have been "Reusable Data Structures." Comment on how each of the following entities or concepts contributes to the reusability of data structures:
   a) classes
   b) class templates
   c) inheritance
   d) private inheritance
   e) composition

20.5 Manually provide the inorder, preorder and postorder traversals of the binary search tree of Fig. 20.24.

Fig. 20.24 | A 15-node binary search tree.

Answers to Self-Review Exercises

20.1 a) referential. b) new. c) stack. d) predicate. e) first-in, first-out (FIFO). f) link. g) delete. h) queue. i) tree. j) last-in, first-out (LIFO). k) binary. l) root. m) child or subtree. n) leaf. o) inorder, preorder, postorder and level order.

20.2 It is possible to insert a node anywhere in a linked list and remove a node from anywhere in a linked list. Nodes in a stack may only be inserted at the top of the stack and removed from the top of a stack.

20.3 A queue data structure allows nodes to be removed only from the head of the queue and inserted only at the tail of the queue. A queue is referred to as a first-in, first-out (FIFO) data structure. A stack data structure allows nodes to be added to the stack and removed from the stack only at the top. A stack is referred to as a last-in, first-out (LIFO) data structure.

20.4 a) Classes allow us to instantiate as many data structure objects of a certain type (i.e., class) as we wish.

   b) Class templates enable us to instantiate related classes, each based on different type parameters—we can then generate as many objects of each template class as we like.

   c) Inheritance enables us to reuse code from a base class in a derived class, so that the derived-class data structure is also a base-class data structure (with public inheritance, that is).

   d) Private inheritance enables us to reuse portions of the code from a base class to form a derived-class data structure; because the inheritance is private, all public base-class member functions become private in the derived class. This enables us to prevent clients of the derived-class data structure from accessing base-class member functions that do not apply to the derived class.

   e) Composition enables us to reuse code by making a class object data structure a member of a composed class; if we make the class object a private member of the composed class, then the class object's public member functions are not available through the composed object's interface.

20.5 The inorder traversal is

    11 18 19 28 32 40 44 49 69 71 72 83 92 97 99

The preorder traversal is

    49 28 18 11 19 40 32 44 83 71 69 72 97 92 99

The postorder traversal is

    11 19 18 32 44 40 28 69 72 71 92 99 97 83 49

Exercises

20.6   Write a program that concatenates two linked list objects of characters. The program should include function concatenate, which takes references to both list objects as arguments and concatenates the second list to the first list.

20.7   Write a program that merges two ordered list objects of integers into a single ordered list object of integers. Function merge should receive references to each of the list objects to be merged and reference to a list object into which the merged elements will be placed.

20.8   Write a program that inserts 25 random integers from 0 to 100 in order in a linked list object. The program should calculate the sum of the elements and the floating-point average of the elements.

20.9   Write a program that creates a linked list object of 10 characters and creates a second list object containing a copy of the first list, but in reverse order.

20.10   Write a program that inputs a line of text and uses a stack object to print the line reversed.

20.11   Write a program that uses a stack object to determine if a string is a palindrome (i.e., the string is spelled identically backward and forward). The program should ignore spaces and punctuation.

20.12   Stacks are used by compilers to help in the process of evaluating expressions and generating machine language code. In this and the next exercise, we investigate how compilers evaluate arithmetic expressions consisting only of constants, operators and parentheses.

Humans generally write expressions like 3 + 4 and 7 / 9 in which the operator (+ or / here) is written between its operands—this is called infix notation. Computers "prefer" postfix notation in which the operator is written to the right of its two operands. The preceding infix expressions would appear in postfix notation as 3 4 + and 7 9 /, respectively.

To evaluate a complex infix expression, a compiler would first convert the expression to postfix notation and evaluate the postfix version of the expression. Each of these algorithms requires only a single left-to-right pass of the expression. Each algorithm uses a stack object in support of its operation, and in each algorithm the stack is used for a different purpose.

In this exercise, you'll write a C++ version of the infix-to-postfix conversion algorithm. In the next exercise, you'll write a C++ version of the postfix expression evaluation algorithm. Later in the chapter, you'll discover that code you write in this exercise can help you implement a complete working compiler.

Write a program that converts an ordinary infix arithmetic expression (assume a valid expression is entered) with single-digit integers such as

```
(6 + 2) * 5 - 8 / 4
```

to a postfix expression. The postfix version of the preceding infix expression is

```
6 2 + 5 * 8 4 / -
```

The program should read the expression into character array infix and use modified versions of the stack functions implemented in this chapter to help create the postfix expression in character array postfix. The algorithm for creating a postfix expression is as follows:

1) Push a left parenthesis '(' onto the stack.
2) Append a right parenthesis ')' to the end of infix.
3) While the stack is not empty, read infix from left to right and do the following:
   If the current character in infix is a digit, copy it to the next element of postfix.
   If the current character in infix is a left parenthesis, push it onto the stack.

If the current character in infix is an operator,
> Pop operators (if there are any) at the top of the stack while they have equal or higher precedence than the current operator, and insert the popped operators in postfix.
> Push the current character in infix onto the stack.

If the current character in infix is a right parenthesis
> Pop operators from the top of the stack and insert them in postfix until a left parenthesis is at the top of the stack.
> Pop (and discard) the left parenthesis from the stack.

The following arithmetic operations are allowed in an expression:

+ addition
- subtraction
* multiplication
/ division
^ exponentiation
% modulus

[*Note:* We assume left-to-right associativity for all operators for the purpose of this exercise.] The stack should be maintained with stack nodes, each containing a data member and a pointer to the next stack node.

Some of the functional capabilities you may want to provide are:

a) function convertToPostfix that converts the infix expression to postfix notation
b) function isOperator that determines whether c is an operator
c) function precedence that determines whether the precedence of operator1 is less than, equal to or greater than the precedence of operator2 (the function returns −1, 0 and 1, respectively)
d) function push that pushes a value onto the stack
e) function pop that pops a value off the stack
f) function stackTop that returns the top value of the stack without popping the stack
g) function isEmpty that determines if the stack is empty
h) function printStack that prints the stack

20.13 Write a program that evaluates a postfix expression (assume it is valid) such as

    6 2 + 5 * 8 4 / -

The program should read a postfix expression consisting of digits and operators into a character array. Using modified versions of the stack functions implemented earlier in this chapter, the program should scan the expression and evaluate it. The algorithm is as follows:

1) Append the null character ('\0') to the end of the postfix expression. When the null character is encountered, no further processing is necessary.
2) While '\0' has not been encountered, read the expression from left to right.
> If the current character is a digit,
>> Push its integer value onto the stack (the integer value of a digit character is its value in the computer's character set minus the value of '0' in the computer's character set).
> Otherwise, if the current character is an *operator*,
>> Pop the two top elements of the stack into variables x and y.
>> Calculate y *operator* x.
>> Push the result of the calculation onto the stack.
3) When the null character is encountered in the expression, pop the top value of the stack. This is the result of the postfix expression.

[*Note:* In *Step 2* above, if the operator is '/', the top of the stack is 2 and the next element in the stack is 8, then pop 2 into x, pop 8 into y, evaluate 8 / 2 and push the result, 4, back onto the stack. This note also applies to operator '-'.] The arithmetic operations allowed in an expression are

+   addition
-   subtraction
*   multiplication
/   division
^   exponentiation
%   modulus

[*Note:* We assume left-to-right associativity for all operators for the purpose of this exercise.] The stack should be maintained with stack nodes that contain an int data member and a pointer to the next stack node. You may want to provide the following functional capabilities:

a) function evaluatePostfixExpression that evaluates the postfix expression
b) function calculate that evaluates the expression op1 operator op2
c) function push that pushes a value onto the stack
d) function pop that pops a value off the stack
e) function isEmpty that determines if the stack is empty
f) function printStack that prints the stack

20.14 Modify the postfix evaluator program of Exercise 20.13 so that it can process integer operands larger than 9.

20.15 *(Supermarket Simulation)* Write a program that simulates a checkout line at a supermarket. The line is a queue object. Customers (i.e., customer objects) arrive in random integer intervals of 1–4 minutes. Also, each customer is served in random integer intervals of 1–4 minutes. Obviously, the rates need to be balanced. If the average arrival rate is larger than the average service rate, the queue will grow infinitely. Even with "balanced" rates, randomness can still cause long lines. Run the supermarket simulation for a 12-hour day (720 minutes) using the following algorithm:

1) Choose a random integer between 1 and 4 to determine the minute at which the first customer arrives.
2) At the first customer's arrival time:
   Determine customer's service time (random integer from 1 to 4);
   Begin servicing the customer;
   Schedule arrival time of next customer (random integer 1 to 4 added to the current time).
3) For each minute of the day:
   If the next customer arrives,
     Say so,
     Enqueue the customer;
     Schedule the arrival time of the next customer;
   If service was completed for the last customer;
     Say so
     Dequeue next customer to be serviced
     Determine customer's service completion time
       (random integer from 1 to 4 added to the current time).

Now run your simulation for 720 minutes, and answer each of the following:

a) What is the maximum number of customers in the queue at any time?
b) What is the longest wait any one customer experiences?
c) What happens if the arrival interval is changed from 1–4 minutes to 1–3 minutes?

20.16 Modify the program of Figs. 20.20–20.22 to allow the binary tree object to contain duplicates.

20.17 Write a program based on Figs. 20.20–20.22 that inputs a line of text, tokenizes the sentence into separate words (you may want to use the strtok library function), inserts the words in a binary search tree and prints the inorder, preorder and postorder traversals of the tree. Use an OOP approach.

20.18 In this chapter, we saw that duplicate elimination is straightforward when creating a binary search tree. Describe how you would perform duplicate elimination using only a one-dimensional array. Compare the performance of array-based duplicate elimination with the performance of binary-search-tree-based duplicate elimination.

20.19 Write a function depth that receives a binary tree and determines how many levels it has.

20.20 (*Recursively Print a List Backward*) Write a member function printListBackward that recursively outputs the items in a linked list object in reverse order. Write a test program that creates a sorted list of integers and prints the list in reverse order.

20.21 (*Recursively Search a List*) Write a member function searchList that recursively searches a linked list object for a specified value. The function should return a pointer to the value if it is found; otherwise, null should be returned. Use your function in a test program that creates a list of integers. The program should prompt the user for a value to locate in the list.

20.22 (*Binary Tree Delete*) In this exercise, we discuss deleting items from binary search trees. The deletion algorithm is not as straightforward as the insertion algorithm. There are three cases that are encountered when deleting an item—the item is contained in a leaf node (i.e., it has no children), the item is contained in a node that has one child or the item is contained in a node that has two children.

If the item to be deleted is contained in a leaf node, the node is deleted and the pointer in the parent node is set to null.

If the item to be deleted is contained in a node with one child, the pointer in the parent node is set to point to the child node and the node containing the data item is deleted. This causes the child node to take the place of the deleted node in the tree.

The last case is the most difficult. When a node with two children is deleted, another node in the tree must take its place. However, the pointer in the parent node cannot be assigned to point to one of the children of the node to be deleted. In most cases, the resulting binary search tree would not adhere to the following characteristic of binary search trees (with no duplicate values): *The values in any left subtree are less than the value in the parent node, and the values in any right subtree are greater than the value in the parent node.*

Which node is used as a *replacement node* to maintain this characteristic? Either the node containing the largest value in the tree less than the value in the node being deleted, or the node containing the smallest value in the tree greater than the value in the node being deleted. Let us consider the node with the smaller value. In a binary search tree, the largest value less than a parent's value is located in the left subtree of the parent node and is guaranteed to be contained in the rightmost node of the subtree. This node is located by walking down the left subtree to the right until the pointer to the right child of the current node is null. We are now pointing to the replacement node, which is either a leaf node or a node with one child to its left. If the replacement node is a leaf node, the steps to perform the deletion are as follows:

1) Store the pointer to the node to be deleted in a temporary pointer variable (this pointer is used to delete the dynamically allocated memory).
2) Set the pointer in the parent of the node being deleted to point to the replacement node.
3) Set the pointer in the parent of the replacement node to null.
4) Set the pointer to the right subtree in the replacement node to point to the right subtree of the node to be deleted.
5) Delete the node to which the temporary pointer variable points.

The deletion steps for a replacement node with a left child are similar to those for a replacement node with no children, but the algorithm also must move the child into the replacement node's position in the tree. If the replacement node is a node with a left child, the steps to perform the deletion are as follows:

1) Store the pointer to the node to be deleted in a temporary pointer variable.
2) Set the pointer in the parent of the node being deleted to point to the replacement node.
3) Set the pointer in the parent of the replacement node to point to the left child of the replacement node.
4) Set the pointer to the right subtree in the replacement node to point to the right subtree of the node to be deleted.
5) Delete the node to which the temporary pointer variable points.

Write member function `deleteNode`, which takes as its arguments a pointer to the root node of the tree object and the value to be deleted. The function should locate in the tree the node containing the value to be deleted and use the algorithms discussed here to delete the node. The function should print a message that indicates whether the value is deleted. Modify the program of Figs. 20.20–20.22 to use this function. After deleting an item, call the `inOrder`, `preOrder` and `postOrder` traversal functions to confirm that the delete operation was performed correctly.

20.23 (*Binary Tree Search*) Write member function `binaryTreeSearch`, which attempts to locate a specified value in a binary search tree object. The function should take as arguments a pointer to the root node of the binary tree and a search key to be located. If the node containing the search key is found, the function should return a pointer to that node; otherwise, the function should return a null pointer.

20.24 (*Level-Order Binary Tree Traversal*) The program of Figs. 20.20–20.22 illustrated three recursive methods of traversing a binary tree—inorder, preorder and postorder traversals. This exercise presents the *level-order traversal* of a binary tree, in which the node values are printed level by level, starting at the root node level. The nodes on each level are printed from left to right. The level-order traversal is not a recursive algorithm. It uses a queue object to control the output of the nodes. The algorithm is as follows:

1) Insert the root node in the queue
2) While there are nodes left in the queue,
   Get the next node in the queue
   Print the node's value
   If the pointer to the left child of the node is not null
      Insert the left child node in the queue
   If the pointer to the right child of the node is not null
      Insert the right child node in the queue.

Write member function `levelOrder` to perform a level-order traversal of a binary tree object. Modify the program of Figs. 20.20–20.22 to use this function. [*Note:* You'll also need to modify and incorporate the queue-processing functions of Fig. 20.16 in this program.]

20.25 (*Printing Trees*) Write a recursive member function `outputTree` to display a binary tree object on the screen. The function should output the tree row by row, with the top of the tree at the left of the screen and the bottom of the tree toward the right of the screen. Each row is output vertically. For example, the binary tree illustrated in Fig. 20.24 is output as shown in Fig. 20.25. Note that the rightmost leaf node appears at the top of the output in the rightmost column and the root node appears at the left of the output. Each column of output starts five spaces to the right of the previous column. Function `outputTree` should receive an argument `totalSpaces` representing the number of spaces preceding the value to be output (this variable should start at zero, so the root node is output at the left of the screen). The function uses a modified inorder traversal to output the tree—it starts at the rightmost node in the tree and works back to the left. The algorithm is as follows:

```
                      99
              97
                      92
       83
                      72
              71
                      69
49
                      44
              40
                      32
       28
                      19
              18
                      11
```

Fig. 20.25 | Result of using `outputTree` to display the tree in Fig. 20.24.

> While the pointer to the current node is not null
> > Recursively call `outputTree` with the right subtree of the current node and
> > > `totalSpaces + 5`
> > Use a for structure to count from 1 to `totalSpaces` and output spaces
> > Output the value in the current node
> > Set the pointer to the current node to point to the left subtree of the current node
> > Increment `totalSpaces` by 5.

Special Section: Building Your Own Compiler

In Exercises 8.18–8.19, we introduced Simpletron Machine Language (SML) and you implemented a Simpletron computer simulator to execute programs written in SML. In this section, we build a compiler that converts programs written in a high-level programming language to SML. This section "ties" together the entire programming process. You'll write programs in this new high-level language, compile these programs on the compiler you build and run them on the simulator you built in Exercise 8.19. You should make every effort to implement your compiler in an object-oriented manner.

20.26 (*The Simple Language*) Before we begin building the compiler, we discuss a simple, yet powerful, high-level language similar to early versions of the popular language BASIC. We call the language *Simple*. Every Simple *statement* consists of a *line number* and a Simple *instruction*. Line numbers must appear in ascending order. Each instruction begins with one of the following Simple *commands*: rem, input, let, print, goto, if...goto and end (see Fig. 20.26). All commands except end can be used repeatedly. Simple evaluates only integer expressions using the +, -, * and / operators. These operators have the same precedence as in C++. Parentheses can be used to change the order of evaluation of an expression.

Our Simple compiler recognizes only lowercase letters. All characters in a Simple file should be lowercase (uppercase letters result in a syntax error unless they appear in a rem statement, in which case they are ignored). A *variable name* is a single letter. Simple does not allow descriptive variable names, so variables should be explained in remarks to indicate their use in a program. Simple uses only integer variables. Simple does not have variable declarations—merely mentioning a variable name in a program causes the variable to be declared and initialized to zero automatically. The syntax of Simple does not allow string manipulation (reading a string, writing a string, comparing strings, etc.). If a string is encountered in a Simple program (after a command other than rem), the compiler generates a syntax error. The first version of our compiler will assume that Simple programs are entered correctly. Exercise 20.29 asks the student to modify the compiler to perform syntax error checking.

Command	Example statement	Description
rem	50 rem this is a remark	Text following rem is for documentation purposes and is ignored by the compiler.
input	30 input x	Display a question mark to prompt the user to enter an integer. Read that integer from the keyboard, and store the integer in x.
let	80 let u = 4 * (j - 56)	Assign u the value of 4 * (j - 56). Note that an arbitrarily complex expression can appear to the right of the equals sign.
print	10 print w	Display the value of w.
goto	70 goto 45	Transfer program control to line 45.
if...goto	35 if i == z goto 80	Compare i and z for equality and transfer control to line 80 if the condition is true; otherwise, continue execution with the next statement.
end	99 end	Terminate program execution.

Fig. 20.26 | Simple commands.

Simple uses the conditional if...goto statement and the unconditional goto statement to alter the flow of control during program execution. If the condition in the if...goto statement is true, control is transferred to a specific line of the program. The following relational and equality operators are valid in an if...goto statement: <, >, <=, >=, == and !=. The precedence of these operators is the same as in C++.

Let us now consider several programs that demonstrate Simple's features. The first program (Fig. 20.27) reads two integers from the keyboard, stores the values in variables a and b and computes and prints their sum (stored in variable c).

The program of Fig. 20.28 determines and prints the larger of two integers. The integers are input from the keyboard and stored in s and t. The if...goto statement tests the condition s >= t. If the condition is true, control is transferred to line 90 and s is output; otherwise, t is output and control is transferred to the end statement in line 99, where the program terminates.

Simple does not provide a repetition statement (such as C++'s for, while or do...while). However, Simple can simulate each of C++'s repetition statements using the if...goto and goto state-

```
 1    10 rem    determine and print the sum of two integers
 2    15 rem
 3    20 rem    input the two integers
 4    30 input a
 5    40 input b
 6    45 rem
 7    50 rem    add integers and store result in c
 8    60 let c = a + b
 9    65 rem
10    70 rem    print the result
11    80 print c
12    90 rem    terminate program execution
13    99 end
```

Fig. 20.27 | Simple program that determines the sum of two integers.

ments. Figure 20.29 uses a sentinel-controlled loop to calculate the squares of several integers. Each integer is input from the keyboard and stored in variable j. If the value entered is the sentinel value -9999, control is transferred to line 99, where the program terminates. Otherwise, k is assigned the square of j, k is output to the screen and control is passed to line 20, where the next integer is input.

Using the sample programs of Fig. 20.27, Fig. 20.28 and Fig. 20.29 as your guide, write a Simple program to accomplish each of the following:

a) Input three integers, determine their average and print the result.

b) Use a sentinel-controlled loop to input 10 integers and compute and print their sum.

c) Use a counter-controlled loop to input seven integers, some positive and some negative, and compute and print their average.

d) Input a series of integers and determine and print the largest. The first integer input indicates how many numbers should be processed.

e) Input 10 integers and print the smallest.

f) Calculate and print the sum of the even integers from 2 to 30.

g) Calculate and print the product of the odd integers from 1 to 9.

```
 1   10 rem    determine the larger of two integers
 2   20 input s
 3   30 input t
 4   32 rem
 5   35 rem    test if s >= t
 6   40 if s >= t goto 90
 7   45 rem
 8   50 rem    t is greater than s, so print t
 9   60 print t
10   70 goto 99
11   75 rem
12   80 rem    s is greater than or equal to t, so print s
13   90 print s
14   99 end
```

Fig. 20.28 | Simple program that finds the larger of two integers.

```
 1   10 rem    calculate the squares of several integers
 2   20 input j
 3   23 rem
 4   25 rem    test for sentinel value
 5   30 if j == -9999 goto 99
 6   33 rem
 7   35 rem    calculate square of j and assign result to k
 8   40 let k = j * j
 9   50 print k
10   53 rem
11   55 rem    loop to get next j
12   60 goto 20
13   99 end
```

Fig. 20.29 | Calculate the squares of several integers.

20.27 (*Building a Compiler; Prerequisite: Complete Exercises 8.18, 8.19, 21.12, 21.13 and 21.26*) Now that the Simple language has been presented (Exercise 20.26), we discuss how to build a Simple compiler. First, we consider the process by which a Simple program is converted to SML and executed by the Simpletron simulator (see Fig. 20.30). A file containing a Simple program is read by the compiler and converted to SML code. The SML code is output to a file on disk, in which SML instructions appear one per line. The SML file is then loaded into the Simpletron simulator, and the results are sent to a file on disk and to the screen. Note that the Simpletron program developed in Exercise 8.19 took its input from the keyboard. It must be modified to read from a file so it can run the programs produced by our compiler.

The Simple compiler performs two *passes* of the Simple program to convert it to SML. The first pass constructs a *symbol table* (object) in which every *line number* (object), *variable name* (object) and *constant* (object) of the Simple program is stored with its type and corresponding location in the final SML code (the symbol table is discussed in detail below). The first pass also produces the corresponding SML instruction object(s) for each of the Simple statements (object, etc.). As we'll see, if the Simple program contains statements that transfer control to a line later in the program, the first pass results in an SML program containing some "unfinished" instructions. The second pass of the compiler locates and completes the unfinished instructions, and outputs the SML program to a file.

Fig. 20.30 | Writing, compiling and executing a Simple language program.

First Pass

The compiler begins by reading one statement of the Simple program into memory. The line must be separated into its individual *tokens* (i.e., "pieces" of a statement) for processing and compilation (standard library function strtok can be used to facilitate this task). Recall that every statement begins with a line number followed by a command. As the compiler breaks a statement into tokens, if the token is a line number, a variable or a constant, it is placed in the symbol table. A line number is placed in the symbol table only if it is the first token in a statement. The symbolTable object is an array of tableEntry objects representing each symbol in the program. There is no restriction on the number of symbols that can appear in the program. Therefore, the symbolTable for a particular program could be large. Make the symbolTable a 100-element array for now. You can increase or decrease its size once the program is working.

Each tableEntry object contains three members. Member symbol is an integer containing the ASCII representation of a variable (remember that variable names are single characters), a line number or a constant. Member type is one of the following characters indicating the symbol's type: 'C' for constant, 'L' for line number and 'V' for variable. Member location contains the Simpletron memory location (00 to 99) to which the symbol refers. Simpletron memory is an array of 100 integers in which SML instructions and data are stored. For a line number, the location is the element in the Simpletron memory array at which the SML instructions for the Simple statement begin. For a variable or constant, the location is the element in the Simpletron memory array in which the variable or constant is stored. Variables and constants are allocated from the end of Simpletron's memory backward. The first variable or constant is stored in location at 99, the next in location at 98, etc.

The symbol table plays an integral part in converting Simple programs to SML. We learned in Chapter 8 that an SML instruction is a four-digit integer composed of two parts—the *operation code* and the *operand*. The operation code is determined by commands in Simple. For example, the simple command `input` corresponds to SML operation code 10 (read), and the Simple command `print` corresponds to SML operation code 11 (write). The operand is a memory location containing the data on which the operation code performs its task (e.g., operation code 10 reads a value from the keyboard and stores it in the memory location specified by the operand). The compiler searches `symbolTable` to determine the Simpletron memory location for each symbol so the corresponding location can be used to complete the SML instructions.

The compilation of each Simple statement is based on its command. For example, after the line number in a `rem` statement is inserted in the symbol table, the remainder of the statement is ignored by the compiler because a remark is for documentation purposes only. The `input`, `print`, `goto` and end statements correspond to the SML *read*, *write*, *branch* (to a specific location) and *halt* instructions. Statements containing these Simple commands are converted directly to SML (note that a `goto` statement may contain an unresolved reference if the specified line number refers to a statement further into the Simple program file; this is sometimes called a forward reference).

When a `goto` statement is compiled with an unresolved reference, the SML instruction must be *flagged* to indicate that the second pass of the compiler must complete the instruction. The flags are stored in 100-element array `flags` of type `int` in which each element is initialized to -1. If the memory location to which a line number in the Simple program refers is not yet known (i.e., it is not in the symbol table), the line number is stored in array `flags` in the element with the same subscript as the incomplete instruction. The operand of the incomplete instruction is set to 00 temporarily. For example, an unconditional branch instruction (making a forward reference) is left as +4000 until the second pass of the compiler. The second pass of the compiler is described shortly.

Compilation of `if...goto` and `let` statements is more complicated than for other statements—they are the only statements that produce more than one SML instruction. For an `if...goto`, the compiler produces code to test the condition and to branch to another line if necessary. The result of the branch could be an unresolved reference. Each of the relational and equality operators can be simulated using SML's *branch zero* or *branch negative* instructions (or a combination of both).

For a `let` statement, the compiler produces code to evaluate an arbitrarily complex arithmetic expression consisting of integer variables and/or constants. Expressions should separate each operand and operator with spaces. Exercise 20.12 and Exercise 20.13 presented the infix-to-postfix conversion algorithm and the postfix evaluation algorithm used by compilers to evaluate expressions. Before proceeding with your compiler, you should complete each of these exercises. When a compiler encounters an expression, it converts the expression from infix notation to postfix notation and then evaluates the postfix expression.

How is it that the compiler produces the machine language to evaluate an expression containing variables? The postfix evaluation algorithm contains a "hook" where the compiler can generate SML instructions rather than actually evaluating the expression. To enable this "hook" in the compiler, the postfix evaluation algorithm must be modified to search the symbol table for each symbol it encounters (and possibly insert it), determine the symbol's corresponding memory location and *push the memory location onto the stack (instead of the symbol)*. When an operator is encountered in the postfix expression, the two memory locations at the top of the stack are popped and machine language for effecting the operation is produced, using the memory locations as operands. The result of each subexpression is stored in a temporary location in memory and pushed back onto the stack so that the evaluation of the postfix expression can continue. When postfix evaluation is complete, the memory location containing the result is the only location left on the stack. This is popped, and SML instructions are generated to assign the result to the variable at the left of the `let` statement.

Second Pass

The second pass of the compiler performs two tasks: Resolve any unresolved references, and output the SML code to a file. Resolution of references occurs as follows:

a) Search the flags array for an unresolved reference (i.e., an element with a value other than -1).

b) Locate the object in array symbolTable, containing the symbol stored in the flags array (be sure that the type of the symbol is 'L' for line number).

c) Insert the memory location from member location into the instruction with the unresolved reference (remember that an instruction containing an unresolved reference has operand 00).

d) Repeat *Steps a*, *b* and *c* until the end of the flags array is reached.

After the resolution process is complete, the entire array containing the SML code is output to a disk file with one SML instruction per line. This file can be read by the Simpletron for execution (after the simulator is modified to read its input from a file). Compiling your first Simple program into an SML file and then executing that file should give you a real sense of personal accomplishment.

A Complete Example

The following example illustrates a complete conversion of a Simple program to SML as it will be performed by the Simple compiler. Consider a Simple program that inputs an integer and sums the values from 1 to that integer. The program and the SML instructions produced by the first pass of the Simple compiler are illustrated in Fig. 20.31. The symbol table constructed by the first pass is shown in Fig. 20.32.

Simple program	SML location & instruction	Description
5 rem sum 1 to x	*none*	rem ignored
10 input x	00 +1099	read x into location 99
15 rem check y == x	*none*	rem ignored
20 if y == x goto 60	01 +2098	load y (98) into accumulator
	02 +3199	sub x (99) from accumulator
	03 +4200	branch zero to unresolved location
25 rem increment y	*none*	rem ignored
30 let y = y + 1	04 +2098	load y into accumulator
	05 +3097	add 1 (97) to accumulator
	06 +2196	store in temporary location 96
	07 +2096	load from temporary location 96
	08 +2198	store accumulator in y
35 rem add y to total	*none*	rem ignored
40 let t = t + y	09 +2095	load t (95) into accumulator
	10 +3098	add y to accumulator
	11 +2194	store in temporary location 94

Fig. 20.31 | SML instructions produced after the compiler's first pass. (Part 1 of 2.)

Simple program	SML location & instruction	Description
	12 +2094	load from temporary location 94
	13 +2195	store accumulator in t
45 rem loop y	*none*	rem ignored
50 goto 20	14 +4001	branch to location 01
55 rem output result	*none*	rem ignored
60 print t	15 +1195	output t to screen
99 end	16 +4300	terminate execution

Fig. 20.31 | SML instructions produced after the compiler's first pass. (Part 2 of 2.)

Symbol	Type	Location
5	L	00
10	L	00
'x'	V	99
15	L	01
20	L	01
'y'	V	98
25	L	04
30	L	04
1	C	97
35	L	09
40	L	09
't'	V	95
45	L	14
50	L	14
55	L	15
60	L	15
99	L	16

Fig. 20.32 | Symbol table for program of Fig. 20.31.

Most Simple statements convert directly to single SML instructions. The exceptions in this program are remarks, the if...goto statement in line 20 and the let statements. Remarks don't translate into machine language. However, the line number for a remark is placed in the symbol table in case the line number is referenced in a goto or an if...goto statement. Line 20 of the program specifies that if the condition y == x is true, program control is transferred to line 60. Because line 60 appears later in the program, the first pass of the compiler has not as yet placed 60 in the symbol table (statement line numbers are placed in the symbol table only when they appear as the first token in a statement). Therefore, it is not possible at this time to determine the operand of the SML *branch zero* instruction at location 03 in the array of SML instructions. The compiler places 60 in location 03 of the flags array to indicate that the second pass completes this instruction.

We must keep track of the next instruction location in the SML array, because there is not a one-to-one correspondence between Simple statements and SML instructions. For example, the if...goto statement of line 20 compiles into three SML instructions. Each time an instruction is produced, we must increment the *instruction counter* to the next location in the SML array. Note that the size of Simpletron's memory could present a problem for Simple programs with many statements, variables and constants. It is conceivable that the compiler will run out of memory. To test for this case, your program should contain a *data counter* to keep track of the location at which the next variable or constant will be stored in the SML array. If the value of the instruction counter is larger than the value of the data counter, the SML array is full. In this case, the compilation process should terminate and the compiler should print an error message indicating that it ran out of memory during compilation. This serves to emphasize that, although you are freed from the burdens of managing memory by the compiler, the compiler itself must carefully determine the placement of instructions and data in memory, and must check for such errors as memory being exhausted during the compilation process.

A Step-by-Step View of the Compilation Process

Let us now walk through the compilation process for the Simple program in Fig. 20.31. The compiler reads the first line of the program

```
5 rem sum 1 to x
```

into memory. The first token in the statement (the line number) is determined using strtok (see Chapter 8 and Chapter 19 for a discussion of C++'s C-style string-manipulation functions). The token returned by strtok is converted to an integer using atoi, so the symbol 5 can be located in the symbol table. If the symbol is not found, it is inserted in the symbol table. Since we are at the beginning of the program and this is the first line, no symbols are in the table yet. So 5 is inserted into the symbol table as type L (line number) and assigned the first location in SML array (00). Although this line is a remark, a space in the symbol table is still allocated for the line number (in case it is referenced by a goto or an if...goto). No SML instruction is generated for a rem statement, so the instruction counter is not incremented.

The statement

```
10 input x
```

is tokenized next. The line number 10 is placed in the symbol table as type L and assigned the first location in the SML array (00, because a remark began the program so the instruction counter is currently 00). The command input indicates that the next token is a variable (only a variable can appear in an input statement). Because input corresponds directly to an SML operation code, the compiler has to determine the location of x in the SML array. Symbol x is not found in the symbol table, so it is inserted into the symbol table as the ASCII representation of x, given type V, and assigned location 99 in the SML array (data storage begins at 99 and is allocated backward). SML code can now be generated for this statement. Operation code 10 (the SML read operation code) is multiplied by 100, and the location of x (as determined in the symbol table) is added to complete the instruction. The instruction is then stored in the SML array at location 00. The instruction counter is incremented by 1, because a single SML instruction was produced.

The statement

```
15 rem    check y == x
```

is tokenized next. The symbol table is searched for line number 15 (which is not found). The line number is inserted as type L and assigned the next location in the array, 01 (remember that rem statements do not produce code, so the instruction counter is not incremented).

The statement

```
20 if y == x goto 60
```

is tokenized next. Line number 20 is inserted in the symbol table and given type L with the next location in the SML array 01. The command if indicates that a condition is to be evaluated. The variable y is not found in the symbol table, so it is inserted and given the type V and the SML location 98. Next, SML instructions are generated to evaluate the condition. Since there is no direct equivalent in SML for the if...goto, it must be simulated by performing a calculation using x and y and branching based on the result. If y is equal to x, the result of subtracting x from y is zero, so the *branch zero* instruction can be used with the result of the calculation to simulate the if...goto statement. The first step requires that y be loaded (from SML location 98) into the accumulator. This produces the instruction 01 +2098. Next, x is subtracted from the accumulator. This produces the instruction 02 +3199. The value in the accumulator may be zero, positive or negative. Since the operator is ==, we want to *branch zero*. First, the symbol table is searched for the branch location (60 in this case), which is not found. So 60 is placed in the flags array at location 03, and the instruction 03 +4200 is generated (we cannot add the branch location, because we have not assigned a location to line 60 in the SML array yet). The instruction counter is incremented to 04.

The compiler proceeds to the statement

```
25 rem   increment y
```

The line number 25 is inserted in the symbol table as type L and assigned SML location 04. The instruction counter is not incremented.

When the statement

```
30 let y = y + 1
```

is tokenized, the line number 30 is inserted in the symbol table as type L and assigned SML location 04. Command let indicates that the line is an assignment statement. First, all the symbols on the line are inserted in the symbol table (if they are not already there). The integer 1 is added to the symbol table as type C and assigned SML location 97. Next, the right side of the assignment is converted from infix to postfix notation. Then the postfix expression (y 1 +) is evaluated. Symbol y is located in the symbol table, and its corresponding memory location is pushed onto the stack. Symbol 1 is also located in the symbol table, and its corresponding memory location is pushed onto the stack. When the operator + is encountered, the postfix evaluator pops the stack into the right operand of the operator, pops the stack again into the left operand of the operator and produces the SML instructions

```
04 +2098    (load y)
05 +3097    (add 1)
```

The result of the expression is stored in a temporary location in memory (96) with instruction

```
06 +2196    (store temporary)
```

and the temporary location is pushed on the stack. Now that the expression has been evaluated, the result must be stored in y (i.e., the variable on the left side of =). So the temporary location is loaded into the accumulator, and the accumulator is stored in y with the instructions

```
07 +2096    (load temporary)
08 +2198    (store y)
```

Notice that SML instructions appear to be redundant. We'll discuss this issue shortly.

When the statement

```
35 rem    add y to total
```

is tokenized, line number 35 is inserted in the symbol table as type L and assigned location 09.

The statement

```
40 let t = t + y
```

is similar to line 30. The variable t is inserted in the symbol table as type V and assigned SML location 95. The instructions follow the same logic and format as line 30, and the instructions 09 +2095, 10 +3098, 11 +2194, 12 +2094 and 13 +2195 are generated. Note that the result of t + y is assigned to temporary location 94 before being assigned to t (95). Once again, note that the instructions in memory locations 11 and 12 appear to be redundant. Again, we'll discuss this shortly.

The statement

```
45 rem    loop y
```

is a remark, so line 45 is added to the symbol table as type L and assigned SML location 14.

The statement

```
50 goto 20
```

transfers control to line 20. Line number 50 is inserted in the symbol table as type L and assigned SML location 14. The equivalent of goto in SML is the *unconditional branch* (40) instruction that transfers control to a specific SML location. The compiler searches the symbol table for line 20 and finds that it corresponds to SML location 01. The operation code (40) is multiplied by 100, and location 01 is added to it to produce the instruction 14 +4001.

The statement

```
55 rem    output result
```

is a remark, so line 55 is inserted in the symbol table as type L and assigned SML location 15.

The statement

```
60 print t
```

is an output statement. Line number 60 is inserted in the symbol table as type L and assigned SML location 15. The equivalent of print in SML is operation code 11 (*write*). The location of t is determined from the symbol table and added to the result of the operation code multiplied by 100.

The statement

```
99 end
```

is the final line of the program. Line number 99 is stored in the symbol table as type L and assigned SML location 16. The end command produces the SML instruction +4300 (43 is *halt* in SML), which is written as the final instruction in the SML memory array.

This completes the first pass of the compiler. We now consider the second pass. The flags array is searched for values other than -1. Location 03 contains 60, so the compiler knows that instruction 03 is incomplete. The compiler completes the instruction by searching the symbol table for 60, determining its location and adding the location to the incomplete instruction. In this case, the search determines that line 60 corresponds to SML location 15, so the completed instruction 03 +4215 is produced, replacing 03 +4200. The Simple program has now been compiled successfully.

To build the compiler, you'll have to perform each of the following tasks:

a) Modify the Simpletron simulator program you wrote in Exercise 8.19 to take its input from a file specified by the user (see Chapter 17). The simulator should output its results to a disk file in the same format as the screen output. Convert the simulator to be an object-oriented program. In particular, make each part of the hardware an object. Arrange the instruction types into a class hierarchy using inheritance. Then execute the program polymorphically by telling each instruction to execute itself with an executeInstruction message.

b) Modify the infix-to-postfix conversion algorithm of Exercise 20.12 to process multi-digit integer operands and single-letter variable name operands. [*Hint:* C++ Standard Library function strtok can be used to locate each constant and variable in an expression, and constants can be converted from strings to integers using standard library function atoi (<csdtlib>).] [*Note:* The data representation of the postfix expression must be altered to support variable names and integer constants.]

c) Modify the postfix evaluation algorithm to process multidigit integer operands and variable name operands. Also, the algorithm should now implement the "hook" discussed previously so that SML instructions are produced rather than directly evaluating the expression. [*Hint:* Standard library function strtok can be used to locate each constant and variable in an expression, and constants can be converted from strings to integers using standard library function atoi.] [*Note:* The data representation of the postfix expression must be altered to support variable names and integer constants.]

d) Build the compiler. Incorporate parts (b) and (c) for evaluating expressions in let statements. Your program should contain a function that performs the first pass of the compiler and a function that performs the second pass of the compiler. Both functions can call other functions to accomplish their tasks. Make your compiler as object oriented as possible.

20.28 (*Optimizing the Simple Compiler*) When a program is compiled and converted into SML, a set of instructions is generated. Certain combinations of instructions often repeat themselves, usually in triplets called *productions*. A production normally consists of three instructions such as *load*, *add* and *store*. For example, Fig. 20.33 illustrates five of the SML instructions that were produced in the compilation of the program in Fig. 20.31. The first three instructions are the production that adds 1 to y. Note that instructions 06 and 07 store the accumulator value in temporary location 96 and load the value back into the accumulator so instruction 08 can store the value in location 98. Often a production is followed by a load instruction for the same location that was just stored. This code can be *optimized* by eliminating the store instruction and the subsequent load instruction that operate on the same memory location, thus enabling the Simpletron to execute the program faster. Figure 20.34 illustrates the optimized SML for the program of Fig. 20.31. Note that there are four fewer instructions in the optimized code—a memory-space savings of 25 percent.

Modify the compiler to provide an option for optimizing the Simpletron Machine Language code it produces. Manually compare the nonoptimized code with the optimized code, and calculate the percentage reduction.

1	04	+2098	*(load)*
2	05	+3097	*(add)*
3	06	+2196	*(store)*
4	07	+2096	*(load)*
5	08	+2198	*(store)*

Fig. 20.33 | Nonoptimized code from the program of Fig. 20.31.

Simple program	SML location & instruction	Description
5 rem sum 1 to x	*none*	rem ignored
10 input x	00 +1099	read x into location 99
15 rem check y == x	*none*	rem ignored
20 if y == x goto 60	01 +2098	load y (98) into accumulator
	02 +3199	sub x (99) from accumulator
	03 +4211	branch to location 11 if zero
25 rem increment y	*none*	rem ignored
30 let y = y + 1	04 +2098	load y into accumulator
	05 +3097	add 1 (97) to accumulator
	06 +2198	store accumulator in y (98)
35 rem add y to total	*none*	rem ignored
40 let t = t + y	07 +2096	load t from location (96)
	08 +3098	add y (98) accumulator
	09 +2196	store accumulator in t (96)
45 rem loop y	*none*	rem ignored
50 goto 20	10 +4001	branch to location 01
55 rem output result	*none*	rem ignored
60 print t	11 +1196	output t (96) to screen
99 end	12 +4300	terminate execution

Fig. 20.34 | Optimized code for the program of Fig. 20.31.

20.29 (*Modifications to the Simple Compiler*) Perform the following modifications to the Simple compiler. Some of these modifications may also require modifications to the Simpletron Simulator program written in Exercise 8.19.

a) Allow the modulus operator (%) to be used in let statements. Simpletron Machine Language must be modified to include a modulus instruction.

b) Allow exponentiation in a let statement using ∧ as the exponentiation operator. Simpletron Machine Language must be modified to include an exponentiation instruction.

c) Allow the compiler to recognize uppercase and lowercase letters in Simple statements (e.g., 'A' is equivalent to 'a'). No modifications to the Simulator are required.

d) Allow input statements to read values for multiple variables such as input x, y. No modifications to the Simpletron Simulator are required.

e) Allow the compiler to output multiple values in a single print statement such as print a, b, c. No modifications to the Simpletron Simulator are required.

f) Add syntax-checking capabilities to the compiler so error messages are output when syntax errors are encountered in a Simple program. No modifications to the Simpletron Simulator are required.

g) Allow arrays of integers. No modifications to the Simpletron Simulator are required.

h) Allow subroutines specified by the Simple commands gosub and return. Command gosub passes program control to a subroutine, and command return passes control back to the statement after the gosub. This is similar to a function call in C++. The same subroutine can be called from many gosub commands distributed throughout a program. No modifications to the Simpletron Simulator are required.

i) Allow repetition statements of the form

```
for x = 2 to 10 step 2
    Simple statements
next
```

This for statement loops from 2 to 10 with an increment of 2. The next line marks the end of the body of the for. No modifications to the Simpletron Simulator are required.

j) Allow repetition statements of the form

```
for x = 2 to 10
    Simple statements
next
```

This for statement loops from 2 to 10 with a default increment of 1. No modifications to the Simpletron Simulator are required.

k) Allow the compiler to process string input and output. This requires the Simpletron Simulator to be modified to process and store string values. [*Hint:* Each Simpletron word can be divided into two groups, each holding a two-digit integer. Each two-digit integer represents the ASCII decimal equivalent of a character. Add a machine-language instruction that will print a string beginning at a certain Simpletron memory location. The first half of the word at that location is a count of the number of characters in the string (i.e., the length of the string). Each succeeding half word contains one ASCII character expressed as two decimal digits. The machine-language instruction checks the length and prints the string by translating each two-digit number into its equivalent character.]

l) Allow the compiler to process floating-point values in addition to integers. The Simpletron Simulator must also be modified to process floating-point values.

20.30 (*A Simple Interpreter*) An interpreter is a program that reads a high-level language program statement, determines the operation to be performed by the statement and executes the operation immediately. The high-level language program is not converted into machine language first. Interpreters execute slowly because each statement encountered in the program must first be deciphered. If statements are contained in a loop, the statements are deciphered each time they are encountered in the loop. Early versions of the BASIC programming language were implemented as interpreters.

Write an interpreter for the Simple language discussed in Exercise 20.26. The program should use the infix-to-postfix converter developed in Exercise 20.12 and the postfix evaluator developed in Exercise 20.13 to evaluate expressions in a let statement. The same restrictions placed on the Simple language in Exercise 20.26 should be adhered to in this program. Test the interpreter with the Simple programs written in Exercise 20.26. Compare the results of running these programs in the interpreter with the results of compiling the Simple programs and running them in the Simpletron Simulator built in Exercise 8.19.

20.31 (*Insert/Delete Anywhere in a Linked List*) Our linked list class template allowed insertions and deletions at only the front and the back of the linked list. These capabilities were convenient for us when we used private inheritance and composition to produce a stack class template and a queue class template with a minimal amount of code by reusing the list class template. Actually, linked lists are more general than those we provided. Modify the linked list class template we developed in this chapter to handle insertions and deletions anywhere in the list.

20.32 (*List and Queues without Tail Pointers*) Our implementation of a linked list (Figs. 20.3–20.5) used both a firstPtr and a lastPtr. The lastPtr was useful for the insertAtBack and removeFromBack member functions of the List class. The insertAtBack function corresponds to the enqueue member function of the Queue class. Rewrite the List class so that it does not use a lastPtr. Thus, any operations on the tail of a list must begin searching the list from the front. Does this affect our implementation of the Queue class (Fig. 20.16)?

20.33 Use the composition version of the stack program (Fig. 20.15) to form a complete working stack program. Modify this program to inline the member functions. Compare the two approaches. Summarize the advantages and disadvantages of inlining member functions.

20.34 *(Performance of Binary Tree Sorting and Searching)* One problem with the binary tree sort is that the order in which the data is inserted affects the shape of the tree—for the same collection of data, different orderings can yield binary trees of dramatically different shapes. The performance of the binary tree sorting and searching algorithms is sensitive to the shape of the binary tree. What shape would a binary tree have if its data were inserted in increasing order? in decreasing order? What shape should the tree have to achieve maximal searching performance?

20.35 *(Indexed Lists)* As presented in the text, linked lists must be searched sequentially. For large lists, this can result in poor performance. A common technique for improving list searching performance is to create and maintain an index to the list. An index is a set of pointers to various key places in the list. For example, an application that searches a large list of names could improve performance by creating an index with 26 entries—one for each letter of the alphabet. A search operation for a last name beginning with 'Y' would first search the index to determine where the 'Y' entries begin and "jump into" the list at that point and search linearly until the desired name was found. This would be much faster than searching the linked list from the beginning. Use the List class of Figs. 20.3–20.5 as the basis of an IndexedList class. Write a program that demonstrates the operation of indexed lists. Be sure to include member functions insertInIndexedList, searchIndexedList and deleteFromIndexedList.

21

Bits, Characters, C Strings and structs

The same old charitable lie
Repeated as the years scoot by
Perpetually makes a hit—
"You really haven't changed a bit!"
—Margaret Fishback

The chief defect of Henry King
Was chewing little bits of string.
—Hilaire Belloc

Vigorous writing is concise. A sentence should contain no unnecessary words, a paragraph no unnecessary sentences.
—William Strunk, Jr.

OBJECTIVES

In this chapter you'll learn:

- To create and use `struct`s.

- To pass `struct`s to functions by value and by reference.

- To use `typedef` to create aliases for previously defined data types and `struct`s.

- To manipulate data with the bitwise operators and to create bit fields for storing data compactly.

- To use the functions of the character-handling library `<cctype>`.

- To use the string-conversion functions of the general-utilities library `<cstdlib>`.

- To use the string-processing functions of the string-handling library `<cstring>`.

21.1 Introduction

We now discuss structures and the manipulation of bits, characters and C-style strings. Many of the techniques we present here are included for the benefit of the C++ programmer who will work with legacy C and C++ code.

The designers of C++ evolved structures into the notion of a class. Like a class, C++ structures may contain access specfiers, member functions, constructors and destructors. In fact, the only differences between structures and classes in C++ is that structure members default to `public` access and class members default to `private` access when no access specifiers are used, and that structures default to `public` inheritance, whereas classes default to `private` inheritance. Classes have been covered thoroughly in the book, so there is really no need for us to discuss structures in detail. Our presentation of structures in this chapter focuses on their use in C, where structures contain only `public` data members. This use of structures is typical of the legacy C code and early C++ code you'll see in industry.

We discuss how to declare structures, initialize structures and pass structures to functions. Then, we present a high-performance card shuffling and dealing simulation in which we use structure objects and C-style strings to represent the cards. We discuss the bitwise operators that allow programmers to access and manipulate the individual bits in bytes of data. We also present bitfields—special structures that can be used to specify the exact number of bits a variable occupies in memory. These bit manipulation techniques are common in C and C++ programs that interact directly with hardware devices that have limited memory. The chapter finishes with examples of many character and C-style string manipulation functions—some of which are designed to process blocks of memory as arrays of bytes.

21.2 Structure Definitions

Structures are aggregate data types—that is, they can be built using elements of several types including other `struct`s. Consider the following structure definition:

```
struct Card
{
    char *face;
    char *suit;
}; // end struct Card
```

Keyword **struct** introduces the definition for structure `Card`. The identifier `Card` is the structure name and is used in C++ to declare variables of the structure type (in C, the type name of the preceding structure is `struct Card`). In this example, the structure type is `Card`. Data (and possibly functions—just as with classes) declared within the braces of the structure definition are the structure's members. Members of the same structure must have unique names, but two different structures may contain members of the same name without conflict. Each structure definition must end with a semicolon.

 Common Programming Error 21.1

Forgetting the semicolon that terminates a structure definition is a syntax error.

The definition of `Card` contains two members of type `char *`—`face` and `suit`. Structure members can be variables of the fundamental data types (e.g., `int`, `double`, etc.) or aggregates, such as arrays, other structures and or classes. Data members in a single structure definition can be of many data types. For example, an `Employee` structure might contain character-string members for the first and last names, an `int` member for the employee's age, a `char` member containing `'M'` or `'F'` for the employee's gender, a `double` member for the employee's hourly salary and so on.

A structure cannot contain an instance of itself. For example, a structure variable `Card` cannot be declared in the definition for structure `Card`. A pointer to a `Card` structure, however, can be included. A structure containing a member that is a pointer to the same structure type is referred to as a self-referential structure. We used a similar construct—self-referential classes—in Chapter 20, Data Structures, to build various kinds of linked data structures.

The `Card` structure definition does not reserve any space in memory; rather, it creates a new data type that is used to declare structure variables. Structure variables are declared like variables of other types. The following declarations

```
Card oneCard;
Card deck[ 52 ];
Card *cardPtr;
```

declare `oneCard` to be a structure variable of type `Card`, `deck` to be an array with 52 elements of type `Card` and `cardPtr` to be a pointer to a `Card` structure. Variables of a given structure type can also be declared by placing a comma-separated list of the variable names between the closing brace of the structure definition and the semicolon that ends the structure definition. For example, the preceding declarations could have been incorporated into the `Card` structure definition as follows:

```
struct Card
{
    char *face;
    char *suit;
} oneCard, deck[ 52 ], *cardPtr;
```

The structure name is optional. If a structure definition does not contain a structure name, variables of the structure type may be declared only between the closing right brace of the structure definition and the semicolon that terminates the structure definition.

Software Engineering Observation 21.1

Provide a structure name when creating a structure type. The structure name is required for declaring new variables of the structure type later in the program, declaring parameters of the structure type and, if the structure is being used like a C++ class, specifying the name of the constructor and destructor.

The only valid built-in operations that may be performed on structure objects are assigning one structure object to another of the same type, taking the address (&) of a structure object, accessing the members of a structure object (in the same manner as members of a class are accessed) and using the `sizeof` operator to determine the size of a structure. As with classes, most operators can be overloaded to work with objects of a structure type.

Structure members are not necessarily stored in consecutive bytes of memory. Sometimes there are "holes" in a structure, because some computers store specific data types only on certain memory boundaries, such as half-word, word or double-word boundaries. A word is a standard memory unit used to store data in a computer—usually two bytes or four bytes and typically four bytes on today's popular 32-bit systems. Consider the following structure definition in which structure objects `sample1` and `sample2` of type `Example` are declared:

```
struct Example
{
    char c;
    int i;
} sample1, sample2;
```

A computer with two-byte words might require that each of the members of `Example` be aligned on a word boundary (i.e., at the beginning of a word—this is machine dependent). Figure 21.1 shows a sample storage alignment for an object of type `Example` that has been assigned the character `'a'` and the integer `97` (the bit representations of the values are shown). If the members are stored beginning at word boundaries, there is a one-byte hole (byte 1 in the figure) in the storage for objects of type `Example`. The value in the one-byte hole is undefined. If the member values of `sample1` and `sample2` are in fact equal, the structure objects are not necessarily equal, because the undefined one-byte holes are not likely to contain identical values.

Common Programming Error 21.2

Comparing structures is a compilation error.

Fig. 21.1 | Possible storage alignment for a variable of type `Example`, showing an undefined area in memory.

Portability Tip 21.1

Because the size of data items of a particular type is machine dependent, and because storage alignment considerations are machine dependent, so too is the representation of a structure.

21.3 Initializing Structures

Structures can be initialized using initializer lists, as is done with arrays. For example, the declaration

```
Card oneCard = { "Three", "Hearts" };
```

creates `Card` variable `oneCard` and initializes member `face` to `"Three"` and member `suit` to `"Hearts"`. If there are fewer initializers in the list than members in the structure, the remaining members are initialized to their default values. Structure variables declared outside a function definition (i.e., externally) are initialized to their default values if they are not explicitly initialized in the external declaration. Structure variables may also be set in assignment expressions by assigning a structure variable of the same type or by assigning values to the individual data members of the structure.

21.4 Using Structures with Functions

There are two ways to pass the information in structures to functions. You can either pass the entire structure or pass the individual members of a structure. By default, structures are passed by value. Structures and their members can also be passed by reference by passing either references or pointers.

To pass a structure by reference, pass the address of the structure object or a reference to the structure object. Arrays of structures—like all other arrays—are passed by reference.

In Chapter 7, we stated that an array could be passed by value by using a structure. To pass an array by value, create a structure (or a class) with the array as a member, then pass an object of that structure (or class) type to a function by value. Because structure objects are passed by value, the array member, too, is passed by value.

Performance Tip 21.1

Passing structures (and especially large structures) by reference is more efficient than passing them by value (which requires the entire structure to be copied).

21.5 typedef

Keyword **typedef** provides a mechanism for creating synonyms (or aliases) for previously defined data types. Names for structure types are often defined with `typedef` to create shorter, simpler or more readable type names. For example, the statement

```
typedef Card *CardPtr;
```

defines the new type name `CardPtr` as a synonym for type `Card *`.

Good Programming Practice 21.1

Capitalize `typedef` names to emphasize that these names are synonyms for other type names.

Creating a new name with `typedef` does not create a new type; `typedef` simply creates a new type name that can then be used in the program as an alias for an existing type name.

Portability Tip 21.2

Synonyms for built-in data types can be created with `typedef` to make programs more portable. For example, a program can use `typedef` to create alias `Integer` for four-byte integers. `Integer` can then be aliased to `int` on systems with four-byte integers and can be aliased to `long int` on systems with two-byte integers where `long int` values occupy four bytes. Then, you simply declare all four-byte integer variables to be of type `Integer`.

21.6 Example: High-Performance Card Shuffling and Dealing Simulation

The program in Figs. 21.2–21.4 is based on the card shuffling and dealing simulation discussed in Chapter 8. The program represents the deck of cards as an array of structures and uses high-performance shuffling and dealing algorithms.

```
1   // Fig. 21.2: DeckOfCards.h
2   // Definition of class DeckOfCards that
3   // represents a deck of playing cards.
4
5   // Card structure definition
6   struct Card
7   {
8      char *face;
9      char *suit;
10  }; // end structure Card
11
12  // DeckOfCards class definition
13  class DeckOfCards
14  {
15  public:
16     DeckOfCards(); // constructor initializes deck
17     void shuffle(); // shuffles cards in deck
18     void deal() const; // deals cards in deck
19
20  private:
21     Card deck[ 52 ]; // represents deck of cards
22  }; // end class DeckOfCards
```

Fig. 21.2 | Header file for `DeckOfCards` class.

```
1   // Fig. 21.3: DeckOfCards.cpp
2   // Member-function definitions for class DeckOfCards that simulates
3   // the shuffling and dealing of a deck of playing cards.
4   #include <iostream>
5   using std::cout;
6   using std::left;
```

Fig. 21.3 | Class file for `DeckOfCards`. (Part 1 of 3.)

```
7    using std::right;
8
9    #include <iomanip>
10   using std::setw;
11
12   #include <cstdlib> // prototypes for rand and srand
13   using std::rand;
14   using std::srand;
15
16   #include <ctime> // prototype for time
17   using std::time;
18
19   #include "DeckOfCards.h" // DeckOfCards class definition
20
21   // no-argument DeckOfCards constructor intializes deck
22   DeckOfCards::DeckOfCards()
23   {
24      // initialize suit array
25      static const char *suit[ 4 ] =
26         { "Hearts", "Diamonds", "Clubs", "Spades" };
27
28      // initialize face array
29      static const char *face[ 13 ] =
30         { "Ace", "Deuce", "Three", "Four", "Five", "Six", "Seven",
31           "Eight", "Nine", "Ten", "Jack", "Queen", "King" };
32
33      // set values for deck of 52 Cards
34      for ( int i = 0; i < 52; i++ )
35      {
36         deck[ i ].face = face[ i % 13 ];
37         deck[ i ].suit = suit[ i / 13 ];
38      } // end for
39
40      srand( time( 0 ) ); // seed random number generator
41   } // end no-argument DeckOfCards constructor
42
43   // shuffle cards in deck
44   void DeckOfCards::shuffle()
45   {
46      // shuffle cards randomly
47      for ( int i = 0; i < 52; i++ )
48      {
49         int j = rand() % 52;
50         Card temp = deck[ i ];
51         deck[ i ] = deck[ j ];
52         deck[ j ] = temp;
53      } // end for
54   } // end function shuffle
55
56   // deal cards in deck
57   void DeckOfCards::deal() const
58   {
```

Fig. 21.3 | Class file for DeckOfCards. (Part 2 of 3.)

```
59        // display each card's face and suit
60        for ( int i = 0; i < 52; i++ )
61           cout << right << setw( 5 ) << deck[ i ].face << " of "
62              << left << setw( 8 ) << deck[ i ].suit
63              << ( ( i + 1 ) % 2 ? '\t' : '\n' );
64     } // end function deal
```

Fig. 21.3 | Class file for `DeckOfCards`. (Part 3 of 3.)

```
1   // Fig. 21.4: fig21_04.cpp
2   // Card shuffling and dealing program.
3   #include "DeckOfCards.h" // DeckOfCards class definition
4
5   int main()
6   {
7      DeckOfCards deckOfCards; // create DeckOfCards object
8
9      deckOfCards.shuffle(); // shuffle the cards in the deck
10     deckOfCards.deal(); // deal the cards in the deck
11     return 0; // indicates successful termination
12  } // end main
```

```
King of Clubs            Ten of Diamonds
 Five of Diamonds        Jack of Clubs
Seven of Spades          Five of Clubs
Three of Spades          King of Hearts
  Ten of Clubs           Eight of Spades
Eight of Hearts           Six of Hearts
 Nine of Diamonds        Nine of Clubs
Three of Diamonds        Queen of Hearts
  Six of Clubs           Seven of Hearts
Seven of Diamonds        Jack of Diamonds
 Jack of Spades          King of Diamonds
Deuce of Diamonds        Four of Clubs
Three of Clubs           Five of Hearts
Eight of Clubs            Ace of Hearts
Deuce of Spades           Ace of Clubs
  Ten of Spades          Eight of Diamonds
  Ten of Hearts           Six of Spades
Queen of Diamonds        Nine of Hearts
Seven of Clubs           Queen of Clubs
Deuce of Clubs           Queen of Spades
Three of Hearts          Five of Spades
Deuce of Hearts          Jack of Hearts
 Four of Hearts           Ace of Diamonds
 Nine of Spades          Four of Diamonds
  Ace of Spades           Six of Diamonds
 Four of Spades          King of Spades
```

Fig. 21.4 | High-performance card shuffling and dealing simulation.

The constructor (lines 22–41 of Fig. 21.3) initializes the Card array in order with character strings representing Ace through King of each suit. Function shuffle implements the high-performance shuffling algorithm. The function loops through all 52 cards (array subscripts 0 to 51). For each card, a number between 0 and 51 is picked randomly. Next, the current `Card` structure and the randomly selected `Card` structure are swapped in the array. A total of 52 swaps are made in a single pass of the entire array, and the array of `Card` structures is shuffled! Unlike the shuffling algorithm presented in Chapter 8, this algorithm does not suffer from indefinite postponement. Because the `Card` structures were swapped in place in the array, the high-performance dealing algorithm implemented in function `deal` requires only one pass of the array to deal the shuffled cards.

21.7 Bitwise Operators

C++ provides extensive bit-manipulation capabilities for programmers who need to get down to the so-called "bits-and-bytes" level. Operating systems, test-equipment software, networking software and many other kinds of software require that you communicate "directly with the hardware." In this and the next several sections, we discuss C++'s bit-manipulation capabilities. We introduce each of C++'s many bitwise operators, and we discuss how to save memory by using bit fields.

All data is represented internally by computers as sequences of bits. Each bit can assume the value 0 or the value 1. On most systems, a sequence of 8 bits forms a byte—the standard storage unit for a variable of type `char`. Other data types are stored in larger numbers of bytes. Bitwise operators are used to manipulate the bits of integral operands (`char`, `short`, `int` and `long`; both `signed` and `unsigned`). Unsigned integers are normally used with the bitwise operators.

Portability Tip 21.3

Bitwise data manipulations are machine dependent.

Note that the bitwise operator discussions in this section show the binary representations of the integer operands. For a detailed explanation of the binary (also called base-2) number system, see Appendix D, Number Systems. Because of the machine-dependent nature of bitwise manipulations, some of these programs might not work on your system without modification.

The bitwise operators are: bitwise AND (&), bitwise inclusive OR (|), bitwise exclusive OR (∧), left shift (<<), right shift (>>) and bitwise complement (~)—also known as the one's complement. (Note that we have been using &, << and >> for other purposes. This is a classic example of operator overloading.) The bitwise AND, bitwise inclusive OR and bitwise exclusive OR operators compare their two operands bit by bit. The bitwise AND operator sets each bit in the result to 1 if the corresponding bit in both operands is 1. The bitwise inclusive-OR operator sets each bit in the result to 1 if the corresponding bit in either (or both) operand(s) is 1. The bitwise exclusive-OR operator sets each bit in the result to 1 if the corresponding bit in either operand—but not both—is 1. The left-shift operator shifts the bits of its left operand to the left by the number of bits specified in its right operand. The right-shift operator shifts the bits in its left operand to the right by the number of bits specified in its right operand. The bitwise complement operator sets all 0 bits in its operand to 1 in the result and sets all 1 bits in its operand to 0 in the result. Detailed discussions of each bitwise operator appear in the following examples. The bitwise operators are summarized in Fig. 21.5.

Operator	Name	Description
&	bitwise AND	The bits in the result are set to 1 if the corresponding bits in the two operands are both 1.
|	bitwise inclusive OR	The bits in the result are set to 1 if one or both of the corresponding bits in the two operands is 1.
^	bitwise exclusive OR	The bits in the result are set to 1 if exactly one of the corresponding bits in the two operands is 1.
<<	left shift	Shifts the bits of the first operand left by the number of bits specified by the second operand; fill from right with 0 bits.
>>	right shift with sign extension	Shifts the bits of the first operand right by the number of bits specified by the second operand; the method of filling from the left is machine dependent.
~	bitwise complement	All 0 bits are set to 1 and all 1 bits are set to 0.

Fig. 21.5 | Bitwise operators.

Printing a Binary Representation of an Integral Value

When using the bitwise operators, it is useful to illustrate their precise effects by printing values in their binary representation. The program of Fig. 21.6 prints an unsigned integer in its binary representation in groups of eight bits each.

```
1   // Fig. 21.6: fig21_06.cpp
2   // Printing an unsigned integer in bits.
3   #include <iostream>
4   using std::cout;
5   using std::cin;
6   using std::endl;
7
8   #include <iomanip>
9   using std::setw;
10
11  void displayBits( unsigned ); // prototype
12
13  int main()
14  {
15     unsigned inputValue; // integral value to print in binary
16
17     cout << "Enter an unsigned integer: ";
18     cin >> inputValue;
19     displayBits( inputValue );
20     return 0;
21  } // end main
22
```

Fig. 21.6 | Printing an unsigned integer in bits. (Part 1 of 2.)

```
23   // display bits of an unsigned integer value
24   void displayBits( unsigned value )
25   {
26      const int SHIFT = 8 * sizeof( unsigned ) - 1;
27      const unsigned MASK = 1 << SHIFT;
28
29      cout << setw( 10 ) << value << " = ";
30
31      // display bits
32      for ( unsigned i = 1; i <= SHIFT + 1; i++ )
33      {
34         cout << ( value & MASK ? '1' : '0' );
35         value <<= 1; // shift value left by 1
36
37         if ( i % 8 == 0 ) // output a space after 8 bits
38            cout << ' ';
39      } // end for
40
41      cout << endl;
42   } // end function displayBits
```

```
Enter an unsigned integer: 65000
    65000 = 00000000 00000000 11111101 11101000
```

```
Enter an unsigned integer: 29
    29 = 00000000 00000000 00000000 00011101
```

Fig. 21.6 | Printing an unsigned integer in bits. (Part 2 of 2.)

Function displayBits (lines 24–42) uses the bitwise AND operator to combine variable value with constant MASK. Often, the bitwise AND operator is used with an operand called a mask—an integer value with specific bits set to 1. Masks are used to hide some bits in a value while selecting other bits. In displayBits, line 27 assigns constant MASK the value 1 << SHIFT. The value of constant SHIFT was calculated in line 26 with the expression

```
8 * sizeof( unsigned ) - 1
```

which multiplies the number of bytes an unsigned object requires in memory by 8 (the number of bits in a byte) to get the total number of bits required to store an unsigned object, then subtracts 1. The bit representation of 1 << SHIFT on a computer that represents unsigned objects in four bytes of memory is

```
10000000 00000000 00000000 00000000
```

The left-shift operator shifts the value 1 from the low-order (rightmost) bit to the high-order (leftmost) bit in MASK, and fills in 0 bits from the right. Line 34 determines whether a 1 or a 0 should be printed for the current leftmost bit of variable value. Assume that variable value contains 65000 (00000000 00000000 11111101 11101000). When value and MASK are combined using &, all the bits except the high-order bit in variable value are "masked off" (hidden), because any bit "ANDed" with 0 yields 0. If the leftmost bit is 1, value & MASK evaluates to

```
00000000 00000000 11111101 11101000      (value)
10000000 00000000 00000000 00000000      (MASK)
-----------------------------------
00000000 00000000 00000000 00000000      (value & MASK)
```

which is interpreted as false, and 0 is printed. Then line 35 shifts variable value left by one bit with the expression value <<= 1 (i.e., value = value << 1). These steps are repeated for each bit variable value. Eventually, a bit with a value of 1 is shifted into the leftmost bit position, and the bit manipulation is as follows:

```
11111101 11101000 00000000 00000000      (value)
10000000 00000000 00000000 00000000      (MASK)
-----------------------------------
10000000 00000000 00000000 00000000      (value & MASK)
```

Because both left bits are 1s, the result of the expression is nonzero (true) and a value of 1 is printed. Figure 21.7 summarizes the results of combining two bits with the bitwise AND operator.

 Common Programming Error 21.3

Using the logical AND operator (&&) for the bitwise AND operator (&) and vice versa is a logic error.

The program of Fig. 21.8 demonstrates the bitwise AND operator, the bitwise inclusive OR operator, the bitwise exclusive OR operator and the bitwise complement operator. Function displayBits (lines 57–75) prints the unsigned integer values.

Bitwise AND Operator (&)

In Fig. 21.8, line 21 assigns 2179876355 (10000001 11101110 01000110 00000011) to variable number1, and line 22 assigns 1 (00000000 00000000 00000000 00000001) to variable mask. When mask and number1 are combined using the bitwise AND operator (&) in the expression number1 & mask (line 27), the result is 00000000 00000000 00000000 00000001. All the bits except the low-order bit in variable number1 are "masked off" (hidden) by "ANDing" with constant MASK.

Bit 1	Bit 2	Bit 1 & Bit 2
0	0	0
1	0	0
0	1	0
1	1	1

Fig. 21.7 | Results of combining two bits with the bitwise AND operator (&).

Bitwise Inclusive OR Operator (|)

The bitwise inclusive-OR operator is used to set specific bits to 1 in an operand. In Fig. 21.8, line 30 assigns 15 (00000000 00000000 00000000 00001111) to variable number1, and line 31 assigns 241 (00000000 00000000 00000000 11110001) to variable

```cpp
1    // Fig. 21.8: fig21_08.cpp
2    // Using the bitwise AND, bitwise inclusive OR, bitwise
3    // exclusive OR and bitwise complement operators.
4    #include <iostream>
5    using std::cout;
6
7    #include <iomanip>
8    using std::endl;
9    using std::setw;
10
11   void displayBits( unsigned ); // prototype
12
13   int main()
14   {
15      unsigned number1;
16      unsigned number2;
17      unsigned mask;
18      unsigned setBits;
19
20      // demonstrate bitwise &
21      number1 = 2179876355;
22      mask = 1;
23      cout << "The result of combining the following\n";
24      displayBits( number1 );
25      displayBits( mask );
26      cout << "using the bitwise AND operator & is\n";
27      displayBits( number1 & mask );
28
29      // demonstrate bitwise |
30      number1 = 15;
31      setBits = 241;
32      cout << "\nThe result of combining the following\n";
33      displayBits( number1 );
34      displayBits( setBits );
35      cout << "using the bitwise inclusive OR operator | is\n";
36      displayBits( number1 | setBits );
37
38      // demonstrate bitwise exclusive OR
39      number1 = 139;
40      number2 = 199;
41      cout << "\nThe result of combining the following\n";
42      displayBits( number1 );
43      displayBits( number2 );
44      cout << "using the bitwise exclusive OR operator ^ is\n";
45      displayBits( number1 ^ number2 );
```

Fig. 21.8 | Bitwise AND, bitwise inclusive-OR, bitwise exclusive-OR and bitwise complement operators. (Part 1 of 2.)

```
46
47      // demonstrate bitwise complement
48      number1 = 21845;
49      cout << "\nThe one's complement of\n";
50      displayBits( number1 );
51      cout << "is" << endl;
52      displayBits( ~number1 );
53      return 0;
54   } // end main
55
56   // display bits of an unsigned integer value
57   void displayBits( unsigned value )
58   {
59      const int SHIFT = 8 * sizeof( unsigned ) - 1;
60      const unsigned MASK = 1 << SHIFT;
61
62      cout << setw( 10 ) << value << " = ";
63
64      // display bits
65      for ( unsigned i = 1; i <= SHIFT + 1; i++ )
66      {
67         cout << ( value & MASK ? '1' : '0' );
68         value <<= 1; // shift value left by 1
69
70         if ( i % 8 == 0 ) // output a space after 8 bits
71            cout << ' ';
72      } // end for
73
74      cout << endl;
75   } // end function displayBits
```

```
The result of combining the following
2179876355 = 10000001 11101110 01000110 00000011
         1 = 00000000 00000000 00000000 00000001
using the bitwise AND operator & is
         1 = 00000000 00000000 00000000 00000001

The result of combining the following
        15 = 00000000 00000000 00000000 00001111
       241 = 00000000 00000000 00000000 11110001
using the bitwise inclusive OR operator | is
       255 = 00000000 00000000 00000000 11111111

The result of combining the following
       139 = 00000000 00000000 00000000 10001011
       199 = 00000000 00000000 00000000 11000111
using the bitwise exclusive OR operator ^ is
        76 = 00000000 00000000 00000000 01001100

The one's complement of
     21845 = 00000000 00000000 01010101 01010101
is
4294945450 = 11111111 11111111 10101010 10101010
```

Fig. 21.8 | Bitwise AND, bitwise inclusive-OR, bitwise exclusive-OR and bitwise complement operators. (Part 2 of 2.)

setBits. When `number1` and `setBits` are combined using the bitwise OR operator in the expression `number1 | setBits` (line 36), the result is 255 (00000000 00000000 00000000 11111111). Figure 21.9 summarizes the results of combining two bits with the bitwise inclusive-OR operator.

Common Programming Error 21.4

Using the logical OR operator (||) for the bitwise OR operator (|) and vice versa is a logic error.

Bitwise Exclusive OR (^)

The bitwise exclusive OR operator (^) sets each bit in the result to 1 if *exactly* one of the corresponding bits in its two operands is 1. In Fig. 21.8, lines 39–40 assign variables `number1` and `number2` the values 139 (00000000 00000000 00000000 10001011) and 199 (00000000 00000000 00000000 11000111), respectively. When these variables are combined with the exclusive-OR operator in the expression `number1 ^ number2` (line 45), the result is 00000000 00000000 00000000 01001100. Figure 21.10 summarizes the results of combining two bits with the bitwise exclusive-OR operator.

Bitwise Complement (~)

The bitwise complement operator (~) sets all 1 bits in its operand to 0 in the result and sets all 0 bits to 1 in the result—otherwise referred to as "taking the one's complement of the value." In Fig. 21.8, line 48 assigns variable `number1` the value 21845 (00000000 00000000 01010101 01010101). When the expression `~number1` evaluates, the result is (11111111 11111111 10101010 10101010).

Figure 21.11 demonstrates the left-shift operator (<<) and the right-shift operator (>>). Function `displayBits` (lines 31–49) prints the `unsigned` integer values.

Bit 1	Bit 2	Bit 1 | Bit 2
0	0	0
1	0	1
0	1	1
1	1	1

Fig. 21.9 | Combining two bits with the bitwise inclusive-OR operator (|).

Bit 1	Bit 2	Bit 1 ^ Bit 2
0	0	0
1	0	1
0	1	1
1	1	0

Fig. 21.10 | Combining two bits with the bitwise exclusive-OR operator (^).

Left-Shift Operator

The left-shift operator (<<) shifts the bits of its left operand to the left by the number of bits specified in its right operand. Bits vacated to the right are replaced with 0s; bits shifted off the left are lost. In the program of Fig. 21.11, line 14 assigns variable number1 the value 960 (00000000 00000000 00000011 11000000). The result of left-shifting variable number1 8 bits in the expression number1 << 8 (line 20) is 245760 (00000000 00000011 11000000 00000000).

```cpp
1   // Fig. 21.11: fig21_11.cpp
2   // Using the bitwise shift operators.
3   #include <iostream>
4   using std::cout;
5   using std::endl;
6
7   #include <iomanip>
8   using std::setw;
9
10  void displayBits( unsigned ); // prototype
11
12  int main()
13  {
14     unsigned number1 = 960;
15
16     // demonstrate bitwise left shift
17     cout << "The result of left shifting\n";
18     displayBits( number1 );
19     cout << "8 bit positions using the left-shift operator is\n";
20     displayBits( number1 << 8 );
21
22     // demonstrate bitwise right shift
23     cout << "\nThe result of right shifting\n";
24     displayBits( number1 );
25     cout << "8 bit positions using the right-shift operator is\n";
26     displayBits( number1 >> 8 );
27     return 0;
28  } // end main
29
30  // display bits of an unsigned integer value
31  void displayBits( unsigned value )
32  {
33     const int SHIFT = 8 * sizeof( unsigned ) - 1;
34     const unsigned MASK = 1 << SHIFT;
35
36     cout << setw( 10 ) << value << " = ";
37
38     // display bits
39     for ( unsigned i = 1; i <= SHIFT + 1; i++ )
40     {
41        cout << ( value & MASK ? '1' : '0' );
42        value <<= 1; // shift value left by 1
43
```

Fig. 21.11 | Bitwise shift operators. (Part 1 of 2.)

```
44          if ( i % 8 == 0 ) // output a space after 8 bits
45              cout << ' ';
46      } // end for
47
48      cout << endl;
49  } // end function displayBits
```

```
The result of left shifting
        960 = 00000000 00000000 00000011 11000000
8 bit positions using the left-shift operator is
     245760 = 00000000 00000011 11000000 00000000

The result of right shifting
        960 = 00000000 00000000 00000011 11000000
8 bit positions using the right-shift operator is
          3 = 00000000 00000000 00000000 00000011
```

Fig. 21.11 | Bitwise shift operators. (Part 2 of 2.)

Right-Shift Operator

The right-shift operator (>>) shifts the bits of its left operand to the right by the number of bits specified in its right operand. Performing a right shift on an unsigned integer causes the vacated bits at the left to be replaced by 0s; bits shifted off the right are lost. In the program of Fig. 21.11, the result of right-shifting number1 in the expression number1 >> 8 (line 26) is 3 (00000000 00000000 00000000 00000011).

Common Programming Error 21.5

The result of shifting a value is undefined if the right operand is negative or if the right operand is greater than or equal to the number of bits in which the left operand is stored.

Portability Tip 21.4

The result of right-shifting a signed value is machine dependent. Some machines fill with zeros and others use the sign bit.

Bitwise Assignment Operators

Each bitwise operator (except the bitwise complement operator) has a corresponding assignment operator. These *bitwise assignment operators* are shown in Fig. 21.12; they are used in a similar manner to the arithmetic assignment operators introduced in Chapter 2.

Bitwise assignment operators	
&=	Bitwise AND assignment operator.
|=	Bitwise inclusive-OR assignment operator.
^=	Bitwise exclusive-OR assignment operator.
<<=	Left-shift assignment operator.
>>=	Right-shift with sign extension assignment operator.

Fig. 21.12 | Bitwise assignment operators.

Figure 21.13 shows the precedence and associativity of the operators introduced up to this point in the text. They are shown top to bottom in decreasing order of precedence.

21.8 Bit Fields

C++ provides the ability to specify the number of bits in which an integral type or enum type member of a class or a structure is stored. Such a member is referred to as a bit field. Bit fields enable better memory utilization by storing data in the minimum number of bits required. Bit field members *must* be declared as an integral or enum type.

> **Performance Tip 21.2**
>
> *Bit fields help conserve storage.*

Consider the following structure definition:

```
struct BitCard
{
    unsigned face : 4;
    unsigned suit : 2;
    unsigned color : 1;
}; // end struct BitCard
```

Operators	Associativity	Type
:: (unary; right to left) :: (binary; left to right)	left to right	highest
( ) [ ] . -> ++ -- static_cast< *type* >( )	left to right	unary
++ -- + - ! delete sizeof	right to left	unary
* ~ & new		
* / %	left to right	multiplicative
+ -	left to right	additive
<< >>	left to right	shifting
< <= > >=	left to right	relational
== !=	left to right	equality
&	left to right	bitwise AND
^	left to right	bitwise XOR
|	left to right	bitwise OR
&&	left to right	logical AND
||	left to right	logical OR
?:	right to left	conditional
= += -= *= /= %= &= |= ^= <<= >>=	right to left	assignment
,	left to right	comma

Fig. 21.13 | Operator precedence and associativity.

The definition contains three unsigned bit fields—face, suit and color—used to represent a card from a deck of 52 cards. A bit field is declared by following an integral type or enum type member with a colon (:) and an integer constant representing the width of the bit field (i.e., the number of bits in which the member is stored). The width must be an integer constant.

The preceding structure definition indicates that member face is stored in 4 bits, member suit in 2 bits and member color in 1 bit. The number of bits is based on the desired range of values for each structure member. Member face stores values between 0 (Ace) and 12 (King)—4 bits can store a value between 0 and 15. Member suit stores values between 0 and 3 (0 = Diamonds, 1 = Hearts, 2 = Clubs, 3 = Spades)—2 bits can store a value between 0 and 3. Finally, member color stores either 0 (Red) or 1 (Black)—1 bit can store either 0 or 1.

The program in Figs. 21.14–21.16 creates array deck containing 52 BitCard structures (line 21 of Fig. 21.14). The constructor inserts the 52 cards in the deck array, and function deal prints the 52 cards. Notice that bit fields are accessed exactly as any other structure member is (lines 18–20 and 28–33 of Fig. 21.15). The member color is included as a means of indicating the card color on a system that allows color displays.

```
1   // Fig. 21.14: DeckOfCards.h
2   // Definition of class DeckOfCards that
3   // represents a deck of playing cards.
4
5   // BitCard structure definition with bit fields
6   struct BitCard
7   {
8      unsigned face : 4; // 4 bits; 0-15
9      unsigned suit : 2; // 2 bits; 0-3
10     unsigned color : 1; // 1 bit; 0-1
11  }; // end struct BitCard
12
13  // DeckOfCards class definition
14  class DeckOfCards
15  {
16  public:
17     DeckOfCards(); // constructor initializes deck
18     void deal(); // deals cards in deck
19
20  private:
21     BitCard deck[ 52 ]; // represents deck of cards
22  }; // end class DeckOfCards
```

Fig. 21.14 | Header file for class DeckOfCards.

```
1   // Fig. 21.15: DeckOfCards.cpp
2   // Member-function definitions for class DeckOfCards that simulates
3   // the shuffling and dealing of a deck of playing cards.
4   #include <iostream>
5   using std::cout;
```

Fig. 21.15 | Class file for DeckOfCards. (Part 1 of 2.)

```
 6   using std::endl;
 7
 8   #include <iomanip>
 9   using std::setw;
10
11   #include "DeckOfCards.h" // DeckOfCards class definition
12
13   // no-argument DeckOfCards constructor intializes deck
14   DeckOfCards::DeckOfCards()
15   {
16      for ( int i = 0; i <= 51; i++ )
17      {
18         deck[ i ].face = i % 13; // faces in order
19         deck[ i ].suit = i / 13; // suits in order
20         deck[ i ].color = i / 26; // colors in order
21      } // end for
22   } // end no-argument DeckOfCards constructor
23
24   // deal cards in deck
25   void DeckOfCards::deal()
26   {
27      for ( int k1 = 0, k2 = k1 + 26; k1 <= 25; k1++, k2++ )
28         cout << "Card:" << setw( 3 ) << deck[ k1 ].face
29              << "  Suit:" << setw( 2 ) << deck[ k1 ].suit
30              << "  Color:" << setw( 2 ) << deck[ k1 ].color
31              << "    " << "Card:" << setw( 3 ) << deck[ k2 ].face
32              << "  Suit:" << setw( 2 ) << deck[ k2 ].suit
33              << "  Color:" << setw( 2 ) << deck[ k2 ].color << endl;
34   } // end function deal
```

Fig. 21.15 | Class file for DeckOfCards. (Part 2 of 2.)

It is possible to specify an unnamed bit field, in which case the field is used as padding in the structure. For example, the structure definition uses an unnamed 3-bit field as padding—nothing can be stored in those 3 bits. Member b is stored in another storage unit.

```
struct Example
{
   unsigned a : 13;
   unsigned   : 3; // align to next storage-unit boundary
   unsigned b : 4;
}; // end struct Example
```

An unnamed bit field with a zero width is used to align the next bit field on a new storage-unit boundary. For example, the structure definition

```
struct Example
{
   unsigned a : 13;
   unsigned   : 0; // align to next storage-unit boundary
   unsigned b : 4;
}; // end struct Example
```

uses an unnamed 0-bit field to skip the remaining bits (as many as there are) of the storage unit in which a is stored and align b on the next storage-unit boundary.

```
1   // Fig. 21.16: fig21_16.cpp
2   // Card shuffling and dealing program.
3   #include "DeckOfCards.h" // DeckOfCards class definition
4
5   int main()
6   {
7      DeckOfCards deckOfCards; // create DeckOfCards object
8      deckOfCards.deal(); // deal the cards in the deck
9      return 0; // indicates successful termination
10  } // end main
```

```
Card:  0  Suit: 0  Color: 0   Card:  0  Suit: 2  Color: 1
Card:  1  Suit: 0  Color: 0   Card:  1  Suit: 2  Color: 1
Card:  2  Suit: 0  Color: 0   Card:  2  Suit: 2  Color: 1
Card:  3  Suit: 0  Color: 0   Card:  3  Suit: 2  Color: 1
Card:  4  Suit: 0  Color: 0   Card:  4  Suit: 2  Color: 1
Card:  5  Suit: 0  Color: 0   Card:  5  Suit: 2  Color: 1
Card:  6  Suit: 0  Color: 0   Card:  6  Suit: 2  Color: 1
Card:  7  Suit: 0  Color: 0   Card:  7  Suit: 2  Color: 1
Card:  8  Suit: 0  Color: 0   Card:  8  Suit: 2  Color: 1
Card:  9  Suit: 0  Color: 0   Card:  9  Suit: 2  Color: 1
Card: 10  Suit: 0  Color: 0   Card: 10  Suit: 2  Color: 1
Card: 11  Suit: 0  Color: 0   Card: 11  Suit: 2  Color: 1
Card: 12  Suit: 0  Color: 0   Card: 12  Suit: 2  Color: 1
Card:  0  Suit: 1  Color: 0   Card:  0  Suit: 3  Color: 1
Card:  1  Suit: 1  Color: 0   Card:  1  Suit: 3  Color: 1
Card:  2  Suit: 1  Color: 0   Card:  2  Suit: 3  Color: 1
Card:  3  Suit: 1  Color: 0   Card:  3  Suit: 3  Color: 1
Card:  4  Suit: 1  Color: 0   Card:  4  Suit: 3  Color: 1
Card:  5  Suit: 1  Color: 0   Card:  5  Suit: 3  Color: 1
Card:  6  Suit: 1  Color: 0   Card:  6  Suit: 3  Color: 1
Card:  7  Suit: 1  Color: 0   Card:  7  Suit: 3  Color: 1
Card:  8  Suit: 1  Color: 0   Card:  8  Suit: 3  Color: 1
Card:  9  Suit: 1  Color: 0   Card:  9  Suit: 3  Color: 1
Card: 10  Suit: 1  Color: 0   Card: 10  Suit: 3  Color: 1
Card: 11  Suit: 1  Color: 0   Card: 11  Suit: 3  Color: 1
Card: 12  Suit: 1  Color: 0   Card: 12  Suit: 3  Color: 1
```

Fig. 21.16 | Bit fields used to store a deck of cards.

Portability Tip 21.5

Bit-field manipulations are machine dependent. For example, some computers allow bit fields to cross word boundaries, whereas others do not.

Common Programming Error 21.6

Attempting to access individual bits of a bit field with subscripting as if they were elements of an array is a compilation error. Bit fields are not "arrays of bits."

Common Programming Error 21.7

Attempting to take the address of a bit field (the & operator may not be used with bit fields because a pointer can designate only a particular byte in memory and bit fields can start in the middle of a byte) is a compilation error.

Performance Tip 21.3

Although bit fields save space, using them can cause the compiler to generate slower-executing machine-language code. This occurs because it takes extra machine-language operations to access only portions of an addressable storage unit. This is one of many examples of the space–time trade-offs that occur in computer science.

21.9 Character-Handling Library

Most data is entered into computers as characters—including letters, digits and various special symbols. In this section, we discuss C++'s capabilities for examining and manipulating individual characters. In the remainder of the chapter, we continue the discussion of character-string manipulation that we began in Chapter 8.

The character-handling library includes several functions that perform useful tests and manipulations of character data. Each function receives a character—represented as an int—or EOF as an argument. Characters are often manipulated as integers. Remember that EOF normally has the value -1 and that some hardware architectures do not allow negative values to be stored in char variables. Therefore, the character-handling functions manipulate characters as integers. Figure 21.17 summarizes the functions of the character-handling library. When using functions from the character-handling library, include the <cctype> header file.

Prototype	Description
`int isdigit( int c )`	Returns true if c is a digit and false otherwise.
`int isalpha( int c )`	Returns true if c is a letter and false otherwise.
`int isalnum( int c )`	Returns true if c is a digit or a letter and false otherwise.
`int isxdigit( int c )`	Returns true if c is a hexadecimal digit character and false otherwise. (See Appendix D, Number Systems, for a detailed explanation of binary, octal, decimal and hexadecimal numbers.)
`int islower( int c )`	Returns true if c is a lowercase letter and false otherwise.
`int isupper( int c )`	Returns true if c is an uppercase letter; false otherwise.
`int tolower( int c )`	If c is an uppercase letter, tolower returns c as a lowercase letter. Otherwise, tolower returns the argument unchanged.
`int toupper( int c )`	If c is a lowercase letter, toupper returns c as an uppercase letter. Otherwise, toupper returns the argument unchanged.
`int isspace( int c )`	Returns true if c is a white-space character—newline ('\n'), space (' '), form feed ('\f'), carriage return ('\r'), horizontal tab ('\t'), or vertical tab ('\v')—and false otherwise.

Fig. 21.17 | Character-handling library functions. (Part 1 of 2.)

Prototype	Description
int iscntrl(int c)	Returns true if c is a control character, such as newline ('\n'), form feed ('\f'), carriage return ('\r'), horizontal tab ('\t'), vertical tab ('\v'), alert ('\a'), or backspace ('\b')—and false otherwise.
int ispunct(int c)	Returns true if c is a printing character other than a space, a digit, or a letter and false otherwise.
int isprint(int c)	Returns true value if c is a printing character including space (' ') and false otherwise.
int isgraph(int c)	Returns true if c is a printing character other than space (' ') and false otherwise.

Fig. 21.17 | Character-handling library functions. (Part 2 of 2.)

Figure 21.18 demonstrates functions `isdigit`, `isalpha`, `isalnum` and `isxdigit`. Function `isdigit` determines whether its argument is a digit (0–9). Function `isalpha` determines whether its argument is an uppercase letter (A-Z) or a lowercase letter (a–z). Function `isalnum` determines whether its argument is an uppercase letter, a lowercase letter or a digit. Function `isxdigit` determines whether its argument is a hexadecimal digit (A–F, a–f, 0–9).

```cpp
1   // Fig. 21.18: fig21_18.cpp
2   // Using functions isdigit, isalpha, isalnum and isxdigit.
3   #include <iostream>
4   using std::cout;
5   using std::endl;
6
7   #include <cctype> // character-handling function prototypes
8   using std::isalnum;
9   using std::isalpha;
10  using std::isdigit;
11  using std::isxdigit;
12
13  int main()
14  {
15     cout << "According to isdigit:\n"
16        << ( isdigit( '8' ) ? "8 is a" : "8 is not a" ) << " digit\n"
17        << ( isdigit( '#' ) ? "# is a" : "# is not a" ) << " digit\n";
18
19     cout << "\nAccording to isalpha:\n"
20        << ( isalpha( 'A' ) ? "A is a" : "A is not a" ) << " letter\n"
21        << ( isalpha( 'b' ) ? "b is a" : "b is not a" ) << " letter\n"
22        << ( isalpha( '&' ) ? "& is a" : "& is not a" ) << " letter\n"
23        << ( isalpha( '4' ) ? "4 is a" : "4 is not a" ) << " letter\n";
24
```

Fig. 21.18 | Character-handling functions `isdigit`, `isalpha`, `isalnum` and `isxdigit`. (Part 1 of 2.)

```
25        cout << "\nAccording to isalnum:\n"
26            << ( isalnum( 'A' ) ? "A is a" : "A is not a" )
27            << " digit or a letter\n"
28            << ( isalnum( '8' ) ? "8 is a" : "8 is not a" )
29            << " digit or a letter\n"
30            << ( isalnum( '#' ) ? "# is a" : "# is not a" )
31            << " digit or a letter\n";
32
33        cout << "\nAccording to isxdigit:\n"
34            << ( isxdigit( 'F' ) ? "F is a" : "F is not a" )
35            << " hexadecimal digit\n"
36            << ( isxdigit( 'J' ) ? "J is a" : "J is not a" )
37            << " hexadecimal digit\n"
38            << ( isxdigit( '7' ) ? "7 is a" : "7 is not a" )
39            << " hexadecimal digit\n"
40            << ( isxdigit( '$' ) ? "$ is a" : "$ is not a" )
41            << " hexadecimal digit\n"
42            << ( isxdigit( 'f' ) ? "f is a" : "f is not a" )
43            << " hexadecimal digit" << endl;
44        return 0;
45   } // end main
```

```
According to isdigit:
8 is a digit
# is not a digit

According to isalpha:
A is a letter
b is a letter
& is not a letter
4 is not a letter

According to isalnum:
A is a digit or a letter
8 is a digit or a letter
# is not a digit or a letter

According to isxdigit:
F is a hexadecimal digit
J is not a hexadecimal digit
7 is a hexadecimal digit
$ is not a hexadecimal digit
f is a hexadecimal digit
```

Fig. 21.18 | Character-handling functions isdigit, isalpha, isalnum and isxdigit. (Part 2 of 2.)

Figure 21.18 uses the conditional operator (?:) with each function to determine whether the string " is a " or the string " is not a " should be printed in the output for each character tested. For example, line 16 indicates that if '8' is a digit—i.e., if isdigit returns a true (nonzero) value—the string "8 is a " is printed. If '8' is not a digit (i.e., if isdigit returns 0), the string "8 is not a " is printed.

Figure 21.19 demonstrates functions islower, isupper, tolower and toupper. Function islower determines whether its argument is a lowercase letter (a–z). Function `isupper` determines whether its argument is an uppercase letter (A–Z). Function `tolower` converts an uppercase letter to lowercase and returns the lowercase letter—if the argument is not an uppercase letter, `tolower` returns the argument value unchanged. Function `toupper` converts a lowercase letter to uppercase and returns the uppercase letter—if the argument is not a lowercase letter, `toupper` returns the argument value unchanged.

```cpp
1   // Fig. 21.19: fig21_19.cpp
2   // Using functions islower, isupper, tolower and toupper.
3   #include <iostream>
4   using std::cout;
5   using std::endl;
6
7   #include <cctype> // character-handling function prototypes
8   using std::islower;
9   using std::isupper;
10  using std::tolower;
11  using std::toupper;
12
13  int main()
14  {
15     cout << "According to islower:\n"
16        << ( islower( 'p' ) ? "p is a" : "p is not a" )
17        << " lowercase letter\n"
18        << ( islower( 'P' ) ? "P is a" : "P is not a" )
19        << " lowercase letter\n"
20        << ( islower( '5' ) ? "5 is a" : "5 is not a" )
21        << " lowercase letter\n"
22        << ( islower( '!' ) ? "! is a" : "! is not a" )
23        << " lowercase letter\n";
24
25     cout << "\nAccording to isupper:\n"
26        << ( isupper( 'D' ) ? "D is an" : "D is not an" )
27        << " uppercase letter\n"
28        << ( isupper( 'd' ) ? "d is an" : "d is not an" )
29        << " uppercase letter\n"
30        << ( isupper( '8' ) ? "8 is an" : "8 is not an" )
31        << " uppercase letter\n"
32        << ( isupper( '$' ) ? "$ is an" : "$ is not an" )
33        << " uppercase letter\n";
34
35     cout << "\nu converted to uppercase is "
36        << static_cast< char >( toupper( 'u' ) )
37        << "\n7 converted to uppercase is "
38        << static_cast< char >( toupper( '7' ) )
39        << "\n$ converted to uppercase is "
40        << static_cast< char >( toupper( '$' ) )
41        << "\nL converted to lowercase is "
42        << static_cast< char >( tolower( 'L' ) ) << endl;
43     return 0;
44  } // end main
```

Fig. 21.19 | Character-handling functions `islower`, `isupper`, `tolower` and `toupper`. (Part 1 of 2.)

```
According to islower:
p is a lowercase letter
P is not a lowercase letter
5 is not a lowercase letter
! is not a lowercase letter

According to isupper:
D is an uppercase letter
d is not an uppercase letter
8 is not an uppercase letter
$ is not an uppercase letter

u converted to uppercase is U
7 converted to uppercase is 7
$ converted to uppercase is $
L converted to lowercase is l
```

Fig. 21.19 | Character-handling functions islower, isupper, tolower and toupper. (Part 2 of 2.)

Figure 21.20 demonstrates functions isspace, iscntrl, ispunct, isprint and isgraph. Function isspace determines whether its argument is a white-space character, such as space (' '), form feed ('\f'), newline ('\n'), carriage return ('\r'), horizontal tab ('\t') or vertical tab ('\v'). Function iscntrl determines whether its argument is a con-

```
1   // Fig. 21.20: fig21_20.cpp
2   // Using functions isspace, iscntrl, ispunct, isprint, isgraph.
3   #include <iostream>
4   using std::cout;
5   using std::endl;
6
7   #include <cctype> // character-handling function prototypes
8   using std::iscntrl;
9   using std::isgraph;
10  using std::isprint;
11  using std::ispunct;
12  using std::isspace;
13
14  int main()
15  {
16     cout << "According to isspace:\nNewline "
17        << ( isspace( '\n' ) ? "is a" : "is not a" )
18        << " whitespace character\nHorizontal tab "
19        << ( isspace( '\t' ) ? "is a" : "is not a" )
20        << " whitespace character\n"
21        << ( isspace( '%' ) ? "% is a" : "% is not a" )
22        << " whitespace character\n";
23
```

Fig. 21.20 | Character-handling functions isspace, iscntrl, ispunct, isprint and isgraph. (Part 1 of 2.)

```
24        cout << "\nAccording to iscntrl:\nNewline "
25            << ( iscntrl( '\n' ) ? "is a" : "is not a" )
26            << " control character\n"
27            << ( iscntrl( '$' ) ? "$ is a" : "$ is not a" )
28            << " control character\n";
29
30        cout << "\nAccording to ispunct:\n"
31            << ( ispunct( ';' ) ? "; is a" : "; is not a" )
32            << " punctuation character\n"
33            << ( ispunct( 'Y' ) ? "Y is a" : "Y is not a" )
34            << " punctuation character\n"
35            << ( ispunct( '#' ) ? "# is a" : "# is not a" )
36            << " punctuation character\n";
37
38        cout << "\nAccording to isprint:\n"
39            << ( isprint( '$' ) ? "$ is a" : "$ is not a" )
40            << " printing character\nAlert "
41            << ( isprint( '\a' ) ? "is a" : "is not a" )
42            << " printing character\nSpace "
43            << ( isprint( ' ' ) ? "is a" : "is not a" )
44            << " printing character\n";
45
46        cout << "\nAccording to isgraph:\n"
47            << ( isgraph( 'Q' ) ? "Q is a" : "Q is not a" )
48            << " printing character other than a space\nSpace "
49            << ( isgraph( ' ' ) ? "is a" : "is not a" )
50            << " printing character other than a space" << endl;
51        return 0;
52    } // end main
```

```
According to isspace:
Newline is a whitespace character
Horizontal tab is a whitespace character
% is not a whitespace character

According to iscntrl:
Newline is a control character
$ is not a control character

According to ispunct:
; is a punctuation character
Y is not a punctuation character
# is a punctuation character

According to isprint:
$ is a printing character
Alert is not a printing character
Space is a printing character

According to isgraph:
Q is a printing character other than a space
Space is not a printing character other than a space
```

Fig. 21.20 | Character-handling functions `isspace`, `iscntrl`, `ispunct`, `isprint` and `isgraph`. (Part 2 of 2.)

trol character such as horizontal tab ('\t'), vertical tab ('\v'), form feed ('\f'), alert ('\a'), backspace ('\b'), carriage return ('\r') or newline ('\n'). Function ispunct determines whether its argument is a printing character other than a space, digit or letter, such as $, #, (,), [,], {, }, ;, : or %. Function isprint determines whether its argument is a character that can be displayed on the screen (including the space character). Function isgraph tests for the same characters as isprint, but the space character is not included.

21.10 Pointer-Based String-Conversion Functions

In Chapter 8, we discussed several of C++'s most popular pointer-based string-manipulation functions. In the next several sections, we cover the remaining functions, including functions for converting strings to numeric values, functions for searching strings and functions for manipulating, comparing and searching blocks of memory.

This section presents the pointer-based string-conversion functions from the general-utilities library <cstdlib>. These functions convert pointer-based strings of characters to integer and floating-point values. Figure 21.21 summarizes the pointer-based string-conversion functions. Note the use of const to declare variable nPtr in the function headers (read from right to left as "nPtr is a pointer to a character constant"). When using functions from the general-utilities library, include the <cstdlib> header file.

Prototype	Description
double **atof**(const char *nPtr)	Converts the string nPtr to double. If the string cannot be converted, 0 is returned.
int **atoi**(const char *nPtr)	Converts the string nPtr to int. If the string cannot be converted, 0 is returned.
long **atol**(const char *nPtr)	Converts the string nPtr to long int. If the string cannot be converted, 0 is returned.
double **strtod**(const char *nPtr, char **endPtr)	Converts the string nPtr to double. endPtr is the address of a pointer to the rest of the string after the double. If the string cannot be converted, 0 is returned.
long **strtol**(const char *nPtr, char **endPtr, int base)	Converts the string nPtr to long. endPtr is the address of a pointer to the rest of the string after the long. If the string cannot be converted, 0 is returned. The base parameter indicates the base of the number to convert (e.g., 8 for octal, 10 for decimal or 16 for hexadecimal). The default is decimal.

Fig. 21.21 | Pointer-based string-conversion functions of the general-utilities library. (Part 1 of 2.)

Prototype	Description
`unsigned long strtoul( const char *nPtr, char **endPtr, int base )`	
	Converts the string `nPtr` to `unsigned long`. `endPtr` is the address of a pointer to the rest of the string after the `unsigned long`. If the string cannot be converted, 0 is returned. The `base` parameter indicates the base of the number to convert (e.g., 8 for octal, 10 for decimal or 16 for hexadecimal). The default is decimal.

Fig. 21.21 | Pointer-based string-conversion functions of the general-utilities library. (Part 2 of 2.)

Function `atof` (Fig. 21.22, line 12) converts its argument—a string that represents a floating-point number—to a `double` value. The function returns the `double` value. If the string cannot be converted—for example, if the first character of the string is not a digit—function atof returns zero.

Function `atoi` (Fig. 21.23, line 12) converts its argument—a string of digits that represents an integer—to an `int` value. The function returns the `int` value. If the string cannot be converted, function atoi returns zero.

Function `atol` (Fig. 21.24, line 12) converts its argument—a string of digits representing a long integer—to a `long` value. The function returns the `long` value. If the string cannot be converted, function atol returns zero. If int and long are both stored in four bytes, function atoi and function atol work identically.

```cpp
1   // Fig. 21.22: fig21_21.cpp
2   // Using atof.
3   #include <iostream>
4   using std::cout;
5   using std::endl;
6
7   #include <cstdlib> // atof prototype
8   using std::atof;
9
10  int main()
11  {
12     double d = atof( "99.0" ); // convert string to double
13
14     cout << "The string \"99.0\" converted to double is " << d
15        << "\nThe converted value divided by 2 is " << d / 2.0 << endl;
16     return 0;
17  } // end main
```

```
The string "99.0" converted to double is 99
The converted value divided by 2 is 49.5
```

Fig. 21.22 | String-conversion function atof.

```
1   // Fig. 21.23: Fig21_26.cpp
2   // Using atoi.
3   #include <iostream>
4   using std::cout;
5   using std::endl;
6
7   #include <cstdlib> // atoi prototype
8   using std::atoi;
9
10  int main()
11  {
12     int i = atoi( "2593" ); // convert string to int
13
14     cout << "The string \"2593\" converted to int is " << i
15        << "\nThe converted value minus 593 is " << i - 593 << endl;
16     return 0;
17  } // end main
```

```
The string "2593" converted to int is 2593
The converted value minus 593 is 2000
```

Fig. 21.23 | String-conversion function atoi.

```
1   // Fig. 21.24: fig21_24.cpp
2   // Using atol.
3   #include <iostream>
4   using std::cout;
5   using std::endl;
6
7   #include <cstdlib> // atol prototype
8   using std::atol;
9
10  int main()
11  {
12     long x = atol( "1000000" ); // convert string to long
13
14     cout << "The string \"1000000\" converted to long is " << x
15        << "\nThe converted value divided by 2 is " << x / 2 << endl;
16     return 0;
17  } // end main
```

```
The string "1000000" converted to long int is 1000000
The converted value divided by 2 is 500000
```

Fig. 21.24 | String-conversion function atol.

Function **strtod** (Fig. 21.25) converts a sequence of characters representing a floating-point value to double. Function strtod receives two arguments—a string (char *) and the address of a char * pointer (i.e., a char **). The string contains the character sequence to be converted to double. The second argument enables strtod to modify a char * pointer in the calling function, such that the pointer points to the location of the

```
1   // Fig. 21.25: fig21_25.cpp
2   // Using strtod.
3   #include <iostream>
4   using std::cout;
5   using std::endl;
6
7   #include <cstdlib> // strtod prototype
8   using std::strtod;
9
10  int main()
11  {
12     double d;
13     const char *string1 = "51.2% are admitted";
14     char *stringPtr;
15
16     d = strtod( string1, &stringPtr ); // convert characters to double
17
18     cout << "The string \"" << string1
19        << "\" is converted to the\ndouble value " << d
20        << " and the string \"" << stringPtr << "\"" << endl;
21     return 0;
22  } // end main
```

```
The string "51.2% are admitted" is converted to the
double value 51.2 and the string "% are admitted"
```

Fig. 21.25 | String-conversion function strtod.

first character after the converted portion of the string. Line 16 indicates that d is assigned the double value converted from string and that stringPtr is assigned the location of the first character after the converted value (51.2) in string.

Function strtol (Fig. 21.26) converts to long a sequence of characters representing an integer. The function receives three arguments—a string (char *), the address of a char * pointer and an integer. The string contains the character sequence to convert. The second argument is assigned the location of the first character after the converted portion of the string. The integer specifies the *base* of the value being converted. Line 16 indicates that x is assigned the long value converted from string and that remainderPtr is assigned the location of the first character after the converted value (-1234567) in string1. Using a null pointer for the second argument causes the remainder of the string to be ignored. The third argument, 0, indicates that the value to be converted can be in octal (base 8), decimal (base 10) or hexadecimal (base 16). This is determined by the initial characters in the string—0 indicates an octal number, 0x indicates hexadecimal and a number from 1–9 indicates decimal.

In a call to function strtol, the base can be specified as zero or as any value between 2 and 36. (See Appendix D for a detailed explanation of the octal, decimal, hexadecimal and binary number systems.) Numeric representations of integers from base 11 to base 36 use the characters A–Z to represent the values 10 to 35. For example, hexadecimal values can consist of the digits 0–9 and the characters A–F. A base-11 integer can consist of the digits 0–9 and the character A. A base-24 integer can consist of the digits 0–9 and the char-

```
1    // Fig. 21.26: fig21_26.cpp
2    // Using strtol.
3    #include <iostream>
4    using std::cout;
5    using std::endl;
6
7    #include <cstdlib> // strtol prototype
8    using std::strtol;
9
10   int main()
11   {
12      long x;
13      const char *string1 = "-1234567abc";
14      char *remainderPtr;
15
16      x = strtol( string1, &remainderPtr, 0 ); // convert characters to long
17
18      cout << "The original string is \"" << string1
19         << "\"\nThe converted value is " << x
20         << "\"\nThe remainder of the original string is \"" << remainderPtr
21         << "\"\nThe converted value plus 567 is " << x + 567 << endl;
22      return 0;
23   } // end main
```

```
The original string is "-1234567abc"
The converted value is -1234567
The remainder of the original string is "abc"
The converted value plus 567 is -1234000
```

Fig. 21.26 | String-conversion function strtol.

acters A–N. A base-36 integer can consist of the digits 0–9 and the characters A–Z. [*Note:* The case of the letter used is ignored.]

Function strtoul (Fig. 21.27) converts to unsigned long a sequence of characters representing an unsigned long integer. The function works identically to strtol. Line 17 indicates that x is assigned the unsigned long value converted from string and that remainderPtr is assigned the location of the first character after the converted value (1234567) in string1. The third argument, 0, indicates that the value to be converted can be in octal, decimal or hexadecimal format, depending on the initial characters.

```
1    // Fig. 21.27: fig21_27.cpp
2    // Using strtoul.
3    #include <iostream>
4    using std::cout;
5    using std::endl;
6
7    #include <cstdlib> // strtoul prototype
8    using std::strtoul;
9
```

Fig. 21.27 | String-conversion function strtoul. (Part 1 of 2.)

```
10   int main()
11   {
12      unsigned long x;
13      const char *string1 = "1234567abc";
14      char *remainderPtr;
15
16      // convert a sequence of characters to unsigned long
17      x = strtoul( string1, &remainderPtr, 0 );
18
19      cout << "The original string is \"" << string1
20         << "\"\nThe converted value is " << x
21         << "\"\nThe remainder of the original string is \"" << remainderPtr
22         << "\"\nThe converted value minus 567 is " << x - 567 << endl;
23      return 0;
24   } // end main
```

```
The original string is "1234567abc"
The converted value is 1234567
The remainder of the original string is "abc"
The converted value minus 567 is 1234000
```

Fig. 21.27 | String-conversion function `strtoul`. (Part 2 of 2.)

21.11 Search Functions of the Pointer-Based String-Handling Library

This section presents the functions of the string-handling library used to search strings for characters and other strings. The functions are summarized in Fig. 21.28. Note that func-

Prototype	Description
char *strchr(const char *s, int c)	
	Locates the first occurrence of character c in string s. If c is found, a pointer to c in s is returned. Otherwise, a null pointer is returned.
char *strrchr(const char *s, int c)	
	Searches from the end of string s and locates the last occurrence of character c in string s. If c is found, a pointer to c in string s is returned. Otherwise, a null pointer is returned.
size_t strspn(const char *s1, const char *s2)	
	Determines and returns the length of the initial segment of string s1 consisting only of characters contained in string s2.
char *strpbrk(const char *s1, const char *s2)	
	Locates the first occurrence in string s1 of any character in string s2. If a character from string s2 is found, a pointer to the character in string s1 is returned. Otherwise, a null pointer is returned.

Fig. 21.28 | Search functions of the pointer-based string-handling library. (Part 1 of 2.)

Prototype	Description

`size_t strcspn( const char *s1, const char *s2 )`

Determines and returns the length of the initial segment of string s1 consisting of characters not contained in string s2.

`char *strstr( const char *s1, const char *s2 )`

Locates the first occurrence in string s1 of string s2. If the string is found, a pointer to the string in s1 is returned. Otherwise, a null pointer is returned.

Fig. 21.28 | Search functions of the pointer-based string-handling library. (Part 2 of 2.)

tions `strcspn` and `strspn` specify return type `size_t`. Type `size_t` is a type defined by the standard as the integral type of the value returned by operator `sizeof`.

Function `strchr` searches for the first occurrence of a character in a string. If the character is found, `strchr` returns a pointer to the character in the string; otherwise, `strchr` returns a null pointer. The program of Fig. 21.29 uses `strchr` (lines 17 and 25) to search for the first occurrences of `'a'` and `'z'` in the string `"This is a test"`.

```
1   // Fig. 21.29: fig21_29.cpp
2   // Using strchr.
3   #include <iostream>
4   using std::cout;
5   using std::endl;
6
7   #include <cstring> // strchr prototype
8   using std::strchr;
9
10  int main()
11  {
12     const char *string1 = "This is a test";
13     char character1 = 'a';
14     char character2 = 'z';
15
16     // search for character1 in string1
17     if ( strchr( string1, character1 ) != NULL )
18        cout << '\'' << character1 << "' was found in \""
19           << string1 << "\".\n";
20     else
21        cout << '\'' << character1 << "' was not found in \""
22           << string1 << "\".\n";
23
24     // search for character2 in string1
25     if ( strchr( string1, character2 ) != NULL )
26        cout << '\'' << character2 << "' was found in \""
27           << string1 << "\".\n";
```

Fig. 21.29 | String-search function `strchr`. (Part 1 of 2.)

```
28        else
29           cout << '\'' << character2 << "' was not found in \""
30              << string1 << "\"." << endl;
31
32        return 0;
33     } // end main
```

```
'a' was found in "This is a test".
'z' was not found in "This is a test".
```

Fig. 21.29 | String-search function strchr. (Part 2 of 2.)

Function strcspn (Fig. 21.30, line 18) determines the length of the initial part of the string in its first argument that does not contain any characters from the string in its second argument. The function returns the length of the segment.

Function strpbrk searches for the first occurrence in its first string argument of any character in its second string argument. If a character from the second argument is found, strpbrk returns a pointer to the character in the first argument; otherwise, strpbrk returns a null pointer. Line 16 of Fig. 21.31 locates the first occurrence in string1 of any character from string2.

```
 1    // Fig. 21.30: fig21_30.cpp
 2    // Using strcspn.
 3    #include <iostream>
 4    using std::cout;
 5    using std::endl;
 6
 7    #include <cstring> // strcspn prototype
 8    using std::strcspn;
 9
10    int main()
11    {
12       const char *string1 = "The value is 3.14159";
13       const char *string2 = "1234567890";
14
15       cout << "string1 = " << string1 << "\nstring2 = " << string2
16          << "\n\nThe length of the initial segment of string1"
17          << "\ncontaining no characters from string2 = "
18          << strcspn( string1, string2 ) << endl;
19       return 0;
20    } // end main
```

```
string1 = The value is 3.14159
string2 = 1234567890

The length of the initial segment of string1
containing no characters from string2 = 13
```

Fig. 21.30 | String-search function strcspn.

```
1   // Fig. 21.31: fig21_31.cpp
2   // Using strpbrk.
3   #include <iostream>
4   using std::cout;
5   using std::endl;
6
7   #include <cstring> // strpbrk prototype
8   using std::strpbrk;
9
10  int main()
11  {
12     const char *string1 = "This is a test";
13     const char *string2 = "beware";
14
15     cout << "Of the characters in \"" << string2 << "\"\n'"
16        << *strpbrk( string1, string2 ) << "\' is the first character "
17        << "to appear in\n\"" << string1 << '\"' << endl;
18     return 0;
19  } // end main
```

```
Of the characters in "beware"
'a' is the first character to appear in
"This is a test"
```

Fig. 21.31 | String-search function `strpbrk`.

Function `strrchr` searches for the last occurrence of the specified character in a string. If the character is found, `strrchr` returns a pointer to the character in the string; otherwise, `strrchr` returns 0. Line 18 of Fig. 21.32 searches for the last occurrence of the character `'z'` in the string `"A zoo has many animals including zebras"`.

Function `strspn` (Fig. 21.33, line 18) determines the length of the initial part of the string in its first argument that contains only characters from the string in its second argument. The function returns the length of the segment.

Function `strstr` searches for the first occurrence of its second string argument in its first string argument. If the second string is found in the first string, a pointer to the location of the string in the first argument is returned; otherwise, it returns 0. Line 18 of Fig. 21.34 uses `strstr` to find the string `"def"` in the string `"abcdefabcdef"`.

```
1   // Fig. 21.32: fig21_32.cpp
2   // Using strrchr.
3   #include <iostream>
4   using std::cout;
5   using std::endl;
6
7   #include <cstring> // strrchr prototype
8   using std::strrchr;
9
10  int main()
11  {
```

Fig. 21.32 | String-search function `strrchr`. (Part 1 of 2.)

```
12      const char *string1 = "A zoo has many animals including zebras";
13      char c = 'z';
14
15      cout << "string1 = " << string1 << "\n" << endl;
16      cout << "The remainder of string1 beginning with the\n"
17         << "last occurrence of character '"
18         << c << "' is: \"" << strrchr( string1, c ) << '\"' << endl;
19      return 0;
20   } // end main
```

```
string1 = A zoo has many animals including zebras

The remainder of string1 beginning with the
last occurrence of character 'z' is: "zebras"
```

Fig. 21.32 | String-search function `strrchr`. (Part 2 of 2.)

```
1    // Fig. 21.33: fig21_33.cpp
2    // Using strspn.
3    #include <iostream>
4    using std::cout;
5    using std::endl;
6
7    #include <cstring> // strspn prototype
8    using std::strspn;
9
10   int main()
11   {
12      const char *string1 = "The value is 3.14159";
13      const char *string2 = "aehils Tuv";
14
15      cout << "string1 = " << string1 << "\nstring2 = " << string2
16         << "\n\nThe length of the initial segment of string1\n"
17         << "containing only characters from string2 = "
18         << strspn( string1, string2 ) << endl;
19      return 0;
20   } // end main
```

```
string1 = The value is 3.14159
string2 = aehils Tuv

The length of the initial segment of string1
containing only characters from string2 = 13
```

Fig. 21.33 | String-search function `strspn`.

```
1    // Fig. 21.34: fig21_34.cpp
2    // Using strstr.
3    #include <iostream>
```

Fig. 21.34 | String-search function `strstr`. (Part 1 of 2.)

```
4   using std::cout;
5   using std::endl;
6
7   #include <cstring> // strstr prototype
8   using std::strstr;
9
10  int main()
11  {
12     const char *string1 = "abcdefabcdef";
13     const char *string2 = "def";
14
15     cout << "string1 = " << string1 << "\nstring2 = " << string2
16        << "\n\nThe remainder of string1 beginning with the\n"
17        << "first occurrence of string2 is: "
18        << strstr( string1, string2 ) << endl;
19     return 0;
20  } // end main
```

```
string1 = abcdefabcdef
string2 = def

The remainder of string1 beginning with the
first occurrence of string2 is: defabcdef
```

Fig. 21.34 | String-search function `strstr`. (Part 2 of 2.)

21.12 Memory Functions of the Pointer-Based String-Handling Library

The string-handling library functions presented in this section facilitate manipulating, comparing and searching blocks of memory. The functions treat blocks of memory as arrays of bytes. These functions can manipulate any block of data. Figure 21.35 summarizes

Prototype	Description
`void *memcpy( void *s1, const void *s2, size_t n )`	
	Copies n characters from the object pointed to by s2 into the object pointed to by s1. A pointer to the resulting object is returned. The area from which characters are copied is not allowed to overlap the area to which characters are copied.
`void *memmove( void *s1, const void *s2, size_t n )`	
	Copies n characters from the object pointed to by s2 into the object pointed to by s1. The copy is performed as if the characters were first copied from the object pointed to by s2 into a temporary array, and then copied from the temporary array into the object pointed to by s1. A pointer to the resulting object is returned. The area from which characters are copied is allowed to overlap the area to which characters are copied.

Fig. 21.35 | Memory functions of the string-handling library. (Part 1 of 2.)

Prototype	Description
`int memcmp( const void *s1, const void *s2, size_t n )`	
	Compares the first n characters of the objects pointed to by s1 and s2. The function returns 0, less than 0, or greater than 0 if s1 is equal to, less than or greater than s2, respectively.
`void *memchr( const void *s, int c, size_t n )`	
	Locates the first occurrence of c (converted to `unsigned char`) in the first n characters of the object pointed to by s. If c is found, a pointer to c in the object is returned. Otherwise, 0 is returned.
`void *memset( void *s, int c, size_t n )`	
	Copies c (converted to `unsigned char`) into the first n characters of the object pointed to by s. A pointer to the result is returned.

Fig. 21.35 | Memory functions of the string-handling library. (Part 2 of 2.)

the memory functions of the string-handling library. In the function discussions, "object" refers to a block of data. [*Note:* The string-processing functions in prior sections operate on null-terminated character strings. The functions in this section operate on arrays of bytes. The null-character value (i.e., a byte containing 0) has no significance with the functions in this section.]

The pointer parameters to these functions are declared void *. In Chapter 8, we saw that a pointer to any data type can be assigned directly to a pointer of type void *. For this reason, these functions can receive pointers to any data type. Remember that a pointer of type void * cannot be assigned directly to a pointer of any other data type. Because a void * pointer cannot be dereferenced, each function receives a size argument that specifies the number of characters (bytes) the function will process. For simplicity, the examples in this section manipulate character arrays (blocks of characters).

Function `memcpy` copies a specified number of characters (bytes) from the object pointed to by its second argument into the object pointed to by its first argument. The function can receive a pointer to any type of object. The result of this function is undefined if the two objects overlap in memory (i.e., are parts of the same object). The program of Fig. 21.36 uses memcpy (line 17) to copy the string in array s2 to array s1.

```cpp
1  // Fig. 21.36: fig21_36.cpp
2  // Using memcpy.
3  #include <iostream>
4  using std::cout;
5  using std::endl;
6
7  #include <cstring> // memcpy prototype
8  using std::memcpy;
9
10 int main()
11 {
```

Fig. 21.36 | Memory-handling function memcpy. (Part 1 of 2.)

```
12      char s1[ 17 ];
13
14      // 17 total characters (includes terminating null)
15      char s2[] = "Copy this string";
16
17      memcpy( s1, s2, 17 ); // copy 17 characters from s2 to s1
18
19      cout << "After s2 is copied into s1 with memcpy,\n"
20          << "s1 contains \"" << s1 << '\"' << endl;
21      return 0;
22   } // end main
```

```
After s2 is copied into s1 with memcpy,
s1 contains "Copy this string"
```

Fig. 21.36 | Memory-handling function memcpy. (Part 2 of 2.)

Function memmove, like memcpy, copies a specified number of bytes from the object pointed to by its second argument into the object pointed to by its first argument. Copying is performed as if the bytes were copied from the second argument to a temporary array of characters, and then copied from the temporary array to the first argument. This allows characters from one part of a string to be copied into another part of the same string.

Common Programming Error 21.8

String-manipulation functions other than memmove that copy characters have undefined results when copying takes place between parts of the same string.

The program in Fig. 21.37 uses memmove (line 16) to copy the last 10 bytes of array x into the first 10 bytes of array x.

```
1    // Fig. 21.37: fig21_37.cpp
2    // Using memmove.
3    #include <iostream>
4    using std::cout;
5    using std::endl;
6
7    #include <cstring> // memmove prototype
8    using std::memmove;
9
10   int main()
11   {
12      char x[] = "Home Sweet Home";
13
14      cout << "The string in array x before memmove is: " << x;
15      cout << "\nThe string in array x after memmove is:  "
16          << static_cast< char * >( memmove( x, &x[ 5 ], 10 ) ) << endl;
17      return 0;
18   } // end main
```

Fig. 21.37 | Memory-handling function memmove. (Part 1 of 2.)

```
The string in array x before memmove is: Home Sweet Home
The string in array x after memmove is:  Sweet Home Home
```

Fig. 21.37 | Memory-handling function `memmove`. (Part 2 of 2.)

Function `memcmp` (Fig. 21.38, lines 19, 20 and 21) compares the specified number of characters of its first argument with the corresponding characters of its second argument. The function returns a value greater than zero if the first argument is greater than the second argument, zero if the arguments are equal, and a value less than zero if the first argument is less than the second argument. [*Note:* With some compilers, function `memcmp` returns –1, 0 or 1, as in the sample output of Fig. 21.38. With other compilers, this function returns 0 or the difference between the numeric codes of the first characters that differ in the strings being compared. For example, when s1 and s2 are compared, the first character that differs between them is the fifth character of each string—E (numeric code 69) for s1 and X (numeric code 72) for s2. In this case, the return value will be 19 (or –19 when s2 is compared to s1).]

```
 1   // Fig. 21.38: fig21_38.cpp
 2   // Using memcmp.
 3   #include <iostream>
 4   using std::cout;
 5   using std::endl;
 6
 7   #include <iomanip>
 8   using std::setw;
 9
10   #include <cstring> // memcmp prototype
11   using std::memcmp;
12
13   int main()
14   {
15      char s1[] = "ABCDEFG";
16      char s2[] = "ABCDXYZ";
17
18      cout << "s1 = " << s1 << "\ns2 = " << s2 << endl
19         << "\nmemcmp(s1, s2, 4) = " << setw( 3 ) << memcmp( s1, s2, 4 )
20         << "\nmemcmp(s1, s2, 7) = " << setw( 3 ) << memcmp( s1, s2, 7 )
21         << "\nmemcmp(s2, s1, 7) = " << setw( 3 ) << memcmp( s2, s1, 7 )
22         << endl;
23      return 0;
24   } // end main
```

```
s1 = ABCDEFG
s2 = ABCDXYZ

memcmp(s1, s2, 4) =   0
memcmp(s1, s2, 7) =  -1
memcmp(s2, s1, 7) =   1
```

Fig. 21.38 | Memory-handling function `memcmp`.

Function memchr searches for the first occurrence of a byte, represented as unsigned char, in the specified number of bytes of an object. If the byte is found in the object, a pointer to it is returned; otherwise, the function returns a null pointer. Line 16 of Fig. 21.39 searches for the character (byte) 'r' in the string "This is a string".

Function memset copies the value of the byte in its second argument into a specified number of bytes of the object pointed to by its first argument. Line 16 in Fig. 21.40 uses memset to copy 'b' into the first 7 bytes of string1.

```cpp
1   // Fig. 21.39: fig21_39.cpp
2   // Using memchr.
3   #include <iostream>
4   using std::cout;
5   using std::endl;
6
7   #include <cstring> // memchr prototype
8   using std::memchr;
9
10  int main()
11  {
12     char s[] = "This is a string";
13
14     cout << "s = " << s << "\n" << endl;
15     cout << "The remainder of s after character 'r' is found is \""
16        << static_cast< char * >( memchr( s, 'r', 16 ) ) << '\"' << endl;
17     return 0;
18  } // end main
```

```
s = This is a string

The remainder of s after character 'r' is found is "ring"
```

Fig. 21.39 | Memory-handling function memchr.

```cpp
1   // Fig. 21.40: fig21_40.cpp
2   // Using memset.
3   #include <iostream>
4   using std::cout;
5   using std::endl;
6
7   #include <cstring> // memset prototype
8   using std::memset;
9
10  int main()
11  {
12     char string1[ 15 ] = "BBBBBBBBBBBBBB";
13
14     cout << "string1 = " << string1 << endl;
15     cout << "string1 after memset = "
16        << static_cast< char * >( memset( string1, 'b', 7 ) ) << endl;
17     return 0;
18  } // end main
```

Fig. 21.40 | Memory-handling function memset. (Part 1 of 2.)

```
string1 = BBBBBBBBBBBBBB
string1 after memset = bbbbbbbBBBBBBB
```

Fig. 21.40 | Memory-handling function `memset`. (Part 2 of 2.)

21.13 Wrap-Up

This chapter introduced `struct` definitions, initializing `struct`s and using them with functions. We discussed `typedef`, using it to create aliases to help promote portability. We also introduced bitwise operators to manipulate data and bit fields for storing data compactly. You also learned about the string-conversion functions in <cstlib> and the string-processing functions in <cstring>. In the next chapter, we continue our discussion of data structures by discussing containers—data structures defined in the C++ Standard Template Library. We also present the many algorithms defined in the STL as well.

Summary

Section 21.2 Structure Definitions

- Structures are collections of related variables (or aggregates) under one name.
- Structures can contain variables of different data types.
- Keyword `struct` begins every structure definition. Between the braces of the structure definition are the structure member declarations.
- Members of the same structure must have unique names.
- A structure definition creates a new data type that can be used to declare variables.

Section 21.3 Initializing Structures

- A structure can be initialized with an initializer list by following the variable in the declaration with an equal sign and a comma-separated list of initializers enclosed in braces. If there are fewer initializers in the list than members in the structure, the remaining members are initialized to zero (or a null pointer for pointer members).
- Entire structure variables may be assigned to structure variables of the same type.
- A structure variable may be initialized with a structure variable of the same type.

Section 21.4 Using Structures with Functions

- Structure variables and individual structure members are passed to functions by value.
- To pass a structure by reference, pass the address of the structure variable or a reference to the structure variable. An array of structures is passed by reference. To pass an array by value, create a structure with the array as a member.

Section 21.5 `typedef`

- Creating a new type name with `typedef` does not create a new type; it creates a name that is synonymous with a type defined previously.

Section 21.7 Bitwise Operators

- The bitwise AND operator (&) takes two integral operands. A bit in the result is set to one if the corresponding bits in each of the operands are one.
- Masks are used with bitwise AND to hide some bits while preserving others.

- The bitwise inclusive-OR operator (|) takes two operands. A bit in the result is set to one if the corresponding bit in either operand is set to one.
- Each of the bitwise operators (except complement) has a corresponding assignment operator.
- The bitwise exclusive-OR operator (∧) takes two operands. A bit in the result is set to one if exactly one of the corresponding bits in the two operands is set to one.
- The left-shift operator (<<) shifts the bits of its left operand left by the number of bits specified by its right operand. Bits vacated to the right are replaced with zeros.
- The right-shift operator (>>) shifts the bits of its left operand right by the number of bits specified in its right operand. Right shifting an unsigned integer causes bits vacated at the left to be replaced by zeros. Vacated bits in signed integers can be replaced with zeros or ones.
- The bitwise complement operator (~) takes one operand and inverts its bits—this produces the one's complement of the operand.

Section 21.8 Bit Fields
- Bit fields reduce storage use by storing data in the minimum number of bits required. Bit-field members must be declared as int or unsigned.
- A bit field is declared by following an unsigned or int member name with a colon and the width of the bit field.
- The bit-field width must be an integer constant.
- If a bit field is specified without a name, the field is used as padding in the structure.
- An unnamed bit field with width 0 aligns the next bit field on a new machine-word boundary.

Section 21.9 Character-Handling Library
- Function islower determines whether its argument is a lowercase letter (a–z). Function isupper determines whether its argument is an uppercase letter (A–Z).
- Function isdigit determines whether its argument is a digit (0–9).
- Function isalpha determines whether its argument is an uppercase (A–Z) or lowercase letter (a–z).
- Function isalnum determines whether its argument is an uppercase letter (A–Z), a lowercase letter (a–z), or a digit (0–9).
- Function isxdigit determines whether its argument is a hexadecimal digit (A–F, a–f, 0–9).
- Function toupper converts a lowercase letter to an uppercase letter. Function tolower converts an uppercase letter to a lowercase letter.
- Function isspace determines whether its argument is one of the following white-space characters: ' ' (space), '\f', '\n', '\r', '\t' or '\v'.
- Function iscntrl determines whether its argument is a control character, such as '\t', '\v', '\f', '\a', '\b', '\r' or '\n'.
- Function ispunct determines whether its argument is a printing character other than a space, a digit or a letter.
- Function isprint determines whether its argument is any printing character, including space.
- Function isgraph determines whether its argument is a printing character other than space.

Section 21.10 Pointer-Based String-Conversion Functions
- Function atof converts its argument—a string beginning with a series of digits that represents a floating-point number—to a double value.
- Function atoi converts its argument—a string beginning with a series of digits that represents an integer—to an int value.

- Function `atol` converts its argument—a string beginning with a series of digits that represents a long integer—to a `long` value.

- Function `strtod` converts a sequence of characters representing a floating-point value to `double`. The function receives two arguments—a string (`char *`) and the address of a `char *` pointer. The string contains the character sequence to be converted, and the pointer to `char *` is assigned the remainder of the string after the conversion.

- Function `strtol` converts a sequence of characters representing an integer to `long`. The function receives three arguments—a string (`char *`), the address of a `char *` pointer and an integer. The string contains the character sequence to be converted, the pointer to `char *` is assigned the location of the first character after the converted value and the integer specifies the base of the value being converted.

- Function `strtoul` converts a sequence of characters representing an integer to `unsigned long`. The function receives three arguments—a string (`char *`), the address of a `char *` pointer and an integer. The string contains the character sequence to be converted, the pointer to `char *` is assigned the location of the first character after the converted value and the integer specifies the base of the value being converted.

Section 21.11 Search Functions of the Pointer-Based String-Handling Library

- Function `strchr` searches for the first occurrence of a character in a string. If found, `strchr` returns a pointer to the character in the string; otherwise, `strchr` returns a null pointer.

- Function `strcspn` determines the length of the initial part of the string in its first argument that does not contain any characters from the string in its second argument. The function returns the length of the segment.

- Function `strpbrk` searches for the first occurrence in its first argument of any character that appears in its second argument. If a character from the second argument is found, `strpbrk` returns a pointer to the character; otherwise, `strpbrk` returns a null pointer.

- Function `strrchr` searches for the last occurrence of a character in a string. If the character is found, `strrchr` returns a pointer to the character in the string; otherwise, it returns a null pointer.

- Function `strspn` determines the length of the initial part of its first argument that contains only characters from the string in its second argument and returns the length of the segment.

- Function `strstr` searches for the first occurrence of its second string argument in its first string argument. If the second string is found in the first string, a pointer to the location of the string in the first argument is returned; otherwise it returns 0.

Section 21.12 Memory Functions of the Pointer-Based String-Handling Library

- Function `memcpy` copies a specified number of characters from the object to which its second argument points into the object to which its first argument points. The function can receive a pointer to any object. The pointers are received as `void` pointers and converted to `char` pointers for use in the function. Function `memcpy` manipulates the bytes of its argument as characters.

- Function `memmove` copies a specified number of bytes from the object pointed to by its second argument to the object pointed to by its first argument. Copying is accomplished as if the bytes were copied from the second argument to a temporary character array, and then copied from the temporary array to the first argument.

- Function `memcmp` compares the specified number of characters of its first and second arguments.

- Function `memchr` searches for the first occurrence of a byte, represented as `unsigned char`, in the specified number of bytes of an object. If the byte is found, a pointer to it is returned; otherwise, a null pointer is returned.

- Function memset copies its second argument, treated as an unsigned char, to a specified number of bytes of the object pointed to by the first argument.

Terminology

& bitwise AND operator	isxdigit
&= bitwise AND assignment operator	mask
<< left-shift operator	memchr
<<= left-shift assignment operator	memcmp
>> right-shift operator	memcpy
>>= right-shift assignment operator	memmove
^ bitwise exclusive-OR operator	memset
^= bitwise exclusive-OR assignment operator	one's complement
| bitwise inclusive-OR operator	padding
|= bitwise inclusive-OR assignment operator	self-referential structure
~ bitwise complement operator	strchr
aggregate data type	strcspn
atof	string-conversion functions
atoi	strpbrk
atol	strrchr
bit field	strspn
bitwise assignment operators	strstr
bitwise operators	strtod
<cstdlib>	strtol
general-utilities library	strtoul
isalnum	struct
isalpha	structure name
iscntrl	structure type
isdigit	tolower
isgraph	toupper
islower	typedef
isprint	unnamed bit field
ispunct	width of a bit field
isspace	zero-width bit field
isupper	

Self-Review Exercises

21.1 Fill in the blanks in each of the following:

a) A(n) _____ is a collection of related variables under one name.

b) The bits in the result of an expression using the _____ operator are set to one if the corresponding bits in each operand are set to one. Otherwise, the bits are set to zero.

c) The variables declared in a structure definition are called its _____.

d) The bits in the result of an expression using the _____ operator are set to one if at least one of the corresponding bits in either operand is set to one. Otherwise, the bits are set to zero.

e) Keyword _____ introduces a structure declaration.

f) Keyword _____ is used to create a synonym for a previously defined data type.

g) Each bit in the result of an expression using the _____ operator is set to one if exactly one of the corresponding bits in either operand is set to one.

h) The bitwise AND operator & is often used to _____ bits (i.e., to select certain bits from a bit string while zeroing others).

i) A structure member is accessed with either operator _____ or _____.

j) The _____ and _____ operators are used to shift the bits of a value to the left or to the right, respectively.

21.2   State whether each of the following is *true* or *false*. If *false*, explain why.

a) Structures may contain only one data type.

b) Members of different structures must have unique names.

c) Keyword `typedef` is used to define new data types.

d) Structures are always passed to functions by reference.

21.3   Write a single statement or a set of statements to accomplish each of the following:

a) Define a structure called `Part` containing int variable `partNumber` and char array `part-Name`, whose values may be as long as 25 characters.

b) Define `PartPtr` to be a synonym for the type `Part *`.

c) Use separate statements to declare variable a to be of type `Part`, array b[10] to be of type `Part` and variable ptr to be of type pointer to `Part`.

d) Read a part number and a part name from the keyboard into the members of variable a.

e) Assign the member values of variable a to element three of array b.

f) Assign the address of array b to the pointer variable ptr.

g) Print the member values of element three of array b, using the variable ptr and the structure pointer operator to refer to the members.

21.4   Find the error in each of the following:

a) Assume that struct `Card` has been defined as containing two pointers to type char—namely, `face` and `suit`. Also, the variable c has been declared to be of type `Card`, and the variable cPtr has been declared to be of type pointer to `Card`. Variable cPtr has been assigned the address of c.

```
cout << *cPtr.face << endl;
```

b) Assume that struct `Card` has been defined as containing two pointers to type char—namely, `face` and `suit`. Also, the array hearts[13] has been declared to be of type `Card`. The following statement should print the member `face` of element 10 of the array.

```
cout << hearts.face << endl;
```

c)
```
struct Person
{
   char lastName[ 15 ];
   char firstName[ 15 ];
   int age;
}
```

d) Assume that variable p has been declared as type `Person` and that variable c has been declared as type `Card`.

```
p = c;
```

21.5   Write a single statement to accomplish each of the following. Assume that variables c (which stores a character), x, y and z are of type int; variables d, e and f are of type double; variable ptr is of type char * and arrays s1[100] and s2[100] are of type char.

a) Convert the character stored in variable c to an uppercase letter. Assign the result to variable c.

b) Determine if the value of variable c is a digit. Use the conditional operator as shown in Figs. 21.18–21.20 to print " is a " or " is not a " when the result is displayed.

c) Convert the string "1234567" to long, and print the value.

d) Determine whether the value of variable c is a control character. Use the conditional operator to print " is a " or " is not a " when the result is displayed.

e) Assign to ptr the location of the last occurrence of c in s1.
f) Convert the string "8.63582" to double, and print the value.
g) Determine whether the value of c is a letter. Use the conditional operator to print " is a " or " is not a " when the result is displayed.
h) Assign to ptr the location of the first occurrence of s2 in s1.
i) Determine whether the value of variable c is a printing character. Use the conditional operator to print " is a " or " is not a " when the result is displayed.
j) Assign to ptr the location of the first occurrence in s1 of any character from s2.
k) Assign to ptr the location of the first occurrence of c in s1.
l) Convert the string "-21" to int, and print the value.

Answers to Self-Review Exercises

21.1 a) structure. b) bitwise AND (&). c) members. d) bitwise inclusive-OR (|). e) struct. f) typedef. g) bitwise exclusive-OR (^). h) mask. i) structure member (.), structure pointer (->). j) left-shift operator (<<), right-shift operator (>>).

21.2 a) False. A structure can contain many data types.
b) False. The members of separate structures can have the same names, but the members of the same structure must have unique names.
c) False. typedef is used to define aliases for previously defined data types.
d) False. Structures are passed to functions by value by default and may be passed by reference.

21.3 a)
```
struct Part
{
    int partNumber;
    char partName[ 26 ];
};
```
b) `typedef Part * PartPtr;`
c)
```
Part a;
Part b[ 10 ];
Part *ptr;
```
d) `cin >> a.partNumber >> a.partName;`
e) `b[ 3 ] = a;`
f) `ptr = b;`
g)
```
cout << ( ptr + 3 )->partNumber << ' '
     << ( ptr + 3 )->partName << endl;
```

21.4 a) *Error:* The parentheses that should enclose *cPtr have been omitted, causing the order of evaluation of the expression to be incorrect.
b) *Error:* The array subscript has been omitted. The expression should be
        hearts[10].face.
c) *Error:* A semicolon is required to end a structure definition.
d) *Error:* Variables of different structure types cannot be assigned to one another.

21.5 a) `c = toupper( c );`
b)
```
cout << '\'' << c << "\' "
     << ( isdigit( c ) ? "is a" : "is not a" )
     << " digit" << endl;
```
c) `cout << atol( "1234567" ) << endl;`
d)
```
cout << '\'' << c << "\' "
     << ( iscntrl( c ) ? "is a" : "is not a" )
     << " control character" << endl;
```

e) `ptr = strrchr( s1, c );`
f) `out << atof( "8.63582" ) << endl;`
g) `cout << '\'' << c << "\' "`
       `<< ( isalpha( c ) ? "is a" : "is not a" )`
       `<< " letter" << endl;`
h) `ptr = strstr( s1, s2 );`
i) `cout << '\'' << c << "\' "`
       `<< ( isprint( c ) ? "is a" : "is not a" )`
       `<< " printing character" << endl;`
j) `ptr = strpbrk( s1, s2 );`
k) `ptr = strchr( s1, c );`
l) `cout << atoi( "-21" ) << endl;`

Exercises

21.6   Provide the definition for each of the following structures:
a) Structure `Inventory`, containing character array `partName[ 30 ]`, integer `partNumber`, floating-point `price`, integer `stock` and integer `reorder`.
b) A structure called `Address` that contains character arrays `streetAddress[ 25 ]`, `city[ 20 ]`, `state[ 3 ]` and `zipCode[ 6 ]`.
c) Structure `Student`, containing arrays `firstName[ 15 ]` and `lastName[ 15 ]` and variable `homeAddress` of type `struct Address` from part (b).
d) Structure `Test`, containing 16 bit fields with widths of 1 bit. The names of the bit fields are the letters a to p.

21.7   Consider the following structure definitions and variable declarations:

```
struct Customer {
    char lastName[ 15 ];
    char firstName[ 15 ];
    int customerNumber;

    struct {
        char phoneNumber[ 11 ];
        char address[ 50 ];
        char city[ 15 ];
        char state[ 3 ];
        char zipCode[ 6 ];
    } personal;

} customerRecord, *customerPtr;

customerPtr = &customerRecord;
```

Write a separate expression that accesses the structure members in each of the following parts:
a) Member `lastName` of structure `customerRecord`.
b) Member `lastName` of the structure pointed to by `customerPtr`.
c) Member `firstName` of structure `customerRecord`.
d) Member `firstName` of the structure pointed to by `customerPtr`.
e) Member `customerNumber` of structure `customerRecord`.
f) Member `customerNumber` of the structure pointed to by `customerPtr`.
g) Member `phoneNumber` of member `personal` of structure `customerRecord`.
h) Member `phoneNumber` of member `personal` of the structure pointed to by `customerPtr`.
i) Member `address` of member `personal` of structure `customerRecord`.
j) Member `address` of member `personal` of the structure pointed to by `customerPtr`.
k) Member `city` of member `personal` of structure `customerRecord`.

l) Member `city` of member `personal` of the structure pointed to by `customerPtr`.

m) Member `state` of member `personal` of structure `customerRecord`.

n) Member `state` of member `personal` of the structure pointed to by `customerPtr`.

o) Member `zipCode` of member `personal` of structure `customerRecord`.

p) Member `zipCode` of member `personal` of the structure pointed to by `customerPtr`.

21.8 Modify the program of Fig. 21.14 to shuffle the cards using a high-performance shuffle, as shown in Fig. 21.3. Print the resulting deck in two-column format, as in Fig. 21.4. Precede each card with its color.

21.9 Write a program that right-shifts an integer variable 4 bits. The program should print the integer in bits before and after the shift operation. Does your system place zeros or ones in the vacated bits?

21.10 Left-shifting an `unsigned` integer by 1 bit is equivalent to multiplying the value by 2. Write function `power2` that takes two integer arguments, `number` and `pow`, and calculates

$$number * 2^{pow}$$

Use a shift operator to calculate the result. The program should print the values as integers and as bits.

21.11 The left-shift operator can be used to pack two character values into a two-byte unsigned integer variable. Write a program that inputs two characters from the keyboard and passes them to function `packCharacters`. To pack two characters into an `unsigned` integer variable, assign the first character to the `unsigned` variable, shift the `unsigned` variable left by 8 bit positions and combine the `unsigned` variable with the second character using the bitwise inclusive-OR operator. The program should output the characters in their bit format before and after they are packed into the unsigned integer to prove that they are in fact packed correctly in the `unsigned` variable.

21.12 Using the right-shift operator, the bitwise AND operator and a mask, write function `unpackCharacters` that takes the `unsigned` integer from Exercise 21.11 and unpacks it into two characters. To unpack two characters from an `unsigned` two-byte integer, combine the unsigned integer with the mask 65280 (11111111 00000000) and right-shift the result 8 bits. Assign the resulting value to a `char` variable. Then, combine the unsigned integer with the mask 255 (00000000 11111111). Assign the result to another `char` variable. The program should print the unsigned integer in bits before it is unpacked, then print the characters in bits to confirm that they were unpacked correctly.

21.13 If your system uses four-byte integers, rewrite the program of Exercise 21.11 to pack four characters.

21.14 If your system uses four-byte integers, rewrite the function `unpackCharacters` of Exercise 21.12 to unpack four characters. Create the masks you need to unpack the four characters by left-shifting the value 255 in the mask variable by 8 bits 0, 1, 2 or 3 times (depending on the byte you are unpacking).

21.15 Write a program that reverses the order of the bits in an `unsigned` integer value. The program should input the value from the user and call function `reverseBits` to print the bits in reverse order. Print the value in bits both before and after the bits are reversed to confirm that the bits are reversed properly.

21.16 Write a program that demonstrates passing an array by value. [*Hint:* Use a `struct`.] Prove that a copy was passed by modifying the array copy in the called function.

21.17 Write a program that inputs a character from the keyboard and tests the character with each function in the character-handling library. Print the value returned by each function.

21.18 The following program uses function `multiple` to determine whether the integer entered from the keyboard is a multiple of some integer X. Examine function `multiple`, then determine the value of X.

```
1    // Exercise 21.18: ex21_18.cpp
2    // This program determines if a value is a multiple of X.
3    #include <iostream>
4
5    using std::cout;
6    using std::cin;
7    using std::endl;
8
9    bool multiple( int );
10
11   int main()
12   {
13      int y;
14
15      cout << "Enter an integer between 1 and 32000: ";
16      cin >> y;
17
18      if ( multiple( y ) )
19         cout << y << " is a multiple of X" << endl;
20      else
21         cout << y << " is not a multiple of X" << endl;
22
23      return 0;
24
25   } // end main
26
27   // determine if num is a multiple of X
28   bool multiple( int num )
29   {
30      bool mult = true;
31
32      for ( int i = 0, mask = 1; i < 10; i++, mask <<= 1 )
33
34         if ( ( num & mask ) != 0 ) {
35            mult = false;
36            break;
37
38         } // end if
39
40      return mult;
41
42   } // end function multiple
```

21.19 What does the following program do?

```
1    // Exercise 21.19: ex21_19.cpp
2    #include <iostream>
3
4    using std::cout;
5    using std::cin;
6    using std::endl;
7    using std::boolalpha;
8
9    bool mystery( unsigned );
10
11   int main()
12   {
13      unsigned x;
14
```

```
15      cout << "Enter an integer: ";
16      cin >> x;
17      cout << boolalpha
18          << "The result is " << mystery( x ) << endl;
19
20      return 0;
21
22  } // end main
23
24  // What does this function do?
25  bool mystery( unsigned bits )
26  {
27      const int SHIFT = 8 * sizeof( unsigned ) - 1;
28      const unsigned MASK = 1 << SHIFT;
29      unsigned total = 0;
30
31      for ( int i = 0; i < SHIFT + 1; i++, bits <<= 1 )
32
33          if ( ( bits & MASK ) == MASK )
34              ++total;
35
36      return !( total % 2 );
37
38  } // end function mystery
```

21.20 Write a program that inputs a line of text with istream member function getline (as in Chapter 15) into character array s[100]. Output the line in uppercase letters and lowercase letters.

21.21 Write a program that inputs four strings that represent integers, converts the strings to integers, sums the values and prints the total of the four values. Use only the C-style string-processing techniques shown in this chapter.

21.22 Write a program that inputs four strings that represent floating-point values, converts the strings to double values, sums the values and prints the total of the four values. Use only the C-style string-processing techniques shown in this chapter.

21.23 Write a program that inputs a line of text and a search string from the keyboard. Using function strstr, locate the first occurrence of the search string in the line of text, and assign the location to variable searchPtr of type char *. If the search string is found, print the remainder of the line of text beginning with the search string. Then use strstr again to locate the next occurrence of the search string in the line of text. If a second occurrence is found, print the remainder of the line of text beginning with the second occurrence. [*Hint:* The second call to strstr should contain the expression searchPtr + 1 as its first argument.]

21.24 Write a program based on the program of Exercise 21.23 that inputs several lines of text and a search string, then uses function strstr to determine the total number of occurrences of the string in the lines of text. Print the result.

21.25 Write a program that inputs several lines of text and a search character and uses function strchr to determine the total number of occurrences of the character in the lines of text.

21.26 Write a program based on the program of Exercise 21.25 that inputs several lines of text and uses function strchr to determine the total number of occurrences of each letter of the alphabet in the text. Uppercase and lowercase letters should be counted together. Store the totals for each letter in an array, and print the values in tabular format after the totals have been determined.

21.27 The chart in Appendix B shows the numeric code representations for the characters in the ASCII character set. Study this chart, and then state whether each of the following is *true* or *false*:

a) The letter "A" comes before the letter "B."
b) The digit "9" comes before the digit "0."
c) The commonly used symbols for addition, subtraction, multiplication and division all come before any of the digits.
d) The digits come before the letters.
e) If a sort program sorts strings into ascending sequence, then the program will place the symbol for a right parenthesis before the symbol for a left parenthesis.

21.28 Write a program that reads a series of strings and prints only those strings beginning with the letter "b."

21.29 Write a program that reads a series of strings and prints only those strings that end with the letters "ED."

21.30 Write a program that inputs an ASCII code and prints the corresponding character. Modify this program so that it generates all possible three-digit codes in the range 000–255 and attempts to print the corresponding characters. What happens when this program is run?

21.31 Using the ASCII character chart in Appendix B as a guide, write your own versions of the character-handling functions in Fig. 21.17.

21.32 Write your own versions of the functions in Fig. 21.21 for converting strings to numbers.

21.33 Write your own versions of the functions in Fig. 21.28 for searching strings.

21.34 Write your own versions of the functions in Fig. 21.35 for manipulating blocks of memory.

21.35 *(Project: A Spelling Checker)* Many popular word-processing software packages have built-in spell checkers. We used spell-checking capabilities in preparing this book and discovered that, no matter how careful we thought we were in writing a chapter, the software was always able to find a few more spelling errors than we were able to catch manually.

In this project, you are asked to develop your own spell-checker utility. We make suggestions to help get you started. You should then consider adding more capabilities. You might find it helpful to use a computerized dictionary as a source of words.

Why do we type so many words with incorrect spellings? In some cases, it is because we simply do not know the correct spelling, so we make a "best guess." In some cases, it is because we transpose two letters (e.g., "defualt" instead of "default"). Sometimes we double-type a letter accidentally (e.g., "hanndy" instead of "handy"). Sometimes we type a nearby key instead of the one we intended (e.g., "biryhday" instead of "birthday"). And so on.

Design and implement a spell-checker program. Your program maintains an array wordList of character strings. You can either enter these strings or obtain them from a computerized dictionary.

Your program asks a user to enter a word. The program then looks up that word in the wordList array. If the word is present in the array, your program should print "Word is spelled correctly."

If the word is not present in the array, your program should print "Word is not spelled correctly." Then your program should try to locate other words in wordList that might be the word the user intended to type. For example, you can try all possible single transpositions of adjacent letters to discover that the word "default" is a direct match to a word in wordList. Of course, this implies that your program will check all other single transpositions, such as "edfault," "dfeault," "deafult," "defalut" and "defautl." When you find a new word that matches one in wordList, print that word in a message such as "Did you mean "default?".".

Implement other tests, such as the replacing of each double letter with a single letter and any other tests you can develop to improve the value of your spell checker.

Standard Template Library (STL)

The shapes a bright container can contain!
—Theodore Roethke

Journey over all the universe in a map.
—Miguel de Cervantes

O! thou hast damnable iteration, and art indeed able to corrupt a saint.
—William Shakespeare

That great dust heap called "history."
—Augustine Birrell

The historian is a prophet in reverse.
—Friedrich von Schlegel

Attempt the end, and never stand to doubt; Nothing's so hard but search will find it out.
—Robert Herrick

OBJECTIVES

In this chapter you'll learn:

- To be able to use the STL containers, container adapters and "near containers."

- To be able to program with the dozens of STL algorithms.

- To understand how algorithms use iterators to access the elements of STL containers.

- To become familiar with the STL resources available on the Internet and the World Wide Web.

22.1 Introduction to the Standard Template Library (STL)

We've repeatedly emphasized the importance of software reuse. Recognizing that many data structures and algorithms commonly are used by C++ programmers, the C++ standard committee added the Standard Template Library (STL) to the C++ Standard Library. The STL defines powerful, template-based, reusable components that implement many common data structures and algorithms used to process those data structures. The STL offers proof of concept for generic programming with templates—introduced in Chapter 14, Templates, and used extensively in Chapter 20, Data Structures. [*Note:* In industry, the features presented in this chapter are often referred to as the Standard Template Library or STL. However, these terms are not used in the C++ standard document, because these features are simply considered to be part of the C++ Standard Library.]

The STL was developed by Alexander Stepanov and Meng Lee at Hewlett-Packard and is based on their research in the field of generic programming, with significant contributions from David Musser. As you'll see, the STL was conceived and designed for performance and flexibility.

This chapter introduces the STL and discusses its three key components—containers (popular templatized data structures), iterators and algorithms. The STL containers are data structures capable of storing objects of almost any data type (there are some restrictions). We'll see that there are three styles of container classes—first-class containers, adapters and near containers.

Performance Tip 22.1

For any particular application, several different STL containers might be appropriate. Select the most appropriate container that achieves the best performance (i.e., balance of speed and size) for that application. Efficiency was a crucial consideration in the STL's design.

Performance Tip 22.2

Standard Library capabilities are implemented to operate efficiently across many applications. For some applications with unique performance requirements, it might be necessary to write your own customized implementations.

Each STL container has associated member functions. A subset of these member functions is defined in all STL containers. We illustrate most of this common functionality in our examples of STL containers vector (a dynamically resizable array which we introduced in Chapter 7, Arrays and Vectors), list (a doubly linked list) and deque (a double-ended queue, pronounced "deck"). We introduce container-specific functionality in examples for each of the other STL containers.

STL iterators, which have properties similar to those of pointers, are used by programs to manipulate the STL-container elements. In fact, standard arrays can be manipulated by STL algorithms, using standard pointers as iterators. We'll see that manipulating containers with iterators is convenient and provides tremendous expressive power when combined with STL algorithms—in some cases, reducing many lines of code to a single statement. There are five categories of iterators, each of which we discuss in Section 22.1.2 and use throughout this chapter.

STL algorithms are functions that perform such common data manipulations as searching, sorting and comparing elements (or entire containers). The STL provides approximately 70 algorithms. Most of them use iterators to access container elements. Each algorithm has minimum requirements for the types of iterators that can be used with it. We'll see that each first-class container supports specific iterator types, some more powerful than others. A container's supported iterator type determines whether the container can be used with a specific algorithm. Iterators encapsulate the mechanism used to access container elements. This encapsulation enables many of the STL algorithms to be applied to several containers without regard for the underlying container implementation. As long as a container's iterators support the minimum requirements of the algorithm, then the algorithm can process that container's elements. This also enables programmers to create new algorithms that can process the elements of multiple container types.

Software Engineering Observation 22.1

The STL approach allows general programs to be written so that the code does not depend on the underlying container. Such a programming style is called generic programming.

In Chapter 20, we studied data structures. We built linked lists, queues, stacks and trees. We carefully wove link objects together with pointers. Pointer-based code is complex, and the slightest omission or oversight can lead to serious memory-access violations and memory-leak errors with no compiler complaints. Implementing additional data structures, such as deques, priority queues, sets and maps, requires substantial extra work. In addition, if many programmers on a large project implement similar containers and algorithms for different tasks, the code becomes difficult to modify, maintain and debug. An advantage of the STL is that programmers can reuse the STL containers, iterators and algorithms to implement common data representations and manipulations. This reuse can save substantial development time, money and effort.

Software Engineering Observation 22.2

Avoid reinventing the wheel; program with the reusable components of the C++ Standard Library. STL includes many of the most popular data structures as containers and provides various popular algorithms to process data in these containers.

Error-Prevention Tip 22.1

When programming pointer-based data structures and algorithms, we must do our own debugging and testing to be sure our data structures, classes and algorithms function properly. It is easy to make errors when manipulating pointers at this low level. Memory leaks and memory-access violations are common in such custom code. For most programmers, and for most of the applications they will need to write, the prepackaged, templatized containers of the STL are sufficient. Using the STL helps programmers reduce testing and debugging time. One caution is that, for large projects, template compile time can be significant.

This chapter introduces the STL. It is by no means complete or comprehensive. However, it is a friendly, accessible chapter that should convince you of the value of the STL in software reuse and encourage further study.

22.1.1 Introduction to Containers

The STL container types are shown in Fig. 22.1. The containers are divided into three major categories—sequence containers, associative containers and container adapters.

Standard Library container class	Description
Sequence containers	
vector	Rapid insertions and deletions at back. Direct access to any element.
deque	Rapid insertions and deletions at front or back. Direct access to any element.
list	Doubly linked list, rapid insertion and deletion anywhere.
Associative containers	
set	Rapid lookup, no duplicates allowed.
multiset	Rapid lookup, duplicates allowed.
map	One-to-one mapping, no duplicates allowed, rapid key-based lookup.
multimap	One-to-many mapping, duplicates allowed, rapid key-based lookup.
Container adapters	
stack	Last-in, first-out (LIFO).
queue	First-in, first-out (FIFO).
priority_queue	Highest-priority element is always the first element out.

Fig. 22.1 | Standard Library container classes.

STL Containers Overview

The sequence containers represent linear data structures, such as vectors and linked lists. Associative containers are nonlinear containers that typically can locate elements stored in the containers quickly. Such containers can store sets of values or key/value pairs. The sequence containers and associative containers are collectively referred to as the first-class containers. As we saw in Chapter 20, stacks and queues actually are constrained versions of sequential containers. For this reason, STL implements stacks and queues as container adapters that enable a program to view a sequential container in a constrained manner. There are other container types that are considered "near containers"—C-like pointer-based arrays (discussed in Chapter 7), bitsets for maintaining sets of flag values and valarrays for performing high-speed mathematical vector operations (this last class is optimized for computation performance and is not as flexible as the first-class containers). These types are considered "near containers" because they exhibit capabilities similar to those of the first-class containers, but do not support all the first-class-container capabilities. Type string (discussed in Chapter 18) supports the same functionality as a sequence container, but stores only character data.

STL Container Common Functions

Most STL containers provide similar functionality. Many generic operations, such as member function size, apply to all containers, and other operations apply to subsets of similar containers. This encourages extensibility of the STL with new classes. Figure 22.2 describes the functions common to all Standard Library containers. [*Note:* Overloaded operators operator<, operator<=, operator>, operator>=, operator== and operator!= are not provided for priority_queues.]

Common member functions for most STL containers	Description
default constructor	A constructor to create an empty container. Normally, each container has several constructors that provide different initialization methods for the container.
copy constructor	A constructor that initializes the container to be a copy of an existing container of the same type.
destructor	Destructor function for cleanup after a container is no longer needed.
empty	Returns true if there are no elements in the container; otherwise, returns false.
insert	Inserts an item in the container.
size	Returns the number of elements currently in the container.
operator=	Assigns one container to another.
operator<	Returns true if the first container is less than the second container; otherwise, returns false.
operator<=	Returns true if the first container is less than or equal to the second container; otherwise, returns false.
operator>	Returns true if the first container is greater than the second container; otherwise, returns false.
operator>=	Returns true if the first container is greater than or equal to the second container; otherwise, returns false.
operator==	Returns true if the first container is equal to the second container; otherwise, returns false.
operator!=	Returns true if the first container is not equal to the second container; otherwise, returns false.
swap	Swaps the elements of two containers.
Functions found only in first-class containers	
max_size	Returns the maximum number of elements for a container.
begin	The two versions of this function return either an iterator or a const_iterator that refers to the first element of the container.
end	The two versions of this function return either an iterator or a const_iterator that refers to the next position after the end of the container.
rbegin	The two versions of this function return either a reverse_iterator or a const_reverse_iterator that refers to the last element of the container.
rend	The two versions of this function return either a reverse_iterator or a const_reverse_iterator that refers to the next position after the last element of the reversed container.
erase	Erases one or more elements from the container.
clear	Erases all elements from the container.

Fig. 22.2 | STL container common functions.

STL Container Header Files

The header files for each of the Standard Library containers are shown in Fig. 22.3. The contents of these header files are all in namespace std.

First-Class Container Common **typedefs**

Figure 22.4 shows the common typedefs (to create synonyms or aliases for lengthy type names) found in first-class containers. These typedefs are used in generic declarations of variables, parameters to functions and return values from functions. For example, value_type in each container is always a typedef that represents the type of value stored in the container.

Standard Library container header files	
<vector>	
<list>	
<deque>	
<queue>	Contains both queue and priority_queue.
<stack>	
<map>	Contains both map and multimap.
<set>	Contains both set and multiset.
<valarray>	
<bitset>	

Fig. 22.3 | Standard Library container header files.

typedef	Description
allocator_type	The type of the object used to allocate the container's memory.
value_type	The type of element stored in the container.
reference	A reference to the type of element stored in the container.
const_reference	A constant reference to the type of element stored in the container. Such a reference can be used only for *reading* elements in the container and for performing const operations.
pointer	A pointer to the type of element stored in the container.
const_pointer	A pointer to a constant element of the type stored in the container.
iterator	An iterator that points to the type of element stored in the container.
const_iterator	A constant iterator that points to the type of element stored in the container and can be used only to *read* elements.

Fig. 22.4 | typedefs found in first-class containers. (Part 1 of 2.)

typedef	Description
reverse_iterator	A reverse iterator that points to the type of element stored in the container. This type of iterator is for iterating through a container in reverse.
const_reverse_iterator	A constant reverse iterator that points to the type of element stored in the container and can be used only to *read* elements. This type of iterator is for iterating through a container in reverse.
difference_type	The type of the result of subtracting two iterators that refer to the same container (operator – is not defined for iterators of lists and associative containers).
size_type	The type used to count items in a container and index through a sequence container (cannot index through a list).

Fig. 22.4 | typedefs found in first-class containers. (Part 2 of 2.)

Performance Tip 22.3

STL generally avoids inheritance and virtual functions in favor of using generic programming with templates to achieve better execution-time performance.

Portability Tip 22.1

Programming with STL will enhance the portability of your code.

When preparing to use an STL container, it is important to ensure that the type of element being stored in the container supports a minimum set of functionality. When an element is inserted into a container, a copy of that element is made. For this reason, the element type should provide its own copy constructor and assignment operator. [*Note:* This is required only if default memberwise copy and default memberwise assignment do not perform proper copy and assignment operations for the element type.] Also, the associative containers and many algorithms require elements to be compared. For this reason, the element type should provide an equality operator (==) and a less-than operator (<).

Software Engineering Observation 22.3

The STL containers technically do not require their elements to be comparable with the equality and less-than operators unless a program uses a container member function that must compare the container elements (e.g., the sort function in class list). Unfortunately, some prestandard C++ compilers are not capable of ignoring parts of a template that are not used in a particular program. On compilers with this problem, you may not be able to use the STL containers with objects of classes that do not define overloaded less-than and equality operators.

22.1.2 Introduction to Iterators

Iterators have many features in common with pointers and are used to point to the elements of first-class containers (and for a few other purposes, as we'll see). Iterators hold state information sensitive to the particular containers on which they operate; thus, iterators are implemented appropriately for each type of container. Certain iterator operations are uniform across containers. For example, the dereferencing operator (*) dereferences an iterator so that you can use the element to which it points. The ++ operation on an iterator moves it to the next element of the container (much as incrementing a pointer into an array aims the pointer at the next element of the array).

STL first-class containers provide member functions begin and end. Function begin returns an iterator pointing to the first element of the container. Function end returns an iterator pointing to the first element past the end of the container (an element that doesn't exist). If iterator i points to a particular element, then ++i points to the "next" element and *i refers to the element pointed to by i. The iterator resulting from end is typically used in an equality or inequality comparison to determine whether the "moving iterator" (i in this case) has reached the end of the container.

We use an object of type iterator to refer to a container element that can be modified. We use an object of type const_iterator to refer to a container element that cannot be modified.

Using *istream_iterator* for Input and Using *ostream_iterator* for Output

We use iterators with sequences (also called ranges). These sequences can be in containers, or they can be input sequences or output sequences. The program of Fig. 22.5 demonstrates input from the standard input (a sequence of data for input into a program), using an istream_iterator, and output to the standard output (a sequence of data for output from a program), using an ostream_iterator. The program inputs two integers from the user at the keyboard and displays the sum of the integers.[1]

Line 15 creates an istream_iterator that is capable of extracting (inputting) int values in a type-safe manner from the standard input object cin. Line 17 dereferences iterator inputInt to read the first integer from cin and assigns that integer to number1. Note that the dereferencing operator * applied to inputInt gets the value from the stream associated with inputInt; this is similar to dereferencing a pointer. Line 18 positions iterator inputInt to the next value in the input stream. Line 19 inputs the next integer from inputInt and assigns it to number2.

Line 22 creates an ostream_iterator that is capable of inserting (outputting) int values in the standard output object cout. Line 25 outputs an integer to cout by assigning to *outputInt the sum of number1 and number2. Notice the use of the dereferencing operator * to use *outputInt as an *lvalue* in the assignment statement. If you want to output another value using outputInt, the iterator must be incremented with ++ (both the prefix and postfix increment can be used, but the prefix form should be preferred for performance reasons).

Error-Prevention Tip 22.2

*The * (dereferencing) operator of any const iterator returns a const reference to the container element, disallowing the use of non-const member functions.*

---

1. The examples in this chapter precede each use of an STL function and each definition of an STL container object with the "std::" prefix rather than placing the using declarations or directives at the beginning of the program, as was shown in most prior examples. Differences in compilers and the complex code generated when using STL make it difficult to construct a proper set of using declarations or directives that enable the programs to compile without errors. To allow these programs to compile on the widest variety of platforms, we chose the "std::" prefix approach.

```
1   // Fig. 22.5: Fig22_05.cpp
2   // Demonstrating input and output with iterators.
3   #include <iostream>
4   using std::cout;
5   using std::cin;
6   using std::endl;
7
8   #include <iterator> // ostream_iterator and istream_iterator
9
10  int main()
11  {
12     cout << "Enter two integers: ";
13
14     // create istream_iterator for reading int values from cin
15     std::istream_iterator< int > inputInt( cin );
16
17     int number1 = *inputInt; // read int from standard input
18     ++inputInt; // move iterator to next input value
19     int number2 = *inputInt; // read int from standard input
20
21     // create ostream_iterator for writing int values to cout
22     std::ostream_iterator< int > outputInt( cout );
23
24     cout << "The sum is: ";
25     *outputInt = number1 + number2; // output result to cout
26     cout << endl;
27     return 0;
28  } // end main
```

```
Enter two integers: 12 25
The sum is: 37
```

Fig. 22.5 | Input and output stream iterators.

Common Programming Error 22.1

Attempting to dereference an iterator positioned outside its container is a runtime logic error. In particular, the iterator returned by end cannot be dereferenced or incremented.

Common Programming Error 22.2

Attempting to create a non-const iterator for a const container results in a compilation error.

Iterator Categories and Iterator Category Hierarchy

Figure 22.6 shows the categories of STL iterators. Each category provides a specific set of functionality. Figure 22.7 illustrates the hierarchy of iterator categories. As you follow the hierarchy from top to bottom, each iterator category supports all the functionality of the categories above it in the figure. Thus the "weakest" iterator types are at the top and the most powerful one is at the bottom. Note that this is not an inheritance hierarchy.

The iterator category that each container supports determines whether that container can be used with specific algorithms in the STL. Containers that support random-access iterators can be used with all algorithms in the STL. As we'll see, pointers into arrays can

Category	Description
input	Used to read an element from a container. An input iterator can move only in the forward direction (i.e., from the beginning of the container to the end) one element at a time. Input iterators support only one-pass algorithms—the same input iterator cannot be used to pass through a sequence twice.
output	Used to write an element to a container. An output iterator can move only in the forward direction one element at a time. Output iterators support only one-pass algorithms—the same output iterator cannot be used to pass through a sequence twice.
forward	Combines the capabilities of input and output iterators and retains their position in the container (as state information).
bidirectional	Combines the capabilities of a forward iterator with the ability to move in the backward direction (i.e., from the end of the container toward the beginning). Bidirectional iterators support multipass algorithms.
random access	Combines the capabilities of a bidirectional iterator with the ability to directly access any element of the container, i.e., to jump forward or backward by an arbitrary number of elements.

Fig. 22.6 | Iterator categories.

Fig. 22.7 | Iterator category hierarchy.

be used in place of iterators in most STL algorithms, including those that require random-access iterators. Figure 22.8 shows the iterator category of each of the STL containers. Note that vectors, deques, lists, sets, multisets, maps, multimaps (i.e., the first-class containers), strings and arrays are traversable with iterators.

Software Engineering Observation 22.4

Using the "weakest iterator" that yields acceptable performance helps produce maximally reusable components. For example, if an algorithm requires only forward iterators, it can be used with any container that supports forward iterators, bidirectional iterators or random-access iterators. However, an algorithm that requires random-access iterators can be used only with containers that have random-access iterators.

Predefined Iterator **typedefs**
Figure 22.9 shows the predefined iterator typedefs that are found in the class definitions of the STL containers. Not every typedef is defined for every container. We use const

Container	Type of iterator supported
Sequence containers (first class)	
vector	random access
deque	random access
list	bidirectional
Associative containers (first class)	
set	bidirectional
multiset	bidirectional
map	bidirectional
multimap	bidirectional
Container adapters	
stack	no iterators supported
queue	no iterators supported
priority_queue	no iterators supported

Fig. 22.8 | Iterator types supported by each Standard Library container.

Predefined typedefs for iterator types	Direction of ++	Capability
iterator	forward	read/write
const_iterator	forward	read
reverse_iterator	backward	read/write
const_reverse_iterator	backward	read

Fig. 22.9 | Iterator typedefs.

versions of the iterators for traversing read-only containers. We use reverse iterators to traverse containers in the reverse direction.

Error-Prevention Tip 22.3

Operations performed on a const_iterator return const references to prevent modification to elements of the container being manipulated. Using const_iterators in preference to iterators where appropriate is another example of the principle of least privilege.

Iterator Operations

Figure 22.10 shows some operations that can be performed on each iterator type. Note that the operations for each iterator type include all operations preceding that type in the figure. Note also that, for input iterators and output iterators, it is not possible to save the iterator and then use the saved value later.

Iterator operation	Description
All iterators	
++p	Preincrement an iterator.
p++	Postincrement an iterator.
Input iterators	
*p	Dereference an iterator.
p = p1	Assign one iterator to another.
p == p1	Compare iterators for equality.
p != p1	Compare iterators for inequality.
Output iterators	
*p	Dereference an iterator.
p = p1	Assign one iterator to another.
Forward iterators	Forward iterators provide all the functionality of both input iterators and output iterators.
Bidirectional iterators	
--p	Predecrement an iterator.
p--	Postdecrement an iterator.
Random-access iterators	
p += i	Increment the iterator p by i positions.
p -= i	Decrement the iterator p by i positions.
p + i *or* i + p	Expression value is an iterator positioned at p incremented by i positions.
p - i	Expression value is an iterator positioned at p decremented by i positions.
p - p1	Expression value is an integer representing the distance between two elements in the same container.
p[i]	Return a reference to the element offset from p by i positions
p < p1	Return true if iterator p is less than iterator p1 (i.e., iterator p is before iterator p1 in the container); otherwise, return false.
p <= p1	Return true if iterator p is less than or equal to iterator p1 (i.e., iterator p is before iterator p1 or at the same location as iterator p1 in the container); otherwise, return false.
p > p1	Return true if iterator p is greater than iterator p1 (i.e., iterator p is after iterator p1 in the container); otherwise, return false.
p >= p1	Return true if iterator p is greater than or equal to iterator p1 (i.e., iterator p is after iterator p1 or at the same location as iterator p1 in the container); otherwise, return false.

Fig. 22.10 | Iterator operations for each type of iterator.

22.1.3 Introduction to Algorithms

STL algorithms can be used generically across a variety of containers. STL provides many algorithms you'll use frequently to manipulate containers. Inserting, deleting, searching, sorting and others are appropriate for some or all of the STL containers.

The STL includes approximately 70 standard algorithms. We provide live-code examples of most of these and summarize the others in tables. The algorithms operate on container elements only indirectly through iterators. Many algorithms operate on sequences of elements defined by pairs of iterators—a first iterator pointing to the first element of the sequence and a second iterator pointing to one element past the last element of the sequence. Also, it is possible to create your own new algorithms that operate in a similar fashion so they can be used with the STL containers and iterators.

Algorithms often return iterators that indicate the results of the algorithms. Algorithm find, for example, locates an element and returns an iterator to that element. If the element is not found, find returns the "one past the end" iterator that was passed in to define the end of the range to be searched, which can be tested to determine whether an element was not found. The find algorithm can be used with any first-class STL container. STL algorithms create yet another opportunity for reuse—using the rich collection of popular algorithms can save programmers much time and effort.

If an algorithm uses less powerful iterators, the algorithm can also be used with containers that support more powerful iterators. Some algorithms demand powerful iterators; e.g., sort demands random-access iterators.

Software Engineering Observation 22.5
The STL is implemented concisely. Until now, class designers would have associated the algorithms with the containers by making the algorithms member functions of the containers. The STL takes a different approach. The algorithms are separated from the containers and operate on elements of the containers only indirectly through iterators. This separation makes it easier to write generic algorithms applicable to many container classes.

Software Engineering Observation 22.6
The STL is extensible. It is straightforward to add new algorithms and to do so without changes to STL containers.

Software Engineering Observation 22.7
STL algorithms can operate on STL containers and on pointer-based, C-like arrays.

Portability Tip 22.2
Because STL algorithms process containers only indirectly through iterators, one algorithm can often be used with many different containers.

Figure 22.11 shows many of the mutating-sequence algorithms—i.e., the algorithms that result in modifications of the containers to which the algorithms are applied.

Mutating-sequence algorithms		
copy	remove	reverse_copy
copy_backward	remove_copy	rotate
fill	remove_copy_if	rotate_copy

Fig. 22.11 | Mutating-sequence algorithms. (Part 1 of 2.)

Mutating-sequence algorithms		
fill_n	remove_if	stable_partition
generate	replace	swap
generate_n	replace_copy	swap_ranges
iter_swap	replace_copy_if	transform
partition	replace_if	unique
random_shuffle	reverse	unique_copy

Fig. 22.11 | Mutating-sequence algorithms. (Part 2 of 2.)

Figure 22.12 shows many of the nonmodifying sequence algorithms—i.e., the algorithms that do not result in modifications of the containers to which they are applied. Figure 22.13 shows the numerical algorithms of the header file <numeric>.

Nonmodifying sequence algorithms		
adjacent_find	find	find_if
count	find_each	mismatch
count_if	find_end	search
equal	find_first_of	search_n

Fig. 22.12 | Nonmodifying sequence algorithms.

Numerical algorithms from header file <numeric>	
accumulate	partial_sum
inner_product	adjacent_difference

Fig. 22.13 | Numerical algorithms from header file <numeric>.

22.2 Sequence Containers

The C++ Standard Template Library provides three sequence containers—vector, list and deque. Class template vector and class template deque both are based on arrays. Class template list implements a linked-list data structure similar to our List class presented in Chapter 20, but more robust.

One of the most popular containers in the STL is vector. Recall that we introduced class template vector in Chapter 7 as a more robust type of array. A vector changes size dynamically. Unlike C and C++ "raw" arrays (see Chapter 7), vectors can be assigned to one another. This is not possible with pointer-based, C-like arrays, because those array names are constant pointers and cannot be the targets of assignments. Just as with C arrays, vector subscripting does not perform automatic range checking, but class template vector does provide this capability via member function at (also discussed in Chapter 7).

Performance Tip 22.4

Insertion at the back of a vector is efficient. The vector simply grows, if necessary, to accommodate the new item. It is expensive to insert (or delete) an element in the middle of a vector—the entire portion of the vector after the insertion (or deletion) point must be moved, because vector elements occupy contiguous cells in memory just as C or C++ "raw" arrays do.

Figure 22.2 presented the operations common to all the STL containers. Beyond these operations, each container typically provides a variety of other capabilities. Many of these capabilities are common to several containers, but they are not always equally efficient for each container. You must choose the container most appropriate for the application.

Performance Tip 22.5

Applications that require frequent insertions and deletions at both ends of a container normally use a deque rather than a vector. Although we can insert and delete elements at the front and back of both a vector and a deque, class deque is more efficient than vector for doing insertions and deletions at the front.

Performance Tip 22.6

Applications with frequent insertions and deletions in the middle and/or at the extremes of a container normally use a list, due to its efficient implementation of insertion and deletion anywhere in the data structure.

In addition to the common operations described in Fig. 22.2, the sequence containers have several other common operations—`front` to return a reference to the first element in a non-empty container, `back` to return a reference to the last element in a non-empty container, `push_back` to insert a new element at the end of the container and `pop_back` to remove the last element of the container.

22.2.1 vector Sequence Container

Class template `vector` provides a data structure with contiguous memory locations. This enables efficient, direct access to any element of a vector via the subscript operator [], exactly as with a C or C++ "raw" array. Class template `vector` is most commonly used when the data in the container must be easily accessible via a subscript or will be sorted. When a `vector`'s memory is exhausted, the `vector` allocates a larger contiguous area of memory, copies the original elements into the new memory and deallocates the old memory.

Performance Tip 22.7

Choose the vector container for the best random-access performance.

Performance Tip 22.8

Objects of class template vector provide rapid indexed access with the overloaded subscript operator [] because they are stored in contiguous memory like a C or C++ raw array.

Performance Tip 22.9

It is faster to insert many elements at once than one at a time.

An important part of every container is the type of iterator it supports. This determines which algorithms can be applied to the container. A `vector` supports random-access iterators—i.e., all iterator operations shown in Fig. 22.10 can be applied to a `vector` iterator. All STL algorithms can operate on a `vector`. The iterators for a `vector` are sometimes implemented as pointers to elements of the `vector`. Each STL algorithm that takes iterator arguments requires those iterators to provide a minimum level of functionality. If an algorithm requires a forward iterator, for example, that algorithm can operate on any container that provides forward iterators, bidirectional iterators or random-access iterators. As long as the container supports the algorithm's minimum iterator functionality, the algorithm can operate on the container.

Using Vector and Iterators

Figure 22.14 illustrates several functions of the `vector` class template. Many of these functions are available in every first-class container. You must include header file `<vector>` to use class template `vector`.

```
1   // Fig. 22.14: Fig22_14.cpp
2   // Demonstrating Standard Library vector class template.
3   #include <iostream>
4   using std::cout;
5   using std::endl;
6
7   #include <vector> // vector class-template definition
8   using std::vector;
9
10  // prototype for function template printVector
11  template < typename T > void printVector( const vector< T > &integers2 );
12
13  int main()
14  {
15     const int SIZE = 6; // define array size
16     int array[ SIZE ] = { 1, 2, 3, 4, 5, 6 }; // initialize array
17     vector< int > integers; // create vector of ints
18
19     cout << "The initial size of integers is: " << integers.size()
20        << "\nThe initial capacity of integers is: " << integers.capacity();
21
22     // function push_back is in every sequence collection
23     integers.push_back( 2 );
24     integers.push_back( 3 );
25     integers.push_back( 4 );
26
27     cout << "\nThe size of integers is: " << integers.size()
28        << "\nThe capacity of integers is: " << integers.capacity();
29     cout << "\n\nOutput array using pointer notation: ";
30
31     // display array using pointer notation
32     for ( int *ptr = array; ptr != array + SIZE; ptr++ )
33        cout << *ptr << ' ';
34
```

Fig. 22.14 | Standard Library `vector` class template. (Part 1 of 2.)

```
35      cout << "\nOutput vector using iterator notation: ";
36      printVector( integers );
37      cout << "\nReversed contents of vector integers: ";
38
39      // two const reverse iterators
40      vector< int >::const_reverse_iterator reverseIterator;
41      vector< int >::const_reverse_iterator tempIterator = integers.rend();
42
43      // display vector in reverse order using reverse_iterator
44      for ( reverseIterator = integers.rbegin();
45         reverseIterator!= tempIterator; ++reverseIterator )
46         cout << *reverseIterator << ' ';
47
48      cout << endl;
49      return 0;
50   } // end main
51
52   // function template for outputting vector elements
53   template < typename T > void printVector( const vector< T > &integers2 )
54   {
55      typename vector< T >::const_iterator constIterator; // const_iterator
56
57      // display vector elements using const_iterator
58      for ( constIterator = integers2.begin();
59         constIterator != integers2.end(); ++constIterator )
60         cout << *constIterator << ' ';
61   } // end function printVector
```

```
The initial size of integers is: 0
The initial capacity of integers is: 0
The size of integers is: 3
The capacity of integers is: 4

Output array using pointer notation: 1 2 3 4 5 6
Output vector using iterator notation: 2 3 4
Reversed contents of vector integers: 4 3 2
```

Fig. 22.14 | Standard Library vector class template. (Part 2 of 2.)

Line 17 defines an instance called integers of class template vector that stores int values. When this object is instantiated, an empty vector is created with size 0 (i.e., the number of elements stored in the vector) and capacity 0 (i.e., the number of elements that can be stored without allocating more memory to the vector).

Lines 19 and 20 demonstrate the size and capacity functions; each initially returns 0 for vector v in this example. Function size—available in every container—returns the number of elements currently stored in the container. Function **capacity** returns the number of elements that can be stored in the vector before the vector needs to dynamically resize itself to accommodate more elements.

Lines 23–25 use function **push_back**—available in all sequence containers—to add an element to the end of the vector. If an element is added to a full vector, the vector increases its size—some STL implementations have the vector double its capacity.

Performance Tip 22.10

It can be wasteful to double a vector's size when more space is needed. For example, a full vector of 1,000,000 elements resizes to accommodate 2,000,000 elements when a new element is added. This leaves 999,999 unused elements. Programmers can use resize and reserve to control space usage better.

Lines 27 and 28 use size and capacity to illustrate the new size and capacity of the vector after the three push_back operations. Function size returns 3—the number of elements added to the vector. Function capacity returns 4, indicating that we can add one more element before the vector needs to add more memory. When we added the first element, the vector allocated space for one element, and the size became 1 to indicate that the vector contained only one element. When we added the second element, the capacity doubled to 2 and the size became 2 as well. When we added the third element, the capacity doubled again to 4. So we can actually add another element before the vector needs to allocation more space. When the vector eventually fills its allocated capacity and the program attempts to add one more element to the vector, the vector will double its capacity to 8 elements.

The manner in which a vector grows to accommodate more elements—a time consuming operation—is not specified by the C++ Standard Document. C++ library implementors use various clever schemes to minimize the overhead of resizing a vector. Hence, the output of this program may vary, depending on the version of vector that comes with your compiler. Some library implementors allocate a large initial capacity. If a vector stores a small number of elements, such capacity may be a waste of space. However, it can greatly improve performance if a program adds many elements to a vector and does not have to reallocate memory to accommodate those elements. This is a classic space–time trade-off. Library implementors must balance the amount of memory used against the amount of time required to perform various vector operations.

Lines 32–33 demonstrate how to output the contents of an array using pointers and pointer arithmetic. Line 36 calls function printVector (defined in lines 53–61) to output the contents of a vector using iterators. Function template printVector receives a const reference to a vector (integers2) as its argument. Line 55 defines a const_iterator called constIterator that iterates through the vector and outputs its contents. Notice that the declaration in line 55 is prefixed with the keyword typename. Because printVector is a function template and vector< T > will be specialized differently for each function-template specialization, the compiler cannot tell at compile time whether or not vector< T >::const_iterator is a type. In particular specialization, const_iterator could be a static variable. The compiler needs this information to compile the program correctly. Therefore, you must tell the compiler that a qualified name, when the qualifier is a dependent type, is expected to be a type in every specialization.

A const_iterator enables the program to read the elements of the vector, but does not allow the program to modify the elements. The for statement in lines 58–60 initializes constIterator using vector member function begin, which returns a const_iterator to the first element in the vector—there is another version of begin that returns an iterator that can be used for non-const containers. Note that a const_iterator is returned because the identifier integers2 was declared const in the parameter list of function printVector. The loop continues as long as constIterator has not reached the end of the vector. This is determined by comparing constIterator to the result of integers2.end(), which returns an iterator indicating the location past the last element of the vector. If constIterator is equal to this value, the end of the vector has been reached. Functions begin and end are available for all first-class containers. The body of the loop dereferences iterator constIterator to get the value in the current element of the vector. Remember that the iterator acts like a pointer to the element and that operator * is overloaded to return a reference to the element. The expression ++constIterator (line 59) positions the iterator to the next element of the vector.

Performance Tip 22.11

Use prefix increment when applied to STL iterators because the prefix increment operator does not return a value that must be stored in a temporary object.

Error-Prevention Tip 22.4

Only random-access iterators support <. It is better to use != and end to test for the end of a container.

Line 40 declares a const_reverse_iterator that can be used to iterate through a vector backward. Line 41 declares a const_reverse_iterator variable tempIterator and initializes it to the iterator returned by function **rend** (i.e., the iterator for the ending point when iterating through the container in reverse). All first-class containers support this type of iterator. Lines 44–46 use a for statement similar to that in function print-Vector to iterate through the vector. In this loop, function **rbegin** (i.e., the iterator for the starting point when iterating through the container in reverse) and tempIterator delineate the range of elements to output. As with functions begin and end, rbegin and rend can return a const_reverse_iterator or a reverse_iterator, based on whether or not the container is constant.

Performance Tip 22.12

For performance reasons, capture the loop ending value before the loop and compare against that, rather than having a (potentially expensive) function call for each iteration.

Vector Element-Manipulation Functions
Figure 22.15 illustrates functions that enable retrieval and manipulation of the elements of a vector. Line 17 uses an overloaded vector constructor that takes two iterators as arguments to initialize integers. Remember that pointers into an array can be used as iterators. Line 17 initializes integers with the contents of array from location array up to—but not including—location array + SIZE.

```
 1   // Fig. 22.15: Fig22_15.cpp
 2   // Testing Standard Library vector class template
 3   // element-manipulation functions.
 4   #include <iostream>
 5   using std::cout;
 6   using std::endl;
```

Fig. 22.15 | vector class template element-manipulation functions. (Part 1 of 3.)

```cpp
7
8   #include <vector> // vector class-template definition
9   #include <algorithm> // copy algorithm
10  #include <iterator> // ostream_iterator iterator
11  #include <stdexcept> // out_of_range exception
12
13  int main()
14  {
15     const int SIZE = 6;
16     int array[ SIZE ] = { 1, 2, 3, 4, 5, 6 };
17     std::vector< int > integers( array, array + SIZE );
18     std::ostream_iterator< int > output( cout, " " );
19
20     cout << "Vector integers contains: ";
21     std::copy( integers.begin(), integers.end(), output );
22
23     cout << "\nFirst element of integers: " << integers.front()
24        << "\nLast element of integers: " << integers.back();
25
26     integers[ 0 ] = 7; // set first element to 7
27     integers.at( 2 ) = 10; // set element at position 2 to 10
28
29     // insert 22 as 2nd element
30     integers.insert( integers.begin() + 1, 22 );
31
32     cout << "\n\nContents of vector integers after changes: ";
33     std::copy( integers.begin(), integers.end(), output );
34
35     // access out-of-range element
36     try
37     {
38        integers.at( 100 ) = 777;
39     } // end try
40     catch ( std::out_of_range &outOfRange ) // out_of_range exception
41     {
42        cout << "\n\nException: " << outOfRange.what();
43     } // end catch
44
45     // erase first element
46     integers.erase( integers.begin() );
47     cout << "\n\nVector integers after erasing first element: ";
48     std::copy( integers.begin(), integers.end(), output );
49
50     // erase remaining elements
51     integers.erase( integers.begin(), integers.end() );
52     cout << "\nAfter erasing all elements, vector integers "
53        << ( integers.empty() ? "is" : "is not" ) << " empty";
54
55     // insert elements from array
56     integers.insert( integers.begin(), array, array + SIZE );
57     cout << "\n\nContents of vector integers before clear: ";
58     std::copy( integers.begin(), integers.end(), output );
59
```

Fig. 22.15 | vector class template element-manipulation functions. (Part 2 of 3.)

```
60      // empty integers; clear calls erase to empty a collection
61      integers.clear();
62      cout << "\nAfter clear, vector integers "
63          << ( integers.empty() ? "is" : "is not" ) << " empty" << endl;
64      return 0;
65   } // end main
```

```
Vector integers contains: 1 2 3 4 5 6
First element of integers: 1
Last element of integers: 6

Contents of vector integers after changes: 7 22 2 10 4 5 6

Exception: invalid vector<T> subscript

Vector integers after erasing first element: 22 2 10 4 5 6
After erasing all elements, vector integers is empty

Contents of vector integers before clear: 1 2 3 4 5 6
After clear, vector integers is empty
```

Fig. 22.15 | vector class template element-manipulation functions. (Part 3 of 3.)

Line 18 defines an ostream_iterator called output that can be used to output integers separated by single spaces via cout. An ostream_iterator< int > is a type-safe output mechanism that outputs only values of type int or a compatible type. The first argument to the constructor specifies the output stream, and the second argument is a string specifying the separator for the values output—in this case, the string contains a space character. We use the ostream_iterator (defined in header <iterator>) to output the contents of the vector in this example.

Line 21 uses algorithm copy from the Standard Library to output the entire contents of vector integers to the standard output. Algorithm copy copies each element in the container starting with the location specified by the iterator in its first argument and continuing up to—but not including—the location specified by the iterator in its second argument. The first and second arguments must satisfy input iterator requirements—they must be iterators through which values can be read from a container. Also, applying ++ to the first iterator must eventually cause it to reach the second iterator argument in the container. The elements are copied to the location specified by the output iterator (i.e., an iterator through which a value can be stored or output) specified as the last argument. In this case, the output iterator is an ostream_iterator (output) that is attached to cout, so the elements are copied to the standard output. To use the algorithms of the Standard Library, you must include the header file <algorithm>.

Lines 23–24 use functions front and back (available for all sequence containers) to determine the vector's first and last elements, respectively. Notice the difference between functions front and begin. Function front returns a reference to the first element in the vector, while function begin returns a random access iterator pointing to the first element in the vector. Also notice the difference between functions back and end. Function back returns a reference to the last element in the vector, while function end returns a random access iterator pointing to the end of the vector (the location after the last element).

Common Programming Error 22.3

The vector *must not be empty; otherwise, results of the* front *and* back *functions are undefined.*

Lines 26–27 illustrate two ways to subscript through a vector (which also can be used with the deque containers). Line 26 uses the subscript operator that is overloaded to return either a reference to the value at the specified location or a constant reference to that value, depending on whether the container is constant. Function at (line 27) performs the same operation, but with bounds checking. Function at first checks the value supplied as an argument and determines whether it is in the bounds of the vector. If not, function at throws an out_of_bounds exception defined in header <stdexcept> (as demonstrated in lines 36–43). Figure 22.16 shows some of the STL exception types. (The Standard Library exception types are discussed in Chapter 16, Exception Handling.)

Line 30 uses one of the three overloaded insert functions provided by each sequence container. Line 30 inserts the value 22 before the element at the location specified by the iterator in the first argument. In this example, the iterator is pointing to the second element of the vector, so 22 is inserted as the second element and the original second element becomes the third element of the vector. Other versions of insert allow inserting multiple copies of the same value starting at a particular position in the container, or inserting a range of values from another container (or array), starting at a particular position in the original container.

Lines 46 and 51 use the two erase functions that are available in all first-class containers. Line 46 indicates that the element at the location specified by the iterator argument should be removed from the container (in this example, the element at the beginning of the vector). Line 51 specifies that all elements in the range starting with the location of the first argument up to—but not including—the location of the second argument should be erased from the container. In this example, all the elements are erased from the vector. Line 53 uses function empty (available for all containers and adapters) to confirm that the vector is empty.

Common Programming Error 22.4

Erasing an element that contains a pointer to a dynamically allocated object does not delete *that object; this can lead to a memory leak.*

Line 56 demonstrates the version of function insert that uses the second and third arguments to specify the starting location and ending location in a sequence of values (pos-

STL exception types	Description
out_of_range	Indicates when subscript is out of range—e.g., when an invalid subscript is specified to vector member function at.
invalid_argument	Indicates an invalid argument was passed to a function.
length_error	Indicates an attempt to create too long a container, string, etc.
bad_alloc	Indicates that an attempt to allocate memory with new (or with an allocator) failed because not enough memory was available.

Fig. 22.16 | Some STL exception types.

sibly from another container; in this case, from array of integers array) that should be inserted into the vector. Remember that the ending location specifies the position in the sequence after the last element to be inserted; copying is performed up to—but not including—this location.

Finally, line 61 uses function `clear` (found in all first-class containers) to empty the vector. This function calls the version of erase used in line 51 to empty the vector.

[*Note:* Other functions that are common to all containers and common to all sequence containers have not yet been covered. We'll cover most of these in the next few sections. We'll also cover many functions that are specific to each container.]

22.2.2 `list` Sequence Container

The `list` sequence container provides an efficient implementation for insertion and deletion operations at any location in the container. If most of the insertions and deletions occur at the ends of the container, the deque data structure (Section 22.2.3) provides a more efficient implementation. Class template `list` is implemented as a doubly linked list—every node in the `list` contains a pointer to the previous node in the `list` and to the next node in the `list`. This enables class template `list` to support bidirectional iterators that allow the container to be traversed both forward and backward. Any algorithm that requires input, output, forward or bidirectional iterators can operate on a `list`. Many `list` member functions manipulate the elements of the container as an ordered set of elements.

In addition to the member functions of all STL containers in Fig. 22.2 and the common member functions of all sequence containers discussed in Section 22.2, class template `list` provides nine other member functions—splice, push_front, pop_front, remove, remove_if, unique, merge, reverse and sort. Several of these member functions are `list`-optimized implementations of STL algorithms presented in Section 22.5. Figure 22.17 demonstrates several features of class `list`. Remember that many of the functions presented in Figs. 22.14–22.15 can be used with class `list`. Header file `<list>` must be included to use class `list`.

```
1   // Fig. 22.17: Fig22_17.cpp
2   // Standard library list class template test program.
3   #include <iostream>
4   using std::cout;
5   using std::endl;
6
7   #include <list> // list class-template definition
8   #include <algorithm> // copy algorithm
9   #include <iterator> // ostream_iterator
10
11  // prototype for function template printList
12  template < typename T > void printList( const std::list< T > &listRef );
13
14  int main()
15  {
16     const int SIZE = 4;
17     int array[ SIZE ] = { 2, 6, 4, 8 };
18     std::list< int > values; // create list of ints
```

Fig. 22.17 | Standard Library `list` class template. (Part I of 3.)

```
19    std::list< int > otherValues; // create list of ints
20
21    // insert items in values
22    values.push_front( 1 );
23    values.push_front( 2 );
24    values.push_back( 4 );
25    values.push_back( 3 );
26
27    cout << "values contains: ";
28    printList( values );
29
30    values.sort(); // sort values
31    cout << "\nvalues after sorting contains: ";
32    printList( values );
33
34    // insert elements of array into otherValues
35    otherValues.insert( otherValues.begin(), array, array + SIZE );
36    cout << "\nAfter insert, otherValues contains: ";
37    printList( otherValues );
38
39    // remove otherValues elements and insert at end of values
40    values.splice( values.end(), otherValues );
41    cout << "\nAfter splice, values contains: ";
42    printList( values );
43
44    values.sort(); // sort values
45    cout << "\nAfter sort, values contains: ";
46    printList( values );
47
48    // insert elements of array into otherValues
49    otherValues.insert( otherValues.begin(), array, array + SIZE );
50    otherValues.sort();
51    cout << "\nAfter insert and sort, otherValues contains: ";
52    printList( otherValues );
53
54    // remove otherValues elements and insert into values in sorted order
55    values.merge( otherValues );
56    cout << "\nAfter merge:\n   values contains: ";
57    printList( values );
58    cout << "\n   otherValues contains: ";
59    printList( otherValues );
60
61    values.pop_front(); // remove element from front
62    values.pop_back(); // remove element from back
63    cout << "\nAfter pop_front and pop_back:\n   values contains: "
64    printList( values );
65
66    values.unique(); // remove duplicate elements
67    cout << "\nAfter unique, values contains: ";
68    printList( values );
69
70    // swap elements of values and otherValues
71    values.swap( otherValues );
```

Fig. 22.17 | Standard Library `list` class template. (Part 2 of 3.)

```
72     cout << "\nAfter swap:\n   values contains: ";
73     printList( values );
74     cout << "\n   otherValues contains: ";
75     printList( otherValues );
76
77     // replace contents of values with elements of otherValues
78     values.assign( otherValues.begin(), otherValues.end() );
79     cout << "\nAfter assign, values contains: ";
80     printList( values );
81
82     // remove otherValues elements and insert into values in sorted order
83     values.merge( otherValues );
84     cout << "\nAfter merge, values contains: ";
85     printList( values );
86
87     values.remove( 4 ); // remove all 4s
88     cout << "\nAfter remove( 4 ), values contains: ";
89     printList( values );
90     cout << endl;
91     return 0;
92  } // end main
93
94  // printList function template definition; uses
95  // ostream_iterator and copy algorithm to output list elements
96  template < typename T > void printList( const std::list< T > &listRef )
97  {
98     if ( listRef.empty() ) // list is empty
99        cout << "List is empty";
100    else
101    {
102       std::ostream_iterator< T > output( cout, " " );
103       std::copy( listRef.begin(), listRef.end(), output );
104    } // end else
105 } // end function printList
```

```
values contains: 2 1 4 3
values after sorting contains: 1 2 3 4
After insert, otherValues contains: 2 6 4 8
After splice, values contains: 1 2 3 4 2 6 4 8
After sort, values contains: 1 2 2 3 4 4 6 8
After insert and sort, otherValues contains: 2 4 6 8
After merge:
   values contains: 1 2 2 2 3 4 4 4 6 6 8 8
   otherValues contains: List is empty
After pop_front and pop_back:
   values contains: 2 2 2 3 4 4 4 6 6 8
After unique, values contains: 2 3 4 6 8
After swap:
   values contains: List is empty
   otherValues contains: 2 3 4 6 8
After assign, values contains: 2 3 4 6 8
After merge, values contains: 2 2 3 3 4 4 6 6 8 8
After remove( 4 ), values contains: 2 2 3 3 6 6 8 8
```

Fig. 22.17 | Standard Library `list` class template. (Part 3 of 3.)

Lines 18–19 instantiate two list objects capable of storing integers. Lines 22–23 use function `push_front` to insert integers at the beginning of values. Function push_front is specific to classes list and deque (not to vector). Lines 24–25 use function push_back to insert integers at the end of values. Remember that function push_back is common to all sequence containers.

Line 30 uses list member function `sort` to arrange the elements in the list in ascending order. [*Note:* This is different from the sort in the STL algorithms.] A second version of function sort allows you to supply a binary predicate function that takes two arguments (values in the list), performs a comparison and returns a bool value indicating the result. This function determines the order in which the elements of the list are sorted. This version could be particularly useful for a list that stores pointers rather than values. [*Note:* We demonstrate a unary predicate function in Fig. 22.28. A unary predicate function takes a single argument, performs a comparison using that argument and returns a bool value indicating the result.]

Line 40 uses list function `splice` to remove the elements in otherValues and insert them into values before the iterator position specified as the first argument. There are two other versions of this function. Function splice with three arguments allows one element to be removed from the container specified as the second argument from the location specified by the iterator in the third argument. Function splice with four arguments uses the last two arguments to specify a range of locations that should be removed from the container in the second argument and placed at the location specified in the first argument.

After inserting more elements in otherValues and sorting both values and other-Values, line 55 uses list member function `merge` to remove all elements of otherValues and insert them in sorted order into values. Both lists must be sorted in the same order before this operation is performed. A second version of merge enables you to supply a predicate function that takes two arguments (values in the list) and returns a bool value. The predicate function specifies the sorting order used by merge.

Line 61 uses list function `pop_front` to remove the first element in the list. Line 62 uses function `pop_back` (available for all sequence containers) to remove the last element in the list.

Line 66 uses list function `unique` to remove duplicate elements in the list. The list should be in sorted order (so that all duplicates are side by side) before this operation is performed, to guarantee that all duplicates are eliminated. A second version of unique enables you to supply a predicate function that takes two arguments (values in the list) and returns a bool value specifying whether two elements are equal.

Line 71 uses function `swap` (available to all containers) to exchange the contents of values with the contents of otherValues.

Line 78 uses list function `assign` to replace the contents of values with the contents of otherValues in the range specified by the two iterator arguments. A second version of assign replaces the original contents with copies of the value specified in the second argument. The first argument of the function specifies the number of copies. Line 87 uses list function `remove` to delete all copies of the value 4 from the list.

22.2.3 deque Sequence Container

Class deque provides many of the benefits of a vector and a list in one container. The term deque is short for "double-ended queue." Class deque is implemented to provide efficient indexed access (using subscripting) for reading and modifying its elements, much like a vector. Class deque is also implemented for efficient insertion and deletion operations at its front and back, much like a list (although a list is also capable of efficient insertions and deletions in the middle of the list). Class deque provides support for random-access iterators, so deques can be used with all STL algorithms. One of the most common uses of a deque is to maintain a first-in, first-out queue of elements. In fact, a deque is the default underlying implementation for the queue adaptor (Section 22.4.2).

Additional storage for a deque can be allocated at either end of the deque in blocks of memory that are typically maintained as an array of pointers to those blocks.[2] Due to the noncontiguous memory layout of a deque, a deque iterator must be more intelligent than the pointers that are used to iterate through vectors or pointer-based arrays.

Performance Tip 22.13

In general, deque has higher overhead than vector.

Performance Tip 22.14

Insertions and deletions in the middle of a deque are optimized to minimize the number of elements copied, so it is more efficient than a vector but less efficient than a list for this kind of modification.

Class deque provides the same basic operations as class vector, but adds member functions **push_front** and **pop_front** to allow insertion and deletion at the beginning of the deque, respectively.

Figure 22.18 demonstrates features of class deque. Remember that many of the functions presented in Fig. 22.14, Fig. 22.15 and Fig. 22.17 also can be used with class deque. Header file **<deque>** must be included to use class deque.

Line 13 instantiates a deque that can store **double** values. Lines 17–19 use functions push_front and push_back to insert elements at the beginning and end of the deque. Remember that push_back is available for all sequence containers, but push_front is available only for class list and class deque.

```
1   // Fig. 22.18: Fig22_18.cpp
2   // Standard Library class deque test program.
3   #include <iostream>
4   using std::cout;
5   using std::endl;
6
7   #include <deque> // deque class-template definition
8   #include <algorithm> // copy algorithm
9   #include <iterator> // ostream_iterator
10
11  int main()
12  {
13     std::deque< double > values; // create deque of doubles
```

Fig. 22.18 | Standard Library deque class template. (Part 1 of 2.)

---

2.   This is an implementation-specific detail, not a requirement of the C++ standard.

```
14         std::ostream_iterator< double > output( cout, " " );
15
16         // insert elements in values
17         values.push_front( 2.2 );
18         values.push_front( 3.5 );
19         values.push_back( 1.1 );
20
21         cout << "values contains: ";
22
23         // use subscript operator to obtain elements of values
24         for ( unsigned int i = 0; i < values.size(); i++ )
25            cout << values[ i ] << ' ';
26
27         values.pop_front(); // remove first element
28         cout << "\nAfter pop_front, values contains: ";
29         std::copy( values.begin(), values.end(), output );
30
31         // use subscript operator to modify element at location 1
32         values[ 1 ] = 5.4;
33         cout << "\nAfter values[ 1 ] = 5.4, values contains: ";
34         std::copy( values.begin(), values.end(), output );
35         cout << endl;
36         return 0;
37      } // end main
```

```
values contains: 3.5 2.2 1.1
After pop_front, values contains: 2.2 1.1
After values[ 1 ] = 5.4, values contains: 2.2 5.4
```

Fig. 22.18 | Standard Library deque class template. (Part 2 of 2.)

The for statement in lines 24–25 uses the subscript operator to retrieve the value in each element of the deque for output. Note that the condition uses function size to ensure that we do not attempt to access an element outside the bounds of the deque.

Line 27 uses function pop_front to demonstrate removing the first element of the deque. Remember that pop_front is available only for class list and class deque (not for class vector).

Line 32 uses the subscript operator to create an *lvalue*. This enables values to be assigned directly to any element of the deque.

22.3 Associative Containers

The STL's associative containers provide direct access to store and retrieve elements via keys (often called search keys). The four associative containers are multiset, set, multimap and map. Each associative container maintains its keys in sorted order. Iterating through an associative container traverses it in the sort order for that container. Classes multiset and set provide operations for manipulating sets of values where the values are the keys—there is not a separate value associated with each key. The primary difference between a multiset and a set is that a multiset allows duplicate keys and a set does not. Classes multimap and map provide operations for manipulating values associated with keys (these values are sometimes referred to as mapped values). The primary difference between a multimap and a map is that a multimap allows duplicate keys with associated values to be stored and a map allows only unique keys with associated values. In addition to the common member functions of all containers presented in Fig. 22.2, all associative containers also support several other member functions, including find, lower_bound, upper_bound and count. Examples of each of the associative containers and the common associative container member functions are presented in the next several subsections.

22.3.1 multiset Associative Container

The multiset associative container provides fast storage and retrieval of keys and allows duplicate keys. The ordering of the elements is determined by a comparator function object. For example, in an integer multiset, elements can be sorted in ascending order by ordering the keys with comparator function object less< int >. We discuss function objects in detail in Section 22.7. The data type of the keys in all associative containers must support comparison properly based on the comparator function object specified—keys sorted with less< T > must support comparison with operator<. If the keys used in the associative containers are of user-defined data types, those types must supply the appropriate comparison operators. A multiset supports bidirectional iterators (but not random-access iterators).

Figure 22.19 demonstrates the multiset associative container for a multiset of integers sorted in ascending order. Header file <set> must be included to use class multiset. Containers multiset and set provide the same basic functionality.

Line 10 uses a typedef to create a new type name (alias) for a multiset of integers ordered in ascending order, using the function object less< int >. Ascending order is the default for a multiset, so std::less< int > can be omitted in line 10. This new type (Ims) is then used to instantiate an integer multiset object, intMultiset (line 19).

Good Programming Practice 22.1

Use typedefs to make code with long type names (such as multisets) easier to read.

The output statement in line 22 uses function count (available to all associative containers) to count the number of occurrences of the value 15 currently in the multiset.

```
1   // Fig. 22.19: Fig22_19.cpp
2   // Testing Standard Library class multiset
3   #include <iostream>
4   using std::cout;
5   using std::endl;
6
7   #include <set> // multiset class-template definition
8
9   // define short name for multiset type used in this program
10  typedef std::multiset< int, std::less< int > > Ims;
11
12  #include <algorithm> // copy algorithm
13  #include <iterator> // ostream_iterator
14
```

Fig. 22.19 | Standard Library multiset class template. (Part 1 of 3.)

```
15   int main()
16   {
17      const int SIZE = 10;
18      int a[ SIZE ] = { 7, 22, 9, 1, 18, 30, 100, 22, 85, 13 };
19      Ims intMultiset; // Ims is typedef for "integer multiset"
20      std::ostream_iterator< int > output( cout, " " );
21
22      cout << "There are currently " << intMultiset.count( 15 )
23         << " values of 15 in the multiset\n";
24
25      intMultiset.insert( 15 ); // insert 15 in intMultiset
26      intMultiset.insert( 15 ); // insert 15 in intMultiset
27      cout << "After inserts, there are " << intMultiset.count( 15 )
28         << " values of 15 in the multiset\n\n";
29
30      // iterator that cannot be used to change element values
31      Ims::const_iterator result;
32
33      // find 15 in intMultiset; find returns iterator
34      result = intMultiset.find( 15 );
35
36      if ( result != intMultiset.end() ) // if iterator not at end
37         cout << "Found value 15\n"; // found search value 15
38
39      // find 20 in intMultiset; find returns iterator
40      result = intMultiset.find( 20 );
41
42      if ( result == intMultiset.end() ) // will be true hence
43         cout << "Did not find value 20\n"; // did not find 20
44
45      // insert elements of array a into intMultiset
46      intMultiset.insert( a, a + SIZE );
47      cout << "\nAfter insert, intMultiset contains:\n";
48      std::copy( intMultiset.begin(), intMultiset.end(), output );
49
50      // determine lower and upper bound of 22 in intMultiset
51      cout << "\n\nLower bound of 22: "
52         << *( intMultiset.lower_bound( 22 ) );
53      cout << "\nUpper bound of 22: " << *( intMultiset.upper_bound( 22 ) );
54
55      // p represents pair of const_iterators
56      std::pair< Ims::const_iterator, Ims::const_iterator > p;
57
58      // use equal_range to determine lower and upper bound
59      // of 22 in intMultiset
60      p = intMultiset.equal_range( 22 );
61
62      cout << "\n\nequal_range of 22:" << "\n   Lower bound: "
63         << *( p.first ) << "\n   Upper bound: " << *( p.second );
64      cout << endl;
65      return 0;
66   } // end main
```

Fig. 22.19 | Standard Library `multiset` class template. (Part 2 of 3.)

```
There are currently 0 values of 15 in the multiset
After inserts, there are 2 values of 15 in the multiset

Found value 15
Did not find value 20

After insert, intMultiset contains:
1 7 9 13 15 15 18 22 22 30 85 100

Lower bound of 22: 22
Upper bound of 22: 30

equal_range of 22:
    Lower bound: 22
    Upper bound: 30
```

Fig. 22.19 | Standard Library multiset class template. (Part 3 of 3.)

Lines 25–26 use one of the three versions of function insert to add the value 15 to the multiset twice. A second version of insert takes an iterator and a value as arguments and begins the search for the insertion point from the iterator position specified. A third version of insert takes two iterators as arguments that specify a range of values to add to the multiset from another container.

Line 34 uses function **find** (available to all associative containers) to locate the value 15 in the multiset. Function find returns an iterator or a const_iterator pointing to the earliest location at which the value is found. If the value is not found, find returns an iterator or a const_iterator equal to the value returned by a call to end. Line 42 demonstrates this case.

Line 46 uses function **insert** to insert the elements of array a into the multiset. In line 48, the copy algorithm copies the elements of the multiset to the standard output. Note that the elements are displayed in ascending order.

Lines 52 and 53 use functions **lower_bound** and **upper_bound** (available in all associative containers) to locate the earliest occurrence of the value 22 in the multiset and the element *after* the last occurrence of the value 22 in the multiset. Both functions return iterators or const_iterators pointing to the appropriate location or the iterator returned by end if the value is not in the multiset.

Line 56 instantiates an instance of class pair called p. Objects of class pair are used to associate pairs of values. In this example, the contents of a pair are two const_iterators for our integer-based multiset. The purpose of p is to store the return value of multiset function **equal_range** that returns a pair containing the results of both a lower_bound and an upper_bound operation. Type pair contains two public data members called **first** and **second**.

Line 60 uses function equal_range to determine the lower_bound and upper_bound of 22 in the multiset. Line 63 uses p.first and p.second, respectively, to access the lower_bound and upper_bound. We dereferenced the iterators to output the values at the locations returned from equal_range.

22.3.2 set Associative Container

The set associative container is used for fast storage and retrieval of unique keys. The implementation of a set is identical to that of a multiset, except that a set must have unique keys. Therefore, if an attempt is made to insert a duplicate key into a set, the duplicate is ignored; because this is the intended mathematical behavior of a set, we do not identify it as a common programming error. A set supports bidirectional iterators (but not random-access iterators). Figure 22.20 demonstrates a set of doubles. Header file <set> must be included to use class set.

```cpp
 1  // Fig. 22.20: Fig22_20.cpp
 2  // Standard Library class set test program.
 3  #include <iostream>
 4  using std::cout;
 5  using std::endl;
 6
 7  #include <set>
 8
 9  // define short name for set type used in this program
10  typedef std::set< double, std::less< double > > DoubleSet;
11
12  #include <algorithm>
13  #include <iterator> // ostream_iterator
14
15  int main()
16  {
17     const int SIZE = 5;
18     double a[ SIZE ] = { 2.1, 4.2, 9.5, 2.1, 3.7 };
19     DoubleSet doubleSet( a, a + SIZE );
20     std::ostream_iterator< double > output( cout, " " );
21
22     cout << "doubleSet contains: ";
23     std::copy( doubleSet.begin(), doubleSet.end(), output );
24
25     // p represents pair containing const_iterator and bool
26     std::pair< DoubleSet::const_iterator, bool > p;
27
28     // insert 13.8 in doubleSet; insert returns pair in which
29     // p.first represents location of 13.8 in doubleSet and
30     // p.second represents whether 13.8 was inserted
31     p = doubleSet.insert( 13.8 ); // value not in set
32     cout << "\n\n" << *( p.first )
33        << ( p.second ? " was" : " was not" ) << " inserted";
34     cout << "\ndoubleSet contains: ";
35     std::copy( doubleSet.begin(), doubleSet.end(), output );
36
37     // insert 9.5 in doubleSet
38     p = doubleSet.insert( 9.5 ); // value already in set
39     cout << "\n\n" << *( p.first )
40        << ( p.second ? " was" : " was not" ) << " inserted";
41     cout << "\ndoubleSet contains: ";
42     std::copy( doubleSet.begin(), doubleSet.end(), output );
```

Fig. 22.20 | Standard Library set class template. (Part 1 of 2.)

```
43        cout << endl;
44        return 0;
45    } // end main
```

```
doubleSet contains: 2.1 3.7 4.2 9.5

13.8 was inserted
doubleSet contains: 2.1 3.7 4.2 9.5 13.8

9.5 was not inserted
doubleSet contains: 2.1 3.7 4.2 9.5 13.8
```

Fig. 22.20 | Standard Library set class template. (Part 2 of 2.)

Line 10 uses typedef to create a new type name (DoubleSet) for a set of double values ordered in ascending order, using the function object less< double >.

Line 19 uses the new type DoubleSet to instantiate object doubleSet. The constructor call takes the elements in array a between a and a + SIZE (i.e., the entire array) and inserts them into the set. Line 23 uses algorithm copy to output the contents of the set. Notice that the value 2.1—which appeared twice in array a—appears only once in doubleSet. This is because container set does not allow duplicates.

Line 26 defines a pair consisting of a const_iterator for a DoubleSet and a bool value. This object stores the result of a call to set function insert.

Line 31 uses function insert to place the value 13.8 in the set. The returned pair, p, contains an iterator p.first pointing to the value 13.8 in the set and a bool value that is true if the value was inserted and false if the value was not inserted (because it was already in the set). In this case, 13.8 was not in the set, so it was inserted. Line 38 attempts to insert 9.5, which is already in the set. The output of lines 39–40 shows that 9.5 was not inserted.

22.3.3 multimap Associative Container

The multimap associative container is used for fast storage and retrieval of keys and associated values (often called key/value pairs). Many of the functions used with multisets and sets are also used with multimaps and maps. The elements of multimaps and maps are pairs of keys and values instead of individual values. When inserting into a multimap or map, a pair object that contains the key and the value is used. The ordering of the keys is determined by a comparator function object. For example, in a multimap that uses integers as the key type, keys can be sorted in ascending order by ordering them with comparator function object less< int >. Duplicate keys are allowed in a multimap, so multiple values can be associated with a single key. This is often called a one-to-many relationship. For example, in a credit-card transaction-processing system, one credit-card account can have many associated transactions; in a university, one student can take many courses, and one professor can teach many students; in the military, one rank (like "private") has many people. A multimap supports bidirectional iterators, but not random-access iterators. Figure 22.21 demonstrates the multimap associative container. Header file <map> must be included to use class multimap.

Performance Tip 22.15

A `multimap` *is implemented to efficiently locate all values paired with a given key.*

Line 10 uses `typedef` to define alias `Mmid` for a `multimap` type in which the key type is `int`, the type of a key's associated value is `double` and the elements are ordered in ascending order. Line 14 uses the new type to instantiate a `multimap` called `pairs`. Line 16 uses function `count` to determine the number of key/value pairs with a key of 15.

```cpp
 1   // Fig. 22.21: Fig22_21.cpp
 2   // Standard Library class multimap test program.
 3   #include <iostream>
 4   using std::cout;
 5   using std::endl;
 6
 7   #include <map> // map class-template definition
 8
 9   // define short name for multimap type used in this program
10   typedef std::multimap< int, double, std::less< int > > Mmid;
11
12   int main()
13   {
14      Mmid pairs; // declare the multimap pairs
15
16      cout << "There are currently " << pairs.count( 15 )
17         << " pairs with key 15 in the multimap\n";
18
19      // insert two value_type objects in pairs
20      pairs.insert( Mmid::value_type( 15, 2.7 ) );
21      pairs.insert( Mmid::value_type( 15, 99.3 ) );
22
23      cout << "After inserts, there are " << pairs.count( 15 )
24         << " pairs with key 15\n\n";
25
26      // insert five value_type objects in pairs
27      pairs.insert( Mmid::value_type( 30, 111.11 ) );
28      pairs.insert( Mmid::value_type( 10, 22.22 ) );
29      pairs.insert( Mmid::value_type( 25, 33.333 ) );
30      pairs.insert( Mmid::value_type( 20, 9.345 ) );
31      pairs.insert( Mmid::value_type( 5, 77.54 ) );
32
33      cout << "Multimap pairs contains:\nKey\tValue\n";
34
35      // use const_iterator to walk through elements of pairs
36      for ( Mmid::const_iterator iter = pairs.begin();
37         iter != pairs.end(); ++iter )
38         cout << iter->first << '\t' << iter->second << '\n';
39
40      cout << endl;
41      return 0;
42   } // end main
```

Fig. 22.21 | Standard Library `multimap` class template. (Part 1 of 2.)

```
There are currently 0 pairs with key 15 in the multimap
After inserts, there are 2 pairs with key 15

Multimap pairs contains:
Key      Value
5        77.54
10       22.22
15       2.7
15       99.3
20       9.345
25       33.333
30       111.11
```

Fig. 22.21 | Standard Library `multimap` class template. (Part 2 of 2.)

Line 20 uses function `insert` to add a new key/value pair to the `multimap`. The expression `Mmid::value_type( 15, 2.7 )` creates a `pair` object in which `first` is the key (15) of type `int` and `second` is the value (`2.7`) of type `double`. The type `Mmid::value_type` is defined as part of the `typedef` for the `multimap`. Line 21 inserts another `pair` object with the key 15 and the value `99.3`. Then lines 23–24 output the number of pairs with key 15.

Lines 27–31 insert five additional `pairs` into the `multimap`. The `for` statement in lines 36–38 outputs the contents of the `multimap`, including both keys and values. Line 38 uses the `const_iterator` called `iter` to access the members of the `pair` in each element of the `multimap`. Notice in the output that the keys appear in ascending order.

22.3.4 map Associative Container

The map associative container performs fast storage and retrieval of unique keys and associated values. Duplicate keys are not allowed—a single value can be associated with each key. This is called a one-to-one mapping. For example, a company that uses unique employee numbers, such as 100, 200 and 300, might have a map that associates employee numbers with their telephone extensions—4321, 4115 and 5217, respectively. With a map you specify the key and get back the associated data quickly. A map is also known as an associative array. Providing the key in a map's subscript operator [] locates the value associated with that key in the map. Insertions and deletions can be made anywhere in a map.

Figure 22.22 demonstrates the map associative container and uses the same features as Fig. 22.21 to demonstrate the subscript operator. Header file <map> must be included to

```
 1   // Fig. 22.22: Fig22_22.cpp
 2   // Standard Library class map test program.
 3   #include <iostream>
 4   using std::cout;
 5   using std::endl;
 6
 7   #include <map> // map class-template definition
 8
 9   // define short name for map type used in this program
10   typedef std::map< int, double, std::less< int > > Mid;
11
```

Fig. 22.22 | Standard Library map class template. (Part 1 of 2.)

```
12   int main()
13   {
14      Mid pairs;
15
16      // insert eight value_type objects in pairs
17      pairs.insert( Mid::value_type( 15, 2.7 ) );
18      pairs.insert( Mid::value_type( 30, 111.11 ) );
19      pairs.insert( Mid::value_type( 5, 1010.1 ) );
20      pairs.insert( Mid::value_type( 10, 22.22 ) );
21      pairs.insert( Mid::value_type( 25, 33.333 ) );
22      pairs.insert( Mid::value_type( 5, 77.54 ) ); // dup ignored
23      pairs.insert( Mid::value_type( 20, 9.345 ) );
24      pairs.insert( Mid::value_type( 15, 99.3 ) ); // dup ignored
25
26      cout << "pairs contains:\nKey\tValue\n";
27
28      // use const_iterator to walk through elements of pairs
29      for ( Mid::const_iterator iter = pairs.begin();
30         iter != pairs.end(); ++iter )
31         cout << iter->first << '\t' << iter->second << '\n';
32
33      pairs[ 25 ] = 9999.99; // use subscripting to change value for key 25
34      pairs[ 40 ] = 8765.43; // use subscripting to insert value for key 40
35
36      cout << "\nAfter subscript operations, pairs contains:\nKey\tValue\n";
37
38      // use const_iterator to walk through elements of pairs
39      for ( Mid::const_iterator iter2 = pairs.begin();
40         iter2 != pairs.end(); ++iter2 )
41         cout << iter2->first << '\t' << iter2->second << '\n';
42
43      cout << endl;
44      return 0;
45   } // end main
```

```
pairs contains:
Key     Value
5       1010.1
10      22.22
15      2.7
20      9.345
25      33.333
30      111.11

After subscript operations, pairs contains:
Key     Value
5       1010.1
10      22.22
15      2.7
20      9.345
25      9999.99
30      111.11
40      8765.43
```

Fig. 22.22 | Standard Library **map** class template. (Part 2 of 2.)

use class map. Lines 33—34 use the subscript operator of class map. When the subscript is a key that is already in the map (line 33), the operator returns a reference to the associated value. When the subscript is a key that is not in the map (line 34), the operator inserts the key in the map and returns a reference that can be used to associate a value with that key. Line 33 replaces the value for the key 25 (previously 33.333 as specified in line 21) with a new value, 9999.99. Line 34 inserts a new key/value pair in the map (called creating an association).

22.4 Container Adapters

The STL provides three container adapters—stack, queue and priority_queue. Adapters are not first-class containers, because they do not provide the actual data-structure implementation in which elements can be stored and because adapters do not support iterators. The benefit of an adapter class is that you can choose an appropriate underlying data structure. All three adapter classes provide member functions **push** and **pop** that properly insert an element into each adapter data structure and properly remove an element from each adapter data structure. The next several subsections provide examples of the adapter classes.

22.4.1 stack Adapter

Class stack enables insertions into and deletions from the underlying data structure at one end (commonly referred to as a last-in, first-out data structure). A stack can be implemented with any of the sequence containers: vector, list and deque. This example creates three integer stacks, using each of the sequence containers of the Standard Library as the underlying data structure to represent the stack. By default, a stack is implemented with a deque. The stack operations are **push** to insert an element at the top of the stack (implemented by calling function push_back of the underlying container), **pop** to remove the top element of the stack (implemented by calling function pop_back of the underlying container), **top** to get a reference to the top element of the stack (implemented by calling function back of the underlying container), **empty** to determine whether the stack is empty (implemented by calling function empty of the underlying container) and **size** to get the number of elements in the stack (implemented by calling function size of the underlying container).

Performance Tip 22.16

Each of the common operations of a stack is implemented as an inline function that calls the appropriate function of the underlying container. This avoids the overhead of a second function call.

Performance Tip 22.17

For the best performance, use class vector as the underlying container for a stack.

Figure 22.23 demonstrates the stack adapter class. Header file <stack> must be included to use class stack.

Lines 20, 23 and 26 instantiate three integer stacks. Line 20 specifies a stack of integers that uses the default deque container as its underlying data structure. Line 23 specifies a stack of integers that uses a vector of integers as its underlying data structure. Line 26 specifies a stack of integers that uses a list of integers as its underlying data structure.

Function pushElements (lines 49–56) pushes the elements onto each stack. Line 53 uses function push (available in each adapter class) to place an integer on top of the stack. Line 54 uses stack function top to retrieve the top element of the stack for output. Function top does not remove the top element.

Function popElements (lines 59–66) pops the elements off each stack. Line 63 uses stack function top to retrieve the top element of the stack for output. Line 64 uses function pop (available in each adapter class) to remove the top element of the stack. Function pop does not return a value.

```cpp
1   // Fig. 22.23: Fig22_23.cpp
2   // Standard Library adapter stack test program.
3   #include <iostream>
4   using std::cout;
5   using std::endl;
6
7   #include <stack> // stack adapter definition
8   #include <vector> // vector class-template definition
9   #include <list> // list class-template definition
10
11  // pushElements function-template prototype
12  template< typename T > void pushElements( T &stackRef );
13
14  // popElements function-template prototype
15  template< typename T > void popElements( T &stackRef );
16
17  int main()
18  {
19     // stack with default underlying deque
20     std::stack< int > intDequeStack;
21
22     // stack with underlying vector
23     std::stack< int, std::vector< int > > intVectorStack;
24
25     // stack with underlying list
26     std::stack< int, std::list< int > > intListStack;
27
28     // push the values 0-9 onto each stack
29     cout << "Pushing onto intDequeStack: ";
30     pushElements( intDequeStack );
31     cout << "\nPushing onto intVectorStack: ";
32     pushElements( intVectorStack );
33     cout << "\nPushing onto intListStack: ";
34     pushElements( intListStack );
35     cout << endl << endl;
36
37     // display and remove elements from each stack
38     cout << "Popping from intDequeStack: ";
39     popElements( intDequeStack );
```

Fig. 22.23 | Standard Library stack adapter class. (Part 1 of 2.)

```
40          cout << "\nPopping from intVectorStack: ";
41          popElements( intVectorStack );
42          cout << "\nPopping from intListStack: ";
43          popElements( intListStack );
44          cout << endl;
45          return 0;
46     } // end main
47
48     // push elements onto stack object to which stackRef refers
49     template< typename T > void pushElements( T &stackRef )
50     {
51          for ( int i = 0; i < 10; i++ )
52          {
53               stackRef.push( i ); // push element onto stack
54               cout << stackRef.top() << ' '; // view (and display) top element
55          } // end for
56     } // end function pushElements
57
58     // pop elements from stack object to which stackRef refers
59     template< typename T > void popElements( T &stackRef )
60     {
61          while ( !stackRef.empty() )
62          {
63               cout << stackRef.top() << ' '; // view (and display) top element
64               stackRef.pop(); // remove top element
65          } // end while
66     } // end function popElements
```

```
Pushing onto intDequeStack: 0 1 2 3 4 5 6 7 8 9
Pushing onto intVectorStack: 0 1 2 3 4 5 6 7 8 9
Pushing onto intListStack: 0 1 2 3 4 5 6 7 8 9

Popping from intDequeStack: 9 8 7 6 5 4 3 2 1 0
Popping from intVectorStack: 9 8 7 6 5 4 3 2 1 0
Popping from intListStack: 9 8 7 6 5 4 3 2 1 0
```

Fig. 22.23 | Standard Library stack adapter class. (Part 2 of 2.)

22.4.2 queue Adapter

Class queue enables insertions at the back of the underlying data structure and deletions from the front (commonly referred to as a first-in, first-out data structure). A queue can be implemented with STL data structure list or deque. By default, a queue is implemented with a deque. The common queue operations are push to insert an element at the back of the queue (implemented by calling function push_back of the underlying container), pop to remove the element at the front of the queue (implemented by calling function pop_front of the underlying container), front to get a reference to the first element in the queue (implemented by calling function front of the underlying container), back to get a reference to the last element in the queue (implemented by calling function back of the underlying container), empty to determine whether the queue is empty (implemented by calling function empty of the underlying container) and size to get the number of elements in the queue (implemented by calling function size of the underlying container).

Performance Tip 22.18

Each of the common operations of a queue is implemented as an inline function that calls the appropriate function of the underlying container. This avoids the overhead of a second function call.

Performance Tip 22.19

For the best performance, use class deque as the underlying container for a queue.

Figure 22.24 demonstrates the queue adapter class. Header file <queue> must be included to use a queue.

Line 11 instantiates a queue that stores double values. Lines 14–16 use function push to add elements to the queue. The while statement in lines 21–25 uses function empty (available in all containers) to determine whether the queue is empty (line 21). While there are more elements in the queue, line 23 uses queue function front to read (but not remove) the first element in the queue for output. Line 24 removes the first element in the queue with function pop (available in all adapter classes).

```cpp
 1  // Fig. 22.24: Fig22_24.cpp
 2  // Standard Library adapter queue test program.
 3  #include <iostream>
 4  using std::cout;
 5  using std::endl;
 6
 7  #include <queue> // queue adapter definition
 8
 9  int main()
10  {
11     std::queue< double > values; // queue with doubles
12
13     // push elements onto queue values
14     values.push( 3.2 );
15     values.push( 9.8 );
16     values.push( 5.4 );
17
18     cout << "Popping from values: ";
19
20     // pop elements from queue
21     while ( !values.empty() )
22     {
23        cout << values.front() << ' '; // view front element
24        values.pop(); // remove element
25     } // end while
26
27     cout << endl;
28     return 0;
29  } // end main
```

```
Popping from values: 3.2 9.8 5.4
```

Fig. 22.24 | Standard Library queue adapter class templates.

22.4.3 priority_queue Adapter

Class `priority_queue` provides functionality that enables insertions in sorted order into the underlying data structure and deletions from the front of the underlying data structure. A priority_queue can be implemented with STL sequence containers vector or deque. By default, a priority_queue is implemented with a vector as the underlying container. When elements are added to a priority_queue, they are inserted in priority order, such that the highest-priority element (i.e., the largest value) will be the first element removed from the priority_queue. This is usually accomplished via a sorting technique called heapsort that always maintains the largest value (i.e., highest-priority element) at the front of the data structure—such a data structure is called a heap. The comparison of elements is performed with comparator function object less< T > by default, but you can supply a different comparator.

There are several common priority_queue operations. push inserts an element at the appropriate location based on priority order of the priority_queue (implemented by calling function push_back of the underlying container, then reordering the elements using heapsort). pop removes the highest-priority element of the priority_queue (implemented by calling function pop_back of the underlying container after removing the top element of the heap). top gets a reference to the top element of the priority_queue (implemented by calling function front of the underlying container). empty determines whether the priority_queue is empty (implemented by calling function empty of the underlying container). size gets the number of elements in the priority_queue (implemented by calling function size of the underlying container).

Performance Tip 22.20

Each of the common operations of a priority_queue is implemented as an inline function that calls the appropriate function of the underlying container. This avoids the overhead of a second function call.

Performance Tip 22.21

For the best performance, use class vector as the underlying container for a priority_queue.

Figure 22.25 demonstrates the priority_queue adapter class. Header file <queue> must be included to use class priority_queue.

```
1   // Fig. 22.25: Fig22_25.cpp
2   // Standard Library adapter priority_queue test program.
3   #include <iostream>
4   using std::cout;
5   using std::endl;
6
7   #include <queue> // priority_queue adapter definition
8
9   int main()
10  {
11      std::priority_queue< double > priorities; // create priority_queue
12
```

Fig. 22.25 | Standard Library priority_queue adapter class. (Part 1 of 2.)

```
13      // push elements onto priorities
14      priorities.push( 3.2 );
15      priorities.push( 9.8 );
16      priorities.push( 5.4 );
17
18      cout << "Popping from priorities: ";
19
20      // pop element from priority_queue
21      while ( !priorities.empty() )
22      {
23         cout << priorities.top() << ' '; // view top element
24         priorities.pop(); // remove top element
25      } // end while
26
27      cout << endl;
28      return 0;
29   } // end main
```

```
Popping from priorities: 9.8 5.4 3.2
```

Fig. 22.25 | Standard Library `priority_queue` adapter class.   (Part 2 of 2.)

Line 11 instantiates a `priority_queue` that stores `double` values and uses a `vector` as the underlying data structure. Lines 14–16 use function `push` to add elements to the `priority_queue`. The `while` statement in lines 21–25 uses function `empty` (available in all containers) to determine whether the `priority_queue` is empty (line 21). While there are more elements, line 23 uses `priority_queue` function `top` to retrieve the highest-priority element in the `priority_queue` for output. Line 24 removes the highest-priority element in the `priority_queue` with function `pop` (available in all adapter classes).

22.5 **Algorithms**

Until the STL, class libraries of containers and algorithms were essentially incompatible among vendors. Early container libraries generally used inheritance and polymorphism, with the associated overhead of `virtual` function calls. Early libraries built the algorithms into the container classes as class behaviors. The STL separates the algorithms from the containers. This makes it much easier to add new algorithms. With the STL, the elements of containers are accessed through iterators. The next several subsections demonstrate many of the STL algorithms.

Performance Tip 22.22

The STL is implemented for efficiency. It avoids the overhead of `virtual` *function calls.*

Software Engineering Observation 22.8

STL algorithms do not depend on the implementation details of the containers on which they operate. As long as the container's (or array's) iterators satisfy the requirements of the algorithm, STL algorithms can work on C-style, pointer-based arrays, on STL containers and on user-defined data structures.

Software Engineering Observation 22.9

Algorithms can be added easily to the STL without modifying the container classes.

22.5.1 fill, fill_n, generate and generate_n

Figure 22.26 demonstrates algorithms fill, fill_n, generate and generate_n. Functions fill and fill_n set every element in a range of container elements to a specific value. Functions **generate** and **generate_n** use a generator function to create values for every element

```cpp
 1   // Fig. 22.26: Fig22_26.cpp
 2   // Standard Library algorithms fill, fill_n, generate and generate_n.
 3   #include <iostream>
 4   using std::cout;
 5   using std::endl;
 6
 7   #include <algorithm> // algorithm definitions
 8   #include <vector> // vector class-template definition
 9   #include <iterator> // ostream_iterator
10
11   char nextLetter(); // prototype of generator function
12
13   int main()
14   {
15      std::vector< char > chars( 10 );
16      std::ostream_iterator< char > output( cout, " " );
17      std::fill( chars.begin(), chars.end(), '5' ); // fill chars with 5s
18
19      cout << "Vector chars after filling with 5s:\n";
20      std::copy( chars.begin(), chars.end(), output );
21
22      // fill first five elements of chars with As
23      std::fill_n( chars.begin(), 5, 'A' );
24
25      cout << "\n\nVector chars after filling five elements with As:\n";
26      std::copy( chars.begin(), chars.end(), output );
27
28      // generate values for all elements of chars with nextLetter
29      std::generate( chars.begin(), chars.end(), nextLetter );
30
31      cout << "\n\nVector chars after generating letters A-J:\n";
32      std::copy( chars.begin(), chars.end(), output );
33
34      // generate values for first five elements of chars with nextLetter
35      std::generate_n( chars.begin(), 5, nextLetter );
36
37      cout << "\n\nVector chars after generating K-O for the"
38         << " first five elements:\n";
39      std::copy( chars.begin(), chars.end(), output );
40      cout << endl;
41      return 0;
42   } // end main
```

Fig. 22.26 | Algorithms fill, fill_n, generate and generate_n. (Part 1 of 2.)

```
43
44   // generator function returns next letter (starts with A)
45   char nextLetter()
46   {
47      static char letter = 'A';
48      return letter++;
49   } // end function nextLetter
```

```
Vector chars after filling with 5s:
5 5 5 5 5 5 5 5 5 5

Vector chars after filling five elements with As:
A A A A A 5 5 5 5 5

Vector chars after generating letters A-J:
A B C D E F G H I J

Vector chars after generating K-O for the first five elements:
K L M N O F G H I J
```

Fig. 22.26 | Algorithms `fill`, `fill_n`, `generate` and `generate_n`. (Part 2 of 2.)

in a range of container elements. The generator function takes no arguments and returns a value that can be placed in an element of the container.

Line 15 defines a 10-element `vector` that stores `char` values. Line 17 uses function `fill` to place the character `'5'` in every element of `vector chars` from `chars.begin()` up to, but not including, `chars.end()`. Note that the iterators supplied as the first and second argument must be at least forward iterators (i.e., they can be used for both input from a container and output to a container in the forward direction).

Line 23 uses function `fill_n` to place the character `'A'` in the first five elements of `vector chars`. The iterator supplied as the first argument must be at least an output iterator (i.e., it can be used for output to a container in the forward direction). The second argument specifies the number of elements to fill. The third argument specifies the value to place in each element.

Line 29 uses function `generate` to place the result of a call to generator function `nextLetter` in every element of `vector chars` from `chars.begin()` up to, but not including, `chars.end()`. The iterators supplied as the first and second arguments must be at least forward iterators. Function `nextLetter` (lines 45–49) begins with the character `'A'` maintained in a `static` local variable. The statement in line 48 postincrements the value of `letter` and returns the old value of `letter` each time `nextLetter` is called.

Line 35 uses function `generate_n` to place the result of a call to generator function `nextLetter` in five elements of `vector chars`, starting from `chars.begin()`. The iterator supplied as the first argument must be at least an output iterator.

22.5.2 equal, mismatch and lexicographical_compare

Figure 22.27 demonstrates comparing sequences of values for equality using algorithms `equal`, `mismatch` and `lexicographical_compare`.

Line 29 uses function **equal** to compare two sequences of values for equality. Each sequence need not necessarily contain the same number of elements—equal returns `false`

```
 1   // Fig. 22.27: Fig22_27.cpp
 2   // Standard Library functions equal, mismatch and lexicographical_compare.
 3   #include <iostream>
 4   using std::cout;
 5   using std::endl;
 6
 7   #include <algorithm> // algorithm definitions
 8   #include <vector> // vector class-template definition
 9   #include <iterator> // ostream_iterator
10
11   int main()
12   {
13      const int SIZE = 10;
14      int a1[ SIZE ] = { 1, 2, 3, 4, 5, 6, 7, 8, 9, 10 };
15      int a2[ SIZE ] = { 1, 2, 3, 4, 1000, 6, 7, 8, 9, 10 };
16      std::vector< int > v1( a1, a1 + SIZE ); // copy of a1
17      std::vector< int > v2( a1, a1 + SIZE ); // copy of a1
18      std::vector< int > v3( a2, a2 + SIZE ); // copy of a2
19      std::ostream_iterator< int > output( cout, " " );
20
21      cout << "Vector v1 contains: ";
22      std::copy( v1.begin(), v1.end(), output );
23      cout << "\nVector v2 contains: ";
24      std::copy( v2.begin(), v2.end(), output );
25      cout << "\nVector v3 contains: ";
26      std::copy( v3.begin(), v3.end(), output );
27
28      // compare vectors v1 and v2 for equality
29      bool result = std::equal( v1.begin(), v1.end(), v2.begin() );
30      cout << "\n\nVector v1 " << ( result ? "is" : "is not" )
31         << " equal to vector v2.\n";
32
33      // compare vectors v1 and v3 for equality
34      result = std::equal( v1.begin(), v1.end(), v3.begin() );
35      cout << "Vector v1 " << ( result ? "is" : "is not" )
36         << " equal to vector v3.\n";
37
38      // location represents pair of vector iterators
39      std::pair< std::vector< int >::iterator,
40         std::vector< int >::iterator > location;
41
42      // check for mismatch between v1 and v3
43      location = std::mismatch( v1.begin(), v1.end(), v3.begin() );
44      cout << "\nThere is a mismatch between v1 and v3 at location "
45         << ( location.first - v1.begin() ) << "\nwhere v1 contains "
46         << *location.first << " and v3 contains " << *location.second
47         << "\n\n";
48
49      char c1[ SIZE ] = "HELLO";
50      char c2[ SIZE ] = "BYE BYE";
51
52      // perform lexicographical comparison of c1 and c2
53      result = std::lexicographical_compare( c1, c1 + SIZE, c2, c2 + SIZE );
```

Fig. 22.27 | Algorithms equal, mismatch and lexicographical_compare. (Part 1 of 2.)

```
54      cout << c1 << ( result ? " is less than " :
55         " is greater than or equal to " ) << c2 << endl;
56      return 0;
57   } // end main
```

```
Vector v1 contains: 1 2 3 4 5 6 7 8 9 10
Vector v2 contains: 1 2 3 4 5 6 7 8 9 10
Vector v3 contains: 1 2 3 4 1000 6 7 8 9 10

Vector v1 is equal to vector v2.
Vector v1 is not equal to vector v3.

There is a mismatch between v1 and v3 at location 4
where v1 contains 5 and v3 contains 1000

HELLO is greater than or equal to BYE BYE
```

Fig. 22.27 | Algorithms equal, mismatch and lexicographical_compare. (Part 2 of 2.)

if the sequences are not of the same length. The == operator (whether built-in or over-loaded) performs the comparison of the elements. In this example, the elements in vector v1 from v1.begin() up to, but not including, v1.end() are compared to the elements in vector v2 starting from v2.begin(). In this example, v1 and v2 are equal. The three iter-ator arguments must be at least input iterators (i.e., they can be used for input from a sequence in the forward direction). Line 34 uses function equal to compare vectors v1 and v3, which are not equal.

There is another version of function equal that takes a binary predicate function as a fourth parameter. The binary predicate function receives the two elements being com-pared and returns a bool value indicating whether the elements are equal. This can be useful in sequences that store objects or pointers to values rather than actual values, because you can define one or more comparisons. For example, you can compare Employee objects for age, social security number, or location rather than comparing entire objects. You can compare what pointers refer to rather than comparing the pointer values (i.e., the addresses stored in the pointers).

Lines 39–43 begin by instantiating a pair of iterators called location for a vector of integers. This object stores the result of the call to mismatch (line 43). Function mismatch compares two sequences of values and returns a pair of iterators indicating the location in each sequence of the mismatched elements. If all the elements match, the two iterators in the pair are equal to the last iterator for each sequence. The three iterator arguments must be at least input iterators. Line 45 determines the actual location of the mismatch in the vectors with the expression location.first - v1.begin(). The result of this calculation is the number of elements between the iterators (this is analogous to pointer arithmetic, which we studied in Chapter 8). This corresponds to the element number in this example, because the comparison is performed from the beginning of each vector. As with function equal, there is another version of function mismatch that takes a binary predicate function as a fourth parameter.

Line 53 uses function lexicographical_compare to compare the contents of two character arrays. This function's four iterator arguments must be at least input iterators. As you know, pointers into arrays are random-access iterators. The first two iterator arguments specify the range of locations in the first sequence. The last two specify the range of locations in the second sequence. While iterating through the sequences, the `lexicographical_compare` checks if the element in the first sequence is less than the corresponding element in the second sequence. If so, the function returns `true`. If the element in the first sequence is greater than or equal to the element in the second sequence, the function returns `false`. This function can be used to arrange sequences lexicographically. Typically, such sequences contain strings.

22.5.3 remove, remove_if, remove_copy and remove_copy_if

Figure 22.28 demonstrates removing values from a sequence with algorithms `remove`, `remove_if`, `remove_copy` and `remove_copy_if`.

Line 26 uses function `remove` to eliminate all elements with the value 10 in the range from `v.begin()` up to, but not including, `v.end()` from `v`. The first two iterator arguments must be forward iterators so that the algorithm can modify the elements in the sequence. This function does not modify the number of elements in the `vector` or destroy the eliminated elements, but it does move all elements that are not eliminated toward the beginning of the `vector`. The function returns an iterator positioned after the last `vector` element that was not deleted. Elements from the iterator position to the end of the `vector` have undefined values (in this example, each "undefined" position has value 0).

Line 36 uses function `remove_copy` to copy all elements that do not have the value 10 in the range from `v2.begin()` up to, but not including, `v2.end()` from `v2`. The elements are placed in `c`, starting at position `c.begin()`. The iterators supplied as the first two arguments must be input iterators. The iterator supplied as the third argument must be an output iterator so that the element being copied can be inserted into the copy location. This function returns an iterator positioned after the last element copied into `vector c`. Note, in line 31, the use of the `vector` constructor that receives the number of elements in the `vector` and the initial values of those elements.

```
1   // Fig. 22.28: Fig22_28.cpp
2   // Standard Library functions remove, remove_if,
3   // remove_copy and remove_copy_if.
4   #include <iostream>
5   using std::cout;
6   using std::endl;
7
8   #include <algorithm> // algorithm definitions
9   #include <vector> // vector class-template definition
10  #include <iterator> // ostream_iterator
11
12  bool greater9( int ); // prototype
13
14  int main()
15  {
16     const int SIZE = 10;
17     int a[ SIZE ] = { 10, 2, 10, 4, 16, 6, 14, 8, 12, 10 };
18     std::ostream_iterator< int > output( cout, " " );
```

Fig. 22.28 | Algorithms remove, remove_if, remove_copy and remove_copy_if. (Part 1 of 3.)

```
19    std::vector< int > v( a, a + SIZE ); // copy of a
20    std::vector< int >::iterator newLastElement;
21
22    cout << "Vector v before removing all 10s:\n    ";
23    std::copy( v.begin(), v.end(), output );
24
25    // remove all 10s from v
26    newLastElement = std::remove( v.begin(), v.end(), 10 );
27    cout << "\nVector v after removing all 10s:\n    ";
28    std::copy( v.begin(), newLastElement, output );
29
30    std::vector< int > v2( a, a + SIZE ); // copy of a
31    std::vector< int > c( SIZE, 0 ); // instantiate vector c
32    cout << "\n\nVector v2 before removing all 10s and copying:\n    ";
33    std::copy( v2.begin(), v2.end(), output );
34
35    // copy from v2 to c, removing 10s in the process
36    std::remove_copy( v2.begin(), v2.end(), c.begin(), 10 );
37    cout << "\nVector c after removing all 10s from v2:\n    ";
38    std::copy( c.begin(), c.end(), output );
39
40    std::vector< int > v3( a, a + SIZE ); // copy of a
41    cout << "\n\nVector v3 before removing all elements"
42       << "\ngreater than 9:\n    ";
43    std::copy( v3.begin(), v3.end(), output );
44
45    // remove elements greater than 9 from v3
46    newLastElement = std::remove_if( v3.begin(), v3.end(), greater9 );
47    cout << "\nVector v3 after removing all elements"
48       << "\ngreater than 9:\n    ";
49    std::copy( v3.begin(), newLastElement, output );
50
51    std::vector< int > v4( a, a + SIZE ); // copy of a
52    std::vector< int > c2( SIZE, 0 ); // instantiate vector c2
53    cout << "\n\nVector v4 before removing all elements"
54       << "\ngreater than 9 and copying:\n    ";
55    std::copy( v4.begin(), v4.end(), output );
56
57    // copy elements from v4 to c2, removing elements greater
58    // than 9 in the process
59    std::remove_copy_if( v4.begin(), v4.end(), c2.begin(), greater9 );
60    cout << "\nVector c2 after removing all elements"
61       << "\ngreater than 9 from v4:\n    ";
62    std::copy( c2.begin(), c2.end(), output );
63    cout << endl;
64    return 0;
65 } // end main
66
67 // determine whether argument is greater than 9
68 bool greater9( int x )
69 {
70    return x > 9;
71 } // end function greater9
```

Fig. 22.28 | Algorithms remove, remove_if, remove_copy and remove_copy_if. (Part 2 of 3.)

```
Vector v before removing all 10s:
   10 2 10 4 16 6 14 8 12 10
Vector v after removing all 10s:
   2 4 16 6 14 8 12

Vector v2 before removing all 10s and copying:
   10 2 10 4 16 6 14 8 12 10
Vector c after removing all 10s from v2:
   2 4 16 6 14 8 12 0 0 0

Vector v3 before removing all elements
greater than 9:
   10 2 10 4 16 6 14 8 12 10
Vector v3 after removing all elements
greater than 9:
   2 4 6 8

Vector v4 before removing all elements
greater than 9 and copying:
   10 2 10 4 16 6 14 8 12 10
Vector c2 after removing all elements
greater than 9 from v4:
   2 4 6 8 0 0 0 0 0 0
```

Fig. 22.28 | Algorithms remove, remove_if, remove_copy and remove_copy_if. (Part 3 of 3.)

Line 46 uses function `remove_if` to delete all those elements in the range from v3.begin() up to, but not including, v3.end() from v3 for which our user-defined unary predicate function greater9 returns true. Function greater9 (defined in lines 68–71) returns true if the value passed to it is greater than 9; otherwise, it returns false. The iterators supplied as the first two arguments must be forward iterators so that the algorithm can modify the elements in the sequence. This function does not modify the number of elements in the vector, but it does move to the beginning of the vector all elements that are not eliminated. This function returns an iterator positioned after the last element in the vector that was not deleted. All elements from the iterator position to the end of the vector have undefined values.

Line 59 uses function `remove_copy_if` to copy all those elements in the range from v4.begin() up to, but not including, v4.end() from v4 for which the unary predicate function greater9 returns true. The elements are placed in c2, starting at position c2.begin(). The iterators supplied as the first two arguments must be input iterators. The iterator supplied as the third argument must be an output iterator so that the element being copied can be inserted into the copy location. This function returns an iterator positioned after the last element copied into c2.

22.5.4 replace, replace_if, replace_copy and replace_copy_if

Figure 22.29 demonstrates replacing values from a sequence using algorithms replace, replace_if, replace_copy and replace_copy_if.

Line 25 uses function `replace` to replace all elements with the value 10 in the range from v1.begin() up to, but not including, v1.end() in v1 with the new value 100. The iterators supplied as the first two arguments must be forward iterators so that the algorithm can modify the elements in the sequence.

```
 1   // Fig. 22.29: Fig22_29.cpp
 2   // Standard Library functions replace, replace_if,
 3   // replace_copy and replace_copy_if.
 4   #include <iostream>
 5   using std::cout;
 6   using std::endl;
 7
 8   #include <algorithm>
 9   #include <vector>
10   #include <iterator> // ostream_iterator
11
12   bool greater9( int ); // predicate function prototype
13
14   int main()
15   {
16      const int SIZE = 10;
17      int a[ SIZE ] = { 10, 2, 10, 4, 16, 6, 14, 8, 12, 10 };
18      std::ostream_iterator< int > output( cout, " " );
19
20      std::vector< int > v1( a, a + SIZE ); // copy of a
21      cout << "Vector v1 before replacing all 10s:\n   ";
22      std::copy( v1.begin(), v1.end(), output );
23
24      // replace all 10s in v1 with 100
25      std::replace( v1.begin(), v1.end(), 10, 100 );
26      cout << "\nVector v1 after replacing 10s with 100s:\n   ";
27      std::copy( v1.begin(), v1.end(), output );
28
29      std::vector< int > v2( a, a + SIZE ); // copy of a
30      std::vector< int > c1( SIZE ); // instantiate vector c1
31      cout << "\n\nVector v2 before replacing all 10s and copying:\n   ";
32      std::copy( v2.begin(), v2.end(), output );
33
34      // copy from v2 to c1, replacing 10s with 100s
35      std::replace_copy( v2.begin(), v2.end(), c1.begin(), 10, 100 );
36      cout << "\nVector c1 after replacing all 10s in v2:\n   ";
37      std::copy( c1.begin(), c1.end(), output );
38
39      std::vector< int > v3( a, a + SIZE ); // copy of a
40      cout << "\n\nVector v3 before replacing values greater than 9:\n   ";
41      std::copy( v3.begin(), v3.end(), output );
42
43      // replace values greater than 9 in v3 with 100
44      std::replace_if( v3.begin(), v3.end(), greater9, 100 );
45      cout << "\nVector v3 after replacing all values greater"
46         << "\nthan 9 with 100s:\n   ";
47      std::copy( v3.begin(), v3.end(), output );
48
49      std::vector< int > v4( a, a + SIZE ); // copy of a
50      std::vector< int > c2( SIZE ); // instantiate vector c2'
```

Fig. 22.29 | Algorithms replace, replace_if, replace_copy and replace_copy_if. (Part 1 of 2.)

```
51        cout << "\n\nVector v4 before replacing all values greater "
52           << "than 9 and copying:\n    ";
53        std::copy( v4.begin(), v4.end(), output );
54
55        // copy v4 to c2, replacing elements greater than 9 with 100
56        std::replace_copy_if(
57           v4.begin(), v4.end(), c2.begin(), greater9, 100 );
58        cout << "\nVector c2 after replacing all values greater "
59           << "than 9 in v4:\n    ";
60        std::copy( c2.begin(), c2.end(), output );
61        cout << endl;
62        return 0;
63    } // end main
64
65    // determine whether argument is greater than 9
66    bool greater9( int x )
67    {
68        return x > 9;
69    } // end function greater9
```

```
Vector v1 before replacing all 10s:
   10 2 10 4 16 6 14 8 12 10
Vector v1 after replacing 10s with 100s:
   100 2 100 4 16 6 14 8 12 100

Vector v2 before replacing all 10s and copying:
   10 2 10 4 16 6 14 8 12 10
Vector c1 after replacing all 10s in v2:
   100 2 100 4 16 6 14 8 12 100

Vector v3 before replacing values greater than 9:
   10 2 10 4 16 6 14 8 12 10
Vector v3 after replacing all values greater
than 9 with 100s:
   100 2 100 4 100 6 100 8 100 100

Vector v4 before replacing all values greater than 9 and copying:
   10 2 10 4 16 6 14 8 12 10
Vector c2 after replacing all values greater than 9 in v4:
   100 2 100 4 100 6 100 8 100 100
```

Fig. 22.29 | Algorithms `replace`, `replace_if`, `replace_copy` and `replace_copy_if`. (Part 2 of 2.)

Line 35 uses function `replace_copy` to copy all elements in the range from `v2.begin()` up to, but not including, `v2.end()` from v2, replacing all elements with the value 10 with the new value 100. The elements are copied into c1, starting at position `c1.begin()`. The iterators supplied as the first two arguments must be input iterators. The iterator supplied as the third argument must be an output iterator so that the element being copied can be inserted into the copy location. This function returns an iterator positioned after the last element copied into c1.

Line 44 uses function `replace_if` to replace all those elements in the range from `v3.begin()` up to, but not including, `v3.end()` in v3 for which the unary predicate function `greater9` returns `true`. Function `greater9` (defined in lines 66–69) returns `true` if the value passed to it is greater than 9; otherwise, it returns `false`. The value 100 replaces each value greater than 9. The iterators supplied as the first two arguments must be forward iterators so that the algorithm can modify the elements in the sequence.

Lines 56–57 use function `replace_copy_if` to copy all elements in the range from `v4.begin()` up to, but not including, `v4.end()` from v4. Elements for which the unary predicate function `greater9` returns `true` are replaced with the value 100. The elements are placed in c2, starting at position `c2.begin()`. The iterators supplied as the first two arguments must be input iterators. The iterator supplied as the third argument must be an output iterator so that the element being copied can be inserted into the copy location. This function returns an iterator positioned after the last element copied into c2.

22.5.5 Mathematical Algorithms

Figure 22.30 demonstrates several common mathematical algorithms from the STL, including `random_shuffle`, `count`, `count_if`, `min_element`, `max_element`, `accumulate`, `for_each` and `transform`.

```cpp
1   // Fig. 22.30: Fig22_30.cpp
2   // Mathematical algorithms of the Standard Library.
3   #include <iostream>
4   using std::cout;
5   using std::endl;
6
7   #include <algorithm> // algorithm definitions
8   #include <numeric> // accumulate is defined here
9   #include <vector>
10  #include <iterator>
11
12  bool greater9( int ); // predicate function prototype
13  void outputSquare( int ); // output square of a value
14  int calculateCube( int ); // calculate cube of a value
15
16  int main()
17  {
18     const int SIZE = 10;
19     int a1[ SIZE ] = { 1, 2, 3, 4, 5, 6, 7, 8, 9, 10 };
20     std::vector< int > v( a1, a1 + SIZE ); // copy of a1
21     std::ostream_iterator< int > output( cout, " " );
22
23     cout << "Vector v before random_shuffle: ";
24     std::copy( v.begin(), v.end(), output );
25
26     std::random_shuffle( v.begin(), v.end() ); // shuffle elements of v
27     cout << "\nVector v after random_shuffle: ";
28     std::copy( v.begin(), v.end(), output );
29
30     int a2[ SIZE ] = { 100, 2, 8, 1, 50, 3, 8, 8, 9, 10 };
31     std::vector< int > v2( a2, a2 + SIZE ); // copy of a2
32     cout << "\n\nVector v2 contains: ";
33     std::copy( v2.begin(), v2.end(), output );
```

Fig. 22.30 | Mathematical algorithms of the Standard Library. (Part 1 of 3.)

```
34
35      // count number of elements in v2 with value 8
36      int result = std::count( v2.begin(), v2.end(), 8 );
37      cout << "\nNumber of elements matching 8: " << result;
38
39      // count number of elements in v2 that are greater than 9
40      result = std::count_if( v2.begin(), v2.end(), greater9 );
41      cout << "\nNumber of elements greater than 9: " << result;
42
43      // locate minimum element in v2
44      cout << "\n\nMinimum element in Vector v2 is: "
45         << *( std::min_element( v2.begin(), v2.end() ) );
46
47      // locate maximum element in v2
48      cout << "\nMaximum element in Vector v2 is: "
49         << *( std::max_element( v2.begin(), v2.end() ) );
50
51      // calculate sum of elements in v
52      cout << "\n\nThe total of the elements in Vector v is: "
53         << std::accumulate( v.begin(), v.end(), 0 );
54
55      // output square of every element in v
56      cout << "\n\nThe square of every integer in Vector v is:\n";
57      std::for_each( v.begin(), v.end(), outputSquare );
58
59      std::vector< int > cubes( SIZE ); // instantiate vector cubes
60
61      // calculate cube of each element in v; place results in cubes
62      std::transform( v.begin(), v.end(), cubes.begin(), calculateCube );
63      cout << "\n\nThe cube of every integer in Vector v is:\n";
64      std::copy( cubes.begin(), cubes.end(), output );
65      cout << endl;
66      return 0;
67   } // end main
68
69   // determine whether argument is greater than 9
70   bool greater9( int value )
71   {
72      return value > 9;
73   } // end function greater9
74
75   // output square of argument
76   void outputSquare( int value )
77   {
78      cout << value * value << ' ';
79   } // end function outputSquare
80
81   // return cube of argument
82   int calculateCube( int value )
83   {
84      return value * value * value;
85   } // end function calculateCube
```

Fig. 22.30 | Mathematical algorithms of the Standard Library. (Part 2 of 3.)

```
Vector v before random_shuffle: 1 2 3 4 5 6 7 8 9 10
Vector v after random_shuffle: 5 4 1 3 7 8 9 10 6 2

Vector v2 contains: 100 2 8 1 50 3 8 8 9 10
Number of elements matching 8: 3
Number of elements greater than 9: 3

Minimum element in Vector v2 is: 1
Maximum element in Vector v2 is: 100

The total of the elements in Vector v is: 55

The square of every integer in Vector v is:
25 16 1 9 49 64 81 100 36 4

The cube of every integer in Vector v is:
125 64 1 27 343 512 729 1000 216 8
```

Fig. 22.30 | Mathematical algorithms of the Standard Library. (Part 3 of 3.)

Line 26 uses function `random_shuffle` to reorder randomly the elements in the range from v.begin() up to, but not including, v.end() in v. This function takes two random-access iterator arguments.

Line 36 uses function `count` to count the elements with the value 8 in the range from v2.begin() up to, but not including, v2.end() in v2. This function requires its two iterator arguments to be at least input iterators.

Line 40 uses function `count_if` to count elements in the range from v2.begin() up to, but not including, v2.end() in v2 for which the predicate function greater9 returns true. Function count_if requires its two iterator arguments to be at least input iterators.

Line 45 uses function `min_element` to locate the smallest element in the range from v2.begin() up to, but not including, v2.end(). The function returns a forward iterator located at the smallest element, or v2.end() if the range is empty. The function's two iterator arguments must be at least input iterators. A second version of this function takes as its third argument a binary function that compares two elements in the sequence. This function returns the bool value true if the first argument is less than the second.

Good Programming Practice 22.2

It is a good practice to check that the range specified in a call to min_element is not empty and that the return value is not the "past the end" iterator.

Line 49 uses function `max_element` to locate the largest element in the range from v2.begin() up to, but not including, v2.end() in v2. The function returns an input iterator located at the largest element. The function's two iterator arguments must be at least input iterators. A second version of this function takes as its third argument a binary predicate function that compares the elements in the sequence. The binary function takes two arguments and returns the bool value true if the first argument is less than the second.

Line 53 uses function `accumulate` (the template of which is in header file <numeric>) to sum the values in the range from v.begin() up to, but not including, v.end() in v. The function's two iterator arguments must be at least input iterators and its third argument represents the initial value of the total. A second version of this function takes as its fourth argument a general function that determines how elements are accumulated. The general function must take two arguments and return a result. The first argument to this function is the current value of the accumulation. The second argument is the value of the current element in the sequence being accumulated.

Line 57 uses function `for_each` to apply a general function to every element in the range from v.begin() up to, but not including, v.end(). The general function takes the current element as an argument and may modify that element (if it is received by reference). Function for_each requires its two iterator arguments to be at least input iterators.

Line 62 uses function `transform` to apply a general function to every element in the range from v.begin() up to, but not including, v.end() in v. The general function (the fourth argument) should take the current element as an argument, should not modify the element and should return the transformed value. Function transform requires its first two iterator arguments to be at least input iterators and its third argument to be at least an output iterator. The third argument specifies where the transformed values should be placed. Note that the third argument can equal the first. Another version of transform accepts five arguments—the first two arguments are input iterators that specify a range of elements from one source container, the third argument is an input iterator that specifies the first element in another source container, the fourth argument is an output iterator that specifies where the transformed values should be placed and the last argument is a general function that takes two arguments. This version of transform takes one element from each of the two input sources and applies the general function to that pair of elements, then places the transformed value at the location specified by the fourth argument.

22.5.6 Basic Searching and Sorting Algorithms

Figure 22.31 demonstrates some basic searching and sorting capabilities of the Standard Library, including `find`, `find_if`, `sort` and `binary_search`.

```
1   // Fig. 22.31: Fig22_31.cpp
2   // Standard Library search and sort algorithms.
3   #include <iostream>
4   using std::cout;
5   using std::endl;
6
7   #include <algorithm> // algorithm definitions
8   #include <vector> // vector class-template definition
9   #include <iterator>
10
11  bool greater10( int value ); // predicate function prototype
12
13  int main()
14  {
15     const int SIZE = 10;
16     int a[ SIZE ] = { 10, 2, 17, 5, 16, 8, 13, 11, 20, 7 };
17     std::vector< int > v( a, a + SIZE ); // copy of a
18     std::ostream_iterator< int > output( cout, " " );
19
20     cout << "Vector v contains: ";
21     std::copy( v.begin(), v.end(), output ); // display output vector
22
```

Fig. 22.31 | Basic searching and sorting algorithms of the Standard Library. (Part 1 of 3.)

```
23      // locate first occurrence of 16 in v
24      std::vector< int >::iterator location;
25      location = std::find( v.begin(), v.end(), 16 );
26
27      if ( location != v.end() ) // found 16
28          cout << "\n\nFound 16 at location " << ( location - v.begin() );
29      else // 16 not found
30          cout << "\n\n16 not found";
31
32      // locate first occurrence of 100 in v
33      location = std::find( v.begin(), v.end(), 100 );
34
35      if ( location != v.end() ) // found 100
36          cout << "\nFound 100 at location " << ( location - v.begin() );
37      else // 100 not found
38          cout << "\n100 not found";
39
40      // locate first occurrence of value greater than 10 in v
41      location = std::find_if( v.begin(), v.end(), greater10 );
42
43      if ( location != v.end() ) // found value greater than 10
44          cout << "\n\nThe first value greater than 10 is " << *location
45              << "\nfound at location " << ( location - v.begin() );
46      else // value greater than 10 not found
47          cout << "\n\nNo values greater than 10 were found";
48
49      // sort elements of v
50      std::sort( v.begin(), v.end() );
51      cout << "\n\nVector v after sort: ";
52      std::copy( v.begin(), v.end(), output );
53
54      // use binary_search to locate 13 in v
55      if ( std::binary_search( v.begin(), v.end(), 13 ) )
56          cout << "\n\n13 was found in v";
57      else
58          cout << "\n\n13 was not found in v";
59
60      // use binary_search to locate 100 in v
61      if ( std::binary_search( v.begin(), v.end(), 100 ) )
62          cout << "\n100 was found in v";
63      else
64          cout << "\n100 was not found in v";
65
66      cout << endl;
67      return 0;
68  } // end main
69
70  // determine whether argument is greater than 10
71  bool greater10( int value )
72  {
73      return value > 10;
74  } // end function greater10
```

Fig. 22.31 | Basic searching and sorting algorithms of the Standard Library. (Part 2 of 3.)

```
Vector v contains: 10 2 17 5 16 8 13 11 20 7

Found 16 at location 4
100 not found

The first value greater than 10 is 17
found at location 2

Vector v after sort: 2 5 7 8 10 11 13 16 17 20

13 was found in v
100 was not found in v
```

Fig. 22.31 | Basic searching and sorting algorithms of the Standard Library. (Part 3 of 3.)

Line 25 uses function find to locate the value 16 in the range from v.begin() up to, but not including, v.end() in v. The function requires its two iterator arguments to be at least input iterators and returns an input iterator that either is positioned at the first element containing the value or indicates the end of the sequence (as is the case in line 33).

Line 41 uses function find_if to locate the first value in the range from v.begin() up to, but not including, v.end() in v for which the unary predicate function greater10 returns true. Function greater10 (defined in lines 71–74) takes an integer and returns a bool value indicating whether the integer argument is greater than 10. Function find_if requires its two iterator arguments to be at least input iterators. The function returns an input iterator that either is positioned at the first element containing a value for which the predicate function returns true or indicates the end of the sequence.

Line 50 uses function sort to arrange the elements in the range from v.begin() up to, but not including, v.end() in v in ascending order. The function requires its two iterator arguments to be random-access iterators. A second version of this function takes a third argument that is a binary predicate function taking two arguments that are values in the sequence and returning a bool indicating the sorting order—if the return value is true, the two elements being compared are in sorted order.

Common Programming Error 22.5

Attempting to sort a container by using an iterator other than a random-access iterator is a compilation error. Function sort requires a random-access iterator.

Line 55 uses function binary_search to determine whether the value 13 is in the range from v.begin() up to, but not including, v.end() in v. The sequence of values must be sorted in ascending order first. Function binary_search requires its two iterator arguments to be at least forward iterators. The function returns a bool indicating whether the value was found in the sequence. Line 61 demonstrates a call to function binary_search in which the value is not found. A second version of this function takes a fourth argument that is a binary predicate function taking two arguments that are values in the sequence and returning a bool. The predicate function returns true if the two elements being compared are in sorted order. To obtain the location of the search key in the container, use the lower_bound or find algorithms.

22.5.7 swap, iter_swap and swap_ranges

Figure 22.32 demonstrates algorithms swap, iter_swap and swap_ranges for swapping elements. Line 20 uses function swap to exchange two values. In this example, the first and second elements of array a are exchanged. The function takes as arguments references to the two values being exchanged.

```cpp
1  // Fig. 22.32: Fig22_32.cpp
2  // Standard Library algorithms iter_swap, swap and swap_ranges.
3  #include <iostream>
4  using std::cout;
5  using std::endl;
6
7  #include <algorithm> // algorithm definitions
8  #include <iterator>
9
10 int main()
11 {
12    const int SIZE = 10;
13    int a[ SIZE ] = { 1, 2, 3, 4, 5, 6, 7, 8, 9, 10 };
14    std::ostream_iterator< int > output( cout, " " );
15
16    cout << "Array a contains:\n   ";
17    std::copy( a, a + SIZE, output ); // display array a
18
19    // swap elements at locations 0 and 1 of array a
20    std::swap( a[ 0 ], a[ 1 ] );
21
22    cout << "\nArray a after swapping a[0] and a[1] using swap:\n   ";
23    std::copy( a, a + SIZE, output ); // display array a
24
25    // use iterators to swap elements at locations 0 and 1 of array a
26    std::iter_swap( &a[ 0 ], &a[ 1 ] ); // swap with iterators
27    cout << "\nArray a after swapping a[0] and a[1] using iter_swap:\n   ";
28    std::copy( a, a + SIZE, output );
29
30    // swap elements in first five elements of array a with
31    // elements in last five elements of array a
32    std::swap_ranges( a, a + 5, a + 5 );
33
34    cout << "\nArray a after swapping the first five elements\n"
35       << "with the last five elements:\n   ";
36    std::copy( a, a + SIZE, output );
37    cout << endl;
38    return 0;
39 } // end main
```

```
Array a contains:
   1 2 3 4 5 6 7 8 9 10
Array a after swapping a[0] and a[1] using swap:
   2 1 3 4 5 6 7 8 9 10
Array a after swapping a[0] and a[1] using iter_swap:
   1 2 3 4 5 6 7 8 9 10
Array a after swapping the first five elements
with the last five elements:
   6 7 8 9 10 1 2 3 4 5
```

Fig. 22.32 | Demonstrating swap, iter_swap and swap_ranges.

Line 26 uses function `iter_swap` to exchange the two elements. The function takes two forward iterator arguments (in this case, pointers to elements of an array) and exchanges the values in the elements to which the iterators refer.

Line 32 uses function `swap_ranges` to exchange the elements from a up to, but not including, a + 5 with the elements beginning at position a + 5. The function requires three forward iterator arguments. The first two arguments specify the range of elements in the first sequence that will be exchanged with the elements in the second sequence starting from the iterator in the third argument. In this example, the two sequences of values are in the same array, but the sequences can be from different arrays or containers.

22.5.8 copy_backward, merge, unique and reverse

Figure 22.33 demonstrates STL algorithms `copy_backward`, `merge`, `unique` and `reverse`. Line 28 uses function `copy_backward` to copy elements in the range from v1.begin() up to, but not including, v1.end(), placing the elements in `results` by starting from the element before results.end() and working toward the beginning of the vector. The function returns an iterator positioned at the last element copied into the `results` (i.e., the beginning of `results`, because of the backward copy). The elements are placed in `results` in the same order as v1. This function requires three bidirectional iterator arguments (iterators that can be incremented and decremented to iterate forward and backward through a sequence, respectively). One difference between `copy_backward` and copy is that the iterator returned from copy is positioned *after* the last element copied and the one returned from copy_backward is positioned *at* the last element copied (i.e., the first element in the sequence). Also, `copy_backward` can manipulate overlapping ranges of elements in a container as long as the first element to copy is not in the destination range of elements.

```cpp
1   // Fig. 22.33: Fig22_33.cpp
2   // Standard Library functions copy_backward, merge, unique and reverse.
3   #include <iostream>
4   using std::cout;
5   using std::endl;
6
7   #include <algorithm> // algorithm definitions
8   #include <vector> // vector class-template definition
9   #include <iterator> // ostream_iterator
10
11  int main()
12  {
13      const int SIZE = 5;
14      int a1[ SIZE ] = { 1, 3, 5, 7, 9 };
15      int a2[ SIZE ] = { 2, 4, 5, 7, 9 };
16      std::vector< int > v1( a1, a1 + SIZE ); // copy of a1
17      std::vector< int > v2( a2, a2 + SIZE ); // copy of a2
18      std::ostream_iterator< int > output( cout, " " );
19
20      cout << "Vector v1 contains: ";
21      std::copy( v1.begin(), v1.end(), output ); // display vector output
22      cout << "\nVector v2 contains: ";
23      std::copy( v2.begin(), v2.end(), output ); // display vector output
```

Fig. 22.33 | Demonstrating copy_backward, merge, unique and reverse. (Part 1 of 2.)

```
24
25        std::vector< int > results( v1.size() );
26
27        // place elements of v1 into results in reverse order
28        std::copy_backward( v1.begin(), v1.end(), results.end() );
29        cout << "\n\nAfter copy_backward, results contains: ";
30        std::copy( results.begin(), results.end(), output );
31
32        std::vector< int > results2( v1.size() + v2.size() );
33
34        // merge elements of v1 and v2 into results2 in sorted order
35        std::merge( v1.begin(), v1.end(), v2.begin(), v2.end(),
36           results2.begin() );
37
38        cout << "\n\nAfter merge of v1 and v2 results2 contains:\n";
39        std::copy( results2.begin(), results2.end(), output );
40
41        // eliminate duplicate values from results2
42        std::vector< int >::iterator endLocation;
43        endLocation = std::unique( results2.begin(), results2.end() );
44
45        cout << "\n\nAfter unique results2 contains:\n";
46        std::copy( results2.begin(), endLocation, output );
47
48        cout << "\n\nVector v1 after reverse: ";
49        std::reverse( v1.begin(), v1.end() ); // reverse elements of v1
50        std::copy( v1.begin(), v1.end(), output );
51        cout << endl;
52        return 0;
53     } // end main
```

```
Vector v1 contains: 1 3 5 7 9
Vector v2 contains: 2 4 5 7 9

After copy_backward, results contains: 1 3 5 7 9

After merge of v1 and v2 results2 contains:
1 2 3 4 5 5 7 7 9 9

After unique results2 contains:
1 2 3 4 5 7 9

Vector v1 after reverse: 9 7 5 3 1
```

Fig. 22.33 | Demonstrating copy_backward, merge, unique and reverse. (Part 2 of 2.)

Lines 35–36 use function **merge** to combine two sorted ascending sequences of values into a third sorted ascending sequence. The function requires five iterator arguments. The first four must be at least input iterators and the last must be at least an output iterator. The first two arguments specify the range of elements in the first sorted sequence (v1), the second two arguments specify the range of elements in the second sorted sequence (v2) and the last argument specifies the starting location in the third sequence (results2) where the elements will be merged. A second version of this function takes as its sixth argument a binary predicate function that specifies the sorting order.

Note that line 32 creates vector `results2` with the number of elements `v1.size()` + `v2.size()`. Using the `merge` function as shown here requires that the sequence where the results are stored be at least the size of the two sequences being merged. If you do not want to allocate the number of elements for the resulting sequence before the `merge` operation, you can use the following statements:

```
std::vector< int > results2;
std::merge ( v1.begin(), v1.end(), v2.begin(), v2.end(),
    std::back_inserter( results2 ) );
```

The argument `std::back_inserter( results2 )` uses function template `back_inserter` (header file `<iterator>`) for the container `results2`. A `back_inserter` calls the container's default `push_back` function to insert an element at the end of the container. More importantly, if an element is inserted into a container that has no more space available, the container grows in size. Thus, the number of elements in the container does not have to be known in advance. There are two other inserters—`front_inserter` (to insert an element at the beginning of a container specified as its argument) and `inserter` (to insert an element before the iterator supplied as its second argument in the container supplied as its first argument).

Line 43 uses function `unique` on the sorted sequence of elements in the range from `results2.begin()` up to, but not including, `results2.end()` in `results2`. After this function is applied to a sorted sequence with duplicate values, only a single copy of each value remains in the sequence. The function takes two arguments that must be at least forward iterators. The function returns an iterator positioned after the last element in the sequence of unique values. The values of all elements in the container after the last unique value are undefined. A second version of this function takes as a third argument a binary predicate function specifying how to compare two elements for equality.

Line 49 uses function `reverse` to reverse all the elements in the range from `v1.begin()` up to, but not including, `v1.end()` in `v1`. The function takes two arguments that must be at least bidirectional iterators.

22.5.9 inplace_merge, unique_copy and reverse_copy

Figure 22.34 demonstrates STL algorithms `inplace_merge`, `unique_copy` and `reverse_copy`. Line 24 uses function `inplace_merge` to merge two sorted sequences of elements in the same container. In this example, the elements from `v1.begin()` up to, but not including, `v1.begin()` + 5 are merged with the elements from `v1.begin()` + 5 up to, but not including, `v1.end()`. This function requires its three iterator arguments to be at least bidirectional iterators. A second version of this function takes as a fourth argument a binary predicate function for comparing elements in the two sequences.

```
1  // Fig. 22.34: Fig22_34.cpp
2  // Standard Library algorithms inplace_merge,
3  // reverse_copy and unique_copy.
4  #include <iostream>
5  using std::cout;
6  using std::endl;
```

Fig. 22.34 | Demonstrating `inplace_merge`, `unique_copy` and `reverse_copy`. (Part 1 of 2.)

```
 7
 8    #include <algorithm> // algorithm definitions
 9    #include <vector> // vector class-template definition
10    #include <iterator> // back_inserter definition
11
12    int main()
13    {
14       const int SIZE = 10;
15       int a1[ SIZE ] = { 1, 3, 5, 7, 9, 1, 3, 5, 7, 9 };
16       std::vector< int > v1( a1, a1 + SIZE ); // copy of a
17       std::ostream_iterator< int > output( cout, " " );
18
19       cout << "Vector v1 contains: ";
20       std::copy( v1.begin(), v1.end(), output );
21
22       // merge first half of v1 with second half of v1 such that
23       // v1 contains sorted set of elements after merge
24       std::inplace_merge( v1.begin(), v1.begin() + 5, v1.end() );
25
26       cout << "\nAfter inplace_merge, v1 contains: ";
27       std::copy( v1.begin(), v1.end(), output );
28
29       std::vector< int > results1;
30
31       // copy only unique elements of v1 into results1
32       std::unique_copy(
33          v1.begin(), v1.end(), std::back_inserter( results1 ) );
34       cout << "\nAfter unique_copy results1 contains: ";
35       std::copy( results1.begin(), results1.end(), output );
36
37       std::vector< int > results2;
38
39       // copy elements of v1 into results2 in reverse order
40       std::reverse_copy(
41          v1.begin(), v1.end(), std::back_inserter( results2 ) );
42       cout << "\nAfter reverse_copy, results2 contains: ";
43       std::copy( results2.begin(), results2.end(), output );
44       cout << endl;
45       return 0;
46    } // end main
```

```
Vector v1 contains: 1 3 5 7 9 1 3 5 7 9
After inplace_merge, v1 contains: 1 1 3 3 5 5 7 7 9 9
After unique_copy results1 contains: 1 3 5 7 9
After reverse_copy, results2 contains: 9 9 7 7 5 5 3 3 1 1
```

Fig. 22.34 | Demonstrating `inplace_merge`, `unique_copy` and `reverse_copy`. (Part 2 of 2.)

Lines 32–33 use function `unique_copy` to make a copy of all the unique elements in the sorted sequence of values from `v1.begin()` up to, but not including, `v1.end()`. The copied elements are placed into vector `results1`. The first two arguments must be at least input iterators and the last must be at least an output iterator. In this example, we did not preallocate enough elements in `results1` to store all the elements copied from `v1`. Instead, we use function back_inserter (defined in header file <iterator>) to add elements to the end of v1. The back_inserter uses class vector's capability to insert elements at the end of the vector. Because the back_inserter inserts an element rather than replacing an existing element's value, the vector is able to grow to accommodate additional elements. A second version of the unique_copy function takes as a fourth argument a binary predicate function for comparing elements for equality.

Lines 40–41 use function **reverse_copy** to make a reversed copy of the elements in the range from v1.begin() up to, but not including, v1.end(). The copied elements are inserted into results2 using a back_inserter object to ensure that the vector can grow to accommodate the appropriate number of elements copied. Function reverse_copy requires its first two iterator arguments to be at least bidirectional iterators and its third to be at least an output iterator.

22.5.10 Set Operations

Figure 22.35 demonstrates Standard Library functions includes, set_difference, set_intersection, set_symmetric_difference and set_union for manipulating sets of sorted values. To demonstrate that Standard Library functions can be applied to arrays and containers, this example uses only arrays (remember, a pointer into an array is a random-access iterator).

Lines 27 and 33 call function **includes** in the conditions of if statements. Function includes compares two sets of sorted values to determine whether every element of the second set is in the first set. If so, includes returns true; otherwise, it returns false. The first two iterator arguments must be at least input iterators and must describe the first set of values. In line 27, the first set consists of the elements from a1 up to, but not including, a1 + SIZE1. The last two iterator arguments must be at least input iterators and must describe the second set of values. In this example, the second set consists of the elements from a2 up to, but not including, a2 + SIZE2. A second version of function includes takes a fifth argument that is a binary predicate function for comparing elements for equality.

```
1   // Fig. 22.35: Fig22_35.cpp
2   // Standard Library algorithms includes, set_difference,
3   // set_intersection, set_symmetric_difference and set_union.
4   #include <iostream>
5   using std::cout;
6   using std::endl;
7
8   #include <algorithm> // algorithm definitions
9   #include <iterator> // ostream_iterator
10
11  int main()
12  {
13     const int SIZE1 = 10, SIZE2 = 5, SIZE3 = 20;
14     int a1[ SIZE1 ] = { 1, 2, 3, 4, 5, 6, 7, 8, 9, 10 };
15     int a2[ SIZE2 ] = { 4, 5, 6, 7, 8 };
16     int a3[ SIZE2 ] = { 4, 5, 6, 11, 15 };
17     std::ostream_iterator< int > output( cout, " " );
18
```

Fig. 22.35 | set operations of the Standard Library. (Part 1 of 3.)

```
19      cout << "a1 contains: ";
20      std::copy( a1, a1 + SIZE1, output ); // display array a1
21      cout << "\na2 contains: ";
22      std::copy( a2, a2 + SIZE2, output ); // display array a2
23      cout << "\na3 contains: ";
24      std::copy( a3, a3 + SIZE2, output ); // display array a3
25
26      // determine whether set a2 is completely contained in a1
27      if ( std::includes( a1, a1 + SIZE1, a2, a2 + SIZE2 ) )
28         cout << "\n\na1 includes a2";
29      else
30         cout << "\n\na1 does not include a2";
31
32      // determine whether set a3 is completely contained in a1
33      if ( std::includes( a1, a1 + SIZE1, a3, a3 + SIZE2 ) )
34         cout << "\na1 includes a3";
35      else
36         cout << "\na1 does not include a3";
37
38      int difference[ SIZE1 ];
39
40      // determine elements of a1 not in a2
41      int *ptr = std::set_difference( a1, a1 + SIZE1,
42         a2, a2 + SIZE2, difference );
43      cout << "\n\nset_difference of a1 and a2 is: ";
44      std::copy( difference, ptr, output );
45
46      int intersection[ SIZE1 ];
47
48      // determine elements in both a1 and a2
49      ptr = std::set_intersection( a1, a1 + SIZE1,
50         a2, a2 + SIZE2, intersection );
51      cout << "\n\nset_intersection of a1 and a2 is: ";
52      std::copy( intersection, ptr, output );
53
54      int symmetric_difference[ SIZE1 + SIZE2 ];
55
56      // determine elements of a1 that are not in a2 and
57      // elements of a2 that are not in a1
58      ptr = std::set_symmetric_difference( a1, a1 + SIZE1,
59         a3, a3 + SIZE2, symmetric_difference );
60      cout << "\n\nset_symmetric_difference of a1 and a3 is: ";
61      std::copy( symmetric_difference, ptr, output );
62
63      int unionSet[ SIZE3 ];
64
65      // determine elements that are in either or both sets
66      ptr = std::set_union( a1, a1 + SIZE1, a3, a3 + SIZE2, unionSet );
67      cout << "\n\nset_union of a1 and a3 is: ";
68      std::copy( unionSet, ptr, output );
69      cout << endl;
70      return 0;
71   } // end main
```

Fig. 22.35 | set operations of the Standard Library. (Part 2 of 3.)

```
a1 contains: 1 2 3 4 5 6 7 8 9 10
a2 contains: 4 5 6 7 8
a3 contains: 4 5 6 11 15

a1 includes a2
a1 does not include a3

set_difference of a1 and a2 is: 1 2 3 9 10

set_intersection of a1 and a2 is: 4 5 6 7 8

set_symmetric_difference of a1 and a3 is: 1 2 3 7 8 9 10 11 15

set_union of a1 and a3 is: 1 2 3 4 5 6 7 8 9 10 11 15
```

Fig. 22.35 | set operations of the Standard Library. (Part 3 of 3.)

Lines 41–42 use function `set_difference` to find the elements from the first set of sorted values that are not in the second set of sorted values (both sets of values must be in ascending order). The elements that are different are copied into the fifth argument (in this case, the array `difference`). The first two iterator arguments must be at least input iterators for the first set of values. The next two iterator arguments must be at least input iterators for the second set of values. The fifth argument must be at least an output iterator indicating where to store a copy of the values that are different. The function returns an output iterator positioned immediately after the last value copied into the set to which the fifth argument points. A second version of function `set_difference` takes a sixth argument that is a binary predicate function indicating the order in which the elements were originally sorted. The two sequences must be sorted using the same comparison function.

Lines 49–50 use function `set_intersection` to determine the elements from the first set of sorted values that are in the second set of sorted values (both sets of values must be in ascending order). The elements common to both sets are copied into the fifth argument (in this case, array `intersection`). The first two iterator arguments must be at least input iterators for the first set of values. The next two iterator arguments must be at least input iterators for the second set of values. The fifth argument must be at least an output iterator indicating where to store a copy of the values that are the same. The function returns an output iterator positioned immediately after the last value copied into the set to which the fifth argument points. A second version of function `set_intersection` takes a sixth argument that is a binary predicate function indicating the order in which the elements were originally sorted. The two sequences must be sorted using the same comparison function.

Lines 58–59 use function `set_symmetric_difference` to determine the elements in the first set that are not in the second set and the elements in the second set that are not in the first set (both sets must be in ascending order). The elements that are different are copied from both sets into the fifth argument (the array `symmetric_difference`). The first two iterator arguments must be at least input iterators for the first set of values. The next two iterator arguments must be at least input iterators for the second set of values. The fifth argument must be at least an output iterator indicating where to store a copy of the values that are different. The function returns an output iterator positioned immediately after the last value copied into the set to which the fifth argument points. A second version of function `set_symmetric_difference` takes a sixth argument that is a binary predicate function indicating the order in which the elements were originally sorted. The two sequences must be sorted using the same comparison function.

Line 66 uses function `set_union` to create a set of all the elements that are in either or both of the two sorted sets (both sets of values must be in ascending order). The elements are copied from both sets into the fifth argument (in this case the array `unionSet`). Elements that appear in both sets are only copied from the first set. The first two iterator arguments must be at least input iterators for the first set of values. The next two iterator arguments must be at least input iterators for the second set of values. The fifth argument must be at least an output iterator indicating where to store the copied elements. The function returns an output iterator positioned immediately after the last value copied into the set to which the fifth argument points. A second version of `set_union` takes a sixth argument that is a binary predicate function indicating the order in which the elements were originally sorted. The two sequences must be sorted using the same comparison function.

22.5.11 `lower_bound`, `upper_bound` and `equal_range`

Figure 22.36 demonstrates functions `lower_bound`, `upper_bound` and `equal_range`. Line 24 uses function `lower_bound` to find the first location in a sorted sequence of values at which the third argument could be inserted in the sequence such that the sequence would still be sorted in ascending order. The first two iterator arguments must be at least forward iterators. The third argument is the value for which to determine the lower bound. The function returns a forward iterator pointing to the position at which the insert can occur. A second version of function `lower_bound` takes as a fourth argument a binary predicate function indicating the order in which the elements were originally sorted.

Line 30 uses function `upper_bound` to find the last location in a sorted sequence of values at which the third argument could be inserted in the sequence such that the sequence would still be sorted in ascending order. The first two iterator arguments must be at least forward iterators. The third argument is the value for which to determine the upper bound. The function returns a forward iterator pointing to the position at which the insert can occur. A second version of `upper_bound` takes as a fourth argument a binary predicate function indicating the order in which the elements were originally sorted.

```cpp
1   // Fig. 22.36: Fig22_36.cpp
2   // Standard Library functions lower_bound, upper_bound and
3   // equal_range for a sorted sequence of values.
4   #include <iostream>
5   using std::cout;
6   using std::endl;
7
8   #include <algorithm> // algorithm definitions
9   #include <vector> // vector class-template definition
10  #include <iterator> // ostream_iterator
11
12  int main()
13  {
14     const int SIZE = 10;
15     int a1[ SIZE ] = { 2, 2, 4, 4, 4, 6, 6, 6, 6, 8 };
```

Fig. 22.36 | Algorithms `lower_bound`, `upper_bound` and `equal_range`. (Part 1 of 3.)

```
16      std::vector< int > v( a1, a1 + SIZE ); // copy of a1
17      std::ostream_iterator< int > output( cout, " " );
18
19      cout << "Vector v contains:\n";
20      std::copy( v.begin(), v.end(), output );
21
22      // determine lower-bound insertion point for 6 in v
23      std::vector< int >::iterator lower;
24      lower = std::lower_bound( v.begin(), v.end(), 6 );
25      cout << "\n\nLower bound of 6 is element "
26         << ( lower - v.begin() ) << " of vector v";
27
28      // determine upper-bound insertion point for 6 in v
29      std::vector< int >::iterator upper;
30      upper = std::upper_bound( v.begin(), v.end(), 6 );
31      cout << "\nUpper bound of 6 is element "
32         << ( upper - v.begin() ) << " of vector v";
33
34      // use equal_range to determine both the lower- and
35      // upper-bound insertion points for 6
36      std::pair< std::vector< int >::iterator,
37              std::vector< int >::iterator > eq;
38      eq = std::equal_range( v.begin(), v.end(), 6 );
39      cout << "\nUsing equal_range:\n   Lower bound of 6 is element "
40         << ( eq.first - v.begin() ) << " of vector v";
41      cout << "\n   Upper bound of 6 is element "
42         << ( eq.second - v.begin() ) << " of vector v";
43      cout << "\n\nUse lower_bound to locate the first point\n"
44         << "at which 5 can be inserted in order";
45
46      // determine lower-bound insertion point for 5 in v
47      lower = std::lower_bound( v.begin(), v.end(), 5 );
48      cout << "\n   Lower bound of 5 is element "
49         << ( lower - v.begin() ) << " of vector v";
50      cout << "\n\nUse upper_bound to locate the last point\n"
51         << "at which 7 can be inserted in order";
52
53      // determine upper-bound insertion point for 7 in v
54      upper = std::upper_bound( v.begin(), v.end(), 7 );
55      cout << "\n   Upper bound of 7 is element "
56         << ( upper - v.begin() ) << " of vector v";
57      cout << "\n\nUse equal_range to locate the first and\n"
58         << "last point at which 5 can be inserted in order";
59
60      // use equal_range to determine both the lower- and
61      // upper-bound insertion points for 5
62      eq = std::equal_range( v.begin(), v.end(), 5 );
63      cout << "\n   Lower bound of 5 is element "
64         << ( eq.first - v.begin() ) << " of vector v";
65      cout << "\n   Upper bound of 5 is element "
66         << ( eq.second - v.begin() ) << " of vector v" << endl;
67      return 0;
68   } // end main
```

Fig. 22.36 | Algorithms `lower_bound`, `upper_bound` and `equal_range`. (Part 2 of 3.)

```
Vector v contains:
2 2 4 4 4 6 6 6 6 8

Lower bound of 6 is element 5 of vector v
Upper bound of 6 is element 9 of vector v
Using equal_range:
   Lower bound of 6 is element 5 of vector v
   Upper bound of 6 is element 9 of vector v

Use lower_bound to locate the first point
at which 5 can be inserted in order
   Lower bound of 5 is element 5 of vector v

Use upper_bound to locate the last point
at which 7 can be inserted in order
   Upper bound of 7 is element 9 of vector v

Use equal_range to locate the first and
last point at which 5 can be inserted in order
   Lower bound of 5 is element 5 of vector v
   Upper bound of 5 is element 5 of vector v
```

Fig. 22.36 | Algorithms `lower_bound`, `upper_bound` and `equal_range`. (Part 3 of 3.)

Line 38 uses function `equal_range` to return a `pair` of forward iterators containing the combined results of performing both a `lower_bound` and an `upper_bound` operation. The first two iterator arguments must be at least forward iterators. The third argument is the value for which to locate the equal range. The function returns a `pair` of forward iterators for the lower bound (`eq.first`) and upper bound (`eq.second`), respectively.

Functions `lower_bound`, `upper_bound` and `equal_range` are often used to locate insertion points in sorted sequences. Line 47 uses `lower_bound` to locate the first point at which 5 can be inserted in order in v. Line 54 uses `upper_bound` to locate the last point at which 7 can be inserted in order in v. Line 62 uses `equal_range` to locate the first and last points at which 5 can be inserted in order in v.

22.5.12 Heapsort

Figure 22.37 demonstrates the Standard Library functions for performing the heapsort sorting algorithm. Heapsort is a sorting algorithm in which an array of elements is arranged into a special binary tree called a heap. The key features of a heap are that the largest element is always at the top of the heap and the values of the children of any node in the binary tree are always less than or equal to that node's value. A heap arranged in this manner is often called a maxheap. Heapsort is discussed in detail in computer science courses called "Data Structures" and "Algorithms."

```
1   // Fig. 22.37: Fig22_37.cpp
2   // Standard Library algorithms push_heap, pop_heap,
3   // make_heap and sort_heap.
4   #include <iostream>
5   using std::cout;
6   using std::endl;
```

Fig. 22.37 | Using Standard Library functions to perform a heapsort. (Part 1 of 3.)

```
7
8   #include <algorithm>
9   #include <vector>
10  #include <iterator>
11
12  int main()
13  {
14     const int SIZE = 10;
15     int a[ SIZE ] = { 3, 100, 52, 77, 22, 31, 1, 98, 13, 40 };
16     std::vector< int > v( a, a + SIZE ); // copy of a
17     std::vector< int > v2;
18     std::ostream_iterator< int > output( cout, " " );
19
20     cout << "Vector v before make_heap:\n";
21     std::copy( v.begin(), v.end(), output );
22
23     std::make_heap( v.begin(), v.end() ); // create heap from vector v
24     cout << "\nVector v after make_heap:\n";
25     std::copy( v.begin(), v.end(), output );
26
27     std::sort_heap( v.begin(), v.end() ); // sort elements with sort_heap
28     cout << "\nVector v after sort_heap:\n";
29     std::copy( v.begin(), v.end(), output );
30
31     // perform the heapsort with push_heap and pop_heap
32     cout << "\n\nArray a contains: ";
33     std::copy( a, a + SIZE, output ); // display array a
34     cout << endl;
35
36     // place elements of array a into v2 and
37     // maintain elements of v2 in heap
38     for ( int i = 0; i < SIZE; i++ )
39     {
40        v2.push_back( a[ i ] );
41        std::push_heap( v2.begin(), v2.end() );
42        cout << "\nv2 after push_heap(a[" << i << "]): ";
43        std::copy( v2.begin(), v2.end(), output );
44     } // end for
45
46     cout << endl;
47
48     // remove elements from heap in sorted order
49     for ( unsigned int j = 0; j < v2.size(); j++ )
50     {
51        cout << "\nv2 after " << v2[ 0 ] << " popped from heap\n";
52        std::pop_heap( v2.begin(), v2.end() - j );
53        std::copy( v2.begin(), v2.end(), output );
54     } // end for
55
56     cout << endl;
57     return 0;
58  } // end main
```

Fig. 22.37 | Using Standard Library functions to perform a heapsort. (Part 2 of 3.)

```
Vector v before make_heap:
3 100 52 77 22 31 1 98 13 40
Vector v after make_heap:
100 98 52 77 40 31 1 3 13 22
Vector v after sort_heap:
1 3 13 22 31 40 52 77 98 100

Array a contains: 3 100 52 77 22 31 1 98 13 40

v2 after push_heap(a[0]): 3
v2 after push_heap(a[1]): 100 3
v2 after push_heap(a[2]): 100 3 52
v2 after push_heap(a[3]): 100 77 52 3
v2 after push_heap(a[4]): 100 77 52 3 22
v2 after push_heap(a[5]): 100 77 52 3 22 31
v2 after push_heap(a[6]): 100 77 52 3 22 31 1
v2 after push_heap(a[7]): 100 98 52 77 22 31 1 3
v2 after push_heap(a[8]): 100 98 52 77 22 31 1 3 13
v2 after push_heap(a[9]): 100 98 52 77 40 31 1 3 13 22

v2 after 100 popped from heap
98 77 52 22 40 31 1 3 13 100
v2 after 98 popped from heap
77 40 52 22 13 31 1 3 98 100
v2 after 77 popped from heap
52 40 31 22 13 3 1 77 98 100
v2 after 52 popped from heap
40 22 31 1 13 3 52 77 98 100
v2 after 40 popped from heap
31 22 3 1 13 40 52 77 98 100
v2 after 31 popped from heap
22 13 3 1 31 40 52 77 98 100
v2 after 22 popped from heap
13 1 3 22 31 40 52 77 98 100
v2 after 13 popped from heap
3 1 13 22 31 40 52 77 98 100
v2 after 3 popped from heap
1 3 13 22 31 40 52 77 98 100
v2 after 1 popped from heap
1 3 13 22 31 40 52 77 98 100
```

Fig. 22.37 | Using Standard Library functions to perform a heapsort. (Part 3 of 3.)

Line 23 uses function `make_heap` to take a sequence of values in the range from v.begin() up to, but not including, v.end() and create a heap that can be used to produce a sorted sequence. The two iterator arguments must be random-access iterators, so this function will work only with arrays, `vectors` and `deques`. A second version of this function takes as a third argument a binary predicate function for comparing values.

Line 27 uses function `sort_heap` to sort a sequence of values in the range from v.begin() up to, but not including, v.end() that are already arranged in a heap. The two iterator arguments must be random-access iterators. A second version of this function takes as a third argument a binary predicate function for comparing values.

Line 41 uses function `push_heap` to add a new value into a heap. We take one element of array a at a time, append that element to the end of vector v2 and perform the push_heap operation. If the appended element is the only element in the vector, the vector is already a heap. Otherwise, function push_heap rearranges the elements of the vector into a heap. Each time push_heap is called, it assumes that the last element currently in the vector (i.e., the one that is appended before the push_heap function call) is the element being added to the heap and that all other elements in the vector are already arranged as a heap. The two iterator arguments to push_heap must be random-access iterators. A second version of this function takes as a third argument a binary predicate function for comparing values.

Line 52 uses pop_heap to remove the top heap element. This function assumes that the elements in the range specified by its two random-access iterator arguments are already a heap. Repeatedly removing the top heap element results in a sorted sequence of values. Function pop_heap swaps the first heap element (v2.begin()) with the last heap element (the element before v2.end() - i), then ensures that the elements up to, but not including, the last element still form a heap. Notice in the output that, after the pop_heap operations, the vector is sorted in ascending order. A second version of this function takes as a third argument a binary predicate function for comparing values.

22.5.13 min and max

Algorithms min and max determine the minimum and the maximum of two elements, respectively. Figure 22.38 demonstrates min and max for int and char values.

22.5.14 STL Algorithms Not Covered in This Chapter

Figure 22.39 summarizes the STL algorithms that are not covered in this chapter.

```cpp
// Fig. 22.38: Fig22_38.cpp
// Standard Library algorithms min and max.
#include <iostream>
using std::cout;
using std::endl;

#include <algorithm>

int main()
{
   cout << "The minimum of 12 and 7 is: " << std::min( 12, 7 );
   cout << "\nThe maximum of 12 and 7 is: " << std::max( 12, 7 );
   cout << "\nThe minimum of 'G' and 'Z' is: " << std::min( 'G', 'Z' );
   cout << "\nThe maximum of 'G' and 'Z' is: " << std::max( 'G', 'Z' );
   cout << endl;
   return 0;
} // end main
```

```
The minimum of 12 and 7 is: 7
The maximum of 12 and 7 is: 12
The minimum of 'G' and 'Z' is: G
The maximum of 'G' and 'Z' is: Z
```

Fig. 22.38 | Algorithms min and max.

Algorithm	Description
inner_product	Calculate the sum of the products of two sequences by taking corresponding elements in each sequence, multiplying those elements and adding the result to a total.
adjacent_difference	Beginning with the second element in a sequence, calculate the difference (using operator –) between the current and previous elements, and store the result. The first two input iterator arguments indicate the range of elements in the container and the third indicates where the results should be stored. A second version of this algorithm takes as a fourth argument a binary function to perform a calculation between the current element and the previous element.
partial_sum	Calculate a running total (using operator +) of the values in a sequence. The first two input iterator arguments indicate the range of elements in the container and the third indicates where the results should be stored. A second version of this algorithm takes as a fourth argument a binary function that performs a calculation between the current value in the sequence and the running total.
nth_element	Use three random-access iterators to partition a range of elements. The first and last arguments represent the range of elements. The second argument is the partitioning element's location. After this algorithm executes, all elements before the partitioning element are less than that element and all elements after the partitioning element are greater than or equal to that element. A second version of this algorithm takes as a fourth argument a binary comparison function.
partition	This algorithm is similar to nth_element, but it requires less powerful bidirectional iterators, making it more flexible than nth_element. Algorithm partition requires two bidirectional iterators indicating the range of elements to partition. The third element is a unary predicate function that helps partition the elements so that all elements in the sequence for which the predicate is true are to the left (toward the beginning of the sequence) of all elements for which the predicate is false. A bidirectional iterator is returned indicating the first element in the sequence for which the predicate returns false.
stable_partition	This algorithm is similar to partition except that this algorithm guarantees that equivalent elements will be maintained in their original order.
next_permutation	Next lexicographical permutation of a sequence.
prev_permutation	Previous lexicographical permutation of a sequence.
rotate	Use three forward iterator arguments to rotate the sequence indicated by the first and last argument by the number of positions indicated by subtracting the first argument from the second argument. For example, the sequence 1, 2, 3, 4, 5 rotated by two positions would be 4, 5, 1, 2, 3.

Fig. 22.39 | Algorithms not covered in this chapter. (Part 1 of 2.)

Algorithm	Description
rotate_copy	This algorithm is identical to rotate except that the results are stored in a separate sequence indicated by the fourth argument—an output iterator. The two sequences must have the same number of elements.
adjacent_find	This algorithm returns an input iterator indicating the first of two identical adjacent elements in a sequence. If there are no identical adjacent elements, the iterator is positioned at the end of the sequence.
search	This algorithm searches for a subsequence of elements within a sequence of elements and, if such a subsequence is found, returns a forward iterator that indicates the first element of that subsequence. If there are no matches, the iterator is positioned at the end of the sequence to be searched.
search_n	This algorithm searches a sequence of elements looking for a subsequence in which the values of a specified number of elements have a particular value and, if such a subsequence is found, returns a forward iterator that indicates the first element of that subsequence. If there are no matches, the iterator is positioned at the end of the sequence to be searched.
partial_sort	Use three random-access iterators to sort part of a sequence. The first and last arguments indicate the sequence of elements. The second argument indicates the ending location for the sorted part of the sequence. By default, elements are ordered using operator < (a binary predicate function can also be supplied). The elements from the second argument iterator to the end of the sequence are in an undefined order.
partial_sort_copy	Use two input iterators and two random-access iterators to sort part of the sequence indicated by the two input iterator arguments. The results are stored in the sequence indicated by the two random-access iterator arguments. By default, elements are ordered using operator < (a binary predicate function can also be supplied). The number of elements sorted is the smaller of the number of elements in the result and the number of elements in the original sequence.
stable_sort	The algorithm is similar to sort except that all equivalent elements are maintained in their original order. This sort is $O(n \log n)$ if enough memory is available; otherwise, it is $O(n(\log n)^2)$.

Fig. 22.39 | Algorithms not covered in this chapter. (Part 2 of 2.)

22.6 Class bitset

Class bitset makes it easy to create and manipulate bit sets, which are useful for representing a set of bit flags. bitsets are fixed in size at compile time. Class bitset is an alternate tool for bit manipulation, discussed in Chapter 21. The declaration

```
bitset< size > b;
```

creates bitset b, in which every bit is initially 0. The statement

```
b.set( bitNumber );
```

sets bit bitNumber of bitset b "on." The expression b.set() sets all bits in b "on."
The statement

```
b.reset( bitNumber );
```

sets bit bitNumber of bitset b "off." The expression b.reset() sets all bits in b "off." The
statement

```
b.flip( bitNumber );
```

"flips" bit bitNumber of bitset b (e.g., if the bit is on, flip sets it off). The expression
b.flip() flips all bits in b. The statement

```
b[ bitNumber ];
```

returns a reference to the bit bitNumber of bitset b. Similarly,

```
b.at( bitNumber );
```

performs range checking on bitNumber first. Then, if bitNumber is in range, at returns a
reference to the bit. Otherwise, at throws an out_of_range exception. The statement

```
b.test( bitNumber );
```

performs range checking on bitNumber first. Then, if bitNumber is in range, test returns
true if the bit is on, false if the bit is off. Otherwise, test throws an out_of_range exception. The expression

```
b.size()
```

returns the number of bits in bitset b. The expression

```
b.count()
```

returns the number of bits that are set in bitset b. The expression

```
b.any()
```

returns true if any bit is set in bitset b. The expression

```
b.none()
```

returns true if none of the bits is set in bitset b. The expressions

```
b == b1
b != b1
```

compare the two bitsets for equality and inequality, respectively.
   Each of the bitwise assignment operators &=, |= and ^= can be used to combine bit-
sets. For example,

```
b &= b1;
```

performs a bit-by-bit logical AND between bitsets b and b1. The result is stored in b.
Bitwise logical OR and bitwise logical XOR are performed by

```
    b |= b1;
    b ^= b2;
```

The expression

```
    b >>= n;
```

shifts the bits in bitset b right by n positions. The expression

```
    b <<= n;
```

shifts the bits in bitset b left by n positions. The expressions

```
    b.to_string()
    b.to_ulong()
```

convert bitset b to a string and an unsigned long, respectively.

Sieve of Eratosthenes with bitset

Figure 22.40 revisits the Sieve of Eratosthenes for finding prime numbers that we discussed in Exercise 7.29. A bitset is used instead of an array to implement the algorithm. The program displays all the prime numbers from 2 to 1023, then allows the user to enter a number to determine whether that number is prime.

Line 20 creates a bitset of size bits (size is 1024 in this example). By default, all the bits in the bitset are set "off." Line 21 calls function **flip** to set all bits "on." Numbers 0 and 1 are not prime numbers, so lines 22–23 call function **reset** to set bits 0 and 1 "off." Lines 29–36 determine all the prime numbers from 2 to 1023. The integer finalBit (line 26) is used to determine when the algorithm is complete. The basic algorithm is that a number is prime if it has no divisors other than 1 and itself. Starting with the number 2, we can eliminate all multiples of that number. The number 2 is divisible only by 1 and itself, so it is prime. Therefore, we can eliminate 4, 6, 8 and so on. The number 3 is divisible only by 1 and itself. Therefore, we can eliminate all multiples of 3 (keep in mind that all even numbers have already been eliminated).

```
1   // Fig. 22.40: Fig22_40.cpp
2   // Using a bitset to demonstrate the Sieve of Eratosthenes.
3   #include <iostream>
4   using std::cin;
5   using std::cout;
6   using std::endl;
7
8   #include <iomanip>
9   using std::setw;
10
11  #include <cmath>
12  using std::sqrt; // sqrt prototype
13
14  #include <bitset> // bitset class definition
15
16  int main()
17  {
18      const int SIZE = 1024;
```

Fig. 22.40 | Class bitset and the Sieve of Eratosthenes. (Part 1 of 3.)

```
19        int value;
20        std::bitset< SIZE > sieve; // create bitset of 1024 bits
21        sieve.flip(); // flip all bits in bitset sieve
22        sieve.reset( 0 ); // reset first bit (number 0)
23        sieve.reset( 1 ); // reset second bit (number 1)
24
25        // perform Sieve of Eratosthenes
26        int finalBit = sqrt( static_cast< double > ( sieve.size() ) ) + 1;
27
28        // determine all prime numbers from 2 to 1024
29        for ( int i = 2; i < finalBit; i++ )
30        {
31           if ( sieve.test( i ) ) // bit i is on
32           {
33              for ( int j = 2 * i; j < SIZE; j += i )
34                 sieve.reset( j ); // set bit j off
35           } // end if
36        } // end for
37
38        cout << "The prime numbers in the range 2 to 1023 are:\n";
39
40        // display prime numbers in range 2-1023
41        for ( int k = 2, counter = 1; k < SIZE; k++ )
42        {
43           if ( sieve.test( k ) ) // bit k is on
44           {
45              cout << setw( 5 ) << k;
46
47              if ( counter++ % 12 == 0 ) // counter is a multiple of 12
48                 cout << '\n';
49           } // end if
50        } // end for
51
52        cout << endl;
53
54        // get value from user to determine whether value is prime
55        cout << "\nEnter a value from 2 to 1023 (-1 to end): ";
56        cin >> value;
57
58        // determine whether user input is prime
59        while ( value != -1 )
60        {
61           if ( sieve[ value ] ) // prime number
62              cout << value << " is a prime number\n";
63           else // not a prime number
64              cout << value << " is not a prime number\n";
65
66           cout << "\nEnter a value from 2 to 1023 (-1 to end): ";
67           cin >> value;
68        } // end while
69
70        return 0;
71    } // end main
```

Fig. 22.40 | Class bitset and the Sieve of Eratosthenes. (Part 2 of 3.)

```
The prime numbers in the range 2 to 1023 are:
    2    3    5    7   11   13   17   19   23   29   31   37
   41   43   47   53   59   61   67   71   73   79   83   89
   97  101  103  107  109  113  127  131  137  139  149  151
  157  163  167  173  179  181  191  193  197  199  211  223
  227  229  233  239  241  251  257  263  269  271  277  281
  283  293  307  311  313  317  331  337  347  349  353  359
  367  373  379  383  389  397  401  409  419  421  431  433
  439  443  449  457  461  463  467  479  487  491  499  503
  509  521  523  541  547  557  563  569  571  577  587  593
  599  601  607  613  617  619  631  641  643  647  653  659
  661  673  677  683  691  701  709  719  727  733  739  743
  751  757  761  769  773  787  797  809  811  821  823  827
  829  839  853  857  859  863  877  881  883  887  907  911
  919  929  937  941  947  953  967  971  977  983  991  997
 1009 1013 1019 1021

Enter a value from 2 to 1023 (-1 to end): 389
389 is a prime number

Enter a value from 2 to 1023 (-1 to end): 88
88 is not a prime number

Enter a value from 2 to 1023 (-1 to end): -1
```

Fig. 22.40 | Class `bitset` and the Sieve of Eratosthenes. (Part 3 of 3.)

22.7 Function Objects

Many STL algorithms allow you to pass a function pointer into the algorithm to help the algorithm perform its task. For example, the `binary_search` algorithm that we discussed in Section 22.5.6 is overloaded with a version that requires as its fourth parameter a pointer to a function that takes two arguments and returns a `bool` value. The `binary_search` algorithm uses this function to compare the search key to an element in the collection. The function returns `true` if the search key and element being compared are equal; otherwise, the function returns `false`. This enables `binary_search` to search a collection of elements for which the element type does not provide an overloaded equality == operator.

STL's designers made the algorithms more flexible by allowing any algorithm that can receive a function pointer to receive an object of a class that overloads the parentheses operator with a function named `operator()`, provided that the overloaded operator meets the requirements of the algorithm—in the case of `binary_search`, it must receive two arguments and return a `bool`. An object of such a class is known as a function object and can be used syntactically and semantically like a function or function pointer—the overloaded parentheses operator is invoked by using a function object's name followed by parentheses containing the arguments to the function. Together, function objects and functions used are know as functors. Most algorithms can use function objects and functions interchangeably.

Function objects provide several advantages over function pointers. Since function objects are commonly implemented as class templates that are included into each source code file that uses them, the compiler can inline an overloaded `operator()` to improve performance. Also, since they are objects of classes, function objects can have data members that `operator()` can use to perform its task.

Predefined Function Objects of the Standard Template Library

Many predefined function objects can be found in the header <functional>. Figure 22.41 lists several of the STL function objects, which are all implemented as class templates. We used the function object less< T > in the set, multiset and priority_queue examples, to specify the sorting order for elements in a container.

Using the STL Accumulate Algorithm

Figure 22.42 demonstrates the accumulate numeric algorithm (discussed in Fig. 22.30) to calculate the sum of the squares of the elements in a vector. The fourth argument to accumulate is a binary function object (that is, a function object for which operator() takes two arguments) or a function pointer to a binary function (that is, a function that takes two arguments). Function accumulate is demonstrated twice—once with a function pointer and once with a function object.

STL function objects	Type	STL function objects	Type
divides< T >	arithmetic	logical_or< T >	logical
equal_to< T >	relational	minus< T >	arithmetic
greater< T >	relational	modulus< T >	arithmetic
greater_equal< T >	relational	negate< T >	arithmetic
less< T >	relational	not_equal_to< T >	relational
less_equal< T >	relational	plus< T >	arithmetic
logical_and< T >	logical	multiplies< T >	arithmetic
logical_not< T >	logical		

Fig. 22.41 | Function objects in the Standard Library.

```cpp
1   // Fig. 22.42: Fig22_42.cpp
2   // Demonstrating function objects.
3   #include <iostream>
4   using std::cout;
5   using std::endl;
6
7   #include <vector> // vector class-template definition
8   #include <algorithm> // copy algorithm
9   #include <numeric> // accumulate algorithm
10  #include <functional> // binary_function definition
11  #include <iterator> // ostream_iterator
12
13  // binary function adds square of its second argument and the
14  // running total in its first argument, then returns the sum
15  int sumSquares( int total, int value )
16  {
17     return total + value * value;
18  } // end function sumSquares
```

Fig. 22.42 | Binary function object. (Part 1 of 2.)

```
19
20    // binary function class template defines overloaded operator()
21    // that adds the square of its second argument and running
22    // total in its first argument, then returns sum
23    template< typename T >
24    class SumSquaresClass : public std::binary_function< T, T, T >
25    {
26    public:
27       // add square of value to total and return result
28       T operator()( const T &total, const T &value )
29       {
30          return total + value * value;
31       } // end function operator()
32    }; // end class SumSquaresClass
33
34    int main()
35    {
36       const int SIZE = 10;
37       int array[ SIZE ] = { 1, 2, 3, 4, 5, 6, 7, 8, 9, 10 };
38       std::vector< int > integers( array, array + SIZE ); // copy of array
39       std::ostream_iterator< int > output( cout, " " );
40       int result;
41
42       cout << "vector integers contains:\n";
43       std::copy( integers.begin(), integers.end(), output );
44
45       // calculate sum of squares of elements of vector integers
46       // using binary function sumSquares
47       result = std::accumulate( integers.begin(), integers.end(),
48          0, sumSquares );
49
50       cout << "\n\nSum of squares of elements in integers using "
51          << "binary\nfunction sumSquares: " << result;
52
53       // calculate sum of squares of elements of vector integers
54       // using binary function object
55       result = std::accumulate( integers.begin(), integers.end(),
56          0, SumSquaresClass< int >() );
57
58       cout << "\n\nSum of squares of elements in integers using "
59          << "binary\nfunction object of type "
60          << "SumSquaresClass< int >: " << result << endl;
61       return 0;
62    } // end main
```

```
vector integers contains:
1 2 3 4 5 6 7 8 9 10

Sum of squares of elements in integers using binary
function sumSquares: 385

Sum of squares of elements in integers using binary
function object of type SumSquaresClass< int >: 385
```

Fig. 22.42 | Binary function object. (Part 2 of 2.)

Lines 15–18 define a function sumSquares that squares its second argument value, adds that square and its first argument total and returns the sum. Function accumulate will pass each of the elements of the sequence over which it iterates as the second argument to sumSquares in the example. On the first call to sumSquares, the first argument will be the initial value of the total (which is supplied as the third argument to accumulate; 0 in this program). All subsequent calls to sumSquares receive as the first argument the running sum returned by the previous call to sumSquares. When accumulate completes, it returns the sum of the squares of all the elements in the sequence.

Lines 23–32 define a class SumSquaresClass that inherits from the class template binary_function (in header file <functional>)—an empty base class for creating function objects in which operator receives two parameters and returns a value. Class binary_function accepts three type parameters that represent the types of the first argument, second argument and return value of operator, respectively. In this example, the type of these parameters is T (line 24). On the first call to the function object, the first argument will be the initial value of the total (which is supplied as the third argument to accumulate: 0 in this program) and the second argument will be the first element in vector integers. All subsequent calls to operator receive as the first argument the result returned by the previous call to the function object, and the second argument will be the next element in the vector. When accumulate completes, it returns the sum of the squares of all the elements in the vector.

Lines 47–48 call function accumulate with a pointer to function sumSquares as its last argument.

The statement in lines 55–56 calls function accumulate with an object of class SumSquaresClass as the last argument. The expression SumSquaresClass< int >() creates an instance of class SumSquaresClass (a function object) that is passed to accumulate, which sends the object the message (invokes the function) operator. The statement could be written as two separate statements, as follows:

```
SumSquaresClass< int > sumSquaresObject;
result = std::accumulate( integers.begin(), integers.end(),
   0, sumSquaresObject );
```

The first line defines an object of class SumSquaresClass. That object is then passed to function accumulate.

22.8 Wrap-Up

In this chapter, we introduced the Standard Template Library and discussed its three key components—containers, iterators and algorithms. You learned the STL sequence containers, vector, deque and list, which represent linear data structures. We discussed associative containers, set, multiset, map and multimap, which represent nonlinear data structures. You also saw that the container adapters stack, queue and priority_queue can be used to restrict the operations of the sequence containers for the purpose of implementing the specialized data structures represented by the container adapters. We then demonstrated many of the STL algorithms, including mathematical algorithms, basic searching and sorting algorithms and set operations. You learned the types of iterators each algorithm requires and that each algorithm can be used with any container that supports the minimum iterator functionality the algorithm requires. You also learned class bitset, which makes it easy to create and manipulate bit sets as a container. Finally, we introduced function objects that work syntactically and semantically like ordinary functions, but offer advantages such as performance and the ability to store data.

In the next chapter, we discuss several more advanced C++ features, including cast operators, namespaces, operator keywords, pointer-to-class-member operators, multiple inheritance and `virtual` base classes.

22.9 STL Web Resources

Our C++ Resource Center (`www.deitel.com/cplusplus/`) focuses on the enormous amount of free C++ content available online. Start your search here for resources, downloads, tutorials, documentation, books, e-books, journals, articles, blogs, RSS feeds and more that will help you develop C++ applications. The C++ Resource Center includes links to many STL resources and tutorials.

Summary

Section 22.1 Introduction to the Standard Template Library (STL)
- The Standard Template Library defines powerful, template-based, reusable components that implement many common data structures, and algorithms used to process those data structures.
- The STL has three key components—containers, iterators and algorithms.
- The STL containers are data structures capable of storing objects of any data type. There are three styles of container classes—first-class containers, container adapters and near containers.
- STL algorithms are functions that perform such common data manipulations as searching, sorting and comparing elements or entire containers.

Section 22.1.1 Introduction to Containers
- The containers are divided into sequence containers, associative containers and container adapters.
- The sequence containers represent linear data structures, such as vectors and linked lists.
- Associative containers are nonlinear containers that quickly locate elements stored in them, such as sets of values or key/value pairs.
- Sequence containers and associative containers are collectively referred to as first-class containers.

Section 22.1.2 Introduction to Iterators
- First-class container function `begin` returns an iterator pointing to the first element of a container. Function `end` returns an iterator pointing to the first element past the end of the container (an element that doesn't exist and is typically used in a loop to indicate when to terminate processing of the container's elements).
- An `istream_iterator` is capable of extracting values in a type-safe manner from an input stream. An `ostream_iterator` is capable of inserting values in an output stream.
- Input and output iterators can move only in the forward direction (i.e., from the beginning of the container to the end) one element at a time.
- A forward iterator combines the capabilities of input and output iterators.
- A bidirectional iterator has the capabilities of a forward iterator and the ability to move in the backward direction (i.e., from the end of the container toward the beginning).

- A random-access iterator has the capabilities of a bidirectional iterator and the ability to directly access any element of the container.

Section 22.1.3 Introduction to Algorithms
- Containers that support random-access iterators, such as vector, can be used with all algorithms in the STL.

Section 22.2 Sequence Containers
- The STL provides sequence containers vector, list and deque. Class templates vector and deque both are based on arrays. Class template list implements a linked-list data structure.

Section 22.2.1 **vector** Sequence Container
- Function capacity returns the number of elements that can be stored in a vector before the vector dynamically resizes itself to accommodate more elements.
- Sequence container function push_back adds an element to the end of a container.
- To use the algorithms of the STL, you must include the header file <algorithm>.
- Algorithm copy copies each element in a container starting with the location specified by the iterator in its first argument and up to—but not including—the location specified by the iterator in its second argument.
- Function front returns a reference to the first element in a sequence container. Function begin returns an iterator pointing to the beginning of a sequence container.
- Function back returns a reference to the last element in a sequence container. Function end returns an iterator pointing to the element one past the end of a sequence container.
- Sequence container function insert inserts value(s) before the element at a specific location.
- Function erase (in all first-class containers) removes specific element(s) from the container.
- Function empty (in all containers and adapters) returns true if the container is empty.
- Function clear (in all first-class containers) empties the container.

Section 22.2.2 **list** Sequence Container
- The list sequence container provides an efficient implementation for insertion and deletion operations at any location in the container. Header file <list> must be included to use class template list.
- The list member function push_front inserts values at the beginning of a list.
- The list member function sort arranges the elements in the list in ascending order.
- The list member function splice removes elements in one list and inserts them into another list at a specific position.
- The list member function unique removes duplicate elements in a list.
- The list member function assign replaces the contents of one list with the contents of another.
- The list member function remove deletes all copies of a specified value from a list.

Section 22.2.3 **deque** Sequence Container
- Class template deque provides the same operations as vector, but adds member functions push_front and pop_front to allow insertion and deletion at the beginning of a deque, respectively. Header file <deque> must be included to use class template deque.

Section 22.3 Associative Containers
- The STL's associative containers provide direct access to store and retrieve elements via keys.

- The four associative containers are `multiset`, `set`, `multimap` and `map`.

- Class templates `multiset` and `set` provide operations for manipulating sets of values where the values are the keys—there is not a separate value associated with each key. Header file `<set>` must be included to use class templates `set` and `multiset`.

- The primary difference between a `multiset` and a `set` is that a `multiset` allows duplicate keys and a `set` does not.

Section 22.3.1 *`multiset` Associative Container*

- The `multiset` associative container provides fast storage and retrieval of keys and allows duplicate keys. The ordering of the elements is determined by a comparator function object.

- A `multiset`'s keys can be sorted in ascending order by ordering the keys with comparator function object `less<T>`.

- The type of the keys in all associative containers must support comparison properly based on the comparator function object specified—e.g., keys sorted with `less<T>` must support comparison with `operator<`.

- A `multiset` supports bidirectional iterators.

- Header file `<set>` must be included to use class `multiset`.

Section 22.3.2 *`set` Associative Container*

- The `set` associative container is used for fast storage and retrieval of unique keys.

- If an attempt is made to insert a duplicate key into a `set`, the duplicate is ignored.

- A `set` supports bidirectional iterators.

- Header file `<set>` must be included to use class set.

Section 22.3.3 *`multimap` Associative Container*

- Class templates `multimap` and `map` provide operations for manipulating values associated with keys.

- The primary difference between a `multimap` and a `map` is that a `multimap` allows duplicate keys with associated values to be stored and a `map` allows only unique keys with associated values.

- Function `count` (available to all associative containers) counts the number of occurrences of the specified value currently in a container.

- Function `find` (available to all associative containers) locates a specified value in a container.

- Functions `lower_bound` and `upper_bound` (available in all associative containers) locate the earliest occurrence of the specified value in a container and the element after the last occurrence of the specified value in a container, respectively.

- Function `equal_range` (available in all associative containers) returns a `pair` containing the results of both a `lower_bound` and an `upper_bound` operation.

- The `multimap` associative container is used for fast storage and retrieval of keys and associated values (often called key/value pairs).

- Duplicate keys are allowed in a `multimap`, so multiple values can be associated with a single key. This is called a one-to-many relationship.

- Header file `<map>` must be included to use class templates `map` and `multimap`.

Section 22.3.4 *`map` Associative Container*

- Duplicate keys are not allowed in a `map`, so only a single value can be associated with each key. This is called a one-to-one mapping.

- A `map` is commonly called an associative array.

Section 22.4 Container Adapters

- The STL provides three container adapters—stack, queue and priority_queue.

- Adapters are not first-class containers, because they do not provide the actual data structure implementation in which elements can be stored and they do not support iterators.

- All three adapter class templates provide member functions push and pop that properly insert an element into and remove an element from each adapter data structure, respectively.

Section 22.4.1 **stack** *Adapter*

- Class template stack is a last-in, first-out data structure. Header file <stack> must be included to use class template stack.

- The stack member function top returns a reference to the top element of the stack (implemented by calling function back of the underlying container).

- The stack member function empty determines whether the stack is empty (implemented by calling function empty of the underlying container).

- The stack member function size returns the number of elements in the stack (implemented by calling function size of the underlying container).

Section 22.4.2 **queue** *Adapter*

- Class template queue enables insertions at the back of the underlying data structure and deletions from the front of the underlying data structure (commonly referred to as a first-in, first-out data structure). Header file <queue> must be included to use a queue or a priority_queue.

- The queue member function front returns a reference to the first element in the queue (implemented by calling function front of the underlying container).

- The queue member function back returns a reference to the last element in the queue (implemented by calling function back of the underlying container).

- The queue member function empty determines whether the queue is empty (implemented by calling function empty of the underlying container).

- The queue member function size returns the number of elements in the queue (implemented by calling function size of the underlying container).

Section 22.4.3 **priority_queue** *Adapter*

- Class template priority_queue provides functionality that enables insertions in sorted order into the underlying data structure and deletions from the front of the underlying data structure.

- The common priority_queue operations are push, pop, top, empty and size.

Section 22.5.1 **fill, fill_n, generate** *and* **generate_n**

- Algorithms fill and fill_n set every element in a range of container elements to a specific value.

- Algorithms generate and generate_n use a generator function or function object to create values for every element in a range of container elements.

Section 22.5.2 **equal, mismatch** *and* **lexicographical_compare**

- Algorithm equal compares two sequences of values for equality.

- Algorithm mismatch compares two sequences of values and returns a pair of iterators indicating the location in each sequence of the mismatched elements.

- Algorithm lexicographical_compare compares the contents of two sequences.

Section 22.5.3 remove, remove_if, remove_copy and remove_copy_if

- Algorithm remove eliminates all elements with a specific value in a certain range.
- Algorithm remove_copy copies all elements that do not have a specific value in a certain range.
- Algorithm remove_if deletes all elements that satisfy the if condition in a certain range.
- Algorithm remove_copy_if copies all elements that satisfy the if condition in a certain range.

Section 22.5.4 replace, replace_if, replace_copy and replace_copy_if

- Algorithm replace replaces all elements with a specific value in certain range.
- Algorithm replace_copy copies all elements with a specific value in a certain range.
- Algorithm replace_if replaces all elements that satisfy the if condition in a certain range.
- Algorithm replace_copy_if copies all elements that satisfy the if condition in a certain range.

Section 22.5.5 Mathematical Algorithms

- Algorithm random_shuffle reorders randomly the elements in a certain range.
- Algorithm count counts the elements with a specific value in a certain range.
- Algorithm count_if counts the elements that satisfy the if condition in a certain range.
- Algorithm min_element locates the smallest element in a certain range.
- Algorithm max_element locates the largest element in a certain range.
- Algorithm accumulate sums the values in a certain range.
- Algorithm for_each applies a general function or function object to every element in a range.
- Algorithm transform applies a general function or function object to every element in a range and replaces each element with the result of the function.

Section 22.5.6 Basic Searching and Sorting Algorithms

- Algorithm find locates a specific value in a certain range.
- Algorithm find_if locates the first value in a certain range that satisfies the if condition.
- Algorithm sort arranges the elements in a certain range in ascending order or an order specified by a predicate.
- Algorithm binary_search determines whether a specific value is in a sorted range of elements.

Section 22.5.7 swap, iter_swap and swap_ranges

- Algorithm swap exchanges two values.
- Algorithm iter_swap exchanges the two elements.
- Algorithm swap_ranges exchanges the elements in a certain range.

Section 22.5.8 copy_backward, merge, unique and reverse

- Algorithm copy_backward copies elements in a range and places the elements into a container starting from the end and working toward the front.
- Algorithm merge combines two sorted ascending sequences of values into a third sorted ascending sequence.
- Algorithm unique removes duplicated elements in a sorted sequence of elements in a certain range.
- Algorithm reverse reverses all the elements in a certain range.

Section 22.5.9 inplace_merge, unique_copy and reverse_copy

- Algorithm inplace_merge merges two sorted sequences of elements in the same container.

- Algorithm `unique_copy` makes a copy of all the unique elements in the sorted sequence of values in a certain range.
- Algorithm `reverse_copy` makes a reversed copy of the elements in a certain range.

Section 22.5.10 Set Operations
- The `set` function `includes` compares two `set`s of sorted values to determine whether every element of the second `set` is in the first `set`.
- The `set` function `set_difference` finds the elements from the first `set` of sorted values that are not in the second `set` of sorted values (both `set`s of values must be in ascending order).
- The `set` function `set_intersection` determines the elements from the first `set` of sorted values that are in the second `set` of sorted values (both `set`s of values must be in ascending order).
- The `set` function `set_symmetric_difference` determines the elements in the first `set` that are not in the second `set` and the elements in the second `set` that are not in the first `set` (both `set`s of values must be in ascending order).
- The `set` function `set_union` creates a set of all the elements that are in either or both of the two sorted `set`s (both `set`s of values must be in ascending order).

Section 22.5.11 `lower_bound`, `upper_bound` and `equal_range`
- Algorithm `lower_bound` finds the first location in a sorted sequence of values at which the third argument could be inserted in the sequence such that the sequence would still be sorted in ascending order.
- Algorithm `upper_bound` finds the last location in a sorted sequence of values at which the third argument could be inserted in the sequence such that the sequence would still be sorted in ascending order.
- Algorithm `equal_range` performs returns the lower bound and upper bound as a `pair`.

Section 22.5.12 Heapsort
- Algorithm `make_heap` takes a sequence of values in a certain range and creates a heap that can be used to produce a sorted sequence.
- Algorithm `sort_heap` sorts a sequence of values in a certain range that are already arranged in a heap.
- Algorithm `pop_heap` removes the top heap element.

Section 22.5.13 `min` and `max`
- Algorithms `min` and `max` determine the minimum of two elements and the maximum of two elements, respectively.

Section 22.6 Class `bitset`
- Class template `bitset` makes it easy to create and manipulate bit sets, which are useful for representing a set of bit flags.

Section 22.7 Function Objects
- A function object is an instance of a class that overloads `operator()`.
- STL provides many predefined function objects, which can be found in header `<functional>`.
- Binary function objects are function objects that take two arguments and return a value. Class template `binary_function` is an empty base class for creating binary function objects that provides standard type names for the function's parameters and result.

Terminology

accumulate algorithm
adapter
algorithm
<algorithm> header file
assign member function of list
associative array
associative container
back member function of sequence containers
back_inserter function template
begin member function of first-class containers
bidirectional iterator
binary function
binary function object
binary_function class template
binary_search algorithm
capacity member function of vector
comparator function object
const_iterator
const_reverse_iterator
container
container adapter
copy_backward algorithm
count algorithm
count_if algorithm
<deque> header file
deque sequence container
empty member function of containers
end member function of containers
equal algorithm
equal_range algorithm
equal_range function of associative container
erase member function of containers
fill algorithm
fill_n algorithm
find algorithm
find function of associative container
find_if algorithm
first data member of pair
first-class container
flip function of bitset
for_each algorithm
forward iterator
front_inserter function template
front member function of sequence container
function object
functor
<functional> header file
generate algorithm
generate_n algorithm

heap
heapsort sorting algorithm
includes algorithm
inplace_merge algorithm
input iterator
input sequence
insert member function of containers
inserter function template
istream_iterator
iterator
iter_swap algorithm
key/value pair
less< int >
lexicographical_compare algorithm
<list> header file
list sequence container
lower_bound algorithm
lower_bound function of associative container
make_heap algorithm
<map> header file
map associative container
max algorithm
max_element algorithm
merge algorithm
min algorithm
min_element algorithm
mismatch algorithm
multimap associative container
multiset associative container
mutating-sequence algorithm
near container
<numeric> header file
one-to-one mapping
ostream_iterator
output iterator
output sequence
pop_back function
pop_front function
pop_heap algorithm
pop member function of container adapters
priority_queue adapter class template
push_heap algorithm
push member function of container adapters
queue adapter class template
<queue> header file
random-access iterator
random_shuffle algorithm
range
rbegin member function of vector

remove algorithm
remove member function of list
remove_copy algorithm
remove_copy_if algorithm
remove_if algorithm
rend member function of containers
replace algorithm
replace_copy algorithm
replace_copy_if algorithm
replace_if algorithm
reset function of bitset
reverse algorithm
reverse_copy algorithm
reverse_iterator
search key
second data member of pair
sequence
sequence container
set associative container
set_difference algorithm

<set> header file
set_intersection algorithm
set_symmetric_difference algorithm
set_union algorithm
size member function of containers
sort algorithm
sort_heap algorithm
sort member function of list
splice member function of list
stack adapter class template
<stack> header file
Standard Template Library (STL)
swap algorithm
swap member function of list
swap_range algorithm
top member function of container adapters
unique algorithm
unique_copy algorithm
unique member function of list
upper_bound algorithm

Self-Review Exercises

State whether the following are *true* or *false* or fill in the blanks. If the answer is *false*, explain why,.

22.1   (T/F) The STL makes abundant use of inheritance and virtual functions.

22.2   The two types of first-class STL containers are sequence containers and _____ containers.

22.3   The five main iterator types are _____, _____, _____, _____ and _____.

22.4   (T/F) An iterator acts like a pointer to an element.

22.5   (T/F) STL algorithms can operate on C-like pointer-based arrays.

22.6   (T/F) STL algorithms are encapsulated as member functions within each container class.

22.7   (T/F) When using the remove algorithm on a vector, the algorithm does not decrease the size of the vector from which elements are being removed.

22.8   The three STL container adapters are _____, _____ and _____.

22.9   (T/F) Container member function end yields the position of the container's last element.

22.10   STL algorithms operate on container elements indirectly, using _____.

22.11   The sort algorithm requires a(n) _____ iterator.

Answers to Self-Review Exercises

22.1   False. These were avoided for performance reasons.

22.2   Associative.

22.3   Input, output, forward, bidirectional, random access.

22.4   False. It is actually vice versa.

22.5   True.

22.6   False. STL algorithms are not member functions. They operate indirectly on containers, through iterators.

22.7   True.

22.8   `stack`, `queue`, `priority_queue`.

22.9   False. It actually yields the position just after the end of the container.

22.10   Iterators.

22.11   Random-access.

Exercises

22.12   Write a function template `palindrome` that takes a `vector` parameter and returns `true` or `false` according to whether the `vector` does or does not read the same forward as backward (e.g., a vector containing 1, 2, 3, 2, 1 is a palindrome, but a vector containing 1, 2, 3, 4 is not).

22.13   Modify Fig. 22.40, the Sieve of Eratosthenes, so that, if the number the user inputs into the program is not prime, the program displays the prime factors of the number. Remember that a prime number's factors are only 1 and the prime number itself. Every nonprime number has a unique prime factorization. For example, the factors of 54 are 2, 3, 3 and 3. When these values are multiplied together, the result is 54. For the number 54, the prime factors output should be 2 and 3.

22.14   Modify Exercise 22.13 so that, if the number the user inputs into the program is not prime, the program displays the prime factors of the number and the number of times each prime factor appears in the unique prime factorization. For example, the output for the number 54 should be

```
The unique prime factorization of 54 is: 2 * 3 * 3 * 3
```

Recommended Reading

Ammeraal, L. *STL for C++ Programmers*. New York: John Wiley, 1997.

Austern, M. H. *Generic Programming and the STL: Using and Extending the C++ Standard Template Library*. Reading, MA: Addison-Wesley, 1998.

Glass, G., and B. Schuchert. *The STL <Primer>*. Upper Saddle River, NJ: Prentice Hall PTR, 1995.

Henricson, M., and E. Nyquist. *Industrial Strength C++: Rules and Recommendations*. Upper Saddle River, NJ: Prentice Hall, 1997.

Josuttis, N. *The C++ Standard Library: A Tutorial and Handbook*. Reading, MA: Addison-Wesley, 1999.

Koenig, A., and B. Moo. *Ruminations on C++*. Reading, MA: Addison-Wesley, 1997.

Meyers, S. *Effective STL: 50 Specific Ways to Improve Your Use of the Standard Template Library*. Reading, MA: Addison-Wesley, 2001.

Musser, D. R., and A. Saini. *STL Tutorial and Reference Guide: C++ Programming with the Standard Template Library*. Reading, MA: Addison-Wesley, 1996.

Musser, D. R., and A. A. Stepanov. "Algorithm-Oriented Generic Libraries," *Software Practice and Experience,* Vol. 24, No. 7, July 1994.

Nelson, M. *C++ Programmer's Guide to the Standard Template Library*. Foster City, CA: Programmer's Press, 1995.

Pohl, I. *C++ Distilled: A Concise ANSI/ISO Reference and Style Guide*. Reading, MA: Addison-Wesley, 1997.

Pohl, I. *Object-Oriented Programming Using C++, Second Edition*. Reading, MA: Addison-Wesley, 1997.

Robson, R. *Using the STL: The C++ Standard Template Library.* New York: Springer Verlag, 2000.

Schildt, H. *STL Programming from the Ground Up*, New York: Osborne McGraw-Hill, 1999.

Stepanov, A., and M. Lee. "The Standard Template Library," *Internet Distribution* 31 October 1995 <www.cs.rpi.edu/~musser/doc.ps>.

Stroustrup, B. "Making a vector Fit for a Standard," *The C++ Report,* October 1994.

Stroustrup, B. *The Design and Evolution of C++.* Reading, MA: Addison-Wesley, 1994.

Stroustrup, B. *The C++ Programming Language, Third Edition.* Reading, MA: Addison-Wesley, 1997.

Vilot, M. J. "An Introduction to the Standard Template Library," *The C++ Report,* Vol. 6, No. 8, October 1994.

23

Game Programming with Ogre

OBJECTIVES

In this chapter you will learn:

- Some basics of game programming.
- Where to find instructions on how to install the Ogre 3D graphics engine to work with your C++ programs on the Windows, Linux and Mac platforms.
- To create games using Ogre.
- To perform collision detection.
- To use Ogre to import and display graphics.
- To use OgreAL to integrate the OpenAL audio library into your games.
- To have Ogre accept keyboard input.
- To create the simple game Pong® with Ogre and OgreAL.
- To use Ogre to regulate the speed of a game.

23.1 Introduction

We now introduce game programming and graphics with the Ogre 3D graphics engine. Created in 2000 by Steve Streeting, Ogre is an open-source project maintained by the Ogre team at `www.ogre3d.org`. First, we discuss basic issues involved in game programming. Then we show how to use Ogre to create a simple game featuring a play mechanic similar to the classic video game Pong®, originally developed by Atari in 1972. We demonstrate how to create a scene with colored 3D graphics, smoothly animate moving objects, use timers to control animation speed, detect collisions between objects, add sound, accept keyboard input and display text output.

23.2 Installing Ogre, OgreAL and OpenAL

Ogre is powerful and easy to use, but the installation is a bit involved and varies for different platforms and compilers. There are two installation options—you can install the Ogre SDK or download the source code and compile it. We use Ogre 1.4 (Eihort) in this text. You must also install OgreAL and the OpenAL audio library. OpenAL handles the sound functionality and OgreAL allows you to integrate the OpenAL capabilities with the Ogre code. We provide detailed instructions for installing the Ogre SDK and all the OgreAL components. The instructions also explain how to configure a Visual C++ 2005 project to use Ogre and OgreAL. You can find the instructions in the Additional Resources section of the book's website at `www.deitel.com/books/cpphtp6`.

23.3 Basics of Game Programming

This section introduces the general fundamentals of game programming. Section 23.4 presents an implementation of the game of Pong, using the Ogre and OgreAL libraries.

Graphics

Graphics are perhaps the most crucial feature of any video game. Once a specialty, graphics programming is becoming more accessible even to novice programmers. There are many 3D graphics engines available—these frameworks hide the often tedious and complex programming required with graphics APIs and allow you to manage graphics more easily.

Ogre (Object-oriented Graphics Rendering Engine), one of the leading graphics engines, has been used in many commercial products including video games. It provides an object-oriented interface for 3D graphics programming. It supports the Direct3D and OpenGL graphics APIs and runs on the Windows, Linux and Mac platforms. Direct3D is Microsoft's Windows 3D graphics API. OpenGL is a graphics specification implemented by many video card vendors across all major platforms, including Windows.

Ogre is strictly a graphics rendering engine—it does not directly support sound, physics, collision detection, networking or other game-related needs. The Ogre community has produced many add-ons that allow users to integrate other libraries with Ogre to support those features.

3D Models

A 3D model is a computer representation of an object which can be drawn on the screen—a process called rendering. Materials determine an object's appearance by setting lighting properties, colors and textures. A texture is an image that is wrapped around the model.

Most objects displayed in 3D graphics, everything from the terrain to the characters and the buildings, are 3D models. Many models are created in 3D modeling tools. Some popular 3D modeling tools are Maya (usa.autodesk.com/adsk/servlet/index?siteID=123112&id=7635018), SoftImage XSI (www.softimage.com/) and Blender (www.blender.org/). They are all available for Windows, Linux and Mac platforms. Blender is free and Maya offers a free version. SoftImage has a free 30-day trial available. The Ogre community has also produced several tools to allow users to export 3D models from these and other popular modeling tools into Ogre.

Materials, Textures and Colors

Colors are determined by red, green and blue light intensities, which can range from 0 to 1.0—a color value of (1.0, 0, 0) will create a bright red color, (0, 1.0, 0) will create a bright green, and (0, 0, 1.0) will make a bright blue. The first value is the red intensity, the second is the green intensity and the third is the blue intensity. To create white, use the maximum intensities of all three color values, (1.0, 1.0, 1.0). To create black—the absence of all color—use (0, 0, 0). Color values sometimes include an alpha channel to represent transparency, also ranging from 0 to 1.0, 0 being completely transparent and 1 completely opaque. Figure 23.1 shows common colors and their red, green, and blue intensity values. You can find color charts on the web as well, such as the color chart at www.tayloredmktg.com/rgb/.

In 3D graphics, materials are used to determine the color of a 3D model. A material determines how the model should reflect different types of light and applies textures to the model. Materials can be set to use different levels of detail (LoD) depending on how far away from the viewer the model is. When close up, the model should be rendered with as much detail as possible. When the object in the scene is far away, there is no point in wasting computing power rendering details that the viewer can't see. To increase performance, the object can be rendered with much less detail.

Color	Red value	Green value	Blue value
Red	1.0	0.0	0.0
Green	0.0	1.0	0.0
Blue	0.0	0.0	1.0
Orange	1.0	0.784	0.0
Pink	1.0	0.686	0.686
Cyan	0.0	1.0	1.0
Magenta	1.0	0.0	1.0
Yellow	1.0	1.0	0.0
Black	0.0	0.0	0.0
White	1.0	1.0	1.0
Gray	0.5	0.5	0.5
Light gray	0.75	0.75	0.75
Dark gray	0.25	0.25	0.25

Fig. 23.1 | Red, green and blue intensities of common colors in Ogre.

Lighting

There are four different types of light in a 3D scene—ambient, diffuse, emissive and specular.[1] Ambient light is the general lighting in the scene that has been reflected off so many surfaces that it doesn't appear to have any definite source. Diffuse light appears to come from a particular direction and is reflected evenly off any surfaces it hits. Emissive light appears to come from an object in the scene. Emissive light won't affect the objects around it but will make the object emitting it seem brighter. Specular light comes from a particular direction and is reflected off an object based on the direction to the viewer. This is used to make an object appear shiny.

Collision Detection and Response

Collision detection is the process of determining whether two objects in a game are touching. You must know which objects to test and must deal with some complex mathematics. Checking whether one square hits another is relatively simple if each is parallel to flat ground. Checking circles and spheres is more difficult—the mathematics of curved surfaces is more complex.

Objects need to react appropriately when they collide with other objects. Some objects, such as walls, are stationary, while others move throughout the scene. Modeling the physics of moving objects can be complex. There are collision detection and physics modeling libraries that handle these complexities for you. Such libraries help to create a realistic game-playing experience.

---

1. D. Astel and K. Hawkins, *Beginning OpenGL: Game Programming*, 2005, pp. 104–110.

Sound

Sound is crucial to the game-playing experience. Gamers want to hear the lasers on their ships blasting away or the engines of their street racers revving up as they "peel out" at the starting line. Audio libraries help you enrich your games with sound. Many of those libraries support 3D sound. In a 3D scene, objects emitting sound may be at various distances and directions from the user. The sound libraries take these factors into account when playing sounds. A sound from an object close to the listener will be louder than the sound from an object farther away. Also, sounds from one side of the listener will be played differently than sounds from the other.

Text

Games often communicate with the user by displaying text. This can range from giving the user instructions, to simply reporting how many points he or she has scored so far. In many games, text is a crucial form of communication between players. You can find free text fonts to use in your games at www.1001freefonts.com.

Timers

The speed at which a game runs can vary between systems due to differences in processor speeds. To solve this problem, game programmers use timers to control animation speed. If an object moves the same distance every frame (each time the screen is redrawn), then it may move at different speeds on different computers. A game running at 100 frames per second (fps) would be twice as fast as the same game running at 50 frames per second. Timers help keep the game play consistent by regulating the speed.

User Experience

Games should be fun to play and should appeal to the player in as many ways as possible. The basics we've discussed contribute to the overall user experience. You can get the player's attention through graphics and sound. Actions in games often have sounds associated with them. Many web sites offer free sounds you can use in your games. Some popular sound sites are Sound Hunter (www.soundhunter.com), Absolute Sound Effects Archive (www.grsites.com/sounds) and the search engine FindSounds (www.findsounds.com). You can also play a sound track in the background. Be sure to get permission to use any copyrighted songs if you plan on releasing your game as a product.

Players need to interact with games. User input devices include the keyboard, mouse, joystick and game controller. Keep the controls simple—the game should be easy to use, but not easy to beat. You can communicate with the player using text.

23.4 The Game of Pong: Code Walkthrough

In the next several sections, we present a complete C++/Ogre implementation of a simple game featuring a play mechanic similar to the classic video game Pong®, originally developed by Atari in 1972. (See the original Pong coin-op game in Fig. 23.2.) We walk through the code, explaining the Ogre capabilities as they are encountered. This is one of the largest example programs in the book. You should test drive the program thoroughly before reading the code walkthrough. You'll find all the files for this program in the ch23 folder of the book's examples. Copy the PongResources folder to the OgreSDK\media folder. Ogre will throw a runtime exception if any of the resources can't be found. Open the

Fig. 23.2 | Atari's Pong coin-op went into commercial production in November of 1972, selling a total of 38,000 machines. The game was designed entirely in TTL circuits, using no CPU or game code software. Its "code" was implemented using simple "gate" chips, timers and counter chips. This simple, fun and addictive game was the cornerstone of what became the video game industry. (PONG® classic video game courtesy of Atari Interactive, Inc. © 2007 Atari Interactive, Inc. All rights reserved. Used with permission.)

Pong Visual C++ project. If you followed the Ogre and OgreAL installation instructions correctly, the project should build successfully. The project's executable file is copied to your `OgreSDK\bin\debug` folder (or `OgreSDK\bin\release` if you build in Release mode). *Important:* Remember to copy the `OgreAL_d.dll` (or `OgreAL.dll` for Release mode) and the `alut.dll` files into the folder containing the Pong executable.

Pong has four major game objects, a ball, two paddles and a rectangular box (Fig. 23.3). The ball will bounce across the screen inside the box while the players control the paddles to keep the ball from hitting the left or right sides. If the ball hits the left or right side of the box, the player "attacking" that side is awarded a point. The score is displayed at the top of the screen.

Play the game for a while, using the *A* and *Z* keys to control the left paddle and the up and down arrow keys to control the right paddle. Notice the colors of the objects, the ball interacting with the other objects and the score displayed at the top of the screen. Hit the *Esc* key to quit—closing the window won't stop the program.

23.4.1 Ogre Initialization

Class `Pong` (Figs. 23.4–23.5) represents the game of Pong. Figure 23.4 contains the `Pong` class definition. Line 6 includes the `Ogre.h` header file. This file automatically includes the most commonly used Ogre header files. Line 23 is the function prototype for the `run` function, which will start and run the game. Lines 26–27 contain the function prototypes for

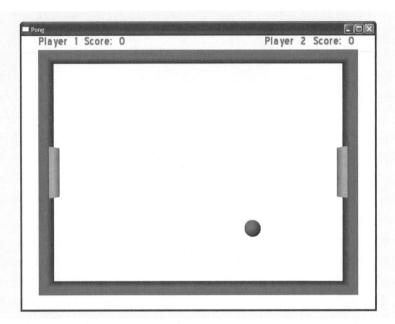

Fig. 23.3 | Pong game objects.

```
1   // Pong.h
2   // Pong class definition (represents a game of Pong).
3   #ifndef PONG_H
4   #define PONG_H
5
6   #include <Ogre.h> // Ogre class definition
7   using namespace Ogre; // use the Ogre namespace
8
9   #include <OIS\OISEvents.h> // OISEvents class definition
10  #include <OIS\OISInputManager.h> // OISInputManager class definition
11  #include <OIS\OISKeyboard.h> // OISKeyboard class definition
12
13  class Ball; // forward declaration of class Ball
14  class Paddle; // forward declaration of class Paddle
15
16  enum Players { PLAYER1, PLAYER2 };
17
18  class Pong : public FrameListener, public OIS::KeyListener
19  {
20  public:
21     Pong(); // constructor
22     ~Pong(); // destructor
23     void run(); // run a game of Pong
24
25     // handle keyPressed and keyReleased events
26     bool keyPressed( const OIS::KeyEvent &keyEventRef );
27     bool keyReleased( const OIS::KeyEvent &keyEventRef );
```

Fig. 23.4 | Pong class definition (represents a game of Pong). (Part 1 of 2.)

```
28
29      // move the game objects and control interactions between frames
30      virtual bool frameStarted( const FrameEvent &frameEvent );
31      virtual bool frameEnded( const FrameEvent &frameEvent );
32      static void updateScore( Players player ); // update the score
33
34   private:
35      void createScene(); // create the scene to be rendered
36      static void updateScoreText(); // update the score on the screen
37
38      // Ogre objects
39      Root *rootPtr; // pointer to Ogre's Root object
40      SceneManager *sceneManagerPtr; // pointer to the SceneManager
41      RenderWindow *windowPtr; // pointer to RenderWindow to render scene in
42      Viewport *viewportPtr; // pointer to Viewport, area that a camera sees
43      Camera *cameraPtr; // pointer to a Camera in the scene
44
45      // OIS input objects
46      OIS::InputManager *inputManagerPtr; // pointer to the InputManager
47      OIS::Keyboard *keyboardPtr; // pointer to the Keyboard
48
49      // game objects
50      Ball *ballPtr; // pointer to the Ball
51      Paddle *leftPaddlePtr; // pointer to player 1's Paddle
52      Paddle *rightPaddlePtr; // pointer to player 2's Paddle
53
54      // variables to control game states
55      bool quit, pause; // did user quit or pause the game?
56      Real time; // used to delay the motion of a new Ball
57      static bool wait; // should the Ball's movement be delayed?
58
59      static int player1Score; // player 1's score
60      static int player2Score; // player 2's score
61   }; // end class Pong
62
63   #endif // PONG_H
```

Fig. 23.4 | Pong class definition (represents a game of Pong). (Part 2 of 2.)

handling user input from the keyboard. Lines 30–31 define the function prototypes for performing game logic between frames. We also declare pointers to important Ogre objects (lines 39–43), input handling objects (lines 46–47) and the game objects (lines 50–52). Lines 55–57 define some variables used to control the behavior of the game—we'll discuss these later.

```
1   // Pong.cpp
2   // Pong class member-function definitions.
3   #include <sstream>
4   using std::ostringstream;
5
```

Fig. 23.5 | Pong class member-function definitions. (Part 1 of 7.)

```
 6   #include <stdexcept>
 7   using std::runtime_error;
 8
 9   #include <Ogre.h> // Ogre class definition
10   using namespace Ogre; // use the Ogre namespace
11
12   #include <OgreAL.h> // OgreAL class definition
13   #include <OgreStringConverter.h> // OgreStringConverter class definition
14   #include <OIS\OISEvents.h> // OISEvents class definition
15   #include <OIS\OISInputManager.h> // OISInputManager class definition
16   #include <OIS\OISKeyboard.h> // OISKeyboard class definition
17   #include "Ball.h" // Ball class definition
18   #include "Paddle.h" // Paddle class definition
19   #include "Pong.h" // Pong class definition
20
21   int Pong::player1Score = 0; // initialize player 1's score to 0
22   int Pong::player2Score = 0; // initialize player 2's score to 0
23   bool Pong::wait = false; // initialize wait to false
24
25   // directions to move the Paddles
26   const Vector3 PADDLE_DOWN = Vector3( 0, -15, 0 );
27   const Vector3 PADDLE_UP = Vector3( 0, 15, 0 );
28
29   // constructor
30   Pong::Pong()
31   {
32      rootPtr = new Root(); // initialize Root object
33
34      // use the Ogre Config Dialog Box to choose the settings
35      if ( !( rootPtr->showConfigDialog() ) ) // user canceled the dialog box
36         throw runtime_error( "User Canceled Ogre Setup Dialog Box." );
37
38      // get a pointer to the RenderWindow
39      windowPtr = rootPtr->initialise( true, "Pong" );
40
41      // create the SceneManager
42      sceneManagerPtr = rootPtr->createSceneManager( ST_GENERIC );
43
44      // create the Camera
45      cameraPtr = sceneManagerPtr->createCamera( "PongCamera" );
46      cameraPtr->setPosition( Vector3( 0, 0, 200 ) ); // set Camera position
47      cameraPtr->lookAt( Vector3( 0, 0, 0 ) ); // set where Camera looks
48      cameraPtr->setNearClipDistance( 5 ); // near distance Camera can see
49      cameraPtr->setFarClipDistance( 1000 ); // far distance Camera can see
50
51      // create the Viewport
52      viewportPtr = windowPtr->addViewport( cameraPtr );
53      viewportPtr->setBackgroundColour( ColourValue( 0, 0, 0 ) );
54
55      // set the Camera's aspect ratio
56      cameraPtr->setAspectRatio( Real( viewportPtr->getActualWidth() ) /
57         ( viewportPtr->getActualHeight() ) );
58
```

Fig. 23.5 | Pong class member-function definitions. (Part 2 of 7.)

```
59      // set the scene's ambient light
60      sceneManagerPtr->setAmbientLight( ColourValue( 0.75, 0.75, 0.75 )
61
62      // create the Light
63      Light *lightPtr = sceneManagerPtr->createLight( "Light" ); // a Light
64      lightPtr->setPosition( 0, 0, 50 ); // set the Light's position
65
66      unsigned long hWnd; // variable to hold the window handle
67      windowPtr->getCustomAttribute( "WINDOW", &hWnd ); // get window handle
68      OIS::ParamList paramList; // create an OIS ParamList
69
70      // add the window to the ParamList
71      paramList.insert( OIS::ParamList::value_type( "WINDOW",
72         Ogre::StringConverter::toString(  hWnd ) ) );
73
74      // create the InputManager
75      inputManagerPtr = OIS::InputManager::createInputSystem( paramList );
76      keyboardPtr = static_cast< OIS::Keyboard* >( inputManagerPtr->
77         createInputObject( OIS::OISKeyboard, true ) ); // create a Keyboard
78      keyboardPtr->setEventCallback( this ); // add a KeyListener
79
80      rootPtr->addFrameListener( this ); // add this Pong as a FrameListener
81
82      // load resources for Pong
83      ResourceGroupManager::getSingleton().addResourceLocation(
84         "../../media/PongResources", "FileSystem", "Pong" );
85      ResourceGroupManager::getSingleton().initialiseAllResourceGroups();
86
87      quit = pause = false; // player has not quit or paused the game
88      time = 0; // initialize the time since Ball was reset to 0
89   } // end Pong constructor
90
91   // Pong destructor erases objects contained in a Pong object
92   Pong::~Pong()
93   {
94      // free dynamically allocated memory for Keyboard
95      inputManagerPtr->destroyInputObject( keyboardPtr );
96      OIS::InputManager::destroyInputSystem( inputManagerPtr );
97
98      // free dynamically allocated memory for Root
99      delete rootPtr; // release memory pointer points to
100     rootPtr = 0; // point pointer at 0
101
102     // free dynamically allocated memory for Ball
103     delete ballPtr; // release memory pointer points to
104     ballPtr = 0; // point pointer at 0
105
106     // free dynamically allocated memory for Paddle
107     delete leftPaddlePtr; // release memory pointer points to
108     leftPaddlePtr = 0; // point pointer at 0
109
110     // free dynamically allocated memory for Paddle
111     delete rightPaddlePtr; // release memory pointer points to
```

Fig. 23.5 | Pong class member-function definitions. (Part 3 of 7.)

```
112     rightPaddlePtr = 0; // point pointer at 0
113   } // end Pong destructor
114
115   // create the scene to be displayed
116   void Pong::createScene()
117   {
118     // get a pointer to the Score Overlay
119     Overlay *scoreOverlayPtr =
120        OverlayManager::getSingleton().getByName( "Score" );
121     scoreOverlayPtr->show(); // show the Overlay
122
123     // make the game objects
124     ballPtr = new Ball( sceneManagerPtr ); // make the Ball
125     ballPtr->addToScene(); // add the Ball to the scene
126     rightPaddlePtr = new Paddle( sceneManagerPtr, "RightPaddle", 90 );
127     rightPaddlePtr->addToScene(); // add a Paddle to the scene
128     leftPaddlePtr = new Paddle( sceneManagerPtr, "LeftPaddle", -90 );
129     leftPaddlePtr->addToScene(); // add a Paddle to the scene
130
131     // create the walls
132     Entity *entityPtr = sceneManagerPtr->
133        createEntity( "WallLeft", "cube.mesh" ); // create the left wall
134     entityPtr->setMaterialName( "wall" ); // set material for left wall
135     entityPtr->setNormaliseNormals( true ); // fix the normals when scaled
136
137     // create the SceneNode for the left wall
138     SceneNode *nodePtr = sceneManagerPtr->getRootSceneNode()->
139        createChildSceneNode( "WallLeft" );
140     nodePtr->attachObject( entityPtr ); // attach left wall to SceneNode
141     nodePtr->setPosition( -95, 0, 0 ); // set the left wall's position
142     nodePtr->setScale( .05, 1.45, .1 ); // set the left wall's size
143     entityPtr = sceneManagerPtr->createEntity( "WallRight", "cube.mesh" );
144     entityPtr->setMaterialName( "wall" ); // set material for right wall
145     entityPtr->setNormaliseNormals( true ); // fix the normals when scaled
146
147     // create the SceneNode for the right wall
148     nodePtr = sceneManagerPtr->getRootSceneNode()->
149        createChildSceneNode( "WallRight" );
150     nodePtr->attachObject( entityPtr ); // attach right wall to SceneNode
151     nodePtr->setPosition( 95, 0, 0 ); // set the right wall's position
152     nodePtr->setScale( .05, 1.45, .1 ); // set the right wall's size
153     entityPtr = sceneManagerPtr->createEntity( "WallBottom", "cube.mesh" );
154     entityPtr->setMaterialName( "wall" ); // set material for bottom wall
155     entityPtr->setNormaliseNormals( true ); // fix the normals when scaled
156
157     // create the SceneNode for the bottom wall
158     nodePtr = sceneManagerPtr->getRootSceneNode()->
159        createChildSceneNode( "WallBottom" );
160     nodePtr->attachObject( entityPtr ); // attach bottom wall to SceneNode
161     nodePtr->setPosition( 0, -70, 0 ); // set the bottom wall's position
162     nodePtr->setScale( 1.95, .05, .1 ); // set bottom wall's size
163     entityPtr = sceneManagerPtr->createEntity( "WallTop", "cube.mesh" );
```

Fig. 23.5 | Pong class member-function definitions. (Part 4 of 7.)

```
164    entityPtr->setMaterialName( "wall" ); // set the material for top wall
165    entityPtr->setNormaliseNormals( true ); // fix the normals when scaled
166
167    // create the SceneNode for the top wall
168    nodePtr = sceneManagerPtr->getRootSceneNode()->
169       createChildSceneNode( "WallTop" );
170    nodePtr->attachObject( entityPtr ); // attach top wall to the SceneNode
171    nodePtr->setPosition( 0, 70, 0 ); // set the top wall's position
172    nodePtr->setScale( 1.95, .05, .1 ); // set the top wall's size
173 } // end function createScene
174
175 // start a game of Pong
176 void Pong::run()
177 {
178    createScene(); // create the scene
179    rootPtr->startRendering(); // start rendering frames
180 } // end function run
181
182 // update the score
183 void Pong::updateScore( Players player )
184 {
185    // increase the correct player's score
186    if ( player == Players::PLAYER1 )
187       player1Score++;
188    else
189       player2Score++;
190
191    wait = true; // the game should wait to restart the Ball
192    updateScoreText(); // update the score text on the screen
193 } // end function updateScore
194
195 // update the score text
196 void Pong::updateScoreText()
197 {
198    ostringstream scoreText; // text to be displayed
199
200    scoreText << "Player 2 Score: " << player2Score; // make the text
201
202    // get the right player's TextArea
203    OverlayElement *textElementPtr =
204       OverlayManager::getSingletonPtr()->getOverlayElement( "right" );
205    textElementPtr->setCaption( scoreText.str() ); // set the text
206
207    scoreText.str( "" ); // reset the text in scoreText
208    scoreText << "Player 1 Score: " << player1Score; // make the text
209
210    // get the left player's TextArea
211    textElementPtr =
212       OverlayManager::getSingletonPtr()->getOverlayElement( "left" );
213    textElementPtr->setCaption( scoreText.str() ); // set the text
214 } // end function updateScoreText
215
```

Fig. 23.5 | Pong class member-function definitions. (Part 5 of 7.)

```
216  // respond to user keyboard input
217  bool Pong::keyPressed( const OIS::KeyEvent &keyEventRef )
218  {
219     // if the game is not paused
220     if ( !pause )
221     {
222        // process KeyEvents that apply when the game is not paused
223        switch ( keyEventRef.key )
224        {
225        case OIS::KC_ESCAPE: // escape key hit: quit
226           quit = true;
227           break;
228        case OIS::KC_UP: // up-arrow key hit: move the right Paddle up
229           rightPaddlePtr->movePaddle( PADDLE_UP );
230           break;
231        case OIS::KC_DOWN: //down-arrow key hit: move the right Paddle down
232           rightPaddlePtr->movePaddle( PADDLE_DOWN );
233           break;
234        case OIS::KC_A: // A key hit: move the left Paddle up
235           leftPaddlePtr->movePaddle( PADDLE_UP );
236           break;
237        case OIS::KC_Z: // Z key hit: move the left Paddle down
238           leftPaddlePtr->movePaddle( PADDLE_DOWN );
239           break;
240        case OIS::KC_P: // P key hit: pause the game
241           pause = true; // set pause to true when the user pauses the game
242           Overlay *pauseOverlayPtr =
243              OverlayManager::getSingleton().getByName( "PauseOverlay" );
244           pauseOverlayPtr->show(); // show the pause Overlay
245           break;
246        } // end switch
247     } // end if
248     else // game is paused
249     {
250        // user hit 'R' on the keyboard
251        if ( keyEventRef.key == OIS::KC_R )
252        {
253           pause = false; // set pause to false when user resumes the game
254           Overlay *pauseOverlayPtr =
255              OverlayManager::getSingleton().getByName( "PauseOverlay" );
256           pauseOverlayPtr->hide(); // hide the pause Overlay
257        } // end if
258     } // end else
259     return true;
260  } // end function keyPressed
261
262  // process key released events
263  bool Pong::keyReleased( const OIS::KeyEvent &keyEventRef )
264  {
265     return true;
266  } // end function keyReleased
267
```

Fig. 23.5 | Pong class member-function definitions. (Part 6 of 7.)

```
268   // return true if the program should render the next frame
269   bool Pong::frameEnded( const FrameEvent &frameEvent )
270   {
271      return !quit; // quit = false if the user hasn't quit yet
272   } // end function frameEnded
273
274   // process game logic, return true if the next frame should be rendered
275   bool Pong::frameStarted( const FrameEvent &frameEvent )
276   {
277      keyboardPtr->capture(); // get keyboard events
278      // the game is not paused and the Ball should move
279      if ( !wait && !pause )
280      {
281         // move the Ball
282         ballPtr->moveBall( frameEvent.timeSinceLastFrame );
283      } // end if
284      // don't move the Ball if wait is true
285      else if ( wait )
286      {
287         // increase time if it is less than 4 seconds
288         if ( time < 4 )
289            // add the seconds since the last frame
290            time += frameEvent.timeSinceLastFrame;
291         else
292         {
293            wait = false; // shouldn't wait to move the Ball any more
294            time = 0; // reset the control variable to 0
295         } // end else
296      } // end else
297
298      return !quit; // quit = false if the user hasn't quit yet
299   } // end function frameStarted
```

Fig. 23.5 | Pong class member-function definitions. (Part 7 of 7.)

Before we can display any graphics, we need to initialize the Ogre engine settings and create certain Ogre objects. The **OGRE Engine Rendering Setup** dialog box (Fig. 23.6) enables the user to choose the rendering settings, including which rendering subsystem to use (Direct3D or OpenGL), resolution, color depth, full-screen mode, and other options that are beyond the scope of this chapter. Direct3D is exclusively for Windows. OpenGL is supported on all major platforms. The resolution is defined by two values, width and height, which determine the number of pixels used to draw the scene. The resolution options for both rendering subsystems can range from 640 × 400 to 1680 × 1050 or higher, depending on your hardware. A higher resolution will produce more detailed graphics. If you choose to turn off full-screen mode, the resolution will also determine the size of the window in which the game is displayed. We run the game at a resolution of 800 × 600. A color depth of n bits means that 2^n possible colors can be displayed on the screen. A lower color depth will make the program require less memory, but the graphics may not be as good. Direct3D and OpenGL each support 16-bit and 32-bit color depths. In 32-bit colors, only 24 bits are used for the color; the other eight bits represent the alpha value (i.e., transparency).

Fig. 23.6 | **OGRE Engine Rendering Setup** dialog box.

To display the dialog box, you must create a Root object (Fig. 23.5, line 32)—the Ogre object used to start the engine. The only Ogre object that can be created before Root is the LogManager—but that is beyond the scope of this book. Next, we call the showConfigDialog function of the Root class (line 35) to display the dialog. Once you hit **OK**, Ogre saves the settings and uses them as the default settings the next time the dialog box is displayed. The program should end if the user selects **Cancel**, because the settings may not be properly configured and could cause errors. We throw a runtime_error if showConfigDialog returns false (i.e., the user selected **Cancel**).

Once the rendering subsystem and window options have been set, we can create the RenderWindow, a window in which Ogre will render graphics, by calling the initialise function of class Root (line 39). The first parameter, true, tells Ogre to create the window with the settings the user chose in the dialog box. Passing false to this parameter allows you to manually create the window at a later time. The second, "Pong", is the name of the window within the engine and will also appear in the title bar of the window if it's not full screen. Notice the British spelling of initialise and of colour in Fig. 23.6, reflecting Ogre's origin in the United Kingdom.

23.4.2 Creating a Scene

Now that we've initialized Ogre and set up a window to render our graphics in, we'll add some objects to create our scene—the collection of images that we display on the screen.

SceneManager

To control the scene we use Ogre's SceneManager object (line 42). The SceneManager manages the scene graph, a data structure that contains all the objects in the scene, both visible and nonvisible. The SceneManager is used to create objects that will be added to the scene graph and determines which objects will be rendered. Excluding objects that are not within the visible scene from being rendered, known as culling, decreases rendering time and increases performance. This is done automatically. We'll keep a pointer to this SceneManager object, as it will be used extensively throughout the game.

Several types of SceneManagers have been designed to handle different types of scenes, such as indoor scenes or expansive landscape scenes. An Ogre application can use more than one SceneManager, separately or at the same time. For the purposes of this chapter, we use only one instance of the generic scene type (ST_GENERIC), a SceneManager that's not optimized for any particular type of scene.

Camera

Once we have a SceneManager, we can start constructing our scene. First we add a Camera. A Camera in Ogre is the eye through which you view the scene. A 3D scene is usually too large to be displayed in one window. The Camera looks into the scene and tells Ogre what part you can actually see. Cameras can be placed at any location in the scene or attached to SceneNodes—we'll discuss these shortly. If attached to a SceneNode, the Camera will follow that node if it moves within the scene. Ogre supports multiple Cameras in a single scene, but we need only one.

We use the SceneManager to create the Camera (line 45), then we set the position, orientation, clip distances and Viewport (lines 46–53). Position is the location of the Camera within the scene. We position the Camera 200 units from the origin along the positive z-axis, toward the player. This places the Camera far enough away from the origin of the scene so that we can center the game around it. We can set all of the z-coordinates to 0 and not have to change them. The orientation is the direction in which the Camera is looking. We have the Camera look at the origin (line 47) because we center the game around that point. The clip distances define how near and how far the Camera can see. If something is closer to the Camera than the near clip distance, or farther away than the far clip distance, then the Camera won't be able to see it. The Viewport is the area of the screen used to display what the Camera can see. We set the Viewport's background color to white. Note that a Camera can have more than one Viewport, but we will use only one for our game. Cameras have many other features and functions, but this is all we need for our game.

Light

One of the most important aspects of a 3D scene is lighting. Ogre has three types of Lights—Point, Spot and Directional. Point lights have a position in space and radiate light in all directions. Spot lights have a position in space like Point lights, but radiate light in only one direction; the strength of the light fades as the distance from the source increases. Directional lights do not have a position in space, they have only a direction in which they shine—the light is assumed to come from the same direction no matter where you are in the scene.

We use a Point light in our game. Lines 63–64 use the SceneManager to create the Light and set its position within the scene. The argument to the createLight function is the name by which we'll refer to the Light. We set the Light's position by specifying its x-, y- and z-coordinates. Our scene is now ready for use.

23.4.3 Adding to the Scene

As we mentioned earlier, Pong has four major game objects—a ball, two paddles and a rectangular box. All of these elements must be added to the scene before they can be displayed.

Add the Ball

Class Ball (Figs. 23.7–23.8) represents the ball that bounces around the screen. We have to add the Ball to the scene before it can be displayed. The member function addToScene (Fig. 23.8, lines 27–52) creates an Entity that represents the Ball, adds it to the scene and creates some sounds associated with the Ball; we'll discuss the sounds later. An Entity is an instance of a mesh within the scene. A mesh is a file that contains the geometry information of a 3D model. Many Entity objects can be based on the same mesh as long as each Entity has a unique name. Lines 30–31 create the Entity, which is referenced through a pointer. The first argument is the name of the Entity. The second argument, "sphere.mesh", is the mesh file used to determine the Entity's shape. We use the sphere mesh provided with the Ogre SDK. You can find the mesh in the OgreSDK\media\models folder on your computer.

```
1   // Ball.h
2   // Ball class definition (represents a bouncing ball).
3   #ifndef BALL_H
4   #define BALL_H
5
6   #include <Ogre.h> // Ogre class definition
7   using namespace Ogre; // use the Ogre namespace
8
9   #include <OgreAL.h> // OgreAL class definition
10
11  class Paddle; // forward declaration of class Paddle
12
13  const int RADIUS = 5; // the radius of the Ball
14
15  class Ball
16  {
17  public:
18     Ball( SceneManager *sceneManagerPtr ); // constructor
19     ~Ball(); // destructor
20     void addToScene(); // add the Ball to the scene
21     void moveBall( Real time ); // move the Ball across the screen
22
23  private:
24     SceneManager *sceneManagerPtr; // pointer to the SceneManager
25     SceneNode *nodePtr; // pointer to the SceneNode
26     OgreAL::SoundManager *soundManagerPtr; // pointer to the SoundManager
27     OgreAL::Sound *wallSoundPtr; // sound played when Ball hits a wall
28     OgreAL::Sound *paddleSoundPtr; // sound played when Ball hits a Paddle
29     OgreAL::Sound *scoreSoundPtr; // sound played when someone scores
30     int speed; // speed of the Ball
31     Vector3 direction; // direction of the Ball
```

Fig. 23.7 | Ball class definition (represents a bouncing ball). (Part 1 of 2.)

```
32
33      // private utility functions
34      void reverseHorizontalDirection(); // change horizontal direction
35      void reverseVerticalDirection(); // change vertical direction
36      void hitPaddle(); // control the Ball hitting the Paddles
37   }; // end class Ball
38
39   #endif // BALL_H
```

Fig. 23.7 | `Ball` class definition (represents a bouncing ball). (Part 2 of 2.)

```
1    // Ball.cpp
2    // Ball class member-function definitions.
3    #include <Ogre.h> // Ogre class definition
4    using namespace Ogre; // use the Ogre namespace
5
6    #include <OgreAL.h> // OgreAL class definition
7    #include "Ball.h" // Ball class definition
8    #include "Paddle.h" // Paddle class definition
9    #include "Pong.h" // Pong class definition
10
11   // Ball constructor
12   Ball::Ball( SceneManager *ptr )
13   {
14      sceneManagerPtr = ptr; // set pointer to the SceneManager
15      soundManagerPtr = new OgreAL::SoundManager(); // create SoundManager
16      speed = 100; // speed of the Ball
17      direction = Vector3( 1, -1, 0 ); // direction of the Ball
18   } // end Ball constructor
19
20   // Ball destructor
21   Ball::~Ball()
22   {
23      // empty body
24   } // end Ball destructor
25
26   // add the Ball to the scene
27   void Ball::addToScene()
28   {
29      // create Entity and attach it to a node in the scene
30      Entity *entityPtr =
31         sceneManagerPtr->createEntity( "Ball", "sphere.mesh" );
32      entityPtr->setMaterialName( "ball" ); // set material for the Ball
33      entityPtr->setNormaliseNormals( true ); // fix the normals when scaled
34      nodePtr = sceneManagerPtr->getRootSceneNode()->
35         createChildSceneNode( "Ball" ); // create a SceneNode
36      nodePtr->attachObject( entityPtr ); // attach the Entity to SceneNode
37      nodePtr->setScale( .05, .05, .05 ); // scale SceneNode
38
39      // attach sounds to Ball so they will play from where Ball is
40      wallSoundPtr = soundManagerPtr->
41         createSound( "wallSound", "wallSound.wav", false );
```

Fig. 23.8 | `Ball` class member-function definitions. (Part 1 of 4.)

```
42      nodePtr->attachObject( wallSoundPtr ); // attach a sound to SceneNode
43      paddleSoundPtr = soundManagerPtr->
44         createSound( "paddleSound", "paddleSound.wav", false );
45      nodePtr->attachObject( paddleSoundPtr ); // attach sound to SceneNode
46      scoreSoundPtr = soundManagerPtr->
47         createSound( "cheer", "cheer.wav", false ); // create a Sound
48
49      // attach the score sound to its own node centered at ( 0, 0, 0 )
50      sceneManagerPtr->getRootSceneNode()->createChildSceneNode( "score" )->
51         attachObject( scoreSoundPtr );
52   } // end function addToScene
53
54   // move the Ball across the screen
55   void Ball::moveBall( Real time )
56   {
57      nodePtr->translate( ( direction * ( speed * time ) ) ); // move Ball
58      Vector3 position = nodePtr->getPosition(); // get Ball's new position
59
60      // get the positions of the four walls
61      Vector3 topPosition = sceneManagerPtr->
62         getSceneNode( "WallTop" )->getPosition();
63      Vector3 bottomPosition = sceneManagerPtr->
64         getSceneNode( "WallBottom" )->getPosition();
65      Vector3 leftPosition = sceneManagerPtr->
66         getSceneNode( "WallLeft" )->getPosition();
67      Vector3 rightPosition = sceneManagerPtr->
68         getSceneNode( "WallRight" )->getPosition();
69
70      const int WALL_WIDTH = 5; // the width of the walls
71
72      // check if the Ball hit the left side
73      if ( ( position.x - RADIUS ) <= leftPosition.x + ( WALL_WIDTH / 2 ) )
74      {
75         nodePtr->setPosition( 0, 0, 0 ); // place Ball in center of screen
76         Pong::updateScore( Players::PLAYER2 ); // update the score
77         scoreSoundPtr->play(); // play a sound when player 2 scores
78      } // end if
79      // check if the Ball hit the right side
80      else if (
81         ( position.x + RADIUS ) >= rightPosition.x - ( WALL_WIDTH / 2 ) )
82      {
83         nodePtr->setPosition( 0, 0, 0 ); // place Ball in center of screen
84         Pong::updateScore( Players::PLAYER1 ); // update the score
85         scoreSoundPtr->play(); // play a sound when player 1 scores
86      } // end else
87      // check if the Ball hit the bottom wall
88      else if (
89         ( position.y - RADIUS ) <= bottomPosition.y + ( WALL_WIDTH / 2 ) &&
90         direction.y < 0 )
91      {
92         // place the Ball on the bottom wall
93         nodePtr->setPosition( position.x,
94            ( bottomPosition.y + ( WALL_WIDTH / 2 ) + RADIUS ), position.z );
```

Fig. 23.8 | `Ball` class member-function definitions. (Part 2 of 4.)

```
 95        reverseVerticalDirection(); // make the Ball start moving up
 96     } // end else
 97     // check if the Ball hit the top wall
 98     else if (
 99        ( position.y + RADIUS ) >= topPosition.y - ( WALL_WIDTH / 2 ) &&
100        direction.y > 0 )
101     {
102        // place the Ball on the top wall
103        nodePtr->setPosition( position.x,
104           ( topPosition.y - ( WALL_WIDTH / 2 ) - RADIUS ), position.z );
105        reverseVerticalDirection(); // make the Ball start moving down
106     } // end else
107
108     hitPaddle(); // check if the Ball hit a Paddle
109  } // end function moveBall
110
111  // reverse the Ball's horizontal direction
112  void Ball::reverseHorizontalDirection()
113  {
114     direction *= Vector3( -1, 1, 1 ); // reverse the horizontal direction
115     paddleSoundPtr->play(); // play the "paddleSound" sound effect
116  } // end function reverseHorizontalDirection
117
118  // reverse the Ball's vertical direction
119  void Ball::reverseVerticalDirection()
120  {
121     direction *= Vector3( 1, -1, 1 ); // reverse the vertical direction
122     wallSoundPtr->play(); // play the "wallSound" sound effect
123  } // end function reverseVerticalDirection
124
125  // control the Ball colliding with the Paddle
126  void Ball::hitPaddle()
127  {
128     // get the position of the Paddles and the Ball
129     Vector3 leftPaddlePosition = sceneManagerPtr->
130        getSceneNode( "LeftPaddle" )->getPosition(); // left Paddle
131     Vector3 rightPaddlePosition = sceneManagerPtr->
132        getSceneNode( "RightPaddle" )->getPosition(); // right Paddle
133     Vector3 ballPosition = nodePtr->getPosition(); // the Ball's position
134
135     const int PADDLE_WIDTH = 2; // width of the Paddle
136     const int PADDLE_HEIGHT = 30; // height of the Paddle
137
138     // is the Ball in range of the left Paddle?
139     if ( ( ballPosition.x - RADIUS ) <
140        ( leftPaddlePosition.x + ( PADDLE_WIDTH / 2 ) ) )
141     {
142        // check for collision with left Paddle
143        if ( ( ballPosition.y - RADIUS ) <
144           ( leftPaddlePosition.y + ( PADDLE_HEIGHT / 2 ) ) &&
145           ( ballPosition.y + RADIUS ) >
146           ( leftPaddlePosition.y - ( PADDLE_HEIGHT / 2 ) ) )
147        {
```

Fig. 23.8 | Ball class member-function definitions. (Part 3 of 4.)

```
148          reverseHorizontalDirection(); // reverse the Ball's direction
149
150             // place the Ball at the edge of the Paddle
151             nodePtr->setPosition(
152                ( leftPaddlePosition.x + ( PADDLE_WIDTH / 2 ) + RADIUS ),
153                ballPosition.y, ballPosition.z );
154          } // end if
155       } // end if
156       // is the Ball in range of the right Paddle?
157       else if ( ( ballPosition.x + RADIUS ) >
158          ( rightPaddlePosition.x - ( PADDLE_WIDTH / 2 ) ) )
159       {
160          // check for collision with right Paddle
161          if ( ( ballPosition.y - RADIUS ) <
162             ( rightPaddlePosition.y + ( PADDLE_HEIGHT / 2 ) ) &&
163             ( ballPosition.y + RADIUS ) >
164             ( rightPaddlePosition.y - ( PADDLE_HEIGHT / 2 ) ) )
165          {
166             reverseHorizontalDirection(); // reverse the Ball's direction
167
168             // place the Ball at the edge of the Paddle
169             nodePtr->setPosition(
170                ( rightPaddlePosition.x - ( PADDLE_WIDTH / 2 ) - RADIUS ),
171                ballPosition.y, ballPosition.z );
172          } // end if
173       } // end else
174    } // end function hitPaddle
```

Fig. 23.8 | Ball class member-function definitions. (Part 4 of 4.)

Line 32 sets the material used to color the Entity. The argument, "ball", is the name of the material used to color the Ball. In Ogre, a material is usually created with a script, though it can also be created directly in the program. A material script (Fig. 23.9) is a text file that Ogre uses to create a material. Save the text file with a .material extension.

```
1    // ball material definition
2    material ball
3    {
4       // define one technique for rendering the Ball
5       technique
6       {
7          // render the Ball in one pass
8          pass
9          {
10             // color the Ball violet
11             ambient 0.58 0 0.827
12             diffuse 0.58 0 0.827
13             specular 0.58 0 0.827 120
14          }
15       }
16    }
```

Fig. 23.9 | ball material script.

Notice that the `ball` material's structure looks similar to C++ code, with curly braces enclosing each section. Line 2 indicates that we're defining a `material` called `ball`. Within the `material`, we define a `technique`—i.e., how to render the object (lines 5–15). You can define multiple `techniques` for a material, but that is beyond our scope. Within each `technique`, one or more `passes` are defined (lines 8–14). Each `pass` defines a single step in the `material`'s rendering process. Using multiple `passes` is beyond our scope. The color is determined in the `pass` by setting color values for the different types of lighting in the scene. We want the `Ball` to be violet, so set the color values to (0.58, 0, 0.827) (lines 11–13). The numbers after each type of light (ambient, diffuse and specular) represent color values. The fourth number in `specular` (120) determines how shiny the `Ball` is. It can be any value greater than 0. The higher the value the shinier the object appears.

Note that "`ball`" is not the name of the file that the `material` is defined in, but rather the name of the `material` within that file. A `material` file can define multiple `materials`. The same `material` can be used for multiple `Entity` objects, but each `material` defined must have a unique name.

We've created the `Entity` for our `Ball`, but it is not part of the scene yet. Lines 34–36 (Fig. 23.8) add it to the scene so it will be rendered on the screen. We use the `Scene-Manager` to create a `SceneNode`—a `Node` within the scene graph that holds information about an object and its position in the scene, visible or nonvisible. A `SceneNode` may have many child `SceneNodes` attached to it, but can have only one parent `Node`. The argument, "`Ball`", is the name by which the `SceneNode` will be referred to in the Ogre engine. Every `SceneNode` in the scene graph must have a unique name. The call to `getRootSceneNode` retrieves the topmost node within the scene graph. The root node is the parent of all other nodes. When you create a child of the root node, its initial position is (0, 0, 0). Line 36 attaches the `Entity` representing the `Ball` to the newly created `SceneNode`. The `Ball` is now part of the scene and will be rendered. Notice that all of the functions used to add the `Ball` to the scene are member functions of the `SceneManager`. That is why the `Ball` constructor takes a pointer to the `SceneManager` as a parameter—the `Ball` object must be able to access the `SceneManager` to add itself to the scene.

The sphere mesh provided with the Ogre SDK has a radius of 100. This is much larger than we need. Line 37 changes the size of the `Entity` attached to the `SceneNode`, but it does not affect the size of the actual mesh that the node's `Entity` is based on. We supply a scaling factor for each axis (*x*, *y* and *z*). We pass `.05` as the scaling factor for all three axes. Using the same scaling factor for all three axes uniformly scales the mesh so it maintains its original shape. The function multiplies the radius of the sphere on each axis by the scaling factor to change the radius from 100 to 5. When you scale a mesh, the lighting effects become somewhat distorted. We fix that by having the `Entity` calculate the new normals for the mesh each time it is scaled (line 33). A normal in this case refers to the direction each facet (i.e., small section) of the object's surface is facing. If the facet is facing toward the light, it is brighter. If it's facing away from the light, it is darker.

There is also a function `scale` that will change the size of the `Entity`. The difference is that `scale` changes the size based on the current size, while `setScale` changes it based on the original size of the node. These functions also scale all children of the `SceneNode` by the same factor. This can be changed by telling each child of the parent node that you do not wish to have it scaled when the parent is scaled—to do that, call the `setInherit-Scale` function and pass it `false`.

Add the *Paddles*

Class Paddle (Figs. 23.10–23.11) represents the Paddles. We add a Paddle to the scene in much the same way that we added the Ball. The member function addToScene (Fig. 23.11, lines 24–35) uses the same first five Ogre functions, but with different arguments.

```
1   // Paddle.h
2   // Paddle class definition (represents a paddle in the game).
3   #ifndef PADDLE_H
4   #define PADDLE_H
5
6   #include <Ogre.h> // Ogre class definition
7   using namespace Ogre; // use the Ogre namespace
8
9   class Paddle
10  {
11  public:
12     // constructor
13     Paddle( SceneManager *sceneManagerPtr, String paddleName,
14     int positionX );
15     ~Paddle(); // destructor
16     void addToScene(); // add a Paddle to the scene
17     void movePaddle( const Vector3 &direction ); // move a Paddle
18
19  private:
20     SceneManager* sceneManagerPtr; // pointer to the SceneManager
21     SceneNode *nodePtr; // pointer to a SceneNode
22     String name; // name of the Paddle
23     int x; // x-coordinate of the Paddle
24  }; // end of class Paddle
25
26  #endif // PADDLE_H
```

Fig. 23.10 | Paddle class definition (represents a paddle in the game).

```
1   // Paddle.cpp
2   // Paddle class member-function definitions.
3   #include <Ogre.h> // Ogre class definition
4   using namespace Ogre; // use the Ogre namespace
5
6   #include "Paddle.h" // Paddle class definition
7
8   // constructor
9   Paddle::Paddle( SceneManager *ptr, String paddleName,
10     int positionX )
11  {
12     sceneManagerPtr = ptr; // set the pointer to the SceneManager
13     name = paddleName; // set the Paddle's name
14     x = positionX; // set the Paddle's x-coordinate
15  } // end Paddle constructor
16
```

Fig. 23.11 | Paddle class member-function definitions. (Part 1 of 2.)

```
17   // destructor
18   Paddle::~Paddle()
19   {
20      // empty body
21   } // end Paddle default destructor
22
23   // add the Paddle to the scene
24   void Paddle::addToScene()
25   {
26      Entity *entityPtr = sceneManagerPtr->
27         createEntity( name, "cube.mesh" ); // create an Entity
28      entityPtr->setMaterialName( "paddle" ); // set the Paddle's material
29      entityPtr->setNormaliseNormals( true ); // fix the normals when scaled
30      nodePtr = sceneManagerPtr->getRootSceneNode()->
31         createChildSceneNode( name ); // create a SceneNode for the Paddle
32      nodePtr->attachObject( entityPtr ); // attach Paddle to the SceneNode
33      nodePtr->setScale( .02, .3, .1 ); // set the Paddle's size
34      nodePtr->setPosition( x, 0, 0 ); // set the Paddle's position
35   } // end function addToScene
36
37   // move the Paddle up and down the screen
38   void Paddle::movePaddle( const Vector3 &direction )
39   {
40      nodePtr->translate( direction ); // move the Paddle
41      if ( nodePtr->getPosition().y > 52.5 ) // top of the box
42         nodePtr->setPosition( x, 52.5, 0 ); // place Paddle at top of box
43      else if ( nodePtr->getPosition().y < -52.5 ) // bottom of the box
44
45         // place the Paddle at the bottom of the box
46         nodePtr->setPosition( x, -52.5, 0 );
47   } // end function movePaddle
```

Fig. 23.11 | `Paddle` class member-function definitions. (Part 2 of 2.)

First we create an `Entity` to represent the `Paddle` on the screen (lines 26–27). Here we use the name supplied to the constructor as the `Entity` name. We can't just use `"Paddle"` as we used `"Ball"` because each `Entity` must have a unique name, and there are two `Paddle`s in the game. We use the cube mesh provided with the Ogre SDK as the model for the `Paddle`. The cube mesh is located in the `OgreSDK\media\models` folder. We color both `Paddle`s dark orange with the same `material` (Fig. 23.12). This `material` script is almost identical to the script used for the ball. The only differences are the name of the `material` (line 2) and the color values (lines 11–13).

Then we create a child `SceneNode` of the root node to hold the data for the `Paddle` (Fig. 23.11, lines 30–31). We use the name provided to the constructor for the `Node`'s name as we did for the `Entity`. This is allowed because `Node`s and `Entity` objects are separate types, so there is not a name conflict.

Next we attach the `Entity` to the node (line 32) and scale the node to an appropriate size (line 33). The cube mesh is $100 \times 100 \times 100$, but we scale it to $2 \times 30 \times 10$ to make it an appropriate size for a `Paddle`. We also set the `Entity` to recalculate its normals (line 29) as we did with the `Ball`. The only new Ogre function we use is `setPosition` (line 34).

```
 1    // paddle material definition
 2    material paddle
 3    {
 4        // define one technique for rendering a Paddle
 5        technique
 6        {
 7            // render a Paddle in one pass
 8            pass
 9            {
10                // color the Paddle dark orange
11                ambient 1 0.549 0
12                diffuse 1 0.549 0
13                specular 1 0.549 0 120
14            }
15        }
16    }
```

Fig. 23.12 | Paddle material script.

This function places the node at the given coordinates in the scene relative to its parent. We didn't need to use this function in the Ball class, because we wanted Ball's SceneNode to start at (0, 0, 0), which is the default position of any node attached to the root node. We want the Paddle to be positioned at the edge of the screen, so we have to move it there. In line 34, x is a data member of class Paddle that defines the Paddle's *x*-coordinate.

Add the Walls

Now we will add the box that contains the bouncing Ball and the moving Paddles. We create this box in the createScene function of class Pong (Fig. 23.5, lines 132–172). We use the same cube mesh, provided with the Ogre SDK, for all four walls—scaling the walls appropriately to make the box and recalculating the normals for lighting. The walls are added to the scene similarly to the Ball and Paddles. We create an Entity using the cube mesh to represent each wall. We use a simple material to color all the walls cyan (Fig. 23.13). The material script looks just like the other two we have seen, only the name and color values differ.

Now position and scale the walls. The left and right walls are each placed 95 units from the origin in the *x*-direction. The top and bottom walls are each placed 70 units from the origin in the *y*-direction. Each wall is then scaled to the correct size. The top and bottom walls are positioned 140 units apart in the *y*-direction. We give both a width of 5 units. This width is an arbitrary value. You can change the width to make the game look as you want it to. If you change this, you'll also have to change the collision detection code—you'll see why when we discuss the collision logic. For the left and right walls to stretch between the top and bottom walls, they must be 145 units long (140 plus the half-width of each wall). So the *x*-scaling factor for the left and right walls is 1.45. The left and right walls are also given a width of 5 units and are positioned 185 units apart in the *x*-direction. For the top and bottom walls to stretch between the left and right walls, they must be 195 units long, so their *y*-scaling factor is 1.95.

```
 1   // wall material definition
 2   material wall
 3   {
 4      // define one technique for rendering a wall
 5      technique
 6      {
 7         // render a wall in one pass
 8         pass
 9         {
10            // color the wall cyan
11            ambient 0 0.545 0.545
12            diffuse 0 0.545 0.545
13            specular 0 0.545 0.545 120
14         }
15      }
16   }
```

Fig. 23.13 | Wall material script.

Add the Text

We use an Ogre Overlay to display the score of the game as text. An Overlay refers to anything you want to render on top of the 3D elements of the scene. We use Overlays only for text in this chapter. The Overlay is defined by a script saved in a .overlay file.

Overlays are composed of OverlayElements. The first element in an Overlay must be an OverlayContainer. An OverlayContainer can hold any type of OverlayElement. A TextAreaOverlayElement holds the text that will be displayed on the screen. Every object in an Overlay has three main attributes—metrics mode, position and size. The position is determined by the top-left corner of the object and is always relative to the parent OverlayContainer of the object. Size is determined by width and height. The metrics mode determines how the object is positioned and sized. Pixel mode will size the object based on the width and height declared in pixels. Relative mode will position and size the object relative to the size of the parent OverlayContainer (or the window if it is the outermost OverlayContainer). In relative mode, size and position values range from 0.0 to 1.0—think of it as a percentage of the parent OverlayElement's size. If you position an element at (0.0, 0.0), it will be at the top-left corner of the parent element; (0.5, 0.0) would be 50 percent across the top.

To display the score, we create an Overlay (Fig. 23.14). Line 2 names the Overlay Score. A single overlay file can hold several Overlay definitions. Ogre will reference each Overlay by the name rather than the file. The z-order of the Overlay (line 5) is used to define what this Overlay should be rendered over. When using multiple Overlays, an Overlay with a higher z-order will be rendered on top of an Overlay with a lower z-order. Lines 8–58 create a PanelOverlayElement container that holds two TextAreaOverlayElements. The OverlayContainer is positioned in the top-left corner of the screen (lines 13–14) and runs along the entire width (line 17). The container is 10 percent of the height of the window (line 18). The first TextAreaOverlayElement (lines 21–38) is positioned at the top of the container 5 percent away from the left side, runs half the width and is the same height as the container (lines 28–31). The other TextAreaOverlayElement (lines 40–57) is positioned 69 percent of the way across the top of the container and runs

```
1    // An Overlay to display the score
2    Score
3    {
4       // set a high z-order, displays on top of anything with lower z-order
5       zorder 500
6
7       // create a PanelOverlayElement container to hold the text areas
8       container Panel(ScorePanel)
9       {
10         // use relative metrics mode to position this container at the
11         // top-left corner of the screen
12         metrics_mode relative
13         left 0.0
14         top 0.0
15
16         // make it 1/10 the height and the full width of the screen
17         width 1.0
18         height .1
19
20         // create a TextAreaOverlayElement to display player 1's score
21         element TextArea(left)
22         {
23            // position and size the element relative to the container
24            metrics_mode relative
25
26            // position it at the top of the container 5% from the left and
27            // make it the same height and half as long as the container
28            left 0.05
29            top 0.0
30            width 0.5
31            height 1.0
32
33            // set font used for caption and set the size and color
34            font_name BlueBold
35            char_height .05
36            colour 1.0 0 0
37            caption Player 1 Score: 0
38         }
39         // create a TextAreaOverlayElement to display player 2's score
40         element TextArea(right)
41         {
42            // position and size the element relative to the container
43            metrics_mode relative
44
45            // position it at the top of the container 69% from the left and
46            // make it the same height as the container, stretch to the end
47            left 0.69
48            top 0.0
49            width 0.5
50            height 1.0
51
52            // set font used for caption and set the size and color
53            font_name BlueBold
```

Fig. 23.14 | Overlay script to display the score. (Part 1 of 2.)

```
54            char_height 0.05
55            colour 1.0 0 0
56            caption Player 2 Score: 0
57        }
58      }
59  }
```

Fig. 23.14 | Overlay script to display the score. (Part 2 of 2.)

to the end. The TextAreaOverlayElements also declare a font to use (which is defined by a script in a .fontdef file in the PongResources folder), the character height, font color (note the British spelling, "colour") and the caption (lines 34–37 and 53–56).

Figure 23.15 is the .fontdef file that defines the BlueBold font. Line 2 gives the font a name that Ogre will refer to. Line 5 tells Ogre what type of font it is. True type is a common font file format (a .ttf file). The source (line 8) is the file that contains the font. We put the .ttf file in the same folder as the .fontdef file. If you place the two files in different locations, you will have to specify the path to the .ttf file in line 8 or add the folder containing the .ttf file as a resource location (discussed in Section 23.4.8).

Lines 119–121 of class Pong (Fig. 23.5) display the score on the screen. We use the static member function getSingleton of class OverlayManager to get a pointer to the OverlayManager object. We use that object to get a pointer to the score Overlay, then we call the show function to display it on the screen. When a player scores, we need to update the text within the Overlay to reflect the change (lines 196–214). First we create the new text. Then we get a pointer to the appropriate TextAreaOverlayElement from the OverlayManager and use the TextAreaOverlayElement member function setCaption to replace the text.

```
1   // define the BlueBold font
2   BlueBold
3   {
4       // define the font type
5       type truetype
6
7       // set the source file for the font
8       source bluebold.ttf
9
10      // set the font size
11      size 16
12
13      // set the font resolution (96 is standard)
14      resolution 96
15  }
```

Fig. 23.15 | BlueBold font definition script.

23.4.4 Animation and Timers

Now that we know how to draw a Ball on the screen, animating it and making it move around the screen is straightforward. The function moveBall (Fig. 23.8, lines 55–109) moves the Ball around the screen. In most Pong games, the ball can travel at many different angles. However, since we are just starting out with Ogre, we want to keep things as simple as possible. For this reason, in our Pong game, the ball has only four possible directions of travel: down-right, up-right, down-left, and up-left—all at 45-degree angles to the x- and y-axes in our program.

Line 57 actually makes the Ball move; the rest of the function controls collisions with various objects within the scene, as we'll see shortly. The translate function takes as an argument a Vector3, which is a three-dimensional vector type defined by Ogre. The vector represents the direction and distance to move the Ball. We pass to the translate function the Ball's direction multiplied by the distance to travel (speed × time) to determine the final vector. The speed parameter is the number of units the ball will move per second. The time parameter is the number of seconds since the last time the Ball was moved. We'll see where this comes from in just a moment. SceneNode translations are done in parent space by default. That means that the node is translated with respect to its parent node's position and orientation (i.e., the direction the node is facing). Translations can also be performed in world or local space by adding another parameter to the translate function (TS_LOCAL or TS_WORLD). Translations in world space are done with respect to the origin of the scene (0, 0, 0). Translations in local space are done with respect to the node's origin (wherever the node is positioned and whichever direction it is facing).[2]

To continuously move the Ball across the screen, call the moveBall function each time a new frame is rendered. Figure 23.4 defines the Pong class, our game's main driving class, which inherits from the Ogre class FrameListener. A FrameListener is a class that processes Ogre::FrameEvents. A FrameEvent occurs every time a frame begins or ends. Every FrameListener has two functions, frameStarted and frameEnded (lines 30–31). These functions both return a bool. Ogre keeps rendering frames until one of these functions returns false. We use the frameStarted function (Fig. 23.5, lines 275–299) to control the animation of our Ball, specifically line 282. This function is called by Ogre before each new frame is rendered. Before every frame, the frameStarted function calls the Ball class member function moveBall, which continuously moves the Ball across the screen. As discussed earlier, controlling the speed of the animation is vital to creating smooth motion. Frame rates (i.e., how quickly the scene gets redrawn) may vary greatly on different machines, so the Ball could move at a different speed on each one. For that reason we pass the FrameEvent's data member timeSinceLastFrame, in seconds, to the moveBall function. We multiply this time by the Ball's speed to determine the distance the Ball should move across the screen. This is an example of using a timer to control animation.

23.4.5 User Input

Now we discuss moving the Paddle up and down on the screen with the movePaddle function of class Paddle (Fig. 23.11, lines 38–47). To move the Paddle, we again use the SceneNode function translate (line 40). Rather than moving the Paddle based on time, we move it based on user input from the keyboard. The user specifies a direction, up or down, by pressing the corresponding key, and the Paddle moves accordingly. The direction is passed to movePaddle as a Vector3.

Ogre does not directly support user input from devices such as the keyboard, mouse or joystick. The Ogre SDK does come with the Object Oriented Input System (OIS) for

---

2.   Junker, Gregory, *Pro OGRE 3D Programming*, 2006, pp. 82—89.

handling user input. It is not required that you use OIS for input with Ogre, but it's a good choice.

We need to create an InputManager, a Keyboard and a KeyListener to handle the user input and control the calls to movePaddle. The InputManager is used to create the various input devices. We create the InputManager in class Pong's constructor (Fig. 23.5, line 75). To create the InputManager we must provide it with a window in which to collect (lines 66–72).

We create a Keyboard object which represents the actual keyboard. To collect KeyEvents, we must call the capture function of class Keyboard. We want to call this function repeatedly, so we place it in the frameStarted function, which is called at the beginning of every frame. Class Pong inherits from class KeyListener, an OIS class that handles input from the keyboard. We register it with the Keyboard (line 78) to receive KeyEvents, i.e., indications that the player has hit a key. A KeyListener defines two member functions (Fig. 23.4, lines 26–27)—we use only one of these (line 26). We must implement the other one, though, because they are both declared pure virtual in the class KeyListener.

The implementation of the key-handling function is in lines 217–260. Every time we capture a key press, the Keyboard sends the KeyEvent to this member function. OIS defines an enumeration of all the keys on the keyboard, which we use to determine which key was pressed. The switch statement (lines 223–246) responds only to certain keys. We extract the key enumeration from the KeyEvent and pass it to the switch statement (line 223). If the *A* or *Z* key is being pressed, the Paddle on the left side should move up or down, respectively. Likewise, if the user presses the up- or down-arrow key, the Paddle on the right side should move in the corresponding direction. The directions passed to the movePaddle function are defined as constant Vector3s (lines 26–27).

We allow the user to pause the game by hitting the *P* key (lines 240–245), which sets the Pong data member pause to true. The if statement (line 220) will skip the switch statement that controls the Paddle movement when pause is true. The pause data member will also stop the Ball from moving when it is true (line 279). We also use an Overlay (Fig. 23.16) to display "Game Paused" on the screen. The game resumes when the player hits the *R* key.

```
1   // An Overlay to display "Game Paused" when the player pauses the game
2   PauseOverlay
3   {
4       // set a high z-order, displays on top of anything with lower z-order
5       zorder 500
6
7       // create a PanelOverlayElement container to hold the text area
8       container Panel(Pause)
9       {
10          // use relative metrics mode to position and size this container
11          metrics_mode relative
12
13          // place the container at the top-left corner of the window
14          left 0.0
```

Fig. 23.16 | Overlay script to display "Game Paused" when player pauses the game. (Part 1 of 2.)

```
15          top 0.0
16
17          // make the container the same size as the window
18          width 1.0
19          height 1.0
20
21          // create a TextAreaOverlayElement to display the text
22          element TextArea(pauseText)
23          {
24              // position and size the element relative to its container
25              metrics_mode relative
26
27              // center it vertically in the container
28              vert_align center
29
30              // put the left corner 4/10 from the left of the container and
31              // make it 2/10 the width of the container and 1/10 the height
32              left 0.4
33              width 0.2
34              height 0.1
35
36              // set the font used for caption and set the size and color
37              font_name BlueBold
38              char_height 0.05
39              colour 0 0 0
40              caption Game Paused
41          }
42      }
43  }
```

Fig. 23.16 | Overlay script to display "Game Paused" when player pauses the game. (Part 2 of 2.)

If the user hits the *Esc* key, the game exits by setting the `quit` data member to `true` (Fig. 23.5 lines 225–227). Recall that Ogre continues to render frames until the `frame-Started` or `frameEnded` function returns `false`. These both return `!quit`, so when we set `quit` to `true`, the functions return `false` and tell Ogre to shut down. If you don't use the *Esc* key to quit, the program won't stop properly; it keeps running in the background. Be sure to use the *Esc* key.

23.4.6 Collision Detection

The `Ball` collides with a number of objects as it bounces around the screen. We need to detect these collisions to make the `Ball` interact correctly with its surroundings. Lines 61–106 of Fig. 23.8 control collisions between the `Ball` and the walls of the playing area. The call to `SceneNode` member function `getPosition` returns a `Vector3` representing the node's position relative to its parent node. Because all of our nodes are direct children of the root node, whose position is (0, 0, 0), the position returned is always relative to the origin. There is also a `_getDerivedPosition` member function that will return the position relative to the origin of any node regardless of its parent's position.

You can retrieve any node within the scene graph by passing the name of the node to the SceneManager member function getSceneNode. We retrieve the nodes of the four walls (lines 61–68) and use their positions to check for collisions with the Ball. If the Ball's x-coordinate (minus the radius) is less than or equal to the left wall's x-coordinate (plus half the wall's width), then the Ball has collided with the left wall. Once the collision is determined, the proper actions are taken. The Ball is placed in the middle of the screen for the next round (line 75). Player 2 is given a point (line 76) by calling the Pong class member function updateScore. We made the updateScore function static so we can call it from the Ball class without a reference to an instance of the Pong class. Finally, a sound is played to indicate that a player has scored (line 77)—we'll explain that function call in Section 23.4.7. The process is the same to determine if the Ball hit the right side. The Ball's x-coordinate is checked against the right wall's x-coordinate. If the Ball hits the right side, the appropriate actions are taken. Figure 23.17 shows player 1 scoring a point. Note that the Ball is not actually going into the wall; it's an illusion caused by the 3D graphics.

The Ball is then checked against the top and bottom walls. The same collision logic is used. If the Ball's y-coordinate (plus or minus the radius, depending on which wall it hits) after being moved would cross the wall's inner y-coordinate (which is physically impossible because they are both solid objects), the Ball has collided with either the top or bottom wall. To prevent the Ball from overlapping the wall, we place it at the edge of the wall after a collision (lines 93–94 and 103–104). Technically this violates the physics of the Ball by changing the distance it moved in the given time interval. To be accurate, we would have to determine the distance and direction it moved after hitting the wall and

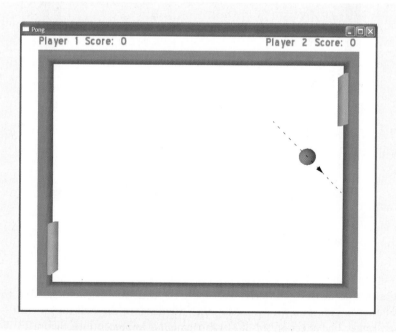

Fig. 23.17 | Player 1 scoring a point. (Part 1 of 2.)

Fig. 23.17 | Player I scoring a point. (Part 2 of 2.)

draw it at that point. In the interest of keeping the code simple, we don't deal with this issue. The scene gets redrawn so quickly that the distance the Ball moves each frame is extremely small. The effect on the Ball's movement is imperceptible. Figure 23.18 shows the Ball bouncing off the top wall.

At the end of moveBall we call the function hitPaddle (lines 126–174) to check for collisions between the Ball and the Paddles and take appropriate actions when one occurs. Lines 129–130 retrieve the node that the left Paddle is attached to, then return the position of the node. Lines 131–132 do the same thing for the right Paddle. We use these positions to detect collisions between the Paddles and the Ball. The logic is similar to the

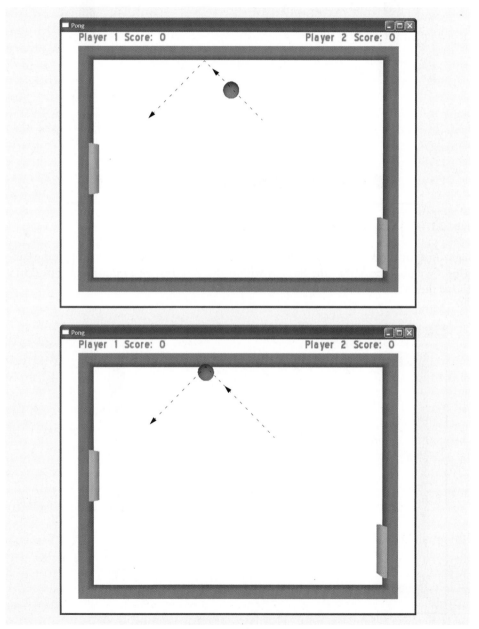

Fig. 23.18 | The Ball bouncing off the top wall. (Part 1 of 2.)

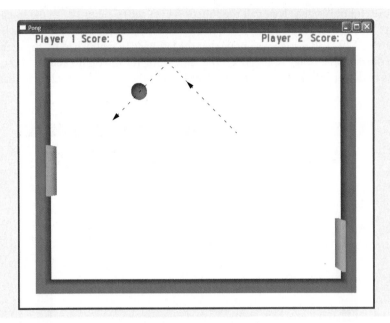

Fig. 23.18 | The Ball bouncing off the top wall. (Part 2 of 2.)

logic used for checking the walls. We first check if the Ball's *x*-coordinate is past the Paddles'. We also check that the Ball is within the Paddles' *y*-coordinates. Figure 23.19 shows the Ball bouncing off a Paddle.

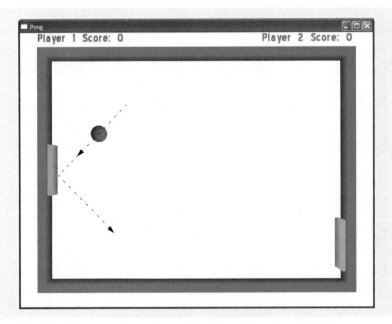

Fig. 23.19 | The Ball bouncing off the left Paddle. (Part 1 of 2.)

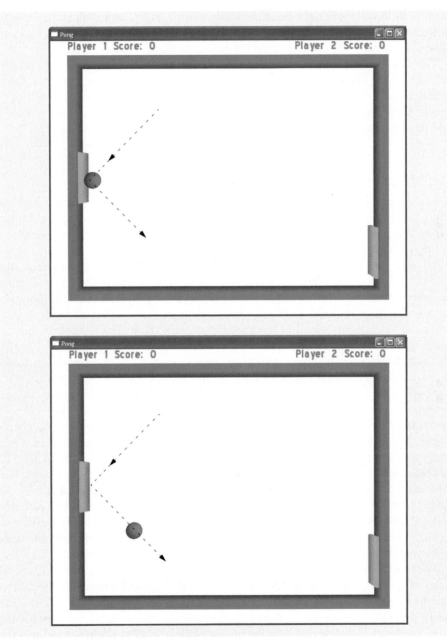

Fig. 23.19 | The Ball bouncing off the left Paddle. (Part 2 of 2.)

Consider the lines that change the ball's direction. Line 114 causes the Ball to start moving left if it's currently moving right, and start moving right if it's currently moving left. Line 121 makes the Ball start moving up if it's currently moving down, and down if it's currently moving up. Why does this work? The direction of the Ball is determined by a Vector3. Each value represents a distance along the x-, y- or z-axis. A positive x-value means the Ball will move right along the *x*-axis, and a negative value will move the Ball left. If the Ball is moving right, multiplying its *x*-value by −1 will change the sign and reverse the direction. We do the same thing to change the vertical direction.

The collisions in our game are fairly simple cases, so we have kept the logic simple. There are whole libraries dedicated to handling collisions and physics, such as Open Dynamics Engine (ODE, www.ode.org/), Bullet (www.continuousphysics.com/Bullet/), Newton Game Dynamics (www.newtondynamics.com/) and PhysX (www.ageia.com/). These libraries have Ogre bindings available on the Ogre Community Add-on page.

23.4.7 Sound

We now discuss importing sounds and playing sound files in Ogre programs, which we will use to "juice up" our Pong game. We play a "boing" sound whenever the Ball hits a wall, we play a different "boing" sound whenever the Ball hits a Paddle and we play a cheering sound whenever a player scores.

We will use OgreAL to add sound to our game. OgreAL is a wrapper around the OpenAL audio library. OgreAL was created and is maintained by Casey Borders (www.mooproductions.org), a member of the Ogre community. The OpenAL library is maintained by Creative Labs, developer.creative.com. The wrapper allows us to integrate sound functionality into the Ogre code by attaching the sounds to nodes within the scene graph. Because all of the sounds we play relate to the Ball, we place the OgreAL code in the Ball class. The OgreAL functions used to import and play sounds are analogous to those used for importing and displaying models in Ogre.

As with Ogre, we include the OgreAL.h header. OgreAL manages the sounds using a SoundManager class, following the Ogre resource management scheme. We create a SoundManager in the Ball constructor (Fig. 23.8, line 15). There can be only one Sound-Manager. The SoundManager is used to create instances of Sounds, the OgreAL objects that contain the sound data. We create three Sounds and attach them to nodes (lines 40–51). The createSound function takes three parameters. The first is an Ogre::String that will be the name of the Sound. The second is the name of the sound file associated with the Sound. The third is a bool that determines if the Sound should be looped to continue playing. Passing false will play the Sound through once, then stop. Passing true will continuously loop the sound until you stop it. We attach the Sounds to a node in the same way we would attach an Entity to a node with the attachObject function.

The first Sound we create (lines 40–41) will be played whenever the Ball bounces off the top or bottom wall. We attach it to the Ball's node. OpenAL supports 3D sound, so when the Sound is attached to the Ball, it will play from wherever the Ball is. Our scene is relatively small, so you may not notice the Sound being played in 3D, but if you listen closely, it will sound slightly different. Because we placed the call to the play function (line 122) inside our function that reverses the Ball's vertical direction, the "boing" sound will play whenever the Ball's vertical direction is reversed—in other words, whenever the ball hits the top or bottom wall.

The second Sound is created the same way as the first, and again is attached to the Ball's node. This sound will play whenever the Ball bounces off one of the Paddles. We play this Sound within the reverseHorizontalDirection function (line 115) for the same reason we play the other sound from reverseVerticalDirection.

The third Sound will play whenever a player scores. There is no particular location to play this Sound from—we attach it directly to the root node of the scene graph, which is positioned at the origin. We play the Sound from the moveBall function every time it is determined that a player has scored (lines 77 and 85).

There are a couple of things to note about Sounds in OgreAL. Each Sound must have a unique name, just like Entity objects and Nodes. A Sound must finish playing before it can be played again.

23.4.8 Resources

As mentioned earlier, Ogre uses scripts to create Materials, Overlays and some other advanced features that are beyond the scope of this text. Ogre also uses .mesh files to represent 3D objects. OgreAL uses sound files. All of these resources must be loaded before we can use them. Ogre will throw a runtime exception if you try to use a resource that hasn't been loaded. To manage the game's resources we use a ResourceGroupManager. To load the resources for our game, we first tell the ResourceGroupManager where to find them. The addResourceLocation function (Figure 23.5, lines 83–84) takes three Ogre::String arguments. The first is the location of the resources. We placed all the resources in a folder called PongResources within the media folder in the Ogre SDK. Normally you would organize the resources in different folders by type, e.g. materials, models and overlays. But for simplicity we maintain one folder to hold all the resources we will need for the game. The second argument is the type of file the resources are in. The third is the resource group these files belong to. We will put these files in the "Pong" group. Now we load the resources in the location we just added (line 83).

23.4.9 Pong Driver

The last step is to write a main function (Fig. 23.20). Ogre supports various platforms, so you should try not to write platform-specific code when you can avoid it. The preprocessor if else wrapper (lines 6–15) will determine whether the program is running on a Windows platform. If it is, it will include the windows.h header and define the WinMain function. If not, it will define the normal main function. This allows the code to run on various platforms without having to be changed. You may not have seen the Windows-specific code before. The preprocessor directive to include the windows.h header gives the program the necessary access to the Windows API to run our program. The definition of WIN32_LEAN_AND_MEAN (line 7) will exclude rarely used headers in the windows.h header. This will speed up the compilation time for our program.

```
1   // PongMain.cpp
2   // Driver program for the game of Pong
3   #include <iostream>
4
5   #include "Pong.h" // Pong class definition
6
7   // If running on Windows, include windows.h and define WinMain function
8   #if OGRE_PLATFORM==PLATFORM_WIN32 || OGRE_PLATFORM==OGRE_PLATFORM_WIN32
9   #define WIN32_LEAN_AND_MEAN
```

Fig. 23.20 | Driver program for the game of Pong. (Part 1 of 2.)

```
10    #include "windows.h"
11
12    int WINAPI WinMain( HINSTANCE hInst, HINSTANCE, LPSTR strCmdLine, INT )
13
14    // If not, define normal main function
15    #else
16    int main( int argc, char **argv )
17    #endif
18    {
19       try
20       {
21          Pong game; // create a Pong object
22          game.run(); // start the Pong game
23       } // end try
24
25       catch ( std::runtime_error &error )
26       {
27    #if OGRE_PLATFORM==PLATFORM_WIN32 || OGRE_PLATFORM==OGRE_PLATFORM_WIN32
28          MessageBoxA( NULL, error.what(), "Exception Thrown!",
29             MB_OK | MB_ICONERROR | MB_TASKMODAL );
30    #else
31          std::cerr << "Exception Thrown: " << error.what() << std::endl;
32    #endif
33       } // end catch
34
35       return 0;
36    } // end main
```

Fig. 23.20 | Driver program for the game of Pong. (Part 2 of 2.)

The main function creates the initial Pong object in a try block (lines 17–21). Recall that the Pong constructor throws an exception if the user cancels the Ogre configuration dialog box. If the user hits **OK** in the dialog box, the Pong object is created and we call the run member function (line 20). Class Pong member function run (Fig. 23.5, lines 176–180) first creates the game's scene (line 178), then calls the startRendering member function (line 179) of class Root to render the scene repeatedly until either the frameStarted or the frameEnded function returns false.

23.5 Wrap-Up

In this chapter you learned the basics of creating computer games with Ogre. We discussed the basic concepts of graphics, briefly describing models, lighting and colors. You saw how to use the free Ogre 3D rendering engine to produce a 3D game. We showed you how to use the SceneManager to create and manage your scene. You learned how to use a Camera to view your scene. We discussed responding to user input from the keyboard with OIS. We demonstrated how to move an object at a constant speed. We covered the basics of collision detection and showed how important it is to game programming. You learned how to display text on the screen using Overlays. We showed how Ogre uses scripts to manage materials and Overlays without having to recompile every time you change them. We also showed how to add sound to your games using the OgreAL wrapper for OpenAL.

This chapter should be viewed only as an introduction. We presented you with a basic example of Pong. Use it as a foundation for your own version. Go out and find your own sounds to use. Add new features to the game. Explore Ogre's other capabilities and create some cool visual effects. Really make this game your own. Game programming is all about being creative.

The next chapter discusses the future of C++. A new standard, known as C++0x, will be released in 2009. You'll learn about the new libraries and core language features being added to C++. You'll also learn about the Boost Libraries, which many of the libraries being added to C++0x are based on. We'll demonstrate how to use two of the new libraries to work with regular expressions and smart pointers.

23.6 Ogre Web Resources

`www.ogre3d.org/`
The Ogre home page. Here you can find the latest Ogre news, download Ogre or Ogre-related tools, browse the documentation or check out projects that use Ogre.

`www.ogre3d.org/index.php?option=com_content&task=view&id=411&Itemid=131`
Prebuilt SDK download page. There are SDKs available for Code::Blocks + MingGW C++ Toolbox, Visual C++ .Net 2003 and Visual C++ .Net 2005 (must install Service Pack 1).

`www.ogre3d.org/index.php?option=com_content&task=view&id=412&Itemid=132`
Ogre source-code download page. Source code available for Windows, Linux and Mac OS X. Also download the third-party dependencies package for your platform. Also has a link to a guide to building Ogre from source.

`www.ogre3d.org/index.php?option=com_content&task=view&id=415&Itemid=144`
Instructions on getting the Ogre source code from the CVS directory.

`www.ogre3d.org/wiki/index.php/Installing_An_SDK`
Installation instructions for the Ogre SDK on Windows with Visual C++, Code::Blocks + MinGW, Code::Blocks + MinGW + STLPort, Eclipse + MinGW + STLPort and GCC & Make/Any IDE. Linux, Debian, Gentoo, Fedora and Ubuntu. Mac OS X.

`www.ogre3d.org/wiki/index.php/Building_From_Source`
Instructions for building the Ogre source code on Windows with Visual C++, Visual C++ Toolkit 2003 & Code::Blocks, and GCC. Linux with GCC & Make, Debian, Fedora, Gentoo, Ubuntu/Kubuntu. Mac OS X with Xcode.

`www.ogre3d.org/wiki/index.php/BuildFAQ`
Solutions to common errors when building from the source code. Errors include not being able to find files, unresolved external symbols and other types of errors.

`www.ogre3d.org/wiki/index.php/SettingUpAnApplication`
Guide to setting up an Ogre Application project on Visual C++, Code::Blocks, GCC, Autotools, Scons, Eclipse, Anjuta IDE, KDevelop IDE.

`www.ogre3d.org/phpBB2addons/viewtopic.php?t=3293`
OgreAL download and installation instructions.

`developer.creative.com/landing.asp?cat=1&sbcat=31&top=38`
OpenAL download and installation links.

`www.openal.org/downloads.html`
OpenAL download page.

`www.wreckedgames.com/wiki/index.php/WreckedLibs:OIS`
Object Oriented Input System (OIS) wiki page includes links to the OIS manual and API reference.

`www.tayloredmktg.com/rgb/`
Color-code chart. Gives RGB values in hex and decimal. Colors are divided into general color range (e.g., grays, blues, greens, oranges).

`www.htmlcenter.com/tutorials/tutorials.cfm/89/General/`
Color chart gives RGB and hex color values.

Tutorials

`www.ogre3d.org/wiki/index.php/Ogre_Tutorials`
Ogre tutorials page. Tutorials range from basic to advanced on topics including introduction to Ogre, FrameListeners, animation multiple SceneManagers and content creation.

`www.blender.org/tutorials-help/`
Blender tutorials page.

`en.wikibooks.org/wiki/Blender_3D:_Noob_to_Pro`
The "Blender 3D: Noob to Pro" wikibook guides new Blender users through the process of 3D modeling. Teaches you how to work with models, lighting, rendering, animation, particles and soft bodies. Also has advanced tutorials on python scripting and advanced animation.

`www.cegui.org.uk/wiki/index.php/Tutorials`
Many tutorials on using Crazy Eddie's GUI System (CEGUI) that is supported by Ogre.

Tools

`www.ogre3d.org/index.php?option=com_content&task=view&id=413&Itemid=133`
Download model export tools for Blender, Maya, Softimage XSI and 3DS Max.

`usa.autodesk.com/adsk/servlet/index?siteID=123112&id=7639525`
Autodesk Maya Personal Learning Edition page. Free version of Maya.

`www.softimage.com/downloads/default.aspx`
SoftImage XSI download page. Free 30-day trial available.

`www.blender.org/download/get-blender/`
Blender download page.

Code Examples

`www.ogre3d.org/wiki/index.php/CodeSnippits#HOWTO`
The Ogre Cookbook contains code samples explaining how to do various tasks relating to geometry, rendering, materials, textures, animation, input GUI and sound.

`www.ogre3d.org/phpBB2/viewtopic.php?t=27326`
Asteroid Wars. A game written using Ogre for graphics. Source code is available.

`www.ogre3d.org/phpBB2/viewtopic.php?t=27806`
Five games written with Ogre. The source code for all the games is available.

Books

`www.amazon.com/Pro-OGRE-3D-Programming/dp/1590597109/ref=pd_bbs_sr_1/102-2583408-2260151?ie=UTF8&s=books&qid=1173888297&sr=1-1`
Pro OGRE 3D Programming, by Gregory Junker.

Forums

`www.ogre3d.org/phpBB2/viewtopic.php?t=5706`
A forum post describing how to install Ogre on Debian GNU/Linux.

`www.ogre3d.org/phpBB2/viewforum.php?f=2`
Ogre Help forum. Get help from Ogre users on any problems you encounter while using Ogre.

www.ogre3d.org/phpBB2/
A number of forums on the Ogre site, including help, using Ogre in practice, content creation, programming basics and more.

www.ogre3d.org/phpBB2addons/
Ogre add-ons forums. A number of forums dedicated to the more popular Ogre add-ons, including OgreAL, OgreODE, NxOgre, PyOgre and more.

www.ogre3d.org/phpBB2addons/viewforum.php?f=10
OgreAL forum on the Ogre site. Information on installing and using OgreAL. Great place to find help.

www.wreckedgames.com/forum/viewforum.php?
f=6&sid=dc5f903554a80ac5194213329f5e46e4
OIS forum. Get help on using OIS.

Summary

Section 23.3 Basics of Game Programming

- 3D graphics engines hide the tedious and complex programming required with graphics APIs.
- Ogre supports the Direct3D and OpenGL graphics APIs and runs on the Windows, Linux and Mac platforms.
- Ogre is strictly a graphics rendering engine. The Ogre community has produced many add-ons that allow users to integrate other libraries with Ogre to support those features.
- A 3D model is a computer representation of an object which can be drawn on the screen.
- Materials determine an object's appearance by setting lighting properties, colors and textures.
- A texture is an image that is wrapped around the model.
- Colors are determined by red, green and blue light intensities and an optional alpha value to represent transparency. Values can range from 0 to 1.0.
- There are four different types of light in a 3D scene—ambient, diffuse, emissive and specular.
- Collision detection is the process of determining whether two objects in a game are touching and reacting appropriately.
- There are collision detection and physics modeling libraries that handle the complexities for you.
- Audio libraries enrich your games with sound. Many of those libraries support 3D sound.
- Games often communicate with the user by displaying text.
- Timers control animation speed and make animations look more natural.
- User input devices include the keyboard, mouse, joystick and the game controller.

Section 23.4.1 Ogre Initialization

- `Root` is the base object used in Ogre used to start the engine. No Ogre calls can be made until the `Root` object has been created.
- Call the `showConfigDialog` function of the `Root` class to display the dialog. The **OGRE Engine Rendering Setup** dialog box enables the user to choose the rendering settings.
- The resolution is defined by two values, width and height, which determine the number of pixels used to draw the scene. A higher resolution will produce more detailed graphics.
- A color depth of n bits means that 2^n possible colors can be displayed on the screen.
- The `RenderWindow` is a window in which Ogre will render graphics.

Section 23.4.2 Creating a Scene

- A scene is a collection of images that make up our graphics.

- The SceneManager manages the scene graph, a data structure that contains all the scene's objects.

- The SceneManager is used to create objects and determine which objects will be rendered. An Ogre application can use more than one SceneManager.

- A Camera is the eye through which you view the scene. Cameras can be placed at any location in the scene or attached to SceneNodes. Ogre supports multiple Cameras in a single scene.

- The Viewport is the area of the screen used to display what the Camera can see. A Camera can have more than one Viewport.

- Ogre has three types of Lights—Point, Spot and Directional. Lights are created with the createLight function of class SceneManager.

Section 23.4.3 Adding to the Scene

- An Entity is an instance of a mesh within the scene. A mesh is a file that contains the geometry information of a 3D model. Many Entity objects can be based on the same mesh, as long as each Entity has a unique name.

- Use the SceneManager to create SceneNodes that hold information about an object and its position in the scene.

- The root node is the parent of all other nodes. When you create a child of the root node, its initial position is (0, 0, 0).

- Attach Entity objects to SceneNodes with the attachObject function of class SceneNode.

- scale changes the size of the Entity attached to the SceneNode, but it does not affect the size of the actual mesh that the node's Entity is based on. setScale changes the size based on the original size of the Entity. These functions also scale all children of the SceneNode by the same factor. To change that, call the setInheritScale function and pass it false.

- setPosition function places the node at the given coordinates in the scene.

- Ogre uses a material script to create a material. Save the file with a .material extension. A material file can define multiple materials; every material must have a unique name.

- An Overlay is defined by a script saved in an .overlay file. A single .overlay file can hold several Overlay definitions. Every object in an Overlay has three main attributes—metrics mode, position and size.

- Overlays are composed of OverlayElements. The first element in an Overlay must be an OverlayContainer. An OverlayContainer can hold any OverlayElement. A TextAreaOverlayElement holds text. Call the show function to display the Overlay on the screen

- Use TextAreaOverlayElement to display text. Call setCaption to change text on the screen.

- An Overlay with a higher z-order will be rendered on top of an Overlay with a lower z-order.

- Fonts are defined by a script in a fontdef file.

- Use the static member function getSingleton of class OverlayManager to get the OverlayManager object.

Section 23.4.4 Animation and Timers

- The translate function moves a SceneNode.

- SceneNode translations are done in parent space by default. Translations in parent space are done with respect to the parent's origin. Translations in world space are done with respect to the origin of the scene (0, 0, 0). Translations in local space are done with respect to the node's origin.

- A `FrameListener` processes `Ogre::FrameEvents`. A `FrameEvent` occurs every time a frame begins or ends.

Section 23.4.5 User Input
- Ogre does not directly support user input from devices such as the keyboard, mouse or joystick.
- Use the Object Oriented Input System (OIS) for handling user input.
- The `InputManager` is used to create the various input devices. To create the `InputManager` we must provide it with a window in which to collect input.
- A Keyboard object collects `KeyEvents` and sends them to a `KeyListener`.
- OIS defines an enumeration of all the keys on the keyboard, which we use to determine which key was pressed.

Section 23.4.6 Collision Detection
- `getPosition` returns a `Vector3` representing the node's position relative to its parent node; `_getDerivedPosition` returns the position relative to the origin.
- The `SceneManager` can retrieve any node within the scene graph by referencing the name given to the node when it was created.
- The direction of the `Ball` is determined by a `Vector3`. A positive *x*-value means the `Ball` will move right along the *x*-axis, and a negative value will move the `Ball` left. If the `Ball` is moving right, multiplying its *x*-value by −1 will change the sign and reverse the direction.
- There are whole libraries dedicated to handling collisions and physics.

Section 23.4.7 Sound
- OgreAL is a wrapper around the OpenAL audio library. The wrapper allows us to integrate sound functionality into the Ogre code by attaching the sounds to nodes within the scene graph.
- We must have the preprocessor directive to include the `OgreAL.h` header.
- Sound is the OgreAL object that contains the sound data. Use the `createSound` function of class `SoundManager` to create sounds. There can be only one `SoundManager`.
- The `createSound` function takes three parameters. The first is an `Ogre::String` that will be the name of the Sound within the OgreAL system. The second is the name of the sound file associated with the Sound. The third is a `bool` that determines whether the Sound should be looped to continue playing. Passing `false` will play the Sound through once, then stop. Passing `true` will continuously loop the sound until you stop it.
- Attach the Sounds to a node with the `attachObject` function.
- Each Sound must have a unique name.
- A Sound must finish playing before it can be played again.

Section 23.4.8 Resources
- All of the resources must be loaded before we can use them.
- Use a `ResourceGroupManager` to manage the game's resources.
- The `addResourceLocation` function takes three `Ogre::String` arguments. The first is the location of the resources. The second is the type of file the resources are in. The third is the resource group these files belong to.

Section 23.4.9 Pong Driver
- Ogre supports various platforms, so you should try not to write platform-specific code when you can avoid it.

Terminology

3D graphics engines
3D model
3D modeling tool
3D sound
add-ons
alpha channel
ambient light
animation
attachObject function of class SceneNode
Camera class
collision detection
color
color depth
createSound function of class SoundManager
culling
diffuse light
Direct3D
Directional lights
emissive light
Entity class
EventProcessor class
frame
FrameEvent class
FrameListener class
getPosition function of class SceneNode
getRootSceneNode function of class
    SceneManager
getWorldPositionfunction of classSceneNode
graphics
initialise function of class Root
InputManager class
Keyboard class
KeyEvent class
KeyListener class
Light class
lighting
local space
LoD (level of detail)
material
mesh
metrics mode
Node class
normal
Ogre
Ogre Application Wizard
OgreAL
OIS (Object Oriented Input System)
OpenAL audio library
OpenGL

Overlay class
OverlayContainer class
OverlayElement class
OverlayManager class
PanelOverlayElement class
parent space
pixel mode
Point light
Pong
relative mode
render
rendering subsystem
RenderWindow class
resolution
ResourceGroupManager class
Root class
root node
scale function of class SceneNode
scaling factor
scene
scene graph
SceneManager class
SceneNode class
scripts
setCaption function of class TextAreaOverlay-
    Element
setInheritScale function of class SceneNode
setPosition function of class SceneNode
setScale function of class SceneNode
showConfigDialog function of class Root
sound
Sound class
SoundManager class
specular light
Spot light
text
TextAreaOverlayElement class
texture
timer
timeSinceLastFrame
translate function of class SceneNode
user input
Vector3
Viewport class
WIN32_LEAN_AND_MEAN
WinMain
world space
z-order

Self-Review Exercises

23.1 Fill in the blanks in each of the following statements:
a) The _____ header includes the most commonly used Ogre header files.
b) The _____ object must be created before any other Ogre function (other than logging) is called.
c) The main type defined by OgreAL for pointing to sound-file data is _____.
d) A(n) _____ object is used to represent a color in Ogre.
e) The _____ header includes the most commonly used OgreAL header files.
f) _____ are used to define materials and overlays for Ogre programs.
g) The _____ object is used to load resources for Ogre programs.
h) Ogre uses a(n) _____ object to manage the scene.
i) A 3D model is defined in an Ogre _____ file.

23.2 State whether each of the following is *true* or *false*. If *false*, explain why.
a) The coordinates (0, 0) refer to the bottom-left corner of an `OverlayContainer`.
b) If Ogre attempts to load an external file that does not exist, a runtime error will occur.
c) Color values in Ogre range from 0 to 255.
d) Passing a value of `false` to the `createSound` function will cause the sound file to play continuously.
e) An `Overlay` that draws text on the screen must specify a font in which that text should be drawn.
f) Every `Entity` must have a unique name.

23.3 Write statements to accomplish each of the following:
a) Attach an `Entity` pointer named `entityPtr` to a `SceneNode` pointer name `nodePtr`.
b) Scale the `Entity` from the previous question to half its original size.
c) Create the `Sound` `sample` that loops the `sound.wav` file.
d) If the spacebar is being pressed, set the value of the `int` `number` to 0.
e) Set an `Overlay` `Element` to position itself relative to the size of its parent `Container`.
f) Add a folder named `sounds` in the `media` folder of the OgreSDK as a "General" resource location.
g) Move a SceneNode 15 units left, 4 units up and 8 units toward you.

23.4 Find the error in each of the following:
a) `SceneNode node;`
b) `ColourValue( 0, 0, 255 );`
c) `Root *rootPtr = new Root();`
   `rootPtr->initialize( true, "Window" );`
d) `viewportPtr = sceneManagerPtr->addViewport( cameraPtr );`

Answers to Self-Review Exercises

23.1 a) `Ogre.h`. b) `Root`. c) `Sound`. d) `ColourValue`. e) `OgreAL.h`. f) scripts. g) `ResourceGroupManager` or `ResourceManager`. h) `SceneManager`. i) `.mesh`.

23.2 a) False. The coordinates (0, 0) refer to the top-left corner of an `OverlayContainer`.
b) True.
c) False. Color values in Ogre range from 0.0 to 1.0.
d) False. The sound will play once, then stop.
e) True.
f) True.

23.3 a) `nodePtr->attachObject( entityPtr );`
b) `nodePtr->setScale( .5, .5, .5 );`

    c) `soundManagerPtr->createSound( "sample", "sound.wav", true );`

    d) `if ( keyEvent.key == OIS::KC_SPACE )`
       `number = 0;`

    e) `metrics_mode relative;`

    f) `ResourceGroupManager::getSingleton().addResourceLocation( "../../media/`
      `sounds", "FileSystem", "General" );`

    g) `sceneNodePtr->translate( -15, 4, 8 );`

23.4   a) The variable node should instead be declared as a pointer to a `SceneNode`. All of Ogre's `SceneNode` functions either take a pointer as a parameter or return a pointer.

    b) The `ColourValue` object can accept parameters only with values between 0 and 1.

    c) Ogre uses British spelling, the function is spelled `initialise`. Also, the render settings must be set before you call `initialise`.

    d) `addViewport` is a function of the `RenderWindow` class, not `SceneManager`.

Exercises

23.5   Look through the resources available in our Game Programming Resource Center at www.deitel.com/computergames/gameprogramming/ and the C++ Game Programming Resource Center at www.deitel.com/CplusplusGameProgramming/.

23.6   Modify the Pong game so that when a player reaches 21 points, the game ends and displays a message that the left or right player has won.

23.7   In most Pong games, when a rally between the two players lasts for a long time, the ball begins to speed up in order to prevent a stalemate. Modify the Pong game so that the ball's speed increases for every ten times that it is hit in a rally. When either player scores, the ball should return to its original speed.

23.8   Some Pong games also modify the speed of one or both players' paddles in an effort to keep the game balanced. Modify the Pong game so that when one player has a lead of at least 5 points, his or her paddle begins to slow down. The greater that player's lead, the slower his or her paddle should move. If the player's lead falls to under 5 points, his or her paddle should return to normal speed.

23.9   Modify the Pong game so that before the game begins, a menu appears on the screen that allows the players to choose from several different ball and paddle speeds.

23.10   Write a program that draws the mesh `sphere.mesh` in the center of the screen. When the user presses one of the arrow keys, the mesh should move ten units in that direction.

23.11   Modify the program from Exercise 23.10 so that if the user holds down an arrow key, the sphere will move only once every second.

23.12   (*The Game of Snake*). The object of the game of snake is to maneuver the snake throughout the game area trying to eat bits of food. The snake is represented with a string of contiguous spheres in the game area, which is a two-dimensional grid. The snake can move up, down, left or right. If the snake eats a piece of food (shown by the "F"), it grows by adding another sphere to the end (Fig. 23.21). If the snake hits a wall of the game area (i.e., would be out of the array), the player loses (Fig. 23.22). If the snake runs into itself, the player loses (Fig. 23.23).

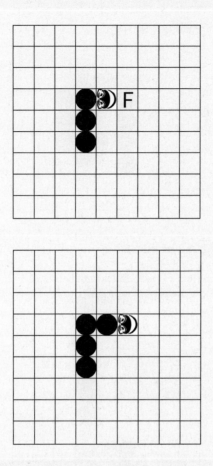

Fig. 23.21 | The snake grows when it eats.

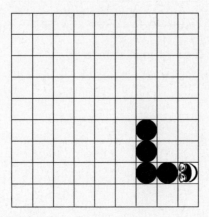

Fig. 23.22 | The snake dies if it hits a wall.

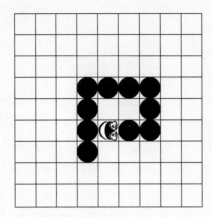

Fig. 23.23 | The snake dies if it hits itself.

23.13 Modify the program from Exercise 23.12 to add obstacles to the game area (Fig. 23.24). If the snake runs into an obstacle, the player loses.

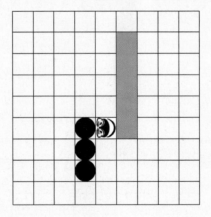

Fig. 23.24 | The snake dies if it hits an obstacle.

Boost Libraries, Technical Report 1 and C++0x

Outstanding leaders go out of their way to boost the self-esteem of their personnel.
—Sam Walton

Practice and thought might gradually forge many an art.
—Virgil

I think "No comment" is a splendid expression.
—Sir Winston Spencer Churchill

So long as you are secure you will count many friends.
—Ovid

The danger from computers is not that they will eventually get as smart as men, but we will meanwhile agree to meet them halfway.
—Bernard Avishai

OBJECTIVES

In this chapter you will learn:

- Future directions for C++.

- What the Boost Libraries are.

- A brief history of the Boost open source project, how new libraries are added to Boost, and how to install Boost.

- To use **Boost.Regex** to search for strings, validate data and replace parts of strings using regular expressions.

- To avoid memory leaks by using **Boost.Smart_ptr** to manage dynamic memory allocation and deallocation.

- What Boost (and other) libraries are included in Technical Report 1 (TR1)—a description of the additions to the C++ Standard Library.

- The changes to the core language and Standard Library coming in the new C++ Standard—C++0x.

- To follow the Deitel online C++ Resource Centers for updates on the evolution of Boost, the Technical Reports and C++0x.

24.1 Introduction

This chapter considers C++'s future. We introduce the Boost C++ Libraries, Technical Report 1 (TR1) and C++0x. The Boost C++ Libraries are free, open source libraries created by members of the C++ community. Boost provides C++ programmers with useful, well-designed libraries that work well with the existing C++ Standard Library. The Boost libraries can be used by C++ programmers working on a wide variety of platforms with many different compilers. We overview the libraries included in TR1 and provide code examples for the regular expression and smart pointer libraries. Technical Report 1 describes the proposed changes to the C++ Standard Library, many of which are based on current Boost libraries. These libraries add useful functionality to C++. C++0x is the working name for the next version of the C++ Standard. It includes some additions to the core language, many of the library additions described in TR1 and other library enhancements.

24.2 Deitel Online C++ and Related Resource Centers

We regularly post online Resource Centers on key programming, software, Web 2.0 and Internet business topics at www.deitel.com/resourcecenters.html. C++0x has not been finalized and new libraries are frequently added to Boost, leaving both in a state of flux. We've created several online Resource Centers that provide links to key information on each of these topics. Visit the C++ Boost Libraries Resource Center at www.deitel.com/CPlusPlusBoostLibraries/ to find current information on the available libraries and new releases. You can find current information on TR1 and C++0x in the C++0x section of the C++ Resource Center at www.deitel.com/cplusplus/ (click **C++0x** in the **Categories** list). We used Visual C++ 2005 Express Edition to compile the code examples in this chapter—for more information on Visual C++, visit our Visual C++ Resource Center at `www.deitel.com/VisualCPlusPlus/`.

24.3 Boost Libraries

The idea for an online repository of free open source C++ libraries was first proposed in a paper by Beman Dawes in 1998.[1] He and Robert Klarer got the idea while attending a C++ Standards Committee meeting. The paper suggested a website where C++ programmers could find and share libraries and foster further C++ development. That idea eventually developed into the Boost Libraries at `www.boost.org`. Boost has grown to over 70 libraries, with more being added frequently. Today there are thousands of programmers in the Boost community.

At the time of this writing, the source code for Boost is hosted on SourceForge (`sourceforge.net`)—the world's largest open source repository, hosting over 140,000 open source projects. SourceForge provides free project development services including revision control such as Subversion (SVN), download services and project website hosting. SourceForge is owned by the Open Source Technology Group (OSTG; `www.ostg.com`), which owns and operates many popular technology websites including `slashdot.org`, `www.linux.com`, `www.newsforge.com` and `www.devchannel.com`. For information about open source software and development check out our Open Source Resource Center at `www.deitel.com/OpenSource/`.

24.4 Adding a New Library to Boost

Boost accepts useful, well-designed, portable libraries from anyone willing to contribute. Potential Boost libraries should conform to the C++ Standard and use the C++ Standard Library—or other appropriate Boost libraries. There is a formal acceptance process to ensure that libraries meet Boost's high quality and portability standards.

The community's interest in a library is determined by posting to mailing lists and reading the responses. If there is interest in a library, a preliminary submission of the library is posted in the Boost Sandbox (`svn.boost.org/svn/boost/sandbox/`)—a code repository for libraries that are under development. The Sandbox allows other users to experiment with the library and provide feedback.

When the library is ready for a formal review, the code submission is posted to the Sandbox Vault and a review manager is selected from a list of approved volunteers. The review manager makes sure the code is ready for formal review, sets up the review schedule, reads all user reviews, and makes the final decision whether or not to accept the library. The review manager may accept the library with certain corrections or improvements that must be implemented before the library is officially added to Boost. Once a library has been accepted, the author is responsible for its maintenance.

The Boost Software License
The Boost Software License (`www.boost.org/more/license_info.html`) grants the rights to copy, modify, use and distribute the Boost source code and binaries for any commercial

1. "Proposal for a C++ Library Repository Web Site," Beman G. Dawes, May 6, 1998, `www.boost.org/more/proposal.pdf`.

or noncommercial use. The only requirement is that the copyright and license information be distributed with any source code that is made public, though it is not required that the source code be released. These conditions allow the Boost libraries to be used in any application. Every Boost library must conform to these conditions.

24.5 Installing the Boost Libraries

The Boost libraries can be used with minimal setup on many platforms and compilers. An installation guide available at `www.boost.org/more/getting_started/index.html` provides setup instructions for many compilers and platforms. We provide Boost installation instructions for Visual C++ 2005 Express on the website for this book at `www.deitel.com/books/cpphtp6`.

24.6 Boost Libraries in Technical Report I (TRI)

Several Boost libraries have been accepted as part of Technical Report 1 (TR1). TR1 is a description of proposed changes and additions to the C++ Standard Library. GCC (GNU Compiler Collection) provides a partial implementation of TR1; the site `gcc.gnu.org/onlinedocs/libstdc++/ext/tr1.html` overviews the TR1 features currently supported. GCC, which is a part of the GNU project, provides free compilers for several programming languages, including C, C++ and Java. Boost has also released a subset of libraries that implement most of the TR1 functionality—this subset is included in the latest release of the Boost libraries. Here we introduce the Boost libraries that the corresponding TR1 extensions are based on. Later, we provide code examples for some of the libraries.

Array [2]
`Boost.Array` is a wrapper for fixed-size arrays that enhances built-in arrays by supporting most of the STL container interface described in Section 22.1. `Boost.Array` allows you to use fixed-size arrays in STL applications rather than `vectors` (dynamically sized arrays), which are not as efficient when there is no need for dynamic resizing.

Bind [3]
`Boost.Bind` extends the functionality of the standard functions `std::bind1st` and `std::bind2nd`. The `bind1st` and `bind2nd` functions are used to adapt binary functions (i.e., functions that take two arguments) to be used with the standard algorithms which take unary functions (i.e., functions that take one argument). `Boost.Bind` enhances that functionality by allowing you to adapt functions that take up to nine arguments. `Boost.Bind` also makes it easy to reorder the arguments passed to the function using placeholders.

Function [4]
`Boost.Function` allows you to store function pointers, member-function pointers and function objects in a function wrapper. You can also store a reference to a function object using the `ref` and `cref` functions added to the `<utility>` header. This allows you to avoid

---

2. Documentation for Boost.Array, Nicolai Josuttis, `www.boost.org/doc/html/array.html`.
3. Documentation for Boost.Bind, Peter Dimov, `www.boost.org/libs/bind/bind.html`.
4. Documentation for Boost.Function, Douglas Gregor, `www.boost.org/doc/html/function.html`.

expensive copy operations. A `boost::function` can hold any function whose arguments and return type can be converted to match the signature of the function wrapper. For example, if the function wrapper was created to hold a function that takes a `string` and returns a `string`, it can also hold a function that takes a `char*` and returns a `char*`, because a `char*` can be converted to a `string`, using a conversion constructor.

Mem_fn [5]

`Boost.mem_fn` enhances the `std::mem_fun` and `std::mem_fun_ref` functions. `mem_fun` and `mem_fun_ref` take a pointer to a member function or a reference to a member function, respectively, and create a function object that calls that member function. The member function can take no arguments or one argument. Function objects are often used with the Standard Library `for_each` function and other STL algorithms. We discussed function objects in Section 22.7. `Boost.mem_fn` enhances the standard functions by allowing you to create the function object with a pointer, reference or smart pointer (Section 24.8) to a member function. It also allows the member functions to take more than one argument. `mem_fn` is a more flexible version of `mem_fun` and `mem_fun_ref`.

Random [6]

`Boost.Random` allows you to create a variety of random number generators and random number distributions. The `std::rand` and `std::srand` functions in the C++ Standard Library generate pseudo-random numbers. A pseudo-random number generator uses an initial state to produce seemingly random numbers—using the same initial state produces the same sequence of numbers. The `rand` function always uses the same initial state, therefore it produces the same sequence of numbers every time. The function `srand` allows you to set the initial state to vary the sequence. Pseudo-random numbers are often used in testing—the predictability enables you to confirm the results. `Boost.Random` provides pseudo-random number generators as well as generators that can produce nondeterministic random numbers—a set of random numbers that can't be predicted. Such random number generators are used in simulations and security scenarios where predictability is undesirable.

Boost.Random also allows you to specify the distribution of the numbers generated. A common distribution is the uniform distribution, which assigns the same probability to each number within a given range. This is similar to rolling a die or flipping a coin—each possible outcome is equally as likely. You can set this range at compile time. `Boost.Random` allows you to use a distribution in combination with any random number generator and even create your own distributions.

Ref [7]

The `Boost.Ref` library provides reference wrappers that enable you to pass references to algorithms that normally receive their arguments by value. The `reference_wrapper` ob-

---

5. Documentation for Boost.Mem_fn, Peter Dimov, `www.boost.org/libs/bind/mem_fn.html`.
6. Jens Maurer, "A Proposal to Add an Extensible Random Number Facility to the Standard Library," Document Number N1452, April 10, 2003, `www.open-std.org/jtc1/sc22/wg21/docs/papers/2003/n1452.html`.
7. Documentation for Boost.Ref, Jaakko Järvi, Peter Dimov, Douglas Gregor and Dave Abrahams, `www.boost.org/doc/html/ref.html`.

ject contains the reference and allows the algorithm to use it as a value. Using references instead of values improves performance when passing large objects to an algorithm.

Regex [8]

`Boost.Regex` provides support for processing regular expressions in C++. Regular expressions are used to match specific character patterns in text. Many modern programming languages have built-in support for regular expressions, but C++ does not. With `Boost.Regex`, you can search for a particular expression in a `string`, replace parts of a `string` that match a regular expression, and split a `string` into tokens using regular expressions to define the delimiters. These techniques are commonly used for text processing, parsing and input validation. We discuss the `Boost.Regex` library in more detail in Section 24.7.

Result_of [9]

The class template `result_of` can be used to specify the return type of a call expression—that is, an expression that calls a function or calls the overloaded parentheses operator of a function object. The call expression's return type is determined based on the types of the arguments passed to the call expression. This can be helpful in templatizing the return types of functions and function objects.

Smart_ptr [10]

`Boost.Smart_ptr` defines smart pointers that help you manage dynamically allocated resources (e.g., memory, files and database connections). Programmers often get confused about when to deallocate memory or simply forget to do it, especially when the memory is referenced by more than one pointer. Smart pointers take care of these tasks automatically. TR1 includes two smart pointers from the `Boost.Smart_ptr` library. `shared_ptrs` handle lifetime management of dynamically allocated objects. The memory is released when there are no `shared_ptrs` referencing it. `weak_ptrs` allow you to observe the value held by a `shared_ptr` without assuming any management responsibilities. We discuss the `Boost.Smart_ptr` library in more detail in Section 24.8.

Tuple [11]

A `tuple` is a set of objects. `Boost.Tuple` allows you to create sets of objects in a generic way and allows generic functions to act on those sets. The library allows you to create tuples of up to 10 objects; that limit can be extended. `Boost.Tuple` is basically an extension to the STL's `std::pair` class template. Tuples are often used to return multiple values from a function. They can also be used to store sets of elements in an STL container where each set of elements is an element of the container. Another useful feature is the ability to set the values of variables using the elements of a tuple.

8. Documentation for `Boost.Regex`, John Maddock, `www.boost.org/libs/regex/doc/index.html`.
9. Documentation for `Boost.Result_of`, Doug Gregor, `www.boost.org/libs/utility/utility.htm#result_of`.
10. Documentation for `Boost.Smart_ptr`, Greg Colvin and Beman Dawes, `www.boost.org/libs/smart_ptr/smart_ptr.htm`.
11. Documentation for `Boost.Tuple`, Jaakko Järvi, `www.boost.org/libs/tuple/doc/tuple_users_guide.html`.

Type_traits [12]

Boost.Type_traits library helps abstract the differences between types to allow generic programming implementations to be optimized. The type_traits classes allow you to determine specific traits of a type (e.g., is it a pointer or a reference type, or does the type have a const qualifier?) and perform type transformations to allow the object to be used in generic code. Such information can be used to optimize generic code. For example, sometimes it is more efficient to copy a collection of objects using the C function memcpy rather than by iterating through all the elements of the collection, as the STL copy algorithm does. With the Boost.Type_traits library, generic algorithms can be optimized by first checking the traits of the types being processed, then performing the algorithm accordingly.

24.7 Regular Expressions with the Boost.Regex Library

Regular expressions are specially formatted strings that are used to find patterns in text. They can be used to validate data to ensure that it is in a particular format. For example, a zip code must consist of five digits, and a last name must start with a capital letter.

The Boost.Regex library provides several classes and algorithms for recognizing and manipulating regular expressions. Class template basic_regex (in the boost namespace) represents a regular expression. The Boost.Regex algorithm regex_match returns true if a string matches the regular expression. With regex_match, the entire string must match the regular expression. Boost.Regex also provides the algorithm regex_search, which returns true if any part of an arbitrary string matches the regular expression. To use the Boost.Regex library, include the header file "boost/regex.hpp". Notice that Boost header files use the .hpp extension.

Regular Expression Character Classes

The table in Fig. 24.1 specifies some character classes that can be used with regular expressions. A character class is not a C++ class—rather it's simply an escape sequence that represents a group of characters that might appear in a string.

A word character is any alphanumeric character or underscore. A whitespace character is a space, tab, carriage return, newline or form feed. A digit is any numeric character. Regular expressions are not limited to the character classes in Fig. 24.1. In Fig. 24.2, you'll see that regular expressions can use other notations to search for complex patterns in strings.

Character class	Matches	Character class	Matches
\d	any decimal digit	\D	any non-digit
\w	any word character	\W	any non-word character
\s	any whitespace character	\S	any non-whitespace character

Fig. 24.1 | Character classes.

---

12. Documentation for Boost.Type_traits, Steve Cleary, Beman Dawes, Howard Hinnant and John Maddock, www.boost.org/doc/html/boost_typetraits.html.

24.7.1 Regular Expression Example

The program in Fig. 24.2 tries to match birthdays to a regular expression. For demonstration purposes, the expression in line 15 matches only birthdays that do not occur in April and that belong to people whose names begin with "J".

Line 15 creates a `regex` (a typedef of the `basic_regex` class template) object by passing a regular expression to the `regex` constructor. Note that we precede each backslash character with an additional backslash. Recall that C++ treats a backslash in a string literal as the beginning of an escape sequence. To insert a literal backslash in a string, you must

```cpp
1   // Fig. 24.2: RegexMatches.cpp
2   // Demonstrating regular expressions.
3   #include <iostream>
4   using std::cout;
5   using std::endl;
6
7   #include <string>
8   using std::string;
9
10  #include "boost/regex.hpp"
11
12  int main()
13  {
14     // create a regular expression
15     boost::regex expression( "J.*\\d[0-35-9]-\\d\\d-\\d\\d" );
16
17     // create a string to be tested
18     string string1 = "Jane's Birthday is 05-12-75\n"
19        "Dave's Birthday is 11-04-68\n"
20        "John's Birthday is 04-28-73\n"
21        "Joe's Birthday is 12-17-77";
22
23     // create a boost::smatch object to hold the search results
24     boost::smatch match;
25
26     // match regular expression to string and print out all matches
27     while ( boost::regex_search( string1, match, expression,
28        boost::match_not_dot_newline ) )
29     {
30        cout << match << endl; // print the matching string
31
32        // remove the matched substring from the string
33        string1 = match.suffix();
34     } // end while
35
36     return 0;
37  } // end function main
```

```
Jane's Birthday is 05-12-75
Joe's Birthday is 12-17-77
```

Fig. 24.2 | Regular expressions checking birthdays.

escape the backslash character with another backslash. For example, the character class \d must be represented as \\d in a C++ string literal.

The first character in the regular expression, "J", is a literal character. Any string matching this regular expression is required to start with "J". In a regular expression, the dot character "." matches any single character. When the dot character is followed by an asterisk, as in ".*", the regular expression matches any number of unspecified characters. In general, when the operator "*" is applied to a pattern, the pattern will match *zero or more* occurrences. By contrast, applying the operator "+" to a pattern causes the pattern to match *one or more* occurrences. For example, both "A*" and "A+" will match "A", but only "A*" will match an empty string.

As indicated in Fig. 24.1, "\d" matches any decimal digit. To specify sets of characters other than those that belong to a predefined character class, characters can be listed in square brackets, []. For example, the pattern "[aeiou]" matches any vowel. Ranges of characters are represented by placing a dash (-) between two characters. In the example, "[0-35-9]" matches only digits in the ranges specified by the pattern—i.e., any digit between 0 and 3 or between 5 and 9; therefore, it matches any digit except 4. You can also specify that a pattern should match anything other than the characters in the brackets. To do so, place ^ as the first character in the brackets. It is important to note that "[^4]" is not the same as "[0-35-9]"; "[^4]" matches any non-digit and digits other than 4.

Although the "-" character indicates a range when it is enclosed in square brackets, instances of the "-" character outside grouping expressions are treated as literal characters. Thus, the regular expression in line 15 searches for a string that starts with the letter "J", followed by any number of characters, followed by a two-digit number (of which the second digit cannot be 4), followed by a dash, another two-digit number, a dash and another two-digit number.

Line 24 creates an smatch (pronounced "ess-match"; a typedef for match_results) object. A match_results object, when passed as an argument to one of the Boost.Regex algorithms, stores the regular expression's match. An smatch stores an object of type string::const_iterator that you can use to access the matching string. There are typedefs to support other string representations such as char* (cmatch).

The while statement (lines 27–34) searches string1 for matches to the regular expression until none can be found. We use the call to regex_search as the while statement condition (lines 27–28). regex_search returns true if the string (string1) contains a match to the regular expression (expression). We also pass an smatch object to regex_search so we can access the matching string. The last argument, match_not_dot_newline, prevents the "." character from matching a newline character. The body of the while statement prints the substring that matched the regular expression (line 30) and removes it from the string being searched (line 33). The call to the match_results member function suffix returns a string from the end of the match to the end of the string being searched. The output in Fig. 24.2 displays the two matches that were found in string1. Notice that both matches conform to the pattern specified by the regular expression.

Quantifiers

The asterisk (*) in line 15 of Fig. 24.2 is more formally called a quantifier. Figure 24.3 lists various quantifiers that you can place after a pattern in a regular expression and the purpose of each quantifier.

We have already discussed how the asterisk (*) and plus (+) quantifiers work. The question mark (?) quantifier matches zero or one occurrences of the pattern that it quantifies. A set of braces containing one number, {n}, matches exactly *n* occurrences of the pattern it quantifies. We demonstrate this quantifier in the next example. Including a comma after the number enclosed in braces matches at least *n* occurrences of the quantified pattern. The set of braces containing two numbers, {n,m}, matches between *n* and *m* occurrences (inclusively) of the pattern that it quantifies. All of the quantifiers are greedy—they will match as many occurrences of the pattern as possible until the pattern fails to make a match. If a quantifier is followed by a question mark (?), the quantifier becomes lazy and will match as few occurrences as possible as long as there is a successful match.

Quantifier	Matches
*	Matches zero or more occurrences of the preceding pattern.
+	Matches one or more occurrences of the preceding pattern.
?	Matches zero or one occurrences of the preceding pattern.
{n}	Matches exactly *n* occurrences of the preceding pattern.
{n,}	Matches at least *n* occurrences of the preceding pattern.
{n,m}	Matches between *n* and *m* (inclusive) occurrences of the preceding pattern.

Fig. 24.3 | Quantifiers used in regular expressions.

24.7.2 Validating User Input with Regular Expressions

The program in Fig. 24.4 presents a more involved example that uses regular expressions to validate name, address and telephone number information input by a user.

```cpp
1   // Fig. 24.4: Validate.cpp
2   // Validating user input with regular expressions.
3   #include <iostream>
4   using std::cin;
5   using std::cout;
6   using std::endl;
7
8   #include <string>
9   using std::string;
10
11  #include "boost/regex.hpp"
12
13  bool validate( const string&, const string& ); // validate prototype
14  string inputData( const string&, const string& ); // inputData prototype
15
16  int main()
17  {
18     // enter the last name
19     string lastName = inputData( "last name", "[A-Z][a-zA-Z]*" );
```

Fig. 24.4 | Validating user input with regular expressions. (Part I of 3.)

```
20
21      // enter the first name
22      string firstName = inputData( "first name", "[A-Z][a-zA-Z]*" );
23
24      // enter the address
25      string address = inputData( "address",
26         "[0-9]+\\s+([a-zA-Z]+|[a-zA-Z]+\\s[a-zA-Z]+)" );
27
28      // enter the city
29      string city =
30         inputData( "city", "([a-zA-Z]+|[a-zA-Z]+\\s[a-zA-Z]+)" );
31
32      // enter the state
33      string state = inputData( "state",
34         "([a-zA-Z]+|[a-zA-Z]+\\s[a-zA-Z]+)" );
35
36      // enter the zip code
37      string zipCode = inputData( "zip code", "\\d{5}" );
38
39      // enter the phone number
40      string phoneNumber = inputData( "phone number",
41         "[1-9]\\d{2}-[1-9]\\d{2}-\\d{4}" );
42
43      // display the validated data
44      cout << "\nValidated Data\n\n"
45         << "Last name: " << lastName << endl
46         << "First name: " << firstName << endl
47         << "Address: " << address << endl
48         << "City: " << city << endl
49         << "State: " << state << endl
50         << "Zip code: " << zipCode << endl
51         << "Phone number: " << phoneNumber << endl;
52
53      return 0;
54   } // end of function main
55
56   // validate the data format using a regular expression
57   bool validate( const string &data, const string &expression )
58   {
59      // create a regex to validate the data
60      boost::regex validationExpression = boost::regex( expression );
61      return boost::regex_match( data, validationExpression );
62   } // end of function validate
63
64   // collect input from the user
65   string inputData( const string &fieldName, const string &expression )
66   {
67      string data; // store the data collected
68
69      // request the data from the user
70      cout << "Enter " << fieldName << ": ";
71      getline( cin, data );
72
```

Fig. 24.4 | Validating user input with regular expressions. (Part 2 of 3.)

```
73      // validate the data
74      while ( !( validate( data, expression ) ) )
75      {
76         cout << "Invalid " << fieldName << ".\n";
77         cout << "Enter " << fieldName << ": ";
78         getline( cin, data );
79      } // end while
80
81      return data;
82   } // end of function inputData
```

```
Enter last name: Doe
Enter first name: John
Enter address: 123 Some Street
Enter city: Some City
Enter state: Some State
Enter zip code: 12345
Enter phone number: 123-456-7890

Validated Data

Last name: Doe
First name: John
Address: 123 Some Street
City: Some City
State: Some State
Zip code: 12345
Phone number: 123-456-7890
```

Fig. 24.4 | Validating user input with regular expressions. (Part 3 of 3.)

The program first asks the user to input a last name (line 19) by calling the `inputData` function. The `inputData` function (lines 65–82) takes two arguments, the name of the data being input and a regular expression that it must match. The function prompts the user (line 70) to input the specified data. Then `inputData` checks whether the input is in the correct format by calling the `validate` function (lines 57–62). That function (lines 57–62) takes two arguments—the `string` to validate and the regular expression it must match. The function first uses the expression to create a `regex` object (line 60). Then it calls `regex_match` to determine whether the `string` matches the expression. If the input isn't valid, `inputData` prompts the user to enter the information again. Once the user enters a valid input, the data is returned as a `string`. The program repeats that process until all the data fields have been validated (lines 19–41). Then we display all the information (lines 44–51).

In the previous example, we searched a `string` for substrings that matched a regular expression. In this example, we want to ensure that the entire `string` for each input conforms to a particular regular expression. For example, we want to accept "Smith" as a last name, but not "9@Smith#". We use `regex_match` here instead of `regex_search`—`regex_match` returns `true` only if the entire `string` matches the regular expression. Alternatively, you can use a regular expression that begins with a "^" character and ends with a "$" character. The characters "^" and "$" represent the beginning and end of a `string`, respectively. Together, these characters force a regular expression to return a match only if the entire string being processed matches the regular expression.

The regular expression in line 19 uses the square bracket and range notation to match an uppercase first letter followed by letters of any case—a-z matches any lowercase letter, and A-Z matches any uppercase letter. The * quantifier signifies that the second range of characters may occur zero or more times in the string. Thus, this expression matches any string consisting of one uppercase letter, followed by zero or more additional letters.

The notation \s matches a single whitespace character (lines 26, 30 and 34). The expression \d{5}, used for the zipCode string (line 37), matches any five digits. The character "|" (lines 26, 30 and 34) matches the expression to its left *or* the expression to its right. For example, Hi (John|Jane) matches both Hi John and Hi Jane. In line 26, we use the character "|" to indicate that the address can contain a word of one or more characters *or* a word of one or more characters followed by a space and another word of one or more characters. Note the use of parentheses to group parts of the regular expression. Quantifiers may be applied to patterns enclosed in parentheses to create more complex regular expressions.

The lastName and firstName variables (lines 19 and 22) both accept strings of any length that begin with an uppercase letter. The regular expression for the address string (line 26) matches a number of at least one digit, followed by a space and then either one or more letters or else one or more letters followed by a space and another series of one or more letters. Therefore, "10 Broadway" and "10 Main Street" are both valid addresses. As currently formed, the regular expression in line 26 doesn't match an address that does not start with a number, or that has more than two words. The regular expressions for the city (line 30) and state (line 34) strings match any word of at least one character or, alternatively, any two words of at least one character if the words are separated by a single space. This means both Waltham and West Newton would match. Again, these regular expressions would not accept names that have more than two words. The regular expression for the zipCode string (line 37) ensures that the zip code is a five-digit number. The regular expression for the phoneNumber string (line 41) indicates that the phone number must be of the form xxx-yyy-yyyy, where the xs represent the area code and the ys the number. The first x and the first y cannot be zero, as specified by the range [1-9] in each case.

24.7.3 Replacing and Splitting Strings

Sometimes it's useful to replace parts of one string with another or to split a string according to a regular expression. For this purpose, the Boost.Regex library provides the algorithm regex_replace and the regex_token_iterator class, which we demonstrate in Fig. 24.5.

Algorithm regex_replace replaces text in a string with new text wherever the original string matches a regular expression. In line 23, regex_replace replaces every instance of "*" in testString1 with "^". Notice that the regular expression ("*") precedes character "*" with a backslash, \. Normally, * is a quantifier indicating that a regular expression should match any number of occurrences of a preceding pattern. However, in this case we want to find all occurrences of the literal character "*"; to do this, we must escape character "*" with character "\". By escaping a special regular expression character with a \, we tell the regular expression matching engine to find the actual character "*" rather than use it as a quantifier. Lines 27–28 use regex_replace to replace the string

```
1   // Fig. 24.5: RegexSubstitution.cpp
2   // Using regex_replace algorithm.
3   #include <iostream>
4   using std::cout;
5   using std::endl;
6
7   #include <string>
8   using std::string;
9
10  #include "boost/regex.hpp"
11
12  int main()
13  {
14     // create the test strings
15     string testString1 = "This sentence ends in 5 stars *****";
16     string testString2 = "1, 2, 3, 4, 5, 6, 7, 8";
17     string output;
18
19     cout << "Original string: " << testString1 << endl;
20
21     // replace every * with a ^
22     testString1 =
23        boost::regex_replace( testString1, boost::regex( "\\*" ), "^" );
24     cout << "^ substituted for *: " << testString1 << endl;
25
26     // replace "stars" with "carets"
27     testString1 = boost::regex_replace(
28        testString1, boost::regex( "stars" ), "carets" );
29     cout << "\"carets\" substituted for \"stars\": "
30        << testString1 << endl;
31
32     // replace every word with "word"
33     testString1 = boost::regex_replace(
34        testString1, boost::regex( "\\w+" ), "word" );
35     cout << "Every word replaced by \"word\": " << testString1 << endl;
36
37     // replace the first three digits with "digit"
38     cout << "\nOriginal string: " << testString2 << endl;
39     string testString2Copy = testString2;
40
41     for ( int i = 0; i < 3; i++ ) // loop three times
42     {
43        testString2Copy = boost::regex_replace( testString2Copy,
44           boost::regex( "\\d" ), "digit", boost::format_first_only );
45     } // end for
46
47     cout << "Replace first 3 digits by \"digit\": "
48        << testString2Copy << endl;
49
50     // split the string at the commas
51     cout << "string split at commas [";
52
```

Fig. 24.5 | Using `regex_replace` algorithm. (Part I of 2.)

```
53     boost::sregex_token_iterator tokenIterator( testString2.begin(),
54        testString2.end(), boost::regex( ",\\s" ), -1 ); // token iterator
55     boost::sregex_token_iterator end;  // empty iterator
56
57     while ( tokenIterator != end ) // tokenIterator isn't empty
58     {
59        output += "\"" + *tokenIterator + "\", "; // add the token to output
60        tokenIterator++; // advance the iterator
61     } // end while
62
63     // delete the ", " at the end of output string
64     cout << output.substr( 0, output.length() - 2 ) << "]" << endl;
65
66     return 0;
67  } // end of function main
```

```
Original string: This sentence ends in 5 stars *****
^ substituted for *: This sentence ends in 5 stars ^^^^^
"carets" substituted for "stars": This sentence ends in 5 carets ^^^^^
Every word replaced by "word": word word word word word word ^^^^^

Original string: 1, 2, 3, 4, 5, 6, 7, 8
Replace first 3 digits by "digit": digit, digit, digit, 4, 5, 6, 7, 8
string split at commas ["1", "2", "3", "4", "5", "6", "7", "8"]
```

Fig. 24.5 | Using `regex_replace` algorithm. (Part 2 of 2.)

"stars" in `testString1` with the string "carets". Lines 33–34 use `regex_replace` to replace every word in `testString1` with the string "word".

Lines 41–45 replace the first three instances of a digit ("\d") in `testString2` with the text "digit". We pass an additional argument, `boost::format_first_only`, to `regex_replace` (lines 43–44). This argument tells `regex_replace` to replace only the first substring that matches the regular expression. Normally `regex_replace` would replace all occurrences of the pattern. We put this call inside a `for` loop that runs three times; each time replacing the first instance of a digit with the text "digit". We use a copy of `testString2` (line 39) so we can use the original `textString2` for the next part of the example.

Next we use a `regex_token_iterator` to divide a `string` into several substrings. A `regex_token_iterator` iterates through the parts of a `string` that match a regular expression. Lines 53 and 55 use `sregex_token_iterator`, which is a `typedef` that indicates the results are to be manipulated with a `string::const_iterator`. We create the iterator (lines 53–54) by passing the constructor two iterators (`testString2.begin()` and `testString2.end()`), which represent the beginning and end of the `string` to iterate over and the regular expression to look for. In our case we want to iterate over the parts of the `string` that *don't* match the regular expression. To do that we pass -1 to the constructor. This indicates that it should iterate over each substring that doesn't match the regular expression. The original `string` is broken at delimiters that match the specified regular expression. We use a `while` statement (lines 57–61) to add each substring to the `output` `string` (line 17). The `regex_token_iterator` end (line 55) is an empty iterator. We've iterated over the entire `string` when `tokenIterator` equals end (line 57).

24.8 Smart Pointers with Boost.Smart_ptr

Many common bugs in C and C++ code are related to pointers. Smart pointers help you avoid errors by providing additional functionality to standard pointers. This functionality typically strengthens the process of memory allocation and deallocation. Smart pointers also help you write exception safe code. If a program throws an exception before `delete` has been called on a pointer, it creates a memory leak. After an exception is thrown, a smart pointer's destructor will still be called, which calls `delete` on the pointer for you.

The C++ Standard Library provides a basic smart pointer, `std::auto_ptr`. An `auto_ptr` is responsible for managing dynamically allocated memory and automatically calls `delete` to free the dynamic memory when the `auto_ptr` is destroyed or goes out of scope. These smart pointers are perfect for automatic variables. Section 16.12 discusses `auto_ptr`.

`auto_ptr`s have some limitations. For example, an `auto_ptr` can't point to an array. When deleting a pointer to an array you must use `delete[]` to ensure that destructors are called for all objects in the array, but `auto_ptr` uses `delete`. Another limitation of `auto_ptr` is that it can't be used with the STL containers—elements in an STL container must be able to be safely copied. When an `auto_ptr` is copied, ownership of the memory is transferred to the new `auto_ptr` and the original is set to `NULL`. An STL container may make copies of its elements, so you can't guarantee that a valid copy of the `auto_ptr` will remain after the algorithm processing the container's elements finishes.

The `Boost.Smart_ptr` library provides additional smart pointers to fill in the gaps where `auto_ptr`s don't work. TR1 includes two of the six types of smart pointers in the `Boost.Smart_ptr` library, namely `shared_ptr` and `weak_ptr`. These smart pointers are not meant to replace `auto_ptr`. Instead, they provide additional options with different functionality.

24.8.1 Reference Counted shared_ptr

`shared_ptr`s hold an internal pointer to a resource (e.g., a dynamically allocated object) that may be shared with other objects in the program. You can have any number of `shared_ptr`s to the same resource. `shared_ptr`s really do share the resource—if you change the resource with one `shared_ptr`, the changes also will be "seen" by the other `shared_ptr`s. The internal pointer is deleted once the last `shared_ptr` to the resource is destroyed. `shared_ptr`s use reference counting to determine how many `shared_ptr`s point to the resource. Each time a new `shared_ptr` to the resource is created, the reference count increases, and each time one is destroyed, the reference count decreases. When the reference count reaches zero, the internal pointer is deleted and the memory is released.

`shared_ptr`s are useful in situations where multiple pointers to the same resource are needed, such as in STL containers. `auto_ptr`s don't work in STL containers because the containers, or algorithms manipulating them, might copy the stored elements. Copies of `auto_ptr`s aren't equal because the original is set to `NULL` after being copied. `shared_ptr`s, on the other hand, can safely be copied and used in STL containers.

`shared_ptr`s also allow you to determine how the resource will be destroyed. For most dynamically allocated objects, `delete` is used. However, some resources require more complex cleanup. In that case, you can supply a custom deleter function, or function object, to the `shared_ptr` constructor. The deleter determines how to destroy the resource. When the reference count reaches zero and the resource is ready to be destroyed, the shared_ptr calls the custom deleter function. This functionality enables a shared_ptr to manage almost any kind of resource.

Example Using shared_ptr

Figures 24.6–24.7 define a simple class to represent a Book with a string to represent the title of the Book. The destructor for class Book (Fig. 24.7, lines 16–19) displays a message on the screen indicating that an instance is being destroyed. We use this class to demonstrate the common functionality of shared_ptr.

The program in Fig. 24.8 uses shared_ptrs to manage several instances of class Book. We include the "boost/shared_ptr.hpp" header file to be able to use shared_ptrs. We

```
 1   // Fig. 24.6: Book.h
 2   // Declaration of class Book.
 3   #ifndef BOOK_H
 4   #define BOOK_H
 5   #include <string>
 6   using std::string;
 7
 8   class Book
 9   {
10   public:
11      Book( const string &bookTitle ); // constructor
12      ~Book(); // destructor
13      string title; // title of the Book
14   };
15   #endif // BOOK_H
```

Fig. 24.6 | Book header file.

```
 1   // Fig. 24.7: Book.cpp
 2   // Member-function definitions for class Book.
 3   #include <iostream>
 4   using std::cout;
 5   using std::endl;
 6
 7   #include <string>
 8   using std::string;
 9
10   #include "Book.h"
11
12   Book::Book( const string &bookTitle ) : title( bookTitle )
13   {
14   }
15
16   Book::~Book()
17   {
18      cout << "Destroying Book: " << title << endl;
19   } // end of destructor
```

Fig. 24.7 | Book member-function definitions.

```cpp
1   // Fig. 24.8: fig24_8.cpp
2   // Demonstrate used of shared_ptrs.
3   #include <iostream>
4   using std::cout;
5   using std::endl;
6
7   #include <vector>
8   using std::vector;
9
10  #include "Book.h"
11  #include "boost/shared_ptr.hpp"
12
13  typedef boost::shared_ptr< Book > BookPtr; // shared_ptr to a Book
14
15  // a custom delete function for a pointer to a Book
16  void deleteBook( Book* book )
17  {
18     cout << "Custom deleter for a Book, ";
19     delete book; // delete the Book pointer
20  } // end of deleteBook
21
22  // compare the titles of two Books for sorting
23  bool compareTitles( BookPtr bookPtr1, BookPtr bookPtr2 )
24  {
25     return ( bookPtr1->title < bookPtr2->title );
26  } // end of compareTitles
27
28  int main()
29  {
30     // create a shared_ptr to a Book and display the reference count
31     BookPtr bookPtr( new Book( "C++ How to Program" ) );
32     cout << "Reference count for Book " << bookPtr->title << " is: "
33        << bookPtr.use_count() << endl;
34
35     // create another shared_ptr to the Book and display reference count
36     BookPtr bookPtr2( bookPtr );
37     cout << "Reference count for Book " << bookPtr->title << " is: "
38        << bookPtr.use_count() << endl;
39
40     // change the Book's title and access it from both pointers
41     bookPtr2->title = "Java How to Program";
42     cout << "The Book's title changed for both pointers: "
43        << "\nbookPtr: " << bookPtr->title
44        << "\nbookPtr2: " << bookPtr2->title <<endl;
45
46     // create a std::vector of shared_ptrs to Books (BookPtrs)
47     vector< BookPtr > books;
48     books.push_back( BookPtr( new Book( "C How to Program" ) ) );
49     books.push_back( BookPtr( new Book( "VB How to Program" ) ) );
50     books.push_back( BookPtr( new Book( "C# How to Program" ) ) );
51     books.push_back( BookPtr( new Book( "C++ How to Program" ) ) );
52
```

Fig. 24.8 | shared_ptr example program. (Part I of 2.)

```
53      // print the Books in the vector
54      cout << "\nBooks before sorting: " << endl;
55      for ( int i = 0; i < books.size(); i++ )
56         cout << ( books[ i ] )->title << "\n";
57
58      // sort the vector by Book title and print the sorted vector
59      sort( books.begin(), books.end(), compareTitles );
60      cout << "\nBooks after sorting: " << endl;
61      for ( int i = 0; i < books.size(); i++ )
62         cout << ( books[ i ] )->title << "\n";
63
64      // create a shared_ptr with a custom deleter
65      cout << "\nshared_ptr with a custom deleter." << endl;
66      BookPtr bookPtr3( new Book( "Small C++ How to Program" ), deleteBook);
67      bookPtr3.reset(); // release the Book this shared_ptr manages
68
69      // shared_ptrs are going out of scope
70      cout << "\nAll shared_ptr objects are going out of scope." << endl;
71
72      return 0;
73   } // end of main
```

```
Reference count for Book C++ How to Program is: 1
Reference count for Book C++ How to Program is: 2

The Book's title changed for both pointers:
bookPtr: Java How to Program
bookPtr2: Java How to Program

Books before sorting:
C How to Program
VB How to Program
C# How to Program
C++ How to Program

Books after sorting:
C How to Program
C# How to Program
C++ How to Program
VB How to Program

shared_ptr with a custom deleter.
Custom deleter for a Book, Destroying Book: Small C++ How to Program

All shared_ptr objects are going out of scope.
Destroying Book: C How to Program
Destroying Book: C# How to Program
Destroying Book: C++ How to Program
Destroying Book: VB How to Program
Destroying Book: Java How to Program
```

Fig. 24.8 | shared_ptr example program. (Part 2 of 2.)

also create a typedef, BookPtr, as an alias for the type boost::shared_ptr< Book > (line 13). Line 31 creates a shared_ptr to a Book titled "C++ How to Program" (using the

BookPtr typedef). The shared_ptr constructor takes as its argument a pointer to an object. We pass it the pointer returned from the new operator. This creates a shared_ptr that manages the Book object and sets the reference count to one. The constructor can also take another shared_ptr, in which case it shares ownership of the resource with the other shared_ptr and the reference count is increased by one. The first shared_ptr to a resource should always be created using the new operator. A shared_ptr created with a regular pointer assumes it's the first shared_ptr assigned to that resource and starts the reference count at one. If you make multiple shared_ptrs with the same pointer, the shared_ptrs won't acknowledge each other and the reference count will be wrong. When the shared_ptrs are destroyed, they both call delete on the resource.

Lines 32–33 display the Book's title and the number of shared_ptrs referencing that instance. Notice that we use the -> operator to access the Book's data member title, as we would with a regular pointer. shared_ptrs provide the pointer operators * and ->. We get the reference count using the shared_ptr member function use_count, which returns the number of shared_ptrs to the resource. Then we create another shared_ptr to the instance of class Book (line 36). Here we use use the shared_ptr constructor with the original shared_ptr as its argument. You can also use the assignment operator (=) to create a shared_ptr to the same resource. Lines 37–38 print the reference count of the original shared_ptr to show that the count increased by one when we created the second shared_ptr. As mentioned earlier, changes made to the resource of a shared_ptr are "seen" by all shared_ptrs to that resource. When we change the title of the Book using bookPtr2 (line 41), we can see the change when using bookPtr (lines 42–44).

Next we demonstrate using shared_ptrs in an STL container. We create a vector of BookPtrs (line 47) and add four elements (recall that BookPtr is a typedef for a shared_ptr< Book >, line 13). This demonstrates a key advantage of using shared_ptr instead of auto_ptr—as mentioned earlier, you can't use auto_ptrs in STL containers. Lines 54–56 print the contents of the vector. Then we sort the Books in the vector by title (line 59). We use the function compareTitles (lines 23–26) in the sort algorithm to compare the title data members of each Book alphabetically.

Line 66 creates a shared_ptr with a custom deleter. We define the custom deleter function deleteBook (lines 16–20) and pass it to the shared_ptr constructor along with a pointer to a new instance of class Book. When the shared_ptr destroys the instance of class Book, it calls deleteBook with the internal Book * as the argument. Notice that deleteBook takes a Book *, not a shared_ptr. A custom deleter function must take one argument of the shared_ptr's internal pointer type. deleteBook displays a message to show that the custom deleter was called, then deletes the pointer. We call the shared_ptr member function reset (line 67) to show the custom deleter at work. The reset function releases the current resource and sets the shared_ptr to NULL. If there are no other shared_ptrs to the resource, it's destroyed. You can also pass a pointer or shared_ptr representing a new resource to the reset function, in which case the shared_ptr will manage the new resource. But, as with the constructor, you should only use a regular pointer returned by the new operator.

All the shared_ptrs and the vector go out of scope at the end of the main function and are destroyed. When the vector is destroyed, so are the shared_ptrs in it. The program output shows that each instance of class Book is destroyed automatically by the shared_ptrs. There is no need to delete each pointer placed in the vector.

24.8.2 weak_ptr: shared_ptr Observer

A weak_ptr points to the resource managed by a shared_ptr without assuming any responsibility for it. The reference count for a shared_ptr doesn't increase when a weak_ptr references it. That means that the resource of a shared_ptr can be deleted while there are still weak_ptrs pointing to it. When the last shared_ptr is destroyed, the resource is deleted and any remaining weak_ptrs are set to NULL. One use for weak_ptrs, as we'll demonstrate later in this section, is to avoid memory leaks caused by circular references.

A weak_ptr can't directly access the resource it points to—you must create a shared_ptr from the weak_ptr to access the resource. There are two ways to do this. You can pass the weak_ptr to the shared_ptr constructor. That creates a shared_ptr to the resource being pointed to by the weak_ptr and properly increases the reference count. If the resource has already been deleted, the shared_ptr constructor will throw a boost::bad_weak_ptr exception. You can also call the weak_ptr member function lock, which returns a shared_ptr to the weak_ptr's resource. If the weak_ptr points to a deleted resource (i.e., NULL), lock will return an empty shared_ptr (i.e., a shared_ptr to NULL). lock should be used when an empty shared_ptr isn't considered an error. You can access the resource once you have a shared_ptr to it. weak_ptrs should be used in any situation where you need to observe the resource but don't want to assume any management responsibilities for it. The following example demonstrates the use of weak_ptrs in circularly referential data, a situation in which two objects refer to each other internally.

Example Using **weak_ptr**
Figures 24.9–24.12 define classes Author and Book. Each class has a pointer to an instance of the other class. This creates a circular reference between the two classes. Note that we use both weak_ptrs and shared_ptrs to hold the cross reference to each class (Fig. 24.9 and 24.10, lines 21–22 in each figure). If we set the shared_ptrs, it creates a memory leak—we'll explain why soon and show how we can use the weak_ptrs to fix this problem.

```cpp
1   // Fig. 24.9: Author.h
2   // Definition of class Author.
3   #ifndef AUTHOR_H
4   #define AUTHOR_H
5   #include <string>
6   using std::string;
7
8   #include "boost/shared_ptr.hpp"
9   #include "boost/weak_ptr.hpp"
10
11  class Book; // forward declaration of class Book
12
13  // Author class definition
14  class Author
15  {
16  public:
17     Author( const string &authorName ); // constructor
18     ~Author(); // destructor
```

Fig. 24.9 | Author class definition. (Part 1 of 2.)

```
19      void printBookTitle(); // print the title of the Book
20      string name; // name of the Author
21      boost::weak_ptr< Book > weakBookPtr; // Book the Author wrote
22      boost::shared_ptr< Book > sharedBookPtr; // Book the Author wrote
23   };
24   #endif // AUTHOR_H
```

Fig. 24.9 | Author class definition. (Part 2 of 2.)

```
1    // Fig. 24.10: Book.h
2    // Definition of class Book.
3    #ifndef BOOK_H
4    #define BOOK_H
5    #include <string>
6    using std::string;
7
8    #include "boost/shared_ptr.hpp"
9    #include "boost/weak_ptr.hpp"
10
11   class Author; // forward declaration of class Author
12
13   // Book class definition
14   class Book
15   {
16   public:
17      Book( const string &bookTitle ); // constructor
18      ~Book(); // destructor
19      void printAuthorName(); // print the name of the Author
20      string title; // title of the Book
21      boost::weak_ptr< Author > weakAuthorPtr; // Author of the Book
22      boost::shared_ptr< Author > sharedAuthorPtr; // Author of the Book
23   };
24   #endif // BOOK_H
```

Fig. 24.10 | Book class definition.

Classes Author and Book define destructors that each display a message to indicate
when an instance of either class is destroyed (Figs. 24.11 and 24.12, lines 19–22). Each
class also defines a member function to print the title of the Book and Author's name
(lines 25–38 in each figure). Recall that you can't access the resource directly through a
weak_ptr, so first we create a shared_ptr from the weak_ptr data member (line 28 in each
figure). If the resource the weak_ptr is referencing doesn't exist, the call to the lock function returns a shared_ptr which points to NULL and the condition fails. Otherwise, the
new shared_ptr contains a valid pointer to the weak_ptr's resource, and we can access the
resource. If the condition in line 28 is true (i.e., bookPtr and authorPtr aren't NULL), we
print the reference count to show that it increased with the creation of the new
shared_ptr, then we print the title of the Book and Author's name. The shared_ptr is
destroyed when the function exits so the reference count decreases by one.

```
1   // Fig. 24.11: Author.cpp
2   // Member-function definitions for class Author.
3   #include <iostream>
4   using std::cout;
5   using std::endl;
6
7   #include <string>
8   using std::string;
9
10  #include "Author.h"
11  #include "Book.h"
12  #include "boost/shared_ptr.hpp"
13  #include "boost/weak_ptr.hpp"
14
15  Author::Author( const string &authorName ) : name( authorName )
16  {
17  }
18
19  Author::~Author()
20  {
21     cout << "Destroying Author: " << name << endl;
22  } // end of destructor
23
24  // print the title of the Book this Author wrote
25  void Author::printBookTitle()
26  {
27     // if weakBookPtr.lock() returns a non-empty shared_ptr
28     if ( boost::shared_ptr< Book > bookPtr = weakBookPtr.lock() )
29     {
30        // show the reference count increase and print the Book's title
31        cout << "Reference count for Book " << bookPtr->title
32           << " is " << bookPtr.use_count() << "." << endl;
33        cout << "Author " << name << " wrote the book " << bookPtr->title
34           << "\n" << endl;
35     } // end if
36     else // weakBookPtr points to NULL
37        cout << "This Author has no Book." << endl;
38  } // end of printBookTitle
```

Fig. 24.11 | Author member-function definitions.

```
1   // Fig. 24.12: Book.cpp
2   // Member-function definitions for class Book.
3   #include <iostream>
4   using std::cout;
5   using std::endl;
6
7   #include <string>
8   using std::string;
9
10  #include "Author.h"
```

Fig. 24.12 | Book member-function definitions. (Part 1 of 2.)

```
11   #include "Book.h"
12   #include "boost/shared_ptr.hpp"
13   #include "boost/weak_ptr.hpp"
14
15   Book::Book( const string &bookTitle ) : title( bookTitle )
16   {
17   }
18
19   Book::~Book()
20   {
21      cout << "Destroying Book: " << title << endl;
22   } // end of destructor
23
24   // print the name of this Book's Author
25   void Book::printAuthorName()
26   {
27      // if weakAuthorPtr.lock() returns a non-empty shared_ptr
28      if ( boost::shared_ptr< Author > authorPtr = weakAuthorPtr.lock() )
29      {
30         // show the reference count increase and print the Author's name
31         cout << "Reference count for Author " << authorPtr->name
32            << " is " << authorPtr.use_count() << "." << endl;
33         cout << "The book " << title << " was written by "
34            << authorPtr->name << "\n" << endl;
35      } // end if
36      else // weakAuthorPtr points to NULL
37         cout << "This Book has no Author." << endl;
38   } // end of printAuthorName
```

Fig. 24.12 | Book member-function definitions. (Part 2 of 2.)

Figure 24.13 defines a main function that demonstrates the memory leak caused by the circular reference between classes Author and Book. Lines 14–16 create shared_ptrs to an instance of each class. The weak_ptr data members are set in lines 19–20. Lines 23–24 set the shared_ptr data members for each class. The instances of classes Author and Book now reference each other. We then print the reference count for the shared_ptrs to show that each instance is referenced by two shared_ptrs (lines 27–30), the ones we create

```
1    // Fig. 24.13: fig24_13.cpp
2    // Demonstrate use of weak_ptr.
3    #include <iostream>
4    using std::cout;
5    using std::endl;
6
7    #include "Author.h"
8    #include "Book.h"
9    #include "boost/shared_ptr.hpp"
10
11   int main()
12   {
```

Fig. 24.13 | shared_ptrs cause a memory leak in circularly referential data. (Part 1 of 2.)

```
13        // create a Book and an Author
14        boost::shared_ptr< Book > bookPtr( new Book( "C++ How to Program" ) );
15        boost::shared_ptr< Author > authorPtr(
16           new Author( "Deitel & Deitel" ) );
17
18        // reference the Book and Author to each other
19        bookPtr->weakAuthorPtr = authorPtr;
20        authorPtr->weakBookPtr = bookPtr;
21
22        // set the shared_ptr data members to create the memory leak
23        bookPtr->sharedAuthorPtr = authorPtr;
24        authorPtr->sharedBookPtr = bookPtr;
25
26        // reference count for bookPtr and authorPtr is one
27        cout << "Reference count for Book " << bookPtr->title << " is "
28           << bookPtr.use_count() << endl;
29        cout << "Reference count for Author " << authorPtr->name << " is "
30           << authorPtr.use_count() << "\n" << endl;
31
32        // access the cross references to print the data they point to
33        cout << "\nAccess the Author's name and the Book's title through "
34           << "weak_ptrs." << endl;
35        bookPtr->printAuthorName();
36        authorPtr->printBookTitle();
37
38        // reference count for each shared_ptr is back to one
39        cout << "Reference count for Book " << bookPtr->title << " is "
40           << bookPtr.use_count() << endl;
41        cout << "Reference count for Author " << authorPtr->name << " is "
42           << authorPtr.use_count() << "\n" << endl;
43
44        // the shared_ptrs go out of scope, the Book and Author are destroyed
45        cout << "The shared_ptrs are going out of scope." << endl;
46
47        return 0;
48     } // end of main
```

```
Reference count for Book C++ How to Program is 2
Reference count for Author Deitel & Deitel is 2

Access the Author's name and the Book's title through weak_ptrs.
Reference count for Author Deitel & Deitel is 3.
The book C++ How to Program was written by Deitel & Deitel

Reference count for Book C++ How to Program is 3.
Author Deitel & Deitel wrote the book C++ How to Program

Reference count for Book C++ How to Program is 2
Reference count for Author Deitel & Deitel is 2

The shared_ptrs are going out of scope.
```

Fig. 24.13 | shared_ptrs cause a memory leak in circularly referential data. (Part 2 of 2.)

in the main function and the data member of each instance. Remember that weak_ptrs don't affect the reference count. Then we call each class's member function to print the information stored in the weak_ptr data member (lines 35–36). The functions also display the fact that another shared_ptr was created during the function call. Finally, we print the reference counts again to show that the additional shared_ptrs created in the print-AuthorName and printBookTitle member functions are destroyed when the functions finish.

At the end of main, the shared_ptrs to the instances of Author and Book we created go out of scope and are destroyed. Notice that the output doesn't show the destructors for classes Author and Book. The program has a memory leak—the instances of Author and Book aren't destroyed because of the shared_ptr data members. When bookPtr is destroyed at the end of the main function, the reference count for the instance of class Book becomes one—the instance of Author still has a shared_ptr to the instance of Book, so it's not deleted. When authorPtr goes out of scope and is destroyed, the reference count for the instance of class Author also becomes one—the instance of Book still has a shared_ptr to the instance of Author. Neither instance is deleted because the reference count for each is still one.

Now, comment out lines 23–24 by placing // at the beginning of each line. This prevents the code from setting the shared_ptr data members for classes Author and Book. Recompile the code and run the program again. Figure 24.14 shows the output. Notice that the initial reference count for each instance is now one instead of two because we don't set the shared_ptr data members. The last two lines of the output show that the instances of classes Author and Book were destroyed at the end of the main function. We eliminated the memory leak by using the weak_ptr data members rather than the shared_ptr data members. The weak_ptrs don't affect the reference count but still allow us to access the resource when we need it by creating a temporary shared_ptr to the resource. When the shared_ptrs we created in main are destroyed, the reference counts become zero and the instances of classes Author and Book are deleted properly.

```
Reference count for Book C++ How to Program is 1
Reference count for Author Deitel & Deitel is 1

Access the Author's name and the Book's title through weak_ptrs.
Reference count for Author Deitel & Deitel is 2.
The book C++ How to Program was written by Deitel & Deitel

Reference count for Book C++ How to Program is 2.
Author Deitel & Deitel wrote the book C++ How to Program

Reference count for Book C++ How to Program is 1
Reference count for Author Deitel & Deitel is 1

The shared_ptrs are going out of scope.
Destroying Author: Deitel & Deitel
Destroying Book: C++ How to Program
```

Fig. 24.14 | weak_ptrs used to prevent a memory leak in circularly referential data.

24.9 **Technical Report I**

Technical Report 1 (TR1) describes proposed additions to the C++ Standard Library. Many of the libraries in TR1 will be accepted by the C++ Standards Committee but they are not considered part of the C++ standard until the next version is finalized. The library additions provide solutions for many common programming problems. We described the 11 Boost libraries in TR1 in Section 24.6; descriptions of the three additional TR1 libraries follow. Many libraries didn't make it into TR1 due to time constraints. Technical Report 2 (TR2), which will be released shortly after C++0x, contains additional library proposals that weren't included in TR1. The release of TR2 will bring even more functionality to the standard library without having to wait for another new standard.

Unordered Associative Containers[13]
The Unordered Associative Containers library defines four new containers—unordered_set, unordered_map, unordered_multiset and unordered_multimap. These associative containers are implemented as hash tables. A hash table is split into sections sometimes called "buckets." A key is used to determine where to store an element in the container. The key is passed to a hash function which returns a size_t. The size_t returned by the hash function determines the "bucket" that the value is placed in. If two values are equal, so are the size_ts returned by the hash function. Multiple values can be placed in the same "bucket." You retrieve an element from the container using the key much as you do with a set or map. The key determines which "bucket" the value was placed in, then the "bucket" is searched for the value.

With unordered_set and unordered_multiset, the element itself is used as the key. unordered_map and unordered_multimap use a separate key to determine where to place the element—the arguments are passed as a pair< const Key, Value >. unordered_set and unordered_map require that all the keys used are unique; unordered_multiset and unordered_multimap don't enforce that restriction. The containers are defined in the <unordered_set> and <undordered_map> headers.

Mathematical Special Functions[14]
This library incorporates mathematical functions added to C99—the C standard published in 1999—that are missing in the C++ Standard. C99 supplies trigonometric, hyperbolic, exponential, logarithmic, power and special functions. This library adds those functions, among others, to C++ in the <cmath> header.

Increased Compatibility with C99[15]
C++ evolved from the C programming language. Most C++ compilers can also compile C programs, but there are some incompatibilities between the languages. The goal of this library is to increase compatibility between C++ and C99. Most of this library involves add-

13. Matthew Austern, "A Proposal to Add Hash Tables to the Standard Library," Document Number N1456=03-0039, April 9, 2003, www.open-std.org/jtc1/sc22/wg21/docs/papers/2003/n1456.html.
14. Walter E. Brown, "A Proposal to Add Mathematical Special Functions to the C++ Standard Library," Document Number N1422=03-0004, February 24, 2003, std.dkuug.dk/jtc1/sc22/wg21/docs/papers/2003/n1422.html.
15. P. J. Plauger, "Proposed Additions to TR-1 to Improve Compatibility With C99," Document Number N1568=04-0008, www.open-std.org/jtc1/sc22/wg21/docs/papers/2004/n1568.htm.

ing items to C++ headers to support C99 features—this is often accomplished by including the corresponding C99 headers.

24.10 C++0x

The C++ Standards Committee is currently revising the C++ Standard. The last standard was published in 1998. Work on the new standard, currently referred to as C++0x, began in 2003. The new standard, likely to be released in 2009, includes the TR1 libraries and additions to the core language. Browse the C++0x section of the Deitel C++ Resource Center at www.deitel.com/cplusplus/ and click **C++0x** in the **Categories** list to find current information on C++0x.

Standardization Process

The International Organization for Standardization (ISO) oversees the creation of international programming language standards, including those for C and C++. Every addition or change to the current C++ standard must be approved by the ISO/IEC JTC 1/SC 22 Working Group 21 (WG21), the committee that maintains the C++ standard. This committee of volunteers from the C++ programming community meets twice a year to discuss issues pertaining to the standard. Smaller, unofficial meetings are held more frequently to consider proposals between official committee meetings. ISO requires at least 5 years between new drafts of a standard.

Goals for C++0x[16]

Bjarne Stroustrup, creator of the C++ programming language, has expressed his vision for the future of C++—the main goals for the new standard are to make C++ easier to learn, improve library building capabilities, and increase compatibility with the C programming language.

24.11 Core Language Changes

A listing of proposed changes to the core language can be found at www.open-std.org/jtc1/sc22/wg21/docs/papers/2007/n2228.html. There are also links to the papers associated with each proposal. We briefly discuss only the core language changes that have been accepted into the working draft of the new standard. The number of proposals that make it into the working draft is likely to increase before the standard is finalized. The GCC C++ compiler has an optional C++0x mode which allows you to experiment with a number of the core language changes (gcc.gnu.org/gcc-4.3/cxx0x_status.html).

Rvalue Reference[17]

The *rvalue* reference type in C++0x allows you to bind an *rvalue* (temporary object) to a non-const reference. An *rvalue* reference is declared as T&& (where T is the type of the object being referenced) to distinguish it from a normal reference T& (now called an *lvalue*

---

16. Bjarne Stroustrup, "The Design of C++0x," May 2005, www.research.att.com/~bs/rules.pdf.
17. Howard E. Hinnant, "A Proposal to Add an *rvalue* Reference to the C++ Language," October 19, 2006, Document Number N2118=06-0188, www.open-std.org/jtc1/sc22/wg21/docs/papers/2006/n2118.html.

reference). An *rvalue* reference can be used to effectively implement move semantics. This improves performance by preventing the compiler from making extra copies of large objects, an expensive operation. *Rvalue* references can also be used in "forwarding functions"—function objects that adapt a function to take fewer arguments (e.g., std::bind1st or function objects created using Boost.Bind). Normally, each reference parameter would need a const and non-const version to account for *lvalues*, const *lvalues* and *rvalues*. With *rvalue* references you need only one forwarding function.

Clarification of Initialization of Class Objects by rvalues[18]

This proposal clarifies the writing in the standard regarding the use of *rvalues* as arguments to functions that receive their arguments by value. The new wording would allow compiler writers to implement move semantics rather than copy semantics if it can be determined that the *rvalue* is going to be removed from memory after the copy. This would increase performance by eliminating an extra copy constructor call.

static_assert[19]

The static_assert declaration allows you to test certain aspects of the program at compile time. A static_assert declaration takes a constant integral expression and a string literal. If the expression evaluates to 0 (false), the compiler reports the error. The error message includes the string literal provided in the declaration. The static_assert declaration can be used at namespace, class or block scope.

The addition of static_assert makes learning C++ easier. The assertions can be used to provide more informative error messages when novice programmers make common mistakes such as using the wrong type of argument in a function call or template instantiation. They're also useful in library development—incorrect usage of the library can be reported much more effectively.

extern template[20]

The keyword extern indicates that a variable or function is defined either later in the current file or in a separate file. This proposal allows the extern keyword to provide the same functionality for templates, which would help prevent extra instantiations of the template. This can improve compilation times and reduce the size of a program's object code.

Extended friend Declarations[21]

This proposal clarifies wording in the C++ standard with respect to friend declarations and templates.

---

18. David Abrahams and Gary Powell, "Clarification of Initialization of Class Objects by *rvalues*," Document Number N1610=04-0050, February 14, 2004, www.open-std.org/jtc1/sc22/wg21/docs/papers/2004/n1610.html.

19. Robert Klarer, Dr. John Maddock, Beman Dawes and Howard Hinnant, "Proposal to Add Static Assertions to the Core Language," Document Number N1720, October 20, 2004, www.open-std.org/jtc1/sc22/wg21/docs/papers/2004/n1720.html.

20. John Spicer, "Adding extern template," Document Number N1987, April 6, 2006, www.open-std.org/jtc1/sc22/wg21/docs/papers/2006/n1987.htm.

21. William M. Miller, "Extended friend Declarations," Document Number N1791, May 1, 2005, www.open-std.org/jtc1/sc22/wg21/docs/papers/2005/n1791.pdf.

Synchronizing the C++ Preprocessor with C99[22]
This proposal is an effort to make C++0x more compatible with C99 by changing the requirements of the C++ preprocessor. The compatibility changes mostly involve copying text directly from the C99 standard and placing it into the C++ standard. The changes affect areas including predefined macros, the `pragma` operator, string concatenation and header and include filenames and translation limit changes. Incorporating these changes into the standard would force complier implementors to create a C++ compiler and preprocessor with the same rules and features as the C99 compiler and preprocessor, making the languages more compatible.

Conditionally Supported Behavior[23]
This proposal adds conditionally supported behavior to C++. Many C++ implementors add optional functionality. Using this functionality with a different implementation that doesn't support it is currently considered undefined behavior. There are no guarantees as to how the program will act when undefined behavior occurs. Currently, compilers aren't required to give warnings in these situations. Under the conditionally supported behavior category, any optional feature that is not supported by the current implementation causes the compiler to return a report that the program uses an unsupported feature. This helps novice programmers who may inadvertently use nonstandard features. They'll receive an informative message rather than having to diagnose the effects of the undefined behavior.

Changing Undefined Behavior into Diagnosable Errors[24]
Another proposal, inspired by the discussions regarding conditionally supported behavior, changes certain situations which cause undefined behavior into diagnosable errors (an error which the compiler can report). The areas that will require a diagnostic report include oversized integers, unsupported character escapes and passing non-POD objects ("plain old data") to variadic functions (functions that take an unspecified number of arguments).

Adding the `long long` Type to C++[25]
The new `long long` type is an integer type that must be at least 64 bits (8 bytes). This type is being introduced to improve compatibility with the C99 Standard, which already includes the `long long` type.

Adding Extended Integer Types to C++[26]
The addition of extended integer types to C++ is part of the effort to add C99 features to C++0x. An extended integer is an integer type defined by an implementation in addition to the integer types required by the C++ Standard. The implementation of an extended

22. Clark Nelson, "Working Draft Changes for C99 Preprocessor Synchronization," Document Number N1653, July 16, 2004, www.open-std.org/jtc1/sc22/wg21/docs/papers/2004/n1653.htm.
23. William M. Miller, "Conditionally-Supported Behavior," Document Number N1627, April 4, 2004, www.open-std.org/jtc1/sc22/wg21/docs/papers/2004/n1627.pdf.
24. William M. Miller, "Changing Undefined Behavior into Diagnosable Errors," Document Number N1727, November 8, 2004, www.open-std.org/jtc1/sc22/wg21/docs/papers/2004/n1727.pdf.
25. J. Stephen Adamczyk, "Adding the `long long` Type to C++," Document Number N1811, April 29, 2005, www.open-std.org/jtc1/sc22/wg21/docs/papers/2005/n1811.pdf.
26. J. Stephen Adamczyk, "Adding Extended Integer Types to C++," Document Number N1988, April 19, 2006, www.open-std.org/jtc1/sc22/wg21/docs/papers/2006/n1988.pdf.

integer type is not required, but certain rules must be followed when a vendor chooses to provide them. Any signed extended integer type must also have a corresponding unsigned type of the same size. Note that explicitly using an extended integer type affects the portability of your program.

Delegating Constructors[27]

This feature allows a constructor to delegate to another of the class's constructors (i.e., call another of the class's constructors). This makes it easier to write overloaded constructors. Currently, an overloaded constructor must duplicate the code that is common to the other constructor. This leads to repetitive and error-prone code. A mistake in one constructor could cause inconsistency in object initialization. By calling another version of the constructor, the common code doesn't need to be repeated and the chance of error decreases.

Right Angle Brackets[28]

It's necessary to put a space between trailing right angle brackets (>) when using nested templates. Without the space, the compiler assumes that the two brackets are the right shift operator (>>). This means that writing vector<class<T>> causes a compiler error. The statement would have to be written as vector<class<T> >. Many novices stumble on this quirk of C++. The proposal is to change the C++ compiler to recognize when >> is part of a template rather than the right-shift operator.

Deducing the Type of Variable from Its Initializer[29]

This proposal defines new functionality for the keyword auto—it automatically determines variable types based on the initializer expression. auto can be used in place of long, complicated types that are unmanageable to type by hand. auto can also be used with const and volatile qualifiers. You can create pointers and references with auto as you would with the full type name. auto supports the declaration of multiple variables in one statement (e.g., auto x = 1, y = 2). The auto keyword is meant to save time, ease the learning process and improve generic programming. The following code creates a vector of instances of a hypothetical Class< T >.

```
vector< Class< T > > myVector;
vector< Class< T > >::const_iterator iterator = myVector.begin();
```

Using auto, the declaration of iterator can be written as

```
auto iterator = myVector.begin();
```

The type of iterator is vector< Class< T > >::const_iterator. You can also create two variables of the same type in one declaration. Both variables in

```
auto iteratorBegin = myVector.begin(), iteratorEnd = myVector.end();
```

27. Herb Sutter and Francis Glassborow, "Delegating Constructors," Document Number N1986=06-0056, April 6, 2006, www.open-std.org/jtc1/sc22/wg21/docs/papers/2006/n1986.pdf.

28. Daveed Vandevoorde, "Right Angle Brackets," Document Number N1857=05-0017, January 14, 2005, www.open-std.org/jtc1/sc22/wg21/docs/papers/2005/n1757.html.

29. Jaakko Järvi, Bjarne Stroustrup and Gabriel Dos Reis, "Deducing the Type of Variable From Its Initializer Expression," Document Number N1984=06-0054, April 6, 2006, www.open-std.org/jtc1/sc22/wg21/docs/papers/2006/n1984.pdf.

are created with the type `vector< Class< T > >::const_iterator`. You can also use `auto` with `const` or `volatile` qualifiers and create pointers or references. The statement

```
const auto & iteratorPtr = myVector.begin();
```

creates a `const` reference to a `vector< Class< T > >::const_iterator`. `auto` can save you a lot of time by automatically determining the type of the variable you're declaring.

Variadic Templates[30]

A variadic template accepts any number of arguments. The template parameters are put in a template type parameter pack. The arguments passed to a function are put in a function parameter pack. These work together to manage the types and values of the parameters, respectively. An ellipsis ("...") to the left of the name of a template or function parameter declares it as a template type parameter pack or function parameter pack, respectively. The parameters must be taken out of the packs before they can be used. An ellipsis to the right of a function parameter extracts all the elements of the parameter pack. The nth element of a template type parameter pack is the type of the nth element in a function parameter pack. Variadic templates make it easier to express classes and functions that may take an arbitrary number of arguments. Many libraries, such as the `tuple` library in TR1, can benefit from using variadic templates.

Template Aliases[31]

Libraries often use templates with many parameters to implement generic programming. There may be situations where it would be useful to be able to specify certain arguments for the template that remain consistent but still be able to vary the rest. This can be done with a template alias. A template alias is similar to a `typedef`—it introduces a name used to refer to a template. In a `typedef`, all the template parameters are specified. Using a template alias, certain parameters are specified and others may still vary. You can use a general-purpose template in a more specific role where many of the arguments are always the same by using a template alias to set the consistent parameters while still being able to vary those that change in each instantiation.

New Character Types[32]

This proposal adds Unicode character support to C++. Unicode is already supported by the C standard, and much of that work is duplicated in the C++ standard. Two new types are introduced, `char16_t` and `char32_t`. These types represent the 16-bit and 32-bit Unicode characters. The prefixes u and U can be used to denote a `char16_t` or `char32_t` character literal, respectively.

---

30. Douglas Gregor, Jaakko Järvi and Gary Powell, "Variadic Templates," Document Number N2080=06-0150, September 9, 2006, `www.osl.iu.edu/~dgregor/cpp/variadic-templates.pdf`.
31. Gabriel Dos Reis and Mat Marcus, "Proposal to Add Template Aliases to C++," Document Number N1449=03-0032, April 7, 2003, `www.open-std.org/jtc1/sc22/wg21/docs/papers/2003/n1449.pdf`.
32. Lawrence Crowl, "New Character Types in C++," Document Number N2149=07-0009, January 10, 2007, `www.open-std.org/jtc1/sc22/wg21/docs/papers/2007/n2149.html`.

Extending *sizeof*[33]

The sizeof operator returns the number of bytes used to store an object. C++0x allows sizeof to be called on a data member without accessing it through an instance of the class it's a part of. sizeof can also be used more naturally with static data members.

Alternative to Sequence Points[34]

The C++ standard describes the order in which operations occur in a program using the term "sequence points." Many C++ experts think the wording fails to clearly describe the required sequence of events in the execution of a program. This proposal changes the wording in the standard to define the sequencing requirements more precisely. This issue is important to C++ because any future attempt to add concurrency (i.e., multithreading) requires a solid understanding of the order of events in a program.

24.12 Wrap-Up

In this chapter we discussed various aspects of the future of C++. We introduced the Boost C++ Libraries and described the Boost libraries that are included in TR1—the additions to the C++ Standard Library.

We discussed the Boost.Regex library and the symbols that are used to form regular expressions. We provided examples of how to use Boost.Regex classes, including regex, match_results and regex_token_iterator. You learned how to find patterns in a string and match entire strings to patterns with Boost.Regex algorithms regex_search and regex_match. We demonstrated how to replace characters in a string with regex_replace and how to split strings into tokens with a regex_token_iterator.

We gave examples of how to use the Boost.Smart_ptr library. We discussed the smart pointers included in TR1, namely shared_ptr and weak_ptr. We showed you how to use these classes to avoid memory leaks when using dynamically allocated memory. We demonstrated how to use custom deleter functions to allow shared_ptrs to manage resources that require special destruction procedures. We also explained how weak_ptrs can be used to prevent memory leaks in circularly referential data.

We overviewed the upcoming revised standard, C++0x, discussing TR1 and the changes to the core language. We introduced each of the libraries accepted into TR1. We described the new core language features including the auto keyword, *rvalue* reference, improvements in compatibility with C99, additional integer types and the new concept of conditionally supported behavior. Remember that Boost, TR1 and C++0x are constantly changing—visit our Resource Centers to stay up to date with all three.

---

33. Jens Maurer, "Extending sizeof to Apply to Non-Static Data Members Without an Object," Document Number N2150=07-0010, January 7, 2007, www.open-std.org/jtc1/sc22/wg21/docs/papers/2007/n2150.html.

34. Clark Nelson, "A Finer-Grained Alternative to Sequence Points," Document Number N1944=06-0014, February 17, 2006, www.open-std.org/jtc1/sc22/wg21/docs/papers/2006/n1944.htm.

Summary

Section 24.2 Deitel Online C++ and Related Resource Centers
- Visit the C++ Boost Libraries Resource Center at www.deitel.com/CPlusPlusBoostLibraries/ to find current information on the available libraries and new releases.
- Find current information on TR1 and C++0x in the **C++0x** category of the C++ Resource Center at www.deitel.com/cplusplus/.
- For more information on Visual C++, visit our Visual C++ Resource Center at www.deitel.com/VisualCPlusPlus/.

Section 24.3 Boost Libraries
- The Boost Libraries at www.boost.org provide free peer-reviewed C++ libraries.
- The source code for Boost is hosted on SourceForge (sourceforge.net).
- For information about open source software and development check out our Open Source Resource Center at www.deitel.com/OpenSource/.

Section 24.4 Adding a New Library to Boost
- Boost libraries must conform to the C++ standard and use the C++ Standard Library—or other appropriate Boost libraries.
- A preliminary submission of each Boost library is posted in the Boost Sandbox Vault.
- The review manager makes sure the code is ready for formal review, sets up the review schedule, reads all user reviews, and makes the final decision whether or not to accept the library.
- The Boost Software License grants the rights to copy, modify, use and distribute the Boost source code and binaries for commercial or noncommercial use.

Section 24.5 Installing the Boost Libraries
- An installation guide is available at www.boost.org/more/getting_started/index.html.
- Download the Boost libraries and the the Boost.Jam build system from sourceforge.net/project/showfiles.php?group_id=7586.
- To install Boost.Jam, extract the archive and copy the bjam.exe file to any folder accessible by the path environment variable on your system.
- Extract the Boost libraries from the archive you downloaded.
- Open a command prompt and change to the directory containing the Boost libraries. To install, type bjam --toolset=msvc install—replace "msvc" with any other toolset you'd like to use.
- Add the include directory, C:\Boost\include\boost-1_34, to the additional include directories.
- Add the library directory, C:\Boost\lib, to the additional library directories.
- Some libraries require that you add the library file as an additional dependency to your project.

Section 24.6 Boost Libraries in Technical Report 1 (TR1)
- TR1 is a description of changes and additions to the C++ Standard Library.
- GCC (GNU Compiler Collection) provides a partial implementation of TR1. For an overview of the supported TR1 features visit gcc.gnu.org/onlinedocs/libstdc++/ext/tr1.html.
- Boost.Array provides fixed-size arrays that support the STL container interface.
- Boost.Bind extends the functionality provided by the standard functions bind1st and bind2nd. It allows you to adapt functions that take up to nine arguments. It also makes it easy to reorder the arguments passed to the function.

- Boost.Function allows you to store function pointers, member-function pointers and function objects in a function wrapper. You can also store a reference to a function object using the ref and cref functions added to the <utility> header. A function can hold any function whose arguments and return type can be converted to match the function wrapper's signature.

- Boost.mem_fn allows you to create a function object with a pointer, reference or smart pointer to a member function. mem_fn is a more flexible version of mem_fun and mem_fun_ref.

- Boost.Random allows you to create a variety of random number generators and distributions.

- A pseudo-random number generator uses an initial state to produce seemingly random numbers—using the same initial state produces the same sequence of numbers.

- The Boost.Ref library provides reference wrappers that allow you to use references in algorithms that normally receive their arguments by value. Using references improves performance when passing large objects to an algorithm.

- Regular expressions are used to match character patterns in text.

- With Boost.Regex, you can search for a particular expression in a string, replace parts of a string that match a regular expression and split a string into tokens using regular expressions.

- Class template result_of determines the return type of a call expression based on the parameters passed to the call expression.

- Boost.Smart_ptr defines smart pointers that help you manage dynamically allocated resources.

- shared_ptrs handle lifetime management of dynamically allocated objects. Memory is released automatically when there are no shared_ptrs referencing it.

- A weak_ptr allows you to observe a shared_ptr's value without any management responsibilities.

- Boost.Tuple allows you to create sets of objects that can be used by generic functions.

- The type_traits classes allow you to determine specific traits of a type and perform type transformations to allow the object to be used in generic code.

Section 24.7 Regular Expressions with the Boost.Regex Library

- Regular expressions are specially formatted strings used to find patterns in text.

- basic_regex represents a regular expression.

- Algorithm regex_match returns true only if an entire string matches the regular expression.

- Algorithm regex_search returns true if any part of a string matches the regular expression.

- To use the Boost.Regex library, include the header file "boost/regex.hpp".

- A character class represents a group of characters.

- A word character (\w) is any alphanumeric character or underscore. A whitespace character (\s) is a space, tab, carriage return, newline or form feed. A digit (\d) is any numeric character.

Section 24.7.1 Regular Expression Example

- You must precede each character class's backslash character with an additional backslash character in C++ strings.

- To specify sets of characters other than those that belong to a predefined character class, list the characters in square brackets, []. Ranges of characters are represented by placing a "-" between two characters. Instances of the "-" character outside [] characters are treated as literals.

- Place ^ as the first character in the brackets to specify that a pattern should match anything other than the characters in the brackets.

- A match_results is an object that holds a match to a regular expression. The typedef smatch represents a match_results that provides access to the match result via a string::const_iterator.

- `match_not_dot_newline` prevents the "`.`" character from matching a newline character.
- `match_results` member function `suffix` returns a `string` from the end of the match to the end of the `string` being searched.
- The "`*`" quantifier will match *zero or more* occurrences.
- The "`+`" quantifier will match *one or more* occurrences.
- The "`?`" quantifier will match *zero or one* occurrences.
- A set of braces containing one number, `{n}`, matches *exactly n* occurrences.
- Including a comma after the number enclosed in braces matches *at least n* occurrences.
- The notation `{n,m}` matches *between n* and *m* occurrences (inclusively).
- Quantifiers are greedy—they will match as many occurrences of the pattern as possible until the pattern fails to make a match.
- A quantifier followed by a question mark (?) becomes lazy and will match as few occurrences as possible as long as there is a successful match.

Section 24.7.2 Validating User Input with Regular Expressions
- The characters "`^`" and "`$`" represent the beginning and end of a `string`, respectively.
- The character "`|`" matches the expression to its left *or* the expression to its right.
- You can apply quantifiers to patterns in parentheses to create more complex regular expressions.

Section 24.7.3 Replacing and Splitting Strings
- Algorithm `regex_replace` replaces text in a `string` with new text wherever the original `string` matches a regular expression.
- Escaping a "`*`" character with a \ tells the regular expression matching engine to find the actual character "`*`" rather than use it as a quantifier.
- `format_first_only` tells `regex_replace` to replace only the first substring that matches the regular expression. Normally `regex_replace` would replace all occurrences of the pattern.
- A `regex_token_iterator` iterates through the parts of a `string` that match the regular expression.
- Create a `regex_token_iterator` by passing the constructor two iterators which represent the beginning and end of the `string` to iterate over, and the regular expression to match.
- Pass `-1` to the `regex_token_iterator` constructor to indicate that it should iterate over each substring that *doesn't* match the regular expression.

Section 24.8 Smart Pointers with **Boost.Smart_ptr**
- Smart pointers avoid errors by strengthening the process of memory allocation and deallocation.
- After an exception is thrown, a smart pointer's destructor will call `delete` on the pointer for you.
- An `auto_ptr` can't point to an array. It also can't be used with the STL containers.
- TR1 includes `shared_ptr` and `weak_ptr`.

Section 24.8.1 Reference Counted **shared_ptr**
- `shared_ptrs` hold an internal pointer to a resource (e.g., a dynamically allocated object) that may be shared with other objects in the program.
- Changes to the resource of a `shared_ptr` will be "seen" by the other `shared_ptrs` to that resource.
- `shared_ptrs` use reference counting to determine how many `shared_ptrs` point to the resource. When the reference count reaches zero, the internal pointer is deleted.
- `shared_ptrs` can safely be copied and can be used in STL containers.

- You can create a shared_ptr with a custom deleter function which specifies how to destroy the resource. A custom deleter function must take one argument of the internal pointer's type.
- Include the "boost/shared_ptr.hpp" header file to use shared_ptrs.
- The shared_ptr constructor takes a pointer to an object. The constructor can also take another shared_ptr, in which case it shares ownership of the resource with the other shared_ptr and the reference count is increased by one.
- The first shared_ptr to a resource should always be created using the new operator.
- shared_ptrs provide the pointer operators * and ->.
- The shared_ptr member function use_count returns the number of shared_ptrs to the resource.
- Function reset releases the current resource and sets the shared_ptr to NULL. You can also pass a pointer or shared_ptr to the reset function; the shared_ptr will manage the new resource.

Section 24.8.2 *weak_ptr: shared_ptr Observer*
- A weak_ptr is used to point to the resource managed by a shared_ptr without assuming any responsibility for it—the reference count for the shared_ptr doesn't increase.
- When the last shared_ptr is destroyed, the resource is deleted and any remaining weak_ptrs are set to NULL.
- A weak_ptr can't access the resource it points to—you must create a shared_ptr from the weak_ptr to access the resource. You can pass the weak_ptr to the shared_ptr constructor. You can also call weak_ptr function lock, which returns a shared_ptr to the weak_ptr's resource.
- Include the "boost/weak_ptr.hpp" header file to use weak_ptrs.

Section 24.9 *Technical Report 1*
- Technical Report 1 (TR1) describes additions to the C++ Standard Library.
- Technical Report 2 (TR2) contains additional library proposals that weren't included in TR1.
- The Unordered Associative Containers library defines four new containers—unordered_set, unordered_map, unordered_multiset and unordered_multimap. These associative containers are implemented as hash tables and are defined in <unordered_set> and <unordered_map>.
- unordered_set and unordered_multiset use the element as the key. unordered_map and unordered_multimap store key–value pairs.
- unordered_set and unordered_map require unique keys; unordered_multiset and unordered_multimap don't enforce that restriction.
- TR1 includes trigonometric, hyperbolic, exponential, logarithmic, power and special functions from C99.
- TR1 includes C99 headers to increase compatibility between C++ and C99.

Section 24.10 *C++0x*
- The new standard, C++0x, includes the TR1 libraries and changes to the core language.
- The International Organization for Standardization (ISO) oversees the creation of international programming language standards. ISO Working Group 21 maintains the C++ standard.
- The main goals for the new standard are to make C++ easier to learn, improve library building capabilities and increase compatibility with the C programming language.

Section 24.11 *Core Language Changes*
- The GNU C++ compiler has an optional C++0x mode which allows you to experiment with several of the core language changes (gcc.gnu.org/gcc-4.3/cxx0x_status.html).

- The *rvalue* reference type in C++0x allows you to bind an *rvalue* (temporary object) to a non-const reference.

- An *rvalue* reference is declared as T&& (where T is the type of the object being referenced).

- An *rvalue* reference can be used to implement move semantics.

- The static_assert declaration allows you to test certain aspects of the program at compile time.

- A static_assert declaration takes a constant integral expression and a string. If the expression evaluates to 0 (false), the compiler reports the error using the string provided in the declaration.

- The keyword extern indicates that a variable, function or template is defined either later in the current file or in a separate file.

- The new long long type (already in C99) is an integer type that is larger than the long type.

- An extended integer is an integer type defined by an implementation but not required by the C++ standard. Any signed extended integer type must have a corresponding unsigned type of the same size. Explicitly using an extended integer type affects the portability of your program.

- A constructor can call another of the class's constructors directly.

- The C++ compiler will recognize when >> is part of a template.

- Keyword auto automatically determines a variable's type based on its initializer expression. auto takes the place of the full type name.

- A variadic template accepts any number of arguments. The template parameters are put in a template type parameter pack. The arguments passed to a function are put in a function parameter pack. The nth element of a template type parameter pack is the type of the nth element in a function parameter pack.

- An ellipsis to the left of a template or function parameter declares it as a template type or function parameter pack. An ellipsis to the right of a function parameter pack extracts the elements.

- char16_t and char32_t represent the 16-bit and 32-bit Unicode characters. The prefixes u and U can be used to denote a char16_t or char32_t character, respectively.

- C++0x allows sizeof to be called on a data member without accessing it through an instance of its class. sizeof can also be used more naturally with static data members.

- The wording in the C++0x standard defines sequencing requirements more precisely. This issue is important to C++, because any future attempt to add concurrency requires a solid understanding of the order of events in a program.

Terminology

* quantifier (0 or more)
+ quantifier (1 or more)
? quantifier (0 or 1)
$ end of a string
^ beginning of a string
\d character class (any decimal digit)
\w character class (any word character)
\s character class (any whitespace character)
\D character class (any non-digit)
\W character class (any non-word character)
\S character class (any non-whitespace character)
{n,} quantifier (at least *n*)
{n,m} quantifier (between *n* and *m*)

{n} quantifier (exactly *n*)
algorithm
auto keyword
auto_ptr
bad_weak_ptr exception
basic_regex class
binary function
bind1st function
bind2nd function
bjam.exe
Boost C++ libraries
Boost.Array library
Boost.Bind library
Boost.Function library

Boost.Jam build system
Boost.mem_fn library
Boost.Random library
Boost.Ref library
Boost.Regex library
Boost.Smart_ptr library
Boost.Tuple library
Boost.Type_traits library
boost namespace
Boost Sandbox Vault
Boost Software License
bucket (hash table)
C++0x
C99
char16_t
char32_t
character classes
circularly referential data
conditionally supported behavior
custom deleter function
delegating constructors
delete function
digit
dynamic memory allocation
extended integer
extern template
format_first_only
friend declaration
function class
function object
function parameter pack
greedy quantifier
hash function
hash table
International Standards Organization
key (hash table)
lazy quantifier
lock member function of class weak_ptr
long long integer type
match_not_dot_newline
match_results class
<math.h>
mem_fun function
mem_fun_ref function
memory leak
Microsoft's Platform SDK

non-deterministic random numbers
pair
pseudo-random number generator
quantifier
rand function
random number distribution
random number generator
reference count
reference counting
reference_wrapper class template
regex typedef
regex_match algorithm
regex_replace algorithm
regex_search algorithm
regex_token_iterator
regular expression
reset member function of class shared_ptr
result_of class template
right angle brackets
rvalue reference
shared_ptr class
sizeof operator
smart pointer
smatch typedef
sourceforge.net
srand function
static_assert declaration
suffix member function of class
    match_results
Technical Report 1 (TR1)
Technical Report 2 (TR2)
template alias
template type parameter pack
tuple
unary function
Unicode character
uniform distribution
unordered_map container
unordered_multimap container
unordered_multiset container
unordered_set container
use_count member function of class shared_ptr
variadic template
weak_ptr class
whitespace character
word character

Self-Review Exercises

24.1 Fill in the blanks in each of the following statements:

    a) The _____ describes proposed changes to the C++ Standard Library.

b) The _____ library helps manage the release of dynamically allocated memory to prevent memory leaks.

c) `Boost.Bind` enhances the _____ and _____ standard library functions.

d) `shared_ptrs` use a _____ to determine when to delete the resource.

e) Class _____ represents a regular expression in `Boost.Regex`.

f) Class `regex_token_iterator` is located in namespace _____.

g) The `Boost.Regex` algorithm _____ changes all occurrences of a pattern in a string to a specified `string`.

h) Regular expression quantifier _____ matches zero or more occurrences of an expression.

i) Regular expression operator _____ inside square brackets will not match any of the characters in that set of brackets.

j) The _____ keyword in C++0x automatically determines the type of a variable when it's initialized.

k) Move semantics and forwarding functions in C++0x can be written using _____.

24.2 State whether each of the following is *true* or *false*. If *false*, explain why.

a) An `auto_ptr` can be used in STL containers.

b) Creating a `weak_ptr` to a resource increases the reference count.

c) A regular expression matches a `string` to a pattern.

d) The expression `\d` in a regular expression denotes all letters.

24.3 Write statements to accomplish each of the following tasks:

a) Create a regular expression to match either a five-letter word or five-digit number.

b) Create a regular expression to match a phone number in the form of (123) 456-7890.

c) Create a `shared_ptr` to the `int` 5 called `intPtr`.

d) Create a `weak_ptr` to `intPtr` called `weakIntPtr`.

e) Access the `int`'s value using `weakIntPtr`.

Answers to Self-Review Exercises

24.1 a) TR1. b) `Boost.Smart_ptr`. c) `bind1st`, `bind2nd`. d) reference count. e) `regex` or `basic_regex`. f) `boost`. g) `regex_replace`. h) `*`. i) `^`. j) `auto`. k) *rvalue* references.

24.2 a) False. An `auto_ptr` can't be safely copied and therefore can't be used in STL containers. b) False. A `weak_ptr` assumes no ownership of its resource and doesn't affect the reference count. c) True. d) False. The expression `\d` in a regular expression denotes all decimal digits.

24.3 a) `boost::regex( "\\w{5}|\\d{5}" );`

b) `boost::regex( "\\(\\d{3}\\)\\s\\d{3}-\\d{4}" );`

c) `boost::shared_ptr< int > intPtr( new int( 5 ) );`

d) `boost::weak_ptr< int > weakIntPtr( intPtr );`

e) `boost::shared_ptr< int > sharedIntPtr = weakIntPtr.lock();`
   `*sharedIntPtr;`

Exercises

24.4 (*Pig Latin*) Write an application that encodes English language phrases into Pig Latin. Pig Latin is a form of coded language often used for amusement. Many variations exist in the methods used to form Pig Latin phrases. For simplicity, use the following algorithm:

To translate each English word into a Pig Latin word, place the first letter of the English word at the end of the word and add the letters "ay." Thus, the word "jump" becomes "umpjay," the word "the" becomes "hetay" and the word "computer" becomes "omputercay." Blanks between words remain blanks. Assume the following: The English phrase consists of words separated by blanks, there are no punctuation marks and all words have two or more letters. Enable the user to input a sentence. Use a `regex_token_iterator` to divide the sentence into separate words. Function `get-PigLatin` should translate a single word into Pig Latin.

24.5 Write a program that uses regular expressions to convert the first letter of all words to uppercase. Have it do this for an arbitrary string input by the user.

24.6 Use a regular expression to count the number of digits, characters and whitespace characters in a string.

24.7 Write a regular expression that will search a string and match a valid number. A number can have any number of digits, but it can have only digits and a decimal point. The decimal point is optional, but if it appears in the number, there must be only one, and it must have digits on its left and its right. There should be whitespace or a beginning- or end-of-line character on either side of a valid number. Negative numbers are preceded by a minus sign.

24.8 Write a program that will take HTML as input and will output the number of HTML tags in the string. The program should use regular expressions to count the number of elements nested at each level. For example, the HTML:

```
<p><strong>hi</strong></p>
```

has a p element (nesting level 0—i.e., not nested in another tag) and a `strong` element (nesting level 1). For simplicity, use HTML in which none of the elements contain nested elements of the same type—for example, a `table` element should not contain another `table` element.

This solution requires a regular expression concept called a back reference to determine the start and end tags of an HTML element. To find these tags, the same word must appear in the start and end tags. A back reference allows you to use a previous match in the expression in another part of the regular expression. When you enclose a portion of a regular expression in parentheses, the match for that subexpression is stored for you. You can then access the result of that expression using the syntax *digit*, where *digit* is a number in the range 1–9. For example, the regular expression

```
^(7*).*\1$
```

matches an entire string that starts and ends with one or more 7s. The strings "777abcd777" and "7abcdef7" both match this regular expression. The \1 in the preceding regular expression is a back reference indicating that whatever matched the subexpression (7*) should also appear at the end of the string. The first parenthesized subexpression is back referenced with \1, the second is back referenced with \2, etc.

You'll need a recursive function so that you can process the nested HTML elements. In each recursive call, you'll need to pass the contents of an element as the string to be processed in that call—for example, the contents of the p element in this example's HTML would be

```
<strong>hi</strong>
```

Use parentheses to store the content that appears between the start and end tags of a string that matches your regular expression. This value is stored in the `match_results` object and can be accessed using the [] operator on that object. As with back references, the subexpression matches are indexed from 1–9.

24.9 Write a program that asks the user to enter a sentence and uses a regular expression to check whether the sentence contains more than one space between words. If so, the program should remove the extra spaces. For example, "Hello   World" should be "Hello World".

24.10 Answer the following questions about smart pointers:
   a) Briefly describe the advantages of `shared_ptr` over `auto_ptr`.
   b) Describe a situation in which a custom deleter function would be used.
   c) Describe a situation in which you'd use a `weak_ptr` that is not responsible for lifetime management of its resource.

25

Other Topics

OBJECTIVES

In this chapter you'll learn:

- To use **const_cast** to temporarily treat a **const** object as a non-**const** object.

- To use **namespace**s.

- To use operator keywords.

- To use **mutable** members in **const** objects.

- To use class-member pointer operators **.*** and **->***.

- To use multiple inheritance.

- The role of **virtual** base classes in multiple inheritance.

25.1 Introduction

We now consider several advanced C++ features. First, you'll learn about the const_cast operator, which allows programmers to add or remove the const qualification of a variable. Next, we discuss namespaces, which can be used to ensure that every identifier in a program has a unique name and can help resolve naming conflicts caused by using libraries that have the same variable, function or class names. We then present several operator keywords that are useful for programmers who have keyboards that do not support certain characters used in operator symbols, such as !, &, ^, ~ and |. We continue our discussion with the mutable storage-class specifier, which enables a programmer to indicate that a data member should always be modifiable, even when it appears in an object that is currently being treated as a const object by the program. Next we introduce two special operators that we can use with pointers to class members to access a data member or member function without knowing its name in advance. Finally, we introduce multiple inheritance, which enables a derived class to inherit the members of several base classes. As part of this introduction, we discuss potential problems with multiple inheritance and how virtual inheritance can be used to solve those problems.

25.2 const_cast Operator

C++ provides the const_cast operator for casting away const or volatile qualification. You declare a variable with the volatile qualifier when you expect the variable to be modified by hardware or other programs not known to the compiler. Declaring a variable volatile indicates that the compiler should not optimize the use of that variable because doing so could affect the ability of those other programs to access and modify the volatile variable.

In general, it is dangerous to use the const_cast operator, because it allows a program to modify a variable that was declared const, and thus was not supposed to be modifiable. There are cases in which it is desirable, or even necessary, to cast away const-ness. For example, older C and C++ libraries might provide functions that have non-const parameters and that do not modify their parameters. If you wish to pass const data to such a function, you would need to cast away the data's const-ness; otherwise, the compiler would report error messages.

Similarly, you could pass non-const data to a function that treats the data as if it were constant, then returns that data as a constant. In such cases, you might need to cast away the const-ness of the returned data, as we demonstrate in Fig. 25.1.

In this program, function maximum (lines 11–14) receives two C-style strings as const char * parameters and returns a const char * that points to the larger of the two strings. Function main declares the two C-style strings as non-const char arrays (lines 18–19); thus, these arrays are modifiable. In main, we wish to output the larger of the two C-style strings, then modify that C-style string by converting it to uppercase letters.

Function maximum's two parameters are of type const char *, so the function's return type also must be declared as const char *. If the return type is specified as only char *, the compiler issues an error message indicating that the value being returned cannot be converted from const char * to char *—a dangerous conversion, because it attempts to treat data that the function believes to be const as if it were non-const data.

```cpp
1   // Fig. 24.1: fig24_01.cpp
2   // Demonstrating const_cast.
3   #include <iostream>
4   using std::cout;
5   using std::endl;
6
7   #include <cstring> // contains prototypes for functions strcmp and strlen
8   #include <cctype> // contains prototype for function toupper
9
10  // returns the larger of two C-style strings
11  const char *maximum( const char *first, const char *second )
12  {
13     return ( strcmp( first, second ) >= 0 ? first : second );
14  } // end function maximum
15
16  int main()
17  {
18     char s1[] = "hello"; // modifiable array of characters
19     char s2[] = "goodbye"; // modifiable array of characters
20
21     // const_cast required to allow the const char * returned by maximum
22     // to be assigned to the char * variable maxPtr
23     char *maxPtr = const_cast< char * >( maximum( s1, s2 ) );
24
25     cout << "The larger string is: " << maxPtr << endl;
26
27     for ( size_t i = 0; i < strlen( maxPtr ); i++ )
28        maxPtr[ i ] = toupper( maxPtr[ i ] );
29
30     cout << "The larger string capitalized is: " << maxPtr << endl;
31     return 0;
32  } // end main
```

```
The larger string is: hello
The larger string capitalized is: HELLO
```

Fig. 25.1 | Demonstrating operator const_cast.

Even though function maximum believes the data to be constant, we know that the original arrays in main do not contain constant data. Therefore, main should be able to modify the contents of those arrays as necessary. Since we know these arrays are modifiable, we use const_cast (line 23) to cast away the const-ness of the pointer returned by maximum, so we can then modify the data in the array representing the larger of the two C-style strings. We can then use the pointer as the name of a character array in the for statement (lines 27–28) to convert the contents of the larger string to uppercase letters. Without the const_cast in line 23, this program will not compile, because you are not allowed to assign a pointer of type const char * to a pointer of type char *.

Error-Prevention Tip 25.1

In general, a const_cast should be used only when it is known in advance that the original data is not constant. Otherwise, unexpected results may occur.

25.3 namespaces

A program includes many identifiers defined in different scopes. Sometimes a variable of one scope will "overlap" (i.e., collide) with a variable of the same name in a different scope, possibly creating a naming conflict. Such overlapping can occur at many levels. Identifier overlapping occurs frequently in third-party libraries that happen to use the same names for global identifiers (such as functions). This can cause compiler errors.

Good Programming Practice 25.1

Avoid identifiers that begin with the underscore character, as these can lead to linker errors. Many code libraries use names that begin with underscores.

The C++ standard solves this problem with namespaces. Each namespace defines a scope in which identifiers and variables are placed. To use a namespace member, either the member's name must be qualified with the namespace name and the binary scope resolution operator (::), as in

MyNameSpace::*member*

or a using declaration or using directive must appear before the name is used in the program. Typically, such using statements are placed at the beginning of the file in which members of the namespace are used. For example, placing the following using directive at the beginning of a source-code file

using namespace *MyNameSpace*;

specifies that members of namespace *MyNameSpace* can be used in the file without preceding each member with *MyNameSpace* and the scope resolution operator (::).

A using declaration (e.g., using std::cout;) brings one name into the scope where the declaration appears. A using directive (e.g., using namespace std;) brings all the names from the specified namespace into the scope where the directive appears.

Software Engineering Observation 25.1

Ideally, in large programs, every entity should be declared in a class, function, block or namespace. This helps clarify every entity's role.

Error-Prevention Tip 25.2

Precede a member with its namespace *name and the scope resolution operator (::) if the possibility exists of a naming conflict.*

Not all namespaces are guaranteed to be unique. Two third-party vendors might inadvertently use the same identifiers for their namespace names. Figure 25.2 demonstrates the use of namespaces.

```cpp
1   // Fig. 25.2: fig24_02.cpp
2   // Demonstrating namespaces.
3   #include <iostream>
4   using namespace std; // use std namespace
5
6   int integer1 = 98; // global variable
7
8   // create namespace Example
9   namespace Example
10  {
11     // declare two constants and one variable
12     const double PI = 3.14159;
13     const double E = 2.71828;
14     int integer1 = 8;
15
16     void printValues(); // prototype
17
18     // nested namespace
19     namespace Inner
20     {
21        // define enumeration
22        enum Years { FISCAL1 = 1990, FISCAL2, FISCAL3 };
23     } // end Inner namespace
24  } // end Example namespace
25
26  // create unnamed namespace
27  namespace
28  {
29     double doubleInUnnamed = 88.22; // declare variable
30  } // end unnamed namespace
31
32  int main()
33  {
34     // output value doubleInUnnamed of unnamed namespace
35     cout << "doubleInUnnamed = " << doubleInUnnamed;
36
37     // output global variable
38     cout << "\n(global) integer1 = " << integer1;
39
40     // output values of Example namespace
41     cout << "\nPI = " << Example::PI << "\nE = " << Example::E
42        << "\ninteger1 = " << Example::integer1 << "\nFISCAL3 = "
43        << Example::Inner::FISCAL3 << endl;
44
```

Fig. 25.2 | Demonstrating the use of namespaces. (Part 1 of 2.)

```
45        Example::printValues(); // invoke printValues function
46        return 0;
47     } // end main
48
49     // display variable and constant values
50     void Example::printValues()
51     {
52        cout << "\nIn printValues:\ninteger1 = " << integer1 << "\nPI = "
53           << PI << "\nE = " << E << "\ndoubleInUnnamed = "
54           << doubleInUnnamed << "\n(global) integer1 = " << ::integer1
55           << "\nFISCAL3 = " << Inner::FISCAL3 << endl;
56     } // end printValues
```

```
doubleInUnnamed = 88.22
(global) integer1 = 98
PI = 3.14159
E = 2.71828
integer1 = 8
FISCAL3 = 1992

In printValues:
integer1 = 8
PI = 3.14159
E = 2.71828
doubleInUnnamed = 88.22
(global) integer1 = 98
FISCAL3 = 1992
```

Fig. 25.2 | Demonstrating the use of `namespaces`. (Part 2 of 2.)

Using the std Namespace

Line 4 informs the compiler that `namespace std` is being used. The contents of header file `<iostream>` are all defined as part of `namespace std`. [*Note:* Most C++ programmers consider it poor practice to write a `using` directive such as line 4 because the entire contents of the namespace are included, thus increasing the likelihood of a naming conflict.]

The `using namespace` directive specifies that the members of a namespace will be used frequently throughout a program. This allows you to access all the members of the namespace and to write more concise statements such as

```
cout << "double1 = " << double1;
```

rather than

```
std::cout << "double1 = " << double1;
```

Without line 4, either every `cout` and `endl` in Fig. 25.2 would have to be qualified with `std::`, or individual `using` declarations must be included for `cout` and `endl` as in:

```
using std::cout;
using std::endl;
```

The `using namespace` directive can be used for predefined namespaces (e.g., `std`) or programmer-defined namespaces.

Defining Namespaces

Lines 9–24 use the keyword `namespace` to define namespace `Example`. The body of a namespace is delimited by braces ({}). Namespace `Example`'s members consist of two constants (`PI` and `E` in lines 12–13), an `int` (`integer1` in line 14), a function (`printValues` in line 16) and a nested namespace (`Inner` in lines 19–23). Notice that member `integer1` has the same name as global variable `integer1` (line 6). Variables that have the same name must have different scopes—otherwise compilation errors occur. A namespace can contain constants, data, classes, nested namespaces, functions, etc. Definitions of namespaces must occupy the global scope or be nested within other namespaces.

Lines 27–30 create an unnamed namespace containing the member `doubleInUnnamed`. The unnamed namespace has an implicit `using` directive, so its members appear to occupy the global namespace, are accessible directly and do not have to be qualified with a namespace name. Global variables are also part of the global namespace and are accessible in all scopes following the declaration in the file.

Software Engineering Observation 25.2

Each separate compilation unit has its own unique unnamed namespace; i.e., the unnamed namespace replaces the `static` linkage specifier.

Accessing Namespace Members with Qualified Names

Line 35 outputs the value of variable `doubleInUnnamed`, which is directly accessible as part of the unnamed namespace. Line 38 outputs the value of global variable `integer1`. For both of these variables, the compiler first attempts to locate a local declaration of the variables in `main`. Since there are no local declarations, the compiler assumes those variables are in the global namespace.

Lines 41–43 output the values of `PI`, `E`, `integer1` and `FISCAL3` from namespace `Example`. Notice that each must be qualified with `Example::` because the program does not provide any `using` directive or declarations indicating that it will use members of namespace `Example`. In addition, member `integer1` must be qualified, because a global variable has the same name. Otherwise, the global variable's value is output. Notice that `FISCAL3` is a member of nested namespace `Inner`, so it must be qualified with `Example::Inner::`.

Function `printValues` (defined in lines 50–56) is a member of `Example`, so it can access other members of the `Example` namespace directly without using a namespace qualifier. The output statement in lines 52–55 outputs `integer1`, `PI`, `E`, `doubleInUnnamed`, global variable `integer1` and `FISCAL3`. Notice that `PI` and `E` are not qualified with `Example`. Variable `doubleInUnnamed` is still accessible, because it is in the unnamed namespace and the variable name does not conflict with any other members of namespace `Example`. The global version of `integer1` must be qualified with the unary scope resolution operator (`::`), because its name conflicts with a member of namespace `Example`. Also, `FISCAL3` must be qualified with `Inner::`. When accessing members of a nested namespace, the members must be qualified with the namespace name (unless the member is being used inside the nested namespace).

Common Programming Error 25.1

Placing `main` in a namespace is a compilation error.

Aliases for Namespace Names

Namespaces can be aliased. For example the statement

```
namespace CPPHTP6E = CPlusPlusHowToProgram6E;
```

creates the alias CPPHTP6E for CPlusPlusHowToProgram6E.

25.4 Operator Keywords

The C++ standard provides operator keywords (Fig. 25.3) that can be used in place of several C++ operators. Operator keywords are useful for programmers who have keyboards that do not support certain characters such as !, &, ∧, ~, |, etc.

Figure 25.4 demonstrates the operator keywords. This program was compiled with Microsoft Visual C++ 2005, which requires the header file <iso646.h> (line 8) to use the operator keywords. In GNU C++, line 8 should be removed and the program should be compiled as follows:

```
g++ -foperator-names Fig24_04.cpp -o Fig24_04
```

The compiler option -foperator-names indicates that the compiler should enable use of the operator keywords in Fig. 25.3. Other compilers may not require you to include a header file or to use a compiler option to enable support for these keywords. For example, the Borland C++ 5.6.4 compiler implicitly permits these keywords.

Operator	Operator keyword	Description
Logical operator keywords		
&&	and	logical AND
||	or	logical OR
!	not	logical NOT
Inequality operator keyword		
!=	not_eq	inequality
Bitwise operator keywords		
&	bitand	bitwise AND
|	bitor	bitwise inclusive OR
∧	xor	bitwise exclusive OR
~	compl	bitwise complement
Bitwise assignment operator keywords		
&=	and_eq	bitwise AND assignment
|=	or_eq	bitwise inclusive OR assignment
∧=	xor_eq	bitwise exclusive OR assignment

Fig. 25.3 | Operator keyword alternatives to operator symbols.

```cpp
1   // Fig. 24.4: fig24_04.cpp
2   // Demonstrating operator keywords.
3   #include <iostream>
4   using std::boolalpha;
5   using std::cout;
6   using std::endl;
7
8   #include <iso646.h> // enables operator keywords in Microsoft Visual C++
9
10  int main()
11  {
12     bool a = true;
13     bool b = false;
14     int c = 2;
15     int d = 3;
16
17     // sticky setting that causes bool values to display as true or false
18     cout << boolalpha;
19
20     cout << "a = " << a << "; b = " << b
21        << "; c = " << c << "; d = " << d;
22
23     cout << "\n\nLogical operator keywords:";
24     cout << "\n   a and a: " << ( a and a );
25     cout << "\n   a and b: " << ( a and b );
26     cout << "\n    a or a: " << ( a or a );
27     cout << "\n    a or b: " << ( a or b );
28     cout << "\n     not a: " << ( not a );
29     cout << "\n     not b: " << ( not b );
30     cout << "\na not_eq b: " << ( a not_eq b );
31
32     cout << "\n\nBitwise operator keywords:";
33     cout << "\nc bitand d: " << ( c bitand d );
34     cout << "\nc bit_or d: " << ( c bitor d );
35     cout << "\n   c xor d: " << ( c xor d );
36     cout << "\n   compl c: " << ( compl c );
37     cout << "\nc and_eq d: " << ( c and_eq d );
38     cout << "\n c or_eq d: " << ( c or_eq d );
39     cout << "\nc xor_eq d: " << ( c xor_eq d ) << endl;
40     return 0;
41  } // end main
```

```
a = true; b = false; c = 2; d = 3

Logical operator keywords:
   a and a: true
   a and b: false
    a or a: true
    a or b: true
     not a: false
     not b: true
a not_eq b: true
```
                                                        (continued ...)

Fig. 25.4 | Demonstrating the operator keywords. (Part 1 of 2.)

```
Bitwise operator keywords:
c bitand d: 2
c bit_or d: 3
   c xor d: 1
   compl c: -3
c and_eq d: 2
 c or_eq d: 3
c xor_eq d: 0
```

Fig. 25.4 | Demonstrating the operator keywords. (Part 2 of 2.)

The program declares and initializes two `bool` variables and two integer variables (lines 12–15). Logical operations (lines 24–30) are performed with `bool` variables a and b using the various logical operator keywords. Bitwise operations (lines 33–39) are performed with the `int` variables c and d using the various bitwise operator keywords. The result of each operation is output.

25.5 mutable Class Members

In Section 25.2, we introduced the `const_cast` operator, which allowed us to remove the "const-ness" of a type. A `const_cast` operation can also be applied to a data member of a `const` object from the body of a `const` member function of that object's class. This enables the `const` member function to modify the data member, even though the object is considered to be `const` in the body of that function. Such an operation might be performed when most of an object's data members should be considered `const`, but a particular data member still needs to be modified.

As an example, consider a linked list that maintains its contents in sorted order. Searching through the linked list does not require modifications to the data of the linked list, so the search function could be a `const` member function of the linked-list class. However, it is conceivable that a linked-list object, in an effort to make future searches more efficient, might keep track of the location of the last successful match. If the next search operation attempts to locate an item that appears later in the list, the search could begin from the location of the last successful match, rather than from the beginning of the list. To do this, the `const` member function that performs the search must be able to modify the data member that keeps track of the last successful search.

If a data member such as the one described above should always be modifiable, C++ provides the storage-class specifier `mutable` as an alternative to `const_cast`. A `mutable` data member is always modifiable, even in a `const` member function or `const` object. This reduces the need to cast away "const-ness."

 Portability Tip 25.1

The effect of attempting to modify an object that was defined as constant, regardless of whether that modification was made possible by a `const_cast` or C-style cast, varies among compilers.

`mutable` and `const_cast` are used in different contexts. For a `const` object with no `mutable` data members, operator `const_cast` must be used every time a member is to be modified. This greatly reduces the chance of a member being accidentally modified because the member is not permanently modifiable. Operations involving `const_cast` are typically hidden in a member function's implementation. The user of a class might not be aware that a member is being modified.

Software Engineering Observation 25.3

mutable members are useful in classes that have "secret" implementation details that do not contribute to the logical value of an object.

Mechanical Demonstration of a mutable Data Member

Figure 25.5 demonstrates using a mutable member. The program defines class Test-Mutable (lines 8–22), which contains a constructor, function getValue and a private data member value that is declared mutable. Lines 16–19 define function getValue as a const member function that returns a copy of value. Notice that the function increments mutable data member value in the return statement. Normally, a const member function cannot modify data members unless the object on which the function operates—i.e.,

```
1    // Fig. 25.5: fig24_05.cpp
2    // Demonstrating storage-class specifier mutable.
3    #include <iostream>
4    using std::cout;
5    using std::endl;
6
7    // class TestMutable definition
8    class TestMutable
9    {
10   public:
11      TestMutable( int v = 0 )
12      {
13         value = v;
14      } // end TestMutable constructor
15
16      int getValue() const
17      {
18         return value++; // increments value
19      } // end function getValue
20   private:
21      mutable int value; // mutable member
22   }; // end class TestMutable
23
24   int main()
25   {
26      const TestMutable test( 99 );
27
28      cout << "Initial value: " << test.getValue();
29      cout << "\nModified value: " << test.getValue() << endl;
30      return 0;
31   } // end main
```

```
Initial value: 99
Modified value: 100
```

Fig. 25.5 | Demonstrating a mutable data member.

the one to which this points—is cast (using const_cast) to a non-const type. Because value is mutable, this const function is able to modify the data.

Line 26 declares const TestMutable object test and initializes it to 99. Line 28 calls the const member function getValue, which adds one to value and returns its previous contents. Notice that the compiler allows the call to member function getValue on the object test because it is a const object and getValue is a const member function. However, getValue modifies variable value. Thus, when line 29 invokes getValue again, the new value (100) is output to prove that the mutable data member was indeed modified.

25.6 Pointers to Class Members (. * and ->*)

C++ provides the .* and ->* operators for accessing class members via pointers. This is a rarely used capability that is used primarily by advanced C++ programmers. We provide only a mechanical example of using pointers to class members here. Figure 25.6 demonstrates the pointer-to-class-member operators.

The program declares class Test (lines 8–17), which provides public member function test and public data member value. Lines 19–20 provide prototypes for the functions arrowStar (defined in lines 32–36) and dotStar (defined in lines 39–43), which demonstrate the ->* and .* operators, respectively. Lines 24 creates object test, and line 25 assigns 8 to its data member value. Lines 26–27 call functions arrowStar and dotStar with the address of the object test.

```cpp
1   // Fig. 25.6: fig24_06.cpp
2   // Demonstrating operators .* and ->*.
3   #include <iostream>
4   using std::cout;
5   using std::endl;
6
7   // class Test definition
8   class Test
9   {
10  public:
11     void test()
12     {
13        cout << "In test function\n";
14     } // end function test
15
16     int value; // public data member
17  }; // end class Test
18
19  void arrowStar( Test * ); // prototype
20  void dotStar( Test * ); // prototype
21
22  int main()
23  {
24     Test test;
25     test.value = 8; // assign value 8
26     arrowStar( &test ); // pass address to arrowStar
27     dotStar( &test ); // pass address to dotStar
```

Fig. 25.6 | Demonstrating the .* and ->* operators. (Part 1 of 2.)

```
28        return 0;
29    } // end main
30
31    // access member function of Test object using ->*
32    void arrowStar( Test *testPtr )
33    {
34        void ( Test::*memPtr )() = &Test::test; // declare function pointer
35        ( testPtr->*memPtr )(); // invoke function indirectly
36    } // end arrowStar
37
38    // access members of Test object data member using .*
39    void dotStar( Test *testPtr2 )
40    {
41        int Test::*vPtr = &Test::value; // declare pointer
42        cout << ( *testPtr2 ).*vPtr << endl; // access value
43    } // end dotStar
```

```
In test function
8
```

Fig. 25.6 | Demonstrating the .* and ->* operators. (Part 2 of 2.)

Line 34 in function arrowStar declares and initializes variable memPtr as a pointer to a member function. In this declaration, Test::* indicates that the variable memPtr is a pointer to a member of class Test. To declare a pointer to a function, enclose the pointer name preceded by * in parentheses, as in (Test::*memPtr). A pointer to a function must specify, as part of its type, both the return type of the function it points to and the parameter list of that function. The function's return type appears to the left of the left parenthesis and the parameter list appears in a separate set of parentheses to the right of the pointer declaration. In this case, the function has a void return type and no parameters. The pointer memPtr is initialized with the address of class Test's member function named test. Note that the header of the function must match the function pointer's declaration—i.e., function test must have a void return type and no parameters. Notice that the right side of the assignment uses the address operator (&) to get the address of the member function test. Also, notice that neither the left side nor the right side of the assignment in line 34 refers to a specific object of class Test. Only the class name is used with the binary scope resolution operator (::). Line 35 invokes the member function stored in memPtr (i.e., test), using the ->* operator. Because memPtr is a pointer to a member of a class, the ->* operator must be used rather than the -> operator to invoke the function.

Line 41 declares and initializes vPtr as a pointer to an int data member of class Test. The right side of the assignment specifies the address of the data member value. Line 42 dereferences the pointer testPtr2, then uses the .* operator to access the member to which vPtr points. Note that the client code can create pointers to class members for only those class members that are accessible to the client code. In this example, both member function test and data member value are publicly accessible.

Common Programming Error 25.2

Declaring a member-function pointer without enclosing the pointer name in parentheses is a syntax error.

Common Programming Error 25.3

Declaring a member-function pointer without preceding the pointer name with a class name followed by the scope resolution operator (::) is a syntax error.

Common Programming Error 25.4

*Attempting to use the -> or * operator with a pointer to a class member generates syntax errors.*

25.7 Multiple Inheritance

In Chapters 9 and 10, we discussed single inheritance, in which each class is derived from exactly one base class. In C++, a class may be derived from more than one base class—a technique known as multiple inheritance in which a derived class inherits the members of two or more base classes. This powerful capability encourages interesting forms of software reuse but can cause a variety of ambiguity problems. Multiple inheritance is a difficult concept that should be used only by experienced programmers. In fact, some of the problems associated with multiple inheritance are so subtle that newer programming languages, such as Java and C#, do not enable a class to derive from more than one base class.

Good Programming Practice 25.2

Multiple inheritance is a powerful capability when used properly. Multiple inheritance should be used when an is-a relationship exists between a new type and two or more existing types (i.e., type A is a type B and type A is a type C).

Software Engineering Observation 25.4

Multiple inheritance can introduce complexity into a system. Great care is required in the design of a system to use multiple inheritance properly; it should not be used when single inheritance and/or composition will do the job.

A common problem with multiple inheritance is that each of the base classes might contain data members or member functions that have the same name. This can lead to ambiguity problems when you attempt to compile. Consider the multiple-inheritance example (Fig. 25.7, Fig. 25.8, Fig. 25.9, Fig. 25.10, Fig. 25.11). Class Base1 (Fig. 25.7) contains one protected int data member—value (line 20), a constructor (lines 10–13) that sets value and public member function getData (lines 15–18) that returns value.

Class Base2 (Fig. 25.8) is similar to class Base1, except that its protected data is a char named letter (line 20). Like class Base1, Base2 has a public member function getData, but this function returns the value of char data member letter.

Class Derived (Figs. 25.9–25.10) inherits from both class Base1 and class Base2 through multiple inheritance. Class Derived has a private data member of type double named real (line 21), a constructor to initialize all the data of class Derived and a public member function getReal that returns the value of double variable real.

To indicate multiple inheritance we follow the colon (:) after class Derived with a comma-separated list of base classes (line 14). In Fig. 25.10, notice that constructor Derived explicitly calls base-class constructors for each of its base classes—Base1 and Base2—using the member-initializer syntax (line 9). The base-class constructors are called in the order that the inheritance is specified, not in the order in which their constructors are mentioned; also, if the base-class constructors are not explicitly called in the member-initializer list, their default constructors will be called implicitly.

```
1   // Fig. 25.7: Base1.h
2   // Definition of class Base1
3   #ifndef BASE1_H
4   #define BASE1_H
5
6   // class Base1 definition
7   class Base1
8   {
9   public:
10     Base1( int parameterValue )
11     {
12        value = parameterValue;
13     } // end Base1 constructor
14
15     int getData() const
16     {
17        return value;
18     } // end function getData
19  protected: // accessible to derived classes
20     int value; // inherited by derived class
21  }; // end class Base1
22
23  #endif // BASE1_H
```

Fig. 25.7 | Demonstrating multiple inheritance—`Base1.h`.

```
1   // Fig. 25.8: Base2.h
2   // Definition of class Base2
3   #ifndef BASE2_H
4   #define BASE2_H
5
6   // class Base2 definition
7   class Base2
8   {
9   public:
10     Base2( char characterData )
11     {
12        letter = characterData;
13     } // end Base2 constructor
14
15     char getData() const
16     {
17        return letter;
18     } // end function getData
19  protected: // accessible to derived classes
20     char letter; // inherited by derived class
21  }; // end class Base2
22
23  #endif // BASE2_H
```

Fig. 25.8 | Demonstrating multiple inheritance—`Base2.h`.

```
1   // Fig. 25.9: Derived.h
2   // Definition of class Derived which inherits
3   // multiple base classes (Base1 and Base2).
4   #ifndef DERIVED_H
5   #define DERIVED_H
6
7   #include <iostream>
8   using std::ostream;
9
10  #include "Base1.h"
11  #include "Base2.h"
12
13  // class Derived definition
14  class Derived : public Base1, public Base2
15  {
16     friend ostream &operator<<( ostream &, const Derived & );
17  public:
18     Derived( int, char, double );
19     double getReal() const;
20  private:
21     double real; // derived class's private data
22  }; // end class Derived
23
24  #endif // DERIVED_H
```

Fig. 25.9 | Demonstrating multiple inheritance—Derived.h.

The overloaded stream insertion operator (Fig. 25.10, lines 18–23) uses its second parameter—a reference to a Derived object—to display a Derived object's data. This operator function is a friend of Derived, so operator<< can directly access all of class Derived's protected and private members, including the protected data member value (inherited from class Base1), protected data member letter (inherited from class Base2) and private data member real (declared in class Derived).

```
1   // Fig. 25.10: Derived.cpp
2   // Member-function definitions for class Derived
3   #include "Derived.h"
4
5   // constructor for Derived calls constructors for
6   // class Base1 and class Base2.
7   // use member initializers to call base-class constructors
8   Derived::Derived( int integer, char character, double double1 )
9      : Base1( integer ), Base2( character ), real( double1 ) { }
10
11  // return real
12  double Derived::getReal() const
13  {
14     return real;
15  } // end function getReal
16
```

Fig. 25.10 | Demonstrating multiple inheritance—Derived.cpp. (Part 1 of 2.)

```
17    // display all data members of Derived
18    ostream &operator<<( ostream &output, const Derived &derived )
19    {
20       output << "    Integer: " << derived.value << "\n  Character: "
21          << derived.letter << "\nReal number: " << derived.real;
22       return output; // enables cascaded calls
23    } // end operator<<
```

Fig. 25.10 | Demonstrating multiple inheritance—Derived.cpp. (Part 2 of 2.)

Now let us examine the main function (Fig. 25.11) that tests the classes in Figs. 25.7–25.10. Line 13 creates Base1 object base1 and initializes it to the int value 10, then creates the pointer base1Ptr and initializes it to the null pointer (i.e., 0). Line 14 creates Base2 object base2 and initializes it to the char value 'Z', then creates the pointer base2Ptr and initializes it to the null pointer. Line 15 creates Derived object derived and initializes it to contain the int value 7, the char value 'A' and the double value 3.5.

```
1     // Fig. 25.11: fig24_11.cpp
2     // Driver for multiple-inheritance example.
3     #include <iostream>
4     using std::cout;
5     using std::endl;
6
7     #include "Base1.h"
8     #include "Base2.h"
9     #include "Derived.h"
10
11    int main()
12    {
13       Base1 base1( 10 ), *base1Ptr = 0; // create Base1 object
14       Base2 base2( 'Z' ), *base2Ptr = 0; // create Base2 object
15       Derived derived( 7, 'A', 3.5 ); // create Derived object
16
17       // print data members of base-class objects
18       cout << "Object base1 contains integer " << base1.getData()
19          << "\nObject base2 contains character " << base2.getData()
20          << "\nObject derived contains:\n" << derived << "\n\n";
21
22       // print data members of derived-class object
23       // scope resolution operator resolves getData ambiguity
24       cout << "Data members of Derived can be accessed individually:"
25          << "\n    Integer: " << derived.Base1::getData()
26          << "\n  Character: " << derived.Base2::getData()
27          << "\nReal number: " << derived.getReal() << "\n\n";
28       cout << "Derived can be treated as an object of either base class:\n";
29
30       // treat Derived as a Base1 object
31       base1Ptr = &derived;
32       cout << "base1Ptr->getData() yields " << base1Ptr->getData() << '\n';
33
```

Fig. 25.11 | Demonstrating multiple inheritance. (Part 1 of 2.)

```
34      // treat Derived as a Base2 object
35      base2Ptr = &derived;
36      cout << "base2Ptr->getData() yields " << base2Ptr->getData() << endl;
37      return 0;
38  } // end main
```

```
Object base1 contains integer 10
Object base2 contains character Z
Object derived contains:
    Integer: 7
  Character: A
Real number: 3.5

Data members of Derived can be accessed individually:
    Integer: 7
  Character: A
Real number: 3.5

Derived can be treated as an object of either base class:
base1Ptr->getData() yields 7
base2Ptr->getData() yields A
```

Fig. 25.11 | Demonstrating multiple inheritance. (Part 2 of 2.)

Lines 18–20 display each object's data values. For objects base1 and base2, we invoke each object's getData member function. Even though there are two getData functions in this example, the calls are not ambiguous. In line 18, the compiler knows that base1 is an object of class Base1, so class Base1's getData is called. In line 19, the compiler knows that base2 is an object of class Base2, so class Base2's getData is called. Line 20 displays the contents of object derived using the overloaded stream insertion operator.

Resolving Ambiguity Issues That Arise When a Derived Class Inherits Member Functions of the Same Name from Multiple Base Classes

Lines 24–27 output the contents of object derived again by using the *get* member functions of class Derived. However, there is an ambiguity problem, because this object contains two getData functions, one inherited from class Base1 and one inherited from class Base2. This problem is easy to solve by using the binary scope resolution operator. The expression derived.Base1::getData() gets the value of the variable inherited from class Base1 (i.e., the int variable named value) and derived.Base2::getData() gets the value of the variable inherited from class Base2 (i.e., the char variable named letter). The double value in real is printed without ambiguity with the call derived.getReal()—there are no other member functions with that name in the hierarchy.

Demonstrating the Is-A Relationships in Multiple Inheritance

The *is-a* relationships of single inheritance also apply in multiple-inheritance relationships. To demonstrate this, line 31 assigns the address of object derived to the Base1 pointer base1Ptr. This is allowed because an object of class Derived *is an* object of class Base1. Line 32 invokes Base1 member function getData via base1Ptr to obtain the value of only the Base1 part of the object derived. Line 35 assigns the address of object derived to the Base2 pointer base2Ptr. This is allowed because an object of class Derived *is an* object of class Base2. Line 36 invokes Base2 member function getData via base2Ptr to obtain the value of only the Base2 part of the object derived.

25.8 Multiple Inheritance and `virtual` Base Classes

In Section 25.7, we discussed multiple inheritance, the process by which one class inherits from two or more classes. Multiple inheritance is used, for example, in the C++ standard library to form class basic_iostream (Fig. 25.12).

Class basic_ios is the base class for both basic_istream and basic_ostream, each of which is formed with single inheritance. Class basic_iostream inherits from both basic_istream and basic_ostream. This enables class basic_iostream objects to provide the functionality of basic_istreams and basic_ostreams. In multiple-inheritance hierarchies, the situation described in Fig. 25.12 is referred to as diamond inheritance.

Because classes basic_istream and basic_ostream each inherit from basic_ios, a potential problem exists for basic_iostream. Class basic_iostream could contain two copies of the members of class basic_ios—one inherited via class basic_istream and one inherited via class basic_ostream). Such a situation would be ambiguous and would result in a compilation error, because the compiler would not know which version of the members from class basic_ios to use. Of course, basic_iostream does not really suffer from the problem we mentioned. In this section, you'll see how using virtual base classes solves the problem of inheriting duplicate copies of an indirect base class.

Fig. 25.12 | Multiple inheritance to form class basic_iostream.

Compilation Errors Produced When Ambiguity Arises in Diamond Inheritance
Figure 25.13 demonstrates the ambiguity that can occur in diamond inheritance. The program defines class Base (lines 9–13), which contains pure virtual function print (line 12). Classes DerivedOne (lines 16–24) and DerivedTwo (lines 27–35) each publicly inherit from class Base and override the print function. Class DerivedOne and class DerivedTwo each contain what the C++ standard refers to as a base-class subobject—i.e., the members of class Base in this example.

Class Multiple (lines 38–46) inherits from both classes DerivedOne and DerivedTwo. In class Multiple, function print is overridden to call DerivedTwo's print (line 44). Notice that we must qualify the print call with the class name DerivedTwo to specify which version of print to call.

Function main (lines 48–64) declares objects of classes Multiple (line 50), DerivedOne (line 51) and DerivedTwo (line 52). Line 53 declares an array of Base * pointers. Each array element is initialized with the address of an object (lines 55–57). An

```cpp
1    // Fig. 25.13: fig24_13.cpp
2    // Attempting to polymorphically call a function that is
3    // multiply inherited from two base classes.
4    #include <iostream>
5    using std::cout;
6    using std::endl;
7
8    // class Base definition
9    class Base
10   {
11   public:
12      virtual void print() const = 0; // pure virtual
13   }; // end class Base
14
15   // class DerivedOne definition
16   class DerivedOne : public Base
17   {
18   public:
19      // override print function
20      void print() const
21      {
22         cout << "DerivedOne\n";
23      } // end function print
24   }; // end class DerivedOne
25
26   // class DerivedTwo definition
27   class DerivedTwo : public Base
28   {
29   public:
30      // override print function
31      void print() const
32      {
33         cout << "DerivedTwo\n";
34      } // end function print
35   }; // end class DerivedTwo
36
37   // class Multiple definition
38   class Multiple : public DerivedOne, public DerivedTwo
39   {
40   public:
41      // qualify which version of function print
42      void print() const
43      {
44         DerivedTwo::print();
45      } // end function print
46   }; // end class Multiple
47
48   int main()
49   {
50      Multiple both; // instantiate Multiple object
51      DerivedOne one; // instantiate DerivedOne object
52      DerivedTwo two; // instantiate DerivedTwo object
53      Base *array[ 3 ]; // create array of base-class pointers
```

Fig. 25.13 | Attempting to call a multiply inherited function polymorphically. (Part 1 of 2.)

```
54
55      array[ 0 ] = &both; // ERROR--ambiguous
56      array[ 1 ] = &one;
57      array[ 2 ] = &two;
58
59      // polymorphically invoke print
60      for ( int i = 0; i < 3; i++ )
61          array[ i ] -> print();
62
63      return 0;
64  } // end main
```

```
C:\Projects\cpphtp5\examples\ch24\Fig24_20\Fig24_20.cpp(55): error C2594:
'=' : ambiguous conversions from 'Multiple *' to 'Base *'
```

Fig. 25.13 | Attempting to call a multiply inherited function polymorphically. (Part 2 of 2.)

error occurs when the address of both—an object of class Multiple—is assigned to array[0]. The object both actually contains two subobjects of type Base, so the compiler does not know which subobject the pointer array[0] should point to, and it generates a compilation error indicating an ambiguous conversion.

Eliminating Duplicate Subobjects with **virtual** *Base-Class Inheritance*
The problem of duplicate subobjects is resolved with virtual inheritance. When a base class is inherited as virtual, only one subobject will appear in the derived class—a process called virtual base-class inheritance. Figure 25.14 revises the program of Fig. 25.13 to use a virtual base class.

The key change in the program is that classes DerivedOne (line 15) and DerivedTwo (line 26) each inherit from class Base by specifying virtual public Base. Since both of these classes inherit from Base, they each contain a Base subobject. The benefit of virtual inheritance is not clear until class Multiple inherits from both DerivedOne and DerivedTwo (line 37). Since each of the base classes used virtual inheritance to inherit class Base's members, the compiler ensures that only one subobject of type Base is inherited into class Multiple. This eliminates the ambiguity error generated by the compiler in Fig. 25.13. The compiler now allows the implicit conversion of the derived-class pointer (&both) to the base-class pointer array[0] in line 56 in main. The for statement in lines 61–62 polymorphically calls print for each object.

```
1   // Fig. 25.14: fig24_14.cpp
2   // Using virtual base classes.
3   #include <iostream>
4   using std::cout;
5   using std::endl;
6
```

Fig. 25.14 | Using virtual base classes. (Part 1 of 3.)

```
7   // class Base definition
8   class Base
9   {
10  public:
11     virtual void print() const = 0; // pure virtual
12  }; // end class Base
13
14  // class DerivedOne definition
15  class DerivedOne : virtual public Base
16  {
17  public:
18     // override print function
19     void print() const
20     {
21        cout << "DerivedOne\n";
22     } // end function print
23  }; // end DerivedOne class
24
25  // class DerivedTwo definition
26  class DerivedTwo : virtual public Base
27  {
28  public:
29     // override print function
30     void print() const
31     {
32        cout << "DerivedTwo\n";
33     } // end function print
34  }; // end DerivedTwo class
35
36  // class Multiple definition
37  class Multiple : public DerivedOne, public DerivedTwo
38  {
39  public:
40     // qualify which version of function print
41     void print() const
42     {
43        DerivedTwo::print();
44     } // end function print
45  }; // end Multiple class
46
47  int main()
48  {
49     Multiple both; // instantiate Multiple object
50     DerivedOne one; // instantiate DerivedOne object
51     DerivedTwo two; // instantiate DerivedTwo object
52
53     // declare array of base-class pointers and initialize
54     // each element to a derived-class type
55     Base *array[ 3 ];
56     array[ 0 ] = &both;
57     array[ 1 ] = &one;
58     array[ 2 ] = &two;
59
```

Fig. 25.14 | Using virtual base classes. (Part 2 of 3.)

```
60      // polymorphically invoke function print
61      for ( int i = 0; i < 3; i++ )
62          array[ i ]->print();
63
64      return 0;
65  } // end main
```

```
DerivedTwo
DerivedOne
DerivedTwo
```

Fig. 25.14 | Using `virtual` base classes. (Part 3 of 3.)

Constructors in Multiple-Inheritance Hierarchies with `virtual` Base Classes

Implementing hierarchies with `virtual` base classes is simpler if default constructors are used for the base classes. The examples in Figs. 25.13 and 25.14 use compiler-generated default constructors. If a `virtual` base class provides a constructor that requires arguments, the implementation of the derived classes becomes more complicated, because the most derived class must explicitly invoke the virtual base class's constructor to initialize the members inherited from the `virtual` base class.

Software Engineering Observation 25.5

Providing a default constructor for `virtual` base classes simplifies hierarchy design.

Additional Information on Multiple Inheritance

Multiple inheritance is a complex topic typically covered in more advanced C++ texts. For more information on multiple inheritance, please visit our C++ Resource Center at

> www.deitel.com/cplusplus/

In the *C++ Multiple Inheritance* category, you'll find links to several articles and resources, including a multiple inheritance FAQ and tips for using multiple inheritance.

25.9 Wrap-Up

In this chapter, you learned how to use the `const_cast` operator to remove the `const` qualification of a variable. We then showed how to use `namespaces` to ensure that every identifier in a program has a unique name and explained how they can help resolve naming conflicts. You saw several operator keywords for programmers whose keyboards do not support certain characters used in operator symbols, such as !, &, ^, ~ and |. Next, we showed how the `mutable` storage-class specifier enables a programmer to indicate that a data member should always be modifiable, even when it appears in an object that is currently being treated as a `const`. We also showed the mechanics of using pointers to class members and the ->* and .* operators. Finally, we introduced multiple inheritance and discussed problems associated with allowing a derived class to inherit the members of several base classes. As part of this discussion, we demonstrated how `virtual` inheritance can be used to solve those problems.

Summary

Section 24.2 `const_cast` Operator

- C++ provides the `const_cast` operator for casting away `const` or `volatile` qualification.

- A program declares a variable with the `volatile` qualifier when that program expects the variable to be modified by other programs. Declaring a variable `volatile` indicates that the compiler should not optimize the use of that variable because doing so could affect the ability of those other programs to access and modify the `volatile` variable.

- In general, it is dangerous to use the `const_cast` operator, because it allows a program to modify a variable that was declared `const`, and thus was not supposed to be modifiable.

- There are cases in which it is desirable, or even necessary, to cast away `const`-ness. For example, older C and C++ libraries might provide functions with non-`const` parameters and that do not modify their parameters. If you wish to pass `const` data to such a function, you would need to cast away the data's `const`-ness; otherwise, the compiler would report error messages.

- If you pass non-`const` data to a function that treats the data as if it were constant, then returns that data as a constant, you might need to cast away the `const`-ness of the returned data to access and modify that data.

Section 24.3 *namespaces*

- A program includes many identifiers defined in different scopes. Sometimes a variable of one scope will "overlap" with a variable of the same name in a different scope, possibly creating a naming conflict. The C++ standard solves this problem with `namespaces`.

- Each `namespace` defines a scope in which identifiers are placed. To use a `namespace` member, either the member's name must be qualified with the `namespace` name and the binary scope resolution operator (`::`) or a `using` directive or declaration must appear before the name is used in the program.

- Typically, `using` statements are placed at the beginning of the file in which members of the `namespace` are used.

- Not all `namespaces` are guaranteed to be unique. Two third-party vendors might inadvertently use the same identifiers for their `namespace` names.

- A `using namespace` directive specifies that the members of a namespace will be used frequently throughout a program. This allows you to access all the members of the namespace.

- A `using namespace` directive can be used for predefined namespaces (e.g., `std`) or programmer-defined namespaces.

- A namespace can contain constants, data, classes, nested namespaces, functions, etc. Definitions of namespaces must occupy the global scope or be nested within other namespaces.

- An unnamed namespace has an implicit `using` directive, so its members appear to occupy the global namespace, are accessible directly and do not have to be qualified with a namespace name. Global variables are also part of the global namespace.

- When accessing members of a nested namespace, the members must be qualified with the namespace name (unless the member is being used inside the nested namespace).

- Namespaces can be aliased.

Section 25.4 *Operator Keywords*

- The C++ standard provides operator keywords that can be used in place of several C++ operators. Operator keywords are useful for programmers who have keyboards that do not support certain characters such as `!`, `&`, `^`, `~`, `|`, etc.

Section 24.5 `mutable` *Class Members*

- If a data member should always be modifiable, C++ provides the storage-class specifier `mutable` as an alternative to `const_cast`. A `mutable` data member is always modifiable, even in a `const` member function or `const` object. This reduces the need to cast away "const-ness."

- `mutable` and `const_cast` are used in different contexts. For a `const` object with no `mutable` data members, operator `const_cast` must be used every time a member is to be modified. This greatly reduces the chance of a member being accidentally modified because the member is not permanently modifiable.

- Operations involving `const_cast` are typically hidden in a member function's implementation. The user of a class might not be aware that a member is being modified.

Section 24.6 Pointers to Class Members (.* *and* ->* *)*

- C++ provides the `.*` and `->*` operators for accessing class members via pointers. This is rarely used capability that is used primarily by advanced C++ programmers.

- Declaring a pointer to a function requires that you enclose the pointer name preceded by an * in parentheses. A pointer to a function must specify, as part of its type, both the return type of the function it points to and the parameter list of that function.

Section 25.7 Multiple Inheritance

- In C++, a class may be derived from more than one base class—a technique known as multiple inheritance, in which a derived class inherits the members of two or more base classes.

- A common problem with multiple inheritance is that each of the base classes might contain data members or member functions that have the same name. This can lead to ambiguity problems when you attempt to compile.

- The *is-a* relationships of single inheritance also apply in multiple-inheritance relationships.

- Multiple inheritance is used, for example, in the C++ Standard Library to form class `basic_iostream`. Class `basic_ios` is the base class for both `basic_istream` and `basic_ostream`, each of which is formed with single inheritance. Class `basic_iostream` inherits from both `basic_istream` and `basic_ostream`. This enables objects of class `basic_iostream` to provide the functionality of both `basic_istream`s and `basic_ostream`s. In multiple-inheritance hierarchies, the situation described here is referred to as diamond inheritance.

- Because classes `basic_istream` and `basic_ostream` each inherit from `basic_ios`, a potential problem exists for `basic_iostream`. If not implemented correctly, class `basic_iostream` could contain two copies of the members of class `basic_ios`—one inherited via class `basic_istream` and one inherited via class `basic_ostream`). Such a situation would be ambiguous and would result in a compilation error, because the compiler would not know which version of the members from class `basic_ios` to use.

Section 24.8 Multiple Inheritance and `virtual` *Base Classes*

- The ambiguity in diamond inheritance occurs when a derived-class object inherits two or more base-class subobjects. The problem of duplicate subobjects is resolved with `virtual` inheritance. When a base class is inherited as `virtual`, only one subobject will appear in the derived class—a process called `virtual` base-class inheritance.

- Implementing hierarchies with `virtual` base classes is simpler if default constructors are used for the base classes. If a `virtual` base class provides a constructor that requires arguments, the implementation of the derived classes becomes more complicated, because the most derived class must explicitly invoke the virtual base class's constructor to initialize the members inherited from the `virtual` base class.

Terminology

.* operator	namespace
->* operator	namespace alias
and operator keyword	namespace keyword
and_eq operator keyword	naming conflict
base-class subobject	nested namespace
bitand operator keyword	not operator keyword
bitor operator keyword	not_eq operator keyword
bitwise assignment operator keywords	operator keyword
bitwise operator keywords	or operator keyword
cast away const-ness	or_eq operator keyword
comma-separated list of base classes	pointer-to-member operators
compl operator keyword	unnamed namespace
const_cast operator	using declaration
diamond inheritance	using namespace declaration
global namespace	virtual base class
inequality operator keywords	virtual inheritance
logical operator keywords	volatile qualifier
most derived class	xor operator keyword
multiple inheritance	xor_eq operator keyword
mutable data member	

Self-Review Exercises

25.1 Fill in the blanks for each of the following:

a) The _____ operator qualifies a member with its namespace.

b) The _____ operator allows an object's "const-ness" to be cast away.

c) Because an unnamed namespace has an implicit using directive, its members appear to occupy the _____, are accessible directly and do not have to be qualified with a namespace name.

d) Operator _____ is the operator keyword for inequality.

e) _____ allows a class to be derived from more than one base class.

f) When a base class is inherited as _____, only one subobject of the base class will appear in the derived class.

25.2 State which of the following are *true* and which are *false*. If a statement is *false*, explain why.

a) When passing a non-const argument to a const function, the const_cast operator should be used to cast away the "const-ness" of the function.

b) namespaces are guaranteed to be unique.

c) Like class bodies, namespace bodies also end in semicolons.

d) namespaces cannot have namespaces as members.

e) A mutable data member cannot be modified in a const member function.

Answers to Self-Review Exercises

25.1 a) binary scope resolution (::). b) const_cast. c) global namespace. d) not_eq. e) multiple inheritance. f) virtual.

25.2 a) False. It is legal to pass a non-const argument to a const function. However, when passing a const reference or pointer to a non-const function, the const_cast operator should be used to cast away the "const-ness" of the reference or pointer

b) False. Programmers might inadvertently choose the namespace already in use.

c) False. namespace bodies do not end in semicolons.

d) False. namespaces can be nested.

e) False. A mutable data member is always modifiable, even in a const member function.

Exercises

25.3 Fill in the blanks for each of the following:

a) Keyword _____ specifies that a namespace or namespace member is being used.

b) Operator _____ is the operator keyword for logical OR.

c) Storage specifier _____ allows a member of a const object to be modified.

d) The _____ qualifier specifies that an object can be modified by other programs.

e) Precede a member with its _____ name and the scope resolution operator if the possibility exists of a scoping conflict.

f) The body of a namespace is delimited by _____.

g) For a const object with no _____ data members, operator _____ must be used every time a member is to be modified.

25.4 Write a namespace, Currency, that defines constant members ONE, TWO, FIVE, TEN, TWENTY, FIFTY and HUNDRED. Write two short programs that use Currency. One program should make all constants available and the other should make only FIVE available.

25.5 Given the namespaces in Fig. 25.15, determine whether each statement is *true* or *false*. Explain any *false* answers.

a) Variable kilometers is visible within namespace Data.

b) Object string1 is visible within namespace Data.

c) Constant POLAND is not visible within namespace Data.

d) Constant GERMANY is visible within namespace Data.

e) Function function is visible to namespace Data.

f) Namespace Data is visible to namespace CountryInformation.

g) Object map is visible to namespace CountryInformation.

h) Object string1 is visible within namespace RegionalInformation.

```
1    namespace CountryInformation
2    {
3       using namespace std;
4       enum Countries { POLAND, SWITZERLAND, GERMANY,
5                        AUSTRIA, CZECH_REPUBLIC };
6       int kilometers;
7       string string1;
8
9       namespace RegionalInformation
10      {
11         short getPopulation(); // assume definition exists
12         MapData map; // assume definition exists
13      } // end RegionalInformation
14   } // end CountryInformation
15
16   namespace Data
17   {
18      using namespace CountryInformation::RegionalInformation;
19      void *function( void *, int );
20   } // end Data
```

Fig. 25.15 | namespaces for Exercise 25.5.

25.6 Compare and contrast `mutable` and `const_cast`. Give at least one example of when one might be preferred over the other. [*Note:* This exercise does not require any code to be written.]

25.7 Write a program that uses `const_cast` to modify a const variable. [*Hint:* Use a pointer in your solution to point to the const identifier.]

25.8 What problem do `virtual` base classes solve?

25.9 Write a program that uses `virtual` base classes. The class at the top of the hierarchy should provide a constructor that takes at least one argument (i.e., do not provide a default constructor). What challenges does this present for the inheritance hierarchy?

25.10 Find the error(s) in each of the following. When possible, explain how to correct each error.

a)
```
namespace Name {
    int x;
    int y;
    mutable int z;
};
```

b)
```
int integer = const_cast< int >( double );
```

c)
```
namespace PCM( 111, "hello" );    // construct namespace
```

Operator Precedence and Associativity Chart

A.1 Operator Precedence

Operators are shown in decreasing order of precedence from top to bottom (Fig. A.1).

Operator	Type	Associativity
::	binary scope resolution	left to right
::	unary scope resolution	
()	parentheses	left to right
[]	array subscript	
.	member selection via object	
->	member selection via pointer	
++	unary postfix increment	
--	unary postfix decrement	
typeid	runtime type information	
dynamic_cast < *type* >	runtime type-checked cast	
static_cast< *type* >	compile-time type-checked cast	
reinterpret_cast< *type* >	cast for nonstandard conversions	
const_cast< *type* >	cast away const-ness	

Fig. A.1 | Operator precedence and associativity chart. (Part 1 of 3.)

Operator	Type	Associativity
++	unary prefix increment	right to left
--	unary prefix decrement	
+	unary plus	
-	unary minus	
!	unary logical negation	
~	unary bitwise complement	
sizeof	determine size in bytes	
&	address	
*	dereference	
new	dynamic memory allocation	
new[]	dynamic array allocation	
delete	dynamic memory deallocation	
delete[]	dynamic array deallocation	
(*type*)	C-style unary cast	right to left
.*	pointer to member via object	left to right
->*	pointer to member via pointer	
*	multiplication	left to right
/	division	
%	modulus	
+	addition	left to right
-	subtraction	
<<	bitwise left shift	left to right
>>	bitwise right shift	
<	relational less than	left to right
<=	relational less than or equal to	
>	relational greater than	
>=	relational greater than or equal to	
==	relational is equal to	left to right
!=	relational is not equal to	
&	bitwise AND	left to right
^	bitwise exclusive OR	left to right
|	bitwise inclusive OR	left to right
&&	logical AND	left to right
||	logical OR	left to right
?:	ternary conditional	right to left

Fig. A.1 | Operator precedence and associativity chart. (Part 2 of 3.)

Operator	Type	Associativity
=	assignment	right to left
+=	addition assignment	
-=	subtraction assignment	
*=	multiplication assignment	
/=	division assignment	
%=	modulus assignment	
&=	bitwise AND assignment	
^=	bitwise exclusive OR assignment	
|=	bitwise inclusive OR assignment	
<<=	bitwise left-shift assignment	
>>=	bitwise right-shift assignment	
,	comma	left to right

Fig. A.1 | Operator precedence and associativity chart. (Part 3 of 3.)

ASCII Character Set

	0	1	2	3	4	5	6	7	8	9
					ASCII character set					
0	nul	soh	stx	etx	eot	enq	ack	bel	bs	ht
1	lf	vt	ff	cr	so	si	dle	dc1	dc2	dc3
2	dc4	nak	syn	etb	can	em	sub	esc	fs	gs
3	rs	us	sp	!	"	#	$	%	&	'
4	(	)	*	+	,	-	.	/	0	1
5	2	3	4	5	6	7	8	9	:	;
6	<	=	>	?	@	A	B	C	D	E
7	F	G	H	I	J	K	L	M	N	O
8	P	Q	R	S	T	U	V	W	X	Y
9	Z	[	\	]	^	_	`	a	b	c
10	d	e	f	g	h	i	j	k	l	m
11	n	o	p	q	r	s	t	u	v	w
12	x	y	z	{	|	}	~	del		

Fig. B.1 | ASCII character set.

The digits at the left of the table are the left digits of the decimal equivalent (0–127) of the character code, and the digits at the top of the table are the right digits of the character code. For example, the character code for "F" is 70, and the character code for "&" is 38.

Fundamental Types

Figure C.1 lists C++'s fundamental types. The C++ Standard Document does not provide the exact number of bytes required to store variables of these types in memory. However, the C++ Standard Document does indicate how the memory requirements for fundamental types relate to one another. By order of increasing memory requirements, the signed integer types are `signed char`, `short int`, `int` and `long int`. This means that a `short int` must provide at least as much storage as a `signed char`; an `int` must provide at least as much storage as a `short int`; and a `long int` must provide at least as much storage as an `int`. Each signed integer type has a corresponding unsigned integer type that has the same memory requirements. Unsigned types cannot represent negative values, but can represent twice as many positive values as their associated signed types. By order of increasing mem-

Integral types	Floating-point types
bool	float
char	double
signed char	long double
unsigned char	
short int	
unsigned short int	
int	
unsigned int	
long int	
unsigned long int	
wchar_t	

Fig. C.1 | C++ fundamental types.

ory requirements, the floating-point types are `float`, `double` and `long double`. Like integer types, a `double` must provide at least as much storage as a `float` and a `long double` must provide at least as much storage as a `double`.

The exact sizes and ranges of values for the fundamental types are implementation dependent. The header files `<climits>` (for the integral types) and `<cfloat>` (for the floating-point types) specify the ranges of values supported on your system.

The range of values a type supports depends on the number of bytes that are used to represent that type. For example, consider a system with 4 byte (32 bit) `int`s. For the signed `int` type, the nonnegative values are in the range 0 to 2,147,483,647 ($2^{31} - 1$). The negative values are in the range -1 to $-2,147,483,648$ (-2^{31}). This is a total of 2^{32} possible values. An `unsigned int` on the same system would use the same number of bits to represent data, but would not represent any negative values. This results in values in the range 0 to 4,294,967,295 ($2^{32} - 1$). On the same system, a `short int` could not use more than 32 bits to represent its data and a `long int` must use at least 32 bits.

C++ provides the data type `bool` for variables that can hold only the values `true` and `false`.

D

Number Systems

Here are only numbers ratified.
—William Shakespeare

Nature has some sort of arithmetic-geometrical coordinate system, because nature has all kinds of models. What we experience of nature is in models, and all of nature's models are so beautiful.
It struck me that nature's system must be a real beauty, because in chemistry we find that the associations are always in beautiful whole numbers—there are no fractions.
—Richard Buckminster Fuller

OBJECTIVES

In this appendix you'll learn:

- To understand basic number systems concepts, such as base, positional value and symbol value.

- To understand how to work with numbers represented in the binary, octal and hexadecimal number systems.

- To abbreviate binary numbers as octal numbers or hexadecimal numbers.

- To convert octal numbers and hexadecimal numbers to binary numbers.

- To convert back and forth between decimal numbers and their binary, octal and hexadecimal equivalents.

- To understand binary arithmetic and how negative binary numbers are represented using two's complement notation.

D. I Introduction

In this appendix, we introduce the key number systems that C++ programmers use, especially when they are working on software projects that require close interaction with machine-level hardware. Projects like this include operating systems, computer networking software, compilers, database systems and applications requiring high performance.

When we write an integer such as 227 or –63 in a C++ program, the number is assumed to be in the decimal (base 10) number system. The digits in the decimal number system are 0, 1, 2, 3, 4, 5, 6, 7, 8 and 9. The lowest digit is 0 and the highest is 9—one less than the base of 10. Internally, computers use the binary (base 2) number system. The binary number system has only two digits, namely 0 and 1. Its lowest digit is 0 and its highest is 1—one less than the base of 2.

As we'll see, binary numbers tend to be much longer than their decimal equivalents. Programmers who work in assembly languages, and in high-level languages like C++ that enable them to reach down to the machine level, find it cumbersome to work with binary numbers. So two other number systems—the octal number system (base 8) and the hexadecimal number system (base 16)—are popular, primarily because they make it convenient to abbreviate binary numbers.

In the octal number system, the digits range from 0 to 7. Because both the binary and the octal number systems have fewer digits than the decimal number system, their digits are the same as the corresponding digits in decimal.

The hexadecimal number system poses a problem because it requires 16 digits—a lowest digit of 0 and a highest digit with a value equivalent to decimal 15 (one less than the base of 16). By convention, we use the letters A through F to represent the hexadecimal digits corresponding to decimal values 10 through 15. Thus in hexadecimal we can have numbers like 876 consisting solely of decimal-like digits, numbers like 8A55F consisting of digits and letters and numbers like FFE consisting solely of letters. Occasionally, a hexadecimal number spells a common word such as FACE or FEED—this can appear strange to programmers accustomed to working with numbers. The digits of the binary, octal, decimal and hexadecimal number systems are summarized in Figs. D.1–D.2.

Each of these number systems uses positional notation—each position in which a digit is written has a different positional value. For example, in the decimal number 937 (the 9, the 3 and the 7 are referred to as symbol values), we say that the 7 is written in the ones position, the 3 is written in the tens position and the 9 is written in the hundreds position. Note that each of these positions is a power of the base (base 10) and that these powers begin at 0 and increase by 1 as we move left in the number (Fig. D.3).

Binary digit	Octal digit	Decimal digit	Hexadecimal digit
0	0	0	0
1	1	1	1
	2	2	2
	3	3	3
	4	4	4
	5	5	5
	6	6	6
	7	7	7
		8	8
		9	9
			A (decimal value of 10)
			B (decimal value of 11)
			C (decimal value of 12)
			D (decimal value of 13)
			E (decimal value of 14)
			F (decimal value of 15)

Fig. D.1 | Digits of the binary, octal, decimal and hexadecimal number systems.

Attribute	Binary	Octal	Decimal	Hexadecimal
Base	2	8	10	16
Lowest digit	0	0	0	0
Highest digit	1	7	9	F

Fig. D.2 | Comparing the binary, octal, decimal and hexadecimal number systems.

Positional values in the decimal number system			
Decimal digit	9	3	7
Position name	Hundreds	Tens	Ones
Positional value	100	10	1
Positional value as a power of the base (10)	10^2	10^1	10^0

Fig. D.3 | Positional values in the decimal number system.

For longer decimal numbers, the next positions to the left would be the thousands position (10 to the 3rd power), the ten-thousands position (10 to the 4th power), the hundred-thousands position (10 to the 5th power), the millions position (10 to the 6th power), the ten-millions position (10 to the 7th power) and so on.

In the binary number 101, the rightmost 1 is written in the ones position, the 0 is written in the twos position and the leftmost 1 is written in the fours position. Note that each position is a power of the base (base 2) and that these powers begin at 0 and increase by 1 as we move left in the number (Fig. D.4). So, $101 = 2^2 + 2^0 = 4 + 1 = 5$.

For longer binary numbers, the next positions to the left would be the eights position (2 to the 3rd power), the sixteens position (2 to the 4th power), the thirty-twos position (2 to the 5th power), the sixty-fours position (2 to the 6th power) and so on.

In the octal number 425, we say that the 5 is written in the ones position, the 2 is written in the eights position and the 4 is written in the sixty-fours position. Note that each of these positions is a power of the base (base 8) and that these powers begin at 0 and increase by 1 as we move left in the number (Fig. D.5).

For longer octal numbers, the next positions to the left would be the five-hundred-and-twelves position (8 to the 3rd power), the four-thousand-and-ninety-sixes position (8 to the 4th power), the thirty-two-thousand-seven-hundred-and-sixty-eights position (8 to the 5th power) and so on.

In the hexadecimal number 3DA, we say that the A is written in the ones position, the D is written in the sixteens position and the 3 is written in the two-hundred-and-fifty-sixes position. Note that each of these positions is a power of the base (base 16) and that these powers begin at 0 and increase by 1 as we move left in the number (Fig. D.6).

For longer hexadecimal numbers, the next positions to the left would be the four-thousand-and-ninety-sixes position (16 to the 3rd power), the sixty-five-thousand-five-hundred-and-thirty-sixes position (16 to the 4th power) and so on.

Positional values in the binary number system			
Binary digit	1	0	1
Position name	Fours	Twos	Ones
Positional value	4	2	1
Positional value as a power of the base (2)	2^2	2^1	2^0

Fig. D.4 | Positional values in the binary number system.

Positional values in the octal number system			
Decimal digit	4	2	5
Position name	Sixty-fours	Eights	Ones
Positional value	64	8	1
Positional value as a power of the base (8)	8^2	8^1	8^0

Fig. D.5 | Positional values in the octal number system.

Positional values in the hexadecimal number system			
Decimal digit	3	D	A
Position name	Two-hundred-and-fifty-sixes	Sixteens	Ones
Positional value	256	16	1
Positional value as a power of the base (16)	16^2	16^1	16^0

Fig. D.6 | Positional values in the hexadecimal number system.

D.2 Abbreviating Binary Numbers as Octal and Hexadecimal Numbers

The main use for octal and hexadecimal numbers in computing is for abbreviating lengthy binary representations. Figure D.7 highlights the fact that lengthy binary numbers can be expressed concisely in number systems with higher bases than the binary number system.

A particularly important relationship that both the octal number system and the hexadecimal number system have to the binary system is that the bases of octal and hexadecimal (8 and 16 respectively) are powers of the base of the binary number system (base 2).

Decimal number	Binary representation	Octal representation	Hexadecimal representation
0	0	0	0
1	1	1	1
2	10	2	2
3	11	3	3
4	100	4	4
5	101	5	5
6	110	6	6
7	111	7	7
8	1000	10	8
9	1001	11	9
10	1010	12	A
11	1011	13	B
12	1100	14	C
13	1101	15	D
14	1110	16	E
15	1111	17	F
16	10000	20	10

Fig. D.7 | Decimal, binary, octal and hexadecimal equivalents.

Consider the following 12-digit binary number and its octal and hexadecimal equivalents. See if you can determine how this relationship makes it convenient to abbreviate binary numbers in octal or hexadecimal. The answers follow the numbers.

Binary number	Octal equivalent	Hexadecimal equivalent
100011010001	4321	8D1

To see how the binary number converts easily to octal, simply break the 12-digit binary number into groups of three consecutive bits each, starting from the right, and write those groups over the corresponding digits of the octal number as follows:

100	011	010	001
4	3	2	1

Note that the octal digit you have written under each group of thee bits corresponds precisely to the octal equivalent of that 3-digit binary number, as shown in Fig. D.7.

The same kind of relationship can be observed in converting from binary to hexadecimal. Break the 12-digit binary number into groups of four consecutive bits each, starting from the right, and write those groups over the corresponding digits of the hexadecimal number as follows:

1000	1101	0001
8	D	1

Notice that the hexadecimal digit you wrote under each group of four bits corresponds precisely to the hexadecimal equivalent of that 4-digit binary number as shown in Fig. D.7.

D.3 Converting Octal and Hexadecimal Numbers to Binary Numbers

In the previous section, we saw how to convert binary numbers to their octal and hexadecimal equivalents by forming groups of binary digits and simply rewriting them as their equivalent octal digit values or hexadecimal digit values. This process may be used in reverse to produce the binary equivalent of a given octal or hexadecimal number.

For example, the octal number 653 is converted to binary simply by writing the 6 as its 3-digit binary equivalent 110, the 5 as its 3-digit binary equivalent 101 and the 3 as its 3-digit binary equivalent 011 to form the 9-digit binary number 110101011.

The hexadecimal number FAD5 is converted to binary simply by writing the F as its 4-digit binary equivalent 1111, the A as its 4-digit binary equivalent 1010, the D as its 4-digit binary equivalent 1101 and the 5 as its 4-digit binary equivalent 0101 to form the 16-digit 1111101011010101.

D.4 Converting from Binary, Octal or Hexadecimal to Decimal

We are accustomed to working in decimal, and therefore it is often convenient to convert a binary, octal, or hexadecimal number to decimal to get a sense of what the number is "really" worth. Our diagrams in Section D.1 express the positional values in decimal. To convert a number to decimal from another base, multiply the decimal equivalent of each digit by its positional value and sum these products. For example, the binary number 110101 is converted to decimal 53 as shown in Fig. D.8.

To convert octal 7614 to decimal 3980, we use the same technique, this time using appropriate octal positional values, as shown in Fig. D.9.

To convert hexadecimal AD3B to decimal 44347, we use the same technique, this time using appropriate hexadecimal positional values, as shown in Fig. D.10.

D.5 Converting from Decimal to Binary, Octal or Hexadecimal

The conversions in Section D.4 follow naturally from the positional notation conventions. Converting from decimal to binary, octal, or hexadecimal also follows these conventions.

Suppose we wish to convert decimal 57 to binary. We begin by writing the positional values of the columns right to left until we reach a column whose positional value is greater than the decimal number. We do not need that column, so we discard it. Thus, we first write:

Positional values: 64   32   16   8   4   2   1

Then we discard the column with positional value 64, leaving:

Positional values: 32   16   8   4   2   1

Converting a binary number to decimal					
Positional values:	32	16	8	4	2	1
Symbol values:	1	1	0	1	0	1
Products:	1*32=32	1*16=16	0*8=0	1*4=4	0*2=0	1*1=1
Sum:	= 32 + 16 + 0 + 4 + 0s + 1 = 53					

Fig. D.8 | Converting a binary number to decimal.

Converting an octal number to decimal			
Positional values:	512	64	8	1
Symbol values:	7	6	1	4
Products	7*512=3584	6*64=384	1*8=8	4*1=4
Sum:	= 3584 + 384 + 8 + 4 = 3980			

Fig. D.9 | Converting an octal number to decimal.

Converting a hexadecimal number to decimal			
Positional values:	4096	256	16	1
Symbol values:	A	D	3	B
Products	A*4096=40960	D*256=3328	3*16=48	B*1=11
Sum:	= 40960 + 3328 + 48 + 11 = 44347			

Fig. D.10 | Converting a hexadecimal number to decimal.

Next we work from the leftmost column to the right. We divide 32 into 57 and observe that there is one 32 in 57 with a remainder of 25, so we write 1 in the 32 column. We divide 16 into 25 and observe that there is one 16 in 25 with a remainder of 9 and write 1 in the 16 column. We divide 8 into 9 and observe that there is one 8 in 9 with a remainder of 1. The next two columns each produce quotients of 0 when their positional values are divided into 1, so we write 0s in the 4 and 2 columns. Finally, 1 into 1 is 1, so we write 1 in the 1 column. This yields:

```
Positional values: 32   16      8      4      2      1
Symbol values:      1    1      1      0      0      1
```

and thus decimal 57 is equivalent to binary 111001.

To convert decimal 103 to octal, we begin by writing the positional values of the columns until we reach a column whose positional value is greater than the decimal number. We do not need that column, so we discard it. Thus, we first write:

```
Positional values:         512         64      8      1
```

Then we discard the column with positional value 512, yielding:

```
Positional values:                     64      8      1
```

Next we work from the leftmost column to the right. We divide 64 into 103 and observe that there is one 64 in 103 with a remainder of 39, so we write 1 in the 64 column. We divide 8 into 39 and observe that there are four 8s in 39 with a remainder of 7 and write 4 in the 8 column. Finally, we divide 1 into 7 and observe that there are seven 1s in 7 with no remainder, so we write 7 in the 1 column. This yields:

```
Positional values: 64      8      1
Symbol values:      1      4      7
```

and thus decimal 103 is equivalent to octal 147.

To convert decimal 375 to hexadecimal, we begin by writing the positional values of the columns until we reach a column whose positional value is greater than the decimal number. We do not need that column, so we discard it. Thus, we first write:

```
Positional values: 4096   256   16      1
```

Then we discard the column with positional value 4096, yielding:

```
Positional values:        256   16      1
```

Next we work from the leftmost column to the right. We divide 256 into 375 and observe that there is one 256 in 375 with a remainder of 119, so we write 1 in the 256 column. We divide 16 into 119 and observe that there are seven 16s in 119 with a remainder of 7 and write 7 in the 16 column. Finally, we divide 1 into 7 and observe that there are seven 1s in 7 with no remainder, so we write 7 in the 1 column. This yields:

```
Positional values: 256     16      1
Symbol values:      1       7      7
```

and thus decimal 375 is equivalent to hexadecimal 177.

D.6 Negative Binary Numbers: Two's Complement Notation

The discussion so far in this appendix has focused on positive numbers. In this section, we explain how computers represent negative numbers using *two's complement notation*. First we explain how the two's complement of a binary number is formed, then we show why it represents the negative value of the given binary number.

Consider a machine with 32-bit integers. Suppose

```
int value = 13;
```

The 32-bit representation of value is

```
00000000 00000000 00000000 00001101
```

To form the negative of value we first form its *one's complement* by applying C++'s bitwise complement operator (~):

```
onesComplementOfValue = ~value;
```

Internally, ~value is now value with each of its bits reversed—ones become zeros and zeros become ones, as follows:

```
value:
00000000 00000000 00000000 00001101

~value (i.e., value's one's complement):
11111111 11111111 11111111 11110010
```

To form the two's complement of value, we simply add 1 to value's one's complement. Thus

```
Two's complement of value:
11111111 11111111 11111111 11110011
```

Now if this is in fact equal to –13, we should be able to add it to binary 13 and obtain a result of 0. Let us try this:

```
 00000000 00000000 00000000 00001101
+11111111 11111111 11111111 11110011
-------------------------------------
 00000000 00000000 00000000 00000000
```

The carry bit coming out of the leftmost column is discarded and we indeed get 0 as a result. If we add the one's complement of a number to the number, the result will be all 1s. The key to getting a result of all zeros is that the two's complement is one more than the one's complement. The addition of 1 causes each column to add to 0 with a carry of 1. The carry keeps moving leftward until it is discarded from the leftmost bit, and thus the resulting number is all zeros.

Computers actually perform a subtraction, such as

```
x = a - value;
```

by adding the two's complement of value to a, as follows:

```
x = a + (~value + 1);
```

Suppose a is 27 and value is 13 as before. If the two's complement of value is actually the negative of value, then adding the two's complement of value to a should produce the result 14. Let us try this:

```
a (i.e., 27)          00000000 00000000 00000000 00011011
+(~value + 1)        +11111111 11111111 11111111 11110011
                     ------------------------------------
                      00000000 00000000 00000000 00001110
```

which is indeed equal to 14.

Summary

- An integer such as 19 or 227 or –63 in a C++ program is assumed to be in the decimal (base 10) number system. The digits in the decimal number system are 0, 1, 2, 3, 4, 5, 6, 7, 8 and 9. The lowest digit is 0 and the highest is 9—one less than the base of 10.

- Internally, computers use the binary (base 2) number system. The binary number system has only two digits, namely 0 and 1. Its lowest digit is 0 and its highest is 1—one less than the base of 2.

- The octal number system (base 8) and the hexadecimal number system (base 16) are popular primarily because they make it convenient to abbreviate binary numbers.

- The digits of the octal number system range from 0 to 7.

- The hexadecimal number system poses a problem because it requires 16 digits—a lowest digit of 0 and a highest digit with a value equivalent to decimal 15 (one less than the base of 16). By convention, we use the letters A through F to represent the hexadecimal digits corresponding to decimal values 10 through 15.

- Each number system uses positional notation—each position in which a digit is written has a different positional value.

- A particularly important relationship of both the octal and the hexadecimal number systems to the binary system is that their bases (8 and 16 respectively) are powers of the base of the binary number system (base 2).

- To convert an octal to a binary number, replace each octal digit with its three-digit binary equivalent.

- To convert a hexadecimal to a binary number, simply replace each hexadecimal digit with its four-digit binary equivalent.

- Because we are accustomed to working in decimal, it is convenient to convert a binary, octal or hexadecimal number to decimal to get a sense of the number's "real" worth.

- To convert a number to decimal from another base, multiply the decimal equivalent of each digit by its positional value and sum the products.

- Computers represent negative numbers using two's complement notation.

- To form the negative of a value in binary, first form its one's complement by applying C++'s bitwise complement operator (~). This reverses the bits of the value. To form the two's complement of a value, simply add one to the value's one's complement.

Terminology

base	base 16 number system
base 2 number system	binary number system
base 8 number system	bitwise complement operator (~)
base 10 number system	conversions

decimal number system
digit
hexadecimal number system
negative value
octal number system

one's complement notation
positional notation
positional value
symbol value
two's complement notation

Self-Review Exercises

D.1 The bases of the decimal, binary, octal and hexadecimal number systems are _____, _____, _____ and _____ respectively.

D.2 In general, the decimal, octal and hexadecimal representations of a given binary number contain (more/fewer) digits than the binary number contains.

D.3 (*True/False*) A popular reason for using the decimal number system is that it forms a convenient notation for abbreviating binary numbers simply by substituting one decimal digit per group of four binary bits.

D.4 The [octal/hexadecimal/decimal] representation of a large binary value is the most concise (of the given alternatives).

D.5 (*True/False*) The highest digit in any base is one more than the base.

D.6 (*True/False*) The lowest digit in any base is one less than the base.

D.7 The positional value of the rightmost digit of any number in either binary, octal, decimal or hexadecimal is always _____.

D.8 The positional value of the digit to the left of the rightmost digit of any number in binary, octal, decimal or hexadecimal is always equal to _____.

D.9 Fill in the missing values in this chart of positional values for the rightmost four positions in each of the indicated number systems:

decimal	1000	100	10	1
hexadecimal	...	256	...	...
binary	...	...	...	...
octal	512	...	8	...

D.10 Convert binary 110101011000 to octal and to hexadecimal.

D.11 Convert hexadecimal FACE to binary.

D.12 Convert octal 7316 to binary.

D.13 Convert hexadecimal 4FEC to octal. [*Hint:* First convert 4FEC to binary, then convert that binary number to octal.]

D.14 Convert binary 1101110 to decimal.

D.15 Convert octal 317 to decimal.

D.16 Convert hexadecimal EFD4 to decimal.

D.17 Convert decimal 177 to binary, to octal and to hexadecimal.

D.18 Show the binary representation of decimal 417. Then show the one's complement of 417 and the two's complement of 417.

D.19 What is the result when a number and its two's complement are added to each other?

Answers to Self-Review Exercises

D.1   10, 2, 8, 16.

D.2   Fewer.

D.3   False. Hexadecimal does this.

D.4   Hexadecimal.

D.5   False. The highest digit in any base is one less than the base.

D.6   False. The lowest digit in any base is zero.

D.7   1 (the base raised to the zero power).

D.8   The base of the number system.

D.9   Filled in chart shown below:

decimal	1000	100	10	1
hexadecimal	4096	256	16	1
binary	8	4	2	1
octal	512	64	8	1

D.10   Octal 6530; Hexadecimal D58.

D.11   Binary 1111 1010 1100 1110.

D.12   Binary 111 011 001 110.

D.13   Binary 0 100 111 111 101 100; Octal 47754.

D.14   Decimal 2 + 4 + 8 + 32 + 64 = 110.

D.15   Decimal 7 + 1 * 8 + 3 * 64 = 7 + 8 + 192 = 207.

D.16   Decimal 4 + 13 * 16 + 15 * 256 + 14 * 4096 = 61396.

D.17   Decimal 177
to binary:

```
256 128 64 32 16 8 4 2 1
128 64 32 16 8 4 2 1
(1*128)+(0*64)+(1*32)+(1*16)+(0*8)+(0*4)+(0*2)+(1*1)
10110001
```

to octal:

```
512 64 8 1
64 8 1
(2*64)+(6*8)+(1*1)
261
```

to hexadecimal:

```
256 16 1
16 1
(11*16)+(1*1)
(B*16)+(1*1)
B1
```

D.18 Binary:

```
512 256 128 64 32 16 8 4 2 1
256 128 64 32 16 8 4 2 1
(1*256)+(1*128)+(0*64)+(1*32)+(0*16)+(0*8)+(0*4)+(0*2)+(1*1)
110100001
```

One's complement: 001011110
Two's complement: 001011111
Check: Original binary number + its two's complement

```
110100001
001011111
---------
000000000
```

D.19 Zero.

Exercises

D.20 Some people argue that many of our calculations would be easier in the base 12 than in the base 10 (decimal) number system because 12 is divisible by so many more numbers than 10. What is the lowest digit in base 12? What would be the highest symbol for the digit in base 12? What are the positional values of the rightmost four positions of any number in the base 12 number system?

D.21 Complete the following chart of positional values for the rightmost four positions in each of the indicated number systems:

decimal	1000	100	10	1
base 6	...	...	6	...
base 13	...	169	...	...
base 3	27	...	...	...

D.22 Convert binary 100101111010 to octal and to hexadecimal.

D.23 Convert hexadecimal 3A7D to binary.

D.24 Convert hexadecimal 765F to octal. [*Hint:* First convert 765F to binary, then convert that binary number to octal.]

D.25 Convert binary 1011110 to decimal.

D.26 Convert octal 426 to decimal.

D.27 Convert hexadecimal FFFF to decimal.

D.28 Convert decimal 299 to binary, to octal and to hexadecimal.

D.29 Show the binary representation of decimal 779. Then show the one's complement of 779 and the two's complement of 779.

D.30 Show the two's complement of integer value −1 on a machine with 32-bit integers.

C Legacy Code Topics

OBJECTIVESc

In this appendix you'll learn

- To redirect keyboard input to come from a file and redirect screen output to a file.
- To write functions that use variable-length argument lists.
- To process command-line arguments.
- To process unexpected events within a program.
- To allocate memory dynamically for arrays, using C-style dynamic memory allocation.
- To resize memory dynamically allocated using C-style dynamic memory allocation.

E.1 Introduction

This chapter presents several topics not ordinarily covered in introductory courses. Many of the capabilities discussed here are specific to particular operating systems, especially UNIX/LINUX/Mac OS X and/or Windows. Much of the material is for the benefit of C++ programmers who will need to work with older C legacy code.

E.2 Redirecting Input/Output on UNIX/Linux/ Mac OS X and Windows Systems

Normally, the input to a program is from the keyboard (standard input), and the output from a program is displayed on the screen (standard output). On most computer systems—UNIX, LINUX, Mac OS X and Windows systems in particular—it is possible to **redirect** inputs to come from a file, and redirect outputs to be placed in a file. Both forms of redirection can be accomplished without using the file-processing capabilities of the standard library.

There are several ways to redirect input and output from the UNIX command line. Consider the executable file sum that inputs integers one at a time, keeps a running total of the values until the end-of-file indicator is set, then prints the result. Normally the user inputs integers from the keyboard and enters the end-of-file key combination to indicate that no further values will be input. With input redirection, the input can be stored in a file. For example, if the data are stored in file input, the command line

```
$ sum < input
```

causes program sum to be executed; the **redirect input symbol** (<) indicates that the data in file input (instead of the keyboard) is to be used as input by the program. Redirecting input in a Windows **Command Prompt** is performed identically.

Note that $ represents the UNIX command-line prompt. (UNIX prompts vary from system to system and between shells on a single system.) Redirection is an operating-system function, not another C++ feature.

The second method of redirecting input is **piping**. A **pipe** (|) causes the output of one program to be redirected as the input to another program. Suppose program random outputs a series of random integers; the output of random can be "piped" directly to program sum using the UNIX command line

```
$ random | sum
```

This causes the sum of the integers produced by random to be calculated. Piping can be performed in UNIX, LINUX, Mac OS X and Windows.

Program output can be redirected to a file by using the **redirect output symbol** (>). (The same symbol is used for UNIX, LINUX, Mac OS X and Windows.) For example, to redirect the output of program random to a new file called out, use

```
$ random > out
```

Finally, program output can be appended to the end of an existing file by using the **append output symbol** (>>). (The same symbol is used for UNIX, LINUX, Mac OS X and Windows.) For example, to append the output from program random to file out created in the preceding command line, use the command line

```
$ random >> out
```

E.3 **Variable-Length Argument Lists**[1]

It is possible to create functions that receive an unspecified number of arguments. An ellipsis (...) in a function's prototype indicates that the function receives a variable number of arguments of any type. Note that the ellipsis must always be placed at the end of the parameter list, and there must be at least one argument before the ellipsis. The macros and definitions of the **variable arguments header** <cstdarg> (Fig. E.1) provide the capabilities necessary to build functions with variable-length argument lists.

Figure E.2 demonstrates function average that receives a variable number of arguments. The first argument of average is always the number of values to be averaged, and the remainder of the arguments must all be of type double.

Function average uses all the definitions and macros of header <cstdarg>. Object list, of type va_list, is used by macros va_start, va_arg and va_end to process the variable-length argument list of function average. The function invokes va_start to initialize object list for use in va_arg and va_end. The macro receives two arguments—object list and the identifier of the rightmost argument in the argument list before the ellipsis—count in this case (va_start uses count here to determine where the variable-length argument list begins).

Next, function average repeatedly adds the arguments in the variable-length argument list to the total. The value to be added to total is retrieved from the argument list by invoking macro va_arg. Macro va_arg receives two arguments—object list and the type of the value expected in the argument list (double in this case)—and returns the value

---

1. In C++, programmers use function overloading to accomplish much of what C programmers accomplish with variable-length argument lists.

Identifier	Description
va_list	A type suitable for holding information needed by macros va_start, va_arg and va_end. To access the arguments in a variable-length argument list, an object of type va_list must be declared.
va_start	A macro that is invoked before the arguments of a variable-length argument list can be accessed. The macro initializes the object declared with va_list for use by the va_arg and va_end macros.
va_arg	A macro that expands to an expression of the value and type of the next argument in the variable-length argument list. Each invocation of va_arg modifies the object declared with va_list so that the object points to the next argument in the list.
va_end	A macro that performs termination housekeeping in a function whose variable-length argument list was referred to by the va_start macro.

Fig. E.1 | The type and the macros defined in header `<cstdarg>`.

```
1   // Fig. E.2: figE_02.cpp
2   // Using variable-length argument lists.
3   #include <iostream>
4   using std::cout;
5   using std::endl;
6   using std::ios;
7
8   #include <iomanip>
9   using std::setw;
10  using std::setprecision;
11  using std::setiosflags;
12  using std::fixed;
13
14  #include <cstdarg>
15  using std::va_list;
16
17  double average( int, ... );
18
19  int main()
20  {
21     double double1 = 37.5;
22     double double2 = 22.5;
23     double double3 = 1.7;
24     double double4 = 10.2;
25
26     cout << fixed << setprecision( 1 ) << "double1 = "
27        << double1 << "\ndouble2 = " << double2 << "\ndouble3 = "
28        << double3 << "\ndouble4 = " << double4 << endl
```

Fig. E.2 | Using variable-length argument lists. (Part 1 of 2.)

```
29              << setprecision( 3 )
30              << "\nThe average of double1 and double2 is "
31              << average( 2, double1, double2 )
32              << "\nThe average of double1, double2, and double3 is "
33              << average( 3, double1, double2, double3 )
34              << "\nThe average of double1, double2, double3"
35              << " and double4 is "
36              << average( 4, double1, double2, double3, double4 )
37              << endl;
38      return 0;
39    }  // end main
40
41    // calculate average
42    double average( int count, ... )
43    {
44       double total = 0;
45       va_list list;  // for storing information needed by va_start
46
47       va_start( list, count );
48
49       // process variable-length argument list
50       for ( int i = 1; i <= count; i++ )
51          total += va_arg( list, double );
52
53       va_end( list ); // end the va_start
54       return total / count;
55    }  // end function average
```

```
double1 = 37.5
double2 = 22.5
double3 = 1.7
double4 = 10.2

The average of double1 and double2 is 30.000
The average of double1, double2, and double3 is 20.567
The average of double1, double2, double3 and double4 is 17.975
```

Fig. E.2 | Using variable-length argument lists. (Part 2 of 2.)

of the argument. Function average invokes macro va_end with object list as an argument before returning. Finally, the average is calculated and returned to main. Note that we used only double arguments for the variable-length portion of the argument list.

Variable-length argument lists promote variables of type float to type double. These argument lists also promote integral variables that are smaller than int to type int (variables of type int, unsigned, long and unsigned long are left alone).

Software Engineering Observation E.1

Variable-length argument lists can be used only with fundamental-type arguments and with arguments of C-style struct types that do not contain C++ specific features such as virtual functions, constructors, destructors, references, const data members and virtual base classes.

Common Programming Error E.1

Placing an ellipsis in the middle of a function parameter list is a syntax error. An ellipsis may be placed only at the end of the parameter list.

E.4 Using Command-Line Arguments

On many systems—Windows, UNIX, LINUX and Mac OS X in particular—it is possible to pass arguments to main from a command line by including parameters int argc and char *argv[] in the parameter list of main. Parameter argc receives the number of command-line arguments. Parameter argv is an array of char *'s pointing to strings in which the actual command-line arguments are stored. Common uses of command-line arguments include printing the arguments, passing options to a program and passing filenames to a program.

Figure E.3 copies a file into another file one character at a time. The executable file for the program is called copyFile (i.e., the executable name for the file). A typical command line for the copyFile program on a UNIX system is

```
$ copyFile input output
```

This command line indicates that file input is to be copied to file output. When the program executes, if argc is not 3 (copyFile counts as one of the arguments), the program

```cpp
1   // Fig. E.3: figE_03.cpp
2   // Using command-line arguments
3   #include <iostream>
4   using std::cout;
5   using std::endl;
6   using std::ios;
7
8   #include <fstream>
9   using std::ifstream;
10  using std::ofstream;
11
12  int main( int argc, char *argv[] )1
13  {
14     // check number of command-line arguments
15     if ( argc != 3 )
16        cout << "Usage: copyFile infile_name outfile_name" << endl;
17     else
18     {
19        ifstream inFile( argv[ 1 ], ios::in );
20
21        // input file could not be opened
22        if ( !inFile )
23        {
24           cout << argv[ 1 ] << " could not be opened" << endl;
25           return -1;
26        } // end if
27
```

Fig. E.3 | Using command-line arguments. (Part 1 of 2.)

```
28              ofstream outFile( argv[ 2 ], ios::out );
29
30              // output file could not be opened
31              if ( !outFile )
32              {
33                 cout << argv[ 2 ] << " could not be opened" << endl;
34                 inFile.close();
35                 return -2;
36              } // end if
37
38              char c = inFile.get(); // read first character
39
40              while ( inFile )
41              {
42                 outFile.put( c );    // output character
43                 c = inFile.get();    // read next character
44              } // end while
45           } // end else
46
47           return 0;
48        } // end main
```

Fig. E.3 | Using command-line arguments. (Part 2 of 2.)

prints an error message (line 16). Otherwise, array argv contains the strings "copyFile", "input" and "output". The second and third arguments on the command line are used as file names by the program. The files are opened by creating ifstream object inFile and ofstream object outFile (lines 19 and 28). If both files are opened successfully, characters are read from file input with member function get and written to file output with member function put until the end-of-file indicator for file input is set (lines 40–44). Then the program terminates. The result is an exact copy of file input. Note that not all computer systems support command-line arguments as easily as UNIX, LINUX, Mac OS X and Windows. Some VMS and older Macintosh systems, for example, require special settings for processing command-line arguments. See the manuals for your system for more information on command-line arguments.

E.5 Notes on Compiling Multiple-Source-File Programs

As stated earlier in the text, it is normal to build programs that consist of multiple source files (see Chapter 9, Classes: A Deeper Look, Part 1). There are several considerations when creating programs in multiple files. For example, the definition of a function must be entirely contained in one file—it cannot span two or more files.

In Chapter 6, we introduced the concepts of storage class and scope. We learned that variables declared outside any function definition are of storage class static by default and are referred to as global variables. Global variables are accessible to any function defined in the same file after the variable is declared. Global variables also are accessible to functions in other files; however, the global variables must be declared in each file in which they are used. For example, if we define global integer variable flag in one file, and refer to it in a second file, the second file must contain the declaration

```
extern int flag;
```

prior to the variable's use in that file. In the preceding declaration, the storage class-specifier extern indicates to the compiler that variable flag is defined either later in the same file or in a different file. The compiler informs the linker that unresolved references to variable flag appear in the file. (The compiler does not know where flag is defined, so it lets the linker attempt to find flag.) If the linker cannot locate a definition of flag, a linker error is reported. If a proper global definition is located, the linker resolves the references by indicating where flag is located.

Performance Tip E.1

Global variables increase performance because they can be accessed directly by any function—the overhead of passing data to functions is eliminated.

Software Engineering Observation E.2

Global variables should be avoided unless application performance is critical or the variable represents a shared global resource such as cin, because they violate the principle of least privilege, and they make software difficult to maintain.

Just as extern declarations can be used to declare global variables to other program files, function prototypes can be used to declare functions in other program files. (The extern specifier is not required in a function prototype.) This is accomplished by including the function prototype in each file in which the function is invoked, then compiling each source file and linking the resulting object code files together. Function prototypes indicate to the compiler that the specified function is defined either later in the same file or in a different file. The compiler does not attempt to resolve references to such a function—that task is left to the linker. If the linker cannot locate a function definition, an error is generated.

As an example of using function prototypes to extend the scope of a function, consider any program containing the preprocessor directive #include <cstring>. This directive includes in a file the function prototypes for functions such as strcmp and strcat. Other functions in the file can use strcmp and strcat to accomplish their tasks. The strcmp and strcat functions are defined for us separately. We do not need to know where they are defined. We are simply reusing the code in our programs. The linker resolves our references to these functions. This process enables us to use the functions in the standard library.

Software Engineering Observation E.3

Creating programs in multiple source files facilitates software reusability and good software engineering. Functions may be common to many applications. In such instances, those functions should be stored in their own source files, and each source file should have a corresponding header file containing function prototypes. This enables programmers of different applications to reuse the same code by including the proper header file and compiling their application with the corresponding source file.

Portability Tip E.1

Some systems do not support global variable names or function names of more than six characters. This should be considered when writing programs that will be ported to multiple platforms.

It is possible to restrict the scope of a global variable or function to the file in which it is defined. The storage-class specifier static, when applied to a file scope variable or a function, prevents it from being used by any function that is not defined in the same file. This is referred to as **internal linkage**. Global variables (except those that are const) and functions that are not preceded by static in their definitions have **external linkage**—they can be accessed in other files if those files contain proper declarations and/or function prototypes.

The global variable declaration

```
static double pi = 3.14159;
```

creates variable pi of type double, initializes it to 3.14159 and indicates that pi is known only to functions in the file in which it is defined.

The static specifier is commonly used with utility functions that are called only by functions in a particular file. If a function is not required outside a particular file, the principle of least privilege should be enforced by using static. If a function is defined before it is used in a file, static should be applied to the function definition. Otherwise, static should be applied to the function prototype. Identifiers defined in the unnamed namespace also have internal linkage. The C++ standard recommends using the unnamed namespace rather than static.

When building large programs from multiple source files, compiling the program becomes tedious if making small changes to one file means that the entire program must be recompiled. Many systems provide special utilities that recompile only source files dependent on the modified program file. On UNIX systems, the utility is called make. Utility make reads a file called Makefile that contains instructions for compiling and linking the program. Systems such as Borland C++ and Microsoft Visual C++ for PCs provide make utilities and "projects." For more information on make utilities, see the manual for your particular system.

E.6 Program Termination with exit and atexit

The general utilities library (<cstdlib>) provides methods of terminating program execution other than a conventional return from main. Function exit forces a program to terminate as if it executed normally. The function often is used to terminate a program when an error is detected or if a file to be processed by the program cannot be opened.

Function **atexit registers** a function in the program to be called when the program terminates by reaching the end of main or when exit is invoked. Function atexit takes a pointer to a function (i.e., the function name) as an argument. Functions called at program termination cannot have arguments and cannot return a value.

Function exit takes one argument. The argument is normally the symbolic constant EXIT_SUCCESS or EXIT_FAILURE. If exit is called with EXIT_SUCCESS, the implementation-defined value for successful termination is returned to the calling environment. If exit is called with EXIT_FAILURE, the implementation-defined value for unsuccessful termination is returned. When function exit is invoked, any functions previously registered with atexit are invoked in the reverse order of their registration, all streams associated with the program are flushed and closed, and control returns to the host environment. Figure E.4 tests functions exit and atexit. The program prompts the user to determine whether the program should be terminated with exit or by reaching the end of main. Note that function print is executed at program termination in each case.

```cpp
1   // Fig. E.4: figE_04.cpp
2   // Using the exit and atexit functions
3   #include <iostream>
4   using std::cout;
5   using std::endl;
6   using std::cin;
7
8   #include <cstdlib>
9   using std::atexit;
10  using std::exit;
11
12  void print();
13
14  int main()
15  {
16     atexit( print ); // register function print
17
18     cout << "Enter 1 to terminate program with function exit"
19          << "\nEnter 2 to terminate program normally\n";
20
21     int answer;
22     cin >> answer;
23
24     // exit if answer is 1
25     if ( answer == 1 )
26     {
27        cout << "\nTerminating program with function exit\n";
28        exit( EXIT_SUCCESS );
29     } // end if
30
31     cout << "\nTerminating program by reaching the end of main"
32          << endl;
33
34     return 0;
35  } // end main
36
37  // display message before termination
38  void print()
39  {
40     cout << "Executing function print at program termination\n"
41          << "Program terminated" << endl;
42  } // end function print
```

```
Enter 1 to terminate program with function exit
Enter 2 to terminate program normally
2

Terminating program by reaching the end of main
Executing function print at program termination
Program terminated
```

Fig. E.4 | Using functions exit and atexit. (Part I of 2.)

```
Enter 1 to terminate program with function exit
Enter 2 to terminate program normally
1

Terminating program with function exit
Executing function print at program termination
Program terminated
```

Fig. E.4 | Using functions `exit` and `atexit`. (Part 2 of 2.)

Terminating a program with function `exit` runs the destructors for only the static and global objects in the program. Terminating with function `abort` ends the program without running any destructors.

E.7 Type Qualifier `volatile`

The `volatile` type qualifier is applied to a definition of a variable that may be altered from outside the program (i.e., the variable is not completely under the control of the program). Thus, the compiler cannot perform optimizations (such as speeding program execution or reducing memory consumption, for example) that depend on "knowing that a variable's behavior is influenced only by program activities the compiler can observe."

E.8 Suffixes for Integer and Floating-Point Constants

C++ provides integer and floating-point suffixes for specifying the types of integer and floating-point constants. The integer suffixes are: u or U for an `unsigned` integer, l or L for a `long` integer, and ul or UL for an `unsigned long` integer. The following constants are of type `unsigned`, `long` and `unsigned long`, respectively:

```
174u
8358L
28373ul
```

If an integer constant is not suffixed, its type is `int`; if the constant cannot be stored in an `int`, it is stored in a `long`.

The floating-point suffixes are f or F for a `float` and l or L for a `long double`. The following constants are of type `long double` and `float`, respectively:

```
3.14159L
1.28f
```

A floating-point constant that is not suffixed is of type `double`. A constant with an improper suffix results in either a compiler warning or an error.

E.9 Signal Handling

An unexpected event, or **signal**, can terminate a program prematurely. Such events include **interrupts** (pressing *<Ctrl> C* on a UNIX, LINUX, Mac OS X or Windows system), **illegal instructions**, **segmentation violations**, **termination orders from the operating system** and **floating-point exceptions** (division by zero or multiplying large floating-point values). The **signal-handling library** provides function `signal` to **trap unexpected events**. Function `signal` receives two arguments—an integer signal number and a pointer to a signal-handling function. Signals can be generated by function `raise`, which takes an integer signal number as an argument. Figure E.5 summarizes the standard signals defined in header file `<csignal>`. The next example demonstrates functions `signal` and `raise`.

Figure E.6 traps an interactive signal (`SIGINT`) with function `signal`. The program calls `signal` with `SIGINT` and a pointer to function `signalHandler`. (Recall that a function's name is a pointer to that function.) When a signal of type `SIGINT` occurs, function `signalHandler` is called, a message is printed and the user is given the option to continue normal program execution. If the user wishes to continue execution, the signal handler is reinitialized by calling `signal` again (some systems require the signal handler to be reinitialized), and control returns to the point in the program at which the signal was detected. In this program, function `raise` is used to simulate an interactive signal. A random number between 1 and 50 is chosen. If the number is 25, then `raise` is called to generate the signal. Normally, interactive signals are initiated outside the program. For example, pressing *<Ctrl> C* during program execution on a UNIX, LINUX, Mac OS X or Windows system generates an interactive signal that terminates program execution. Signal handling can be used to trap the interactive signal and prevent the program from terminating.

Signal	Explanation
SIGABRT	Abnormal termination of the program (such as a call to abort).
SIGFPE	An erroneous arithmetic operation, such as a divide by zero or an operation resulting in overflow.
SIGILL	Detection of an illegal instruction.
SIGINT	Receipt of an interactive attention signal.
SIGSEGV	An invalid access to storage.
SIGTERM	A termination request sent to the program.

Fig. E.5 | Signals defined in header `<csignal>`.

```
1   // Fig. E.6: figE_06.cpp
2   // Using signal handling
3   #include <iostream>
4   using std::cout;
5   using std::cin;
6   using std::endl;
7
8   #include <iomanip>
9   using std::setw;
10
11  #include <csignal>
12  using std::raise;
13  using std::signal;
14
```

Fig. E.6 | Using signal handling. (Part 1 of 3.)

```
15    #include <cstdlib>
16    using std::exit;
17    using std::rand;
18    using std::srand;
19
20    #include <ctime>
21    using std::time;
22
23    void signalHandler( int );
24
25    int main()
26    {
27       signal( SIGINT, signalHandler );
28       srand( time( 0 ) );
29
30       // create and output random numbers
31       for ( int i = 1; i <= 100; i++ )
32       {
33          int x = 1 + rand() % 50;
34
35          if ( x == 25 )
36             raise( SIGINT ); // raise SIGINT when x is 25
37
38          cout << setw( 4 ) << i;
39
40          if ( i % 10 == 0 )
41             cout << endl; // output endl when i is a multiple of 10
42       } // end for
43
44       return 0;
45    } // end main
46
47    // handles signal
48    void signalHandler( int signalValue )
49    {
50       cout << "\nInterrupt signal (" << signalValue
51          << ") received.\n"
52          << "Do you wish to continue (1 = yes or 2 = no)? ";
53
54       int response;
55
56       cin >> response;
57
58       // check for invalid responses
59       while ( response != 1 && response != 2 )
60       {
61          cout << "(1 = yes or 2 = no)? ";
62          cin >> response;
63       } // end while
64
65       // determine if it is time to exit
66       if ( response != 1 )
67          exit( EXIT_SUCCESS );
```

Fig. E.6 | Using signal handling. (Part 2 of 3.)

```
68
69      // call signal and pass it SIGINT and address of signalHandler
70      signal( SIGINT, signalHandler );
71   } // end function signalHandler
```

```
    1    2    3    4    5    6    7    8    9   10
   11   12   13   14   15   16   17   18   19   20
   21   22   23   24   25   26   27   28   29   30
   31   32   33   34   35   36   37   38   39   40
   41   42   43   44   45   46   47   48   49   50
   51   52   53   54   55   56   57   58   59   60
   61   62   63   64   65   66   67   68   69   70
   71   72   73   74   75   76   77   78   79   80
   81   82   83   84   85   86   87   88   89   90
   91   92   93   94   95   96   97   98   99
Interrupt signal (2) received.
Do you wish to continue (1 = yes or 2 = no)? 1
   100
```

```
    1    2    3    4
Interrupt signal (2) received.
Do you wish to continue (1 = yes or 2 = no)? 2
```

Fig. E.6 | Using signal handling. (Part 3 of 3.)

E.10 Dynamic Memory Allocation with calloc and realloc

In Chapter 10, we discussed C++-style dynamic memory allocation with new and delete. C++ programmers should use new and delete, rather than C's functions malloc and free (header <cstdlib>). However, most C++ programmers will find themselves reading a great deal of C legacy code, and therefore we include this additional discussion on C-style dynamic memory allocation.

The general utilities library (<cstdlib>) provides two other functions for dynamic memory allocation—calloc and realloc. These functions can be used to create and modify **dynamic arrays**. As shown in Chapter 8, Pointers and Pointer-Based Strings, a pointer to an array can be subscripted like an array. Thus, a pointer to a contiguous portion of memory created by calloc can be manipulated as an array. Function calloc dynamically allocates memory for an array and initializes the memory to zeros. The prototype for calloc is

```
void *calloc( size_t nmemb, size_t size );
```

It receives two arguments—the number of elements (nmemb) and the size of each element (size)—and initializes the elements of the array to zero. The function returns a pointer to the allocated memory or a null pointer (0) if the memory is not allocated.

Function realloc changes the size of an object allocated by a previous call to malloc, calloc or realloc. The original object's contents are not modified, provided that the memory allocated is larger than the amount allocated previously. Otherwise, the contents are unchanged up to the size of the new object. The prototype for realloc is

```
void *realloc( void *ptr, size_t size );
```

Function realloc takes two arguments—a pointer to the original object (ptr) and the new size of the object (size). If ptr is 0, realloc works identically to malloc. If size is 0 and ptr is not 0, the memory for the object is freed. Otherwise, if ptr is not 0 and size is greater than zero, realloc tries to allocate a new block of memory. If the new space cannot be allocated, the object pointed to by ptr is unchanged. Function realloc returns either a pointer to the reallocated memory or a null pointer.

Common Programming Error E.2

Runtime errors may occur if you use the delete operator on a pointer resulting from malloc, calloc or realloc, or if you use realloc or free on a pointer resulting from the new operator.

E.11 Unconditional Branch: goto

Throughout the text we have stressed the importance of using structured programming techniques to build reliable software that is easy to debug, maintain and modify. In some cases, performance is more important than strict adherence to structured-programming techniques. In these cases, some unstructured programming techniques may be used. For example, we can use break to terminate execution of a repetition structure before the loop-continuation condition becomes false. This saves unnecessary repetitions of the loop if the task is completed before loop termination.

Another instance of unstructured programming is the **goto statement**—an unconditional branch. The result of the goto statement is a change in the flow of control of the program to the first statement after the **label** specified in the goto statement. A label is an identifier followed by a colon. A label must appear in the same function as the goto statement that refers to it. Figure E.7 uses goto statements to loop 10 times and print the counter value each time. After initializing count to 1, the program tests count to determine whether it is greater than 10. (The label start is skipped, because labels do not per-

```
1   // Fig. E.7: figE_07.cpp
2   // Using goto.
3   #include <iostream>
4   using std::cout;
5   using std::endl;
6
7   #include <iomanip>
8   using std::left;
9   using std::setw;
10
11  int main()
12  {
13     int count = 1;
14
15     start: // label
16        // goto end when count exceeds 10
17        if ( count > 10 )
18           goto end;
```

Fig. E.7 | Using goto. (Part 1 of 2.)

```
19
20          cout << setw( 2 ) << left << count;
21          ++count;
22
23          // goto start on line 17
24          goto start;
25
26     end: // label
27          cout << endl;
28
29          return 0;
30  }  // end main
```

```
1  2  3  4  5  6  7  8  9  10
```

Fig. E.7 | Using goto. (Part 2 of 2.)

form any action.) If so, control is transferred from the goto to the first statement after the label end. Otherwise, count is printed and incremented, and control is transferred from the goto to the first statement after the label start.

In Chapters 4–5, we stated that only three control structures are required to write any program—sequence, selection and repetition. When the rules of structured programming are followed, it is possible to create deeply nested control structures from which it is difficult to escape efficiently. Some programmers use goto statements in such situations as a quick exit from a deeply nested structure. This eliminates the need to test multiple conditions to escape from a control structure.

Performance Tip E.2

The goto statement can be used to exit deeply nested control structures efficiently but can make code more difficult to read and maintain. Its use is strongly discouraged.

Error-Prevention Tip E.1

The goto statement should be used only in performance-oriented applications. The goto statement is unstructured and can lead to programs that are more difficult to debug, maintain, modify and understand.

E.12 Unions

A **union** (defined with keyword **union**) is a region of memory that, over time, can contain objects of a variety of types. However, at any moment, a union can contain a maximum of one object, because the members of a union share the same storage space. It is your responsibility to ensure that the data in a union is referenced with a member name of the proper data type.

Common Programming Error E.3

The result of referencing a union member other than the last one stored is undefined. It treats the stored data as a different type.

Portability Tip E.2

If data are stored in a union as one type and referenced as another type, the results are implementation dependent.

At different times during a program's execution, some objects might not be relevant, while one other object is—so a union shares the space instead of wasting storage on objects that are not being used. The number of bytes used to store a union will be at least enough to hold the largest member.

Performance Tip E.3

Using unions conserves storage.

Portability Tip E.3

The amount of storage required to store a union is implementation dependent.

A union is declared in the same format as a struct or a class. For example,

```
union Number
{
    int x;
    double y;
};
```

indicates that Number is a union type with members int x and double y. The union definition must precede all functions in which it will be used.

Software Engineering Observation E.4

Like a struct or a class declaration, a union declaration simply creates a new type. Placing a union or struct declaration outside any function does not create a global variable.

The only valid built-in operations that can be performed on a union are assigning a union to another union of the same type, taking the address (&) of a union and accessing union members using the structure member operator (.) and the structure pointer operator (->). unions cannot be compared.

Common Programming Error E.4

Comparing unions is a compilation error, because the compiler does not know which member of each is active and hence which member of one to compare to which member of the other.

A union is similar to a class in that it can have a constructor to initialize any of its members. A union that has no constructor can be initialized with another union of the same type, with an expression of the type of the first member of the union or with an initializer (enclosed in braces) of the type of the first member of the union. unions can have other member functions, such as destructors, but a union's member functions cannot be declared virtual. The members of a union are public by default.

Common Programming Error E.5

Initializing a union in a declaration with a value or an expression whose type is different from the type of the union's first member is a compilation error.

A union cannot be used as a base class in inheritance (i.e., classes cannot be derived from unions). unions can have objects as members only if these objects do not have a constructor, a destructor or an overloaded assignment operator. None of a union's data members can be declared static.

Figure E.8 uses the variable value of type union Number to display the value stored in the union as both an int and a double. The program output is implementation dependent. The program output shows that the internal representation of a double value can be quite different from the representation of an int.

An **anonymous** union is a union without a type name that does not attempt to define objects or pointers before its terminating semicolon. Such a union does not create a type but does create an unnamed object. An anonymous union's members may be accessed directly in the scope in which the anonymous union is declared just as are any other local variables—there is no need to use the dot (.) or arrow (->) operators.

Anonymous unions have some restrictions. Anonymous unions can contain only data members. All members of an anonymous union must be public. And an anonymous union declared globally (i.e., at file scope) must be explicitly declared static. Figure E.9 illustrates the use of an anonymous union.

```cpp
1   // Fig. E.8: figE_08.cpp
2   // An example of a union.
3   #include <iostream>
4   using std::cout;
5   using std::endl;
6
7   // define union Number
8   union Number
9   {
10      int integer1;
11      double double1;
12  };  // end union Number
13
14  int main()
15  {
16      Number value; // union variable
17
18      value.integer1 = 100; // assign 100 to member integer1
19
20      cout << "Put a value in the integer member\n"
21           << "and print both members.\nint:    "
22           << value.integer1 << "\ndouble: " << value.double1
23           << endl;
24
25      value.double1 = 100.0;   // assign 100.0 to member double1
26
27      cout << "Put a value in the floating member\n"
28           << "and print both members.\nint:    "
29           << value.integer1 << "\ndouble: " << value.double1
30           << endl;
31
```

Fig. E.8 | Printing the value of a union in both member data types. (Part 1 of 2.)

```
32        return 0;
33   }  // end main
```

```
Put a value in the integer member
and print both members.
int:    100
double: -9.25596e+061
Put a value in the floating member
and print both members.
int:    0
double: 100
```

Fig. E.8 | Printing the value of a union in both member data types. (Part 2 of 2.)

E.13 Linkage Specifications

It is possible from a C++ program to call functions written and compiled with a C compiler. As stated in Section 6.17, C++ specially encodes function names for type-safe linkage. C, however, does not encode its function names. Thus, a function compiled in C will not be recognized when an attempt is made to link C code with C++ code, because the C++ code expects a specially encoded function name. C++ enables you to provide linkage specifications to inform the compiler that a function was compiled on a C compiler and to prevent the name of the function from being encoded by the C++ compiler. Linkage specifications are useful when large libraries of specialized functions have been developed, and the user either does not have access to the source code for recompilation into C++ or does not have time to convert the library functions from C to C++.

```
 1   // Fig. E.9: figE_09.cpp
 2   // Using an anonymous union.
 3   #include <iostream>
 4   using std::cout;
 5   using std::endl;
 6
 7   int main()
 8   {
 9      // declare an anonymous union
10      // members integer1, double1 and charPtr share the same space
11      union
12      {
13         int integer1;
14         double double1;
15         char *charPtr;
16      };  // end anonymous union
17
18      // declare local variables
19      int integer2 = 1;
20      double double2 = 3.3;
21      char *char2Ptr = "Anonymous";
```

Fig. E.9 | Using an anonymous union. (Part 1 of 2.)

```
22
23        // assign value to each union member
24        // successively and print each
25        cout << integer2 << ' ';
26        integer1 = 2;
27        cout << integer1 << endl;
28
29        cout << double2 << ' ';
30        double1 = 4.4;
31        cout << double1 << endl;
32
33        cout << char2Ptr << ' ';
34        charPtr = "union";
35        cout << charPtr << endl;
36
37        return 0;
38   }  // end main
```

```
1 2
3.3 4.4
Anonymous union
```

Fig. E.9 | Using an anonymous union. (Part 2 of 2.)

To inform the compiler that one or several functions have been compiled in C, write the function prototypes as follows:

```
extern "C" function prototype     // single function

extern "C"   // multiple functions
{
    function prototypes
}
```

These declarations inform the compiler that the specified functions are not compiled in C++, so name encoding should not be performed on the functions listed in the linkage specification. These functions can then be linked properly with the program. C++ environments normally include the standard C libraries and do not require you to use linkage specifications for those functions.

E.14 Wrap-Up

This appendix introduced a number of C legacy-code topics. We discussed redirecting keyboard input to come from a file and redirecting screen output to a file. We also introduced variable-length argument lists, command-line arguments and processing of unexpected events. You also learned about allocating and resizing memory dynamically. In the next appendix, you'll learn about using the preprocessor to include other files, define symbolic constants and define macros.

Summary

Section E.2 Redirecting Input/Output on UNIX/Linux/Mac OS X and Windows Systems

- On many systems—UNIX, LINUX, Mac OS X or Windows systems in particular—it is possible to redirect input to a program and output from a program. Input is redirected from the UNIX, LINUX, Mac OS X or Windows command lines using the redirect input symbol (<) or a pipe (|). Output is redirected from the UNIX, LINUX, Mac OS X or Windows command lines using the redirect output symbol (>) or the append output symbol (>>). The redirect output symbol simply stores the program output in a file, and the append output symbol appends the output to the end of a file.

Section E.3 Variable-Length Argument Lists

- The macros and definitions of the variable arguments header <cstdarg> provide the capabilities necessary to build functions with variable-length argument lists.

- An ellipsis (…) in a function prototype indicates that the function receives a variable number of arguments.

- Type va_list is suitable for holding information needed by macros va_start, va_arg and va_end. To access the arguments in a variable-length argument list, an object of type va_list must be declared.

- Macro va_start is invoked before the arguments of a variable-length argument list can be accessed. The macro initializes the object declared with va_list for use by macros va_arg and va_end.

- Macro va_arg expands to an expression of the value and type of the next argument in the variable-length argument list. Each invocation of va_arg modifies the va_list object so that the object points to the next argument in the list.

- Macro va_end facilitates a normal return from a function whose variable argument list was referred to by the va_start macro.

Section E.4 Using Command-Line Arguments

- On many systems—UNIX, LINUX, Mac OS X and Windows in particular—it is possible to pass command-line arguments to main by including in main's parameter list the parameters int argc and char *argv[]. Parameter argc is the number of command-line arguments. Parameter argv is an array of char *'s containing the command-line arguments.

Section E.5 Notes on Compiling Multiple-Source-File Programs

- A function definition must be entirely contained in one file—it cannot span two or more files.

- Global variables must be declared in each file in which they are used.

- Function prototypes can be used to declare functions in other program files. (The extern specifier is not required in a function prototype.) This is accomplished by including the function prototype in each file in which the function is invoked, then linking the compiled files together.

- The storage-class specifier static, when applied to a file scope variable or a function, prevents it from being used by any function that is not defined in the same file. This is referred to as internal linkage. Global variables and functions that are not preceded by static in their definitions have external linkage—they can be accessed in other files if those files contain proper declarations and/ or function prototypes.

- The static specifier is commonly used with utility functions that are called only by functions in a particular file. If a function is not required outside a particular file, the principle of least privilege should be enforced by using static.

- When building large programs from multiple source files, compiling the program becomes tedious if making small changes to one file means that the entire program must be recompiled. Many systems provide special utilities that recompile only the modified program file. On UNIX systems, the utility is called make. Utility make reads a file called Makefile that contains instructions for compiling and linking the program.

Section E.6 Program Termination with `exit` and `atexit`

- Function exit forces a program to terminate as if it had executed normally.

- Function atexit registers a function to be called upon normal termination of the program—i.e., either when the program terminates by reaching the end of main, or when exit is invoked.

- Function atexit takes a pointer to a function (e.g., a function name) as an argument. Functions called at program termination cannot have arguments and cannot return a value.

- Function exit takes one argument—normally the symbolic constant EXIT_SUCCESS or the symbolic constant EXIT_FAILURE. If exit is called with EXIT_SUCCESS, the implementation-defined value for successful termination is returned to the calling environment. If exit is called with EXIT_FAILURE, the implementation-defined value for unsuccessful termination is returned.

- When function exit is invoked, any functions registered with atexit are invoked in the reverse order of their registration, all streams associated with the program are flushed and closed and control returns to the host environment.

Section E.7 Type Qualifier `volatile`

- The volatile qualifier is used to prevent optimizations of a variable, because it can be modified from outside the program's scope.

Section E.8 Suffixes for Integer and Floating-Point Constants

- C++ provides integer and floating-point suffixes for specifying the types of integer and floating-point constants. The integer suffixes are u or U for an unsigned integer, l or L for a long integer and ul or UL for an unsigned long integer. If an integer constant is not suffixed, its type is determined by the first type capable of storing a value of that size (first int, then long int). The floating-point suffixes are f or F for a float and l or L for a long double. A floating-point constant that is not suffixed is of type double.

Section E.9 Signal Handling

- The signal-handling library provides the capability to register a function to trap unexpected events with function signal. Function signal receives two arguments—an integer signal number and a pointer to the signal-handling function.

- Signals can also be generated with function raise and an integer argument.

Section E.10 Dynamic Memory Allocation with `calloc` and `realloc`

- The general-utilities library (cstdlib) provides functions calloc and realloc for dynamic memory allocation. These functions can be used to create dynamic arrays.

- Function calloc receives two arguments—the number of elements (nmemb) and the size of each element (size)—and initializes the elements of the array to zero. The function returns a pointer to the allocated memory or if the memory is not allocated, the function returns a null pointer.

- Function realloc changes the size of an object allocated by a previous call to malloc, calloc or realloc. The original object's contents are not modified, provided that the amount of memory allocated is larger than the amount allocated previously.

- Function realloc takes two arguments—a pointer to the original object (ptr) and the new size of the object (size). If ptr is null, realloc works identically to malloc. If size is 0 and the pointer received is not null, the memory for the object is freed. Otherwise, if ptr is not null and size is greater than zero, realloc tries to allocate a new block of memory for the object. If the new space cannot be allocated, the object pointed to by ptr is unchanged. Function realloc returns either a pointer to the reallocated memory or a null pointer.

Section E.11 Unconditional Branch: goto

- The result of the goto statement is a change in the program's flow of control. Program execution continues at the first statement after the label in the goto statement.

- A label is an identifier followed by a colon. A label must appear in the same function as the goto statement that refers to it.

Section E.12 Unions

- A union is a data type whose members share the same storage space. The members can be almost any type. The storage reserved for a union is large enough to store its largest member. In most cases, unions contain two or more data types. Only one member, and thus one data type, can be referenced at a time.

- A union is declared in the same format as a structure.

- A union can be initialized only with a value of the type of its first member or another object of the same union type.

Section E.13 Linkage Specifications

- C++ enables you to provide linkage specifications to inform the compiler that a function was compiled on a C compiler and to prevent the name of the function from being encoded by the C++ compiler.

- To inform the compiler that one or several functions have been compiled in C, write the function prototypes as follows:

```
extern "C" function prototype    // single function

extern "C"   // multiple functions
{
    function prototypes
}
```

These declarations inform the compiler that the specified functions are not compiled in C++, so name encoding should not be performed on the functions listed in the linkage specification. These functions can then be linked properly with the program.

- C++ environments normally include the standard C libraries and do not require you to use linkage specifications for those functions.

Terminology

append output symbol >>	exit
argv	EXIT_FAILURE
atexit	EXIT_SUCCESS
calloc	extern "C"
command-line arguments	extern storage-class specifier
const	external linkage
<csignal>	float suffix (f or F)
<cstdarg>	floating-point exception
dynamic arrays	free
event	goto statement

I/O redirection	segmentation violation
illegal instruction	`signal`
internal linkage	signal-handling library
interrupt	static storage-class specifier
`long double` suffix (`1` or `L`)	trap
`long integer` suffix (`1` or `L`)	`union`
`make`	unsigned integer suffix (`u` or `U`)
`Makefile`	unsigned long integer suffix (`u1` or `UL`)
`malloc`	`va_arg`
pipe `|`	`va_end`
piping	`va_list`
`raise`	`va_start`
`realloc`	variable-length argument list
redirect input symbol `<`	`volatile`
redirect output symbol `>`	

Self-Review Exercises

E.1 Fill in the blanks in each of the following:

a) Symbol _____ redirects input data from the keyboard to come from a file.

b) The _____ symbol is used to redirect the screen output to be placed in a file.

c) The _____ symbol is used to append the output of a program to the end of a file.

d) A(n) _____ is used to direct the output of a program as the input of another program.

e) A(n) _____ in the parameter list of a function indicates that the function can receive a variable number of arguments.

f) Macro _____ must be invoked before the arguments in a variable-length argument list can be accessed.

g) Macro _____ is used to access the individual arguments of a variable-length argument list.

h) Macro _____ performs termination housekeeping in a function whose variable argument list was referred to by macro `va_start`.

i) Argument _____ of `main` receives the number of arguments in a command line.

j) Argument _____ of `main` stores command-line arguments as character strings.

k) The UNIX utility _____ reads a file called _____ that contains instructions for compiling and linking a program consisting of multiple source files. The utility recompiles a file only if the file (or a header it uses) has been modified since it was last compiled.

l) Function _____ forces a program to terminate execution.

m) Function _____ registers a function to be called upon normal termination of the program.

n) An integer or floating-point _____ can be appended to an integer or floating-point constant to specify the exact type of the constant.

o) Function _____ can be used to register a function to trap unexpected events.

p) Function _____ generates a signal from within a program.

q) Function _____ dynamically allocates memory for an array and initializes the elements to zero.

r) Function _____ changes the size of a block of dynamically allocated memory.

s) A(n) _____ is an entity containing a collection of variables that occupy the same memory, but at different times.

t) The _____ keyword is used to introduce a union definition.

Answers to Self-Review Exercises

E.1　　a) redirect input (<).　b) redirect output (>).　c) append output (>>).　d) pipe (|).
e) ellipsis (...).　f) va_start.　g) va_arg.　h) va_end.　i) argc.　j) argv.　k) make, Makefile.　l) exit.
m) atexit.　n) suffix.　o) signal.　p) raise.　q) calloc.　r) realloc.　s) union.　t) union.

Exercises

E.2　　Write a program that calculates the product of a series of integers that are passed to function
product using a variable-length argument list. Test your function with several calls, each with a different number of arguments.

E.3　　Write a program that prints the command-line arguments of the program.

E.4　　Write a program that sorts an integer array into ascending order or descending order. The
program should use command-line arguments to pass either argument -a for ascending order or -d
for descending order. [*Note:* This is the standard format for passing options to a program in UNIX.]

E.5　　Read the manuals for your system to determine what signals are supported by the signal-
handling library (<csignal>). Write a program with signal handlers for the signals SIGABRT and SIG-
INT. The program should test the trapping of these signals by calling function abort to generate a
signal of type SIGABRT and by pressing *<Ctrl> C* to generate a signal of type SIGINT.

E.6　　Write a program that dynamically allocates an array of integers using a function from
<cstdlib>, not the new operator. The size of the array should be input from the keyboard. The elements of the array should be assigned values input from the keyboard. Print the values of the array.
Next, reallocate the memory for the array to half of the current number of elements. Print the values
remaining in the array to confirm that they match the first half of the values in the original array.

E.7　　Write a program that takes two filenames as command-line arguments, reads the characters
from the first file one at a time and writes the characters in reverse order to the second file.

E.8　　Write a program that uses goto statements to simulate a nested looping structure that prints
a square of asterisks as shown in Fig. E.10. The program should use only the following three output
statements:

```
cout << '*';
cout << ' ';
cout << endl;
```

E.9　　Provide the definition for union Data containing char charcter1, short short1, long
long1, float float1 and double double1.

E.10　　Create union Integer with members char c, short s, int i and long l. Write a program
that inputs values of type char, short, int and long and stores the values in union variables of type
union Integer. Each union variable should be printed as a char, a short, an int and a long. Do the
values always print correctly?

E.11　　Create union FloatingPoint with members float float1, double double1 and long double
longDouble. Write a program that inputs values of type float, double and long double and stores
the values in union variables of type union FloatingPoint. Each union variable should be printed as
a float, a double and a long double. Do the values always print correctly?

E.12　　Given the union

```
union A
{
   double y;
   char *zPtr;
};
```

which of the following are correct statements for initializing the union?

a) `A p = b;` `// b is of type A`
b) `A q = x;` `// x is a double`
c) `A r = 3.14159;`
d) `A s = { 79.63 };`
e) `A t = { "Hi There!" };`
f) `A u = { 3.14159, "Pi" };`
g) `A v = { y = -7.843, zPtr = &x };`

```
*****
*   *
*   *
*   *
*****
```

Fig. E.10 | Example for Exercise E.8.

F

Preprocessor

OBJECTIVES

In this appendix you'll learn:

- To use #include for developing large programs.
- To use #define to create macros and macros with arguments.
- To understand conditional compilation.
- To display error messages during conditional compilation.
- To use assertions to test if the values of expressions are correct.

F.1 Introduction

This chapter introduces the preprocessor. Preprocessing occurs before a program is compiled. Some possible actions are inclusion of other files in the file being compiled, definition of symbolic constants and macros, conditional compilation of program code and conditional execution of preprocessor directives. All preprocessor directives begin with #, and only whitespace characters may appear before a preprocessor directive on a line. Preprocessor directives are not C++ statements, so they do not end in a semicolon (;). Preprocessor directives are processed fully before compilation begins.

Common Programming Error F.1

Placing a semicolon at the end of a preprocessor directive can lead to a variety of errors, depending on the type of preprocessor directive.

Software Engineering Observation F.1

Many preprocessor features (especially macros) are more appropriate for C programmers than for C++ programmers. C++ programmers should familiarize themselves with the preprocessor, because they might need to work with C legacy code.

F.2 The #include Preprocessor Directive

The #include preprocessor directive has been used throughout this text. The #include directive causes a copy of a specified file to be included in place of the directive. The two forms of the #include directive are

```
#include <filename>
#include "filename"
```

The difference between these is the location the preprocessor searches for the file to be included. If the filename is enclosed in angle brackets (< and >)—used for standard library header files—the preprocessor searches for the specified file in an implementation-dependent manner, normally through predesignated directories. If the file name is enclosed in quotes, the preprocessor searches first in the same directory as the file being compiled, then in the same implementation-dependent manner as for a file name enclosed in angle brackets. This method is normally used to include programmer-defined header files.

The #include directive is used to include standard header files such as <iostream> and <iomanip>. The #include directive is also used with programs consisting of several source files that are to be compiled together. A header file containing declarations and definitions common to the separate program files is often created and included in the file. Examples of such declarations and definitions are classes, structures, unions, enumerations and function prototypes, constants and stream objects (e.g., cin).

F.3 The #define Preprocessor Directive: Symbolic Constants

The #define preprocessor directive creates symbolic constants—constants represented as symbols—and macros—operations defined as symbols. The #define preprocessor directive format is

```
#define identifier replacement-text
```

When this line appears in a file, all subsequent occurrences (except those inside a string) of *identifier* in that file will be replaced by *replacement-text* before the program is compiled. For example,

```
#define PI 3.14159
```

replaces all subsequent occurrences of the symbolic constant PI with the numeric constant 3.14159. Symbolic constants enable you to create a name for a constant and use the name throughout the program. Later, if the constant needs to be modified throughout the program, it can be modified once in the #define preprocessor directive—and when the program is recompiled, all occurrences of the constant in the program will be modified. [*Note:* Everything to the right of the symbolic constant name replaces the symbolic constant. For example, #define PI = 3.14159 causes the preprocessor to replace every occurrence of PI with = 3.14159. Such replacement is the cause of many subtle logic and syntax errors.] Redefining a symbolic constant with a new value without first undefining it is also an error. Note that const variables in C++ are preferred over symbolic constants. Constant variables have a specific data type and are visible by name to a debugger. Once a symbolic constant is replaced with its replacement text, only the replacement text is visible to a debugger. A disadvantage of const variables is that they might require a memory location of their data type size—symbolic constants do not require any additional memory.

Common Programming Error F.2

Using symbolic constants in a file other than the file in which the symbolic constants are defined is a compilation error (unless they are #included from a header file).

Good Programming Practice F.1

Using meaningful names for symbolic constants makes programs more self-documenting.

F.4 The #define Preprocessor Directive: Macros

[*Note:* This section is included for the benefit of C++ programmers who will need to work with C legacy code. In C++, macros can often be replaced by templates and inline functions.] A macro is an operation defined in a #define preprocessor directive. As with symbolic constants, the macro-identifier is replaced with the replacement-text before the program is compiled. Macros may be defined with or without arguments. A macro without arguments is processed like a symbolic constant. In a macro with arguments, the arguments are substituted in the *replacement-text*, then the macro is expanded—i.e., the *replacement-text* replaces the macro-identifier and argument list in the program. There is no data type checking for macro arguments. A macro is used simply for text substitution.

Consider the following macro definition with one argument for the area of a circle:

```
#define CIRCLE_AREA( x ) ( PI * ( x ) * ( x ) )
```

Wherever CIRCLE_AREA(y) appears in the file, the value of y is substituted for x in the replacement text, the symbolic constant PI is replaced by its value (defined previously) and the macro is expanded in the program. For example, the statement

```
area = CIRCLE_AREA( 4 );
```

is expanded to

```
area = ( 3.14159 * ( 4 ) * ( 4 ) );
```

Because the expression consists only of constants, at compile time the value of the expression can be evaluated, and the result is assigned to area at runtime. The parentheses around each x in the replacement text and around the entire expression force the proper order of evaluation when the macro argument is an expression. For example, the statement

```
area = CIRCLE_AREA( c + 2 );
```

is expanded to

```
area = ( 3.14159 * ( c + 2 ) * ( c + 2 ) );
```

which evaluates correctly, because the parentheses force the proper order of evaluation. If the parentheses are omitted, the macro expansion is

```
area = 3.14159 * c + 2 * c + 2;
```

which evaluates incorrectly as

```
area = ( 3.14159 * c ) + ( 2 * c ) + 2;
```

because of the rules of operator precedence.

 Common Programming Error F.3

Forgetting to enclose macro arguments in parentheses in the replacement text is an error.

Macro CIRCLE_AREA could be defined as a function. Function circleArea, as in

```
double circleArea( double x ) { return 3.14159 * x * x; }
```

performs the same calculation as CIRCLE_AREA, but the overhead of a function call is associated with function circleArea. The advantages of CIRCLE_AREA are that macros insert code directly in the program—avoiding function overhead—and the program remains readable because CIRCLE_AREA is defined separately and named meaningfully. A disadvantage is that its argument is evaluated twice. Also, every time a macro appears in a program, the macro is expanded. If the macro is large, this produces an increase in program size. Thus, there is a trade-off between execution speed and program size (if disk space is low).

Note that `inline` functions (see Chapter 3) are preferred to obtain the performance of macros and the software engineering benefits of functions.

Performance Tip F.1

Macros can sometimes be used to replace a function call with `inline` code prior to execution time. This eliminates the overhead of a function call. Inline functions are preferable to macros because they offer the type-checking services of functions.

The following is a macro definition with two arguments for the area of a rectangle:

```
#define RECTANGLE_AREA( x, y ) ( ( x ) * ( y ) )
```

Wherever `RECTANGLE_AREA( a, b )` appears in the program, the values of a and b are substituted in the macro replacement text, and the macro is expanded in place of the macro name. For example, the statement

```
rectArea = RECTANGLE_AREA( a + 4, b + 7 );
```

is expanded to

```
rectArea = ( ( a + 4 ) * ( b + 7 ) );
```

The value of the expression is evaluated and assigned to variable `rectArea`.

The replacement text for a macro or symbolic constant is normally any text on the line after the identifier in the `#define` directive. If the replacement text for a macro or symbolic constant is longer than the remainder of the line, a backslash (\\) must be placed at the end of each line of the macro (except the last line), indicating that the replacement text continues on the next line.

Symbolic constants and macros can be discarded using the `#undef` preprocessor directive. Directive `#undef` "undefines" a symbolic constant or macro name. The scope of a symbolic constant or macro is from its definition until it is either undefined with `#undef` or the end of the file is reached. Once undefined, a name can be redefined with `#define`.

Note that expressions with side effects (e.g., variable values are modified) should not be passed to a macro, because macro arguments may be evaluated more than once.

Common Programming Error F.4

Macros often replace a name that wasn't intended to be a use of the macro but just happened to be spelled the same. This can lead to exceptionally mysterious compilation and syntax errors.

F.5 Conditional Compilation

Conditional compilation enables you to control the execution of preprocessor directives and the compilation of program code. Each of the conditional preprocessor directives evaluates a constant integer expression that will determine whether the code will be compiled. Cast expressions, `sizeof` expressions and enumeration constants cannot be evaluated in preprocessor directives because these are all determined by the compiler and preprocessing happens before compilation.

The conditional preprocessor construct is much like the `if` selection structure. Consider the following preprocessor code:

```
#ifndef NULL
    #define NULL 0
#endif
```

which determines whether the symbolic constant NULL is already defined. The expression `#ifndef NULL` includes the code up to `#endif` if NULL is not defined, and skips the code if NULL is defined. Every `#if` construct ends with `#endif`. Directives `#ifdef` and `#ifndef` are shorthand for `#if defined(` *name* `)` and `#if !defined(` *name* `)`. A multiple-part conditional preprocessor construct may be tested using the `#elif` (the equivalent of `else if` in an `if` structure) and the `#else` (the equivalent of `else` in an `if` structure) directives.

During program development, programmers often find it helpful to "comment out" large portions of code to prevent it from being compiled. If the code contains C-style comments, `/*` and `*/` cannot be used to accomplish this task, because the first `*/` encountered would terminate the comment. Instead, you can use the following preprocessor construct:

```
#if 0
    code prevented from compiling
#endif
```

To enable the code to be compiled, simply replace the value 0 in the preceding construct with the value 1.

Conditional compilation is commonly used as a debugging aid. Output statements are often used to print variable values and to confirm the flow of control. These output statements can be enclosed in conditional preprocessor directives so that the statements are compiled only until the debugging process is completed. For example,

```
#ifdef DEBUG
    cerr << "Variable x = " << x << endl;
#endif
```

causes the `cerr` statement to be compiled in the program if the symbolic constant DEBUG has been defined before directive `#ifdef DEBUG`. This symbolic constant is normally set by a command-line compiler or by settings in the IDE (e.g., Visual Studio) and not by an explicit `#define` definition. When debugging is completed, the `#define` directive is removed from the source file, and the output statements inserted for debugging purposes are ignored during compilation. In larger programs, it might be desirable to define several different symbolic constants that control the conditional compilation in separate sections of the source file.

Common Programming Error F.5

Inserting conditionally compiled output statements for debugging purposes in locations where C++ currently expects a single statement can lead to syntax errors and logic errors. In this case, the conditionally compiled statement should be enclosed in a compound statement. Thus, when the program is compiled with debugging statements, the flow of control of the program is not altered.

F.6 The #error and #pragma Preprocessor Directives

The `#error` directive

```
#error tokens
```

prints an implementation-dependent message including the *tokens* specified in the directive. The tokens are sequences of characters separated by spaces. For example,

```
#error 1 - Out of range error
```

contains six tokens. In one popular C++ compiler, for example, when a `#error` directive is processed, the tokens in the directive are displayed as an error message, preprocessing stops and the program does not compile.

The `#pragma` directive

```
#pragma tokens
```

causes an implementation-defined action. A pragma not recognized by the implementation is ignored. A particular C++ compiler, for example, might recognize pragmas that enable you to take advantage of that compiler's specific capabilities. For more information on `#error` and `#pragma`, see the documentation for your C++ implementation.

F.7 Operators # and

The `#` and `##` preprocessor operators are available in C++ and ANSI/ISO C. The `#` operator causes a replacement-text token to be converted to a string surrounded by quotes. Consider the following macro definition:

```
#define HELLO( x ) cout << "Hello, " #x << endl;
```

When `HELLO(John)` appears in a program file, it is expanded to

```
cout << "Hello, " "John" << endl;
```

The string `"John"` replaces `#x` in the replacement text. Strings separated by whitespace are concatenated during preprocessing, so the above statement is equivalent to

```
cout << "Hello, John" << endl;
```

Note that the `#` operator must be used in a macro with arguments, because the operand of `#` refers to an argument of the macro.

The `##` operator concatenates two tokens. Consider the following macro definition:

```
#define TOKENCONCAT( x, y )   x ## y
```

When `TOKENCONCAT` appears in the program, its arguments are concatenated and used to replace the macro. For example, `TOKENCONCAT( O, K )` is replaced by `OK` in the program. The `##` operator must have two operands.

F.8 Predefined Symbolic Constants

There are six predefined symbolic constants (Fig. F.1). The identifiers for each of these begin and (except for `__cplusplus`) end with *two* underscores. These identifiers and preprocessor operator `defined` (Section F.5) cannot be used in `#define` or `#undef` directives.

Symbolic constant	Description
`__LINE__`	The line number of the current source-code line (an integer constant).
`__FILE__`	The presumed name of the source file (a string).
`__DATE__`	The date the source file is compiled (a string of the form `"Mmm dd yyyy"` such as `"Aug 19 2002"`).

Fig. F.1 | The predefined symbolic constants. (Part 1 of 2.)

Symbolic constant	Description
__STDC__	Indicates whether the program conforms to the ANSI/ISO C standard. Contains value 1 if there is full conformance and is undefined otherwise.
__TIME__	The time the source file is compiled (a string literal of the form `"hh:mm:ss"`).
__cplusplus	Contains the value 199711L (the date the ISO C++ standard was approved) if the file is being compiled by a C++ compiler, undefined otherwise. Allows a file to be set up to be compiled as either C or C++.

Fig. F.1 | The predefined symbolic constants. (Part 2 of 2.)

F.9 Assertions

The assert macro—defined in the <cassert> header file—tests the value of an expression. If the value of the expression is 0 (false), then assert prints an error message and calls function abort (of the general utilities library—<cstdlib>) to terminate program execution. This is a useful debugging tool for testing whether a variable has a correct value. For example, suppose variable x should never be larger than 10 in a program. An assertion may be used to test the value of x and print an error message if the value of x is incorrect. The statement would be

```
assert( x <= 10 );
```

If x is greater than 10 when the preceding statement is encountered in a program, an error message containing the line number and file name is printed, and the program terminates. You may then concentrate on this area of the code to find the error. If the symbolic constant NDEBUG is defined, subsequent assertions will be ignored. Thus, when assertions are no longer needed (i.e., when debugging is complete), we insert the line

```
#define NDEBUG
```

in the program file rather than deleting each assertion manually. As with the DEBUG symbolic constant, NDEBUG is often set by compiler command-line options or through a setting in the IDE.

Most C++ compilers now include exception handling. C++ programmers prefer using exceptions rather than assertions. But assertions are still valuable for C++ programmers who work with C legacy code.

F.10 Wrap-Up

This appendix discussed the #include directive, which is used to develop larger programs. You also learned about the #define directive, which is used to create macros. We introduced conditional compilation, displaying error messages and using assertions. In the next appendix, you'll implement the design of the ATM system from the Software Engineering Case Study found in Chapters 1–7, 9 and 13.

Summary

Section F.2 The `#include` Preprocessor Directive
- All preprocessor directives begin with # and are processed before the program is compiled.
- Only whitespace characters may appear before a preprocessor directive on a line.
- The `#include` directive includes a copy of the specified file. If the filename is enclosed in quotes, the preprocessor begins searching in the same directory as the file being compiled for the file to be included. If the filename is enclosed in angle brackets (< and >), the search is performed in an implementation-defined manner.

Section F.3 The `#define` Preprocessor Directive: Symbolic Constants
- The `#define` preprocessor directive is used to create symbolic constants and macros.
- A symbolic constant is a name for a constant.

Section F.4 The `#define` Preprocessor Directive: Macros
- A macro is an operation defined in a `#define` preprocessor directive. Macros may be defined with or without arguments.
- The replacement text for a macro or symbolic constant is any text remaining on the line after the identifier (and, if any, the macro argument list) in the `#define` directive. If the replacement text for a macro or symbolic constant is too long to fit on one line, a backslash (\) is placed at the end of the line, indicating that the replacement text continues on the next line.
- Symbolic constants and macros can be discarded using the `#undef` preprocessor directive. Directive `#undef` "undefines" the symbolic constant or macro name.
- The scope of a symbolic constant or macro is from its definition until it is either undefined with `#undef` or the end of the file is reached.

Section F.5 Conditional Compilation
- Conditional compilation enables you to control the execution of preprocessor directives and the compilation of program code.
- The conditional preprocessor directives evaluate constant integer expressions. Cast expressions, `sizeof` expressions and enumeration constants cannot be evaluated in preprocessor directives.
- Every `#if` construct ends with `#endif`.
- Directives `#ifdef` and `#ifndef` are provided as shorthand for `#if defined(`*name*`)` and `#if !defined(`*name*`)`.
- A multiple-part conditional preprocessor construct is tested with directives `#elif` and `#else`.

Section F.6 The `#error` and `#pragma` Preprocessor Directives
- The `#error` directive prints an implementation-dependent message that includes the tokens specified in the directive and terminates preprocessing and compiling.
- The `#pragma` directive causes an implementation-defined action. If the pragma is not recognized by the implementation, the pragma is ignored.

Section F.7 Operators # and ##
- The # operator causes the following replacement text token to be converted to a string surrounded by quotes. The # operator must be used in a macro with arguments, because the operand of # must be an argument of the macro.
- The ## operator concatenates two tokens. The ## operator must have two operands.

Section F.8 Predefined Symbolic Constants

- There are six predefined symbolic constants. Constant __LINE__ is the line number of the current source-code line (an integer). Constant __FILE__ is the presumed name of the file (a string). Constant __DATE__ is the date the source file is compiled (a string). Constant __TIME__ is the time the source file is compiled (a string). Note that each of the predefined symbolic constants begins (and, with the exception of __cplusplus, ends) with two underscores.

Section F.9 Assertions

- The assert macro—defined in the <cassert> header file—tests the value of an expression. If the value of the expression is 0 (false), then assert prints an error message and calls function abort to terminate program execution.

Terminology

\ (backslash) continuation character	__FILE__
abort	header file
argument	#if
assert	#ifdef
<cassert>	#ifndef
concatenation preprocessor operator ##	#include "filename"
conditional compilation	#include <filename>
conditional execution of preprocessor	__LINE__
convert-to-string preprocessor directive	macro
__cplusplus	macro with arguments
<cstdio>	operator #
<cstdlib>	#pragma
__DATE__	predefined symbolic constants
debugger	preprocessing directive
#define	preprocessor
directives	replacement text
#elif	scope of a symbolic constant or macro
#else	standard library header files
#endif	symbolic constant
#error	__TIME__
expand a macro	#undef

Self-Review Exercises

F.1 Fill in the blanks in each of the following:

a) Every preprocessor directive must begin with _____.

b) The conditional compilation construct may be extended to test for multiple cases by using the _____ and the _____ directives.

c) The _____ directive creates macros and symbolic constants.

d) Only _____ characters may appear before a preprocessor directive on a line.

e) The _____ directive discards symbolic constant and macro names.

f) The _____ and _____ directives are provided as shorthand notation for #if defined(*name*) and #if !defined(*name*).

g) _____ enables you to control the execution of preprocessor directives and the compilation of program code.

h) The _____ macro prints a message and terminates program execution if the value of the expression the macro evaluates is 0.

i) The _____ directive inserts a file in another file.

j) The _____ operator concatenates its two arguments.

k) The _____ operator converts its operand to a string.

l) The character _____ indicates that the replacement text for a symbolic constant or macro continues on the next line.

F.2 Write a program to print the values of the predefined symbolic constants __LINE__, __FILE__, __DATE__ and __TIME__ listed in Fig. F.1.

F.3 Write a preprocessor directive to accomplish each of the following:

a) Define symbolic constant YES to have the value 1.

b) Define symbolic constant NO to have the value 0.

c) Include the header file common.h. The header is found in the same directory as the file being compiled.

d) If symbolic constant TRUE is defined, undefine it, and redefine it as 1. Do not use #ifdef.

e) If symbolic constant TRUE is defined, undefine it, and redefine it as 1. Use the #ifdef preprocessor directive.

f) If symbolic constant ACTIVE is not equal to 0, define symbolic constant INACTIVE as 0. Otherwise, define INACTIVE as 1.

g) Define macro CUBE_VOLUME that computes the volume of a cube (takes one argument).

Answers to Self-Review Exercises

F.1   a) #. b) #elif, #else. c) #define. d) whitespace. e) #undef. f) #ifdef, #ifndef.
g) Conditional compilation. h) assert. i) #include. j) ##. k) #. l) \.

F.2   (See below.)

```
1   // exF_02.cpp
2   // Self-Review Exercise F.2 solution.
3   #include <iostream>
4
5   using std::cout;
6   using std::endl;
7
8   int main()
9   {
10      cout << "__LINE__ = " << __LINE__ << endl
11           << "__FILE__ = " << __FILE__ << endl
12           << "__DATE__ = " << __DATE__ << endl
13           << "__TIME__ = " << __TIME__ << endl
14           << "__cplusplus = " << __cplusplus << endl;
15
16      return 0;
17
18   } // end main
```

```
__LINE__ = 9
__FILE__ = c:\cpp4e\ch19\ex19_02.CPP
__DATE__ = Jul 17 2002
__TIME__ = 09:55:58
__cplusplus = 199711L
```

F.3   a) #define YES 1

b) #define NO 0

c) `#include "common.h"`
d) `#if defined(TRUE)`
   `    #undef TRUE`
   `    #define TRUE 1`
   `#endif`
e) `#ifdef TRUE`
   `    #undef TRUE`
   `    #define TRUE 1`
   `#endif`
f) `#if ACTIVE`
   `    #define INACTIVE 0`
   `#else`
   `    #define INACTIVE 1`
   `#endif`
g) `#define CUBE_VOLUME( x )  ( ( x ) * ( x ) * ( x ) )`

Exercises

F.4   Write a program that defines a macro with one argument to compute the volume of a sphere. The program should compute the volume for spheres of radii from 1 to 10 and print the results in tabular format. The formula for the volume of a sphere is

$$(4.0 / 3) * \pi * r^3$$

where π is `3.14159`.

F.5   Write a program that produces the following output:

```
The sum of x and y is 13
```

The program should define macro SUM with two arguments, x and y, and use SUM to produce the output.

F.6   Write a program that uses macro MINIMUM2 to determine the smaller of two numeric values. Input the values from the keyboard.

F.7   Write a program that uses macro MINIMUM3 to determine the smallest of three numeric values. Macro MINIMUM3 should use macro MINIMUM2 defined in Exercise F.6 to determine the smallest number. Input the values from the keyboard.

F.8   Write a program that uses macro PRINT to print a string value.

F.9   Write a program that uses macro PRINTARRAY to print an array of integers. The macro should receive the array and the number of elements in the array as arguments.

F.10   Write a program that uses macro SUMARRAY to sum the values in a numeric array. The macro should receive the array and the number of elements in the array as arguments.

F.11   Rewrite the solutions to Exercises F.4–F.10 as `inline` functions.

F.12   For each of the following macros, identify the possible problems (if any) when the preprocessor expands the macros:
a) `#define SQR( x ) x * x`
b) `#define SQR( x ) ( x * x )`
c) `#define SQR( x ) ( x ) * ( x )`
d) `#define SQR( x ) ( ( x ) * ( x ) )`

ATM Case Study Code

G.1 ATM Case Study Implementation

This appendix contains the complete working implementation of the ATM system that we designed in the Software Engineering Case Study sections found at the ends of Chapters 1–7, 9 and 13 . The implementation comprises 877 lines of C++ code. We consider the classes in the order in which we identified them in Section 3.11:

- ATM
- Screen
- Keypad
- CashDispenser
- DepositSlot
- Account
- BankDatabase
- Transaction
- BalanceInquiry
- Withdrawal
- Deposit

We apply the guidelines discussed in Section 9.11 and Section 13.10 to code these classes based on how we modeled them in the UML class diagrams of Fig. 13.28 and Fig. 13.29. To develop the definitions of classes' member functions, we refer to the activity diagrams presented in Section 5.11 and the communication and sequence diagrams presented in Section 7.12. Note that our ATM design does not specify all the program logic and may not specify all the attributes and operations required to complete the ATM implementation. This is a normal part of the object-oriented design process. As we implement the system, we complete the program logic and add attributes and behaviors as necessary to construct the ATM system specified by the requirements specification in Section 2.8.

We conclude the discussion by presenting a C++ program (`ATMCaseStudy.cpp`) that starts the ATM and puts the other classes in the system in use. Recall that we are developing a first version of the ATM system that runs on a personal computer and uses the computer's keyboard and monitor to approximate the ATM's keypad and screen. We also only simulate the actions of the ATM's cash dispenser and deposit slot. We attempt to implement the system, however, so that real hardware versions of these devices could be integrated without significant changes in the code.

G.2 Class ATM

Class ATM (Figs. G.1–G.2) represents the ATM as a whole. Figure G.1 contains the ATM class definition, enclosed in #ifndef, #define and #endif preprocessor directives to ensure that this definition gets included only once in a program. We discuss lines 6–11 shortly.

```
1   // ATM.h
2   // ATM class definition. Represents an automated teller machine.
3   #ifndef ATM_H
4   #define ATM_H
5
6   #include "Screen.h" // Screen class definition
7   #include "Keypad.h" // Keypad class definition
8   #include "CashDispenser.h" // CashDispenser class definition
9   #include "DepositSlot.h" // DepositSlot class definition
10  #include "BankDatabase.h" // BankDatabase class definition
11  class Transaction; // forward declaration of class Transaction
12
13  class ATM
14  {
15  public:
16     ATM(); // constructor initializes data members
17     void run(); // start the ATM
18  private:
19     bool userAuthenticated; // whether user is authenticated
20     int currentAccountNumber; // current user's account number
21     Screen screen; // ATM's screen
22     Keypad keypad; // ATM's keypad
23     CashDispenser cashDispenser; // ATM's cash dispenser
24     DepositSlot depositSlot; // ATM's deposit slot
25     BankDatabase bankDatabase; // account information database
26
27     // private utility functions
28     void authenticateUser(); // attempts to authenticate user
29     void performTransactions(); // performs transactions
30     int displayMainMenu() const; // displays main menu
31
32     // return object of specified Transaction derived class
33     Transaction *createTransaction( int );
34  }; // end class ATM
35
36  #endif // ATM_H
```

Fig. G.1 | Definition of class ATM, which represents the ATM.

Lines 16–17 contain the function prototypes for the class's public member functions. The class diagram of Fig. 13.29 does not list any operations for class ATM, but we now declare a public member function run (line 17) in class ATM that allows an external client of the class (i.e., ATMCaseStudy.cpp) to tell the ATM to run. We also include a function prototype for a default constructor (line 16), which we discuss shortly.

Lines 19–25 of Fig. G.1 implement the class's attributes as private data members. We determine all but one of these attributes from the UML class diagrams of Fig. 13.28 and Fig. 13.29. Note that we implement the UML Boolean attribute userAuthenticated in Fig. 13.29 as a bool data member in C++ (line 19). Line 20 declares a data member not found in our UML design—an int data member currentAccountNumber that keeps track of the account number of the current authenticated user. We'll soon see how the class uses this data member.

Lines 21–24 create objects to represent the parts of the ATM. Recall from the class diagram of Fig. 13.28 that class ATM has composition relationships with classes Screen, Keypad, CashDispenser and DepositSlot, so class ATM is responsible for their creation. Line 25 creates a BankDatabase, with which the ATM interacts to access and manipulate bank account information. [*Note:* If this were a real ATM system, the ATM class would receive a reference to an existing database object created by the bank. However, in this implementation we are only simulating the bank's database, so class ATM creates the BankDatabase object with which it interacts.] Note that lines 6–10 #include the class definitions of Screen, Keypad, CashDispenser, DepositSlot and BankDatabase so that the ATM can store objects of these classes.

Lines 28–30 and 33 contain function prototypes for private utility functions that the class uses to perform its tasks. We'll see how these functions serve the class shortly. Note that member function createTransaction (line 33) returns a Transaction pointer. To include the class name Transaction in this file, we must at least include a forward declaration of class Transaction (line 11). Recall that a forward declaration tells the compiler that a class exists, but that the class is defined elsewhere. A forward declaration is sufficient here, as we are using a Transaction pointer as a return type—if we were creating or returning an actual Transaction object, we would need to #include the full Transaction header file.

ATM *Class Member-Function Definitions*
Figure G.2 contains the member-function definitions for class ATM. Lines 3–7 #include the header files required by the implementation file ATM.cpp. Note that including the ATM header file allows the compiler to ensure that the class's member functions are defined correctly. This also allows the member functions to use the class's data members.

Line 10 declares an enum named MenuOption that contains constants corresponding to the four options in the ATM's main menu (i.e., balance inquiry, withdrawal, deposit and

```
1   // ATM.cpp
2   // Member-function definitions for class ATM.
3   #include "ATM.h" // ATM class definition
4   #include "Transaction.h" // Transaction class definition
5   #include "BalanceInquiry.h" // BalanceInquiry class definition
6   #include "Withdrawal.h" // Withdrawal class definition
7   #include "Deposit.h" // Deposit class definition
```

Fig. G.2 | ATM class member-function definitions. (Part 1 of 4.)

```
8
9    // enumeration constants represent main menu options
10   enum MenuOption { BALANCE_INQUIRY = 1, WITHDRAWAL, DEPOSIT, EXIT };
11
12   // ATM default constructor initializes data members
13   ATM::ATM()
14      : userAuthenticated ( false ), // user is not authenticated to start
15        currentAccountNumber( 0 ) // no current account number to start
16   {
17      // empty body
18   } // end ATM default constructor
19
20   // start ATM
21   void ATM::run()
22   {
23      // welcome and authenticate user; perform transactions
24      while ( true )
25      {
26         // loop while user is not yet authenticated
27         while ( !userAuthenticated )
28         {
29            screen.displayMessageLine( "\nWelcome!" );
30            authenticateUser(); // authenticate user
31         } // end while
32
33         performTransactions(); // user is now authenticated
34         userAuthenticated = false; // reset before next ATM session
35         currentAccountNumber = 0; // reset before next ATM session
36         screen.displayMessageLine( "\nThank you! Goodbye!" );
37      } // end while
38   } // end function run
39
40   // attempt to authenticate user against database
41   void ATM::authenticateUser()
42   {
43      screen.displayMessage( "\nPlease enter your account number: " );
44      int accountNumber = keypad.getInput(); // input account number
45      screen.displayMessage( "\nEnter your PIN: " ); // prompt for PIN
46      int pin = keypad.getInput(); // input PIN
47
48      // set userAuthenticated to bool value returned by database
49      userAuthenticated =
50         bankDatabase.authenticateUser( accountNumber, pin );
51
52      // check whether authentication succeeded
53      if ( userAuthenticated )
54      {
55         currentAccountNumber = accountNumber; // save user's account #
56      } // end if
57      else
58         screen.displayMessageLine(
59            "Invalid account number or PIN. Please try again." );
60   } // end function authenticateUser
```

Fig. G.2 | ATM class member-function definitions. (Part 2 of 4.)

```cpp
61
62   // display the main menu and perform transactions
63   void ATM::performTransactions()
64   {
65      // local pointer to store transaction currently being processed
66      Transaction *currentTransactionPtr;
67
68      bool userExited = false; // user has not chosen to exit
69
70      // loop while user has not chosen option to exit system
71      while ( !userExited )
72      {
73         // show main menu and get user selection
74         int mainMenuSelection = displayMainMenu();
75
76         // decide how to proceed based on user's menu selection
77         switch ( mainMenuSelection )
78         {
79            // user chose to perform one of three transaction types
80            case BALANCE_INQUIRY:
81            case WITHDRAWAL:
82            case DEPOSIT:
83               // initialize as new object of chosen type
84               currentTransactionPtr =
85                  createTransaction( mainMenuSelection );
86
87               currentTransactionPtr->execute(); // execute transaction
88
89               // free the space for the dynamically allocated Transaction
90               delete currentTransactionPtr;
91
92               break;
93            case EXIT: // user chose to terminate session
94               screen.displayMessageLine( "\nExiting the system..." );
95               userExited = true; // this ATM session should end
96               break;
97            default: // user did not enter an integer from 1-4
98               screen.displayMessageLine(
99                  "\nYou did not enter a valid selection. Try again." );
100              break;
101        } // end switch
102     } // end while
103  } // end function performTransactions
104
105  // display the main menu and return an input selection
106  int ATM::displayMainMenu() const
107  {
108     screen.displayMessageLine( "\nMain menu:" );
109     screen.displayMessageLine( "1 - View my balance" );
110     screen.displayMessageLine( "2 - Withdraw cash" );
111     screen.displayMessageLine( "3 - Deposit funds" );
112     screen.displayMessageLine( "4 - Exit\n" );
```

Fig. G.2 | ATM class member-function definitions. (Part 3 of 4.)

```
113      screen.displayMessage( "Enter a choice: " );
114      return keypad.getInput(); // return user's selection
115   } // end function displayMainMenu
116
117   // return object of specified Transaction derived class
118   Transaction *ATM::createTransaction( int type )
119   {
120      Transaction *tempPtr; // temporary Transaction pointer
121
122      // determine which type of Transaction to create
123      switch ( type )
124      {
125         case BALANCE_INQUIRY: // create new BalanceInquiry transaction
126            tempPtr = new BalanceInquiry(
127               currentAccountNumber, screen, bankDatabase );
128            break;
129         case WITHDRAWAL: // create new Withdrawal transaction
130            tempPtr = new Withdrawal( currentAccountNumber, screen,
131               bankDatabase, keypad, cashDispenser );
132            break;
133         case DEPOSIT: // create new Deposit transaction
134            tempPtr = new Deposit( currentAccountNumber, screen,
135               bankDatabase, keypad, depositSlot );
136            break;
137      } // end switch
138
139      return tempPtr; // return the newly created object
140   } // end function createTransaction
```

Fig. G.2 | ATM class member-function definitions. (Part 4 of 4.)

exit). Note that setting BALANCE_INQUIRY to 1 causes the subsequent enumeration constants to be assigned the values 2, 3 and 4, as enumeration constant values increment by 1.

Lines 13–18 define class ATM's constructor, which initializes the class's data members. When an ATM object is first created, no user is authenticated, so line 14 uses a member initializer to set userAuthenticated to false. Likewise, line 15 initializes currentAccountNumber to 0 because there is no current user yet.

ATM member function run (lines 21–38) uses an infinite loop (lines 24–37) to repeatedly welcome a user, attempt to authenticate the user and, if authentication succeeds, allow the user to perform transactions. After an authenticated user performs the desired transactions and chooses to exit, the ATM resets itself, displays a goodbye message to the user and restarts the process. We use an infinite loop here to simulate the fact that an ATM appears to run continuously until the bank turns it off (an action beyond the user's control). An ATM user has the option to exit the system, but does not have the ability to turn off the ATM completely.

Inside member function run's infinite loop, lines 27–31 cause the ATM to repeatedly welcome and attempt to authenticate the user as long as the user has not been authenticated (i.e., !userAuthenticated is true). Line 29 invokes member function displayMessage-Line of the ATM's screen to display a welcome message. Like Screen member function displayMessage designed in the case study, member function displayMessageLine (declared in line 13 of Fig. G.3 and defined in lines 20–23 of Fig. G.4) displays a message to the user, but this member function also outputs a newline after displaying the message. We have added this member function during implementation to give class Screen's clients more control over the placement of displayed messages. Line 30 of Fig. G.2 invokes class ATM's private utility function authenticateUser (lines 41–60) to attempt to authenticate the user.

We refer to the requirements specification to determine the steps necessary to authenticate the user before allowing transactions to occur. Line 43 of member function authenticateUser invokes member function displayMessage of the ATM's screen to prompt the user to enter an account number. Line 44 invokes member function getInput of the ATM's keypad to obtain the user's input, then stores the integer value entered by the user in a local variable accountNumber. Member function authenticateUser next prompts the user to enter a PIN (line 45), and stores the PIN input by the user in a local variable pin (line 46). Next, lines 49–50 attempt to authenticate the user by passing the accountNumber and pin entered by the user to the bankDatabase's authenticateUser member function. Class ATM sets its userAuthenticated data member to the bool value returned by this function—userAuthenticated becomes true if authentication succeeds (i.e., accountNumber and pin match those of an existing Account in bankDatabase) and remains false otherwise. If userAuthenticated is true, line 55 saves the account number entered by the user (i.e., accountNumber) in the ATM data member currentAccountNumber. The other member functions of class ATM use this variable whenever an ATM session requires access to the user's account number. If userAuthenticated is false, lines 58–59 use the screen's displayMessageLine member function to indicate that an invalid account number and/or PIN was entered and the user must try again. Note that we set currentAccountNumber only after authenticating the user's account number and the associated PIN—if the database could not authenticate the user, currentAccountNumber remains 0.

After member function run attempts to authenticate the user (line 30), if userAuthenticated is still false, the while loop in lines 27–31 executes again. If userAuthenticated is now true, the loop terminates and control continues with line 33, which calls class ATM's utility function performTransactions.

Member function performTransactions (lines 63–103) carries out an ATM session for an authenticated user. Line 66 declares a local Transaction pointer, which we aim at a BalanceInquiry, Withdrawal or Deposit object representing the ATM transaction currently being processed. Note that we use a Transaction pointer here to allow us to take advantage of polymorphism. Also note that we use the role name included in the class diagram of Fig. 3.20—currentTransaction—in naming this pointer. As per our pointer-naming convention, we append "Ptr" to the role name to form the variable name currentTransactionPtr. Line 68 declares another local variable—a bool called userExited that keeps track of whether the user has chosen to exit. This variable controls a while loop (lines 71–102) that allows the user to execute an unlimited number of transactions before choosing to exit. Within this loop, line 74 displays the main menu and obtains the user's menu selection by calling an ATM utility function displayMainMenu (defined in lines 106–115). This member function displays the main menu by invoking member functions of the ATM's screen and returns a menu selection obtained from the user through the ATM's keypad. Note that this member function is const because it does not modify the contents of the object. Line 74 stores the user's selection returned by displayMainMenu in local variable mainMenuSelection.

After obtaining a main menu selection, member function `performTransactions` uses a `switch` statement (lines 77–101) to respond to the selection appropriately. If `mainMenuSelection` is equal to any of the three enumeration constants representing transaction types (i.e., if the user chose to perform a transaction), lines 84–85 call utility function `createTransaction` (defined in lines 118–140) to return a pointer to a newly instantiated object of the type that corresponds to the selected transaction. Pointer `currentTransactionPtr` is assigned the pointer returned by `createTransaction`. Line 87 then uses `currentTransactionPtr` to invoke the new object's `execute` member function to execute the transaction. We'll discuss `Transaction` member function `execute` and the three `Transaction` derived classes shortly. Finally, when the `Transaction` derived class object is no longer needed, line 90 releases the memory dynamically allocated for it.

Note that we aim the `Transaction` pointer `currentTransactionPtr` at an object of one of the three `Transaction` derived classes so that we can execute transactions polymorphically. For example, if the user chooses to perform a balance inquiry, `mainMenuSelection` equals `BALANCE_INQUIRY`, leading `createTransaction` to return a pointer to a `BalanceInquiry` object. Thus, `currentTransactionPtr` points to a `BalanceInquiry`, and invoking `currentTransactionPtr->execute()` results in `BalanceInquiry`'s version of `execute` being called.

Member function `createTransaction` (lines 118–140) uses a `switch` statement (lines 123–137) to instantiate a new `Transaction` derived class object of the type indicated by the parameter `type`. Recall that member function `performTransactions` passes `mainMenuSelection` to this member function only when `mainMenuSelection` contains a value corresponding to one of the three transaction types. Therefore `type` equals either `BALANCE_INQUIRY`, `WITHDRAWAL` or `DEPOSIT`. Each case in the `switch` statement aims the temporary pointer `tempPtr` at a newly created object of the appropriate `Transaction` derived class. Note that each constructor has a unique parameter list, based on the specific data required to initialize the derived class object. A `BalanceInquiry` requires only the account number of the current user and references to the ATM's `screen` and the `bankDatabase`. In addition to these parameters, a `Withdrawal` requires references to the ATM's `keypad` and `cashDispenser`, and a `Deposit` requires references to the ATM's `keypad` and `depositSlot`. Note that, as you'll soon see, the `BalanceInquiry`, `Withdrawal` and `Deposit` constructors each specify reference parameters to receive the objects representing the required parts of the ATM. Thus, when member function `createTransaction` passes objects in the ATM (e.g., `screen` and `keypad`) to the initializer for each newly created `Transaction` derived class object, the new object actually receives *references* to the ATM's composite objects. We discuss the transaction classes in more detail in Sections G.9–G.12.

After executing a transaction (line 87 in `performTransactions`), `userExited` remains `false` and the `while` loop in lines 71–102 repeats, returning the user to the main menu. However, if a user does not perform a transaction and instead selects the main menu option to exit, line 95 sets `userExited` to `true`, causing the condition of the `while` loop (`!userExited`) to become `false`. This `while` is the final statement of member function `performTransactions`, so control returns to the calling function `run`. If the user enters an invalid main menu selection (i.e., not an integer from 1–4), lines 98–99 display an appropriate error message, `userExited` remains `false` and the user returns to the main menu to try again.

When `performTransactions` returns control to member function `run`, the user has chosen to exit the system, so lines 34–35 reset the ATM's data members `userAuthenticated` and `currentAccountNumber` to prepare for the next ATM user. Line 36 displays a goodbye message before the ATM starts over and welcomes the next user.

G.3 **Class Screen**

Class Screen (Figs. G.3–G.4) represents the screen of the ATM and encapsulates all aspects of displaying output to the user. Class Screen approximates a real ATM's screen with a computer monitor and outputs text messages using cout and the stream insertion operator (<<). In this case study, we designed class Screen to have one operation—displayMessage. For greater flexibility in displaying messages to the Screen, we now declare three Screen member functions—displayMessage, displayMessageLine and displayDollarAmount. The prototypes for these member functions appear in lines 12–14 of Fig. G.3.

Screen *Class Member-Function Definitions*

Figure G.4 contains the member-function definitions for class Screen. Line 11 #includes the Screen class definition. Member function displayMessage (lines 14–17) takes a string as an argument and prints it to the console using cout and the stream insertion operator (<<). The cursor stays on the same line, making this member function appropriate for displaying prompts to the user. Member function displayMessageLine (lines 20–23) also prints a string, but outputs a newline to move the cursor to the next line. Finally, member function displayDollarAmount (lines 26–29) outputs a properly formatted dollar amount (e.g., $123.45). Line 28 uses stream manipulators fixed and setprecision to output a value formatted with two decimal places. See Chapter 15, Stream Input/Output, for more information about formatting output.

```
1   // Screen.h
2   // Screen class definition. Represents the screen of the ATM.
3   #ifndef SCREEN_H
4   #define SCREEN_H
5
6   #include <string>
7   using std::string;
8
9   class Screen
10  {
11  public:
12     void displayMessage( string ) const; // output a message
13     void displayMessageLine( string ) const; // output message with newline
14     void displayDollarAmount( double ) const; // output a dollar amount
15  }; // end class Screen
16
17  #endif // SCREEN_H
```

Fig. G.3 | Screen class definition.

```
1   // Screen.cpp
2   // Member-function definitions for class Screen.
3   #include <iostream>
4   using std::cout;
5   using std::endl;
6   using std::fixed;
7
```

Fig. G.4 | Screen class member-function definitions. (Part 1 of 2.)

```
 8   #include <iomanip>
 9   using std::setprecision;
10
11   #include "Screen.h" // Screen class definition
12
13   // output a message without a newline
14   void Screen::displayMessage( string message ) const
15   {
16      cout << message;
17   } // end function displayMessage
18
19   // output a message with a newline
20   void Screen::displayMessageLine( string message ) const
21   {
22      cout << message << endl;
23   } // end function displayMessageLine
24
25   // output a dollar amount
26   void Screen::displayDollarAmount( double amount ) const
27   {
28      cout << fixed << setprecision( 2 ) << "$" << amount;
29   } // end function displayDollarAmount
```

Fig. G.4 | Screen class member-function definitions. (Part 2 of 2.)

G.4 Class Keypad

Class Keypad (Figs. G.5–G.6) represents the keypad of the ATM and is responsible for receiving all user input. Recall that we are simulating this hardware, so we use the computer's keyboard to approximate the keypad. A computer keyboard contains many keys not found on the ATM's keypad. However, we assume that the user presses only the keys on the computer keyboard that also appear on the keypad—the keys numbered 0–9 and the *Enter* key. Line 9 of Fig. G.5 contains the function prototype for class Keypad's one member function getInput. This member function is declared const because it does not change the object.

```
 1   // Keypad.h
 2   // Keypad class definition. Represents the keypad of the ATM.
 3   #ifndef KEYPAD_H
 4   #define KEYPAD_H
 5
 6   class Keypad
 7   {
 8   public:
 9      int getInput() const; // return an integer value entered by user
10   }; // end class Keypad
11
12   #endif // KEYPAD_H
```

Fig. G.5 | Keypad class definition.

Keypad *Class Member-Function Definition*
In the Keypad implementation file (Fig. G.6), member function getInput (defined in lines 9–14) uses the standard input stream cin and the stream extraction operator (>>) to obtain input from the user. Line 11 declares a local variable to store the user's input. Line 12 reads input into local variable input, then line 13 returns this value. Recall that get-Input obtains all the input used by the ATM. Keypad's getInput member function simply returns the integer input by the user. If a client of class Keypad requires input that satisfies some particular criteria (i.e., a number corresponding to a valid menu option), the client must perform the appropriate error checking. [*Note:* Using the standard input stream cin and the stream extraction operator (>>) allows noninteger input to be read from the user. Because the real ATM's keypad permits only integer input, however, we assume that the user enters an integer and do not attempt to fix problems caused by noninteger input.]

```
 1   // Keypad.cpp
 2   // Member-function definition for class Keypad (the ATM's keypad).
 3   #include <iostream>
 4   using std::cin;
 5
 6   #include "Keypad.h" // Keypad class definition
 7
 8   // return an integer value entered by user
 9   int Keypad::getInput() const
10   {
11      int input; // variable to store the input
12      cin >> input; // we assume that user enters an integer
13      return input; // return the value entered by user
14   } // end function getInput
```

Fig. G.6 | Keypad class member-function definition.

G.5 Class CashDispenser

Class CashDispenser (Figs. G.7–G.8) represents the cash dispenser of the ATM. The class definition (Fig. G.7) contains the function prototype for a default constructor (line 9). Class CashDispenser declares two additional public member functions—dispenseCash (line 12) and isSufficientCashAvailable (line 15). The class trusts that a client (i.e., Withdrawal) calls dispenseCash only after establishing that sufficient cash is available by calling isSufficientCashAvailable. Thus, dispenseCash simply simulates dispensing the requested amount without checking whether sufficient cash is available. Line 17 declares private constant INITIAL_COUNT, which indicates the initial count of bills in the cash dispenser when the ATM starts (i.e., 500). Line 18 implements attribute count (modeled in Fig. 13.29), which keeps track of the number of bills remaining in the CashDispenser at any time.

CashDispenser *Class Member-Function Definitions*
Figure G.8 contains the definitions of class CashDispenser's member functions. The constructor (lines 6–9) sets count to the initial count (i.e., 500). Member function dispense-Cash (lines 13–17) simulates cash dispensing. If our system were hooked up to a real hardware cash dispenser, this member function would interact with the hardware device

```
1   // CashDispenser.h
2   // CashDispenser class definition. Represents the ATM's cash dispenser.
3   #ifndef CASH_DISPENSER_H
4   #define CASH_DISPENSER_H
5
6   class CashDispenser
7   {
8   public:
9      CashDispenser(); // constructor initializes bill count to 500
10
11     // simulates dispensing of specified amount of cash
12     void dispenseCash( int );
13
14     // indicates whether cash dispenser can dispense desired amount
15     bool isSufficientCashAvailable( int ) const;
16  private:
17     const static int INITIAL_COUNT = 500;
18     int count; // number of $20 bills remaining
19  }; // end class CashDispenser
20
21  #endif // CASH_DISPENSER_H
```

Fig. G.7 | CashDispenser class definition.

```
1   // CashDispenser.cpp
2   // Member-function definitions for class CashDispenser.
3   #include "CashDispenser.h" // CashDispenser class definition
4
5   // CashDispenser default constructor initializes count to default
6   CashDispenser::CashDispenser()
7   {
8      count = INITIAL_COUNT; // set count attribute to default
9   } // end CashDispenser default constructor
10
11  // simulates dispensing of specified amount of cash; assumes enough cash
12  // is available (previous call to isSufficientCashAvailable returned true)
13  void CashDispenser::dispenseCash( int amount )
14  {
15     int billsRequired = amount / 20; // number of $20 bills required
16     count -= billsRequired; // update the count of bills
17  } // end function dispenseCash
18
19  // indicates whether cash dispenser can dispense desired amount
20  bool CashDispenser::isSufficientCashAvailable( int amount ) const
21  {
22     int billsRequired = amount / 20; // number of $20 bills required
23
24     if ( count >= billsRequired )
25        return true; // enough bills are available
26     else
27        return false; // not enough bills are available
28  } // end function isSufficientCashAvailable
```

Fig. G.8 | CashDispenser class member-function definitions.

to physically dispense cash. Our simulated version of the member function simply decreases the count of bills remaining by the number required to dispense the specified amount (line 16). Note that line 15 calculates the number of $20 bills required to dispense the specified amount. The ATM allows the user to choose only withdrawal amounts that are multiples of $20, so we divide amount by 20 to obtain the number of billsRequired. Also note that it is the responsibility of the client of the class (i.e., Withdrawal) to inform the user that cash has been dispensed—CashDispenser cannot interact directly with Screen.

Member function isSufficientCashAvailable (lines 20–28) has a parameter amount that specifies the amount of cash in question. Lines 24–27 return true if the CashDispenser's count is greater than or equal to billsRequired (i.e., enough bills are available) and false otherwise (i.e., not enough bills). For example, if a user wishes to withdraw $80 (i.e., billsRequired is 4), but only three bills remain (i.e., count is 3), the member function returns false.

G.6 Class DepositSlot

Class DepositSlot (Figs. G.9–G.10) represents the deposit slot of the ATM. Like the version of class CashDispenser presented here, this version of class DepositSlot merely simulates the functionality of a real hardware deposit slot. DepositSlot has no data members and only one member function—isEnvelopeReceived (declared in line 9 of Fig. G.9 and defined in lines 7–10 of Fig. G.10)—that indicates whether a deposit envelope was received.

```
1  // DepositSlot.h
2  // DepositSlot class definition. Represents the ATM's deposit slot.
3  #ifndef DEPOSIT_SLOT_H
4  #define DEPOSIT_SLOT_H
5
6  class DepositSlot
7  {
8  public:
9     bool isEnvelopeReceived() const; // tells whether envelope was received
10 }; // end class DepositSlot
11
12 #endif // DEPOSIT_SLOT_H
```

Fig. G.9 | DepositSlot class definition.

```
1  // DepositSlot.cpp
2  // Member-function definition for class DepositSlot.
3  #include "DepositSlot.h" // DepositSlot class definiton
4
5  // indicates whether envelope was received (always returns true,
6  // because this is only a software simulation of a real deposit slot)
7  bool DepositSlot::isEnvelopeReceived() const
8  {
9     return true; // deposit envelope was received
10 } // end function isEnvelopeReceived
```

Fig. G.10 | DepositSlot class member-function definition.

Recall from the requirements specification that the ATM allows the user up to two minutes to insert an envelope. The current version of member function isEnvelope-Received simply returns true immediately (line 9 of Fig. G.10), because this is only a software simulation, and we assume that the user has inserted an envelope within the required time frame. If an actual hardware deposit slot were connected to our system, member function isEnvelopeReceived might be implemented to wait for a maximum of two minutes to receive a signal from the hardware deposit slot indicating that the user has indeed inserted a deposit envelope. If isEnvelopeReceived were to receive such a signal within two minutes, the member function would return true. If two minutes elapsed and the member function still had not received a signal, then the member function would return false.

G.7 Class Account

Class Account (Figs. G.11–G.12) represents a bank account. Lines 9–15 in the class definition (Fig. G.11) contain function prototypes for the class's constructor and six member functions, which we discuss shortly. Each Account has four attributes (modeled in Fig. 13.29)—accountNumber, pin, availableBalance and totalBalance. Lines 17–20 implement these attributes as private data members. Data member availableBalance represents the amount of funds available for withdrawal. Data member totalBalance represents the amount of funds available, plus the amount of deposited funds still pending confirmation or clearance.

Account *Class Member-Function Definitions*
Figure G.12 presents the definitions of class Account's member functions. The class's constructor (lines 6–14) takes an account number, the PIN established for the account, the

```
1   // Account.h
2   // Account class definition. Represents a bank account.
3   #ifndef ACCOUNT_H
4   #define ACCOUNT_H
5
6   class Account
7   {
8   public:
9      Account( int, int, double, double ); // constructor sets attributes
10     bool validatePIN( int ) const; // is user-specified PIN correct?
11     double getAvailableBalance() const; // returns available balance
12     double getTotalBalance() const; // returns total balance
13     void credit( double ); // adds an amount to the Account balance
14     void debit( double ); // subtracts an amount from the Account balance
15     int getAccountNumber() const; // returns account number
16  private:
17     int accountNumber; // account number
18     int pin; // PIN for authentication
19     double availableBalance; // funds available for withdrawal
20     double totalBalance; // funds available + funds waiting to clear
21  }; // end class Account
22
23  #endif // ACCOUNT_H
```

Fig. G.11 | Account class definition.

initial available balance and the initial total balance as arguments. Lines 8–11 assign these values to the class's data members using member initializers.

Member function `validatePIN` (lines 17–23) determines whether a user-specified PIN (i.e., parameter `userPIN`) matches the PIN associated with the account (i.e., data member `pin`). Recall that we modeled this member function's parameter `userPIN` in the UML class diagram of Fig. 6.37. If the two PINs match, the member function returns `true` (line 20); otherwise, it returns `false` (line 22).

Member functions `getAvailableBalance` (lines 26–29) and `getTotalBalance` (lines 32–35) are *get* functions that return the values of `double` data members `availableBalance` and `totalBalance`, respectively.

```
1   // Account.cpp
2   // Member-function definitions for class Account.
3   #include "Account.h" // Account class definition
4
5   // Account constructor initializes attributes
6   Account::Account( int theAccountNumber, int thePIN,
7      double theAvailableBalance, double theTotalBalance )
8      : accountNumber( theAccountNumber ),
9        pin( thePIN ),
10       availableBalance( theAvailableBalance ),
11       totalBalance( theTotalBalance )
12  {
13     // empty body
14  } // end Account constructor
15
16  // determines whether a user-specified PIN matches PIN in Account
17  bool Account::validatePIN( int userPIN ) const
18  {
19     if ( userPIN == pin )
20        return true;
21     else
22        return false;
23  } // end function validatePIN
24
25  // returns available balance
26  double Account::getAvailableBalance() const
27  {
28     return availableBalance;
29  } // end function getAvailableBalance
30
31  // returns the total balance
32  double Account::getTotalBalance() const
33  {
34     return totalBalance;
35  } // end function getTotalBalance
36
37  // credits an amount to the account
38  void Account::credit( double amount )
39  {
40     totalBalance += amount; // add to total balance
41  } // end function credit
```

Fig. G.12 | Account class member-function definitions. (Part I of 2.)

```
42
43   // debits an amount from the account
44   void Account::debit( double amount )
45   {
46      availableBalance -= amount; // subtract from available balance
47      totalBalance -= amount; // subtract from total balance
48   } // end function debit
49
50   // returns account number
51   int Account::getAccountNumber() const
52   {
53      return accountNumber;
54   } // end function getAccountNumber
```

Fig. G.12 | Account class member-function definitions. (Part 2 of 2.)

Member function credit (lines 38–41) adds an amount of money (i.e., parameter amount) to an Account as part of a deposit transaction. Note that this member function adds the amount only to data member totalBalance (line 40). The money credited to an account during a deposit does not become available immediately, so we modify only the total balance. We assume that the bank updates the available balance appropriately at a later time. Our implementation of class Account includes only member functions required for carrying out ATM transactions. Therefore, we omit the member functions that some other bank system would invoke to add to data member availableBalance (to confirm a deposit) or subtract from data member totalBalance (to reject a deposit).

Member function debit (lines 44–48) subtracts an amount of money (i.e., parameter amount) from an Account as part of a withdrawal transaction. This member function subtracts the amount from both data member availableBalance (line 46) and data member totalBalance (line 47), because a withdrawal affects both measures of an account balance.

Member function getAccountNumber (lines 51–54) provides access to an Account's accountNumber. We include this member function in our implementation so that a client of the class (i.e., BankDatabase) can identify a particular Account. For example, BankDatabase contains many Account objects, and it can invoke this member function on each of its Account objects to locate the one with a specific account number.

G.8 Class BankDatabase

Class BankDatabase (Figs. G.13–G.14) models the bank's database with which the ATM interacts to access and modify a user's account information. The class definition (Fig. G.13) declares function prototypes for the class's constructor and several member functions. We discuss these momentarily. The class definition also declares the BankDatabase's data members. We determine one data member for class BankDatabase based on its composition relationship with class Account. Recall from Fig. 13.28 that a BankDatabase is composed of zero or more objects of class Account. Line 24 of Fig. G.13 implements data member accounts—a vector of Account objects—to implement this composition relationship. Lines 6–7 allow us to use vector in this file. Line 27 contains the function prototype for a private utility function getAccount that allows the member functions of the class to obtain a pointer to a specific Account in the accounts vector.

```
 1   // BankDatabase.h
 2   // BankDatabase class definition. Represents the bank's database.
 3   #ifndef BANK_DATABASE_H
 4   #define BANK_DATABASE_H
 5
 6   #include <vector> // class uses vector to store Account objects
 7   using std::vector;
 8
 9   #include "Account.h" // Account class definition
10
11   class BankDatabase
12   {
13   public:
14      BankDatabase(); // constructor initializes accounts
15
16      // determine whether account number and PIN match those of an Account
17      bool authenticateUser( int, int ); // returns true if Account authentic
18
19      double getAvailableBalance( int ); // get an available balance
20      double getTotalBalance( int ); // get an Account's total balance
21      void credit( int, double ); // add amount to Account balance
22      void debit( int, double ); // subtract amount from Account balance
23   private:
24      vector< Account > accounts; // vector of the bank's Accounts
25
26      // private utility function
27      Account * getAccount( int ); // get pointer to Account object
28   }; // end class BankDatabase
29
30   #endif // BANK_DATABASE_H
```

Fig. G.13 | BankDatabase class definition.

BankDatabase *Class Member-Function Definitions*

Figure G.14 contains the member-function definitions for class BankDatabase. We implement the class with a default constructor (lines 6–15) that adds Account objects to data member accounts. For the sake of testing the system, we create two new Account objects with test data (lines 9–10), then add them to the end of the vector (lines 13–14). Note

```
 1   // BankDatabase.cpp
 2   // Member-function definitions for class BankDatabase.
 3   #include "BankDatabase.h" // BankDatabase class definition
 4
 5   // BankDatabase default constructor initializes accounts
 6   BankDatabase::BankDatabase()
 7   {
 8      // create two Account objects for testing
 9      Account account1( 12345, 54321, 1000.0, 1200.0 );
10      Account account2( 98765, 56789, 200.0, 200.0 );
11
```

Fig. G.14 | BankDatabase class member-function definitions. (Part 1 of 3.)

```
12     // add the Account objects to the vector accounts
13     accounts.push_back( account1 ); // add account1 to end of vector
14     accounts.push_back( account2 ); // add account2 to end of vector
15  } // end BankDatabase default constructor
16
17  // retrieve Account object containing specified account number
18  Account * BankDatabase::getAccount( int accountNumber )
19  {
20     // loop through accounts searching for matching account number
21     for ( size_t i = 0; i < accounts.size(); i++ )
22     {
23        // return current account if match found
24        if ( accounts[ i ].getAccountNumber() == accountNumber )
25           return &accounts[ i ];
26     } // end for
27
28     return NULL; // if no matching account was found, return NULL
29  } // end function getAccount
30
31  // determine whether user-specified account number and PIN match
32  // those of an account in the database
33  bool BankDatabase::authenticateUser( int userAccountNumber,
34     int userPIN )
35  {
36     // attempt to retrieve the account with the account number
37     Account * const userAccountPtr = getAccount( userAccountNumber );
38
39     // if account exists, return result of Account function validatePIN
40     if ( userAccountPtr != NULL )
41        return userAccountPtr->validatePIN( userPIN );
42     else
43        return false; // account number not found, so return false
44  } // end function authenticateUser
45
46  // return available balance of Account with specified account number
47  double BankDatabase::getAvailableBalance( int userAccountNumber )
48  {
49     Account * const userAccountPtr = getAccount( userAccountNumber );
50     return userAccountPtr->getAvailableBalance();
51  } // end function getAvailableBalance
52
53  // return total balance of Account with specified account number
54  double BankDatabase::getTotalBalance( int userAccountNumber )
55  {
56     Account * const userAccountPtr = getAccount( userAccountNumber );
57     return userAccountPtr->getTotalBalance();
58  } // end function getTotalBalance
59
60  // credit an amount to Account with specified account number
61  void BankDatabase::credit( int userAccountNumber, double amount )
62  {
```

Fig. G.14 | BankDatabase class member-function definitions. (Part 2 of 3.)

```
63        Account * const userAccountPtr = getAccount( userAccountNumber );
64        userAccountPtr->credit( amount );
65    } // end function credit
66
67    // debit an amount from Account with specified account number
68    void BankDatabase::debit( int userAccountNumber, double amount )
69    {
70        Account * const userAccountPtr = getAccount( userAccountNumber );
71        userAccountPtr->debit( amount );
72    } // end function debit
```

Fig. G.14 | BankDatabase class member-function definitions. (Part 3 of 3.)

that the Account constructor has four parameters—the account number, the PIN assigned to the account, the initial available balance and the initial total balance.

Recall that class BankDatabase serves as an intermediary between class ATM and the actual Account objects that contain users' account information. Thus, the member functions of class BankDatabase do nothing more than invoke the corresponding member functions of the Account object belonging to the current ATM user.

We include private utility function getAccount (lines 18–29) to allow the Bank-Database to obtain a pointer to a particular Account within vector accounts. To locate the user's Account, the BankDatabase compares the value returned by member function getAccountNumber for each element of accounts to a specified account number until it finds a match. Lines 21–26 traverse the accounts vector. If the account number of the current Account (i.e., accounts[i]) equals the value of parameter accountNumber, the member function immediately returns the address of the current Account (i.e., a pointer to the current Account). If no account has the given account number, then line 28 returns NULL. Note that this member function must return a pointer, as opposed to a reference, because there is the possibility that the return value could be NULL—a reference cannot be NULL, but a pointer can.

Note that vector function size (invoked in the loop-continuation condition in line 21) returns the number of elements in a vector as a value of type size_t (which is usually unsigned int). As a result, we declare the control variable i to be of type size_t, too. On some compilers, declaring i as an int would cause the compiler to issue a warning message, because the loop-continuation condition would compare a signed value (i.e., an int) and an unsigned value (i.e., a value of type size_t).

Member function authenticateUser (lines 33–44) proves or disproves the an ATM user's identity. This function takes a user-specified account number and user-specified PIN as arguments and indicates whether they match the account number and PIN of an Account in the database. Line 37 calls utility function getAccount, which returns either a pointer to an Account with userAccountNumber as its account number or NULL to indicate that userAccountNumber is invalid. We declare userAccountPtr to be a const pointer because, once the member function aims this pointer at the user's Account, the pointer should not change. If getAccount returns a pointer to an Account object, line 41 returns the bool value returned by that object's validatePIN member function. Note that Bank-Database's authenticateUser member function does not perform the PIN comparison itself—rather, it forwards userPIN to the Account object's validatePIN member function to do so. The value returned by Account member function validatePIN indicates whether the user-specified PIN matches the PIN of the user's Account, so member function authenticateUser simply returns this value to the client of the class (i.e., ATM).

BankDatabase trusts the ATM to invoke member function authenticateUser and receive a return value of true before allowing the user to perform transactions. BankDatabase also trusts that each Transaction object created by the ATM contains the valid account number of the current authenticated user and that this is the account number passed to the remaining BankDatabase member functions as argument userAccountNumber. Member functions getAvailableBalance (lines 47–51), getTotalBalance (lines 54–58), credit (lines 61–65) and debit (lines 68–72) therefore simply retrieve a pointer to the user's Account object with utility function getAccount, then use this pointer to invoke the appropriate Account member function on the user's Account object. We know that the calls to getAccount within these member functions will never return NULL, because user-AccountNumber must refer to an existing Account. Note that getAvailableBalance and getTotalBalance return the values returned by the corresponding Account member functions. Also note that credit and debit simply redirect parameter amount to the Account member functions they invoke.

G.9 Class Transaction

Class Transaction (Figs. G.15–G.16) is an abstract base class that represents the notion of an ATM transaction. It contains the common features of derived classes BalanceInquiry, Withdrawal and Deposit. Figure G.15 expands upon the Transaction header file first developed in Section 13.10. Lines 13, 17–19 and 22 contain function prototypes for the class's constructor and four member functions, which we discuss shortly. Line 15 defines a virtual destructor with an empty body—this makes all derived-class destructors virtual (even those defined implicitly by the compiler) and ensures that dynamically allocated derived-class objects get destroyed properly when they are deleted via a base-class pointer. Lines 24–26 declare the class's private data members. Recall from the class diagram of Fig. 13.29 that class Transaction contains an attribute accountNumber (implemented in line 24) that indicates the account involved in the Transaction. We derive data members screen (line 25) and bankDatabase (line 26) from class Transaction's associations modeled in Fig. 13.28—all transactions require access to the ATM's screen and the bank's database, so we include references to a Screen and a BankDatabase as data members of class Transaction. As you'll soon see, Transaction's constructor initializes these references. Note that the forward declarations in lines 6–7 signify that the header file contains references to objects of classes Screen and BankDatabase, but that the definitions of these classes lie outside the header file.

```
1   // Transaction.h
2   // Transaction abstract base class definition.
3   #ifndef TRANSACTION_H
4   #define TRANSACTION_H
5
6   class Screen; // forward declaration of class Screen
7   class BankDatabase; // forward declaration of class BankDatabase
8
```

Fig. G.15 | Transaction class definition. (Part 1 of 2.)

```
9   class Transaction
10  {
11  public:
12     // constructor initializes common features of all Transactions
13     Transaction( int, Screen &, BankDatabase & );
14
15     virtual ~Transaction() { } // virtual destructor with empty body
16
17     int getAccountNumber() const; // return account number
18     Screen &getScreen() const; // return reference to screen
19     BankDatabase &getBankDatabase() const; // return reference to database
20
21     // pure virtual function to perform the transaction
22     virtual void execute() = 0; // overridden in derived classes
23  private:
24     int accountNumber; // indicates account involved
25     Screen &screen; // reference to the screen of the ATM
26     BankDatabase &bankDatabase; // reference to the account info database
27  }; // end class Transaction
28
29  #endif // TRANSACTION_H
```

Fig. G.15 | Transaction class definition. (Part 2 of 2.)

```
1   // Transaction.cpp
2   // Member-function definitions for class Transaction.
3   #include "Transaction.h" // Transaction class definition
4   #include "Screen.h" // Screen class definition
5   #include "BankDatabase.h" // BankDatabase class definition
6
7   // constructor initializes common features of all Transactions
8   Transaction::Transaction( int userAccountNumber, Screen &atmScreen,
9      BankDatabase &atmBankDatabase )
10     : accountNumber( userAccountNumber ),
11       screen( atmScreen ),
12       bankDatabase( atmBankDatabase )
13  {
14     // empty body
15  } // end Transaction constructor
16
17  // return account number
18  int Transaction::getAccountNumber() const
19  {
20     return accountNumber;
21  } // end function getAccountNumber
22
23  // return reference to screen
24  Screen &Transaction::getScreen() const
25  {
26     return screen;
27  } // end function getScreen
28
```

Fig. G.16 | Transaction class member-function definitions. (Part 1 of 2.)

```
29   // return reference to bank database
30   BankDatabase &Transaction::getBankDatabase() const
31   {
32      return bankDatabase;
33   } // end function getBankDatabase
```

Fig. G.16 | Transaction class member-function definitions. (Part 2 of 2.)

Class Transaction has a constructor (declared in line 13 of Fig. G.15 and defined in lines 8–15 of Fig. G.16) that takes the current user's account number and references to the ATM's screen and the bank's database as arguments. Because Transaction is an abstract class, this constructor will never be called directly to instantiate Transaction objects. Instead, the constructors of the Transaction derived classes will use base-class initializer syntax to invoke this constructor.

Class Transaction has three public *get* functions—getAccountNumber (declared in line 17 of Fig. G.15 and defined in lines 18–21 of Fig. G.16), getScreen (declared in line 18 of Fig. G.15 and defined in lines 24–27 of Fig. G.16) and getBankDatabase (declared in line 19 of Fig. G.15 and defined in lines 30–33 of Fig. G.16). Transaction derived classes inherit these member functions from Transaction and use them to gain access to class Transaction's private data members.

Class Transaction also declares a pure virtual function execute (line 22 of Fig. G.15). It does not make sense to provide an implementation for this member function, because a generic transaction cannot be executed. Thus, we declare this member function to be a pure virtual function and force each Transaction derived class to provide its own concrete implementation that executes that particular type of transaction.

G.10 Class BalanceInquiry

Class BalanceInquiry (Figs. G.17–G.18) derives from abstract base class Transaction and represents a balance-inquiry ATM transaction. BalanceInquiry does not have any data members of its own, but it inherits Transaction data members accountNumber, screen and bankDatabase, which are accessible through Transaction's public *get* functions. Note that line 6 #includes the definition of base class Transaction. The BalanceInquiry constructor (declared in line 11 of Fig. G.17 and defined in lines 8–13 of Fig. G.18) takes arguments corresponding to the Transaction data members and simply forwards them to Transaction's constructor, using base-class initializer syntax (line 10 of Fig. G.18). Line 12 of Fig. G.17 contains the function prototype for member function execute, which is required to indicate the intention to override the base class's pure virtual function of the same name.

Class BalanceInquiry overrides Transaction's pure virtual function execute to provide a concrete implementation (lines 16–37 of Fig. G.18) that performs the steps involved in a balance inquiry. Lines 19–20 get references to the bank database and the ATM's screen by invoking member functions inherited from base class Transaction. Lines 23–24 retrieve the available balance of the account involved by invoking member function getAvailableBalance of bankDatabase. Note that line 24 uses inherited member function getAccountNumber to get the account number of the current user, which it then passes to getAvailableBalance. Lines 27–28 retrieve the total balance of the current user's account. Lines 31–36 display the balance information on the ATM's

```
 1   // BalanceInquiry.h
 2   // BalanceInquiry class definition. Represents a balance inquiry.
 3   #ifndef BALANCE_INQUIRY_H
 4   #define BALANCE_INQUIRY_H
 5
 6   #include "Transaction.h" // Transaction class definition
 7
 8   class BalanceInquiry : public Transaction
 9   {
10   public:
11      BalanceInquiry( int, Screen &, BankDatabase & ); // constructor
12      virtual void execute(); // perform the transaction
13   }; // end class BalanceInquiry
14
15   #endif // BALANCE_INQUIRY_H
```

Fig. G.17 | BalanceInquiry class definition.

```
 1   // BalanceInquiry.cpp
 2   // Member-function definitions for class BalanceInquiry.
 3   #include "BalanceInquiry.h" // BalanceInquiry class definition
 4   #include "Screen.h" // Screen class definition
 5   #include "BankDatabase.h" // BankDatabase class definition
 6
 7   // BalanceInquiry constructor initializes base-class data members
 8   BalanceInquiry:: BalanceInquiry( int userAccountNumber, Screen &atmScreen,
 9      BankDatabase &atmBankDatabase )
10      : Transaction( userAccountNumber, atmScreen, atmBankDatabase )
11   {
12      // empty body
13   } // end BalanceInquiry constructor
14
15   // performs transaction; overrides Transaction's pure virtual function
16   void BalanceInquiry::execute()
17   {
18      // get references to bank database and screen
19      BankDatabase &bankDatabase = getBankDatabase();
20      Screen &screen = getScreen();
21
22      // get the available balance for the current user's Account
23      double availableBalance =
24         bankDatabase.getAvailableBalance( getAccountNumber() );
25
26      // get the total balance for the current user's Account
27      double totalBalance =
28         bankDatabase.getTotalBalance( getAccountNumber() );
29
30      // display the balance information on the screen
31      screen.displayMessageLine( "\nBalance Information:" );
32      screen.displayMessage( " - Available balance: " );
33      screen.displayDollarAmount( availableBalance );
```

Fig. G.18 | BalanceInquiry class member-function definitions. (Part 1 of 2.)

```
34        screen.displayMessage( "\n - Total balance:        " );
35        screen.displayDollarAmount( totalBalance );
36        screen.displayMessageLine( "" );
37   } // end function execute
```

Fig. G.18 | BalanceInquiry class member-function definitions. (Part 2 of 2.)

screen. Recall that displayDollarAmount takes a double argument and outputs it to the
screen formatted as a dollar amount. For example, if a user's availableBalance is 700.5,
line 33 outputs $700.50. Note that line 36 inserts a blank line of output to separate the
balance information from subsequent output (i.e., the main menu repeated by class ATM
after executing the BalanceInquiry).

G.11 Class Withdrawal

Class Withdrawal (Figs. G.19–G.20) derives from Transaction and represents a withdrawal ATM transaction. Figure G.19 expands upon the header file for this class developed in Fig. 13.31. Class Withdrawal has a constructor and one member function
execute, which we discuss shortly. Recall from the class diagram of Fig. 13.29 that class
Withdrawal has one attribute, amount, which line 16 implements as an int data member.
Figure 13.28 models associations between class Withdrawal and classes Keypad and Cash-
Dispenser, for which lines 17–18 implement references keypad and cashDispenser, respectively. Line 19 is the function prototype of a private utility function that we soon
discuss.

```
1    // Withdrawal.h
2    // Withdrawal class definition. Represents a withdrawal transaction.
3    #ifndef WITHDRAWAL_H
4    #define WITHDRAWAL_H
5
6    #include "Transaction.h" // Transaction class definition
7    class Keypad; // forward declaration of class Keypad
8    class CashDispenser; // forward declaration of class CashDispenser
9
10   class Withdrawal : public Transaction
11   {
12   public:
13      Withdrawal( int, Screen &, BankDatabase &, Keypad &, CashDispenser & );
14      virtual void execute(); // perform the transaction
15   private:
16      int amount; // amount to withdraw
17      Keypad &keypad; // reference to ATM's keypad
18      CashDispenser &cashDispenser; // reference to ATM's cash dispenser
19      int displayMenuOfAmounts() const; // display the withdrawal menu
20   }; // end class Withdrawal
21
22   #endif // WITHDRAWAL_H
```

Fig. G.19 | Withdrawal class definition.

```
1    // Withdrawal.cpp
2    // Member-function definitions for class Withdrawal.
3    #include "Withdrawal.h" // Withdrawal class definition
4    #include "Screen.h" // Screen class definition
5    #include "BankDatabase.h" // BankDatabase class definition
6    #include "Keypad.h" // Keypad class definition
7    #include "CashDispenser.h" // CashDispenser class definition
8
9    // global constant that corresponds to menu option to cancel
10   const static int CANCELED = 6;
11
12   // Withdrawal constructor initialize class's data members
13   Withdrawal::Withdrawal( int userAccountNumber, Screen &atmScreen,
14      BankDatabase &atmBankDatabase, Keypad &atmKeypad,
15      CashDispenser &atmCashDispenser )
16      : Transaction( userAccountNumber, atmScreen, atmBankDatabase ),
17        keypad( atmKeypad ), cashDispenser( atmCashDispenser )
18   {
19      // empty body
20   } // end Withdrawal constructor
21
22   // perform transaction; overrides Transaction's pure virtual function
23   void Withdrawal::execute()
24   {
25      bool cashDispensed = false; // cash was not dispensed yet
26      bool transactionCanceled = false; // transaction was not canceled yet
27
28      // get references to bank database and screen
29      BankDatabase &bankDatabase = getBankDatabase();
30      Screen &screen = getScreen();
31
32      // loop until cash is dispensed or the user cancels
33      do
34      {
35         // obtain the chosen withdrawal amount from the user
36         int selection = displayMenuOfAmounts();
37
38         // check whether user chose a withdrawal amount or canceled
39         if ( selection != CANCELED )
40         {
41            amount = selection; // set amount to the selected dollar amount
42
43            // get available balance of account involved
44            double availableBalance =
45               bankDatabase.getAvailableBalance( getAccountNumber() );
46
47            // check whether the user has enough money in the account
48            if ( amount <= availableBalance )
49            {
50               // check whether the cash dispenser has enough money
51               if ( cashDispenser.isSufficientCashAvailable( amount ) )
52               {
```

Fig. G.20 | Withdrawal class member-function definitions. (Part 1 of 3.)

```
53                  // update the account involved to reflect withdrawal
54                  bankDatabase.debit( getAccountNumber(), amount );
55
56                  cashDispenser.dispenseCash( amount ); // dispense cash
57                  cashDispensed = true; // cash was dispensed
58                      '
59                  // instruct user to take cash
60                  screen.displayMessageLine(
61                      "\nPlease take your cash from the cash dispenser." );
62              } // end if
63              else // cash dispenser does not have enough cash
64                  screen.displayMessageLine(
65                      "\nInsufficient cash available in the ATM."
66                      "\n\nPlease choose a smaller amount." );
67          } // end if
68          else // not enough money available in user's account
69          {
70              screen.displayMessageLine(
71                  "\nInsufficient funds in your account."
72                  "\n\nPlease choose a smaller amount." );
73          } // end else
74      } // end if
75      else // user chose cancel menu option
76      {
77          screen.displayMessageLine( "\nCanceling transaction..." );
78          transactionCanceled = true; // user canceled the transaction
79      } // end else
80  } while ( !cashDispensed && !transactionCanceled ); // end do...while
81 } // end function execute
82
83 // display a menu of withdrawal amounts and the option to cancel;
84 // return the chosen amount or 0 if the user chooses to cancel
85 int Withdrawal::displayMenuOfAmounts() const
86 {
87     int userChoice = 0; // local variable to store return value
88
89     Screen &screen = getScreen(); // get screen reference
90
91     // array of amounts to correspond to menu numbers
92     int amounts[] = { 0, 20, 40, 60, 100, 200 };
93
94     // loop while no valid choice has been made
95     while ( userChoice == 0 )
96     {
97         // display the menu
98         screen.displayMessageLine( "\nWithdrawal options:" );
99         screen.displayMessageLine( "1 - $20" );
100        screen.displayMessageLine( "2 - $40" );
101        screen.displayMessageLine( "3 - $60" );
102        screen.displayMessageLine( "4 - $100" );
103        screen.displayMessageLine( "5 - $200" );
104        screen.displayMessageLine( "6 - Cancel transaction" );
105        screen.displayMessage( "\nChoose a withdrawal option (1-6): " );
```

Fig. G.20 | Withdrawal class member-function definitions. (Part 2 of 3.)

```
106
107        int input = keypad.getInput(); // get user input through keypad
108
109        // determine how to proceed based on the input value
110        switch ( input )
111        {
112           case 1: // if the user chose a withdrawal amount
113           case 2: // (i.e., chose option 1, 2, 3, 4 or 5), return the
114           case 3: // corresponding amount from amounts array
115           case 4:
116           case 5:
117              userChoice = amounts[ input ]; // save user's choice
118              break;
119           case CANCELED: // the user chose to cancel
120              userChoice = CANCELED; // save user's choice
121              break;
122           default: // the user did not enter a value from 1-6
123              screen.displayMessageLine(
124                 "\nIvalid selection. Try again." );
125        } // end switch
126     } // end while
127
128     return userChoice; // return withdrawal amount or CANCELED
129  } // end function displayMenuOfAmounts
```

Fig. G.20 | Withdrawal class member-function definitions. (Part 3 of 3.)

Withdrawal *Class Member-Function Definitions*

Figure G.20 contains the member-function definitions for class Withdrawal. Line 3 #includes the class's definition, and lines 4–7 #include the definitions of the other classes used in Withdrawal's member functions. Line 11 declares a global constant corresponding to the cancel option on the withdrawal menu. We'll soon discuss how the class uses this constant.

Class Withdrawal's constructor (defined in lines 13–20 of Fig. G.20) has five parameters. It uses a base-class initializer in line 16 to pass parameters userAccountNumber, atm-Screen and atmBankDatabase to base class Transaction's constructor to set the data members that Withdrawal inherits from Transaction. The constructor also takes references atmKeypad and atmCashDispenser as parameters and assigns them to reference data members keypad and cashDispenser using member initializers (line 17).

Class Withdrawal overrides Transaction's pure virtual function execute with a concrete implementation (lines 23–81) that performs the steps involved in a withdrawal. Line 25 declares and initializes a local bool variable cashDispensed. This variable indicates whether cash has been dispensed (i.e., whether the transaction has completed successfully) and is initially false. Line 26 declares and initializes to false a bool variable transactionCanceled that indicates whether the transaction has been canceled by the user. Lines 29–30 get references to the bank database and the ATM's screen by invoking member functions inherited from base class Transaction.

Lines 33–80 contain a do...while statement that executes its body until cash is dispensed (i.e., until cashDispensed becomes true) or until the user chooses to cancel (i.e., until transactionCanceled becomes true). This loop continuously returns the user to the start of the transaction if an error occurs (i.e., the requested withdrawal amount is greater than the user's available balance or greater than the amount of cash in the cash dispenser). Line 36 displays a menu of withdrawal amounts and obtains a user selection by calling private utility function displayMenuOfAmounts (defined in lines 85–129). This function displays the menu of amounts and returns either an int withdrawal amount or the int constant CANCELED to indicate that the user has chosen to cancel the transaction.

Member function displayMenuOfAmounts (lines 85–129) first declares local variable userChoice (initially 0) to store the value that the member function will return (line 87). Line 89 gets a reference to the screen by calling member function getScreen inherited from base class Transaction. Line 92 declares an integer array of withdrawal amounts that correspond to the amounts displayed in the withdrawal menu. We ignore the first element in the array (index 0) because the menu has no option 0. The while statement in lines 95–126 repeats until userChoice takes on a value other than 0. We'll see shortly that this occurs when the user makes a valid selection from the menu. Lines 98–105 display the withdrawal menu on the screen and prompt the user to enter a choice. Line 107 obtains integer input through the keypad. The switch statement in lines 110–125 determines how to proceed based on the user's input. If the user selects a number between 1 and 5, line 117 sets userChoice to the value of the element in amounts at index input. For example, if the user enters 3 to withdraw $60, line 117 sets userChoice to the value of amounts[3] (i.e., 60). Line 118 terminates the switch. Variable userChoice no longer equals 0, so the while in lines 95–126 terminates and line 128 returns userChoice. If the user selects the cancel menu option, lines 120–121 execute, setting userChoice to CANCELED and causing the member function to return this value. If the user does not enter a valid menu selection, lines 123–124 display an error message and the user is returned to the withdrawal menu.

The if statement in line 39 in member function execute determines whether the user has selected a withdrawal amount or chosen to cancel. If the user cancels, lines 77–78 execute to display an appropriate message to the user and set transactionCanceled to true. This causes the loop-continuation test in line 80 to fail and control to return to the calling member function (i.e., ATM member function performTransactions). If the user has chosen a withdrawal amount, line 41 assigns local variable selection to data member amount. Lines 44–45 retrieve the available balance of the current user's Account and store it in a local double variable availableBalance. Next, the if statement in line 48 determines whether the selected amount is less than or equal to the user's available balance. If it is not, lines 70–72 display an appropriate error message. Control then continues to the end of the do...while, and the loop repeats because both cashDispensed and transactionCanceled are still false. If the user's balance is high enough, the if statement in line 51 determines whether the cash dispenser has enough money to satisfy the withdrawal request by invoking the cashDispenser's isSufficientCashAvailable member function. If this member function returns false, lines 64–66 display an appropriate error message and the do...while repeats. If sufficient cash is available, then the requirements for the withdrawal are satisfied, and line 54 debits amount from the user's account in the database. Lines 56–57 then instruct the cash dispenser to dispense the cash to the user and set cashDispensed to true. Finally, lines 60–61 display a message to the user that cash has been dispensed. Because cashDispensed is now true, control continues after the do...while. No additional statements appear below the loop, so the member function returns control to class ATM.

In the function calls in lines 64–66 and lines 70–72, we divide the argument to Screen member function displayMessageLine into two string literals, each placed on a separate line in the program. We do so because each argument is too long to fit on a single line. C++ concatenates (i.e., combines) string literals adjacent to each other, even if they are on separate lines. For example, if you write "Happy " "Birthday" in a program, C++ will view these two adjacent string literals as the single string literal "Happy Birthday". As a result, when lines 64–66 execute, displayMessageLine receives a single string as a parameter, even though the argument in the function call appears as two string literals.

G.12 Class Deposit

Class Deposit (Figs. G.21–G.22) derives from Transaction and represents a deposit ATM transaction. Figure G.21 contains the Deposit class definition. Like derived classes BalanceInquiry and Withdrawal, Deposit declares a constructor (line 13) and member function execute (line 14)—we discuss these momentarily. Recall from the class diagram of Fig. 13.29 that class Deposit has one attribute amount, which line 16 implements as an int data member. Lines 17–18 create reference data members keypad and depositSlot that implement the associations between class Deposit and classes Keypad and DepositSlot modeled in Fig. 13.28. Line 19 contains the function prototype for a private utility function promptForDepositAmount that we'll discuss shortly.

***Deposit* Class Member-Function Definitions**
Figure G.22 presents the Deposit class implementation. Line 3 #includes the Deposit class definition, and lines 4–7 #include the class definitions of the other classes used in Deposit's member functions. Line 9 declares a constant CANCELED that corresponds to the value a user enters to cancel a deposit. We'll soon discuss how the class uses this constant.

```
1   // Deposit.h
2   // Deposit class definition. Represents a deposit transaction.
3   #ifndef DEPOSIT_H
4   #define DEPOSIT_H
5
6   #include "Transaction.h" // Transaction class definition
7   class Keypad; // forward declaration of class Keypad
8   class DepositSlot; // forward declaration of class DepositSlot
9
10  class Deposit : public Transaction
11  {
12  public:
13     Deposit( int, Screen &, BankDatabase &, Keypad &, DepositSlot & );
14     virtual void execute(); // perform the transaction
15  private:
16     double amount; // amount to deposit
17     Keypad &keypad; // reference to ATM's keypad
18     DepositSlot &depositSlot; // reference to ATM's deposit slot
19     double promptForDepositAmount() const; // get deposit amount from user
20  }; // end class Deposit
21
22  #endif // DEPOSIT_H
```

Fig. G.21 | Deposit class definition.

```
1    // Deposit.cpp
2    // Member-function definitions for class Deposit.
3    #include "Deposit.h" // Deposit class definition
4    #include "Screen.h" // Screen class definition
5    #include "BankDatabase.h" // BankDatabase class definition
6    #include "Keypad.h" // Keypad class definition
7    #include "DepositSlot.h" // DepositSlot class definition
8
9    const static int CANCELED = 0; // constant representing cancel option
10
11   // Deposit constructor initializes class's data members
12   Deposit::Deposit( int userAccountNumber, Screen &atmScreen,
13      BankDatabase &atmBankDatabase, Keypad &atmKeypad,
14      DepositSlot &atmDepositSlot )
15      : Transaction( userAccountNumber, atmScreen, atmBankDatabase ),
16        keypad( atmKeypad ), depositSlot( atmDepositSlot )
17   {
18      // empty body
19   } // end Deposit constructor
20
21   // performs transaction; overrides Transaction's pure virtual function
22   void Deposit::execute()
23   {
24      BankDatabase &bankDatabase = getBankDatabase(); // get reference
25      Screen &screen = getScreen(); // get reference
26
27      amount = promptForDepositAmount(); // get deposit amount from user
28
29      // check whether user entered a deposit amount or canceled
30      if ( amount != CANCELED )
31      {
32         // request deposit envelope containing specified amount
33         screen.displayMessage(
34            "\nPlease insert a deposit envelope containing " );
35         screen.displayDollarAmount( amount );
36         screen.displayMessageLine( " in the deposit slot." );
37
38         // receive deposit envelope
39         bool envelopeReceived = depositSlot.isEnvelopeReceived();
40
41         // check whether deposit envelope was received
42         if ( envelopeReceived )
43         {
44            screen.displayMessageLine( "\nYour envelope has been received."
45               "\nNOTE: The money deposited will not be available until we"
46               "\nverify the amount of any enclosed cash, and any enclosed "
47               "checks clear." );
48
49            // credit account to reflect the deposit
50            bankDatabase.credit( getAccountNumber(), amount );
51         } // end if
52         else // deposit envelope not received
53         {
```

Fig. G.22 | Deposit class member-function definitions. (Part 1 of 2.)

```
54              screen.displayMessageLine( "\nYou did not insert an "
55                 "envelope, so the ATM has canceled your transaction." );
56          } // end else
57       } // end if
58       else // user canceled instead of entering amount
59       {
60          screen.displayMessageLine( "\nCanceling transaction..." );
61       } // end else
62    } // end function execute
63
64    // prompt user to enter a deposit amount in cents
65    double Deposit::promptForDepositAmount() const
66    {
67       Screen &screen = getScreen(); // get reference to screen
68
69       // display the prompt and receive input
70       screen.displayMessage( "\nPlease enter a deposit amount in "
71          "CENTS (or 0 to cancel): " );
72       int input = keypad.getInput(); // receive input of deposit amount
73
74       // check whether the user canceled or entered a valid amount
75       if ( input == CANCELED )
76          return CANCELED;
77       else
78       {
79          return static_cast< double >( input ) / 100; // return dollar amount
80       } // end else
81    } // end function promptForDepositAmount
```

Fig. G.22 | Deposit class member-function definitions. (Part 2 of 2.)

Like class Withdrawal, class Deposit contains a constructor (lines 12–19) that passes three parameters to base class Transaction's constructor using a base-class initializer (line 15). The constructor also has parameters atmKeypad and atmDepositSlot, which it assigns to its corresponding data members (line 16).

Member function execute (lines 22–62) overrides pure virtual function execute in base class Transaction with a concrete implementation that performs the steps required in a deposit transaction. Lines 24–25 get references to the database and the screen. Line 27 prompts the user to enter a deposit amount by invoking private utility function promptForDepositAmount (defined in lines 65–81) and sets data member amount to the value returned. Member function promptForDepositAmount asks the user to enter a deposit amount as an integer number of cents (because the ATM's keypad does not contain a decimal point; this is consistent with many real ATMs) and returns the double value representing the dollar amount to be deposited.

Line 67 in member function promptForDepositAmount gets a reference to the ATM's screen. Lines 70–71 display a message on the screen asking the user to input a deposit amount as a number of cents or "0" to cancel the transaction. Line 72 receives the user's input from the keypad. The if statement in lines 75–80 determines whether the user has entered a real deposit amount or chosen to cancel. If the user chooses to cancel, line 76 returns the constant CANCELED. Otherwise, line 79 returns the deposit amount after converting from the number of cents to a dollar amount by casting input to a double, then dividing by 100. For example, if the user enters 125 as the number of cents, line 79 returns 125.0 divided by 100, or 1.25—125 cents is $1.25.

The if statement in lines 30–61 in member function execute determines whether the user has chosen to cancel the transaction instead of entering a deposit amount. If the user cancels, line 60 displays an appropriate message, and the member function returns. If the user enters a deposit amount, lines 33–36 instruct the user to insert a deposit envelope with the correct amount. Recall that Screen member function displayDollarAmount outputs a double formatted as a dollar amount.

Line 39 sets a local bool variable to the value returned by depositSlot's isEnvelopeReceived member function, indicating whether a deposit envelope has been received. Recall that we coded isEnvelopeReceived (lines 7–10 of Fig. G.10) to always return true, because we are simulating the functionality of the deposit slot and assume that the user always inserts an envelope. However, we code member function execute of class Deposit to test for the possibility that the user does not insert an envelope—good software engineering demands that programs account for all possible return values. Thus, class Deposit is prepared for future versions of isEnvelopeReceived that could return false. Lines 44–50 execute if the deposit slot receives an envelope. Lines 44–47 display an appropriate message to the user. Line 50 then credits the deposit amount to the user's account in the database. Lines 54–55 will execute if the deposit slot does not receive a deposit envelope. In this case, we display a message to the user stating that the ATM has canceled the transaction. The member function then returns without modifying the user's account.

G.13 Test Program ATMCaseStudy.cpp

ATMCaseStudy.cpp (Fig. G.23) is a simple C++ program that allows us to start, or "turn on," the ATM and test the implementation of our ATM system model. The program's main function (lines 6–11) does nothing more than instantiate a new ATM object named atm (line 8) and invoke its run member function (line 9) to start the ATM.

```
1   // ATMCaseStudy.cpp
2   // Driver program for the ATM case study.
3   #include "ATM.h" // ATM class definition
4
5   // main function creates and runs the ATM
6   int main()
7   {
8      ATM atm; // create an ATM object
9      atm.run(); // tell the ATM to start
10     return 0;
11  } // end main
```

Fig. G.23 | ATMCaseStudy.cpp starts the ATM system.

G.14 Wrap-Up

Congratulations on completing the entire Software Engineering ATM Case Study! We hope you found this experience to be valuable and that it reinforced many of the concepts that you learned in Chapters 1–13. We would sincerely appreciate your comments, criticisms and suggestions. You can reach us at deitel@deitel.com. We'll respond promptly.

UML 2: Additional Diagram Types

H.1 Introduction

If you have read the optional Software Engineering Case Study sections in Chapters 2–7, 9 and 13, you should now have a comfortable grasp of the UML diagram types that we use to model our ATM system. The case study is intended for use in first- or second-semester courses, so we limit our discussion to a concise subset of the UML. The UML 2 provides a total of 13 diagram types. The end of Section 2.8 summarizes the six diagram types that we use in the case study. This appendix lists and briefly defines the seven remaining diagram types.

H.2 Additional Diagram Types

The following are the seven diagram types that we have chosen not to use in our Software Engineering Case Study.

- Object diagrams model a "snapshot" of the system by modeling a system's objects and their relationships at a specific point in time. Each object represents an instance of a class from a class diagram, and several objects may be created from one class. For our ATM system, an object diagram could show several distinct Account objects side by side, illustrating that they are all part of the bank's account database.

- Component diagrams model the artifacts and components—resources (which include source files)—that make up the system.

- Deployment diagrams model the system's runtime requirements (such as the computer or computers on which the system will reside), memory requirements, or other devices the system requires during execution.

- Package diagrams model the hierarchical structure of packages (which are groups of classes) in the system at compile time and the relationships that exist between the packages.

- Composite structure diagrams model the internal structure of a complex object at runtime. New in UML 2, they allow system designers to hierarchically decompose a complex object into smaller parts. Composite structure diagrams are beyond the scope of our case study. They are more appropriate for larger industrial applications, which exhibit complex groupings of objects at execution time.

- Interaction overview diagrams, new in UML 2, provide a summary of control flow in the system by combining elements of several types of behavioral diagrams (e.g., activity diagrams, sequence diagrams).

- Timing diagrams, also new in UML 2, model the timing constraints imposed on stage changes and interactions between objects in a system.

To learn more about these diagrams and advanced UML topics, please visit www.uml.org and the web resources listed at the ends of Section 1.21 and Section 2.8.

Using the Visual Studio Debugger

OBJECTIVES

In this appendix you'll learn:

- To set breakpoints to debug programs.
- To run a program through the debugger.
- To set, disable and remove a breakpoint.
- To use the **Continue** command to continue execution.
- To use the **Locals** window to view and modify the values of variables.
- To use the **Watch** window to evaluate expressions.
- To use the **Step Into**, **Step Out** and **Step Over** commands to control execution.
- To use the **Autos** window to view variables that are used in the surrounding statements.

I.1 Introduction

In Chapter 2, you learned that there are two types of errors—compilation errors and logic errors—and you learned how to eliminate compilation errors from your code. Logic errors (also called bugs) do not prevent a program from compiling successfully, but can cause the program to produce erroneous results when it runs. Most C++ compiler vendors provide software called a debugger, which allows you to monitor the execution of your programs to locate and remove logic errors. The debugger will be one of your most important program development tools. This appendix demonstrates key features of the Visual Studio debugger. Appendix J discusses the features and capabilities of the GNU C++ debugger. Our C++ Resource Center (www.deitel.com/cplusplus/) provides links to tutorials that can help students and instructors familiarize themselves with the debuggers provided with various other development tools.

I.2 Breakpoints and the Continue Command

We begin our study of the debugger by investigating breakpoints, which are markers that can be set at any executable line of code. When program execution reaches a breakpoint, execution pauses, allowing you to examine the values of variables to help determine whether a logic error exists. For example, you can examine the value of a variable that stores the result of a calculation to determine whether the calculation was performed correctly. Note that attempting to set a breakpoint at a line of code that is not executable (such as a comment) will actually set the breakpoint at the next executable line of code in that function.

To illustrate the features of the debugger, we use the program listed in Fig. I.3, which creates and manipulates an object of class Account (Figs. I.1–I.2). Execution begins in main (lines 12–30 of Fig. I.3). Line 14 creates an Account object with an initial balance of $50.00. Account's constructor (lines 10–22 of Fig. I.2) accepts one argument, which specifies the Account's initial balance. Line 17 of Fig. I.3 outputs the initial account balance using Account member function getBalance. Line 19 declares a local variable withdrawalAmount, which stores a withdrawal amount read from the user. Line 21 prompts the user for the withdrawal amount, and line 22 inputs the amount into withdrawalAmount. Line 25 subtracts the withdrawal from the Account's balance using its debit member function. Finally, line 28 displays the new balance.

```
1   // Fig. I.1: Account.h
2   // Definition of Account class.
3
4   class Account
5   {
6   public:
7      Account( int ); // constructor initializes balance
8      void credit( int ); // add an amount to the account balance
9      void debit( int ); // subtract an amount from the account balance
10      int getBalance(); // return the account balance
11   private:
12      int balance; // data member that stores the balance
13   }; // end class Account
```

Fig. I.1 | Header file for the **Account** class.

```
1   // Fig. I.2: Account.cpp
2   // Member-function definitions for class Account.
3   #include <iostream>
4   using std::cout;
5   using std::endl;
6
7   #include "Account.h" // include definition of class Account
8
9   // Account constructor initializes data member balance
10   Account::Account( int initialBalance )
11   {
12      balance = 0; // assume that the balance begins at 0
13
14      // if initialBalance is greater than 0, set this value as the
15      // balance of the account; otherwise, balance remains 0
16      if ( initialBalance > 0 )
17         balance = initialBalance;
18
19      // if initialBalance is negative, print error message
20      if ( initialBalance < 0 )
21         cout << "Error: Initial balance cannot be negative.\n" << endl;
22   } // end Account constructor
23
24   // credit (add) an amount to the account balance
25   void Account::credit( int amount )
26   {
27      balance = balance + amount; // add amount to balance
28   } // end function credit
29
30   // debit (subtract) an amount from the account balance
31   void Account::debit( int amount )
32   {
33      if ( amount <= balance ) // debit amount does not exceed balance
34         balance = balance - amount;
35
```

Fig. I.2 | Definition for the **Account** class. (Part 1 of 2.)

```
36      else // debit amount exceeds balance
37          cout << "Debit amount exceeded account balance.\n" << endl;
38   } // end function debit
39
40   // return the account balance
41   int Account::getBalance()
42   {
43      return balance; // gives the value of balance to the calling function
44   } // end function getBalance
```

Fig. I.2 | Definition for the Account class. (Part 2 of 2.)

```
1    // Fig. I.3: figI_03.cpp
2    // Create and manipulate Account objects.
3    #include <iostream>
4    using std::cin;
5    using std::cout;
6    using std::endl;
7
8    // include definition of class Account from Account.h
9    #include "Account.h"
10
11   // function main begins program execution
12   int main()
13   {
14      Account account1( 50 ); // create Account object
15
16      // display initial balance of each object
17      cout << "account1 balance: $" << account1.getBalance() << endl;
18
19      int withdrawalAmount; // stores withdrawal amount read from user
20
21      cout << "\nEnter withdrawal amount for account1: "; // prompt
22      cin >> withdrawalAmount; // obtain user input
23      cout << "\nattempting to subtract " << withdrawalAmount
24          << " from account1 balance\n\n";
25      account1.debit( withdrawalAmount ); // try to subtract from account1
26
27      // display balances
28      cout << "account1 balance: $" << account1.getBalance() << endl;
29      return 0; // indicate successful termination
30   } // end main
```

Fig. I.3 | Test class for debugging.

In the following steps, you'll use breakpoints and various debugger commands to examine the value of the variable withdrawalAmount declared in Fig. I.3.

1. *Enabling the debugger.* The debugger is normally enabled by default. If it is not enabled, you have to change the settings of the *Solution Configurations* combo box (Fig. I.4) in the toolbar. To do this, click the combo box's down arrow, then select **Debug**.

Fig. I.4 | Enabling the debugger.

2. *Inserting breakpoints in Visual Studio 2005.* To insert a breakpoint in Visual Studio 2005, click inside the margin indicator bar (the gray margin at the left of the code window in Fig. I.5) next to the line of code at which you wish to break or right click that line of code and select **Breakpoint > Insert Breakpoint**. You can set as many breakpoints as necessary. Set breakpoints at lines 21 and 25 of your code. A red circle appears in the margin indicator bar where you clicked, indicating that a breakpoint has been set (Fig. I.5). When the program runs, the debugger pauses execution at any line that contains a breakpoint. The program is said to be in break mode when the debugger pauses the program. Breakpoints can be set before running a program, in break mode and while a program is running.

3. *Starting to debug.* After setting breakpoints in the code editor, select **Build > Build Solution** to compile the program, then select **Debug > Start Debugging** to begin the debugging process. [*Note:* If you do not compile the program first, it will still be compiled when you select **Debug > Start Debugging**.] When you debug a console application, a **Command Prompt** window appears (Fig. I.6) in which you can specify program input and view program output. The debugger enters break mode when execution reaches the breakpoint at line 21.

Fig. I.5 | Setting two breakpoints.

Fig. I.6 | **Inventory** program running.

4. ***Examining program execution.*** Upon entering break mode at the first breakpoint (line 21), the IDE becomes the active window (Fig. I.7). The yellow arrow to the left of line 21 indicates that this line contains the next statement to execute.

5. ***Using the Continue command to resume execution.*** To resume execution, select **Debug > Continue**. The Continue command resumes program execution until the next breakpoint or the end of main is encountered, whichever comes first. The program continues executing and pauses for input at line 22. Enter 13 as the withdrawal amount. The program executes until it stops at the next breakpoint (line 25). Notice that when you place your mouse pointer over the variable name withdrawalAmount, the value stored in the variable is displayed in a *Quick Info box* (Fig. I.8). As you'll see, this can help you spot logic errors in your programs.

6. ***Setting a breakpoint at the return statement.*** Set a breakpoint at line 29 in the source code by clicking in the margin indicator bar to the left of line 29. This will prevent the program from closing immediately after displaying its result. When there are no more breakpoints at which to suspend execution, the program will execute to completion and the **Command Prompt** window will close. If you do not set this breakpoint, you won't be able to view the program's output before the console window closes.

7. ***Continuing program execution.*** Use the **Debug > Continue** command to execute the code up to the next breakpoint. The program displays the result of its calculation (Fig. I.9).

Yellow arrow that
indicates the next ——
statement to execute

Fig. I.7 | Program execution suspended at the first breakpoint.

Quick Info box

Fig. I.8 | *Quick Info* box showing the value of a variable.

Fig. I.9 | Program output.

8. ***Disabling a breakpoint.*** To disable a breakpoint, right click a line of code on which a breakpoint has been set (or the breakpoint itself) and select **Disable Breakpoint**. The disabled breakpoint is indicated by a hollow circle (Fig. I.10). Disabling rather than removing a breakpoint allows you to reenable the breakpoint later by clicking the hollow circle or by right-clicking the hollow circle and selecting **Enable Breakpoint**.

9. ***Removing a breakpoint.*** To remove a breakpoint that you no longer need, right click a line of code on which a breakpoint has been set and select **Breakpoint > Delete Breakpoint**. You also can remove a breakpoint by clicking the breakpoint in the margin indicator bar.

10. ***Finishing program execution.*** Select **Debug > Continue** to execute the program to completion.

In this section, you learned how to enable the debugger and set breakpoints so that you can examine the results of code while a program is running. You also learned how to continue execution after a program suspends execution at a breakpoint and how to disable and remove breakpoints.

Fig. I.10 | Disabled breakpoint.

I.3 Locals and Watch Windows

In the preceding section, you learned that the *Quick Info* feature allows you to examine a variable's value. In this section, you'll learn to use the Locals window to assign new values to variables while your program is running. You'll also use the Watch window to examine the value of more complex expressions.

1. ***Inserting breakpoints.*** Clear the existing breakpoints. Then, set a breakpoint at line 25 in the source code by clicking in the margin indicator bar to the left of

line 25 (Fig. I.11). Set another breakpoint at line 28 by clicking in the margin indicator bar to the left of line 28.

2. *Starting debugging.* Select **Debug > Start**. Type 13 at the **Enter withdrawal amount for account1:** prompt and press *Enter* so that your program reads the value you just entered. The program executes until the breakpoint at line 25.

3. *Suspending program execution.* The debugger enters break mode at line 25 (Fig. I.12). At this point, line 22 has input the withdrawalAmount that you entered (13), lines 23–24 have output that the program will attempt to withdraw money and line 25 is the next statement that will execute.

4. *Examining data.* In break mode, you can explore the values of your local variables using the debugger's **Locals** window. To view the **Locals** window, select **Debug > Windows > Locals**. Figure I.13 shows the values for main's local variables account1 and withdrawalAmount (13).

Fig. I.11 | Setting breakpoints at lines 25 and 28.

Fig. I.12 | Program execution suspended when debugger reaches the breakpoint at line 25.

Name	Value	Type
account1	{balance=50 }	Account
withdrawalAmount	13	int

Fig. I.13 | Examining variable withdrawalAmount.

5. *Evaluating arithmetic and boolean expressions.* You can evaluate arithmetic and boolean expressions using the **Watch** window. You can display up to four **Watch** windows. Select **Debug > Windows > Watch > Watch 1**. In the first row of the **Name** column, type (withdrawalAmount + 3) * 5, then press *Enter*. The value of this expression (80 in this case) is displayed in the **Value** column (Fig. I.14). In the next row of the **Name** column, type withdrawalAmount == 3, then press *Enter*. This expression determines whether the value of withdrawalAmount is 3. Expressions containing the == operator (or any other relational or equality operator) are treated as bool expressions. The value of the expression in this case is false (Fig. I.14), because withdrawalAmount currently contains 13, not 3.

6. *Resuming execution.* Select **Debug > Continue** to resume execution. Line 25 debits the account by the withdrawal amount, and the debugger reenters break mode at line 28. Select **Debug > Windows > Locals** or click the **Locals** tab at the bottom of Visual Studio to redisplay the **Locals** window. The updated balance value in account1 is now displayed in red (Fig. I.15) to indicate that it has been modified since the last breakpoint. Click the plus box to the left of account1 in the **Name** column of the **Locals** window. This allows you to view each of account1's data member values individually—this is particularly useful for objects that have several data members.

7. *Modifying values.* Based on the value input by the user (13), the account balance output by the program should be $37. However, you can use the **Locals** window to change the values of variables during the program's execution. This can be valuable for experimenting with different values and for locating logic errors. In the **Locals** window, click the **Value** field in the balance row to select the value 37. Type 33, then press *Enter*. The debugger changes the value of balance and displays its new value in red (Fig. I.16).

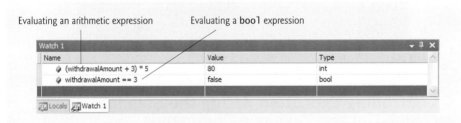

Evaluating an arithmetic expression   Evaluating a bool expression

Name	Value	Type
(withdrawalAmount + 3) * 5	80	int
withdrawalAmount == 3	false	bool

Fig. I.14 | Examining the values of expressions.

Name	Value	Type
account1	{balance=37}	Account
withdrawalAmount	13	int

Value of account1's balance data member displayed in red

Fig. I.15 | Displaying the value of local variables.

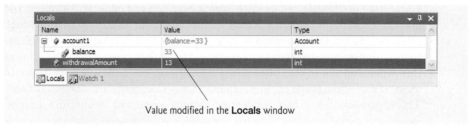

Fig. I.16 | Modifying the value of a variable.

8. *Setting a breakpoint at the **return** statement.* Set a breakpoint at line 29 in the source code to prevent the program from closing immediately after displaying its result. If you do not set this breakpoint, you won't be able to view the program's output before the console window closes.

9. *Viewing the program result.* Select **Debug > Continue** to continue program execution. Function main executes until the return statement in line 29 and displays the result. Notice that the result is $33 (Fig. I.17). This shows that *Step 7* changed the value of balance from the calculated value (37) to 33.

10. *Stopping the debugging session.* Select **Debug > Stop Debugging**. This will close the **Command Prompt** window. Remove all remaining breakpoints.

In this section, you learned how to use the debugger's **Watch** and **Locals** windows to evaluate arithmetic and boolean expressions. You also learned how to modify the value of a variable during your program's execution.

```
c:\Account\debug\Account.exe
account1 balance: $50

Enter withdrawal amount for account1: 13

attempting to subtract 13 from account1 balance

account1 balance: $33
```

Fig. I.17 | Output displayed after modifying the account1 variable.

I.4 Controlling Execution Using the Step Into, Step Over, Step Out and Continue Commands

Sometimes executing a program line by line can help you verify that a function's code executes correctly, and can help you find and fix logic errors. The commands you learn in this section allow you to execute a function line by line, execute all the statements of a function at once or execute only the remaining statements of a function (if you have already executed some statements within the function).

1. *Setting a breakpoint.* Set a breakpoint at line 25 by clicking in the margin indicator bar to the left of the line.

2. *Starting the debugger.* Select **Debug > Start**. Enter the value 13 at the **Enter withdrawal amount for account1:** prompt. Execution will halt when the program reaches the breakpoint at line 25.

3. *Using the Step Into command.* The Step Into command executes the next statement in the program (the one that the yellow arrow points to in line 25 of Fig. I.18), then immediately halts. If that statement is a function call (as is the case here), control transfers into the called function. This enables you to execute each statement inside the function individually to confirm the function's execution. Select **Debug > Step Into** to enter the debit function. Then, Select **Debug > Step Into** again so the yellow arrow is positioned at line 33, as shown in Fig. I.19.

Fig. I.18 | Using the **Step Into** command to execute a statement.

Fig. I.19 | Stepping into the debit function.

4. *Using the Step Over command.* Select **Debug > Step Over** to execute the current statement (line 33 in Fig. I.19) and transfer control to line 34 (Fig. I.20). The Step Over command behaves like the **Step Into** command when the next statement to execute does not contain a function call. You'll see how the **Step Over** command differs from the **Step Into** command in *Step 10.*

Control transfers to the next statement

Fig. I.20 | Stepping over a statement in the debit function.

5. *Using the* Step Out *command.* Select **Debug > Step Out** to execute the remaining statements in the function and return control to the next executable statement (line 28 in Fig. I.3). Often, in lengthy functions, you'll want to look at a few key lines of code, then continue debugging the caller's code. The **Step Out** command enables you to continue program execution in the caller without having to step through the entire called function line by line.

6. *Setting a breakpoint.* Set a breakpoint at the `return` statement of `main` at line 29 of Fig. I.3. You'll make use of this breakpoint in the next step.

7. *Using the* Continue *command.* Select **Debug > Continue** to execute until the next breakpoint is reached at line 29. Using the **Continue** command is useful when you wish to execute all the code up to the next breakpoint.

8. *Stopping the debugger.* Select **Debug > Stop Debugging** to end the debugging session. This will close the **Command Prompt** window.

9. *Starting the debugger.* Before we can demonstrate the next debugger feature, you must start the debugger again. Start it, as you did in *Step 2*, and enter 13 in response to the prompt. The debugger enters break mode at line 25.

10. *Using the* Step Over *command.* Select **Debug > Step Over** (Fig. I.21) Recall that this command behaves like the **Step Into** command when the next statement to execute does not contain a function call. If the next statement to execute contains a function call, the called function executes in its entirety (without pausing execution at any statement inside the function), and the yellow arrow advances to the next executable line (after the function call) in the current function. In this case, the debugger executes line 25, located in `main` (Fig. I.3). Line 25 calls the `debit` function. The debugger then pauses execution at line 28, the next executable line in the current function, `main`.

11. *Stopping the debugger.* Select **Debug > Stop Debugging**. This will close the **Command Prompt** window. Remove all remaining breakpoints.

In this section, you learned how to use the debugger's **Step Into** command to debug functions called during your program's execution. You saw how the **Step Over** command can be used to step over a function call. You used the **Step Out** command to continue execution until the end of the current function. You also learned that the **Continue** command continues execution until another breakpoint is found or the program exits.

The `debit` function call executes to completion when the **Step Over** command is selected

Fig. I.21 | Using the debugger's **Step Over** command.

I.5 Autos Window

The **Autos window** displays the variables used in the previous statement executed (including the return value of a function, if there is one) and the variables in the next statement to execute.

1. *Setting breakpoints.* Set breakpoints at lines 14 and 22 in `main` by clicking in the margin indicator bar.

2. *Using the* **Autos** *window.* Start the debugger by selecting **Debug > Start**. When the debugger enters break mode at line 14, open the **Autos** window (Fig. I.22) by selecting **Debug > Windows > Autos**. Since we are just beginning the program's execution, the **Autos** window lists only the variables in the next statement that will execute—in this case, the `account1` object, its value and its type. Viewing the values stored in an object lets you verify that your program is manipulating these variables correctly. Notice that `account1` contains a large negative value. This value, which may be different each time the program executes, is `account1`'s uninitialized value. This unpredictable (and often undesirable) value demonstrates why it is important to initialize all C++ variables before they are used.

3. *Using the* **Step Over** *command.* Select **Debug > Step Over** to execute line 14. The **Autos** window updates the value of `account1`'s `balance` data member (Fig. I.23) after it is initialized. The value of `balance` is displayed in red to indicate that it just changed.

4. *Continuing execution.* Select **Debug > Continue** to execute the program until the second breakpoint at line 22. The **Autos** window displays uninitialized local variable `withdrawalAmount` (Fig. I.24), which has a large negative value.

Fig. I.22 | **Autos** window displaying the state of `account1` object.

Fig. I.23 | **Autos** window displaying the state of `account1` object after initialization.

Fig. I.24 | **Autos** window displaying local variable `withdrawalAmount`.

5. *Entering data.* Select **Debug > Step Over** to execute line 22. At the program's input prompt, enter a value for the withdrawal amount. The **Autos** window updates the value of local variable withdrawalAmount with the value you entered (Fig. I.23).

6. *Stopping the debugger.* Select **Debug > Stop Debugging** to end the debugging session. Remove all remaining breakpoints.

Fig. I.25 | **Autos** window displaying updated local variable withdrawalAmount.

I.6 Wrap-Up

In this appendix, you learned how to insert, disable and remove breakpoints in the Visual Studio debugger. Breakpoints allow you to pause program execution so you can examine variable values. This capability will help you locate and fix logic errors in your programs. You saw how to use the **Locals** and **Watch** windows to examine the value of an expression and how to change the value of a variable. You also learned debugger commands **Step Into**, **Step Over**, **Step Out** and **Continue** that can be used to determine whether a function is executing correctly. Finally, you learned how to use the **Autos** window to examine variables used specifically in the previous and next commands.

Summary

Section I.1 Introduction

- Most C++ compiler vendors provide software called a debugger, which allows you to monitor the execution of your programs to locate and remove logic errors.

- Breakpoints are markers that can be set at any executable line of code. When program execution reaches a breakpoint, execution pauses.

- The debugger is enabled by default. If it is not enabled, you have to change the settings of the *Solution Configurations* combo box.

Section I.2 Breakpoints and the Continue Command

- To insert a breakpoint, either click inside the margin indicator bar next to the line of code or right click that line of code and select **Breakpoint > Insert Breakpoint**. A red circle appears where you clicked, indicating that a breakpoint has been set.

- When the program runs, it suspends execution at any line that contains a breakpoint. It is then said to be in break mode.

- A yellow arrow indicates that this line contains the next statement to execute.

- When you place your mouse pointer over a variable name, the value that the variable stores is displayed in a *Quick Info* box.

- To disable a breakpoint, right click a line of code on which a breakpoint has been set and select **Breakpoint > Disable Breakpoint**. The disabled breakpoint is indicated by a hollow circle.

- To remove a breakpoint that you no longer need, right click a line of code on which a breakpoint has been set and select **Breakpoint > Delete Breakpoint**. You also can remove a breakpoint by clicking the circle in the margin indicator bar.

Section I.3 Locals and Watch Windows

- Once the program has entered break mode, you can explore the values of your variables using the debugger's **Locals** window. To view the **Locals** window, select **Debug > Windows > Locals**.

- You can evaluate arithmetic and boolean expressions using the **Watch** window.

- Updated variables are displayed in red to indicate that they have been modified since the last breakpoint.

- Clicking the plus box next to an object in the **Name** column of the **Locals** window allows you to view each of object's data member values individually.

- You can click the **Value** field of a variable to change its value in the **Locals** window.

Section I.4 Controlling Execution Using the Step Into, Step Over, Step Out and Continue Commands

- The **Step Into** command executes the next statement (the yellow highlighted line) in the program. If the next statement is to execute a function call and you select **Step Into**, control is transferred to the called function.

- The **Step Over** command behaves like the **Step Into** command when the next statement to execute does not contain a function call. If the next statement to execute contains a function call, the called function executes in its entirety, and the yellow arrow advances to the next executable line in the current function.

- The **Step Over** command executes the remaining statements in the function and returns control to the function call.

- The **Continue** command will execute any statements between the next executable statement and the next breakpoint or the end of main, whichever comes first.

Section I.5 Autos Window

- The **Autos** window allows you to view the contents of the variables used in the last statement that was executed. The **Autos** window also lists the values in the next statement to be executed.

Terminology

Autos window	margin indicator bar
break mode	*Quick Info* box
breakpoint	*Solution Configurations* combo box
bug	**Step Into** command
Continue command	**Step Out** command
debugger	**Step Over** command
disabling a breakpoint	**Watch** window
Locals window	yellow arrow in break mode

Self-Review Exercises

I.1   Fill in the blanks in each of the following statements:
   a) When the debugger suspends program execution at a breakpoint, the program is said to be in _____ mode.
   b) The _____ feature in Visual Studio 2005 allows you to look at the value of a variable by positioning the mouse over the variable name in the code.

c) You can examine the value of an expression by using the debugger's _____ window.

d) The _____ command behaves like the **Step Into** command when the next statement to execute does not contain a function call.

I.2 State whether each of the following is *true* or *false*. If *false*, explain why.

a) When program execution suspends at a breakpoint, the next statement to be executed is the statement after the breakpoint.

b) When a variable's value is changed, it becomes yellow in the **Autos** and **Locals** windows.

c) During debugging, the **Step Out** command executes the remaining statements in the current function and returns program control to the place where the function was called.

Answers to Self-Review Exercises

I.1 a) break. b) *Quick Info* box. c) **Watch**. d) **Step Over**.

I.2 a) False. When program execution suspends at a breakpoint, the next statement to be executed is the statement at the breakpoint. b) False. A variable turns red when its value is changed. c) True.

J

Using the GNU C++ Debugger

OBJECTIVES

In this appendix you'll learn:

- To use the **run** command to run a program in the debugger.
- To use the **break** command to set a breakpoint.
- To use the **continue** command to continue execution.
- To use the **print** command to evaluate expressions.
- To use the **set** command to change variable values during program execution.
- To use the **step**, **finish** and **next** commands to control execution.
- To use the **watch** command to see how a data member is modified during program execution.
- To use the **delete** command to remove a breakpoint or a watchpoint.

J.1   Introduction

In Chapter 2, you learned that there are two types of errors—compilation errors and logic errors—and you learned how to eliminate compilation errors from your code. Logic errors do not prevent a program from compiling successfully, but they can cause the program to produce erroneous results when it runs. GNU includes software called a debugger that allows you to monitor the execution of your programs so you can locate and remove logic errors.

The debugger is one of the most important program development tools. Many IDEs provide their own debuggers similar to the one included in GNU or provide a graphical user interface to GNU's debugger. This appendix demonstrates key features of GNU's debugger. Appendix I discusses the features and capabilities of the Visual Studio debugger. Our C++ Resource Center (www.deitel.com/cplusplus/) provides links to tutorials that can help students and instructors familiarize themselves with the debuggers provided with various other development tools.

J.2   Breakpoints and the `run`, `stop`, `continue` and `print` Commands

We begin our study of the debugger by investigating breakpoints, which are markers that can be set at any executable line of code. When program execution reaches a breakpoint, execution pauses, allowing you to examine the values of variables to help determine whether a logic error exists. For example, you can examine the value of a variable that stores the result of a calculation to determine whether the calculation was performed correctly. Note that attempting to set a breakpoint at a line of code that is not executable (such as a comment) will actually set the breakpoint at the next executable line of code in that function.

To illustrate the features of the debugger, we use class `Account` (Figs. J.1–J.2) and the program listed in Fig. J.3, which creates and manipulates an object of class `Account`. Execution begins in `main` (lines 12–30 of Fig. J.3). Line 14 creates an `Account` object with an initial balance of $50.00. `Account`'s constructor (lines 10–22 of Fig. J.2) accepts one argument, which specifies the `Account`'s initial `balance`. Line 17 of Fig. J.3 outputs the initial account balance using `Account` member function `getBalance`. Line 19 declares a local variable `withdrawalAmount` which stores a withdrawal amount input by the user. Line 21 prompts the user for the withdrawal amount; line 22 inputs the `withdrawalAmount`. Line 25 uses the `Account`'s `debit` member function to subtract the `withdrawalAmount` from the `Account`'s `balance`. Finally, line 28 displays the new `balance`.

```
 1   // Fig. J.1: Account.h
 2   // Definition of Account class.
 3
 4   class Account
 5   {
 6   public:
 7      Account( int ); // constructor initializes balance
 8      void credit( int ); // add an amount to the account balance
 9      void debit( int ); // subtract an amount from the account balance
10      int getBalance(); // return the account balance
11   private:
12      int balance; // data member that stores the balance
13   }; // end class Account
```

Fig. J.1 | Header file for the Account class.

```
 1   // Fig. J.2: Account.cpp
 2   // Member-function definitions for class Account.
 3   #include <iostream>
 4   using std::cout;
 5   using std::endl;
 6
 7   #include "Account.h" // include definition of class Account
 8
 9   // Account constructor initializes data member balance
10   Account::Account( int initialBalance )
11   {
12      balance = 0; // assume that the balance begins at 0
13
14      // if initialBalance is greater than 0, set this value as the
15      // balance of the Account; otherwise, balance remains 0
16      if ( initialBalance > 0 )
17         balance = initialBalance;
18
19      // if initialBalance is negative, print error message
20      if ( initialBalance < 0 )
21         cout << "Error: Initial balance cannot be negative.\n" << endl;
22   } // end Account constructor
23
24   // credit (add) an amount to the account balance
25   void Account::credit( int amount )
26   {
27      balance = balance + amount; // add amount to balance
28   } // end function credit
29
30   // debit (subtract) an amount from the account balance
31   void Account::debit( int amount )
32   {
33      if ( amount <= balance ) // debit amount does not exceed balance
34         balance = balance - amount;
35
```

Fig. J.2 | Definition for the Account class. (Part 1 of 2.)

```
36          else // debit amount exceeds balance
37              cout << "Debit amount exceeded account balance.\n" << endl;
38     } // end function debit
39
40     // return the account balance
41     int Account::getBalance()
42     {
43          return balance; // gives the value of balance to the calling function
44     } // end function getBalance
```

Fig. J.2 | Definition for the Account class. (Part 2 of 2.)

```
 1     // Fig. J.3: figJ_03.cpp
 2     // Create and manipulate Account objects.
 3     #include <iostream>
 4     using std::cin;
 5     using std::cout;
 6     using std::endl;
 7
 8     // include definition of class Account from Account.h
 9     #include "Account.h"
10
11     // function main begins program execution
12     int main()
13     {
14         Account account1( 50 ); // create Account object
15
16         // display initial balance of each object
17         cout << "account1 balance: $" << account1.getBalance() << endl;
18
19         int withdrawalAmount; // stores withdrawal amount read from user
20
21         cout << "\nEnter withdrawal amount for account1: "; // prompt
22         cin >> withdrawalAmount; // obtain user input
23         cout << "\nattempting to subtract " << withdrawalAmount
24             << " from account1 balance\n\n";
25         account1.debit( withdrawalAmount ); // try to subtract from account1
26
27         // display balances
28         cout << "account1 balance: $" << account1.getBalance() << endl;
29         return 0; // indicate successful termination
30     } // end main
```

Fig. J.3 | Test class for debugging.

In the following steps, you'll use breakpoints and various debugger commands to examine the value of the variable withdrawalAmount declared in line 19 of Fig. J.3.

1. *Compiling the program for debugging.* To use the debugger, you must compile your program with the -g option, which generates additional information that the debugger needs to help you debug your programs. To do so, type

```
g++ -g -o figJ_03 figJ_03.cpp Account.cpp
```

2. ***Starting the debugger.*** Type gdb figJ_03 (Fig. J.4). The gdb command starts the debugger and displays the (gdb) prompt at which you can enter commands.

3. ***Running a program in the debugger.*** Run the program through the debugger by typing run (Fig. J.5). If you do not set any breakpoints before running your program in the debugger, the program will run to completion.

4. ***Inserting breakpoints using the GNU debugger.*** Set a breakpoint at line 17 of FigJ_03.cpp by typing break 17. The break command inserts a breakpoint at the line number specified as its argument (i.e., 17). You can set as many breakpoints as necessary. Each breakpoint is identified by the order in which it was created. The first breakpoint is known as Breakpoint 1. Set another breakpoint at line 25 by typing break 25 (Fig. J.6). This new breakpoint is known as Breakpoint 2. When the program runs, it suspends execution at any line that contains a breakpoint and the debugger enters break mode. Breakpoints can be set even after the debugging process has begun. [*Note:* If you do not have a numbered listing for your code, you can use the list command to output your code with line numbers. For more information about the list command type help list from the gdb prompt.]

5. ***Running the program and beginning the debugging process.*** Type run to execute your program and begin the debugging process (Fig. J.7). The debugger enters

```
$ gdb FigJ_03
GNU gdb 6.3-debian
Copyright 2004 Free Software Foundation, Inc.
GDB is free software, covered by the GNU General Public License, and you are
welcome to change it and/or distribute copies of it under certain conditions.
Type "show copying" to see the conditions.
There is absolutely no warranty for GDB.  Type "show warranty" for details.
This GDB was configured as "i486-linux-gnu"...Using host libthread_db
library "/ lib/tls/i686/cmov/libthread_db.so.1".

(gdb)
```

Fig. J.4 | Starting the debugger to run the program.

```
(gdb) run
Starting program: /home/nuke/AppJ/FigJ_03
account1 balance: $50

Enter withdrawal amount for account1: 13

attempting to subtract 13 from account1 balance

account1 balance: $37

Program exited normally.
(gdb)
```

Fig. J.5 | Running the program with no breakpoints set.

```
(gdb) break 17
Breakpoint 1 at 0x80486f6: file FigJ_03.cpp, line 17.
(gdb) break 25
Breakpoint 2 at 0x8048799: file FigJ_03.cpp, line 25.
(gdb)
```

Fig. J.6 | Setting two breakpoints in the program.

```
(gdb) run
Starting program: /home/nuke/AppJ/FigJ_03

Breakpoint 1, main () at FigJ_03.cpp:17
17          cout << "account1 balance: $" << account1.getBalance() << endl;
(gdb)
```

Fig. J.7 | Running the program until it reaches the first breakpoint.

break mode when execution reaches the breakpoint at line 17. At this point, the debugger notifies you that a breakpoint has been reached and displays the source code at that line (17), which will be the next statement to execute.

6. *Using the **continue** command to resume execution.* Type continue. The **continue command** causes the program to continue running until the next breakpoint is reached (line 25). Enter 13 at the prompt. The debugger notifies you when execution reaches the second breakpoint (Fig. J.8). Note that figJ_03's normal output appears between messages from the debugger.

7. *Examining a variable's value.* Type print withdrawalAmount to display the current value stored in the withdrawalAmount variable (Fig. J.9). The **print command** allows you to peek inside the computer at the value of one of your variables. This can be used to help you find and eliminate logic errors in your code. In this case, the variable's value is 13—the value you entered that was assigned to variable withdrawalAmount in line 22 of Fig. J.3. Next, use print to display the contents of the account1 object. When an object is displayed with print, braces are placed

```
(gdb) continue
Continuing.
account1 balance: $50

Enter withdrawal amount for account1: 13

attempting to subtract 13 from account1 balance


Breakpoint 2, main () at FigJ_03.cpp:25
25          account1.debit( withdrawalAmount ); // try to subtract from
account1
(gdb)
```

Fig. J.8 | Continuing execution until the second breakpoint is reached.

```
(gdb) print withdrawalAmount
$2 = 13
(gdb) print account1
$3 = {balance = 50}
(gdb)
```

Fig. J.9 | Printing the values of variables.

around the object's data members. In this case, there is a single data member—balance—which has a value of 50.

8. *Using convenience variables.* When you use print, the result is stored in a convenience variable such as $1. Convenience variables are temporary variables created by the debugger that are named using a dollar sign followed by an integer. Convenience variables can be used to perform arithmetic and evaluate boolean expressions. Type print $1. The debugger displays the value of $1 (Fig. J.10), which contains the value of withdrawalAmount. Note that printing the value of $1 creates a new convenience variable—$3.

9. *Continuing program execution.* Type continue to continue the program's execution. The debugger encounters no additional breakpoints, so it continues executing and eventually terminates (Fig. J.11).

10. *Removing a breakpoint.* You can display a list of all of the breakpoints in the program by typing info break. To remove a breakpoint, type delete, followed by a space and the number of the breakpoint to remove. Remove the first breakpoint by typing delete 1. Remove the second breakpoint as well. Now type info break to list the remaining breakpoints in the program. The debugger should indicate that no breakpoints are set (Fig. J.12).

11. *Executing the program without breakpoints.* Type run to execute the program. Enter the value 13 at the prompt. Because you successfully removed the two breakpoints, the program's output is displayed without the debugger entering break mode (Fig. J.13).

```
(gdb) print $1
$3 = 13
(gdb)
```

Fig. J.10 | Printing a convenience variable.

```
(gdb) continue
Continuing.
account1 balance: $37

Program exited normally.
(gdb)
```

Fig. J.11 | Finishing execution of the program.

```
(gdb) info break
Num Type           Disp Enb Address    What
1    breakpoint     keep y   0x080486f6 in main at FigJ_03.cpp:17
         breakpoint already hit 1 time
2    breakpoint     keep y   0x08048799 in main at FigJ_03.cpp:25
         breakpoint already hit 1 time
(gdb) delete 1
(gdb) delete 2
(gdb) info break
No breakpoints or watchpoints.
(gdb)
```

Fig. J.12 | Viewing and removing breakpoints.

```
(gdb) run
Starting program: /home/nuke/AppJ/FigJ_03
account1 balance: $50

Enter withdrawal amount for account1: 13

attempting to subtract 13 from account1 balance

account1 balance: $37

Program exited normally.
(gdb)
```

Fig. J.13 | Program executing with no breakpoints set.

12. *Using the quit command.* Use the quit command to end the debugging session (Fig. J.14). This command causes the debugger to terminate.

In this section, you used the gdb command to start the debugger and the run command to start debugging a program. You set a breakpoint at a particular line number in the main function. The break command can also be used to set a breakpoint at a line number in another file or at a particular function. Typing break, then the filename, a colon and the line number will set a breakpoint at a line in another file. Typing break, then a function name will cause the debugger to enter the break mode whenever that function is called.

Also in this section, you saw how the help list command will provide more information on the list command. If you have any questions about the debugger or any of its commands, type help or help followed by the command name for more information.

Finally, you examined variables with the print command and remove breakpoints with the delete command. You learned how to use the continue command to continue execution after a breakpoint is reached and the quit command to end the debugger.

```
(gdb) quit
$
```

Fig. J.14 | Exiting the debugger using the quit command.

J.3 print and set Commands

In the preceding section, you learned how to use the debugger's print command to examine the value of a variable during program execution. In this section, you'll learn how to use the print command to examine the value of more complex expressions. You'll also learn the set command, which allows you to assign new values to variables. We assume you are working in the directory containing this appendix's examples and have compiled for debugging with the -g compiler option.

1. *Starting debugging.* Type gdb figJ_03 to start the GNU debugger.

2. *Inserting a breakpoint.* Set a breakpoint at line 25 in the source code by typing break 25 (Fig. J.15).

3. *Running the program and reaching a breakpoint.* Type run to begin the debugging process (Fig. J.16). This will cause main to execute until the breakpoint at line 25 is reached. This suspends program execution and switches the program into break mode. The statement in line 25 is the next statement that will execute.

4. *Evaluating arithmetic and boolean expressions.* Recall from Section J.2 that once the debugger enters break mode, you can explore the values of the program's variables using the print command. You can also use print to evaluate arithmetic and boolean expressions. Type print withdrawalAmount - 2. This expression returns the value 11 (Fig. J.17), but does not actually change the value of withdrawalAmount. Type print withdrawalAmount == 11. Expressions containing the == symbol return bool values. The value returned is false (Fig. J.17) because withdrawalAmount withdrawalAmount still contains 13.

5. *Modifying values.* You can change the values of variables during the program's execution in the debugger. This can be valuable for experimenting with different

```
(gdb) break 25
Breakpoint 1 at 0x8048799: file FigJ_03.cpp, line 25.
(gdb)
```

Fig. J.15 | Setting a breakpoint in the program.

```
(gdb) run
Starting program: /home/nuke/AppJ/FigJ_03
account1 balance: $50

Enter withdrawal amount for account1: 13

attempting to subtract 13 from account1 balance


Breakpoint 1, main () at FigJ_03.cpp:25
25          account1.debit( withdrawalAmount ); // try to subtract from
account1
(gdb)
```

Fig. J.16 | Running the program until the breakpoint at line 25 is reached.

```
(gdb) print withdrawalAmount - 2
$1 = 11
(gdb) print withdrawalAmount == 11
$2 = false
(gdb)
```

Fig. J.17 | Printing expressions with the debugger.

values and for locating logic errors. You can use the debugger's set command to change a variable's value. Type set withdrawalAmount = 42 to change the value of withdrawalAmount, then type print withdrawalAmount to display its new value (Fig. J.18).

6. *Viewing the program result.* Type continue to continue program execution. Line 25 of Fig. J.3 executes, passing withdrawalAmount to Account member function debit. Function main then displays the new balance. Note that the result is $8 (Fig. J.19). This shows that the preceding step changed the value of withdrawalAmount from the value 13 that you input to 42.

7. *Using the quit command.* Use the quit command to end the debugging session (Fig. J.20). This command causes the debugger to terminate.

In this section, you used the debugger's print command to evaluate arithmetic and boolean expressions. You also learned how to use the set command to modify the value of a variable during your program's execution.

```
(gdb) set withdrawalAmount = 42
(gdb) print withdrawalAmount
$3 = 42
(gdb)
```

Fig. J.18 | Setting the value of a variable while in break mode.

```
(gdb) continue
Continuing.
account1 balance: $8

Program exited normally.
(gdb)
```

Fig. J.19 | Using a modified variable in the execution of a program.

```
(gdb) quit
$
```

Fig. J.20 | Exiting the debugger using the quit command.

J.4 Controlling Execution Using the step, finish and next Commands

Sometimes you'll need to execute a program line by line to find and fix errors. Walking through a portion of your program this way can help you verify that a function's code executes correctly. The commands in this section allow you to execute a function line by line, execute all the statements of a function at once or execute only the remaining statements of a function (if you have already executed some statements within the function).

1. *Starting the debugger.* Start the debugger by typing gdb figJ_03.

2. *Setting a breakpoint.* Type break 25 to set a breakpoint at line 25.

3. *Running the program.* Run the program by typing run, then enter 13 at the prompt. After the program displays its two output messages, the debugger indicates that the breakpoint has been reached and displays the code at line 25. The debugger then pauses and wait for the next command to be entered.

4. *Using the step command.* The step command executes the next statement in the program. If the next statement to execute is a function call, control transfers to the called function. The step command enables you to enter a function and study its individual statements. For instance, you can use the print and set commands to view and modify the variables within the function. Type step to enter the debit member function of class Account (Fig. J.2). The debugger indicates that the step has been completed and displays the next executable statement (Fig. J.21)—in this case, line 33 of class Account (Fig. J.2).

5. *Using the finish command.* After you have stepped into the debit member function, type finish. This command executes the remaining statements in the function and returns control to the place where the function was called. The finish command executes the remaining statements in member function debit, then pauses at line 28 in main (Fig. J.22). In lengthy functions, you may want to look at a few key lines of code, then continue debugging the caller's code. The finish command is useful for situations in which you do not want to step through the remainder of a function line by line.

6. *Using the continue command to continue execution.* Enter the continue command to continue execution until the program terminates.

7. *Running the program again.* Breakpoints persist until the end of the debugging session in which they are set. So, the breakpoint you set in *Step 2* is still set. Type run to run the program and enter 13 at the prompt. As in *Step 3*, the program runs until the breakpoint at line 25 is reached, then the debugger pauses and waits for the next command (Fig. J.23).

```
(gdb) step
Account::debit (this=0xbff81700, amount=13) at Account.cpp:33
33            if ( amount <= balance ) // debit amount does not exceed balance
(gdb)
```

Fig. J.21 | Using the step command to enter a function.

```
(gdb) finish
Run till exit from #0  Account::debit (this=0xbff81700, amount=13) at
    Account.cpp:33
0x080487a9 in main () at FigJ_03.cpp:25
25          account1.debit( withdrawalAmount ); // try to subtract from account1
(gdb)
```

Fig. J.22 | Using the `finish` command to complete execution of a function and return to the calling function.

```
(gdb) run
Starting program: /home/nuke/AppJ/FigJ_03
account1 balance: $50

Enter withdrawal amount for account1: 13

attempting to subtract 13 from account1 balance


Breakpoint 1, main () at FigJ_03.cpp:25
25          account1.debit( withdrawalAmount ); // try to subtract from
account1
(gdb)
```

Fig. J.23 | Restarting the program.

8. *Using the next command.* Type `next`. This command behaves like the `step` command, except when the next statement to execute contains a function call. In that case, the called function executes in its entirety and the program advances to the next executable line after the function call (Fig. J.24). In *Step 4*, the `step` command enters the called function. In this example, the `next` command executes `Account` member function `debit`, then the debugger pauses at line 28.

9. *Using the quit command.* Use the `quit` command to end the debugging session (Fig. J.25). While the program is running, this command causes the program to immediately terminate rather than execute the remaining statements in `main`.

```
(gdb) next
28          cout << "account1 balance: $" << account1.getBalance() << endl;
(gdb)
```

Fig. J.24 | Using the `next` command to execute a function in its entirety.

```
(gdb) quit
The program is running.  Exit anyway? (y or n) y
$
```

Fig. J.25 | Exiting the debugger using the `quit` command.

In this section, you used the debugger's step and finish commands to debug functions called during your program's execution. You saw how the next command can step over a function call. You also learned that the quit command ends a debugging session.

J.5 watch Command

The watch command tells the debugger to watch a data member. When that data member is about to change, the debugger will notify you. In this section, you'll use the watch command to see how the Account object's data member balance is modified during execution.

1. *Starting the debugger.* Start the debugger by typing gdb figJ_03.
2. *Setting a breakpoint and running the program.* Type break 14 to set a breakpoint at line 14. Then, run the program with the command run. The debugger and program will pause at the breakpoint at line 14 (Fig. J.26).
3. *Watching a class's data member.* Set a watch on account1's balance data member by typing watch account1.balance (Fig. J.27). This watch is labeled as watchpoint 2 because watchpoints are labeled with the same sequence of numbers as breakpoints. You can set a watch on any variable or data member of an object currently in scope. Whenever the value of a watched variable changes, the debugger enters break mode and notifies you that the value has changed.
4. *Executing the constructor.* Use the next command to execute the constructor and initialize the account1 object's balance data member. The debugger indicates that the balance data member's value changed, shows the old and new values and enters break mode at line 20 (Fig. J.28).
5. *Exiting the constructor.* Type finish to complete the constructor's execution and return to main.
6. *Withdrawing money from the account.* Type continue to continue execution and enter a withdrawal value at the prompt. The program executes normally. Line 25 of Fig. J.3 calls Account member function debit to reduce the Account

```
(gdb) break 14
Breakpoint 1 at 0x80486e5: file FigJ_03.cpp, line 14.
(gdb) run
Starting program: /home/nuke/AppJ/FigJ_03

Breakpoint 1, main () at FigJ_03.cpp:14
14          Account account1( 50 ); // create Account object
(gdb)
```

Fig. J.26 | Running the program until the first breakpoint.

```
(gdb) watch account1.balance
Hardware watchpoint 2: account1.balance
(gdb)
```

Fig. J.27 | Setting a watchpoint on a data member.

```
(gdb) next
Hardware watchpoint 2: account1.balance

Old value = 0
New value = 50
Account (this=0xbfcd6b90, initialBalance=50) at Account.cpp:20
20          if ( initialBalance < 0 )
(gdb)
```

Fig. J.28 | Stepping into the constructor.

object's balance by a specified amount. Line 34 of Fig. J.2 inside function debit
changes the value of balance. The debugger notifies you of this change and enters break mode (Fig. J.29).

7. *Continuing execution.* Type continue—the program will finish executing function main because the program does not attempt any additional changes to balance. The debugger removes the watch on account1's balance data member
because the account1 object goes out of scope when function main ends. Removing the watchpoint causes the debugger to enter break mode. Type continue
again to finish execution of the program (Fig. J.30).

```
(gdb) continue
Continuing.
account1 balance: $50

Enter withdrawal amount for account1: 13

attempting to subtract 13 from account1 balance

Hardware watchpoint 2: account1.balance

Old value = 50
New value = 37
0x0804893b in Account::debit (this=0xbfcd6b90, amount=13) at Account.cpp:34
34          balance = balance - amount;
(gdb)
```

Fig. J.29 | Entering break mode when a variable is changed.

```
(gdb) continue
Continuing.
account1 balance: $37

Watchpoint 2 deleted because the program has left the block in
which its expression is valid.
0xb7da0595 in exit () from /lib/tls/i686/cmov/libc.so.6
(gdb) continue
Continuing.

Program exited normally.
(gdb)
```

Fig. J.30 | Continuing to the end of the program.

8. *Restarting the debugger and resetting the watch on the variable.* Type run to re-start the debugger. Once again, set a watch on account1 data member balance by typing watch account1.balance. This watchpoint is labeled as watchpoint 3. Type continue to continue execution (Fig. J.31).

9. *Removing the watch on the data member.* Suppose you want to watch a data member for only part of a program's execution. You can remove the debugger's watch on variable balance by typing delete 3 (Fig. J.32). Type continue—the program will finish executing without reentering break mode.

In this section, you used the watch command to enable the debugger to notify you when the value of a variable changes. You used the delete command to remove a watch on a data member before the end of the program.

```
(gdb) run
Starting program: /home/nuke/AppJ/FigJ_03

Breakpoint 1, main () at FigJ_03.cpp:14
14              Account account1( 50 ); // create Account object
(gdb) watch account1.balance
Hardware watchpoint 3: account1.balance
(gdb) continue
Continuing.
Hardware watchpoint 3: account1.balance

Old value = 0
New value = 50
Account (this=0xbfd8eb90, initialBalance=50) at Account.cpp:20
20              if ( initialBalance < 0 )
(gdb)
```

Fig. J.31 | Resetting the watch on a data member.

```
(gdb) delete 3
(gdb) continue
Continuing.
account1 balance: $50

Enter withdrawal amount for account1: 13

attempting to subtract 13 from account1 balance

account1 balance: $37

Program exited normally.
(gdb)
```

Fig. J.32 | Removing a watch.

J.6 Wrap-Up

In this appendix, you learned how to insert and remove breakpoints in the debugger. Breakpoints allow you to pause program execution so you can examine variable values with the debugger's print command, which can help you locate and fix logic errors. You used the print command to examine the value of an expression, and you used the set command to change the value of a variable. You also learned debugger commands (including the step, finish and next commands) that can be used to determine whether a function is executing correctly. You learned how to use the watch command to keep track of a data member throughout the scope of that data member. Finally, you learned how to use the info break command to list all the breakpoints and watchpoints set for a program and the delete command to remove individual breakpoints and watchpoints.

Summary

Section J.1 Introduction
- GNU includes software called a debugger, which allows you to monitor the execution of your programs to locate and remove logic errors.

Section J.2 Breakpoints and the *run*, *stop*, *continue* and *print* Commands
- The GNU debugger works only with executable files that were compiled with the -g compiler option, which generates information that is used by the debugger to help you debug your programs.
- The gdb command will start the GNU debugger and enable you to use its features. The run command will run a program through the debugger.
- Breakpoints are markers that can be set at any executable line of code. When program execution reaches a breakpoint, execution pauses.
- The break command inserts a breakpoint at the line number specified after the command.
- When the program runs, it suspends execution at any line that contains a breakpoint and is said to be in break mode.
- The continue command causes the program to continue running until the next breakpoint is reached.
- The print command allows you to peek inside the computer at the value of one of your variables.
- When the print command is used, the result is stored in a convenience variable such as $1. Convenience variables are temporary variables that can be used in the debugging process to perform arithmetic and evaluate boolean expressions.
- You can display a list of all of the breakpoints in the program by typing info break.
- To remove a breakpoint, type delete, followed by a space and the number of the breakpoint to remove.

Section J.3 *print* and *set* Commands
- Use the quit command to end the debugging session.
- The set command allows you to assign new values to variables.

Section J.4 Controlling Execution Using the *step*, *finish* and *next* Commands
- The step command executes the next statement in the program. If the next statement to execute is a function call, control transfers to the called function. The step command enables you to enter a function and study the individual statements of that function.

- The finish command executes the remaining statements in the function and returns control to the place where the function was called.
- The next command behaves like the step command, except when the next statement to execute contains a function call. In that case, the called function executes in its entirety and the program advances to the next executable line after the function call.

Section J.5 watch Command
- The watch command sets a watch on any variable or data member of an object currently in scope during execution of the debugger. Whenever the value of a watched variable changes, the debugger enters break mode and notifies you that the value has changed.

Terminology

break command	info break command
break mode	next command
breakpoint	print command
continue command	quit command
debugger	run command
delete command	set command
finish command	step command
-g compiler option	watch command
gdb command	

Self-Review Exercises

J.1   Fill in the blanks in each of the following statements:
   a) A breakpoint cannot be set at a(n) _____.
   b) You can examine the value of an expression by using the debugger's _____ command.
   c) You can modify the value of a variable by using the debugger's _____ command.
   d) During debugging, the _____ command executes the remaining statements in the current function and returns program control to the place where the function was called.
   e) The debugger's _____ command behaves like the step command when the next statement to execute does not contain a function call.
   f) The watch debugger command allows you to view all changes to a(n) _____.

J.2   State whether each of the following is *true* or *false*. If *false*, explain why.
   a) When program execution suspends at a breakpoint, the next statement to be executed is the statement after the breakpoint.
   b) Watches can be removed using the debugger's remove command.
   c) The -g compiler option must be used when compiling programs for debugging.

Answers to Self-Review Exercises

J.1   a) non-executable line. b) print. c) set. d) finish. e) next. f) data member.

J.2   a) False. When program execution suspends at a breakpoint, the next statement to be executed is the statement at the breakpoint. b) False. Watches can be removed using the debugger's delete command. c) True.

Bibliography

For additional C++ books, articles and more, please visit the Deitel C++ Resource Center at

`www.deitel.com/cplusplus`

Abrahams, D. and A. Gurtovoy. *C++ Template Metaprogramming: Concepts, Tools, and Techniques from Boost and Beyond.* Boston, MA: Addison-Wesley Professional, 2004.

Alexandrescu, A. *Modern C++ Design: Generic Programming and Design Patterns Applied.* Boston, MA: Addison-Wesley Professional, 2001.

Alhir, S. *UML in a Nutshell.* Cambridge, MA: O'Reilly & Associates, Inc., 1998.

Almarode, J. "Object Security." *Smalltalk Report* Vol. 5, No. 3 November/December 1995, 15–17.

American National Standard, Programming Language C++. (ANSI Document ISO/IEC 14882), New York, NY: American National Standards Institute, 1998.

Anderson, A. E. and W. J. Heinze. *C++ Programming and Fundamental Concepts.* Englewood Cliffs, NJ: Prentice Hall, 1992.

Arciniegas, F. *C++ XML.* Indianapolis, IN: Sams, 2001.

Arlow, J. and I. Neustadt. *UML 2 and the Unified Process: Practical Object-Oriented Analysis and Design, Second Edition.* Boston, MA: Addison-Wesley Professional, 2005.

Astle, D. and K. Hawkins. *Beginning OpenGL Game Programming.* Boston, MA: Course Technology PTR, 2004.

Bar-David, T. *Object-Oriented Design for C++.* Englewood Cliffs, NJ: Prentice Hall, 1993.

Beck, K. "Birds, Bees, and Browsers—Obvious Sources of Objects." *The Smalltalk Report* Vol. 3, No. 8, June 1994,13.

Becker, P. "Shrinking the Big Switch Statement." *Windows Tech Journal* Vol. 2, No. 5, May 1993, 26–33.

Becker, P. "Conversion Confusion." *C++ Report* October 1993, 26–28.

Berard, E. V. *Essays on Object-Oriented Software Engineering: Volume I.* Englewood Cliffs, NJ: Prentice Hall, 1993.

Binder, R. V. "State-Based Testing." *Object Magazine* Vol. 5, No. 4, August 1995, 75–78.

Binder, R. V. "State-Based Testing: Sneak Paths and Conditional Transitions." *Object Magazine* Vol. 5, No. 6, October 1995, 87–89.

Blum, A. *Neural Networks in C++: An Object-Oriented Framework for Building Connectionist Systems.* New York, NY: John Wiley & Sons, 1992.

Booch, G. *Object Solutions: Managing the Object-Oriented Project.* Reading, MA: Addison-Wesley, 1996.

Booch, G. *Object-Oriented Analysis and Design with Applications, Third Edition.* Reading: MA: Addison-Wesley, 2005.

Booch, G., J. Rumbaugh, and I. Jacobson. *The Unified Modeling Language User Guide*. Reading, MA: Addison-Wesley, 1999.

Cargill, T. *C++ Programming Style*. Reading, MA: Addison-Wesley, 1993.

Carroll, M. D. and M. A. Ellis. *Designing and Coding Reusable C++*. Reading, MA: Addison-Wesley, 1995.

Chonoles, M. J. and J. A. Schardt. *UML 2 for Dummies*. New York, NY: Wiley Publishing, Inc., 2003.

Coplien, J. O. and D. C. Schmidt. *Pattern Languages of Program Design*. Reading, MA: Addison-Wesley, 1995.

Dawson, M. *Beginning C++ Game Programming*. Boston, MA: Course Technology PTR, 2004.

Deitel, H. M, P. J. Deitel and D. R. Choffnes. *Operating Systems, Third Edition*. Upper Saddle River, NJ: Prentice Hall, 2004.

Deitel, H. M and P. J. Deitel. *Java How to Program, Seventh Edition*. Upper Saddle River, NJ: Prentice Hall, 2007.

Deitel, H. M. and P. J. Deitel. *C How to Program, Fifth Edition*. Upper Saddle River, NJ: Prentice Hall, 2007.

Dennis, A., B. H. Wixom and D. Tegarden. *Systems Analysis and Design with UML Version 2.0: An Object-Oriented Approach, Second Edition*. New York, NY: Wiley Publishing, Inc., 2004.

Dewhurst, S. C. *C++ Common Knowledge: Essential Intermediate Programming*. Boston, MA: Addison-Wesley Professional, 2005.

Donovan, S. *C++ Example*. Indianapolis, IN: Que, 2001.

Duncan, R. "Inside C++: Friend and Virtual Functions, and Multiple Inheritance." *PC Magazine* 15 October 1991, 417–420.

Ellis, M. A. and B. Stroustrup. *The Annotated C++ Reference Manual*. Reading, MA: Addison-Wesley, 1990.

Embley, D. W., B. D. Kurtz and S. N. Woodfield. *Object-Oriented Systems Analysis: A Model-Driven Approach*. Englewood Cliffs, NJ: Yourdon Press, 1992.

Eriksson, H., D. Fado, B. Lyons and M. Penker. *UML 2 Toolkit*. New York, NY: Wiley Publishing, Inc., 2003.

Firesmith, D.G. and B. Henderson-Sellers. "Clarifying Specialized Forms of Association in UML and OML." *Journal of Object-Oriented Programming* May 1998: 47–50.

Flamig, B. *Practical Data Structures in C++*. New York, NY: John Wiley & Sons, 1993.

Fowler, M. *UML Distilled: A Brief Guide to the Standard Object Modeling Language, Third Edition*. Reading, MA: Addison-Wesley, 2004.

Giancola, A. and L. Baker. "Bit Arrays with C++." *The C Users Journal* Vol. 10, No. 7, July 1992, 21–26.

Glass, G. and B. Schuchert. *The STL <Primer>*. Upper Saddle River, NJ: Prentice Hall PTR, 1995.

Gooch, T. "Obscure C++." *Inside Microsoft Visual C++* Vol. 6, No. 11, November 1995, 13–15.

Henricson, M. and E. Nyquist. *Industrial Strength C++: Rules and Recommendations*. Upper Saddle River, NJ: Prentice Hall, 1997.

International Standard: Programming Languages—C++. ISO/IEC 14882:1998. New York, NY: American National Standards Institute, 1998.

Jacobson, I. "Is Object Technology Software's Industrial Platform?" *IEEE Software Magazine* Vol. 10, No. 1, January 1993, 24–30.

Jaeschke, R. *Portability and the C Language.* Indianapolis, IN: Sams Publishing, 1989.

Johnson, L.J. "Model Behavior." *Enterprise Development* May 2000: 20–28.

Josuttis, N. *The C++ Standard Library: A Tutorial and Reference.* Boston, MA: Addison-Wesley, 1999.

Karlsson, B. *Beyond the C++ Standard Library: An Introduction to Boost.* Boston, MA: Addison-Wesley Professional, 2005.

Koenig, A. "What is C++ Anyway?" *Journal of Object-Oriented Programming* April/May 1991, 48–52.

Koenig, A. "Implicit Base Class Conversions." *The C++ Report* Vol. 6, No. 5, June 1994, 18–19.

Koenig, A. and B. Stroustrup. "Exception Handling for C++ (Revised)," *Proceedings of the USENIX C++ Conference,* San Francisco, CA, April 1990.

Koenig, A. and B. E. Moo. *Accelerated C++: Practical Programming Example.* Boston, MA: Addison-Wesley Professional, 2000.

Koenig, A. and B. E. Moo. *Ruminations on C++: A Decade of Programming Insight and Experience.* Reading, MA: Addison-Wesley, 1997.

Kruse, R. L. and A. J. Ryba. *Data Structures and Program Design in C++.* Upper Saddle River, NJ: Prentice Hall, 1999.

Lajoie, J., S. B. Lippman, and B. E. Moo. *C++ Primer, Fourth Edition.* Boston, MA: Addison-Wesley Professional, 2005.

Langer, A. and K. Kreft. *Standard C++ IOStreams and Locales: Advanced Programmer's Guide and Reference.* Reading, MA: Addison-Wesley, 2000.

Larman, C. *Applying UML and Patterns: An Introduction to Object-Oriented Analysis and Design and Iterative Development, Third Edition.* Upper Saddle River, NJ: Prentice Hall PTR, 2004.

Lee, L., A. Lumsdaine and J. G. Siek. *The Boost Graph Library User Guide and Reference Manual.* Boston, MA: Addison-Wesley Professional, 2001.

Lippman, S. B. and J. Lajoie. *C++ Primer, Third Edition,* Reading, MA: Addison-Wesley, 1998.

Lorenz, M. *Object-Oriented Software Development: A Practical Guide.* Englewood Cliffs, NJ: Prentice Hall, 1993.

Lorenz, M. "A Brief Look at Inheritance Metrics." *The Smalltalk Report* Vol. 3, No. 8 June 1994, 1, 4–5.

Malik, D.S. *C++ Programming: From Problem Analysis to Program Design, Third Edition.* Boston, MA: Course Technology, 2006.

Martin, J. *Principles of Object-Oriented Analysis and Design.* Englewood Cliffs, NJ: Prentice Hall, 1993.

Martin, R. C. *Designing Object-Oriented C++ Applications Using the Booch Method.* Englewood Cliffs, NJ: Prentice Hall, 1995.

Matsche, J. J. "Object-Oriented Programming in Standard C." *Object Magazine* Vol. 2, No. 5, January/February 1993, 71–74.

McCabe, T. J. and A. H. Watson. "Combining Comprehension and Testing in Object-Oriented Development." *Object Magazine* Vol. 4, No. 1, March/April 1994, 63–66.

McGrath, M. *C++ Programming in Easy Steps.* Southam, Warwickshire, United Kingdom: Computer Step, 2005.

McLaughlin, M. and A. Moore. "Real-Time Extensions to the UML." *Dr. Dobb's Journal* December 1998: 82–93.

Melewski, D. "UML Gains Ground." *Application Development Trends* October 1998: 34–44.

Melewski, D. "UML: Ready for Prime Time?" *Application Development Trends* November 1997: 30–44.

Melewski, D. "Wherefore and What Now, UML?" *Application Development Trends* December 1999: 61–68.

Meyer, B. *Object-Oriented Software Construction, Second Edition.* Englewood Cliffs, NJ: Prentice Hall, 1997.

Meyer, B. and D. Mandrioli. *Advances in Object-Oriented Software Engineering.* Englewood Cliffs, NJ: Prentice Hall, 1992.

Meyers, S. *Effective C++: 55 Specific Ways to Improve Your Programs and Designs, Third Edition.* Boston, MA: Addison-Wesley Professional, 2005.

Meyers, S. *Effective STL: 50 Specific Ways to Improve Your Use of the Standard Template Library.* Reading, MA: Addison-Wesley, 2001.

Muller, P. *Instant UML.* Birmingham, UK: Wrox Press Ltd, 1997.

Murray, R. *C++ Strategies and Tactics.* Reading, MA: Addison-Wesley, 1993.

Musser, D. R. and A. A. Stepanov. "Algorithm-Oriented Generic Libraries." *Software Practice and Experience* Vol. 24, No. 7, July 1994.

Musser, D. R., G. J. Derge and A. Saini. *STL Tutorial and Reference Guide: C++ Programming with the Standard Template Library, Second Edition.* Reading, MA: Addison-Wesley, 2001.

Nierstrasz, O., S. Gibbs and D. Tsichritzis. "Component-Oriented Software Development." *Communications of the ACM* Vol. 35, No. 9, September 1992, 160–165.

Pender, T. *UML Bible.* Wiley Publishing, Inc., 2003.

Perry, P. "UML Steps to the Plate." *Application Development Trends* May 1999: 33–36.

Pilone, D. and N. Pitman. *UML 2.0 in a Nutshell, Second Edition.* Sebastopol, CA: O'Reilly Media, Inc., 2005.

Pittman, M. "Lessons Learned in Managing Object-Oriented Development." *IEEE Software Magazine* Vol. 10, No. 1, January 1993, 43–53.

Plauger, D. "Making C++ Safe for Threads." *The C Users Journal* Vol. 11, No. 2, February 1993, 58–62.

Podeswa, H. *UML for the IT Business Analyst: A Practical Guide to Object-Oriented Requirements Gathering.* Boston, MA: Course Technology PTR, 2005.

Pohl, I. *C++ Distilled: A Concise ANSI/ISO Reference and Style Guide.* Reading, MA: Addison-Wesley, 1997.

Prata, S. *C++ Primer Plus, Fifth Edition.* Indianapolis, IN: Sams, 2004.

Prieto-Diaz, R. "Status Report: Software Reusability." *IEEE Software* Vol. 10, No. 3, May 1993, 61–66.

Prosise, J. "Wake Up and Smell the MFC: Using the Visual C++ Classes and Applications Framework." *Microsoft Systems Journal* Vol. 10, No. 6, June 1995, 17–34.

Ritchie, D. M. "The UNIX System: The Evolution of the UNIX Time-Sharing System." *AT&T Bell Laboratories Technical Journal* Vol. 63, No. 8, Part 2, October 1984, 1577–1593.

Rosler, L. "The UNIX System: The Evolution of C—Past and Future." *AT&T Laboratories Technical Journal* Vol. 63, No. 8, Part 2, October 1984, 1685–1699.

Robson, R. *Using the STL: The C++ Standard Template Library.* New York, NY: Springer Verlag, 2000.

Rubin, K. S. and A. Goldberg. "Object Behavior Analysis." *Communications of the ACM* Vol. 35, No. 9, September 1992, 48–62.

Rumbaugh, J., M. Blaha, W. Premerlani, F. Eddy and W. Lorensen. *Object-Oriented Modeling and Design*. Englewood Cliffs, NJ: Prentice Hall, 1991.

Rumbaugh, J., Jacobson, I. and G. Booch. *The Unified Modeling Language Reference Manual, Second Edition*. Reading, MA: Addison-Wesley, 2005.

Saks, D. "Inheritance." *The C Users Journal* May 1993, 81–89.

Schildt, H. *STL Programming from the Ground Up*. Berkeley, CA: Osborne McGraw-Hill, 1999.

Schildt, H. *The Art of C++*. Berkeley, CA: McGraw-Hill Osborne Media, 2004.

Schlaer, S. and S. J. Mellor. *Object Lifecycles: Modeling the World in States*. Englewood Cliffs, NJ: Prentice Hall, 1992.

Sedgwick, R. *Bundle of Algorithms in C++, Parts 1–5: Fundamentals, Data Structures, Sorting, Searching, and Graph Algorithms (Third Edition)*. Reading, MA: Addison-Wesley, 2002.

Skelly, C. "Pointer Power in C and C++." *The C Users Journal* Vol. 11, No. 2, February 1993, 93–98.

Snyder, A. "The Essence of Objects: Concepts and Terms." *IEEE Software Magazine* Vol. 10, No. 1, January 1993, 31–42.

Stepanov, A. and M. Lee. "The Standard Template Library." 31 October 1995 <www.cs.rpi.edu/~musser/doc.ps>.

Stroustrup, B. "The UNIX System: Data Abstraction in C." *AT&T Bell Laboratories Technical Journal* Vol. 63, No. 8, Part 2, October 1984, 1701–1732.

Stroustrup, B. "What is Object-Oriented Programming?" *IEEE Software* Vol. 5, No. 3, May 1988, 10–20.

Stroustrup, B. "Parameterized Types for C++." *Proceedings of the USENIX C++ Conference* Denver, CO, October 1988.

Stroustrup, B. "Why Consider Language Extensions?: Maintaining a Delicate Balance." *The C++ Report* September 1993, 44–51.

Stroustrup, B. "Making a vector Fit for a Standard." *The C++ Report* October 1994.

Stroustrup, B. *The Design and Evolution of C++*. Reading, MA: Addison-Wesley, 1994.

Stroustrup, B. *The C++ Programming Language, Special Third Edition*. Reading, MA: Addison-Wesley, 2000.

Taylor, D. *Object-Oriented Information Systems: Planning and Implementation*. New York, NY: John Wiley & Sons, 1992.

Urlocker, Z. "Polymorphism Unbounded." *Windows Tech Journal* Vol. 1, No. 1, January 1992, 11–16.

Van Camp, K. E. "Dynamic Inheritance Using Filter Classes." *The C/C++ Users Journal* Vol. 13, No. 6, June 1995, 69–78.

Vilot, M. J. "An Introduction to the Standard Template Library." *The C++ Report* Vol. 6, No. 8, October 1994.

Voss, G. "Objects and Messages." *Windows Tech Journal* February 1993, 15–16.

Wang, B. L. and J. Wang. "Is a Deep Class Hierarchy Considered Harmful?" *Object Magazine* Vol. 4, No. 7, November/December 1994, 35–36.

Weisfeld, M. "An Alternative to Large Switch Statements." *The C Users Journal* Vol. 12, No. 4, April 1994, 67–76.

Weiskamp, K. and B. Flamig. *The Complete C++ Primer, Second Edition*. Orlando, FL: Academic Press, 1993.

Wiebel, M. and S. Halladay. "Using OOP Techniques Instead of `switch` in C++." *The C Users Journal* Vol. 10, No. 10, October 1993, 105–112.

Wilde, N. and R. Huitt. "Maintenance Support for Object-Oriented Programs." *IEEE Transactions on Software Engineering* Vol. 18, No. 12, December 1992, 1038–1044.

Wilde, N., P. Matthews and R. Huitt. "Maintaining Object-Oriented Software." *IEEE Software Magazine* Vol. 10, No. 1, January 1993, 75–80.

Wilson, G. V. and P. Lu. *Parallel Programming Using C++*. Cambridge, MA: MIT Press, 1996.

Wilt, N. "Templates in C++." *The C Users Journal* May 1993, 33–51.

Wirfs-Brock, R., B. Wilkerson and L. Wiener. *Designing Object-Oriented Software*. Englewood Cliffs, NJ: Prentice Hall PTR, 1990.

Wyatt, B. B., K. Kavi and S. Hufnagel. "Parallelism in Object-Oriented Languages: A Survey." *IEEE Software* Vol. 9, No. 7, November 1992, 56–66.

Yamazaki, S., K. Kajihara, M. Ito and R. Yasuhara. "Object-Oriented Design of Telecommunication Software." *IEEE Software Magazine* Vol. 10, No. 1, January 1993, 81–87.

Yuzwa, E. *Game Programming In C++: Start To Finish*. Boston, MA: Charles River Media, 2006.

Index

The DEITEL® Suite of Products...

HOW TO PROGRAM BOOKS

C++ How to Program
Sixth Edition

BOOK / CD-ROM

©2008, 1400 pp., paper
(0-13-615250-3)

The complete authoritative DEITEL® LIVE-CODE introduction to programming with C++! The Sixth Edition takes an easy-to-follow, carefully developed early classes and objects approach to programming in C++. The text includes comprehensive coverage of the fundamentals of object-oriented programming in C++. It includes an optional automated teller machine (ATM) case study that teaches the fundamentals of software engineering and object-oriented design with the UML 2.0 in Chapters 1-7, 9 and 13. Additional integrated case studies appear throughout the text, including the `Time` class (Chapter 9), the `Employee` class (Chapters 12 and 13) and the `GradeBook` class (Chapters 3-7). This new edition includes a chapter on C++ game programming with the OGRE and OpenAL libraries, and a chapter on the Boost C++ Libraries, Technical Report 1 (TR1) and the forthcoming C++0X standard.

Java™ How to Program
Seventh Edition

BOOK / CD-ROM

©2007, 1596 pp., paper
(0-13-222220-5)

The complete authoritative DEITEL® LIVE-CODE introduction to programming with the new Java™ Standard Edition 6! *Java How to Program, Seventh Edition* is up-to-date with Java™ SE 6 and includes comprehensive coverage of the fundamentals of object-oriented programming in Java; an early classes and objects approach; and an optional automated teller machine (ATM) case study that teaches the fundamentals of software engineering and object oriented design with the UML 2.0 in Chapters 1-8 and 10. Additional integrated case studies appear throughout the text, including GUI and graphics (Chapters 3-12), the `Time` class (Chapter 8), the `Employee` class (Chapters 9 and 10) and the `GradeBook` class (Chapters 3-8). New topics covered include Java Desktop Integration Components, Ajax Web application development with JavaServer Faces, web services and more.

Small C++
How to Program
Fifth Edition

BOOK / CD-ROM

©2005, 773 pp., paper
(0-13-185758-4)

Based on chapters 1-13 (except the optional OOD/UML case study) and appendices of *C++ How to Program, Fifth Edition, Small C++* features a new early classes and objects approach and comprehensive coverage of the fundamentals of object-oriented programming in C++. Key topics include applications, variables, memory concepts, data types, control statements, functions, arrays, pointers and strings, inheritance and polymorphism.

📖 **Now available for both *C++ How to Program, 6/e* and *Small C++ How to Program, 5/e:* C++** Web-based *Cyber Classroom* included with the purchase of a new textbook. The *Cyber Classroom* includes a complete e-book, audio walkthroughs of the code examples, a Lab Manual and selected student solutions. See the *Cyber Classroom* section of this advertorial for more information.

Small Java™
How to Program
Sixth Edition

BOOK / CD-ROM

©2005, 540 pp., paper
(0-13-148660-8)

Based on chapters 1-10 of *Java™ How to Program, Sixth Edition* (not Seventh), *Small Java* is for use with J2SE™ 5.0, features an early classes and objects approach and comprehensive coverage of the fundamentals of object-oriented programming in Java. Key topics include applications, variables, data types, control statements, methods, arrays, object-based programming, inheritance and polymorphism.

📖 **Now available for both *Java How to Program, 7/e* and *Small Java How to Program, 6/e:* Java** Web-based *Cyber Classroom* included with the purchase of a new textbook. The *Cyber Classroom* includes a complete e-book, audio walkthroughs of the code examples, a Lab Manual and selected student solutions. See the *Cyber Classroom* section of this advertorial for more information.

Sign up now for the FREE *DEITEL® Buzz Online* newsletter at:
www.deitel.com/newsletter/subscribe.html

Visual Basic® 2005 How to Program Third Edition

BOOK / CD-ROM

*©2006, 1513 pp., paper
(0-13-186900-0)*

The complete authoritative DEITEL® LIVE-CODE introduction to Visual Basic programming. *Visual Basic® 2005 How to Program, Third Edition* is up-to-date with Microsoft's Visual Basic 2005. The text includes comprehensive coverage of the fundamentals of object-oriented programming in Visual Basic including a new early classes and objects approach and a new optional automated teller machine (ATM) case study that teaches the fundamentals of software engineering and object-oriented design with the UML 2.0 in Chapters 1, 3–9 and 11. Additional integrated case studies appear throughout the text, including the Time class (Chapter 9), the Employee class (Chapters 10 and 11) and the Gradebook class (Chapters 4–9). This book also includes discussions of more advanced topics such as XML, ASP.NET, ADO.NET and Web services. New Visual Basic 2005 topics covered include partial classes, generics, the My namespace and Visual Studio's updated debugger features.

Visual C#® 2005 How to Program Second Edition

BOOK / CD-ROM

*©2006, 1591 pp., paper
(0-13-152523-9)*

The complete authoritative DEITEL® LIVE-CODE introduction to C# programming. *Visual C#® 2005 How to Program, Second Edition* is up-to-date with Microsoft's Visual C# 2005. The text includes comprehensive coverage of the fundamentals of object-oriented programming in C#, including a new early classes and objects approach and a new optional automated teller machine (ATM) case study that teaches the fundamentals of software engineering and object-oriented design with the UML 2.0 in Chapters 1, 3–9 and 11. Additional integrated case studies appear throughout the text, including the Time class (Chapter 9), the Employee class (Chapters 10 and 11) and the Gradebook class (Chapters 4–9). This book also includes discussions of more advanced topics such as XML, ASP.NET, ADO.NET and Web services. New Visual C# 2005 topics covered include partial classes, generics, the My namespace, .NET remoting and Visual Studio's updated debugger features.

Visual C++ .NET® How To Program

BOOK / CD-ROM

*©2004, 1319 pp., paper
(0-13-437377-4)*

Written by the authors of the world's best-selling introductory/intermediate C and C++ textbooks, this comprehensive book thoroughly examines Visual C++® .NET 2003. *Visual C++® .NET How to Program* begins with a strong foundation in the introductory and intermediate programming principles students will need in industry, including fundamental topics such as arrays, functions and control statements. Readers learn the concepts of object-oriented programming, then the text explores such essential topics as networking, databases, XML and multimedia. Graphical user interfaces are also extensively covered, giving students the tools to build compelling and fully interactive programs using the "drag-and-drop" techniques provided by Visual Studio .NET 2003.

C How to Program Fifth Edition

BOOK / CD-ROM

*©2007, 1130 pp., paper
(0-13-240416-8)*

C How to Program, Fifth Edition—the world's best-selling C text—is designed for introductory through intermediate courses and programming languages survey courses. This comprehensive text is aimed at readers with little or no programming experience through intermediate audiences. Highly practical in approach, it introduces fundamental notions of structured programming and software engineering and gets up to speed quickly. The Fifth Edition features new chapters on the C99 standard and an introduction to game programming with the Allegro C Library.

Advanced Java™ 2 Platform How to Program

BOOK / CD-ROM

©2002, 1811 pp., paper
(0-13-089560-1)

Expanding on the world's best-selling Java text-book—*Java™ How to Program*—*Advanced Java™ 2 Platform How To Program* presents advanced Java topics for developing sophisticated, user-friendly GUIs; significant, scalable enterprise applications; wireless applications and distributed systems. Primarily based on Java 2 Enterprise Edition (J2EE) 1.2.1, this textbook integrates technologies such as XML, JavaBeans, security, JDBC™, JavaServer Pages (JSP™), servlets, Remote Method Invocation (RMI), Enterprise JavaBeans™ (EJB), design patterns, Swing, J2ME™, Java 2D and 3D, XML, design patterns, CORBA, Jini™, JavaSpaces™, Jiro™, Java Management Extensions (JMX) and Peer-to-Peer networking with an introduction to JXTA.

Internet & World Wide Web How to Program
Fourth Edition

BOOK / CD-ROM

©2008, 1500 pp., paper
(0-13-175242-1)

This book introduces students with little or no programming experience to the exciting world of Web-based applications. It has been substantially reworked to reflect today's Web 2.0 rich Internet application-development methodologies. The book teaches the skills and tools for creating dynamic Web applications. Topics include introductory programming principles, markup languages (XHTML/XML), scripting languages (JavaScript, PHP, Ruby/Ruby on Rails and Perl), Ajax, web services, web servers (IIS/Apache), relational databases (MySQL/SQL Server 2005 Express/Apache Derby/Java DB), ASP .NET 2.0 and JavaServer™ Faces (JSF). You'll build Ajax-enabled rich Internet applications (RIAs)—using Ajax frameworks, Adobe® Flex™ and Microsoft® Silverlight—with the look-and-feel of desktop applications. The Web 2.0 and Internet business chapter exposes readers to many other topics associated with Web 2.0 applications and businesses. After mastering the material in this book, students will be well prepared to build real-world, industrial-strength, Web-based applications.

Python How to Program

BOOK / CD-ROM

©2002, 1376 pp., paper
(0-13-092361-3)

This exciting textbook provides a comprehensive introduction to Python—a powerful object-oriented programming language with clear syntax and the ability to bring together various technologies quickly and easily. This book covers introductory programming techniques and more advanced topics such as graphical user interfaces, databases, wireless Internet programming, networking, security, process management, multithreading, XHTML, CSS, PSP and multimedia. Readers will learn principles that are applicable to both systems development and Web programming.

XML How to Program

BOOK / CD-ROM

©2001, 934 pp., paper
(0-13-028417-3)

This book is a comprehensive guide to programming in XML. It teaches how to use XML to create customized tags and includes chapters that address markup languages for science and technology, multimedia, commerce and many other fields. Concise introductions to Java, JavaServer Pages, VBScript, Active Server Pages and Perl/CGI provide readers with the essentials of these programming languages and server-side development technologies to enable them to work effectively with XML. The book also covers topics such as XSL, DOM™, SAX, a real-world e-commerce case study and a complete chapter on Web accessibility that addresses Voice XML. Other topics covered include XHTML, CSS, DTD, schema, parsers, XPath, XLink, namespaces, XBase, XInclude, XPointer, XSLT, XSL Formatting Objects, JavaServer Pages, XForms, topic maps, X3D, MathML, OpenMath, CML, BML, CDF, RDF, SVG, Cocoon, WML, XBRL and BizTalk™ and SOAP™ Web resources.

Perl How to Program

©2001, 1057 pp., paper (0-13-028418-1)

This comprehensive guide to Perl programming emphasizes the use of the Common Gateway Interface (CGI) with Perl to create powerful, dynamic multi-tier Web-based client/server applications. The book begins with a clear and careful introduction to programming concepts at a level suitable for beginners, and proceeds through advanced topics such as references and complex data structures. Key Perl topics such as regular expressions and string manipulation are covered in detail. The authors address important and topical issues such as object-oriented programming, the Perl database interface (DBI), graphics and security. Also included is a treatment of XML, a bonus chapter introducing the Python programming language, supplemental material on career resources and a complete chapter on Web accessibility.

e-Business & e-Commerce How to Program

BOOK / CD-ROM

©2001, 1254 pp., paper (0-13-028419-X)

This book explores programming technologies for developing Web-based e-business and e-commerce solutions, and covers e-business and e-commerce models and business issues. Readers learn a full range of options, from "build-your-own" to turnkey solutions. The book examines scores of the top e-businesses (examples include Amazon, eBay, Priceline, Travelocity, etc.), explaining the technical details of building successful e-business and e-commerce sites and their underlying business premises. Learn how to implement the dominant e-commerce models—shopping carts, auctions, name-your-own-price, comparison shopping and bots/intelligent agents—by using markup languages (HTML, Dynamic HTML and XML), scripting languages (JavaScript, VBScript and Perl), server-side technologies (Active Server Pages and Perl/CGI) and database (SQL and ADO), security and online payment technologies.

> "In my courses, I've read several Deitel books. I really enjoy reading and learning from them because they're written in a fashion that's very easy to follow. It's almost like someone is speaking to you, and you don't get lost in a lot of unnecessarily complicated paragraphs. There are sections that have some humor and the real world examples they use help you understand why some things that are good in theory don't work as well in practice. I think Paul and Harvey Deitel have done an amazing job researching the latest technologies and then presenting them in a very understandable way. Whenever I take a new class and find out that we are to use a Deitel book, I'm very happy about that because they're my favorite. I know I can rely upon the book to explain the subject clearly."
>
> — Christine Spencer, Graduate of MIT

For ordering information,
visit us on the Web at www.prenhall.com.

INTERNATIONAL ORDERING INFORMATION

CANADA:
Pearson Education Canada
26 Prince Andrew Place
PO Box 580
Don Mills, Ontario M3C 2T8 Canada
Tel.: 416-925-2249; Fax: 416-925-0068
e-mail: phcinfo.pubcanada@pearsoned.com

EUROPE, MIDDLE EAST, AND AFRICA:
Pearson Education
Edinburgh Gate
Harlow, Essex CM20 2JE UK
Tel: 01279 623928; Fax: 01279 414130
e-mail: enq.orders@pearsoned-ema.com

BENELUX REGION:
Pearson Education
Concertgebouwplein 25
1071 LM Amsterdam
The Netherlands
Tel: 31 20 5755 800; Fax: 31 20 664 5334
e-mail: amsterdam@pearsoned-ema.com

ASIA:
Pearson Education Asia Pte. Ltd.
23/25 First Lok Yang Road
Jurong, 629733 Singapore
Tel: 65 476 4688; Fax: 65 378 0370

JAPAN:
Pearson Education Japan
Ogikubo TM Bldg. 6F. 5-26-13 Ogikubo
Suginami-ku, Tokyo 167-0051 Japan
Tel: 81 3 3365 9001; Fax: 81 3 3365 9009

INDIA:
Pearson Education
Indian Branch
482 FIE, Patparganj
Delhi – 110092 India
Tel: 91 11 2059850 & 2059851
Fax: 91 11 2059852

AUSTRALIA:
Pearson Education Australia
Unit 4, Level 2, 14 Aquatic Drive
Frenchs Forest, NSW 2086, Australia
Tel: 61 2 9454 2200; Fax: 61 2 9453 0089
e-mail: marketing@pearsoned.com.au

NEW ZEALAND/FIJI:
Pearson Education
46 Hillside Road
Auckland 10, New Zealand
Tel: 649 444 4968; Fax: 649 444 4957
E-mail: sales@pearsoned.co.nz

SOUTH AFRICA:
Maskew Miller Longman
Central Park   Block H
16th Street Midrand 1685
South Africa
Tel: 27 21 686 6356; Fax: 27 21 686 4590

LATIN AMERICA:
Pearson Education Latin America
Attn: Tina Sheldon
1 Lake Street
Upper Saddle River, NJ 07458

The SIMPLY SERIES!

The Deitels' *Simply Series* takes an engaging new approach to teaching programming languages from the ground up. The pedagogy of this series combines the DEITEL® signature *LIVE-CODE Approach* with an *APPLICATION-DRIVEN Tutorial Approach* to teach programming with outstanding pedagogical features that help students learn. They have merged the notion of a lab manual with that of a conventional textbook, creating a book in which readers build and execute complete applications from start to finish, while learning the fundamental concepts of programming!

Simply Visual Basic® 2005 An APPLICATION-DRIVEN Tutorial Approach

©2007, 795 pp., paper
(0-13-243862-3)

Simply Visual Basic® 2005 An APPLICATION-DRIVEN Tutorial Approach guides readers through building real-world applications that incorporate Visual Basic 2005 programming fundamentals. Learn GUI design, controls, methods, functions, data types, control statements, procedures, arrays, object-oriented programming, strings and characters, sequential files and more in this comprehensive introduction to Visual Basic 2005. Higher-end topics include ADO .NET 2.0, ASP .NET 2.0, Visual Web Developer 2005 Express, database programming, multimedia and graphics and Web applications development.

Simply Java™ Programming An APPLICATION-DRIVEN Tutorial Approach

©2004, 971 pp., paper
(0-13-142648-6)

Simply Java™ Programming An APPLICATION-DRIVEN Tutorial Approach guides readers through building real-world applications that incorporate Java programming fundamentals. Learn GUI design, components, methods, event-handling, types, control statements, arrays, object-oriented programming, exception-handling, strings and characters, sequential files and more in this comprehensive introduction to Java. We also include higher-end topics such as database programming, multimedia, graphics and Web applications development.

Simply C# An APPLICATION-DRIVEN Tutorial Approach

©2004, 924 pp., paper
(0-13-142641-9)

Simply C# An APPLICATION-DRIVEN Tutorial Approach guides readers through building real-world applications that incorporate C# programming fundamentals. Learn GUI design, controls, methods, functions, data types, control statements, procedures, arrays, object-oriented programming, strings and characters, sequential files and more in this comprehensive introduction to C#. We also include higher-end topics such as database programming, multimedia and graphics and Web applications development.

Simply C++ An APPLICATION-DRIVEN Tutorial Approach

©2005, 644 pp., paper
(0-13-142660-5)

Simply C++ An APPLICATION-DRIVEN Tutorial Approach guides readers through building real-world applications that incorporate C++ programming fundamentals. Learn methods, functions, data types, control statements, procedures, arrays, object-oriented programming, strings and characters, pointers, references, templates, operator overloading and more in this comprehensive introduction to C++.

MULTIMEDIA CYBER CLASSROOMS

Premium content available with *Java™ How to Program, Seventh Edition* and *C++ How to Program, Sixth Edition!*

Java How to Program, 7/e and *C++ How to Program, 6/e* are now available with 12-month access to the Web-based *Multimedia Cyber Classroom* for students who purchase new copies of these books! The *Cyber Classroom* is an interactive, multimedia, tutorial version of DEITEL textbooks. *Cyber Classrooms* are a great value, giving students additional hands-on experience and study aids.

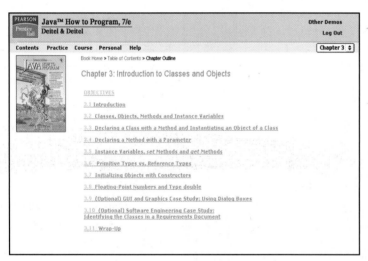

DEITEL® Multimedia Cyber Classrooms *feature an e-book with the complete text of their corresponding* How to Program *titles.*

Unique audio "walkthroughs" of code examples reinforce key concepts.